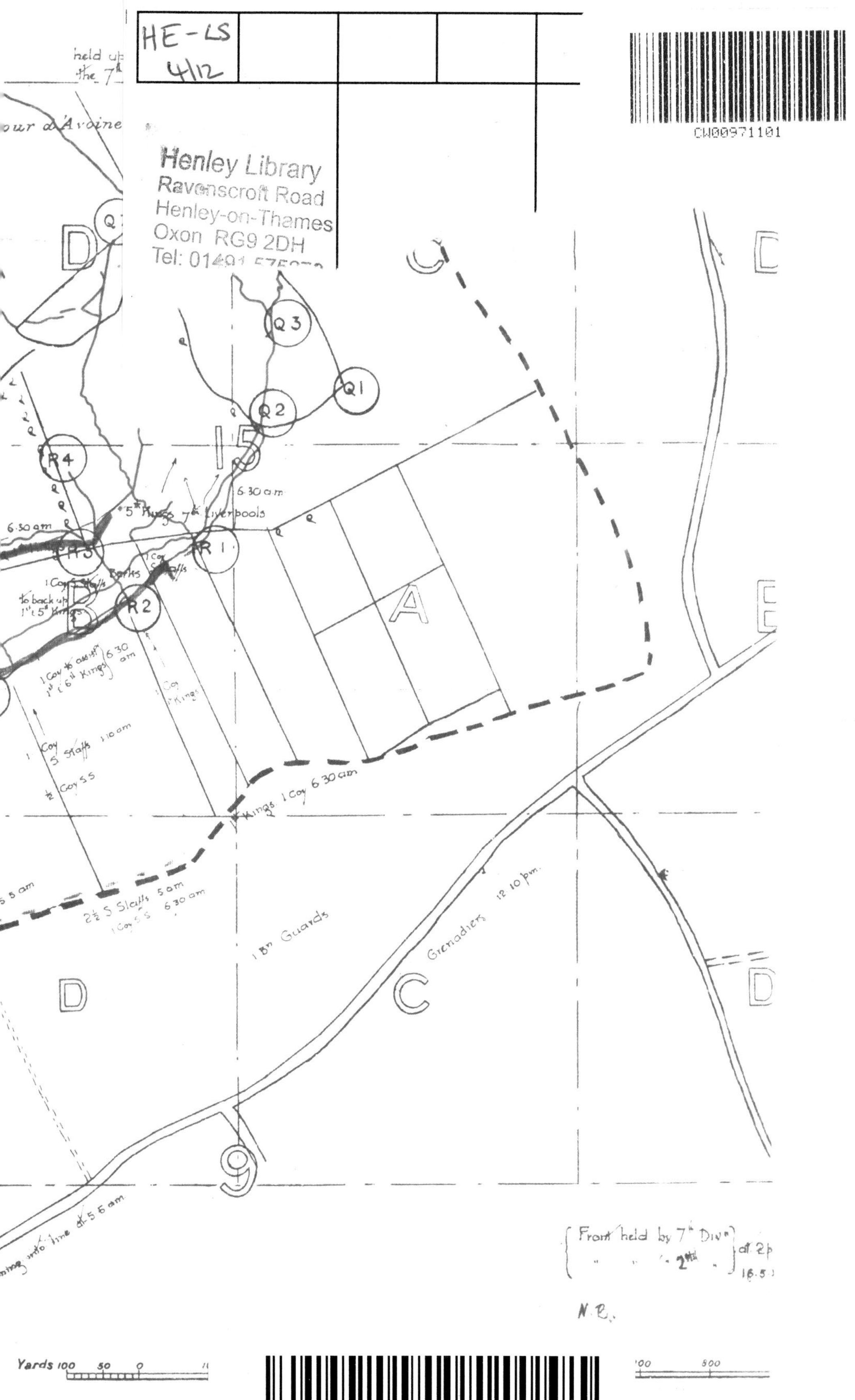

r Diary. [National Archiv

The 52nd Light Infantry in France and Belgium

'It's rather like our Colonel – who, when a huge shell landed within 10 feet of his dug out and shook half of it down said – "Crosse, I think you'd better cover up the butter," then readjusted his specs and went on with his paper'.

[The imperturbable Lieutenant-Colonel Henry Davies to his Adjutant Captain Richard Crosse. Recorded by Lieutenant Geoffrey Titherington in December 1914].

HISTORY of the 43rd and 52nd (Oxfordshire and Buckinghamshire) LIGHT INFANTRY in the GREAT WAR, 1914 – 1918

Volume II

THE 52nd LIGHT INFANTRY IN FRANCE AND BELGIUM

By Simon Harris

ROOKE PUBLISHING
Clenchwarton

ISBN 978-0-9548640-1-9

Published in the UK in 2012 by
Rooke Publishing
Porch Farm
Clenchwarton
King's Lynn
Norfolk PE34 4AG
Tel 01553 766409

Printed and bound by CPI Group (UK) Ltd, Croydon, CR0 4YY

In Memory of Lieutenant-Colonel Richard Banastre Crosse D.S.O. and bar. A great commanding officer and veritable Achilles.

1916-1919.

[Achilles was the hero of Homer's *Iliad*: he was the bravest and swiftest of Greek soldiers.]

Lieutenant-Colonel Robert Fanshawe 1907-1911.

Lieutenant-Colonel Henry Davies 1911-1915.

Lieutenant-Colonel Archibald Eden 1915-1916.

The 52nd Light Infantry defeating the Prussian Guards in Nonne Bosschen Wood on November 11th 1914.
Painting by William Barnes Wollen 1857-1936. [Courtesy of the Royal Green Jackets Museum]

Contents

Maps

Illustrations

[Many of the photographs are around 100 years old and some are of poor quality. They have been retained to give as complete a photographic record as is possible].

Acknowledgements

I am indebted to a large number of individuals and institutions in the preparation of the First World War history of the 52nd Light Infantry.

The Residual Regimental Committee and the Darell-Brown Memorial Fund have supported the book financially and I am very grateful to the members of the two committees for their backing: particularly so in the cases of Lieutenant-Colonel George Elliott, Brigadier Nigel Mogg, General Sir Robert Pascoe K.C.B., M.B.E. and Colonel John Tillett.

In alphabetical order three persons have played an important part in the preparation of the book. My brother, Ralph Harris, has allowed me free access to the 750 letters, documents and artefacts relating to our great-uncle, Captain Ralph Kite, to be found in the Kite archive. In addition, Ralph has been my companion in walking virtually all the 52nd's battlefields on the 'Old Western Front'. He has also commented on the manuscript. Lieutenant-Colonel David Stanley O.B.E., recently retired from the Oxfordshire and Buckinghamshire Light Infantry Archives [Research Section], first pointed out to me that although the history of the 43rd Light Infantry in World War I had been written by Sir Edmond Neville, no companion work on the 52nd Light Infantry had been undertaken. As well as being the primary instigator of this history, he has reviewed my manuscript and maps from the military angle. My friend Professor Hughie Young has spent months of his time correcting and polishing my written work and has been invaluable in checking the maps and their scales. To these three men I owe the greatest debt of gratitude.

Colonel John Tillett and Lieutenant-Colonel George Elliott, both former members of the Oxfordshire and Buckinghamshire Light Infantry [43rd/52nd] and the 52nd Light Infantry, gave me a long tour of the Royal Green Jackets' Museum and have been greatly supportive of my efforts to produce a companion history. John Tillett, of whom it can be said that there is something of the aura of Richard Crosse about him, has given me his memories of former World War I officers, and has also advised me on photographs for the book. Tom Donovan produced Geoffrey Titherington's vivid wartime letters and also Charles Colvill's album with rare photographs of the 52nd Light Infantry's officers from 1917-18. Captain Colin Edgar kindly provided me with a copy of the book he edited, *'The Humf*

Letters 1910-15'. The niece of Humf [Douglas Humfrey], Jane Humfrey, has recalled memories of her family. Christopher Dobson related to me the story of Jack Hardcastle's father having his dead son's evening clothes laid out each night for many years after his boy's demise. The Mayor of Hersin-Coupigny, Jean-Marie Caramiaux, has given me details of his eccentric predecessor who was entertained by the 52nd in his own house.

Mrs Georgina Barclay, the daughter of one of the 52nd Light Infantry's most distinguished soldiers, Guy Blewitt, entertained me to lunch and gave me illuminating memories of her father and his contemporaries. In addition, she allowed me to read the five volumes of her father's war diaries which she has now most generously presented to the Regimental Archives. Richard Booth, son of Philip 'Blig' Booth, and like Georgina Barclay a godchild of Richard Crosse, also helped me with an account of his late father's era. Rosalind Gorton, daughter of Sir Edmond 'Jim' Neville, recalled her father to me in a long telephone conversation. Lieutenant-Colonel Fergus Higgins has given me his recollections of his father, Brigadier-General Charles 'Buggins' Higgins. The late Ben Ruck Keene provided me with interesting information about that most engaging of sportsmen, his kinsman, Lancie Ruck Keene. Geoff Mawer has generously allowed me to quote from his grandfather's letters from the trenches.

I am indebted to Lieutenant-Colonel Graham Parker O.B.E. who with Tony and Teddy Noyes stimulated my interest and increased my knowledge of the First World War over the last 25 years. Indeed it was Graham Parker who first introduced me to Nonne Bosschen Wood. My other brother Timothy and his wife Geli undertook some German translation for me and have visited a number of the 52nd's battlefields. Laurence Morlaàs also did some French translation. Dino Lemonofides, formerly of the Regimental Archives, helped me with some of the officers' Christian names and gave a useful hypothesis for the capture of Private Walter Hancox during the retreat from Mons. Mike Marr, the Assistant Regimental Secretary, Oxford, was most supportive in giving me ready access to Slade Barracks, in order to collect material. Also, he has been very helpful with advice on marketing the book. Major Hugh Babington Smith, Mike Cross and Steve Berridge of the Soldiers of Oxfordshire Trust produced copies of a number of illustrations. Stanley Jenkins provided me with photographs relating to Lionel Dashwood. Vivian Emamooden, Churchwarden of St. Aidan's Anglican Church, Longueville, N.S.W., made great efforts to obtain a photograph of their former Rector, Morris Fielding. The Reverend Mark Abrey of All Saints' Church, Spelsbury, Oxfordshire, has kindly allowed me to publish a photograph of the Harry Dillon memorial window. Willie Townsend's advice concerning medals awarded to the 52nd Light Infantry and his permission to publish photographs of some of them has been much appreciated. Derek Stone has once again produced the excellent maps. Mark Bowler, David Browne, Robin Elliott and Ken Fricker of the printers CPI Antony Rowe have been particularly helpful in the preparation of the manuscript and photographs.

I am grateful to the National Archives for permission to quote at length from the *Battalion, 5th Infantry Brigade and 2nd Division War Diaries.* In addition they have allowed me to reproduce parts of the trench maps of Richebourg l'Avoué and the Redan Ridge. The Imperial War Museum has permitted the publication of extracts from Harry Dillon's important war letters and also several photographs. The Regimental Archives formerly in the Slade Barracks, Oxford have been a great source of material – from journals and manuscripts to rare photographs. Leeds University Library's Special Collections have provided rich material on Sir Edmond Neville in the form of a manuscript and audiotape. John D'Arcy on behalf of the Neville estate has agreed to the publication of extracts from *'The Letters of a Light Infantryman',* and material in the Norfolk Record Office in the form of letters, diaries and photograph albums. The Curator of the Royal Green Jackets Museum, Christine Pullen, has allowed me to use photographs of a number of their pictures and artefacts. These include Wollen's action in Nonne Bosschen Wood and Northcote's portrait of Sir John Moore. The Society for Promoting Christian Knowledge [S.P.C.K.] has kindly agreed to my using their photograph of Bishop Llewellyn Gwynne.

The following institutions have provided me with information: Buckingham Studies, Hampshire Record Office, National Army Museum, Norfolk Record Office, North Yorkshire County Record Office, Oxfordshire Record Office, Royal Archives Windsor, Royal Artillery Museum, Royal Hospital Chelsea, Royal Regiment of Fusiliers, Royal Highland Fusiliers, Staffordshire Regiment, Waterford County Museum and the Worcestershire History Centre.

I have tried to contact all the relevant people whose works I have used in the preparation of this book. If I have omitted any individual or institution, they have my apologies and I will correct matters in any future editions of the book.

Finally, a thank you to my wife, Clare, for putting up with my trips to France following in the footsteps of the 52nd Light Infantry and for allowing me to spend so many years in my study working on this book.

Introduction

The following chapters recount the story of the Second Battalion of the Oxfordshire and Buckinghamshire Light Infantry in the First World War 1914-18. They had a proud record extending as far back as the middle of the eighteenth century. Initially, the Regiment was known as the 52nd Foot until 1803 when Sir John Moore chose them to be the first Light Infantry Regiment, the 52nd Light Infantry. In 1881, the Cardwell reforms led to an amalgamation with the 43rd Light Infantry, the two regiments becoming the 1st [43rd] and 2nd [52nd] Battalions of the Oxfordshire Light Infantry. This was a most unpopular union and the author, following others [see below], has adhered to the older nomenclature. A further reorganization took place in 1908 with the Battalions becoming the 1st and 2nd Battalions of the Oxfordshire and Buckinghamshire Light Infantry.

The 52nd saw service in the Light Brigade under Sir John Moore, and they were with him in early 1809, when he was tragically killed in the final stages of his retreat to Corunna. Later in the Peninsular War, the 52nd would serve with another inspirational leader Robert 'Black Bob' Craufurd until his untimely demise at Ciudad Rodrigo. The 52nd further distinguished themselves at the Battle of Waterloo in 1815, when under the command of Sir John Colborne their musket volleys and charge into the flank of Napoleon's Imperial Guard routed them.

The *History of the 43rd and 52nd Light Infantry in the Great War 1914-1919 Volume 1* by Sir Edmond Neville was published in 1938. This covers solely the 43rd and there was every intention to publish a companion history of the 2nd Battalion or, as they still liked to be known, the 52nd Light Infantry. However, lack of finance and the coming of Hitler's War put a stop to it. Just after the Second World War, Lieutenant-Colonel Richard Crosse wrote that he did not think it would ever be written or published, as interest at that time was mainly in the recent war, and the first one had been forgotten. Crosse was saddened by this turn of events, as he felt in a hundred years time people would be as interested in the exploits of his men in the Great War as he himself was in the Peninsular War of over a century before.

Why write the First World War History of the 52nd now nearly a century after the event? The *Regimental Chronicles* give a detailed account of the war but they are scattered amongst the records of the other battalions of the Regiment and are far from comprehensive. Certainly Richard Crosse felt that a history of his war should be written at least as a record for posterity. The author concurs with this view and has had a personal interest in the project as his great-uncle, Captain Ralph Kite, was mortally wounded fighting with the 52nd in 1916. In retrospect it is a great shame that neither Richard Crosse nor Sir Edmond 'Jim' Neville were able to write their own histories of the 52nd as they had all the facts to hand, and the survivors of the Great War were readily available to them until they gradually died out by the 1960s. The last surviving officer lived until the early 1980s.

As well as the *Regimental Chronicles,* Richard Crosse's articles written from the 1930s-50s have been a rich source of material. Crosse's own book *A Record of H.M. 52nd Light Infantry in 1914* which covers the period of the then Lieutenant-Colonel Henry Davies' command, and Sir Edmond 'Jim' Neville's *The War Letters of a Light Infantryman* are not widely known and have been drawn upon extensively. In addition much fresh information has been gleaned from a study of the *Battalion, 5th Infantry Brigade,* and the *Second Division's War Diaries.* The finding of Richard Crosse's annotated trench map for the abortive attack on Guillemont Station on July 30th 1916 was a seminal discovery in the National Archives, and allows a better understanding of that action than was previously available.

The 52nd in August 1914 was a superbly efficient, elite fighting unit which was still imbued with the training and spirit of their greatest Colonel, Sir John Moore. There is no doubt whatever that the Regiment was first-class in the field, but drill – either manoeuvre or ceremonial – was not its strong point. The officer corps was very much the product of their class and time. Almost exclusively they were drawn from the former pupils of the major Victorian and Edwardian Public Schools. Pre-war, one company was officered by old boys of Winchester, another company by Radley, and a third by Marlborough/Wellington. Eton was also well represented with some 50 Old Etonians serving in the Regiment as a whole during the Great War and, of these, twelve served with 52nd. Private means of at least £200 a year was necessary. Many of the officers had had fathers or other relations who had served in the 52nd before them, some going back as far as the Peninsular War. Relatives in the Church were also well represented amongst the officers of 1914, which may explain the underlying Christian ethics in their outlook on life. Surprisingly, the 52nd had several literary connections with descendants of Samuel Pepys the diarist, Robert Southey the poet, and Thomas Hughes author of '*Tom Brown's Schooldays*', amongst the ranks of their pre-war/wartime officers.

The interests of the pre-war 52nd officer, apart from soldiering, were those of the country gentleman which at heart he was. All could ride capably, and fox-hunting, polo ['snob's hockey'], pig-sticking, and steeple-chasing were popular pursuits. There was a fine cricket side but tennis was looked upon as licensed 'poodle-faking' and golf was played if there was nothing else to do. The 52nd was a regiment of the gentry rather than the aristocracy, although Ashley Ponsonby was a nephew of the third Baron De Mauley and, two wartime officers, Edmond 'Jim' Neville and Philip Whitehead, would become baronets. A few had had university educations at Oxford or Cambridge before training at Sandhurst. Pride in their Regimental history and its traditions were at the very core of their beings. They were truly a band of brothers and there was a spirit of comradeship amongst all ranks. The spirit engendered in their predecessors by Sir John Moore and Robert Craufurd was still very much a living part of the 52nd Light Infantry in 1914. No officer or man of the Regiment would do anything to harm the reputation of the 52nd Light Infantry. The Oxfordshire and Buckinghamshire Light Infantry were one of a small number of Regiments in the First World War not to have executed any of its members.

The 52nd were indeed fortunate in their Commanding Officers in the immediate pre-war period and during the war itself. Robert Fanshawe was the son of a clergyman who was imbued with the traditions and spirit of the Peninsula. He was a kind man, likened to Lord Roberts and led a Spartan life whilst following the path of duty. Fanshawe's successor, Henry Davies, the son of a lieutenant-general whose grandfather and great-uncle had also served in the 52nd, took the Regiment to war in August 1914. Fluent in several oriental languages, Davies was brave, determined, imperturbable, with a high sense of honour and justice. Despite a slightly stiff air, perhaps due to shyness, he was a kind Christian gentleman who was never heard to speak ill of anyone. It was Davies who held the 52nd together during the long retreat from Mons. Archibald Eden was a more demonstrative leader who was renowned for his calmness under fire. In the war he was aged 42-46 years, wounded twice, and seldom out of the line, but the strain never broke him. Eden always put the service before himself.

Perhaps the greatest and certainly the most interesting man in the 52nd during the Great War, was the redoubtable Richard Banastre Crosse who followed Eden in command during the summer of 1916. Crosse started the war as a super-efficient adjutant nicknamed 'Energy' who knew all his men's regimental numbers by heart. As Commanding Officer, Crosse guided by the celestial presence of Sir John Moore, was the very embodiment of the Regiment. Whereas Davies and Eden had at least a core of pre-war officers, Crosse had to train his newly commissioned officers who had volunteered for service, and then later in the war, reluctant conscripted men. In this he was successful and the efficacy of the 52nd in 1917-18 was largely a manifestation of his training capabilities. Crosse looked upon everyone as an individual: men did not serve under him, they served with him. Unmarried, the Regiment became a surrogate family to him. Tall, handsome, Crosse had an engaging personality with a fine sense of humour, but above all else he was a compassionate man. In August 1918, Crosse had to choose an officer to become an instructor safely behind the lines. He selected Harry Dashwood whose three brothers had already been killed in the war. Crosse was without question a very brave man who served throughout the four and a third years of the war in or near the front line. If a Military General Service Medal had been awarded for the Great War, he would have had no less than 28 clasps. The highest number of clasps given in the Peninsular War was fourteen. There was consternation in the Regiment when he was seriously wounded at Triangle Copse in August 1918. In order not to lose the command of his beloved 52nd, Crosse returned to the fray still with a gaping wound in his back, and for a time, had to be lifted into the saddle of his horse. Above all else, Crosse had immense pride in his Regiment, and what Sir John Moore initiated he carried on unswervingly. It is not too much to say that in the Great War Richard Crosse was the Regiment.

During the four and a third years of the Kaiser's War the 52nd would serve on all the major British battlefields from Ypres to the Somme. The Regiment was at the height of its powers in 1914, with its ranks largely made up of pre-war professional soldiers. The advance to Mons and the subsequent retreat was an enormous strain on all concerned and this was followed by the vicious actions at Soupir Farm on the Aisne and then in the environs of Ypres. The slaughter of the German innocents at Langemarck followed by action in the woods south of the Menin Road, did much to stop the German enemy from taking Ypres and the Channel ports. On November 11th 1914, the 52nd fought their most celebrated action of the war in Nonne Bosschen Wood when the Prussian Guards were routed. 1914 found the 52nd at the very height of its powers as a most formidable fighting unit.

In May 1915, the 52nd fought in the first British night action of the war at the Battle of Festubert, where there were heavy casualties amongst the pre-war officers and men. The autumn saw the subsidiary action, at Givenchy, a part of the Battle of Loos. Here the 52nd attacked after the release of chlorine gas which did more damage to themselves than to the enemy. After Givenchy few pre-war officers remained; they were either dead, wounded or promoted to command other units, leaving the 52nd with an inexperienced officer corps. The Regiment was fortunate to miss the debacle of July 1st 1916 on the Somme, although it had the misfortune to be involved with the ill-conceived operation against Guillemont Station on July 30th. At the end of 1916, the 52nd fought bravely during the final Battle of the Somme, on the Ancre.

After one of the coldest winters since records began, the 52nd played a significant part in the Battle of Arleux, in late April 1917, part of the Battles of Arras. Here by protecting the right flank of the Canadians, the Regiment allowed their Dominion comrades to take and hold the vital village of Arleux. In the late autumn, the 52nd were anticipating being thrown into the battles for the

Passchendaele ridge. At the eleventh hour they were switched to the south and took part in the later stages of the Battle of Cambrai 1917. Here their stout defence around Lock 6 allowed a successful British withdrawal to a better defensive line. Thanks to the foresight of Richard Crosse, the 'Commander', as he was known, the 52nd survived the vicissitudes of the March 1918 retreat as a relatively intact unit. In August, the Regiment captured the important village of Sapignies, near Bapaume, and in the early autumn took part in some of the battles for the Hindenburg Line. September/early October saw the 52nd fighting in the Battles of Havrincourt and the Canal du Nord, as the demoralized Germans were pushed back towards their homeland. In mid-October 1918, the Regiment took part in their final battle of the war, the Battle of the Selle. After the Armistice, the 52nd marched proudly into Germany and became part of the army of occupation.

It may be invidious to highlight the achievements of some members of the 52nd above those of others, as their performance in the Great War was essentially that of a team. However, some names shine more brightly than others in the coming pages. Of the pre-war officers the exploits of Harry 'Rabbit' Dillon and Cuthbert 'Bingo' Baines in Nonne Bosschen Wood are rightly looked upon as the highlights of 52nd's most celebrated action of the whole war. It was at least the equal of Sir John Colborne's dispatch of Napoleon's Imperial Guard at Waterloo, and the exploits of John Howard and his men at Pegasus Bridge in 1944.

Other pre-war officers who served the 52nd valiantly were the dour Charles 'Buggins' Higgins, later to command a brigade, and the fastidious George Colvile [formerly of the 43rd] who found time to change his wet socks whilst in no man's land, under fire, at Richebourg l'Avoué in 1915. The gifted Guy Blewitt served his Regiment with great distinction before being seriously wounded at Soupir Farm in 1914. Later he would be awarded the D.S.O. and the M.C. and went on to the staff of a brigade. The much admired Ashley Ponsonby combined courage with coolness and clearness of thought before being shot dead in 1915. Then there was the irrepressible Rupert Brett whose infectious laughter and 'good hunting old cock' did so much to keep up the spirits of the Regiment in the dark days of early 1918. The feisty Reggie Owen tried to sue the Army authorities for the damage to his clothing, which the R.A.M.C cut away to get at his wounds on the Aisne! Sadly Owen's demise in August 1916 put an end to a nascent fine career. Ernest 'Whitters' Whitfeld gave outstanding service first at Richebourg l'Avoué with the annihilation of a machine-gun team, and then later as Adjutant.

Of the officers who joined the 52nd later in the war a number stand out. Jack Hardcastle and Ralph Kite were singled out by Philip Booth in his book *The Oxfordshire and Buckinghamshire Light Infantry.* As Booth had little contact with either man, the views that the former was 'a young man of great promise' and the latter 'another young man of outstanding ability' are likely to have been Richard Crosse's assessments. David Barnes' brilliant front line leadership at Arleux led to a well deserved D.S.O., even if Richard Crosse had to use irregular means to obtain it. Tom 'Twitt' Tyrwhitt-Drake and the gentle William Giles were awarded M.C.s and bars, two in the former case, and stand out prominently. William 'Billy' Barnard, Dick 'Puff Ball' Warren, Jim Neville, and Charles Colvill also gave outstanding service to the 52nd in the final years of the war. In 1940, Colvill would become a member of a very select band who won gallantry awards in both World Wars.

Almost certainly the two most intelligent officers in the Regiment during the war were Leslie Johnston and Nick Hill. Pre-war Johnston was a Fellow and Senior Dean of Arts at Magdalen College Oxford. He was a brilliant theologian, author of *Some Alternatives to Jesus Christ,* and tutor to the future Edward VIII. Johnston was wounded near the enemy's wire in May 1916, and it is likely that he was summarily executed by the Germans. Nick Hill was awarded scholarships to both Winchester and New College, Oxford. Although the war precluded him from going up to Oxford, Hill became an exemplary soldier with an M.C. and possessed great charm and wit. He had the great misfortune to be killed by a chance shell in early 1917. Both Johnston and Hill were men their country could ill-afford to lose.

A number of the other ranks stand out from the roll of the 52nd. George Field began the war as a company serjeant-major, was commissioned, won the M.C. and bar, and as a major commanded the 52nd after Richard Crosse was wounded at Triangle Copse in 1918. Frederick 'Old Alf' Barnes, the Quartermaster of the 52nd with Richard Crosse was at the very heart of the Regiment. Somehow in the March Retreat of 1918, he contrived to feed the 52nd whilst some other regiments starved. The executioner-in-chief in the culvert of the Lekkerbotenbeek, the former tram-driver, Private Henry Hastings, and that bible-carrying Serjeant, Tom Hudson, in Nonne Bosschen Wood, are both worthy of recognition. Serjeant Ernest Constable was put forward for the V.C. after his exploits at Lock 6, on the Canal du Nord, in 1917. Second only to Constable's bravery were the actions of the unassuming Serjeant Cecil Bailey at the Battle of the Ancre. Bailey was the first man into Munich Trench and, despite being injured himself, held a trench block during the retiral so that the wounded could be evacuated. Serjeant Henry 'Nicky' Lay was one of the most highly decorated members of the 52nd with the D.C.M., M.M. and bar. He was described as 'the very best of best non commissioned officers'.

With the possible exception of George Field, perhaps the greatest non-commissioned officer in the 52nd, at the time of the Great War, was Fred Clare, who was made a serjeant in August 1914, and ended the war as the Regimental Serjeant-Major with the D.C.M. Post-war, he was commissioned and retired as a lieutenant-colonel. Standing a little over six feet in height, he was a fine figure of a man, and had great strength of character and powers of organization. Clare has been likened to that pillar of the Regiment in the Peninsular War, the legendary John Winterbottom. There can be no higher praise.

Other non-fighting men have left their mark on the 1914-18 52nd Light Infantry. Not least among this group was Llewellyn Gwynne, Bishop of Khartoum, who started the war as a humble Fourth Class Chaplain at the 5th Infantry Brigade. In the late summer of 1915, no less a man than Earl Kitchener promoted him to be the Deputy Chaplain General, the senior clergyman on the Western Front. Despite his exalted position, Gwynne was frequently to be found visiting, as he called them, 'the 52nd Foot'. Perhaps Gwynne's greatest gift was his easy familiarity and identification with the ordinary soldier. Well into his nineties he was regularly attending the Regimental reunions. The other clergyman who was looked upon 'as a 52nd man apart from his cloth' was the Reverend Edward Montmorency Guilford known as 'Monty' who was to be awarded the M.C. He deemed it an honour to serve with Richard Crosse, and was with the Regiment from September 1916 until April 1919 apart from a short break at the 2nd Division. During the Battle of Arleux, 'Monty' was working in the Regimental Aid Post close to Crosse's headquarters, and had to be reminded of his ecclesiastical position so keen was he to join in the fighting!

The 52nd's doctors came and went with great regularity during the war. Indeed in 1917-18, there was a grave shortage of medical staff and Americans had to be drafted in to fill the gap. One doctor who served the 52nd in an exemplary fashion was Ernest Scott who was with them in 1915-16. 'Doctor Scott' endeared himself to all ranks and, in 1915, he had the difficult task of dealing with the large number of casualties at Richebourg l'Avoué and Givenchy where he was wounded during the course of his duties. Later in the war Scott won the D.S.O.

Before leaving the personnel of the 52nd in the Great War, mention must be made of the 'characters' in the Regiment. John Murray of the Pioneer Platoon was certainly one of these: whether it was cut-out figures of German soldiers to pop up in front of the trenches to confuse the enemy, or illicit materials to build a church, he came up trumps leaving poor Richard Crosse agonizing over the morality of the transaction. Laurence Goodwyn, a solicitor in private life, was a fine amateur actor who regularly entertained the Regiment. Cyril 'Shiny' Horley nicknamed after the Bruce Bairnsfather character, 'Shinio' the juggler, was not only a fine soldier but also an expert in practical jokes. Whether it was setting fire to the bottom of *The Times* newspaper while it was being read, or arranging for the cap of a Very cartridge to be thrown into the fire-place behind a garrulous doctor, 'Shiny' was your man.

No member of the 52nd was to be awarded the V.C. in the Great War, although Serjeant Ernest Constable, as was recorded earlier, was recommended for one. Early in the war D.S.O.s were awarded to Richard Crosse, Cuthbert Baines, Francis Pepys, Hugh Pendavis, Vere Spencer, and Harry Dillon. After the institution of the M.C. in late 1914, it became rare for company officers to be awarded the D.S.O. which appeared to be reserved for battalion commanders and those on the staff of brigades and above. For example, Jasper 'Tiger' Wyld, who was wounded with the 52nd at Richebourg l'Avoué, joined the staff and was awarded the M.C. as a staff captain in 1917 and the D.S.O. as a brigade-major in 1918. The staff appropriated most of the foreign decorations handed out by Allied Governments. Not that they were always well-received. Unsurprisingly, Guy Blewitt, as a brigade-major, 'was not particularly flattered' to be presented with the 5th Class Order of Danilo of Montenegro by his corps commander! Only the occasional French or Belgian Croix de Guerre reached battalions of infantry or field gunners. Fine officer that Jasper Wyld undoubtedly was, it is not surprising that there was so much resentment at company level. Only David Barnes of the company officers would receive the D.S.O. in the final years of the war, and considerable pressure and bluff was required for even that.

The officers of the 52nd had a low opinion of staff officers. 'Shits in shatoos' or 'velvet bottoms' were some of the kinder comments. Jim Neville wrote: 'to us in the 52nd all who were bedizened with red tabs and hatbands were objects of scorn, ridicule and contempt'. 'I am on the Staff' – Answer 'you make me laugh'. The gilded Staff travelled by a special train at a civilized time from Victoria Station, unlike the ordinary troops. As Jim Neville succinctly put it 'after all they were the butchers and cattle had no choices'. During his time in the trenches he only saw his Brigadier-General G.M. 'Humpty Dumpty' Bullen-Smith on two occasions. The first time Neville successfully stimulated the Germans into firing mortar bombs on to the position of the Brigadier-General and, the second time, he was collapsed on a tree stump during the March 1918 retreat. Perhaps the 52nd were unfortunate to serve under such a man.

The 52nd of the Great War era had a number of idiosyncrasies. Although there was a regular interchange of officers between the 43rd and 52nd Light Infantries, rivalries going back into the nineteenth century still existed. No doubt they recalled the tale of the 52nd officer who would strop his razor 52 times before shaving. After the Cardwell reorganization of 1881, when he got to the 43rd strop he would turn his head and spit! The officers' Sam Browne belts had double shoulder-straps unlike those of most other regiments. Boots had plain toe-caps.

The rank of sergeant was always spelt with a j – thus serjeant. Abbreviations were frowned upon and it would be Lieutenant-Colonel rather than Lt.-Col; Richard Crosse was a stickler for this. It was never mufti but always civilian clothes.

Two unsavoury episodes during the war have not been glossed over. The allegation that Captain Laurence 'Pullthrough' Fullbrook-Leggatt falsified his report giving details of his company's retirement from Lock 6 in 1917, and the death of the inexperienced Joseph Sears on a daylight patrol in August 1918 have been reluctantly included. The author was more shocked than virtually anything he has read about the Great War by the fact that the British authorities deducted 12/6d from the pay of the nineteen-year-old Second-Lieutenant Edward Barclay for the blanket he was buried in. So little was this only son's life worth to his King and Country.

Finally, the author has had a comprehensive list of maps drawn, mainly based on original trench maps so that all the 52nd's battles can be followed. A number of trench map references have been added to the text so that those wishing to follow the precise movements of the 52nd can do so. The National Archives have produced an excellent CD, *The Western Front 1914-18,* which illustrates more than 700 trench maps, scale 1 in 10,000, and is available from the Naval and Military Press Ltd. Finally, the vast majority of times have been recorded using the twelve hour clock and the terms a.m. and p.m. In late 1918, the British army switched to the 24 hour clock. However, with the exception of the timings of the Armistice, times have been altered to the twelve hour clock for the sake of consistency.

Read on to discover the exploits of the young men of a previous generation who were so proud to serve with the 52nd Light Infantry and to whose sacrifice we owe so much. As they march on into history we shall not see their like again.

Chapter I

The Outbreak of War, Mobilization, and the Advance to and Battle of Mons.

August 4th - August 24th 1914

[Maps: page 13, 16.]

The assassination of Archduke Franz Ferdinand of Austria and his wife, Sophie, in Sarajevo on June 28th 1914 triggered the onset of World War I. During the afternoon of August 4th, the British Ambassador in Berlin was instructed to seek assurances concerning Germany's respect of Belgium's neutrality. When these were summarily rejected the British Government declared that the two countries were at war from midnight[1] on August 4th 1914. The order to mobilize went out at 4 p.m. on the 4th. In fact the timing was inauspicious as the day before was a bank holiday Monday, and many Territorial units were in the process of travelling to their summer camps. The Government decided on a short delay, until the 9th, before the British Expeditionary Force should embark for France. The command of the B.E.F. was given to Sir John French an experienced cavalry officer with a legendary amorous life. French was a brave, dedicated officer, with unsurpassed powers of leadership; however events would show that he was out of his depth commanding a large army in 1914-5.

The first German troops invaded Belgium on August 4th and started to put into effect the Schlieffen Plan[2]. This involved advancing the bulk of the German forces through neutral Belgium while leaving screening forces on their own frontier with France, and a further small force on their border to the east with Russia. Once through Belgium the German armies would swing like a ball on a chain, to the left of the French line, to the west of Paris, masking the capital and trapping the French against their own line of fortresses on their border with Germany and the Swiss frontier.

The Second Battalion of the Oxfordshire and Buckinghamshire Light Infantry [52nd Light Infantry] had been stationed at Albuhera barracks, Aldershot since September 29th 1911. They were part of the 5th Infantry Brigade of the 2nd Division and would remain so for the duration of the war. The division was the key unit of the war as it was self-sufficient in all arms, and rotated through a succession of corps and army commands, both of which were headquarters formations only. Commanding the 5th Brigade was Brigadier-General Richard 'Dicky' Haking, who would gain the unenviable reputation of being something of

---

[1] 11 p.m. Greenwich mean time.

[2] The original plan had been drawn up by Graf Alfred von Schlieffen in 1905.

a 'thruster' and 'butcher' later in the war. Technically at mobilization Major-General Archibald 'Old Archie' Murray was in command of the 2nd Division although, on August 5th, he was replaced by the heavily built Major-General Charles Monro[3]. Murray was an intelligent and able officer whose excitability and lack of physical strength were a handicap in a senior commander. He became the Chief of the General Staff of the British Expeditionary Force in France. Monro was very much a soldier's general and would eventually command firstly the Third Army, and then the First Army, later in the war. His father was Scottish and his mother Irish and it was said of him that he was Scottish on duty and Irish off duty. Monro was an excellent speaker, fluent in French, and a superb diplomat. Sadly, most unjustly, he is remembered for Winston Churchill's withering comment when he recommended the withdrawal from the Gallipoli peninsula – 'he came, he saw, he capitulated'[4].

At the outbreak of war the other battalions in the 5th Brigade were the 2nd Battalion of the Worcestershire Regiment [36th Foot], the 2nd Battalion of the Highland Light Infantry [74th Highlanders] and the 2nd Battalion of the Connaught Rangers [94th Foot]. In 1914 the old system of eight companies [A-H] to a battalion was changed to four [A-D]. Initially each battalion was supposed to consist of 30 officers and 977 other ranks.

The 52nd had been commanded by Lieutenant-Colonel Henry Rodolf Davies for nearly three years. He had replaced the then Lieutenant-Colonel Robert Fanshawe in September 1911. The 48-year-old Davies was an outstanding commanding officer by any standard. He was physically and morally brave, imperturbable come what may, with a deep sense of duty and discipline, and universally kind to all he came into contact with. He was never heard to speak an ill word of anyone. The 52nd were indeed fortunate to have such a man to take them to war. Henry Davies' predecessor, Robert Fanshawe, was another great Light Infantryman whose training during 1907-11, his years of command, had done so much to prepare the 52nd for the rigours of war. Fanshawe and Davies would become the two 52nd generals of World War 1.

Until July 31st 1914 the 52nd led the normal life of a busy member of the Aldershot garrison. The previous week, winter leave arrangements were made for all the companies and a training programme was laid down until the early autumn.

[3] Harshly Sir Douglas Haig thought that Monro had become corpulent serving pre-war with the Territorials. Richard Crosse, Adjutant and then Commanding Officer of the 52nd, described Monro as an old-fashioned 'soldiers' general' and much beloved by the troops.

[4] At 5 a.m. on October 22nd 1915, Monro left London by train. Winston Churchill was on the platform at this early hour and tossed a bundle of papers through the window as the train departed. His final words were 'remember that a withdrawal from Gallipoli would be as great a disaster as Corunna'. History has shown that Monro was right and Churchill wrong.

The last few days of peace were not wasted as instructions were given out on various matters. Provision was given for carrying officers' greatcoats, rubbing feet with methylated spirit, carriage of a plate, mug, jersey, in the pack and hair cutting so beloved of all armies.

On July 27th a test mobilization of the 2nd Division[5] was carried out and on the evening of the 29th Major-General Archibald Murray inspected the mobilized 2nd Division. The following morning the 52nd, as part of the 2nd Division, marched to near Frensham and bivouacked there. The first real sign that war was in the air occurred on the 31st when some of the officers' horses that were loaned to them by the army were called in for duty. That same day, a Friday, the Divisional exercise ended and the 52nd returned to their barracks.

The next morning, Saturday August 1st, there was consternation in the ranks as the much anticipated Bank Holiday Monday leave was cancelled. This was the first of many privations suffered by the troops that could be laid at the Kaiser's door. The Sunday church parade took place as normal but, most unusually for the Sabbath, regimental orders were published postponing future field operations. Suspense and an air of mystery enveloped Aldershot for the day.

Captain Harry Dillon of the 52nd recorded his views on the situation that Sunday in a letter to an uncle[6]. It is clear that the officers were expecting to mobilize at any minute.

> This war has come so suddenly one hardly realises it – I expect they will get us, the two Aldershot divisions across within a few days as the effect of the announcement that British troops have landed will be very encouraging to France. I want to ask you could you put my kit away for me, it only consists of about 6 boxes….. I think this war will be fearful still it will clear the atmosphere for many years to come and the situation has been impossible for so long. I would strongly advise you to lay in a lot of provisions now as everything will be famine prices in no time and there will be crowds of starving people about. Personally I am so thankful that I shall be one of the first to go as if the war goes on for long it will be fearful at home. We have not yet actually started mobilizing but I expect we shall tomorrow.

---

[5] The personnel and animals of the 1st Division represented the reservists who would report for duty on definitive mobilization.

[6] Letter written on August 2nd 1914.

On Bank Holiday Monday, the 3rd, Albuhera barracks was in a state of tension, which was relieved to a degree by an order in the early afternoon to carry out a medical inspection immediately. All officers and men had to be passed medically fit for active service abroad. Not only did it give the men something to do but it also allowed a quicker mobilization proper. The next day, the 52nd paraded at 8.20 a.m., the Adjutant, Lieutenant Richard Crosse, noting in his diary, 'we are merely waiting for the order to mobilise'. It was with a quiet sense of relief that at 6 p.m. the official order to mobilize arrived. In fact two keen members of the 52nd reported for duty before mobilization had been ordered. They were Privates E. Pearce and E. Crompton who had special duties.

August 5th became the first day of mobilization and the regimental Colours[7], the symbols of their history and loyalty, were taken to the Cowley Depot for safe keeping by Second-Lieutenants Francis Pepys, Aubrey Barrington-Kennett, and F.W.C. 'Chips' Chippindale. Two of these three fine young men would be dead before the autumn was out. On this day the strength of the battalion stood at 22 officers, 486 men and 10 horses. To complete mobilization a further 9 officers, 590 men and 48 horses were required. Captain Edward Kirkpatrick was appointed to command a detail of 116 men not proceeding on service. They were mainly underage or unfit for a variety of reasons. Lieutenant Gladwyn Turbutt and Second-Lieutenant Hugh Pendavis were to be left behind to assist Kirkpatrick.

A number of officers arrived on August 5th. A former 43rd officer, [1st Battalion Oxfordshire and Buckinghamshire Light Infantry], Captain Guy Blewitt resigned his staff appointment[8] to join the 52nd on active service. Another former 43rd officer who joined that day was Captain Stephen Hammick. In addition, Lieutenant R.H.G. Tatton and Second-Lieutenant G.T. Button from the Special Reserve also joined. A party of 134 reservists from Oxford arrived at North Camp Station where they were greeted by buglers and were then played into barracks.

Harry Dillon wrote again to his uncle on the first day of mobilization.

> I really think the Germans must have gone mad, anyhow the sooner we get across and to work the better. I think we can keep them going on the French frontier until the Russians come along, in fact it is hoped that with France and Belgium we may do a good deal more. – Everything is being kept dead secret this time I am glad to say and so

---

[7] Richard Crosse insisted that the Colours should have a capital letter.

[8] He was acting as A.D.C. to his father Major-General W.E. Blewitt G.O.C. South Coast Defences at Portsmouth.

> everything is pure speculation. Our mobilization is going off like clockwork so far and if they want they can shift some 200,000 troops by midday Saturday. – I expect a good deal will depend on what the Navy do in the next 24 hours and what sort of show Belgium will put up.

Between August 6th, the second day of mobilization, and August 8th, the fourth day of mobilization, 599 reservists returned to the Colours. Further officers joined the 52nd. They were Second-Lieutenants C.F.R. Hanbury-Williams, John Boardman and Charles Fowke. The mature reservists impressed the current, youthful men of the 52nd when they marched into Albuhera barracks. Company training began at once and arrangements were made to bring the reservists up to speed with a course of musketry. Each man was required to fire ten rounds on the range. On the 7th, three officers, Captain Stephen Hammick, Lieutenant R.H.G. Tatton and Second-Lieutenant Francis 'Jimmie' Riddle, were ordered back to the depot at Cowley to help with training. Ninety nine men were to be left behind to become the first reinforcements when needed. A reserve machine-gun section was selected and all drafts for India and the Colonies were cancelled.

Saturday August 8th was a wet day but by the end of it, with the exception of four officers still to join, mobilization was complete. Two mobilization staff appointments upset the arrangements of the 52nd. Captain Geoffrey 'Mulligan' Sullivan became Assistant Provost Marshal at the 2nd Division headquarters and Lieutenant W.E.C. Terry became staff captain of the 5th Brigade. Captain Harry Dillon took over command of A Company and Lieutenant John Southey became Machine-Gun Officer. Each company commander was given £5 by Henry Davies to spend on his men. Harry Dillon spent it 'on nailing reservists' boots[9], buying dubbin to take out, also cotton wool, lint, boracic powder and tincture of iodine for sore feet, clippers for hair. – String for bivies'. Dillon also recorded that 'they have shot two Germans here this morning, trying to poison the water. One of the brutes cut my hair about a month ago'. Next day, Sunday the 9th, church parades were held in the normal way except service dress was worn. The day passed peacefully with many officers taking the opportunity to pack their private effects. The presence of so many reservists made Albuhera barracks crowded.

Training continued on Monday August 10th with a route march. Captain Evelyn Villiers, aged 39 years, of the 1st Royal Sussex joined and as an

[9] Each soldier in the B.E.F. was supposed to have two pairs of boots, but in most cases one pair was retained for the formation of new units. Later this was to have serious consequences during the long retreat from Mons when boots started to wear out.

experienced officer with a D.S.O. [Distinguished Service Order][10] took over Harry Dillon's two-day command of A Company. During this period Lieutenant George Tolson, who was on leave from the 43rd, reported for duty. A number of N.C.O.s [Non-Commissioned Officers] were promoted to bring the 52nd up to war strength. They included Corporal Fred Clare to be serjeant and Lance-Corporal C.T. Moody to be corporal[11]. Clare was to become one of the outstanding soldiers in the history of the 52nd. He has been likened to the legendary John Winterbottom of the Peninsular War and Waterloo. That evening the bandmaster, boys and unfit men left Aldershot by train for Cambridge barracks, Portsmouth where the reserve 3rd Battalion had relocated on the 8th.

King George V and Queen Mary made an informal inspection of the regiment on Tuesday, August 11th[12]. In effect it was an opportunity to say goodbye to the 52nd before they went overseas. George V had written a moving message for his army as they went off to war[13].

> You are leaving home to fight for the safety and honour of my Empire.
>
> Belgium, whose country we are pledged to defend, has been attacked and France is about to be invaded by the same powerful foe.
>
> I have implicit confidence in you my soldiers. Duty is your watchword, and I know your duty will be nobly done.
>
> I shall follow your every movement with deepest interest and mark with eager satisfaction your daily progress; indeed your welfare will never be absent from my thoughts.
>
> I pray God to bless you and guard you and bring you back victorious.

Having received orders on the 12th, Thursday August 13th saw the 52nd depart from Aldershot for France. A and B Companies paraded at 10.50 a.m. and C and D, under Major Archibald Eden, at 12.30 p.m., but no inkling of their destination was given to them. The 52nd entrained at the Government siding,

---

[10] D.S.O. for his service in the South African War. London Gazette, September 27th 1901. Villiers' own battalion spent the whole of the war on the North-West Frontier much to their disgust. He commanded the 3rd Battalion of the Royal Sussex Regiment in 1919.

[11] Clare and Moody would eventually be commissioned as quartermasters in 1924 and 1928 respectively.

[12] The *Regimental Chronicles* and Harry Dillon's diary give the date as the 12th. Richard Crosse, the Royal Archives, Windsor and a newspaper report correctly give the date of their Majesties' visit as August 11th.

[13] Written on August 9th 1914.

Aldershot station, in two trains at 12.38 p.m. and 2.02 p.m., bound for the docks at Southampton. The port was packed with troops all in transit, and loaded ships were constantly putting to sea and then steering for the French coast. The men of the 52nd had tea in the harbour sheds before embarking on their ship at 8 p.m. that evening. Earlier in the day meat had been cooked and this plus the remains of the bread ration were carried by each man. Preserved meat and biscuit were also taken on the person for the next two days.

The ship, the *S.S. Lake Michigan*, belonged to the Canadian Pacific Railway Company and usually carried emigrants and cattle. As well as the 52nd, the ship carried the 2nd H.L.I., 2nd Worcestershire, some Argyll and Sutherland Highlanders, Royal Engineers and the chief baker of the Expeditionary Force. As they progressed down Southampton Water there was great cheering from other ships, and in response the pipers of the 2nd H.L.I. gathered aft. As darkness came, the whole ship's company joined in a rendering of '*On the Bonnie, Bonnie Banks o' Loch Lomond'*. The men were packed tightly together on the upper deck without shelter and many of them had room to sit but were unable to lie down. Even the ship's boats were full. The officers were a little better off on the small bridge deck. Henry Davies slept in his greatcoat and Burberry lying on the deck and had a fairly good night. Most tightly packed in of all were the horses with their saddlery and harnesses on. The one advantage was that with space being so limited they could not fall and hurt themselves. Fortunately the weather was kind and the sea calm, so that the crossing was a smooth one without anyone suffering from sea sickness which, in such a confined space, would have been difficult to deal with.

Probably the man who had the most comfortable voyage was Harry Dillon, who managed a whiskey and soda and a bunk to sleep in! In a diary entry for the day he recorded his experiences.

> At about 8 p.m. we weighed anchor. The whole harbour was searched in every direction with search lights, and it was rather a wonderful sight when our crowded decks were lit up to see the mass of men crowded together. I thought it was now time to look after No. 1 as I foresaw it would be very cold later, 2/6 and a few kind words to an intelligent steward procured me a whiskey and soda and a bunk. This was a great piece of luck and I shortly afterwards dossed down. – At about 11 p.m. there was a great deal of noise and all the lamps were put out. Remained on deck about an hour and

then told Tylden-Pattenson[14] I had found a place to sleep. We had some difficulty getting down, over the men, but did so and got to sleep.

Towards 5 a.m., on the 14th, most of the 52nd were woken by the cold and the men ate their breakfasts soon afterwards. There was plenty of hot water available and the piping hot tea soon warmed them up. The officers were better off in that they were able to shave in the cabins of the ship. Beachy Head was passed at 8 a.m. and Eastbourne at 9.30 a.m. as the ship crept at a snail's pace for their destination, Boulogne. Harry Dillon espied '8 warships presumably British on our starboard and later two to port'. There was somewhat of a queue of ships at Boulogne waiting to disembark the Expeditionary Force. At 2.30 p.m., the 52nd began to disembark, and started the two-mile uphill march over the cobbled streets to a rest camp at No. 3 Base. Bell tents had already been pitched here in a grass field close to the Colonne de la Grande Armée[15]. Despite the fact that this was the fourth day of troop arrivals in Boulogne, the 52nd received a rapturous welcome from the local population. There was much begging of buttons and ribbons. The town of Boulogne is an ancient one with its citadel situated on a lofty hill.

One private soldier missed the hot and sweaty march to the camp. He was the groom to the second-in-command major[16] and had insisted in travelling with the horses whilst on board ship. The unfortunate man had succumbed to the high temperature and it is said an unfamiliar abstinence from alcohol! Richard Crosse, the Adjutant, putting his schoolboy French to good use persuaded two nuns from a local hospital to take charge of the ailing man. To the irritation of the men of the 52nd, as they struggled up the steepest part of the climb to their camp, an ancient taxi cab swept past them. In the back seat comfortably ensconced between the two nuns was their sick comrade. A string of ribald remarks poured forth from the ranks of the 52nd to the discomfort of the unfortunate groom. He would return to the Regiment the following month fully recovered.

---

[14] Second-Lieutenant Arthur Tylden-Pattenson.

[15] Memorial to the army that was intended to invade England in 1804.

[16] The post was vacant as Major Lancie Ruck Keene D.S.O. was at home medically unfit. He was a great loss to the 52nd. A born raconteur and mimic. His contemporary Rupert Brett wrote: 'I forget how many horses he claimed to have ridden in his life; he was a rather better than average shot, an enthusiastic fisherman and in his earlier days fond of cricket. He had lived most of his life in South Oxfordshire, was usually accompanied by a pack of dogs, and was wont to take orderly room at the Depot on hunting mornings in a great-coat that barely concealed the pink colour of the garment underneath'. It is likely that he would have commanded the 52nd in February 1915, when Henry Davies was promoted, if he had been fit enough.

The 52nd were lucky that their camp was pitched on grass, as some of the other battalions had their tents in a stubble field which was much less comfortable to sleep on. Two French interpreters, Emil Sartorius and René Flament were taken on to the strength of the regiment. Money was changed at a rate of 25 francs to the pound sterling. The restriction on smoking under arms or on fatigues was quietly dropped to the great pleasure of many of the men. The only complaint that the men had about their rations was the lack of milk, fresh or tinned. Surprisingly this did not feature as part of field service ration. However, the next day the 52nd were assured of fresh meat, bread and cheese. In the evening of August 14th, Field-Marshal Sir John French, Commander-in-Chief of the British Expeditionary Force, who had crossed to France that afternoon, visited the camp. French noted 'officers and men looked fit and well, and were full of enthusiasm and cheer'. He continued 'as I walked around the camps and bivouacs, I could not think of the many fine fellows around me who had said goodbye to Old England for ever'. After French's visit the men of the 52nd, who were all exhausted by the journey, were soon fast asleep in their bell tents. Captain Guy Blewitt recorded in his diary: 'the baggage didn't arrive till 11.30 p.m. and we were very glad to get it and turn in as we had had little sleep on board the night before'.

The following day, Saturday the 15th, was treated by the 52nd as a rest day and the men were allowed to sleep in until 'rouse' at 7 a.m. Various inspections were carried out and George V's and Earl Kitchener's messages were read out to the Regiment. As well as calling on the men to do their duty for king and country, Kitchener put them on their guard against 'excesses'. 'In this new experience you may find temptations in wine and women. You must entirely resist both temptations, and while treating all women with perfect courtesy, you should avoid all intimacy'[17]. Despite Kitchener's strictures, a popular move that day was Henry Davies getting two issues of beer from a local café.

Harry Dillon has left an account of the day in his diary.

> Finished various jobs in camp by 12.30……. Walked about the town for a bit. Nothing to be seen except old men, boys and women, most of the latter in black. Went to see the Cathedral of Notre Dame which was packed. The whole land is in mourning. 5 p.m. returned to camp which was much more cheerful. The men are making great

[17] Later in the war brothels would become available. Those for officers were marked by a blue lamp and for other ranks with a red one. The R.A.M.C. inspected prostitutes to reduce the incidence of venereal disease. An official brothel in Rouen was visited by 171,000 men in its first year. Pressure from home led to its closure.

> friends everywhere, carrying the children about in their arms, and nearly every French girl seems to have a badge or souvenir of some sort. The supply of which I see will very soon be finished. All these friendships quite "comme il faut" which is good. Tomorrow we leave for concentration camp.

On Sunday 16th, the 52nd left camp at 8 a.m. and marched down the hill into Boulogne. Entrainment began at 9 a.m. and, although four hours had been allowed for it, the 52nd were safely aboard by 10.30 a.m. Eventually the train set off at the original time of 1 p.m. and the journey was to last almost twelve hours. Their route took them through Amiens, Albert, Arras, Douai, Cambrai and then via a branch line to Caudry, Busigny and finally to their destination, Wassigny. Long halts were made at Amiens and Arras where souvenir hunters invaded their carriages seeking cap badges and insignia. One young officer was so alarmed by this that he managed to rescue his platoon with a pack of playing cards with the regimental crest on their backs which delighted the local inhabitants.

Henry Davies described the day.

> Our journey was a sort of triumphal progress. At every station, bridge, and level crossing there were cheering crowds, and wherever we stopped the whole population appeared to be there, offering us bouquets, chocolate, bread, fruit, sweets, scent, wine, beer, cigarettes, newspapers, and every sort of thing. I was presented with several bouquets at different stations, with a short speech from someone – usually in English. At Arras there was an enormous crowd. Extraordinary enthusiasm everywhere, shouting, cheering, and hand-shaking. Sentries all along the line waved their caps, some of them doing their bayonet exercise and sticking imaginary Germans.
>
> Such scenes in France between Englishmen and Frenchmen can certainly never have been witnessed before. The whole thing was most exciting and amusing. Our men enjoyed it immensely, and entered into the enthusiasm of the French most thoroughly. Nearly every man was wearing a tricolor ribbon in his jacket or was waving a tricolor flag.

It was close on midnight when the 52nd finally reached the large village of Wassigny, which had become the detraining point for the 2nd Division who were to concentrate in the vicinity. Wassigny, where the 2nd Division Headquarters was established, lies about eight miles north of Guise and about the same distance south of Le Cateau. On detraining the 52nd bivouacked in a grass field close to the station. Here on the sodden grass they got a few hours sleep in their greatcoats before being awakened by the cold. Today the station at Wassigny has long been closed and is an overgrown wilderness[18]. However, the field next to the former station, where the 52nd lay down on the night of August 16th/17th can still be seen.

Breakfast was taken at 7 a.m. and the men were pleased with their hot tea as they had been unable to cook since breakfast the previous day. Captain Guy Blewitt and Second-Lieutenant Pierce Newton-King, a fine linguist, were sent ahead on bicycles to the neighbouring village of Mennevret to find billets for the 52nd. The remainder of the 5th Brigade was placed in the surrounding villages. Mennevret was a comfortable three and a half miles march away to the south-west. Blewitt had secured good billets for the 52nd with the men able to stay together in barns. There was plenty of hay and straw to lie comfortably on, but great care had to be taken with matches. Guy Blewitt recorded: ‘the farm at which D Coy billeted was in charge of a poor woman whose husband and her four brothers were at the front and she had only been married four months’.

The Commanding Officer, Henry Davies, and the Adjutant, Richard Crosse, were in a small inn whose large outer room was used as the officers' mess. According to Guy Blewitt the old man who owned the pub sometimes used to ‘go off’ with a patriotic harangue at meals ‘courage mes braves’ etc. There were warnings of these outbursts such as a laurel branch placed before the Colonel's place at dinner! Besides their rations the 52nd were able to buy eggs, vegetables, milk, butter, wine and beer. The thoughtful Davies made arrangements for the supply of beer on a twice daily basis. The British soldiers were struck by the fact that there were no young men in the towns and villages as they were all now serving in the French army.

Harry Dillon reflected on the day in his own characteristic manner.

> Slept remainder of night in a field in our great coats and marched off into billets 3½ miles at (Mennevret). A. Coy is billeted in a farm, the men in two barns which are clean and they have lots of straw. Most of the officers in other Coys are in barns but we have been lucky and have got two rooms in the farm house. – Our hostess Mme. --- is a dear old lady, she has a son at the front and has done all she can to make everybody comfortable. – Crosse and the Col. went round the billets each morning bearing a large bouquet. – Fancy if they had done this at Aldershot a few days ago.

---

[18] By 2005 a timber merchant had taken over some of the station buildings.

The 52nd remained at Mennevret over the period August 17th-20th and their time was taken up with recovering from the journey and in training. The weather was very hot and some of the reservists fell out of a ten-mile route march suffering from heat stroke and the unaccustomed pack. A number of them had been reservists for nine years and it took a little time for them to readjust to service life. After training for the day was over, some of the men helped with getting in the harvest, as all the young French men were away with their own army. Private William Cheshire wrote in his diary on the 18th: 'nothing to cuddle about 100 inhabitants mostly old women about 70-80'.

Harry Dillon has left further comments on this period[19].

> Mme. --- gave the men a lot of coffee and salad and they are to help her get in the harvest all the men of the place being away. Practically no news from the front, but what there is good. –The "Petit Parisien" states German Crown Prince wounded[20]. – If true I hope it hurts. – Hope we shall be going forward now the fighting is only 60 miles off.

During the period August 12th-17th the various units of the British Expeditionary Force had crossed the English Channel to France. Although no formal alliance between Great Britain and France existed before the war, the development of 'Entente' resulted in arrangements being made for joint action. The B.E.F. was expected to act in a semi-independent capacity. On the 14th and the following days they moved by train to the areas of concentration between Mauberge and Le Cateau. The area involved was pear-shaped and was about 25 miles long from north-east to south-west, and averaging ten miles wide. The B.E.F. consisted of I Corps [1st and 2nd Divisions], II Corps [3rd and 5th Divisions], and the Cavalry. Sir Douglas Haig commanded I Corps and the fiery-tempered Sir Horace Smith-Dorrien[21] commanded II Corps. The B.E.F. was to advance on

---

[19] Diary entry on August 17th 1914.

[20] Crown Prince Frederick Wilhelm Victor August [1882-1951], the eldest son of the German Emperor Wilhelm II and, as the war progressed, mockingly called 'Little Willie' in British newspapers. He commanded the German Fifth Army in 1914-16. In November 1914, the Crown Prince gave an interview to a foreign correspondent describing the war 'the most stupid and unnecessary war of modern times'. Initially, on the rise of the Nazi Party, 'Little Willie' supported Adolf Hitler but, in the Second World War he lived as a private citizen on his family's estates.

[21] The original commander of II Corps, reputedly Britain's most able general, Sir James Grierson [1859-1914], died suddenly on a train in France, from an aneurysm of the heart, on August 17th. He was only 55 years of age at the time of his untimely death. Sir Horace Smith-Dorrien replaced him.

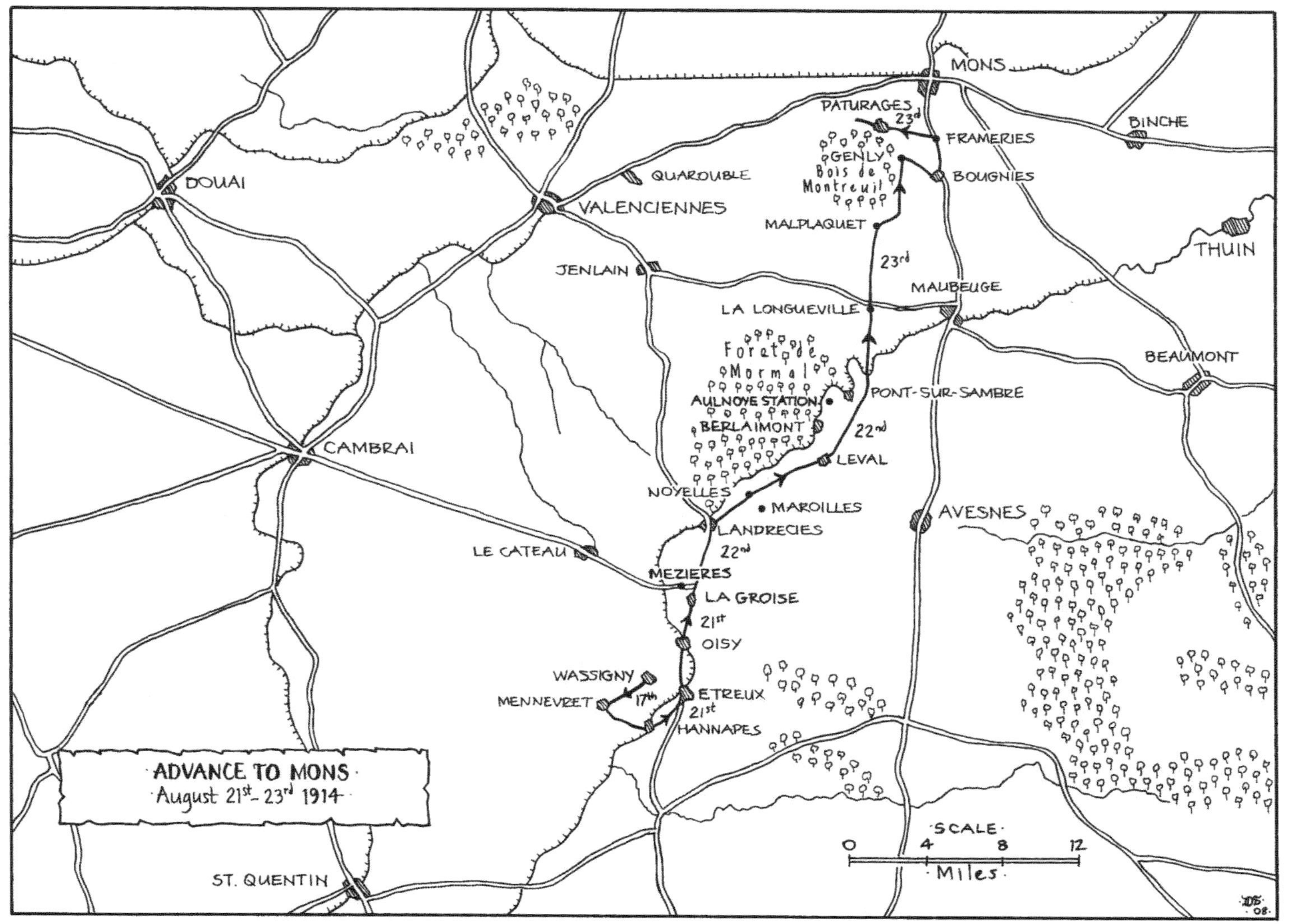
ADVANCE TO MONS
August 21st–23rd 1914
MONS
PATURAGES
23rd
FRAMERIES
BINCHE
GENLY
Bois de Montreuil
BOUGNIES
QUAROUBLE
DOUAI
VALENCIENNES
MALPLAQUET
THUIN
23rd
JENLAIN
MAUBEUGE
LA LONGUEVILLE
Forêt de Mormal
BEAUMONT
PONT-SUR-SAMBRE
AULNOYE STATION
BERLAIMONT
22nd
CAMBRAI
LEVAL
NOYELLES
MAROILLES
AVESNES
LANDRECIES
22nd
LE CATEAU
MEZIERES
LA GROISE
21st
OISY
WASSIGNY
MENNEVRET
17th
ETREUX
21st
HANNAPES
SCALE
0 4 8 12
Miles
ST. QUENTIN

the left of General Charles Lanrezac's Fifth Army into Belgium. The Germans were not anticipated to get much beyond Mons, and the B.E.F. could then wheel eastward to envelop them, once Lanrezac's men had crossed the Sambre. As part of the 2nd Division, the 52nd were in Haig's I Corps.

In the late evening of August 20th, the 52nd received orders that they were to advance in the morning. At 8.30 a.m., the 52nd paraded and then marched out of Mennevret with all the inhabitants of the village turned out to give them a rousing send off. The officers received large bouquets mostly of dahlias, which were distributed to the men; a dahlia in the cap became a popular adjunct of apparel. Fortunately the weather was cooler and the march of about twelve miles not a long one with many halts on the road. A partial eclipse of the sun added interest to the march and made them a little less hot. The general direction was to the north-east and the route took them through Tupigny, Hannapes, Etreux, Oisy and La Groise to Mézières. Near La Groise, Major-General Charles Monro, commanding the 2nd Division, watched them march by and sent word to say that he was impressed with their turnout. The 52nd went into moderate billets and were able to sleep. On arrival at Mézières, Guy Blewitt and the other D Company officers managed to bath with elderly women dodging in and out of the room!

The following day, August 22nd, the 52nd were up at 4.55 a.m. and started their fifteen miles march to Pont-sur-Sambre while it was still cool. The general direction was still to the north-east and took them just short of Landrecies, and then along a poor road through Maroilles, Noyelles, Leval, Aulnoye Station, to better billets than the night before. This was in Pont-sur-Sambre where they arrived at 12.30 p.m. In view of the fact that they were uncertain of the position of the enemy the side roads were picketed. Many of the men availed themselves of the opportunity to bathe in the River Sambre. According to Guy Blewitt, the officers of C and D Companies were billeted in quite a nice house, the owner of which had a wound in his stomach supposedly inflicted by a 'spy'. He insisted in exposing his abdomen for each officer in turn to admire, until finally he had a row with Second-Lieutenant Paul Giradot and retired to bed. The officers slept downstairs to be ready 'at a moment's notice' and only the bolder one's removed their boots and puttees.

As the 52nd were beginning their march to Pont-sur-Sambre, the British fired their first shots of the war. A patrol under Major Tom Bridges of the 4th Royal Irish Dragoon Guards advanced on the road from Obourg to Soignies and fired on a German piquet. During the day the main British forces reached Mons. Haig's I Corps was positioned along the Mons to Beaumont road and Smith-Dorrien's II Corps in front of Mons along the Mons-Condé canal, with cavalry between the two corps and around Binche. This line of defence left a great deal to be desired as there was an unwanted and vulnerable salient in it. The original intention had been a joint Anglo/French operation to attack the German forces facing them and perhaps envelop them. However, the French force that should have been on the left of II Corps failed to show up leaving the British flank in the air. Matters were made worse when the Germans made a thrust between I Corps and General Charles Lanrezac's Fifth French Army on their right, which proceeded to withdraw leaving both British flanks open. At first the British dug in on their defence line thinking the French would return. When they failed to do so the British were forced to withdraw.

The German opponent of Smith-Dorrien's II Corps was Generaloberst Alexander von Kluck's First Army, and Haig's I Corps was opposed by Generaloberst Karl von Bulow's Second Army. At the time of the Battle of Mons which lasted for the two days of August 23rd-24th, the cautious von Bulow was in overall command of the two armies. Indeed the allies were considerably outnumbered by the German enemy. The Germans had no less than three armies in the vicinity [von Kluck's, von Bulow's, von Hausen's[22]] and were opposed by a small Belgian army of six divisions, Lanrezac's Fifth French Army, and the four divisions of the B.E.F. Some 34 Divisions against 20, a frontier lacking natural obstacles, guarded by obsolete forts and with the direct road to Paris ahead of them.

At daybreak on August 23rd, the Germans began shelling Mons and the heaviest of the fighting took place along the Mons-Condé canal where the unfortunate 3rd Division [II Corps] was in position. I Corps on the right of II Corps took little active part in the two days fighting in the Battle of Mons. The 5th Brigade [including the 52nd] at Smith-Dorrien's urgent request went to the aid of the hard-pressed 3rd Division. At dawn on the 24th, the remainder of the 2nd Division made a powerful demonstration against Binche which was now in German hands. This allowed II Corps to retire to the line Quarouble-Dour-Frameries, although they suffered heavy casualties in the process as the Germans had by then taken Mons.

On the afternoon of August 23rd Sir John French, commanding the B.E.F., was informed that no less than three German corps were advancing on his front and another was turning towards his left flank from the direction of Tournai. To his great surprise he was also informed that General Charles Lanrezac's Fifth Army was withdrawing on his right. It was a precarious position to find himself in and he resolved to withdraw his forces to a line from south-east of Valenciennes on the left to Mauberge on his right. During the 24th, Smith-Dorrien's II Corps got as far as the line Dour-Frameries and made an attempt to

[22] General Max von Hausen commanded the Third Army.

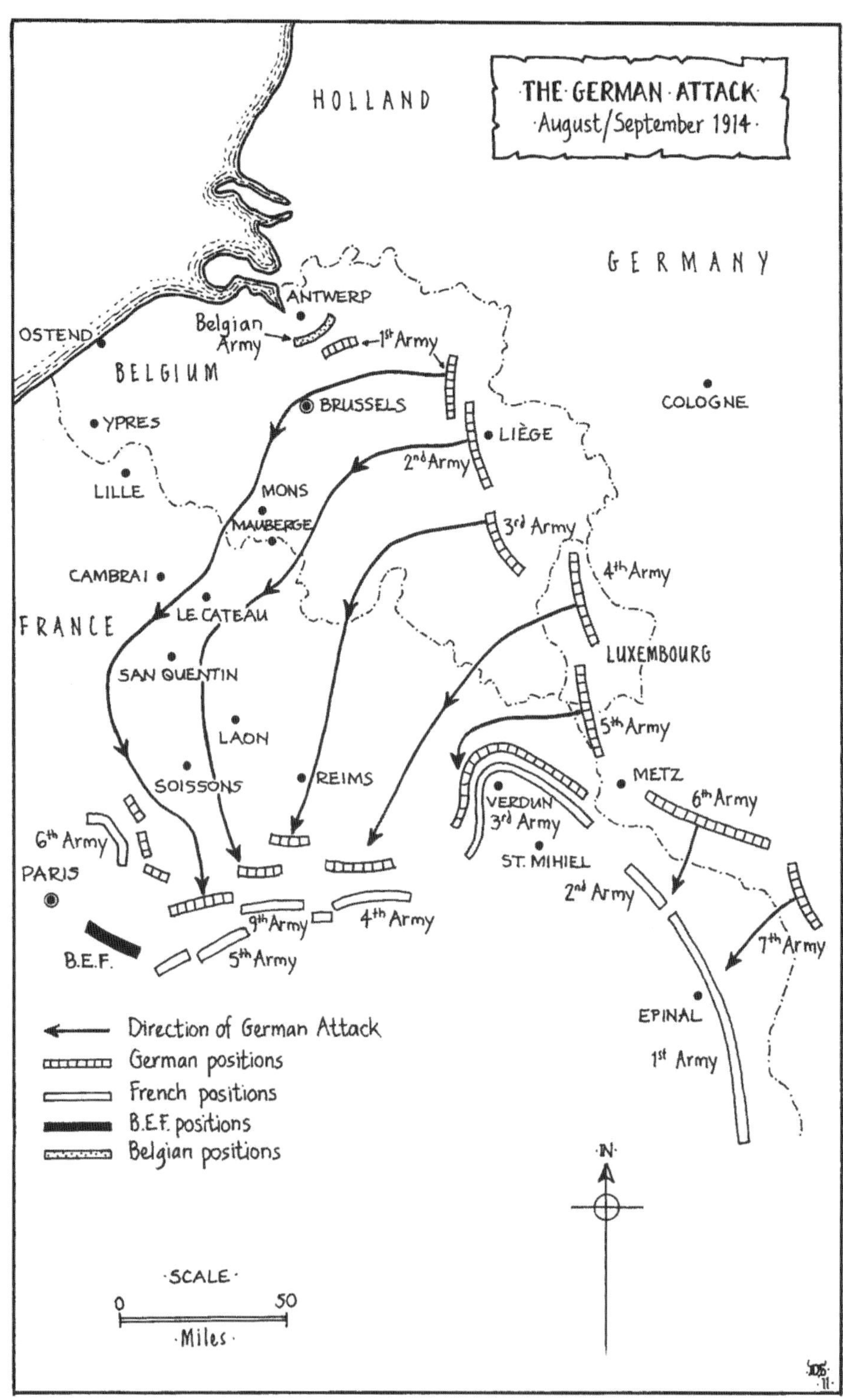
THE GERMAN ATTACK
August/September 1914
HOLLAND
GERMANY
BELGIUM
FRANCE
LUXEMBOURG
ANTWERP
Belgian Army
1st Army
OSTEND
BRUSSELS
COLOGNE
YPRES
LIÈGE
2nd Army
LILLE
MONS
MAUBERGE
3rd Army
CAMBRAI
4th Army
LE CATEAU
SAN QUENTIN
LAON
5th Army
SOISSONS
REIMS
METZ
VERDUN
3rd Army
6th Army
6th Army
PARIS
ST. MIHIEL
2nd Army
9th Army
4th Army
B.E.F.
5th Army
7th Army
EPINAL
1st Army
Direction of German Attack
German positions
French positions
B.E.F. positions
Belgian positions
N
SCALE
0
50
Miles

dig in. Meanwhile Haig's I Corps withdrew carefully to the line Mauberge on the right to Bavai[23] on the left. The 5th Brigade [of which the 52nd was a part] was ordered to cover the withdrawal of the 3rd Division. In doing so it held positions at La Bouverie, then Sars-la-Bruyère and finally rejoined the 2nd Division at Bavai. The severe pressure on Smith-Dorrien's II Corps from two German corps attacking its front, and another one its flank, forced the British back to the line of Bavai by nightfall.

On the night of August 24th the B.E.F. found I Corps in positions from Mauberge to Bavai, II Corps from Bavai to Jehlain and cavalry on the left flank. However, Sir John French had no intention of holding this line as he was informed that the French were still retreating on his right flank making his position untenable. It seemed to the British Commander-in-Chief that the Germans with their much greater numbers intended to trap and surround his exhausted forces in the vicinity of Mauberge. Therefore he ordered a retirement on Le Cateau and before daylight on August 25th the British forces were on the move once again.

At 1.30 a.m. August 23rd, the 52nd were awoken in their billets in Pont-sur-Sambre and at 3.30 a.m. they marched towards Genly. Their twelve and a half miles route to the north took them through Hargnies, La Longueville, over the battlefield of Malplaquet[24], across the border between France and Belgium, Blaregnies and finally to Genly. The march was an unpleasant one in the most intense heat with many checks and blocks on the way. At 9 a.m. in a field near Malplaquet the 52nd had a long halt for breakfast. It was their first food of the day. Here the men first heard the sound of gunfire and this was intermingled with the ringing of church bells from the surrounding villages as it was Sunday. Private William Cheshire noted: 'it is a pitiful sight to see the people come in crying from the villages'. Genly was at last reached at 3 p.m. and the 52nd settled into billets and had their dinner.

At 5 p.m., no sooner had the 52nd finished their meal when they were ordered to march two and a quarter miles to the east to Bougnies, where they found the rest of the 2nd Division busy digging in. This was to entrench a back position in order to cover a retirement. The reason for the sudden move from Genly was a fear that the village was about to be shelled. The 52nd believed that they would be advancing into Belgium with the French on their right. They were a little taken aback, as it was clear to them that things were not going well. Ahead of the 2nd Division, the 1st Division was in contact with the enemy. The 52nd

---

[23] The modern spelling is Bavay.

[24] On September 11th 1709, the Duke of Marlborough and Prince Eugene defeated the French under Marshal Claude-Louis-Hector Villars.

settled down to dig, when a further order instructed them to follow the 2nd Worcestershire and the 2nd H.L.I. to Frameries, and to fill a gap that had developed between the 3rd and 5th Divisions of II Corps. It was feared that the Germans would advance into the gap splitting the British line. In addition they were to clear out any of the enemy that had penetrated as far as Frameries. Most of the 5th Brigade was going at Sir Horace Smith-Dorrien's urgent request to plug the hole in his line. Only the 2nd Connaught Rangers were left at Bougnies.

The bulk of the 5th Brigade set off at 9 p.m. and passed through Noirchain before reaching Frameries, where they found no Germans but Brigadier-General F.C. Shaw and the Headquarters of the 9th Brigade [3rd Division] instead. Frameries was an ugly mining village with slag heaps and tangled streets. Shaw told them that II Corps had been forced back from their position in front of Mons to their present position, and it was the gap in this new line that the 5th Brigade was to fill. The 5th Brigade was led across the gap and dropped off first the 2nd Worcestershire and then the 2nd H.L.I., company by company, to plug it. By the time it came to the 52nd the gap had been filled and they moved into reserve in the cobbled square of the small town of Paturages, having marched twenty miles that day. By now it was the early hours of August 24th, as the 52nd settled down to a meagre one hour's sleep on the cobbles, between 3-4 a.m. On awaking, local women gave the men whisky. The cobbled square can be seen to this day in the small industrial area of Paturages, which is now a suburb of Mons. The 2nd Worcestershire and 2nd H.L.I. had great difficulty in finding defensive positions and a reasonable field of fire in the built up area with its numerous houses. They were sure to be shelled as soon as it was light.

Harry Dillon continued his account of the previous few days in his diary.

> Started for Mons but when we reached Paturage [sic] encountered the enemy. – We went through Malplaquet where the 52nd fought[25], soon after passing the old battlefield I was sent off with some N.C.O.s to arrange billets. I did this but we never occupied them[26]. The sound of guns we heard in the distance grew louder and by 2 p.m. the battle approached to within about 5 miles, we could see the town of –[27] in flames and our people deployed across the plain. About 6 p.m. we moved with the brigade into a field and later started to dig trenches. We hardly got to work when we were ordered to close in order to counter attack the enemy in occupation of

[25] Dillon was wrong about this point, the Regiment was not formed until later in the 18th century.
[26] Genly.
[27] Mons.

> (Frameries). We marched and marched through the live long night walking 100 yards and then stopping, everybody was most fearfully tired and dozens of men fell out. About 2 a.m. I came across an officer of some regiment who told me he had been in action all the afternoon, he thought they had lost in his regiment 600 out 1000 men and said our guns had not come up and they were plastered with shrapnel for hours. – He said the enemy were quite close. – Soon afterwards we passed crowds of men asleep on pavements. – I heard afterwards they were corpses. – Soon after this the other 3 battns. of the Bde. began to line out in the gardens of the houses we were reserve in the big square in the town. (Paturages). At 3 a.m. the owner of a café asked me if I would like some coffee. – He gave me any amount and cigarettes and brandy. When daylight broke we marched to the outside of the town and put a bit of rising ground in a state of defence, meanwhile a great cannonade commenced and the Germans bombarded the town which very soon caught fire. We did not come into action but a battery close by had the shells among them all day.

Paturages was as close to Mons as the 52nd and Harry Dillon would get, as they would soon be retreating all the way back to and beyond the River Marne. Although the 52nd had been a part of the 5th Brigade in the closing of the gap between the 3rd and 5th Divisions, they had been held in reserve in the square of Paturages. They were well and truly within the sound and sight of the guns, but there was no direct contact with the enemy.

Chapter II

The Retreat from Mons and the Battle of the Marne.

August 24th - September 11th 1914

[Maps: pages 16, 21, 33, 40.]

On August 24th 1914, the 52nd Light Infantry started the long retreat back from Paturages. They stood to arms at 4 a.m., and shortly afterwards marched the one and a half miles southwards to near La Bouverie where they started to dig a defensive position. The 52nd had been ordered to cover the withdrawal of troops in front of them. The position was far from ideal, with a poor field of fire, but the men applied themselves assiduously to digging trenches, despite the fact they had had no food and very little sleep. Brigadier-General Richard Haking, commanding the 5th Infantry Brigade, appeared at the nearby cross-roads and informed Lieutenant-Colonel Henry Davies, commanding the 52nd, that the French[28] on their right had retired exposing the right flank of the 1st Division. Haking said that the 5th Brigade was to proceed to Sars-la-Bruyère to cover the retirement of the 1st Division.

The 2nd Worcestershire and the 2nd Highland Light Infantry were ordered to move back first, and they came through the 52nd's entrenched positions near La Bouverie. These two battalions had been holding the same ground, between the 3rd and 5th Divisions, that they had taken up the night before. The task of getting away from their entrenched positions under shellfire was somewhat simplified as the houses of Paturages were close up to the trench line, so that the men were able to withdraw fairly quickly under cover of the buildings. However, there were a number of casualties from shell shards and shrapnel amongst the two battalions who were moving back. The 52nd themselves did not fire a shot as the Germans failed to follow up quickly, although a few desultory shells were aimed in their general direction. The 2nd Connaught Rangers were still holding a position near Bougnies.

At approximately 9.30 a.m., the Worcestershire and the H.L.I. having retired through them, the 52nd took their turn to go back with Captain Allan Harden and D Company bringing up the rear and covering the retirement. The route they took was initially to the south, touching the corner of the Bois Royal, and then past the hamlet of Eugies to a second rearguard position. By 11 a.m., they occupied a line from the village of Sars-la-Bruyère on their right to the

[28] General Charles Lanrezac's Fifth Army.

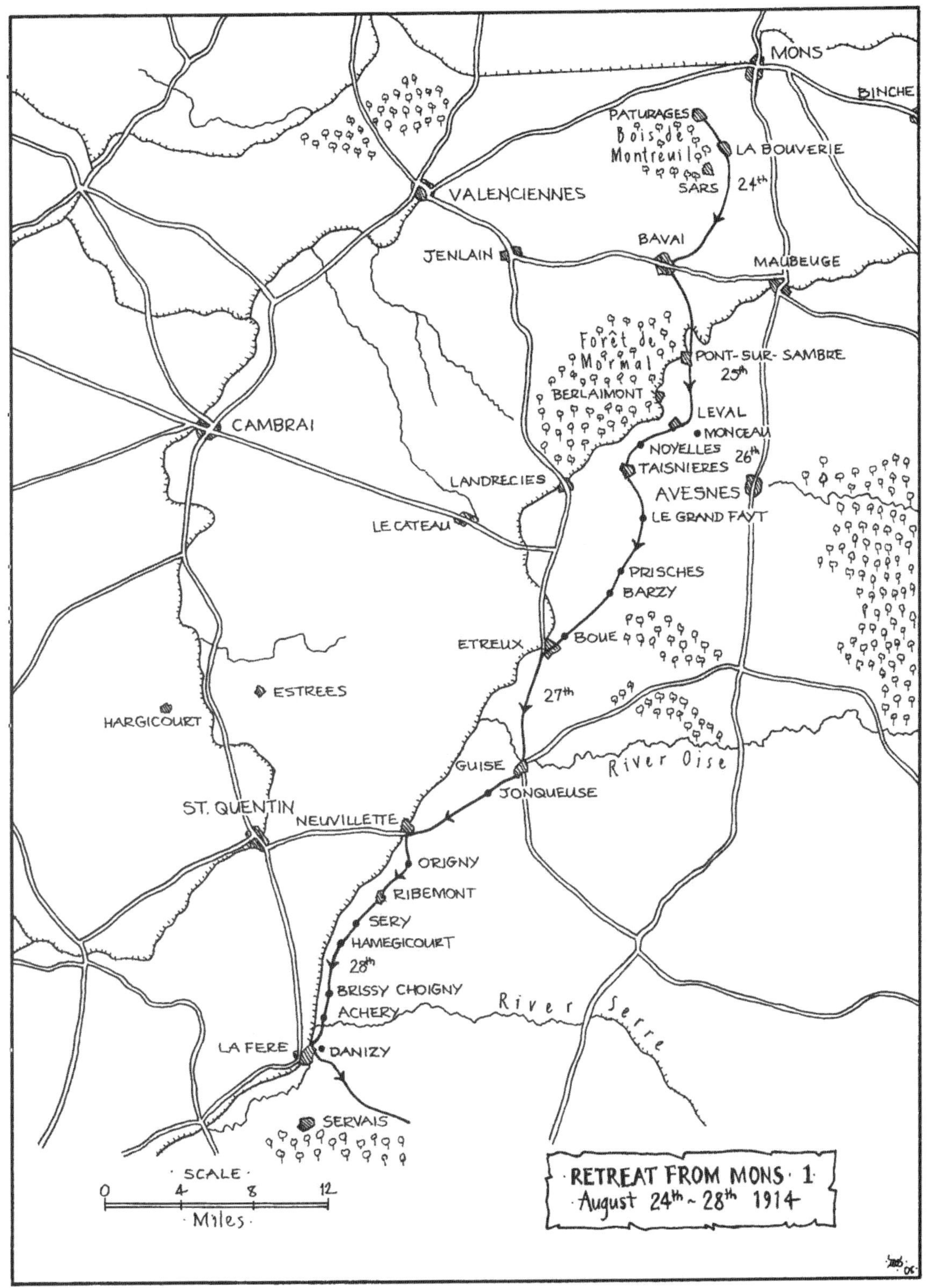
MONS
BINCHE
PATURAGES
Bois de Montreuil
LA BOUVERIE
SARS
24th
VALENCIENNES
BAVAI
JENLAIN
MAUBEUGE
Forêt de Mormal
PONT-SUR-SAMBRE
25th
BERLAIMONT
LEVAL
MONCEAU
CAMBRAI
NOYELLES
26th
TAISNIERES
LANDRECIES
AVESNES
LE GRAND FAYT
LE CATEAU
PRISCHES
BARZY
ETREUX
BOUE
ESTREES
27th
HARGICOURT
GUISE
River Oise
JONQUEUSE
ST. QUENTIN
NEUVILLETTE
ORIGNY
RIBEMONT
SERY
HAMEGICOURT
28th
BRISSY CHOIGNY
ACHERY
River Serre
LA FERE
DANIZY
SERVAIS
SCALE
0 4 8 12
Miles
RETREAT FROM MONS 1
August 24th – 28th 1914

western edge of the Bois de Montreuil on their left. The defensive positions on the right were extended by the 2nd H.L.I. It was here that the 52nd had the novelty of seeing their first German soldier, a prisoner taken by men of the 1st Dorsetshire[29], who had become detached from their own regiment and came into the line in the Bois de Montreuil. Henry Davies noted that both the 3rd and 5th Divisions had considerably more difficulty extricating themselves from the fighting than did the 5th Brigade.

The 52nd remained in their positions until 5 p.m. when the march to the south was resumed with the regiment acting as rearguard to the 5th Brigade. The road that crossed the Franco/Belgian border was a fairly good one, and ran parallel to and west of the main road they had taken the day before as they went north. It was an odd sight bordered by a mass of abandoned greatcoats, entrenching tools and general equipment. At every cross-road the hindmost company, with their bayonets fixed, halted and turned about. Although they saw a few German cavalrymen in the distance they were not molested. It was well after dark when the 52nd arrived at their destination, Bavai. Here in this town they were once more in France. It was packed with soldiers of both the I and II Corps who were wandering around and blocking the streets.

Captain Guy Blewitt of D Company described the scene[30].

> We didn't get to Bavai till 11 p.m. I have never been so tired as in the last 46 hours I had no sleep covered 40 miles besides having the anxiety of a rearguard. At nearing Bavai it was evident that things were serious the road being packed, cavalry with their horses, cavalry men who had lost their horses, ambulance wagons, refugees, bicycles, perambulators, guns, infantry in fours, infantry men who had lost their units and infantrymen whose units didn't know where they were required and were sleeping by the side of the road. The cobbles of Bavai and its vicinity made one's feet sorer and we were very glad to be turned into a stubble field to bivouac, here fires were soon burning and we got some food to eat and straw to sleep on.

The roads had been full of large numbers of pathetic civilians fleeing from the advancing Germans. What was particularly galling to the civilian population of both France and Belgium was that they had only recently welcomed the British troops as they had gone forward to meet the German foe. A few days later, it was quite clear that things had gone badly as the British were in headlong

---

[29] 15th Brigade, 5th Division.

[30] Diary entry for August 24th 1914.

retreat. During this day the 52nd lost their first man, Private Walter Hancox, who was posted missing, and was subsequently found to be a prisoner-of-war.

Captain Harry Dillon recorded his observations at that time. The view given to the 52nd that the retreat was preconceived, to lead the enemy on, does not fit with the facts. No doubt the commanders did not wish their men to become disheartened.

> Still reserve behind a wood and saw no fighting. The condition of the inhabitants was most pitiable and saw then, and since then, the most pitiable sights I ever have seen. One poor old man in a dying condition being taken away in a cart just had strength to raise his hand and say “Vive l’Angleterre”. – The fighting this day was very severe. We know now this was a very bold dash of ours to delay the enemy and we never intended to stop. We had nine German corps up against is [sic], about 360,000 men to our 4 divisions about 90,000 by our action we delayed the enemy probably 4 days. – In the evening we got orders to leave and I had the rear guard a most anxious job. The men are not pleased at having to go back, in fact everybody was fed up but were told it was a preconcerted [sic] plan to draw the Germans on. – In reality the fall of Namur laid Paris open and it was the British Army who saved France thank God.

In the early hours of August 25th the B.E.F. continued to march to the south, towards the Le Cateau position where the 4th Division under Major-General Thomas Snow had arrived from Britain. The Le Cateau position extended from Cambrai in the west, through Le Cateau, to Landrecies in the east. It was to reach this line that Sir Horace Smith-Dorrien’s beleaguered II Corps marched by the roads to the west of the Forest of Mormal, covered by the Cavalry, while Sir Douglas Haig’s I Corps used less direct routes to the east of the forest. To make matters more difficult the roads to the east of the forest were full of civilian fugitives from Mauberge and its surrounding districts. The disorder produced by the civilians made the retreat of I Corps, at any speed and in any order, difficult, with the constant blocking of the roads, and the troops were lucky to manage two miles an hour.

At dusk on the 25th, I Corps was scattered along the line Taisnières-Maroilles-Landrecies, with the 5th Brigade holding the bridges and entrenched around Leval and Pont-sur-Sambre. Unfortunately, a gap of ten miles had opened up between I and II Corps, partly due to the lie of the land and partly due to the exhausted state of the troops[31]. Throughout the day German troops pursued rapidly and in a relentless fashion the exhausted I and II Corps. During the night of August 25th/26th the Germans, who approached through the Forest of Mormal, attacked Landrecies and Maroilles heavily. This was repulsed and the right flank of I Corps was protected once contact was made with French cavalry at Avesnes. Further to the west the Germans were preparing to attack II Corps at Le Cateau, and Sir John French, realising that I Corps was too distant to assist, intended II Corps to fall back on a line running east-west through San Quentin.

In the early hours of August 26th, the brigades of I Corps marched south from the various positions they had halted at. Realising that II Corps was too far away to interfere, the enemy followed relentlessly and managed to capture most of the Munster Fusiliers from 1st Brigade. The other brigades were luckier and managed to reach Hannappes, Etreux, Oisy, and in the case of the 52nd and the 2nd Worcestershire, Barzy. Meanwhile II Corps was in danger of being annihilated by Generaloberst Alexander von Kluck's men. In fact he was so certain of victory that he sent a telegram to Berlin announcing that the British Army was encircled.

Sir Horace Smith-Dorrien found himself in a very tricky situation in his Le Cateau position. His II Corps, consisting of three divisions, was faced by no less than seven enemy divisions and his artillery had only a quarter of the strength of his opponents. Despite the fact that Sir John French wanted him to retire on St. Quentin, Smith-Dorrien had little choice but to stand and fight as his troops were pinned down by artillery fire. Although the British artillery took a heavy toll on the advancing German infantry formations, at about midday, the British line was gradually pushed back. Some battalions who had held on too long were cut off and captured. So well had Smith-Dorrien's men fought that their temporary stand at Le Cateau and the damage that they had done to their German opponents allowed them to withdraw relatively intact.

By nightfall on the 26th, II Corps had reached Vermaud, Hargiecourt and Estrées and was approximately in line with Haig's I Corps, although they were some distance apart. Sir John French never forgave Smith-Dorrien for his stand at Le Cateau and for not falling back on St. Quentin. It was one of his excuses for sacking his potential rival, Smith-Dorrien, the following year. Most authorities now consider that the irascible Smith-Dorrien was justified in his actions, and may well have saved the whole B.E.F. from destruction.

---

[31] According to Sir James Edmonds in a revised edition of his *Official History* the reason for the divergence between I and II Corps, was a brief period of panic at Haig's Headquarters. 'Haig momentarily lost his head – a remarkable lapse for so stout hearted a fellow'. Edmonds noted a gap in the records about this incident.

The proposed line through St. Quentin was now considered too far forward on which to fight the superior forces of the enemy and so, on August 27th and 28th, the whole B.E.F. was united and stabilized on a line east and west through La Fère. The pursuit slackened and the British were able to rest and reorganize. The French Sixth Army came up on their left and the Fifth Army on their right.

We left the 52nd bivouacked in their stubble field to the south of Bavai. At 4 a.m. on August 25th they marched to the south once more. A German aeroplane flew over and observed them. It was a very hot day and the men were worn out by the time Pont-sur-Sambre was reached via the direct road route. Here the 52nd were instructed to set up positions to defend four bridges over the River Sambre. From north to south the bridges were Aymeries [road over river] D Company, Aulnoye [road over river] A Company, Berlaimont [railway over river] B Company, and Sassegnies [railway over river] C Company. Regimental headquarters were set up close to the railway station at Aulnoye. Although this was roughly in the centre of the 52nd's operational area, it was less than ideal as the station was full of civilian refugees desperate to escape from the German army's advance. Despite the fact that a train had left Aulnoye station at this time, the platform remained packed. Also defending the Sambre were the 2nd Worcestershire on the right of the 52nd and the 2nd H.L.I. on their left.

The companies set up excellent defensive positions around each bridge, and Lieutenant-Colonel Henry Davies rather hoped that an attack would be forthcoming so that the enemy might be given a bloody nose. However, they were not attacked and were ordered, at about 4 p.m., to hand over the bridges at Aymeries and Aulnoye, to the care of a French reserve division who had arrived on the scene. B and C Companies remained in their positions on the two railway bridges, and A and D Companies were ordered to form a defensive outpost line, from Leval to Monceau, to the south. As darkness came down, at around 6 p.m., A Company took up a position on the left at Leval where the Regimental headquarters had moved to, and D Company established itself in the right sector at Monceau. The distance from Bavai to Leval is ten miles. During the early part of the night there was a constant stream of British troops and artillery passing through Leval in their retreat to the south.

In Leval, Guy Blewitt recorded[32]: 'Suddenly a mounted French soldier galloped ventre a lévee through the village "Les Allemands les Allemands" followed by the transport and a certain amount of firing. There was somewhat of a panic the transport retiring at the gallop threatening to be more dangerous than

[32] Diary entry for August 25th 1914.

the charge of the Uhlans which was expected to follow'. The 2nd H.L.I. restored order and the only casualty was a Scot bayoneted in the leg by a comrade.

As soon as the 52nd had made preparations to spend the night in their new positions, on the two railway bridges and defensive outpost line, further orders came in, one after the other. Henry Davies had found a bed with sheets when three minutes after turning in, at 10 p.m., the first order arrived at the Leval headquarters of the 52nd. It instructed them to get ready to continue the march with the rest of the 5th Brigade, to the south, at 1 a.m. on the 26th. Shortly afterwards this was cancelled and a further order to reoccupy the bridges over the Sambre arrived. Mystery surrounds the sending of the order to reoccupy the bridges, and Davies was later told by Brigadier-General Richard Haking, commanding the 5th Brigade, that the 2nd Division had not intended to send this order. However, Haking undoubtedly received the order from the Division, which was forwarded to the 52nd. B and C companies were still holding their bridges, but A and D had to be called in from their outpost line which took some time. Before daylight on August 26th, the imperturbable Henry Davies had collected A and D Companies at Leval and marched to Aulnoye once more. This was not the end of his problems as he and the 52nd [A and D Companies] came across members of the French reserve division and did not know their password. Some time was lost in convincing the French that they were not Germans, and that the 52nd were to take over the road bridges once more. Davies was horrified that their French allies were guarding the bridge at Aulnoye in such a desultory fashion and that the one at Aymeries was left unattended. A nearby French officer denied any knowledge of its existence, and Davies thought that a regular French division would not have been so casual.

Henry Davies escorted D Company to the bridge at Aymeries and returned to Aulnoye to discover that the situation had changed, as the Germans had taken the bridge over the Sambre, at Maroilles, to their south. Further orders for the 52nd instructed them to make haste to the south for fear that they would be cut off from the rest of the 5th Brigade at Noyelles. In the event, the Germans did not move quickly and the 52nd were not cut off. B and C Companies were recalled from their bridges and joined A and D on the march from Aulnoye via Leval to Noyelles.

Unfortunately, the 52nd received their first officer casualties of the war in the blowing up of the railway bridge at Berlaimont by the French. Captain Lindsay Wood[33], commanding B Company had been told of the French intention to destroy the bridge, but not the time of the explosion. Two of his officers were seriously wounded by high velocity stone projectiles from the bridge as it blew

[33] Henry Lindsay Wood. Known by his second name.

up. Captain Philip Godsal[34] was injured in the leg and Second-Lieutenant G.T. Button suffered a lung contusion. A most unfortunate loss of two valuable officers so early in the campaign and ironically from 'friendly fire' too. Earlier that night a signaller, Private F. Giles, had been hit in the groin by a rifle bullet, giving him the dubious distinction of being the first casualty that the 52nd suffered in the war. The three wounded men were last seen three miles south of Pont-sur-Sambre being carried to hospital in the French van that had been used to bring up explosives to blow up the bridges. That same evening they fell into German hands when the enemy overran the hospital at Avesnes Nord.

The 52nd's first line transport was at Leval and by sending a message ahead, Henry Davies was able to arrange for the men to have a hasty breakfast of hot tea and biscuit on their arrival. It was here, at Leval, that the 52nd received further orders not to go to Noyelles, but to turn more to the east through Taisnières and Marbaix. Soon after leaving Leval, the 52nd caught up with the 2nd Connaught Rangers who were acting as the rearguard of the 5th Brigade and passed through them. The road that the 5th Brigade was using and the adjacent ones were full of French soldiers also retreating to the south and near Taisnières there was a long delay as the 52nd allowed some of them to pass. All day long could be heard the continuous artillery fire from the west where II Corps were fighting to save themselves and the B.E.F., at the Battle of Le Cateau. Also on a lesser scale could be heard firing from near Landrecies where the 4th and 6th Brigades were also in action. However, the Germans did not follow the 52nd too closely.

On the high ground to the north-east of Le Grand Fayt, the 52nd had a long rest as French troops and artillery passed them by. Here rations were issued and the first mail from home miraculously arrived. Orders to proceed to Barzy via Prisches and bivouac there were received. The 52nd arrived at Barzy with the 2nd Worcestershire, shortly before dark, after a journey of some seventeen miles from Leval via Aymeries, and settled down in an orchard. There was no sign of the 5th Brigade headquarters or of the other two regiments. Henry Davies had just gone to sleep in the open at 10 p.m. and was awoken at midnight by Lieutenant-Colonel Claude Westmacott, Commanding Officer of the Worcestershire, with the unwelcome news that the French, who should have been covering their right or eastern flank, were all retiring. In addition the rearguard of the 5th Brigade, the

[34] Captain Philip Godsal made a successful escape from a German prisoner-of-war camp in March-April 1917. Subsequently he was awarded a M.C. for his efforts. A particularly fine rifle shot who was in both the Eton and Oxford University Eights and had also represented England. The son of a former 52nd officer, he would have been in his element in the coming action at Langemarck the following October.

hapless 2nd Connaught Rangers, had been severely dealt with by enemy action when on the march that evening. They had lost their colonel and some 300 men. Claude Westmacott, in the absence of Brigadier-General Richard Hacking, decided that it would be better to march to Boué to gain information of the whereabouts of the 5th Brigade or 2nd Division[35]. It was clear that Barzy would not be an easy place to defend.

Major Archibald Eden, commanding C Company, recorded in his diary his perspective on August 26th.

> Owing to the constant blocking of the road by French troops, there were many halts. At the long mid-day halt, we got our first mail from home sorted out, and some rations issued to the men. During the day our route was continually altered. Altogether it was a most trying march, and the men felt the weight of their equipment. Saw unmistakable signs on the road of the exhausted condition of the troops preceding us. In two places we found large collections of British greatcoats piled up and left behind.

The 52nd continued their march to the south, at 2 a.m., on August 27th, and reached Boué at dawn. While Westmacott and Davies were collecting information from retreating French troops and their general, the two regiments rested in a field and were able to make breakfast with restorative hot tea. At this juncture Brigadier-General Richard Haking appeared, having been with the 2nd H.L.I. and not very far away from the 52nd when they were at Barzy. Haking confirmed the bad news that the 2nd Connaught Rangers had become isolated and received many casualties at the enemy's hands the evening before. On arrival at Boué, Henry Davies had sent Lieutenant Reginald Worthington on to Etreux in search of the 2nd Division's headquarters. He found it there and was sent back with orders for the 52nd to move to Etreux as swiftly as possible. At Etreux rations were issued and the march continued almost immediately, so that the loaves of bread were carried on stretchers.

Less than a week earlier the 52nd had passed through Etreux in the opposite direction on the way from the concentration area towards Mons. Their route took them through Guise, Jonquese, Mont d'Origny to Neuvillette. As the 52nd passed through the deserted fine old town of Guise, they imagined that they might halt a little beyond it. This was not to be the case, and a report came in to

---

[35] In the *Records of the Worcestershire Regiment in the First World War* the impression is given that this was a joint decision of the two battalion commanders. However, Davies in his diary made it clear that Westmacott took the decision. In any case it was a sensible one.

the effect that German infantry was ahead of them. The 52nd prepared for action, but fortunately for the exhausted men this proved to be false information. A little further on, while crossing some hills, they were soaked by a heavy storm. This increased the weight of the men's packs considerably, but the sun came out and they were nearly dry by the time they reached their destination, Neuvillette. As Henry Davies put it, 'we arrived with everyone dead beat from fatigue and want of sleep'. It was not surprising that they were exhausted as between 2 a.m. and 6 p.m., exclusive of manoeuvring, they had covered 22 miles under fraught service conditions. Most of the men were billeted in the houses of Neuvillette although outposts had to be found in the hill which overlooked the village. The 5th Brigade were now all together again as the 2nd H.L.I. had rejoined them.

At midnight on August 27th/28th the 52nd were ordered to pack up all their baggage and to send it off on the transport train. Rouse was at 3 a.m., and breakfast taken with a view to moving off at 4 a.m. However, the 52nd were ordered by the 5th Brigade to find further outposts in the hills above the village of Neuvillette to cover the right flank on the march of the 1st and 2nd Divisions. Eventually the outposts were reduced just to B and C Companies, under Captain Lindsay Wood. At 10 a.m., A and D Companies followed their Commanding Officer, Henry Davies, on the 20 miles march to Servais via Mont d'Origny, Ribemont, Sery, Hamégicourt, Brissay Choigny, Achery, Danizy, and La Fère.

The weather was fine and a powerful sun beat down on the weary and footsore men. Davies was forced to call a halt after each half hour of marching, and he allowed more water to be drunk than usual. Many of the men were limping badly, but stuck to the march bravely. Guy Blewitt was grateful for a sun flap on his cap which he had been given by his brother Ralph serving with the Royal Field Artillery. By chance the brothers had met in Neuvillette. At one point the 52nd halted close to some apple trees and Davies allowed the men to refresh themselves on the succulent fruit. As they passed through the deserted La Fère the men hoped that this would be their destination, but this was not to be the case; they had to go on to Servais, which they reached just as darkness came down at 7 p.m. Despite the fact that some of the men had difficulty putting one leg in front of the other, A and C Companies came in singing. B and D Companies, under Captain Lindsay Wood, who had been relieved of their rearguard responsibility by troops of the 1st Division, did not arrive until 9 p.m., but they too came in in fine style singing lustily. Wood had used his initiative by hiring a French wagon at one of the villages to carry the packs of the most tired men. In all, the 52nd had marched 59 miles in the previous 64 hours, beginning in the middle of an entirely sleepless night, and getting no more than eight hours sleep on the other two nights.

Saturday August 29th 1914 was not a day to be forgotten by the survivors of the 52nd in their retirement from Mons. It was a blessed day of rest for them as they bivouacked in their stubble field at Servais. Their rest was not as good as it might have been as the sun was unremitting in its intensity, but rest of any sort was better than no rest at all. Guy Blewitt's servant made him a bed of sheaves of corn and with an india rubber pillow that he carried in his pocket was very comfortable. The men took the opportunity to write and send off letters to their families. Lindsay Wood's wagon was retained to convey the men's greatcoats and they carried waterproof ground sheets to protect themselves in the event of rain.

Harry Dillon took the opportunity to write up his diary in the stubble field at Servais.

> Today a rest day, the French have come up and their guns have been going all day. – Saw proclamation explaining reasons for our retreat also news of Russian advance. It was pitiable yesterday coming in, everybody limping and crowds of men who could not keep up coming in by themselves. Hope today's rest will have put them right. Our casualties so far are Batten [sic] severely wounded[36], Godsall [sic] slightly, 4 men.

The same day, August 29th, Harry Dillon also wrote to his family.

> I am very fit and everything is going top hole. We have done a great march — it has been fearful work, 25 hours with hardly a stop once and it has been going on so far almost continuously for days. One's feet throb so one can hardly stick it at times. We have bumped into absolutely the flower of the German army and have laid them out absolutely in thousands. In one place they lie in heaps of 50 to 100 for 3 miles. Of course we have had some losses but I think there are probably 20 or more Germans to every Englishman. The swine are doing all sorts of low things. In one case they drove civilian women and children in front of them, – our men would not fire but rushed at them with their bayonets and fought till they were all killed, which was inevitable on account of the numbers. On another occasion they dressed in French uniforms and came up shouting 'Vive l'Angleterre' and actually started talking French to our people and

[36] Second-Lieutenant G.T. Button had suffered a lung contusion in the blowing up of the railway bridge at Berlaimont.

when they were all up they suddenly opened fire. This happened to a picket of about 50 men so it was not very serious. We have had the best of them everywhere.

Meanwhile, Sir John French, commanding the B.E.F., was in a more comfortable position from August 29th as French armies had been brought up to protect his flanks. However, he was concerned about the safety of his lines of communication with the port of Le Havre. Amiens had been evacuated and the Germans had promptly moved in. French made his main base St. Nazaire with an advanced base at Le Mans. The enemy pushed on with great vigour and General Joseph Joffre, the French Commander-in-Chief, continued the retreat of the allied forces to the line of the River Marne, awaiting a favourable moment to go on the offensive. Thus, on August 30th, the allied troops kept up their retirement, and on the 30th were approximately on the line through Crépy and Villers-Cotterêts. Various local actions took place, but on September 2nd the British forces reached the Marne, and on the 3rd crossed to the south bank. The bridges were blown up and the troops took up a position between Lagny and Signy-Signets. A further march to the south of twelve miles brought the British on September 5th to the point where they turned around and went on the offensive. Air reconnaissance showed that the German enemy had suspended their advance on Paris and changed direction to the south-east and were intending to break the line of the allies between Château-Thierry and Vitry-le-Francois. On September 5th some German troops had halted on the River Ourcq and others had crossed the Marne between Chagnis and Mezy.

Returning to the activities of the 52nd, after their day of rest in the stubble field at Servais, they and the rest of the 5th Brigade were on the move again, at 4.30 a.m. on the 30th, in a southerly direction. Their route in a very tiring march of fifteen miles took them through Barisis, the fine fortified old town of Couchy-le-Château to Terny, where they bivouacked, on the west side of the road, in a field close to the village. The wooded countryside was beautiful but the roads were rough ones and the heat exhausting and unrelenting. The march had been made a little easier by having their greatcoats carried in the hired cart. There was no sign of the enemy this day. In Terny the 52nd requisitioned some potatoes which they were able to cook. On the retreat from Mons food was not really a problem although there was a shortage of vegetables. Often the company officers were able to supplement the diet of their men with milk and bread purchased from the local inhabitants. The Regiment had not been provided with maps south of Terny an omission which Guy Blewitt felt made the marching rather dull. He also commented: ‘The fact of having no maps of these parts made us slow to believe that our retirement was the preconceived strategic plan of campaign which hitherto we had rather been led to believe'[37].

The next day, August 31st, the 52nd were off to an early start at 5 a.m. once more. The day's march of fifteen miles was on a route to the south again, through the northern suburbs of Soissons and across the River Aisne by the bridge at Pommiers. The men of the 5th Brigade had their first view of the river and valley of the Aisne, where, in just over two weeks later, the 52nd did their first serious fighting of the war. There was a long delay at the bridge because of a mistaken order given to the brigade transport. Having eventually crossed the Aisne at Pommiers to the west of Soissons, the 52nd moved further westwards along the south bank of the river before making a final turn southward up a side valley through Pernant, to Cutry and Laversine. Here, at 1.30 p.m., to the south side of the village, in a closed-in ravine, the 52nd bivouacked. All of C Company and part of B were required to provide protective outposts against a surprise attack by the enemy. The train wagons remained here for a time before being ordered to continue the march, for fear that they would find the roads blocked on the following day. Perhaps the greatest joy for the men was a small stream which ran through the valley and allowed them to wash themselves.

At 2.30 a.m. September 1st, the 52nd set off once more, while it was still dark, into the forest country to the south of Laversine. Their route took them via Coevres, through the pretty old town of Villers-Cotterêts with its fine arch over the main street, Boursonne and Ivors to Cuvergnon, a distance of some seventeen miles in all. In Villers-Cotterêts the 5th Brigade, including the 52nd, passed through the entrenched position of the 4th Brigade [Guards] who were there to check the enemy's pursuit. Around 10 a.m., the leading troops of the enemy came into contact with the Guards in the woods of Villers-Cotterêts and a sharp firefight took place. As a result of this attack the 5th Brigade lay in a wood at Villers-en-Potées, listening to the firing. It was thought that the 5th Brigade would be sent back to assist the Guards, but the action was soon over and they were ordered to continue the retreat and to entrench a position at Cuvergnon instead. Brigadier-General R. Scott-Kerr, commanding the 4th Brigade, was wounded and the commanding officer of the 1st Irish Guards killed in this vigorous little action.

The 6th Brigade had halted just to the south of Villers-Cotterêts to cover the retreat of the Guards, and the 5th Brigade were to act as a rallying point to the other two Brigades at Cuvergnon. The 52nd in their trenches across the road at Cuvergnon spent a miserably cold night awaiting the enemy who never came. Allan Harden and Guy Blewitt of D Company slept just in the rear of the trenches, 'taking it in turns to go down the trench and see that every fourth man

---

[37] Diary entry August 30th 1914.

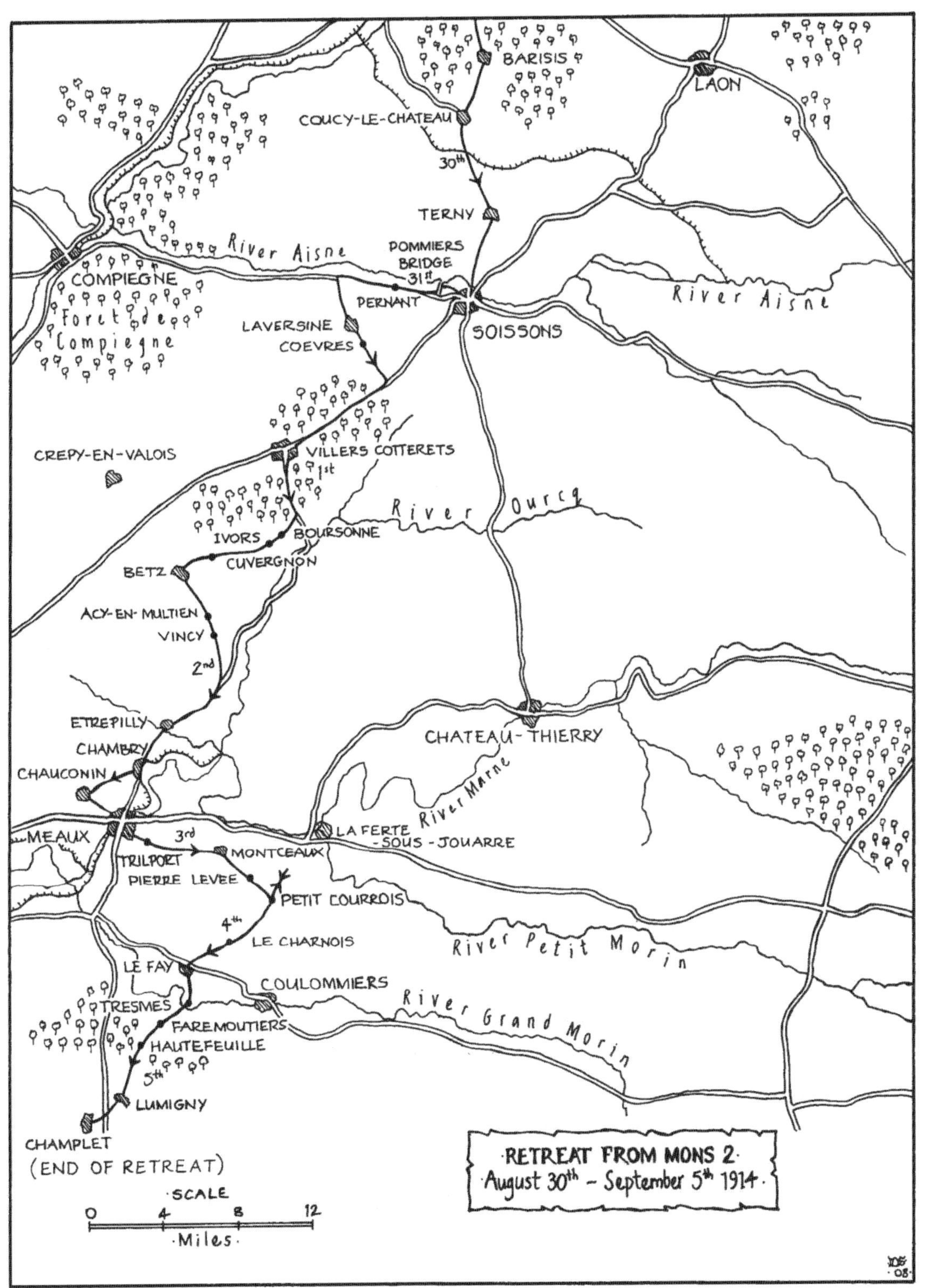
BARISIS
LAON
COUCY-LE-CHATEAU
30th
TERNY
River Aisne
POMMIERS BRIDGE
31st
PERNANT
SOISSONS
River Aisne
COMPIEGNE
Foret de Compiegne
LAVERSINE
COEVRES
CREPY-EN-VALOIS
VILLERS COTTERETS
1st
River Ourcq
IVORS
BOURSONNE
CUVERGNON
BETZ
ACY-EN-MULTIEN
VINCY
2nd
ETREPILLY
CHAMBRY
CHAUCONIN
CHATEAU-THIERRY
River Marne
MEAUX
3rd
LA FERTE -SOUS-JOUARRE
MONTCEAUX
TRILPORT
PIERRE LEVEE
PETIT COURROIS
4th
LE CHARNOIS
River Petit Morin
LE FAY
COULOMMIERS
River Grand Morin
TRESMES
FAREMOUTIERS
HAUTEFEUILLE
5th
LUMIGNY
CHAMPLET
(END OF RETREAT)
·RETREAT FROM MONS 2·
·August 30th – September 5th 1914·
·SCALE
0 4 8 12
·Miles·

was on sentry during the night'. Some of the wounded of the Guards came through their positions followed by the rest of the 4th Brigade.

September 2nd was one of the very worst days of the retreat from Mons with stifling heat and the Germans expected to attack at any moment. The 52nd were to take their turn as the rearguard of the 2nd Division, covered by the 4th Cavalry Brigade in the extreme rear. Orders were issued that the rearguard must hold on at all costs until the bridge at Betz had been cleared by the main body of the 2nd Division. In the event only enemy patrols were seen as, the previous day, the Guards had taken the sting out of the enemy. At 7.45 a.m., the 52nd accompanied by the 2nd Worcestershire filed out of their trenches and began their 20 miles march via Betz, Acy-en-Multien, Vincy, Etrépilly, Chambry to Chauconin. Some of the 52nd's men temporarily lost contact with their Regiment. Guy Blewitt and the billeting party had gone ahead on bicycles, selecting part of the Château's park for the Regiment to bivouac in. After dinner on a beautiful moonlight night, Blewitt and Lieutenant John Southey found the strength to look at the Château and its gardens.

Henry Davies described the day in his diary.

> This was one of the worst marches we had. The 1st Line Transport had to be sent off the night before, and as in the early morning we were standing to arms in the trenches, it was not possible to get any tea, so our breakfast was biscuit and water. The sun was very hot indeed, and after a few miles it began to tell on the men. Several fell down unconscious from heat stroke, and others were quite unable to keep up. We had no ambulances and no transport, but some of the worst cases were taken on by the artillery who were with us.
>
> Our orders were to hurry on as quickly as possible, the reason of this being, I believe, so as not to keep back the cavalry, as it seems to have been expected that the Germans would press in on the rear. I went to the Brigadier[38], and told him that too much hurrying would result in our leaving a number of men on the road. I pointed out that it was not a question of unwillingness on the men's part, but simply their inability to march fast with empty stomachs under a hot sun, after all the previous hard marching they had done, and on top of a night in the trenches with little if any sleep. The Brigadier quite agreed with me, but said that orders were to push on as quickly as possible. However, he gave us one or two halts, which saved us a good deal; and fortunately, between Etrépilly and Chambry, we came

[38] Brigadier-General Richard Haking.

up with our 1st Line Transport, when we found Brett (Transport Officer)[39] had with great foresight, made tea for the whole Regiment. This really saved us. We were allowed half an hour (which was subsequently extended to three-quarters), and after some tea, with something to eat, the Regiment marched excellently – well closed up in their fours, and in good spirits, for another three hours to a bivouac in a pleasant field.

Once again the 52nd were off to an early start on September 3rd, as they set out, at 3 a.m., on the fourteen miles march to Petit Courrois. This movement of the 5th Brigade to the east was intended to close the gap that had developed between the British right and the left flank of the nearest French troops. Until the turn to the east, the Regiment was convinced that Paris was to be their destination. The journey took them from Chauconin through the town of Meaux with its magnificent cathedral, via Trilport, Montceaux, Pierre Levée and finally at midday to Petit Courrois. The medieval town of Meaux was reached at 4 a.m. and the River Marne was crossed just before 6 a.m. The exact spot at Petit Courrois was three quarters of a mile west of the La Ferté-sous-Jouarre to Coulommiers road, and roughly midway between these two places. The remainder of the day was spent in resting in another corn field. Henry Davies managed a good long night's sleep under a haystack. That evening Captain Allan Harden and D Company occupied an outpost line to the east of the bivouac. They spent a great deal of time looking into French staff cars, amongst Belgian and local refugees for German spies. In this they were unsuccessful. Nearby, the 2nd Worcestershire succeeded in shooting down an enemy aircraft that evening.

On September 4th, yet another day of oppressive heat, the 1st Division and a Cavalry Brigade moved off southwards from La Ferté across the front of the 52nd. Reports came in to the effect that the enemy was crossing the River Marne by the partially destroyed bridge at La Ferté. By this time the 1st Division had passed through the 52nd, and at about 10 a.m. Henry Davies was ordered to use his men as an outpost and rearguard, and to move towards La Ferté. Davies was told that if the enemy advanced he was to make some resistance, but to retire if heavily engaged. Davies placed A Company about L'Hôtel des Bois where there was an excellent field of fire. C Company was at La Fingle on the left of the road and part of B Company on the right. The remainder of B Company was to the south of this, facing east and D Company remained at Petit Courrois. However, the Germans were seen to be marching away to the east on the road to Montmirail, and only a few cavalry patrols came in the direction of the 52nd.

[39] Lieutenant Rupert Brett.

During the afternoon of the 4th, the 52nd received orders to move back on Petit Courrois at 5 p.m., and to form the rearguard while the 5th Brigade retreated during the hours of darkness through Giremontiers. As the 52nd began to withdraw they were followed by a small body of German cavalry. Lieutenant Reggie Owen of A Company described what happened.

> At about 6 p.m. the Company was ordered to withdraw, and I to do rearguard with my Platoon. Soon after the Company had moved off, I saw two mounted men coming along the road towards us. I got my glasses on to them, but could not make up my mind for certain whether they were Germans or our own troopers, but I thought they must be the former. I had my men across the road with bayonets fixed and rifles loaded. Meanwhile the two horsemen had come within a few hundred yards, and there was no further doubt that they were Germans of the Death's Head Hussars. They were quite by themselves, although I could see a few others about a half mile behind them. They continued to come along quite unconcernedly, until they got within about forty yards, when I called out to them, and held up my arms, with the idea of trying to convey to them that they better surrender. They, thereupon, threw their lances on to the road, and we immediately doubled forward and bagged them. Two of my men took possession of the lances, and were very pleased with themselves; while I, having selected the better horse of the two, immediately mounted it. As this was our first capture, there was naturally a certain amount of excitement. By this time we were getting rather left behind, and a few more Germans were coming along, so I gave the order to open fire on them. We knocked one fellow out, also killing his horse, and wounding another, whose rider scuttled like a hare into a wood which bordered the road. We then joined up with the Company feeling quite happy. When I examined the holsters of my newly acquired charger, I found several boxes of matches, towels, sponges, tins of preserved meat, and various odds and ends, which I distributed amongst the men of the Platoon.

The 52nd marched out of Petit Courrois at 7.30 p.m., on the 4th, and followed the rest of the 5th Brigade. Led by Allan Harden on a bright moonlight night, their nine and a half mile route took them through Le Gros Chêne, Pré aux Rats, Le Charnois and to bivouac in yet another stubble field at Le Fay Farm, at 1.30 a.m. the following day. Their rest period was short-lived as they were on the road again at 6 a.m. [5th], once more as Brigade rearguard, with another nine miles march ahead of them. The River Morin was crossed at Tresmes and then via Faremoutiers to the Avenue of the Château at Lumigny. Here there was a long halt before the 52nd bivouacked at nearby Champlet. Fastidious Guy Blewitt managed a bath in a canvas bucket. The rest of 5th Brigade went on to Marles. A and B Companies were sent as outposts to face north on the Marles to Lumigny road with, on their right, the 1st Division, and on the left, the 2nd Connaught Rangers. The night was a quiet one except for one brief episode of firing, and it was here in Champlet that the 52nd's retreat from the vicinity of Mons came to an end.

The 52nd's Commanding Officer, Henry Davies wrote the following at the end of the retreat.

> Between 24th August and the 5th September we have done 178 miles in 12 marches, and had one halt day. Not a very long distance, but very long hours under arms; hardly any sleep, and broiling hot weather. Never in my life have I felt anything like the degree of tiredness that I felt on this retreat. Everyone suffered in the same way. We often wondered if we should ever feel rested again, and whether it would have any permanent effect on us[40]. The worst thing was the want of sleep; next came the heat of the sun and the thirst. I think the extreme fatigue brought on a sort of unnatural thirst. Hunger I do not think one felt to any great extent. Once or twice I tried to eat some biscuit and bully beef at a halt on the march, but failed to manage more than a few mouthfuls. Apples helped us more than anything; and whenever we happened to halt near apple trees, I always ordered the apples to be picked and eaten.
>
> More than half the men were reservists, who, in spite of some route marches, had not got into proper condition for marching, and consequently, there were a good many sore feet. A few of these were so bad that they had to be sent to hospital, but the large majority of the sore-footed men stuck to it splendidly. We usually had no ambulances with us, so that even the men who fell down unconscious with sunstroke had to be got along on transport of some kind, or on artillery limbers. In spite of all this, the Regiment had only one man missing during the whole retreat. The officers all worked magnificently; tired to death as they themselves were, they

[40] After the war, Henry Davies was of the opinion that no one suffered permanent ill effects from the horrendous retreat in the searing August heat.

> kept their companies together all through. Whenever there was a halt, men dropped down and slept on the road, and one had to allow extra time at each halt to wake them up before we could get on the move again. Sometimes a company commander, going down his company to wake men, would find at the end that some of the men whom he had awakened first had dropped asleep again.
>
> Though having to begin the war with a long retirement undoubtedly came as an unpleasant surprise, we did not feel any real depression or loss of confidence. Every day we expected to be the last of retiring, and we always imagined that we should turn round and advance the following day. The retreat was certainly carried farther than we expected, but this only made it all the more pleasant when we did eventually turn round and chase the Germans.

Major Archibald Eden's memories and the distance covered during the retreat from Mons were a little different from those of Henry Davies.

> C Company was on outpost near a large farm and market garden, and close to a fine shooting lodge; so plenty of good vegetables, as well as jam and some excellent red wine, were to be had. A quiet night. In the last 16 days we have marched 227 miles, and I have had 45 hours sleep (excluding the rest day, when some of us managed 8 or 10 solid hours). The actual distance of march since the retirement began is 173 miles in 12 marching days. Lumigny was the most southerly point reached by the 5th Brigade. Weather still very hot.

A member of the 5th Brigade Signals' staff[41] held the view that during the retreat from Mons, the Connaught Rangers had struggled most followed by the 52nd. He felt the reason for this was that the 52nd's officers were inclined to do everything themselves and thus became exhausted. The Regiment that coped best with the rigours of the long retreat was the 1st King's Royal Rifle Corps of the 6th Brigade. Their officers delegated much more to the N.C.O.s and were less worn out.

Between September 6th and 10th 1914[42], was fought the First Battle of the Marne or as it is sometimes called the Miracle of the Marne, in which the 52nd

---

[41] Personal communication from the late Colonel Robin Evelegh, whose father was an officer with the 5th Brigade's Signal Staff, during the Retreat from Mons.

[42] According to the Battles Nomenclature Committee the battle began on September 7th. Edmonds, in the *Official History,* gave the date of the start of the offensive as September 6th.

were to play a small part. It ended in a victory for the Anglo-French forces under Sir John French and General Joseph Joffre over the German armies of Generalobersten Alexander von Kluck and Karl von Bulow. The allies numbered some 1,071,000 against the Germans 1,485,000 and the casualties suffered were 263,000 against 250,000. On September 6th, the B.E.F. had on its left the Sixth French Army, under General M.J. Manoury, and on its right the French Fifth Army, now under General Franchet d'Espèrey[43]. When the German armies altered their original plans and swung away from Paris to the south-east, General Joseph Joffre, the French Commander-in-Chief, saw his opportunity to attack the enemy's exposed right flank. The German's apparent intention had been to fall on the French Fifth Army in great strength. The French Sixth Army under General Manoury was ordered to wheel up and to attack the enemy on the River Ourcq, cross the river and attack Generaloberst von Kluck's First German army in the flank. The B.E.F. was also to swing to the right and join in the general offensive. This was put into effect on September 6th, and by midday the enemy, having realized the predicament they were in, began to withdraw to the north.

The next day September 7th saw the French Fifth and Sixth Armies push the enemy back towards the Rivers Ourcq and Petit Morin, and inflict considerable casualties on him. The British Cavalry and some infantry were also involved. On the 8th the Germans were still retreating, but the fighting remained severe all day. The following day, the 9th, the River Marne was crossed with some difficulty as the bridges had been destroyed and the Germans were stubborn in their resistance. The two French armies, after long and fierce fighting, drove the enemy northwards. The pursuit of the Germans resumed at dawn, and the B.E.F. pushed the enemy back across the River Ourcq, taking large numbers of prisoners and much military equipment. On September 11th, the British crossed the Ourcq with little opposition and the same day the cavalry reached the River Aisne. It was here that the Germans chose to stand and fight.

Sunday, September 6th, opened quietly for the 52nd in their bivouacs at Champlet. Early in the morning, the 52nd were ordered to be ready to move at any moment, but did not actually do so until 7 p.m. The delay was said to be due to the 3rd Division coming up into the line. To the east was artillery fire and the enemy was reported to be in the Forêt de Crécy and the Forêt de Malvoisine to the

[43] General Franchet d'Espèrey [1856-1942] had replaced General Charles Lanrezac in command of the Fifth Army and was called by the British troops 'Desperate Frankie'. In May 1918, he would be badly defeated by the Germans at the Battle of Chemin des Dames and was removed from the Western Front. Subsequently he commanded the Allied Armies in Salonika. In 1919, he entered Constantinople and would cause lasting resentment amongst the local population by riding his white horse over the Turkish flag in the Galata district.

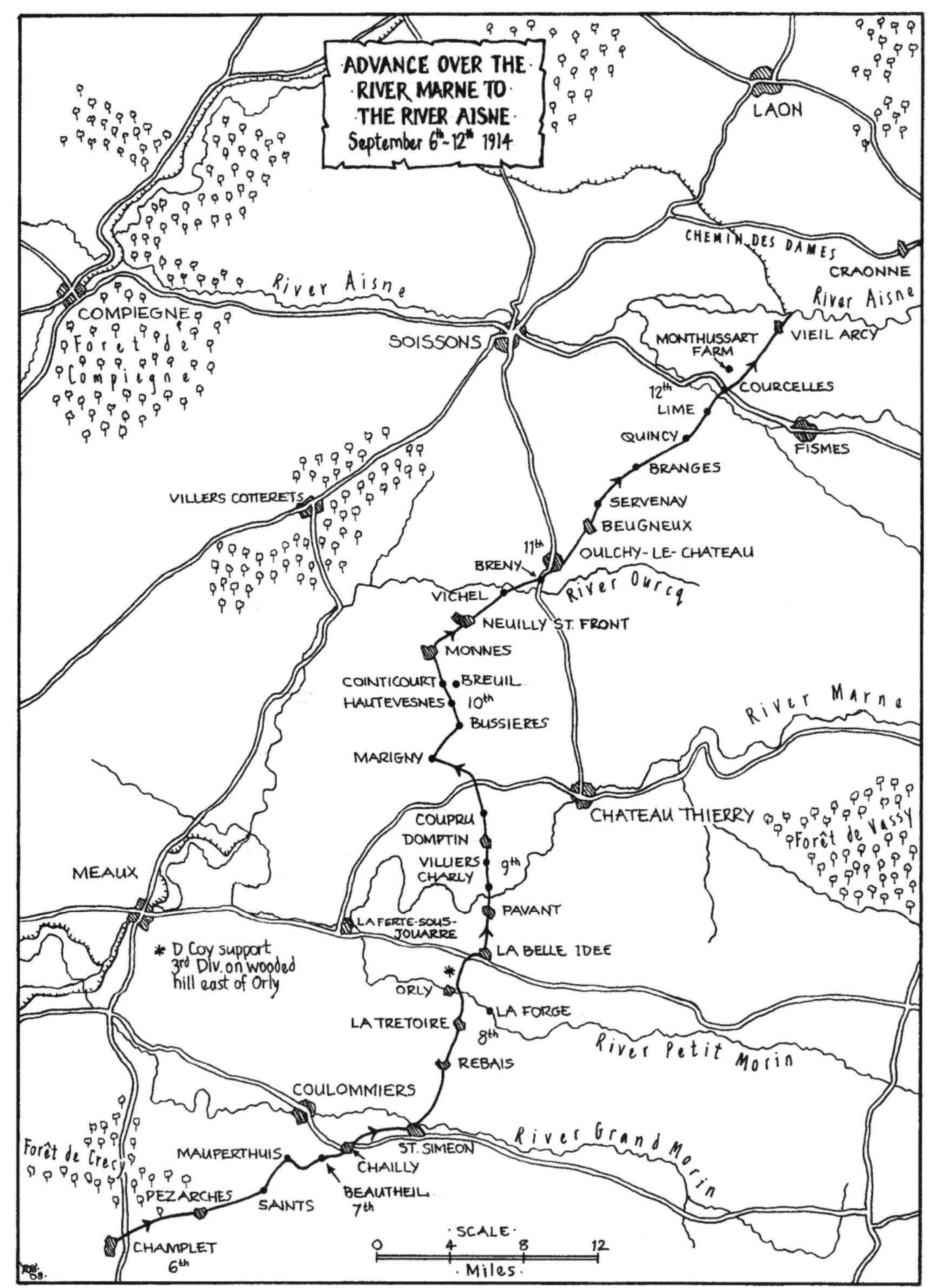
ADVANCE OVER THE RIVER MARNE TO THE RIVER AISNE
September 6th–12th 1914
LAON
CHEMIN DES DAMES
CRAONNE
River Aisne
COMPIEGNE
Forêt de Compiègne
SOISSONS
MONTHUSSART FARM
VIEIL ARCY
COURCELLES
12th
LIME
QUINCY
FISMES
BRANGES
VILLERS COTTERETS
SERVENAY
BEUGNEUX
11th
OULCHY-LE-CHATEAU
BRENY
River Ourcq
VICHEL
NEUILLY ST. FRONT
MONNES
COINTICOURT
BREUIL
HAUTEVESNES
10th
BUSSIERES
River Marne
MARIGNY
CHATEAU THIERRY
Forêt de Vassy
COUPRU
DOMPTIN
VILLIERS CHARLY
9th
MEAUX
PAVANT
LA FERTE-SOUS-JOUARRE
LA BELLE IDEE
* D Coy support 3rd Div. on wooded hill east of Orly
ORLY
LA FORGE
LA TRETOIRE
8th
REBAIS
River Petit Morin
COULOMMIERS
River Grand Morin
ST. SIMEON
Forêt de Crecy
MAUPERTHUIS
CHAILLY
BEAUTHEIL
7th
PEZARCHES
SAINTS
SCALE
0 4 8 12
Miles
CHAMPLET
6th

north of the 52nd. There was some light artillery shelling which forced the 5th Brigade, including the 52nd, to dig trenches at Champlet, while D Company was occupied in outposts in the woods around the Château of Lumigny. The long range shelling of their positions around Champlet proved to be the high water mark of the German advance. To the east and west the Germans were being pushed back and about 2.30 p.m. word went down the line that the enemy was retreating. Eventually, at 7 p.m., the 52nd were able to march the three miles to a damp field just north-east of Pézarches, where they were able to bivouac uncomfortably.

The next day, the 7th, was the first day of significant advance to the Marne and their march began at 8.45 a.m. As Guy Blewitt put it: 'very thankful to be pursuing instead of pursued, the miles did not seem so long and weary and everyone was in high spirits'[44]. In the 2nd Division column, the 4th Brigade [Guards] led the way with the 5th Brigade following them and the 6th Brigade bringing up the rear. A halt from 9 a.m. to midday was called for at Mauperthuis, where the presence of dead horses made the air malodorous. On they went again from Mauperthuis to Saints, Beautheil, Le Fahy-Banchelin and Chailly-en-Brie to bivouac in yet another stubble field at St. Simeon, at 7 p.m., a distance of fourteen miles for the day. There were concerns about water for both men and horses as the Germans had supposedly poisoned the water supply. To add to the general paranoia, tin tacks were found in some of the bags of oats, and this again was attributed to the devious enemy.

Henry Davies in his diary entry for the day recorded further underhand activities of the Germans.

> On this march we passed numerous old German bivouacs, in which the most conspicuous feature was the number of empty bottles. Evidently they issue wine as a ration, or else the troops help themselves. In all the villages through which we are passing now a lot of damage has been done to houses and furniture by German troops. Shops are often looted, and the French inhabitants complain bitterly of their conduct.

The 52nd set off again at 6.45 a.m. September 8th for Rebais, which was full of British troops, and then to a little short of La Trétoire where they had a long wait. During this halt they were joined by Captain Charles 'Buggins' Higgins and the second reinforcement of 80 men. They had gone by train to Coulommiers and marched from there. Charles Higgins took over C Company

---

[44] Diary entry for September 7th 1914.

from Archibald Eden who now acted as senior major. The cause of the delay was a sharp fire fight between the 4th Brigade [Guards] who were again leading the 2nd Division, and the Germans holding the line of the Petit Morin River with its steep banks. From Le Trétoire a winding road led northwards towards the river through a thickly wooded valley, which the German machine-gunners made great use of, and the Guards were soon in action. The 2nd Worcestershire and the 2nd H.L.I. from the 5th Brigade were sent up to assist the Guards. The 52nd were not involved in this action. Eventually, by 2 p.m. the Petit Morin had been forced at La Forge and Becherelle.

To the west, the 3rd Division had been trying to force the Germans out of Orly and this was achieved by 3 p.m. with assistance from the 2nd Connaught Rangers and the 52nd which had by this time passed through La Trétoire, crossed the river and approached Orly from the east. Meanwhile D Company of the 52nd was sent up a wooded hill to the east of Orly and ran into some Germans. In the thick wood, a scout, Private Arthur Allen aged 25 years, from Stoke Newington, was killed and became the first 52nd man of the war to be killed in action[45]. D Company pushed on and succeeded in killing five Germans including an officer belonging to the Guards Jäger Battalion[46]. A bicycle, two ponies and a complete packet of maps were captured from the enemy. For gallantry during this little action Private A. Kippax was later awarded the French Médaille Militaire. As the objective of the advance, Orly, had been taken, Brigadier-General Richard Haking ordered the recall of D Company. The march was then resumed to La Belle Idée, on the La Ferté to Montmirail road, about two miles north-east of Orly, where well after dark the 52nd bivouacked, having covered eleven and three quarters miles that day.

September 9th was to be the day when the B.E.F. forced the passage of the River Marne. The 2nd Division, of which the 52nd were a part, was on the left flank of I Corps, and advanced on Charly, and the 3rd Division, on the right flank of II Corps, advanced on Nanteuil. A stiff resistance by the enemy was expected, but this was not to be the case. At 4.30 a.m., the 6th Brigade, who had replaced the 4th Brigade [Guards] as the advanced guard of the 2nd Division, set off for the bridge at Charly. Cautiously approaching the bridge they found it barricaded with carts and furniture. Loop-holes had been made in the walls of the adjacent buildings and it seemed that the 6th Brigade were in for a difficult time. However,

---

[45] Private Arthur Allen was buried by the side of the La Trétoire to Orly road, close to the spot where he was killed. He is commemorated on the La Ferté-sous-Jouarre memorial.

[46] Richard Crosse recorded that four Germans were killed. Guy Blewitt who unlike Crosse was present at the action recorded in his diary entry for September 8th 1914 that five Germans were killed.

the bridge was undefended and the local inhabitants reported that the Germans had got drunk and had gone away. The 6th Brigade crossed to the north bank of the Marne unopposed.

Meanwhile, the 5th Brigade and the 52nd did not march until 11.30 a.m., as there was a delay in the supply wagons coming up, and the subsequent issuing of rations. When they reached Pavant, less than half way to the river, the Brigade was ordered to entrench on the south bank of the Marne. The reason for this was that large numbers of enemy were north of Château-Thierry and there was a lack of support on the right from the French. Consequently Sir Douglas Haig ordered I Corps to halt until the position became clearer. Hence those units of the 2nd Division who had not yet crossed the Marne were to remain in observation on the south bank. The 52nd had just started to dig trenches when the order was cancelled and the march was resumed once more. The 5th Brigade crossed the River Marne at Charly around 5 p.m. unopposed.

The main difficulty was the number of troops wishing to use the bridge including those of II Corps. A German soldier had written on a wall in Charly the date on which they expected to enter Paris! The march continued to the north by Villiers-sur-Marne, and they went into bivouac near Domptin. The bivouac was cold, damp and uncomfortable. Worse still there was little available water and the animals could have none that night. This was particularly distressing for the grooms who were inclined to water the horses before themselves. Guy Blewitt's insides were upset and he put this down to bitter red wine. Many of the Regiment had suffered from similar problems during the retreat from Mons. The 52nd had covered nine miles during the day.

Harry Dillon wrote to his family again[47].

> I am perfectly fit and well but we all want rest and boots. Will you please send me 3 tins Gold Flake cigarettes and 2 boxes of matches a week. We have had no letters for 3 weeks but I hope they will be coming regularly soon. We get the best of it everywhere we meet the Germans but there are not enough of us to do much good. I think everything is going satisfactorily. The Germans are behaving in a most brutal manner and appear to take no notice of the Geneva convention. We got two of their horses the other day and have been allowed to keep one so far which Owen[48] Pepys[49] and myself share and he is a great blessing and carries a lot of our things besides one

[47] Probably written from Domptin on September 9th 1914.
[48] Lieutenant Reggie Owen.
[49] Second-Lieutenant Francis Pepys.

> of us. Not at all a bad looking Grey. They took the other away but he was not much good as he was on his last legs. It is one of the worst things in the war, dead horses everywhere and the stink is fearful. The corpses of the men get moved or disposed of somehow but there is no time to deal with the horses. The battle goes on more or less continuously and God knows when it will end, the enemy's losses must be enormous.

On the final day of the Battle of the Marne, the 10th, rouse was at 3.30 a.m., and Henry Davies left the cover of his apple tree which had kept off the dew, and the 52nd were on the road at 4.20 a.m. Their route took them via Coupru, Marigny-en-Orxois to Bussières. Just short of Bussières heavy firing was heard where the advanced guard, in the form of the 6th Brigade, attacked an enemy column which was caught between them and the 3rd Division on the left. The German column was retiring up a narrow valley, and the 52nd's B and half C Companies were able to join in, by moving on to the right flank of the 6th Brigade north of Hautevesnes. Later, the 5th Brigade was ordered to advance on the left of the 1st Division, which was moving on Priez, across country west of Couchamps, through Montmenjon, Breuil, and Cointicourt, to attack the ridge behind. The 52nd led the 5th Brigade, advanced on the ridge, and the few Germans they found soon retired. However, on the ridge they were subjected to shellfire, as were all the companies at some point in the day. It was the first vigorous shelling of the war that the 52nd had been subjected to. In Montmenjon, Private Sidney Beldon from Great Marlow, and the pack animal he was leading were killed by a shell. Beldon was the second 52nd man of the war to be killed. Four other men were wounded during the day. At 4 p.m. the 5th Brigade, including the 52nd, reached the small village of Monnes, but it was 7 p.m. before they bivouacked and then in a small and wet field. The 52nd had covered twelve miles during a miserably wet day.

The 2nd Division continued to march to the north-east, at 5 a.m. on the 11th. The 52nd passed through Neuilly, Vichel, Nanteuil, Rozet-St. Albin, Grand Menil and Oulchy-la-Ville to Beugneux, which they reached at 1 p.m., and bivouacked in a field on the windward side of a hill in pouring rain. Some of the 5th Brigade found billets, but the 52nd were the unlucky ones. The hot weather of the retreat from Mons had gone. They had marched thirteen miles.

Guy Blewitt recorded in his diary.

> All the villages we came through were in an awful state after the Germans had looted them. I went into various houses, the German

> system of looting is extraordinary, everything is destroyed, nothing left on the walls, all cupboards and drawers pulled open and the contents thrown on the floor, it was even the same in a house chalked up "Offiziere Kaserne. Kein eintrilt [sic][50]."

It was clear by nightfall on September 10th 1914 that the First Battle of the Marne had been won by the allies. Both east and west, principally the French armies had beaten back the German enemy who were in full retreat. The British had played their part in thrusting into the enemy's weakened line and had driven them back. The 52nd had played but a small part and had been involved in little serious fighting, as is shown by only two deaths since the campaign started. In the retreat from Mons whenever the 52nd were rearguard the enemy were not very active, whereas the 2nd Connaught Rangers were decimated on August 26th. In the advance across the Marne other units seemed to come into action more frequently than the 52nd Light Infantry. This was through no fault of the 52nd, but was part of the lottery of war and was soon to change in the vicinity of the river Aisne.

[50] Officers Barracks. No entry. [eintritt].

Chapter III

The Battle of the Aisne and La Cour de Soupir.

September 12th - October 19th 1914

[Maps: pages 49, 54.]

The Battle of the Aisne was officially designated as having taken place between September 12th-15th 1914. This included the final day, the 12th, of advance towards the river, the crossings on the 13th, 14th and the attempted push forward on the 15th. The 12th had been a disappointing day for the allies with no Aisne bridges taken and their forces still some two miles from the river. The nature of the country with its numerous streams and valleys favoured the delaying tactics of the enemy. Heavy rain with the inevitable muddy roads did not help either. The British forces had advanced some 50-60 miles against the retreating German enemy. At the Aisne, the Germans had prepared a line of defence, but it was not clear whether this was merely to allow rearguard delaying tactics or as a solid line of defence. Sir John French, commanding the British Expeditionary Force, believed that there were a minimum of three German army corps guarding the passage of the Aisne. On the morning of September 13th French ordered his troops to force this passage.

The valley of the Aisne runs approximately east and west, and is a flat bottomed depression whose width varies from half a mile to two miles and down which the river runs following a winding course towards the west. Both sides of the valley are about 400 feet high and consist of numerous spurs and re-entrants. The slopes are steep in places with woods, quarries and ravines. Several villages and small towns are scattered along the floor of the valley and between the spurs. The principal town is Soissons and the British sector stretched from here to Villers, about 30 miles to the east. The Aisne is a sluggish river 50 yards in width and fifteen feet deep in the centre. In the British sector there were eleven crossing points, all of which were under German artillery fire from the northern bank. In addition, for much of the sector, the Aisne canal runs parallel to the river and formed an additional watery barrier to the British troops. About five miles to the north of the valley of the Aisne lies the Chemin des Dames or 'Ladies Way'[51]. This road runs along the chalky ridge, which separates the valley of the Aisne in the south from that of the Ailette to the north, and is nearly nineteen miles long.

[51] Acquired this name in the 18th century as it was the route taken by the daughters, Adélaide and Victoire, of Louis XV, between Paris and the Château de La Bove, home of Louis' former mistress, Countess of Narbonne-Lara, whom the two women used to visit. To make the journey easier Louis XV had the road surfaced and it then gained the name Chemin des Dames.

The British forces used in the assault across the Aisne were the I, II, and III Corps plus cavalry. I Corps was on the right of the line with the French Fifth Army on its right. To the left of the I Corps were in succession the II, III Corps and finally the Sixth French Army. The crossing of the Aisne was difficult as the Germans had taken care to destroy all the bridges bar one and this was kept under artillery and machine-gun fire. On September 13th, British forces moved up to first the canal and then the river and proceeded to repair the bridges and put pontoons into position in order to effect a crossing. They met with mixed fortunes but in general those on the right or east of the line progressed better than the others. Further crossings were made on the 14th and once across the river the various brigades pushed on and endeavoured to reach the all-important commanding heights of the Chemin des Dames. Elements of the 1st Division [I Corps] reached this key ridge near Cerny, but elsewhere the British became bogged down under intense German artillery fire. Despite every effort to push forward, the war became a static one of trench warfare.

Later in September, while the British held down the valley of the Aisne, General Joseph Joffre, the French Commander-in-Chief, ordered the French Sixth Army to drive the German right flank back. By the end of the month this had been done and the Germans were facing westwards with their extreme right on St. Quentin. The Germans realized that they had been foiled in their bid to take Paris and that they were faced with a stalemate. Hence, whilst leaving a holding force in position, the enemy moved the centre of his attention to the north-east and the plains of Flanders. The British and French followed suit and the race to the sea started.

The 52nd Light Infantry began their approach to the Aisne by marching out of Beugneux at 5.30 a.m. September 12th. Their route took them through Servenay, Arcy, Branges, Jouaignes, Quincy to Lime where a long halt took place. This allowed the bridge over the River Vesle at Courcelles to be repaired so that infantry could cross it. The 5th Infantry Brigade led by the 2nd Worcestershire and the 52nd were the advance guard of the 2nd Division for the day. During the afternoon the 2nd Worcestershire crossed the bridge and marched to the high ground to the north of Courcelles and occupied Monthussart Farm beyond it. They were followed across the bridge by the 52nd who advanced towards the Braine-Dhuizel road.

Meanwhile on the left of the 2nd Division's advance, the cavalry was driving back the enemy across the same high ground. Suddenly, just beyond Monthussart Farm, a large party of Germans[52] came into sight and D Company,

[52] Crosse in *A Record of H.M. 52nd Light Infantry in 1914* stated that they were members of the 13th Landwehr Division. As the division was not formed until 1915, this cannot be correct.

under Captain Allan Harden, leading the 52nd, opened fire. Immediately, the Germans put up white flags of surrender, but remembering how the enemy had not always respected the use of a white flag, D Company made them abandon their arms, whilst covering them with rifles. Seven officers and about 107 other ranks were made prisoner. A Company, under Captain Evelyn Villiers[53], had only just come up beside D Company when five Uhlans[54] on horseback came galloping up as if lost. A Company opened fire killing one and capturing two more, one of whom was wounded. By crossing the Vesle at Courcelles, the 5th Brigade had struck the flank of the retreating Germans. This little excitement was followed by a delay before the 52nd continued their progress to Vieil Arcy, arriving at 8 p.m., having marched sixteen miles without suffering casualties in their minor forays with the enemy. Billeting was much complicated by pouring rain.

The 52nd were in the 5th Brigade, 2nd Division, of Sir Douglas Haig's I Corps. At 5 a.m. on September 13th they witnessed Divisional cavalry passing through the 5th Brigade outposts at Vieil Arcy, to reconnoitre the canal and river bridges. The canal bridge at Pont Arcy had been partially destroyed and had a gap of six to eight feet in its centre. The river bridge at Pont Arcy had been virtually destroyed apart from one twisted girder which allowed men to cross in single file. Without delay the 2nd Connaught Rangers, the vanguard of the 2nd Division, crossed the damaged canal bridge and then used the surviving girder to cross the river bridge. They were then able to cover the repair of the canal bridge and the bringing up of pontoons. Between 11.15 a.m. and 4.30 p.m., the 11th Field Company R.E. repaired the canal bridge with wooden planking and sleepers, making it fit for ordinary military traffic. The arrival of the 1st Division's pontoons allowed a bridge of six barges and one trestle to be placed over the river 100 yards downstream and to the west of the old river bridge. Details of how the 52nd spent the morning of the 13th are sparse. Lieutenant-Colonel Henry Davies recorded that prisoners were sent back, the mail arrived and he had time to shave and write letters himself. Captain Guy Blewitt managed another canvas bucket bath and a haircut.

Lieutenant Reggie Owen of A Company recorded in his diary some memories of the day.

---

[53] Captain Evelyn Villiers of the 1st Royal Sussex Regiment was attached to A Company.

[54] The name Uhlan is derived through Polish from Turkish-Tartar and was originally given to light cavalry armed and clothed in semi-oriental fashion. But the word became best known as a term for German heavy cavalry armed with a ten foot five inches long rolled steel lance. The four edged point was twelve inches long. The distinction between Uhlans and other cavalry became only one of uniform and tradition. In 1914, the Imperial German Army had no less than 26 Uhlan Regiments. All were disbanded in 1918-19.

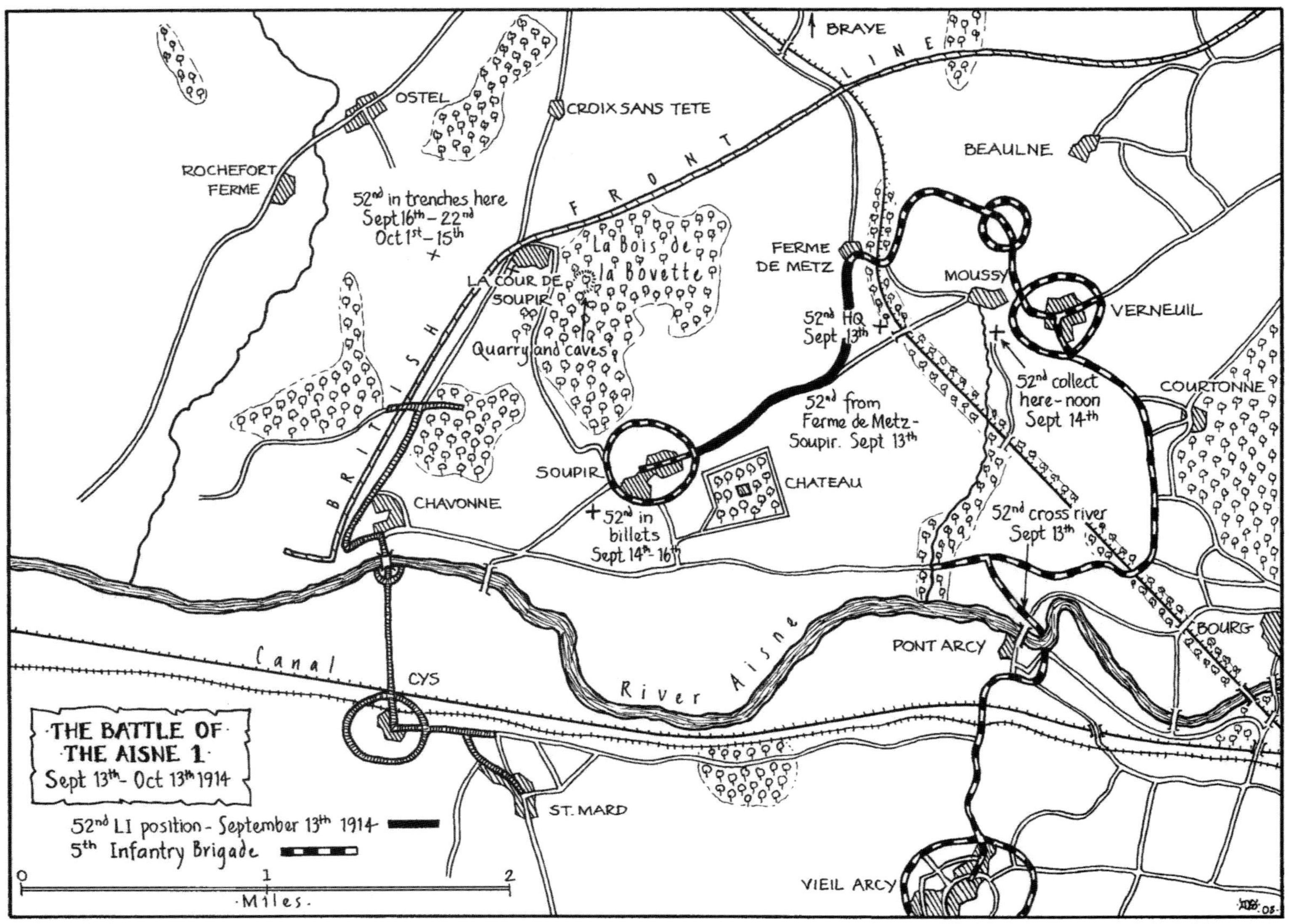
BRAYE
OSTEL
CROIX SANS TETE
ROCHEFORT FERME
BEAULNE
BRITISH FRONT LINE
52nd in trenches here Sept 16th - 22nd Oct 1st - 15th
La Bois de la Bovette
LA COUR DE SOUPIR
Quarry and caves
FERME DE METZ
MOUSSY
VERNEUIL
52nd HQ Sept 13th
52nd collect here - noon Sept 14th
COURTONNE
52nd from Ferme de Metz - Soupir. Sept 13th
SOUPIR
CHATEAU
CHAVONNE
52nd in billets Sept 14th - 16th
52nd cross river Sept 13th
BOURG
PONT ARCY
Canal
CYS
River Aisne
THE BATTLE OF THE AISNE 1
Sept 13th - Oct 13th 1914
ST. MARD
52nd LI position - September 13th 1914
5th Infantry Brigade
0
1
2
Miles
VIEIL ARCY

> We tumbled out of bed, found our socks, etc, while the good lady brewed us some coffee, and we had quite a good breakfast of eggs and sardines; the latter we got from the mess.
>
> However, no actual order to move came, and at about 11.30 a.m. we had a substantial meal all together, which improved matters very considerably. This turned out to be a red letter day, as a mail arrived during the morning, and also a parcel for me which contained a khaki shirt among other things, which I was thankful to get. I changed at once in the middle of the yard, and as I had been wearing the other shirt day and night ever since we left Aldershot, i.e. five weeks, I thought it better to burn it----. After this excitement I went back to the cottage and put in about three hours' sleep, after which I wrote some letters. We had another good meal and eventually left our billets at 4.30 p.m.

About 5 p.m., the 52nd crossed to the northern bank of the Aisne on the newly made pontoon bridge under desultory shellfire and fortunately suffered no casualties. After a brief hold up on the Bourg to Chavonne road, the 5th Brigade formed an outpost line from near Verneuil to Soupir. The 52nd were responsible for the section from the Ferme de Metz to Soupir [exclusive], which corresponded roughly with the gentle curve of the road between Soupir and Moussy. The 2nd Worcestershire was on their right and the 2nd Connaught Rangers on their left. The remaining battalion of the brigade, the 2nd H.L.I., was in reserve at Verneuil. Lieutenant-Colonel Henry Davies positioned the 52nd's headquarters in an estaminet close to the canal bridge west of Moussy and managed a few hours welcome sleep in a real bed. D Company was nearby in reserve, A to the right around the Ferme de Metz, B was in the centre, and C on the left as far as the beginning of the village of Soupir.

Captain Harry Dillon continued his correspondence with his family[55].

> Everything is going well and I think the Germans are done. Yesterday after sleeping out in the rain we came up with them. We were under pretty sharp infantry fire for some time but no casualties, the regiment captured 116 prisoners including 5 officers how many of them we killed and wounded and were taken away I don't know. – Our bullets make fearful wounds. – I spent some time trying to help a poor devil who had half his inside out and an arm ripped off but he died so we chucked him into an old trench and covered him

[55] Letter written on September 13th 1914.

> up. Many of the sights are ghastly. – I captured another horse the day before but had to let him go as he was so done. The day before that again we nearly got some horses that were running loose but the shelling was rather heavy and as we were some way ahead they stopped us. I suppose we shall be chasing them now for some time which means marching all day and coming into action in the evening. One hears the guns incessantly all round but does not really often come into action although they may be shelling some place only 100 yards off on one side or the other. We have not lost a man yet in my Coy. which is extraordinary the rest all have, but we have captured bicycles, horses and Germans galore so there is no cause to complain. I don't mind this show except for marching and being always wet and short of sleep etc.

The night of September 13th was wet and cold, but trouble-free apart from the rumbling of wheels on the ridge in front of them. In the early morning [14th] a German cavalry patrol approached the Ferme de Metz.

Lieutenant Reggie Owen recorded in his diary.

> As soon as it was daylight we were suddenly shelled by the enemy. A cavalry patrol had come up almost to the farm about half an hour before and had been fired on by our piquets, and I suppose this patrol took back the news that we were holding the farm. At any rate their shells made it too hot for us, and we had to leave the buildings, taking up a position two or three hundred yards behind it. We are now under terrific shellfire, which never slackened for a moment. All we could do was to try and dig ourselves in, lying down as we were; if we started walking about they seemed to spot us at once. More than once fragments of shell fell at my feet. It is now about noon and this had been going on since daylight. What made it so bad was that there seemed to be no support from our own guns behind us. I suppose they had not crossed the river.

One hour after writing this, at 1 p.m., Owen was seriously wounded by shrapnel. He had no less than four gunshot wounds to his shoulder and chest. Reggie Owen, the son of the Dean of Ripon Cathedral, was taken to the Regimental Aid Post situated in out-houses of the estaminet west of Moussy, which had been used as the headquarters of the 52nd the night before. The Regimental Aid Post continued to fill up with wounded until they could be evacuated on the night of the 16th. Owen was taken to the Australian Hospital at St. Nazaire, survived his penetrating chest wounds and returned to the regiment in 1915, still with a shrapnel ball in his thorax. He was a resolute, feisty character who asked the military authorities to pay for his shirt, cardigan, jacket and Burberry, which the Royal Army Medical Corps had cut off him to get at his wounds! Later he would write again asking for his sword, revolver and haversack to be replaced at their expense as they had been lost during his hospital transfers. It is unlikely that he succeeded[56]. During September 14th, the 52nd suffered 45 casualties, four were killed and 41 wounded.

On September 14th, British forces were to continue the pursuit and to act vigorously against the retreating enemy. I Corps was to make the Chemin des Dames its prime objective with the 1st Division making for the sector Cerny-Courtecon, and the 2nd Division from there westwards to Ostel. The 2nd Division's 4th [Guards] and 6th Brigades were to attack in the direction of La Croix sans Tête and Courtecon respectively. The 5th Brigade, including the 52nd, was to hold its outpost line until the 4th and 6th Brigades had passed through and then to follow up. By 10 a.m. the 6th Brigade had passed through the 52nd's outpost line and was engaged in heavy fighting at Braye.

The 4th Brigade [Guards] was to advance through the village of Soupir and La Cour de Soupir [a large farm situated on the edge of a plateau, one and a half miles north-west of the village][57], to secure La Croix sans Tête, whose alternative name was Point 197. The Guards passed through the 2nd Connaught Rangers on the 5th Brigade's left and advanced up the densely wooded slope towards La Cour de Soupir. The commanding officer of the Connaught Rangers had used his initiative and decided to assist the Guards by taking the high ground at La Cour de Soupir with his own men. At 5.30 a.m. they succeeded in doing so and held the farm and the ground up to La Croix sans Tête. According to Harry Dillon, the Irish regiment 'fought like nothing on earth'[58]. The 2nd Grenadier Guards[59] arrived at 10 a.m. and almost simultaneously the Germans attacked. In the absence of the 6th Brigade, who had been unable to get forward, the defenders of the farm's right flank were almost turned. Heavy fighting continued until the afternoon before the British line was firmly established just to the north of La Cour de Soupir Farm. Without the initiative of the Connaught Rangers, I Corps might only have had a precarious hold on the north bank of the Aisne and the

[56] At the Battle of Cambrai, in 1917, a British tank commander lost his wig when his tank sank in a canal. He tried to sue the War Office for the loss of the wig!

[57] Known to the French as La Ferme de la Cour Soupir. The British called the farm La Cour de Soupir.

[58] Letter from Dillon to his family written on September 23rd 1914.

[59] The first battalion of the 4th Brigade to reach La Cour de Soupir.

Germans might have been able to drive for the Aisne and separate I and II Corps. The 52nd would soon become very familiar with the English-styled buildings of La Cour de Soupir and its trenches. The German opponents of the 2nd Division were the right half of the 14th Reserve Division from Westphalia and part of the 6th Division from Brandenburg.

The 52nd remained in their outpost line during the morning under fire of both high explosive and shrapnel shells. Major Archibald Eden, second-in-command of the 52nd recorded that 'the enemy's fire was very heavy, and did us a great deal of damage. A and B Companies were in the open, with their firing line so situated that they could not use their rifles, and suffered several casualties. One H.E. shell, bursting at one spot, killed four men and wounded another four'. Private William Cheshire of A Company wrote in his diary: 'we dig rabbit holes to hide our heads, we lay quite still until the firing eased up, many are getting killed and wounded'.

In the early afternoon the 52nd were ordered to assemble at Moussy and to advance up the slope with the 2nd Worcestershire. Later this order was cancelled, and at around 5 p.m., a further order placed them in reserve at the disposal of the Guards Brigade, and they marched to Soupir. Although they were shelled on route, casualties were avoided by staying to the south of the Moussy to Soupir road. Brigadier-General E.M. Percival, C.R.A.[60] of the 2nd Division, in command at Soupir, sent them to billets in the village. D Company's officers found themselves in a most comfortable farm house 'where the good lady prepared a most excellent feed----'[61]. However, at about 11 p.m., they were roused from their slumbers and ordered up the hill to support the Guards at La Cour de Soupir. Wearily in the rain the 52nd made their way up the zigzagged road, partly through a deep and heavily-wooded valley, to the farm situated on the plateau above. The German attack proved to be against the 3rd Division on their left, and thankfully the 52nd were able to return down the hill to their billets, and three more hours of blessed sleep.

Harry Dillon of A Company, in a letter to his family gave a more personal account of the 52nd's experiences on September 14th[62].

> We had a fearful day yesterday. My Coy. were on outpost and at dawn some German Cavalry appeared a few minutes later shells began coming. This was about 4.30 a.m. We left the shed we were in and extended in a turnip field only one man being hit. – At about

[60] Commanding Royal Artillery.
[61] Guy Blewitt's diary entry for September 14th 1914.
[62] Dillon's letter was almost certainly written on September 15th 1914.

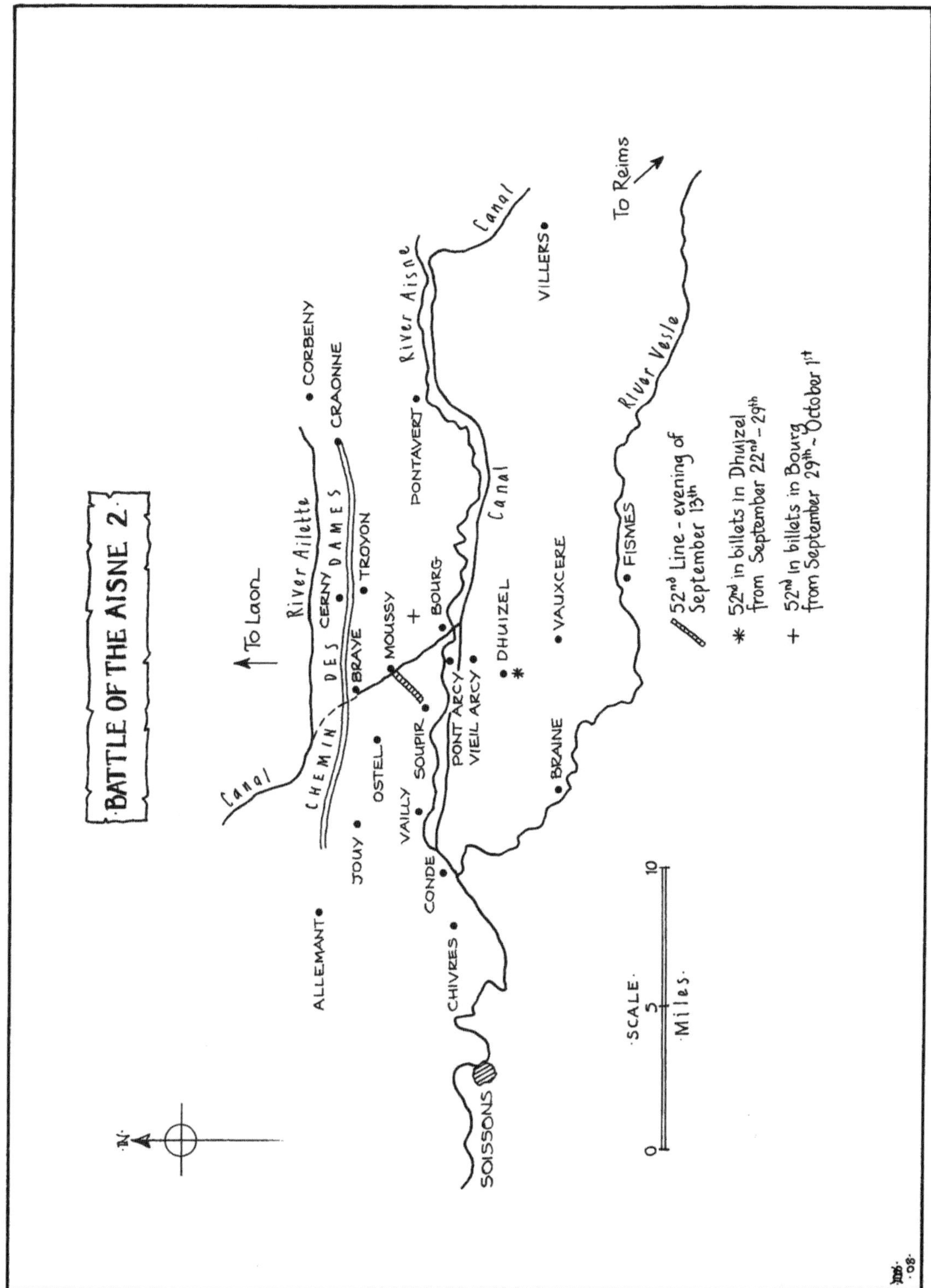
BATTLE OF THE AISNE 2
N
To Laon
To Reims
Canal
River Ailette
CHEMIN DES DAMES
CORBENY
CRAONNE
CERNY
TROYON
BRAYE
MOUSSY
BOURG
PONTAVERT
River Aisne
Canal
Canal
Canal
VILLERS
River Vesle
FISMES
VAUXCERE
DHUIZEL
PONT ARCY
VIEIL ARCY
SOUPIR
OSTEL
VAILLY
JOUY
CONDE
ALLEMANT
CHIVRES
SOISSONS
BRAINE
SCALE
0 5 10
Miles
52nd Line - evening of September 13th
52nd in billets in Dhuizel from September 22nd - 29th
52nd in billets in Bourg from September 29th - October 1st

6 a brigade began to attack[63]. It was a wonderful sight as they swept up the valley among the bursting shells. – These however got more and more and eventually for miles right and left there was nothing but bursting shells. In the meantime our guns could not get across the river and consequently we could not return the compliment, at about 1 o'clock we had to withdraw about 200 yards into a cutting about 4 feet deep. They must have seen us as from then on it was absolute hell let loose, one could not move a finger and the opposite bank was plastered with shell and shrapnel. One high explosive shell burst right above where I was and the 2 poor devils on my right got a piece of it between them. It tore the flesh clean away from the bone of one of their legs, and there was a piece of bone 6 inches long with the flesh hanging over the heel. – We bandaged him up but I expect he will lose his leg, the other one was pretty bad too. – A few minutes later Owen[64] got hit in the shoulder, I think it was a rather nasty one but hope he will be alright. This went on for some time the shells coming at short intervals 8 or 9 together. – I could see down the cutting some men retiring and we were warned to look out for a counter attack by the infantry. – It was not very pleasant as we did not know if we were left alone. – However the firing slackened a bit later on and we managed to move to another place. – By an extraordinary piece of luck the firing stopped in our direction for a bit and we all got away but only just as they sent down again without stopping for a moment for something like ¼ hour. – This beats anything I have ever seen. – All the hollows and orchards where our guns have been (they came into action eventually) were full of dead horses and men and blood and filth. We got to the village where I am now at about 7 p.m. but were turned out again at 11.30 to support a night attack but were not wanted when we got to the place[65] so returned to the village[66]. The fight has been going on continuously ever since but the firing is getting further away and the Germans I hope have got another knock they will not forget. – It is I believe their 3rd crack corps (the iron corps of Brandenburg) we are fighting. – I expect we will turn out later on and pursue them through the

[63] 6th Brigade.
[64] Lieutenant Reggie Owen.
[65] La Cour de Soupir.
[66] Soupir village.

night. The French did well on our left[67] this day so it was a good day for us really. – The worst of it from our point of view that the enemy were too far off for us to use our rifles and so we just had to lie in the rain and mud all day and be hammered wet through and nothing to eat. – It was fair bloody. – I am awfully glad the Russians have come as it will have great moral effect on the Germans. – The swine are up to their old tricks again. The cavalry I mentioned who advanced on us in the morning had on English great coats and caps. – In the advance of one of the Guards regiments some Germans dropped apparently wounded and as the Guards advanced over them they jumped up and shot the officers. – In another case they hoisted a white flag and then opened fire[68]. It was annoying to lose men without firing a shot back. We never let off a rifle all day. Anyhow we are up on them as far as our losses are concerned. I am hoping to get some cigarettes as soon as there is tobacco to be got hold of but it is filth and I have a continual sore mouth. – I would like a Weekly Times as we know very little of what goes on except in our own part. I will go back to bed for a week when I get home. I don't think we average over 2 hours sleep in the 24 and as for washing I have not brushed my hair or done such a thing for days as any water we get we drink and brushes are never seen. Well if I get through this unpunctured I shall have a jolly good bust and I shall not be the only one. Everybody is in good spirits and we are hammering the swine and the men go along with a will and don't seem to think much about getting outed.

September 15th was a day of relative rest for the 52nd in their billets in Soupir and a certain amount of reorganization of the companies was carried out. Although the Germans shelled the 4th Brigade[69] at La Cour de Soupir at 6 a.m., the village of Soupir was free of artillery attention until later in the morning. Lieutenant-Colonel Henry Davies managed seven hours sleep and described it as the first real rest since August 20th when the 52nd were at Mennevret. Captains Guy Blewitt and Charles Higgins walked to Soupir Château, owned by a millionaire Monsieur Calmet, and admired the lake and charming gardens.

[67] French Sixth Army.

[68] Some of these incidents may have been due to the 'fog' of war. However, there were so many reports of this nature that some of them must have been true.

[69] By this stage the 2nd Grenadier Guards had been joined by the 2nd and 3rd Coldstream Guards and the 1st Irish Guards.

Shellfire would see that neither the Château nor the gardens would remain intact for much longer. The 16th was also a fairly peaceful day in the village although there was a lot of shelling all round them. However, at about noon C and D Companies were sent up to La Cour de Soupir in support of the 4th Brigade.

The day before, the 15th, the Guards [4th Brigade], as well as being heavily shelled at La Cour de Soupir from artillery in the vicinity of Ostel, were subjected to vigorous counter-attacks by the enemy. The line that the Guards were holding was too long for them with the number of men that they had available. Under a heavy bombardment they had withdrawn to the nearby woods and watched with quiet satisfaction their erstwhile trenches being plastered with shrapnel. Early in the morning of the 16th, stretcher parties sent out by the Guards to bring in German wounded were shelled deliberately and they had to stop their humanitarian work. Even Red Cross brassards, British or German, were no protection. The enemy wounded that they had managed to bring in were housed in the farm and its outhouses. Neither side were taking many unwounded prisoners. At 11 a.m., a haystack on the right of the farm was set on fire. This acted as a marking point for the enemy's artillery to bring down accurate fire on the farm itself. Eventually the farm was set alight and battalion headquarters was transferred to the quarry, a few yards from the farm, on the east side of the road. There followed a scene of hopelessly illogical chivalry with the British troops rescuing the wounded Germans from burning to death in the farm as a result of their own guns. It was into this horrendous scene that the 52nd's C and D Companies were thrown.

On arriving at La Cour de Soupir the men of C Company were sent into a large cave on the northern edge of the stone quarry which was about 50 yards to the east of the farm. The cave had been used for cattle. D Company was positioned still further to the east of the farm and avoided the impending disaster. Here the men of D Company lay with fixed bayonets on an inky black night in pouring rain unaware of the drama that had unfolded in the quarry. There were several massive caves under the northern side of the quarry, which were used to house the battalion headquarters of the Guards and the wounded of both sides. At about 5 p.m. on the 16th, Major George 'Ma' Jeffreys[70], commanding the 2nd Grenadier Guards received a report that the enemy were advancing, and he ordered his No. 2 Company to come up from the quarry. He positioned his men just below the top edge of the quarry as shells roared over and crashed into the woods further down the slope. Jeffreys and three other officers sat on a ledge near the top of the quarry's bank so that they could occasionally look over the top.

[70] George Jeffreys was described by the former Prime Minister Harold Macmillan, who served with him in the Grenadier Guards, as 'the supreme example of a great regimental officer'.

C Company was also ordered out of the cave so that they would be ready to act. Just as the officers at the head of C Company left the entrance of the cave and entered the quarry there was a tremendous explosion. An eight inch high explosive shell just missed the farm, grazing the roof, and pitched on the edge of the quarry. The trees on the bank fell down with a crash and the whole place was filled with a dense yellow-black smoke.

The shell killed or wounded 59 out of the 103 Grenadier Guards on the edge of the quarry. In addition, it killed three officers and eight men of the 52nd's C Company, and wounded three further officers and eight men of the Regiment. These were the first officer deaths of the war and effectively eliminated the leaders of C Company. The unfortunate officers who died were: Lieutenant Reginald Worthington, the Battalion Scout Officer. Lieutenant Hugh Mockler-Ferryman, whose father and uncle had both served in the 52nd[71]. He had also played minor counties cricket for Berkshire. Second-Lieutenant Paul Giradot, who lived for ten minutes, was the only son of Lieutenant-Colonel J.F. Giradot of the 43rd Light Infantry, a survivor of the *Birkenhead*[72]. The wounded officers were Captain Charles Higgins with shrapnel wounds to his face, Captain Rosslyn Evelegh, and Second-Lieutenant Arthur Tylden-Pattenson.

To make matters even worse the disastrous shot also killed Lieutenant James Huggan[73], the only medical officer in the vicinity. George Jeffreys shouted, 'Where's that Doctor?' Someone said, 'Here Sir', and Jeffreys saw that he was dead. This meant that there was no qualified person to look after the wounded who were packed into the caves. The scene was reminiscent of *Dante's Inferno* with the only light that of a single candle, and both German and British men writhing in agony with their limbs smashed to pieces. The survivors did their best to bind up the wounds and comfort friend and foe alike. Perhaps the luckiest men present in the quarry were three Grenadier Guards officers, including the Commanding Officer Major George Jeffreys, who were sitting close to the centre of the explosion but were left untouched. For some inexplicable reason they were not injured despite the fact that men on every side of them, including those under cover, were killed or wounded.

Captain Harry Dillon was sent up the hill to take command of the officer-depleted C Company. He described the scene that he found in a letter to his

---

[71] Lieutenant-Colonel A.F. Mockler-Ferryman [father] and Major G.F. Mockler-Ferryman [uncle].
[72] The ship sank, on February 26th 1852, off South Africa, with the loss of 23 officers and 468 sailors and soldiers.
[73] Lieutenant James Huggan R.A.M.C. attached to the 3rd Coldstream Guards had been recommended for the Victoria Cross.

brother. It is a very early description of formal trench warfare, which would occupy millions of men for four long years[74].

> ...... at 10 p.m. night before last got a message to say that 3 officers were killed and 3 wounded in one Coy. leaving only a 2nd Lt. The Coy was on top of a big hill and the Col. sent me up to take command. On arrival I found them and a Coy of Guards in a farmyard. One high explosive shell had killed 5 officers and wounded 3 and killed and wounded 80 men. The trenches were just to our front and it was the only place we could be put. It was awful. Some big caves in the hill were filled with dead and wounded the Germans wounded were put in the farm house and this was soon set on fire and they were burnt cattle were also burnt in the out houses [sic][75]. At 4 a.m. I relieved the Guards in the trenches. Hundreds of German dead and wounded lie in thick clusters within a few yards but we cannot come out to collect them. It pelted all day and the trenches got inches deep in mud but one could not move hand or foot for the shells, at 4 o'clock another Coy relieved me and I go again at 4 a.m. tomorrow morning. The moans and groans of the wounded Germans are fearful and you can imagine the filth after all this rain with thousands of troops in a small space.

Another soldier of the 52nd, Private Ernest Wallington, recorded the details of his day, on September 16th.

> On the 16th I was put on sentry by the hospital doors. The Church was the hospital, and it was full of wounded, mostly serious cases, while in the yard outside there were 74 German prisoners, 70 of whom were wounded, but able to walk about. These we had to watch; and our wounded, who were arriving fairly often, had to find another place, the Church being crowded. I went on sentry for a second time at 5 p.m. and had not been on five minutes before my Captain[76] was carried in. They had left the village scarcely an hour before for the firing line, and were standing in the mouth of a cave, where they were ready to reinforce the trenches if required, when a

[74] Harry Dillon's letter was written from Chavonne on September 18th 1914.

[75] It is likely that only the cattle and not the German wounded were burnt to death.

[76] Charles Higgins.

> shell dropped over the bank, and killed two officers of my company (besides the Battalion Scout Officer[77]), wounded the Captain and two others, and left one officer absolutely unhurt. One of the others was my platoon officer[78]. I learnt he did not speak after, whilst the other lived only ten minutes[79]. Three days later our other Captain[80] and another officer were killed[81], which made four officers killed and two wounded – all the six that we had in the Company, and all, you might say, sheer bad luck.

The 52nd were roused at 2 a.m., on September 17th, to relieve the 2nd Grenadier Guards, in the trenches at 4.30 a.m. B and D Companies climbed the hill to the La Cour de Soupir, and A Company was sent independently to Chavonne on the River Aisne, and to the west of Soupir. It was to relieve a detached company of the Grenadier Guards. The 52nd's Headquarters were at the farm, whose fine buildings had been badly damaged by artillery fire. However, at 11.30 a.m., several shells screamed into the farm buildings and forced the Headquarters to be transferred from the forge into the caves in the stone quarry. Luckily, the only casualty that day was Lance-Corporal Hobson who was wounded in the arm.

Henry Davies described the 17th in his diary.

> It was a good place to hold, and we were able to make those men who were not actually in the trenches very comfortable in caves and elsewhere under cover. We found trenches already dug, and at once set to work to improve them.
>
> The place was full of German wounded, who had had a very poor time, as most of them had been hit three days before. Their wounds had been dressed, but many of them were becoming gangrened, and they wanted getting away to hospital badly. They were originally put in a cow-house, but yesterday this was set on fire by German shells. The Grenadiers succeeded in getting all the German wounded out of the barn at considerable risk to themselves, but some unfortunate cows (chained up) were all burned to death, and their charred carcases [sic] remained there during the whole time

[77] Reginald Worthington.
[78] Hugh Mockler-Ferryman.
[79] Paul Giradot.
[80] Rosslyn Evelegh.
[81] Aubrey Barrington-Kennett.

S.S. Lake Michigan. In August 1914, transported the 52nd from Southampton to Boulogne. Later during the war, in 1918, the ship was torpedoed and sank.
[Private Collection]

La Place de la Gare, Wassigny where the 52nd detrained prior to the advance on Mons. Photograph circa 1908.
[Private Collection]

The main square at Paturages. Here, in the early hours of August 24th 1914, the 52nd rested briefly, before the retreat from Mons. Photograph circa 1920.
[Private Collection]

The bridge over the river Sambre at Berlaimont. The 52nd briefly took up defensive positions around it during the retreat from Mons. Photograph circa 1913.
[Private Collection]

On August 31st 1914, the 52nd crossed the bridge over the river Aisne at Pommiers during the retreat from Mons.
[Private Collection]

On September 13th 1914, the 52nd were unable to use this damaged bridge over the river Aisne at Pont Arcy. Photograph circa 1915.
[Private Collection]

At this site the 52nd crossed the river Aisne using a pontoon bridge on September 13th 1914.
[Author's Collection 2008]

Reggie Owen. Severely wounded near La Ferme de Metz on September 14th 1914. On recovery he fought with the 52nd again, before dying of further wounds on August 2nd 1916.
[Regimental Chronicles]

La Ferme de Metz, Moussy which had been damaged by German artillery fire. The farm was not rebuilt after the war. La Bois de la Bovette can be seen in the background. Photograph circa 1915.
[Private Collection]

> we were in those trenches, and had to be constantly covered with earth to stop the smell.
>
> Ambulances could not come up in the day-time owing to shelling, but after dark we got all the German wounded away into hospitals which had been established in the Church and château in Soupir village.

At 6.30 p.m., on the 17th, the three dead officers of C Company [Giradot, Mockler-Ferryman and Worthington] were buried in the churchyard of Soupir Church where they lie to this day. Private Ernest Wallington of their company described the events of that day from his perspective.

> I came off guard early next morning and went to join my Company on the hill where all this had happened. As soon as it was light, shells were flying in all directions, from quite short range, too. There were only two wounded close to us, luckily, that day, and at dusk the fire of the Germans slackened down, so I, with others went to the cave mouth, and made a stretcher of my waterproof sheet, and carried our officer[82] down to Soupir churchyard, where, in company of the other officers who were killed, he was buried. He was a nice chap, and was dearly liked by everybody, although we reservists had known him only a matter of six weeks. But there he lies, with a small wooden cross above him, and my waterproof over him.

The next day, the 18th, was a quiet one for the 52nd in the trenches at La Cour de Soupir. The weather for the time of year was wet, making the trenches muddy and unpleasant. At dawn, Captain Allan Harden, commanding D Company, started making a bomb proof shelter behind the trenches, while Guy Blewitt superintended the digging of graves and burying corpses. He recorded that 'most bodies had been dead 4 days and it was a horrible job'[83]. Private William Cheshire buried fifteen cows that had been burnt to death. It was an odoriferous job. Later in the day, D Company dug a communication trench and put out obstacles consisting of wire, harrows, and harvesting implements from the farm. Rosslyn Evelegh and Arthur Tylden-Pattenson had recovered sufficiently from their wounds from two days earlier to rejoin the Regiment. A Company returned from Chavonne where, the day before, they had engaged the enemy and inflicted 20-30 casualties on them without loss to themselves.

[82] Lieutenant Hugh Mockler-Ferryman.

[83] Diary entry for September 18th 1914.

September 19th opened quietly enough until, at 1.15 p.m., the German artillery blasted the farm, the mouths of the caves, the stone quarry and the road between the farm and the quarry. Guy Blewitt had been enjoying a bath found in the dairy and filled with hot water from the kitchens of the farmhouse. The succession of officers enjoying their ablutions was abruptly stopped by the shellfire. A and D Companies were holding trenches which ran around the farm at about 100 yards distance from it. They started in the south-west from the direction of Chavonne and continued to the north-east around La Bois de la Bovette. They were not the continuous trench lines that became so familiar later in the war, but were a line of pits or holes in the ground that allowed one or more men shelter. The position of the trenches was less than ideal with those at the junction of the woods and the turnip fields looking up a slope. The field of fire was only 200 yards in places.

Henry Davies stayed in the caves with B and C Companies in reserve. At about 3.30 p.m. Davies heard infantry fire from the fields above and suspected that the Germans were attacking. He sent Captain Lindsay Wood and B Company around the south side of the farm to support the men who were in trenches to the left of the farm. Davies took one and a half platoons from C Company, under Lieutenant Gladwyn Turbutt and Second-Lieutenant George Marshall, to the forge, to act as a reserve for A Company in the trenches to the right of the farm. Eventually, these men lay down behind the trenches with fixed bayonets, ready to meet any German infantry who broke through the sparse barbed wire entanglements in front of the trenches. Here in the forge, Davies was in a better position to control his forces than hidden away in the caves.

The German attack was not pressed home, although on the right a Maxim machine-gun was brought up near some hay-stacks but fortunately the firing was always high. During the afternoon and early evening, the 52nd suffered 35 casualties all from shellfire, of whom nine were killed and 26 wounded. Amongst the dead was Captain Rosslyn Evelegh who had been wounded on the 16th only to return to duty and be killed instantly three days later. Evelegh had bravely left his cover to release animals that were fastened in a burning building[84].

Second-Lieutenant Aubrey Barrington-Kennett was hit in the jaw, neck and back and suffered terribly, although he put on a brave face and remained very cheerful. Initially, he refused to be carried to the dressing station in the cave where Captain Lionel Thurston R.A.M.C.[85] was doing his best to look after the

---

[84] Richard Crosse's footnote in the *Regimental Journal* for 1954, page 514. According to Guy Blewitt's diary entry for September 19th 1914: 'I afterwards learnt that Evelegh was killed by a shell that day when out of the trench putting a wounded pig out of its agony'.
[85] Royal Army Medical Corps.

casualties. The third officer casualty, Captain Guy Blewitt, was struck by a shrapnel ball below the right eye and could not close his mouth. In the cave he lay down next to the wounded Barrington-Kennett and did his best to make him comfortable. 'Here I found poor "B.K." terribly wounded and lay down beside him as he preferred me to the orderly and I did what I could for him'[86]. Henry Davies visited the two wounded officers and was very kind to them. At 11 p.m. a horse-drawn ambulance carried the two men to Vieil Arcy where, on the 21st, Barrington-Kennett died, having had his arm amputated[87]. Blewitt had the shrapnel ball removed from his right jaw muscles in Paris, and returned to the Regiment the following December.

Captain Lionel Thurston recorded his impressions of La Cour de Soupir and the caves in a letter to his relatives written the next day[88].

> Our army continued its advance until a week ago, when we came up against the Germans in a prepared position and, since then, we have not budged an inch, it has been HELL. Our (the Regiments) only means of cover are three caves, and these are dark, and offensive and full of wounded and dying, with their groans reaching surely to heaven. The Germans bombard us suddenly with high explosive, which is staggering in its concussion. There is a farmhouse near by the caves and although highly dangerous the officers come over for meals. i.e. bully beef and biscuit and perhaps hot tea. Yesterday at our midday meal, we were suddenly saluted by a tremendous artillery fire right on the buildings and in trying to get to the caves, one officer was killed and two wounded. The place here is a regular cockpit; 150 oxen were roasted to death two days ago, and all the cows have been shot and yesterday, out of the remaining five pigs only two escaped. There are about 500 dead Germans lying about 800 yards from our trenches and I really think something should be done about it as they have been there for four days. Some of the wounded crawl in among the turnips with the most awful wounds I have ever seen. I saw two yesterday with half their heads blown off, and we have 150 of them lying near the caves, wounded – moaning all day, with most of their wounds septic. I have not had any medical appliances to treat them but thank God they were removed yesterday.

[86] Guy Blewitt's diary entry for September 19th 1914.

[87] Aubrey Hapderi Barrington-Kennett was the youngest of four brothers, three of whom were killed in the war. He was reputed to have been struck by shell fragments.

[88] September 20th 1914.

> I am writing this to you from a barn not completely destroyed, where I sleep, which is preferable to Dante's Inferno in the caves, but more risky; but the crashes of the shells (one hundred yards away now) is more nerve shaking and distressing, to say the least. With it all the men keep their spirits and officers of course show duty's way.

During a period of particularly heavy shelling, on the 19th, Privates Carter and Payne carried a badly wounded comrade Private Hambling to shelter. For their bravery they were awarded the Military Medal [M.M.]. Both men worked in the officers' mess where they continued their work until the end of the war.

On September 20th, the 52nd were still holding the trenches at La Cour de Soupir. The day was generally a quiet one with little shelling, but at dusk small parties of the enemy fired at them with rifles and machine-guns. Earlier in the day, two men were hit and wounded by rifle bullets, which was unusual at La Cour de Soupir where nearly all the casualties resulted from artillery rather than rifle fire. The best shots in the Regiment retaliated and a number of the enemy appeared to have been hit. Harry Dillon formally took over command of C Company this day.

There was still some sniping and shelling on the 21st. The Germans dug some new trenches, the nearest being 700 yards away from the British lines. During the day Private Walter Warner, one of four brothers serving with the Regiment, was killed and Bugler Lovelace, one of two brothers also serving with the Regiment was wounded. That night the 52nd were relieved by the 2nd Leinster, and were ordered to march the six and a half miles back to Dhuizel, to rejoin the 5th Brigade, having been detached for more than a week. The actual relief did not take place until 2 a.m. on the 22nd.

The 52nd crossed the Aisne at Chavonne and marched via Vieil Arcy to Dhuizel. Finding the 5th Brigade there they went into billets and slept. Brigadier-General Richard Haking, commanding the 5th Brigade, had been wounded on September 16th and Lieutenant-Colonel Claude Westmacott of the Worcestershire was in temporary command. Whilst at Dhuizel, Lieutenant Douglas Humfrey and the third reinforcement of 120 men arrived to replace those men who had become casualties. A large number of gifts from friends of the Regiment were delivered, including 1,000 cigarettes from Lord Orkney[89]. The children of Great Hampden had raised £1-5s-6d from blackberry picking.

---

[89] Edmond Walter Fitz-Maurice, 7th Earl of Orkney. Former Lieutenant-Colonel in the 3rd Battalion Oxfordshire Light Infantry.

Captain Harry Dillon while resting at Dhuizel reflected on the recent action at La Cour de Soupir in a vivid account for his family[90]. In the second letter he dealt with German morale.

> At 9 p.m. we received a message to say 3 officers in one Coy were killed and 3 wounded only leaving one, a 2nd Lieut, so the Colonel sent me up to take over command. It was an appalling show when I got up there, but in the darkness I did not see all until morning. There was a large farm on top where our Coy was, it was pelting with rain and everything knee-deep in mud and filth. 50 yds. down the hill were two caves and just in front of the farm our trenches. – All the farm buildings were full of wounded, and the caves outside, on the road, in the yard, every-where were German dead and wounded and their shrieks and groans went on all night. Then the shells set fire to a portion of the farm and the poor devils there were burnt alive[91]. – At 4 a.m. the rest of the Regt. arrived and we all went into the trenches and relieved the Guards. They have lost frightfully over two thirds of their officers in every regiment. – I have lost count of the days after this we could only lie in the trenches drenched with rain at night a portion of the trenches went into support in the caves. – Personally I almost perferred [sic] the trenches as one did not get so much smell of dead German. – Yesterday 22nd a Regiment relieved us and I have never been more glad to leave a place. – The Germans lie in hundreds in front of the trenches and a whole herd of cattle all killed and they are all going bad and it was beastly. We lost 5 officers killed and 5 wounded in the time we were there, I don't know how many men but not nearly so many in proportion. I had some extraordinary escapes and in the end have got off with nothing worse than a lump of earth in the face – so I think I may consider myself very lucky. We have had a very nice message from the Guards thanking us for the help we gave them. Our whole Brigade has suffered very severely in the battle, one regt. have only 250 men and 6 officers left out of 1000 men and 30 officers. – We are now out of harm's way and may not be sent back into action until tomorrow. I hope when we go again it will not be in such a confined space. It is rather nice sitting here in the sun

[90] Letters written on September 23rd and 28th 1914 at Dhuizel.

[91] This is unlikely to be correct. The Grenadier Guards had carried all the German wounded to safety. See the *Regimental Journal* 1934 the Regiment at War XXII page 137.

> having washed and shaved and to hear the guns thundering away a couple of miles off. Every one of our casualties bar two have been from shells. The German gunners are really good but their infantry is no good at all and we have absolutely annihilated them every time we have had the luck to come across them. If it was not for their guns we would very soon sweep their wretched infantry off the face of God's earth. I don't know if some of this letter is a bit gruesome but I can tell you there are a good many things I have not and could not put on paper, but I think it a mistake to gloss everything over and that people at home should imagine war lightly as a sort of picnic.
>
> Anyhow for every one we have lost I think we can safely say we accounted for at least 10 Germans. They came on with great dash in the 1st battles but as they got the worst of it on every occasion with the most appalling slaughter I think they are now cooling off and their attacks have no longer got the determination in them they had. I also think they have lost heart a lot whereas our men are as keen to get at them as ever. I really think their losses must be tremendous and one gets so used to seeing the grey bundles on the ground one almost forgets they are men.

For the next two days, 23rd-24th, the 52nd rested at Dhuizel, in I Corps reserve, away from the machine-gun bullet and the shell. The men took the opportunity to clean themselves up and to wash their clothes. Henry Davies made a point of addressing the officers and then the N.C.O.s, thanking them for the good work that they had done during the retreat and later on the Aisne. He asked his words to be passed on to the men as it was not possible for him to hold a regimental parade. The 52nd got some exercise by digging trenches, as a precautionary measure, on a ridge south of Dhuizel, on September 25th. Also the same day, Second-Lieutenant F.W.C. 'Chips' Chippindale joined the regiment from England. Five men who had been court martialled[92] for sleeping on sentry duty had their sentences of one year's imprisonment with hard labour confirmed. In the event the sentences were suspended. Whilst recognizing the dangers of sentries not being awake, it is hard not to have sympathy for the exhausted men.

The following day, the 26th, there was considerable artillery and infantry fire on the northern heights of the Aisne. That night the 52nd were put on fifteen minutes notice to move, and remained so until 8 a.m. on the 28th. During the 27th,

---

[92] These were Field General Courts Martial which were simplified versions of a General Court Martial. However death sentences could be imposed.

Captain Ashley Ponsonby joined the 52nd and was given command of C Company. Ponsonby [pronounced Punsunby] was an outstanding and popular officer who had resigned his position, as Assistant Military Secretary to the Commander-in-Chief, in South Africa, to return to the Regiment. During this time the 52nd were pleased to hear that their former Commanding Officer, Colonel Robert Fanshawe [Fanny][93] had been promoted to command the 6th Brigade which was also a part of the 2nd Division. Fanshawe had commanded the 52nd from 1907-11 and had done so much to prepare them for war.

During the afternoon of September 29th, the 52nd were ordered to cross the Aisne to Bourg, a distance of three and a half miles. They took over good billets from the 2nd Connaught Rangers and then did little more than clean the streets and provide a few sentries. In effect it was really a continuation of their rest period. On the 30th, a regimental order was made known that on September 24th, a soldier of another regiment was tried by Field General Court Martial for 'misbehaviour before the enemy in such a way as to show cowardice' and was sentenced 'to suffer death by being shot', and the sentence was duly carried out two days later. According to Richard Crosse this promulgation made a profound impression on the Regiment. Everyone had heard of these things but few then serving had known it in reality. What Crosse does not make clear was whether it was the cowardice or the execution or perhaps both that affected the 52nd so much.

The unfortunate man was Private George Ward of the 1st Berkshire who, as part of the 6th Brigade, was in the 2nd Division with the 52nd. After a mere three days of active service, Ward had gone back during an uphill advance, under shellfire, towards the Chemin des Dames, and was not seen again for six days. Sir Douglas Haig, commanding I Corps, felt he should be executed to prevent further cases occurring and Sir John French concurred. Robert Fanshawe had only taken command of the 6th Brigade on the day before the court martial, and the papers must have been some of the first that he saw in his new command. In the late afternoon of September 26th Ward was shot. It was unusually late in the day for an execution as they were normally held at dawn. The unfortunate Ward was the second of 346 British men executed for military offences in the Great War and its aftermath[94]. The Oxfordshire and Buckinghamshire Light Infantry were one of the few units not to have a man executed during the war, which says

---

[93] Colonel Robert Fanshawe [Later Major-General Sir Robert] 1863-1946; G.S.O.1 1st Division 1914; G.O.C. 6th Brigade, 1914-15; G.O.C. 48th Division, 1915-18; G.O.C. 69th Division, 1918-19. His brothers were Lieutenant-General Sir Edward Fanshawe and Lieutenant-General Sir Hew Fanshawe. Richard Crosse described Robert Fanshawe as a very great light infantryman and commanding officer, who in appearance and manner often reminded him of Lord Roberts. As well as 'Fanny' he was also known as the 'Chocolate Soldier'.

[94] The number of men executed from August 4th 1914-March 31st 1920. *Statistics 1914-1920.*

much for their esprit de corps[95]. The vast majority of British soldiers sentenced to death were justly condemned by the law as it then stood.

The end of September found the weather getting much colder, and at 7.30 p.m., on October 1st, the 52nd trekked the four miles from Bourg back to La Cour de Soupir, where they relieved the Leinster in their former trenches. Considerable work had been carried out on the trenches and a support trench system was in the making. The nearest German trenches were now 550-600 yards away. To the right of the 52nd, in the trenches, was the 2nd H.L.I., whose line was a long one. The 52nd's B Company was sent to help them, which allowed three companies in the front line and one in reserve. October 2nd was a misty morning and Private Sidney Hurst[96], a regimental scout, was shot dead having got too close to the enemy's trenches. The next day, accurate German shelling on B Company, in front of the woods to the right of the farm, killed three and wounded nineteen more. That night A Company relieved B in accordance with the arrangement whereby D Company on the left remained permanently in the line, whilst the other three companies rotated on the right, with two days in the front line and then one day in reserve. On October 3rd the owners of the La Cour de Soupir briefly returned to collect some of their treasures that had been buried in the ground.

Harry Dillon continued to write to his family from La Cour de Soupir. He discussed the difficulty of living in a trench and the morale of his own men and that of the enemy[97].

> We have gone back into the battle line again at the same old farm and I am writing this in the trenches with a new pair of socks on. Today is comparatively quiet so far. They are shelling the batteries on either side and behind us and they [sic] are returning the compliment so there are shells backwards and forwards the whole time. We had 9 men hit this morning which is bad luck, and is out of proportion to the amount they have expended on us. There is plenty of time yet as it has only just gone 10 o'clock and they may switch on to the trenches again presently. I believe the regiment on our left have had more of it. We have now 48 hours in the trenches and 24 out. Personally I prefer the trenches as they are cleaner than the farm and from the point of view of safety it does not matter a bit where

[95] The other units were; Grenadier Guards, Welsh Guards, Honourable Artillery Company, Bedfordshire, Royal Irish Regiment, Gloucestershire, Shropshire, Monmouthshire, Cambridgeshire, Herefordshire, Hertfordshire, Royal Army Medical Corps and the Cavalry.

[96] Recorded as being killed in action on September 1st 1914. This is likely to be wrong as the *Battalion War Diary* makes no mention of any casualties on this date.

[97] Letter written on October 3rd 1914.

one is as the shells go through everything up here except into the caves and they are so filthy that I would rather go through anything than stop in them. I hope we shall soon go on as this is the 19th day we have fought round this spot and it fairly reeks.

I came across Gordon Ives's[98] grave in the garden of the farm. I had no idea he was here. He was the man who was a friend of Arthur's and used to come out hunting. It is getting beastly cold now but the trenches are deep and we have got straw down and if it is dry it is bearable, when it rains it is beastly and of course we have no change of clothes and just have to stick it. When we are behind we get our valises in which one has spare shirts and blankets but when in the battle line of course nothing but what one can carry and one does not want to carry too much as it hinders one when advancing. I always have my sword, revolver and ammunition, emergency ration of biscuits and bully, field glasses, haversack in which I carry a woolly and cape. Then if the ammunition mule can be got up he carries one's greatcoat. This is the most one can manage. I did try and carry some washing things but it is impossible and everybody has given it up and one simply goes with-out or does as much as one can with one's hands and drying with a handkerchief. One does not really feel this sort of discomfort as much as one would think. The fighting takes one's mind off it a bit for one thing and now the situation seems satisfactory it does not matter having a few hardships. The Russians should have had time to get well started by now and it would be great if we could smash them here and there at the same time. The trouble is that the armies are so huge it takes such a long time. I think however the German soldiers have had enough and I am sure they have not the guts of our men. Our people are perfectly happy and I think only are keen to get on as it is difficult for them to understand that one portion of the line can't go on by itself. If they had their way we should very soon be across the 500 yards which separate us and drive them out but it would be no good. I went out the other night a little way and one could hear them talking quite close. We also shoot at them occasionally and they back, but it does not do much good. I expect we shall soon have them out of it and back into their own country.

---

[98] No Gordon Ives appears on the *Soldiers Died in the Great War 1914-19* CD.

On October 4th, there was further shelling on the same part of the trenches as the day before. A Company was now the unlucky recipient of this most accurate fire. One man was killed and nine more were wounded including Serjeant Dunn and Corporal Millgate. Millgate was particularly unlucky as he was taking cover under an overhanging rock at the time. The Germans had started using high explosive shrapnel shells which burst fairly high but backwards as well as forwards. Serjeant Thomas Hudson would later receive the Distinguished Conduct Medal for his gallantry this day. Telephone wires having been cut, he volunteered to carry a message, under heavy shellfire, and later removed a severely wounded man from the trenches under the same fire. To the north the Germans could be heard singing hymns on their side of the line.

The following day there were no casualties in the trenches, but six men were wounded in the farmyard. Because of this, orders were issued that everyone not on duty must be under cover from 10 a.m. to noon. The lack of casualties in the trenches owed much to the 52nd having improved the overhead cover, as the original trench that they had taken over was too wide, and made them susceptible to high explosive shrapnel. No more than five men were to be around the farm pump at any one time. The 52nd settled into a routine in the trenches at La Cour de Soupir: 6.30 a.m., breakfast; 7 a.m., collection of letters from home; 9 a.m., orderly room; 12 noon, sick parade in the medical inspection cave; 12.30 p.m., dinner; 4.30 p.m., tea; 8 p.m., roll call. They were now on good rations with fresh meat and bread each day and also bacon, cheese, and a regular rum ration.

The officers used the cellar of the farm as a mess and the Headquarters' officers slept on its floor on straw. As the furthest British trenches were only 200 yards from the farm, all the officers were able to come in turn there to eat. Captain Evelyn Villiers, who had been commanding A Company since mobilization, left to rejoin his own regiment, the Royal Sussex.

Harry Dillon continued his letters home[99]. In this letter he described being shelled in the trenches, sniping and conditions in the cellar of La Cour de Soupir.

> I came out of the trenches at 4 a.m. this morning and go on tomorrow for another 48 hours. – I had a lucky escape yesterday. I left my trench with my coat in it and got into the next one which was not such a good one but at that moment they started the worst shelling I have yet seen which went on for 14 minutes. – When I could come back I found my coat with 15 holes in it, one 4 inches long, in fact if I had been there another minute I should have been blown to pieces.

[99] Letter written on October 6th 1914 from the cellar of La Cour de Soupir.

One man was killed and 9 others injured so I was well out of it[100]. In this place the trenches are on the edge of a wood and shells have ripped everything to ribbons. I had rather a better view of it than I wanted as there was no head cover to my trench and I thought I might just as well keep my eyes open as shut them, we were all smothered in dust and leaves and some of the stones hit very hard but not enough to go through my hide that journey. I am glad to say we have not lost any more officers these last few days but a certain amount of men. In a way it is worse in a permanent position like this as they have got the range to these trenches to the inch and as they have a lot of very heavy guns which they brought up for the siege of Paris and as that never came off they are using them on us. However it does not matter so long as we slate them well and judging by the din today from our guns they must have been having a good time in their trenches. I could not see them as there is a slight rise in front but where I am tomorrow I am only 500 yards off and amuse myself having pots at them if they put their heads up. If they pot back I can walk along the bottom of the trench a little further on. We have our 24 hours off in a cellar which I am in now. I think it is shell proof but rather dull and cold and smelly and the lamps are so bad one can hardly see so I shall be glad to get back to the trenches tomorrow. We can't take any clothes off here which is a nuisance and one gets absolutely filthy. Today is the fifth without taking my boots off and washing, as for my teeth they have gone to glory already, so I shall have them out if I get back and have a clean lot put in.

The final week in the trenches from October 6th to 13th was fairly uneventful with some intermittent shelling. One man was wounded on the 8th. The autumnal nights had become cold with a white frost in the mornings and the days bright with warm sunshine. Lieutenant-Colonel Henry Davies admired the beauty of the surrounding countryside and wished that he could go walking in the nearby woods without the fear of a German shell dropping on him. On the 8th no less than six fresh officers arrived to fill the places of the dead and wounded. These included the experienced Captain Edward Kirkpatrick who had remained behind at Aldershot on mobilization, Lieutenants Christopher Murphy from the 43rd Light Infantry and Maurice ffolliott Wingfield formerly of the 52nd, and

[100] Although the letter implied that he was discussing October 5th, no one was killed that day according to the *Battalion War Diary*. However, on the 4th one man was killed and nine wounded so that it was likely that Dillon was describing the scene on October 4th.

Second-Lieutenants Hugh Pendavis, Geoffrey 'Tithers' Titherington and Leonard Filleul.

Whilst travelling by train in France, Titherington had witnessed the French obsession with obtaining military insignia which had been such a feature of the 52nd's journey to Wassigny six weeks earlier[101].

> Every time one gets out anywhere ladies rush up with scissors drawn to pinch buttons. A Highlander had his whole coat collared this morning while washing. Great chase down platform – Cameronian in kilt, stockings and Glengarry – naked from waste [sic] up – lady running like a hare with skirts to her knees – he caught her alright.

In a later letter to his parents, Geoffrey Titherington described life at La Cour de Soupir towards the end of the 52nd's time there. It is surprising that the farm was still standing[102].

> We're in a most beautiful farm – one of the biggest and best I've ever seen with everything quite modern. Fortunately it's built very solid of thick stone and we can live in the cellars and back rooms instead of dug out caves like a lot of folk. The trenches are just out in front a little bit higher than us. Of course the whole place is absolutely shot to blazes and as I write bullets are smacking into the walls of the first story [sic] – as you can imagine it is an unhealthy place. They come in 10 or 12 per minute. It is 'sniping' and nothing more and of course can't hurt us in the farm. This morning we were all sitting in the garden (i.e. 'all' = the newly joined officers and about 3 off trench duty) when there was a bang and up went a bit of roof – we all broke records to the cellar and they shelled the farm for 2 hrs – damage further dilapidation of buildings – two pigeons killed.

Also on October 8th a list of the 52nd's missing was recorded: Privates Ambrose, Baylis, Gunter, Harris, Hurst, Lewis, Osborne, Taylor and Hancox[103]. The last named was the only man missing on the retreat from Mons and had

---

[101] Postcard from Geoffrey Titherington to his mother dated Monday [by inference September 28th 1914].

[102] Unheaded letter probably to his parents written on October 9th 1914.

[103] Taken from Crosse's *A Record of H.M. 52nd Light Infantry in 1914* page 53. It is not clear whether they were accounted for locally or were prisoners-of-war. How Walter Hancox was captured during the retreat from Mons is also something of a mystery. He was a member of D Company which was acting as the rearguard and he may simply have got left behind.

become a prisoner-of-war. The remainder were eventually accounted for. In their final days at La Cour de Soupir a large number of parcels arrived mainly from the counties of Oxfordshire and Buckinghamshire. Captain Richard Crosse recalled the donation of a very special sandbag.

> It had become known that there was a temporary shortage of sandbags at the front, and a semi-official hint was dropped that these would be acceptable. From London an old lady sent her gifts packed in a remarkable sandbag, upon which she had worked "52" and which was secured with rifle-green ribbon, and begged that it might be built into the parapet on the Regimental front, which it duly was, greatly to her satisfaction. "I have loved the 52nd," she wrote, "for more than sixty years. I first saw the Regiment at Liverpool in 1850. Three of my brothers have served with it since then, and my nephew is with it now".

On the 9th, Serjeant Sam Moulder of C Company wrote two letters to his family in England[104]. Less than a month later he would be killed in action at Langemarck.

> I am writing this in the trenches (tell you when I see you). I am in a hole not much bigger than (well just big enough to creep in) – we are 600 yards from the German trenches, and they keep sniping or shooting at us and of course we have shot at them. It is very seldom they hit any of our chaps and I don't know what luck we have in hitting them but there is a few saucy ones among them for when we have shot at them they signal back (with a white flag) a miss (cheeky devils aye?). We had a lively hour this morning as there was an Artillery duel shells screaming and bursting all around us, I don't think we had anyone hit as soon as they start shelling we creep into our holes, in fact we were telling tales and laughing and singing this morning and shells busting over our heads one knocked the water-proof sheet up over our heads, all we said was, My eye, that was a near go. All our troops are in the best of health and I don't believe we have had a case of fever. Of course we have had a few killed and wounded by shellfire for when they start (well I don't know how to express it). The Germans have got a gun we call Black Maria, which fires a shell we call a coal box (when the shell bursts there is a cloud

[104] Both letters were written on October 9th 1914.

of black smoke) shell I think about 120 lb. So when Black Maria[105] empties her coal box it makes us bob a bit. I don't think she has killed or wounded many, although where the shell bursts in some places it makes a hole big enough to bury 7 or 8 men.

I am writing this in a trench or hole in the ground, just large enough to creep in 600 yards from the German trenches, we can see the Germans digging their trenches. And we send them a souvenir now and then (our souvenir is a bullet) just to let them know we are awake. The Germans also send a few souvenirs in fact they are sending some along while I am writing this. But they can carry on, as they are wasting their Bullets. We had a lively hour this morning when our Artillery and the German Artillery had a duel. But no one was hurt of ours (as far as I know). But I think the Germans must lose a lot of men and Guns, as our Artillery Gunners are the best in the world, and they are firing at the Germans all day, and have been doing so for weeks. We can see the shells burst in the German trenches. Aeroplanes are flying over us all day (Ours and Germans). And we can see the shells bursting in the air, when the artillery fires shrapnel (shells?) at them. But I have not seen one fetched down yet. A Frenchman fired three shots with his rifle the other day and brought a German Aeroplane down. I heard it from one of the chaps that saw it come down.

I must close now as my chum (Ginger Sgt. King) Major King's from Cowley Barracks son) [sic] is worrying the life out of me as he wants to have a sleep (poor thing) he's all sleep, and I am disturbing him for the hole we are in was only meant for one, but we stick together.

Moulder's two letters confirm that the trench system at La Cour de Soupir, in October 1914, was largely a line of holes capable of giving protection to several men, rather than the continuous trench lines of 1915 onwards. Second-Lieutenant Geoffrey Titherington also gave further details of the excavations which were described as a 'Boer Trench' with no head cover and a shelter

[105] A German 15 cm. shell. An alternative nickname was a Jack Johnson named after the contemporary black heavyweight boxing champion. Here Moulder has described the gun as a Black Maria. Other nicknames for individual types of shell were Pissing Jenny and Whistling Percy.

hollowed out under the parapet[106]. Also it is interesting that even at this early stage of the war aeroplanes were so active.

Between October 11th-12th, the 52nd began their preparations to hand over to the French and for their move to the north. In their final action on the Aisne, one of the 52nd's sentry groups shot dead a German scout in front of the trenches. He was a fine specimen of a man and must have been six feet four in height. He was thought to be a member of the 8th Grenadier Guard Regiment. The 52nd would soon destroy the equally huge Potsdam Guards in Nonne Bosschen Wood. The 13th was their last day on the Aisne, and at 11 p.m. the French 254th Regiment arrived to relieve them. The Germans in their trenches facing the 52nd's positions were clearly suspicious of an attack and sent up lights, which were to become so familiar to those in the trenches. The 52nd were also supplied for the first time with their own means of illumination, Very lights[107]. Soon after midnight the 52nd marched away from La Cour de Soupir for the very last time. They were not sorry to leave.

Today, at Pont Arcy, the modern bridges over the Aisne river and canal are in the same position as 100 years ago. The site of the pontoon bridge over the river is easily found although the banks are covered in thick undergrowth. The Ferme de Metz, near where Reggie Owen was so badly wounded, has long since vanished and there is no trace of the building, although a little to the north a thicket of trees and bushes may mark the site of an outhouse or barn. Soupir Church which was used as a reception area for the wounded is still there, although it was badly damaged in the Great War. The graves of the four 52nd officers lie in a line to the south of the churchyard. The gates of Soupir Château are still standing proudly in a ploughed field although the château itself was destroyed in the war. La Cour de Soupir was rebuilt slightly to the south of its original site. Just to the north and east the fields slope upwards towards the former German front line. The stone quarry to the east of the farm is easily found and is now a mass of undergrowth and pitted with shell holes. Some of the caves in the north face of the quarry can be seen. The largest one, the scene of so much suffering, is massive and can accommodate to this day a battalion of troops, and extends under La Cour de Soupir. It is protected by an iron gate.

In the early hours of October 14th, the 52nd marched via Soupir and St. Mard to Vauxcéré, arriving at 3.30 a.m. and going into billets after a seven mile march. That afternoon, after a brief sleep, the 52nd marched to Fismes and departed by train at 6.20 p.m. The train's accommodation left a great deal to be

[106] Letter written by Geoffrey Titherington to his mother or father on October 5th 1914. He had been given the information by a wounded corporal of the 52nd on the way to Soupir.
[107] Patented by Edward Very in the U.S.A. in 1877.

desired as 45 men had to be crammed into a space designed for only 40 and the roof was festooned with them. B Company under Captain Lindsay Wood had to stay behind to follow with the 2nd Worcestershire. Part of the reason for the lack of space was that 5th Brigade Headquarters were travelling in the 52nd's train. The 29-hour-journey continued throughout the night as they passed through Amiens, Boulogne, Calais, St. Omer to Hazebrouck. The only official stop was at Amiens and as the train entered the tunnel north of Boulogne, Private Thomas King climbed out on to the look-out of his truck and suffered a fatal head injury. Two horses also escaped from a truck. Perhaps, Captain Harry Dillon had the most comfortable journey as he was appointed billeting officer at 2nd Division's Headquarters, and travelled across France by car, managing 'a most excellent lunch in Beauvais' on the way!

At 11.30 p.m. on the 15th, the train finally reached Hazebrouck and the weary 52nd climbed down on to the platform. A further march of four miles to Morbeck[108] followed and then into clean billets and hot coffee. Second-Lieutenant Geoffrey Titherington described his quarters: 'I've got a pile of 3 v. comfy French feather beds on the floor they are bliss after the trench which had the disadvantage among others that every time one turned or moved a lot of clay descended upon one's head. I found a sleeping cap very useful and have contracted the habit of lying very still'[109]. October 16th, a raw damp day, was a very welcome rest period while the 5th Brigade assembled at Morbeck. During the hours of daylight the 52nd bathed. Once more Titherington described the scene: 'The whole mess has seized the opportunity this morning and all the village laundry tubs and have all had capital baths we all look several shades more blonde and several people complain of feeling chilly owing to the absence of the film of dirt accumulated in the trench'[110]. That night, Major Archibald Eden also enjoyed a good sleep in a comfortable bed and breakfasted on eggs, brown bread, butter and fresh milk.

At 8 p.m. orders were given to move at dawn. Regimental orders recorded this day that the late Lieutenant Reginald Worthington had been awarded the French Légion d'honneur for gallantry during operations between August 21st-30th, and Private A. Kippax the Médaille Militaire. At 7 a.m., on the 17th, a twelve mile march to Godewaersvelde was begun. By 11.30 a.m., the 52nd had reached their destination and went into billets shortly after. During the afternoon Major-General Charles Monro visited them. The 18th was a rest day with plenty of food but no mail. The following day again opened quietly with the

---

108 Morbeck is the Flemish spelling and Morbecque the French version.
109 Letter to his parents written on October 16th 1914.
110 As above.

Regiment spending the morning opening no less than 40 boxes of gifts from England. Expecting another quiet night, the 52nd were ordered in the late afternoon, to march the seven miles to Poperinghe, across the Belgian border. Then into billets again. A challenging two months awaited them in the environs of Ypres.

Chapter IV

The Battle of Langemarck.

October 20th – 23rd 1914

[Maps: pages 79, 81, 148.]

In 1920, the Battles Nomenclature Committee decreed that the Battles of Ypres 1914, fought in the environs of the city, took place from October 19th-November 22nd and were to be subdivided. The subdivisions were the Battle of Langemarck October 21st-24th, the Battle of Gheluvelt October 29th-31st, and the Battle of Nonne Bosschen on November 11th. The subdivisions were in some measure arbitrary and fighting occurred during the whole period. The Battles of Ypres 1914 are more commonly known as the First Battle of Ypres. Great Britain's small professional army, supposedly described by the Kaiser as contemptible, plus their French and Belgian allies, prevented a far superior German force taking Ypres and breaking through to the Channel ports. This would have been catastrophic for Britain and her allies and possibly meant the loss of the war. As will be seen the 52nd Light Infantry would play a significant role in the forthcoming battles.

Following their efforts on the Aisne, the initial action of the 52nd Light Infantry in the First Battle of Ypres [Battle of Langemarck] was to be along and around the St. Julien - Poelcappelle road to the north-east of the city. General Sir Douglas Haig's I Corps was to advance towards Thorout with the 2nd Division crossing the Langemarck to Zonnebeke road to attack in the direction of the village of Passchendaele. On their left would be the 1st Division moving forward from Langemarck to attempt to take Poelcappelle from the occupying Germans. On the right of the 2nd Division would the 7th Division. Optimistically, it was hoped that the British advance might even reach Bruges. If the Germans could be pushed back seven miles from Ypres they would lose the commanding ridges which overlooked the town. Twelve miles would see the allies take the important communication centre of Roulers.

The 2nd Division arranged to have the 5th Brigade on the left and the 4th Brigade [Guards] on the right. In the 5th Brigade, the 52nd were in the front line on the left and the 2nd Worcestershire on the right. The second line consisted of the 2nd Highland Light Infantry supporting the 52nd and the 2nd Connaught Rangers the Worcestershire. Their inexperienced German opponents were the 52nd Reserve Division of the German Fourth Army, supported by heavy artillery, 8 inch howitzers being observed in the action. This division had been formed

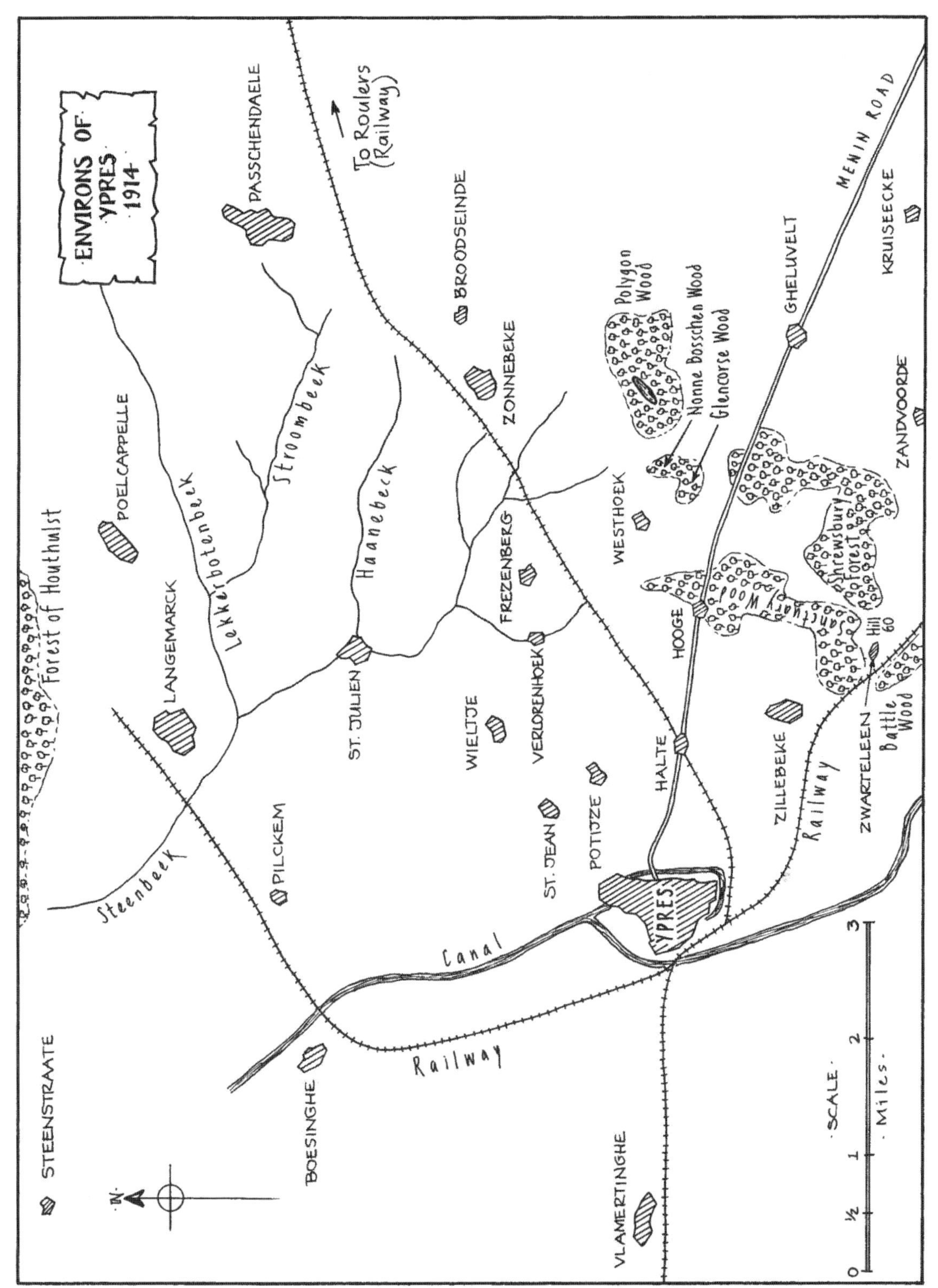
ENVIRONS OF YPRES 1914
PASSCHENDAELE
To Roulers (Railway)
BROODSEINDE
MENIN ROAD
KRUISEECKE
GHELUVELT
Polygon Wood
Nonne Bosschen Wood
Glencorse Wood
ZONNEBEKE
ZANDVOORDE
POELCAPPELLE
Stroombeek
Lekkerbotenbeek
Haanebeek
WESTHOEK
FREZENBERG
Forest of Houthulst
LANGEMARCK
St. JULIEN
VERLORENHOEK
WIELTJE
HOOGE
Sanctuary Wood
Shrewsbury Forest
Hill 60
Battle Wood
ZWARTELEEN
ZILLEBEKE
Railway
HALTE
POTIJZE
St. JEAN
PILCKEM
Steenbeek
YPRES
Canal
STEENSTRAATE
BOESINGHE
Railway
VLAMERTINGHE
N
SCALE
Miles
0
½
1
2
3

between August and October 1914 and came from the Rhine Province. They had only left their training camp at Senne on October 12th and would receive huge numbers of casualties against the cream of the regular British Divisions in the ensuing battle. This phase of the battle was known to the Germans as the 'Kindermord bei Ypern', the massacre of the innocents at Ypres.

On October 20th, Lieutenant-Colonel Henry Davies marched the 52nd the nine miles from Poperinghe to Pilckem via Elverdinghe. The 5th Brigade outpost line stretched from Pilckem to two thirds of the way to Steenstraate with the 52nd placed in the centre of it. At 3 a.m. on the 21st, Henry Davies was given orders to have the 52nd rendezvous in the orchard of a farm, Maison du Hibou, west of the St. Julien to Langemarck road. Davies accompanied by the Adjutant, Lieutenant Richard Crosse, had difficulty finding their way and only just had time to get the 52nd into position. Wearily, in the early hours of the morning they made their way to the rendezvous and then deployed along the Langemarck to Zonnebeke road with their left on the Lekkerbotenbeek. By now it was 6.30 a.m.

In the front line, the 52nd had Captain Ashley Ponsonby's C Company on the left and Captain Allan Harden's D Company on the right. The second line consisted of Captain Lindsay Wood's B Company on the left and Captain Edward Kirkpatrick's A Company on the right. Between 8-9 a.m., contact was made with the 1st South Wales Borderers of the 1st Division who reported that they were at last advancing. Unfortunately, the three hours delay in the 1st Division coming up allowed their German opponents to approach closer to the 5th Brigade. Lieutenant-Colonel Henry Davies went back to see the temporary commander of the 5th Brigade, Lieutenant-Colonel Claude Westmacott of the Worcestershire, to inform him and was given orders to advance. Soon after 9 a.m. Davies returned to his men and the 52nd moved forward in skirmishing order. Serjeant H.C. Gutteridge recorded that they went forward in short rushes of 30 yards at a time with six yards between each man.

The 52nd, in the words of their commanding officer advanced 'quickly and steadily'. Shrapnel was falling and desultory rifle and machine-gun fire came in from their left front. Initially this caused little damage but as the day progressed the enfilade fire, particularly from the north bank of the Lekkerbotenbeek, became heavier and the number of casualties increased. Heavy artillery was seen to knock down a row of elm trees like matchsticks. B Company's commander Captain Lindsay Wood and Second-Lieutenant George Marshall had been badly wounded at the outset by a shell. Two days later Marshall was to die of his wounds, but Wood would recover from his severe back wound. The senior major of the 52nd, Archibald Eden, was wounded in the hand by a bullet. He received attention in the Regimental Aid Post or Dressing Station

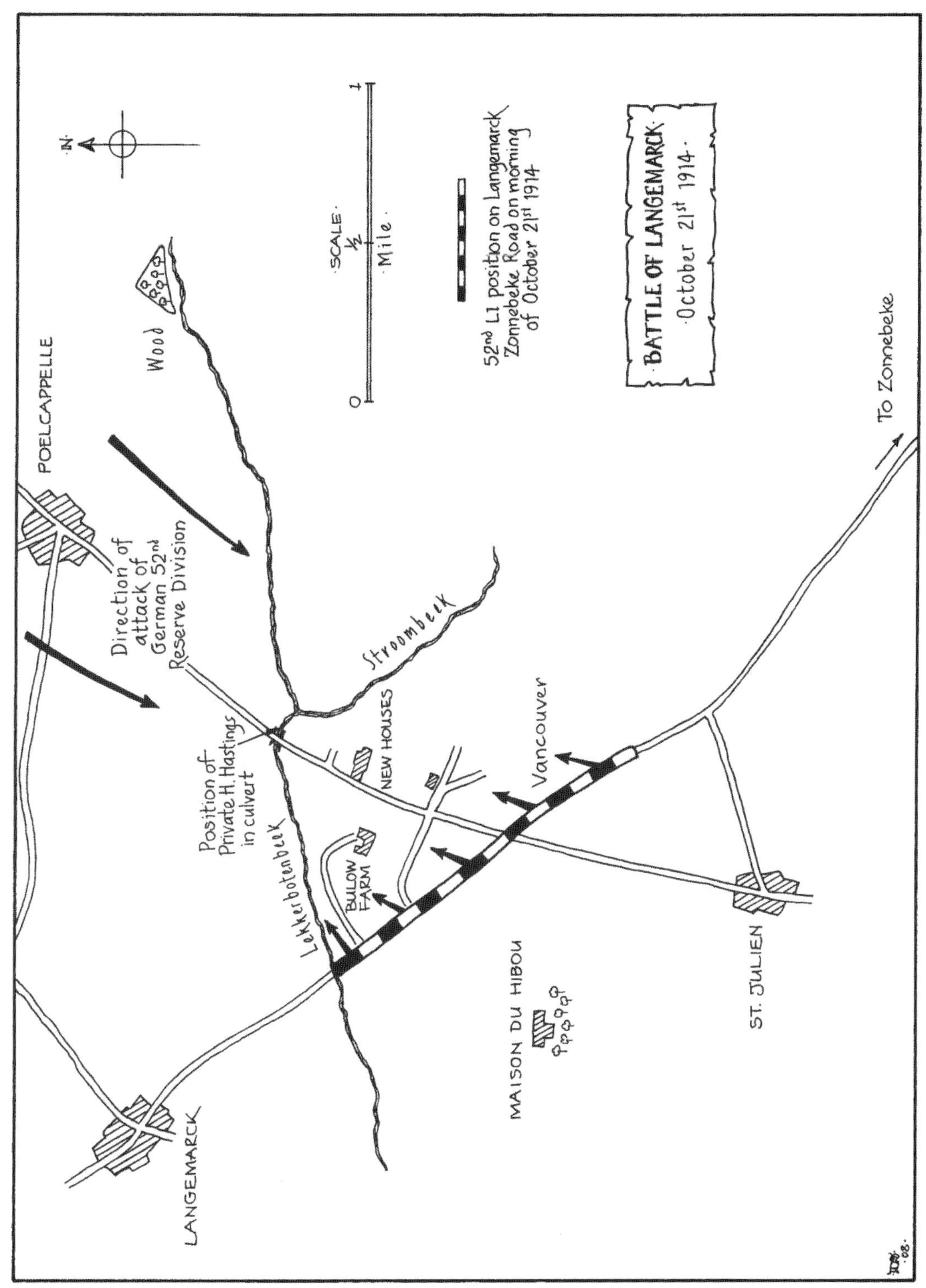

BATTLE OF LANGEMARCK
October 21st 1914
N
SCALE
0
½
1
Mile
52nd LI position on Langemarck Zonnebeke Road on morning of October 21st 1914
POELCAPPELLE
Wood
Direction of attack of German 52nd Reserve Division
Stroombeek
NEW HOUSES
Vancouver
Position of Private H. Hastings in culvert
Lekkerbotenbeek
BULOW FARM
MAISON DU HIBOU
ST. JULIEN
LANGEMARCK
To Zonnebeke

which had been set up in an estaminet south of the seven kilometre post on the poplar-bordered St. Julien to Poelcappelle road.

The ground ahead of the 52nd was relatively flat and the few low ridges failed to show up. Thick hedges and dykes divided the land up and were a hindrance to observation and movement. Visibility was further obstructed by labourers' cottages, trees in the hedgerows and small copses. Just short of the Lekkerbotenbeek the 52nd's advance was held up by a hedge interwoven with barbed wire. Eventually Lieutenants George Tolson and Vere Spencer ran the gauntlet of the only gate at the same time as the hedge was broken down in several places. A contemporary account reported that there were 200 casualties [including ten officers] in fifteen minutes trying to negotiate the gate[111]. This was far from accurate as Henry Davies recorded that the number of casualties at the gate was 30 and few if any of the officers were killed or wounded there.

Lieutenant-Colonel Henry Davies had accompanied A Company on the right of the second line. Just north of the seven kilometre post on the St. Julien to Poelcappelle road, Davies climbed to the upper floor of a farmhouse, later known as New Houses which was situated a few yards to the east of the road. From this vantage point he could see to a degree in three directions. To his left he looked in vain for the infantry of the 1st Division and ahead was his own front line some 200 hundred yards away. German movement could be seen to the right towards the positions of the 2nd Worcestershire but this was curtailed by the shrapnel of the British artillery. The 5th Brigade's artillery support was from the XXXVIth Brigade Royal Field Artillery. Eventually, the captain of the South Wales Borderers' company, on the 52nd's immediate left, sent a message to say that he was ahead of the rest of the 1st Division who were not coming on. It transpired that a French cavalry unit protecting their flank had been moved away towards Houthulst Forest. This led to their front being so wide that they could no longer advance. Henry Davies was of the opinion that if the 1st Division had been able to move forward and had protected the 52nd's own flank, it was likely that the German trenches would have been taken.

The 52nd's initial advance had gained some 1,500 yards of ground but as Archibald Eden, the senior major, put it 'the whole road and neighbourhood was plastered with shell and rifle bullets'[112]. During the day much of the firing died down and at times ceased completely. The battle had become a static one and remained so for the rest of the day with the 52nd unable to get forward in view of their exposed left flank. Their position was some 200 yards north of New Houses with the German trenches a further 300 yards ahead. The nearest ran from the

---

[111] *The First Seven Divisions* by Lord Ernest Hamilton. Published 1916.
[112] Eden's diary entry for October 21st 1914.

junction of the Lekkerbotenbeek and the Stroombeek via a track leading towards Langemarck.

The 52nd had no continuous trench line but small parties of men were scattered around using whatever cover they could find. On the left of the St. Julien - Poelcappelle road the 52nd's positions were in front of the Lekkerbotenbeek and to the right behind that stream. In addition, on the left of the road, twenty yards ahead of the Regiment's other positions, was a small trench where Edward Kirkpatrick and Cuthbert Baines were in command. This vulnerable trench linked the 52nd's positions on either side of the road, but as well as being exposed to the enemy's front, it was subject to sniper fire from behind the nearby poplar trees, and also enfiladed from a wood down the valley to the east. An attack from this wood along the valley would allow the enemy a clear run on to this trench. To mitigate against this possibility, a further small trench was dug along the edge of the road at right angles to the advanced trench. Finally, a forward pit was dug to accommodate two sharpshooters who successfully picked off the German snipers hidden by the poplars along the St. Julien - Poelcappelle road.

Henry Davies sent messages asking the 1st Division to get forward but to no avail. He was joined on the upper floor of New Houses by the Commanding Officer of the 2nd H.L.I., Lieutenant-Colonel Arthur Wolfe-Murray, and his adjutant as it was such an excellent vantage point and they stayed until dusk.

At one point during the day Henry Davies accompanied by the adjutant of the 52nd, Richard Crosse, left New Houses and went along a hedge to visit D Company. On the way they were informed that Lieutenant Christopher Murphy, 'a wild man from Galway'[113], had just died of his wounds and that his body was 50 yards away under a haystack. On reaching D Company their commander Captain Allan Harden crossed the road to speak to Davies and Crosse. Davies had told him not to come as it was too dangerous. But come Harden would and as he was explaining the disposition of his men, he was shot through the head and died instantly. Harden was an experienced soldier who had served throughout the South African War with the Militia and the 1st Battalion of the Regiment. It was to be the first of three occasions in the war that Crosse was actually speaking to a man when he was killed in front of his eyes.

Captain Harry Dillon of A Company has left a graphic description of the fighting written on the following day to his family. These letters were passed on to the War Office where they were greatly valued and led to some changes in military training. Later Dillon would record his sadness at the loss of his grey

[113] Letter from Second-Lieutenant Geoffrey Titherington to his mother written on September 24th 1914.

horse, which he had captured earlier from the enemy, in the day's fighting. He was one of the very best officers in the 52nd and, according to Richard Crosse, would have been given command of the 52nd in July 1916 if he had been fit and available. He was known as 'rabbit Dillon' probably because of his prominent front teeth. Dillon was subject to recurrent chest infections and would die from pneumonia in early 1918.

October 22nd

We are in the middle of the most furious battle it is possible to imagine, but I have got a few men of 3 regiments entrenched which I managed to do the night before last, and we have got well in; and as I can do no more for the present, here goes.

We attacked yesterday with about 9 divisions (of about 20,000 men each), so something decisive ought to be the result; but I only know what happened in my brigade. We got under fire almost at once. I was the right hand coy. of the second line, and as soon as we got into line ready to advance they turned their guns on to us like a hose, we had to wait a bit to let the first line get on and a good many people got hit. When the first line got on I went forward at once and ran until I got to a ditch and put 50 men into it. All the officers of the first line coy. in front of me bar one, were down by now, so the only thing was to get on at all costs and get our rifles into the devils. Went on again, but the men fell fast as we advanced. Collected about 200 men at some hay-stacks but the wounded were rushing in from all sides for cover, so went on again. Got to farm buildings with 12 men and had a few minutes' rest. Went on again into lane where I found 4 officers (Ashley Ponsonby was one) and it seemed impossible to get on and I found only 3 of my men had got on. I had to go back to the farm to try to collect some men, but when I got there could find nobody and I don't know where they got to. Started coming back when I saw there was a deep furrow in a field on my right with some men in it which I thought must be them, so went through. There was no shellfire now, but we were fairly snowed on by rifles and machine-guns from God knows where, and had to crawl on elbows. When I got on about 60 yards I found that they were not my men but some of Ashley's Coy. and another regiment[114]. While I was debating what to do a man ran to me; he had six holes in him

[114] Probably from the 2nd Worcestershire.

and asked me to bandage him. He had no dressing, but I covered all the wounds bar one for which I had no dressing – not a very good start for a battle as I got covered in blood and shall not get a chance to wash for perhaps a week. Got on to hedge and at last discovered German position. Wingfield was there with some men. The other officer, Murphy, and most of his men killed. Opened fire at I suppose about 10 a.m. 20th [21st] and am still in the same spot at 1 p.m. 22nd. One could not move hand or foot all day, but in the evening went down and got some men of a Scotch regiment[115]. This made 3 different lots under my command. If we could have got another hundred men we could have rushed the Germans, but they did not want us to, as the next troops on our left were behind. A great pity, as the Germans evidently had had enough and we could have got through. Dug deep trenches all night. The fire this first day was beyond belief – high explosives, shrapnel, machine guns and rifles blended into one unending roar. I was completely deaf through the first part of the night, but a good deal has worn off now. To hark back to about 8, the fire slackened a good deal. I left Wingfield in charge and went to find out what had happened. Found the Colonel who was all right, thank God, but seven other officers gone west[116]. He told me to take command of all the troops I had with me, get the wounded away if possible and dig. We did dig and got the wounded away before morning. The dead we pulled out into a field and covered them up, also got some rations and water. There was nothing to be done but await events. At dawn the guns opened again, but in the trenches "c'est tout different," and had a bit of sleep. At about 5 p.m. hell was absolutely let loose again and continued all night.

At dusk the 52nd began to further entrench and used the night hours to deepen and extend their trenches. A company of the 2nd H.L.I. came up on their left to fill the gap between them and the South Wales Borderers of the 1st Division. During the night Henry Davies organised that rations and ammunition were brought up plus the big entrenching tools. Water bottles were filled in New Houses and the wounded were eventually evacuated. They had been collecting at

---

[115] 2nd Highland Light Infantry.

[116] In fact four officers were killed and six others wounded on the 21st. Second-Lieutenant George Marshall was to die of his wounds on the 23rd.

the farm all day and were some fifty in number. Davies was fearful that New Houses would be shelled and was greatly relieved when the final casualty was evacuated shortly before dawn. The original convoy of ambulances had mistakenly been ordered to turn back before reaching them. A bearer sub-division of the 5th Field Ambulance was responsible for the care of the casualties. At 8.30 p.m., Archibald Eden who had been shot in the right hand led a party of walking wounded some 36 strong down the road to St. Julien, where they were well looked after in a clearing hospital. Eden was soon to recover from his injury and would command the 52nd for much of 1915-16.

The night of October 21st-22nd 1914 was a quiet one from the fighting point of view. Henry Davies reflected that 'that this was our first big fight. The men advanced splendidly, and the officers and n.c.o.s did their duty magnificently. There was always an absolute readiness to advance on the part of the men'. Corporal J.W. Hodges' gallant conduct in the attack of the 21st typified many in the regiment. He was awarded the Distinguished Conduct Medal [D.C.M.].

The 52nd had suffered heavy casualties on the 21st: in total, 217 for the day.[117] Four officers and 61 other ranks had been killed. The officers were Captain Allan Harden, Lieutenant Gladwyn Turbutt, Lieutenant Christopher Murphy, and Second-Lieutenant Leonard Filleul. Six officers and 143 other ranks were wounded. Three men were missing. The wounded officers were Major Archibald Eden [gunshot wound right hand], Captain Lindsay Wood [gunshot wound back][118], Captain Edward Kirkpatrick [bullet wound shoulder and neck][119], Second-Lieutenant George Marshall [died of his wounds October 23rd 1914], Second-Lieutenant Pierce Newton-King [gunshot wound forearm] and Second-Lieutenant F.W.C. 'Chips' Chippindale [gunshot wound arm].

Dawn came on October 22nd with Lieutenant-Colonel Henry Davies still able to live in the farm – New Houses. During the day there was little fire on the 52nd's trenches. In front of Davies the 52nd had dug in and the men of the four companies were much mixed up following the previous day's assault. This meant that officers were commanding some of their own men and some from other companies. Sensibly, Davies made no attempt to reorganise them feeling that it was better for the men to remain in familiar trenches that they had dug themselves.

---

117 The *Battalion War Diary* gave a higher figure of 226. Killed 65, wounded 146 [149], missing 15[3]. The post-war figures quoted in the text are more likely to be accurate.

118 Lindsay Wood survived his wounds to become a Brigade-Major in 1915. In 1917 he commanded the 5th Battalion Oxfordshire and Buckinghamshire Light Infantry.

119 The 52nd's casualty book stated upper arm. Henry Davies' diary recorded shoulder and neck.

To the right of the St. Julien to Poelcappelle road were Harry Dillon and his men. On the main road itself was George Tolson with Cuthbert 'Bingo' Baines to its left and Edward Kirkpatrick beyond him. Kirkpatrick continued in action for 24 hours after receiving wounds in his neck and shoulder. In the fields on the extreme left was Ashley Ponsonby. Late in the afternoon the Germans restarted shelling and concentrated on the farm, soon setting it on fire. Henry Davies had prepared for this by having a trench dug about 25 yards behind the farm and into this his Regimental Headquarters were able to move without suffering any casualties. When the fire started, several regimental scouts, and in particular Private Hart, retrieved vital ammunition from a store close to the farm at great personal risk to themselves.

Shortly afterwards at about 5.30 p.m., with the light fading, a fairly heavy attack was made on the 52nd's trenches near the main road. The German attack at around battalion strength concentrated on the trenches just to the east of the road. However, George Tolson and his men lying on the road enfiladed it to great effect. Three of his men, under Private Henry Hastings, a former tram driver, on their own initiative, actually lay in the culvert where the small stream of the Lekkerbotenbeek crossed the road and executed large numbers of Germans with deadly precision. The enemy came on in thick lines singing and shouting but the 52nd remained steady under fire. The leading Germans got to within 25 yards of the British positions, but could stand it no more and retreated at speed. By the day's end, 70 German dead could be counted in front of them although the numbers were undoubtedly greater. Four enemy wounded from the attack were also brought in the next morning. The 52nd in their prepared positions lost only one man killed and another wounded during the action. A further six men were killed and eight wounded at other times of the day. Much of the night was spent in burying the dead.

A description of the actions of Private Henry Hastings and his brave companions in the culvert appeared in '*Deeds That Thrilled The Empire*'[120]. For his gallantry Hastings was awarded the D.C.M.

> It had been a day of desperately hard fighting; the Germans, for the most part new levies, though mown down in swathes by our fire, coming on again and again with the utmost courage and determination, and it was not expected that the night would pass

[120] The book gave the date as October 23rd. In fact Hastings went out to the culvert on both the 22nd and 23rd. His D.C.M. citation stated that he killed 23 Germans personally on the 23rd. He was later transferred to the Royal Engineers.

without a renewal of their attacks. Private Hastings had already made a name for himself by his cool courage and the excellence of his marksmanship, and he and two other men were entrusted with the task of holding a culvert over a brook and a narrow footpath connecting the enemy's line with ours, from which position they would be able to enfilade the Germans as they advanced. A bush growing over the brook screened the mouth of the brook in direct front, but they had to hold the gaps on each flank. Hastings, having been given a free hand, put up some barbed wire over their side and across the brook and built a sod barricade.

Scarcely had these preparations been completed, when two companies of the enemy advanced to the attack. He waited until they were almost level with him and he had them black against the sky, and then opened fire. One of his comrades stood by to keep him supplied with ammunition, but by the time he had fired twenty six rounds, the Germans had had enough of it and retreated. On going out to ascertain the loss he had inflicted on them, he found nine Huns, one of whom was an officer, lying dead, and another wounded. They were all from the 223rd and 235th Regiments[121] – two corps raised since the outbreak of war – and most of them mere lads in new uniforms. With the assistance of another man he carried the wounded German into the British lines next day, together with five others, who had fallen in a previous attack. They were very grateful, and one of them called him: "Kind Kamerad!" Their friends in the German trenches were much less appreciative, for they fired on Hastings and the other soldier[122].

During the 22nd, Henry Davies received orders that the 52nd and the Worcestershire were to retire at nightfall to a position about half a mile to the rear. Understandably incensed by orders that meant giving up ground gained with the blood of so many of his men, he protested vehemently to the temporary commander of the 5th Brigade, Lieutenant-Colonel Claude Westmacott. Davies

[121] The 235th Regiment was in the area at about this time, but the 223rd was reportedly concentrated near Metz in the middle of October and on the 25th it was transferred to the area between Armentières and La Bassée. It is far more likely that the men killed by Hastings came from the 52nd Reserve Division, whose 240th Reserve Infantry Regiment, were definitely in the correct area and posted casualties of 28 officers and 1,360 men for the period October 18th-28th 1914.

[122] Hastings brought in the German wounded in a wheelbarrow.

felt well able to hold his own position and did not think that it would be difficult for the 1st Division to come up in line with the 52nd. His protest was forwarded by Westmacott to Major-General Charles Monro commanding the 2nd Division. Monro replied that he appreciated their reluctance to retire from ground gained at such cost, but that it was necessary to maintain the general line of the army. Fortunately, to the great relief of Davies, the order was cancelled that night, possibly because of the German attack that day.

The 52nd's casualties on the 22nd were surprisingly light. Seven killed and eight wounded. During the evening attack only one man was killed and another wounded and these losses occurred in parts of the line not being directly assaulted. The enemy's artillery fire continued on other trenches not being directly attacked. The remaining casualties took place at other times in the day. The Germans had suffered great losses; Harry Dillon recorded that he had personally killed with his rifle seven on the 21st and 30-40 on the 22nd. He believed that the 52nd were killing ten of the enemy for the loss of every man of their own.

On October 23rd there was a considerable amount of artillery fire plus at times rifle and machine-gun fire from the Germans. In the afternoon both the farm and the 52nd's trenches received artillery fire. Just to the west of the main road, where the redoubtable Cuthbert Baines was in command of his advanced trench, high explosive shells smashed in the trench, burying him to the waist, and killing many of his men. Cleverly, Baines withdrew his surviving men during the shelling to the steep bank of a stream some 50 yards to the rear. If the Germans attacked, the men would immediately return to the trench that they had retired from. Baines' wise action reduced casualties significantly.

During the day two men were killed and seven wounded[123], amongst them Captain Ashley Ponsonby [gunshot wound shoulder] and Lieutenant Douglas Humfrey [wound calf right leg]. In a letter to his young friend, Betty Dawes, Humfrey gave a few details of his part in the action[124].

> Don't be alarmed if you see my name in the casualty list. I only got a bullet thro' my leg and the wound has almost healed but the muscle won't let me put my leg down yet. I rather hope to leave this place on Monday either for home or some private hospital or home in London where I can get a massage. We had some awful hard

[123] Private William Cheshire was wounded in the leg by a German sniper and lay in a pig sty for three days. He died in Bedford Hospital on October 27th 1914. It is not clear on which of the three days October 21st, 22nd, 23rd he was actually wounded.

[124] Letter written from the Royal Naval Hospital, Plymouth on October 31st 1914.

> fighting in Belgium last week and lost a lot of officers. I lost all the things I was carrying such as sword, overcoat, burbery [sic], revolver etc. I only got myself and men out of a trench a few seconds before a huge shell fell in and smothered the whole trench and I expect my things are now reposing under 10 ft of soil and a tree. When I got my wound we were going at the Deutchers with the bayonet but they turned back as they always do when we......at them.

At 5.30 p.m. the German infantry attacked again with a larger force than the night before. The principle thrust was to the east of the main St. Julien - Poelcappelle road with thick lines of the enemy getting up close to the 52nd's trenches. As the Commanding Officer, Henry Davies recorded 'our men were absolutely cool and steady and fired well. The attack appearing to be more formidable than that of yesterday, I reinforced the line with every man, until the firing line was as full as it could be. I also succeeded in getting up ammunition, and after the attack every man was again well supplied'.

The result was the same as the previous evening; the Germans broke and retired to the nearest hedge 150 yards to the rear. There shouting could be heard, officers apparently trying to get their men to go forward again. In this they were unsuccessful and they all retired to their own trenches. As on the night before, Private Hart did excellent work in bringing up ammunition to the firing line from a store close to the farm which was still ablaze.

Harry Dillon continued his vivid account of the action and the 52nd's relief by the French in a letter to his family.

> 3 p.m.[125]. Have just driven back an attack, but to continue where I left off. The Germans attacked 2 times during the night, but we drove them off. This morning the ground is dotted with thick clusters of their dead. Just as I got to where I put the dots a tremendous shelling started followed half an hour later by swarms of Germans, and we have been blazing away for all we have been worth. I think I dropped 6 myself, and we must have knocked over a lot. No casualties in my lot, owing to our good trenches. No more for the present.

---

[125] The *Regimental Chronicles* gave the date as the 23rd. Dillon's original letter merely stated 3 p.m. with no date given.

October 24th [126]. Since writing many things have happened, and I am still unwashed, but in another trench some miles from where I was. To continue where I left off. Far the most exciting thing that has happened to me happened on the evening of the 22nd. In my section about 200 yards I had about 150 men, and just where I was myself was the thinnest portion. The night came on rather misty and dark, and I thought several times of asking for reinforcements, but I collected a lot of rifles off the dead, and loaded them and put them along the parapet instead. All of a sudden about a dozen shells came down and almost simultaneously 2 machine guns and a tremendous rifle fire opened on us. It was a most unholy din. The shells ripped open the parapet and trees came crashing down. However I was well underground and did not care much, but presently the guns stopped, and I knew we were in for it. I had to look over the top for about 10 minutes however under their infernal maxims before I saw what I was looking for. It came with a suddenness that was the most startling thing I have ever known. The firing stopped, and I had been straining my eyes so for a moment I could not believe them, but fortunately I did not hesitate long. A great grey mass of humanity was charging straight on us not 50 yards off, – about as far as the summer-house to the coach-house. Everybody's nerves were pretty well on edge as I had warned them what to expect, and as I fired my rifle the rest went off almost simultaneously. One saw the great mass of Germans quiver. In reality some fell, and others came on. I have never shot so much in such a short time, [it] could not have been more than a few seconds and they were down. Suddenly one man, I expect an officer, jumped up and came on; I fired and missed, seized the next rifle and dropped him a few yards off. Then the whole lot came on again and it was the most critical moment of my life. Twenty yards more and they would have been over us in thousands, but our fire must have been fearful, and at the very last moment they did the most foolish thing they possibly could have done. Some of the leading people turned to the left for some reason, and they all followed like some great flock of sheep. We did not lose much time I can give you my oath. My right hand is one huge bruise from banging the bolt up and down. I don't think one could have missed at that distance and for one short minute or two we poured

[126] Dillon's original letter stated the 24th, however the *Regimental Chronicles* in their copy of the letter stated the 25th.

the ammunition into them in boxfuls. My rifles were red hot at the finish, I know, and that was the end of the battle for me. The firing died down and out of the darkness a great moan came. People with their arms and legs off trying to crawl away; others who could not move gasping out their last moments with the cold night wind biting into their broken bodies and the lurid red glare of a farm house showing up clumps of grey devils killed by the men on my left further down. A weird awful scene; some of them would raise themselves on one arm or crawl a little distance, silhouetted as black as ink against the red glow of the fire. Well, I suppose if there is a God, Emperor Bill will have to come to book some day. When one thinks of the misery of these wounded and later on, wives, mothers and friends, and to think that this great battle where there may have been half a million on either said [side], is only on a front of about 25 miles, and that this sort of thing is now going on on a front of nearly 400. To think that this man could have saved it all. The proposition is almost too vast to get a grip of. It is ruining thousands of lives, from France, Germany, Russia, India, and right to Serbia, poor wives and people waiting to hear. It really is the greatest calamity the world has ever seen. Our losses in the battle were 6 officers killed and five wounded[127], and we have not had time to find out how many men, but I should think about 400. There are not many of the original lot left now. Our Colonel is all right. I am the only Captain and the rest subalterns. It fills me with a great rage. I know I have got to stop my bullet some time, and it is merely a question of where it hits one whether it is dead or wounded. We fight every day and I am in support today in a trench with the shells coming along at intervals. The order may come at any minute to support an attack which is going on, and then it is just a chance. I don't care a farthing as far as I am concerned, but the whole thing is an outrage on civilisation. The whole of this beautiful country is devastated. Broken houses, broken bodies, blood, filth and ruin everywhere. Can any unending Hell fire for the Kaiser, his son, and the party who caused this war repair the broken bodies and worse broken hearts which are being made? – Being made this very minute within a few hundred yards of where I am sitting. Well, there's my sentiments, so back to my story.

---

[127] In the fighting between October 21st-24th 1914, the 52nd had four officers killed, one died of his wounds, and seven wounded.

At about 11 o'clock we were told some French troops were to relieve us and that we were to go to another part of the line. I was the first to be relieved and started off. I got a good shelling on my way but no damage. We got assembled at about 4.30 a.m. and I learnt who the dead were; poor George Marshall was one you would know. Ashley Ponsonby wounded – that is 20 officers we have lost, and we only started with 26. We marched until 6, then had some breakfast and were hurried on here. Something had happened which I can't put down. Yesterday we had an uncomfortable job. I had 2 killed and 8 wounded in my coy. Pepys got another bullet through his sword hilt; he is a very lucky young man as it is the third time he has been the only one out of a bunch of six[128]. I forgot to take any biscuit in the morning, so had nothing to eat all day and got very exhausted. We got four hours' sleep, and this morning I have been detached with my coy. on the right of my brigade, which is in support to an attack going on in front. The firing is very heavy and I can't see what is happening from my place as there are woods all round.

Again dead Germans wherever one goes. I suppose 5,000,000 men take a lot of killing, but we ought to have accounted for a good few by now. I suppose this is one big battle that has been going on for about 6 days. It is certainly bloody enough for anything. I am now 2nd in command of the regiment, so if the Colonel gets hit I take command – rather too much responsibility for my liking; still it might be a chance of doing something. I do hope the old man will be all right, but he moves about too much and I am always in terror that he will get hit. I have had 2 men wounded today up to date. Well, will finish now. I only wish I could wash and get a comfortable bed. Not so much as washed my hands since the 20th and only 4 hours' sleep. My trench is so narrow I can't sleep here. I will dig it deeper after dark; but then one is always anxious in case they should attack. So long.

Harry Dillon's four hours sleep in three nights of battle illustrates just how exhausted the men of I Corps had become. It is not surprising Dillon was apprehensive of having to take over command of the 52nd in the event of Henry Davies becoming a casualty, as he had only had command of A Company for

[128] Pepys' luck was about to run out, he would be killed on November 12th 1914.

three days following Harden's death on the 21st[129]. It is interesting that Pepys was still carrying his sword. Dillon took a rifle and bayonet rather than his sword into battle. His letters are supposed to have provoked a debate whether officers should be trained to use the rifle and bayonet rather than spending precious time in learning sword exercises[130].

Second-Lieutenant Geoffrey Titherington, a platoon commander in Ashley Ponsonby's C Company, has also left a contemporaneous account of the action[131].

> We had quite a hot fight advancing against an entrenched village and the 52nd did very well. We pushed ahead in the morning and got a fair position about 300 yards from them and dug ourselves in under fire. We were shrapnelled rather heavily. My trench was under a hedge – a beautiful range mark – so every Deutcher in the district had a go at it. On the second day they made another attack on us and we counted over 700 of their dead in front. Their method is to sleep till 1, then shell and rifle fire gradually putting in more and more as it gets dusk when their infantry come on sometimes silently, sometimes making a great deal of noise and shouting "don't shoot, English" or "we've had enough". They had a white flag up in front of me one morning. Of course why losses are heavy is because the country is so very thick. But "you can't make omelettes without breaking eggs". The villages literally seem to run into one another and the average farm appears to be about 20 acres. It's good in one way – one can get straw easily.

The 52nd as a whole had fought splendidly and they had lived up to the great traditions of the Regiment. The next day the French counted no less than 740 dead Germans in front of the trenches heroically defended by the 52nd. This included the 70 whom they had killed on the evening of the 22nd of October.

Early in the evening of the 23rd the Regiment was informed that they would be relieved by the French 125th Regiment. This took place between 10 and 11 p.m. with the first part taking place uneventfully. When it came to the relief of the trenches to the west of the main road, the Germans opened fire with rifles,

---

129 Dillon also had brief experience as a company commander just after mobilization and again on the Aisne.

130 In January 1915, officers' swords were replaced by rifles. Perhaps Dillon's views played a small part in the debate.

131 Letter to his father written on October 24th 1914 [Titherington thought].

machine-guns and shrapnel. This interrupted matters as the men were forced to seek cover by lying down. Fortunately no men of the 52nd were killed during the relief. They were clear of the trenches by 1 a.m. and moved by St. Julien via St. Jean-Potijze to the Halte, a distance of five miles. In later years this crossing of the Ypres-Roulers railway by the Ypres-Menin road would become known as the notorious Hellfire Corner.

During the relief, Privates Francis Upperton and Daniel Piggott showed great courage by bringing up their limbered wagons to retrieve the tools from the Regimental Headquarters. This act of devotion to duty took place while there was intermittent shellfire on their route up from Ypres. Despite the chaos in the pitch darkness resulting from the intermingling of French and British troops, they kept their frightened horses calm. Eventually in 1916, Upperton received the D.C.M. and Piggott the M.M. for further acts of gallantry. Another man to be awarded the D.C.M. for his actions that night was a stretcher bearer Private E.D. Stock who carried out his duties under heavy fire[132].

By the autumn of 1917, Henry Davies had risen to be the Major-General commanding the 11th Division [Northern], which attacked over the same ground as the 52nd on October 21st 1914. He was able to inspect the ground that had been left intact to the French on October 23rd 1914. It did not remain permanently in their hands as French Colonial troops broke under the first gas attack of the war in April 1915. The Germans held the ground for two and a half years until Poelcappelle was retaken in October 1917. Six months later the allies were forced to withdraw to the line of the Pilckem Ridge and the 52nd's old battlefield again fell into the enemy's possession and remained so until the final advance in the autumn of 1918.

Henry Davies found that the countryside had changed greatly by 1917. In 1914, there were flourishing farmhouses with pleasant gardens and fields with crops divided from each other by high, strong fences, which had formed a significant obstacle to their attack. These farmhouses, gardens, fields and fences had vanished from the face of the earth. All that remained was a brown desert of shell holes. Artillery fire had so broken up the drainage system that the shell holes were full of water and the small streams had become a series of swampy pools.

Some landmarks remained to enable Davies to follow the line of the October 21st attack. The main Ypres to Poelcappelle road was open to motor vehicles and the Zonnebeke to Langemarck road, along which the 52nd had formed up, was still in existence. Henry Davies had the Sappers of the 11th Division make a wooden cross to commemorate the 52nd's fallen of October 21st-

---

[132] Awarded December 17th 1914.

23rd 1914. On October 11th 1917, the cross was placed on the site where some of the 52nd's dead had been buried on October 22nd 1914. The map reference was U.30d.40.55. Davies accompanied by his wife paid a further visit to the place in April 1919, and was pleased to find the cross still in existence although damaged by shellfire. The cross with its inscription, 'In memory of 5 officers, 70 N.C.O.s and men, 52nd Light Infantry, killed in action 21st-23rd Oct. 1914, some of whom are buried near this spot', was later removed to the cemetery at Poelcappelle with the bodies of the men buried there.

Today, it is not difficult to follow the course of the 52nd's movements on the ground during the period October 21st-23rd 1914. The most obvious landmark in the area is the Canadian memorial at Vancouver Farm, which is sited close to the cross-roads at the junction of the Langemarck - Zonnebeke and St. Julien - Poelcappelle roads. To the north of the memorial lies the rebuilt farm at the site of New Houses from where Henry Davies commanded the 52nd during the battle. In 1919 there was a German bunker here but this has long since been demolished. Bulow Farm, where the 2nd H.L.I. had their Headquarters during the battle, has been replaced. Further up the road to Poelcappelle, with its flat and featureless fields on either side, can be seen the culvert where Private Henry Hastings did such deadly execution of the advancing German infantry on those long ago October days.

Chapter V

Fighting in the Woods around Ypres: the Battle of Gheluvelt.

October 24th – November 10th 1914

[Maps: pages 99, 105, 111, 148.]

The 52nd Light Infantry reached the Halte [Hellfire Corner] at 5 a.m. on October 24th and had time for a short sleep in a field before the cold awoke them. Breakfast was taken and the mail from home was distributed and read. After their exertions of the previous three days they were entitled to expect a short time in reserve and a well-earned rest. It was not to be as the commander of the 2nd Division, Major-General Charles Monro, ordered the 5th Infantry Brigade to go to the assistance of the beleaguered 7th Division whose eight mile front had been breached a little earlier that morning. The 7th Division was formed after the outbreak of war from the three remaining regular battalions in England and nine brought back from overseas. They were experienced professional soldiers and were commanded by Major-General Thompson Capper[133]. To the east of Polygon Wood, the 2nd Wiltshire had been obliterated by an attack on their trenches around the Reutel Spur from both the flank and rear. The German Reserve Infantry Regiment No. 244, consisting of three battalions, had penetrated into Polygon Wood and the situation was critical.

At 9 a.m., the 5th Brigade, led by the unfortunate 2nd Worcestershire, set off in a hurry for Polygon Wood. The previous night the battalion had been the last to be relieved, as they had been covering the withdrawal of the British guns, and there was no time for breakfast and only twenty minutes of rest. The 2nd Worcestershire and the 2nd Highland Light Infantry cleared Polygon Wood, largely with the bayonet, as they feared using firearms with British troops still thought to be ahead of them in the wood. Polygon Wood consisted of a thick mass of pine trees with a dense undergrowth of oak, beech and chestnut. The 52nd would become familiar with it over the next few weeks. The 52nd were fortunate to be kept out of the bayonet fighting and were held in reserve to the west end of Polygon Wood. However, Captain Cuthbert Baines and his B Company were sent to support the 2nd Scots Guards in trenches to the north-east of the Wood.

Whilst in reserve Second-Lieutenant Geoffrey Titherington wrote a letter to his father[134]. He had not washed or shaved for five days and was 'filthy'.

---

[133] 'Tommy' Capper commanded the 7th Division 1914–15. He died of wounds received at the Battle of Loos.

[134] Letter written to his father on October 24th 1914. [Titherington thought].

> We were relieved after 3 days and at present I am sitting in a trench in a pine wood in support – we've just relieved the Scots guards. Its [sic] well hidden and we only get chance bullets and a very occasional shell. About ½ an hour ago one actually hit the ground just in front of my trench i.e. about 5 feet from my ear. I am glad it was not a Jack Johnson or I should now doubtless be giving someone the trouble of collecting bits of me and putting them underground.

In the same letter Titherington gave an insight into the 52nd's night fighting technique.

> We are getting rather hot at night fighting and I think we puzzle the Deutchers. Most regiments if they are shot at get up and reply and pandemonium reigns: next the guns wake up and everything is noisy and uncomfortable. We let them shoot and lie doggo with of course one man in 4 to look out but don't fire. Then suddenly we fire 5 rounds per man 'rapid' in case anyone is out in front – then stop completely and I find the Deutchers generally take the hint and shut up if they are not doing a genuine attack.

Like so many of the 52nd, Titherington was fond of animals, particularly horses and dogs. He continued his letter.

> Give my love to the dogs – I've made lots of dog friends here for every deserted house has a wretched tike locked up in it and other beasts – of course no one has time to feed them I loose all I can. There's a little Dachshund now with the ammunition cart but I daren't adopt her for her German master was slain and 2 successive English one's so that she seems a bit unlucky.

At about 3.30 p.m., Lieutenant-Colonel Henry Davies was ordered to take the remainder of the 52nd to the cross-roads near the 9th kilometre mark on the Ypres to Menin road, where a further German attack was expected at any moment. Here he was to meet a staff officer of the 7th Division who would give him further orders. Davies was told to avoid going through the village of Gheluvelt, which was being shelled, and to go to the north of it and to come out close to the 8th kilometre mark on the road. A cross-country journey without knowing the positions of friend or foe was difficult for the 52nd. Davies led from

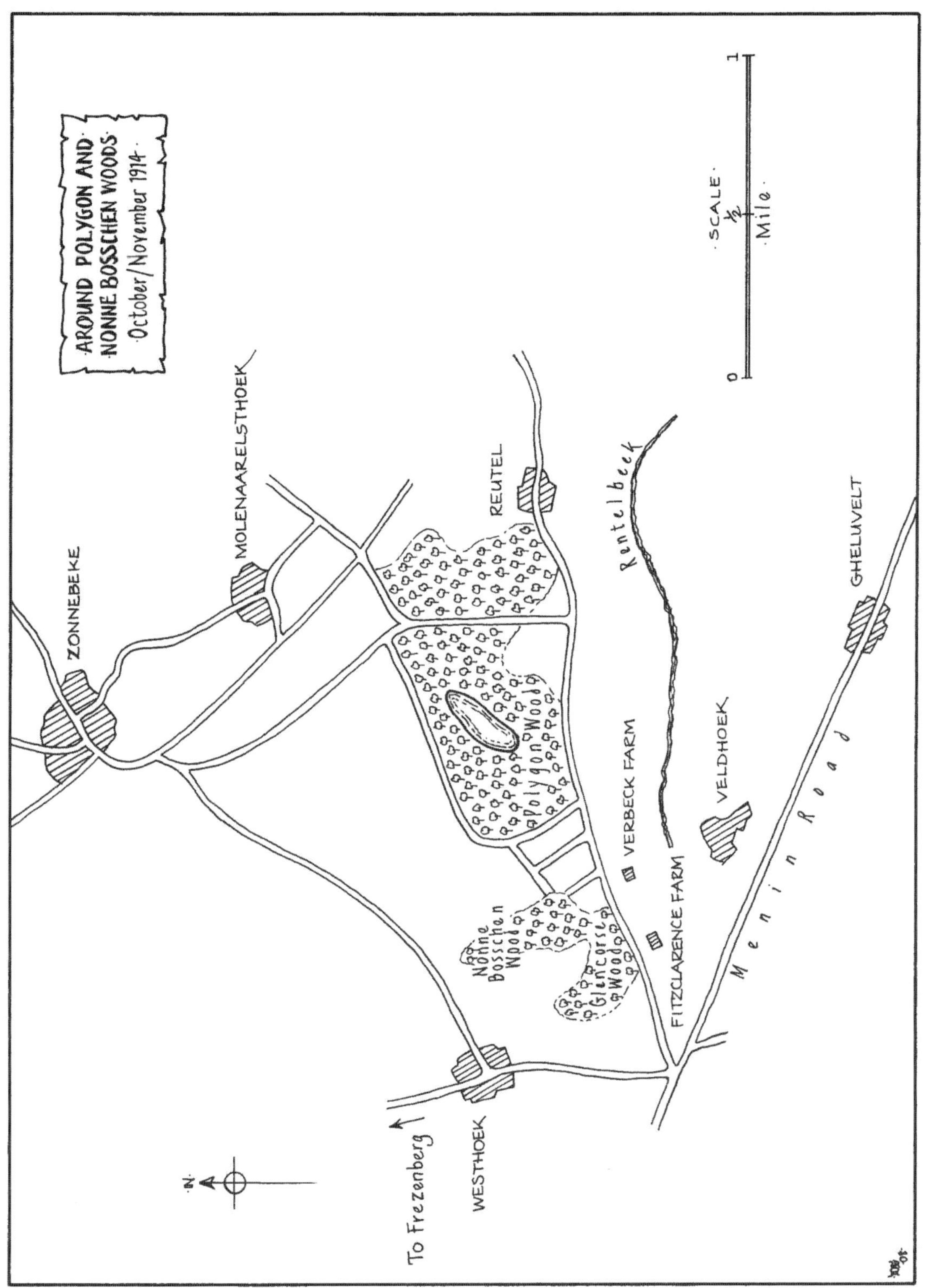
AROUND POLYGON AND
NONNE BOSSCHEN WOODS
October/November 1914
SCALE
0
½
1
Mile
ZONNEBEKE
MOLENAARELSTHOEK
REUTEL
Reutelbeek
GHELUVELT
VELDHOEK
VERBECK FARM
FITZCLARENCE FARM
Polygon Wood
Nonne Bosschen Wood
Glencorse Wood
Menin Road
WESTHOEK
To Frezenberg
N

the front himself, and after taking advice from the 2nd Bedfordshire, who were in trenches close to Gheluvelt, as to the safest ground, he was able to reach the 8th kilometre mark without many casualties. A Company who were bringing up the rear did lose one man killed and four others wounded from machine-gun fire, but Davies felt that they had got off lightly. The haziness of the late October evening helped them to move unobserved.

Although an odd shell was falling on the road there was no other evidence of any fighting. Davies left the 52nd under the cover of a steep bank and went on with two buglers as far as the appointed cross-roads near the 9th kilometre mark. There was no sign of any staff officer from the 7th Division or indeed any fighting. Eventually Davies found Lieutenant-Colonel C.A.C. King of the 2nd Green Howards who said that nothing was happening and reinforcements were not needed. Finding he was not required, Davies wearily retraced his steps and rejoined his men. The 52nd then marched down the road to Veldhoek and bivouacked for the night in some buildings and an orchard to the south of the Ypres to Menin road. Here Davies was able to make contact with the Headquarters of the 21st Brigade[135] under whose orders they had temporarily come. The 52nd had covered some fifteen miles, mainly across country, since leaving the Halte that morning. They were able to get a few hours sleep. On October 24th, Lieutenant Pierce Newton-King and Second-Lieutenant F.W. 'Chips' Chippindale received gunshot wounds of the forearm and arm respectively.

The reason for the delay in making contact with the Headquarters of the 21st Brigade until so late in the day was a very odd one. Whilst looking for them, the Adjutant of the 52nd, Richard Crosse, was arrested as a suspected German spy. An overzealous officer of the Royal Horse Guards took him into protective custody until various individuals were able to vouch for him. It seems ludicrous at this distance of time that this quintessential Englishman and old boy of Rugby School could have been taken to be a German!

During the night of the 24th-25th, it was decided that the 2nd Division would attack the enemy's positions to the east of Polygon Wood, in support of a French attack towards Passchendaele. The 4th Brigade [Guards] was to pass through the 5th Brigade's positions and attack the Reutel Spur and the 6th Brigade was to attack at the same time on their left.

Next day, October 25th was St. Crispin's Day. A day of mixed fortunes in the history of England and her armies. In 1415, Agincourt had been a great victory for Henry V over the French. But it was also the day of the charge of the unfortunate Light Brigade at Balaclava, in 1854. The 52nd again came under the

[135] 7th Division.

orders of the 5th Brigade and was sent to relieve the 2nd Scots Guards in the north-eastern part of Polygon Wood. The move was made early in the morning. C and D Companies were placed on the wood's edge with the 2nd Worcestershire and the 2nd H.L.I. on their right. B Company under Cuthbert Baines rejoined them and A Company was situated on the right of the H.L.I. Part of the 6th Brigade was in front of them, so that only half the 52nd's men were actually in the front line. Although a few shells and bullets came over in the afternoon, it was relatively quiet.

The Guards' attack in the morning was delayed and eventually took place at dusk. They were unable to get further than the western slopes of the Reutel Spur. As darkness came down, it started to pour with rain, soaking the attacking force and also the 52nd who were watching, from their trenches, the gun flashes on the slope 300 yards ahead of them. The Guards were reputed to have captured two guns.

October 26th was to be a frustrating day for the 52nd. It started with them in trenches to the eastern end of Polygon Wood. At 1 p.m. they were sent back into Divisional Reserve to join the rest of the 5th Brigade, in a wood to the south-east of Westhoek [Eksternest]. Later in the war it would be called Glencorse Wood. Under the general pressure exerted by the Germans and the organisational chaos of that October, they were almost immediately sent back to where they had come from. This was to support an abortive attack by the 6th Brigade to follow up pressure exerted by the French further north, where it was thought that the Germans were on the point of collapse. However, by the time the 52nd reached their former positions at the eastern end of Polygon Wood, it was dark and they were sent back again into reserve. Regimental Headquarters found a small house close to Glencorse Wood and the men obtained some shelter from the elements in the wood. Hot tea was served for only the second time since the 20th [the first being at breakfast on the 24th]. A quiet night followed.

The experience was repeated on the next day, the 27th, with the 52nd bivouacked in Glencorse Wood and subject to some desultory shelling from time to time. At 3 p.m., the 52nd and the rest of the 5th Brigade retraced their steps once more to the north-east end of Polygon Wood. The latest attack by the 6th Brigade was cancelled and the 52nd returned to the shelters that they had made in Glencorse Wood.

The morning of October 28th was bright and clear making artillery observation easier, and Major-General Charles Monro, commanding the 2nd Division, wasted no time in ordering his divisional artillery to soften up the enemy. The long-awaited attack of the 5th and 6th Brigades would begin that afternoon. At 8 a.m., the 52nd returned once again to the trenches at the north-east corner of Polygon Wood and set about improving them. The attack started at 3 p.m. with the 2nd Connaught Rangers supported by the 2nd H.L.I. leading the 5th Brigade with the 52nd and the 2nd Worcestershire remaining in reserve in a clearing in the wood. The attack did not get very far before it was broken up by devastating shellfire from the German artillery. For the first time in several days the 52nd suffered casualties from the enemy shelling. One man was killed and eighteen more wounded including Lieutenant Maurice Wingfield. Wingfield known as 'Tolly'[136] received a serious head injury and although he recovered from it, never fought with the 52nd again. He was a colourful character who in later life married a showgirl.

Captain Harry Dillon recounted to his relatives his experiences in Polygon Wood on the morning of the 28th[137].

> I was sent out yesterday morning with 2 scouts to reconnoitre a line to attack a position and had rather an exciting time. Our own people were so well hidden we did not see them and mistook a German trench for them, at about 200 yards they opened on us and we got back all right and did our job. On the way back I heard a poor kitten mewing in a cottage and went to its rescue. I found the little beast starving also lots of rabbits and pigs and goats all of which I let out and took the poor kitten to some friendly gunners who gave her of the best that they had. The whole ground round the place was covered with dead etc, but I don't know why, perhaps because one has got so used to this sight one did not feel it. It does seem hard though that these poor creatures should suffer because men are such foul creatures. – Well I suppose I am very lucky to be here fit and well. – I do hope however that before the inevitable bullet or shell comes my way I shall get my bayonet into a German. We never carry swords now which are quite useless but collar a rifle bayonet from a dead man and throw it away at the end of the battle.

Dillon's comments about the uselessness of swords in battle are interesting. As we have seen earlier, he was not alone in the 52nd with his compassion for animals; Rosslyn Evelegh had even given his life attempting to release cattle in a barn at La Cour de Soupir on the Aisne.

---

[136] The nickname originated in his taste for Tolly Cobbold beer. The 52nd's wounds and movements book has a final entry 'In South Cork Infirmary. Whereabouts unknown'.

[137] The letter was written from Polygon Wood on October 29th 1914.

In a further letter to his family Dillon requested a torch[138].

> The electric torch arrived all right but unfortunately is too big and I can't carry it. Could you send me another same make if possible and small enough to put in my pocket. You might do this as soon as you get this as it is most important. One is always wanting to read one's map or a message. Three nights ago in fact I had a message when 200 yds off the Germans, by putting a great coat down and carefully shading the light from a torch I might have read it – As a matter of fact I tried twice with wet matches and then gave it up – Fortunately it was not very important. ....I hope when my bullet comes if it does not do the trick will not make me a cripple. That is the only thing that makes one care. We have been through it so much now everybody is quite callous and indifferent. The men are splendid.

At 3.30 p.m. on the 28th, Sir Douglas Haig, commanding I Corps, was informed by Sir John French that an intercepted German wireless transmission indicated that the German XXVII Reserve Corps was to attack in the direction of Kruiseecke-Gheluvelt at 5.30 a.m., the following morning. Brigades were warned in confidence and rifles were cleaned to remove dust and grit so that they were fit for rapid fire. Despite this news Haig was determined to continue with the 2nd Division's attack with the 1st Division in support, whilst the hard-pressed 7th Division held on. The Battle of Gheluvelt would officially last from October 29th-31st 1914.

At 8 a.m. October 29th, the 2nd Division received a report that enemy troops were massing near a cross-roads south-east of Gheluvelt opposite the point of junction of the 1st and 7th Divisions. Under cover of the early morning mist, the Germans at army corps strength broke through at this point and rolled up the flanks of the Divisions. Divisional reserves were able to close the gap although the enemy had been able to occupy the advanced trenches in front of the cross-roads. Meanwhile further reports indicated that there was a German build-up of troops in the château grounds west of Poezelhoek. The position in the vicinity of the Menin road was becoming uncomfortable for the British.

The 52nd had started the misty morning of the 29th in their positions to the north-east of Polygon Wood. During the afternoon they were withdrawn to form

138 Written on October 29th 1914.

a reserve under Brigadier-General the Earl of Cavan[139], with the 4th Brigade [Guards], the 2nd Worcestershire and the 1st King's [Liverpool] from the 6th Brigade. Casualties were light during the day with only one man wounded. The night was spent in the north-west corner of Polygon Wood. Geoffrey Titherington noted: 'The country is almost identical with Wolmer [sic] Forest[140] – sand and pines'.

The morning of October 30th was a quiet one for the officers and men of the 52nd, but in the early afternoon they were included with the Irish Guards and 2nd Grenadier Guards in a force under Lord Cavan, 'Fatty', to come to the assistance of the 7th Division south of the Ypres to Menin road. The 7th Division on the night of the 29th was holding only a fraction of its previous line, about 3,000 yards from just east of Zandvoorde to a point on the Gheluvelt to Tenbrielen road, south of the 8th kilometre stone. On the 30th the Germans attacked again and Cavan's force was needed to stop a breakthrough. The 52nd set off at 2.30 p.m. from their reserve position, at the north-west corner of Polygon Wood, to cover the four miles to just west of Zwarteleen. Arriving in the dark, they set about digging trenches to cover the Ypres road and the railway from the south-east, as a possible back position. Meanwhile the Irish and Grenadier Guards had dug trenches to the east of Klein Zillebeke to fill a gap in the line.

Once the trenches near Zwarteleen were dug, Henry Davies took the 52nd to a small wood near the railway and their Regimental Headquarters shared a farm with that of the 10th Hussars. Davies had just put his head down for a well-earned sleep when he was ordered at 10 p.m. to take two companies to fill a further gap in the line between the Irish Guards and the 7th Division. A Company under Harry Dillon and B Company under Cuthbert Baines were the unfortunate ones to be selected. Davies and the Adjutant, Richard Crosse, accompanied them in person for the march in the moonlight. They woke up sleepy officers of the Irish Guards and the 2nd Gordon Highlanders [7th Division] who had no idea of the position they were supposed to take up and in the end Davies put Dillon and his company into trenches at Groenenberg Farm [east of Klein Zillebeke], where they found some sappers who were expecting to be relieved. Baines and his company were placed in a small wood to the farm's north-west, where in places new trenches had to be dug. Wearily Davies and Crosse retraced their steps to rejoin the other two companies in their original farm, and had time for one hour of sleep starting at 4.30 a.m. on the 31st. Luckily the 52nd had no casualties on October 30th. The 31st was to be one of the critical days of the war.

---

139 Frederick Rudolf Lambart, 10th Earl of Cavan. Later in the war he was Commander-in-Chief in Italy.

140 Woolmer Forest lies on the border of Hampshire and Sussex.

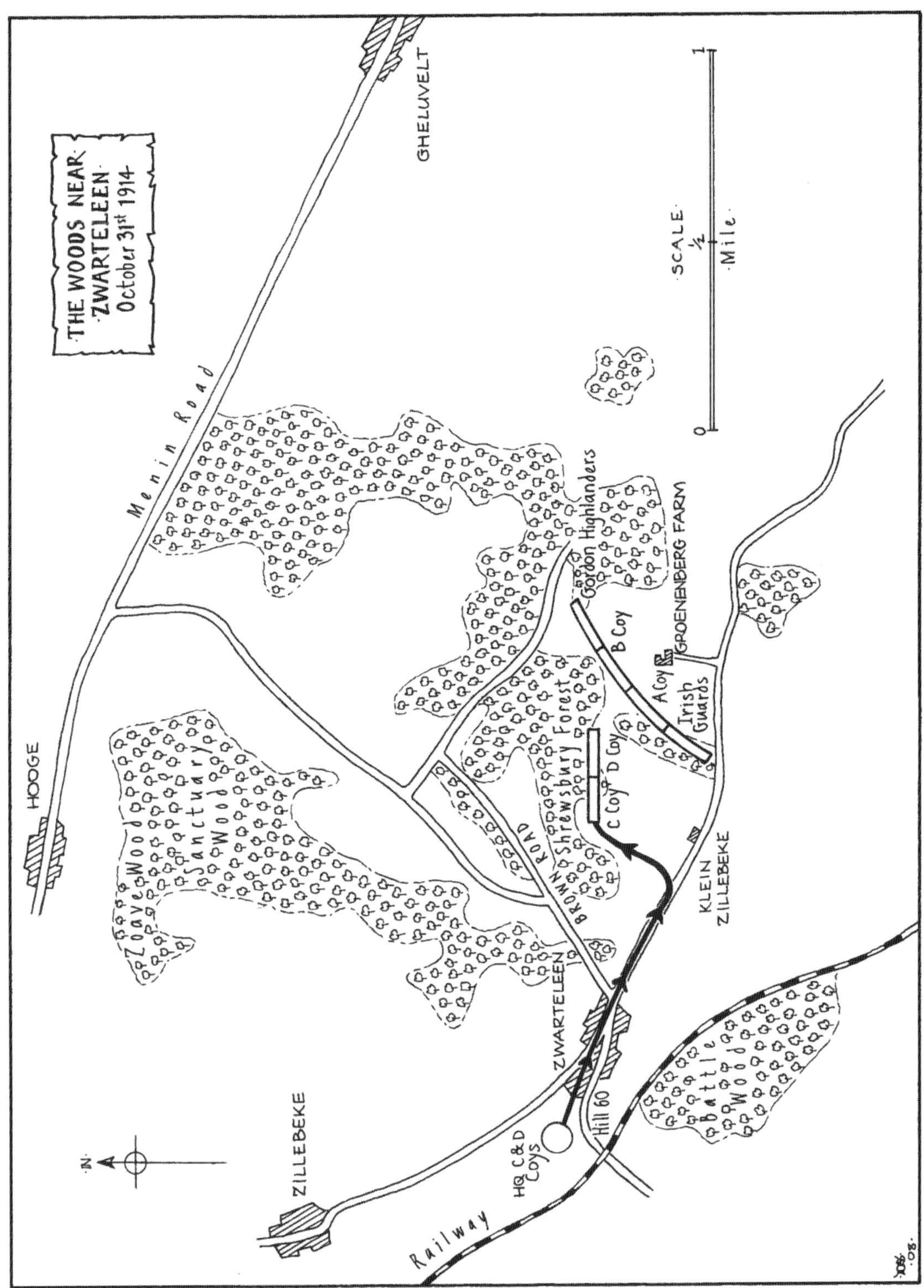
THE WOODS NEAR
ZWARTELEEN
October 31st 1914
GHELUVELT
Menin Road
HOOGE
Zouave Wood
Sanctuary Wood
SCALE
0
½
1
Mile
Gordon Highlanders
GROENENBERG FARM
B Coy
A Coy
Irish Guards
D Coy
C Coy
Shrewsbury Forest
BROWN ROAD
KLEIN ZILLEBEKE
ZWARTELEEN
Hill 60
Battle Wood
HQ C&D Coys
ZILLEBEKE
N
Railway

When the morning of October 31st broke, it was clear that the enemy was collecting along the I Corps front with a view to an imminent attack on the British line and hoping to break through to Ypres itself. The Germans had brought up the fresh troops of Army Group Fabeck[141]. North of the Ypres to Menin road they outnumbered the British three to two and south of it three to one. The 6th Brigade, on the 2nd Division's front, would not be attacked in force that day, which was just as well as they were ordered to stand where they were whatever the cost. At 12.45 p.m., Major-General Charles Monro, commanding the 2nd Division, was rendered unconscious by two high-explosive shells landing on his Headquarters at Hooge Château which he was sharing with the 1st Division. Although Monro rapidly recovered, other members of his staff and also some of those of the 1st Division were killed and wounded, making command and control more difficult. Monro retired to an isolated farm two miles closer to the front where, after a prolonged discussion with an elderly, crusty, French General, he lay down to sleep in the straw on the floor. Later that night, he awoke to a loud cry. Thinking the alarm had been sounded he jumped up, only to discover it came from one of his staff who had been awoken by a goat coming into the room and sitting down on his face! The period between 2 and 3 p.m. was critical with the 1st Division retiring and thus exposing the flank of the 7th Division to the south. Meanwhile the Germans managed to capture Gheluvelt, the key village on the Menin road. Fortunately, the 2nd Worcestershire retook it with the bayonet in a famous action that was for them the equivalent of the 52nd's actions at Nonne Bosschen and Waterloo.

At the height of the action on the 31st, Sir Douglas Haig, commanding I Corps, in full immaculate uniform, rode down the Menin road with a small escort of lancers. Near the small hamlet of Veldhoek, he dismounted and personally rallied the shattered men who were streaming back towards Ypres. Haig's calm and courageous demeanour amongst the hail of shells did much to restore the spirits of his men. Richard Crosse has made an interesting comment on this episode. Perhaps he was thinking of Field-Marshal Bernard Montgomery's unusual adornment of his beret in the Second World War.

> It is refreshing and inspiring now, to read this story of the days before commanders in more recent campaigns adopted varieties of dress which would have engaged the attention of the Military Police forty years ago. The effect on discipline is not far to seek. Sir John Moore "was enabled to establish a characteristic order and regularity

[141] Commanded by General Max von Fabeck.

of conduct *because the troops found in their leader a striking example of the discipline which he enforced in others."*

What of the role of the 52nd on this critical day? The weather was kind and this last day of October was fine and warm. At about 10 a.m., the early morning mist cleared from the woods near Zwarteleen and allowed the Germans to use barrage balloons for the first time in the war to direct their heavy artillery. Later in the morning Henry Davies received a report that the Germans had broken into Battle Wood to the south-west of Klein Zillebeke, and the 52nd were ordered to dig trenches facing the wood with their left on a small mound. The French were busy entrenching on the mound which subsequently became known the following spring as the infamous Hill 60. The report that the Germans were in Battle Wood was incorrect and before the 52nd had even started digging they were urgently summoned away. Davies was ordered to take his two remaining companies, C Company under Lieutenant Arthur Tylden-Pattenson and D Company under Lieutenant George Tolson, to a threatened point north of Groenenberg Farm.

Henry Davies took his two companies by the minor road from a point just south-east of Zwarteleen and followed it for half a mile to a farmhouse in a small gap between the woods. Here they turned eastward back into the large wood which was subsequently known as Shrewsbury Forest. Davies has left a record in his own words of the movements and fighting of the 52nd that afternoon.

> I could not find anyone to tell me the situation, but soon saw Gordon Highlanders[142] retiring to the north-east of Groenenberg Farm, as other troops on their left had already retired. The result of this was to make the position of "A" and "B" Companies insecure, since the Germans following up the Gordon Highlanders were looking into the left rear of the two companies. Soon afterwards therefore they began to withdraw. I now put "C" and "D" Companies into position where we were, to stop any further advance of the Germans south of the big wood; and as soon as "A" and "B" Companies came back, I lined them up along a ride facing eastward. I also sent two platoons of "C" and some Regimental Scouts to the north, to prevent any of the enemy getting round our left flank, as that was the direction in which the main German advance was said to have taken place.

[142] 2nd Gordon Highlanders of the 7th Division.

Some of the Irish Guards had retired with our "A" and "B" Companies, but the position which we took up now enabled all their right companies to remain where they were. After a little time I received information from the party which I had sent northward that the Northamptonshire[143] and Royal Sussex[144] were advancing on our left. So I told "A" and "B" Companies to get in touch with them, advance eastward through the wood, and clear it of Germans. This movement, I think, took the enemy by surprise for, at the beginning of the advance, we could see some of them, only a short distance ahead, crossing from our right to left, evidently quite unaware of what was impending. Others were running about in a confused manner, and though a few of them stood and fought, we had the best of them, killing a considerable number – some with the bayonet – and clearing the wood to the edge. "C" Company also followed through the wood in this advance, while "D" was kept back to look after the right flank, where they had a pretty good field of fire.

In the evening I got most of the Regiment collected at the south edge of the wood, and after much consultation with the Irish Guards and Gordon Highlanders, it was decided to take up our old line of trenches of last night.

Our casualties today were nine men killed and 36 wounded, two of whom were captured. No officer was hit, for we had not many left. "A" and "B" Companies were shelled considerably in the morning, before the German infantry attack, but they had dug in so well that they suffered little. On the whole it was a good day for us.

The counter-attack through Shrewsbury Forest had been at the behest of Brigadier-General Edward Bulfin[145] who was in temporary command of the 1st Division. In every direction German spiked helmets could be seen advancing and the British position seemed desperate. The 2nd Gordon Highlanders, who were three quarters of a mile in the rear, were sent back. Bulfin informed the 1st Northamptonshire and the 2nd Royal Sussex that reinforcements were arriving and ordered them, when they heard cheering behind them, to give the Germans the "mad minute". This meant one minute of rapid rifle fire and then to clear the enemy out of the wood at the point of the bayonet. To the surprised Germans the

143 1st Northamptonshire of the 1st Division.

144 2nd Royal Sussex of the 1st Division.

145 Bulfin later commanded the 28th and 60th Divisions and finally XXI Corps. His performance in 1914 was greatly admired by Haig.

rapid rifle fire sounded as if they were faced by a large number of machine-guns and the trees hid the weakness of the attackers. As the Gordons, Northamptonshire, and Royal Sussex came up to them, so A and B Companies of the 52nd joined in with a relish. C Company also followed up but D was kept back to cover the right flank, where they had an excellent field of fire. A few Germans resisted and were easily despatched, but the majority fled leaving their dead in heaps behind them. In the excitement Bulfin feared that his men would never stop. However, after just under half a mile they did so. Not only did the counter-attack recover ground locally but, further to the north, pressure on the 7th Division was eased.

During the evening Henry Davies collected his men at the south edge of Shrewsbury Forest and, after consultation with the Irish Guards and the Gordon Highlanders, it was decided to take up their old line of trenches from the night before[146]. At this juncture Davies was sent for by Brigadier-General Edward Bulfin who wanted a further attack on part of the woods still in German hands. The commanding officers of the other nearby battalions thought that their men were too exhausted for this undertaking. Davies was in full agreement and the plan was aborted. It was arranged for the 52nd to fill the gap between the left of the Irish Guards and the right of the Northamptonshire. The Gordon Highlanders, who were reduced to one officer and 100 men, were placed in reserve. However, this was not quite possible to carry out as the Germans were still occupying part of the Gordon Highlanders' trenches. Davies was suspicious about the presence of the enemy in these trenches and undertook a reconnaissance in person accompanied by his soldier-servant Flowers and Second-Lieutenant Francis Pepys. Approaching cautiously, they were challenged in German and had to run for it with rifle bullets whizzing after them. Fortunately they escaped unhurt.

In the end C Company held the south and east edges of the little wood, and D Company the south-east corner and part of the eastern edge of Shrewsbury Forest. A Company was a little behind D, and B was in reserve near the Regimental Headquarters some 700 yards further west. Initially Davies put some men into Groenenberg Farm, but soon withdrew them as they were under observation of the Germans from the left rear. October 31st had been an exhausting and eventful day for the 52nd. It would not get easier the following day.

Although the Battles Nomenclature Committee decreed that the Battle of Gheluvelt ended on October 31st, fierce fighting in the woods south of the Ypres to Menin road continued into November. On the first day of November, the Germans, in the form of the XV Corps, attacked the Earl of Cavan's force and

[146] The position of A and B Companies the previous night.

gradually extended the action to the north and the 7th Division. In the early afternoon the enemy made a very determined onslaught on the 2nd Irish Guards, the 1st Northamptonshire and the 52nd. It was met with great resolution.

Early on November 1st, Sir Douglas Haig, commanding I Corps, informed the Earl of Cavan that the Kaiser in person was expected to conduct operations against the British Army that day. The morning was misty, but once this cleared, Henry Davies recorded that the 52nd were heavily shelled. At about 1 p.m., Davies was visiting D Company on the eastern edge of Shrewsbury Forest when the enemy's shelling became even more intense and accurate. The bombardment concentrated on the left of the Irish Guards, gradually blowing in their trenches bit by bit with high explosive shells, and silencing their machine-guns. This necessitated part of the Irish Guards, on the 52nd's right, retiring under a hail of shrapnel balls which left them with a large number of casualties. Realising that this exposed C Company in the nearby small wood, Davies immediately withdrew them into the southern edge of the big wood, Shrewsbury Forest, where they lined up along with A Company. Their left joined on to the right of D Company at the south-eastern corner of the wood and all three companies were ordered to stand fast.

Soon afterwards Lieutenant George Tolson, commanding D Company, reported to Davies that the 1st Northamptonshire on his company's left were withdrawing further into the wood with the Germans in hot pursuit of them. Henry Davies quickly appreciated that, with both flanks unprotected, he was open to attack from the rear and ordered Tolson and his company to withdraw into the wood by a more northerly track. At the same time Davies, with A and C Companies, withdrew down a track along the southern edge of Shrewsbury Forest.

Over eight years later, in 1923, after publication of Edmonds' *Official History*, Henry Davies was in correspondence with three members of D Company on the events of November 1st 1914. Edmonds wrote 'But now, about 1.30 p.m., the flank company of the Northamptonshire was also forced back by heavy shelling and, exposed on both flanks, the Oxfordshire were ordered back to the line of their reserve company, where the whole line rallied'. The three were George Tolson who commanded D Company that day, Lieutenant Vere Spencer, and George Field. As might be expected the three accounts differ somewhat. Tolson was particularly upset by the withdrawal of the 1st Northamptonshire without their informing him of their intention. The first he knew about the withdrawal was being told by a Royal Engineers' Officer, some of whose men were in the line to the left of D Company, that the Northamptonshire had gone back. Tolson had every right to be upset as his left flank had been left in the air

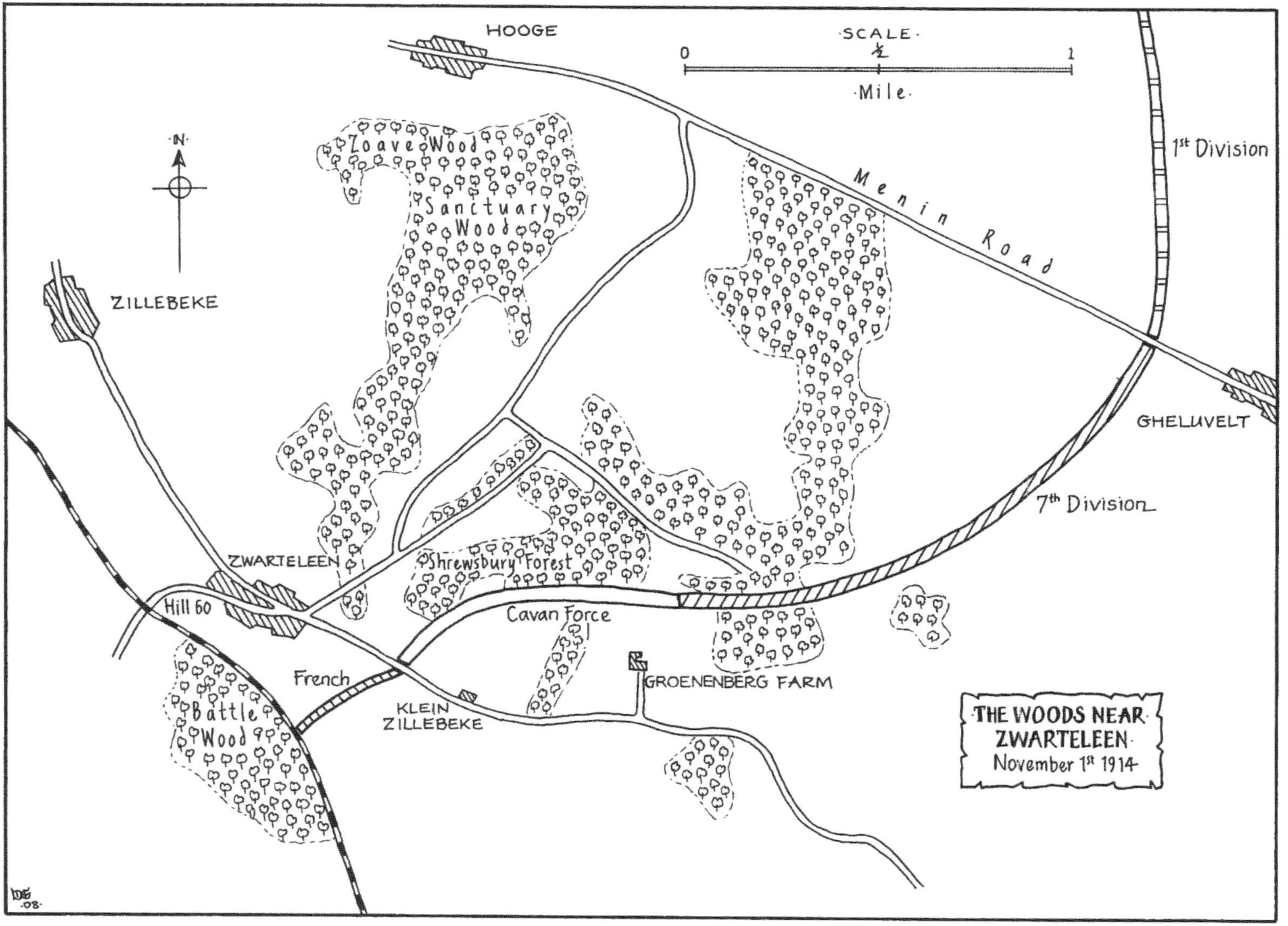
THE WOODS NEAR ZWARTELEEN
November 1st 1914
SCALE ½ Mile
0
1
HOOGE
1st Division
Menin Road
GHELUVELT
7th Division
Zoave Wood
Sanctuary Wood
ZILLEBEKE
N
ZWARTELEEN
Shrewsbury Forest
Hill 60
Cavan Force
GROENENBERG FARM
French
KLEIN ZILLEBEKE
Battle Wood

for 45 minutes before he was ordered to withdraw by Davies. When Tolson met the commanding officer of the Northamptonshire further back in Shrewsbury Forest a brisk conversation took place.

> When I got back a bit to the coy. the first person I saw was the C.O. of the Northamptons, he asked me why I had come back, and I being rather hot and bothered at the moment I said "Because the Irish Guards have gone on our right and your adjective regiment on our left and without letting us know." He said he knew his regt. had gone but he was collecting them and about to send them forward – he seemed interested, not to say pleased, that the Guards had gone too!

Having reached a track running north-east along the north-west of the wood [Brown Road], Davies with the two companies of the 52nd, found the 2nd Grenadier Guards from reserve with orders to advance to the east. The Grenadier Guards had been ordered to clear the wood of the enemy, at the point of the bayonet, by the Earl of Cavan, now commanding the whole sector in the absence of Brigadier-General Edward Bulfin, who had been wounded a little earlier that day. Cavan was calmness personified, carefully selecting a cigar from his cigar-case, seeing that it was evenly lighted, before issuing his orders. During the advance the Grenadier Guards came under fire from the south and wheeled in that direction to deal with it. This put an end to their advance and their second line went no further either. In actual fact on November 1st, although British troops in this sector had been pushed back the line was not completely broken.

To the north of the Grenadier Guards, Tolson's D Company ran into the 2nd Gordon Highlanders and the 1st Northamptonshire who were moving towards the trenches that had been vacated earlier in the day. D Company joined them and their position was a little to the north and behind the Grenadier Guards' second line. The 52nd received orders to dig trenches cutting off the exposed south-eastern corner of Shrewsbury Forest. This protected them to a degree from shellfire as they could not be directly seen in their new position by the German artillery observers.

At the end of the day D Company moved a little to the right to link up with the left of the Grenadier Guards' first line where they entrenched facing east. One company of the Guards' second line replaced the Gordon Highlanders and linked up with the right of the Northamptonshire. A platoon of B Company moved up to fill a gap between the Irish Guards and the Grenadier Guards. The remainder of B Company plus A and C Companies dug in on a road in reserve.

That night the Germans tried to set the wood on fire without a great deal of success although there were a few isolated fires. The Germans were very close and it was not an easy position to hold. Trenches were improved although the fields of fire were limited to fifteen to twenty yards by the trees. This was against all normal infantry principles but the troops had had no choice of terrain.

Although some ground had been lost at the south-east corner of Shrewsbury Forest, the Earl of Cavan's force was in a better position than on the night before. The 52nd suffered 64 casualties during the day with 17 killed, 48 wounded and 9 missing. Fortunately no officers were amongst the casualties as their number was already much depleted, but a number of valuable N.C.O.s including Serjeant James Jeffery had fallen. Richard Crosse held the view that in two ways the 52nd were largely responsible for stabilising the line and allowing the 2nd Grenadier Guards to go forward again. Firstly, they had speedily formed a defensive flank in response to the Irish Guards being shelled out of their trenches and secondly, the local retirement was halted on B Company in Shrewsbury Forest.

The regimental medical officer, Captain Lionel Thurston, aged 33 years, who had been with the 52nd from the beginning of the war and had served them so devotedly in the horrors of the caves under La Cour de Soupir left the Regiment to join a field ambulance. One of his last sick parades was unlikely to be forgotten by some members of the regiment. 'On October 30th half the battalion attended sick parade. With the exception of castor oil my meagre store of drugs was soon exhausted in treating the first 20 or 30; thereafter castor oil was administered upon which the remainder of the sick parade rapidly dissolved, and all took a hero's place in the battle'. In Thurston's view the whole battalion was unfit by peace-time standards. In 1918, as an acting Lieutenant-Colonel with the D.S.O. he would command 53 Casualty Clearing Station. Thurston was replaced by Lieutenant T.L. Hardy R.A.M.C. Nearby, at Zonnebeke, during the period October 29th-November 8th Lieutenant Arthur Martin-Leake R.A.M.C. won a bar to his Victoria Cross for conspicuous gallantry in repeatedly rescuing wounded men whilst under fire.

Without doubt the two days October 31st-November 1st 1914 were of supreme importance in the First Battle of Ypres and indeed to the war as a whole. The brunt of the Germans' attack had fallen on Haig's I Corps of which the 52nd were a part. The men had had no rest by day or night and were exhausted. However, by their courage and fortitude they had fought a far larger German force to a standstill and saved the British Expeditionary Force from the indignity of being thrown back on to the Channel ports and defeat. November 1st was the day that the Secretary of State for War, Earl Kitchener, met the French President,

Raymond Poincaré, and General Joseph Joffre[147] at Dunkirk. Kitchener told the French that he would not send untrained recruits into action as it would be little short of murder. Trained British troops would be ready by the late spring of 1915 and that the army would be at full capacity by mid-1917.

Field-Marshal Sir John French has left us his views on these crucial two days.

> October 31st and November 1st will remain for ever memorable in the history of our country; for during those two days no more than one thin and straggling line of tired-out British soldiers stood between the Empire and its practical ruin as an independent first-class power. I still look back in wonder on that thin line of defence, stretched, out of sheer necessity, far beyond its natural and normal power for defence. Right, centre, and left, our men were tried and pressed as troops were never tried and pressed before.

Fortunately for the 52nd, November 2nd was somewhat quieter for the sorely tried troops. During the day the Germans made a number of attacks on D Company and the 2nd Grenadier Guards at 8.45 a.m., 11 a.m., 2 p.m. and 5.45 p.m. Henry Davies looked upon the attacks as half-hearted, although the Guards considered them vigorous. D Company was surrounded by fir trees and Germans kept crossing their front and several were shot. At 5.45 p.m., just as it was getting dark, was the most serious attack with the enemy advancing with the beating of drums and the blowing of horns. That night the 52nd sent two companies, A and B, to relieve a Grenadier Guards company between their D Company and the Northamptonshire, so that they had three companies in the front line and one in reserve. This arrangement continued for several days allowing a rotation of men with each company getting a night in reserve every fourth night. The Grenadier Guards and the 52nd had become a little intermingled. During the day the trenches were improved and a few strands of barbed wire fixed between trees as a simple obstacle. Shelling was light and the 52nd only had one man wounded during the day.

At about this time, Second-Lieutenant Geoffrey Titherington recorded a description of wood fighting[148].

---

[147] Commander-in-Chief of the French army.

[148] Letter to his father written on November 5th 1914. He ended the letter with a PS: 'This paper was "made in Germany".' Presumably it had been removed from a prisoner or a corpse.

The country is almost identical with Wolmer [sic] forest – sand and pines. I am forcibly reminded again and again of home. You can imagine how absolutely desperate fighting in such country is. But we are doing well. You know the slope which runs up from the top of Wagner's Walk towards Kingswood firs? Imagine a line of deep trenches dug across that facing up hill. The trees are all knocked about and broken by shell fire. The ground is 'clayey' and very wet – the trench all mud. About 80 yards towards the top of the hill you glimpse patches of fresh earth – the German trench. Between us the ground is absolutely grey with their dead of the 126th regt.[149] – there are patches of foxy brown – their cow-skin 'packs' with the hair left on the leather. In our trench men in a state of filth which you at home can't imagine. – colour of clothes indistinguishable, hair long and beards unkempt faces and hands foul. Outside in the fields it is warm and the sun is out but here it is damp and cold – every coat etc is wet from a soaking night and apparently will stay wet for some time yet. Shells go over all the time but up to date have troubled us little. I think their own men are too close to allow them to go for us but every now and then a low one hits the trees and bursts all over the wood. But in spite of all the men are very cheerful and confident and full of contempt for the Deutcher. They are well supplied with food and tobacco but all want a wash and a hot meal. However we all know we've got a job before us to do first. We were just relieving the Grenadiers when they made their attack 2 days ago. It was just dark with a little moon. They made 2 rushes and only one man got into the trench but 10 yards and less outside they are strewn thick in every sort of attitude. We sneak out and collect wounded at night and have brought in a lot of unfortunate devils that way of course one can't go far or in large parties because they open fire if they see or hear us. The men who are sent out always bring in a pack or two and everyone has a bed of G.[150] overcoats (we've no straw here). The regiment is evidently fairly fresh up for their packs are full of new things – tremendously appreciated by our grubby fellows needless to say. They have all treated themselves to new underclothes and very badly some of them wanted them. I don't know what we can do about burying the people – at present its [sic] impossible owing to fire. In the actual rush our own losses were nil,

[149] 126th Regiment of the German 39th Division.

[150] German.

> tho we had a man or two hit in the preliminary firing – we've wiped out that regiment – I suppose they failed to realize our numbers and exact position for the trench bends about and a lot of them were infiladed [sic]. Personally I am fit tho' sleepy and filthy. I have got a touch of rheumatism in my back and knees in fact few of us are free from it. Another great trouble is that one's hands are full of little scratches and these get filled with mud and go rather nasty but I am keeping mine fairly well with carbolated vaseline. I don't think there is anything I very much want besides what I have already asked you for. The torch has taken a new lease of life since I put in the new refill this morning. It's worth its weight in gold. I want a new little one as a reserve in case this one breaks. Officer's pattern puttees are what I want most now but I believe I have asked you for those. Keep the boots in oil for me I'll write for them soon if I'm spared and also some new breeches but I'll write my tailor direct for those. The raisins were much appreciated.

Later in this letter to his father, Titherington described an odd nocturnal adventure with a goat. A rude awakening in the middle of the night, an experience not dissimilar to that of his divisional commander, Major-General Charles Monro, described earlier.

> Give little Hester my love – say that this is a wonderful country for goats. There are lots of pretty little ones set free by our men from deserted houses. A sweet little grey kid fell into my trench the other night when I was asleep and gave me an awful start. Then when I looked up having settled the goat I saw a man standing on the edge of the trench peering down with a bayonet held out ready. In my confused state I really thought that he was a Deutcher and was just going to shoot him with my pistol when he spoke – it was a sentry come to see what the noise was all about.

There was intermittent shelling on November 3rd and the snipers on both sides were active. Trenches were improved and deepened and the troops of the Earl of Cavan's force were told that they must rely on their own reserve companies for support. There was a cavalry brigade in reserve but Cavan did not want to use it unless it was absolutely essential. I Corps warned the troops of the enemy's deceptive tricks.

> First Cavalry Division reports that in the attacks on them the Germans wore British uniforms, especially kilts, and when approaching our trenches shouted, "Don't fire; we are short of ammunition," and similar expressions. All troops in the trenches are to be warned of this practice by the enemy.

The trenches of the 52nd in the wood, with the exception of those on the left where one man was wounded, escaped damage. During the day, in front of A Company, a party of Germans started digging a trench about 30 yards away. Second-Lieutenants Francis Pepys and Hugh Pendavis, plus Privates G. 'Skinner' Hall and H. Merry, stood on the edge of the trench and shot at the enemy group. They plus some other members of A Company rushed the Germans, driving them back and killing about 30 of them as they retired. In fact the Germans were very frightened and hardly returned fire. Later, Pepys and Pendavis would be awarded the Distinguished Service Order [D.S.O.] and Hall and Merry the Distinguished Conduct Medal [D.C.M.] for their bravery. A contemporary illustration of the action, based on an oil painting by Alan Stewart, shows Merry leading the men, but makes no mention of Hall or the two officers in the caption!

Harry Dillon in a further letter to his family gave more details of the 52nd's recent fighting and in particular the bravery of Francis Pepys[151].

> The fighting here has been absolutely desperate up to yesterday when it slackened a bit. We have been fighting alongside the Grenadiers who are a splendid lot, and I am glad as they always seem very pleased to see us come along. Date I can't remember as we have not had our clothes off or washed or a regular sleep since the 21st. Just fighting like hell, then lie down and sleep to wake up and fight again or find rations have been issued, or to hurry off somewhere. I said I had been sent out to reconnoitre a line of attack and nearly walked into a German trench. After we were sent off to act with the Guards and help hold the line previously held by -------- [Northamptonshire] who have been almost annihilated; we came in on the Guards left with these people I will call X on our left again. I did not get my men in till 3.30 and very soon saw why we were losing so heavily, the reason being that their trenches were not deep enough. We worked like anything and were four feet deep by daylight. My Coy.

[151] The letter was written on November 4th 1914.

was 136 strong (full strength 240). As soon as it was light the Germans opened with all guns, lots of men were buried in their trenches but were got out and into others, and remarkably little damage was done; but about 3 p.m. to my horror I saw X retiring. This was the absolute devil as it meant I had to get out and report. They told me to retire and try to stop the Germans getting past a certain road. From this on it was awful; as soon as we left the trenches they opened up with every gun and rifle, we got back luckily neither of my officers were hit and I got the new position and collected about 150 men. Things looked real nasty as the Germans by this time were pouring through the gap and filling the wood we were in. Under the circumstances I thought to do something unexpected might upset their apple-cart, so fixed bayonets and went straight in; we soon came across them and had the finest fight that ever was fought. I make no pretence at liking the ordinary battle, and anybody who says they do is a liar; but this was quite different. We first came on some fifty of the grey swine, went straight in and annihilated them. We were very quickly into the next lot and in a few minutes we were shooting, bayoneting and annihilating everything that we came across. I got a sharp sting on my leg and shoved my hand there and found a bullet which I think I threw at a German and myself after it. To cut a long story short, we drove the whole crowd back and by 2 a.m. we were back in our trenches again. Five holes in my coat as a souvenir, but only 23 of my company left. This fight has done me more good than I can say. Another 40 came in later on. We went on occupying this position which was vitally important, for it might be about three days. I know the next thing I can remember was coming on here – when I again had a narrow shave, a bullet cut clean through Ashley Ponsonby's equipment which I have now got, and just grazed my arm inside. In fact it was between my arm and body and cut the clothes both sides. Yesterday the German trenches were 25 yds in front of us, i.e. about the length of a tennis court, with a fairly thick wood in between. Pepys was the hero of the day. It was very uncomfortable having them so close with our men reduced one could not see how to rush them out without losing a lot. Pepys now had a brain wave; by looking carefully at the ground he found a bit of a hump which he got behind with Pendavis, the other subaltern, and the two soldiers, and placed himself so skilfully that he saw down the whole length of a trench.

He got four rifles loaded and then let drive with the result that he stampeded the lot and killed forty ---- We still could not make out if there were any left, so I took 25 meaning to reconnoitre about 150 in and if the ground was not occupied put up some wire entanglements; sure enough there was nothing in the trench but the 40 dead Germans. Another twenty yards more trenches and more dead – in fact in this 150 yards there may have been four to five hundred dead. I told Pendavis to remain out with this covering party and Pepys to start putting up the wire, and I went to search the dead to see what they belonged to, and get any wire cutters off them which we were short of. I was just in the middle of this pleasing job when on looking into a trench I found it full of alive Germans who at once opened fire. How they missed me I can't imagine as I was absolutely on the point of stepping across the trench. The thing gave me such a shock that unfortunately most of them got away, in fact we only bagged two out of about eight. It was a pity we let them get away, but the staff are awfully pleased at us having cleared them out at all. It was awfully good work on Pepys's part, and I hope he will get a mention, not that that appeals to him much, but I am sure he deserves it. This was yesterday, and today I am back in reserve at the bottom of a trench being shelled. This is the normal state of affairs which I frankly admit I simply hate. Well, I think these Germans can't hold out much longer; I can't say why, but that is my opinion I mean here. Their losses are enormous, and their men give me the impression that they try to get wounded or taken prisoner, the only means of getting away from the incessant nerve racket. Our men are fortunately a tougher more fighting lot, and in spite of fearful casualties we have had, are always ready. In fact, with hardly an exception, they are splendid. I should like a wash, bed and dinner, still now we are at it, let's make a good job of it and be finished with Germany for good and all, and we shall.

The enemy were not very enterprising on the 3rd with a certain amount of shelling but made no attack. During the day the 52nd suffered a grievous loss by shelling of its rearward services and transport which had been established at the Halte [Hellfire Corner]. The majority of the 52nd's casualties for the day occurred here. The Transport Officer, Lieutenant Rupert Brett, Regimental Quartermaster-

Serjeant A.J. Saker, Pioneer-Serjeant F.C. Sibley, Bugle-Major J.E.C. Martin[152], and the Orderly Room Clerk Serjeant A.J. Smith were wounded. Rupert Brett suffered gunshot wounds to his head and Sibley and Smith had legs amputated. The total number of casualties for the day was eleven with one killed and ten wounded.

Among the wounded that day at the Halte was the Adjutant's groom, Private A. Watson. Rupert Brett's general factotum, Private G. Holtom, escaped unharmed. George Holtom was a taciturn man with a stern sense of duty and no sense of humour. On the next occasion the Adjutant, Richard Crosse, wanted one of his horses, Holtom appeared with both of them. The second being a German troop horse captured on September 4th. When Holtom was asked what he was doing there, he gravely replied: "You've lost your groom and I've lost my officer, so I thought that I better take you over." So "George" remained with his horses until he left the 52nd in Germany in 1919. Crosse was well served by his servants during the war. Private J. Cobbold cleaned his buttons and kept him respectable from Aldershot to Lichfield in 1920, practically the whole of his colour service after recruits training.

On the night of November 3rd, the fourth reinforcement arrived under Second-Lieutenant Jack Ward, a young officer straight from the Royal Military College, Sandhurst. The 120 replacements were very welcome. Sadly the young officer, Ward, would meet an heroic death three days later.

An artillery duel between the two sides took place over the next two days as a result of a German aeroplane having identified the position of the British trenches. On November 4th, the 52nd were shelled from 11 a.m. until 5 p.m. with nine men being wounded. By sticking strictly to their trenches the 52nd kept their casualties to a minimum. At nightfall there was a welcome respite from the constant bombardment and the men settled down to a pitch-black, miserable, wet night in the trenches. The ground beneath their feet was marsh and wet clay. Private A.J. Tyrell would later [16-1-15] be awarded the D.C.M. for volunteering to carry messages through half a mile of heavy shellfire on no less than four occasions during the previous two days.

The next day, November 5th, it was thought that the Germans had given up the idea of breaking the British line. This was not the case at all as in reality they were awaiting reinforcements before hurling in their superior numbers, in a further effort to take Ypres. The 52nd had no casualties this day with only their Headquarters being shelled but not their trenches in the edge of Shrewsbury Forest.

---

[152] Died of his wounds as a company serjeant-major on April 30th 1916.

November 6th was to be another important day in the defence of the city of Ypres. Having dented the Allies' line near Messines, the Germans chose the junction of General De Moussy's French Division and the four battalions of the Earl of Cavan's force at Klein Zillebeke, for their point of attack. Any meeting place between two divisions was likely to be a weak spot let alone those of different nationality. At this juncture the German Chief of the General Staff, General Erich von Falkenhayn, thought that a little more perseverance would lead to a complete success and the taking of Ypres and a breakthrough to the Channel ports. He was to be proved wrong but only just.

Shelling of the British line began as soon as the morning mist had cleared at 11 a.m. and by 12 noon its effect on the 1st Irish Guards and 2nd Grenadier Guards, on the right of the 52nd, was reported to be serious. However, the front remained intact until, at 2.30 p.m., four German columns emerged from sap-heads driven forward under cover of the mist, close to the allied line. General De Moussy's French were forced back and the Germans poured into the resulting gap. The position of the 1st Irish Guards and most of the 2nd Grenadier Guards became untenable. The 52nd, to the left of the Grenadier Guards, were not directly threatened although their right flank was effectively in the air.

Henry Davies, has left an account of the day in his diary.

> Reports came in that some Germans were working through on our right flank, and tolerably close. As I had to keep most of my reserve company ("B") facing the front (to take the place of the right company of the Grenadiers, who had lost a good many men from shell-fire, and whose right had been exposed by the retirements on their right), I was only able to spare one platoon, and this I sent out on our right. The Grenadiers were also able to send out one platoon, which eventually joined up with some of the 2nd Life Guards (dismounted), who had been sent up from reserve and did some very good work. They succeeded in pushing back the Germans, who had got up to the farm at K.23.c.2.7. and the road to the south-west of it[153].
>
> About this time just before dark, two companies of the Sussex Regiment (2nd Brigade) also came up, and this reinforcement finally stopped the German advance. They had, however, gained a little ground on our right, as owing to the French retirement it was not possible to get back to the trenches which had been held by the Irish

[153] Near Zillebeke.

Guards. But we were able to establish quite a good line, the Grenadiers being a little behind their former position, our reserve company digging a new line on their right, and the Sussex joining up farther on the right so as to fill the gap between us and the 2nd Life Guards.

Our three companies on the left of the Grenadiers had been left undisturbed. Their trenches, being inside the wood, were not shelled, and the companies were some distance from the part of the line against which the German attack had come. During the night there was a certain amount of firing, and some of the enemy, creeping up to reconnoitre the Sussex trenches, were shot, but no further attack was made.

The allied line in the vicinity of Klein Zillebeke was stabilised by the Earl of Cavan summoning the Household Cavalry [2nd Life Guards] to come out of reserve in Sanctuary Wood and to drive the Germans back. Dismounting close to the action and led in person by their Colonel, Gordon Wilson, they fixed bayonets and tore into the enemy with all the precision of an infantry battalion. The Germans could not stand up to the Life Guards in hand-to-hand fighting and they were gradually driven back at the point of the bayonet. The 2nd Grenadier Guards, 2nd Sussex and the 52nd also played a supporting role in the stabilisation of the allied line. By the end of the day, most but not all of the trenches had been regained. The Earl of Cavan believed that the bravery and drive of the Life Guards had saved his force from annihilation and more importantly had saved Ypres. However, the night closed with the Germans in possession of Zwarteleen and close to St. Eloi, both less than two miles from Ypres. The enemy had driven a deep wedge between the French and British. It was an uncomfortable position to be in.

The 52nd's casualty list for the day was two killed and six wounded. Killed in action that day was Second-Lieutenant Jack Ward, fresh from Sandhurst, who had brought up reinforcements just three days before. Ward had been sent by his company commander, Cuthbert Baines, to find out what was happening as the Germans started to push around the 52nd's right flank. The youthful Ward, observing the enemy in front of him, collected a party composed mainly of Sussex men, a few Grenadier Guards, and two of his own men and charged the enemy with his revolver in his hand. At their head, Jack Ward was shot dead a few yards from a fence held by the Germans. Baines ran out alone and tried to bring the body in, but that was not possible until the darkness came down. Later, Baines overheard two Grenadiers discussing how well the young Ward had led

The pre 1914 La Cour de Soupir.
[Private Collection]

Guy Blewitt D.S.O. M.C.
Wounded at La Cour de Soupir
on September 19th 1914.
[Blewitt's Diaries]

Aubrey Barrington-Kennett. Mortally wounded at La Cour de Soupir on September 19th 1914.
[Blewitt's Diaries]

Shrapnel ball removed from Guy Blewitt's face. Depressions made by his facial bones are visible. Now a bangle in the possession of his daughter.
[Author's Collection 2010]

Paul Giradot. Killed in action near La Cour de Soupir on September 16th 1914. [Regimental Chronicles]

Officers and men of the 52nd close to the mouth of the cave in the quarry near La Cour de Soupir. [Regimental Chronicles]

Reginald Worthington. Killed in action near La Cour de Soupir on September 16th 1914. [Regimental Chronicles]

Rosslyn Evelegh. Killed in action near La Cour de Soupir on September 19th 1914. [Regimental Chronicles]

The mouth of the main cave in the quarry near La Cour de Soupir. [Author's Collection 2008]

Hugh Mockler-Ferryman. Killed in action near La Cour de Soupir on September 16th 1914. [Regimental Chronicles]

The damaged La Cour de Soupir seen in a photograph of 1915 after its capture by the Germans.
[Private Collection]

Men of the 52nd Light Infantry sheltering from shrapnel behind the Headquarters of the 20th Infantry Brigade 7th Division during the First Battle of Ypres.
[Imperial War Museum. Q57205]

Allan Harden. D Company commander, killed in action near the St. Julien-Poelcappelle road on October 21st 1914.
[Blewitt's Diaries]

Henry Hastings D.C.M. used this culvert to execute many Germans on October 22nd and 23rd 1914.
[Author's Collection 2008]

Christopher Murphy. Killed in action near Langemarck on October 21st 1914.
[Regimental Chronicles]

George Marshall was mortally wounded near Langemarck on October 21st 1914.
[Regimental Chronicles]

In 1917, Henry Davies arranged for this wooden cross to be raised over the site of the graves of the officers and men who were killed with the 52nd near Langemarck between October 21st and 23rd 1914.
[Regimental Archives]

Geoffrey 'Tithers' Titherington, Oxford rowing blue and copious letter writer. Wounded at Richebourg l'Avoué on May 16th 1915.
[Titherington Collection]

them. Although he was mentioned in Sir John French's dispatches, his bravery warranted more than that. One man whose courage during this period was recognised was Acting Serjeant E. Ashby. Over the first week in November he had constantly undertaken dangerous work, often in close proximity to the enemy, and a well deserved D.C.M. [16-1-15] was his reward.

For the next three days, November 7th-9th, the 52nd remained in their trenches without a direct attack being made on them. The shelling continued with parts of the trenches being blown in by the German howitzers. The nights were quiet apart from some sniping and the mornings were misty. Bad weather was welcomed by the men as it precluded any artillery observation of their positions. On the 7th one man was killed and another wounded and on the 8th one man was wounded.

Henry Davies' diary gave a flavour of the life of the 52nd during these bleak days on the edge of Shrewsbury Forest.

> We have now been about three weeks without changing our clothes or boots, and with our feet generally wet, but every one has kept very fit. Our work in these woods has been, I think, satisfactory, and we have not lost heavily; but we have been made uncomfortable by a good deal of rain.
>
> My usual day, on quiet days, has been to get up out of my hole in the ground at daylight, go round our trenches, and then come back to breakfast. On some days we have been lucky enough to have fog, and then shelling did not start until late, but ordinarily it began at about 10 a.m., when we retired into our holes which we had dug, taking with us some bread and jam, or something of the kind, to eat during the day. In the evening, when the shelling slackened, we could issue out again; and then I made another tour of the trenches. After dark the rations would come up, when we had a meal of whatever there happened to be, and washed it down with tea. Sometimes the meal was interrupted by an outburst of firing, when the bullets would crack unpleasantly through the wood, and we lay flat, or, perhaps, even crept into our holes until the uproar was over, and we could finish our meal. Our cooks were based in a farmhouse, so we were able to send out hot tea to the companies morning and evening.

Before these feeding arrangements were perfected, Richard Crosse has given a characteristically whimsical account of meeting a 'curious procession'.

> I went out and met a curious procession. At its head was the acting Regimental Quartermaster-serjeant, "Alf" Barnes, later Quartermaster, with bayonet fixed, prepared to use that on the enemy and the butt on anyone else who got in the way. Behind him came a string of soldiers carrying tea and even stew. They stumbled along through shell-holes and mud, relieving their feelings in that energetic language at which British soldiers were then – I hope they are still – such adepts. But they fed us and we were grateful.

Dawn was breaking on November 9th when the 52nd were relieved by the London Scottish. Leaving at 4 a.m., by a track they proceeded to Zillebeke, and then north to an area close to the Headquarters of the 2nd Division near Verlonenhoek. At about this time, Second-Lieutenant W. Wooding who had embarked as a serjeant with the 52nd in August, received a gunshot wound of his thigh on the very day of his promotion. The 52nd arrived at about 6 a.m. after a journey of three miles and settled into some old French trenches. The officers' mess and Regimental Headquarters were situated in a barn, called the White House, which also contained the Headquarters of the 2nd Division. During the next 48 hours the 52nd were in first divisional and then corps reserve, effectively at the beck and call of any general who was in difficulty. On the 10th the regiment received a visit from their Divisional commander Major-General Charles Monro and Sir Douglas Haig commanding I Corps. Monro told Henry Davies that the men looked fit and cheerful. The 52nd had time to clean up and rest, although it was too cold for much sleep.

Safely ensconced in the White House, Second-Lieutenant Geoffrey Titherington reflected on his recent experiences in an informative letter to his father. The topics covered were a narrow escape from a shell, difficulties with his laundry, the magnificent spirit of his men, the despair of the enemy and his own 'horrible dreams'. The letter ended with the inspiring words 'Tell M. [Mother] to write soon and not to think of me or the regt: but the cause in which we fight'. Just what his father, the Reverend A.F. Titherington, made of his son's latest war experiences while reading this letter in his quiet Hampshire rectory is difficult to imagine.

Just got yours of Nov 2 in an old barn where we are putting in a day's sleep!! Of course we're still in easy reach of the Deutcher guns and only this morning they went for a battery ½ mile behind us but they leave us in peace so really we are not under fire – 1st time for 18 days. Sleep in straw just heavenly after 19 nights running in trenches. I've had my hair cut a shave and a partial wash and feel better. They left us in some peace after my last letter except for some shells – I think we rather put the fear of God into the infantry opposite us for tho' they hung on 100 yards in front they didn't do much. I had the narrowest escape yet yesterday it was raining and I had just got up to stretch (there had been no shells for ½ hour) when a shrapnel hit the tree in front of me. It deafened me and a bit cut my face – it felt hot but that was all. I really thought the Kaiser had got me but as one soon discovers here a miss is as good as several miles.

It's got awfully cold: this is damp clay soil and winter here's going to be proper beastly I fear but I've got all the warm things I can possibly carry at present. If I lose any thing [sic] I'll write to you to replace and of course I'd like a fairly steady stream of clean under-clothes for needless to say laundrying [sic] is not poss[ible] When a parcel arrives people put on the new and bury the old (indeed its all they're good for usually). The fighting continues severe – you in England will be amazed when you hear the full loses but the Deutchers lose more in their massed attacks and losses seem to make no difference to our men they are truly magnificent in the way they cheerfully carry on in spite of everything. Here they are dirty, ragged and frequently lousy but simply full of an unconquerable spirit. If K's army[154] do ¼ as well they'll be splendid. Its going obviously to be a question of the side which has the last reserve pulling it off – it'll be us all right I know but one wishes our Army were a bit bigger and we cd. have more frequent reliefs. The letters we've looted off the G. dead were full of woe and despair and had the most deluded ideas of how things are going. They are marvellously equipped infantry but slow. I don't think the pattern of their kit better than ours but the material is, tho' it's rather heavy, and the cloth they wear is excellent. Their rifle is less likely to jam than ours but they can't use it. I don't know why they carry a

[154] Earl Kitchener's New Armies.

ayonet at all[155]. I enclose the snout of a shell. 3 bayonet knots (I don't know what the colours mean), 1st Jaeger's[156] strap and officer's of the 172nd regiment[157]. All off men who were in front of us. I had a lot of very interesting trophies but no means of carrying them. 9 Iron Crosses were collected! A lot of excellent watches were got by the men (but we don't descend quite to that). They are evidently a freshly arrived regiment.

Well I expect tomorrow or the next day we shall relieve some regiment that's had a bad time today and a new position is always interesting. If its in a wood you see little and its cold. If its in the open you may get your trench blown in yard by yard by their heavy guns so both have disadvantages. They tried a new 'stink' shell on us the other day – it bust quite close and turned everyone black but quite failed to asphyxiate anyone. I'm awful glad to have got some sleep anyway. I was beginning to have most horrible dreams everytime I dozed for a minute – result of strain I suppose, but it's all right now. There being so few officers it means a good deal of work for each. I daresay you'll have noticed I'm the only reinforcement offr. left to this rgt.

The 52nd Light Infantry were not to rest for long, as the very next day, Wednesday November 11th, would find them fighting in their most celebrated engagement of the whole of the First World War at Nonne Bosschen Wood.

---

155 The inference was that they were either not trained or frightened to use the bayonet.

156 German light infantry. 1st Jäger Battalion. The Jäger Division was not formed until about November 1917: prior to this date individual Jäger battalions were attached to divisions.

157 Part of the German 39th Division.

Chapter VI

Action in Nonne Bosschen Wood.

November 11th – December 22nd 1914

[Maps: pages 130, 148.]

On November 8th, I Corps Headquarters believed that in their area of operations the German offensive was breaking down. In this they were sadly mistaken as the Germans were collecting for a further onslaught on the hapless British and French forces in order to try, yet again, to take Ypres and then the Channel ports. The German General Staff came to the conclusion, after their lack of success in late October and early November, that the fresh troops of Army Group Fabeck[158] on and south of the Menin road were not going to succeed. In particular, the 52nd Light Infantry had played a significant part in containing the enemy with their actions in and around Shrewsbury Forest. But the enemy had a great superiority as regards men and equipment over the allies and, in the relatively quiet northern sector of I Corps, the Germans had been reorganising their troops; their very finest soldiers, the Prussian Guard, had been brought up to attempt what their colleagues had singularly failed to achieve.

The blow fell on the misty morning of November 11th, when the Germans attacked from Messines in the south to Zonnebeke further north, with no less than six and a half corps against the British and French line. To the south and centre the battle had gone reasonably well for the allies with Sir Douglas Haig, commanding I Corps, having to use few of his reserves on maintaining the line. However, to the north of the Menin road between Veldhoek and Polygon Wood, Brigadier-General Charles FitzClarence's 1st Guards Brigade of the 1st Division had been particularly heavily shelled. FitzClarence was an inspiring leader of men, with a colourful ancestry. He was the great-grandson of King William IV and his mistress, the actress Dorothy Jordan[159]. He had been awarded the Victoria Cross [V.C.] for acts of bravery around Mafeking in 1899 and gained the sobriquet of the "Demon" for his gallantry. The V.C. was eventually awarded to FitzClarence after he had been recommended for it no less than three times.

The German bombardment had started at 6.30 a.m. and slowly worked up to its greatest fury, becoming the most severe yet experienced in the war. Except for a few small farms, orchards and hedges, most of the 1,100 yards of ground that FitzClarence's 1st Brigade occupied was open and exposed to observation from the nearby Reutel ridge which was some 30 feet higher. Telephone cables to

---

[158] General Max von Fabeck.

[159] Her real name was Dorothea Bland, but she used the stage name Mrs Jordan.

the artillery batteries in the rear, at this stage of the war unburied, were repeatedly cut and a number of officers went back on foot to warn the batteries. Outnumbered, reduced to 800 men, living on rum and biscuits without a hot meal for days, the exhausted 1st Brigade gave way.

Nearby, during the German bombardment of November 11th, an incident occurred which was made famous in *Punch.* Count Albert 'Glick' Gleichen's Brigade-Major, Captain J.T. Weatherby, a 52nd officer, appeared in the Brigadier-General's bedroom at Beukenhorst Château [Stirling Castle] with nothing but a towel around his waist and his clothes draped over his arm. "May I finish my dressing here. They're shelling the bathroom."[160]

Just before 9 a.m. a German plane flew over the 1st Brigade, followed by thick lines of Germans coming out of the mist about 50 yards away at a jog. Their officers had drawn swords and the men with rifles at the port. The few defenders of the shallow front line trenches were cleared out at the point of a bayonet without a shot being fired. At this stage of the war the trenches allowed cover by kneeling and a few strands of barbed wire were put up between the trees. The continuous trench systems with their comprehensive barbed wire entanglements were a thing of the future. Although the line was overwhelmed, the men in the support trenches fought so well that the Germans lost their cohesion. The two regiments of the German 1st Guard Brigade[161], the 3rd Foot Guard Regiment to the north and 1st Foot Guard Regiment to the south, some six battalions in total, had been ordered to advance north-westwards into the gap between Polygon and the Veldhoek Woods. The dividing line between the regiments was at the south-western corner of the triangularly shaped Nonne Bosschen Wood [Nuns Wood].

The right flank of the 3rd Foot Guard Regiment was shot at by the 400 men of the 1st King's, of the 6th Brigade, from the southern edge of Polygon Wood. They turned towards their assailants and were decisively beaten off leaving piles of their dead in a turnip field. The 1st Foot Guard Regiment to the south of the 3rd swept over the front and support trenches and received heavy fire from left and right. The two leading companies turned right towards Nonne Bosschen Wood and others went to the left towards Veldhoek Château with only a weak section going straight on. The German second line troops were held up by the defenders of Verbeck Farm, the 1st Black Watch and 1st Cameron Highlanders, and the supporting battalions suffered heavy casualties on the old German front

---

[160] *Punch* December 23rd 1914. Count Albert Edward Gleichen commanded the 15th Brigade in the 5th Division.

[161] 1st Guard Division. In November 1914, the 1st Brigade was in the vicinity of Ypres. They were part of the Prussian Guards.

line from accurate allied artillery fire. The first report that the enemy were in Nonne Bosschen Wood was timed at 10.30 a.m. in a message from the Northamptonshire to the 1st Brigade[162]. Later in the afternoon, the Prussian Guard would meet their nemesis in the form of Sir John Moore's military descendants – the 52nd Light Infantry. It was to be an extremely unpleasant if not fatal afternoon for most of these German elite[163].

The news that the Germans had broken through the ground held by the 1st Brigade gradually trickled back to the various divisional and brigade headquarters in the vicinity. Lieutenant-Colonel Claude Westmacott, still temporarily commanding the 5th Brigade[164], from his headquarters at the north-western corner of Polygon Wood, was told by a member of the Black Watch that the enemy were in the trenches of his battalion. The 1st King's, holding the southern edge of Polygon Wood, recorded accurately in their *Battalion War Diary*, 'supported on the right by the Prussian Guard'. All that lay between them and the Germans was a ruined house. Westmacott immediately ordered the 2nd Connaught Rangers and the 5th Field Company Royal Engineers to form a defensive flank on the right rear of the 1st King's opposite Nonne Bosschen Wood and facing south and west.

Major-General Charles Monro, commanding the 2nd Division, on being informed by Westmacott of the situation, brought up further troops to stabilise the situation. Amongst them were the 52nd who, soon after 10 a.m., left Verlorenhoek for Westhoek to the north-west of Nonne Bosschen Wood. Their movement in a winding column of single file took some time as heavy artillery fire on them led to delays. However, they reached their destination miraculously without loss of life and were greeted enthusiastically by a bearded commander of an artillery brigade. He was Lieutenant-Colonel Stephen Lushington of the XLI Brigade, Royal Field Artillery [R.F.A.], part of the 2nd Division's artillery. 'Thank God you've come,' he said. Standing in front of the silent guns, armed with rifles, were a motley collection of gunners and cooks awaiting the advance of the German infantry across the open ground in front of Nonne Bosschen Wood, which they had taken unopposed. On reaching Westhoek, Lieutenant-Colonel

---

162 Brigadier-General E.M.Percival, C.R.A. [Commander Royal Artillery] 2nd Division, was said to have received a report that the enemy were in Nonne Bosschen Wood at 10 a.m. This is the earliest time recorded for a German presence in the wood.

163 Sir Douglas Haig believed that they had been especially brought up from Arras as other troops had failed to break the British line. The Guards Division throughout the war was considered to be one of the very best German shock divisions.

164 Claude Westmacott continued in command until November 20th when he was replaced by the returning Brigadier-General Richard Haking, who had recovered from the wounds that he had received on September 16th. On November 23rd Westmacott took command of the 2nd Brigade in the 1st Division.

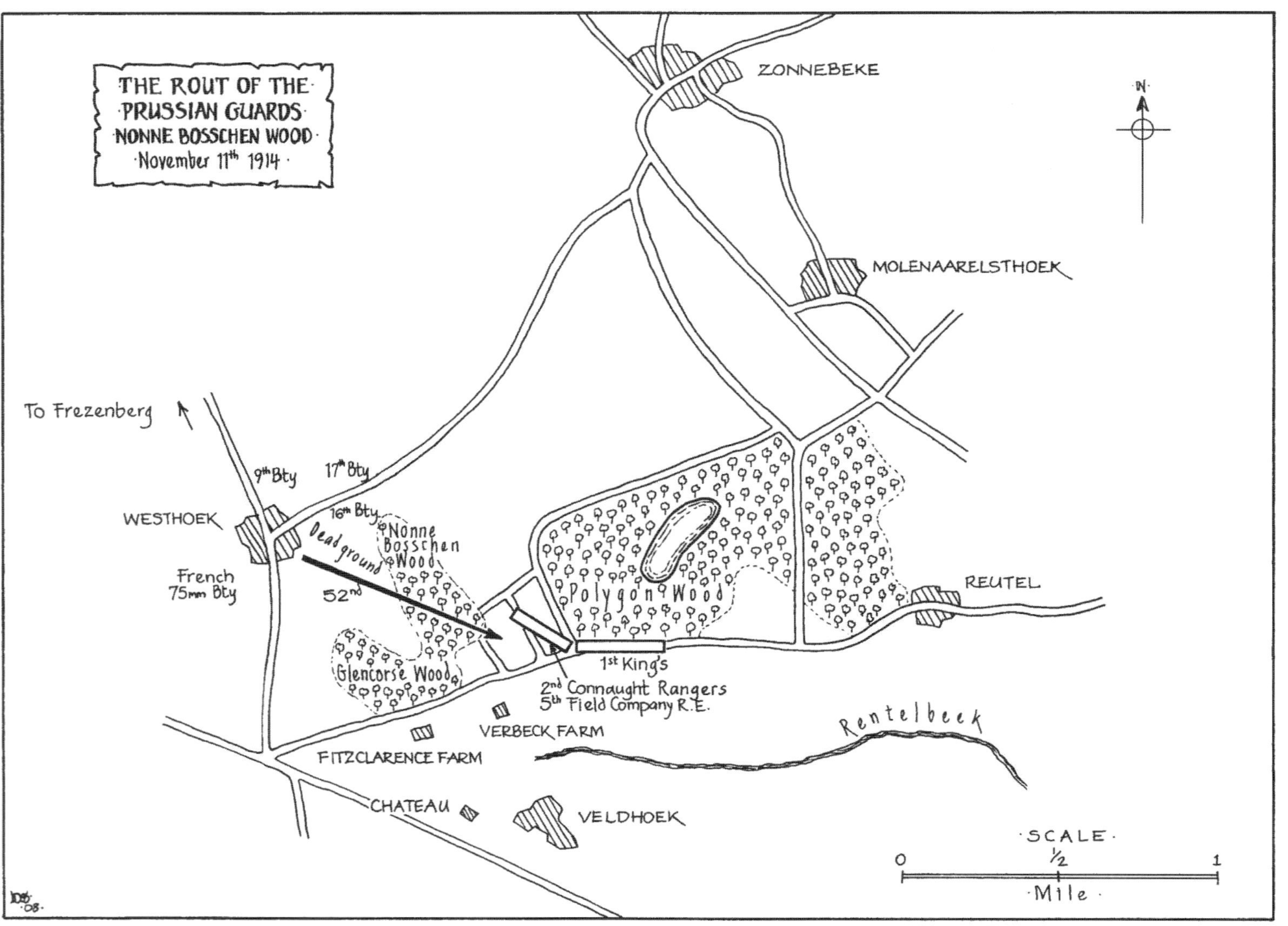
THE ROUT OF THE PRUSSIAN GUARDS
NONNE BOSSCHEN WOOD
November 11th 1914
N
ZONNEBEKE
MOLENAARELSTHOEK
REUTEL
Polygon Wood
1st Kings
2nd Connaught Rangers
5th Field Company R.E.
VERBECK FARM
VELDHOEK
Reutelbeek
SCALE
0
½
1
Mile
FITZCLARENCE FARM
CHATEAU
Glencorse Wood
Nonne Bosschen Wood
Dead ground
52nd
16th Bty
17th Bty
9th Bty
WESTHOEK
French 75mm Bty
To Frezenberg

Henry Davies, commanding the 52nd, watched the 1st Northamptonshire of the 1st Division advancing on their right into the south of Glencorse Wood[165].

Lushington's XLI Brigade consisted of the 9th, 16th, and 17th batteries, each of six eighteen-pounder guns. The headquarters and batteries were all in the vicinity of Westhoek. Brigade headquarters was in a splinter-proof dug-out close to the chapel and cross-roads. 9th Battery was in the garden of a cottage with the guns screened by branches of apple trees stuck in the ground in front of them to give the appearance of saplings. 16th Battery was situated along a fence in a grass field sheltered by more apple trees. 17th battery was just behind a line of willow trees. Also in the area was a French battery of 75 mm. guns south of Westhoek in a bend on the road leading to Clapham Junction. These French guns continued to fire all day despite the proximity of the Germans, demonstrating remarkable Gallic sang-froid. The French battery commander did not seem to be the slightest bit put out by the nearby presence of the enemy, but he did protest with great vehemence when shelled by a British battery.

In all probability German guardsmen of the 3rd and 1st Foot Guard Regiments were taking shelter, from British shells, in Nonne Bosschen Wood, soon after 9 a.m. Certainly by 9.30 a.m. hostile rifle fire broke out on the western side of the wood and small parties of infantry were working their way forward towards Lushington's batteries. There was a certain amount of dead ground between the guns and the edge of the wood, which made it difficult to judge just how close the enemy actually were. The ground also fell from the south-west to north-east. The batteries of the XLI Brigade continued to fire shrapnel and high explosive shells into Nonne Bosschen Wood, covered by the hastily assembled firing line of clerks, cooks and spare artillery men.

Once Lieutenant-Colonel Stephen Lushington had given the 52nd a warm welcome, he proceeded to explain the situation to Henry Davies. Davies was told that the enemy were in Nonne Bosschen Wood, a few hundred yards ahead of him, and the guns' only protection was the hastily improvised line of spare soldiers. A little later, around noon, Davies was ordered by the 5th Brigade to clear Nonne Bosschen of Germans, and to join up with the 2nd Highland Light Infantry who were holding the western side of Polygon Wood. Both battalions would then attack the trenches that the enemy had taken which extended southwards from Polygon Wood.

Almost at the same moment Davies was ordered by the 1st Guards Brigade to take the 52nd to the south-eastern corner of Nonne Bosschen Wood to aid troops of the 1st Division who were still holding out there. The orders were mutually exclusive and Davies had to think quickly. The Germans were in

[165] Glencorse Wood was not taken by the Germans during the Battle of Nonne Bosschen.

possession of Nonne Bosschen Wood and were behind the right of the 2nd Division, placing themselves in a vulnerable position. In addition, the enemy were close to Westhoek, where British and French batteries were still in action only covered by an exiguous firing line. Correctly, Davies decided that Nonne Bosschen must be cleared and that the 5th Brigade order must take priority. He formed up the 52nd for an attack on Nonne Bosschen Wood. The 1st Brigade was informed of his decision.

Shortly before 3 p.m., Henry Davies sent A Company under Captain Harry Dillon and Second-Lieutenant Francis Pepys, and B Company under Lieutenant Cuthbert Baines, into the wood. They were supported by C Company under Lieutenant Arthur Tylden-Pattenson and Second-Lieutenant Geoffrey Titherington, and D Company under Lieutenant George Tolson and Lieutenant Vere Spencer[166]. Numbering less than 400 men and led by the redoubtable 'Rabbit' Dillon, the 52nd charged into Nonne Bosschen and attacked the giant Prussian guardsmen[167] of the 1st and 3rd Foot Guard Regiments. Amounting to approximately 800 men, the Germans, some in spiked helmets and some in caps, appeared disorientated and lacked fight probably because of the artillery fire that they had been subjected to. In the wood, the effect of the shellfire was magnified by the vibration and crashing of broken trees. The XLI Brigade and other allied units had plastered Nonne Bosschen with shrapnel and high explosive shells. In addition to this their own artillery had been firing at them accidently. Nonne Bosschen Wood consisted of small oaks and chestnuts with an undergrowth of maple and hazel. The 52nd entered the wood at the north western end and advanced in a south-easterly direction killing and taking prisoner the demoralised Prussian Guardsmen[168].

On coming out of the wood A and B Companies, still led by Dillon, charged the unfortunate guardsmen out of the trenches south of Polygon Wood. Earlier in the day they had been the support trenches of the British 1st Brigade.

---

166 Sir Henry Newbolt in *The Story of The Oxfordshire and Buckinghamshire Light Infantry* stated that B Company [Baines], on the left and, C Company [Tylden-Pattenson], on the right, went into the Nonne Bosschen Wood first under covering fire from A Company [Dillon], who were on the extreme left. Once B and C Companies had reached the wood, A Company joined them, followed by D Company [Tolson] in the second line. Both Crosse in *A Record of H.M. 52nd Light Infantry in 1914* and the *Battalion War Diary* are at variance with this, and they have been followed in the text.

167 Lieutenant Geoffrey Titherington is reputed to have buried three who were over seven feet in height. If this sounds unlikely, a German soldier of seven and a half feet was captured by a five feet three inch Canadian corporal in World War II! Nicknamed 'The Great Uranus' whilst with a circus, he later acted on Broadway.

168 The casualties of the Prussian Guard on November 11th 1914 are not known with absolute certainty. A report in 1924 for the 1st Foot Guard Regiment gave the figures of 10 officers and 310 other ranks killed on the day. This would mean with the usual proportion about 900 wounded.

The 52nd were joined in this assault on the right by the 1st Northamptonshire from the southern edge of Glencorse Wood, and on the left by some Connaught Rangers and the 5th Field Company Royal Engineers. The Rangers and the Engineers attacked down the gap between Polygon and Nonne Bosschen Woods and showed great bravery. The Prussian Guards had lost the will to stand and fight and many ran when the 52nd were 30 or 40 yards away. Most of those that ran were shot.

Dillon and his men might well have been able to retake the former 1st Brigade front line trenches if a French battery at Frezenberg had not peppered the 52nd's front line with shrapnel. The gunners were unaware that the attack had progressed so quickly and by the time they were informed it was pouring with rain and getting dark. Acting Serjeant H. Edwards would later be awarded the D.C.M. [16-1-15] for his action in the counter-attack by taking a house which allowed the German trenches to be enfiladed.

A fine example of the fighting spirit of the 52nd that day was Serjeant Tom Hudson. He was in B Company with Cuthbert Baines and the two of them went through the wood together side by side as if on a pheasant shoot. Hudson was a great character, a deeply religious man who wielded the Bible and bayonet with equal enthusiasm. Later he would win the D.C.M. and would be killed in action at Givenchy on September 25th 1915. Hudson was a great loss to the regiment. 'Bingo' Baines was one of the best, if not the best, pistol shot in the regiment, and firing at less than 30 yards range, he was the executioner-in-chief of the unfortunate Prussian Guards.

The role of the 5th Field Company Royal Engineers in blocking the gap between Polygon and Nonne Bosschen Woods, and the protection they afforded the left flank of the 52nd during their clearing of the wood should not be forgotten. Whilst ensconced in a disused trench to the right rear of the 1st King's they suffered many casualties, including Captain Arthur Collins, who in 1899 scored 628 not out in a cricket house match at Clifton[169]. Later, as the 52nd went through the wood, they bravely charged in the open and helped to retake the 1st Brigade's support trenches.

Soon after the 52nd entered Nonne Bosschen Wood, a German force of some 1,200 strong were seen by the 5th Brigade advancing westward past the south of Polygon Wood. Probably they were the reserve battalion of the 1st Guard

[169] Collins was killed in the action and he is commemorated on the Menin Gate. Young Collins was only thirteen years old when he achieved the highest individual score ever recorded. His seven hour innings was spread over four afternoons from June 22nd-26th, 1899. Enormous crowds gathered and reports of his great feat appeared daily in *The Times.*

Brigade and if they had not been scattered by rifle and artillery fire might have saved their comrades in Nonne Bosschen Wood.

At dusk, Lieutenant-Colonel Henry Davies collected his men at two or three houses at the south edge of Nonne Bosschen Wood and reported back to the headquarters of 5th Brigade on the north edge of Polygon Wood. Their casualties for the day were remarkably light: twenty seven in number, of whom five were killed and 22 wounded. Amongst the dead was Colour-Serjeant Jesse Jones who had just been promoted to Second-Lieutenant although sadly he never knew it[170]. Cuthbert Baines, with a gunshot wound to his right arm, was one of the wounded. He was escorted to the rear by a Prussian officer and five other prisoners, who carried his equipment for him. To an English officer of another regiment, who met them on the way back, it was one of the most surprising sights of his life. The butcher's bill for the 52nd's most renowned action of the whole First World War was indeed a remarkably light one.

One of the disappointing features of the records of the 52nd is that Captain Harry 'Rabbit' Dillon, who was at their head in Nonne Bosschen Wood on November 11th 1914, has left only a brief written account of the action. Dillon was a fine soldier by any standard, but he suffered from a chronic chest weakness and died from pneumonia in January 1918, no doubt a victim of the great influenza pandemic of that year.

> .... on the previous day we had a furious attack on the Potsdam Guards. The best infantry that Germany can produce. They had rushed some trenches of another Regt. and were on the point of capturing a battery of our guns. The counter attack consisted of my Coy. A. and B. Coy. 52nd and some sappers. Baines of B. Coy was wounded and all the sapper officers killed and half our men and only Pepys and myself were left at the finish, out of the officers. Not one of the Germans got back and so prisoners mostly wounded were all that lived[171].

Sadly these few lines appear to be all that Harry Dillon wrote about his actions at Nonne Bosschen. However, his fellow company commander, Cuthbert 'Bingo' Baines, at the head of B Company that day, did put down on paper his memories of that day of glory for the Regiment. The much wounded Baines, who

[170] Promoted on November 9th 1914.

[171] Dillon's brief account of Nonne Bosschen was written on November 19th 1914.

nearly lost his life with an appalling groin wound in 1919[172], lived until 1972 and wrote this vivid account of the action, in 1932. It is reprinted in full.

A Personal Account of the Battle of Nonne Bosschen

As I am the sole surviving officer who was in the front line of the counter attack against the Prussian Guard in November, 1914[173], it may be of interest to the Regiment if I record my impressions of the fight before my memory of them completely fails. I remember little of the tactics and not much of the sequence of events, as I was in a state of considerable excitement at the time, and very tired after three weeks of continuous fighting, marching and counter marching, attacking and counter attacking since October 21st. I do not know how much "C" Company (under Tylden Pattenson and Titherington[174]) and "D" Company (under Tolson and Spencer) saw of the fighting. Both officers of "A" Company, Dillon and Pepys, were killed afterwards, and I was the only officer in "B" Company. "A" and "B" were in the front line, and "C" and "D", I believe, in support.

I probably saw more of the fight than any surviving officer. But my memory has become dimmed, though many incidents stand out very vividly.

We had a peaceful night in a French redoubt and some farm sheds on November 10th, and started the morning of the 11th by washing and cleaning up. Before we had done much, as usual in those days, we were ordered up to the front. It was a nasty, grey, raw day and there was a lot of noise going on somewhere in the distance. Such noise always filled me with awe, as I had quite long enough experience to know what it meant. My dislike for shells had started on first acquaintance; the Aisne and then Ypres had intensified my dislike into a positive hatred.

172 Cuthbert Baines was wounded again, in North Russia, at Ignatovskaya, in 1919. After developing an aneurysm of his femoral artery, he was subjected in turn to amputation through his ankle, then his knee and finally his hip. It was ironic that 'Bingo' Baines should survive World War I before being seriously wounded in this insignificant action.

173 Francis Pepys was killed the very next day, November 12th. Harry Dillon was not killed by the Germans, but died of pneumonia in 1918.

174 In a card to his father, on November 15th 1914, Titherington wrote: 'We had a great fight with the Prussian Grenadiers 2 days ago and pushed them back. My coy was not in 1st line but saw something of the show'. In a later letter, written on November 20th, he wrote: 'I wish I c[oul]d have been in the first line that day we cleared the Imperial Guard out'.

We packed up, and off we went. I have no idea how far, and no recollection of the march until we came to some of our six inch guns pulling out, which struck me as odd.

Later we came to some French "75"s – silent, which struck me as odder still, because the noise of battle was now quite close, and generally the French were all out to see how many rounds they could get through their guns before they became red hot. Soon after, we came to some of our own guns, 4.5 Howitzers I think, apparently deserted, we halted near them. I remember seeing the Commanding Officer (Davies) and Crosse looking for an artillery officer and eventually unearthing Colonel Lushington. Colonel Davies assembled the Company Commanders and told us that the Germans had broken through the trenches of another Brigade and were in a wood just over the brow of a hill behind which we were halted. He told us that there were only a few gunners and sappers, fighting as infantry, lined out between us and the Germans. We were to charge over the open between us and the wood and clear the wood of the Germans with the object of recovering the lost trenches. "A" and "B" Companies were to be in the front line, "C" and "D" in reserve.

My heart quickened. I had no wish to run over the open in full view of the Germans, nor to do any more wood fighting, of which I had had quite enough during the past few days.

However, orders were orders, and the machine produced by years of discipline pushed me on. I told my platoon serjeants (having no other officers in the company) what we had to do, and we set off. When we topped the ride we saw a big stretch of open field, with a few khaki figures lying about – whether alive or dead I don't know to this day. Beyond, was a huge wood, and looking through my glasses I could see Germans wandering about in it. More were lining the edge and shooting at us. My heart sank still further and I decided that I at any rate would not reach that wood – and I was not sure that I wanted to. If I became a casualty Sjt Hudson would have his chance of leading "B" Company in action which was his ambition.

However, the machine worked again and I decided that what had to be done was best done quickly. We all did a sprint and then lay down and shot at the Germans. Up and on again as hard as we could down and shooting, up and into the wood, sweating in every pore, more from fright than exertion!

I don't know how many were hit running across the open, but the men went like hell and shot between times. I believe that "C" Company were shooting at the wood from somewhere or other. When we got into the wood I was bewildered to find so many Germans there. But, thank God, not so bewildered as they appeared to be, as they put up no fight at all. There seemed to be crowds of them – literally crowds – because they were in no sort of formation and were wandering aimlessly about and most of them put their hands up as soon as they saw us. I did not know what to do with them all, so passed the word down to send all the prisoners down the centre where I was, on a ride through the wood. The picture left in my memory is of a few little men in khaki making noises like wild animals, very hot and out of breath, shouting and swearing at a mob of the most enormous men in field grey that I have ever seen. But the Germans gave no trouble at all and urged by the bayonets of our men collected on the ride. Eventually, I think, we detailed one slightly injured man to take them all back. I have no idea how many there were or what happened to them. Starting through the wood, we strung out into a very thin line, two men at intervals of twelve to fifteen yards. Many of the trees had had their branches knocked off by shells, which together with thick undergrowth made progress difficult. We moved slowly forward like a line of beaters and kept on coming on bunches of Germans. Some loosed off their rifles without bothering to take careful aim, thank goodness, and then turned tail and ran. Others surrendered without more ado. I took pot shots with my revolver at those that ran. I must mention here, for the sake of the incredulous, that there were, I think, three officers in the 52nd in 1914 at Aldershot, who had been known to hit the target at 30 yards or was it fifteen? – at the officers' annual revolver shoot, and I was one of them. In fact I have been known to hit the target more often than to miss it, and what is more, with the left hand as well as the right. I only mention this in the hope that those that read this will believe me when I say that I don't think I missed one German that I fired at on this day. I fired fifty-two rounds through my revolver, and burn't my left hand on the barrel in reloading. It is not difficult to understand when I say that the longest range at which I fired at a German was about thirty yards and the enormous bulk of the average Prussian Guardsman made an easy target, even on the run.

We struggled on, Sjt Hudson roaring like a bull, and doing great execution with the bayonet. The Boches kept breaking cover just in front of me up the ride and giving wonderful shooting.

Hudson was up with me on the ride and had shots when a bunch came out. But if a single one appeared he invariably shouted "Your bird, Sir". I don't think he had ever been out shooting before! I was so excited by this time that the sweat was streaming down my face and pouring off the points of my collar which, having no tie-pin, were outside my jacket. I was wet through, but I had almost forgotten to be frightened.

About this time we got held up on the left and I took a dive into the undergrowth. I broke through a thick bit and stumbled right on top of a bunch of about thirty Boches, who promptly put up their hands (before I had time to do so myself!). By a stroke of luck, out of the corner of my eye I saw one German getting up from the ground a little apart from the rest. He seemed different from the rest and as I looked at him he raised his revolver, but I was just before him and shot him dead at ten yards range. The only effect that this had on his men – he was their officer – was that their hands seemed to go a bit higher in the air than usual. They had all dropped their arms. I herded them on the ride to be received by Hudson, who nearly bayoneted the first of them, before he realised the situation.

Having got back on the ride I found a big bunch of Germans collected there, and was conferring with Hudson, what to do with them, when a slightly wounded man came along most conveniently and took charge of the fifty odd hulking Prussians. We still went on collecting more Boches, and left a party of them sitting on the ride because we had no spare man to send back with them. Hudson kept on looking back on them to see that they were still there, when suddenly I saw him take a dozen leaps back and he was amongst them with his bayonet, yelling like a madman. I dashed back, and he swore he had seen them collecting rifles. My own view was that they were far too frightened and much too thankful to be out of the fight to wish to arm themselves even if they had the chance. However, eventually we were able to detail one man to stay with them and collect any others that were sent back. A lot of shells were bursting over head and the noise was terrific. Suddenly I had a colossal blow on my right shoulder which sent me reeling. I was furious and turned on Hudson and said: "What the hell hit me?" I was getting rather stupid with excitement and exertion. "He said you have been hit, Sir". I said, "I know that, but who hit me?" He said, "You're wounded". "Oh!" I replied, "I thought somebody had hit me with a stick". I could not move my arm, it hung useless, so I carried on with my revolver in my left hand. Hudson telling me all the time that I ought to go back.

There was only one thing left that I wanted to do from now onwards and that was to get out of it. But the machine worked again and much against my will, I heard myself saying to Hudson: "I am not going back yet - I am alright," and cursing myself for a fool at the same time.

So we went on again and I actually forgot my wound for a time. I heard a ghastly noise coming from the right and taking a plunge into the undergrowth I came across a little man in khaki, cursing and swearing and crying all at once and making the most agonising noises. He was trying to get his bayonet out of a huge Boche. I gathered that the Boche had surrendered and then had picked up a rifle and tried to shoot his captor, who was so frightened that he shoved his bayonet right into a bony part of the Boche and then got still more frightened when he found that he could not get his bayonet out again.

He was simply howling with fright and rage and tugging like a maniac. I told him to leave his bayonet where it was and take the German's rifle and bayonet, and pick another English one when he could find one.

I got back to the ride again and had some more good shooting, but the shells overhead were damnable and branches of trees were falling all around us. The artillery seemed to be concentrating on us, but as it was just as bad behind as in front, we decided to push on. After a bit, I saw the end of the wood and an open space beyond. Just as we got to it, I received a message from "Rabbit" Dillon to say that French "75s" were shelling our line and we were to stay where we were, until he had sent a message back. Just at that moment a big shell landed somewhere behind us and turning round I saw a German Officer walk out onto the ride. He had one look at me and then ran towards our rear. It was the last shot I had that day and the best – running at thirty yards and a bull. When we got to the edge of the wood, we saw a few Germans disappearing across the open, but when they had gone we could see no sign of life although there seemed to be a lot of bullets flying about and the shells were terrifying. I began to feel sick and then the trees went up into the sky and the sky came down to the earth. I found Hudson bending over me and saying in the gentlest tones, "This is no place for you, Sir, I'll get the men to line the edge of the wood. They'll be all right and I have got some nice Boches to help you. It will be dark before you get back if you don't go now".

I do not remember more. Loss of blood had made me rather stupid. I remember walking back up the ride we had come up, with some Boches, one of whom was an officer. Another, who talked English fluently, carried my equipment for me. The officer gave me his field glasses with his name and regiment – 1st Battalion, 1st Guard Corps – engraved on it. They were all over 6ft 4ins, and the one carrying my equipment 6ft 7ins. As we passed the officer I had shot last, he pointed at him and said: "My officer, you shot him. I saw it. It was a very good shot," and grinned. I still had my revolver in my left hand and felt inclined to shoot the blighter for that bestial grin, but I had only two rounds of ammunition left, having started the day with fifty four, and he could not stop talking. He told me the Germans had captured Paris, Calais and Boulogne and that the British Army were surrounded round Ypres. He said they had mounted a gun at Calais which was shelling Dover and one was being brought up that would reach London. When I told him we should all be in England very soon, he told the officer, who smiled a pitying smile. They all believed the story and were rather sorry for me! I got back to Regimental Headquarters eventually, although I remember very little of the journey. From there by horse and ambulance from Ypres to the Château Blanc. Then by motor ambulance to Poperinghe, where I was put into a children's hospital and nursed by nuns. Afterwards to Hazebrouck, and Boulogne, and so to Southampton and finally to London, the Mecca of all wounded men.

Although written some eighteen years after the event, Cuthbert Baines gave a vivid account of the 52nd's most famous action of the war. He was one of the three best pistol shots in the regiment, and there is little doubt that he killed and wounded a large number of the demoralised Prussian Guardsmen that day. However, Baines' claim of 52 successful shots out of 52, seems to be a little too much of a coincidence, as the regimental number had also been 52 and the battalion still thought of themselves as the 52nd Light Infantry. The relatively small men of the 52nd so comprehensively defeating the giant Prussian Guardsmen, in Nonne Bosschen Wood that grey November afternoon, has an almost David versus Goliath air about it. Certainly driving the premier German regiment out of the wood in such a decisive manner was of inestimable importance in stopping the enemy break through to the north of the Menin road. The action certainly bears comparison with that of their forefathers in the 52nd, in overwhelming Napoleon's Imperial Guard at the Battle of Waterloo, nearly 100 years earlier.

We left the 52nd in some houses just east of the southern edge of Nonne Bosschen Wood and the 5th Brigade Headquarters on the northern edge of Polygon Wood. In the late afternoon Brigadier-General Charles FitzClarence, whose 1st Brigade had virtually disappeared, went to 5th Brigade Headquarters to see Lieutenant-Colonel Claude Westmacott, still in temporary command of the Brigade. A plan was formulated for the 52nd and the 2nd H.L.I. to make a surprise attack, without artillery preparation, from the south-west corner of Polygon Wood, to retake the lost 1st Brigade front line trenches. As it was pitch black, it was decided to delay the assault from 9 p.m. until 1 a.m. on the 12th, when the moon should have come up making it easier to see where they were going. Lieutenant-Colonel Henry Davies returned to the 52nd from the 5th Brigade Headquarters just as it started to pour with rain and hail. He got all the 52nd under cover in the houses, although he was drenched through himself. The night of November 11th/12th 1914 was reputed to be one of the most miserable experienced by the troops in Flanders. The torrential rain had filled the old trenches and shell holes with water and the ground was a quagmire.

At about 11 p.m., Henry Davies accompanied the staff captain of the 1st Brigade to see Brigadier-General Charles FitzClarence in his Headquarters[175] to the south of Glencorse Wood. Davies was told by FitzClarence that he had had further troops put under his command and he would co-operate in the 52nd's proposed attack. FitzClarence also had orders to attack from the south-west corner of Polygon Wood at 4 a.m. the following morning and he was determined to regain his brigade's former front line trenches come what may. The troops concerned were the 2nd Grenadier Guards, the 1st Irish Guards both of the 2nd Division and some Munster Fusiliers from the 1st Division. It is surprising that there was to be a two and a half hour gap between the two British assaults.

175 On November 11th this was in a farm on the edge of Glencorse Wood where the track from the south enters it. FitzClarence Farm was never his headquarters and is shown as such in error on the 1914 maps.

At 1.30 a.m. on the 12th, Henry Davies and the 52nd moved up to the south-west corner of Polygon Wood. As best he could, Davies reconnoitred the enemy's trench in the dark[176]. It did not seem possible to enfilade the trench for any great distance, and to make matters worse the Germans had another line behind it, which would allow them to fire into the flank of the 52nd as they progressed down the enemy trench. In addition, it was far from clear whether or not the 9th Brigade, on the Menin road, was still in the prolongation of the trench the 52nd were to attack. For all these reasons and also because he was uncertain of the ground he was to attack over, Davies thought that the assault should not take place. The Brigade-Major of the 5th Brigade who had accompanied Davies in his reconnaissance returned to his headquarters and informed Lieutenant-Colonel Claude Westmacott, in command of the brigade, of Davies' view. Westmacott fully supported the view of Davies and the attack was cancelled. Today their decision seems to have been an eminently sensible one. The 52nd were ordered to return to their former position just to the east of the southern edge of Nonne Bosschen Wood.

While all this was happening between 2-3 a.m. there was considerable firing from the German-held trench, and on their way back, the 52nd ran into FitzClarence's force along the western edge of Polygon Wood. In moving across the wood, this force had lost some men by approaching too close to the enemy's trench. At the moment the 52nd met the 2nd Grenadier Guards, a report came through that Charles FitzClarence had been killed. He was showing the men of his old Regiment, the Irish Guards, the way over ground familiar to him but not to them, when the moon suddenly came out and he immediately threw up his arms, having been shot by a single rifle bullet. It was a sad end to an inspirational commander who had been determined to fully regain the front line trenches his own 1st Brigade had lost earlier in the day. After FitzClarence's almost immediate death, the attack was abandoned.

Today, Polygon and Nonne Bosschen Woods still exist in much the same position as 100 years ago. The A 19 motorway separates the two woods. Unfortunately the Belgian authorities have allowed private houses to be scattered all over Nonne Bosschen Wood, which makes it virtually impossible to follow the route taken by the 52nd from north-west to south-east on that grey November 11th nearly a century ago. However it is possible to visualise the open ground that the 52nd charged across to overwhelm the Prussian Guards in the wood.

In the early hours of November 12th, Lieutenant-Colonel Henry Davies left the 52nd in the houses just to the east of the southern edge of Nonne Bosschen

---

176 According to Edmonds in his *Official History* the ground was being swept by rifle fire and it was impossible to collect the wounded.

Wood and reported again to the 5th Brigade headquarters. He was ordered to dig trenches with their left on Polygon Wood and passing in front of the houses, which they were currently occupying, to the south-east corner of Nonne Bosschen. To the 52nd's right in front of Verbeck Farm were the 1st Northamptonshire and then the 1st Gloucestershire and Guards, extending the line towards Veldhoek Château. To the left near the south-west corner of Polygon Wood were the 2nd Connaught Rangers and the 2nd H.L.I. Fortunately, the trench line had just been completed by dawn. C and D Companies were in this new trench line and A and B were in support in some partly dug trenches behind them.

During the daylight hours of the 12th, the 52nd were shelled in their new trench line, and nine men were killed and fourteen wounded[177]. Amongst the dead was Second-Lieutenant Francis Pepys who was killed by a single shrapnel ball whilst out of his trench for an instant. Harry Dillon was particularly upset by Pepys' untimely death. 'I was awfully cut up about poor Pepys who was killed getting back into the trench which he and I shared. He was the only other officer in my Company and now I have to sit frozen to death all day alone........I have never been so upset about anything'. He was a great loss to the regiment and Henry Davies considered him to be a very good leader in action. The following month the *London Gazette* announced the award of the D.S.O. for his actions on November 3rd. Pepys was a fine cricketer, a descendant of the celebrated diarist, Samuel Pepys, and a great-grandson of Major John Woodgate, a 52nd Peninsular officer. It was clear that the Germans had suffered heavy casualties. In the 1st Brigade area, 700 bodies were found in the recovered British line with many more visible in front of it.

November 13th was a relatively quiet day for the 52nd in their trench line with only light shelling. One bugler was killed during the day and that night Captain Claude Chichester brought a very welcome fifth reinforcement some 140 strong. The following day, the 14th, the 52nd were heavily shelled in the morning and this resulted in one man killed. Colour-Serjeant William Fossey was the unfortunate man; he had served with the regiment on the north-west frontier of India in 1897-8 and throughout the summer and autumn of 1914. In the evening, the 52nd were relieved by the Hertfordshire Territorials [1/1st Battalion], who had only been in France since November 6th. Henry Davies and his weary men marched to Molenaarelsthoek, one and a half miles away to the north-east of Polygon Wood. Here they went into the 6th Brigade's reserve under Brigadier-General Robert Fanshawe, who had commanded the 52nd from 1907-11.

177 The casualty figures are taken from the *Regimental Chronicle* of *1914*. The *Battalion War Diary* for November 12th quoted 23 casualties. Seven dead plus Pepys, fourteen wounded, and one missing.

Fanshawe was known as the "chocolate soldier" as he regularly handed it out to his men. On this occasion it was soup that he provided for the officers.

During the evening of the 14th, Field-Marshal Lord Roberts had died in St. Omer within hearing of the guns of Ypres. Roberts had landed at Boulogne on the 11th and been visiting his former Indian troops. He caught a chill and was soon dead of the old man's friend, pneumonia. In his book, *Forty-one years in India,* Roberts described the 52nd's attack on the Cashmere Gate at Delhi. Thus ended the link between the Indian Mutiny of 1857 and Ypres 1914. Richard Crosse, then aged nine, recalled being lifted to see the little Field-Marshal, "Bobs", in Queen Victoria's Diamond Jubilee Procession in 1897[178].

Snow fell on the 15th and that night the 52nd was relieved by the French 109th Regiment, under an arrangement whereby the British troops were to be replaced by French ones, to allow the former to recover from their heroic endeavours of the last few weeks. Lieutenant-Colonel Henry Davies led his men to a point just beyond Westhoek. He had intended to take the road towards Zonnebeke and then turn left for Westhoek, but the Germans were shelling the road between Zonnebeke and Westhoek so heavily that they turned about and retraced their steps. Once more and for the last time they marched along the track to the north of Polygon Wood, which was ankle deep in mud and slush. The road from the wood to Westhoek was equally bad and it was 1 a.m. on the 16th before they reached the village. During the 15th, Lance-Serjeant J. Millgate, who had been wounded on the Aisne, arrived with the sixth reinforcement of 46 men.

In the early hours of November 16th the 52nd moved on to take over trenches, from Ferme Verbeck southwards, from the Northamptonshire and Gloucestershire regiments. A Company was left in reserve at Westhoek and B, C, D were in the line. Regimental Headquarters were in a small farmhouse half a mile south of Westhoek. These trenches were immediately to the right of those the 52nd had occupied from November 12th-14th. The 2nd H.L.I. was on the right and Davies took command of both regiments as the acting 5th Brigade's commanding officer was still in Polygon Wood. The rest of the day was fairly quiet apart from some sniping which left two men dead and three wounded. Geoffrey Titherington commented: 'It was a perfectly dreadful day – all trenches had 4-6 inches of water in them. The Deutchers shelled various people but left our particular bit alone they only sniped viciously all day'[179]. In the evening the 52nd were relieved by the French 158th Regiment and marched by Potijze to Ypres where their forefathers had been billeted 100 years earlier.

---

[178] Crosse's uncle Charles Kenrick Crosse was the first man through the Cashmere Gate in 1857.
[179] Letter written to his father on November 20th 1914.

On arrival in Ypres the 52nd should have been met by a staff officer to show them their billets. Unfortunately no one was there to meet them and they were forced to remain in the open in pouring rain with heavy shells falling in the vicinity. Eventually, at 2 a.m., the Headquarters of the 2nd Division showed them to their billet, in a timber warehouse near the canal, to the north-west of the town. Geoffrey Titherington 'slept like the dead'. Henry Davies found a comfortable house for his Headquarters and was able to sleep in a real bed for the first time in weeks. Unsurprisingly he had difficulty waking up in the morning.

Most of the 52nd spent the 17th resting in Ypres. Occasional shells fell into the town, some houses had been destroyed but at this stage in the war the damage was not great. Henry Davies even managed a bath at Captain Geoffrey Sullivan's house. Sullivan, a first-class pianist who had on occasion accompanied Dame Nellie Melba, was a provost marshal with the 2nd Division and had served with the 52nd before the outbreak of war. Geoffrey Titherington wrote: '- - but everyone wants a bath and clean clothes. Our present ones are in some cases what the men call 'fresh' '[180]. The only members of the Regiment who were unable to rest were the unfortunate Machine-Gun Section under Lieutenant John Southey who were sent up the Menin road to assist the 3rd Division against a final German attack. During the day the astonishing news came of home leave, initially for officers and shortly afterwards for the N.C.O.s and men. This could be taken over the next few weeks/months as the situation allowed. No one could believe this wonderful news, but it was true. Henry Davies recorded in his diary just how few officers who had come out to France with the Regiment there now were: Richard Crosse, A.S. Field [quartermaster], Harry Dillon, George Tolson, John Southey, Vere Spencer, and Arthur Tylden-Pattenson.

The Adjutant, Richard Crosse, had some unusual views about leave. His ancestor, John Cross [no e], had taken no leave for six years during the Peninsular War a century before, and Crosse intended to follow his example. Eventually, Crosse felt the need to take leave, but this was not until 1917. According to his own account his colleagues thought that he was "mentally afflicted"[181]. One man who made the most of his leave was Harry Dillon. On November 22nd he sent a telegram informing his family and then travelled to London where he was stared at by the population. They were not used to seeing a man home from the trenches particularly one with his greatcoat shot through!

At 5 a.m. on November 18th the 52nd marched, with the 2nd H.L.I., the fourteen miles to Bailleul via Westoetre and Locre. Breakfast was taken at an

---

180 Card written to his mother on November 17th 1914.

181 The story is told incorrectly in Robert Graves' *Goodbye to All That.* Crosse described the book as unpleasant.

empty convent at Locre. At last the bedraggled 52nd were out of the range of shells and were able to take a well-earned rest. Apart from a brief excursion to the trenches near Wytschaete from the 25th-27th, they were to remain in Bailleul until December 23rd. The 52nd had good billets and a brasserie with a plentiful supply of barrels. Once the barrels were cut in half they made excellent bath tubs. Equipment was checked, boots and clothing were exchanged and some drill carried out. Geoffrey Titherington reported a visit by the commanders of the 2nd Division and 5th Brigade: 'Both Gen. [sic] Haking and Munro [sic] have been here and both had very high praise for the 52nd and indeed I think the regiment has earned it'[182].

According to Edmonds' *Official History*, bathing and the changing of underclothes left a great deal to be desired.

> There was not sufficient to give everyone a change. Divisional schemes were therefore devised by which a first batch of men, after getting a bath in tubs provided in washhouses, factories and other large buildings taken over for the purpose, received new underclothing. Their original garments were then washed and issued to the next succeeding batch, and so on.
>
> There was no change of uniform to be had, so the khaki jackets, trousers and great coats were ironed, in order to destroy insect life, whilst the men were in the baths. Warm clothing in the shape of "Coats warm British" and goat-skin jerkins, and "comforts" were received in good quantities. Much appreciated ration of rum was issued. Entertainments for the men were also started, the first being inaugurated in Armentières with the help of artistes from Paris.

Even under the conditions of war, the thought of communal underpants, particularly as they had been worn for many weeks, is not a happy one for the 21st century mind to accept, but perhaps there was no alternative. Richard Crosse recorded a related story of the 52nd's time in Bailleul.

> We had been warned that some of our accommodation might have to be given up. The Commanding Officer had made up his mind that his men could be comfortable in no less, and therefore that none of it

[182] Letter to his father written on November 20th 1914.

should be given up. It must have been on one of our first three days in Bailleul that there arrived in [the] orderly room a very important field officer in command of an A.S.C.[183] (as it was then) reinforcement. He had been told, he said, to see the adjutant of the 52nd and get some accommodation from us. I did all I could to persuade him that we had none to spare, but he continued to press his demand. I looked helplessly towards the Commanding Officer, who had been listening attentively, in the characteristic attitude – hands clasped behind his head. He joined in the fray at once. There was a lengthy argument, and when every reason had been urged, for and against crowding our men up, Colonel Davies said very quietly: "Have your men got lice?" "No sir: certainly not: they are all newly from Base." "My men are from beyond Ypres, and they have *all* got lice." Not another word was spoken, and the major vanished. We kept our billets. The Commanding Officer remained perfectly still for some minutes. I bent my head low over my writing. Nobody will ever know what I have suffered, at times like these, in trying to maintain the official solemnity proper to the occasion.

Changes were made to the 5th Brigade on November 19th; the 2nd Connaught Rangers who were numerically weak and had lost many of their officers were amalgamated with their 1st Battalion. The 52nd were sad to see the Irishmen depart with their fine record in the Peninsular War when they were affectionately known as the "Connaught Robbers". They were replaced by the 9th Highland Light Infantry [Glasgow Highlanders], a kilted Territorial Force battalion from England. They would work closely with the 52nd over the coming months and would soon earn their respect.

Two days later, the 21st, the imperturbable Lieutenant John Southey and his machine-gun section, returned from duty on the Menin road with the 3rd Division. One of his men had been wounded. Southey, a descendant of the poet, Robert Southey, was one of only three of the original 52nd, 1914 officers, not to be wounded during the war[184]. Leave for seven days to England, for officers and

183 Army Service Corps.

184 The other two were the Medical Officer, Lionel Thurston, and the Quartermaster, A.S. Field, who was soon invalided home medically unfit. Southey spent most of the war in front line positions and commanded the 9th Cheshire Regiment, the South Nottinghamshire Hussars, the 1st Royal Berkshire Regiment and the 9th Durham Light Infantry. He was Mentioned in Dispatches in 1918. Poor recognition for a gallant officer. Ironically, having survived the war unscathed, Southey suffered a fractured pelvis in collision with a skidding London taxi.

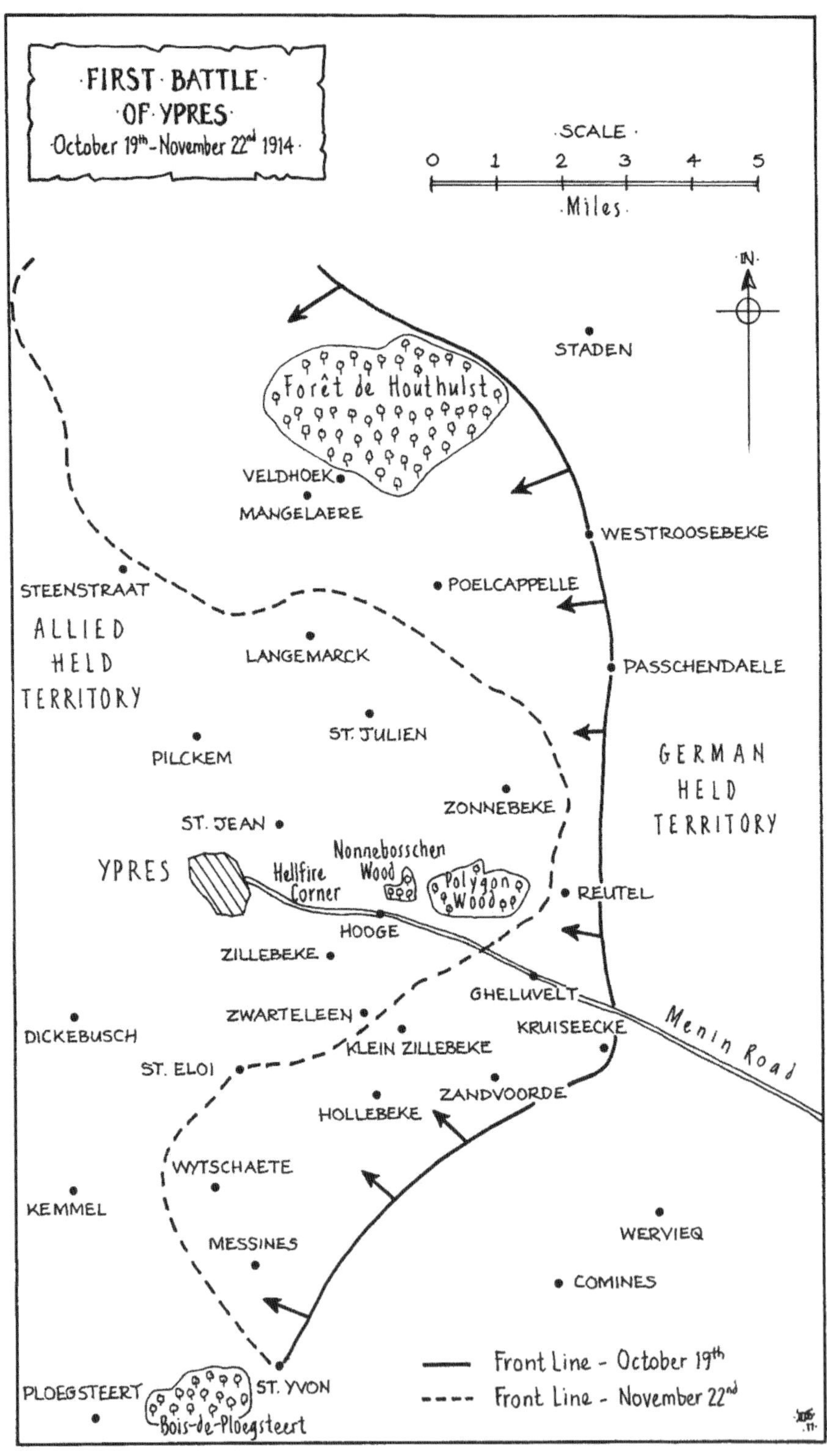
·FIRST·BATTLE·
·OF·YPRES·
·October 19th - November 22nd 1914·
·SCALE·
0 1 2 3 4 5
·Miles·
·N·
STADEN
Forêt de Houthulst
VELDHOEK
MANGELAERE
WESTROOSEBEKE
STEENSTRAAT
POELCAPPELLE
ALLIED
HELD
TERRITORY
LANGEMARCK
PASSCHENDAELE
ST. JULIEN
PILCKEM
GERMAN
HELD
TERRITORY
ZONNEBEKE
ST. JEAN
Nonnebosschen
Wood
YPRES
Hellfire
Corner
Polygon
Wood
REUTEL
HOOGE
ZILLEBEKE
GHELUVELT
ZWARTELEEN
KRUISEECKE
Menin Road
DICKEBUSCH
KLEIN ZILLEBEKE
ST. ELOI
ZANDVOORDE
HOLLEBEKE
WYTSCHAETE
KEMMEL
WERVIEQ
MESSINES
COMINES
Front Line - October 19th
Front Line - November 22nd
PLOEGSTEERT
ST. YVON
Bois-de-Ploegsteert

N.C.O.s, had opened and on the 23rd in bitterly cold weather with frost and snow on the ground, Lieutenant-Colonel Henry Davies went on leave. No man deserved it more after his calm and sensible leadership of the 52nd throughout the First Battle of Ypres, a seminal battle of the First World War.

The 52nd's rest and recuperation was rudely interrupted on November 25th when, quite unexpectedly, they were ordered to relieve the 1st Gloucestershire in trenches near Wytschaete. This they carried out in moonlight and took over shallow, imperfect trenches at the foot of Mount Kemmel. Captain Claude Chichester was in temporary command in the absence of Henry Davies. Only D Company had more than one officer. A, C, and D Companies were in the front line with B in reserve. One man was wounded. Although there was little shelling the next day, the 26th, the German trenches were very close and there was considerable sniping. Three men were killed and three more wounded. Amongst the wounded was Lieutenant Vere Spencer with severe gunshot wounds to the chest. Spencer would survive his serious injuries and become the Adjutant of the 3rd Battalion of the Oxfordshire and Buckinghamshire Light Infantry[185]. The 27th was an altogether quieter day although three further men were wounded. That evening the 52nd were relieved by the 10th Lincolnshire and got back to their billets in Bailleul at 2 a.m.

The 52nd continued their time at Bailleul with a mixture of rest, drill, musketry and route marches. Further reinforcements arrived to replace the officers and men who had been lost in the First Battle of Ypres. On November 30th, Captain Stephen Hammick and Lieutenant T.C. Tanner arrived with the seventh reinforcement of 80 men. Some of these included 43rd men who had served with the 33-year-old Hammick in the Mounted Infantry Company in South Africa. They all wanted to "get with the Captain again, if possible, sir". They had their way and C Company became a lively and happy one. The next day, December 1st, Captain A.K. North joined. Information of the promotions of Colour-Serjeants Jesse Jones [already K.I.A.], George Field, C. Dean, and Serjeant W. Wooding [gunshot wound to thigh on November 4th] to be Second-Lieutenants dated November 9th was received.

On December 3rd, the 52nd paraded and lined part of the Meterin road for inspection by King George V in person, who shook hands with the commanding officers. Information was also received of the award of the Distinguished Service Order to Lieutenants R.B. Crosse, C.S. Baines, A.V. Spencer, and Second-Lieutenants F. Pepys[186] and H.V. Pendavis. Distinguished Conduct Medals were

---

[185] Whilst the Adjutant of the 3rd Battalion Vere Spencer was reputed to have terrified the subalterns.

[186] Francis Pepys was dead by this time.

awarded to Corporal J.W. Hodges and Privates E.D. Stock, H.J. Hastings, H. Merry, and G. Hall. Serjeant A. Kippax received the Médaille Militaire. The King presented Crosse with the D.S.O. and Merry and Hall with the D.C.M. at Divisional Headquarters. Captain Harry Dillon went with Crosse to see the King and to collect a D.S.O. himself. However, as he put it 'I was in a later lot and they had not got it so I had to come back without'. Undoubtedly Dillon deserved the medal then and there and he had been recommended for it by Henry Davies 'for consistently bold leading in action'. He would have to wait until June 23rd 1915 before he was gazetted for it[187].

The same day, the 3rd, the eighth reinforcement consisting of 206 men and four officers arrived. The officers were Captains Francis 'Boovey' Beaufort, and H.W. Jackson, Second-Lieutenants Reggie Rendel and Jasper 'Tiger' Wyld. The next day Second-Lieutenant Francis 'Jimmie' Riddle joined and on the 13th Captain Lionel Folliott 'Sweeny' Scott also joined. The numbers of officers and men of the 52nd were rising to an acceptable level.

On December 10th, one man from each platoon was sent for training, under the commander of the 5th Field Company, Royal Engineers, in throwing bombs or, as they were later called, hand-grenades. The "jam pot" consisted of a tin jam pot filled with shredded guncotton and nails with a detonator and a short length of fuse. "Clay up the lid, light with a match and throw for all you're worth". The Battye consisted of a cylinder filled with explosive, detonator and fuse. It was ignited by a light blow. The hairbrush bomb had a slab of guncotton made fast by wires to a flat piece of wood which was used as a handle for throwing. The early bombs or hand-grenades were unreliable. In a demonstration, of one such device, before 40 generals and their staffs, only the handle went forward and the charge fell to the ground. Some fled, others crouched to the ground, but there was no explosion. A search was made and the charge found beneath the person of a general! Initially the Germans' bombs were much superior to those of the allies.

The training of the 52nd was enlivened on the 12th by a divisional order for the carrying of sandbags by every soldier. 'One sandbag is issued to each soldier for tactical purposes: the bag to be carried on the soldier, and in very cold weather permission is given for these to be used as foot muffs'. Richard Crosse recalled a rather dull training period being brightened by the men experimenting with their

---

[187] Letter from Henry Davies to Harry Dillon written on November 25th 1914. 'My dear Dillon – I meant to thank you before you left Bailleul for all the splendid work you have done, especially for the two occasions lately when you have cleared Germans out of woods. I have twice sent in your name, so I hope you will at least find your name mentioned in dispatches'.

foot warming sandbags. Later, for tactical purposes, each man in the 52nd would carry two sandbags.

Geoffrey Titherington was unimpressed with the expensive food and poor water in Bailleul: 'The inhabitants here must be making fortunes for everything is ruinously dear and it is too much to expect human nature to live on rations in the midst of plenty. I wish I could send you a sample of the water its [sic] green and very 'tasty' but apparently harmless. However after some of the ditch water I've drunk nothing in that line will do me much harm'.

Brigadier-General Richard Haking had received a serious head wound, on the Aisne, in September, and had returned to command the 5th Brigade on November 20th. A month later, on December 20th, he departed from his brigade for the last time and went to command the 1st Division as a major-general. Lieutenant-Colonel Henry Davies stepped up to take temporary command of the 5th Brigade before the arrival of Brigadier-General A.A. Chichester on the 31st. Richard Haking wrote a generous letter to Henry Davies on his departure from the brigade.

> On handing over command of the 5th Brigade, which I have held over three years, I wish to express to all ranks of the Battalion under your command my appreciation of the work they have done during this campaign. It is unnecessary for me to go into any details, because the rapid and skilful manoeuvring of the Battalion during the retirement from Mons, and the subsequent advance to the Aisne, their defence during the long occupation of the latter, and, above all, their splendid attacks and defence round Ypres, is well known throughout the Army, and later on will become a matter of history. The Battalion has always been celebrated for its attack at Waterloo, but, in my opinion, it will in future be distinguished, above others, for its magnificent attack near Ypres.
>
> Your Battalion has been in the Brigade during the whole time I have been in command, and consequently, I feel more closely attached to it than to the others. I cannot tell you what satisfaction it gives me to be able to record in this brief manner the heroic doings of the Battalion during the present campaign, which cannot be exaggerated.

The First Battle of Ypres was the last period of open fighting before the two sides settled down into the attrition of trench warfare. Although the battle had started as an encounter battle, it developed into a defensive one for the allies. Trenches were shallow and did not form a continuous line, and wiring was in its infancy. The artillery had little protection except that provided by the wooded countryside. Aeroplane observation of the ground was being gradually developed.

Although Britain and her allies were outnumbered two to one over the whole of the Ypres front, in local sectors the odds against them were even greater[188]. The German enemy also had a great superiority in heavy artillery, trench mortars, and machine-guns. Each British battalion had only two machine-guns when they took the field and many were damaged. The British compensated for the lack of machine-guns by the rapidity of their rifle fire. So effective was it that the enemy was convinced the British had large numbers of machine-guns. In 1909, the School of Musketry at Hythe, had urged that each battalion should have six machine-guns. When this was turned down for financial reasons rapid rifle fire was introduced as a substitute. Among the pre-war commandants at Hythe had been Charles Monro, now commanding the 2nd Division in which the 52nd was serving. In the early years of the twentieth century, Monro's reforms at Hythe had laid the basis for the prowess of the British Expeditionary Force in rapid, accurate rifle fire.

The German enemy, with their greater resources in men and material, really should have overcome the allies and taken Ypres. Their troops were well disciplined and for the main part had fought bravely. Perhaps the blame should lie with the leaders of the German forces, who attacked on too wide a front instead of concentrating their forces on one place such as Langemarck. They may have overestimated the number of allied troops facing them, and believed that when they made a dent in the allied line that they had only overcome outposts rather than the actual defensive line. At times they broke into but never completely through the allied line. In truth it was the tenacity of the British troops, and the rapidity and accuracy of their rifle fire, plus the French 75 mm. field guns which kept the Germans at bay around Ypres in the autumn 1914.

---

188 The Germans had about 600,000 men in the field.

Chapter VII

The Onset of Trench Warfare.

December 23rd 1914 - April 30th 1915

[Maps: pages 161, 237.]

At midnight, on December 23rd, the 52nd Light Infantry with the rest of the 5th Infantry Brigade left the Grand Place Bailleul in buses for the fourteen miles journey to La Couture. Second-Lieutenant Geoffrey Titherington observed the Grand Place: 'At present it is packed with cars mostly Daimlers and Rolls such beauties and so dirty'[189]. Their route took them through Hazebrouck and Merville and was an eventful one as some of the buses got lost and others broke down. Their hasty move was the result of a German attack on the Indian Corps and its trenches around Cuinchy and Givenchy. It was midday before the 52nd was safely ensconced in their billets at La Couture. In the event they were not required to support the Indians. During the day, reinforcements of 70 men arrived. Captain Francis Beaufort acted as the temporary Commanding Officer of the 52nd as Lieutenant-Colonel Henry Davies was away at 5th Brigade.

Christmas Eve and Day were spent quietly in their billets at La Couture, and a service was held by the recently appointed Chaplain to the 5th Brigade, the Bishop of Khartoum, Llewellyn Gwynne. Bishop Gwynne[190] was to become much loved by the men of the 52nd who knew him as 'our Bishop'. He was a fine sportsman, and regularly played centre forward for Derby County, including in a F.A. Cup semi-final, during the 1880s. Sadly for the 52nd, at the end of the summer of 1915, he would be taken away from them to become the Deputy Chaplain-General, with the rank of major-general, at the personal insistence of Earl Kitchener. As the Chaplain-General was based in London, this made Gwynne the senior clergyman in France and Kitchener, the then all-powerful War Minister, could not have picked a better man. After the First World War, Gwynne returned to the Sudan and it is said that no other man had such a long and influential term in that country, which he saw developed from destitution to a modern state.

The British Expeditionary Force was reorganised with effect from Boxing Day 1914. It now consisted of eleven infantry and five cavalry divisions. The new order of battle consisted of the First Army under Sir Douglas Haig and the

---

[189] Card showing the Grand Place Bailleul sent to his father in December 1914.

[190] Llewellyn Gwynne [1862-1957] was Bishop in Egypt and Sudan 1920-45 and Bishop in Egypt 1945-6. He died in his 95th year in 1957. The Bishop was a great supporter of the 52nd, and regularly attended the annual Regimental reunions. His last appearance at one of these was in 1957, just seven weeks before his death.

Second Army under Sir Horace Smith-Dorrien. The First Army had no less than three corps, and the 52nd remained in I Corps, under their former divisional commander, Sir Charles Monro, who had become a lieutenant-general. Monro's place at the 2nd Division was taken by Major-General Henry Horne[191]. He had started the war as Haig's artillery advisor at I Corps and was a deeply religious Scot with a strong sense of duty. Horne was not a great soldier, although he was careful and professional in what he undertook, and relied heavily on his able staff officers.

During Boxing Day, Captain Guy Blewitt returned to the Regiment at La Couture having recovered from the facial wound that he had received on the Aisne. He was accompanied by a young barrister, and would-be Liberal Member of Parliament for Salisbury, Lieutenant Jack Warner. The day before, at St. Omer, Blewitt had discovered that his draft was one man short: 'Arrived one man short at which I was rather ashamed but the authorities only remarked "what only one out of 120 the last fellow lost 7 and an officer out of 38" '. Blewitt, as senior officer present took over temporary command of the 52nd from Francis Beaufort. At this time, Guy Blewitt was described as 'a capital fellow and an excellent soldier'[192].

On December 27th, the 5th Brigade was sent to relieve Indian troops from Neuve Chapelle southwards. Brigade Headquarters was situated in Richebourg St. Vaast, and the 52nd, having relieved the 39th Garhwal Rifles, was placed in the centre of the brigade line. The 52nd positioned three companies in the front line, near Richebourg l'Avoué, and had their remaining company in billets. The Indian troops had suffered severely in the sleet and frost which followed Christmas. The trenches were in an appalling state, and the men had to wade through knee or waist-deep freezing water and slime. Here the clayey sub-soil held up the water two feet or less below the surface, so that the trenches were always water-logged. Eventually, later in the winter, these flooded trenches were abandoned and breastworks[193] were built further back near the Rue du Bois. The official history of the 2nd Worcestershire Regiment[194], whose men were in the adjoining trenches, recorded the scene.

> The fighting of the previous fortnight had left the ground littered with unburied dead and had shattered the defences. With the utmost

[191] General Sir Henry Horne [1861-1929] [Lord Horne of Stirkoke]. He commanded XV Corps in 1916 and First Army in 1916-19.
[192] Second-Lieutenant Geoffrey Titherington in a letter to his father written on January 6th 1915.
[193] A parapet above ground and usually made of sandbags.
[194] *The Worcestershire Regiment in the Great War.*

> difficulty, and under continuous fire, officers and men laboured to effect improvements. It was most difficult to bring material for revetting the trenches up to the front line. Even sandbags were difficult to obtain, tools were scarce, and the overburdened ration parties found it almost impossible to make their way up the flooded communication trenches.

The 52nd had a slightly quieter time in their section of the trenches, although the following day, the 28th, one man was killed and another wounded by a British shell falling short. In the evening of December 29th, the 52nd were pleased to be relieved by the 9th Highland Light Infantry [Glasgow Highlanders] and went into billets at nearby Richebourg St. Vaast. During the day, Captain Calvert FitzGerald[195] rejoined for duty and a further man was wounded. The Regiment spent the 30th resting, washing and drying clothes.

Private Jack Mawer had become the soldier servant of Jack Warner, and in a letter to his family, he described his life at this time[196].

> I have a busy time in the trenches I cook three officers [sic] meals and look after my officer. We are in billets again for a day or two and then move off to some more trenches. I can tell you the trenches are in a terrible state up to your knees in mud and water. So you can guess what sort of state we are in. We earn all the rest we get. Where we are staying now there are several young girls I have a bit o fun with them. I can tell you it is a sight to see the villages we go through with most of the houses blown down by shells. There are [sic] some splendid furniture knocking about.

As 1914 came to an end the 52nd were able to take stock of their four months of fierce fighting. Their total casualties were 632, consisting of 31 officers and 601 men, over 60% of the battalion establishment. Of these 13 officers and 150 other ranks had been killed. Except for one other rank, who had been taken prisoner, the remainder had been wounded. Many of its cream had become casualties, and the 52nd would never be quite the same again.

During the first winter of the war, Germany and her allies had taken the offensive against Czarist Russia. Although the enemy had failed to achieve a major breakthrough, they decided to go on the defensive in the west during 1915

---

195 Calvert FitzGerald had originally retired from the 52nd in 1910. He transferred to the 43rd in 1917 and survived the war.

196 Undated letter written at about this time.

so that a forward push might be made in the east. Thus the German Supreme Command shifted forces from the Western Front to the east. Once Russia was crushed, the vast majority of their troops could be shifted back to overwhelm Britain, France and Belgium. This almost came to fruition in 1918. General Joseph Joffre foresaw the German intentions and decided to attack in the west during the spring of 1915. The New Year would see the British and French forces, on the Western Front, making repeated attempts to effect a breakthrough, failing, and the fighting degenerating into attritional warfare.

On December 31st, the 52nd went back into the line to relieve the 2nd H.L.I., immediately to the right of the trenches that they had previously occupied. Here they spent a miserable New Year's Eve before, the next day, Henry Davies returned from the 5th Brigade to resume command of the Regiment. At this juncture, Guy Blewitt took over command of B Company. The 52nd was to remain in the water-logged trenches, near Richebourg l'Avoué, until January 5th, when they were relieved by the 9th H.L.I. and retired into brigade reserve, with billets in Richebourg St. Vaast. Whilst in the trenches they had two companies in the front line, one in support, and one in reserve.

During this spell in the trenches, Second-Lieutenant Geoffrey Titherington described his experiences in a ruined cottage on the Rue du Bois and then on the final evening digging a new trench[197]. He found 'the trenches are muddy and wet and where some idiot dug them along the line of a ditch of course they fill with water'.

> Fit and well in spite of weather which is still wet. At present in a row of ruined cottages about 500 yds from G. Trench so have to keep very quiet by day. Near my place is bike shop all blown to bits. Looks very forlorn – ruined bikes and walls all covered with gaudy French posters it reminds me of H.G. Wells' book 'The War in the Air' and "Bert Smallways" something very undignified about bikes in war. No roof on my house owing to shell fire so rather damp at present. Anxious moment this morning thought Gs were going to shell but they contented themselves with 3 shells and stopped. I believe we go to trench tonight. Horrid wet and we're digging new ones in front. One can see Gs baling water out of theirs all day long.

---

[197] Card to his father written on January 2nd and a letter dated January 6th 1915. Titherington's letters were published by his old school Radley. He wrote: 'for heaven's sake don't send them any more of my letters – I didn't write them to be published and everyone of course knows who wrote them'.

> We finished up last night with some navvying. On our right between us and the 60th there was a gap of 500 yds. It was decided we should close it. We kicked off at 5.15 – pitch dark – and extended right across the gap. We had of course taped out the line first. We carried rifles 1 bandolier and spades and you can imagine how flat we lay when the Gs turned the searchlight on for we were only 250 yards from their trench. They never discovered us and we made the trench – handed it over about 1 a.m. and came back here and slept the sleep of the just. It was about 300 yds – I suppose – of advance. We unearthed 2 very dead Frenchmen in the process which was unfortunate but we planted them again in a shell hole. We had no men hit in the digging – an amazing thing for we were right in the open – tho' a bullet removed the heel of my boot. This was at Richebourg l'Avoué.

Although these few days in the trenches were relatively quiet, on the 4th, one man was wounded by rifle fire from the enemy's line, some 300-400 yards away. Sadly on the 5th, Lieutenant Arthur Tylden-Pattenson was killed, most unluckily, by a stray rifle shot on the Rue du Bois. The 20-year-old officer had been slightly wounded on the Aisne, and like so many other officers in the 52nd, had a strong family connection with the Regiment[198]. Tylden-Pattenson had served with the 52nd for barely a year when he was killed, but in this short time he had greatly impressed his colleagues. Richard Crosse, the Adjutant, wrote 'he had shown himself a Regimental soldier of a very high order when, more than once in the 1914 campaign, finding himself in command of his company in situations which might have baffled a more experienced officer, he had risen magnificently to the occasion'.

Geoffrey Titherington described finding the body of Tylden-Pattenson[199]. He was greatly shaken by the death of his friend: 'I think sooner or later we shall most of us stop some odd bullet some day – I fear me just like poor T.P'.

> I am sorry to say Tylden Pattenson was killed last night about 5. I had gone up from my company which was in reserve and bridged a little river we had to cross. I reached the house where T.P. was while it was still light and so I went in and had tea with him. Toast and

[198] His great-grandfather Cooke Tylden-Pattenson served with the 43rd throughout the Peninsular War. Another ancestor, Sir John Tylden, served with the 43rd from 1804-11 and the 52nd from 1811-26.

[199] Letter to his father written on January 6th 1915.

sardines. Then I went and did my bridge. On my way back I found him shot through the head just outside his house. Some unaimed bullet had hit him or at least a bullet meant for someone else for he was a long way behind the trenches. His going has hit me more than anyone else's for he and I were left alone with the coy after Oct 21st and went through all the Ypres business together in charge of our coy. He was a cheery soul and always saw the best side of things – age 20. We buried him in a little churchyard this morning – the church just a pile of stones and the top 6 feet of the spire with its weather-cock neatly planted downwards in the earth just where it fell: blown off by some shell. He had left Aldershot with the 52nd in Aug.

Also on January 5th, Major Archibald Eden returned to the 52nd after recovering from the hand wound that he had received at Langemarck. Little happened on January 6th, although Guy Blewitt took over his old company, D. The company became known, in accordance with regimental tradition, as D or Captain G. Blewitt's Company. Captain C. FitzGerald took command of the ever expanding Headquarters Company, and also became the second machine-gun officer, as the establishment of machine-guns per battalion in the B.E.F. had been increased from two to four. Captain Lionel 'Sweeny' Scott became the Regimental Transport Officer. On the following day the Bishop of Khartoum, Llewellyn Gwynne, conducted the burial service of the unfortunate Tylden-Pattenson, who was laid to rest, in the shell-battered churchyard of Richebourg St. Vaast. The simple and impressive service was conducted to the sound of distant artillery fire.

On January 8th, the 5th Brigade, including the 52nd, moved into corps reserve, in the vicinity of Locon, three miles to the north-east of Béthune. The Regiment were not sorry to leave Richebourg l'Avoué as 'trenches on both sides will soon be uninhabitable. One can't use communication trenches as it is 4ft water in some or even more'[200]. A reinforcement of a serjeant and nineteen men arrived. Guy Blewitt and his fellow officers found a useful billet, in a farmhouse, living with the farmer and his wife. Blewitt had a certain amount of difficulty in getting a nearby estaminet opened as an officers' mess, with the old lady who owned it objecting on the grounds that 'mon mari est mort'. In due course she relented and enjoyed having them there. However, Blewitt, George Tolson, George Field, Jasper Wyld and the other D Company officers were unable to

---

[200] Letter from the newly promoted Lieutenant Geoffrey Titherington to his parents written on January 9th 1915.

persuade her that they were not interested in her late husband's vest, which she produced each morning at breakfast! Francis Beaufort had earnest conversations with her debating whether her clock was Louis XIV or Jeanne d'Arc! Life was made more bearable with whisky sent from Paris.

In a letter to his parents Geoffrey Titherington described this period in reserve[201].

> Just had a birthday lunch. Melon soup. Cold pheasant and chip potatoes. Cape fresh butter – blackberry jam – raisins and cigars also café – excellently made by madame (who has a lunatic daughter loose on the premises). A great treat. I shot a hare 2 days ago and hoped we'd have a great feed but it had a shell wound and was too thin to eat – great disappointment – I hit it moving with my revolver a fluke.

The following day the men had baths. On the 10th, at 11.15 a.m., the Bishop of Khartoum took a service in D Company's farmyard. The afternoon was spent on stand-by to move, at half an hour's notice, because the 1st Division was attempting to retake some trenches, at Cuinchy, and it was thought that a general action might ensue. January 11th was spent digging and practicing attacking trenches. The Medical Officer of the 52nd, Lieutenant T.L. Hardy, was admitted to hospital and he was replaced by Lieutenant Ernest Scott, who was to do such sterling service for the Regiment in 1915. In the afternoon, Guy Blewitt rode to Loisne, and then walked to Gorre Château, where a shell landing in the courtyard had killed and wounded a large number of Indians. Two days later, the 52nd undertook a route march to Paradis and got very wet, and in the afternoon Blewitt rode into Béthune where things went on much as before.

Early in January, Captain Harry Dillon, whose gallant conduct in the woods around Ypres had been greatly admired by the Regiment, was taken ill and he was invalided to Versailles. In 1912, he had been seriously ill, in Nigeria, with malaria, and the hardships of the war, particularly the cold, broke him down again. Soon he was sent to Nice, in the south of France, to recuperate. In letters to his family he made some pertinent comments. 'I have asked not to be sent home as I am frightened of getting kept and put into Kitchener's Army[202] and I

[201] Letter to his parents written on January 9th 1915.

[202] The name applied to the volunteer armies raised at the outbreak of war by Earl Kitchener. Within a year over two million men had come forward and three new armies were in existence.

want as soon as possible to get back to the Regt'[203]. Most sick or wounded officers of the 52nd were desperate to get back to their own Regiment.

Harry Dillon commented on the Christmas 'truce' of 1914. 'On Xmas I hear our people got out and talked to the Germans and exchanged cigarettes etc. The German authorities were angry and changed the Saxon Regt. for a Prussian Jaegar Regt. and we fight them continually. Not much love lost between us and the Prussians'[204]. The 52nd were out of the line in billets when the brief Yule-tide fraternization took place and were thus not involved. Dillon also appears to have suffered from shell-shock, although at this stage of the war, it was not recognized as such. 'My memory is bad and I get fearful fits of depression which I personally think is due to being so often shelled as I used to get headaches and of course one must be continually having slight concussions'[205]. Shell-shock could strike even the bravest of men as Dillon unquestionably was.

The 52nd returned to the trenches on the evening of January 14th and were to remain there until the evening of the 20th. They relieved the Meerut Cavalry Brigade, in the line to the south of Festubert, in front of the village of Le Plantin. Festubert was a small village four and a half miles east by north of the town of Béthune. The original front line had been several hundred yards in front of the village, but the water-logged trenches had to be abandoned. A line of breastworks made of sandbags was set up along the edge of the village. The 52nd held them with two companies in the front line, and headquarters and the remaining two companies in the houses of Le Plantin. In practice, even the front line companies could place the majority of their men undercover in the village, leaving a few sentries behind the breastworks to keep an eye on the enemy. However, the flimsy breastworks were fully-manned at night. There appeared to be a tacit agreement that neither side use their artillery to destroy each others' breastworks[206]. They were all too easily damaged by frost and rain and required constant repair. The enemy trenches were nearly half a mile away with the intervening land something of a swamp.

This six day period in the trenches was to be a relatively quiet time for the 52nd. The enemy sniped a little and their artillery fired the odd shell, but they were not as active as their British counterparts. The casualties of the 52nd for the period were light, with one man killed, on the 14th, and two more wounded, on the 20th. Invariably, usually after dark, when movement was possible, the Bishop of Khartoum came up to the line to take funeral services in person. The houses that

[203] Letter written from Versailles on January 11th 1915.
[204] Letter written from Versailles on January 17th 1915.
[205] Letter written from Nice on January 4th 1915.
[206] *The Worcestershire Regiment in the Great War.*

FROM FROMELLES TO VIMY
1915-16
N
Approximate Trench Line
1915 / early 1916
Canal d'Aire
To Delettes
FROMELLES
AUBERS
RICHEBOURG
-ST. VAAST
NEUVE CHAPELLE
RICHEBOURG L'AVOUE
ST. HILAIRE
COTTES
LILLERS
GONNEHEM
OBLINGHEM
CHOCQUES
ESSARS
FESTUBERT
LA BASSEE
BETHUNE
GORRE
VENDIN
LE PLANTIN
Canal
ANNEZIN
LE QUESNOY
GIVENCHY
BEUVRY
Bois des Dames
LE PREOL
CUINCHY
CAMBRIN
VERQUIN
RAIMBERT
ANNEQUIN
PERNES
LA BOURSE
VERMELLES
CAMBLAIN-CHATELAIN
PHILOSOPHE
MAZINGARBE
DIVION
LOOS
HERSIN
GRENAY
BULLY-LES-MINES
LENS
NOTRE DAME
DE LORETTE
ANGRES
SERVINS
GIVENCHY-
EN-GOHELLE
ESTREE
CAUCHY
ABLAIN ST. NAZAIRE
Zoave
Valley
SOUCHEZ
CABARET ROUGE
CAMBLAIN
L'ABBE
CARENCY
VIMY
NEUVILLE ST. VAAST
SCALE
0
2
4
6
8
Miles

the 52nd found in Le Plantin were in a filthy state and much time was spent in making them habitable for the men. To their left in the line of breastworks were the 2nd Worcestershire and to their right the 1st South Wales Borderers of the 1st Division. Although the tour was a quiet one, it was made uncomfortable by snow which fell on the 18th and lay three inches deep, until it melted on the 20th. Guy Blewitt's billet had no doors or windows so that he and George Tolson had the novel idea of sleeping in a wardrobe laid on its back on the floor! Probationary Second-Lieutenants, Cyril Baker and Victor Martin, joined the Regiment from the Artists' Rifles, on January 16th, and were confirmed in their ranks a month later. On the evening of the 20th, the 52nd were relieved by the 9th H.L.I. and went into brigade reserve at Essars.

Geoffrey Titherington has left a record of this time at Le Plantin[207]. Clearly he held a dim view of the Indians and our French allies.

> I spent a very comfy birthday in a big house which we occupied and loopholed etc because the trenches were full – it was a very easy place really for the country in front is full of water and at present they can only come up the roads. Of course these want v. careful guarding at night. They shelled us a bit but as usual. Their shrapnel is not dangerous if one can get behind 2 walls one to burst the shell the other to stop the bits. They have one howitzer near – a v. big one; indeed we are still in its reach. It threw 2 shells along this afternoon and got 6 sappers about 200 yards from here up the road. At present we are in regimental reserve i.e. 2 coys up in the firing line and two behind to do any odd dirty work. This place is an island in the midst of a swamp and all the houses have recently been occupied by Indians – that is to say they are incredibly filthy. The Indian seems not to have any ideas upon sanitation whatever and appears to all of us to be a hopeless helpless timid sort of beast.-------
> ------------------------------
>
> We shall be very glad to go from here tho' its better than trenches for its horribly dirty and smelly. You see – there's been fighting here since September and things have gone backwards and forwards – between us and the Gs there were lying Indian infantry Cavalry, French, Gl'osters. 1st Bedfords, London Scottish and dead Gs – add to this horses and cows and you'll understand we are glad the prevailing winds are west. Things looked better today when the sun came out between snow storms. Even the dump-heaps at the pit-

[207] Letters to his father written on January 19th and 23rd 1915.

heads look quite pretty with snow on them – like piles of granulated sugar in a gigantic grocer's window.

Glad to get out of last spot – a dismal swamp also it got a bit wearing perpetually seeing that the soldier showed no smoke by day or light by night. He's such an awful d'-d fool especially as we have him now in the shape of the ancient reservist. Someone's vigilance relaxed a bit the last day – up went a column of smoke and bang went 4 shells right into farm I'd been in but handed over to another coy. on Jan 17. Only 2 hurt so perhaps the lesson's cheap – one hit with a 6 in nail – query was it the shell or in the roof?----------------------------- Possibly some [men] are going to put backbone into the Fr. at Soissons? Isn't it funny how they wont fight if they haven't got a way out behind? After où fait-on la cuisine?[208] They usually asked Montrez la ligne de retraite[209]. If you can retire a big force over groggy bridges seems tho' you can shove re-inforcements up to 'em equally easily.--

We had some great ferreting our last day up there. The Rabbit = the 'Un: the ferret = 90 lb lyddite shells: the guns = us. Their trench was blown in – they ran and we shot them. Its not bad shooting at 750 yds to hit a man crawling. Its getting a bit of our own back after Ypres only we can't go and pinch the trench: everyone can't swim with rifle etc.

The period January 21st-24th, in Essars, was comfortable for the 52nd in good billets and with friendly inhabitants. Headquarters were in the local school and the large school-room made an excellent officers' mess. Guy Blewitt managed a bed with clean sheets, the first since he left England. The Curé even gave the Bishop of Khartoum permission to hold an Anglican Church Parade in his Roman Catholic Church. Sadly, either his bishop objected or the Curé himself had a change of heart. At the time of the Church Parade, the men of the 52nd found themselves locked out of the church. Richard Crosse, the Adjutant, has left an account of this unhappy episode[210].

---

208 Where does one cook it.

209 Show the retirement line.

210 Henry Davies recorded that the service took place in the church, but was not repeated. However, Crosse's account rings true.

> The Bishop could be angry too. Once, about the same time, in early 1915, I went with him in the capacity of interpreter (!) to call upon M. le Curé of Essars, where our billets were. There was a most friendly conversation in shocking French, during which we drank a powerful yellow beverage, and at the close of which we were promised the use of the church for a C of E Service on the following Sunday. This was a great achievement and the Bishop was much pleased.
>
> But meanwhile the Reverend Father had changed his mind, and on arrival at the church on Sunday we found we had been locked out. Our Bishop was very angry indeed. A fellow minister of God had broken faith. We had thought that we were dealing with one of a different kind: with one who sweareth unto his neighbour and disappointeth him not, and the Bishop saw it as a violation of an honourable obligation, like old Blucher's 'Soldiers, I have promised my brother Wellington, and will you have me break my word?' as he urged his weary warriors towards Waterloo: and that was inexcusable.
>
> But we were not defeated. The Bishop found some steps which he mounted. 'This will be my pulpit', he said. His 'flock, the 52nd Foot', as he called us, gathered around him, and the service was held in the churchyard.

At 7.30 a.m. on January 25th, the 52nd heard artillery fire from the region of the La Bassée Canal. The 1st Division had been attacked on either side of the canal, at Givenchy and Cuinchy. The 52nd was sent to be in reserve for the 3rd Brigade, at Givenchy, and was placed on the canal bank in a wood to the south of Marais. Here they suffered from the bitterly cold weather. The 2nd H.L.I., two battalions of the Coldstream Guards, and the North Lancashire Regiment were also present, and all ready to go into action. In the event, the 3rd Brigade cleared their trenches, retook Givenchy, and none of the reserve battalions were required to fight. By 7.30 p.m., the 52nd were back in their billets, where they were joined by Lieutenant Rupert Brett, with the 11th reinforcement of 153 men. Brett had been wounded at the Halte, the previous November, and was now said to be fully recovered. However, he would have to be invalided back to England again the next month suffering from concussion after a shell exploded close to him. Geoffrey Titherington wrote: 'he'd only just come back having got a bit of shell in the head near Ypres. I think he returned a bit too soon. A lump of scrap iron in the head can't be good for one's nerves'[211].

The 52nd remained in reserve, at Essars, ready to move at fifteen minutes notice, from January 26th-28th. January 27th was the Kaiser's birthday and the recent attack had been in honour of this auspicious occasion. Geoffrey Titherington wrote: 'The Kaiser's birthday attack has come off and fizzled out with great loss to the Gs and the gain of not one single yard'[212]. The 2nd Royal Inniskilling Fusiliers joined the 5th Brigade on the 26th[213]. The 52nd returned to their old trenches at Le Plantin, on January 29th, when they relieved the 9th H.L.I., and remained there until February 6th. This was a quiet period with desultory shelling and a little sniping. Although, on the 6th, the 5th Brigade supported the successful 4th Brigade [Guards] attack, on Cuinchy brickstacks, by rapid machine-gun and rifle fire, north of the canal. The enemy did not reply. Guy Blewitt wrote: 'we had nothing to fire at and our fire was not returned and we felt quite shy rather like arriving at a dance before anyone else, however things soon warmed up on our right'[214]. The casualties for the eight days were two killed and eight wounded. At night, a new line of breastworks was made in front of the present line, and close to the original trenches, which had had to be abandoned because they were waterlogged. The flat low-lying ground was intersected by dykes, making a continuous line of breastworks impossible. The weather was a little warmer and there was not a great deal of rain.

During this tour of the trenches, there was a certain amount of change of personnel amongst the officers. On the 4th, the experienced Captain Edward Kirkpatrick rejoined, having been wounded at Langemarck the previous October. Lieutenant Ernest Whitfeld, known as 'Ernie' or 'Whitters', the grandson of a former commanding officer[215], came with Kirkpatrick, and would soon distinguish himself in battle. The 5th saw the arrival of 47-year-old Major George Colvile who, for many years, had served in the 43rd Light Infantry[216]. Lieutenant T.C. Tanner, the 'Shropshire Lad', left to join the 2nd Shropshire Light Infantry on the 6th. On the same day the 52nd returned to their billets in Essars to be in reserve.

---

[211] Letter to his parents written on February 1st 1915.

[212] Letter to his parents written on January 27th 1915.

[213] The 5th Brigade now had five battalions.

[214] Diary entry for February 6th 1915.

[215] Colonel the Hon. E.G. Curzon, who served with the 52nd from 1844-77 and was in command 1870-77.

[216] George Northcote Colvile was born on July 9th, 1867, son of Lieutenant-General Sir Fiennes Colvile. He served in the South African War, 1899-1901, being severely wounded, and winning the D.S.O. In 1917, he was given the honary rank of Brigadier-General, having commanded the 7th Duke of Cornwall's Light Infantry since July 1915.

George Colvile was a very good friend of Llewellyn Gwynne, the 5th Brigade's Chaplain, from their time together in the Nottingham area. Gwynne had been Vicar of Emmanuel and Colvile had been involved with the Sherwood Forester Volunteers [7th Sherwood Foresters]. By the time Colvile joined the Regiment, he had found himself a horse and, as an ex-mounted infantryman from his days in South Africa, he was proficient in the saddle. Colvile had a taste for exploring the line on horseback, 'to take some interest in the war', but wishing to see Ypres, which was too far away for the horse, he enlisted the aid of his good friend the Bishop. Richard Crosse related the story.

> Once, when the Bishop visited the Regiment, the comfortable car placed at his disposal, did not escape the notice of his old friend, whose voice, during a meal in our mess, boomed across the table; 'I say my Lord Bishop, I want to go and see Ypres: couldn't we go and confirm someone up there.' The Bishop laughed loudest of all. But the journey was performed. What part if any the Major took in the Service of Confirmation, if there was one, is not recorded. The story will mean more to those who remember the imperturbable, undefeatable Brigadier-General George Colvile than those who do not.

The 52nd made the most of their six days in reserve, from February 7th-13th, in Essars. Training was undertaken and the men were drilled and route marched. Each day, a party undertook road mending in the vicinity of Le Plantin. The 52nd visited the divisional baths at Béthune, bathed, and were given clean underwear. On February 8th, Lieutenant Douglas Humfrey returned to duty, having recovered from his leg wound, sustained near Langemarck the previous October. He was accompanied by the 20-year-old Second-Lieutenant Robert Bull, the elder son, of a Buckingham brewer, who at school was reported to be quick-tempered. Just over three months later both young men would be killed in action.

Whilst resting in front of a coal fire in a biscuit tin, at Essars, Geoffrey Titherington wrote again to his parents. He gave a graphic description of building a breastwork in the dark and finding the body of a member of the 1st South Wales Borderers[217].

> Imagine a flat plain with water courses all about it with pollard willows along them and much mud. A much battered village in the

[217] Letter written to his parents on February 9th 1915.

> background from which there crept out after dark 30 men laden with shovels sandbags etc with their rifles slung: They staggered through the mud for ¼ mile (they looked as if they were drunk for the muds sticky to a degree). They all stop and squat down while a place is chosen for the breastwork for an advanced-post which we've come out to build. To dig down is impossible so one must build up instead. Then they all get to work meanwhile I've gone to the front a bit with two groups to post them to cover us. You can imagine us cowering along and squatting whenever a 'flare' goes up a lot of these and they make things very light. Suddenly in the light of one of these we all see a man sitting down quite close against a willow. We stalked him with care but its obvious he wants to be captured or else is in a bad way. As a fact he was dead and had been about a fortnight. Evidently he'd thought a pollard willow bullet-proof and had tried to hide behind it. I suppose he was a scout or patrol or something like that. We could find no identity disk or papers and so buried him there in the wet clay as we found him in his equipment. All the volley he got was the occasional 'spock' of a sniper's bullet and the continual splutter of rifles away on the right where some one had got the jumps. I took his cap in and found he belonged to the S.W.B. I expect if we'd gone further we'd have found a lot like him.

Another officer took the opportunity to write home. Douglas Humfrey in a letter to a young friend, reflected on how warfare had changed in the few months he had been away[218].

> We are off to the trenches to-morrow (Sunday). I am sorry to leave my nice comfortable billet in a cottage 5 mis. [sic] behind the firing line. There is not nearly as much firing going on and the times are not nearly as hard as they were on the Aisne and in Belgium in Sept. and Oct. We have many more guns and troops and now get relieved more frequently. There are only 7 of us officers out here now with the Regt. the day I left before, October 23rd. Only 3 have been thro' the whole show. The water has gone down 6ft but the country is very wet. You will be pleased to hear all the horses that I see belonging to our troops out here look very well. All have long shaggy coats. I will send you a German souvenir for the museum directly. I can pluck a small one. I hope you received the small

[218] Letter from Humfrey to Betty Dawes February 12th 1915. Mrs Dawes was her mother.

> buttons all right which I sent you from Southampton. I wear the equipment of a Tommy now, to be less conspicuous, no sword or belt. Tell Mrs Dawes I have her glasses safe. They are splendid for distinguishing German and our aeroplanes.

Between February 14th and 21st, the 52nd returned for a further eight days, in the now familiar trenches, in front of Le Plantin, taking the place of the 2nd R. Inniskilling Fusiliers. It was to be a very quiet period with little enemy activity. Small strong points or redoubts were built into the front line breastworks, at night, and larger, self-contained ones were placed in the breastworks of the second line just in front of the village. Guy Blewitt explained the makeup of the breastworks: 'the breastworks which we were making now consisted of bullet proof sand bag work of about 30 yards in length connected to one another by hurdles which afforded partial cover from view'. He even braved going round the breastworks in daylight without being shot at.

Geoffrey Titherington described a minor action during this period[219].

> With the aid of Dryden's really excellent little glass I spotted 3 Gs coming along to their breastworks in front of us yesterday about 4 p.m. They'd come out a lot too early, for it was still light. I think we sent one to Kingdom come from the way he fell and we certainly frightened his pals for they leapt into the trench along whose side they were walking. They made a huge splash so I hope they enjoyed the remainder of the night out under the stars. I fear they may have been chilly. It was nemesis for they'd slain a Highlander on the road I mentioned the night before.

Casualties during this tour of the trenches were light, with two men killed and three more wounded. Second-Lieutenants Cyril 'Shiny' Horley and J.B. Solomon joined the Regiment on the 17th and the following day another Second-Lieutenant W.J. Eighteen arrived. Yet another Second-Lieutenant, Leslie Johnston, with the twelfth reinforcement of one serjeant and 29 others, strengthened the Regiment on the 21st. The 29-year-old Johnston joined from the 3rd Battalion, and had had a brilliant university career, at Magdalen College, Oxford, where he was tutor to the Prince of Wales[220]. The young Prince would occasionally visit the Regiment to see his old tutor. For a while the Prince of Wales was attached to Lieutenant-General Charles Monro's I Corps and, from

---

219 Letter written to his parents on February 16th 1915.

220 Later briefly Edward VIII.

time to time, he headed towards the front line. On one occasion Monro chased after him in his car. "I heard what you said, Prince," said Sir Charles, "Here is that damned old general after me again". "Jump into the car or you will spoil my appetite for breakfast". Laughingly the Prince did so.

Lieutenant Douglas Humfrey wrote another letter to his young friend Betty Dawes[221].

> I came in late last night when it was dark enough to change over from my 24 hours turn in the trenches. Now till 10.30 tonight I am resting in a cottage a little way behind, then I go down with my 56 men to fill sandbags and improve the breastworks, come in at 2 a.m. and the next night do another 24 hours in the line of breastworks. The mud is indescribable. Just those 24 hours is misery but they go by alright and leave me none the worse. It's heavenly to come back and have a good snooze in a battered old cottage on a bundle of straw. Another officer has just treated me to a nice mid-morning lunch – a hunk of cake and a tiddly of cherry brandy his mama had sent him. The Germans in their trenches are very near – we keep their heads down. One sergeant was sniped through the head for putting his head too high for 3 secs. We had to bury him in an orchard but always leave if possible a cross with his name etc on, on the grave. We have no parsons with us. It's a pity I was not qualified before the war to fulfill [sic] the two posts, wasn't it?[222]
>
> We are all eager to capture Iron Crosses. One of our Captains is the only one who has secured one and the man who wore it thoroughly deserved it. He held his post to the last very bravely. He was wearing two pairs of trousers and had the cross for safety in a pocket of the inner pair.
>
> We now have mules for our maxim guns[223]. They are awfully naughty beasts. They love chewing blankets.

---

221 Letter written on February 19th 1915.

222 Humfrey's late father had been a clergyman, and Douglas himself, intended to become ordained, when the family living became vacant. Five generations of the Humfrey's family were rectors of Thorpe Mandeville, Northamptonshire, for 157 years, between 1727-1902, with one gap of nineteen years. A 1,000 year old yew tree, which must have been familiar to Douglas can still be seen in the churchyard. The Bishop of Khartoum often came up at night to take burial services for the 52nd.

223 Machine-gun used by most of the belligerents in World War I. In 1912, the British replaced it with the Vickers, a modification of the Maxim.

> My old servant has been killed I have a capital new one who is splendid looking after my "health". He runs up a cup of cocoa or soup at most unexpected moments. He can get a small fire going and water boiling in a few minutes. When out all night I oil my feet to keep out the cold and wear three pairs of socks under my big Russian top boots[224].

On the 22nd, the Regiment was relieved by the 2nd R. Inniskilling Fusiliers, and marched to Les Choquaux, about a mile from Essars. They had lost two men killed and three more wounded during their time in the trenches. On the same day news came that Lieutenant-Colonel Henry Davies had been appointed to command the 3rd Brigade. The following day, Davies left his Regiment for the last time, after more than 30 years service, to take up his new command, the 3rd Brigade. Technically, he remained commanding the 52nd, until September 17th 1915, when he had completed his four-year tenure. In practice his regimental days were over. The 52nd were indeed fortunate to have been taken to war by such a man. Every inch the light infantryman, Davies' inspirational, yet calm, and undemonstrative leadership, had carried the 52nd through those traumatic and vital first months of the war. His country and his regiment were in his debt.

Davies wrote his final regimental order.

> Colonel H.R. Davies, on giving up his command, wishes to again thank all ranks for the splendid manner in which they have maintained the good name of the Regiment during this war. He is quite confident that they will continue to fight with the same courage and coolness that they have already shewn, and to remember always the great traditions of the 52nd and of the Light Division, which is the duty of all of us to keep up.

In addition to sending this order out for publication, Henry Davies wrote a more personal letter to the Adjutant, Richard Crosse. The two men had always got on well, and Davies was very much the role model for Crosse, and Crosse very much the protégé of Davies.

> I feel so very sorry that our time of working together has come to an end. I can't tell you how much I think of the extraordinarily good work you have done as adjutant both at Aldershot and in the war.

[224] Humfrey had been tutor to Prince Vladimir Galitzen, in St. Petersburg, from 1912-13. Vladimir's father had been Master of the Czar's Horse. No doubt he brought the boots home with him.

> You have done so much to keep the regiment together in bad times always by being so cheerful yourself. I know there is no one more devoted to the regiment than you are and you have done great service to the regiment by being adjutant in this war. I indeed have been lucky in having you as adjutant. It has made commanding easy.
> When you have time will you write to me occasionally. I shall always be glad of the smallest piece of news about the regiment. I shall come and see you sometimes if I ever have the chance.
> It is indeed a sad day when one has to leave, but of course it has to come sooner or later. It is always something to look back on for the rest of my life that I have had the great honour to have commanded the 52nd. When the war is over we shall hope to see you often. My wife has as much admiration for you as I have.

Richard Crosse cherished this letter for the rest of his days. There is no doubt that Crosse was an outstanding adjutant, and in the fullness of time would become a truly great commanding officer of the Regiment. Major Archibald Eden took over command of the 52nd, and became a temporary, and then Brevet Lieutenant-Colonel. Lieutenant-Colonel C.H. Cobb, formerly of the 43rd, and now commanding the 5th [Service] Battalion, joined the Regiment, on a short attachment, that same day.

Geoffrey Titherington commented on Davies' promotion and Eden's succession to the command. As the Commanding Officer, Henry Davies was universally respected and, indeed, admired by the Regiment[225].

> I am sorry to say we've lost the Colonel. He's gone to 3rd Brigade I can't say how sorry we all are to lose him. In every way he was ideal and everyone has the most complete confidence in him and besides that absolutely devoted to him. Of course we are glad he's a brigadier and I think after him Eden who now has the regiment is the best man for the job.

On February 25th, the 52nd marched from Les Choquaux, the two and a quarter miles, to Béthune under their new commanding officer, Archibald Eden. The men were billeted in the empty Ecole de Jeunes Filles, which consisted of a large building on three sides of a square. Like so many of the other buildings that the 52nd used as billets, the school was destroyed in the German bombardment of

[225] Undated letter written to his parents at this time.

1918[226]. The officers were accommodated in the surrounding private houses. The school dining-hall became the mess, and there was an excellent kitchen, allowing a life of relative luxury after the misery of the open air, and the breastworks at Le Plantin. Eden and his new second-in-command, George Colvile, still wearing a uniform of the Sherwood Foresters, were staying in a house on the main boulevard. Their host was a keen fisherman, and the house was festooned with stuffed fish in display cases, and the paraphernalia of fishing. His wife provided chocolate and excellent rolls.

The 52nd was based in Béthune until the end of the month. The three days were a pleasant rest after their exertions, although a certain amount of drill and route marching was carried out. Good baths in the girls' school allowed all ranks to have a welcome bath and to generally clean up during these three days[227]. On the 27th, the 52nd attended an entertaining concert, put on at the instigation of the 5th Brigade, in the nearby Town Theatre. The prospective Liberal Member of Parliament, Lieutenant Jack Warner of the 52nd and Ralph Blewitt, the younger brother of Guy, surpassed themselves in excellent costumes, as Mordkin and Pavlova[228], bringing the house of 1,500 officers and men down. On the final day of the month, the 52nd marched the two miles, east-south-east, to new billets, in nearby Beuvry. They had now moved into brigade reserve. Beuvry was to become very familiar to the 52nd, over the next few months, as they were frequently billeted there. During one of these visits, the Prince of Wales walked into the orderly room in Beuvry school house and asked an astonished Richard Crosse to conduct him to the officers' mess. The little Prince had come to visit his former Oxford tutor Leslie Johnston. Today, the 52nd would recognize the central square, and the roads in the vicinity of the church, as they have changed little over the last 95 or so years.

From March 1st-3rd, the 52nd remained in their billets in Beuvry, with either drill practice or a route march each day. On the 2nd, the whole Regiment again had baths in Béthune, and 'all' their blankets were washed. In the *Battalion War Diary*, written up each day, by the Adjutant, Richard Crosse, the word 'all' has been underlined, and it is likely that an attempt was being made to get rid of

---

226 The ancient town of Béthune was almost razed to the ground, by the German bombardment, of April 13th-18th 1918. Major Guy Blewitt's diary entry for July 27th 1918: 'and went for a joy ride in an aeroplane with Pau 16th Squadron in the evening. We went and saw Bethune [sic], Beuvry, Hinges etc. Poor old Bethune [sic] a heap of ruins it makes one very sad when one thinks of the happy times we had there in 1915, now the place and most of the fellows are gone!'

227 The girls had been evacuated!

228 Renowned Russian ballet dancers. Anna Pavlova [1881-1931] and Mikhail Mordkin [1880-1944]. Guy Blewitt's diary entries for February 26th/27th 1915 do not record which man played the part of the ballerina!

parasitic lice. The 52nd had had an infestation of lice while at Ypres, the previous autumn, and no doubt, as with all other armies of the period, they were suffering again. On the 3rd, Archibald Eden and George Colvile rode over to Vermelles, to the south of the La Bassée canal, to look closely at the area. In November 1914, there had been heavy fighting here, until the French drove the Germans out. The line at Vermelles was still occupied by the French, although a few months later in 1915, the 52nd themselves would be in the trenches there. The dividing line between the French and British, at this time, was the Béthune to La Bassée road, just south of the canal, and the following day Eden and his men were to occupy the right sector of the Cuinchy trenches close to the road. The same day the thirteenth reinforcement of fifteen men arrived.

Private Jack Mawer, and his officer, Jack Warner, found a particularly good billet in Beuvry. Mawer described it[229].

> I am pleased to say I am going on first rate. I didn't think the lady would send you a PC from France. She is the person where my officer and I stop. Her and her husband treated me first rate. The very best place we have ever stopped at since I have been out here. I used to help her wash up and light her fire in the morning and generally potter about send her a nice card and also if you can manage a piece of china with the Oxford crest on.

The following day, March 2nd, Second-Lieutenant Leslie Johnston, wrote to his mother, commenting on the contents of the men's letters that he had to censor. It is unlikely that he read Jack Mawer's letter as they were in different companies. Having recently arrived in the trenches, Johnston was a little taken aback by the heartiness and the sense of humour of his fellow officers. However, it was clear that some of them were feeling the strain.

> 1. The apparent carelessness and cursing jests of the men with the very emotional character of their epistles, which we have to read (Neville Talbot had not done that[230]). I fancy they do lay it on a bit thick writing home, *pour encourager les autres,* etc but it does correspond to a very real strain of sentimentality in their make-up, which the other is partly assumed to disguise.

[229] Letter to his wife written on March 1st 1915.

[230] Rev. Neville Talbot, who became Bishop of Pretoria, in 1920. In 1911, he had criticized the Theological College, at Cuddeston, where Leslie's father had been the Principal.

2. The complete comfort a short way behind the firing-line and its opposite in the trenches – a great difference one gathers, from South Africa.
3. The childish heartiness of officers and the scenes they have been through – the more they've seen, the less they seem to care. E.g. going up to the breastworks the other day, a partially buried corpse stretched up a more or less skeleton hand, which was seized and warmly shaken with 'Well, and how are you, old boy?' – not assumed, but quite natural humour, however grim it may seem to us new hands. On the other hand there are a few fellows whose nerves are quite obviously shaken and who yet were the boldest of the bold a month or two ago, and men have aged perceptibly, even in white hairs. I fancy a steady healthy life turns up trumps here, as the rackety have mostly disappeared already.

During the afternoon of March 4th, the 52nd took over trenches at Cuinchy from the 2nd R. Inniskilling Fusiliers. This was a much more active part of the line, than the scene of their previous activities around Richebourg l'Avoué and Le Plantin. On their right were the French, south of the Béthune to La Bassée road, and to their left the 2nd H.L.I. All four companies were in the trenches, two in the front line and two in close support nearby. Eden's Headquarters were in the cellar of the most prominent house in the area, half a mile behind the front line trenches. It was called Kingsclere, but known to the 52nd as the Dovecote, as it had a pigeon loft. The trenches that the 52nd were now occupying were those taken by the 4th Brigade [Guards], on February 6th, while the 52nd provided support, in the form of rapid machine-gun and rifle fire from north of the canal. The ground at Cuinchy allowed trenches to be dug, unlike the waterlogged area in front of Le Plantin, where breastworks, above the ground, had to suffice. Eden considered that the Guards had done an excellent job in clearing up the area and improving the trenches they were now occupying, which were old German ones. Captain Guy Blewitt, commanding D Company, described the lay-out in his diary[231].

> Our trenches, old German ones, have communication trenches leading to the present German trenches. They are doubly barricaded, and we have posts behind our barricades about 40 yards down them. The Germans are about 20 yards off, behind their barricade. Our main trench is about 70 yards from the Germans in some parts. A lot

[231] Diary entry for March 5th 1915.

of sniping goes on. We have every other man on sentry, and two officers on duty at night.

The next day, the 6th, Guy Blewitt and his company moved from the front line into the support trenches, and his snipers accounted for two of the enemy. As the French, south of the La Bassée road, were attacking, the 52nd attracted a certain amount of artillery fire. That evening Blewitt went down a number of mines, one of which was 25 yards long with a T, to listen for evidence of enemy mining operations. The British miners had only been in France for a week. The ground at Cuinchy was suitable for mining operations, unlike the 52nd's former haunts at Le Plantin. Blewitt spent his nights in the 'Guards Club' dug-out accompanied by George 'the Colonel' Tolson[232] and Robert Bull. Tolson was lucky enough to have the top birth, while Blewitt and Robert Bull made do with the floor. The other part of the dug-out had a table and chairs, which they used for eating and games of bridge. Young Bull sang loudly to add to the entertainment.

Archibald Eden has recorded that for the first time, the trenches had been named after well-known streets and roads in England. The practice of naming trenches in this way would become widespread as the war progressed [see map on page 237]. Hence, the main routes into and out of the Cuinchy trenches were Old Kent Road and Coldstream Lane. Other important trenches were Oxford Street, Praed Street and Regent Street. The road running through nearby Cambrin village was Harley Street. Any native Londoners amongst the British troops would have felt quite at home. Although rain made the trenches muddy, unlike those north of the La Bassée Canal, they dried quickly.

Geoffrey Titherington recorded his first impressions of the trenches at Cuinchy[233].

The brickstacks are not attractive – the place is an absolute cemetery but the trenching is rather wonderful nearly 1½ miles underground before it reaches the firing line and a regular maze too all nicely brick-paved and very deep 8-10 feet. There are many souvenirs lying about – the most interesting we found were G cartridges loaded with a bullet butt forward – this makes them turn over and act like a small shell tho' of course their range is short – one man was hit (and

---

[232] Guy Blewitt's diary entry for March 7th 1915. 'Tolson, now known as "the Colonel" (a name given him by "the Nursery" (Robert Bull and Jasper Wyld) because he has rheumatism and a liver in the morning) ----'. Clearly a relaxed atmosphere pertained amongst the D Company officers.

[233] Letter to his parents written on March 10th 1915.

> was not a very pretty sight) almost certainly by one of these things. If ever we catch a Hun carrying such ammunition he will be most abruptly prevented from doing such a thing again. I found 13 – I sent mine all to Brigade for the General's inspection. Such things seem so objectless don't they? But the Gs are such swine.

The Germans were very vigilant in the area and a great deal of sniping took place. Until they got used to it, the 52nd found the noise of bullets ricocheting off Cuinchy brickstacks disconcerting. To the east of the village of Cuinchy, was the site of a former brickworks, with piles of bricks still in place. The solid, sturdy stacks of bricks stood up to eighteen feet in height and covered about 35 square feet. They were remarkably resistant to artillery fire. This heavily fought over area was the infamous Cuinchy brickstacks. Today, an abandoned Electricity Generating Station occupies the site, and there is no evidence of the brickworks.

During this brief tour of the trenches the 52nd lost one man killed and eight wounded. Unfortunately, they lost the use of two of their machine-guns from the attention of a German 77 mm. field gun or 'whizz-bang'. The British soldier called them 'whizz-bangs' because their velocity was greater than the speed of sound, so that the unfortunate person underneath one, heard the whizz of the shell before the bang of the gun, and consequently had no chance to take cover. The shell was reputed to burst with 500 splinters. On their final day in the trenches, March 8th, Guy Blewitt and Robert Bull paid a further visit to the French, on their right, before the 2nd R. Inniskilling Fusiliers relieved the 52nd, and they retired to billets in Beuvry.

From March 9th-11th, the 52nd were in brigade reserve. This period of time corresponded with the start of the Battle of Neuve Chapelle, on March 10th, in which the 52nd played no part in the actual fighting. Sir John French intended the First Army, of Sir Douglas Haig, to attack and take the village of Neuve Chapelle, before pushing on to capture the village of Aubers, a mile to the east. In the event of success, the First Army might move on and press the defences of Lille. Forty thousand men attacked, at 7.30 a.m., on March 10th, after a short artillery barrage of 30 minutes duration. It has been said that more shells were fired by the 342 guns, in this 30 minutes, than in the whole of the Boer War. Initially the British and Indian troops were successful in taking Neuve Chapelle, but were unable to progress to Aubers. Lack of heavy artillery ammunition and ready availability of reserves and a failure to follow up the initial success had led to only a very limited gain. Crown Prince Rupprecht's Sixth Army counter-attacked on March 12th, but the British managed to cling on to their gains. The

British called off their attack on March 13th. The experience of Neuve Chapelle was to become a reoccurring theme throughout much of the First World War: the Allies broke into the German line, but were unable to break out from it into open country. The failure at Neuve Chapelle led to Earl Kitchener, the War Minister, confiding in the Prime Minister, Herbert Asquith, that Sir John French was not up to the job of commanding the B.E.F.

The 2nd Division played a part in the Battle of Neuve Chapelle with their "holding attack" on Givenchy, on March the 10th. Their 6th Brigade put in a vigorous attack on the enemy, just to the north of the La Bassée Canal. Although it achieved nothing in the way of capture of ground, it did hold German reserve troops, from going the few miles to the north, to reinforce their fellow countrymen, at Neuve Chapelle. While these dramatic events were taking place, the 52nd were on stand-by, to move at short notice to support the 6th Brigade, at Givenchy. This interfered with their period of rest, but at least they were allowed to sleep in their billets at night.

Despite being on stand-by, the 52nd used the first day out of the line to clean themselves and their equipment. The Headquarters Company dealt with back correspondence and wrote up the *Battalion War Diary*. Drill was carried out close to their billets. Private Jack Mawer wrote a further letter to his wife, Midge, from his billet in Beuvry[234].

> Well I am pleased to say that I am in a perfect state of health. We have just returned from the trenches once again safe and sound. We have had one or two wounded again. I have not complained about suffering with the cold, but, this turn of trenches. We all suffered a terrible lot. My poor old feet got cold the first night and kept cold of four days I could not get them warm and to make matters worse no sleep and what with the rain and one thing and another it was a very miserable time. I shall be pleased to get a parcel from you but the one thing I want you to send is some fags. I have run right out of them I had to go round my chums and get them to get me some, fags are begin [sic] to get short amongst us. I don't suppose you can picture me. Just you go and dig a trench about 2 ft 6 inches wide and 6 ft deep in the garden and stand in that all day and night long and then you will be able to picture me. We manage to burrow ourselves under a little so as to lie down, but musn't burrow to [sic] much or else if you do the earth keeps falling on top of you.

---

[234] Letter written on March 9th 1915.

Douglas Humfrey wrote another letter to his young friend Betty Dawes[235].

> I found your parcel after 4 awful days in the most important trenches we've ever been in. I took the cherry brandy round to the officers mess last night. It would make your head swell if I told you the nice things they said about you. Cherry Brandy is one of those things you hear about but very seldom see.
> We walking masses of mud when we marched back from the trenches. I have not time for a long letter. We are under orders to move on any moment. A huge battle is going on to the left. The whole line hopes to get on now. The noise of artillery at the present moment is terrific. "Mother" is using awful language. This a 9.2.
> I may be in a Deutcher trench before nightfall. The fight started at 7.30 a.m. this morning[236].

On March 11th, Guy Blewitt and some of his fellow officers got their horses into a nearby field where jumps were put up and all went through their paces. Even the poor old mess-cart horse performed in blinkers, and without its saddle. The other officers involved were George Colvile, Jasper Wyld, Reggie Rendel, Francis 'Jimmie' Riddle, and Stephen Hammick.

On March 12th, the 52nd returned to the trenches at Cuinchy, carrying out their customary swop with the 2nd R. Inniskilling Fusiliers. The German trenches were 100-200 yards away on their right side, but only 60-120 yards on the left. Guy Blewitt took Private Ayres to make a reconnaissance of the right communication trench leading directly to the enemy's line. These two intrepid men climbed out of the trench to get around the barricade, before climbing in once more on the enemy's side, hoping to catch a German. The German barricade was only about 25 yards from their trench, and some 15-20 yards from our own block. Blewitt and Ayres were unsuccessful. The following day the irrepressible Private Ayres accompanied on this occasion by Private Hayes, returned to the enemy's side of the barrier, and sat there to await the German snipers. This took great courage in view of the close proximity of the enemy. No one came and it was thought that snipers were not using that section of the trench.

During their four-day stint in the trenches at Cuinchy, the 52nd were shelled in an irregular manner, and the German snipers were not only active, but very accurate with their shooting. Their activities were particularly brisk after dark. Private Holmes was hit in the wrist, Serjeant Chandler in the face, and

---

[235] Letter written on March 10th 1915, the first day of the Battle of Neuve Chapelle.

[236] The Battle of Neuve Chapelle.

Private Haymer in the hand. By day, many trench periscopes were destroyed by the enemy snipers. The German shooting was so accurate they quickly hit the lids of cigarette boxes when they were put up in lieu of periscopes. On March 15th, Second-Lieutenant Lionel Dashwood, formerly a Royal Engineers' Motor-Cyclist Corporal, reported for duty. That evening the officers of D Company 'had a great dinner, liqueurs, chrystalized [sic] fruit and band. Cpl Emmett and three men of Jasper's platoon on mouth organs'[237]. The casualties sustained in this tour of the trenches were two killed and twelve wounded.

On March 16th, the 52nd once more left their Cuinchy trenches on relief by the 2nd R. Inniskilling Fusiliers: 'which openly expressed its intention of "giving 'em 'ell" tomorrow night by way of celebration of the 17th' [St. Patrick's Day][238]. The Regiment marched to the strains of their mouth-organ band: the passing French were suitably moved by a rendition of the La Marseillaise and a Scottish Regiment was greeted with Lochiel. Their rest period at Beuvry continued until the 20th, when they once more exchanged positions with the R. Inniskilling Fusiliers. Unlike their last rest period this proved to be a quiet one. Private Jack Mawer sent a parcel home to his wife[239]. Soldiers frequently sent home the souvenirs of war.

> Well hope this parcel of souvenirs will reach you safe. The silver cup is for Master Roy[240]. My officer[241] gave it to me. The Jack knife is for Syd[242] when he is a boy Scout. It is what was issued out to me. The piece of iron are what the German(s) send over us inside shells one piece nearly killed me it fell just the side of my head.

On the 18th, Captain and Quartermaster A.S. Field retired on the grounds of ill-health [bronchitis] and he was replaced, the next day, by Serjeant-Major Arthur Warnock who became an honorary Lieutenant. The Quartermaster was responsible for seeing that rations were brought up to the trenches, when the Regiment was in the line. Each morning, the Quartermaster would take his small convoy of horse-drawn carts, from Beuvry to the refilling depot in the Marché des Chevaux in Béthune. From there the rations would be carried to Harley Street,

---

[237] Guy Blewitt's diary entry for March 15th 1915. Jasper 'Tiger' Wyld.
[238] Geoffrey Titherington's letter to his parents written on March 16th 1915.
[239] March 19th 1915.
[240] Son.
[241] Lieutenant Jack Warner. Mawer and Warner got on well together and would talk for hours. The following month Mawer was admitted to hospital with influenza, but his main concern was to get back to his officer in case he was replaced.
[242] Elder son.

the road running north to south through Cambrin village. Here the individual companies took over responsibility for their own rations. As the 5th was relieved by the 6th Brigade on the 21st, the 52nd spent a brief 24 hours in the trenches at Cuinchy before the 1st King's Royal Rifle Corps [K.R.R.C.] relieved them. They marched back to familiar billets in the Ecole de Jeunes Filles[243] in Béthune. One man was wounded that day.

On March 22nd, the 52nd returned to their former trenches in the Festubert-Le Plantin sector, replacing the 2nd K.R.R.C. of the 2nd Brigade. Since their previous tour, the breastworks had been converted into a continuous line. As before, two companies were put in the front line, one in support in the village and the final company in reserve. Much patrolling was required. The following day, three further officers joined them: Second-Lieutenants William Barnard, Ralph Kite and Hugh Pendavis. Barnard and Kite were new to the Regiment, but Pendavis had won a D.S.O., in the autumn fighting in Ypres. The young men had come up from the base camp at Harfleur, near Le Havre, by train. Perhaps the primitive conditions of the base camp prepared them for the rigours of the trenches. At Harfleur, the camp consisted of one tin hut for a mess, a canvas hut in which to sleep and the rest of the place was a muddy swamp. The canvas hut kept out the rain but was very cold to sleep in at night. The new officers were warmly welcomed by the Germans with shelling of the breastworks.

March 24th saw the return of Lieutenant Cuthbert 'Bingo' Baines, one of the great heroes of the action in Nonne Bosschen Wood, the previous November. He had recovered from his arm wound and had been waiting patiently for a recall to the Regiment, at Harfleur. The other great hero of Nonne Bosschen, Harry Dillon, was also still at the base camp at Harfleur. Dillon was still not himself; 'it is a wretched existence. – I hate the place and have one of the worst colds I ever had and rheumatism ever since I have been here…'. Dillon was still not fit enough for a return to the Regiment. The next day 'Bingo' Baines was joined by Lieutenant Charles Fowke and Second-Lieutenant Douglas Sewell as further officer replacements. Although there was some shelling during their six days in the trenches, it was not very heavy. Water was found at a depth of six inches making the digging of trenches impossible. At night working parties lengthened and put new arms on the breastworks. Two platoons of the 17th London Regiment, Territorial Force, joined the 52nd for 24 hours of instruction of trench duties. During this tour of the trenches, the 52nd had two men killed and eight wounded. Amongst the wounded was Second-Lieutenant Cyril 'Shiny' Horley who had a gunshot wound of his heel.

---

243 Archibald Eden's diary, as quoted in the *Regimental Chronicles* stated that the billets were in Beuvry. The *Battalion War Diary* has been followed above.

Geoffrey Titherington has recorded: comments on the Territorial Force [Terriers], some illuminating words on the foibles of the men of the 52nd in the line at Festubert and a serious practical 'joke' on a German sniper[244].

> I was in v. uncomfortable trenches on the anniversary of the Boat Race[245] we spent the night "gingering up" the Deutscher working party. I think with some success for they shelled us all next day with 4.2″ shells. However about £200 worth of shell only bagged about 5/- worth of sandbags and no men so we got the best of the exchange. We had a lot of Terriers attached that time and they had a most instructive day – I think. They didn't like the shells much at first but the attitude of our funny old boys soon reassured them. They are getting very war hardened. I wish you cd: see them going to trenches – all laden with fuel. They cook all day and when they can temporarily hold no more they stew tea and wash it down. If a pal's hit they leave the meal in preparation and go and do what they can for him and bear no ill-will if the bacon's spoilt but if its bagged while their backs were turned there's the devil to pay. Its not considered good form to get killed over your friends' meal tho' you may splash his person with your blood and he'll bear you no ill-will. They get dreadfully shirty if a shell comes close enough to splash mud into the tea. They really are a comic lot. We put up rather a good gag for a sniper a day or 2 ago. He was very close but no one could find him and he kept hitting our periscopes which are little mirrors 3″ by 1″ on sticks. So I had a biscuit tin cut into pieces of the same size and mounted on sticks. We put all up together 45 in number. The sniper put holes in 5 and then chucked it in absolute disgust and we lost no more periscopes.

The 52nd came out of the Festubert trenches, on March 28th, on relief by their old friends the 2nd R. Inniskilling Fusiliers, and went into billets at Gorre, just behind the line. They would remain here until April 5th. It was to be a period of company training, with route-marching, musketry, bomb-throwing and negotiating obstacles across country. During this period, Captain Claude Chichester left the 52nd for duties at base, and Lieutenant Douglas Humfrey went

---

[244] Letter to his father written on March 30th 1915.

[245] On March 28th 1914, Cambridge won the Boat Race by four and a half lengths. It was their first victory after five successive defeats. Geoffrey Titherington rowed at No. 7 in the Oxford boat. Forty two rowing blues would lose their lives in the First World War.

on a course of instruction for the trench mortar, at St. Venant. On returning to the Regiment, Humfrey recorded that he hoped 'he would soon have a battery to command and how much they hated serving in the trenches'. While they were at Gorre one man on a working party was injured, and further reinforcements joined them. On April 1st, the fifteenth reinforcement of 26 men and, on the 4th, the sixteenth reinforcement of 30 men arrived. Second-Lieutenant Leslie Johnston, feeling in need of some solitude, spent Good Friday, the 2nd, on a long walk to the nearest wooded heights[246], and found himself amongst the French Reserves behind Notre Dame de Lorette. Here he watched their guns in action, before returning home again chastened but cheerful.

During this period, in Brigade reserve, at Gorre, Leslie Johnston wrote again to his mother[247]. He described his first experience of being under fire, the behaviour of the men, and his efforts to discover which German units were facing them.

> We were relieved on Saturday night by another Company and went back into Reserve half a mile back, but I had to take a working party up that night at 12, to make breastworks in front of our line – it was my first experience of being under fire in the open and was odd – a clear night with a moon and few clouds, men with rifles and bandoliers shovelling for dear life to fill up a double line of hurdles, knowing that they're getting more cover each spadeful. No sound but grunts, and low commands from me. I found one really didn't mind a bit and had rather a laughing pity for the men who did. As a matter of fact, we didn't get many shots, as the Deutchers[248] had a party out too and were afraid of stirring us up, and we lost no one. It's odd how men seem to rely on you in that sort of case – I found that as long as I strolled about upright, with my hands in my pockets, they worked all right, but if I started working they got jumpy. It's not healthy, but has to be done, and is good in a way, as it gets the men used to war out of cover. The effect of rifle fire is curious – when shots come over, you only hear them when they're no longer dangerous and the tendency is to laugh and then duck.

---

[246] Johnston wrote in a letter: 'and walked some twenty or thirty miles to the nearest hills, ---'. He must have meant a round trip of 20 or 30 miles. The distance as the crow flies between Gorre and Notre Dame de Lorette is no more than ten miles. It is most unlikely that Johnston could have walked 40-60 miles in a day.

[247] Letter written on March 30th 1915.

[248] Known to the men as 'Dodgers'.

Jack Ward. Killed at the head of his men charging the enemy in the woods near Ypres on November 6th 1914. [Regimental Chronicles]

Shrewsbury Forest. Here the 52nd were heavily engaged with the enemy from October 31st-November 1st 1914. [Author's Collection 2008]

Francis Pepys D.S.O. Killed in action in the woods near Ypres on November 12th 1914. [Regimental Chronicles]

The war medals of Thomas Hudson D.C.M. He was prominent in Nonne Bosschen Wood on November 11th 1914. [Townsend Collection]

Bishop Llewellyn Gwynne of Khartoum as the Deputy Chaplain-General. Looked upon by the 52nd as their chaplain. [Society for the Propagation of the Christian Gospel]

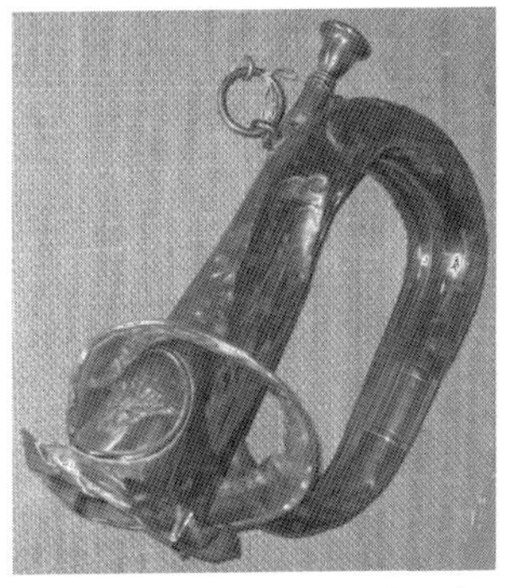

German bugle taken by the 52nd on November 11th 1914 in Nonne Bosschen Wood. [Royal Green Jackets Museum]

The ground covered by the 52nd on November 11th 1914 with Nonne Bosschen Wood in the distance.
[Author's Collection 2008]

Cuthbert 'Bingo' Baines D.S.O., hero of Nonne Bosschen Wood on November 11th 1914.
[Colvill Collection]

Harry Dillon's memorial window in All Saints Church, Spelsbury Oxfordshire.
[Author's Collection 2011]

Harry 'Rabbit' Dillon D.S.O., hero of Nonne Bosschen Wood on November 11th 1914. Died in early 1918 of natural causes.
[Regimental Archives]

A waterlogged shell crater at Le Plantin.
[Imperial War Museum Q50316]

George Field M.C. and bar at Le Plantin in 1915.
[Blewitt's Diaries]

George 'the Colonel' Tolson M.C. in 1915.
[Blewitt's Diaries]

Arthur Tylden-Pattenson unluckily shot through the head by a stray bullet on the Rue du Bois on January 5th 1915.
[Regimental Chronicles]

Robert Bull in early 1915.
[Blewitt's Diaries]

Gorre Château. On Easter Day 1915, the Bishop of Khartoum conducted a service for the 52nd in the grounds. Photograph circa 1916.
[Private Collection]

Charles Fowke's dug-out at Festubert. March 30th 1915.
[Regimental Archives]

Officers' billet at Festubert. March 25th 1915.
[Regimental Archives]

Shelling on breastworks at Festubert. April 19th 1915.
[Regimental Archives]

I had another and rather more enterprising go the next night, as the Brigade Office wanted to know who were opposite us, and our C.O., knowing I knew a little German, told me to go and talk to them, also to listen, if I could, to their working parties[249]. So I got a megaphone off the Artillery and went to the nearest place to their lines – 100 yards or so – and called them up, 'Hoch, meine Herren, guten Abend. Sind Sie da? Es thut mir Leid dass Sie sind alle gestorben, etc'[250]. – till they answered. And then we chatted, calling each other 'Kameraden'. I told them some lies about us and tried to get the name of their corps; but they wouldn't tell me, though they agreed that 'Saxonen' were 'gute Menshen,'[251] but would not agree that the Prussians were not. However, I heard the soft *ch* quite distinctly, and deduced that they were Saxons or Bavarians with a Prussian officer[252] (as my brother told me he's heard at the Christmas truce[253]). After that came the listening – they didn't fire at all when I was talking to them and were altogether most friendly, but one couldn't expect that, if one stalked them. I hoped they'd have a working party out, and left our breastworks with a scout to find them. We got fifty yards or so, though the moon was very bright, and then lay down to look with glasses; but I think the moon must have shone on our glasses, and they opened fire – first with a machine gun and then rifles. As we lay flat in a little hollow, the shots went over and only hotted up the people in the breastworks behind. But it meant no further advance, but a very muddy and wet retreat like a serpent. They didn't open at all again with machine gun – for which I was grateful – as it's a nasty persevering instrument and requires no rest, and is not subject to deflection by human error if once trained on a spot. As we had been able to see that there were no working parties out (the night being too clear) and it seemed hopeless to get near enough their breastworks to overhear their talk, I had to come back and could not report much, but shall have another shot on a cloudy night.

---

[249] Leslie Johnston had spent the spring and early summer of 1909 studying Theology, in Marburg, Germany. It was here that he learnt to speak German.

[250] Good evening gentlemen. Are you there? I am sorry that they are all dead etc. Johnston was trying to use irony to stimulate the Germans into conversing with him.

[251] Saxons are good people.

[252] The Germans were likely to have been members of the 55th Regiment of the 13th Division. They were largely recruited from Westphalia.

[253] Hugh Johnston.

Geoffrey Titherington described further use of the megaphone: 'Leslie Johnston has made himself a megaphone and holds long conversations with the Deutschers – they swear their regiment never uses bullets butt-end foremost. L.J. promised them many rifle-grenades in exchange if ever we have reason to suspect them of it'[254]. Earlier, some of the 52nd's officers had thought the Germans were guilty of using this vile practice which led to more destructive wounds. Certainly, ammunition with the bullet reversed had been found.

Easter Day, April 4th, was celebrated by a parade service held by Llewellyn Gwynne, the Bishop of Khartoum, in Gorre Château. Guy Blewitt had a billet in the château itself but there was no glass in the room's windows. Today the red-brick entrance block with a small central tower is all that remains of the once grand château's buildings. The grass and tree-covered grounds, surrounded in the main by water, where the church parade took place on that long ago Easter Day, can still be seen and surreptitiously walked upon. Nearby, through the trees, is Gorre Cemetery where so many of the casualties of 1915 lie.

On April 5th, the 52nd returned to their old haunts at Le Plantin, replacing the 2nd R. Inniskilling Fusiliers. They would remain here until the 12th, a full week in the front line, which was made possible by the less cold weather. In fact the first night was a wet one and Captain Guy Blewitt managed to fall into a hole with his greatcoat on. It was his only previously dry piece of clothing and he was not best pleased, particularly as he was dripped on all night in his dug-out. The next day, the 6th, the 2nd Worcestershire, whose working party had been joining the Le Plantin breastworks to the trenches at Givenchy, suffered two killed and three wounded, and the 52nd had difficulty getting them away.

Despite the casualties taken by the 2nd Worcestershire, it was a relatively quiet time with little shelling. On the 8th-10th, the 19th London Regiment, Territorial Force, were intermingled with the 52nd, so that they might become familiar with front line warfare. Leslie Johnston's, impression of the Terriers, was that 'they're too young, and their officers not strict enough'. Guy Blewitt undertook a little sniping. The 52nd had the use of one rifle with telescopic and another with magnifying sights. Both were privately owned[255]. In Great Britain there was a shortage of suitable rifles with telescopic sights, as the pre-war supplier of this type of weapon had been Germany. Sportsmen in Britain were asked to donate their guns and telescopic sights to the army. On April 7th, Captain Harry 'Rabbit' Dillon, of Nonne Bosschen fame, brought up the seventeenth

[254] Letter to his father written on March 30th 1915.

[255] Second-Lieutenants Robert Bull and Ralph Kite sent home for them.

reinforcement of 30 men. The casualties for this period in the trenches were two killed and six wounded.

The following day, April 8th, Leslie Johnston wrote to his mother once more. In this letter, he described the first casualties in his platoon, and gave details of an original luminous night sight.

> Came out of the breastworks late last night after a rather horrid two days and nights – drenching rain on and off (mostly on) which turned all the floor into a quagmire and brought down a good deal of dry weather work; incessant and rather accurate sniping, though very little shelling, and clothes and boots soaked throughout – for the men worse than for ourselves. I got two men in my platoon hit – the first two I'd lost at all – which made me rather sad. One, a most capital fellow, was sniping at a German who was firing through a loophole (they never fire over) got his shot and came down under cover, thinking he'd hit his man, went up with his glasses again to see if the fellow's rifle was still there, and got it in the left hand – fortunately not serious, but what's called a 'duration of war' wound. The other was killed almost straight out: he was working, beating down sand-bags with a spade, which got above the parapet – the German sniper hit him through the top sand-bag – the bullet turning and making an awful mess of his head. It was a sad business collecting his little possessions (old pipes, some letters, etc) from his pockets, and preparing him for burial[256]. It made one realize danger more than before – I fear I had let my platoon and myself get careless, though his being hit was purely bad luck (as they say) it made me wonder at the safety one granted before – and even after, as I had to do some fixing of rifles on certain spots of the enemy trenches, 150 yards off, which necessarily meant a lot of exposure; and though I was at work on it in one place for three-quarters of an hour four times, mercifully I only got a shot or two, and those not really close. I am sure if the Germans exposed themselves as we do they'd lose an awful lot, but they don't. You now and then see the top of a hat or helmet, but always moving – they never fire but through iron plates, which it's very hard to knock out. Now, however, we've got one telescopic-sighted rifle (of German make, of course) with which you practically

[256] The man killed was either Private Thomas Horn, aged 35 years or Private Samuel Insall, age unknown. Both men were killed on April 6th 1915 and are buried in Brown's Road Military Cemetery, Festubert.

can't miss a steady shot, and have managed to get shots through most of them in time, which keeps that one quiet for a bit. The marvel is that as they've had this apparatus in plenty all the time we've ever been missed. The night, of course, is a fairly safe time, as aimed fire, except from fixed rifles, is practically impossible, though I'm getting a little done with luminous-painted sights (a dodge I don't think the Germans have, and I wonder we haven't tried before), but then we have working parties out (as I told you last time) only behind wattled hurdles, and though if you make the men keep quiet and extend them properly you may not attract attention – as we've proved by only getting one man hit so far – the other regiments, who provoke them and don't take precautions, lose rather heavily – the night before last five per cent. I don't know whether all this of one's everyday thoughts and insistent interests has any meaning for you, but I thought I'd write it, as there is nothing else to say, and you may as well realize.

Yet again the 52nd were relieved, on the 13th, by the 2nd R. Inniskilling Fusiliers, and retired into Divisional Reserve at Les Choquaux and Essars. Here they would remain in billets until April 22nd. The weather was glorious with the crops and trees coming out and swallows on the wing. Training was continued on a daily basis. Second-Lieutenant Leslie Johnston recorded; 'practised bombing and bayoneting our way along a trench – a very exciting game'. Soon it would become a reality. On the 18th, Lieutenant J.B. Solomon left to join the Royal Flying Corps as a probationary observer. That same day the 52nd's Commanding Officer, Archibald Eden, took a car with Edward Kirkpatrick and Richard Crosse, to visit the 1/4th Oxfordshire and Buckinghamshire, and the 1/1st Bucks Battalions who had only just arrived in France. Both battalions were close to Ploegsteert [Plugstreet] Wood near Ypres. During this period in billets Lieutenant Douglas Humfrey had a novel gourmet experience; 'My French is most disappointing. I asked an old woman (in French) to do me two eggs to have with my coffee the other morning. She thought I said "dans" and not "avec" and she brought a large cup of coffee with the two eggs beaten into it. However it was tres [sic] bon all the same'[257]. On the 21st, the eighteenth reinforcement of three serjeants and 57 men joined the 52nd for duty.

During this period, a successful inter-platoon football tournament was contested on brick-hard grounds. Eighteen teams entered, and up to three games at a time were played on separate grounds. Many of the games were keenly

[257] Letter to Betty Dawes postmarked April 21st 1915.

contested with one game having to be played no less than three times in order to get a result. The recent influx of officers allowed many of the subalterns to play for their platoons. In the final, No. 12 platoon beat No. 3 by an only goal. Undoubtedly the tournament was good for morale, although one officer thought that a bayonet charge would be safer. The officers entertained themselves with polo and poker. Geoffrey Titherington used his company pack horse as a polo pony: 'he refuses to get excited or be dictated to but barges after the ball in a most sedate way'[258]. Titherington told an amusing anecdote about two men from the Territorial Force[259].

> We suffer much from the callow Terrier at present. It was too funny the other day to see a Regular old skin catching up 2 Ts creeping along a road. It is a place which is sniped a bit. My old man had about ½ a house on his back (to boil tea with) and a pipe in his mouth and told the 2 cautious gents it was all right because they hit a bloke here last night and now it will be 3 weeks before they hit another "'cos just here they never get more than 1 every 3 weeks."

On the afternoon of April 23rd, the 52nd replaced the 17th London in the trenches near Festubert. The next 24 hours were quiet, with no casualties, before the 52nd were relieved by the 19th London and marched to poor billets in the Rue d'Aire quarter of Béthune[260]. Between April 25th and 30th, the whole of the 5th Brigade was out of the line in the environs of Béthune. The nineteenth replacement of two serjeants and 43 men arrived on the 27th. Company training was carried out in an area between Béthune and Beuvry. Guy Blewitt recorded in his diary: 'the mess is quite good now, a nice room, French chef, flowers on the table and champagne every night'[261]. The weather was now warmer, and although working parties were required at night, it was a relatively restful period for the Regiment. Lieutenant Charles Fowke recorded his memories of one of these working parties, which set off on the evening of April 28th.

> Last night we paraded at 5.15 p.m., and started for a seven-mile march, with Captain Hammick, of C Company, in command. He was riding, and we had a tool-cart drawn by two horses, so we were

---

[258] Letter to his mother written on April 19th 1915.
[259] Letter to his parents written on April 29th 1915.
[260] As stated in the *Regimental Chronicles.* It housed Béthune prison. However, the *Battalion War Diary* recorded the Rue d'Arras quarter.
[261] Diary entry for April 28th 1915.

> making a fair amount of noise. When we had nearly reached the place, he halted us in the road, and ordered us to issue picks and shovels, while he went on to meet an officer of the R.E.[262], who was to show him where the trench was to be dug. In two minutes he was back again, saying, "A German sniper had the cheek to have three shots at me." Meanwhile a Sapper had arrived and seemed worried. Eventually he said that troops were forbidden to use the road by which we had come up in daylight, but since we were there, we could not go back. All horses, however, must be got rid of at once. Hammick wanted to keep his horse, but, after some discussion, all the horses were sent away, and the men (150) took cover as much as possible. The Sapper asked me and five others to go with him, to see what work was to be done. Just as we stopped to look at a trench, dug correctly on the previous night, the Germans turned a machine-gun on to us, and we dived into that trench like rabbits. Two bullets whizzed between my head and the next man's, but no one was hurt. There we lay until it got darker, when the men were brought up to dig the new trench. We were shot at there, too, but not before we had got some cover, and we finished the job without any casualties. On the way back we met a field-kitchen, sent up to meet us by the Bishop of Khartoum (our Brigade Chaplain), and everyone got a cup of hot Oxo or cocoa, for which we were most grateful.

Lieutenant Douglas Humfrey in a further letter to his young friend, Betty Dawes, summed up the achievements of the 52nd in the first nine months of the war[263].

> Only a line to prove the Deutchers have not given me gas. All that business is going on round Langmark [sic][264] where I was wounded last October not far from Wypers. Now at the other end of the line that the English hold, I expect my regiment's turn for a bit of fun will come round again soon. During the whole war, it has never given a yard to the Germans tho' once we got left by the Northamptons on our left[265] and the Gordons on our right. We stuck it and came out

[262] Royal Engineers.
[263] Letter written on April 29th 1915.
[264] French colonial troops broke under the first gas attack of the war at Langemarck, on April 22nd 1915.
[265] The 52nd were still sore at the behaviour of the 1st Northamptonshire, in the woods near Zwarteleen, on November 1st 1914.

top. Not many regiments can say they never retired during the last eight months, not counting the Mons retreat.

On April 22nd, the Second Battle of Ypres had opened with the Germans releasing chlorine gas, near Langemarck, leading to a large gap developing in the allied lines[266]. This was the first substantiated use of gas in the war, although the Germans had accused the French of using it near Verdun, a week earlier. Reserves were used to stabilize the front, but the British were hard pressed and forced to reduce the length of their front line, making the salient more compact. The Gallipoli landings took place three days later, on the 25th, leading to a loss of potential manpower and particularly artillery ammunition on the Western Front.

Geoffrey Titherington commented on the use of gas: 'I think the idea of bolting men from trenches by stink-gas is good and distinctly Prussian. It is well the prevalent wind is west. It must be very annoying to be fumigated like wasps in to semi-insensibility and then bayoneted by a fat Deutscher'[267]. Titherington also had an inkling that the 52nd were shortly to be involved in a major attack: '-- we expect to be launched into a show any day now for there is a distinct liveliness at present which is rather more than local vide Daily Papers'. His instincts were correct, the Battle of Aubers Ridge would open shortly.

---

[266] Lord Cavan, commanding the 4th Brigade, had a novel way of detecting gas. On May 5th he wrote, "I am arranging for Lieutenant Daish (a University Honours in Chemistry man) to go tonight to the same place and have a good sniff and report back." No doubt Daish had a sensitive olfactory organ!

[267] Letter to his parents written on April 26th 1915.

Chapter VIII

The Battles of Aubers Ridge and Festubert.

May 1st - May 18th 1915

[Maps: pages 161, 203, inside front cover.]

On May Day 1915, it became clear to Lieutenant-Colonel Archibald Eden, commanding the 52nd Light Infantry, that further offensive operations were being planned. As early as March 24th, General Joseph Joffre, the French Commander-in-Chief, enquired of Sir John French, whether the B.E.F. would co-operate in an offensive, five to six weeks later. Joffre received an answer in the affirmative, and, on April 6th, preliminary orders went out for the French Tenth Army and the British First Army to make an important attack north of Arras, with a view to breaking the enemy's line[268]. Part of the rationale behind French's decision was that a successful offensive on Aubers Ridge would put a stop to further resources being sent to Gallipoli.

French forces were to assault Vimy Ridge and the northern foothills of the Artois plateau between Lens and La Bassée. Meanwhile the British First Army would endeavour to take the Aubers Ridge from La Bassée towards Lille. The ridge was some 20 miles long, with a flat plateau of arable land, and never rose more than 40 feet above the plain. However, it was drier than the surrounding area, making it an excellent site for observation. Once this continuous barrier had been secured, preparations could be made for an offensive into the plain of Douai. If this was successful, it might be possible to interfere with German rail and road communications, in the Noyon salient, between Arras and Reims.

The British First Army was to launch a two-pronged pincer movement on German forces to the north and south of Neuve Chapelle. This attack was to become known as the Battle of Aubers Ridge. The northern attack was to be made by the 8th Division in order to take the line Fromelles to La Cliqueterie. To the south, the 1st and Meerut Divisions would advance in an easterly direction, on a front of 2,400 yards, from Chocolate Menier Corner to Port Arthur. The 2nd Division, including the 5th Infantry Brigade and the 52nd, was to be in reserve to these two attacking divisions. Hence the 52nd could claim the Battle of Aubers Ridge amongst their battle honours[269]. One of the fatal flaws in the plan was the

---

[268] The French Tenth Army should have been involved with an offensive, in the Artois, at the time of the Battle of Neuve Chapelle, but this had had to be postponed as it had not been possible to transfer men from the Ypres sector, to give them sufficient force.

[269] On May 9th 1915, the 52nd were in the designated area: Road la Quinque Rue (exclusive) - le Touret - Lacouture - Croix Barbée: thence a line to the Bois du Biez (South-West Corner).

6,000 yards between the start points of the northern and southern attacking British divisions.

General Joseph Joffre decided that the French attacks, to the south, would have a prolonged artillery bombardment lasting several days. General Sir Douglas Haig's First Army depended on a short sharp 40 minute "hurricane bombardment". The reason for this was partly the initial success that they had had at Neuve Chapelle, and also the shortage of artillery ammunition. The inclement weather, alternating between steamy heat and heavy rain, delayed the attacks from May 6th until the 9th which was a sunny day. The British bombardment started at 5 a.m. and the troops moved forward forty minutes later. Both the northern and southern prongs of the British attack suffered huge numbers of casualties from both artillery and machine-gun and failed.

As will be seen, the 52nd was placed in reserve, to the 1st Division, behind breastworks, at Gorre. The 2nd, 3rd, and Dehra Dun Brigades pushed into no man's land, where they were cut to pieces by machine-guns placed just above ground level. Few gaps in the wire were found and here the bunching of men led to further slaughter. Some men of the 1st Northamptonshire and 2nd Royal Munster Fusiliers managed to reach the enemy's front line trench, where they were either killed or taken prisoner. The advance came to a halt and many men were stuck in no man's land unable to go forward or back. Further artillery bombardments were made in the early morning. At 8 a.m., Sir Douglas Haig, underestimating the difficulties of the attacking troops, called up his reserves. During the afternoon, a further bombardment was followed by a new attempt to take the German line by the 1st Black Watch, of the 1st Brigade, and 1st Gloucestershire and 1st South Wales Borderers, both fresh battalions of the 3rd Brigade. They failed and again suffered large number of casualties.

The Northern attack had some minor successes, in that part of the German line was captured, but had to be given up. The next day lack of artillery ammunition led to further attacks being called off[270]. The Battle of Aubers Ridge was disastrous for the British and her Empire troops. Total casualties were about 11,500 and no ground was won or tactical advantage gained. Ironically, the French, fifteen miles to the south, overran the German front line trenches and

---

[270] The failure of the Neuve Chapelle offensive had been blamed on the shortage of munitions. The shell scandal helped the Liberal Government to fall, and David Lloyd George became responsible for a newly created Ministry of Munitions. Lloyd George was so concerned with drunkenness amongst munition workers that he advocated rigorous control over the alcohol trade. There were calls for total prohibition. Finally, in July 1915, the Central Control Board was created and, in the following December, licensing hours restricted the times of sale of alcohol, which remained until recently.

pushed on to the heights of Vimy Ridge, without taking its summit. Over the next week they captured Carency and Ablain St. Nazaire.

On May 1st, Lieutenant-Colonel Archibald Eden took the 52nd from their billets in Béthune to some practice trenches about six miles away. Here they practiced getting out of the trenches and attacking from them. On the return journey they came across General Sir Douglas Haig, commanding the First Army, who complimented them on their turn out, and recalled how well they had fought in the woods, near Ypres, the previous November. On the 3rd, the 52nd moved their billets from the Rue d'Aire area of Béthune to better ones in the Tobacco Factory. The officers' quarters were also an improvement and with each company having six officers, the mess had become quite large. A new mess-cart, the third of the war, had been purchased and the officers were well-served in the culinary sense by Sergeant Ward. The mess-cart was known as the 'Cathedral'. Opposite their quarters was a sausage factory which afforded endless interest, particularly to Major George Colvile.

In an undated entry in his diary, Captain Guy Blewitt described the fascinating factory.

> The Sausage Factory opposite the mess causes us daily amusement; the most enormous old Frenchwoman [sic] with a heavy grey beard discourses on the value of the miserable cripples of horses, which are to end their days in sausages or pig food. Pigs are kept but they are sold in Paris and the sausages are pure, or rather impure, horse. The machine for pressing the meat into the cows gut covering is a work of art and the division of the gut into sausages by means of string, the colouring process and cooking are all equally horrible. They sell from 800 to 1000 a day to the French and Belgian Troops; Colville [sic] revels in the show was seen one day throwing sausages at Jimmie Riddle the next day he took the Bishop of Kartoum [sic] for a personally conducted tour round the works.

On May 4th, Archibald Eden took the 52nd for a field day near the Bois des Dames, a few miles to the west of Béthune. Here they trained with an 18-pounder battery, and put into practice some of the lessons that had been learned at Neuve Chapelle. The humidity was high and there was a severe thunderstorm leading to a soaking on the return march. The following day Captain Harry Dillon wrote home to his family. 'We have all got respirators now to stop the effects of the poisonous gas'. This followed the Germans' use of chlorine, the previous month, at Langemarck. Guy Blewitt obtained flasks for his men to carry lime water in to put on their masks as protection against the asphyxiating gas. On the 8th Harry Dillon assumed command of C Company and Captain Francis Beaufort resumed command of B Company. The following day Second-Lieutenant Hugh Pendavis, who had won a D.S.O., in the autumn fighting at Ypres, left to join the Royal Flying Corps, as a probationer.

The disastrous Battle of Aubers Ridge took place on May 9th and, at 1.30 a.m., the 52nd, as part of the 2nd Division, marched out of Béthune for Gorre, two and three quarters miles away to the east by north. Here they were situated behind a line of breastworks and acted as a reserve to the 1st Division, who had formed part of the southern prong of the attack on the enemy trenches, near Richebourg St. Vaast. Both this and a later attack failed. During the afternoon, Archibald Eden took his company commanders to reconnoitre further breastworks south of the Rue du Bois, near Richebourg l'Avoué. At 8 p.m., the 5th Brigade, including the 52nd, was ordered to proceed through Le Touret, La Couture, and Richebourg St. Vaast, to relieve the 2nd Brigade of the 1st Division. However, it was not until 1 a.m., on the 10th, that they received final orders to relieve the 1st Loyal North Lancashire Regiment, in the previously reconnoitred breastworks, near Richebourg l'Avoué. The relief had to be carried out quickly as there were only two hours before daylight. Narrow communication trenches with unburied dead made the relief more difficult, but it was successfully completed before daylight.

May 10th was a busy day in the trenches for the 52nd. Two companies were placed in the front line breastworks, with the other ones in lines north and south of the Rue du Bois. Mayhem existed in no man's land where there was a grim carpet of the 1st Division's wounded and dead. Guy Blewitt recorded in his diary[271].

> Rested in support breastworks and moved at 8 p.m. into the firing line. Was out 8.30 p.m. to 12.30 a.m. bringing in wounded from between the lines, we found 7 including an officer [? Munro] Northants, "A" Coy got 6 a difficult job finding wounded amongst the dead with German flares continually going up. I stupidly walked into German wire thinking it was our own.

Lieutenant Geoffrey Titherington has left a short account of his part in the Battle of Aubers Ridge and its immediate aftermath[272].

---

[271] Diary entry for May 10th 1915.

[272] Letter to his father written in the early morning of May 11th 1915. Incongruously, Titherington wrote this letter of death and destruction on a 'simply glorious day – the white lilac of which there

> There has been a big attack in which to date I'm glad we've had no share. We were waiting behind all yesterday and they turned a most terrific bombardment on the Ds and then loosed the infantry who were more or less outed by machine-gun fire pretty quick. We came in after messing round all night and took over in the early morning and tho' I think I am absolutely hardened I was nearly sick. I don't care a curse for the Deutscher dead the more there are the better I like them but our poor devils are different – it really was a sad sight. All day we spotted wounded and got them I'm glad to say all last night. There was some magnificent work done yesterday by really brave men crawling out and dragging in wounded. The cultured Bosche needless to add amused himself by shooting at any one who wagged an arm or a leg. One of ours stripped and half swam or waded up a ditch about 250 yards and dragged one in.

To make matters worse there was a good deal of shelling and the 52nd were fortunate to have only one man killed and three wounded during the day, considerably less than the rest of the 5th Brigade. The next day, the 11th, they were shelled again and Second-Lieutenant Cyril Baker and three men were wounded. Baker suffering a gunshot injury of the shoulder. Guy Blewitt wrote in his diary on the 11th: ' "The Colonel" [George Tolson] and Sgt Ashby kept us very anxious 5 a.m. to 11.30 a.m.'. Blewitt's report of the great valour of three of his men is still in existence[273].

> I have the honour to report the actions of Captain W.G. Tolson[274], 8645 Sergeant E. Ashby, 12141 Private E.H. Gamble witnessed by me this morning and to request that you will bring this to the notice of the Commanding Officer.
>
> At 5 a.m. Sergt Ashby pointed out to me a living man lying on the edge of a ditch, and asked me if he could go out and bring him in. I gave him permission to try; he got to him and carried him back about 30 yards out of the 120 yards he had to come. The man was too heavy and he could get him no further.

---

is a regular thicket close to – smells lovely. I've got a big bunch in my dug-out in an empty shell for a vase'.

[273] Blewitt's report dated May 12th 1915 was addressed to the Adjutant Richard Crosse.

[274] Tolson did not become a substantive captain until June 10th 1915.

> Captain Tolson then went out to help him and after Capt. Tolson and Sergt. Ashby had carried him another 30 yards they were fired upon: eventually Sergt. Ashby was hit in the back. Captain Tolson cut his coat off and dressed his wound, and got him more or less under cover. He then asked me to sap the remaining 60 yards along the ditch towards them, starting under the parapet. This took longer than we expected and before we had got through Pte. Gamble went out to help Captain Tolson. Between them they first carried Sergt. Ashby back, then went back and carried the man who had been wounded on the 9th inst. back: in the latter case they were again fired upon. Capt. Tolson and Private Gamble had brought Sgt. Ashby and the man who was wounded on the 9th inst. in by 11.30 a.m.

The rest of Guy Blewitt's day was busy with visits from officers of the Royal Artillery and Royal Engineers plus Major Archibald Eden all in connection with the impending attack. On the 11th, another courageous man, Private R.G. Jones, had gone out alone under heavy shell and rifle fire to bring a wounded man in. That evening Second-Lieutenant Leslie Johnston received a visit in his dug-out from Llewellyn Gwynne, the Bishop of Khartoum. It was expected that the attack would be renewed the following morning, and the two men discussed the chances of the next day. The perceptive Johnston was quite prepared and half expected to die in the service of his country. 'For myself, except for the people who would be left behind for the time, I think I can say honestly that I am not afraid to die, though still rather fearing that one might be struck by panic – but this is lessened by the little experience one has had'. In the presence of the Bishop, Johnston made his confession and received the Absolution from the Communion Service and the Blessing. Afterwards, Llewellyn Gwynne wrote to Johnston's father. 'I shall never forget his bowed head and huge shoulders'. When he looked up, the Bishop looked gloomy and Johnston said; 'It's all right, Bishop, it must be all right'. Then Johnston walked the Bishop down the communication trench and put him on his way home.

Later, that evening, volunteers were called for, to go out again into no man's land, to bring in further wounded, some of whom had been lying there for two days, without food or water. These were mainly men of the 1st Black Watch and the 2nd Sussex, both of the 1st Division. Leslie Johnston was one of those who offered to go out to bring the casualties in. Before his search party set forth, Johnston, a devout Christian, was seen kneeling as if in prayer. Three times his search party returned, from their dangerous mission, with a wounded man on a stretcher. The circumstances of their fourth errand of mercy are uncertain with differing accounts having been recorded. What is certain, is that Johnston thought he saw a wounded man moving, in close proximity, to the enemy's wire. Well aware of the risks his party was taking, Johnston went to investigate and they were fired on by the enemy. Johnston was shot, probably in the abdomen, and was unable to crawl back to the British lines. One of Johnston's companions was unwounded, and he was sent back for help, leaving Johnston and the other injured man, close to the enemy's wire. Eventually, once it was deemed safe, a search party went out and found the wounded stretcher bearer, who had managed to crawl part of the way back. However, of Leslie Johnston there was no sign. Next day a careful examination of the ground was made with field-glasses, but without success.

Captain Guy Blewitt has also left us a description of the scene that day, in his report giving further evidence, in the mystery of Leslie Johnston's disappearance[275]. The battle-hardened Blewitt was obviously distressed by the loss of Johnston as he wrote in his diary 'it is most worrying and one gets little sleep'[276].

> Johnston went out last night with two stretcher bearers to look for two men he had seen during the day. One of his stretcher bearers – Pte. Hickman – returned saying they had been within 60 yards of the German trenches, and he had been challenged; the sentry had also said: "Hands up". A flare went up while they were crawling away, the sentry shouted to his men, who fired wounding one stretcher bearer, Pte. Angel, in the side, and Johnston in the stomach. Hickman spoke to Johnston, who told him to come back and take a party to fetch them in. Firing continued and I did not allow the search party to go for one hour. They brought in the stretcher bearer Angel, who had crawled some way, and returned for Johnston and after a long search returned without him. I concluded the Germans had taken him in and decided not to allow further search. Pte. Stock and Inglefield led by Pte. Hickman formed the search party for Johnston. I believe them to have been very thorough in their search.

Geoffrey Titherington recorded his thoughts on the Johnston affair[277].

---

[275] Report written for Major Archibald Eden on May 12th 1915.
[276] Diary entry for May 11th 1915.
[277] Letter to his parents written on May 13th 1915.

> I am sorry to say Leslie Johnston is missing – he was out looking for wounded and got too close to the Gs who saw and shot him (It is very easy to go too far as one goes along from group to group one forgets how many paces towards the Gs one's taken). He had two men with him and a stretcher and was picked up by the Gs. I don't think he was very badly hit (by the account of one of the bearers who got away) and he could talk German well so should be all right.

Initially, the wounded Leslie Johnston was listed as missing and was thought to be a prisoner in the hands of the German enemy. Indeed, his parents, in vain, studied photographs of men in prisoner-of-war camps, hoping to find their son. Several months after Johnston vanished, his parents received a parcel, from the agents Cox and Co. It contained their son's two leather identification tags and his pocket book. Evidently, the book had been upon him, when he was shot, as some of the pages were blood-stained. The agents were unable to explain how the objects had come into their hands, adding further to the mystery. Johnston was never seen again, and the book recording the movements and wounds of the officers of the 52nd has this entry.

> Private Martin states that this officer was shot in the back at Richebourg when they were getting the wounded in, and as he could not move they left him, intending to go back and fetch him, but in the meantime the Prussian Guards[278] had been and when they got back he was gone. Martin does not think he is alive as the Prussian Guards were killing our wounded.

Leslie 'Johno or Johnner' Johnston was a theologian, devout Christian, brilliant academic and a fellow of Magdalen College, Oxford, when he vanished[279]. He had been the senior Dean of Arts at the College when the Prince of Wales [the future Edward VIII] was a student there. Occasionally, as was recorded earlier, in 1915 the young Prince would visit the 52nd. A fellow officer, Captain A.K. North, described Johnston as: 'one of the finest fellows I have ever known, as brave as a lion and gentle as a child, one of those religious men who

[278] The men, likely to have been responsible, were drawn from Westphalia, a province of Prussia. Perhaps the officers were Prussian. However, they were not Prussian Guards. Six weeks earlier, Johnston, by listening to the voices of a working party, deduced that they were Saxons or Bavarians with Prussian Officers.

[279] As with a number of other officers in the 52nd, Johnston was the son of a clergyman. His father was Canon John Octavius Johnston, former Principal of Cuddesdon College, and later Chancellor of Lincoln Cathedral.

are not always thrusting it at the men. He was one I have the greatest admiration for'. Johnston was a fine example of the very best type of Christian man, who was lost to the nation, in the war to end all wars. If true, the behaviour of the Prussians, in executing the helpless wounded was disgraceful, but it was not unknown for the British to take no prisoners. Both sides had signed the Geneva Convention and captured wounded should have been safe.

On May 13th, Captain Harry Dillon gave his perspective on the last few days in a graphic letter to his uncle, Frank Dillon.

> Just a line to let you know I am alive and kicking. The greatest battle the world has ever seen is in full swing and it would take a much more expert writer than me to describe it but it is terrific[280]. We were in reserve when it started on Sunday morning[281]. Went with Commanding officer to the battle line that evening[282] but eventually were marched all through the night to an entirely different point[283]. Here we stopped some time and the cold was awful as we had nothing on practically ready to go into the attack, eventually we came back and went into trenches. I was again in the 2nd line and so had rather a dull time simply being shelled and lost one subaltern I am sorry to say[284]. Our front line companies had great excitement getting in the wounded as the whole of no man's land some 300 yards was full of them and the Germans kept on sending up their flares and shooting our people with their machine guns. We got in great numbers and unfortunately lost another officer – Johnston who before the war was Dean of Magdalen. He was shot in the stomach right up on the Hun's barbed wire and the man with him through the thigh but the soldier managed to crawl back, a search party went out but he was gone. There were some wonderfully plucky rescues and the condition of the wounded who had been out 48 hours was fearful. Many of them have dozen bullets through them. We came out yesterday and are a mile back. Hope to be at them tomorrow. An interesting thing to me is the change in our men. The poisoned gas episode etc have at last disgusted them and there is a deep feeling of hatred growing. If I know anything of Englishmen it has grown

280 The Battle of Aubers Ridge.
281 Breastworks at Gorre.
282 Near Richebourg l'Avoué.
283 Richebourg St. Vaast.
284 Second-Lieutenant Cyril Baker was the wounded officer. He joined the R.F.C. in 1917 and lived until 1975.

slowly but will die more slowly still and Germany has only herself to blame if this hatred does not go on for 100 years. The French have done wonders on our right, the dust of their 75's hangs all along the line of their attack. Well it is business this time cost what may and I have never seen men in a better frame of mind to go through with it than the old 52nd.

Harry Dillon's letter showed that the use of poisonous gas by the Germans had at last produced a real enmity in the men of the 52nd. Despite the appalling wounds of the men of the 1st Division lying out in no man's land, the morale of the 52nd, on the eve of the Battle of Festubert was still excellent.

At 2.30 a.m. May 12th, Guy Blewitt and his men stood to arms after having been woken up continuously during the night. Blewitt made a personal reconnaissance of the British wire and obstacles before it was light. Later, he went around the lines with the 52nd's former commanding officer, the now Brigadier-General Robert Fanshawe of the 6th Brigade. The 12th proved to be the last day the Regiment spent in this section of the line. Despite a great deal of shelling they concentrated on bringing in the unfortunate wounded, from the 1st Division[285], who had been lying between the breastwork lines for three days and were in an unimaginable state. By now the 52nd had developed a technique of marking the position of the wounded by day and then bringing them in under the cover of darkness. However, Lieutenant Charles Fowke did not follow this principle as he crawled to within 150 yards of the German line to carry in on his back another wounded man whilst under constant rifle fire. Private Jack Mawer had a close encounter with a Jack Johnson. 'There was [sic] five of us sitting in our dug-out. But my luck was in it never exploded. We felt the thud and it made me tremble but alright now. I jumped up and went to see if my officer [Jack Warner] was alright'[286]. Four men were wounded during the day, and that evening the 2nd R. Inniskilling Fusiliers relieved them, and they returned to billets in Richebourg St. Vaast.

The next day the 52nd were in brigade reserve, but thoroughly disturbed by the roar of British artillery firing from positions in close proximity to the village. The German artillery replied in kind wounding Lieutenant Charles Fowke in the head. Guy Blewitt managed to sleep in a cellar. Geoffrey Titherington wrote to his parents: 'We're had the devil of a shelling these last few days – almost like Ypres but I find I don't mind it half as much as I used – I think

---

[285] Some of these men were from the 3rd Brigade, commanded by Henry Davies, who until two months before was in charge of the 52nd.

[286] German 15 cm. shell. Clearly a close bond had developed between Jack Mawer and his officer.

we are all getting very fatalistic which does not mean we fail to lie pretty flat if they are coming our way'[287]. On the 14th there was a divisional conference at which it was decided to make a night attack from their present lines. The attack was scheduled for May 15th and the roar of the guns in their preparatory bombardment of the Germans' positions was reaching a crescendo.

Lieutenant Douglas Humfrey wrote his final letter to Betty Dawes[288]. Within 24 hours he would be killed in action.

> We are in a nasty quarter just now. We came out of the most uninviting trenches on Wednesday. And have since lived in the only house in this village with a roof. It has no doors or windows.
>
> Excuse bad writing but mother making an awful noise and makes me jump out of my skin every two minutes. She is just outside in the garden, 9.2 round the waist and 100 lbs in weight[289].
>
> I have come to the conclusion I don't like war. We all attended an open air communion this morning in an orchard. The Bishop of Khartoum took it. You could hardly hear his voice for the noise of ours and the enemies [sic] guns. It was like a snow storm as the blossom was all shaken down by the shocks.

Douglas Humfrey and the rest of the officers and men on the 52nd were about to become involved in the opening night action of the Battle of Festubert, which would last from May 15th-25th 1915. Sir John French, the British Commander-in-Chief, was put under great pressure by his French counterpart, General Joseph Joffre, to continue the offensive despite the disastrous Battle of Aubers Ridge, with no ground gained and so many casualties. Joffre was perturbed by the fact that the Germans had moved such reserves as they had opposite the British, to the south to deal with the French Tenth Army's offensive in the Artois. French was in a difficult position with the Second Battle of Ypres still raging in the north, fresh divisions either being held back in England, to prevent a possible invasion, or being sent to Gallipoli, and there was also a shortage of ammunition. On May 12th, Sir John French had a trying meeting with Generals Joffre and Ferdinand Foch, at which he was pressurized into either relieving a French Division south of the La Bassée Canal or attacking again. Joffre believed that if the allies did not defeat the Germans in 1915, while the enemy was occupied in Russia, the war could be lost. French reserved his

[287] Letter to his parents written on May 13th 1915.

[288] Letter written on May 15th 1915.

[289] 'Mother' was a 9.2 inch and 'Granny' a 15 inch artillery piece.

decision until he had consulted with Sir Douglas Haig, commanding the First Army.

Sir Douglas Haig's plans for a renewed offensive north of Festubert were already well advanced. He had quickly learnt some lessons from the debacle at Aubers Ridge. The German positions were so strongly built, and their machine-guns so well-positioned, that a rapid infantry attack with distant objectives, preceded by a brief "hurricane" artillery barrage, would no longer work. Haig proposed to follow the French principle of a prolonged barrage with his heavy artillery, before the infantry advance on limited objectives.

The final details for this new offensive were settled at I Corps Headquarters, on May 12th, by Haig, in consultation with his corps and divisional commanders. The underlying principle of the infantry attack was similar to the one used on May 9th, although the objectives were to be more limited. The attacking divisions, the 7th, north of Festubert, and, the 2nd and Meerut, from the Rue du Bois, north of Chocolat Menier Corner, would have a gap of only 600 yards between them, as opposed to the 6,000 yards between the attacking divisions, on the 9th. The assault on Aubers Ridge had required an advance of 3,000 yards, but the initial objectives of the new attack were much closer at about 1,000 yards. Combined with a three-day prolonged artillery bombardment, in the French style, Haig and his commanders could be more confident of success.

The artillery barrage on the 5,000 yards between Festubert and Port Arthur began on the morning of May 13th, and continued throughout the next two days, until the start of the attack. The bombardment of 36 hours originally intended was eventually prolonged to 60 hours. A total of 433 guns and howitzers were used to soften up the enemy and his emplacements. They consisted of howitzers: 15 inch-2; 9.2 inch-9; 6 inch-36; 5 inch-20; 4.5 inch-54 and guns: 6 inch-4; 60 pounders-12; 4.7 inch-4; 18 pounders-210; 13 pounders-48; 15 pounders-16; 75 mm.-18. The two must common pieces, the 4.5 inch howitzer and the 18 pounder, had ranges of 7,300 and 6,525 yards respectively. The French 75 mm. field guns were found to be particularly useful firing on fixed lines perpendicular to the breastworks. The bombardment followed a set pattern, with the 6 inch howitzers being allotted approximately 250 yards of breastworks, and the 4.5 howitzers concentrating on the support and communication trenches. Artillery observers carefully followed the effects of the bombardment. The total expenditure of ammunition of the I Corps' artillery bombardment was over 100,000 rounds. Despite the best efforts of the British gunners, the enemy's batteries remained active throughout the coming battle.

The weather had been fine on May 10th and 11th, but on the afternoon of the 12th it clouded over and rain fell during the night. This continued during the next 24 hours, but it began to clear on the 14th, leaving the ground saturated. The inclement weather made observation of the shellfire difficult and the wet ground reduced the effect of high explosive shells. Major G. Chambers, of the 2nd Worcestershire, reported to 5th Brigade, on the 15th, that in his front line sector not a single howitzer shell fired by the British had exploded. He also stated that the German front line was untouched by our artillery fire. The sodden ground was not the only cause of the shells failing to explode; by the admission of Sir Douglas Haig, 'much of the artillery ammunition was very faulty until 1917'. The attack should have started on the 14th, but the wet ground and the fact that the artillery, supporting the Meerut Division, had still not started cutting the enemy's wire, led Haig to postpone the attack by 24 hours. In order to deceive the enemy, artillery feints were made on the 14th, and again on the 15th, at 10 a.m. and 3 p.m. The infantry joined in with cheering as if an assault was intended. Saturday May 15th was a beautiful early summer's day with bright sunshine which helped to dry the ground.

The 52nd and the other units taking part in the offensive were well aware that the Germans might inflict toxic chlorine gas on them and were prepared for it. Geoffrey Titherington recorded: 'We're all well prepared for gassing tactics now with masks and lime-water and ammonia sprayers etc but to date have had no need to use them as they haven't made a real effort with it here but no doubt they will I have got Allen and Hanbury to send me a very good pattern mask with a talc eye piece etc so should be alright'[290].

On May 15th, the day of the attack, 5th Brigade sent down their orders to the 52nd. Haig's First Army was resuming the offensive that night with the aim of pressing forward on Violaines and Beau Puits. The first phase of the assault on the German breastworks would begin that evening, at 11.30 p.m., with the Meerut Division of the Indian Corps attacking simultaneously with the 2nd Division, from the Rue du Bois. In the second phase, the 7th Division[291] would assault the enemy's line from north of Festubert, at 3.15 a.m., on May 16th. It was anticipated that the 2nd Division would take the Ferme du Bois and the 7th Division the Ferme Cour d'Avoué, before the three divisions moved on to the line Festubert - La Quinque Rue - La Tourelle cross-roads - Port Arthur. If all went well they could push on to Violaines and Beau Puits, with a defensive flank along the La Bassée to Estaires road on the left, and maintaining the right on Givenchy.

---

[290] Letter to his parents written on May 13th 1915. Allen and Hanbury, a pharmaceutical firm, were founded in 1715 and absorbed into Glaxo in 1958. In World War I they produced anaesthetic equipment and gas masks.

[291] Both the 2nd and 7th Divisions were part of the now Lieutenant-General Sir Charles Monro's I Corps.

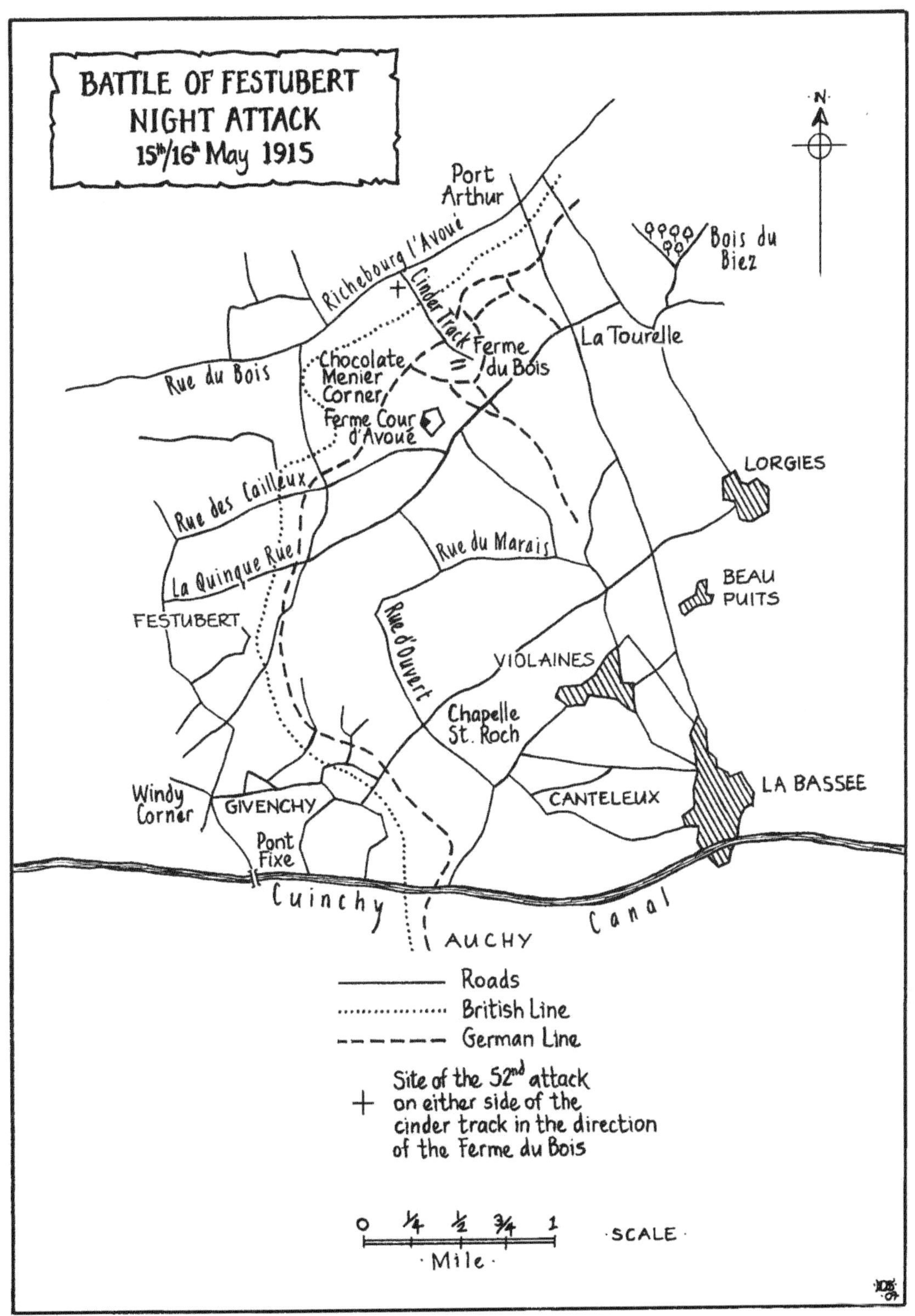
BATTLE OF FESTUBERT
NIGHT ATTACK
15th/16th May 1915
N
Port Arthur
Richebourg l'Avoué
Cinder Track
Bois du Biez
La Tourelle
Ferme du Bois
Rue du Bois
Chocolate Menier Corner
Ferme Cour d'Avoué
LORGIES
Rue des Cailleux
Rue du Marais
La Quinque Rue
BEAU PUITS
FESTUBERT
Rue d'Ouvert
VIOLAINES
Chapelle St. Roch
LA BASSEE
Windy Corner
GIVENCHY
CANTELEUX
Pont Fixe
Cuinchy
Canal
AUCHY
Roads
British Line
German Line
Site of the 52nd attack on either side of the cinder track in the direction of the Ferme du Bois
0 1/4 1/2 3/4 1
SCALE
Mile

The commander of the 2nd Division, Major-General Henry Horne, suggested that the Meerut and 2nd Divisions should attack at night, as they were familiar with the area, and it might enable them to get close to the German line undetected. It would become the first night attack of the war[292] made by British troops on the Western Front. The 7th Division, to their right, was new to the region and it was thought they would require some early morning light, to find their way in their unfamiliar surroundings. It was hoped that the Meerut and 2nd Divisions could co-ordinate their actions with those of the 7th Division with a renewed thrust at 3.15 a.m.

The 2nd Division would have the 6th Brigade under Brigadier-General Robert Fanshawe, a former commanding officer of the 52nd, assaulting the enemy's breastworks from R1 to the bend in the German line between R6 and V1 inclusive. [See trench map inside the front cover]. To their right was a gap and then units of the 7th Division, whose assault would begin some three hours and 45 minutes after their own. The 5th Brigade was on the left of the 6th, and it would assault the enemy from the bend in the German line between R6 and V1 exclusive, to the north-west corner of the salient, between V3 and V6. The frontage that the 5th and 6th Brigades were to attack over was 1,300 yards long. The 4th Brigade [Guards] was in reserve. It was hoped that at the same time as the 7th Division's attack, at 3.15 a.m., the 5th Brigade would be able to capture the German strong point at the fortified Ferme du Bois. The Meerut Division was on the left of the 5th Brigade with a frontage of 400 yards. At 11.30 p.m., it would assault the German first and second line trench systems in the vicinity of V5 and V6, before making a defensive flank from V6 back to their own front line breastworks. V6 was a small redoubt in the vicinity of the enemy's support trench. In 1921 it was noted to still have concrete dug-outs for machine-guns. As the 2nd Division's attack progressed it was hoped that the Meerut Division would take the Port Arthur to La Tourelle road.

Brigadier-General A.A. Chichester, commanding the 5th Brigade, arranged for the 2nd Worcestershire to be on the left, and the 2nd Royal Inniskilling Fusiliers on the right, to carry out the assault of the German line. The 9th H.L.I. [Glasgow Highlanders] would support the 2nd Worcestershire and the 52nd the R. Inniskilling Fusiliers. The fifth battalion of the brigade, the 2nd H.L.I., was kept in reserve, in a position between Richebourg St. Vaast and Richebourg l'Avoué. The 5th Brigade Headquarters were nearby, as was an Advanced Dressing Station at a cross-roads between the two villages.

[292] The German Fifth Army made a disastrous night attack on the French Third Army, to the west and south-west of Verdun, on the night of September 9th/10th 1914. This action was the first night attack of the war.

During the daytime on May 15th, Geoffrey Titherington scrawled a final letter and an addendum to his parents before the action[293].

> 'Tonights the night' as they say and we're all glad its coming off at last after many postponements. Its been rather like the few days before Boat Race day lately only not so terrifying as that was. The things been hatched very elaborately and tho' I don't think it will be a surprise it might be a success I think. We've had a great many six inch shells lately but nearly all harmless missing by those few blessed yards which mean so much to the badgered but fairly cheerful soldiers. I wish I could have walked with you. The country here in its new clothes it not so bad and only man is vile but he is very vile indeed a disturber of the peace. Love to you all.
>
> G
>
> We've sat still for so long that I've got quite a needle about this show. Perhaps the sight of your predecessors in the attack has not been encouraging. However we always find we can go where the 1st Div. can't write soon.

The officers of the 52nd had a final meal together in their mess at Richebourg St. Vaast, and were then addressed by their Commanding Officer Lieutenant-Colonel Archibald Eden. As he put it: 'This was the last opportunity that I ever had of even seeing so many of these excellent fellows'. The Regiment paraded at 8.45 p.m. and passed the starting point, Auberge de la Mairie, at 9 p.m., in order of companies A, C, D, and B. The entry of the various battalions into the battle area had been carefully staggered, with those leading the assault, the 2nd Worcestershire and 2nd R. Inniskilling Fusiliers, positioned on the front line breastworks and in two freshly-dug cover trenches by 9 p.m. The support battalions, the 9th H.L.I. and the 52nd, were ordered to pass a specific house on the way into Richebourg l'Avoué at 9 and 9.45 p.m. respectively. Water-bottles had been filled and great care had been taken to standardize the time between companies. At 7.15 p.m., the official time was given out in the Orderly Room with one N.C.O. per company and signallers, issued with watches, ordered to attend.

---

[293] Letter to his parents written on May 15th 1915. The tension engendered by the coming attack is almost palpable in this letter. It is interesting that Titherington was more nervous before the Boat Race than here at Richebourg l'Avoué. What is surprising is that the 52nd were prepared to leave their trenches, having seen the carnage, in no man's land, produced by the Aubers Ridge fiasco. Only unwavering regimental esprit de corps would carry them forward to the Germans' line.

The 52nd arrived at the Rue du Bois, with the men carrying shovels and sandbags as well as their rifles, and took up position behind the breastworks. At nightfall, the assaulting brigades moved up to the four lines of breastworks from which they were to advance. Accompanying the 52nd to their assembly positions was Llewellyn Gwynne, the Bishop of Khartoum, and now Chaplain to the 5th Brigade. During a long wait with Regimental Headquarters, he went to sleep in a ditch, telling Richard Crosse to wake him if he snored! It is not surprising that the men of the 52nd loved the man they called their bishop.

In the fading light, Llewellyn Gwynne, hearing how the chaplain of another religious persuasion had blessed his flock before battle[294], devotedly took up a position at the foot of the communication trench. Here he spoke words of encouragement that were worth many blessings to the men as they passed him by. His kindly 'God bless you my lads' was appreciated when a solid countryman feeling called upon to reply, said 'the same to 'ee sir'. Earlier in the day, a Saturday, Gwynne took a communion service for the 52nd, in an orchard at Richebourg St. Vaast. His voice was intermittently drowned out by the roar of the guns, which made the apple blossom fall on to the heads of the 52nd like snowflakes. Despite this, Gwynne continued with the service knowing full well that many of his congregation were going to their deaths.

The sky was overcast, the moon being barely 36 hours old and it was quite dark. To avoid confusion each man wore a white patch on his chest and back. The 52nd took up positions either side of the cinder track, so that they were in a position to support the 2nd R. Inniskilling Fusiliers in their assault of the German line, from the bend in the wire between V1 and R6, to the north-west corner of the salient between V3 and V6. The 52nd supplied the 2nd R. Inniskilling Fusiliers with three platoons carrying shovels and sandbags to act as working parties. Immediately to their left was the 2nd Worcestershire, supported by the 9th H.L.I. Still further to their left was the Indian Garhwal Brigade [of the Meerut Division], under their commander Brigadier-General C.G. Blackader. To their right was the 6th Brigade whose units were to attack the German line between R1 and R6. The battalion closest to the 5th Brigade on their right was the 1st King's Royal Rifle Corps of the 6th Brigade. The total strength of the 6th, 5th, and Garhwal Brigades in the first assault was 10,000 men. They were faced by some 2,200 men of the German 55th Regiment, of the 13th Division, who were recruited largely from Westphalia. The division was a good one and had been heavily attacked, at Neuve Chapelle, the previous March. It would fight valiantly on the Aisne from June to July 1916, and the following September put up a vigorous defence on the Somme, not yielding any ground. There is no doubt that the 52nd

[294] This was the Roman Catholic Chaplain of the 2nd Royal Inniskilling Fusiliers.

were faced by formidable opponents. The apparent discrepancy in numbers signified nothing, as the enemy had a large number of machine-guns, and the advantage lay with the defenders behind their breastworks.

The attack was to start at 11.30 p.m., by which time some of the leading British troops were lying out, in no man's land, in front of their lines. Unfortunately there was little chance of surprise, as the Indian Lahore Division, just northwards of the line of attack, had been ordered to assist with rifle and machine-gun fire during the artillery bombardment, in order to mislead the Germans[295]. Consequently they had fired intermittently throughout the evening. This was most unusual and had alerted the enemy to the imminence of an attack. The Germans with the aid of light-ball grenades spotted men of the 5th and Garhwal Brigades, putting light bridges over the dyke in front of the British breastworks, and forming up for the attack. The dyke was twelve feet wide and had four feet of water in it. When the British field batteries ceased firing, the enemy opened heavy machine-gun and rifle fire, raking no man's land, in anticipation of an attack. In a moment the ground between the two lines was illuminated by further light-ball grenades, flares and even a searchlight. As the 2nd R. Inniskilling Fusiliers moved forward they were met with a withering fire into their flanks, particularly the left one. Their difficulties were compounded by the Germans firing rocket signals to bring down a rain of artillery shells on them.

At 11.55 p.m., Archibald Eden reported to the 5th Brigade, that the Commanding Officer, Lieutenant-Colonel C.A. Wilding, and the last of the 2nd R. Inniskilling Fusiliers were leaving the British lines, and that the German infantry fire appeared to be coming from their second line. Five minutes later, at midnight, Eden reported: 'I believe first line taken', and at 12.20 a.m., an orderly reported that the strong point at V1 had also been taken. This was no mean feat as reports indicated that there were no less than five machine-guns in the vicinity of V1. The 52nd were called upon to reinforce the 2nd R. Inniskilling Fusiliers, as the opposition was considerable, and it was difficult to judge precisely the results of the Irishmen's onslaught. At around 12.30 a.m., on this Sunday morning, the 52nd moved out over the breastworks in lines into a hail of fire, with C Company [Captain Harry Dillon], supported by B [Captain Francis Beaufort], on the right, and A Company [Major Edward Kirkpatrick], supported by D [Captain Guy Blewitt], on the left. A cinder track ran between the two lines of breastworks and through the area they were to advance over. The flat ground between them and the German front line, approximately three hundred yards away, was mostly fallow, covered by a crop of weeds and grass about a foot high. In the dark and

[295] Lieutenant-General Charles Monro, commanding I Corps, was the originator of the order. With the benefit of hindsight, it was a mistake.

general confusion it was difficult to see in which direction to advance but, in places, furrows pointing directly ahead to the enemy breastwork were a guide as to the direction to go.

Archibald Eden was able to report, at 12.45 a.m., that half his battalion were now in the enemy's first line. Twenty-three minutes later, he asked the 5th Brigade to arrange for British heavy artillery to counter-barrage German field artillery, in the region of La Tourelle, which was shelling the area occupied by his men. Soon after 1 a.m., the 2nd Worcestershire, on the immediate left of the 52nd, began to retire towards their own breastworks. This was a serious turn of events for the 52nd as it left their left flank totally exposed. Some of the men of the 9th H.L.I., who had attacked with the Worcestershire, reported that the Germans were shouting 'come on you Scotch bastards, we have been waiting for you all week'.

Why had the 2nd Worcestershire failed to advance across no man's land and take their allotted section of the enemy's breastworks? Their frontage was about 320 yards long and the right flank of the battalion was about 100 yards north of the cinder track. Orders had been given that the attack was timed for 11.30 p.m. and was to be undertaken in absolute silence. The night was dark and close and it was not until 11.15 p.m. that the last men of the Worcestershire where in position. The *Official History of the Regiment* states that the watches of the Worcestershire officers were still several minutes short of "zero" hour, 11.30 p.m., when there was a chorus of wild Irish yells, as the 2nd R. Inniskilling Fusiliers charged into the night[296]. Unless the R. Inniskilling Fusiliers attacked prematurely, this is disingenuous as the 5th Brigade had ordered a representative with at least two watches, to report to their headquarters, at 7 p.m., to get the correct time. If they did not know the correct time, it could be attributed to their own negligence.

The 2nd Worcestershire had expected to walk across no man's land in absolute silence, and then make a final rush for the enemy's line, before bayoneting the defenders. However, they had little choice but to follow the example of the 2nd R. Inniskilling Fusiliers and charge the enemy's line at the double. It is difficult to believe that they really thought that they could surprise the enemy, as an Indian Division[297] to their north had been ordered to fire intermittently throughout the evening, putting the Germans on guard. The Worcestershire had two hundred yards to cover to reach the German breastworks. Men of their right sub-sector were also held up by an old British trench, full of the dead and smelling most horribly. Flares had gone up and they were subjected to a

---

[296] *The Worcestershire Regiment In The Great War* also stated that synchronisation of watches had not been instituted. Other evidence is to the contrary.

[297] Lahore Division.

torrid fire from the enemy. Companies and platoons became separated and command and control was difficult. Many men fell, although a small number of groups reached the wire entanglements. Fewer still got into the German line and these were soon forced out again. Chaos reigned in no man's land, and the Commanding Officer of the Worcestershire, Major G.C. Lambton, ordered his men back to their own breastworks. Few officers and men obeyed, as they searched no man's land for their fallen and missing comrades. It was not until dawn broke that the survivors of the Worcestershire finally returned to their own line. Matters were not helped by the fact that communications with the 5th Brigade had broken down. For all these reasons the Worcestershire had failed to take their section of the German breastworks, and the consequence of this, from the 2nd R. Inniskilling Fusiliers' and 52nd's points of view, was that their left flank was completely unprotected.

At 1.15 a.m., the Worcestershire reported that they had retired to their own breastworks. This was not strictly true as many men were still milling about in no man's land looking for their comrades. Archibald Eden asked the Worcestershire: 'Are you attacking again at 1.30 a.m.?' 'Please reply.' Almost immediately 5th Brigade asked Eden to comment on the situation. He replied that he had sent his bombers forward, was uncertain where the left of the R. Innisklllling Fusiliers rested, and was intending to use his last company in conjunction with a further attack of the Worcestershire at 1.30 a.m. Shortly afterwards, the Worcestershire notified Eden that they were not attacking at that time. Not unnaturally Eden asked the 5th Brigade for further instructions. There followed two messages from brigade to the 52nd. The first stated that the Worcestershire would renew their attack at 3.15 a.m. after an artillery bombardment at 2.45 a.m. It also stated that a working party of the 2nd H.L.I. was endeavouring to make a defensive flank up a ditch leading to V2. The second message warned Eden that it was essential to provide protection to the captured left section of the German front line, and to warn the men holding it that fire from the left rear might be expected after daylight.

Archibald Eden, reported to the 5th Brigade, at 2.10 a.m.: 'I now feel pretty certain that we have not got the front of German line from V1 eastwards'. He followed this at 2.20 a.m.: 'Inniskilling officer just returned reports we are in occupation of German second line trench about R7. Am sending two platoons to reinforce them'. Ten minutes later, in a message dispatched at 2.30 a.m., by the 5th Brigade, Eden received his first authentic information as to how the attack had been going.

Sixth Brigade attack has been successful. Inniskillings have captured front line. Glasgows[298] will carry out assault on the line V2 to north-west corner of salient east of V3. Gharwal [sic] Brigade are assaulting at same time. At 2.45 a.m. artillery will bombard German first and second line trenches. The assault will be delivered at 3.15 a.m. Glasgows must have two lines out in front by that time. Arrangements for attack as for Worcesters to-day'.

At 2.50 a.m. Eden was told that the 2nd H.L.I. was moving up behind his position. He informed the 5th Brigade, at 3.05 a.m., that V1 was definitely the furthest point on the left held by the British and that the Maxim machine-guns between V1 and 2 were still undamaged. Also that part of the enemy's second line around R7 was still in our hands[299]. The brigade's next message, at 3.10 a.m., asked Eden if he was still in touch with the new front line and whether they required further troops. If this was the case, he was to send his own men and to call upon the 2nd H.L.I. which was in reserve. To this Eden replied, at 3.21 a.m., stating that he had no contact by wire with the front line, and that if a further advance was required, the 2nd H.L.I. would have to be used as he had only two platoons of his own men left. In addition there was heavy shellfire in his area. Four minutes later, Eden enquired of Captain Arratoon Gaussen, Commanding Officer of the 2nd H.L.I.[300], whether they had been asked to support the 52nd's attack as he had no men left. Eden requested the Commanding Officer to come and join him behind his barricade for consultations.

Archibald Eden's dialogue with the 5th Brigade Headquarters continued in the early hours of the morning. He reported, at 4.15 a.m. that yellow flags were being waved at V1, where Second-Lieutenant Ralph Kite and his bombers were hard at work behind their block, keeping the enemy at bay. The yellow flags were for use in daylight to indicate that V1 was held by men of the 2nd Division. The 7th Division's recognition flag was red with a white horizontal bar. Eden could see little signs of life east of V1 which was not surprising as the 2nd Worcestershire and Garhwal Brigade had failed to take their objectives. At 4.45 a.m. 5th Brigade asked Eden if the 9th H.L.I. had attacked. They were supposed to have assaulted the enemy's line, to the east of the position of the 52nd, in place of

298 Glasgow Highlanders, the 9th Highland Light Infantry.

299 The 2nd R. Inniskilling Fusiliers and the 52nd had captured approximately half their allotted area of the German front line.

300 Gaussen was the senior officer and had command of the battalion. He was to be killed during the battle on May 17th.

the routed 2nd Worcestershire. The 3.15 a.m. attack by the 9th H.L.I. should have been co-ordinated with that of the 7th Division further to the south.

At 4.50 a.m., Eden informed 5th Brigade that he was handing over his barricade to the 2nd H.L.I., and was taking his Headquarters over to the former enemy front line. At this stage the 9th H.L.I. were occupying the Worcestershires' breastwork, but they had not attacked as there was so much congestion that they were unable to form up. In addition Eden informed brigade that he was taking one company of the 2nd H.L.I. with him across no man's land. In the event it was to be another two hours before Eden moved his Headquarters. Just over an hour later, at 6 a.m., Eden informed 5th Brigade that he was endeavouring to get across to the west of the cinder track, but was under fire from near V2. It is possible that he had elected to go to the west of the cinder track because the 1st K.R.R.C., of the 6th Brigade, on their immediate right, were well established in the enemy line. At this point, 5th Brigade ordered the 2nd H.L.I. to send bombs from their store to the left of the front line, where Second-Lieutenant Ralph Kite, at V1, and his bombing party were running short.

At about this time, it became clear to Archibald Eden that the attack by the 6th Brigade to his right had succeeded, and that they had taken their allotted section of the German line. The 6th Brigade had gone across no man's land at a walk with bayonets fixed, and the leading companies took the front line with barely a shot fired. The intermittent rifle fire of the Lahore Division to the north, had not put the Germans in front of them on their guard. Indeed, about a mile further to the west, at dawn, the 7th Division had made a successful attack and had taken a minimum of two German trench lines. Their opponents, the 57th Regiment of the 14th Division, had less than two companies of infantrymen in the front line, against the men of two brigades of the 7th Division. The 5th Brigade had had a partial success in taking sections of the enemy's front and second line. However, to the east, on Eden's left, there had been no success for the 2nd Worcestershire and Garhwal Brigade[301], and no successful second assault had been launched. At 3.15 a.m. the 5th Brigade, with their heavy losses, had not been in a position to push on again. To their left fresh units of the Garhwal Brigade had made a further attempt to attack, but the losses of the leading lines were so great that the remainder were held back. Hence the attack of the 2nd and Meerut Divisions, at dawn, to coincide with that of the 7th Division, came to nothing. At 5.40 a.m., Sir Douglas Haig took stock of the situation and the failure of the

[301] The German trenches were particularly well fortified in front of the Garhwal Brigade. In 1921, the then Brigadier-General D.H. Drake-Brockman, whose troops had been involved in the attack, noted the heavily constructed concrete dug-outs all along the front, and also steel mantlets for the observers. In retrospect he was not surprised the attack failed.

assault by the 2nd Worcestershire and Garhwal Brigade. He ordered that the left position gained by the 6th Brigade and part of the 5th, should become the left boundary of the offensive front. Troops to the north of it were to go on the defensive.

Eventually, around 7 a.m., Eden got his Headquarters across the 200 yards to the captured German lines. They were lucky to get across as the enemy plastered them with shrapnel, which stopped most of the machine-gun section, apart from Lieutenant John Southey, from joining them. Over 50 years later, the former Lieutenant Ernest Whitfeld, recalled; 'he [Eden] was very calm and collected under fire and, in my mind's eye I can see him advancing across no-man's land on May 16th 1915, in broad daylight, to join those of us who had survived the previous night's operations and were sitting in front of the German parapet'. Eden and Richard Crosse, the Adjutant, became separated from Major George Colvile on the way over. Twenty minutes later, the fastidious Colvile arrived having got wet feet and then changed his socks using dry ones from a casualty's kit! At this point Eden was able to get an idea about how much line had been taken, and the number of casualties they had sustained. He also came to appreciate just why so many platoons had had such difficulty crossing the two to three hundred yards on a very dark night[302].

Soon after reaching the captured German line, Eden spoke to Captain Francis Beaufort, the B Company commander, and gave him orders about consolidating their position. No sooner had Beaufort gone two paces from Eden, than a German sniper shot him through the head, killing him instantly. The 31-year-old Francis 'Boovey' Beaufort was a career soldier who had joined the Regiment from Oxford, in 1905, and was a fine polo player. Most of his service was spent with the 43rd in India and Burma. Eden gave instructions for the men to clean their rifles, which had been choked with mud. They were not totally dependent on their own weapons as they managed to retrieve both rifles and bombs from the captured German trench.

The 52nd were occupying some 120 yards of the enemy's line, and the men were packed into a relatively small space, and with daylight now upon them there was no chance of reducing the numbers safely. However, a fresh fire trench was dug on the British side of the German breastworks and this allowed a reduction in numbers. Thankfully, the enemy's artillery spared them although they continued to plaster the original British breastworks. No major counter-attack was made by the German infantry on the ground held by the 52nd. Communication back to their own lines was through runners who braved

---

[302] Captain Guy Blewitt described the section of no man's land that he had had to cross as being 400 yards wide.

everything to take messages in both directions. There were no intact field telephone wires.

At 8.45 a.m., on the morning of Sunday, May 16th, Archibald Eden received a message from 5th Brigade via the 2nd H.L.I. The H.L.I. was to continue with a trench in the process of being dug out, from the British lines to V1, and a defensive flank was to be formed along this line. This would protect the 52nd and the 2nd R. Inniskilling Fusiliers after the failure of the 2nd Worcestershire and Garhwal Brigade in their abortive attack on the German line. The 52nd and R. Inniskilling Fusiliers were told to dig in and to consolidate their position. The morning passed and at 2 p.m. Eden reported again to 5th Brigade.

> We are in a good position in the German front line, but rather too crowded. 6th Infantry Brigade is on our right and in German second line. Bombs, Véry pistols[303], and ammunition very essential. If a pair of machine-guns could reach here it would greatly strengthen our left flank. No wire between first and second lines, or in gap north-east of R7. Have been trying to get visual signalling with H.L.I. and Z.E. Station, but failed. My signaller at transmitting station was wounded.

At 3.30 p.m. Eden received a message sent by 5th Brigade, at 12.35 p.m., via the 9th H.L.I.

> It is intended to attack the German lines from R7 northwards. Oxfords to carry out attack from German first line V1 southwards after bombardment. When will Oxfords be ready, and have troops organized for the attack? Pass this message to H.L.I., and for report to Oxfords, so that the bombardment can be arranged. H.L.I. and Glasgows will support from our trenches and get battalions in depth. H.L.I. and Glasgows will at once send someone to repair telegraph wire.

Five minutes later, at 3.35 p.m., Eden replied to this message stating that the 52nd would be ready to attack again at 4.45 p.m., and giving a list of his officer casualties. At this time he estimated that his other ranks had suffered 50% of their men either killed or wounded, and that the 2nd R. Inniskilling Fusiliers had suffered similarly. Soon afterwards Eden received two notes from Captain Arratoon Gaussen, the Commanding Officer of the 2nd H.L.I. In the first he

303 Fired cartridges producing coloured illumination.

sought clarification whether he was to support the 52nd by assault or only by fire. Gaussen queried whether Eden still wanted machine-guns as it would be an offensive rather than a defensive flank. In the second note Eden was informed that 5th Brigade's instructions had changed once more. They wanted to know whether the 52nd could hold the line if the R. Inniskilling Fusiliers withdrew, their exact position, and if their men were in the German second line at R7. They were also instructed to regroup. The new attack was off the agenda. As Eden had no easy means of communication with 5th Brigade, he should send a runner to the 2nd H.L.I. who would telephone his reply through.

Archibald Eden in due course answered these questions.

> We can hold our position alone, allowing the Inniskilling to withdraw, provided our two Maxims, and plenty of bombs, tools, Véry pistols and ammunition, and S.A. ammunition[304], are sent to us. We and Inniskillings occupy from V1 to communication trench 100 yards south, occupying both sides of the parados. Only the Sixth Infantry Brigade occupy R7. A communication trench to our first line is very necessary, as is also telephone communication, or failing that, signalling. I now have no operators or instruments available.

The 52nd continued to hold their position until that night [Sunday May 16th], when they were relieved by two companies of the 2nd H.L.I., and returned to their original front line breastworks. The relief proved to be difficult for the H.L.I., as the few communication trenches were full of wounded men and corpses, and the 52nd were only occupying part of the trench system. As one H.L.I. officer put it, he was concerned that they were so close to the neighbouring Germans, that they might try relieving the enemy rather than the 52nd! The two sides were only separated by a narrow barricade. Eden and Richard Crosse made their way back to the original British line by a rather circuitous route, and to their dismay discovered the fate of many of their fallen colleagues. They identified some of the bodies of men who had been reported missing. The stretcher bearers of the 52nd were kept busy all night and they could have used three times the number that were actually available to them. Lieutenant Ernest Scott, their Medical Officer, did sterling work looking after the wounded. Later in the war he would be awarded a D.S.O.

What of the men of the 52nd who had left the relative safety of their own lines for an uncertain future in the wet, shell-pocked no man's land and the German trenches? A number of accounts of the heroism of the officers and men

---

304 Small arms ammunition.

of the 52nd during that critical day, May 16th, have been recorded. No man's land was full of dead and wounded R. Inniskilling Fusiliers. Lieutenant Ernest 'Ernie' or 'Whitters' Whitfeld of A Company, with a small party of men, had got into the German front line and after killing the seven- or eight-man gun detachment had captured a machine-gun and set up a strong point. After the war, Whitfeld made a name for himself by killing man-eating tigers in India, and at the beginning of World War II commanded the 43rd Light Infantry[305]. Second-Lieutenant Ralph Kite had also gone across no man's land with A Company and he probably witnessed the death of his fellow company officer and friend, Second-Lieutenant Lionel Dashwood. Having been wounded in the leg, Dashwood was putting a dressing on it when he was shot again and killed[306]. Kite was deeply affected by his friend's death and sought retribution from the Germans, as will be seen later.

Kite defended the part of the trench where the now wounded Whitfeld had captured the machine-gun and he held it throughout the day with a scratch party of bombers. According to one report 'Kite remained with six men. He took command, piled sandbags across the trench as we were fighting in the same trench as the Germans and all night long kept the position till help came in the morning'[307]. Amongst the men with Kite at V1 was the then Company Serjeant-Major Fred Clare, a fine figure of a man, standing over six feet in height and every inch a fighting soldier. He was one of the finest men ever to grace the ranks of the 52nd. Clare recorded his impression of the 20-year-old Kite, in his first action, after a mere six weeks in the trenches[308].

> The first time I got to know him was in the fight at Richebourg, on the 15th and 16th of May last year.
>
> I finished up in the same bit of trench that he did, on the extreme left of our line.
>
> He was at that time a subaltern in A Coy. I shall never forget the night we spent in that bit of trench. Possibly he has told you of it.
>
> I thought at the time he had the making of a good Officer, as he quickly organized the defence of the trench, and took command of the situation, which was a most unpleasant one for us.

---

[305] Whitfeld was wounded near Comines during the withdrawal to Dunkirk in 1940.

[306] The Army Headquarters in the field believed that Lionel Dashwood was buried near breastworks north of the Rue du Bois.

[307] *RBK A Very Parfit Gentil Knight.*

[308] Letter from Fred Clare to Edith Kite written on December 27th 1916.

V1 marked the extreme left of the 52nd's gains in the early hours of May 16th. Whitfeld and Kite were two of the few to be mentioned by name, in the account of the battle, to be found in the *Battalion War Diary*. Kite recorded some of his experiences that day in a letter to his relatives[309].

> We stormed the Hunnish trenches by night on the 15th/16th this month. You may have seen in the list what it cost us, but our particular attack was a complete success. I survived by some extraordinary fortune, I am not sure whether good or bad. The Hunnish booby hutches were of extreme luxury; one fellow had a bed pyjamas and sheets. Stoves, chimneys, washing stands and glass windows were the rule. Each booby hutch had a bolt-hole at the back, which, when our men discovered it, one would prod in the door while another hared off round the back and wait for Hun to shove out his head. It takes a lot to stir the ordinary man but our fellows are beginning to feel a dull hatred of the Germans, which the Germans have only themselves to thank for. Hence we took three prisoners. The Huns yelled for mercy when our fellows got in amongst them. My poor pal was hit in the leg and got out his field dressing when he was shot again[310]. Next time we get into them, I will take good care, if god spares me that no prisoners are taken, not even three.
>
> 'Eye-Witness' says Germans were using explosive bullets. He lies. The reason for men catching fire in action is because a man under fire leans forward and thus the ammunition in his pouches presents his cap towards the enemy. A bullet hits cap, explodes one cartridge, whose heat explodes chest and man is fairly ablaze in three seconds. This also happens lying down. I have seen, so I know.

The prospective Liberal Member of Parliament, Lieutenant Jack Warner, also of A Company, was reported missing early on in the action and his body was never found. His servant Private Jack Mawer was wounded while accompanying his officer across no man's land. He made his way back to a field hospital and had the gross misfortune to be blown up there. Captain Guy Blewitt, the D Company commander, was on the left in support of Edward Kirkpatrick's A Company. He reported that when his platoons went out, they had to form up on the enemy's side of the breastworks, as the British side was teeming with

---

309 Letter written on May 28th 1915 to his sister and brother-in-law Muriel and Bernard Watts.

310 Second-Lieutenant Lionel Dashwood. Fifth son of Sir George [6th Baronet] and Lady Mary Dashwood. Grandson of the 5th Marquess of Hertford.

wounded. As Blewitt started to advance, he received a gunshot wound of the left shoulder, and had to hand over command of his company to Second-Lieutenant Robert Bull. The 20-year-old Bull took D Company across the open ground, but was checked at some uncut wire, when he was killed instantly by a bullet in the head[311]. Blewitt then walked back to Richebourg St. Vaast, a journey he found both painful and perilous. He had to pass through the Rue du Bois which he described as hell.

From his bed in the London Hospital, Captain Harry Dillon, the C Company commander, described his experiences in the early hours of May 16th to Archibald Eden[312].

> My career was very short after I saw you behind the A barricade. I sent Sewell over as soon as his, the leading platoon, was closed up; and as soon as Humfrey came up I went over the top with him and his platoon, and we all got forward. After about 100 yards we lay down for a minute, to get our wind and collect, and here poor Humfrey was killed next to, and almost touching me[313].
>
> We went on again, and I was blown up by a shell and have an indistinct recollection of what happened. Eventually I found I lost all strength in my left leg, and here I am with a hole 3 inches deep in it. Our losses again have been dreadful but it is a great consolation to know that the regiment got there. I thought the men were splendid, all seemed keen to go on, and, in fact, unless Sewell led them, C Company must have gone on under their N.C.O.s after I was hit.
>
> I suppose A Company got mixed up in the redoubt on the left. I was rather puzzled at first when I got over our barricade, how to keep direction, as the flanks seemed to come round in a semicircle, and I know that I started to go too much to the left; but I corrected the mistake after the first advance. I came to the conclusion that the Germans must have had machine-guns in advance of their barricade to our left front. I wish I had been able to reach their barricade to our left front. However, better luck next time.

---

[311] Robert Bull was reported to be buried near breastworks north of the Rue du Bois. There was a close bond between Bull and his company commander Blewitt. The *Daily Mail* published this letter in the summer of 1915. 'Sir,- While in action on the morning of Friday, August 20, 1915, I found a large cigarette case, badly damaged and with these words engraved on it: "Robert, from Guy D, 52nd Light Infantry." I will return it to the owner if he applies to me. R.G. Saunders, Sergeant'.

[312] Letter written from the London Hospital on May 29th 1915.

[313] Lieutenant Douglas Humfrey.

In a further letter to a relative, Harry Dillon gave more details of the action and his wounding[314].

> Our attack of the 15th was a most desperate affair. Others of our best troops had failed and the 2nd Division swore they would get through and so we did, which is some satisfaction. I don't know who is left of the Regt. but not many.
>
> I was knocked out by a high explosive shell 50 yds from the German barbed wire, it killed several of my men and ripped the legs off another and threw what was left of him[315] and me some distance. How I got back God knows. I was so dazed and deaf I did not know I was wounded for a time but had the sense to crawl along over a mile and here I am. And can assure you I have had enough for a long time.

Other men from Dillon's C Company have left a record of their experiences of the night May 15th/16th. After Harry Dillon and Lieutenant Douglas Sewell were wounded, the men were taken on by their N.C.O.s in the form of Serjeant William French and Corporal Maguire. Two months after the battle Corporal Maguire gave this account of the action[316].

> I am pleased to say there are a good many men returned and quite recovered from their wounds, and hope to rejoin the Regiment as soon as possible. Their only fear is that they may be drafted to another regiment. You will excuse me if I did not explain fully in my last letter that I belonged to C Company – Mr Sewell's Platoon – Number Eleven. I am sorry to say that we lost sight of Mr Sewell going across to the attack, but Sergeant French and myself managed to keep the men together fairly well, though by the time we got into the left portion of the enemy trench there were only a few left. The right portion was still occupied by the enemy with a machine gun.
>
> I think Mr Whitfeld was the officer who took a few men with him and put the gun out of action, and I think accounted for all the Germans with it. I did not see anything more of Mr Whitfeld, but I believe he went back to the dressing station. About that time Sergeant French was killed, which left me in charge and in very poor

---

[314] Letter written from a hospital in Park Lane on May 23rd 1915.

[315] This may well have been the unfortunate Lieutenant Douglas Humfrey.

[316] Letter to Major Archibald Eden.

straits for men, with only four and myself – all being wounded – one badly. Private Howard, who I had placed on sentry duty in the German communication trench, reported that a large body of the enemy had come through and got into an unoccupied portion of the line on our left. Shortly afterwards they tried to bomb us from the trench. I asked for a volunteer to go back and report to you how we were situated, and Private Howard volunteered to go. What I mean by unoccupied portion is that it was not occupied by our men, but I do not think that it was ever really empty, as the Germans were continually bombing from it, until you sent reinforcements across, when the enemy retired. My idea in sending back Private Howard to you was to explain our exact position, as I could not ascertain if the enemy had any machine-guns with them. I wanted more men to get the enemy out of it and to make it as safe as possible for any future reinforcements coming across to us.

I am very glad to hear from you, Sir, that things turned out the reverse of what I thought. I think the idea of the enemy in trying to bomb us out was to get back to the machine-gun and use it against the supports coming across to us. I am pleased to say that the men with me held on very well, and I think it was only their well directed fire that kept the enemy back. I can only give you the names of my men Lance-Corporal G. Stokes and Private Howard both of C Company. The other two men belonged to the Inniskilling Fusiliers. Lance-Corporal G. Stokes was wounded again, and, I believe, has since died[317]. Private Howard I have seen here.

I think the time was near as possible between 6 a.m. and 6.30 a.m. when I sent back for reinforcements. I might add that I am almost certain that it was near that time, because I remember asking the officer who came across and took command of the trench, just after I sent back for reinforcements. I do not remember his name, but I believe he belonged to A Company. He told me he had been out attending to some wounded during the night.

Richard Crosse, the Adjutant of the 52nd, has reported an unlikely arrival at the cinder track in the later stages of the action.

Those who witnessed it will never forget the sight of an ancient French pony trap, drawn by an animal to match, which appeared

[317] Lance-Corporal George Stokes died on May 16th 1915.

> during the later phase of the action, on the once famous cinder track, where movement by day had been forbidden. On the floor of the pony trap were its furnishings, two chairs of Windsor variety, upon which sat the driver, the Bishop's orderly, 'my church-warden', he called him, and the Bishop himself [Llewellyn Gwynne]. They had brought a very welcome urn of tea, and they were determined to reach the troops[318].

We left the 52nd, on the night of May 16th, in the breastworks of the original British front line. They spent an unpleasant night in this position with little rest had by anyone. At 6 a.m., the 52nd were given orders to support an attack to be made by the 2nd H.L.I., with the aid of the 9th H.L.I. and the 6th Brigade, on the north-west corner of the fortified farmhouse of the Ferme du Bois. The attack was timed to start at 10.30 a.m. on the 17th, but was brought forward by an hour, when a large number of Germans, in front of the 6th Brigade, surrendered. The Commanding Officer of the 2nd H.L.I., Captain Arratoon Gaussen, was killed in the communication trench between the lines before he could issue his orders. The 52nd was to occupy the trenches vacated by the 2nd H.L.I. This was all part of an attempt being made, by their own 2nd Division, to link up with the 7th Division on their right.

Despite their exhausted state, Archibald Eden, Richard Crosse, Second-Lieutenant George Field and about twenty others went forward to reconnoitre the best line of advance to the 2nd H.L.I.'s trenches. Although some Indian Pioneers had dug a communication trench three quarters of the way to the recently captured line, Eden described it as one of the most difficult and trying journeys he had ever made. The trench was only waist deep before petering out completely, well short of the German line. On reaching the Headquarters of the 2nd H.L.I., they found that matters were not going well with the attack, and the shelling of all areas was very heavy and accurate. However Eden, and the few men who had crossed to the old German front line with him, remained with the 2nd H.L.I., awaiting the opportunity to summon the remainder of the Regiment to their side.

The attack on the Ferme du Bois gradually petered out, and three companies of the 52nd spent most of the day in the front line breastworks, where they were also subjected to heavy enemy shellfire. The remaining company was sheltering in the new communication trench dug by the Indian Pioneers. The senior Major, George Colvile, in the absence of Archibald Eden, did his best to see that the men were protected as much as possible from the German artillery

---

[318] Without wishing to doubt Richard Crosse, it is difficult to believe that a pony trap could have got anywhere near the cinder track while the 52nd were in the vicinity.

fire. Despite this there were still numerous casualties. At dusk Archibald Eden went down to the 5th Brigade Headquarters to report in person. The stretcher bearers continued to bring in the wounded, and shortly after midnight the 52nd was relieved by the 15th Sikhs and retired into billets at Richebourg St. Vaast. The 15th Sikhs of the Sirhind Brigade [Meerut Division] had great difficulty in carrying out the relief as the communication trenches were blocked by wounded and were also knee-deep in mud and water. The Meerut Division had failed in its attacks at 11.30 p.m., on the 15th, and again at 3.15 a.m. on the 16th. It was decided to use it to exploit the successes on their right, and thus the Sirhind Brigade had been put under the orders of the 2nd Division. In their official history, *The Indian Corps in France,* the state of the trenches found by the Sikhs is described.

> The whole area of the support and fire trenches bore witness to the terrible fighting which had taken place there on the previous day. The parapets were in many places levelled and the trenches filled up; the ground was everywhere pitted with huge shell holes, and might be described as carpeted with dead bodies.

Another battalion of the Sirhind Brigade, the 1st H.L.I., described an even worse scene in the German front line trenches, formerly occupied by the 2nd R. Inniskilling Fusiliers and the 52nd.

> The Germans had buried many bodies in the parapet from which our shelling had unearthed them; mangled remains were trodden into the deep mud at the bottom of the trenches, and it was some days before they could be extricated. The conditions in the meantime cannot with decency be described.

The 52nd were now able to count the cost of their taking, with the 2nd R. Inniskilling Fusiliers, of about 120 yards of the German front line and a small section of the second line, on the night of May 15th and 16th. The total number of casualties, for the period May 15th-18th, was 395. Five officers and 42 men were killed. Twelve officers and 272 men [including two from the R.A.M.C.] were wounded. Three officers and 61 men were missing. Most of the missing were likely to be dead, as part of the area fought over was not won and was much swept by shellfire. It proved almost impossible to search it even after dark. Many bodies were entirely destroyed by shellfire. The missing were unlikely to have been taken prisoner because, as we have seen earlier with the case of Second-

Lieutenant Leslie Johnston, it was reported that the Germans were killing the British wounded. The 52nd themselves took few prisoners, with Second-Lieutenant Ralph Kite recording that they only took three. Not since the storming of Badajoz, in 1812, during the Peninsular War, had the 52nd lost a comparable number of men[319].

The officers killed were: Captain Francis Beaufort; Lieutenants Robert Bull, Douglas Humfrey; Second-Lieutenants Lionel Dashwood, Francis Riddle. Wounded: Captains Harry Dillon [gunshot wound buttock], Guy Blewitt [gunshot wound left shoulder], Stephen Hammick [gunshot wound leg and contusion of left foot][320]; Lieutenants George Tolson [gunshot wound leg], Cuthbert Baines [gunshot wound hand and leg], Douglas Sewell [concussion], Geoffrey Titherington [gunshot wound right forearm][321], Jasper Wyld [gunshot wound abdomen], Ernest Whitfeld [gunshot wound back and head]; Second-Lieutenants W.J. Eighteen [gunshot wound arm], C. Dean [gunshot wound right leg][322], William 'Billy' Barnard [gunshot wound right shoulder]. Missing: Brevet-Major Edward Kirkpatrick; Lieutenants Jack Warner, Reggie Rendel [known to have been wounded].

On May 17th, soon after the battle, using his left hand, the wounded Geoffrey Titherington wrote to his parents. The style of his writing is reminiscent of Horatio Nelson's immediately after the amputation of his right arm in 1797.

> I have got a very cushy little wound – a bit of shell clean through just below right elbow hence left handed writing. I am crossing to England tomorrow I hope if there's a boat. We had a very fierce little show on Sat: night and captured some G. Trenches. About 20 52nd offrs got hit altogether. Will you please pack a compl-ete [sic] suit of things (civilian clothes I mean) ready to send me when I know what Hospital I go to. I shall want everything from the skin outwards for at present owing to my clothes being covered with mud and blood (some of it made in Germany). I am living in Government pyjamas tho' of course I am not a lying down case at all. You might

---

[319] Badajoz was a Spanish City taken by the Duke of Wellington in April 1812. In fact the 52nd's casualties for this action were 19 officers and 334 other ranks, of whom 5 officers and 53 men were killed. Somewhat less than at Richebourg l'Avoué.

[320] Captain Stephen Hammick was invalided to England. In February 1916, he joined the 43rd L.I. and was mortally wounded at Sannaiyat on April 6th 1916, and died at Basra on April 16th 1916. His father, Sir St. Vincent Hammick, was a former 43rd officer.

[321] Lieutenant Geoffrey 'Tithers' Titherington, an Oxford rowing blue, also joined the Provisional Battalion of the 43rd, in 1916. He survived the war and died of natural causes in 1951, aged 58 years, whilst out shooting in Cumberland.

[322] Dean had been promoted from Colour-Serjeant on November 9th 1914.

> put in a silk scarf for a sling. I have not been X rayed but my arm does not feel as if any bones were broken or touched tho I can't do much with my right fingers yet. Just going to have a glorious and much needed bath. Au revoir.

Other battalions in the 5th Brigade had suffered heavy casualties on May 16th. The 2nd R. Inniskilling Fusiliers lost 19 officers and 630 other ranks; the 2nd Worcestershire 6 officers and 305 other ranks; the 52nd lost 20 officers and 375 other ranks. Casualties in the Meerut Division were also of a similar magnitude.

Major Archibald Eden put forward a number of men for gallantry awards. Not all of the officers and men were to receive them.

Lieutenant Charles Fowke: on May 12th, bringing in a wounded man from within 150 yards of the German line [received the M.C.].

Lieutenant George Tolson: on May 11th [received the M.C.], Serjeant E. Ashby[323], and Private E.A. Gamble, bringing in a wounded man.

Private R.G Jones: on May 11th, going out in broad daylight, to bring in a wounded man, under heavy shell and rifle fire [received the D.C.M.].

Lieutenant Ernest Whitfeld: despite being wounded on May 16th, capturing a German machine-gun at V1 and killing its operators [received the M.C.].

Second-Lieutenant Ralph Kite: on May 16th, guarding the left flank at V1, with a party of bombers, for over fifteen hours.

Lieutenant Ernest Scott [R.A.M.C.]: over the period May 16th-18th, searching for and treating the wounded.

Privates H. Fuzzens and H. Rowe: on May 16th, carrying messages under fire between the lines.

Privates E. Zeacle and F. W. Wykes: on May 16th, both were wounded within 30 yards of the captured German line, whilst bringing up a box of bombs, under shellfire [both received the D.C.M.].

Private E. Howard: on May 16th, bringing back a report on the situation in the front line when information was scarce.

During the afternoon of May 16th, Sir Douglas Haig decided that a further advance, on the left of the battle front, towards the Ferme Cour d'Avoué and the Ferme du Bois, would be difficult as the enemy's batteries at Lorgies and Beau Puits were still active. He decided that it would be more profitable to attempt a more southerly line of advance from his right wing near Festubert. Haig's actions were supported by the Commander-in-Chief, Sir John French, who reiterated that

[323] Earlier in the year, Ashby had already been awarded the D.C.M. for his gallantry in the woods near Ypres, between November 1st-8th 1914.

their main object remained the wearing down of the Germans, and to prevent the detachment of their troops to oppose the French. Orders were issued for the next day, the 17th, with the intention of closing the gap between the 2nd and 7th Divisions, and to secure a line from Festubert along the La Quinque Rue to the Ferme Cour d'Avoué. Once this position had been obtained, a defensive left flank was to be made from Ferme Cour d'Avoué - Ferme du Bois - the Cinder Track - the original front line breastworks. Subsequent operations were aimed at advancing to the line Givenchy - Chapelle St. Roch - Rue d'Ouvert. On the 17th, Haig told the 2nd and 7th Divisional commanders that their ultimate objective was no longer Aubers Ridge, but now had become La Bassée and the railway triangle so as to gain access to the south of the canal. Both divisions made further efforts to get forward and failed. At night on May 18th, the Canadian Division began the relief of the 7th Division, and the following night, the 19th, the 51st [Highland] Division relieved the 2nd Division. While these changes were taking place, the Germans were hard at work consolidating their positions. During the period May 19th-22nd, a Canadian Brigade advanced in a number of places. Again, on May 23rd, Sir Douglas Haig made arrangements for a combined attack by the 47th and Canadian Divisions towards Chapelle St. Roch and the Rue Ouvert. Although some minor gains were made, the Battle of Festubert came to an end on May 25th. The Germans attacked the British line over the next two days, but without success.

Sir John French summed up the results of the Battle of Festubert in a dispatch.

> The enemy was driven from a position which was strongly fortified, and ground won on a front of four miles to an average depth of 600 yards. The enemy is known to have suffered very heavy losses, and in the course of the battle 785 prisoners and 10 machine guns have been captured.

The losses in the Battle of Festubert had been heavy. From the night of May 15th/16th, 710 officers and 15,938 other ranks had become casualties. The figures for the 2nd Division were 178 officers and 5,267 other ranks, 7th Division 167 and 3,956, and for the Meerut Division 102 and 2,419. In the Battle of Aubers Ridge, on May 9th, no German reserves had been brought into the battle. However, for Festubert every conceivable German who could be spared had been drawn into the defence of their line. Naturally this took the pressure off the French forces further to the south. The 52nd had fought tenaciously in support of the 2nd R. Inniskilling Fusiliers, at Richebourg l'Avoué, on the night of May

15th/16th, and had suffered heavy losses. In the end the Battle of Festubert once more saw local gains without a significant breakthrough of the German lines.

Today, the 52nd's battlefield at Richebourg l'Avoué can still be seen and walked upon. A bituminised agricultural road leading from the Rue du Bois towards the site of the Ferme du Bois has replaced the cinder track[324]. To either side lie flat arable fields and water filled ditches, which are reminiscent of Holland or the Cambridgeshire fens. With the aid of a trench map it is possible to accurately position the British and German front lines. Also the key positions of V1 and R7 can be placed within a few feet. An artificial lake has been dug out over part of the old German front line at R6, which the 52nd and R. Inniskilling Fusiliers held on May 16th 1915. The site of the Ferme du Bois beyond R7, can be clearly seen. A few red bricks from the old farmhouse and its outbuildings are still on the surface, amongst the grass covered undulations produced by shellfire. Beyond the farm is a copse, which is heavily waterlogged. The copse is very typical of those that now mark the sites of strong points on the old Western Front. Towards the south-west is the site of the Ferme Coeur d'Avoué, which is again covered in trees and virtually surrounded by water. Neither farm was taken by the British in 1915 and they were not rebuilt after the war. Looking over the flat fields of Richebourg it is salutary to remember that they contain the mortal remains of so many of the officers and men of the 52nd Light Infantry. Much of the land they fought over was never taken and their bodies, broken by shellfire, could not be brought in.

[324] The entrance leading to La Ferme du Bois was on the La Tourelle-Festubert road. The cinder track led to a house called La Corretière which was destroyed.

Chapter IX

Trench Warfare at Mazingarbe, Vermelles, Givenchy, and Cuinchy.

May 18th - September 23rd 1915

[Maps: pages 161, 237, 250, 252, 479.]

We left the 52nd Light Infantry, on May 18th, on relief by the 15th Sikhs, and they went into billets at Richebourg St. Vaast. An unknown clergyman who witnessed the 52nd marching away from Richebourg recorded the scene: 'the old 52nd Light Infantry are marching down the road. They went in at full strength in front of Richebourg. They are marching out 150 strong. They gained their objective. They are undefeated. They hold their heads high. They are whistling their regimental march[325]. That is the spirit of the old country at its best – unquenchable. It is the spirit divine'.

The Regiment was much depleted by the recent fighting, with only one officer per company, as twenty of them had become casualties. Lieutenant-Colonel Archibald Eden's Headquarters staff had been miraculously untouched. The exhausted men were able to sleep until the early afternoon when they paraded with the rest of the 5th Infantry Brigade. Then they set off for new billets ten miles away in the village of Bellerive, near Gonnehem, to the north-west of Béthune. Despite the fact that their numbers were considerably depleted, their quarters were cramped and poor. The 20th reinforcement of a welcome 130 men joined to fill some of the gaps left by their recent casualties.

The billets at Bellerive being too small for the Regiment, after dinner they proceeded on the half-mile march to the pretty village of Gonnehem. However, late at night, the 52nd were informed that the 5th Brigade was to move out, the next day, as the 7th Division had been allotted their current billets. The following day, the 20th, the 52nd paraded at 8 a.m. before marching the seven and a half miles to Raimbert [now Rimbert-les-Auchel]. This was a mining village without the usual facilities for billeting such as schools and barns. The men were accommodated in twos and threes, in miners' cottages and very comfortable they were too. Raimbert was peaceful and away from the incessant roar of the artillery.

From May 20th until the 29th, the 52nd remained in their comfortable billets in the long lines of miners' cottages in Raimbert. On the 21st, Major-General Henry Horne, commanding the 2nd Division, came to thank the 52nd for their excellent work at Richebourg l'Avoué. The following day the Regiment bathed in a facility available in one of the mines. That day they were able to

[325] The Lower Castle Yard.

welcome the return of Captain Charles Higgins and Lieutenant Reggie Owen, who had both been wounded on the Aisne, and also Lieutenant Pierce Newton-King who had been a casualty at Langemarck. Second-Lieutenant P.C. Webster from the 3rd Battalion also arrived that day. The 23rd was Whit Sunday and Llewellyn Gwynne, Bishop of Khartoum, conducted an open-air service for the 52nd, followed by communion in an estaminet. During their rest period Gwynne conducted short memorial services for the fallen, in each of the company billets. As Richard Crosse recorded, how much these were appreciated, only those who attended could tell. The Bishop would conclude: 'And now, boys, let us pray for peace, a just peace and a lasting peace; but, mind you', here he waged a chubby finger at an admiring congregation, 'mind you must beat the enemy first'. Here was a soldier's padre indeed[326].

On May 24th company training began and chiefly took the form of route marching and work in woods. Their Corps commander, Lieutenant-General Sir Charles Monro, visited the Regiment and told Archibald Eden that they had behaved admirably throughout the current campaign. Although Eden thought that this was nice, Monro could have been a little more fulsome with his praise after the recent fighting. His comments were passed on to the 52nd. The next day, the 25th, Eden went with some of the 5th Brigade's staff to view a line of trenches that they were expecting to take over. Second-Lieutenant Thomas Withington reported for duty from the 3rd Battalion. General Sir Douglas Haig also joined the list of commanders thanking the troops for their gallantry and hard work. He passed on the thanks of General Joseph Joffre, the French Commander-in-Chief, for drawing the enemy away from his men, this having been one of the salient requirements of the Battle of Festubert.

The following day, the 26th, company training continued in the vicinity of Raimbert, whilst, in the afternoon, Archibald Eden and Brigadier-General A.A. Chichester visited yet another line of trenches, this time near Mazingarbe, well to the south of the La Bassée Canal. The French were in occupation and the weather was very hot indeed. At 8.15 a.m., on the 27th, Eden took his four company

---

[326] Gwynne's remarks were surely more measured on the subject of war, than those of his brother bishop, Arthur Foley Winnington-Ingram, Bishop of London, who would give his addresses in uniform from a platform decked in 'Union Jacks' calling on the audience to fight the great crusade. '- - we cannot deny it – to kill Germans. To kill them not for the sake of killing but to save the world: to kill the good as well as the bad; to kill the young men as well as the old; to kill those who have shown kindness to our wounded as well as those fiends who crucified the Canadian sergeant. - - to kill lest the civilisation of the world be killed itself'. Winnington-Ingram served as a much-loved Bishop of London from 1901-39, and was Chaplain to the London Rifle Brigade. An imperialist by nature, he was invited out to France by Sir John French. French wrote, 'Five minutes of you cheers me up. Come out for ten days'. In 1916, Ingram was asked to visit the Grand Fleet by Admirals John Jellicoe and David Beatty.

commanders, Lieutenant Reggie Owen [A], Captain Charles Higgins [B], Captain Calvert FitzGerald [C], and Lieutenant Pierce Newton-King [D], on horseback, to view the new line of trenches. All four company commanders were new to the job, as their predecessors had all been killed or wounded at Richebourg l'Avoué. The French brigade commander at Philosophe was bemused by the ministerial changes in London, and particularly Winston Churchill's role as Chancellor of the Duchy of Lancaster! Then Eden spoke to the elderly commander of the French 281st Regiment, and finally the major commanding the battalion they were relieving. The French gave the 52nd's officers a complete tour of their trenches, which meant that they rode 30 miles and walked several more in addition, before they returned to Raimbert late in the evening.

On May 28th, a further draft of reinforcements, the 21st, of 270 men and six officers arrived. The officers were Lieutenant J.H. Boardman, Temporary Lieutenant C.A. Barran, and Second-Lieutenants J.W. Meade, S.M. Minifie-Hawkins, C.T. Chevallier, A.N. Carew Hunt. Lieutenant Reggie Owen wrote in his diary: 'a draft of 270 men arrived of which I had 70. Some officers also arrived, my company consists of self, Kite, Carew Hunt, Withington and Ch….all good uns – except the last'. The last was Second-Lieutenant Clement Chevallier who was known as 'Shoveller'. As the officers had only arrived that day, Owen did not take long to sum them up. He was a man who expected the highest standards in his company. In due course Chevallier would prove himself and would become a regular at the post war-reunions.

The next day, the 29th, the 52nd marched the fourteen miles to their new trenches at Mazingarbe, well to the south of the La Bassée Canal. They paraded at 1.45 p.m., at Raimbert, and set off on their long march with the 2nd H.L.I. for company. The route took them through Auchy, Marles-les-Mines, Bruay, Labuissière to Houchin where a halt lasting one and a half hours was made. Then it was on again through Noeux-les-Mines and Mazingarbe to the small village of Philosophe. At 11.30 p.m. that night, the 52nd began the relief of the French 281st Infantry Regiment in what became the right half of the 5th Brigade's front. The relief was not finally completed until 2.30 a.m. the following morning. The 52nd were distributed as follows. Right Section – B Company with one platoon in support. Centre Section – D Company with one platoon in support. Left Section – A Company with all four platoons in the firing line. Regimental Headquarters plus half of C Company were situated in miners' cottages at Fosse 7[327]. The remainder of C Company was in further miners' cottages at Fosse 3, whilst the Regimental Transport was at Houchin.

---

[327] A Fosse was a main mine shaft.

As the Adjutant, Richard Crosse, recorded in the *Battalion War Diary*, the trenches were deep, cut out of chalk, and there were many dug-outs, those for the supports being extremely well made. However, some parts of the fire trench had very long stretches without traverses, which made them vulnerable to artillery fire. It was French practice to use wooden loop-holes in all their fire trenches. The communication trenches behind the firing line were numerous, but were rather straight and broad, which again made them vulnerable to shelling. The machine-gun emplacements were well made. The 52nd were fortunate to find their new trenches in such a reasonable condition. Many trenches dug by the French were poorly constructed and filthy, with discarded food and excreta scattered randomly around[328].

The German trenches were along a crest line which commanded the greater part of the 52nd's area, but they were invisible to the Regiment's left centre. The distance between the lines was 200-300 yards on the flanks and 200 yards in the right centre. It was typical of the Germans to be situated on the high ground overlooking the allies' trenches. Several saps had been dug out towards the enemy's line, but none, with the exception of one on the extreme right, which had been captured from the Germans, came within 120 yards. During the morning the 52nd were subjected to fairly persistent shelling by small calibre guns on their right. Second-Lieutenant John 'Bunjie' Littledale[329] joined for duty and was assigned to B Company.

Late in the afternoon of the last day of May, Major-General Henry Horne, the commander of the 2nd Division, plus Brigadier-General A.A. Chichester, of the 5th Brigade, visited the Regiment to review the situation. Archibald Eden who accompanied them, found the walk hot, and the glare thrown up by the white chalk trying. Although the sniping was reported to be light the 52nd suffered one man killed and seven more wounded. Further officer replacements in the form of Second-Lieutenants A.G. Cardy, J.G. Grant, and James Belgrave reported for duty.

Lieutenant Reggie Owen commented in his diary:

> At about 4.30 the Div: and Brigade Commanders came round they seemed quite pleased with what we had done, I then managed a shave and quite a good wash. Quite a peaceful day. Beautiful calm sky and sun. A good deal of aeroplane shelling in the evening. C Company relieved us at 9 p.m. I got to bed about midnight in a cellar with Kite and Chevallier, quite comfortable.

---

[328] There were no sanitary squads in the French army until November 1916.

[329] Willoughby John Littledale.

Meanwhile, at home in England, Captain Harry Dillon was struggling to overcome the wound that he had received at Richebourg l'Avoué. He reported to a relative: 'my wound is going on all right but it is 3½ inches deep and as big as a duck's egg and they say it will be some time and require massage before I can do much walking'. Dillon had been wounded in the buttock and the sciatic nerve had been involved. It would be some time before he could get back to active service again.

By June 1st, the 52nd had been joined by a trench mortar battery, which turned out to be something of a mixed blessing, as their offensive efforts on the German line usually brought down retaliatory fire. This was particularly unpopular with those occupying the front line trenches. The next day, the 2nd, the 52nd was relieved by the 2nd R. Inniskilling Fusiliers and went into billets in nearby Philosophe. The mining village was absolutely filthy and it was still difficult to walk around as the German trenches overlooked them. Reggie Owen recorded: 'the regt came out of the trenches in the eve. Kite and I were billeted in a room together – quite good'.

Second-Lieutenant Ralph Kite took the opportunity to write home to request a sniping rifle[330]. He had asked his uncle to arrange for a sniping rifle to be sent to him nearly a month before the Battle of Richebourg l'Avoué, and the demise of Second-Lieutenant Lionel Dashwood and his other friends, had merely hardened his intention of making the Germans pay for their deaths. At the end of the month a suitable rifle reached him, costing him £12-3-4, out of his own pocket.

> As regards the rifle, a carbine sounds very nice (I'm rather vague on the subject). I would willingly give the fourteen pounds for a light rifle which will enable me to shoot through a loophole 3" x 2" at 300. In our present position the Deutchers are on a hill above us and overlook our position and snipe like the devil. I hope to instill a holy terror.

From June 3rd until the 6th, the 52nd remained in Brigade Reserve, in billets at Philosophe. French artillery of all calibres surrounded them, and the resulting shellfire occurred at irregular intervals. As they were overlooked by the enemy, it was very difficult for the 52nd to move around in daylight. Nearby was a château, belonging to a wealthy mine owner, still with its furniture, and with its

[330] Letter to Henry Kite written on June 3rd 1915.

grounds well laid out[331]. The grass was still being mown and the immaculate gardens, as good as anything Archibald Eden had seen before, were still being tended by twelve gardeners instead of the peacetime twenty. The French had used it as a divisional headquarters, but when British divisional staff moved in, the enemy gave it even more attention. On the 5th, the 22nd reinforcement of 30 men arrived. Their casualties during this period in Philosophe were light with one man killed and another wounded.

Today, there is no sign of the trenches at Mazingarbe as the area has been built over and slag heaps from the mines are still very much in evidence. Philosophe has not improved much in the last 100 years and is now a rather seedy industrial suburb of Lens. At dusk the neon lights of the shops intermingled with old piles of detritus makes a most unattractive sight.

On June 7th, the 52nd were ordered to move into divisional reserve around Fouquières. They were delighted to leave Philosophe, where they had been uncomfortable, and subjected to shelling at irregular times, which precluded any training being undertaken. The 141st Brigade of the 47th Division[332] relieved them, at 8.30 a.m., and three hours later they went into billets at Verquin. Second-Lieutenants C. Hurst-Brown and P.M. Ridout joined for duty. The only drawback to Verquin was that the Headquarters of the 47th Division was in the same village making accommodation scarce.

For the week June 7th-14th, the 52nd remained in their billets in Verquin. The weather was warm and they were able to undertake a considerable amount of training, including night work. This allowed the numerous replacements who had joined the Regiment since the night action at Richebourg l'Avoué, to be brought up to speed. On the 10th, information was received that Colour-Serjeant Thomas Hudson, one of the heroes of Nonne Bosschen Wood, the preceding autumn, and Serjeant P. Breach had been awarded the Distinguished Conduct Medal. Hudson received his award for an earlier action on the Aisne, and Breach for gallant conduct, as a scout serjeant, chiefly on the Aisne and also at Festubert. At Festubert his night patrolling brought in a great deal of useful information. Second-Lieutenant Edward Hughes, 'Little Hughes', the elder son of a former commanding officer of the 52nd[333], joined the Regiment during this period.

Second-Lieutenant Ralph Kite took the opportunity of the rest period in Verquin to write to his parents[334]. His comments about clergymen had a certain

---

[331] Mazingarbe Château.

[332] A 1st Line Territorial Force Division. Until May 11th 1915, it was called the 2nd London Division.

[333] Lieutenant-Colonel Reginald George Hutton Hughes who commanded the 52nd from 1904-7. Later in World War I, he would command the 7th [Service] Battalion.

[334] Letter to his parents written on June 13th 1915.

insight as he was the son of one himself. Llewellyn Gwynne, the Bishop of Khartoum was universally respected.

> The weather is very hot now – quite different to March when I arrived. The dust is so fearful that it is impossible to move by day for miles behind the line as it gives the position away to the Huns. We have a first class padre – the Bishop of Khartoum – he is a thoroughly good fellow and until he was stopped was frequently to be seen in the trenches. The men all like him and he is quite in their confidence. The old fellow is on leave in England at present (he has earned it) and today Sunday we had an appalling service from a parson of the usual sort.

On June 14th, Lieutenant-Colonel Archibald Eden accompanied the 5th Brigade staff in a reconnaissance of the trenches at nearby Vermelles, which the 52nd were to occupy themselves next day. Early the following morning Eden took his company commanders to view their new trench line. They arrived back at Verquin at 1.30 p.m., and in the evening, at 8 p.m., marching via Sailly-Labourse, took over the right section, Y1, of the Brigade sector, from the 1st King's Regiment. Archibald Eden checked his line immediately after the relief and did not get to bed until 3.30 a.m. The following morning he had to go around the trenches yet again with Brigadier-General A.A. Chichester, commanding the 5th Brigade.

The 52nd's Battalion Headquarters were at La Retoire Farm. The line at Vermelles had been captured by the French, in November 1914, when the Germans in typical fashion retired to the high ground, which dominated most of the land between them and Vermelles. Here both sides had settled down for a quiet time with the trenches far apart. In the early summer of 1915, the 1st Division took over this line of trenches from the French, and immediately put an end to this cosy co-existence by pushing the trench lines forward. However, the trench lines were still 250 yards apart on the left and 500-600 yards on the right[335]. The trenches were deep and usually well made, with many dug-outs, where the French had been in occupation.

The 52nd had two companies in the front line, dug by the 1st Division, and the other two companies in the support line, which had originally been the French front and reserve lines. In continuance of the policy of reducing the distance between the two front lines, the Brigade commenced a new trench 100 yards in front. After the 52nd moved on to fresh pastures the advancement of the trench

[335] *The Battalion War Diary* stated 500-1,000 yards.

line continued, so that at the time of the Battle of Loos, the gap was down to 150-200 yards. This period in the trenches, at Vermelles, was a quiet one with little shelling or sniping by the Germans, and most unusually there were no casualties. The 52nd's snipers and observers put in some excellent practice, between 5 and 7 p.m., when the light was wonderful for accurate aiming. Night patrolling was also carried out.

On June 18th, Lieutenant Charles Fowke of B Company recorded, in a letter, his impressions of the Vermelles trenches. The 'up market' dug-out demonstrated the 'live and let live' attitude of the French and German forces on that section of the front. The British would soon change all that.

> The trenches were originally made by the Germans, captured by the French, and finally handed over to the British. They are now a complete maze, each set of occupants having altered them to their own liking. They are made in a cornfield, and are six or seven feet deep. Corn growing on the banks gives them the appearance from within of deep Devonshire lanes, while from outside they are quite invisible. If one stands up (at a safe moment) to look at the country the scene is really a wonderful one; there is no sign of any other trenches, as they are covered by self-sown ripe corn; and the whole country is divided up into patches of brilliant yellow, red, and blue – corn which cannot be gathered in, poppies, and cornflowers.
>
> Higgins, Boardman[336], and I are living in a dug-out, with four or five feet of timber, corrugated iron, and earth on top of it. Inside it measures about fourteen feet by nine, and is seven feet high. It has a wooden floor, two glass windows (which open), and a door, while the walls and the ceiling are papered. The furniture consists of two tables, four chairs, a bookcase full of French books, two beds of a sort (I prefer the floor), and a stove. Lace curtains adorn the windows, and there are even two flower vases made of old shell-cases. It is quite the smartest dug-out that we have yet come across.

At 8.30 a.m., on June 19th, the 9th H.L.I. of their own 5th Brigade, relieved the 52nd, in the Vermelles trenches, and they marched the short distance to Labourse. The 52nd would remain in Brigade reserve here until June 23rd. June 18th 1915 marked the centenary of the Battle of Waterloo in which the 52nd had played a significant part. Unfortunately they had been in the line on the anniversary, but this time in reserve gave them the opportunity to have a

[336] Captain Charles Higgins, the B company commander, and Lieutenant John Boardman.

celebration. This was to take the form of the usual Waterloo Sports, on a suitable grass field opposite a farmhouse they were using as a mess. The 22nd was a warm day with a cool wind which was ideal for athletic pursuits. Appreciating that they were to be celebrating in the land of their former foes and not wishing to upset French sensibilities, the 52nd avoided a gaudy programme. Instead a few copies were run off in the orderly room. At the bottom of the simple programme was the following order: 'Should a hostile aeroplane appear, a bugler will sound three G's as a signal to take cover under the wall or the trees'. Fortunately the Germans left them undisturbed during their athletic exertions.

The following events took place during the afternoon: half mile; pack fighting in teams of six; bomb throwing of dummies; 220 yards; tug-of-war; dispatch riders competition; quarter mile; transport horses' turn out; inter-company relay race; blindfold crawl; stretcher bearers' competition; one mile; officers' and serjeants' relay race; band race; boat race; machine-gun competition; veterans' race [men over 35 years were given an eighteen yards start]; officers' chargers' turnout prize. The events showed a suitable balance between athletic prowess and training for war. The fitter serjeants were to beat the officers in the relay race.

The day was graced by the presence of their former Brigade Commander, Major-General Richard Haking, and by their former Regimental Commanding Officer, Brigadier-General, Henry Davies. Archibald Eden arranged for the London Field Ambulance Band to play, which was quite a feat as not many bands were out in France. In the middle of the afternoon there was an hour's interval for tea. Serjeant Hazel and his cooks had baked cakes in the village baker's oven. The day was a great success and allowed the 52nd to relax a little.

During June 23rd, the 23rd reinforcement of 25 men arrived, and in the evening the 52nd marched to Vermelles, in relief of the 2nd R. Inniskilling Fusiliers, but they went into billets, still in reserve. The accommodation was poor and the village required cleaning. While in their Vermelles billets, news came of the promotion of Archibald Eden from Temporary to Brevet-Lieutenant-Colonel, and the award of the D.S.O. for the wounded Captain Harry Dillon, and a M.C. for Captain George Tolson. Dillon's D.S.O. was long overdue after his gallantry at Langemarck and Nonne Bosschen Wood; surely there must have been an oversight. Just over a month later, Harry Dillon wrote[337]: '----- my wound is

[337] Letter written to a relative on July 3rd 1915. At the end of October 1915, Dillon was passed fit for home duty and sent to Portsmouth. He was passed fit for general service in June 1916, over a year after being wounded. Later, Dillon commanded the 1st West Yorkshire Light Infantry in the capture of the Quadrilateral and Les Boeufs. On April 27th 1917, he took command of the 6th (Service) Battalion of the Oxfordshire and Buckinghamshire Light Infantry. Sadly he died of

completely healed but the leg is very stiff still. P.S. they gave me the D.S.O. after all but whether for the fighting before Xmas or this last show I don't know. If it was for the last show I did not deserve it'. He was correct in thinking that the medal was not deserved for his actions at Richebourg l'Avoué, but his gallantry in the autumnal fighting around Ypres, in 1914, warranted it several times over. Sadly Harry Dillon would not fight with the 52nd again. He was one of their most outstanding officers of the war.

At the end of June, Second-Lieutenant Ralph Kite wrote again to his parents from Vermelles[338]. Like Charles Fowke he recognized the beauty of his surroundings.

> We are living in a large village at present, living in cellars. The Huns took it in November and shelled it. The French shelled and took it after most bloody fighting in December. Now Allybosh shell it fitfully. It is a splendid ruin – the chateau[339] a mere heap of ruins and the church clean blown away. We are quite happy living in it; though we live a rather mole like existence. The trenches are in a plain now thick with green corn, poppies and cornflower. It looks awfully pretty. My dug-out has been decorated with cornflower.

Shelling on June 27th and 28th killed one man and wounded twelve more. One shell penetrated a house in Vermelles, and accounted for the dead man and eight of the wounded. At 10 p.m., the 52nd was relieved by the 2nd Welsh Regiment, of 3rd Infantry Brigade[340], and marched the six and a half miles to familiar billets, in the Ecole de Jeunes Filles, at Béthune. The 29th was spent at Béthune in divisional reserve. The following day, the 30th, the 52nd relieved the 2nd Border Regiment of the 7th Division, in trenches to the north of the La Bassée Canal, at Givenchy [see maps pages 252 and 479]. For the next three days they would remain in the same trenches. Two companies were placed in the front line, in well-constructed trenches, and a further company was in support, close to the canal. The remaining company was situated in the vicinity of the Orchard and the old Keep, close to the church. A new second line was in the process of being constructed. The German trenches were 200 yards away on the canal bank, and only 50 yards away on the extreme left of the sector. However, the British line

---

pneumonia on January 13th 1918 aged 36 years and, was buried in Spelsbury [All Saints] churchyard, Oxfordshire. Dillon's grave can be seen to this day.

338 Letter to his parents written on June 27th 1915.

339 Vermelles Château.

340 1st Division.

formed a large re-entrant, just to the north of the canal, with its maximum point about 600 yards from it. During this period in the trenches, as a result of desultory shelling, one man was killed on July 1st and a further man killed and another wounded on the 4th.

Second-Lieutenants Aubrey Carew Hunt and Ralph Kite nearly joined the list of casualties, on the 1st, when they had a narrow escape. Their company commander, Reggie Owen, described it in a letter to his parents.

> I forgot if I've told you of the narrow escape 2 of my subalterns got the day before yesterday. About 5.30 p.m. they started sending Jack Johnsons into us and they caught the extreme left of my company. One of them reduced to ashes the dugout in which Hunt and Kite lived in, if they had been in it they would have been done for. They are both awfully nice fellows and good at their jobs.

In the afternoon of July 4th, the 2nd R. Inniskilling Fusiliers relieved the 52nd in their trenches at Givenchy, and they went into billets at Le Preol on the banks of the Beuvry Canal. For the next few days the 52nd were required to find 200 men per day for working parties in connection with the mines at Givenchy. One man was killed during this work. On the 8th, the 52nd returned to the trenches at Givenchy, having relieved the 2nd R. Inniskilling Fusiliers. This tour of the trenches was to prove a relatively quiet one, though occasional shells and rifle grenades, mainly against the front line trenches, spoilt the calm. However, there were two officer casualties, Lieutenant John Meade was only slightly wounded in the left knee on the 9th[341], and Second-Lieutenant Shirley 'Minnie' Minifie-Hawkins seriously, by a mortar bomb, on the 11th. Minifie-Hawkins received a severe head injury from a gunshot, which required trephining, and he was lucky to survive[342].

The 24th reinforcement of 25 men under Captain Ashley Ponsonby arrived on July 9th. Ashley Ponsonby, a most popular member of the Regiment, had recovered from his wounded shoulder that he suffered at Langemarck, the previous autumn. A further reinforcement, the 25th, consisting of eight men, all machine-gunners, arrived three days later. Between 8 and 9 a.m., the Germans fired 30-40 large shells at Pont Fixe, the bridge which crossed the La Bassée

---

[341] John Windam Meade was invalided to England with the gunshot wound of his knee. In December 1915, he took a draft of 350 men to Mesopotamia for the 97th Regiment. Later Meade was wounded for the second time with the 43rd and in 1919 he took command of that regiment.

[342] Shirley Minifie-Hawkins was ordained after the war and was still alive in 1955 as the Chaplain to Holy Trinity, Madeira. Much of his life was spent as a schoolmaster or chaplain in various far-flung parts of the British Empire.

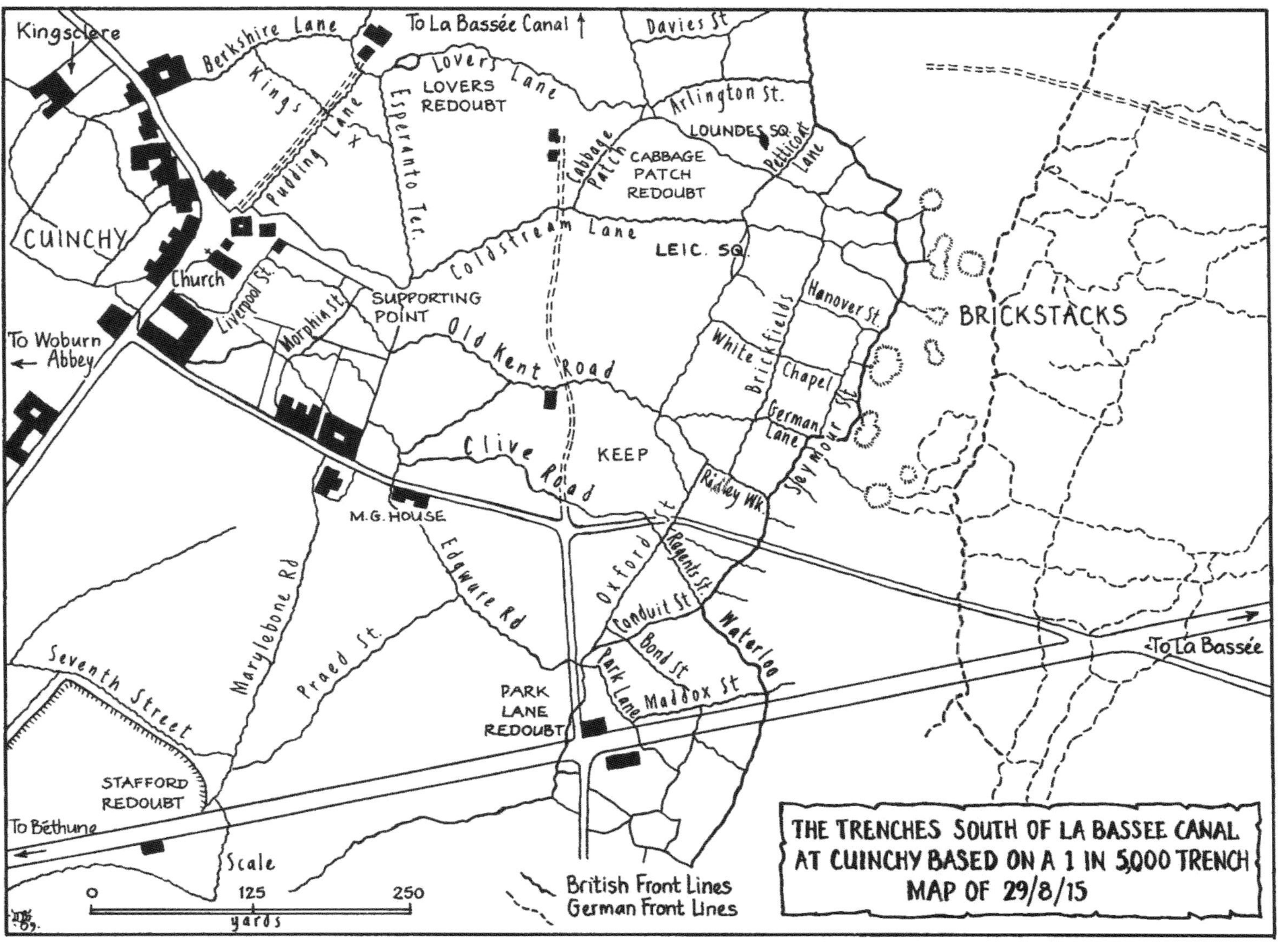
Kingsclere
Berkshire Lane
To La Bassée Canal
Davies St
Kings
Lovers Lane
LOVERS REDOUBT
Esperanto Ter.
Pudding Lane
Arlington St.
LOUNDES SQ.
Petticoat Lane
Cabbage Patch
CABBAGE PATCH REDOUBT
CUINCHY
Coldstream Lane
LEIC. SQ.
Church
Liverpool St.
Morphia St.
SUPPORTING POINT
Old Kent Road
Hanover St.
BRICKSTACKS
To Woburn Abbey
White Chapel
Brickfields
German Lane
Seymour St
Clive Road
KEEP
Ridley Wk.
M.G. HOUSE
Edgware Rd
Oxford St
Regents St.
Conduit St
Waterloo
Bond St
Marylebone Rd
Praed St.
Seventh Street
Park Lane
Maddox St
To La Bassée
PARK LANE REDOUBT
STAFFORD REDOUBT
To Béthune
Scale
0
125
250
yards
British Front Lines
German Front Lines
THE TRENCHES SOUTH OF LA BASSEE CANAL
AT CUINCHY BASED ON A 1 IN 5,000 TRENCH
MAP OF 29/8/15

Canal at Cuinchy. That afternoon the 1/7th King's [Liverpool] Regiment, of the 6th Brigade, relieved the 52nd and they moved into billets in the Rue du Tir area of Béthune.

The 52nd remained in Béthune, as part of the brigade in corps reserve, ready to move at two hours notice, from July 14th until the 20th. Training continued with the usual route marching and musketry, and the grenadiers exercised with the Battye bomb. Major Basil Condon Battye, of the 21st Field Company R.E., designed this emergency bomb, which was made locally in Béthune. It consisted of a cylinder four inches in length and two in diameter, which was filled with explosive, usually ammonal. The 52nd made use of the swimming baths in Béthune, taking part in a brigade swimming competition, in which Second-Lieutenant P.C. Webster excelled. During this period of relative rest three significant changes in personnel took place. Brigadier-General A.A. Chichester left the 5th Brigade to join the staff of III Corps, and he was replaced by Brigadier-General Charles Corkran from the Grenadier Guards. Also Captain Guy Blewitt, another outstanding officer of the 52nd, having recovered from his shoulder wound at Richebourg l'Avoué, joined the 5th Brigade as Staff Captain[343]. The 5th Brigade Chaplain, Llewellyn Gwynne, Bishop of Khartoum, with accelerated promotion became the Deputy Chaplain-General to the B.E.F., the senior clerical post in France. Although he continued to visit the 52nd throughout the war, he was no longer a constant presence and was sorely missed.

July 21st saw the 52nd return once more to the trenches south of the La Bassée Canal at Cuinchy, where they relieved the 3rd Coldstream Guards in the southern part of the sector. The trenches were in a much better state of repair than during their last tour in the area in March. Three companies were in the trenches with the remaining one in reserve, in Harley Street. Archibald Eden's Headquarters was in a rebuilt house known as Woburn Abbey, whose walls were covered with cuttings from the *Daily Sketch* and other newspapers. The three and a half days in the Cuinchy trenches proved to be relatively quiet for the 52nd, although shelling on the 22nd wounded three men. A further two men were wounded on the 24th. The 26th reinforcement of 30 men arrived on the 23rd.

The 52nd were relieved on the morning of July 25th, by the 1st Queen's [Royal West Surrey Regiment] who had replaced the 2nd R. Inniskilling Fusiliers, in the 5th Brigade. The R. Inniskilling Fusiliers were transferred to the Third Army. From the Cuinchy trenches, the 52nd moved to the Tobacco Factory at Béthune, where they went into billets at 2 p.m. Major George Colvile, the senior

[343] Guy Blewitt spent the rest of the war in staff appointments or as a Chief Instructor at the Senior Officers' School at Aldershot. He was awarded the D.S.O. in 1917, and retired as a Lieutenant-Colonel in 1922 to farm and hunt. He died in 1969.

major, left the 52nd that day on promotion to command the 7th Duke of Cornwall's Light Infantry. The Regiment remained in brigade reserve until the 29th, when they returned to the southern Cuinchy trenches in place of the 1st Queens. The relief took place in the afternoon, and some shelling around the Regimental Headquarters wounded one man. The next period in the trenches was another quiet one, although there was an intermittent bombardment by rifle grenades and mortars which wounded five men. The weather was very hot and the ever-present mosquitoes were an irritation. A series of dug-outs were constructed in the bank alongside the road for the Headquarters staff to sleep in. The house Woburn Abbey had only room for a mess.

During the morning of August 2nd, the 52nd was relieved by the 1st Queen's, with two and a half companies going into billets. The remaining companies were stationed in Cuinchy support post and Cambrin supporting point, with a machine-gun in each position. Between the 3rd and 6th they were based in billets, at Annequin, and undertook work in musketry, drill and physical training. The 27th reinforcement of 25 men arrived, and one man was wounded. At midday on August 7th, the 52nd marched to new billets in the Cemetery area of Béthune, as part of the corps reserve, and training was continued. The arrangements for baths were not as efficient as in the early months of the year. Only 350 men could be washed in a day, in place of the previous 1,000. The weather was very hot, but cooled significantly in the evening when riding became pleasant. Many of the officers had little or no experience of riding a horse, and Captain Ashley Ponsonby ran a riding class for those that needed it. The ability to ride was a requisite for an infantry officer in World War I.

On August 9th, Second-Lieutenant Ralph Kite was sent off to take over the 5th Brigade School of Bombing. Each brigade ran its own school to train its men how to throw bombs efficiently and safely at the enemy. The schools were mobile ones and normally sited close to the Brigade Headquarters. Under Kite's direction, about twenty men per course spent ten days learning how to use bombs. A soldier with a strong arm could throw a grenade about 35-40 yards. Later smoke and gas grenades were produced and used to clear trenches. Kite gave his impressions of running the school: 'I am away from the regiment horrible dictum, running a bombing school, which the powers that be have been pleased to honour me with: I call it a suicide club'[344].

August 13th saw the first anniversary of the 52nd's arrival, as part of the B.E.F., in France. Of those who had left England a year ago there were still serving with the 52nd: 7 officers, 3 warrant officers, 27 serjeants, 4 buglers, and 228 rank and file, including 2 attached R.A.M.C. men. Only 2 officers, 1 warrant

[344] An undated letter written to his sister, Muriel Watts, at about this time.

officer, 12 serjeants, 2 buglers, and 133 rank and file had served continuously. During the year there had been 1,023 admissions to hospital at an average of 2.8 per day. The first year of the war had been costly for the 52nd, with 23 officers and 268 men killed, and 35 officers and 811 men wounded. There was one other-rank unwounded prisoner, giving a total of 1,138 casualties for the calendar year.

In the evening of the 13th, some enthusiastic officers decided to put on an anniversary dinner at the Hôtel de France in Béthune. Initially, their Commanding Officer, Lieutenant-Colonel Archibald Eden, refused to attend out of respect for the large number of casualties over the last year. However, at the last moment, he relented and went to the dinner. The Hôtel de France was considered to be a great institution, which remained open most of the time except when Béthune was bombarded. Sadly it did not survive the war.

On the morning of August 14th, Eden took his company commanders to view a new sector of trenches for the 52nd, at Givenchy. Later in the day, Second-Lieutenant Keith Peploe joined for duty. In the afternoon of the following day, the 15th, the 52nd took over the B 2 section of the Givenchy trenches, to the north of the La Bassée Canal. They replaced the 1st Irish Guards, whose Commanding Officer, the 36-year-old Lieutenant-Colonel J.F.H.F.S. 'Jack Tre' Trefusis, had just been appointed to command the 20th Brigade, in the 7th Division[345]. Second-Lieutenant Laurence Goodwyn joined from the 2nd King's Own Yorkshire Light Infantry.

From August 16th-19th, the 52nd remained in the B2 section of the Givenchy trenches [see map on page 252]. They were now in the left sector extending from the Shrine on the right, to the low ground and the extension of Scottish trench to the left. Two other 5th Brigade battalions continued the line to the canal. The 52nd had two companies in the front line, one in support, less one platoon in Herts Redoubt, and the Regimental Headquarters and the remaining company were in houses at Windy Corner[346]. Both sides' trench mortars were very active, but although the British artillery was in action by day and night, the enemy troubled them little in this respect. Opposite the right front line company were numerous mine craters, some made by the British and others by the enemy. The craters formed two distinct groups, northern and southern. Three saps led out to the southern ones and four to the northern. In places the enemy was only 30-40 yards away, almost within bombing range. In practice, the 52nd were using about 200 bombs per night, principally to keep the Germans from getting into the craters and then rushing the British-held saps. For once the enemy did not reply

---

[345] Trefusis was soon to be killed on October 24th 1915.

[346] Archibald Eden, in the *Regimental Chronicles,* stated that two companies were in support, and only the Regimental Headquarters was at Windy Corner.

with anything like the same number of bombs. Both sides were very active in their mining activities at Givenchy, and this led to numerous men and much working material in the communication trenches.

The close proximity of the enemy meant that the front line companies of the 52nd had to double the number of subalterns on duty, which resulted in reduced rest periods for the junior officers. Archibald Eden and Ashley Ponsonby visited their old breastwork line at Festubert, and were able to see at close quarters the old German front line breastworks which had been captured earlier in the summer. Two men were wounded on the 15th and a further two on the 16th.

Lieutenant Reggie Owen, commanding A Company, described his recent experiences in a letter written on August 19th 1915[347].

> The particular bit of trench where I am now is probably the worst bit of any around here until you get right up to Ypres. I have half the company in front and the other half in support behind. There are a lot of mines all over the place, and the wretched sappers and fatigue parties go up and down miles and pump water all day long, bringing up filthy sandbags etc. Between my front and the Germans the ground is very complicated. It really consists of two main mine craters, i.e. where mines have blown up, the result being a huge hole, exactly like an ordinary gravel pit. We have sapped up to the edge of the pit on this side, and the Hun have done exactly the same on the other side; so we are really sitting opposite each other on the edges of this chasm. At various points we have bombers, who throw bombs all through the night, one bomb about every ¼ hour. I have seven points from which they throw, and last night they threw more than 400 bombs. It is too dangerous to throw much by day, as the bombs can be seen coming through the air, and this would be a signal to the Huns to turn their trench mortars on to our saps.
>
> It is largely luck if you ever actually hit anyone with a bomb, and you very rarely do so, as in most cases the distance between the two saps is just too far for hand-thrown bombs. But you keep on throwing them in order to prevent the enemy from creeping over his edge of the crater, getting down into it, and then crawling up your side, so as to rush your saps. They cannot do much of this if you are constantly chucking bombs.

[347] Quoted in the *Regimental Chronicles*. It was probably written to his parents, Susan and Charles Owen or to his naval officer brother, Basil.

Yesterday evening the Colonel (Eden) and Crosse (Adjutant) came up at about 9.30, and we started going round the trenches and visiting the saps, which took us until about 11.30 p.m. Then I started out again, and did not get back to my dug-out until 2 a.m. I knocked up my servant, and, after he had made me a cup of cocoa, I turned in again and slept until 7.30 a.m.; so since Tuesday night I reckon I have not had much more than 6 hours' sleep, but I am not feeling so very tired. This morning at 10.50 some officers of the Regiment who are relieving us tomorrow came up, and I had to take them all round and show them everything, which kept me on the go until 1 o'clock. I was feeling a bit desperate then, so after lunch I gave orders that no one was to come near me unless absolutely necessary, and I got about 3 hours' sleep.

I have been around to-night with Colonel Eden, and shall be starting round again on my own very shortly. We ought to get out of these trenches about 5 to-morrow afternoon, and I shall not be sorry. They are very old and crumbling, so if there is any heavy rain (like that of yesterday) the sides will fall in, which is a great bore, and often men get buried in that way. There is (or I should say was) a Highlander lying a few yards outside my trench at one place. He must have been there a very long time, as there is not much of him left except his kilt. I got a couple of my sanitary squad to spray him with creosote this evening, and to-night I hope we shall be able to cover him up. There is what is practically a skeleton just a little way from my dug-out, and in one of the sap trenches a man's knees and feet are actually sticking out of the trench.

Reggie Owen's letter illustrates the monotony of officers' rounds of the trenches, the constant tiredness, and the problems associated with respectfully disposing of corpses. It is difficult not to have sympathy for Reggie's soldier servant, who was awoken in the early hours of the morning to make his officer's cup of cocoa.

In the evening of August 20th, the 52nd left the Givenchy trenches and marched to billets at Le Quesnoy. Their replacement was once again the 1st Queen's also of the 5th Brigade[348]. The same day Second-Lieutenant Victor Jacob reported for duty with the Regiment, and the following day he was joined by Second-Lieutenant A.E.S. Riddle. The next three days were restful for the 52nd

[348] The 1st Queen's [Royal West Surrey Regiment] joined the 5th Brigade from I Corps troops on July 21st 1915 and was transferred to the 33rd Division on December 15th 1915.

after their exertions in the trenches. August 24th saw the 52nd exchanging positions with the 1st Queen's and returning to the Givenchy trenches. Although the day started quietly, the Germans made a persistent bombing attack between 8 p.m. and 9 p.m. on the northern craters. Three men were killed and four were wounded during the day. A Radley schoolmaster, Second-Lieutenant Lancelot Vidal, joined for duty.

In the early hours of the 25th the enemy blew up a small mine at the sap head of the most northern crater. Three men were interred in the debris, but the enemy gained no ground at all. The digging out of the men successfully avoided their asphyxiation, but the restoration of the sap took time. The physical labour of digging was made worse by the stifling heat of a hot August day. One man who came out of this little action with great credit was Lance-Corporal William Watkins, who on hearing the noise of the explosion, on his own initiative, took two bombers to the sap to assist. On August 26th, Lieutenant-General Hubert Gough, the I Corps commander, and Brigadier-General Alexander Cobbe V.C. inspected the new strong points that were being constructed. During the day the 28th reinforcement of 40 other ranks arrived.

The night of the 26th was quiet, but on the 27th, shortly after midnight, the Germans made a determined bombing attack on the northern craters at the Sunken Road, but they were repulsed after considerable bombing on the British side. At one time, the enemy approached closely, with the result that several of their bombs fell into the 52nd's trenches causing casualties. Seven men were killed and thirteen more were wounded by this bombing attack. Understandably, at 4 a.m., Lieutenant-Colonel Archibald Eden was distressed by the sight of so many of his men laid out by the action. The Germans gained no ground anywhere. This was the first real chance that the Regiment's grenadiers had had of showing their mettle, and according to Richard Crosse, the Adjutant, they acquitted themselves admirably. Again this was particularly so in the case of Lance-Corporal William Watkins[349] of C Company, who volunteered to stay on duty all night, and, at times, climbed out of his trench in order to pitch bombs into the attacking enemy. The night of the 27th/28th passed quietly, although every night there was a considerable amount of firing from the trenches on both sides, and the British artillery shelled from time to time.

In a further letter, Lieutenant Reggie Owen described his own experience of the early hours of August 27th in the Givenchy trenches[350].

---

[349] Awarded the D.C.M. for his brave actions on August 25th and 26th 1915. On the following September 10th, he was killed in action at Givenchy unaware that he had been awarded the medal.

[350] Quoted in the *Regimental Chronicles*. Letter written on August 29th 1915.

We had a regular doing in the trenches this time. You remember we went up on Tuesday last, and I spent the first two nights in reserve – not in the trenches at all. Then on Thursday afternoon I moved up to the craters to relieve Ponsonby. The usual sort of bombing began about 8 p.m. I had just got back to my dug-out, at about 11.30, from my usual first round, when a man dashed in and said that we were having a hot time in the saps, and that several men had been wounded; so I went down there, and found that the Huns had managed to lob a bomb or two into our sap-heads. At one place I found two men lying dead in the trench and two more a little further on. However, our bombers did splendidly, never hesitating to take a man's place directly he went down. We had several badly wounded, and I managed to give morphine to two or three; but, of course, a Company Commander has to be hard-hearted on an occasion like this, and cannot spend time in attending to wounded while the Huns are trying to get into his trenches, as they undoubtedly were that night. I am sure that they came out and crept round the edge of the crater, but we managed to put them off it. We threw about 800 bombs.

This went on until 3 a.m., when I came back and got a little rest. The net result was 7 killed and about 14 wounded[351]. One of the former was the best corporal I had in my company – a rare good fellow, and he died a very gallant death. I was talking to him only a few minutes before[352].

The next morning we were busy getting the bodies out of the way, reorganizing the Company, etc, and the night (Friday) was not nearly so bad. The Germans did not actually damage us with their bombs, but one of our bombers unfortunately blew himself to bits with his own bomb, which exploded just before he threw it. He was showing another man how to throw it when it went off, killing him and wounding the other man. I also had a man killed by a trench mortar shell, which burst right in the trench; so my Company suffered badly. I think the Colonel was quite pleased with what we did, but I hate having men killed.

During this tour of the trenches Lieutenant-Colonel Archibald Eden recorded his daily routine. Accompanied by Richard Crosse, he visited each

[351] The *Battalion War Diary* stated thirteen wounded.

[352] Probably Corporal Arthur Inson who was killed on August 27th 1915.

Ecole de Jeunes Filles, Béthune. The 52nd were billeted here in 1915 and 1917. Photograph circa 1913.
[Private Collection]

View from Festubert to Givenchy in 1915.
[Imperial War Museum Q50315]

Francis Beaufort. Killed in action on May 16th 1915. [Blewitt's Diaries]

The Battle of Festubert. May 1915. [Imperial War Museum Q17307]

Lionel Dashwood. Killed in action on May 16th 1915. [Regimental Chronicles]

Lionel Dashwood's memorial plaque. [Regimental Archives]

Jack Warner. Missing in action on May 16th 1915, presumed killed. [Regimental Chronicles]

Francis Riddle. Killed in action on May 16th 1915. [Regimental Chronicles]

Douglas Humfrey. Killed in action on May 16th 1915. [Regimental Chronicles]

Robert Bull. Killed in action on May 16th 1915. [Blewitt's Diaries]

Leslie Johnston. Wounded and missing on May 11th 1915. Possibly executed by the Germans. [Regimental Chronicles]

Guy Blewitt's horse, Siam, at Beuvry in 1915. [Blewitt's Diaries]

Edward Kirkpatrick. Missing in action on May 16th 1915, presumed killed. [Regimental Chronicles]

After the Battle of Festubert, the 52nd were billeted in miners' cottages in Raimbert. Photograph circa 1910. [Private Collection]

French in the Mazingarbe trenches. May 27th 1915. [Regimental Archives]

Dug-out in the Mazingarbe trenches. June 1st 1915. [Regimental Archives]

French trenches Mazingarbe. June 1st 1915. [Regimental Archives]

Waterloo Sports at Labourse: bomb throwing contest on June 22nd 1915. [Regimental Archives]

52nd's billets at Labourse. June 19th 1915. [Regimental Archives]

German grave at Le Rutoir on June 24th 1915. [Regimental Archives]

The ruined Vermelles Château on June 27th 1915. [Regimental Archives]

John Boardman outside a dug-out on June 23rd 1915. Later, as second-in-command of the 9th Rifle Brigade, he was wounded during the German onslaught of March 1918 and died as a prisoner-of-war. [Regimental Archives]

John Littledale in a small mine crater at Vermelles. June 27th 1915. He was to be wounded at the Battle of the Ancre and eventually killed in action near Vélu Wood on March 23rd 1918. [Regimental Archives]

company during the morning, often again in the afternoon, and always once more between 9 and 11 p.m. The evening tour of the trenches never took less than two hours, and if there had been rain, with the trenches full of sticky mud, much longer. Even in the darkness, Eden and Crosse were inclined to stick to the communication trenches as many stray bullets were flying around. The temptation to use the open road was great, and was often the quicker route, but one that they resisted. Eden found that the early morning was the best time to observe the enemy from the sap heads. It was possible in the first glimmer of dawn to move around in the open behind the front line, although enemy snipers had to be watched for. In general, dawn was the best time for the German snipers, but the late afternoon light favoured the allies. Eden was lucky to have a comfortable Regimental Headquarters, in a house, at Windy Corner. They were careful not to advertise their presence there by keeping smoke down to a minimum, and watching for enemy aircraft. Hence they had not been subject to much shelling.

The 52nd was relieved during the afternoon of August 28th by the 2nd Royal Scots of the 21st Brigade, and moved into familiar billets in the Rue du Tir area of Béthune. Archibald Eden was lucky enough to find a comfortable billet in a private house with an old lady and her daughter. He gleaned that something of importance was in the air, as there were frequent conferences, in the lead up to the Battle of Loos. The 52nd remained in brigade reserve from the 29th until September 2nd, which allowed them to carry out the usual drills and training. They had the use of the baths, at Béthune, for a whole day which allowed them to clean up after the filth and mud of the trenches.

As was recorded earlier, twenty men at a time were sent to the Brigade Bomb School, for a six to seven day course, which was run by Second-Lieutenant Ralph Kite from August 9th until early October 1915. During this time there were no accidents at all. On average, the records show that there was one accident per 3,000 bombs used by the B.E.F. Kite recorded an attempt by the German enemy to spread propaganda which he did not take very seriously. The usual attitude of the troops was to collect the paper for use in the latrines[353].

> The Hun played a great joke on us not long ago. He sent over a shell which burst into pink papers on which was found to be written a list of all his ‘victories’ and a panegyric to his own virtues in English. This was, no doubt, a great moral victory, as you can imagine how depressed the average stolid soldier would be, who probably could

[353] Letter written to his mother on September 6th 1915.

not read the pink paper and wouldn't, if he could – everything German being 'taboo'.

On a very wet September 3rd, the 52nd moved to billets at Le Quesnoy, in relief of the 2nd Royal Scots Fusiliers. New waterproof capes proved most beneficial to the men as protection from the rain. The next day, the 4th, large fatigue parties were found by the Regiment. Lieutenant-Colonel Archibald Eden recorded in his diary that in the forthcoming offensive the British were to use gas, although everyone was sworn to secrecy. The chlorine cylinders, known as 'rats' were brought up to within a mile of Le Quesnoy by rail. They were then transported in wagons to a rendezvous about two miles from the front line, and finally carried manually over a man's shoulder with a further man in relief[354]. Needless to say great care was taken with the carriage of the 'rats'. On the 5th, the 29th reinforcement of 85 men arrived.

The 52nd returned to their familiar trenches at Givenchy on September 6th, relieving the 1st Queen's. The night proved to be a fairly quiet one with little bombing to trouble them. The next day, the 7th, the Germans blew a small mine, in the early morning, with the result that the British had an obstructed view from their sap-heads, close to the southern craters. Although it was a quiet night, some premature bomb explosions wounded a number of men, including Lieutenant C.A. Barran and Second-Lieutenant A.E.S. Riddle[355]. Barran suffered multiple wounds to his thighs, leg, arm, feet, and required an amputation of a leg. To clear the obstruction made by the enemy's mine, British miners blew a mine of their own at 5 a.m., the following morning. This resulted in a much improved position for the 52nd. Archibald Eden, Ashley Ponsonby and Richard Crosse visited the sap-head soon after the explosion, and were congratulating themselves on the success of the explosion, when Ponsonby dropped dead. He had been shot by a sniper through the head and fell across Eden's knees stone-dead. In the poor light the three men thought they were well under cover, and it was a tremendous shock to the surviving men. However, Ponsonby was a tall man and his silhouette must have shown clearly to the German marksman, in the early morning light.

Of all the 52nd's officers, Ashley Ponsonby was perhaps the most respected and liked. Eden wrote 'we have lost one of our very best friends, and the Regiment one of the very finest gentlemen and officers who have ever worn its uniform'. Guy Blewitt commented in his diary 'it was an awful blow to us all

---

[354] The cylinders were transported first to Gorre by train and then to Cambrin Church by lorry or wagon.

[355] After recovering from the gunshot wound to his head, Riddle joined the 43rd L.I. in Mesopotamia.

and an irreparable loss to the regiment'[356]. Reggie Owen recorded 'it was a fearful shock to us, for we all loved him; I suppose he was almost the most popular officer in the whole Regiment'. Poor Ponsonby was buried, at 3 p.m., in the Military Cemetery, near Windy Corner, where his grave can be seen to this day. The respect that he was held in is indicated by the fact both the 5th Brigade's commander, Brigadier-General Charles Corkran, and the Colonel of the 2nd H.L.I., Lieutenant-Colonel Arthur Wolfe-Murray, attended his funeral in person.

In the afternoon of the 8th, the 52nd returned to their usual billets in Le Quesnoy, on relief by the 1st Queen's. Here they rested for the next 48 hours before exchanging positions with the Queen's again. The following two days, 11th-12th, in the Givenchy trenches, proved to be quiet except that the Germans were more active with the minenwerfer[357]. Casualties during this spell in the trenches were light with one man killed on the 10th, one killed and another wounded on the 12th, and a further two wounded on the 13th.

In the afternoon of September 13th, the 52nd was relieved by the 2nd Royal Welsh Fusiliers of the 19th Brigade, and marched the four miles to new billets in Oblinghem and Vendin. The billets were considered to be good, although scattered, and the officers had an excellent mess in a farm-house. From the 14th-16th, the whole of the 5th Brigade remained in reserve, and the usual drills and classes were undertaken. This included an adjutant's drill conducted by Richard Crosse. On the 14th, Archibald Eden and one of the other officers rode over to Laventie to visit their 6th Battalion[358], and found them well.

On September 17th, the 5th Brigade was on the move again, and the 52nd returned to billets in Le Quesnoy after a march of three to four miles. The following day, the 18th, the officers staged a primitive sort of steeplechase over flat ground with a few ditches. Second-Lieutenant P.M. Ridout won the race on a transport horse in a field of twelve starters. On the 19th, the 52nd relieved the 2nd Worcestershire, in the right sector of the Givenchy trenches. The night was quiet but warm, and the same conditions prevailed the following day, which saw the arrival of the 31st reinforcement of sixteen men. They were all machine-gunners or signallers. One man was killed this day.

As a prelude to the new offensive, the British artillery bombardment began on September 21st. In anticipation of German artillery retaliation, the 52nd reduced their front and second line strength by half, and one company returned to

---

356 Diary entry for September 8th 1915.

357 The original minenwerfers were breech loading short range howitzers. Later in the war, a muzzle loading short range trench mortar was developed which took the same name. The name meant literally a mine thrower used to destroy barbed wire and bunkers that the artillery might find difficult to sight on.

358 The 6th [Service] Battalion of the Oxfordshire and Buckinghamshire Light Infantry.

billets at dawn. In the afternoon the Regiment was relieved by the 2nd Worcestershire and returned to billets at Le Quesnoy. Two men were wounded during the day. On the 22nd, the 52nd remained in reserve, while the artillery bombardment continued with little reply from the enemy. Heavy rain fell on the 23rd, but the bombardment of the German trenches continued unabated throughout the day. During the afternoon, the 52nd returned to the Givenchy trenches in place of the 2nd Worcestershire and the night was a quiet one. Shortly, the Regiment would be sorely tested in the major British action of 1915, the Battle of Loos.

Chapter X

The Battle of Loos: the Subsidiary Attack at Givenchy.

September 23rd – October 18th 1915

[Maps: pages 250, 252, 269.]

In mid-September, General Joseph Joffre, the French Commander-in-Chief, gave a final exposition of his offensive plans to Sir John French and the commanders of Groups of French Armies, Generals Noel de Castelnau, Ferdinand Foch and Auguste Dubail. Joffre pointed out that the French Army manpower was now as high as it was ever likely to be, and that Kitchener's New Armies, raised in Britain, were beginning to come on line. The Germans had up to one third of their forces fighting on the Eastern Front and unable to directly influence events in the west. It was calculated that the Germans had 800,000 rifles on the Western Front opposed by 1,185,000 of the Allies'. Not unreasonably, Joffre considered that it was a propitious moment for a major assault on the enemy in the west. Already, he had a near three to two superiority in manpower, but by weakening parts of his front and strengthening others where the attacks were to be launched, he would increase his numerical advantage. In addition, since the last offensive in the summer, the allied artillery capacity, particularly in heavy ordnance, had increased. Joffre felt that after a preliminary artillery bombardment of great severity, his numerical superiority in infantry would carry the day.

Joseph Joffre's offensive plans had been raised earlier in the year, and consisted of a two-pronged assault from the Artois and the Champagne, both in the direction of Namur. However, the new plan had one great difference from the earlier one; the Champagne would become the principal area of action, at the expense of the Artois. The reason for this was that the French had failed to capture Vimy Ridge in their attacks of May and June. The Germans occupied the high ground on the ridge, overlooking the Artois plateau, where the French would have placed the bulk of their infantry and artillery. For this reason, Joffre felt obliged to change the weight of his attack from the Artois to the Champagne. In the Artois, a Franco-British assault would be delivered across the plain of Douai against the German Sixth Army, under the command of Crown Prince Rupprecht of Bavaria. From the Champagne, the French were to attack northwards against the German Third Army. If both offensives were successful, no less than three German Armies would be trapped inside the Noyon Salient. The enemy's divided forces could then be defeated one unit at a time.

The Artois offensive was to be overseen by General Ferdinand Foch, and be undertaken by the French Tenth Army and the British First Army, on the

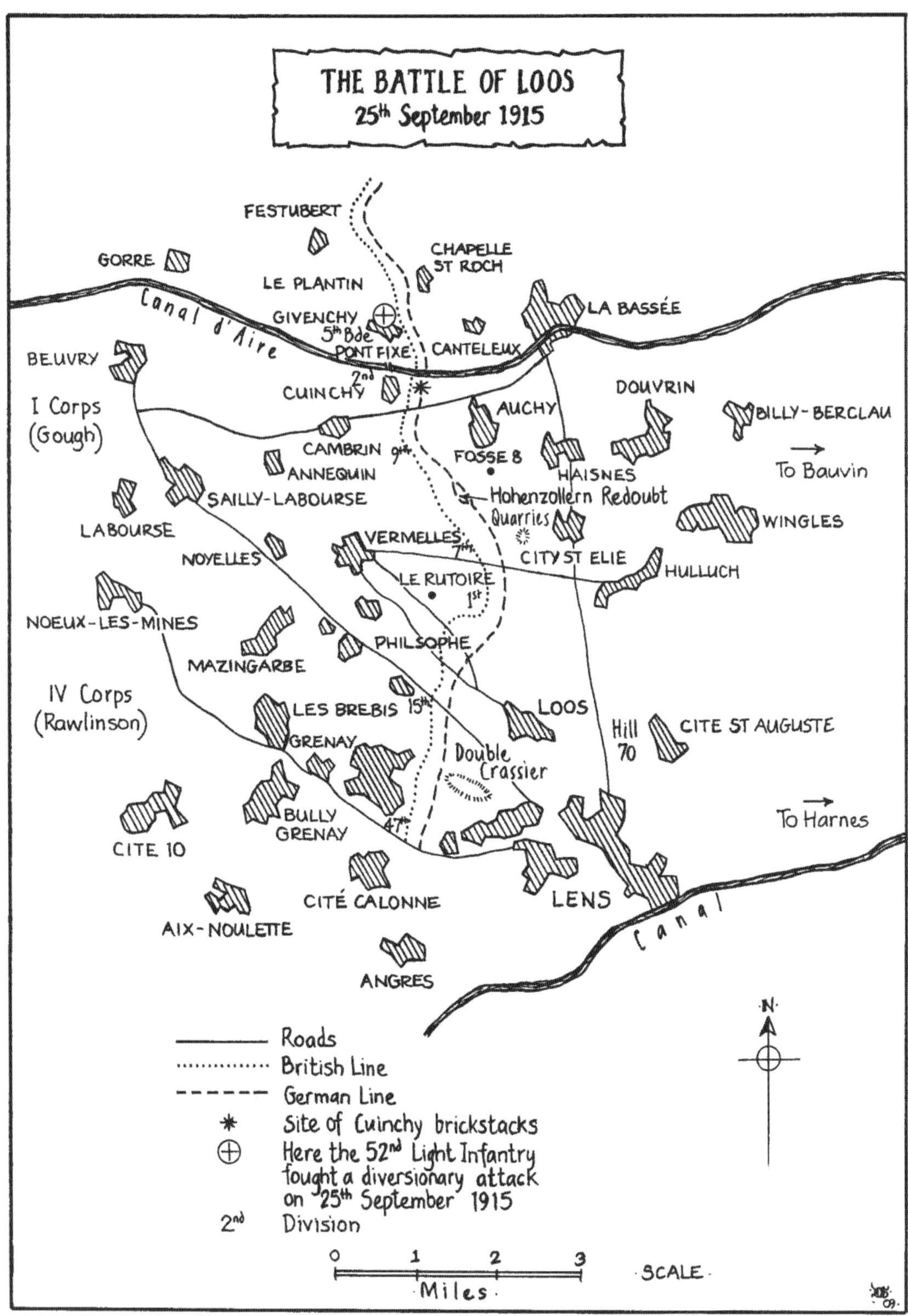
THE BATTLE OF LOOS
25th September 1915
FESTUBERT
GORRE
CHAPELLE ST ROCH
LE PLANTIN
Canal d'Aire
GIVENCHY
5th Bde
LA BASSÉE
PONT FIXE
CANTELEUX
BEUVRY
2nd
CUINCHY
DOUVRIN
I Corps (Gough)
AUCHY
BILLY-BERCLAU
CAMBRIN
9th
FOSSE 8
ANNEQUIN
HAISNES
To Bauvin
Hohenzollern Redoubt
SAILLY-LABOURSE
Quarries
WINGLES
LABOURSE
VERMELLES
7th
CITY ST ELIE
NOYELLES
HULLUCH
LE RUTOIRE
1st
NOEUX-LES-MINES
PHILSOPHE
MAZINGARBE
IV Corps (Rawlinson)
LES BREBIS
15th
LOOS
Hill 70
CITE ST AUGUSTE
GRENAY
Double Crassier
BULLY GRENAY
47th
To Harnes
CITE 10
CITÉ CALONNE
LENS
AIX-NOULETTE
Canal
ANGRES
N
Roads
British Line
German Line
Site of Cuinchy brickstacks
Here the 52nd Light Infantry fought a diversionary attack on 25th September 1915
2nd Division
0 1 2 3
Miles
SCALE

twenty mile front from Arras in the south to the La Bassée canal in the north. In order to support the main assault, various subsidiary attacks north of the La Bassée canal and in the vicinity of Ypres were to take place simultaneously. For the British main attack, on the six miles from the La Bassée canal to the village of Grenay, General Sir Douglas Haig's First Army was to be used. This consisted of Lieutenant-General Henry Rawlinson's IV Corps and Lieutenant-General Hubert Gough's I Corps. In reserve were the 3rd Cavalry Division and XI Corps. From north to south, the Divisions were part of the 2nd, the 9th, 7th, 1st, 15th, and the 47th. In the Ypres sector's subsidiary attack, the 3rd and 14th Divisions of General Herbert 'Plum' Plumer's Second Army, were to undertake the operation. For the subsidiary attacks north of the La Bassée canal, the III Corps, Indian Corps, and the remainder of the 2nd Division were to be used. These three units were also all part of General Sir Douglas Haig's First Army.

As has been related above, the 2nd Division was to be positioned astride the La Bassée canal. Its principal task was to form a defensive flank, facing north-east, to cover the main assault in the south. In addition, they were to push forward vigorously, with a view to tying in the forces facing them, so that they could not be withdrawn for use in a counter-attack against the main British assault. The 5th Infantry Brigade [Brigadier-General C.E. Corkran], of which the 52nd Light Infantry was a part, was to be north of the canal, at Givenchy, the 6th Brigade [Brigadier-General A.C. Daly], south of it, at Cuinchy, and the 19th Brigade [Brigadier-General P.R. Robertson], south of the La Bassée to Béthune road as far as Sims Keep. The 5th Brigade would attempt to advance to a line through Canteleux to Chapelle St. Roch, the right to prolong the line south of the La Bassée canal, and the left thrown back to join the right of the Indian Corps in the original British front line.

The 5th Brigade would have in the front line from north to south: the 52nd, from the northern end of the northern craters to Berkeley Street [about 100 yards south of the Shrine]; the 1st Queen's, between Berkeley Street and Shaftesbury Avenue; the 2nd Highland Light Infantry, from Shaftesbury Avenue along the front of the Duck's Bill to Corunna Road; two companies of the 9th Highland Light Infantry, just north of the La Bassée canal. Although, the 52nd, 1st Queen's and 2nd H.L.I. were to be in a continuous formation in the front line trenches, there was to be a significant half mile gap between the 2nd and 9th H.L.I. battalions. However, the inner companies of these two battalions were to link up as the attack progressed. The 2nd Worcestershire was held in reserve.

The instructions for Haig's First Army were to advance from between Lens and the La Bassée canal towards the line Henin - Lietard - Carvin. Initially, the line Loos - Hulluch and the ground extending towards the La Bassée canal

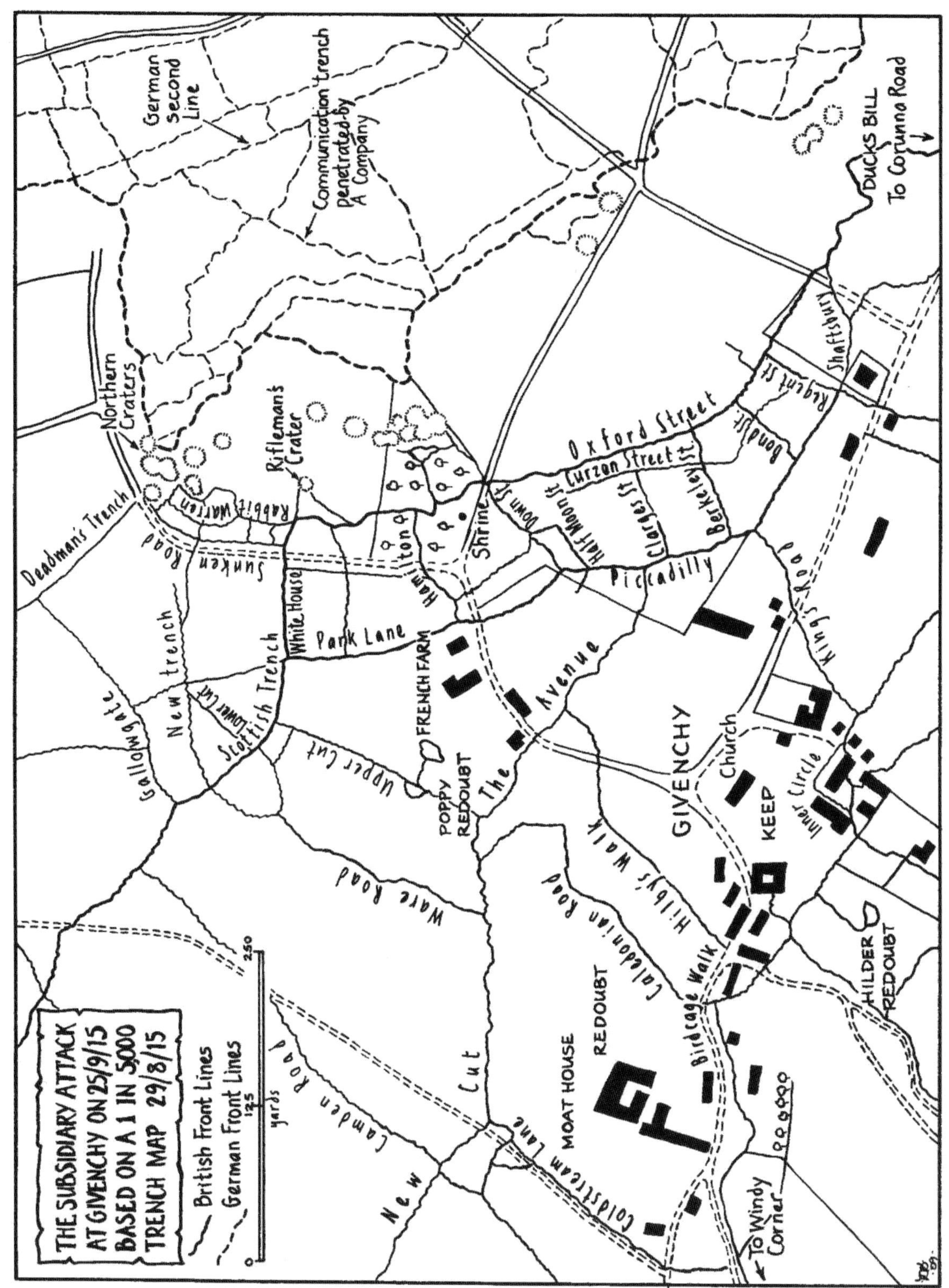
THE SUBSIDIARY ATTACK
AT GIVENCHY ON 25/9/15
BASED ON A 1 IN 5,000
TRENCH MAP 29/8/15
British Front Lines
German Front Lines
0
125
250
yards
German Second Line
Communication trench penetrated by A Company
DUCKS BILL
To Corunna Road
Northern Craters
Rifleman's Crater
Deadman's Trench
Rabbit Warren
Sunken Road
Oxford Street
Regent St
Shaftsbury
Bond St
Curzon Street
Berkeley St
Clarges St
Half Moon St
Down St
Shrine
Hamilton
Piccadilly
White House
Park Lane
New trench
Lower Cut
Scottish Trench
Gallowgate
FRENCH FARM
The Avenue
Upper Cut
POPPY REDOUBT
Kings Road
GIVENCHY
Church
KEEP
Inner Circle
Hilby's Walk
Caledonian Road
Ware Road
HILDER REDOUBT
Birdcage Walk
REDOUBT
MOAT HOUSE
Cut
New
Camden Road
Coldstream Lane
To Windy Corner

was to be their objective. Immediately after piercing this line, units were to be pushed forward, to gain crossings of the Haute-Deule canal, between Harnes and Bauvin. North of the La Bassée canal, the enemy was to be engaged vigorously in order to prevent him from withdrawing troops for a counter-attack. Wherever, the Germans gave up ground they were to be followed up with the greatest energy.

The key to any significant breakthrough on the Western Front was the preparatory artillery barrage. As Edmonds in the *Official History* stated:

> The Battle of Loos is a landmark in the history of artillery development. It was the first British attack on a large scale (11,250 yards of front), although, owing to the employment of cloud gas, the total force of artillery in proportion to the frontage was much weaker than at Neuve Chapelle (frontage 1,450 yards) and Festubert (bombardment frontage 5,080 yards). In spite of the fact that there was a prolonged and systematic bombardment, the number of guns and amount of ammunition (although nearly three times as much per yard as Festubert) available were not sufficient to make it formidable.

Edmonds clearly recognised that there were insufficient guns and ammunition for a formidable bombardment. On September 25th, the total number of guns used in action with the First Army was 897: consisting of siege and heavy artillery, 47; counter battery, 62; divisional field artillery, 788. The most numerous artillery piece was the 18-pounder, of the divisional field artillery, of which there were 832 in total. Throughout 1915 both the quality and the quantity of ammunition was a problem for the Allies. In the preliminary bombardment for Festubert [three days] 31,221 shells were used. Here at Loos [four days] 255,883 shells, and, at Messines, in 1917 [twelve days] no less than 3,561,530 shells were expended. In the assault on Messines ridge, the much heavier barrage combined with nineteen huge mines, allowed a significant breach of the German line.

Sir Douglas Haig believed that, with the limited artillery at his disposal, the inability to lay down a formidable bombardment could be compensated for by the use of gas, just prior to the start of the assault. Chlorine would incapacitate the enemy by blinding them or leaving them drowning in the secretions of their own lungs. In high concentrations a rapid death could follow from asphyxia. However, the efficacy of the chlorine gas was very much dependent on the direction and strength of the wind for it to drift over the German trenches in sufficient quantities to harm the enemy. In order to be effective, the wind needed to be in an arc from south-west to north-west, and if from any other direction would afflict the friendly forces rather than the enemy. The strength of the wind was crucial – too strong and the gas would disperse, and if too weak the gas would hang over the British trenches. Ideally it should be of the order of ten to fifteen miles per hour. Indeed, if it was deemed impractical to use gas, then the British would launch a much-reduced main attack south of the La Bassée canal.

By September 19th, no less than 5,500 cylinders, containing 150 tons of chlorine gas, had been sent to France in great secrecy. I Corps was allotted 2,568 cylinders for its 259 trench bays, with 199 south of the La Bassée canal and 60 north of it[359]. The cylinders for the northern sector were sent by train to Gorre, and then by lorry to Cambrin Church for temporary storage. Large numbers of men carried the 140 lb cylinders to the front line trenches where they were placed in special recesses dug under the parapet. Here they were protected from incoming shells by sandbags and, in the event, no cylinder was damaged during its transit to the front line. The cylinders were operated by Royal Engineers Gas officers, who were responsible for turning the gas on. The delivery system, connecting the cylinder to metal pipes projecting beyond the parapet, was made of rubber hose.

It was reported that the German gas mask would protect the enemy for only 40 minutes, and that if they were to be disabled, the gas would have to flow for at least this length of time. A cylinder emptied in two minutes and therefore at least 20 cylinders per trench bay were required to achieve this objective. Unfortunately, there were insufficient cylinders for the purpose and it was proposed to turn them intermittently on and off, and to use smoke to simulate gas in the intervals. Single smoke candles made of phosphorus were used for this purpose, and triple ones to form a thick smoke curtain behind which the attacking troops could advance. However, for the 52nd's attack, gas would be started at the same time as the smoke, and both would be run continuously for only ten minutes. In the event the gas was only run for six to eight minutes and only two thirds of the available cylinders were used.

The key to a successful gas attack, to make up for the limited artillery bombardment, was the direction and strength of the wind. The more accurate the weather forecast the more likely the efficacy of the gas attack. The man with the unenviable task of making that forecast was Captain Ernest Gold, a Cambridge don, and Britain's leading meteorologist. On the night of September 24th, Gold

---

[359] Lieutenant-Colonel Louis 'Father' Vaughan, G.S.O. 1, of the 2nd Division, sent instructions to the 5th Brigade, on September 8th, to the effect that each of their 60 trench bays would have three cylinders of chlorine, making a total of 180. This was considerably less than the fifteen cylinders per bay for use south of the La Bassée canal.

was present at Sir Douglas Haig's army headquarters, and in almost constant contact with him throughout the night. At 3 a.m., the south-westerly wind was one mile per hour, but Gold felt that it would be stronger at sunrise. Haig fixed zero hour for 5.50 a.m. which meant that the main attack, south of the La Bassée canal, would commence at 6.30 a.m. At 5 a.m., it was almost calm, as one of Haig's staff officers lit a cigarette and watched the smoke drift away to the north-east[360]. However, at 5.15 a.m., Haig gave the order to carry on, and the die was cast. Clouds of toxic chlorine gas were about to be unleashed on the unsuspecting Germans. Sadly, in the northern sector of the battlefield, the chlorine would harm the British soldier more than the enemy.

We left the 52nd in their Givenchy trenches on September 23rd. The preparatory bombardment continued heavily all the next day. This led to two men being killed and three more wounded during the day. In the evening they took up their battle positions, for the subsidiary attack to the forthcoming Battle of Loos, at Givenchy. Their role, with the remainder of the 5th Brigade, was to keep the enemy occupied, so that they were unable to go to the support of their comrades, south of the La Bassée canal. I Corps orders required the 5th Brigade to follow the enemy up vigorously if they should retire, but they could not push on too far, as there were no reserves available to them. The Germans facing them were from the 56th Regiment, with the supporting battalion in Canteleux. They were part of the German 14th Division from Westphalia. Earlier in 1915, they had suffered considerable losses at Neuve Chapelle and Festubert, and had had to be reinforced. The 56th Regiment was reported by Brigadier-General Charles Corkran, commanding the 5th Brigade, to be very well turned out and in full marching order. The inference was that an attack was expected.

The 52nd's Regimental Headquarters moved to deep shelters behind the support trenches. Although they had been purpose built, Lieutenant-Colonel Archibald Eden, Commanding Officer of the 52nd, was not impressed as, safe and deep as they were, space was limited and the staff were on top of one another. The 52nd's frontage extended from the north end of the northern craters to about 100 yards south of the Shrine, at Berkeley Street. As described earlier, to their right were the 1st Queen's, 2nd H.L.I. and 9th H.L.I. respectively. In addition, a party of the 5th Field Company, Royal Engineers, was ready to assist in the event of a successful attack, and a working party of 100 men, from the 7th King's [Liverpool] Regiment, was employed to dig out a communication trench. But in the event, the work did not proceed very far. Later in the attack, in one part of the line, a party thus employed very much impeded the advance of reinforcements on

[360] The 2nd *Division's War Diary* recorded 'Wind was S.S.W., very light, estimated rate about 2 miles per hour. Day was wet with heavy rain at times'.

this line of little cover. The 5th Brigade Headquarters was moved to Fanshawe Castle, between Pont Fixe and Windy Corner. Captain Guy Blewitt, now Staff Captain 5th Brigade, 'drank success to our arms in a bottle of fiz'.

Prior to the assault, packs and waterproof coats were stored, and haversacks were worn in the middle of the back, with a waterproof ground-sheet and cardigan rolled on the belt below. Every man carried 220 rounds of ammunition and two sandbags. Smoke helmets, made of felt, and each with a rectangular formica eye-piece, were to be worn to protect the men from the effects of the chlorine gas. However, this limited their vision and every member of the Regiment had a recognition patch sewn on to the upper left arm. Company commanders had their appropriate company letter, the platoon commanders the number of their platoon [large], and the men their platoon number [small]. Medical orderlies wore a red and white band on one arm, and the five men carrying vermoral sprayers[361] had an armlet with a V on it. Eden and Richard Crosse, the Adjutant, had small pieces of regimental ribbon pinned on their shoulders.

Archibald Eden had positioned A Company, under Captain Reggie Owen, on the right, supported by C Company, and Lieutenant Pierce Newton-King's D Company[362], on the left, with B Company in support. Major Charles Higgins was withdrawn from command of B Company to become second-in-command to Eden. Corps orders limited the number of officers allowed to go into action to twenty, and Second-Lieutenant Keith Peploe remained behind in reserve, at Windy Corner. In addition, reserve signallers and machine-gunners, company N.C.O.s in excess of one platoon serjeant and two N.C.O.s per section were left behind.

At about 2 a.m., in the early hours of September 25th, the 52nd was informed that the "accessory" cylinders of chlorine gas, would be opened at 5.50 a.m., and that their attack would begin ten minutes later at 6 a.m. These timings would also apply to most of the 5th Brigade, in their positions north of the La Bassée canal. The exception was the Glasgow Highlanders [9th H.L.I.], situated immediately to the north of the canal, who would attack 30 minutes later, at 6.30

---

361 To disperse the gas.

362 On September 1st 1915, the *Regimental Chronicles* recorded Captain John Southey as the senior officer in D Company [until August he had been the Machine-Gun Officer when he was replaced by Captain Calvert FitzGerald]. However, Newton-King's obituary, also in the *Chronicles,* stated that he was the company commander, at the time of his death, here at Givenchy. Possibly, Southey had been temporarily moved to take command of B Company after Charles Higgins became second-in-command of the Regiment. Southey was quoted by Archibald Eden as describing the Germans lighting a line of fires in front of their second line. He could have seen this with B Company which was supporting D. The other possibility was that Southey remained in command of D Company and that Newton-King's obituary in the *Chronicles* is inaccurate.

a.m. This was at the same time that the principal assault, south of the La Bassée canal, from Cuinchy to Grenay started. The 9th H.L.I.'s attack was co-ordinated with that of the 6th Brigade situated just to the south of the canal at Cuinchy. The Royal Engineers Gas Officer opened his gas cylinders promptly at the appointed hour, and clouds of the toxic yellowish-green chlorine gas poured forth into the atmosphere. Unfortunately, the air above the 52nd's trenches was almost motionless, with the result that the gas hung very considerably in their portion of the line. The chlorine did more harm to the 52nd, despite their primitive respirators, than to the enemy, who only in a very few cases were found to have been affected by the gas, much to the chagrin of the men of the 52nd.

Captain Reggie Owen's A Company was on the right of the Regimental area, from approximately the Shrine to Berkeley Street, just to the east of what remained of the ruined village of Givenchy. The German front line was some 200 yards away and parallel to the British line. Owen decided to attack on a frontage of one platoon and at 6 a.m. his first line advanced and reached the German front line without opposition. The first of his men to get into the German trench were certain that no Germans had been gassed, although several of the enemy had been recently killed by shellfire. Those Germans still alive in the German front line were dispatched with the bullet or bayonet. After his first two platoons were ensconced in the German line, Reggie Owen negotiated the 200 yards of no man's land, safely, with his third and fourth platoons. Owen's men pushed up a communication trench, running in a north-easterly direction, and certainly reached the German second line, a fact confirmed by Lieutenant Clement Chevallier who was with them. Those men on the right became mixed up with men of the 1st Queen's, and they were led by an officer of that Regiment, who was subsequently wounded. On the way to the German second line they killed about six Germans in a dug-out, and passed several more dead ones in the trench. However, these men were attacked by the enemy from cross-communication trenches and, eventually driven out of their position by a lack of bombs, beat a hasty retreat, apparently without loss, back to the German front line. It was reported that some men of the 52nd had penetrated as far as 150 yards beyond the German second line.

The key weapon in this brisk little trench action was the bomb. A Company had about 20 bombers, who carried 200 bombs of the new Ball pattern. Each man carried five in a belt and each pair shared a box of two dozen more. In the event, the number of bombs available to the 52nd proved to be inadequate, both in number and quality. The damp atmosphere made the ignition of the bombs, by a striker on an armlet, difficult or impossible. Owen had the foresight to take a dozen boxes of matches with his company, which allowed more bombs to be detonated. In addition, his men successfully used captured German bombs on the enemy. There was no doubt that the German bomb was superior to that of the British, in reliability and the distance it could be thrown. The wooden handle of the German bomb allowed it to be hurled a prodigious distance in comparison with the ball grenade.

Reggie Owen had taken a telephone plus wire across to the enemy line, with A Company, and for a while he was able to communicate directly with his Commanding Officer, Archibald Eden. However, this did not last for long as Owen was reported to be away on the German second line. Eden felt that communications between Battalion Headquarters and the companies worked 'wonderfully well' during the action, principally with runners.

Efforts were made to support Owen's A Company during the early morning. Two machine-guns followed them across and were thought to have been lost. The serjeant in charge of the first gun was seen to be blown up by a shell. The former schoolmaster Second-Lieutenant Lancelot Vidal tried to take a second gun over no man's land but was killed in the vain attempt. Both machine-guns were later recovered. At one point during the morning, it was reported that A Company was almost surrounded, and as a last resort Lieutenant Victor Jacob was allowed, with the remainder of the battalion's bombs, to make a counter-attack. This failed and poor Jacob, having served with the 52nd for just over a month, was added to the list of the missing. Between 8-9 a.m., Owen asked for reinforcements from his supporting company, C. One platoon with the young and energetic Second-Lieutenant Edward Hughes, went over the parapet to A Company's assistance. However, it could make little headway across no man's land under intense German artillery fire. The exact fate of this platoon was unrecorded, but its commander 'Little' Hughes was missing and presumed killed.

Reggie Owen's A Company was gradually driven back to a thirty-yard section of the German front line trench, where they managed to isolate themselves with the aid of barricades. Eventually, lack of bombs forced them to withdraw once more to their own front line, via Lone Tree Sap. Whilst retiring, Owen came across a crater which he was unaware existed. Using it as a redoubt, he tried to rally his men without much success. However, he did gain five minutes for his wounded's retirement. By 10.25 a.m., Owen and the survivors of A Company were back in their own front line. Later, it was established that they were the last men of the 5th Brigade to leave the German trenches. Owen estimated that his men had accounted for certainly 50 dead Germans, although his men thought that the minimum number of enemy dead, in this set of trenches, was 70. The initial casualties in A Company were thought to be fifteen, known to have been killed in the German trench, with 45 wounded, and 49 missing. A high casualty rate of 64%.

A few days after the battle Reggie Owen wrote an account of it for his parents at home in Ripon[363].

> The German front-line trench was about 200 yards in front of us and parallel to ours. The two front lines of my company (i.e., half the company) appeared to get into the German trench without many casualties, and then I went over myself. I negotiated the 200 yards all right, and was then held up for a minute or two by the barbed wire, but I managed to reach the trench. In it I found a good many dead Germans lying, also some of our own men. The Germans were holding their second-line trenches, only about 30 yards away, and it was simply a bombing competition the whole time.
>
> We soon ran out of bombs, but fortunately found German ones, which we used with good effect. It was impossible to get up reinforcements, and eventually, when we had no bombs left and the Germans were on top of us, I gave the order to retire. Somehow or other we managed to get back to our original front line trench, from which we had started. Afterwards I found out that the two regiments on our right had retired some time before we did, and that we had been left there entirely by ourselves. God knows how I escaped. I was in the German trench the whole time, and got back again to our own unscratched. Out of about 170 of my Company who started, I have now about 60 odd unhurt. The Regiment has had 9 officers killed and wounded, I believe.
>
> The gas failed absolutely with us, and so the whole 2nd Division attack failed, but we hear that, further south, Vermelles way, we have been successful, and that the French have got on a lot.

At 6 a.m., at the same time as A Company attacked, on their left, Lieutenant Pierce Newton-King, led his D Company out of the Warren Trenches, to the west of the northern group of craters, towards the German front line. A Company had 200 yards to cross to the enemy line, but D Company had a shorter distance to go, as the lines were much closer together on the left. In addition, the craters formed an obstruction, and the firing of a mine further confused matters. Despite wearing smoke helmets, men of D Company were affected by the lingering gas, but managed to remain in position. Amongst those gassed was

---

[363] Letter written to his parents on September 26th 1915.

Second-Lieutenant George Field, who started the war as a company serjeant-major, and would, in 1918, command the Regiment for several weeks. D Company received a very warm reception from the enemy. They advanced in two parties, each of two sections; the southern one under Pierce Newton-King immediately came under severe machine-gun fire and practically no advance could be made. Boldly, Newton-King, with his men, tried to outflank the craters, but on rounding one corner of them, nearly all the 30 men and their company commander were killed by machine-gun fire. The northern party fared no better as, on advancing to the edge of the craters, they found the enemy ready prepared for them, and for some little time a bombing and fire encounter took place in which they were able to kill many Germans, but no ground could be gained. Intact wire entanglements and numerous machine-guns stopped them in their tracks. The Germans had heavily fortified the craters and had many machine-guns in position. Later, the remnants of three platoons, from D Company, managed to join their A Company comrades to the right. The original D Company assault was a fiasco and achieved nothing at considerable expense in men's lives.

An unnamed company serjeant-major of the 52nd who took part in the attack has left a description of it[364].

> I believe we have done very well in some parts of the line. Where our Bgde: attacked we made no progress at all and indeed were not expected to. Its about the strongest part of the G. Line and wd: want some taking. In time now they will be forced to evacuate it.
>
> We attacked at 6 am last Saturday 25/9/15 after giving them 6 mins: of "smelling salts" [gas]. The wind blew being in the wrong direction we got the full benefit of it. 'D' was set an impossible task as we were relying on the stuff to do the work for us. At 30 yards it took no effect on them so it couldn't possibly have done so where 'A' attacked as the distance was 150-250 yds there. 'A' got into the G. first line with very little opposition and a few got to the 2nd line. On the right of 'A' the whole Bgde got the 1st line and in some places the 2nd. I afterwards went over to reinforce 'A'. After we'd been in the trench ½ an hour or so the G:s counter-attacked from the left flank with a strong bombing party. They also enfiladed us from the high position which 'D' was set to take. Having used all the bombs

364 A 'Copy of a letter from C.S.M. – 52nd Light Infantry' which was found amongst Geoffrey Titherington's letters. It was written on September 30th 1915, almost certainly by C.S.M. Fred Clare of D Company.

> we took over in the first place and not being able to get further supplies they simply doubled us up from the flank and it was a case of every man for himself, back to our own lines. In the scrimmage to get back we had most of the casualties. Eventually the whole Bgde: had to retire to its original line. Having to retire cast no reflection on us, for we accomplished what was expected namely to draw G. Reserves. ---
>
> Well, I have managed to dodge them once more but I suppose I shall meet my Waterloo one of these times. Poor Tom Hudson went this time. He has stuck it right through: he was hit by a whiz-bang and got the full weight of it: he was standing in a communication trench at the time.

One man who had a grandstand view of the operations that morning, was Captain Guy Blewitt, the former 52nd officer, now Staff Captain of the 5th Brigade. At 4 a.m., he was awoken with the news that zero hour was 5.50 a.m., and he made his way to their observation platform at Belle Vue near the remains of the church in Givenchy. The morning was stuffy and rain during the night had made the trenches treacherous to move along. At 5.25 a.m., Blewitt reached the post, and looking across towards the German's line saw that a gentle south-westerly wind was wafting away the smoke from their fires. He believed that the wind was too light for the gas to be let off. However, on the dot of 5.50 a.m., Blewitt witnessed jets of white smoke from the north of the Orchard down to the Duck's Bill. This was followed by barrages of smoke, fired from the Sunken road and to the south of the Duck's Bill, to protect the flanks of the assault. In due course, the smoke barrage around the Duck's Bill had to be stopped, as it blew north into the faces of the attacking British battalions. All along the intervening front smoke candles were lit, under cover of which the 52nd, 1st Queen's and 2nd H.L.I. advanced.

To Guy Blewitt, from his vantage point it was 'a grand sight', and the opposition appeared to be light. The enemy had lit fires on their parapet to disperse the gas. British soldiers could be seen walking about on the edge of the German trenches and firing down into them. At 6.50 a.m., Blewitt walked back to the 5th Brigade Headquarters to report what he had seen, and on the way met men who had been gassed by leaking cylinders. He also noted that his first impression about the strength of the wind had been correct, and some of their own men had been gassed. An hour later he returned to Belle Vue, but there was little to be seen, apart from a working party digging from Lone Tree Sap towards the German line, under machine-gun fire. The village of Givenchy was under heavy shellfire, and around 8.50 a.m., a shell hit the bottom of the observation tower. When Blewitt called down the speaking-tube to the basement, where the signallers were situated, all he got was a puff of smoke up the tube. On going down to see what had happened, he found out that the men had been killed. Once more, at 9.50 a.m., Blewitt returned to the Brigade Headquarters, in Fanshawe Castle, and was astonished to hear that there had been a general retreat north of the La Bassée canal, although news from further south was better.

All the surviving men of the 52nd were back in their front line by 10.25 a.m. and the other battalions of the 5th Brigade fared no better. The 2nd H.L.I., at the Duck's Bill, and the 1st Queen's, between them and the 52nd, each managed to get two companies into the German line, but were forced out by 10 a.m., prior to Reggie Owen's withdrawal with A Company. The German artillery was very active between 6-11 a.m. with 'whizz bangs'[365], on the British trenches, and heavier ordnance firing about Givenchy Church. The 9th H.L.I., positioned close to the north bank of the La Bassée canal, whose attack was co-ordinated with that of the 6th Brigade south of the canal, never left their trenches in any force. They had the misfortune to be seriously gassed by chlorine blown across the canal from the south. The officer responsible for the release of this gas, in the 6th Brigade area, was reluctant to open the valves on his cylinders, as he judged that the direction and strength of the wind was inappropriate, but was ordered to do so. However, he was allowed to switch off, if the gas was harming his own men, and after ten minutes did so. Unfortunately, many of the 6th Brigade and also of the 9th H.L.I. would suffer badly at the hands of their own gas. A patrol of volunteers from the 9th H.L.I. was sent out to test the defences of the enemy. They were annihilated to a man, by heavy rifle and machine-gun fire from the Tortoise Redoubt, one of their original objectives.

The *Official History* of the Worcestershire Regiment, the 5th Brigade's reserve battalion, gave a graphic summary of the actions of the rest of their Brigade, on September 25th.

> Very soon rumours of disaster began to filter back from the front line to the 2nd Worcestershire in their reserve position. Disabled men trickled past, either wounded or choking from gas fumes. It became known that the wind had proved too light to carry the gas forward from our trenches to those of the enemy. The dense cloud of gas and smoke had hung motionless in front of our parapet. The attacking troops had emerged half-blinded by their gas masks, into broad

[365] German 77 mm. field guns. The whistle of the shell's arrival almost coincided with the sound of its explosion. An alternative name was a pip-squeak.

daylight on the further side of the stationary cloud, and had fallen in swathes before the enemy's fire. No ground had been gained and the attack of the 5th Brigade was at a standstill.

Major-General Henry Horne, commanding the 2nd Division, has left on the record his views why it was not possible for the 5th Brigade to establish themselves in the German trenches.

> Considering that the gas had failed to affect the Germans, that the attack was no surprise, that the rain had interfered with the action of the ball grenades, and that no support was available, I am of the opinion that it was not possible for us to establish ourselves in the German trenches.

On September 25th, the remainder of the 2nd Division, the 6th and 19th Brigades, although they fought bravely, achieved even less than the 5th Brigade. The 6th Brigade suffered from its own chlorine gas, despite using smoke hoods, which did not protect them fully. In many places the 6th Brigade's battalions found the wire uncut in front of them and were unable to seriously threaten the German front line trench. The 19th Brigade fared little better, and also suffered from the effects of their own gas blowing back on them. They went forward in fine order, as if on exercise, but without protective smoke, they were met by a hail of rifle and heavy machine-gun fire, which decimated them in front of the enemy's wire. Edmonds in the *Official History* recorded that 'the 2nd Division (Major General H.S. Horne) awoke to a day of tragedy, unmitigated by any gleam of success'. While it was indeed a day of tragedy, it is arguable that the 2nd Division's offensive actions, helped to pin down the enemy troops in front of them, who might otherwise have been used to great effect further south, towards the village of Loos.

Fortunately for the British, the opening day of the Battle of Loos, was a much more successful one for them in the southern part of the battlefield. Units of the I and IV Corps moved with great dash and captured the enemy's front line from the formidable Hohenzollern Redoubt southwards, and also the village of Loos, which gave its name to the battle. In places the German second line was penetrated, and by the evening Hulluch and Haisnes were under threat. In the south, the wind was more favourable, and the gas more effective. All day the fighting was severe with frequent counter-attacks in poor weather conditions. The position of the British line, on the night of September 25th, was promising. That night, Sir John French succinctly described the British dispositions, in his dispatch. 'From the Double Crassier, south of Loos, by the western part of Hill 70, to the western exit of Hulluch, thence by the quarries and western end of Cité St. Elie, east of Fosse 8, back to our original line'.

At the end of September 25th, the 52nd were able to count the cost of their action at Givenchy. Three officers and 33 men had been killed, and six officers and 124 men had been wounded. The following day, one of the wounded officers, the 21-year-old Second-Lieutenant Cecil Hurst-Brown, who had only been with the Regiment for four months, died of his wounds. In addition, 69 men were missing, including the brave Lieutenant Victor Jacob who had tried to get bombs to A Company when they were almost surrounded. The dead officers were: Lieutenant Pierce Newton-King was the son of a former 52nd officer, who commanded the 7th Battalion during the Great War[366], and was also a fine linguist. Second-Lieutenant Edward Hughes, known as 'Little Hughes' in view of his short stature, was the elder son of a former commanding officer of the 52nd, Lieutenant-Colonel R.G.H. Hughes, who also commanded the 7th Battalion in the war. The younger Hughes was a fine schoolboy boxer, at Rugby School, and was said to have had 'a very large heart encased in a not very large body'. The 28-year-old Second-Lieutenant Lancelot Vidal, the machine-gun officer, had been a master at Radley, and was a fine sportsman and keen botanist. He had served with the Regiment for just two months. Among the dead men was Serjeant-Major Tom Hudson, one of the heroes of Nonne Bosschen Wood, who had survived the war, so far, without a scratch.

The wounded officers were: Lieutenant George Field [gassed]. Second-Lieutenants; Thomas Withington [gunshot wound back - slight], Aubrey Carew Hunt [gunshot wound buttock and right knee], P.C. Webster [gunshot wound left wrist], and James Belgrave [gassed - facial wounds]. The Medical Officer, Captain Ernest Scott was among the wounded, and he was temporarily replaced by Lieutenant R. Clark. Lieutenant-Colonel Archibald Eden wrote of 'Scott's untiring energy and searching for and tending wounded on the battlefield and in organizing the stretcher bearers..........on September 25th he tended the wounded under fire until slightly wounded himself. On both occasions [Festubert and Givenchy] all the arrangements he had made for collecting and evacuating the wounded proved extremely satisfactory'. In March 1916 Scott would be promoted to D.A.D.M.S. 2nd Division[367].

---

366 Lieutenant-Colonel F.J. Newton-King.

367 "Doctor Scott" left the Regiment, in March 1916, to become D.A.D.M.S., 2nd Division, a post he held until the following October when he was transferred to England sick. On January 1st 1917 he was awarded the D.S.O.

The initial success of Sir Douglas Haig's army, on the opening day of the Battle of Loos, was to be marred by the lack of available reserves to exploit the situation. The Commander-in-Chief, Sir John French, had kept the general reserve, consisting of XI Corps, under Lieutenant-General Richard Haking, and the Cavalry Corps, in his own hands. To make matters worse, the general reserve was situated in the vicinity of Lillers, many miles from the battlefield. Haig had wanted the general reserve to be placed under his own direct orders, and much closer to the front. General friction between French and Haig exacerbated matters. The three divisions of XI Corps were the Guards, 21st, and 24th Divisions. The 21st and 24th Divisions were new, and had never been in the line before, let alone under fire. When they arrived at the front, early on September 26th, they were soaked to the skin by heavy rain, and exhausted by the long march. It had only been intended to use these inexperienced troops to follow up a German rout, and not to place them in a difficult position such as they found themselves in. The elite Guards Division, of experienced men, had been expected to lead the 21st and 24th Divisions into action, but the reverse took place. There is no doubt that Sir John French had made an error of the greatest magnitude, in having his general reserve so far back, and for not swopping his inexperienced divisions with more experienced ones from the Somme. At the start of operations, French had been reluctant to attack into the industrial hinterland around Loos. Before the year was out, the Battle of Loos would cost him his position as Commander-in-Chief.

The night of September 25th was wet and stormy, with the Germans making a number of counter-attacks. The next day, the advance was held up despite the general reserve coming into the action. No great headway was made on the 27th, although some ground was won back. The 28th was used to consolidate the position and the British line changed little. Further to the south, the French had run into difficulties, leaving the British right flank exposed, and Sir John French persuaded General Joseph Joffre to relieve British troops, holding part of Hill 70, and the village of Loos. This was carried out on September 29th and 30th. Over the early days of October, the Germans attempted to regain the ground that they had lost. A particularly violent counter-attack, by the Germans, on October 8th, from Fosse 8 in the north, to the French IX Corps in the south, was repulsed at great cost to the enemy. Only at the Double Crassier and to the north-east of the Hohenzollern Redoubt, had the enemy made any ground, in exchange for the thousands of dead that lay unburied in front of the British trenches. Officially, the Battle of Loos was deemed to end on October 8th, but in practice the fighting continued.

The 52nd remained in their trenches, at Givenchy, for the next three days [September 26th-28th]. It was a very much depleted Regiment, A and C Companies having received the most casualties. During the day, on September 26th, it rained steadily, and the exhausted men laboured to repair the damage done to their trenches by the heavy shellfire. Fortunately, the enemy's artillery was not very active, although the trench mortars fired from time to time. In the evening, the Regimental Headquarters moved back to Windy Corner. Second-Lieutenant Cyril 'Shiny' Horley returned to the 52nd, having recovered from a gunshot wound to his heel, six months earlier.

The 27th proved to be a quiet day, although three men were wounded. The next day was fine, until the evening when it poured with rain, and at 10 p.m., the 52nd were relieved by the 1st Seaforth Highlanders, attached to the Sirhind Brigade. Archibald Eden felt pity for their replacements, in that they were taking over such a complicated system of trenches, for the first time, in such filthy weather. The Regiment then marched the five miles west to the Orphanage in Béthune.

In the afternoon of September 29th, the 52nd marched the one and a half miles to billets in Essars. Other units were present and it was a tight fit to get everyone placed. The following day was a restful one for the Regiment and they used the time to regain their strength and to clean themselves up. The next day, October 1st, at 8 a.m., Archibald Eden was summoned to the 5th Brigade's Headquarters, at Annequin, and then went with the Brigade Staff to reconnoitre their new trenches, in the vicinity of Vermelles. Meanwhile, at 8.30 a.m., the 52nd received orders to march, at 11 a.m., the eight miles from Essars to Vermelles. The journey took them three hours and they reached Vermelles at 2 p.m. At 5 p.m., they were rejoined by their Commanding Officer, Archibald Eden. Three hours later, the 52nd started their long trek through the recent battlefield to relieve the 2nd Royal Scots Fusiliers of the 7th Division. In this section of the line, the 7th Division had made a considerable advance, since September 25th. The Regiment marched up the Vermelles to Hulluch road, past the former British front line trenches, into the old German front line, and on to a gun line trench. Owing to the distance being three miles, and with many delays in the incompletely organized communication trenches, the relief did not start until 2 a.m. [October 2nd], and was not completed until an hour later. It was a most trying time.

In the early morning autumnal light of October 2nd, the men of the 52nd were able to survey their new surroundings. They were occupying a gun line trench [Gun Trench] which, prior to the fighting, was the site of an eight-gun German emplacement, from which the enemy had been driven out. They had left behind several guns, which the Royal Artillery was not slow to claim. The ground was covered with artillery ammunition and new gun sights. As was usual, the 52nd found excellent officer dug-outs with tables, chairs, beds, fire-places, and an elaborate system of electrical communication. However, the latter had been destroyed by the retreating Germans. Invariably, the enemy's dug-outs were better constructed and better furnished than those of the allies. To their left was the 2nd H.L.I., also in the Gun Trench, but with the enemy occupying a 200 yards section of the trench in their centre. This had been lost by the 7th Division, prior to the arrival of the 5th Brigade. Blocks had been placed at either end of the trench to isolate the enemy, who had free access to their section via a communication trench. That evening, the 2nd H.L.I. was ordered to drive the enemy out of their position in the trench.

In their positions to the east of Vermelles little could be seen of the German infantry facing the 52nd, and the enemy's shelling was light during the day, but heavier that night. This was in response to the attack, by the 2nd H.L.I., on the 200 yards of enemy trench to their left, in which they had captured a foothold the day before. The assault was only partly successful[368]. The 52nd had B and D Companies in the front line Gun Trench, with A, now only 70 men, 120 yards behind in a support trench, and C, 100 strong, in reserve, in the old German front line trench. During the day the 52nd deepened their trenches, although these were strongly built with deep dug-outs for shelter. One irritation was attempting to keep their candles alight as each explosion of an artillery shell blew them out. Guy Blewitt walked around the area in the morning and noted 'there are an appalling amount of dead men and horses and equipment lying about the result of the 25th fighting'.

On October 3rd, the 52nd maintained the same company positions in the trenches as for the previous day. There was little rifle fire from the enemy, who were not far away and could be seen walking around in small groups. The morning was fairly quiet, but in the afternoon there was heavy shelling, from both field and heavy artillery. Archibald Eden counted no less than 400 shells falling on their trenches during the afternoon. Fortunately these did little damage, although an unlucky shell fell directly into a trench, killing two good serjeants[369]. Three further men were wounded during the day. The 32nd reinforcement of 149 men arrived that night, and went some way to replacing the men lost at Givenchy, on September 25th. In the early hours of the following day, the 4th, the 52nd was

[368] Brigadier-General Charles Corkran, in a confidential memorandum, of October 6th, to the 2nd Division, reported that his Brigade was tired and there "was a lack of sufficient devil and drive to carry things through." Probably he was referring to this attack.

[369] Serjeant Herbert Knight Roberts, who was killed in action on the 3rd, was likely to have been one of them. No other named serjeant appeared in the records as having been killed that day.

relieved by the 1st Grenadier Guards of the Guards Division, and they marched wearily to billets in Beuvry, with their last company arriving at 6 a.m. Their Commanding Officer, Lieutenant-Colonel Archibald Eden, took the opportunity to catch up on his sleep, and in this he was joined by many in the Regiment.

No less than eight officer replacements joined the 52nd on October 5th. They were Lieutenant Hubert Rawson; Second-Lieutenants W.L. 'Billy' Barnard, C.H.B. 'Ben' Slocock, Reginald Strickland, C.G. Stephens, Archibald Ramsay, Thomas Tyrwhitt-Drake, and Jack Hardcastle. Two days later, a further three officers Lieutenants Ernest Whitfeld, Jasper Wyld and Douglas Sewell returned to the Regiment. Like Billy Barnard they had recovered from wounds received at Richebourg l'Avoué the previous May. On October 7th, the 52nd went into reserve to the 7th Division and fourteen machine-gunners reported for duty. Company training for the new drafts began, with the usual classes in wiring, drill and bombing. In addition, special attention was given to attacking tactics by small parties; these would become more sophisticated over the final years of the war. The 52nd was coming up to full muster, but it was a very different 52nd from the one that had gone to war, on August 13th 1914. Many of the best officers and men had become casualties, or had been promoted to staff appointments, or had left to lead the new Kitchener volunteer battalions. The Regiment would never be the same again.

If Sir Douglas Haig's First Army was to advance further, the Hohenzollern Redoubt, Fosse 8, and the Quarries had to be taken and held by British forces. An assault on these formidable areas of defence was intended for October 10th, but inclement weather led to a postponement until 2 p.m. on the 13th. Only the 5th Brigade of the 2nd Division was to play a small part in the attack. The principal divisions involved were the 1st, 11th, 12th, and 46th.

On October 10th, Archibald Eden was out early to reconnoitre a new area of trenches for the 52nd, and found them to be a perfect maze. They were situated close to Auchy, just south of the La Bassée to Béthune road. The Regiment rejoined the 5th Brigade, moved to Cambrin, and took over the second line trenches from the 2nd Yorkshire Regiment [Green Howards] at 5 p.m. They were in support of the 1st Queen's and the 9th H.L.I., who were in the front line. A and C Companies were in Headquarter Trench, near Lewis Keep, Sim's Keep, and Railway Keep. B Company was in Cambrin and D nearby.

The next two days saw the British artillery pounding the German line, around Fosse 8[370], Corons de Pekin[371], and the Hohenzollern Redoubt. This

[370] A Fosse was a principal pit-head. The iron girders forming the wheel-houses of lift cages, rising high above the ground, were useful observation points. Puits were auxillary mine-shafts.

[371] Corons or miner's cottages were built identically, in red brick, in parallel rows around pit-heads.

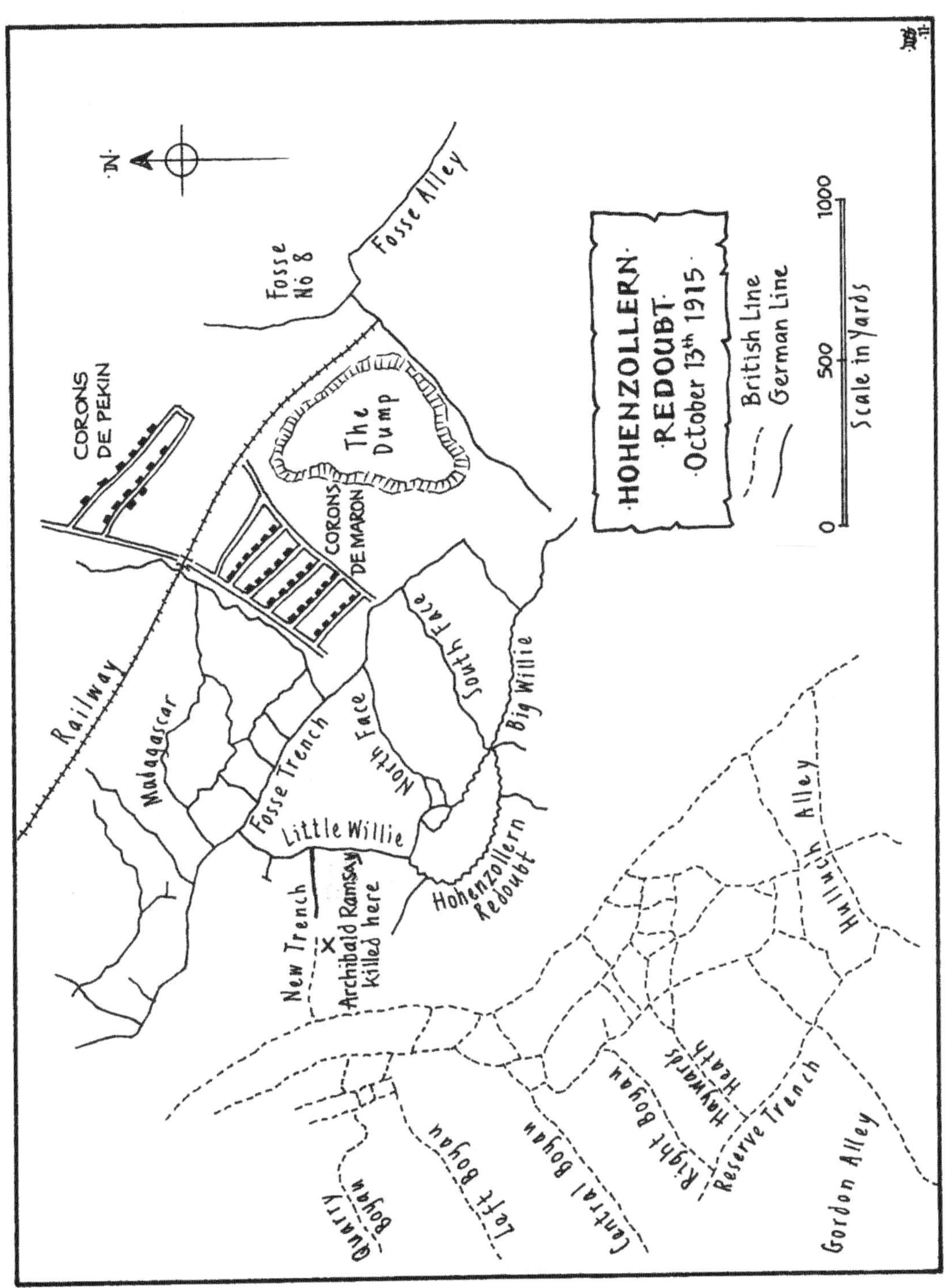
N
CORONS DE PEKIN
Fosse No 8
Fosse Alley
The Dump
CORONS DE MARON
Railway
Madagascar
Fosse Trench
North Face
South Face
Big Willie
Little Willie
Hohenzollern Redoubt
New Trench
Archibald Ramsay Killed here
HOHENZOLLERN REDOUBT
October 13th 1915
British Line
German Line
0
500
1000
Scale in Yards
Hulluch Alley
Haywards Heath
Reserve Trench
Right Boyau
Central Boyau
Left Boyau
Quarry Boyau
Gordon Alley

redoubt or keep was a German strong point, 300 yards long and slightly convex, and connected to the rest of the enemy's front line system by the Big Willie and Little Willie trenches[372]. British planners considered the Hohenzollern Redoubt to have been the strongest point of the front on the first day of the Battle of Loos. It jutted out into a wide stretch of no man's land and was designed to protect the all-important flat topped slag heap known as 'the Dump'. Despite only being twenty feet in height, it gave excellent views in all directions.

Lieutenant Ralph Kite, in a letter to his mother, described the aerial combat that was going on in the sky above the 52nd[373]. The next day, the 12th, he became acting Staff Captain 5th Infantry Brigade.

> Early this morning I heard a lot of shooting and put my head out of the window to see what was doing. Two of our planes were hustling a big Hun plane. All three were banging away with machine guns and didn't seem to mind where the bullets went, so I brought in my head. When I looked out again the whole sky was thick in our planes and the wretched Hun was fairly being hounded out of the sky. He had come down to within a couple of hundred feet and was dodging just like a three-quarter trying to avoid being collared. All our planes were circling round him in great swoops and one fellow finally steered straight for him. Needless to say the Hun flunked it and came down, with his three occupants all untouched.

A further bombardment was carried out by the British, between 12-1 p.m., on October 13th. Gas and smoke were used to cover an assault by the 46th [North Midland] Division, at 2 p.m., on the formidable Hohenzollern Redoubt. The 5th Brigade assisted the 46th Division with a bombing attack up a communication trench, New Trench, to its junction with Little Willie, but unfortunately this made little headway. At the same moment that the 46th Division started their assault, 2 p.m., the 52nd sent one officer, two N.C.O.s and 24 men to take part in the bombing attack. Boldly, the officer in question, Second-Lieutenant Archibald Ramsay, who had been attached to the Brigade bombers, led his men up New Trench supported by further men from the 1st Queen's. Sadly, Ramsay and most of his men were annihilated by heavy rifle and machine-gun fire concentrated on the sap head. Only a single officer of the Queen's, in a second party, managed to reach Little Willie trench. Poor Archibald Ramsay had only been with the Regiment for just over a week, and was one of the 52nd men

---

372 The irreverent names given to the Kaiser and his eldest son by the British troops.

373 Letter written to Edith Kite on October 11th 1915.

killed that day. His body was not recovered. The assault on the German line achieved little.

During the afternoon of October 14th, the 52nd moved up to the front line near Auchy and took over a section of the trenches from the 1st Queen's, with the 46th Division on their immediate right. B and D Companies were in the front line with A and C in support. The trenches that they were now occupying had been badly damaged during the recent attack, and a great deal of cleaning up and repair work had to be carried out. A new sap, Guildford Trench, was being dug out towards the German line, and an effort was made to link up with the troops holding part of the Hohenzollern Redoubt. A party from C Company had started this sap on the night of the 13th, and in the early hours of the next morning, while coming away, Lieutenants P.M. Ridout [buttock, pelvis, abdomen] and W.G. Mills [thigh] were wounded. Ultimately, Guildford Trench was linked up with the Hohenzollern Redoubt, and the Guards Division who were holding part of it.

Early in the morning of October 15th, a party from A and B Companies was working on Guildford Trench, when two German soldiers, an officer and a private, strayed into their vicinity. Captain Charles Fowke described what happened.

> We were ordered to barb-wire the head of the sap, as it was only 25 yards from the German trench. During this operation we were observed and fired on from close quarters, with the sole result of one man wounded and none killed. After this the men went back for more wire, and Hardcastle[374] and I remained at the top of the sap to await their return. While waiting I saw two men coming across the open, and I went to find out who they were, but before I reached them they greeted Hardcastle in German. He had not noticed their approach, but with great presence of mind drew his wire cutters and covered the leading German, who promptly threw up his hands. The other raised his rifle, but finding himself covered by my revolver, threw up his hands also. I took them back to our front trench, where one of them proved to be an officer. The other, who was slightly wounded, explained that he was "Blessé dans la viande!"

The 52nd remained in their front line trenches until October 18th. On all three days they were subject to shelling, which destroyed their mess kitchen. At noon on the 18th, the 52nd were grateful to leave the trenches and march to good accommodation in Montmorency Barracks in Béthune. It had been a grim five

[374] Second-Lieutenant Jack Hardcastle.

days and they had suffered ten men killed and a further seventeen wounded during the period October 14th-18th.

So the Battle of Loos came to an end. In 1920, the Battles Nomenclature Committee decided that it had run from September 25th-October 8th 1915, with subsequent actions on the Hohenzollern Redoubt from October 13th-19th. *The Principal Events of 1914–1918,* published in 1922, gave the same dates. However, Edmonds' *Official History* gives the casualty lists for the Battle of Loos for the period September 25th-October 16th, implying that this was the true duration. The casualties suffered by the 2nd Division, during the Battle of Loos, were 131 officers and 3,234 men. Of these the 52nd had had seven officers and 107 men killed, with a total number of wounded of 157. The bulk of their casualties had occurred at Givenchy on September 25th.

Neither Sir John French nor Sir Douglas Haig had wanted to assault the fortified German line at the Battle of Loos; they were obeying Earl Kitchener's orders. Kitchener wanted the British forces to do their utmost to support the French offensive, in the Artois and Champagne, even if heavy casualties were the result. He was well aware that the continuance of the Entente might depend on this support. Haig had hoped that the use of gas might mitigate the insufficient numbers of artillery and shells. In the event, the gas was a mixed blessing, effective in the south of the battlefield, and harming British forces more than the enemy in the north. The ground over which the French wished Haig to attack was flat and open, and the German defences strong and well sited. The old Regular divisions were much changed from those of 1914, in view of the high number of casualties that they had suffered. The Territorial Force's divisions were new to war and did not have professional officers and N.C.O.s. Kitchener's New Army divisions were not fully trained, and also had no experience of war. The initial successes of September 25th were not exploited, because Sir John French had allotted inexperienced divisions to his general reserve, and compounded this error by placing it too far to the rear, so that it could not quickly come into the line, to turn a break-in into a break-out. The failure to break out was a bitter disappointment for the British, although the French achieved no more on their right. In the Champagne, the French had an initial brilliant success, taking much of the enemy's front line, but were unable to do the same with the formidable second line defences. The failure of the offensive both in the Artois and Champagne precluded the possibility of encircling three German armies, as had been originally envisaged.

What of the 52nd's part in the Battle of Loos? They had taken their place in the subsidiary attack, at Givenchy, and had performed with great credit. Despite being more hindered than helped by the chlorine gas, the men of the 52nd had got beyond the enemy's second line, holding his forces in place, even if they did not break through to the line Canteleux - Chapelle St. Roch. The Commanding Officer of the 52nd, Lieutenant-Colonel Archibald Eden, took pride in Captain Reggie Owen's A Company being the last unit of the 5th Brigade to leave the German line. Major-General Henry Horne, commanding the 2nd Division, made clear in his report for the I Corps that the failure of the gas, lack of surprise, poor performance of the ball bomb and lack of support, made it impossible for the men of the 5th Brigade to establish themselves in the Germans' trenches. The role of the 52nd may not have had the glory of the main attack, but it was still an important one.

Chapter XI

A Wet Second Winter of the War in the Trenches.

October 19th 1915 - March 31st 1916

[Maps: pages 161, 237, 288, 463.]

The war on the Western Front began to close down for the winter months, and no major offensive by either side would be made before the German attack, at Verdun, in late February 1916. It was difficult enough to survive in the waterlogged trenches of these winter months, let alone undertake major offensive operations. The Second Battle of the Champagne, which had opened so promisingly, on September 25th, at the same time as the British attack at Loos, lost momentum and came to a stop without the enemy's second line being taken. The Germans counter-attacked at the end of October and reclaimed most of the territory gained by the French. The offensive was restarted without much success, and was finally abandoned in the first week of November.

Elsewhere the undertakings of the Allies were not going well. In Gallipoli, the August 6th landings, at Suvla Bay, had been a failure[375] and, in October 1915, the whimsical Commander-in-Chief, General Sir Ian Hamilton was replaced by the more pragmatic General Sir Charles Monro, the erstwhile commander of the 52nd Light Infantry's own 2nd Division. After studying the situation, Monro came to the conclusion that the Gallipoli Peninsula should be abandoned and, in November, Earl Kitchener, the War Minister, went out to see for himself and decided that Monro was right. Anzac Cove and Suvla Bay were evacuated on December 19th and 20th, and the final departure from Cape Helles took place on January 8th 1916. Miraculously, the withdrawal of the British and Anzac[376] troops went undetected. In addition, an Anglo-French expedition was sent to Salonika, in October, in an unsuccessful attempt to support Serbia against a combined attack by Germany, Austria-Hungary, and Bulgaria. Having failed to assist the Serbs, it was decided to keep the force in being, and the strength was increased to five British and three French divisions. The force would remain there until 1918[377].

Following the Battle of Loos, the position of the Commander-in-Chief, Sir John French, came under close scrutiny. At home there was considerable

---

[375] The original landings of British, Australian, New Zealand, and French troops had taken place on April 25th 1915.

[376] Australian and New Zealand Army Corps.

[377] The 7th [Service] and 8th [Pioneer] Battalions of the Oxfordshire and Buckinghamshire L.I. would serve in Salonika.

concern at the lack of success in the campaign of 1915. Neuve Chapelle, the Second Battle of Ypres, Aubers Ridge, Festubert, and Loos had led to a huge number of casualties, without the enemy's line being broken. French's failure to position his reserves close enough to the front to exploit the early successes of the Battle of Loos was rightly held against him, particularly by his leading subordinate, Sir Douglas Haig. In fact Haig believed that French should have been replaced immediately after the retreat from Mons, because he did not have the experience and intellectual capacity to command a large modern army in the field. By this stage of the war, French was 63-years-old and needed regular bed rest for a supposed heart condition. The die was cast, and on December 17th, Sir John French resigned his command, returned to England, and became Field-Marshal Commanding-in-Chief Home Forces with a viscountcy. His replacement was long overdue.

We left the 52nd in Montmorency Barracks, Béthune, on October 18th. The following day, the 35th reinforcement of 80 N.C.O.s and men arrived to help increase the numbers in the battalion. The Regiment was required to furnish working parties, of 450 men in the day and another 100 at night, to remove the empty chlorine gas cylinders from the trenches. The parties were taken to Cambrin and back in motor-lorries, but it was still back-breaking work. On the 21st, the 52nd moved to scattered billets in farm-houses to the west of Gonnehem, and the following day, they moved once more, to new billets, about two miles to the west, in an area called Censé la Vallée. For the next six days the 52nd remained here, in atrocious weather which led to the ground becoming waterlogged. The sodden ground interfered with company training, although the men were able to practice a new method of bombing attack. Major Charles 'Buggins' Higgins assumed temporary command of the Regiment, on October 25th, when Lieutenant-Colonel Archibald Eden was admitted to hospital with a bladder infection, in Béthune. During this period 20 further reinforcements arrived. From October 29th until November 2nd, the 52nd moved again, this time to billets at Annequin and Cambrin. The weather remained very wet, soaking the working parties that were sent on fatigues to the trenches.

On November 2nd, the 52nd paraded, at 8.30 a.m., and took over a sector of the Boyau trenches [see map page 463], south of the La Bassée to Béthune road and facing Auchy. Each company placed two platoons in the front line, and the remaining two in support. The German line was 200-300 yards away. D Company garrisoned the strong point of Sim's Keep and C Company took over Arthur's Keep. In front of them was a crater which they sapped out to, leaving the enemy sap-head 50 yards away. The trenches were in a poor state in view of the heavy rain, and a great deal of building up, revetting, and trench flooring was necessary before they were usable. One hundred and seventy pairs of thigh-length trench boots were issued to the men and were invaluable to them. On this first day, in the Boyau trenches, the 52nd was fortunate that the enemy was inactive and did not interfere with the Regiment. The weather improved over the next three days, which were occupied by more work on the trenches, and an officer's patrol went out to the crater. The Germans did little shelling and sniping and were generally quiet during this time. The Regiment remained here, in the Boyau trenches, until November 6th, when they were relieved by the 9th Highland Light Infantry, and marched to billets in Beuvry.

On November 5th, the now Lieutenant-General Henry Horne left the 2nd Division. He wrote a generous letter to Archibald Eden.

> I wish I had the opportunity of seeing you to thank all ranks of the 52nd for all that they have done for me. It has been a great honour to be associated with a battalion with such grand traditions, and I cannot say more than that. I am confident that you have all not only maintained but added to these traditions. I am very grateful for the good side, gallant fighting and loyal support of the 52nd, and I wish you farewell and all good fortune. I hope we may be associated again before long.

On November 7th, the 52nd moved one mile west of Béthune, to billets in Annezin, and remained there until the morning of November 11th. Archibald Eden returned to the Regiment from hospital and leave, on November 8th, and resumed command. Major Charles Higgins became the official senior major on the 10th. On the morning of November 11th, the 52nd marched to Annequin, four miles east-south-east of Béthune, and went into billets there. Garrisons, of one platoon each, were found for Russel's and Lewis' Keeps, which were local fortified strong points. The following day the 5th Infantry Brigade moved back for a rest period, and the Regiment found themselves, in familiar billets, in the Béthune Orphanage. They were on the move again on the 13th, marching to quarters in Gonnehem. It was a wet and blustery day and the 52nd was pleased to try out the new Divisional showers, and there was also a theatre in the area where films could be shown.

By November 15th, the whole of the 2nd Division was out of the line resting. The rest period would last until November 20th. A suitable field was found near Chocques, where adjutant's and company drills could be undertaken. Special courses in wiring, musketry, and bombing were run. The firing practice took place, on a small 50 yards range, near the Bois des Dames, and each man fired five rounds. The 52nd was visited by Major-General William George Walker V.C.[378], who had replaced Henry Horne in command of the 2nd Division, on November 5th. Walker had won his V.C., in East Africa in 1903, and he had commanded the Sirhind Brigade in 1915. Each 52nd officer, in turn, was introduced to his new Divisional commander. Archibald Eden considered that this six-day period of rest was one of the best that the Regiment had had for some time. The small theatre was used to entertain the men, with shows run by Lieutenant Laurence Goodwyn and Serjeant Benford, on a nightly basis. A minstrel troupe was formed and the Divisional band put on two performances. Laurence Goodwyn, in particular, was a fine amateur actor, and his performances were always well-received. The food during this period was considerably better than normal, with the standard stew replaced by regular roast meat, cooked in cottage ovens.

At 9.30 a.m., November 21st, the rest period came to an end, with the 52nd leaving for their familiar haunts, at Annequin, which was reached at 12.30 p.m. At 9 a.m. the following morning, the 52nd began to relieve the 1st South Staffordshire, of the 7th Division, in the right Cuinchy Sector [see map page 237]. The area was now somewhat different from their last tour there, in the preceding July. The ground to be occupied now stretched for almost a company frontage, south of the La Bassée to Béthune road, and on the left just reached the infamous brickstacks. The trenches were in a poor state of repair, partly caused by the inclement weather and partly by the reduced number of men occupying the front and support trenches. This latter strategy was done to reduce casualties and had been the policy of the Germans for some time. The number of men in the front area was dependent on how many were required to keep the trenches in a decent state of repair, rather than the number required for defence purposes. Captain Guy Blewitt now of the 5th Brigade made a pertinent comment in his diary: 'rain and trenches going from bad to worse, Gum boot Store and Soup Kitchen seem to have assumed the utmost importance'.

A Company was in the front line trenches, south of the La Bassée to Béthune road, with two platoons in the front line and the other two in support. C Company occupied the front line trenches, from the road on the right, to Ridley Walk on the left, at which point the 2nd H.L.I. took over the line. C Company's men were distributed in the same fashion as those of A Company, in the front and support positions. B Company was in support in Praed Street and Marylebone Road. D Company placed two platoons in the Cuinchy Support[ing] Point, one platoon in Park Lane Redoubt, and the remaining platoon in Stafford Redoubt. Regimental Headquarters was at Woburn Abbey.

[378] Major-General William George Walker 1863-1936.

The Regiment remained in the Cuinchy trenches until November 26th. The Germans were not very active, although there was a certain amount of sniping. However, the 52nd's own snipers claimed to have downed no less than three of the enemy in the trenches opposite them. Earl Kitchener's New Army Divisions were being introduced to 'trench craft' by the more experienced and battle-hardened Divisions. During this period the 33rd Division was attached to the 2nd Division. The 52nd instructed first the 20th and then the 24th Royal Fusiliers on a company by company basis. These fresh men, as well as gleaning 'trench craft', were an enormous help in keeping the trench in some sort of orderly state.

At 9 a.m., on November 26th, the 52nd was relieved by the 1st Queen's, whose billets they took over in Harley Street, Cambrin. The Regiment would remain in this area for the next four days. The companies were distributed; A Company, in the street south of Pont Fixe; B Company had three platoons at Braddell Point, two sections at Cambrin Support Point, one section in Carter's Keep, and one section in Tourbières Keep; C Company was in huts at Beuvry; D Company at Pont Fixe, south of the canal. Captain John Southey, Lieutenant Douglas Sewell and four N.C.O.s were temporarily attached to the 24th Royal Fusiliers, to further their trench education. On the 30th, it was back to the Cuinchy trenches [A 1 section] again on a wet day, but at least the enemy was inactive. The first three days of December were spent in the line, with the initiation of a company, from the 17th Royal Fusiliers, being undertaken. At first, a platoon from the newcomers was attached to each company of the 52nd, before the 17th R.F.'s full company was allowed to occupy the front line for the final two days. On December 1st, Lieutenants A.G. Cardy and George Field were posted to the Mediterranean Expeditionary Force[379], and on the 3rd, Second-Lieutenants Robert and David Barnes joined for duty.

At 9 a.m. on December 4th, the 9th H.L.I. relieved the 52nd, which proceeded to billets in the Rue d'Aire area of Béthune. The actual relief proved to be difficult, as the mud slowed everything down, so that five hours were required instead of the usual two. The men wore gum-boots, which took time to get out of store in the local village school and, after use, cleaning was necessary, making it a lengthy process. The washing of the boots meant a large number of men congregating in a small area, making them vulnerable to artillery fire or attack from the air. Archibald Eden was always relieved when the boot-washing operation took place on a cloudy day. On their first day in Béthune, they were

[379] George Field served in Egypt from December 11th 1915 until March 18th 1916. Following a brief attachment as a temporary captain with the Hampshire Regiment, he contrived to return to the 52nd in the summer of 1916. On January 1st 1916, Field was awarded the M.C., and a bar to it, on July 26th 1918. He was twice wounded during the war.

visited by their former Commanding Officer, Brigadier-General Henry Davies, who was now with the 3rd Brigade. He was joined by Lieutenant-Colonel George Colvile, then commanding the 7th Duke of Cornwall's Light Infantry. Also that day, Lieutenant Douglas Sewell was transferred to No. 2 Infantry Base, Rouen, which he was to become the Adjutant of, on February 10th 1916. Clearly Sewell had not recovered fully from the head injury that he had received at Richebourg l'Avoué, the previous May.

At 8 a.m. on December 6th, the first companies of the 52nd moved off, preparatory to taking over another part of the Cuinchy trenches, [B 1 sector], from the 1st Queen's. This area was low-lying, very wet and required continuous pumping to keep the water down. The Regiment remained in this sector until the 10th, continuing with the instruction of the 24th R.F., who were by now capable of having an unsupervised company in the front line. Further rain on the 9th made life even more miserable, although only the flanks in the front line were occupied. Some of the communication trenches were in a shocking state, with sections of up to twenty yards being blocked by cave-ins.

Lieutenant Ralph Kite has left a record of this short period in the Cuinchy trenches[380].

> The trenches are very muddy and wet and the weather is far from genial. We don't get on so badly though, in spite of difficulties. I have got a first class fur lined coat and several woolly waistcoats, so I don't suffer much from the cold. Nothing short of a suit of corrugated iron will keep the wet out. The country has changed since the summer. Where we used to have green fields we now have mud flats. It is very misty and dreary.

On December 10th, the 52nd came out of the line, on being relieved by the 9th H.L.I., and retired to Beuvry. The following day, Second-Lieutenants Cyril Horley and Jack Hardcastle, travelled to Wisques, for a six day course of instruction on the Lewis gun. This was a most effective British light machine-gun that was gas operated, air cooled, and fed from a rotating drum of 47 or 97 rounds. Manufacture started in Belgium during 1913 and in Birmingham in 1914. The Lewis gun could be used for ground attack or defence, and as an anti-aircraft weapon, often lashed on to a cartwheel. When the Lewis gun was first demonstrated to the 52nd, their Commanding Officer, Lieutenant-Colonel Archibald Eden had a painful experience[381].

---

[380] Letter written to Edith Kite on December 11th 1915.

[381] Recollection of the former Lieutenant Ernest Whitfeld.

> Another recollection is of the day the Regiment received its first Lewis gun (the first light automatic that the Army ever possessed) and of the evening, when it was dark enough, this new weapon was placed on the parapet to demonstrate how it worked. The Commanding Officer stood on the firestep on the right-hand side of the drum. No one had told him that the practically red-hot empties came out at right angles on that side. It must have been quite a painful experience!

It was back to the Cuinchy trenches [A 1 section], on December 12th, when the 52nd, once more, relieved the 1st Queen's [see map page 237]. Regimental Headquarters had been moved from Woburn Abbey to Harley Street, as the sleeping dug-outs had become uninhabitable. The state of the trenches was such that company positions had had to be rearranged. One company had a platoon south of the La Bassée road, a second platoon in Waterloo Place and Oxford Street, a third platoon in Stafford Redoubt, and the final one in Park Lane Redoubt. A second company placed two platoons in the area around Ridley Walk, and two further platoons in Cuinchy Support Point. The third company had two platoons in Braddell Point, one and a half platoons in Cambrin Support Point, and sections in Carter's Redoubt and Tourbières Redoubt. The final company was held in reserve in Harley Street. One company of the 13th Essex was brought into the line for 24-hour periods. The rain had made the upkeep of the trenches so difficult that fewer of them were ordered to be maintained.

On the morning of December 14th, the 52nd was relieved by the 24th R. F., and retired to billets in north Beuvry. After the rain and cold of the trenches, the men were able to get baths, which cheered them up. At 2 p.m., on the 16th, the 52nd returned to a new section [A 2] for them, of the Cuinchy trenches, closer to the railway embankment, and relieved the 2nd H.L.I. This tour of the trenches would last for four days and it rained for three of them. The enemy was quiet but alert, and the 52nd's companies were spread out. One company was on the right front, with its Headquarters in Brickfield Keep, and one platoon in Cabbage Patch Redoubt. A second company on the left flank, with its headquarters and two platoons around the railway embankment, and a further two platoons were in and about Lovers Keep. The remaining two companies were in houses in Harley Street, near Pont Fixe. Regimental Headquarters was situated at Kingsclere House. The positions taken up by the companies reflected the appalling state of the trenches. In fact there was an unoccupied gap of 150 yards in the front line between the two companies.

On December 17th, the Scout Serjeant, P. Breach, took out a patrol to find out the state of the enemy's wire. Breach and his men crossed two lines of deserted trenches, which they thought were old British ones, and found a German working party putting up wire in front of their trench. Lewis gun fire was brought down on the enemy, and was continued intermittently throughout the night. Later Breach and his party were fired on at short range. Archibald Eden thought that this fire had come from a sniper's or listening post, 30-50 yards in front of the German line. It was foggy on the 20th and it was possible to walk around outside the trenches. The able and feisty, Captain Reggie Owen, left for a stint as G.S.O.3[382], at the 2nd Division Headquarters, and it was clear that if he did not become a casualty, Owen was destined for a battalion command. Casualties, during this period, were not heavy, with one man killed and an officer, Second-Lieutenant Billy Barnard [gunshot wound of left forearm with compound fracture of radius][383] and two men wounded. At 5 p.m. on the 20th, the 52nd was relieved by the 2nd H.L.I. and moved to new billets in north Annequin.

The weather did not relent, in their time in reserve in Annequin, as it continued to rain. Their rest was disturbed by the constant firing of the British heavy artillery, which was pounding the German trenches. In the evening of the 21st some gas was let off, but the result was not good as the vigilance of the enemy stopped an infantry advance. On this day the number of men in each company was A 126, B 123, C 127, and D 111, making a total of 487. On the 22nd, Archibald Eden was instructed, by the 2nd Division, to send a captain to the 5th Oxfordshire and Buckinghamshire Light Infantry. Having just lost Reggie Owen to the 2nd Division, it must have been difficult for Eden to have to send away yet another experienced officer. The unlucky Captain Charles Fowke was the man selected, and he recorded in his diary 'handed over company to Goodwyn and feel like an exile'[384].

At 10 a.m. on December 22nd, the 52nd once more relieved the 9th H.L.I. in the trenches at Cuinchy [A 1 section]. One company had three platoons south of the La Bassée to Béthune road, and the remaining platoon in Stafford Redoubt. On their left, the second company had three of their platoons north of the road and

[382] General Staff Officer Third Grade.

[383] Second-Lieutenant Billy Barnard had only returned to the Regiment two and a half months earlier, having recovered from a wound received at Richebourg l'Avoué the previous May. He would be wounded again in 1917. On each of the three occasions that Barnard was wounded, he was about to go on leave.

[384] From the photographic point of view, it was a great pity that Eden picked Fowke, as it was his camera and subsequent photographs that gave such a fine record of the 52nd during 1915. Photographs of the Regiment taken later in the war, are not as common. Fowke's active war would come to an end on March 24th 1916 after an abdominal wound. Captain Laurence Goodwyn took over his company in the 52nd.

one in Park Lane Redoubt. The third company had its headquarters and two platoons in Cuinchy Support Point, and two further ones at Braddell Point. The fourth company was with the Regimental Headquarters in Harley Street. The enemy was quiet, though the British artillery was very active. For once the trenches were clean, although further rain led to much repair work being required on them. The 52nd had the misfortune to be in the trenches on Christmas Day 1915. Lieutenant Ralph Kite briefly recorded his impression of it; 'we spent a wet Xmas in the trenches and no more about it. I will not attempt to describe the existence in the ditches, because my humble pen would be quite inadequate to such a mighty task. No-one who has not experienced it could conceive a tenth part of it'[385]. The 52nd remained in the Cuinchy trenches for four days until the 26th.

On Christmas Day, Major Charles 'Buggins' Higgins[386] left the Regiment to take command of the 17th Royal Fusiliers, who were also part of the 5th Brigade[387]. One of Higgins' new company commanders, in the 17th Royal Fusiliers, gave an illuminating account of the new commanding officer's arrival, which illustrated his character and particularly his sang-froid. Clearly, Higgins was not over-keen on taking command of one of Kitchener's New Army battalions.

> He was wary of the stories of many new battalions who were pretty bad. So he took out for a walk his four company commanders on a road near Festubert, to show them the war. We were obviously seen, and had a small artillery barrage to ourselves. The road seemed to disappear in blast, fire, and smoke, I crouched into the ditch. Higgins stalked on. When it was over he was some way ahead. Ashamed, I caught him up and he said, 'Never do that again, Hole.' I believe I never did. Such was his personal magnetism[388].

Also on Christmas Day, the 37th reinforcement of 28 men joined from base. Just prior to the festive season, the 2nd and 33rd Divisions were

---

385 Letter to Henry Kite written on January 8th 1915.

386 Charles Higgins was an able, brave, but rather dour officer. He commanded the 17th Royal Fusiliers, throughout the Battles of the Somme and Beaumont Hamel, in 1916, and then aged 38 years, in April 1917, he commanded the 174th Brigade, which captured Bullecourt and the Langemarck Ridge, in the Third Battle of Ypres. During 1917 and 1918, he frequently commanded the 58th Division, due to the ill-health of Major-General A.B. Cator. Higgins was awarded the D.S.O. for his actions with the 52nd at Loos, and a bar to it in 1918. In 1924, he returned to command the 52nd for a few months.

387 Higgins was replaced as second-in-command by Captain L.F. 'Sweeny' Scott.

388 Major John Hole, later High Sheriff of Nottinghamshire.

reconstituted. The 19th Brigade[389], the 1st Queen's, and the 2nd Worcestershire[390] departed from the 2nd Division, and in return it received six service battalions from the 33rd Division. The 5th Brigade was now made up of the 52nd, 2nd H.L.I., 17th and 24th Royal Fusiliers[391].

On Boxing Day morning at 11, the 52nd came out of the line, on relief by the 2nd H.L.I., and moved back to billets at Annequin north. Here they received the sad news that on Christmas Day, at night, the 23-year-old Second-Lieutenant Reginald Strickland had died in hospital, at Béthune, after a short illness. This was described as 'acute ascending paralysis', in modern parlance a form of Guillain-Barré syndrome[392]. Strickland had been on a fourteen-day course, with the 2nd Division, when he was taken ill. Next day, the 27th, the whole of the 2nd Division was relieved by the 33rd, and marched the five miles to Béthune, where the 52nd went into billets in the now familiar Rue d'Aire area. This brought to a welcome, although temporary, end to a prolonged period of unrelenting trench life. The normal brigade rotational system of battalions, in and out of the line, had to be suspended because of this. Each division and brigade had its own system, but the 2nd Division worked on the basis of each brigade being in the trenches for sixteen days, with each battalion in the line for four days and then four days out. A pair of battalions relieved each other twice. This was followed by the brigade going back away from the trenches for eight days.

The following day, the 52nd paraded at 9 a.m., and then marched the twelve miles, to the north-west of Béthune through Chocques, and Lillers, until they reached Cottes St. Hilaire. They arrived in this pleasant little village at 2.30 p.m., having had dinners from cookers on the way. Perhaps it was the thought of a prolonged rest that made the men march well to their new quarters. The billets were said to be good, although scattered, with most men accommodated in farm buildings and a few lucky ones in houses. Two officers' messes were set up so that they could be close to the men.

1915 came to a close for the 52nd, in their comfortable billets, in Cottes St. Hilaire. It had been an eventful year for the Regiment, with heavy fighting for them, at Richebourg l'Avoué, on May 15th/16th, and then the subsidiary action at Givenchy, on September 25th. The year had started with Lieutenant-Colonel Henry Davies in command, but he had been promoted to the 3rd Brigade, leaving

389 Transferred from the 27th Division, on August 19th 1915, to replace the 4th Brigade [Guards], and moved again to the 33rd Division, on November 25th 1915.

390 The 1st Queen's and 2nd Worcestershire transferred to the 33rd Division on December 15th 1915.

391 The 17th and 24th Royal Fusiliers transferred from the 99th Brigade on December 13th 1915.

392 In 1915 it would have been called Landry's Paralysis. Guillain-Barré Syndrome was first described in 1916. The unfortunate Strickland would have had an unpleasant asphyxial death. Today it would be eminently survivable.

his former deputy, Lieutenant-Colonel Archibald Eden to take the Regiment into the New Year. If 1915 had been a disappointing year for the Allies, in that they had failed to break through the Germans' line, let alone expel them from the occupied areas of France and Belgium, the 52nd had never failed to give anything but their very best.

From the Regimental viewpoint the first six months of 1916 were to be relatively uneventful. The second winter in the trenches was every bit as bad as the first. However, for the 52nd the New Year opened happily enough in billets, at Cottes St. Hilaire. The 2nd Division was taking its turn in corps reserve and would remain so deployed until January 16th. New Year's Day was kept as Christmas Day, and the men had their rations supplemented through the generosity of the wife of their former Commanding Officer, Henry Davies and her Regimental Comfort's Fund. All the members of the 52nd, both officers and men, had sausages for breakfast and roast beef, ham and half a pound of plum pudding for dinner. On the 3rd, the 39th reinforcement of 139 men arrived. The leave allotment had improved as the two service battalions who were now with them were not yet on the leave roster.

The fortnight at Cottes St. Hilaire was relatively restful for the 52nd, although a certain amount of exercise and training was undertaken. Each morning opened with three quarters of an hour of physical training, followed by short range musketry, grenade[393] throwing classes, and drill. A six mile Brigade route march took place on the 7th. The following day the 52nd played the 2nd H.L.I. at football, which ended in a two-all draw after extra time. In the return game, played on the 10th, the 2nd H.L.I. were the eventual winners, by two goals to one. On January 8th, Second-Lieutenants A.G. Gibbons and A.W. Middleditch, both from the 9th Battalion, joined for duty. The latter was soon invalided out and died of a cerebral haemorrhage, on June 19th, 1916. The 14th saw the arrival of the 40th reinforcement of 25 men.

The well-deserved rest period came to an end on January 17th, with the men parading at 7.45 a.m., before marching the three miles to Lillers. There, at 9 a.m., the 52nd entrained for the short journey to Béthune. Detraining at 9.45 a.m., the Regiment marched the two and a quarter miles to billets in Essars, arriving at 10.45 a.m. Archibald Eden was delighted to be back in his old billet in the local school-mistress's house. The officers' mess was opened in the Curé's house. The 5th Brigade, of which the 52nd was a part, was now out of the line in reserve, and would remain so until January 26th. On the 18th, four hundred men were required for mining fatigues. Three days later, Eden took temporary command of the 5th

[393] As the war progressed the term 'bomb' for a hand-delivered explosive device was changed to 'grenade'.

Brigade, in the absence of Brigadier-General Charles Corkran. That evening Eden attended the Divisional cinema show, where the band played excellently. On January 23rd, he rode over to Richebourg St. Vaast and found that the village had been severely damaged, with hardly a house still inhabited. Eden spent the evening in the company of a former 52nd officer, Captain Guy Blewitt, listening to the Royal Artillery band playing in the theatre at Béthune.

Archibald Eden returned to the 52nd in time for their return to the Festubert trenches on January 26th. At 7 p.m., the Regiment began the relief of the 1st King's Royal Rifle Corps, which took until 6 a.m. the following morning, mainly because of the lack of efficient guides. The ground was saturated with water, making it impossible to have a continuous front line of breastworks, let alone trenches. Instead, part of two companies occupied sixteen island posts which formed the forward position of the 52nd. Men from these companies, not providing the garrison for the island posts, were placed in billets in the village of Festubert. Headquarters and the remaining two companies occupied the old British front line breastworks which, after the advance at the Battle of Festubert in May 1915, were now well behind the current front line. It was possible to get around behind the island posts, but it took time. Eden visited the whole of the front line before daylight and then again at night. However, it was a long job, taking three and a half hours, as it was difficult to find the way from one post to the next. On the left of the 52nd was the 24th R.F. of their own brigade and, on the right, in the direction of Givenchy, the 1st Hertfordshire of the 6th Brigade. The weather was dull and foggy and three men were wounded during this tour of the trenches.

On January 30th, a foggy day, Archibald Eden explored the old German front line that the Regiment had faced in February 1915, and which was now behind the British line. At 7.30 p.m., the 52nd was relieved by the 17th R. F., who they now usually worked with. The well-organized relief took until 9.30 p.m. and the men occupied keeps and rather poor billets in Festubert. This was a quiet period in support, with the time spent in providing 250 men for working parties, chiefly to unload the stores of the Royal Engineers and also to undertake general fatigues in the trenches and keeps. This uneventful period came to an end on February 3rd, when the 52nd returned to the Festubert trenches in the place of the 17th R. F. The front line islands had been improved and an attempt to join them up was being made. B and D Companies were on the left and right of the front line respectively and they were supported by C and A Companies in the old British line. The companies swopped positions on February 5th. The following day, the 6th, the Regiment undertook work, under the supervision of the East Anglian Field Company, to improve the second line around Baintin Road. The number of casualties during this time in the Festubert trenches amounted to four men wounded.

On February 7th, the 52nd once more exchanged positions with the 17th R. F. and returned to the so-called 'village line' in Festubert. The companies were distributed: B and C less two platoons in the Rue de l'Epinette; two platoons of A Company in Cailloux Keep; the rest of A Company in Festubert including the Keep; D Company in Estaminet Corner. During this short period in support, the 52nd had one man killed. On the 11th, the 6th Brigade relieved the 5th, and the Regiment marched to billets in the Tobacco Factory at Béthune. Archibald Eden, who had returned from leave the night before, found himself once again in temporary command of the 5th Brigade, firstly at Loignies and then Les Choquaux. On the 14th, Eden, Richard Crosse, John Southey and Hubert Rawson watched a demonstration for military attachés by 100 of the brigade bombers. That same day, Eden returned to the Regiment, and Second-Lieutenant J.E.V. Rathbone joined the Regiment from the 3rd Dorsetshire.

The Regiment marched, on the 15th, for two and a half hours to poor billets in Les Harrisoirs and its vicinity. It rained heavily and a hurricane blew. The gale was still blowing on the 16th, and the 17th saw the commencement of the relief of the 2nd Division by the 38th Division of XI Corps. At 9 a.m., the 52nd marched to new and good billets at Busnes, with the officers' mess in a farmhouse. Archibald Eden watched a demonstration of the Stokes mortar on the 20th, and Llewellyn Gwynne, the Bishop of Khartoum, their former 5th Brigade chaplain, visited the Regiment on the 23rd. Training was interfered with by the water-logged ground, which was made worse by snow and then a rapid thaw. A party of 40 men had some preliminary training in grenade throwing.

On the evening of February 23rd, the 52nd received orders to be ready to move at short notice. Officers were summoned back from courses and schools of instruction. The following day the 41st reinforcement of seventeen N.C.O.s and men arrived. Over the next few days Second-Lieutenants William Chown, F.C. Dixon, both of the 3rd Dorsetshire, and E.H. Vigars, a former sergeant in the 19th Hussars, joined the Regiment. The 52nd were unable to train or take exercise during this frustrating period on stand-by. The reason for the Regiment being ordered to be ready to move at such short notice was the German Army's onslaught against the French, at Verdun, on February 21st. Operation Gericht or 'Law Court', as it was called, would turn into a charnel-house for both the French and Germans and, over the next ten months, become one of the seminal battles of the First World War.

In order to free up French divisions for the defence of Verdun, British divisions were made responsible for a greater share of the trench line. Hence, the

2nd Division took over the Calonne sector with the 6th Brigade and the Angres sector with the 5th Brigade. The 52nd, as part of the 5th Brigade, was to occupy a part of the Angres trenches, thus relieving the French. Their new area of operations lay just to the north of the infamous Lorette Ridge, where so much French and German blood had been spilt in 1915. The countryside consisted of a series of ridges with hills to the south and a good deal of chalk in the soil.

At 3.30 p.m. on February 26th, the 52nd marched to Lillers station and entrained for Noeux-les-Mines. Having completed their short train journey to the south, the Regiment then marched the two miles to billets in Petit Sains. At 6 a.m. the following morning, Archibald Eden, Richard Crosse, and the four company commanders went to Bully-Grenay, where they were joined by guides who took them to view their new area of operations in the right half of the Angres sector of trenches. They met the Commandant of the 3rd Battalion of the 66th Regiment[394], whose men were currently holding the sector. The French Commandant was very pleasant, and described the topography of the area carefully. There was a long communication trench between the village and the Commandant's Headquarters, which Eden thought was in a poor spot. The Headquarters dug-out was deep and safe enough, but rather cramped allowing space for only five men. At 7 p.m., the relief of the French began and was completed without incident just after midnight. They seemed only too pleased to be leaving the area and scuttled off over the top in every direction, making scant use of the communication trenches.

Many years later, the former Lieutenant Ernest Whitfeld recalled their relief of the French.

> It was about the 28th February, and I was due to become Adjutant on the 1st of March that the Regiment took over the line at Bully-Grenay from the French. It was a new sector as far as we were concerned. The approach was by very long communication trenches, so we arrived at the Command Post rather tired. Although the hand-over was well carried out the take-over, in French, was a little trying to the Commanding Officer, who was not, I think, exactly a fluent French scholar! Added to the 'jabber' I remember there was a noisy telephone bell attached to a very antiquated machine, which rang almost incessantly and there was a lot more 'jabbering' as a result.
>
> Eventually the French left and the Commanding Officer decided that he had had enough for one day and would lie down on, I think, the only bunk in the dug-out.

---

394 French 18th Division.

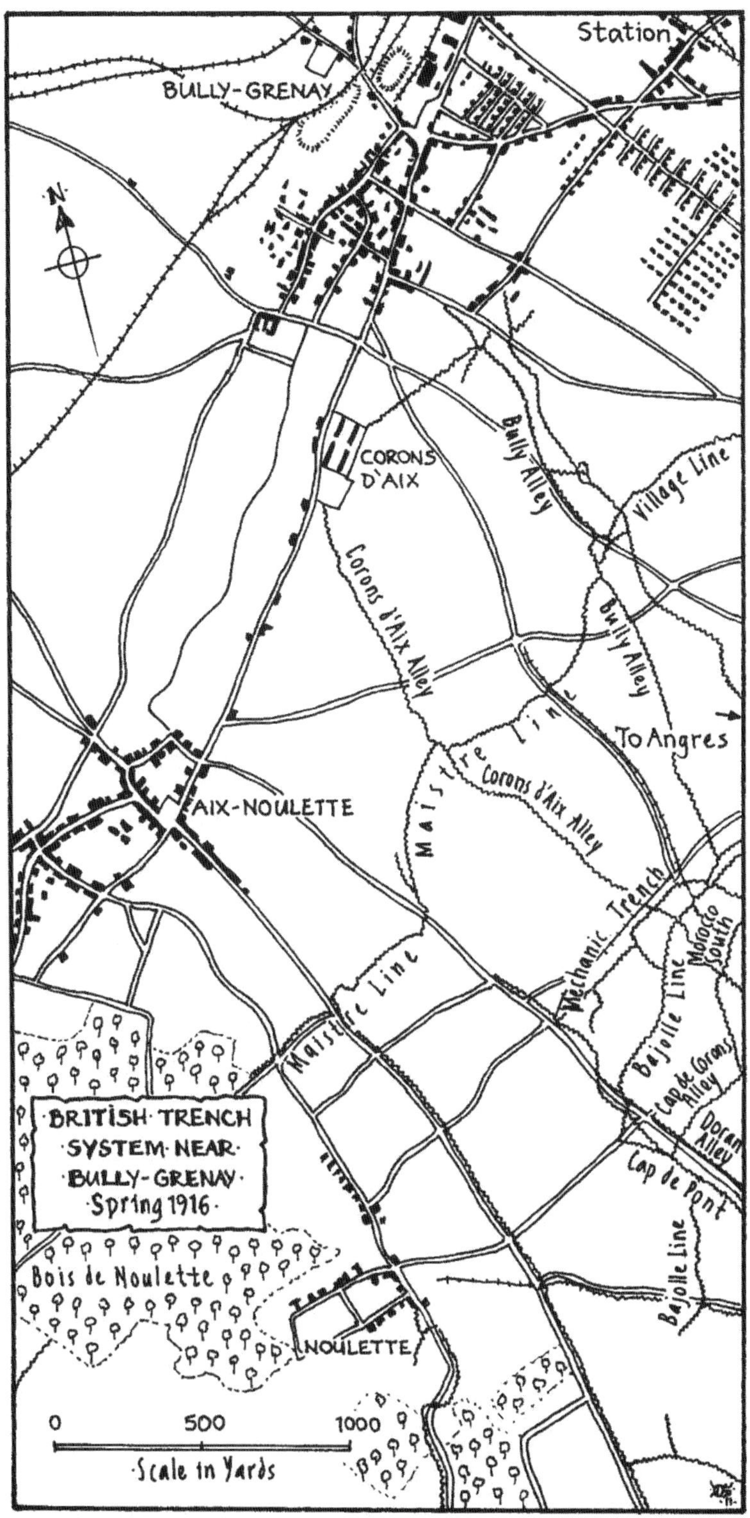
Station
BULLY-GRENAY
N
CORONS
D'AIX
Bully Alley
Village Line
Corons d'Aix Alley
Bully Alley
To Angres
Maistre Line
Corons d'Aix Alley
AIX-NOULETTE
Mechanic Trench
Morocco South
Maistre Line
Bajolle Line
Cap de Corons Alley
Doran Alley
Cap de Pont
BRITISH TRENCH SYSTEM NEAR BULLY-GRENAY Spring 1916
Bois de Noulette
Bajolle Line
NOULETTE
0
500
1000
Scale in Yards

> The trenches we had taken over were dug in chalk which, as everyone knows, is porous and water percolated through the ceiling; the French had hung the equivalent of our bully-beef tins up on the ceiling to catch the water. Unfortunately as our respected Commander got into the bunk, his head came in contact with a particularly well filled tin and he received a very adequate but unpleasant showerbath! Crosse and I decided that the front line was a more desirable spot for the time being than Regimental H.Q.

The 5th Brigade had three battalions in the front line of the Angres trenches. On the left was the 24th R. F., in the centre the 17th R. F., and the 52nd on the right, closest to the Lorette Ridge. Archibald Eden positioned his men as follows. Three companies in the front line; the right company with three platoons in the front line and one in support; the centre company with two platoons in the front line and two in support; the left company with the same arrangements as the centre company; the remaining company in reserve about 300 yards from Corons d'Aix. At the end of 48 hours the reserve company relieved the right company, but the other two companies had to remain in their original positions. On the immediate right of the 52nd was the French 77th Regiment, later replaced by the 7th Hussars. The frontage that the Regiment was responsible for was wide, but fortunately the enemy was quiet.

The next day, the 29th, was a bright one with much activity by aeroplanes in the skies above. The Brigade frontage had to be reduced to two battalions, which necessitated the left battalion extending further to the left and thus thinning out its line. A vast amount of work was required to bring up ammunition and grenades, which Archibald Eden always noted was the case when the French were relieved. The front line trenches were well-constructed, with deep dug-outs, and there was a support line 30-60 yards behind. However, the second line, further back, was an indefinite one which, from the practical point of view, only existed on the trench maps! This meant a great deal of extra labour for the battalions who were supposed to be resting.

The first day of March ended the tenure of Captain Richard Crosse as Adjutant and he was replaced by Lieutenant Ernest Whitfeld. Crosse had proved to be a super-efficient adjutant, with an encyclopaedic knowledge of the men in the 52nd. In due course, a little later in the year, he would command the Regiment. Although he had served with equal loyalty both Henry Davies and Archibald Eden, the two Commanding Officers of the 52nd, during his time as Adjutant, it is apparent that he was more comfortable under Davies than Eden. Perhaps this was related to the fact that Eden had only joined the 52nd in 1911 and was consequently a less familiar figure. The day proved to be quiet with some shelling behind the front line and the occasional rifle grenade fired at the 52nd. Three men were wounded during that day.

In the evening of the following day, the 52nd was relieved by the 17th Royal Fusiliers and moved to billets in Corons d'Aix, close to Bully-Grenay. The relief was long and tedious, in consequence of the very wet condition of the trenches, and was not completed until midnight. In the event, only the Headquarters and two companies were housed in billets at Corons d'Aix. The corons were poor quality miners' cottages, some of which were still occupied by miners, and others badly damaged by shellfire. The remaining two companies were placed in strong points, at Maroc Sud [Morocco South] and Metro Cap De Pont, in the reserve line.

The following day, March 3rd, Brigadier-General Henry Davies, their former Commanding Officer, visited the Regiment. His 3rd Brigade Headquarters were nearby, just north of Calonne. The weather remained bitterly cold and there was snow during the night. The next day there was more snow and all the 52nd moved back into billets at Fosse 10. The countryside that the Regiment was now in, was very much mining country, and indeed one of the mines continued to work during daylight hours. It was not unheard of for mining operations to be continued actually under and even beyond the front lines. At Fosse 10, the billets of the 52nd, in miners' semi-detached villas were much more satisfactory than their former ones at Corons d'Aix. The 42nd reinforcement of 41 men joined for duty. On March 5th, Captain Reggie Owen returned from his temporary attachment at the Headquarters of the 2nd Division.

On March 6th, the 52nd relieved the 2nd H.L.I., in the centre sub-section of the Angres trenches. The first company reached the trenches at 8.45 a.m., the last at 3.45 p.m., and the relief was finally completed at 6.30 p.m. The countryside in this area was hillier than encountered previously, and the Germans commanded a view of some of the roads leading up to the trenches. To reduce the possibility of casualties, the strength of parties moving to the front was reduced to that of a platoon. All this, added to the length of the communication trenches, made for a slow relief. Captain John Southey left to take up a post at General Headquarters, as an instructor at the Cadet's School.

The 7th was a misty day and Archibald Eden and the commander of the 5th Brigade, Brigadier-General Charles Corkran, took the opportunity to explore more of the trenches. The 24th R. F. was on the 52nd's left and the 17th R. F. on their right. Beyond the latter, the 99th Brigade was occupying a frontage down to the Souchez River. The next day, March 8th, was bright and sunny, but more snow fell at night. During the 7th and 8th the enemy's rifle grenades were active, but the 52nd was able to reply in kind, as their own supplies had been recently increased. The German snipers were inactive, but the 52nd's own got down to work although their opportunities to kill the enemy were few and far between. The Regiment's night patrols found little evidence that the enemy was using the hours of darkness to maintain their own barbed wire defences.

On the 9th, the Regimental Headquarters was moved back to some dug-outs, where previously the French had had a pioneer company. At about this time, the 5th Brigade had set up its own sapping company, with each regiment providing a platoon of some 36 men, under an officer, and it was commanded overall by Lieutenant Hubert Rawson, who also commanded the 52nd's constituent platoon. The sapping company complemented the work of the Royal Engineers in revetting trenches and performing work of a similar nature. The great advantage of the sapping company was that they were always available and this was not the case with the R.E.

The 2nd H.L.I. relieved the 52nd on March 10th. This short period in the trenches had been relatively quiet, with the German artillery largely inactive, except on the afternoons of the 7th and 10th, when some 4.2 shells fell around the front line. During this time, two men had been killed and eleven more wounded. Second-Lieutenant Richard Maul reported for duty. The 52nd was billeted once more at Fosse 10. Until this point in the war, the 2nd Division with the 52nd, had been part of the I Corps, but at this juncture they became part of the IV Corps under the command of General Sir Henry Wilson[395].

There were good baths at Fosse 10 and every man got one during the four-day spell out of the trenches. The *London Gazette,* of March 11th, published the citation for the D.C.M. awarded to Company Serjeant-Major Fred Clare, one of the greatest servants of the 52nd in that era. The citation read; 'for conspicuous good work throughout the whole campaign, notably on one occasion, when he led on two platoons, into the enemy trench[396]. He has great initiative and power of

---

[395] General [later Field-Marshal] Sir Henry Hughes Wilson [1864-1922]. Sub-Chief of Staff, B.E.F., 1914-5; Chief Liaison Officer with the French Army, 1915; Commanded IV Corps 1915-16; Chief Liaison Officer with the French Army 1917; General Officer Commanding Eastern Command 1917; C.I.G.S. 1918-22. Highly intelligent, fluent in French, Wilson was distrusted by many in the Army and was seen as an intriguer. On June 22nd 1922, he was assassinated, in full field-marshal's uniform, with his sword in his hand, by the Irish Republican Brotherhood, near his home in London. The following day the celebrated pathologist, Bernard Spilsbury, conducted a post-mortem in the Field-Marshal's study, in deference to the widow's feelings, and to allow the military funeral procession to start from the house! Wilson, in his only senior command in the field, was not seen as a success with IV Corps.

[396] On January 14th 1916, a supplement to the *London Gazette* announced that a D.C.M. had been awarded to Clare. Normally, notification of an award for gallantry took place about three months after the event. Therefore, 'when he led on two platoons, into the enemy trench', is likely to refer

command, and has set a fine example'. On the afternoon, of March 12th, Archibald Eden accompanied by Lieutenant Jack Hardcastle rode down to the south, to view the ruins of Ablain St. Nazaire. The 15th century church and, most of the houses of the place, had been destroyed in the heavy fighting around the Lorette Ridge, during 1914-5. The unchanged ruins of the church can be seen to this day. Second-Lieutenants Noel Harrison and W.I.B. Ware joined the Regiment for duty.

Lieutenant Ralph Kite gave a first-hand account of this last tour of the Angres trenches in a letter to his mother[397].

> We have just ended our rest after one of the worst turns in the trenches I have ever known. The cold has been so intense and it has snowed hard. Our dugout dripped hard and it was so cold it froze the heart out of me. However with frequent hot drinks just tinged with rum, we managed to hold out for four days. The men were splendid through all this wet and cold as usual. This burst of cold weather was just the final touch of winter: today we went about without coats, so hot did it get.
>
> I am at present in command of a company[398] and have a horse which I have called The Crump. He is a lazy old brute, but we jog along together somehow.

On March 14th, the 52nd returned once again to the Angres trenches, when they exchanged places with the 2nd H.L.I. Companies moved at intervals of two and a half hours, and some enemy shelling in the vicinity of Corons d'Aix interfered slightly with the relief. Each of the other two battalions of the 5th Brigade remained in the line all the time, but with only two-thirds of their men actually in the trenches. During this period, the weather was fine, but the visibility was not good and consequently the enemy's artillery was not too troublesome. German snipers were becoming more active, but had not caused casualties so far. Hard labour on repairing the trenches and parapets was carried out, and the full supply of small arms ammunition and grenades was brought up. There were some lighter moments. Lieutenant Ralph Kite explained how rats in his dug-out were dealt with. 'We had rather a humorous incident in our dugout the other night. I complained of the rats and my servant when he went to fetch

---

to the subsidiary attack at Givenchy, although Clare had also been prominent, at Richebourg l'Avoué, on May 16th 1915. The actual citation was published on March 11th 1916.

[397] Letter written on March 13th 1916.

[398] D Company.

Russians from the village collared five and put them in a sandbag and suddenly released five rather angry very ruffled cats upon us'. The 43rd reinforcement of 53 men joined the Regiment. The *Battalion War Diary* recorded that their quality was deteriorating somewhat[399]. The following day, the 15th, the weather was brighter and there was a great deal of aeroplane activity in the skies above them. For the present, the Allies appeared to have the upper hand and few German planes got near to the British lines. Reggie Owen was seconded once more; this time he travelled to Pernes, for duty at the 2nd Divisional School.

The 52nd was relieved, at 6 p.m. on March 19th, by the 10th West Riding Regiment [69th Brigade, 23rd Division] and the operation was carried out well. The Regiment was then billeted at Hersin for the night, before the next day marching through Barlin and Bruay to Divion. The day was hot and muggy making the seven miles march to Divion an unpleasant one. However, the billets at Divion although good, were scattered, so that two officers' messes had to be set up to allow close supervision of the men. The village of Divion lay in a hollow and the 52nd shared its facilities with the 24th R. F. The countryside was very pretty with rolling hills and valleys. The young officers were taught to ride which was an essential requisite in the First World War. Few of them excelled at it, in contrast with the pre-war regulars. Officers' rides were irreverently known as 'the Wild West Show'. Much of their week in Divion was spent in cleaning up, refitting and on route marches. On the 52nd's last day in Divion, March 27th, the 5th Brigade was inspected by their corps commander Lieutenant-General Sir Henry Wilson.

On March 28th, the 52nd marched the one and a half miles to Houdain station and, accompanied by the 2nd H.L.I., travelled by train to Hersin. After a 50 minutes journey, they were billeted in excellent quarters in the Convent School at Hersin. The pupils were not present, and the buildings can be seen to this day and are now a museum. That night 400 men of the 52nd were sent as a night fatigue to improve the second line trenches in the Angres sector. On the 30th and 31st, each night, 250 men were sent for fatigues on the same sector trenches. Unfortunately for the Regiment, these nightly fatigues greatly upset training. However, Archibald Eden did find enough time to take ten young officers for further riding instruction on waste ground on the Lorette Ridge. On the 30th, Second-Lieutenant Basil Warde reported for duty.

---

[399] In January 1916, a Military Service Act had been passed by Parliament, allowing all unmarried men between the ages of 18-41 to be conscripted, unless they were considered to be in a reserved occupation. Within four months, the act was modified to allow married men to be called up as well. The fall off in quality of the recruits to the 52nd, at the end of March 1916, was more likely to indicate the reaching of the 'bottom of the barrel' of volunteer recruits, as it took several months to train men up to fight in the trenches.

During this time at Hersin, some of the officers and men watched a demonstration of a 'flammenwerfer' or flame-thrower, which had been captured from the Germans near Ypres. The hideous stream of fire was terrifying to see, but it was said not to do too much harm if you lay at the bottom of the trench. Archibald Eden described it as 'a delightful instrument of war'. The German Army had experimented with flame-throwers as early as 1900 and they had first been used on the Western Front in October 1914. They were operated by two men and were used principally to clear front line trenches. A petrol tank was attached to the back of a man with a hose pipe and nozzle projecting forwards. When the nozzle was lit, a roaring hissing flame was projected forward, swelling at the end to an oily fiery rose, six feet in diameter. Initially, their range was only 25 metres but later this was increased to 40 metres. Flame-throwers were difficult to move around and only contained enough fuel to burn for 40 seconds at a time. Flame-thrower operators were marked men, who immediately attracted fire and frequently ended up being incinerated, as the petrol tanks that were strapped on their backs were prone to being hit by rifle or machine-gun bullets and ignited.[400]

[400] The British experimented with flame-throwers, but found the short range of the hoses inefficient. They developed huge two-ton flame-throwers that were introduced in 1916. Initially, these weapons caused panic with the German foe, but they were soon knocked out and the British abandoned their use for the rest of the war.

Chapter XII

The Spring and early Summer of 1916 in the Trenches of Angres and Zoave Valley.

April 1st - July 19 1916th

[Maps: pages 161, 288, 302.]

April 1st still found the 52nd Light Infantry in their comfortable billets in the Convent at Hersin. During the day, a mine shaft, 100 yards from the Convent, was accurately shelled and severely damaged by the enemy. So accurate was the bombardment that no member of the Regiment was injured. In the afternoon, Sir Henry Wilson, commanding IV Corps, gave an excellent lecture, at Bruay, entitled 'The Situation in Europe'. Wilson was a brilliant lecturer and had started his series of lectures on this topic, earlier in the year, with the 1st Division. So popular was the talk that Wilson repeated it for several of the other Divisions in his Corps. One present at the original lecture for the 1st Division has left his impressions of it[401].

> Standing well forward on the stage, leaning on a pointer, with a vast sketch map of Europe arranged on a curtain behind him, he began his lecture, speaking very slowly and distinctly as though carefully weighing each word. He said:-
>
> A distinguished officer of your division has told me that I ought to inflict this lecture upon you, because the general view of all young officers is that Corps Commanders are fat, old pot-bellied blighters, who live back in safety in 'chattoos,' eat and drink a great deal, and know nothing of the realities of war. This being the case, I felt that if any of you were kind enough to avail yourselves of my invitation to come here this evening, you would at least realize that I am *not pot-bellied.* And I venture to hope that when I have finished the few observations that I propose to make, you may perhaps believe me when I say that I have given some time to the thought and time to the study of this war, and I am not altogether without experience of our allies, our antagonists, and the theatre of operations in which it is being waged.
>
> These prefatory remarks produced a wild burst of applause, during which Henry stood, tall, gaunt, and whimsical, propped up by the

[401] Quoted in *Field-Marshal Sir Henry Wilson, His Life And Diaries* by Major-General Sir C.E. Callwell. Volume I, page 275.

> pointer and regarding his audience with affected surprise. He then proceeded to grip the three or four hundred assembled officers and to keep them spellbound for an hour, while he traced the causes which had led up to the war, and the course of operations that had followed. To show them his knowledge was not merely gained from books and reports, he mentioned that he had made no less than 17 trips up and down the Franco-German and Belgian frontiers on a bicycle during the years preceding the War and added, 'On a *push*-bike – a *push*-bike. I did not say a *buzz*-bike.'
>
> The lecture created tremendous interest, and the discussion over it lasted several days. A very clever young chemical engineer, who had just become my adjutant and who, up to the War, had devoted his time to science and had never so much as heard of Henry's existence, remarked to me, 'I could not have believed that any man in one short lecture could have so imbued his audience with a sense of his profound mastery of his subject, and could at the same time have made an even greater impression on them by the magnetism of his personality.'

Such were Sir Henry Wilson's abilities as an orator and no doubt he delivered a similar lecture to the officers of the 2nd Division. In truth Wilson was a better staff officer and strategist than he was a corps commander. He was considered to be both an intriguer and too close to our French allies, whose liaison officer he had been. This may have been unfair, and one of the reasons that he was close to the French, was that he spoke their language almost perfectly, thanks to a French governess in his childhood.

The next day, April 2nd, the 52nd were on the move once more, this time to Camblain-Châtelain, known to the troops as 'Charlie Chaplin'. Initially the Regiment marched the one and a quarter miles to Barlin, and then proceeded on a 20 minute train journey to Bruay. This was followed by a five miles march through Divion to good billets in Camblain-Châtelain. During these short journeys the First Line Transport and chargers[402] proceeded by road. The 2nd Division provided two motor lorries which carried the two blankets per man. April 3rd was spent in their new billets and, on the afternoon of the 4th, the 52nd was inspected in musketry exercises by their divisional commander at the beginning of the war, Sir Charles Monro, now commanding the First Army. Monro had recently returned from Gallipoli, and was an expert in musketry,

402 Horses.

having commanded the School of Musketry at Hythe, for a time in the pre-war period.

At 12.30 p.m. on April 5th, the 52nd entrained at Calonne-Ricourt Station, about half a mile from their billets, and arrived at Aire at 1.45 p.m. Then they had a nine and a half miles march, through Therouanne to Delettes, where their Regimental predecessors, almost a century before, had been billeted whilst part of the Army of Occupation of France. The First Line Transport and the Regimental chargers went separately by road, a journey of some nineteen and a half miles through Estrée Blanche. The next day the Regiment spent from 9 a.m. to 3.20 p.m. in battalion training, in beautiful countryside with high hills and deep valleys, with very few landmarks to guide them. There were a few villages, but they were tucked away from view down in the hollows.

On April 7th, the 5th Infantry Brigade with the 52nd took part in a training exercise largely for the benefit of General Joseph Joffre, the French Commander-in-Chief, who had expressed a wish to see British troops on manoeuvre. Lieutenant-Colonel Archibald Eden, commanding the 52nd, thought privately that it was a waste of time as a stereotyped form of attack was delivered. The 8th was spent in training in another part of the area, with the 52nd in reserve for most of the time. The following day, the 52nd retraced their steps to their old billets at Camblain-Châtelain, on foot to Aire and then by train. In the absence of a band, the buglers were a great help in keeping up spirits on the march.

The 52nd spent April 10th-11th at Camblain-Châtelain. The two days were occupied in company fire-control exercises and in scout and sniper training. Each member of the Regiment also managed a welcome bath. Two hundred men were also away on fatigues, which interfered with training. On the 12th, the 52nd marched through Divion to Bruay and entrained for the 20 minute journey to Hersin. They were not too pleased to be billeted in small cottages, away from the Convent School, where previously they had been very comfortable. That night another 200 hundred men had to be found for fatigues. Further fatigues during the next three days seriously upset training, but time was found to give N.C.O.s instruction in the latest methods of physical training and bayonet fighting. A church parade service was held on April 15th, a Saturday, as so many Sunday services had been missed. That afternoon, Archibald Eden and his new Adjutant, Ernest Whitfeld, took the opportunity to ride around their old positions at Mazingarbe, Philosophe, and Vermelles. The last two places had been seriously damaged since the Regiment was last there in June 1915.

On April 16th, the 52nd moved into billets in Bully-Grenay, on the commencement of the relief of the 23rd Division by the 2nd Division. The 5th Brigade front was now to be held by two battalions instead of three. The

Regiment was placed in support, with Headquarters and two companies in Bully. A further company was at Metro Cap de Pont, in trenches 300 yards from the west end of Corons d'Aix alley. The final company was situated in Mechanics Trench, at the disposal of the commanding officer of the right battalion. The 17th was a day without incident and, on the 18th, the 44th reinforcement of sixteen men arrived. The next few days proved to be quiet, with wet and windy weather.

On April 20th, the 52nd relieved the 17th Royal Fusiliers as the right battalion in the Angres trenches, and having their Headquarters, as before, in a good but not deep dug-out in Mechanics Trench. Once more, this was a quiet period, apart from a certain amount of hostile rifle grenade activity. On the 22nd, heavy rain flooded the trenches and Archibald Eden had difficulty getting around them. Four Royal Navy petty officers from the Grand Fleet spent several days with the Regiment to gain experience of the trenches. The following day, the 23rd, was Easter Sunday, and their Chaplain William Dallas arranged two Holy Communion services for the officers and men in the line. Ernest Whitfeld recorded an unfortunate Easter experience for Archibald Eden.

> As Adjutant I always accompanied the Commanding Officer on his nightly or early morning rounds of the Companies. He always insisted on leading the way chiefly, I think, because he loved slashing at the big trench rats which he could see silhouetted on the parapets. He also "found" all the holes or broken duckboards which saved me many a fall. A particular case of this was on, I think, Easter Day. We were doing an early morning trip and were nearing home when my commander fell flat on his face in several inches of water. I am afraid I found it very difficult to conceal my features as, unpleasant though it was for the chief actor, there was a certain humorous side to it from the spectator's point of view.

Two precious days without rain dried out the trenches. This period in the trenches had been uneventful with just one man killed and one more wounded. The 52nd was relieved in the afternoon of the 24th by the 17th R. F. and retired to good billets in Fosse 10.

On April 25th, while in their billets in Fosse 10, the 52nd was joined by Second-Lieutenant M.F.M. Parkes from the 9th Battalion. Archibald Eden was in temporary command of the 5th Brigade as its commander, Charles Corkran, was away with the 2nd Division[403]. Little of note occurred over the next few days, although Eden took the opportunity to view the right sector of the Angres trenches

[403] Eden returned to the 52nd on April 30th 1916.

with Charles Higgins[404] and, the following day, the left sector. It was the first time Eden had seen the Bully craters and he noted that light trench mortar missiles always seemed to be flying around the area. On April 28th, once again, the 52nd relieved the 17th R. F., in the same sector of the Angres trenches. Three companies were in the front line, each with a platoon in the support line. The fourth company had three platoons in the support line on the extreme right, with the remaining platoon close to the advanced brigade headquarters. As before, the Regimental Headquarters was in Mechanics Trench. During the day, three men were wounded, including the recently promoted C.S.M. John Martin, who died of his wounds on April 30th. Archibald Eden held Martin, who had actually been born near the Regimental Depot at Cowley, in high esteem and recorded that he was a great loss to the Regiment.

If the front was quiet for the 52nd, on either side of them there was enemy activity. To the north, near Hulluch, on the 1st Division's front there was a gas attack and, to the south, near Givenchy-en-Gohelle, on the 47th Division's front, there was heavy shelling. Second-Lieutenants John Holland and R.G. Pluckrose arrived for duty on April 29th. The following day, April 30th, news reached the Regiment of the fall of Kut, in Mesopotamia, with the capture and eventual death of so many officers and men of their 1st Battalion, the 43rd Light Infantry[405].

The 52nd spent May Day in the Angres trenches with the German artillery fairly active. The next day they were relieved by the 17th R. F. and, once more, moved into billets in Bully-Grenay. As before, one company was in Cap de Pont and Mechanics Trenches. Little of note happened on the 3rd and, on the 4th, the 45th reinforcement of seventeen men arrived. On May 5th, it was back to the trenches again, in relief of the 17th R. F. Two days later, Lieutenant-Colonel Archibald Eden visited an artillery observation-post, which gave him an excellent view over Liévin, a western suburb of Lens, with the enemy's trench system clearly visible in the foreground. That same day the 46th reinforcement of one serjeant and 37 men arrived. This short tour of the trenches was a very quiet one, and gave the 52nd ample opportunity to deepen and generally improve the trenches. Unusually there were no casualties.

Once again, on May 10th, the 17th Royal Fusiliers relieved the 52nd who retired to billets at Fosse 10. The weather was now warm and pleasant and, on the 11th, Archibald Eden paid another visit to the artillery observation post on the Lorette Heights. From this magnificent vantage point, he had an interesting time watching the British trench mortars blasting the German trenches. Needless to

[404] Now commanding the 17th Royal Fusiliers.
[405] Nine officers and 300 men of the 43rd were captured at Kut.

say the enemy retaliated in kind later in the day. That night C Company provided 100 men to repair the communication trenches.

On May 12th, the 69th Brigade of the 23rd Division relieved the 5th Brigade, who moved into excellent billets at their old haunt, the Convent, at Hersin. The day was fine but cloudy and no hostile aircraft or balloons were to be seen. Regimental Headquarters was set up in the Mayor of Hersin's house, leaving him a mere two rooms to live in. There was a pleasant garden in which the Mayor, Monsieur Guislain Decrombecque, kept a wild boar. Before the war, he also had a tame fox and the two animals used to follow him around like faithful dogs! The Mayor was a great sportsman and kept valuable horses, but as they were now behind the enemy's lines, at Lille, it was most unlikely that he would ever see them again. On May 15th, the Mayor of Hersin came to dinner with the Regiment in his own house!

On the same day as the Mayoral dinner, Brigadier-General Charles Corkran, Grenadier Guards, was transferred to the 3rd Guards Brigade. He was replaced in command of the 5th Brigade by Brigadier-General George Moultrie 'Humpty Dumpty' Bullen-Smith of the Leinsters. The following day, May 16th, Archibald Eden took the new Brigadier-General around his brigade and introduced him to its various constituent regiments. During their time in Hersin, the 52nd provided working parties of about two companies in the areas occupied by the 23rd and 47th Divisions. On May 18th, the 52nd marched via Maisnil-les-Ritz, Houdain, and Divion to Camblain-Châtelain, in the Bruay part of the IV Corps rest area. The march was a very hot one, with three men falling out, despite a 45 minute break for tea, near Houdain. The overcoats of the men were carried on motor-lorries. Some time on the 19th was spent in cleaning their billets which were in a poor state of cleanliness. Apart from this, the 19th and 20th were spent in ordinary drills and musketry. The 52nd marched to Divion on the 21st and moved into new scattered billets there. This day, the Regiment narrowly avoided being directly implicated in a minor defeat, which would sully the reputation of their corps commander, as a field officer, Lieutenant-General Sir Henry Wilson.

On the nights of May 19th and 20th, IV Corps, under the command of Sir Henry Wilson, had taken over some of the line around the western slopes, at the northern end of Vimy Ridge, from Lieutenant-General Sir Julian 'Bungo' Byng's XVII Corps. This was an awkward section of the line to hold as it was full of craters, generally overlooked, and constantly under fire. The German opposition, the IX Reserve Corps, under General Alexander von Freytag-Loringhoven[406], had suffered from the superior mining operations of the British. The constant thought of either suddenly being blown to bits from below, or an equally unpleasant death

[406] General Alexander von Freytag-Loringhoven [1849-1926].

from being buried alive, was undermining the morale of his men. Alexander von Freytag-Loringhoven, was Deputy Chief of the General Staff of the Supreme Command and, being keen to gain front line experience, had been given six weeks leave to take the place of a temporarily sick officer in a field command. He determined that the British mine shafts must be taken, to put an end to the sudden entombment of his front line troops. Following a very heavy artillery barrage, on the evening of May 21st, the Germans overran the 47th Division, occupying the Berthonval sector of trenches, and part of Sector P to the south[407] and the Carency Sector to the north[408]. Although Sir Henry Wilson wished to counter-attack on the following day, he was overruled by the Commander-in-Chief Sir Douglas Haig, to allow more artillery to be brought up. Eventually, on the evening of May 23rd, a counter-attack involving the 2nd Division was made and managed to retake some of the trenches. The 2nd Division used its 99th Brigade and to a lesser extent its 6th Brigade in this endeavour to retake the lost trenches. The 5th Brigade and the 52nd were held in reserve for the operation.

In Sir Douglas Haig's eyes, Henry Wilson had come out of this minor loss of trenches in a bad light. He wrote in his diary: 'The IV Corps was the most efficient one in the Army when Sir H. Wilson took over the Command. Since then it had much decreased in military value. There is no doubt that he has failed as a Commander in the field'. Wilson's IV Corps had only just taken over responsibility for the lost trenches and Haig had stopped him from launching a counter-attack on the first day, when the enemy was at his most vulnerable. At this juncture of the war, Haig was not enamoured of Wilson, but their relationship would improve later in the war. It is difficult not to believe that Sir Henry Wilson was hard done by in this matter, and his reputation as a commander in the field was unnecessarily tarnished.

Just before dawn on May 22nd, the 52nd received information that from 8 a.m. they must be ready to move at one hour's notice. This was in response to the bombardment of the 47th Division and the line south of it, resulting in the loss of some trenches, and the move forward of the 6th and 99th Brigades. The Regiment remained at one hour's notice to move throughout the next 37 hours, until 9 p.m. on the 23rd, when the 'ready to move' was extended to two hours. On the evening of May 24th, it looked as if the 52nd would soon be in action, as orders were received to be prepared to move, but they were subsequently cancelled.

On May 25th, the Regiment marched at 9 a.m., via Houdain, Rebreuve, and Fresnicourt, to tents in the Bois de Verdrel. At the start, the march was particularly unpleasant, because of heavy rain, this demonstrating the regimental

---

407 Actually held by the 7th Brigade of the 25th Division, but temporarily under the 47th Division.

408 The Berthonval Sector extended from Central Avenue to Ersatz Avenue.

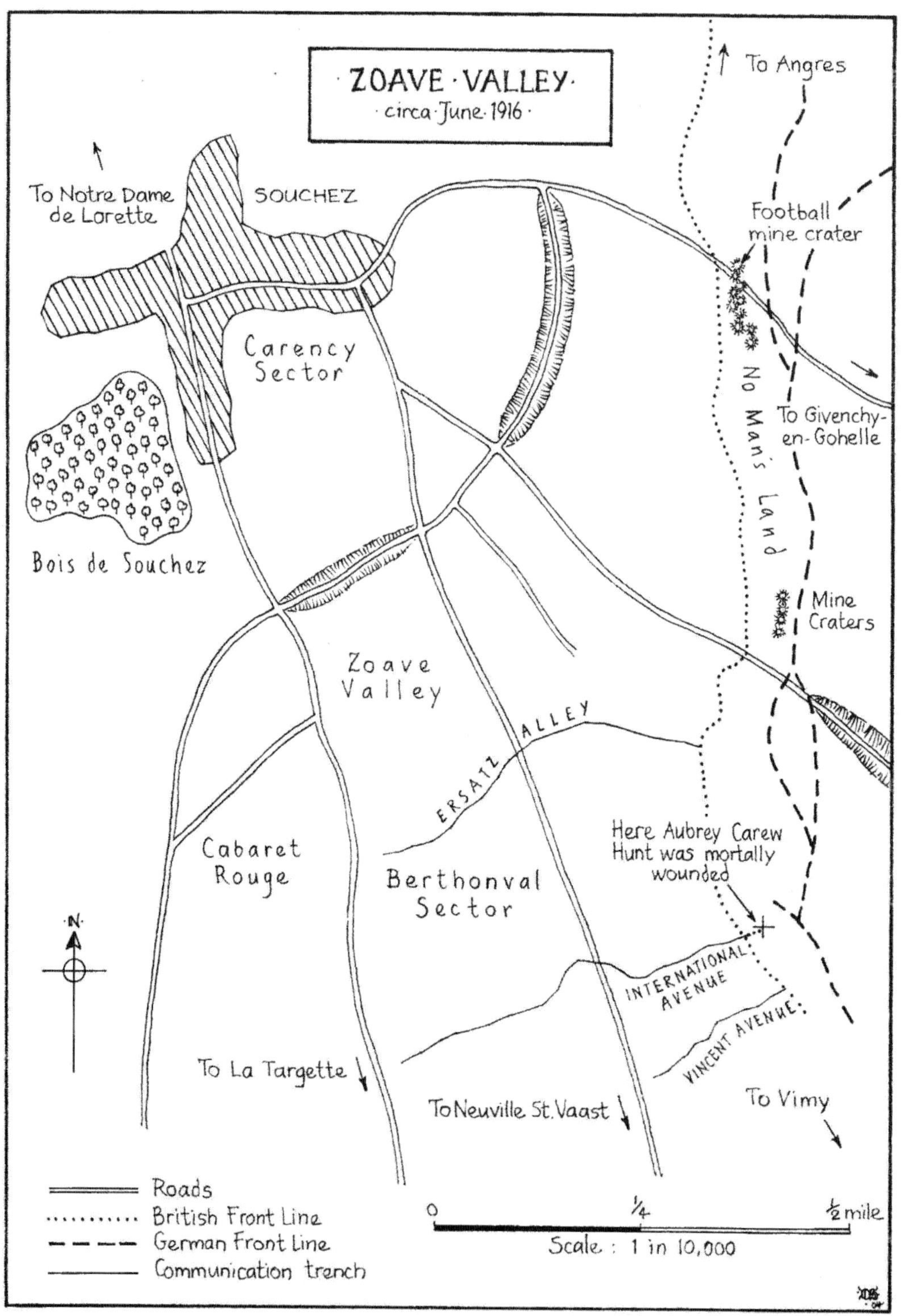
·ZOAVE·VALLEY·
·circa·June·1916·
To Angres
To Notre Dame de Lorette
SOUCHEZ
Football mine crater
Carency Sector
No Man's Land
To Givenchy-en-Gohelle
Bois de Souchez
Mine Craters
Zoave Valley
ERSATZ ALLEY
Here Aubrey Carew Hunt was mortally wounded
Cabaret Rouge
Berthonval Sector
N
INTERNATIONAL AVENUE
VINCENT AVENUE
To La Targette
To Neuville St. Vaast
To Vimy
Roads
British Front Line
German Front Line
Communication trench
0
¼
½ mile
Scale : 1 in 10,000

value of carrying waterproof sheets. At 1.30 p.m. the following day, the 52nd marched to Gouy Servins via Grand Servins and Petit Servins. The 5th Brigade was reserve to the 2nd Division, which was in the process of replacing the badly battered 47th Division in the line. The battle position assigned to the 52nd, if necessary, was the Maitre, and the position further forward was the line between the rivers Carency and Souchez, with the left flank approximately on the ruined village of Ablain Saint Nazaire. From May 27th until the 31st, the 52nd furnished working parties, and carried out training in the vicinity of their billets. Familiarisation with their new line was made daily by officers and N.C.O.s. Lieutenant-Colonel Archibald Eden, having missed the recent excitement, returned from leave on May 29th and resumed his command of the Regiment.

On June 1st, a beautiful day, Archibald Eden took his company commanders to view their new trenches opposite Vimy. Optimistically, he wrote in his diary; 'They do not seem to be as bad as people make out'. Few would agree with Eden's first impression, as it was generally seen as a very unpleasant part of the line to be in. Vimy Ridge extended for nine miles from the valley of the river Scarpe, in front of Arras, to the valley of the Souchez river, in which lay the villages of Souchez and Carenchy. Beyond the Souchez Valley was the Lorette Ridge facing north. Today the chapel of Notre Dame de Lorette stands on its eastern end. In 1916, only a small section of the brick wall of the original chapel was still in existence after the heavy fighting of 1915. The western slope of Vimy Ridge was slight, but just behind the British front line of 1916, it was cut into by a branch of the Souchez Valley running to the south. This was known as Zoave Valley, which narrowed and accentuated the end of the ridge. In 1915, there had been heavy fighting in Zoave Valley and large numbers of French Colonial troops or Zoaves had been killed in the action. Their unburied bodies, in brightly coloured uniforms, lay decomposing in no man's land for months on end, and were to give the valley its name. The eastern slope of the ridge dropped sharply away to the plain of Douai. The summit of Vimy Ridge was held almost in its entirety by the Germans, giving them an excellent view of the British positions. Only at the northern end of the ridge did the British line lie near the top and even here the crest was in no man's land, with the two adversaries in trenches on the slopes of either side.

On June 1st, the 47th reinforcement of 20 men arrived. The following day, the 52nd was reinforced by the return of four officers who had recovered from wounds, received whilst serving with the Regiment. They were Captain Aubrey Carew Hunt, Lieutenants F.W.C. 'Chips' Chippindale, P.C. Webster, and James

Belgrave[409]. The 52nd left their billets in Gouy-Servins, at 8 p.m. on June 2nd, and made their way to the left sub-sector of the Berthonval trenches, opposite the infamous Vimy Ridge, where they relieved the 1st Royal Berkshire of the 99th Brigade.

Although the battlefield had been well cleaned up, the trench system was in a poor state of repair, partly from damage by the enemy's artillery fire, and because the trenches had originally been part of the British support line. The front line trenches had been lost by the 47th Division during the German attack on May 21st, and the support line trenches, 300-400 yards further back, had not been fully developed. The front of the Regiment extended from Vincent Avenue inclusive, in the south, to Ersatz Avenue exclusive, to the north. Three companies were in the line, A, B, and D. B Company spent daytime in the second line, only venturing into the front line at night, as it was unfinished and in a rudimentary state. The left front company had no second line, and the right front company had only the semblance of a second line. The Regimental Headquarters were in Zoave Valley, and the 5th Brigade had its own Headquarters, about half an hour's walk away, near the Cabaret Rouge. Cabaret Rouge was a ruined house, one mile south of Souchez, on the Arras road. On the right of the 52nd were the 24th Royal Fusiliers of their own brigade, and on the left were the 1st King's of the 6th Brigade.

The men of the 52nd spent the night of June 2nd and the following day endeavouring to improve their positions. Trenches were deepened and connected up, and the wire, of which there was a distinct lack, was increased. Sixteen chevaux-de-frise[410] were carried to the front, via the long communication trenches through Zoave Valley, and placed into position by dawn. The enemy's wire was little better than that of the British, and the Germans were hard at work improving it. Until the 52nd had completed their own relief, no effort was made to interfere with the German wiring parties for fear of retaliation. From 9 to 11 a.m., on June 3rd, there was heavy shellfire which reduced the amount of work that could be done on the trenches. Forty heavy shrapnel and high explosive shells fell to the east and west of Zoave Valley. On the 3rd, one man from A Company was killed, and another from B Company was wounded.

Work continued, on June 4th, with the enemy said to be very quiet despite the fact that one man was killed and five more were wounded. It was at this point the 52nd heard the first reports of the epic sea battle of World War One, the Battle

---

[409] James Belgrave joined the R.F.C. on July 20th 1916. As a captain with seventeen victories, a M.C. and bar, he was killed in a 'dog-fight' with a German plane on July 13th 1918.

[410] A defensive structure consisting of a moveable obstacle, composed of barbed wire, or a spike attached to a wooden frame. Originally they were intended as an obstruction to cavalry.

of Jutland, which had been fought on May 31st. These reports indicated that there had been heavy losses on both sides[411]. The 5th was reported to be quiet with no trench mortaring and no mining. As much progress as possible was made with wiring and deep dug-outs, but the work was hampered by the lack of, and the difficulty of getting up, material for their protection. At 10 p.m. on June 5th, Captain Aubrey Carew Hunt was mortally wounded while getting out of the International Avenue Sap-head, with a wiring party, before it was quite dark, and died a few minutes later. It was reported that he had been hit by a stray bullet, but it seems to be more likely that it was a deliberate sniper's shot[412]. The 24-year-old Carew Hunt had only just returned to the 52nd, three days before, following his recovery from serious wounds received at Givenchy on September 25th 1915. Perhaps he had forgotten his trench craft, as he had been away from the Regiment for many months. That same day Second-Lieutenants Nick Hill and Theodore Ionides, joined the Regiment. Lieutenant Robert Barnes returned from duties at No. 2 Infantry Base, and his place there was taken by Second-Lieutenant Keith Peploe.

In the evening of June 6th, the 52nd was relieved by the 17th R. F., and they became the support battalion in and around Cabaret Rouge, Alhambra, and Coliseum Redoubts. The men were crowded and the officers' quarters filthy. One man was killed and two wounded during the day. The following afternoon, the Regiment heard of the death of Earl Kitchener, the Secretary of State for War, who was drowned when his cruiser, H.M.S. Hampshire, struck a mine, off the Orkneys, on the way to Russia. Although the 'all powerful' War Minister's influence had declined in recent months, particularly after the Gallipoli debacle, he was still a man to be reckoned with. To Archibald Eden, Kitchener's demise was 'very mysterious', but the facts speak for themselves; the Hampshire was unlucky enough to hit a mine and sank. The only mystery was that the distinguished Field-Marshal and Minister was reputed to have made little effort to save himself. 'Make way for Lord Kitchener' rang out as he made his way to the

---

411 The British Fleet, under Sir John Jellicoe, lost their only chance of the war to annihilate the German High Seas Fleet. In fact, the British lost more men and ships than the enemy, who slunk away to the safety of their own harbours during the night. It can be argued that strategically the British had the advantage, as the German foe never ventured, in any force, far from the safety of their own ports, for the remainder of the war.

412 Aubrey Carew Hunt was an excellent officer, the son of a clergyman as were so many other officers in the 52nd. A product of Merton College, where he was an exhibitioner, and the Oxford University O.T.C, he was a fine oarsman and was destined to command a company if he had not been killed. The site of Carew Hunt's death is close to the present Zoave Valley Military Cemetery, and he was buried at Ecoivres Military Cemetery, Mont St. Eloi. As with so many other young officers, he had made no will and died intestate, leaving £140.7.6.

bridge, where the commander of the ship urged him to take to the lifeboats. Kitchener appears to have refused.

At 'Stand-to' on June 8th, Lieutenant-Colonel Archibald Eden and the now Major Richard Crosse visited the garrisons in the Coliseum and Alhambra strong points. The garrisons had been reduced in strength as there was not a great deal to do, and three or four officers at a time went back to Petit Servins, for a bath and a good night's rest. It was fortunate that the Germans did not attack, as they had on May 21st, or the 52nd would have been embarrassed at the very least. At night time, trucks were drawn up a light railway by mules, with rations and other materials of war.

After drawing food and water, at 9 p.m. on June 10th, the 52nd relieved the 17th R. F. in the same Berthonval trenches as they had occupied before. The Regiment would remain here until June 15th, a period described in the *Battalion War Diary* as 'nothing occurred out of the ordinary course'. Both British and Germans, particularly at night, were far too busy improving their own trench lines to have time to interfere with each other. Certainly the 52nd was making rapid progress with their defences. On the 12th, the 48th reinforcement of 52 men arrived, and two serjeants joined at Petit Servins from the Base. Second-Lieutenant T.G.C. Caulfield-Stoker also reported for duty and was sent to Captain John Boardman's C Company. The following day, Second-Lieutenant William Goffe joined the Regiment, from the Motor Machine-Gun Corps, and was sent to Captain Ralph Kite's D Company. The night of June 13th was wet and this interfered with the work in progress. Archibald Eden got no rest before 12.30 a.m., as the working parties had to be inspected and new defences laid out. Stand-to was at 2.30 a.m., just before first light, when the enemy might be expected to attack. Thus the nights were very short and rest in short supply.

One of the areas of construction that the 52nd had been working on, during this tour of the trenches, was the building of deep, protective, dug-outs. The work continued for 20 out of the 24 hours, with the use of regular reliefs. The entrances were difficult to construct as only a few men at a time could be used. A great deal of timber had to be carried up by working parties, as regular shoring up was needed as the excavations continued. Over four days, the 52nd put in no less than 200 steps into the new dug-outs, under the supervision of Richard Crosse, acting as a 'foreman of works'. One of Crosse's nicknames was 'Energy', which seems to have been particularly suitable under the circumstances[413].

In the early hours of June 15th, the 17th R. F. completed the relief of the 52nd, who moved to Camblain l'Abbé with the last company getting in at 4.30

---

[413] Crosse's other nicknames were 'The Commander' and 'Achilles'. Achilles was the hero of Homer's *Iliad,* the bravest and swiftest of Greek soldiers.

a.m. An early breakfast was taken and then everyone went to bed and slept until midday. Their new billets were good ones, in huts originally put up by the French, for the use of their own troops. The officers had a hut to themselves, which was divided into two, allowing sleeping quarters and a mess. The 52nd was to remain at Camblain l'Abbé until June 18th. It was to be a period of rest, bathing and training, although about 200 men had to be found each night for Brigade fatigue parties in the area about the trenches. June 18th saw the arrival of the 49th reinforcement of 45 men including Acting Quarter-Master Serjeant Andrews who joined from the Base. That evening, on the anniversary of the Battle of Waterloo, the Regiment moved back to small and uncomfortable billets, in Estree-Cauchy.

The 52nd was to remain at Estree-Cauchy until June 27th. Close to the village was a 50 yards shooting-range, which allowed each company to be given a short course in grouping and rapid fire. On the 19th, 500 men were required for fatigues, and Second-Lieutenant A.G. Gibbons transferred to the Royal Engineers, before posting to 170 Tunnelling Company. The other half of the village was taken by a Royal Naval Battalion, and Archibald Eden was interested in that a soldier held the command, but most of the officers were sailors and they saluted in naval fashion. On June 21st, Eden took nine officers for a reconnaissance near Villars, from 6.30 a.m. until 9.30 a.m. Later he was informed that he was to leave on the 23rd for special duty in the Fourth Army Area. The delayed Waterloo Sports were held, on June 22nd, in front of a large number of spectators, including the commander of the 2nd Division, Major-General William Walker V.C., and the new 5th Brigade commander, Brigadier-General George Bullen-Smith. The weather was very good and the event was held in a flat field close to the billets. An excellent bombing competition was put on by Second-Lieutenant Percy Bobby and, in the evening, a concert was organized by Lieutenant Laurence Goodwyn. The day was deemed to have been a great success.

A printed programme from the night's entertainment is still in existence. The front page shows a trooper of the 52nd in 1815, shaking hands with one from 1916. The band of the 17th Royal Fusiliers played and a number of men from the Regiment sang songs. Captain Jack Hardcastle gave a rendition of '*The Duck Pond*', Corporal Harris played a selection on his violin, Private Hollingdale sang '*She Pushed Me Into The Parlour*' and Lieutenant Nicholas Hill assisted by friends sang '*Another Little Drink*'. Despite the short time he had been with the Regiment, Hill was well recognized for his wit and his ability to keep the mess going in periods of general depression. The advertisements on the back of the programme suggested 'Don't Scratch Use Vermin Jelly' and that 'The Audience Are Requested To Refrain From Throwing Nose Caps or Bases of Shells At The

Artistes'. The vermin jelly referred to the fact that the troops' clothing was never free from lice for any length of time. Ironically, the audience was informed that 'The Fire Proof Curtain Will Be Lowered At Least Three Times During The Performance'.

On June 23rd, Lieutenant-Colonel Archibald Eden departed from the 52nd, leaving them in the most capable of hands, those of Major Richard Crosse, and proceeded for special duty at the Fourth Army Headquarters. The 44-year-old Eden had been a fine commanding officer, although in a more demonstrative style than his predecessor, the more self-effacing but equally successful Henry Davies. Earlier in June, Eden had been awarded a well-merited D.S.O., an award that Davies unfathomably never received. Initially, Richard Crosse's command was a temporary one; however, it would soon become permanent [on July 8th] and he would lead the 52nd, apart from a three week period in 1918, when he was wounded, for the remainder of the war. From Senior Subaltern to Commanding Officer in less than two years was rapid progress by any standard. His first Commanding Officer in the 52nd, then Major-General Robert Fanshawe, wrote some kindly words of advice. It was generous of Fanshawe to have found the time to write to Crosse, as eight days later, his 48th Division was to be involved in the first catastrophic day of the Somme battles.

> 23 June 1916 ----- this morning I met Eden and he told me you were left in command. I am very glad to hear you are in the best position in the British Army and I write to remind you that now you are in that position you must remember that your first duty is to keep yourself as fit and fresh as you can, and above all in a fight to be where you can best look after the Regiment as a whole, including its rearward services, so that it may be fed and rested as much as possible, and you can put in your services in a fight when and where they will have most effect. You are now the most important man in the Regiment, and you must use others to do their different jobs. The faults I usually see Battn. and other Comdrs. make is to be too far back and not doing enough reconnaissance *before* the fighting begins *and too far forward after* the fighting has begun, to best control their command as a whole.
>
> I apologise for my lecture but it will do no harm. Good luck to you and the Regiment.

On the 27th, the 52nd marched to new billets at Villers au Bois, where training continued, and the 50th reinforcement of 30 men arrived. The last two

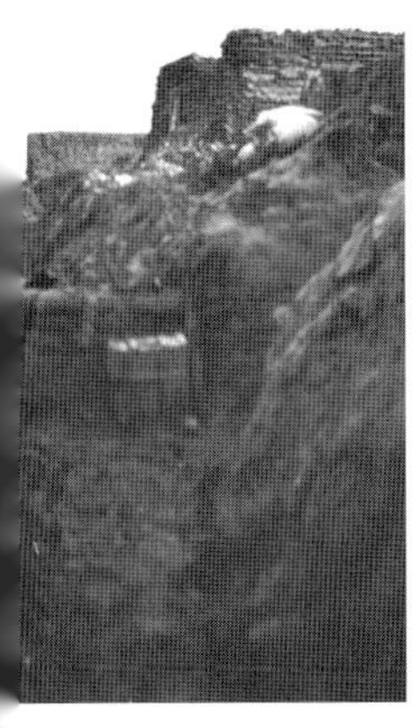

Brickstacks opposite La Bassée. 1915. [Imperial War Museum Q56233]

George Field, Robert Bull, and Guy Blewitt at the Guards Club, Cuinchy. 1915. [Blewitt's Diaries]

Claude Chichester and Robert Bull. 1915. [Blewitt's Diaries]

52nd at Cuinchy in 1915. [Blewitt's Diaries]

52nd at Cuinchy Brickstacks. 1915. [Blewitt's Diaries]

Cuinchy trenches in 1915. [Blewitt's Diaries]

French at Cuinchy. 1915. [Blewitt's Diaries]

German Brickstacks Cuinchy. August 1st 1915. [Regimental Archives]

Charles Fowke in the Guards Club, Cuinchy. August 1st 1915. [Regimental Archives]

Writing home from the Givenchy front line. August 24th 1915.
[Regimental Archives]

Making tea in the front line Givenchy. August 24th 1915.
[Regimental Archives]

Memorial Cross at Givenchy Cemetery. August 29th 1915.
[Regimental Archives]

Ashley Ponsonby was shot dead by a sniper at Givenchy on September 8th 1915. He had the reputation of being the most popular officer of his era in the 52nd.
[Blewitt's Diaries]

Ashley Ponsonby's grave is on the far left of the picture. Windy Corner Military Cemetery.
[Blewitt's Diaries]

Charles Fowke's platoon at Hearts Redoubt. September 11th 1915.
[Regimental Archives]

Givenchy Church. September 10th 1915.
[Regimental Archives]

The able Charles Higgins who was second-in-command of the 52nd at the Battle of Loos. Later a brigadier-general at 38 years of age. [Regimental Chronicles]

Pierce Newton-King. Son of a former 52nd officer, wounded at Langemarck. Killed in action on September 25th 1915. [Regimental Chronicles]

Lancelot Vidal. Radley schoolmaster, botanist. Killed in action on September 25th 1915. [Regimental Chronicles]

Givenchy from the air. Circa September 1915. [Blewitt's Diaries]

Cecil Hurst-Brown. Died of wounds, received the previous day, on September 26th 1915. [Regimental Chronicles]

Edward Hughes. Killed in action on September 25th 1915. Small of body, big of heart. [Regimental Chronicles]

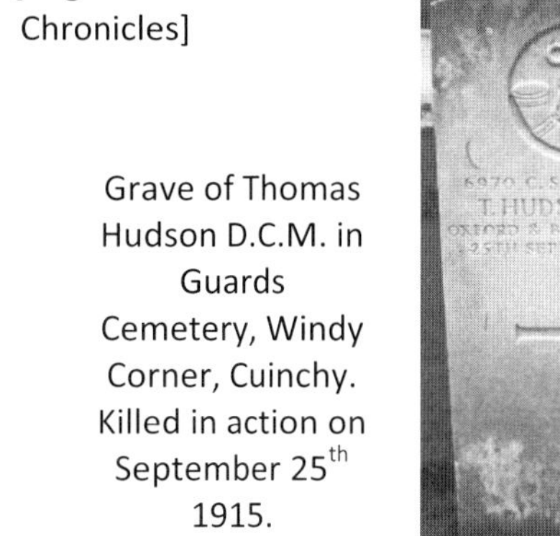

Grave of Thomas Hudson D.C.M. in Guards Cemetery, Windy Corner, Cuinchy. Killed in action on September 25th 1915. [Author's Collection 2008]

Grave of Edward Hughes in Guards Cemetery, Windy Corner, Cuinchy. [Author's Collection 2008]

Montmorency Barracks, Béthune. The 52nd were billeted here after the Battle of Loos and again in 1917. Photograph circa 1918.
[Private Collection]

Aubrey Carew Hunt. Shot by a sniper whilst getting out of International Avenue Sap-Head with a wiring party on June 5th 1916.
[Regimental Chronicles]

Zoave Valley looking towards Notre Dame de Lorette. The scene of the 52nd's fighting in June/July 1916.
[Author's Collection 2006]

reinforcements were given separate training under Lieutenant Cyprien 'Ben' Slocock. One man from D Company was wounded on the 29th. July 1st found the 52nd still in Brigade Reserve at Villers au Bois, and the 51st reinforcement of one serjeant and 25 other ranks arrived. The following day, the Regiment moved to the trenches at Carency, in relief of the 17th R. F. July 3rd and 4th were quiet days with little activity on either side. On the 4th, a wet day, the 52nd was visited by officers of the 2nd South Staffordshire, of the 6th Brigade, who were keen to take over the line. At 11.30 a.m. on the 5th, the 52nd's trench mortars registered on the enemy line. The Germans responded in kind at 1.15 p.m., leading to the sentry at Regimental Headquarters, Private William Clark, a cockney, being killed, and Private Tustain of the officers' mess being wounded. At 11 a.m. the next day, the British trench mortars began wire cutting and, one and a half hours later, the enemy retaliated for an hour by plastering the Regimental Headquarters with mortar bombs.

At night on the 6th, the Regiment was relieved by the 17th R. F., and became the support battalion. B Company was put at the disposal of the left battalion; C Company at the disposal of the right battalion; D Company at Cabaret Rouge; A Company at Carency. The 7th saw a trench raid made by the 17th R. F., and the 52nd's Regimental Headquarters and Zoave Valley in general were bombarded by the enemy. The following day was a quiet one, the only notable event being the temporary promotion of Richard Crosse, who was now commanding the 52nd, to Lieutenant-Colonel. His substantive rank was captain and brevet-major and he would soon be affectionately known in the Regiment as the 'Commander'.

On Sunday July 9th, at 8.30 a.m., the enemy blew up a mine under the Football Crater, damaging the lip on the British side. Later in the day, at 11 p.m., the 52nd relieved the 17th Royal Fusiliers, and the Regimental Headquarters were established in a new place, Rever Terra South. Captain Hubert Rawson, whose defective eyesight had originally precluded him from joining the Army or Navy, was in his element as the sapping officer. He had been working on the new Headquarters for the previous two days, and his sapping platoon had done a great deal of excellent work. The old Headquarters, Holloway, was being shelled so regularly that it had been expedient to find a new site. D and C Companies were in their old positions on the right and centre respectively; B Company was on the left; A Company was in support in the Quarry. Second-Lieutenant Percy Bobby was required at 5th Brigade Headquarters, and Lieutenant Noel Harrison became the grenade officer.

July 10th proved to be a quiet day; although the 52nd expected the enemy to set off another mine, nothing happened. The next day, Brigadier-General

George Bullen-Smith, of the 5th Brigade, paid an early morning visit, at 5.30 a.m., to view the 52nd's trenches. Hostile trench mortars were fired at 6 a.m. and 11 a.m.; otherwise the day was quiet. At 11.30 p.m. on the 12th, a German patrol suddenly appeared around the north side of the Football Crater, and bombed the 52nd's wiring party in front of the right picket. The men of the wiring party retaliated vigorously with bombs, which saw off the enemy. The British Mills bomb[414] was now considered by Lieutenant-Colonel Richard Crosse to be superior to the German bomb. Once peace had been restored the wiring proceeded uneventfully. Earlier in the day, information had been received that their former Commanding Officer, Lieutenant-Colonel Archibald Eden had been appointed to the temporary command of 24th Brigade[415]. In fact he would retain command of the Brigade until January 14th 1917.

At 4 a.m. on July 13th, Brigadier-General George Bullen-Smith paid a further early morning visit to the 52nd and had the situation in the Football Crater explained to him. In the late afternoon, at 4.30 p.m., Richard Crosse was told by telephone to "clear up" the situation in the Football Crater and later to write a report on it. The report timed at 7.30 p.m. was done but withheld, as further verbal orders by telephone instructed Crosse to carry out the operation in the crater "PRIOR TO RELIEF tonight". At 9 p.m., he received a written order to patrol the crater. Crosse recorded in the *Battalion War Diary* that the crater was patrolled at 10.40 p.m. The 52nd was relieved that night by the 13th Essex, of the 6th Brigade, and the relief was complete by 1.30 a.m. on the 14th[416].

The trench notebook of Captain Ralph Kite, commanding D Company, is still in existence and covers the period in the Souchez trenches. The notes that he made were of instructions from Eden, Crosse, and the Adjutant, Ernest Whitfeld. They give a flavour of Regimental life during this period. 'Lice. N.C.O.s must report men who are really bad'. Lice, pediculus vestimentii, were a constant irritation in the trenches and the only way of getting rid of the eggs was by burning the seams of their clothing with a candle. A 1916 study showed an average lice count of 10.5 per shirt and 4.2 per pair of trousers. In one extreme

---

[414] The Mills bomb had been invented, in 1915, by William Mills of Birmingham. It could be modified to be fired from a rifle as a rifle grenade. Mills bombs were still used by the British Army until the 1960s.

[415] When Eden joined the 24th Brigade, it was in the 23rd Division [New Army Division], but three days later it returned to the 8th Division, from whence it had come on October 18th 1915.

[416] Reading between the lines, it looks as though some sort of altercation had taken place between Crosse and Bullen-Smith. The *Regimental Chronicles* made no mention of the incident which is most unusual. Crosse went to great lengths to put the timings in the *Battalion War Diary*. In addition, he stated in it that 'all details of this operation are contained in a separate file which is retained with Regt. Office Copy of War Diary'. Perhaps Bullen-Smith wanted the Football Crater patrolled immediately and Crosse felt that it should be left to the incoming 13th Essex.

case 10,428 lice and 10,253 eggs were found housed in a single shirt! Typhus, the scourge of all armies in the field, was carried by the louse. Many of the anti-lice agents of that era were ineffective. At this very time, Kite sent home for a strong disinfectant soap after an outbreak of parasites among the D Company officers. Lice were not the only parasites to affect the 52nd. Early in 1917 scabies infected some of the officer corps.

'Firing over parapet sentries must not put sandbags on the firestep as every man must be able to shoot over the parapet'. 'Raids: N.C.O. on duty. Usually posts sentries and must know where bomb store is. All sentries must know where enemy line is and where the ammunition store is. Sentries must not talk'. 'Platoon Commanders must live more with their platoons'. 'Official time must be regarded. All company watches must be set to this'. 'One or two of my officers must be kept back'. Certainly in the big attacks it was customary to keep back a number of officers and N.C.O.s, so that in the event of heavy casualties some leaders were still alive. 'Protection of food. Muslin bags'. In the warm weather of an average French summer, flies and other insects getting on to the men's food might lead to illness. Kite got his mother to make the muslin bags for his own D Company.

Kite's notebook continued: 'Company latrine paper'. Latrines were sited close to the front line in small saps [short blind-ending trenches] dug through the parados [the elevation of earth along the back of the trench]. They consisted of buckets or deep holes in the ground each with a pole across the top. It was known for troops to fire captured German artillery signal rockets down them to see what colours they were. The sanitary corporal who was responsible for the latrines was inevitably known as 'the shit-wallah'. A little later, in 1916, the Second Division's Assistant Director of Medical Services described the type of latrines used by the division, including those of the 52nd.

> The latrine system is unsuitable for summer use, and under present conditions is completely unsanitary, consisting of open buckets with disinfectant and periodically buried in the waste ground behind the trenches. In most cases this can only be done during the hours of darkness.
>
> This system is in the process of being replaced by deep pits covered with fly-proof boarding, the centre board being hinged and capable of being swung back. This type of latrine has been in general use in the Division throughout the present summer and proved extremely satisfactory, both in the Souchez area and Vimy Ridge.

Kite had further entries in his notebook: 'Wounded men should have their hands tied behind their backs'. Presumably this referred to wounded Germans, who had been known to feign death, before attacking their opponents when they were not looking. 'Telephones not to be used at all except by officers between Regt:HQ. Coy HQ'. The telephone or runners were the prime means of communication in the trenches. Unfortunately telephone wires were frequently cut by artillery fire. 'hair cut'. Hair was worn short because of lice. 'Serg:Broughton to lecture on gas'. Gas was first used by the Germans in 1915, and from 1916 onwards gas was routinely added to bombardments. The main agents used were chlorine [from April 1915], phosgene [late 1915] and mustard gas [1917]. Chlorine and the odourless phosgene could lead to an asphyxial death. Fatalities with mustard gas were usually from secondary infection of the skin lesions. German tear-gas or 'sneezer' was chloropicrin. Some soldiers called gas the 'Devil's Breath'. It was particularly effective against horses as the equine gas mask was primitive.

In the early hours of July 14th, the Regiment marched to Estree-Cauchy. The following day, it was on to billets in Camblain-Châtelain, where they were joined by their new second-in-command, Captain Reggie Owen, who had been on attachment to General Staff Headquarters, IV Corps. No doubt, Richard Crosse was pleased to see the return of such a fine and experienced officer as Owen. Sadly, he would survive less than three weeks in the post. The 52nd was to remain at Camblain-Châtelain until they entrained, at Pernes, at 10.52 a.m. on July 20th, bound for the Somme. The 17th was quiet and on the 18th there was a practice ceremonial parade, for the following day's inspection, by Lieutenant-General Sir Henry Wilson, commander of IV Corps. However, on the 19th, the inspection was cancelled and the 52nd was ordered to stand by in billets ready to entrain for an unknown destination.

As Captain Ralph Kite wrote to his mother; 'we have just come out after an exciting twelve days. The last spot was just about as bad as I have known. We are thankful to have seen the last of it'[417]. Their as yet unknown destination was to be even more of a challenge to the 52nd than the Souchez trenches that they had just left. They were destined for the Somme, an even more dangerous and unpleasant sector. Lieutenant-Colonel Richard Crosse looked upon their time in the vicinity of Vimy Ridge as a useful step up from routine trench life to the active warfare of the Somme. After the war, he wrote, 'the disturbed and anxious six weeks in June-July, 1916, spent by the 52nd on Vimy Ridge, usefully filled the transition from the security and orderly arrangements of an established system of

[417] Letter to Edith Kite written on July 16th 1916.

trenches to the rough and tumble of the Somme'. How right he was, as we will see.

Chapter XIII

The Somme: the Assaults on Guillemont Station and towards the Village of Ginchy.

July 20th - August 13th 1916

[Maps: pages 315, 317, 323, 326, 332, 340.]

Late in 1915, the Allies decided that in the New Year their interests were best served by attacking Germany on all sides. The French and the British would take part in an offensive on the Somme, while the Russian and Italian armies would attack in their own theatres. Assaulted from several directions at once, the Germans would find it difficult to switch their forces at each new threat. Sir Douglas Haig would have liked British efforts to be in the region of Ypres, with the possibility of clearing the Belgium coast of U-boat bases. But with good grace he had bowed to French wishes. However, as more and more French soldiers were sucked into the charnel-house of Verdun, the British would become the senior partner on the Somme.

In early 1916, soon after taking over command of the B.E.F., Haig had directed General Sir Edmund Allenby to make a study of an attack, to the north of the Somme, in the Third Army area. On March 6th, five days after taking command of the new Fourth Army front, which stretched from the Somme to Foncquevillers, General Sir Henry Rawlinson held a conference with his corps commanders[418]. He had taken over responsibility for the Somme offensive. Rawlinson explained to them that Fourth Army would probably be reinforced by another corps, and by heavy artillery. The offensive would be in June or July, although it might have to be brought forward to April, in view of German pressure on the French at Verdun. Eventually, the area to be attacked was agreed upon. The Fourth Army would attack on a 25,000 yards front from Hébuterne, in the north, to Maricourt in the south. The Third Army would be responsible for a subsidiary attack at Gommecourt.

The German front line to be assaulted ran from Serre, through the Redan Ridge, and west of Beaumont Hamel, Thiepval, Ovillers, La Boisselle and Fricourt. At this point, the enemy's line turned east for four miles, covering Mametz, before turning south once more, to cross the river Somme just to the west of Curlu. South of the river it ran to the east of Frise and to the west of Dompierre and Fay. Behind the front system, a second system had been constructed 2,000-5,000 yards from it, mainly on the Guillemont - Pozières ridge.

[418] Sir Edmund Allenby would replace Archibald Murray as Commander-in-Chief of the Egyptian Expeditionary Force in June 1917.

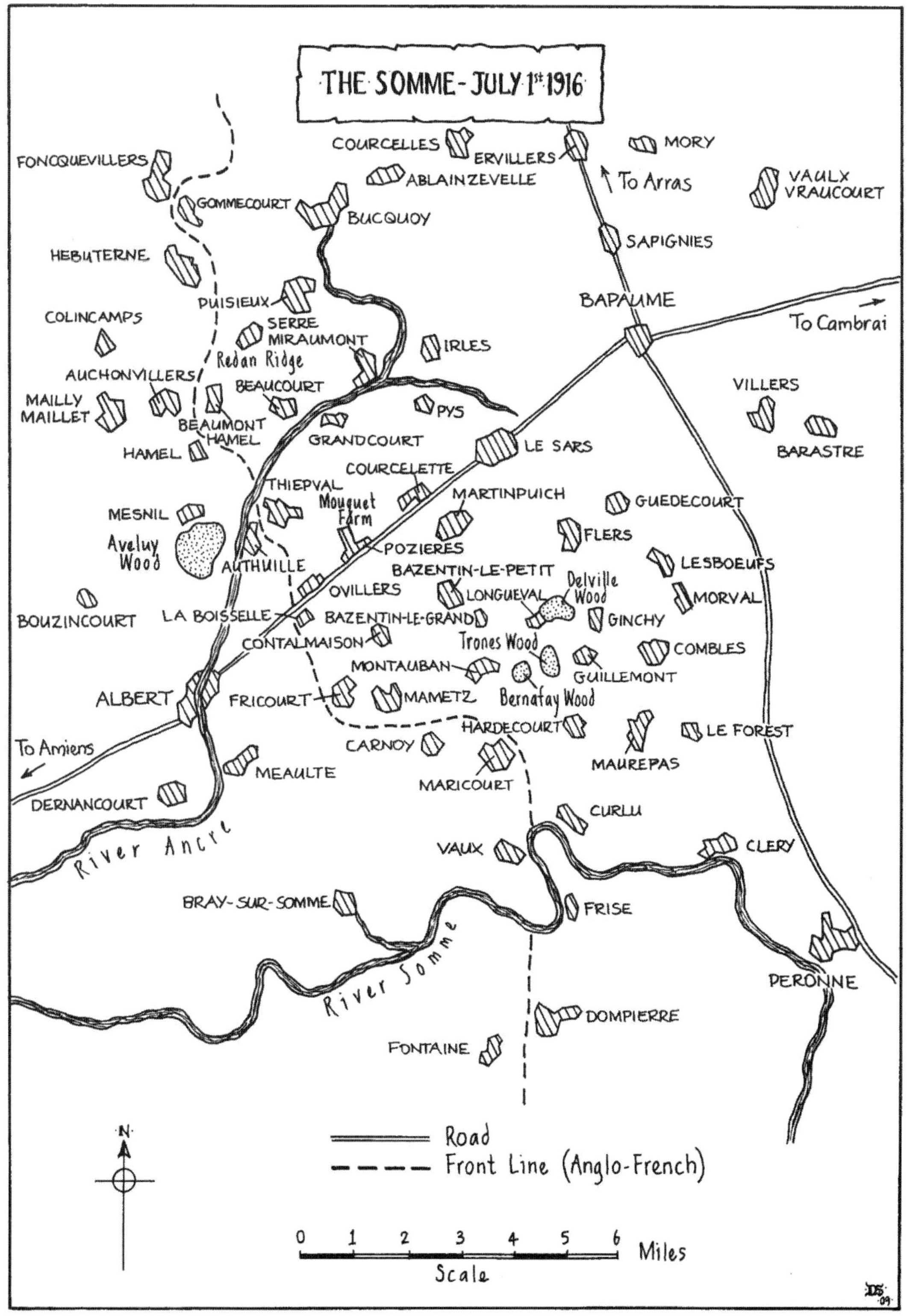
THE SOMME - JULY 1st 1916
FONCQUEVILLERS
GOMMECOURT
HEBUTERNE
COLINCAMPS
PUISIEUX
SERRE
MIRAUMONT
Redan Ridge
AUCHONVILLERS
MAILLY MAILLET
BEAUCOURT
BEAUMONT HAMEL
HAMEL
MESNIL
Aveluy Wood
AUTHUILLE
THIEPVAL
BOUZINCOURT
LA BOISSELLE
ALBERT
To Amiens
DERNANCOURT
MEAULTE
COURCELLES
ERVILLERS
ABLAINZEVELLE
BUCQUOY
MORY
To Arras
VAULX VRAUCOURT
SAPIGNIES
BAPAUME
To Cambrai
IRLES
PYS
GRANDCOURT
LE SARS
COURCELETTE
Mouquet Farm
MARTINPUICH
POZIERES
OVILLERS
BAZENTIN-LE-PETIT
BAZENTIN-LE-GRAND
CONTALMAISON
LONGUEVAL
Delville Wood
GINCHY
Trones Wood
MONTAUBAN
FRICOURT
MAMETZ
Bernafay Wood
GUILLEMONT
CARNOY
HARDECOURT
MARICOURT
VILLERS
BARASTRE
GUEDECOURT
FLERS
LESBOEUFS
MORVAL
COMBLES
LE FOREST
MAUREPAS
CURLU
VAUX
CLERY
FRISE
BRAY-SUR-SOMME
River Ancre
River Somme
PERONNE
DOMPIERRE
FONTAINE
N
Road
Front Line (Anglo-French)
0 1 2 3 4 5 6 Miles
Scale

It crossed the Ancre near Grandcourt, before running to the north past Puisieux[419]. Between the two positions, a number of villages like Montauban, Contalmaison, Pozières and Serre had been fortified. The first and second systems each consisted of several lines of deep trenches, with numerous communication trenches connecting them. Both these first and second line positions had been heavily protected with barbed wired, in many cases in two belts forty yards broad, built of iron stakes interlaced with barbed wire as thick as a man's finger. The chalk subsoil allowed dug-outs to be built, which were both deep and strongly constructed. Concrete machine-gun emplacements had also been built by the enemy, so that he might sweep his own trenches should they be taken. The numerous valleys and depressions made the concealment of artillery batteries, of both sides, relatively easy. In summary, the Germans had built not just a series of defensive lines, but a composite system of mutual support and of enormous depth and strength.

Facing the German line from north to south were the following British corps. The VIIIth [Lieutenant-General Aylmer Hunter-Weston, 'Hunter-Bunter']; Xth [Lieutenant-General Thomas Morland[420]]; IIIrd [Lieutenant-General William Pulteney, 'Putty']; XVth [Lieutenant-General Henry Horne]; XIIIth [Lieutenant-General Walter Congreve, 'Squibs']. To the south of XIII Corps was the French Sixth Army, under General Marie Emile Fayolle, which was positioned astride the river Somme, facing east, opposite Curlu, Dompierre and Fay.

The river Somme takes a westerly course between Péronne and Amiens, cutting into the great plain of northern France. The banks of the river on the south side make a gentle slope, whilst the northern banks are steep. The valley of the Somme is half to three quarters of a mile wide, consisting of water-meadows and marshes. The river was unfordable and, with its surrounding water-meadows and marsh, made a significant military obstacle. The slopes of the northern bank are broken by numerous small valleys with spurs between them. In the most prominent of these valleys runs, a tributary of the Somme, the river Ancre, some twenty to thirty feet wide and three to four feet deep. The valley of the Ancre was a miniature version of the Somme, about 200-300 yards wide, with marshy surrounds.

South of the Somme the ground is flat, but to the north it undulates, rising to a ridge 300 feet above the river valley, on which are situated from south to north, Guillemont, Longueval, Bazentin-le-Petit, Pozières, and Thiepval. Here

[419] The distance between the two positions was 4,000 yards on the right, less than 2,000 yards at Thiepval, and widening again north of the Ancre.

[420] Despite being over 50 years of age, on July 1st 1916, Morland gained fame of a sort by climbing a tree to watch the fighting!

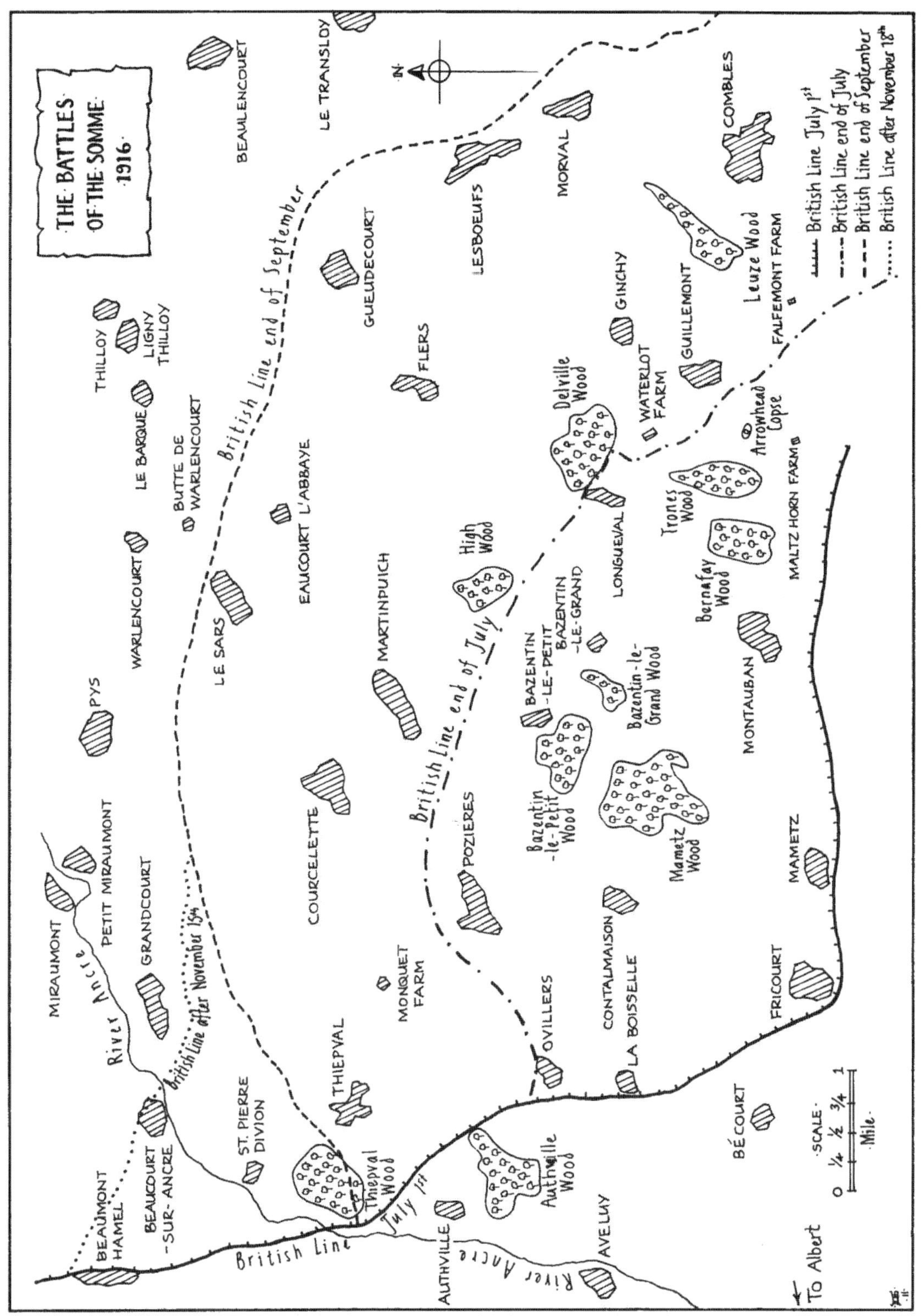
THE BATTLES OF THE SOMME 1916
N
BEAULENCOURT
LE TRANSLOY
COMBLES
MORVAL
LESBOEUFS
GUEUDECOURT
British Line end of September
THILLOY
LIGNY THILLOY
FLERS
GINCHY
GUILLEMONT
Leuze Wood
FALFEMONT FARM
British Line July 1st
British Line end of July
British Line end of September
British Line after November 18th
LE BARQUE
BUTTE DE WARLENCOURT
EAUCOURT L'ABBAYE
Delville Wood
WATERLOT FARM
Arrowhead Copse
MALTZ HORN FARM
Trones Wood
High Wood
LONGUEVAL
WARLENCOURT
LE SARS
MARTINPUICH
BAZENTIN -LE-GRAND
BAZENTIN -LE-PETIT
Bernafay Wood
British Line end of July
PYS
Bazentin-le-Grand Wood
MONTAUBAN
COURCELETTE
PETIT MIRAUMONT
MIRAUMONT
GRANDCOURT
POZIERES
Bazentin -le-Petit Wood
Mametz Wood
MAMETZ
British Line after November 15th
River Ancre
MONQUET FARM
CONTALMAISON
FRICOURT
THIEPVAL
OVILLERS
LA BOISSELLE
ST. PIERRE DIVION
BÉCOURT
SCALE 0 ¼ ½ ¾ 1 Mile
BEAUMONT HAMEL
BEAUCOURT -SUR- ANCRE
Thiepval Wood
July 1st
Authuille Wood
AUTHVILLE
AVELUY
British Line
River Ancre
To Albert

the ridge reaches the river Ancre, before continuing as further high ground marked by Beaucourt, Hébuterne, Gommecourt, and Foncquevillers. To the north of this ridge the ground falls away, before rising again towards Bapaume. In the area as a whole were a number of large villages, but surprisingly few isolated farm-houses. A few large woods, such as Delville [known as 'Devil's Wood'] and Mametz Wood, would play a significant role in the coming battle, and whose names are forever etched into the English mind. The ground between the woods was intensively cultivated and had a chalk undersoil. A main road ran from Amiens through Albert to Bapaume. There was a double railway line from Albert along the Ancre valley towards Arras, with a branch from Albert up the Fricourt valley towards Combles.

One of the main problems that bedevilled the July 1st attack was a fundamental disagreement between the Commander-in-Chief, Sir Douglas Haig, and the Fourth Army Commander, Henry Rawlinson ['Rawly' or 'the Cad' to his contemporaries], about what might reasonably be achieved with the resources available to them. Haig and the French Commander-in-Chief, General Joseph Joffre, were convinced that it was possible to break through all the three German positions[421], before the cavalry destroyed the enemy's communications, and rolled up his line to the north. Rawlinson was more cautious in wanting to take small steps at a time, resembling siege warfare, in much the same manner as General Herbert Plumer would use at Messines, in 1917. Another subject of debate was the length of the preliminary artillery barrage. A short barrage of great intensity would have the value of surprise. A prolonged bombardment would destroy the enemy's morale and have a much better chance of destroying the protective belts of barbed wire. Rawlinson correctly thought that there would be a problem with cutting the wire, and in this he was proved to be correct despite a seven-day preliminary barrage. The failure to cut the wire would have tragic consequences.

The artillery available to Rawlinson's Fourth Army consisted of – Field artillery: 18 pounders, 808; 4.5 inch howitzers, 202. Heavy guns: 4.7 inch, 32; 60 pounders, 128; 6 inch, 20; 9.2 inch, 1; 12 inch, 1. Heavy howitzers: 6 inch, 104; 8 inch, 64; 9.2 inch, 60; 12 inch, 11; 15 inch, 6. French artillery: 220 mm. howitzers, 16; 75 mm., 60; 120 mm., 24. Total number 1,537. The artillery barrage was intended to devastate the German defences to such an extent that the British battalions expected to face little opposition when they reached the enemy's line. Although one and a half million shells were fired during the seven day bombardment, they did not consistently cut the belts of barbed wire in front of the enemy's trenches. In addition, many of the German machine-gunners, who

[421] The German third line, which ran from the west of Irles, Pys, Le Sars, Eaucourt l'Abbayé, Flers, Lesboeufs, and Morval, to the south, was still under construction.

wreaked such carnage on the morning of July 1st, were out of harm's way, in their deep dug-outs, ready to pour murderous fire into the advancing British infantry, the moment the barrage ceased. There were a number of reasons why the artillery barrage did not have the desired effect. There were insufficient guns per yard, the ammunition was still unreliable, and there was a lack of high explosive shells. Shrapnel was effective against personnel in the open, but high explosive shells were required to kill the German machine-gunners in their deep dug-outs. The number of artillery pieces used, here on the Somme, was about three times the number used at the Battle of Loos, but still considerably fewer than was used in later battles, such as at Messines.

The 1916 battles of the Somme can be conveniently divided into four chronological stages. The 2nd Division and the 52nd Light Infantry were not involved in the opening phase, but in order to fully follow their part, it is important to consider the initial actions of the battle.

The first stage, from July 1st until the 13th [Battle of Albert], was an assault on the first German position. At 7.30 a.m. on July 1st, a beautiful day, the British Fourth Army attacked from Serre, in the north, to Maricourt, in the south. Two miles to the north of Serre, a subsidiary attack was delivered by units of the Third Army, at Gommecourt. It failed to take any ground, but did hold the enemy's troops in place, so that they could not go to the aid of their comrades in the south. To the north of the river Ancre, little progress was made; however, further to the south, the British achieved much more with their offensive action. The villages of Montauban and Mametz fell, the outskirts of Ovillers and La Boisselle were reached, and ground to the north of Fricourt was taken. However, the limited success was at a fearful cost, with nearly 20,000 dead and total casualties of just under 60,000, on the first day alone[422]. July 1st was the single most catastrophic day in the history of the British army. A failure of the artillery to consistently breach the enemy's wire, and to kill or incapacitate the German machine-gunners were the two most important reasons for the debacle. Still further to the south, the French had been more successful, taking Dompierre, Becquincourt, Bussu, and Fay. At nightfall on the 1st, a fourteen mile stretch of the enemy's first position, from Mametz to Fay had been taken, but at a terrible cost to the British army.

On July 2nd, slight progress was made at Ovillers and La Boisselle; the notorious German salient at Fricourt fell; Bernafay Wood was entered and appeared to be unoccupied; the French made further progress in the south. The

[422] On July 1st, the total number of casualties for the Fourth Army plus those of VII Corps was 57,470, of whom 19,240 were killed or died of their wounds. The majority of the casualties occurred in the first two hours of the action.

3rd saw Bernafay Wood occupied; the advance pressed forward towards Mametz Wood, which was potentially a difficult position to take and virtually unguarded on this day; the village of La Boisselle was entered; the French moved on in the direction of Péronne. The 4th was a stormy day; the capture of La Boisselle, apart from a few ruins at the northern end, was completed; Mametz Wood was entered for the first time by a small number of British troops. On July 5th, the difficult advance continued towards Contalmaison. Then a pause followed on the 6th, to allow the artillery to prepare for further assaults. During the next few days, heavy fighting resulted in: on July 7th, a footing being gained in the outer defences of Ovillers, a village considered to be impregnable by the Germans; most of Mametz Wood was taken, it being finally cleared of the enemy on the 12th; the southern end of Trones Wood was occupied including a trench along the south-eastern edge and the wood was totally in British hands on July 9th. A German counter-attack on the 9th/10th threw the British troops out, but on the 11th, the enemy was forcibly removed from the wood, except from its northern corner. Trones Wood was finally cleared on July 14th and Contalmaison was captured on July 10th.

The second stage, from July 14th to September 13th, [Battles of Bazentin Ridge, Delville Wood, Pozières Ridge, Guillemont, and Ginchy], was an assault on the German second position. The 52nd would play a part, on July 30th, in this the second phase of the 1916 Somme battles. In the early morning of July 14th, a new attack was made leading to the occupation of all Trones Wood, and a footing was gained in the village of Longueval. Later in the day, Bazentin-le-Grand, Bazentin-le-Petit, and High Wood were captured. This meant that a three mile section of the enemy's second line was now in British hands. Further fighting, on the 15th, saw Delville Wood almost taken by the South Africans, and Waterlot Farm entered, but the British were driven out of High Wood.

The following day, the 16th, Ovillers finally fell after a stubborn resistance, and progress was made towards Pozières, on the Albert to Bapaume road. On the 17th, the ruined sugar refinery at Waterlot Farm was finally captured. A German counter-attack, on July 18th, retook the northern and north-eastern section of Delville Wood, and the British troops in Longueval were forced out of the northern part of the village. On the 20th, the southern part of High Wood was back in British hands again. Two days of artillery bombardment followed, and on the 23rd, an assault was made extending from Guillemont to near Pozières. Initially little ground was taken, but Pozières finally fell on the 25th. Two days later, the enemy was driven out of most of Delville Wood by the 99th Brigade of the 2nd Division, and on the 29th, Longueval and its orchards to the north-west were captured. On July 30th, Guillemont was unsuccessfully attacked by the 30th Division, although the village itself was held for a time. The 52nd was very much involved in this action, in their attempted assault of Guillemont Station to protect the left flank of the 30th Division, this costing the Regiment so dearly in casualties.

Early August saw a lull in the fighting until the night of August 4th/5th, when the windmill on the ridge behind Pozières was captured. On the same day, a further attempt was made on the village of Guillemont, again without a successful outcome. A combined Anglo-French attack from the flanks, to squeeze Guillemont from both sides, was planned and put into place. This assault took place on August 18th, leading to the capture of Guillemont Station, and further progress was made in the environs of Guillemont, without the village being actually taken. Intermittent fighting continued over the next few days, with the British line moving ever closer to Thiepval. On the 24th, Hindenburg Trench was taken and Delville Wood was finally cleared of the enemy. The Germans counter-attacked vigorously but failed to regain the ground that they had so recently lost.

At noon, on September 3rd, a general Anglo-French assault was delivered all along the line. The stubborn village of Guillemont was stormed and captured, followed by part of nearby Ginchy. The French were successful in taking Cléry-sur-Somme and Le Forest, and pushed on to the outskirts of Combles. However, Falfemont Farm, to the south of Ginchy, although rushed by British soldiers, could not be held. Two days later, it fell when Leuze Wood to its north was occupied, bringing the line within three-quarters of a mile of Combles. On September 9th, the capture of Ginchy was completed, and a further advance was made east of Delville Wood, and to the south and east of High Wood. By September 10th, the whole of the German second position between Thiepval and Estrées had been taken, and the Allies now held the high ground.

For their actions on the Somme, in the summer and autumn of 1916, the 52nd could claim three battle honours. They were Somme 1916 [present during part of the period July 1st-November 18th], Delville Wood [July 15th-September 3rd], and the Ancre 1916 [November 13th-18th]. As will be seen, on July 30th, the Regiment fought bravely at Guillemont Station and in the trenches towards Ginchy. Strangely this did not give them the battle honour for Guillemont, which only applied to units in the area of the destroyed village from September 3rd-6th. The 52nd's actions, on July 30th, were covered by the battle honour for Delville Wood.

We left the 52nd, at Camblain-Châtelain, awaiting their summons to travel to the Somme. The Regiment paraded at 9.20 a.m. on July 20th, entrained at Pernes Station, leaving at 10.52 a.m. precisely. At 4.40 p.m. they arrived at Saleux, south of Amiens, before marching the sixteen miles to Corbie, not arriving until after midnight. Their packs were carried in lorries, and the men were said to have marched well with only two falling out. The 52nd got into their billets at 12.25 a.m., which were considered to be very fair, except those of the officers. On that subject the Town Major was at first troublesome, but the matter was eventually settled to everyone's satisfaction.

After their long march of the day before, the Regiment spent the 21st resting in their billets, on what turned out to be a very hot day. Rest was difficult with the constant stream of lorries passing through the town by both day and night. Major Reggie Owen thought that it was just like Piccadilly Circus. Corbie was a small town at the junction of the rivers Somme and Ancre, about 25 miles behind the front trenches. It was an important medical centre with both No. 5 and No. 21 Casualty Clearing Stations [C.C.S.] set up there. Wounded men were given immediate treatment here before they were evacuated by ambulance train or barge down the river Somme. During this day of rest for the 52nd, Major William Congreve, of the Rifle Brigade, who had won a posthumous V.C., was buried in Corbie Cemetery[423].

While his men were regaining their strength on the 21st, their restless Commanding Officer, Lieutenant-Colonel Richard Crosse, and the Adjutant Ernest Whitfeld, were out reconnoitring the country to the north-west of Bray, including their next destination, Happy Valley. The following day, the 22nd, the Regiment managed an early bathing parade, but then stood by all day, awaiting orders to move to the front. At 9.15 a.m., Richard Crosse held a conference of his company commanders, and Brigadier-General George Bullen-Smith, commanding the 5th Brigade, visited Regimental Headquarters. At 10.30 a.m. on July 23rd, the 52nd set off on their march to Happy Valley, which they reached at 4.30 p.m. It was packed with an enormous number of horses and vehicles, all standing out in the open.

Happy Valley[424] was situated just to the north-west of Bray, in the direction of Méaulte, and was a reserve area for battalions of the Fourth Army, who were out of the line. The military historian, Basil Liddell Hart, who was briefly based there, after action at Fricourt, in early July 1916, described the valley as a sheltered hollow behind the original British front line. By mid-July,

---

423 William La Touche Congreve won the V.C. for his bravery during the period July 6th-20th 1916. At the time of his death he had already been awarded the D.S.O. and the M.C. for earlier actions. He was the first officer to receive the V.C., D.S.O., and M.C. Six weeks before his death, aged 25 years, he had married the daughter of Cyril Maude, the actor-manager, and his wife, the celebrated actress Winifred Emery. William Congreve's father, Lieutenant-General Sir Walter Congreve, had himself won the V.C. for his bravery in the South African war, in 1899.

424 There were other Happy Valleys, including one near Mametz Wood which was also appropriately known as Death Valley.

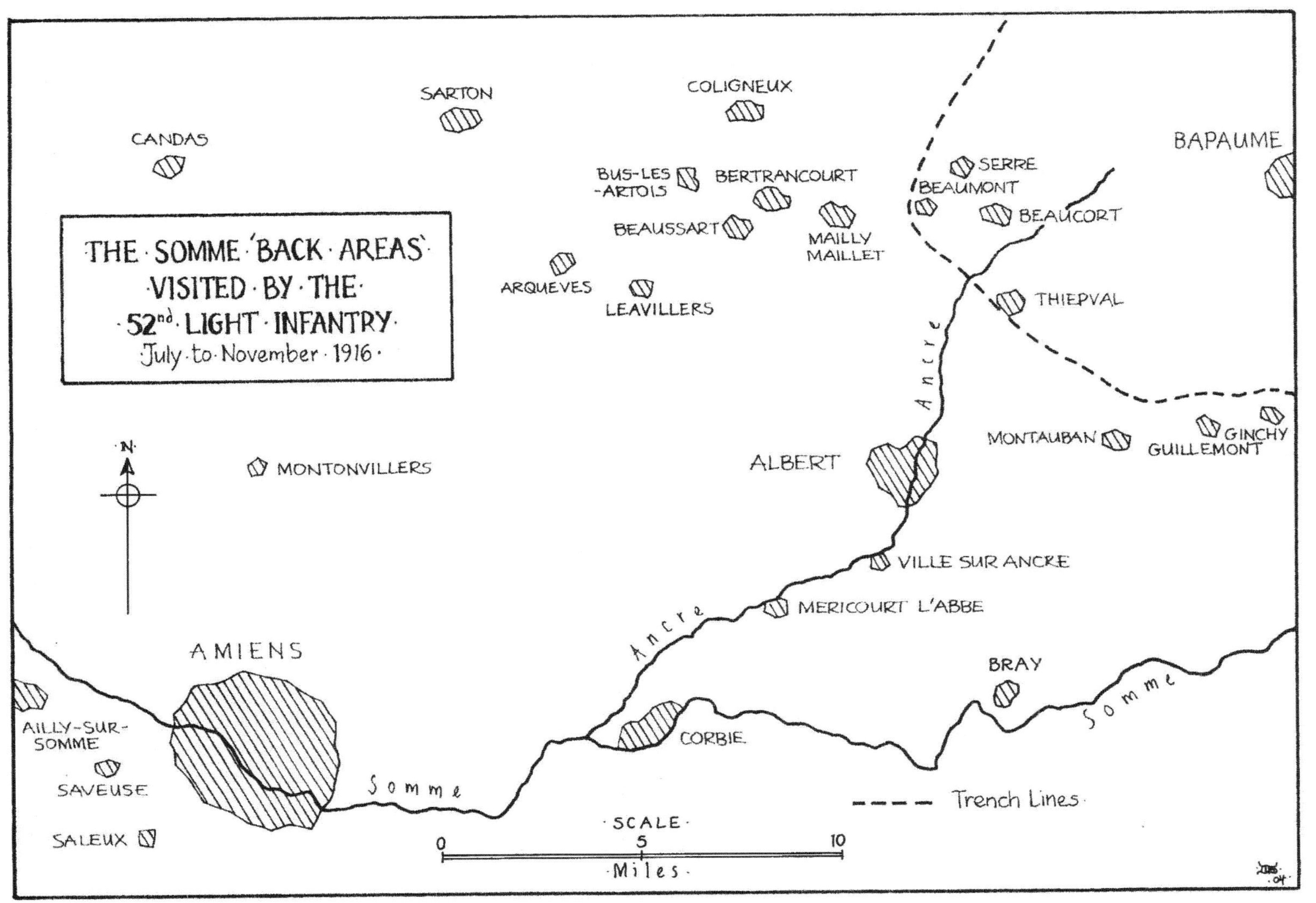
THE · SOMME · 'BACK · AREAS'
VISITED · BY · THE ·
· 52nd · LIGHT · INFANTRY ·
July · to · November · 1916 ·
SARTON
COLIGNEUX
CANDAS
BAPAUME
BUS-LES -ARTOIS
BERTRANCOURT
SERRE
BEAUMONT
BEAUCORT
BEAUSSART
MAILLY MAILLET
ARQUEVES
LEAVILLERS
THIEPVAL
Ancre
MONTAUBAN
GINCHY
GUILLEMONT
N
MONTONVILLERS
ALBERT
VILLE SUR ANCRE
MERICOURT L'ABBE
Ancre
AMIENS
BRAY
Somme
AILLY-SUR-SOMME
CORBIE
SAVEUSE
Somme
Trench Lines
SALEUX
· SCALE ·
0
5
10
· Miles ·

there were ranks of artillery, which blasted away continuously from the north-eastern exit of the valley, towards Montauban, Delville Wood and Longueval. Happy Valley was described at the time as a monstrous fairground with everyone going to the fair. The trees of the valley were dead, as horses had torn off their bark. The valley had become something of a desert with its grassless brown earth, compressed by thousands of military feet and horses' hooves. The sides of the valley were a mass of tents where doctors and others were stationed. No wells were present in Happy Valley and water had to be brought up from Bray by cart. A sadly depleted body of South Africans, back from their exertions and the slaughter of Delville Wood, were bivouacked next to the 2nd Highland Light Infantry, of the 52nd's own 5th Brigade.

On July 24th, Richard Crosse and Brigadier-General George Bullen-Smith spent the whole day, starting at 4 a.m., reconnoitring the front line, while the Regiment remained in Happy Valley. The next day, Crosse took his A and D company commanders on a reconnaissance to the reserve and support trenches. The second-in-command, Major Reggie Owen, walked up as far as Carnoy during the morning. Carnoy was just within the allied lines on July 1st, and lies to the south-west of Montauban and north-west of Maricourt. It was near here, on July 1st 1916, that the 22-year-old Captain Wilfred Nevill, of the 8th East Surrey, had provided footballs for his platoons to kick, as they attacked over no man's land.

At 8 p.m. on the 25th, the 52nd left their bivouacs in Happy Valley and moved to the south of the village of Montauban, as the battalion in the 5th Brigade's reserve. The 5th Brigade had relieved a brigade of the 3rd Division[425]. Reggie Owen got in about midnight, and with the rest of the Headquarters' officers had to share a dug-out with the officers of B Company. At 3 a.m. the following morning, Richard Crosse and Reggie Owen started a tour of their battalion's trenches, getting back at 5 a.m. Owen described the British shelling that day as terrific. There was little enemy shelling in reply. On the morning of the 27th, Owen was up early again, at 4 a.m., to visit C Company, under Captain Jack Hardcastle, and D Company, under Captain Ralph Kite. The enemy had been firing heavy shells all night, and the 52nd's men had had a bad time of it. This led to Lieutenant John Murray suffering from concussion and Second-Lieutenant Edward Vigars being gassed. It was on this day, that their fellow Brigade in the 2nd Division, the 99th, started the clearance of Delville Wood[426].

---

[425] The *Battalion War Diary* stated '8th or 9th I forget which but not Br Genl. Potter's Brigade'. Wyrall in *The History of the Second Division* stated that it was the 8th Brigade. Presumably 'Potter's Brigade' meant Porter's Brigade, the 76th. However, Brigadier-General C.L. Porter did not take command of the brigade until the following October 1st.

[426] Lieutenant-Colonel H.A. Vernon, Commanding Officer of the 23rd Royal Fusiliers, reported the finding of a South African soldier who had been wounded on the 18th, some nine days before. The

The daytime was relatively quiet for the 52nd, apart from some shelling in the vicinity of their Regimental Headquarters. Fortunately, Captain Hubert Rawson, the Sapping Officer, had improved its defences as well as making it more comfortable. Very late that night, the 52nd received orders that on the morrow they were to relieve the 2nd H.L.I. in the front line trenches about Waterlot Farm.

In the early morning of July 28th, Richard Crosse, Captain Ernest Whitfeld, the Adjutant, Lieutenant Percy Bobby, the Grenade Officer, and Lieutenant Cyril Horley, the Lewis gun officer, went round the trenches at Waterlot Farm. Later in the day Bobby received an accidental gunshot wound of his left leg and, Second-Lieutenant W.I.B. Ware a gunshot wound of his loins. At 7 p.m. that same evening, the 52nd moved up to relieve the 2nd H.L.I. in the front line trenches around Waterlot Farm. Their route took them via Bernafay Wood, Trones Wood, up Longueval Alley, to the south-western edge of Delville Wood, and then past Waterlot Farm. Longueval Alley was a trench extending from the north of Bernafay Wood, around the Quarry, and on to the north of Trones Wood. It was to the south of the straggling village of Longueval [see map page 326]. Major Reggie Owen described their route to the front as 'a horrible walk', with the ground strewn with the dead of the recent fighting, in grotesque positions and much decomposed. The constant fire of the German artillery, particularly on Longueval Alley, had not allowed the dead to be collected, let alone buried. On arrival there was a scare, which stopped the 52nd's companies getting into position, and the unfortunate 2nd H.L.I. did not get away until after midnight. The relief had started at 5 p.m. in the afternoon. In the darkness of the summer night it must have been all rather unnerving. Bernafay and Trones Woods formed an obstacle on the way to the front line. The artillery barrages had brought about a chaotic tangle of trees and branches and the former German communication trenches and the light railway tracks were the easiest lines of passage. In order to keep direction, a compass was a necessity. At some point, on the 28th, Richard Crosse and the other commanding officers were informed verbally of plans for an offensive on July 30th.

Fortunately for the 52nd, July 29th was a quiet day from the point of view of enemy activity, although the weather was very hot. Richard Crosse and Reggie Owen were busy all day promulgating orders for the morrow's attack. The

---

unfortunate man had been living in a shell hole and had survived on water and iron rations taken from the numerous dead. The South African soldier reported seeing some of his comrades compelled to surrender and then being shot by the Germans. A German officer found him and proceeded to torment him by showing him his water bottle and then refusing him a drink. Vernon not unreasonably wrote; 'these facts were not known to me at the time or my Battalion would not have taken 2 German Officer prisoners!!'. It is not difficult to understand the meaning of his words.

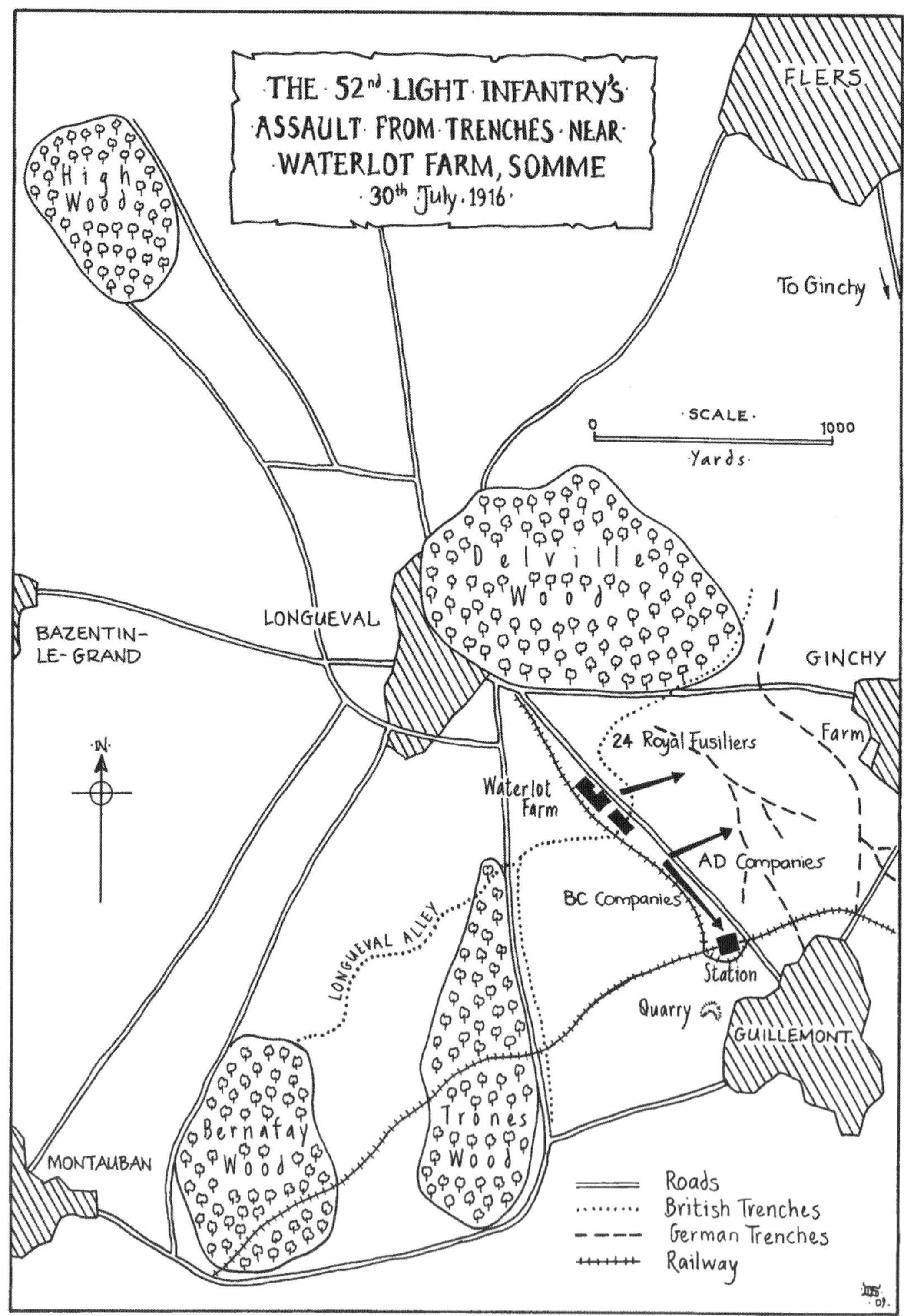
THE 52nd LIGHT INFANTRY'S
ASSAULT FROM TRENCHES NEAR
WATERLOT FARM, SOMME
30th July 1916
FLERS
High Wood
To Ginchy
SCALE
0
1000
Yards
Delville Wood
LONGUEVAL
BAZENTIN-LE-GRAND
GINCHY
Farm
24 Royal Fusiliers
N
Waterlot Farm
AD Companies
BC Companies
LONGUEVAL ALLEY
Station
Quarry
GUILLEMONT
Bernafay Wood
Trones Wood
MONTAUBAN
Roads
British Trenches
German Trenches
Railway

Regimental Headquarters of the 52nd were moved to the 2nd Division's Headquarters.

Three days earlier, on July 26th, General Henry Rawlinson visited General Emile Fayolle, commanding the French Sixth Army, on the Somme, to discuss their next move. Later that day they were joined by Sir Douglas Haig and by General Ferdinand Foch. Foch intended to attack south of the Somme from Lihons to Barleux, after a three-day barrage, once the weather had improved sufficiently. North of the Somme, he was prepared to attack immediately, as soon as the weather was sufficiently clear to allow reasonable observation during the attack itself. Haig wanted the village of Guillemont taken expeditiously to enable his forces to advance further. Out of the deliberations of Rawlinson and Foch came the decision to attack along the whole front from the Somme, to Maurepas, Falfemont Farm, and Guillemont. It was hoped that the British would be in Guillemont before the French reached their objectives, which were more distant. Rawlinson also promised the French that his Fourth Army would make several subsidiary offensive operations along their front, both to confuse the enemy and to tie down their forces.

On July 28th, Henry Rawlinson met his corps commanders, and it was agreed that III and XV Corps would assist XIII [2nd, 3rd, 9th, 18th, 24th Divisions] in its operations. In particular, XV Corps would attempt to clear the orchards to the north-west of Longueval, and use its artillery resources to defend Delville Wood, and to bombard the villages of Flers, Lesboeufs, and Morval. At 11 a.m., on the 29th, Rawlinson's Fourth Army instructions were issued to the men under his command, giving 4.45 a.m. on July 30th as zero hour. However, a delayed zero hour of 6.10 a.m. was allowed for the units of the III and XV Corps, who required as much time as possible to make their arrangements.

In XIII Corps, the 30th Division, a New Army Division, would use its 89th and 90th Brigades to attack on the left of the French Sixth Army[427]. The objectives of the 89th Brigade, on the immediate left of the French, would be Falfemont Farm and the German second position north-west of it, as far as the southern edge of Guillemont. The 90th Brigade would endeavour to capture the strongly held village of Guillemont itself. The 5th Brigade of the 2nd Division, including the 52nd, would support and protect the left flank of the 90th Brigade, by capturing Guillemont Railway Station and the enemy's trenches to the north-west and north-east of it. The 89th Brigade would advance from trenches to the south

[427] The 17th Earl of Derby was mainly responsible for raising the units which formed the 30th [originally the 37th] Division. He gave permission for the 30th Division to adopt the Stanley crest as its Divisional sign. Indeed, Brigadier-General Hon. Ferdinand Stanley commanded the 89th Brigade in this action. He was a younger brother of the Earl.

of Trones Wood, and on their right, Maltz Horn Farm, with its trenches running to the north of it, would have to be taken at the outset of the attack. The 90th Brigade was to advance astride the Trones Wood to Guillemont track. Unfortunately the 89th, and to a lesser extent the 90th Brigade, were heavily bombarded with both gas and high explosive shells during the night of July 29th, when they were forming up. The 5th Brigade would use the 24th Royal Fusiliers, on the left, advancing from front line trenches stretching from the southern edge of Delville Wood to Waterlot Farm. Their objective was a German trench 600 yards east of Waterlot Farm. The 52nd would be on the right, in trenches facing east and south-east, around Waterlot Farm[428], for their attack on Guillemont Station and the trenches towards Ginchy.

Waterlot Farm and the trenches in its environs, from which the 52nd would launch their attack on July 30th, was a misnomer as it was a ruined sugar refinery, originally with a tall chimney, and not a farm. As Richard Crosse pointed out, in the early maps, the name Waterlot Farm was placed between the ruined sugar refinery, which came to be known as Waterlot Farm, and the real farm further to the east, Ginchy Farm. Hence the confusion came about. Waterlot Farm had been a strong point in the German second position between Longueval and Guillemont. It had finally been captured and consolidated on July 17th, and was used as a British base. Pigeons were kept there for communication with Bernafay Wood and Corbie. Lack of dug-outs and copious mud made it an uncomfortable place to be based in, and also very dangerous. However, the cellars at Waterlot Farm could accommodate 40-60 men.

As with most First World War offensives, the key to a successful outcome was the preliminary artillery barrage to neutralize the enemy's defences by cutting the barbed wire and incapacitating their machine-guns. Indeed, for the 2nd and 30th Divisions' operations on July 30th, there was a barrage, starting at 9 p.m. on the 29th and provided by both the heavy and field artillery. The 2nd Division's artillery consisted of the XXXIV, XXXVI, and the XLI Brigades, Royal Field Artillery. In addition, French 75 mm. guns fired gas shells into the village of Guillemont. After zero hour, at 4.45 a.m., a rolling barrage, with lifts at set times, was organized to isolate parts of the German line and to stop reserves being brought up. The artillery commanders were well aware of the important part they must play, if there was to be a successful outcome, on July 30th.

---

[428] Richard Crosse recorded that the 52nd were 'in the trenches facing south-east and east around the so-called Waterlot Farm and astride the Longueval to Ginchy road upon which the southern edge of Delville Wood lay'. On the 30th, it seems likely that the 24th Royal Fusiliers were in these latter trenches and the 52nd solely around Waterlot Farm. On Crosse's trench map, for July 30th, now attached to the *5th Brigade War Diary,* in the National Archives, the position of the 52nd is shown well to the south-east of Waterlot Farm.

Brigadier-General L.W.P. East, commanding the XIII Corps' Heavy Artillery, wrote at the end of the orders he issued to his subordinates: 'all guns must be as active as possible – a great deal is being asked of us and a very great deal depends on our efforts to-day and to-night and I am sure the officers will play up to their utmost'.

The precise objectives of the 5th Brigade were laid down in the 2nd Division's orders of July 29th.

> The objective of the 5th Inf. Brigade is the capture of the enemy's defences between WATERLOT FARM and GUILLEMONT (exclusive) including the trench which runs parallel to the LONGUEVAL - GUILLEMONT road through T.19.a., S.24.b., and S.18.d.[429]
>
> The establishment of touch with the 30th Division on its right and the joining up of the German trench in S.18.d with SOUTH STREET (boundary between S.18. b. and d.).
>
> The boundary between the 5th Inf. Bde. and the 30th Division for the infantry attack will be the road through the WATERLOT FARM chimney to GUILLEMONT as far as level crossing at S.24.d.4.9. (road inclusive to 5th Inf. Bde.) and thence line just South of trench junction at B.M. 138.6. to cross-roads at T.19.c.2.8. (exclusive to 2nd Division) thence the road (exclusive to 2nd Division) to railway T.19.a.8.3.
>
> After capture and consolidation of the objectives given, the railway will become the boundary (the Station inclusive to the 5th Inf. Bde.): time when this boundary will come into force will be notified later.

The 2nd Division's orders of July 29th continued.

> The infantry of the 30th Division will assault from 1st objective just after 0 plus 8 at which hour the barrage will move to the second line. G.O.C. 5th Inf. Bde.will arrange for his attack so that the infantry arrive at their objectives at -
>
> a) GUILLEMONT STATION.
>
> b) Trench South of it.

429 According to Richard Crosse the 5th Brigade's orders stated that the 52nd's objectives included the German trench from T.19.a.7 ½ - T.19.c.4.9 ½. This did not appear in the original 2nd Division orders. [See trench map: 57cSW3 Longueval. Edition 2D. Trenches to 24/7/16].

c) The portion of the German trench situated in S.18.d. at the same time as the infantry of the 30th Division reach their first objective. He will arrange for his attack on the remainder of the trench T 19.a to S.24.b. to be delivered so that his infantry reach it immediately after the barrages lift at 0 plus 25.

The G.O.C., 5th Inf. Bde. will arrange for machine-guns in the S.E. corner of DELVILLE WOOD to sweep the ground between GINCHY VILLAGE and the German trenches during and subsequent to the attack, arranging with the G.O.C. 6th Inf. Bde. if he wishes to place any guns in the 6th Inf. Bde. line.

After the infantry have reached their final objective the 5th Inf. Bde. will establish strong points at the Railway Station and about T 19.a.4.2. and also about S 18.d. central. [see trench map 57cSW3 Longueval. Edition 2D. Trenches to 24/7/16].

Various other matters had to be arranged. Communications during the assault were to be by telephone, visual, runners, and pigeons. Telephone wires were difficult to run out under active service conditions and were frequently cut by shell-fire. Visual signalling communication was to be via sites just to the north of Waterlot Farm, and in the vicinity of Bernafay Wood[430]. Green flares were only to be used to indicate that objectives had been reached at 0 plus 8 minutes and 0 plus 25 minutes. Runners were often killed whilst carrying messages. Pigeons were to form an essential method of communication. Four birds were kept at Waterlot Farm and a further four at Bernafay. They flew to Corbie with their attached messages and the contents were then wired back to the 5th Brigade Headquarters. The whole process took about 30-45 minutes to accomplish. The pigeons and their handlers were to lead to a rare criticism, by the 5th Brigade, of the Commanding Officer of the 52nd, Lieutenant-Colonel Richard Crosse. 'It has been noticed that both pigeons and pigeon-flyers have been left, without a scrap of cover, sitting outside Battalion H.Q. Both should be given a corner of a dug-out'[431]. It was out of character for the eagle-eyed Crosse not to have noticed their plight, but he had a great deal on his mind, as this was the first significant action in which he had commanded the 52nd. However, the handlers themselves must take some responsibility of their own by not seeking cover.

[430] Visual signalling was usually conducted with the heliograph using the sun and mirrors. Flags were used, but rarely so.

[431] By 1918, 20,000 pigeons had been made available for communication purposes on the Western Front. No less than 380 experts had trained 90,000 men to look after them. 'Pigeoneers' went over the top with pigeons in assault baskets. One corps used 532 birds in a single day and received 92 messages in return.

Two Stokes mortars were placed at the disposal of the 52nd for the duration of the assault. Such a mortar consisted of a smooth-bore steel barrel with a screw mechanism to allow adjustment of angles of elevation. A cylindrical bomb was fired with a range of about 1,000 yards. The Stokes mortars would play a vital part in the attack by neutralizing the enemy's bombing posts, which were on the line of advance. Each soldier was to have a full water-bottle, a day's rations, plus iron rations. They were ordered to have two bandoliers and three grenades per man. Picks and shovels were also taken.

Brigadier-General George Bullen-Smith sent a note to Richard Crosse with the 5th Brigade's orders for the 52nd.

> Plan of action as discussed by us yesterday has been approved by the Divisional Commander. You will notice in the Orders sent herewith that the actual forming-up places for your battalion are left to your discretion, as you must be a better judge than I can be of what is most suitable.
>
> The Divisional Commander desired me to impress on you the importance of your right flank. It is possible that the 30th Division may meet very stubborn resistance, and, naturally your advance to the second objective cannot proceed with the right flank in the air.
>
> By holding the station you can very materially assist the main operation.
>
> In case I am not able to come and see you, I wish you and your fine battalion the best of luck.

Richard Crosse's post-war accounts of the action, on July 30th, do not record exactly which part of the trenches, at Waterlot Farm, that he chose as the start point for the 52nd to advance from. However, the trench map that he used that day is to be found in the National Archives[432], and clearly shows that the trenches that they attacked from were well to the south-east of Waterlot Farm. In the event, part of the 90th Brigade of the 30th Division did manage to get into Guillemont, and it was mainly the failure of the 52nd to secure their flank, that led to the withdrawal.

A little before 4.45 a.m. on July 30th, the 52nd left their trenches to the south-east of Waterlot Farm to take part in the attack on Guillemont Station and the trenches south of it. Also, as a second objective, they were to assault part of the trench which ran parallel to the Longueval to Guillemont Road, in the direction of Ginchy, from T.19.c.4.9½. to S.24.b.8.8. To their left were units of

---

[432] In the *5th Brigade's War Diary.* WO 95 1344.

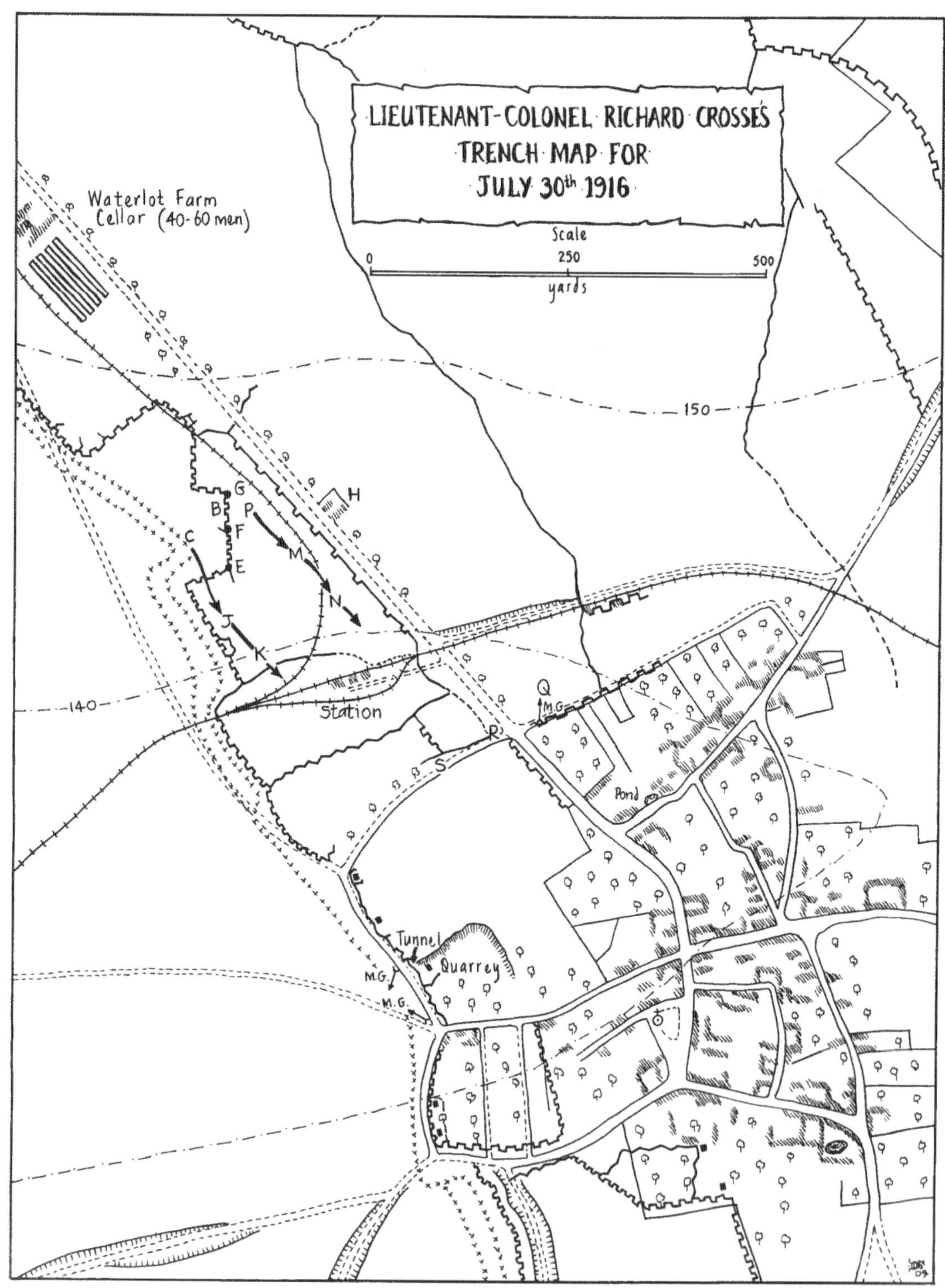
LIEUTENANT-COLONEL RICHARD CROSSE'S
TRENCH MAP FOR
JULY 30th 1916
Scale
0
250
500
yards
Waterlot Farm
Cellar (40-60 men)
150
140
G
H
B
P
F
C
M
E
N
J
K
Station
Q
M.G.
R
S
Pond
Tunnel
Quarrey
M.G.
M.G.

the 24th Royal Fusiliers, who were attacking the same trench, but a little further to the north, from S.24.b.8.8. to S.18.d.5.5. The 52nd was scheduled to reach Guillemont Station behind the barrage at zero plus 8 minutes, and the trench from T.19.c.4.9½. to S.24.b.8.8., at zero plus 25 minutes. Their comrades of the 24th Royal Fusiliers were expected to reach their section of the trench, from S.24.b.8.8. to S.18.d.5.5 at zero plus 8 minutes, again behind the barrage.

Richard Crosse had ordered B, C Companies to undertake the attack on Guillemont Station, plus the trench to the south of it and A, D Companies to attack the German trench system towards Ginchy. Both assaults were at one and a half companies' strength. Just before 4.45 a.m., on a misty morning, the dawn had already broken, when the men of the 52nd, who were involved in the attack, lay in front of their trenches to the south-east of Waterlot Farm, as the artillery barrage roared overhead, ready to move off at zero hour. Although, the B and C Company Commanders, Captains Laurence Goodwyn and Jack Hardcastle respectively, attacked with their men, the D Company Commander, Captain Ralph Kite, was ordered to stay behind. It was an order that he found particularly difficult to obey as he knew that he was sending many men of his D Company to a certain death. It was standard practice, by this stage of the war, to keep some of the officers and experienced N.C.O.s out of the attack, with its inevitable casualties, so that there were some able instructors for the replacements.

At precisely 4.45 a.m., the men of the 5th, 89th and 90th Brigades left their start points at the same time, the 2nd Division having synchronised all their watches on July 28th. The first wave of the 52nd's A and D Companies' attack, at three platoons' strength, moved off in a north-easterly direction towards Ginchy, and their enemy trench line objective. Twenty five minutes had been allotted for them to reach the enemy's line. To their left, men of the 24th Royal Fusiliers progressed in a more easterly direction towards their section of the same German trench. As they had a shorter distance to cover, only eight minutes had been allowed for them to reach their objective. Despite protective machine-gun fire from Delville Wood, both the A, D Companies and the 24th R.F. attack faltered under the withering enemy fire. Both Regiments reached the uncut German wire, but got no further. The British bombardment, whose efficacy was difficult to judge on that misty morning, failed, leaving the unfortunate men of the 52nd and the R.F.s, at the mercy of enemy machine-gun fire from their right. Crosse, very wisely, did not send the second wave of three platoons, from A and D Companies, into action as only a few men and no officers had returned from the first wave. Their right flank as Crosse put it 'would have been in the air'.

The 24th Royal Fusiliers had fared no better. Their Regimental History, *The Royal Fusiliers in the Great War,* by H.C. O'Neill, gave an account of their fortunes that day.

> On July 30th C Company of the 24th Battalion was engaged. On the previous evening the battalion had taken over the front line from the southern edge of Delville Wood to Waterlot Farm, and on the 30th they advanced against a German trench some 600 yards away from Waterlot Farm. A thick mist lay over the ground as the men went forward, and it was very difficult to keep direction. When this initial and serious handicap had been overcome, it was found that the German wire was uncut. "The king of the war," as the French called barbed wire, exercised its sovereignty once again. Captain C.S. Meares was killed on the wire, leading his men, and the company fought valiantly, but to no purpose. C Company attacked with three officers and 114 other ranks. One wounded officer and 11 other ranks remained at the end of the day. Such was the price paid for co-operation in the attack on Guillemont.

On July 31st, Lieutenant-Colonel H.E. Walsh, Commanding Officer of the 24th Royal Fusiliers, described his Regiment's attack, the previous day, for the 5th Brigade. More details of the assault appear in his report.

> At 4.30 a.m. on the 30th July the Company of the 24th R.F. occupying the ANGLE TRENCH moved out and crawled out to top of ridge facing the German trench at 0.8. owing to the mist they could not [see] sun after they left our trenches. From the survivors I have gained the following information. The Coy lay down about 200 yards from the German trench. The Barrage did not lift till considerably after 0.8. When they advanced they were fired on by m guns and rifles. On the right Captain Meares and a few men reached the enemy's wire but never reached the trench. I am of the opinion that the Coy during the advance diverged too much to the right and did not strike the N end of the trench owing to the ground being all [unintelligible] holes and it was difficult to keep touch in the mist.
>
> The trench was strongly held with many sentries and M guns mounted on the parapet. It is stated that the N end of the German trench was not wired but further south it was, but not strong wire.

At the same time as the A and D Companies' attack on the German trench, to the east of the Longueval to Guillemont road [High Holborn], Captain Jack Hardcastle led the men of B and C Companies, at one and a half companies' strength, down towards Guillemont Station. The assault was interrupted at its inception by enemy bombing posts, situated between their positions south-east of Waterlot Farm and the Station. The Stokes mortars were supposed to have neutralized the German bombers, but had failed dismally. Instead of the assault sweeping over the bombing posts unopposed, the 52nd's men became briefly disorganized before pushing on in two columns. Machine-gun fire from enemy strong points just to the south of the station, and a machine-gun house to the east of High Holborn, decimated the attackers, particularly those in the rear. Jack Hardcastle and many of his men were cut down, although some were seen to reach the north face of the station, and none returned. One of Hardcastle's men named Gladwin went out and brought him in to the British lines. Another of his men who went out at the same time to assist was killed.

Both the 52nd's attacks on the enemy had failed in the first few minutes, although this was not clear at the time because of the misty morning which would clear later in the day. At 6 a.m., the Commanding Officer of the 52nd, Lieutenant-Colonel Richard Crosse, sent a message to the 5th Brigade. 'Attack on station at first held up by line of bombing posts is now getting forward, but I cannot tell whether it has reached objective. Heavy casualties'. Later, in the early afternoon, the 5th Brigade [Fruit] sent in a report to the 2nd Division [Heart].

> Situation as follows at 12.45 p.m. aaa Coy of Pear [24th R.F.] attacked and reached hostile trench in S 18d at 0.8 aaa It is believed that company are still holding on there aaa Grape [52nd] attacked station but were held up by bombing posts and MG fire at 0.8 aaa A proportion of one wave rushed trenches in vicinity of station and aeroplane reports mirrors flashing at T19a00 aaa. At 0.25 three platoons attacked second objective and no information regarding this attack has been obtainable aaa. Hostile arty. are maintaining an exceedingly heavy barrage on Longueval Alley and Bernafay Wood in vicinity of Western edge aaa No digging of trench connecting enemy's line with SE corner of Delville Wood has yet been possible hitherto. Fruit [5th Brigade] 12.50 p.m.

The information that the 24th R.F. were holding their objective, a section of an enemy trench, was incorrect. The attack had got no further than the enemy's wire and, naturally, the new trench to link up with the southern edge of

Delville Wood was never dug. It is interesting that mirrors were seen flashing at T.19.a.00., which is a point just to the east of Guillemont Station. Perhaps, they were survivors of the 52nd's attack on the station who were later overwhelmed by the enemy, or possibly the report was an error[433].

As is not unusual in battle there was considerable confusion as to the reality of the situation. On July 30th, Major-General William Walker V.C., commanding the 2nd Division, sent this rather irritated message to the 5th Brigade.

> I wish to call your attention to the fact that no message was received from the 2/Ox. and Bucks L. I. for 4 hours after ZERO and none has been received from the 24th Royal Fusiliers as far as I am aware, all day.
>
> Even now I am uncertain whether the trench at S.18.d. [section of trench attacked by 24th R.F.] is held by us or not.
>
> In view of the fact that I have been receiving constant reports all day by runner from the Artillery O. P. [Observation Post] near WATERLOT FARM, I consider that more information and reports should have been forthcoming, and would like you to report what efforts were made to get them through.

Richard Crosse had sent in an initial report to 5th Brigade at 6 a.m., and this later one, which is quoted below in full, may have been triggered by the divisional commander's complaint. On August 10th, Crosse attached this report to the *Battalion War Diary.*

> To Fruit [5th Brigade]. 30/7/16.
>
> We have made as great an effort as is possible to attack Station but have not got there aaa. The Stokes Mortars failed to deail [sic] with the bombing posts and evidently the bombardment had no effect on hostile machine guns from straight and almost straight down the main road aaa I can get no information of Division on our right and the present position is as follows: [original sketch by Richard Crosse].

[433] Richard Crosse thought that this might be German deception.

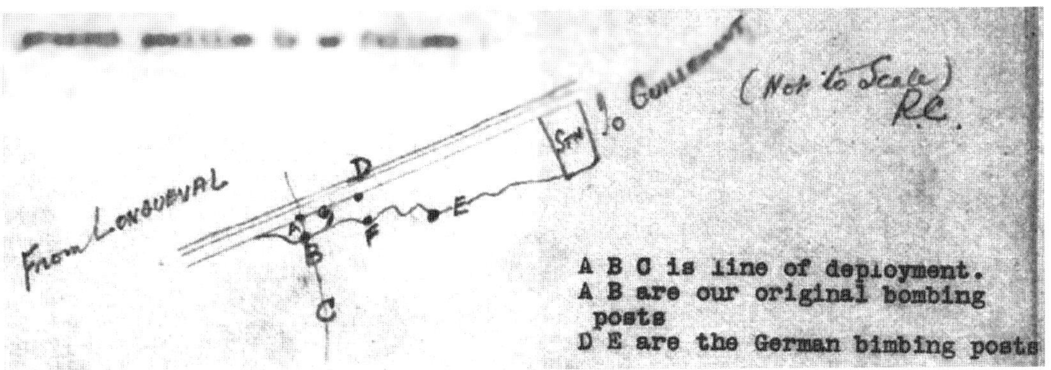

A B C is line of deployment.
A B are our original bombing posts
D E are the German bimbing [sic] posts
which our Stokes Mortars were to destroy and did not aaa

Our advance got to within bombing distance of line D E after a loss from a M.G. fire which I cannot at present estimate aaa Our men were bombed from these places and the remainder of them were formed up in Old Trench B F aaa I propose to consolidate this and make another bombing post out to G aaa I can get no information back but I know that our leading party got well up to the North face of the Station, but I think they must have been shot aaa If the 30th Division or other Troops succeed in taking the Station or getting near it hostile bombing posts D and E will have to go and I can meet them by prolonging trench B F E towards the Station aaa

As regards the other operation, or "second objective" attack on Right of PEAR [24th R.F.], of a first wave of 3 platoons only a few men and no Officers have come back aaa It appears they were enfiladed by M.G. fire from the right aaa In accordance with the Brigadier-General's letter I did not send forward the second waive [sic] because my right would have been in the air aaa Casualties Officers Killed Captain J.B. Hardcastle, 2nd Lieut. W.L. CHOWN [sic], and wounded Captain L.J. Goodwin [sic], Lieut F.W. Chippindale, 2nd Lieut R.G. Pluckrose, 2nd Lieut M.G. Fielding, 2nd Lieut T.G.C. Caulfield-Stoker, and Missing Lieut N.S. Harrison, 2nd Lieut B.C. Warde, 2nd Lieut W.R. Goffe, 2nd Lieut R.S. Maul also wounded 2nd Lieut J.E.V. Rathbone 3rd Dorset Regt attached aaa Others "heavy" but I cannot tell at present.

Lieutenant-Colonel Richard Crosse followed up this report to the 5th Brigade, with a further one the following day July 31st, at 4.15 p.m. [see map on page 332][434].

> Ref map 1/5,000 Ginchy and Guillemont also my sketch and report of yesterday. (which please read in conjunction).
>
> I have made certain marks on the map as desired by the Brigade and would like to add a few remarks because I think I am in possession of several useful pieces of information about the locality which will be of use in further offensive operations, also to supplement my yesterdays [sic] reports as regards my Regiment's unsuccessful attack.
>
> 1. I taken [sic] (what I have marked) H to be a ruined cottage or building which is easily identifiable by three long pieces of timber that stick up from it. In my opinion a German machine gun fires from this.
>
> My reasons for this are.
>
> (1) A great deal of M.G. fire came from this very direction.
>
> (2) The nature of the wounds inflicted by fire from 'this very direction' is absolute proof that the bullets were fired at very short range.
>
> (3) I think I know German habits pretty well and I am sure that they would not fail to make use of such a place, as they wd realise its value for denying to us the ground SE of Waterlot Fm.
>
> 2. I am sure the vicinity of the Station and NOT the Station itself is an exceedingly strong position which wd suffer not at all from a bombardment far more violent than the one it received yesterday. The ground from my line of deployment ABC SW towards the station is generally down hill undulating, and exceedingly broken and affords ample scope for the methods of use [of] machine guns in defence so successfully employed by the enemy:- chiefly:-
>
> (1) concealed emplacement from gun firing at ground level.
>
> (2) guns in the open pushed forward in shell holes.
>
> It is also very favourable for sniping.
>
> 3. Yesterdays attack. [see Crosse's trench map on page 332]. Everything was based on the supposition that hostile bombers posts

[434] It is surprising that Richard Crosse made no mention of this fascinating report in any of his accounts of July 30th 1916. It is mentioned in neither the *Battalion War Diary* for 1916 nor the *Regimental Chronicles* for 1916/17. The report and Crosse's annotated trench map can be seen in the *5th Brigade's War Diary,* WO 95 1344.

D and E would have been silenced by the Stokes Mortars and that the infantry attack would sweep clean over them. This was not the case. Points D and E disorganized the attack as a line it broke through in 2 columns

Right C - J - K ⟶

Left P - M - N ⟶

and became lost to me.

Machine gun fire opened from H and from directions Q. R. S. and the rear wave such as did not break through got into trench B F towards E. Our post B is thus carried forward and its prolongation BF was handed over by me in a state of being consolidated.

If mirrors were flashed at aeroplane from close to the station it may have been either (1) our furthest forward line from inside shell holes or under other cover. (2) The enemy's trick to deceive our aeroplanes. I will continue this but have reached the time limit given me. I would be glad of the loan of the attached map again or a tracing of area I have added to.

The operations of the 5th Brigade on July 30th, can only be described as a complete failure, with its units eventually withdrawing to their assembly positions under heavy shellfire. In retrospect, their German opponents felt that they had the situation under control by 7.30 a.m. After the attack, the rest of the day was quiet for the 52nd, although they had a disturbed night. Meanwhile the two brigades of the 30th Division, the 89th and 90th, and units of the French Sixth Army on their right, had attacked at 4.45 a.m., the same zero hour as the 5th Brigade [see map on page 340]. At the outset, despite thick fog, Maltz Horn Farm fell to the 89th Brigade, aided by the French from the south. Their commander, Brigadier-General F.C. Stanley recorded that: 'of course there was a lot of "Kamerad" business, but that is not thought much of now and only one was taken prisoner'. The battalions of the 89th Brigade moved on to the line of the Hardecourt to Guillemont road, and a few men of the 19th King's penetrated as far as an orchard on the south-eastern outskirts of Guillemont.

The 90th Brigade, on the left of the 89th, attacked astride the axis of the Trones Wood to Guillemont track, and entered the village from the south-west, without many casualties. The 2nd Royal Scots, of the 90th Brigade, followed the lifts of the barrage through Guillemont to its north-eastern edge, where consolidation was begun, keeping in touch with a party of the 18th Manchester [90th Brigade] on the left. The 18th Manchester had advanced with its left on the Trones Wood - Guillemont railway, and managed to reach the German front line

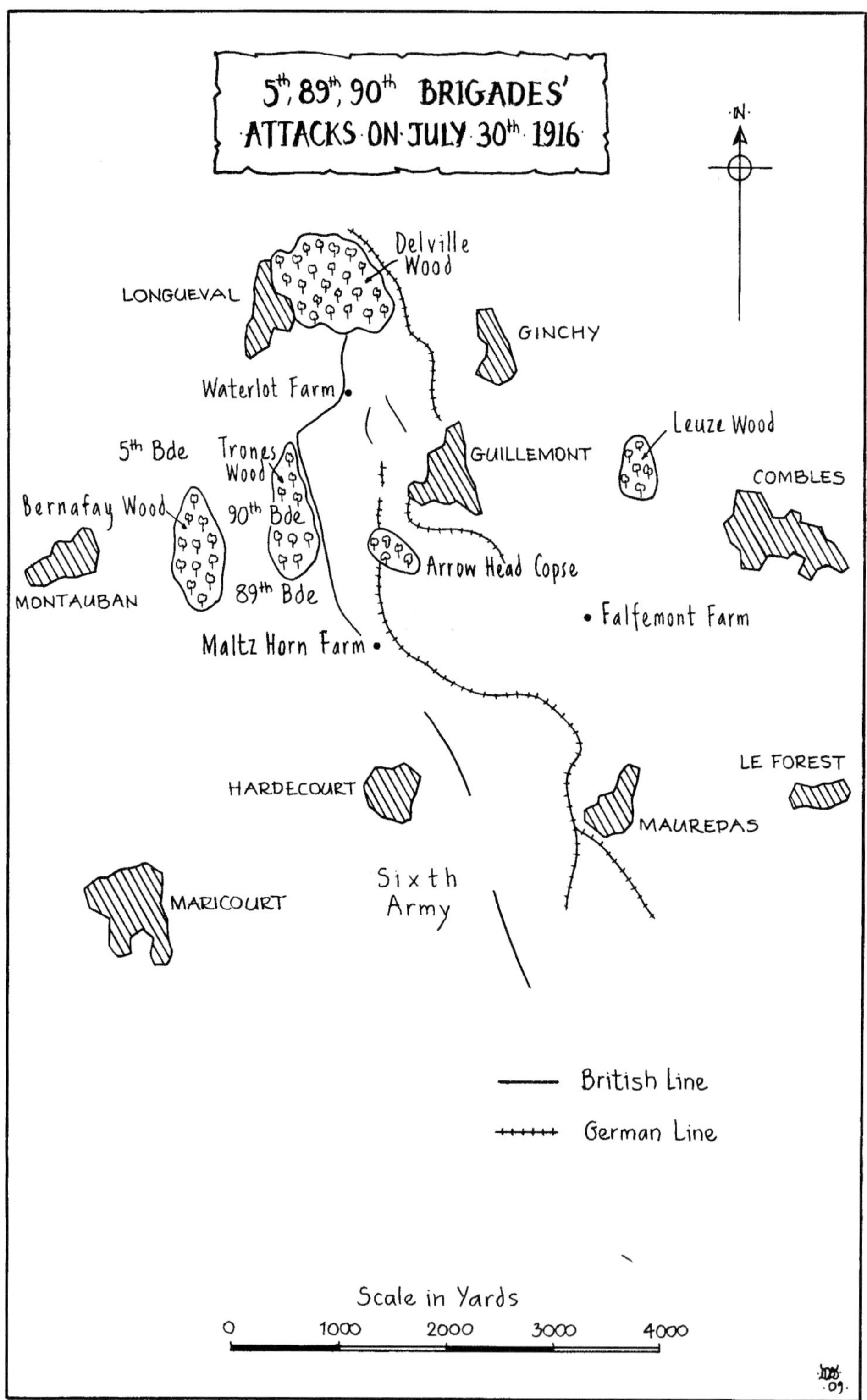
5th, 89th, 90th BRIGADES'
ATTACKS ON JULY 30th 1916
N
Delville Wood
LONGUEVAL
GINCHY
Waterlot Farm
Leuze Wood
5th Bde
Trones Wood
GUILLEMONT
COMBLES
Bernafay Wood
90th Bde
Arrow Head Copse
MONTAUBAN
89th Bde
Falfemont Farm
Maltz Horn Farm
LE FOREST
HARDECOURT
MAUREPAS
Sixth Army
MARICOURT
British Line
German Line
Scale in Yards
0
1000
2000
3000
4000

trench, taking many prisoners in the process. Most of the battalion was unable to advance further under cross-fire from the Quarry and Guillemont Station. A further attack, by the 16th and 17th Manchester [both 90th Brigade], came to nothing in front of the uncut wire to the south of Guillemont Station. Here they were forced to retire by machine-gun fire in enfilade.

As with the 5th Brigade's attack, information at brigade and divisional level was difficult to come by as the telephone wires were cut by artillery fire. Early in the afternoon, the left of the 19th King's [89th Brigade], believing itself to be isolated in the orchard near Guillemont, withdrew. Further parties of the 19th King's, in the road beyond the German front line, followed them a little later. In spite of a heavy artillery barrage being laid on the cross-roads east of Guillemont, round Ginchy, and on Leuze Wood, the Germans counter-attacked. Three unfortunate companies of the 2nd Royal Scots [90th Brigade] were trapped in the village of Guillemont, where they were eventually overwhelmed by the enemy, selling their lives dearly in the process. The early morning mist had cleared, much improving the visibility, and it became a hot day with full sunshine. The two brigades of the 30th Division spent the remainder of the day restoring the line. The 89th Brigade consolidated the only ground captured, which was from Arrow Head Copse, along the sunken Hardecourt - Guillemont road, to Maltz Horn Farm.

The attack of the French Sixth Army, to the north of the Somme, on July 30th, was also a disappointment. Their objectives included Maurepas and the German defences along the Maurepas to Cléry road as far as the river. Although the French assault started well enough, the Germans regained much of the ground and Maurepas was never taken. The artillery was hampered by the mist, and the failure of the attack was thought to be due to the enemy's effective method of defence. The front trenches were lightly held with an abundance of machine-guns and snipers firing at close range. The bulk of the defending force was held further back, ready to counter-attack at a moment's notice. This they undertook with great effect on July 30th.

The principal opponent of the 30th Division and the 5th Brigade was the German 24th Reserve Division, whose sphere of operations, at this juncture, extended from about Maltz Horn Farm northward to Guillemont and the trenches to the west of Ginchy. The 24th Reserve Division was Saxon in origin, and had entered Belgium on August 19th 1914. In 1915, the Division was in the Champagne, where it was badly mauled by the French offensive in September. At the beginning of July 1916, in response to the Franco-British offensive, it had been transferred to the Somme and became responsible for the line between Longueval to Hardecourt. The 52nd's abortive attack on Guillemont Station, under the unfortunate Captain Jack Hardcastle, broke in at approximately the junction of the 107th Reserve Regiment, of the 24th Reserve Division, and the I./22nd Bavarian Reserve Regiment, which was attached to the same Division. The Germans believed that this combined force of Saxons and Bavarians had matters under control in the environs of Guillemont Station by 7.30 a.m. on July 30th. Guillemont village was cleared of the remnants of the British 30th Division by companies from the 104th and 107th Reserve Regiments, both from the 24th Reserve Division, and by Jäger units, including the 13th Reserve Jäger.

July 30th 1916 was indeed a bleak day in the history of the 52nd Light Infantry. Despite great fortitude, their twin attacks on Guillemont Station and towards Ginchy had achieved nothing, and their casualties had been heavy. The Regiment had lost fourteen officers and 205 men as casualties[435]. The casualties amounted to about a third of the men taking part in the attack. This might be considered light by the standards set on July 1st, but is still very heavy for an abortive assault. Major Reggie Owen, second-in-command of the 52nd, wrote in his diary, ‘this is just like the Givenchy show last year’. The officers killed were: Captain Jack Hardcastle; Lieutenant Noel Harrison[436]; Second-Lieutenants Richard Maul [initially reported missing], William Chown, William Goffe [initially reported missing], and Basil Warde [initially reported missing]. The wounded officers were: Captain Laurence Goodwyn [gunshot wound left arm][437]; Lieutenants F.W.C. ‘Chips’ Chippindale [gunshot wound to face with fractured maxilla], C.T. Chevallier [gunshot wound back], P.C. Webster [shell shock – first described as a medical condition in January 1915]; Second Lieutenants Morris Fielding [gunshot wound eye], R.G. Pluckrose [gunshot wound right shoulder],

---

[435] The *Battalion War Diary* gave the casualties for July 30th as twelve officers and 205 other ranks. The *Regimental Chronicles for 1916-1917* listed twelve officer casualties by name. However, Second-Lieutenant William Reginald Goffe had been omitted, although Richard Crosse, in his articles, in the *Regimental Journals,* of 1936 and 1956, stated that Goffe, on July 30th, was reported missing, in the former, and missing presumed killed, in the latter. The confusion is added to by Goffe’s obituary in the *Regimental Chronicles for 1919-1920,* which stated that he was reported wounded and missing on July 7th 1916, and subsequently reported to have been killed in action on that date. No casualties are recorded for July 7th in either the *Battalion War Diary* or the *Regimental Chronicles* for 1916-1917. In addition, William Goffe’s name appears with Jack Hardcastle’s and others, killed on July 30th, on the original grave marker, now in Broughton Poggs Church. The digital database *Soldiers Died In The Great War 1914-19* states that William Goffe was killed in action on July 30th. This last statement should conclude the matter. Further, Lieutenant C.T. Chevallier was also wounded on July 30th and was sent to No. 21 C.C.S, although his name was not included in the wounded list in the *Regimental Chronicles for 1916-1917.* This makes a total of fourteen officer casualties for the day.

[436] The grenade officer.

[437] Laurence Goodwyn was to be wounded again on May 3rd 1917, whilst serving with the 5th Battalion Oxfordshire and Buckinghamshire Light Infantry, at the Third Battle of the Scarpe, near Arras.

T.G.C. Caulfield-Stoker [gunshot wound right forearm], J.E.V. Rathbone [gunshot wound right shoulder].

A little more needs to be recorded about Captain Jack Balfour Hardcastle, the brave C Company commander, who died on July 30th, leading his men in an almost suicidal attack on Guillemont Station. The 23-year-old Hardcastle was a slim young man with widely-set eyes and a finely clipped moustache on his upper lip. He had tried to get into Sandhurst in 1912, but had failed the mathematics section of the examination. Hardcastle spent the next two years at Wye Agricultural College, with a view to running the family estate in Gloucestershire. When war broke out, he was again turned down for a commission as his chest measurement at 32½ inches was no less than nine inches below the minimum allowed! A few months later, Hardcastle was finally admitted for training at Sandhurst, and ironically was soon made the Under Officer. Both Archibald Eden and Richard Crosse rapidly recognized Jack Hardcastle's leadership qualities, as within six months of joining the Regiment, he had been given the command of a company. His greatest Regimental friend, Captain Ralph Kite in a letter to his own mother said; 'I lost a very dear friend Jack Hardcastle, who threw his life away through inexperience. It is very hard to forget our losses, but I know that he is waiting on the other side'[438]. Just what Kite meant by 'threw his life away through inexperience' is far from clear. Perhaps, this was the prevailing view of Crosse and the other officers in the Regiment, and may be related to the foolhardiness of continuing the attack when the enemy's bombers and machine-gunners were still active. It is surprising that Jack Hardcastle received no award for his gallantry that day. In *The Oxfordshire and Buckinghamshire Light Infantry* by Philip Booth, written in 1971, Hardcastle was one of two young officers who were singled out as being of great promise[439].

The other young officer singled out by Philip Booth as being of great promise was the D Company commander, Captain Ralph Kite. Although Kite briefly served with Philip Booth in the 52nd, Jack Hardcastle did not, as he was already dead by the time Booth joined the Regiment. It is likely that the view of both young men showing great promise before their deaths was that of their Commanding Officer, Lieutenant-Colonel Richard Crosse. Crosse and Booth were close friends, and no doubt the former influenced the latter, in the book's brief section on World War I. If Hardcastle was not rewarded for his gallantry on July 30th, Ralph Kite was, as he received the Military Cross. *The London Gazette*

[438] Letter written to Edith Kite on August 17th 1916.

[439] John Hardcastle, the father of Jack, was devastated by his son's death. At the family home, Broughton Hall, the servants laid out Jack's evening clothes in his room every night of the year until the old man finally died in 1946, some thirty years after his son.

of October 20th 1916, recorded his citation; 'for conspicuous gallantry during operations. He did fine work organizing the attack, and displayed great coolness and utter disregard for danger. When the bombers holding one of our saps became casualties, he went at once to the spot, organized the defence, and threw bombs himself'. Although Richard Crosse himself, in a letter to Kite's parents, in 1917, stated the award was for the young man's actions, at Waterlot Farm on July 30th/31st, in reality it was principally for his gallantry at Richebourg l'Avoué, on the night of May 15th/16th 1915[440].

The attack on Guillemont village by the 30th Division, on July 30th, was a complete failure. At the end of the day, little ground had been taken from the enemy and the village itself was still in German hands. Guillemont had been turned into a veritable fortress by the enemy. Trenches and strong points, bristling with machine-guns, dominated in every direction. In fact shellfire had so destroyed the village that it was difficult to tell where the fields ended and houses began. As Edmonds in the *Official History* recorded, there was no great surprise that the assault had failed, in much the same way as a previous one, on July 23rd. On this day, it was once more the unfortunate 30th Division who had attempted to take Guillemont, while the 3rd Division concentrated on Guillemont Station, Delville Wood and Longueval. After their experiences in this first attack, the local commanders felt that a further attempt, on Guillemont, from the west, was unlikely to succeed. As Edmonds put it; 'Up the exposed shallow trough which marked the termination of Caterpillar Valley[441] - and from the south-west - over a crest and down a slope, both devoid of cover - had little chance of success'. Although some men of the 30th Division had, on July 30th, managed to get into the village of Guillemont, with their flanks unsecured, they were unable to establish themselves.

Writing an account in 1936 of the 52nd's attempt on Guillemont Station, Lieutenant-Colonel Richard Crosse was scathing in his criticism of the operational plan[442]. He wrote, 'the operation was graded as a "side show" was based on a remarkable scheme which, had it been propounded by a candidate for examination in "Tactical Fitness for Command," would have caused him

---

[440] In an article written in 1935, Crosse implied that the award was for Kite's actions at Richebourg l'Avoué, in 1915. It will be recalled that he was ordered to remain in the trenches at Waterlot Farm while his company attacked the trenches towards Ginchy. However, on July 30th, he did play a part in a bombing duel with the Germans. Kite would be mortally wounded on November 13th 1916 at the Battle of the Ancre.

[441] Caterpillar Valley was so named in view of its shape. It extended from west to east, in front of Mametz Wood, across the Montauban - Longueval road, to the north of Bernafay Wood, and towards Trones Wood and Guillemont.

[442] *Regimental Journal* January-November 1936, page 110.

promptly to be failed'. Twenty years later, in a further account of the action, Crosse was more measured in his view of the operational plan. 'The operation which was graded as 'a side show', was based upon a scheme which inspired nobody with confidence from the start, and made no provision for any supporting troops available to go through and exploit a success. There were, in fact, no such troops'[443]. In both articles, Crosse also described Everard Wyrall's account of the action, in *The History of the Second Division 1914 – 1918*, as being one with 'characteristic inaccuracy'. Indeed Wyrall had confused which of the 52nd's companies were used in the attack on Guillemont Station. Crosse felt that Edmonds' account in the *Official History* was more accurate.

It is difficult not to have some sympathy with Richard Crosse's views. The key to a successful assault by the 5th Brigade on July 30th 1916 was the artillery barrage. The barrage had to make gaps in the barbed wire for the troops to go through, and also had to knock out the enemy bombing posts and machine-guns. This it manifestly failed to do. The early morning mist and the resulting inability to see the effects of the barrage did not help matters. Fourth Army, XIII Corps, 2nd Division, and the 5th Brigade were all aware or should have been aware of the strength of the German positions around Guillemont Station. A week earlier, on July 23rd, the 2nd Royal Scots, of the 8th Brigade, had attempted to bomb down the trenches from Waterlot Farm, on either side of the Guillemont road and railway, in order to capture the station. Although some progress was made, the ground could not be held under machine-gun fire from the direction of Ginchy and from the north-east. This should have been a stark warning as to the strength of the enemy's positions. By the time of the 52nd's attack, on July 30th, there were further machine-guns to the right of the Guillemont road and to the south of the station. The 52nd was initially held up by bombing posts, which disrupted their formation, forcing them into two lines. It had been anticipated that the bombing posts would have been neutralized by the Stokes mortars, but they had failed. It is true that there were no reinforcements to exploit a successful advance. However, in the event, this did not matter as there was no success to exploit.

Major Reggie Owen wrote in his diary, 'zero was at 4.45 a.m., i.e., daylight, and much too late'. It seems reasonable to think that Richard Crosse held a similar view to Owen's, although he has not recorded this specific criticism. An attack in the darkness might have given the 52nd a small degree of protection against the bombers and also the enemy's machine-guns. However, it was more difficult, at night, to get troops on to the correct start line for an assault. Indeed, on July 1st 1916, zero hour was even later, at 7.30 a.m., so that an attack

---

[443] *Regimental Journal* May 1956, page 118.

in daylight was not out of the ordinary for the British or indeed the French. Crosse's main complaints about the July 30th attack can be summarized as a zero hour in daylight, an inadequate barrage, and a lack of reserves to exploit any initial territorial gains. The plan of attack had been drawn up by Brigadier-General George Bullen-Smith, and accepted by Major-General William Walker V.C., commanding the 2nd Division. Crosse had had some input to the plan, but as a new battalion commander, perhaps he had felt unable to have it modified.

At 2 a.m. on July 31th, the 52nd received orders that they were to be relieved by the 2nd H.L.I., with the exception of D Company. By 7 a.m., the rest of the Regiment was back in its old haunts to the south of Montauban. The men hoped for a peaceful night's rest, but considerable shelling put a stop to that. The rest period was short-lived as, at 5 p.m. on August 1st, the Regiment proceeded from Brigade Reserve back to the trenches at Waterlot Farm, where the 2nd H.L.I. was relieved. Here Second-Lieutenant H.J. Ellam was buried in a dug-out by a shell. On release he was found to have fractured his right clavicle and some ribs.

Tragedy struck the 52nd on the following day, August 2nd, when their newly appointed second-in-command, Major Reggie Owen, was mortally wounded at Waterlot Farm. He had already been severely wounded, near the Ferme de Metz, on the Aisne, in 1914, and had escaped untouched at Givenchy, in the autumn of 1915, and again more recently, on July 30th, here at Waterlot Farm. At 9 a.m., Owen suffered severe gunshot wounds to his back, left arm, and left foot as the result of an exploding shell. The back wound had led to a penetrating wound of his chest, which almost certainly led to his demise. The 25-year-old Reggie Owen was evacuated to the Advanced Dressing Station at Dive Copse[444], where he died a few hours later. The serious nature of his wounds precluded any possibility of his transfer to a Casualty Clearing Station, where surgery might have been undertaken. Amongst his belongings that were sent home were a gold ring, a broken watch, no doubt from his left wrist, and an acclaimed romantic novel '*The Happy Warrior*' by A.S.M. Hutchinson. What distressed his mother, Susan Owen, so much, was the fact that he had died without anyone he knew by his side. She wrote 'and yet one of the biggest bits of my trouble seems to be that my darling boy died alone in the little clearing hospital of his wounds – without one soul who knew him near. Not even a sister or nurse – merely a strange orderly'[445].

[444] Named after Captain Dive who commanded the dressing station. It was situated to the north of Sailly. There was a Motor Ambulance Convoy based here and it was also a Divisional Rest Station. Owen was buried in the nearby Dive Copse British Cemetery, and his weather-beaten gravestone can be seen to this day. Dive Copse is a lonely, unattractive, windswept place.

[445] Letter to Edith Kite written on February 3rd 1917.

Richard Crosse must have been devastated by the death of his young second-in-command, who was so steeped in the traditions of the Regiment[446], as his cadre of officers was now very inexperienced . The unfortunate Owen was the only casualty in the 52nd that day.

In the early hours of August 3rd, the 52nd was forced to deal with an incursion by ten Germans into Delville Wood. Crosse reported the matter to 5th Brigade.

> At 3 a.m. today a party of 10 Germans made what maybe a "raid" on, or an attempt to enter DELVILLE WOOD Via [sic], the bombing post on the left of my platoon holding the South face aaa They were dealt with as follows:-
>
> Shot by the Lewis gunners 4 or 5
> Otherwise killed 2
> Wounded and taken prisoners 2
> of whom one died
> Taken prisoner 1
>
> The last mentioned was brought to these Head Quarters shortly before the Brigadier General came and being unaware of the above information merely sent him on without taking further interest aaa Since I have received his papers (forwarded herewith) and the above information aaa I also send the papers taken from the wounded prisoner who died in ANGLE TRENCH aaa It is noticeable that these men had what we estimate at 3 day's rations about them and therefore it is possible they were coming into the Wood for several days sniping aaa They had full equipment aaa The delay in receipt of information was due to excessive shelling of DELVILLE WOOD area Via [sic] which orderly had to pass aaa It is noticeable that a few hours previous to this the DELVILLE WOOD End [sic] of ANGLE TRENCH was so shelled that we withdrew the platoon next on the right to the one I have referred to above.

Later, at 8 p.m. on August 3rd, the 52nd was relieved by the 17th R. F. and returned, once more, to their reserve position south of Montauban. During the day Serjeant P. Barlow, a scout, was wounded and three men were killed while out on patrol. The following day proved to be quiet, and, on August 5th, the 52nd

[446] Reggie Owen was the great-grandson of Captain W.S. Moorsom, who wrote the *Historical Record of the Regiment,* and the great-nephew of Captain W.R. Moorsom, who served with the 52nd from 1853 to 1858 and was killed at Lucknow.

reinforcement of one serjeant and 65 other ranks joined the Regiment in Happy Valley. Also on this day, the 5th Brigade as a whole was relieved by the 6th Brigade from divisional reserve.

August 6th and 7th, proved to be quiet, but on the 8th, the 5th Brigade and Regimental Headquarters were shelled, in an unpleasant manner, for five hours. On the same day, the 55th Division and the 6th Brigade of the 2nd Division made a further attempt on Guillemont and its station. As on July 30th, the village was entered but German counter-attacks retook it before the day was out. Sir Douglas Haig was unhappy that this further assault on Guillemont had failed and questioned whether sufficient forces had been used by XIII Corps who were responsible for the operation. The upshot of this was that the commander of XIII Corps, Sir Walter Congreve, relinquished his command, on August 10th; he had been suffering from ill-health for some time. Poor Congreve had lost his son on the Somme less than a month before. In view of the 6th Brigade's attack on Guillemont Station, the relief of the 5th Brigade from divisional reserve was cancelled, and the 52nd found itself lent to the 6th Brigade. The Regiment took up positions in support between Trones and Bernafay Woods.

Although, on the next day, August 9th, the 6th Brigade renewed their attack, and B, C Companies of the 52nd moved up, they were not required. Later in the day the 6th Brigade was relieved by the 17th Brigade and the 52nd returned to the 5th Brigade. The night proved to be a wet one. On the 10th, the Regiment and the rest of their Brigade went into bivouac in the Sandpit area. The next day, the 52nd marched to Ville-sur-Ancre. Here the men rested and were joined, on the 12th, by the 53rd reinforcement of a serjeant and 38 other ranks. On August 13th, the Regiment was on the move once more, as it marched to Mericourt l'Abbé, and then travelled by train to Saleux, to the south-west of Amiens. A further march via Saveuse took them to their destination at Ailly-sur-Somme and into comfortable billets. By now the 52nd were well away from the rubble that was all that remained of Guillemont and its station. The Regiment had not finished with the Somme battlefields as a whole, but in future their involvement would be further north, opposite Serre and then Beaumont Hamel.

Chapter XIV

The Somme: the Battle of the Ancre.

August 14th - December 31st 1916

[Maps: pages 315, 317, 365, inside back cover.]

August 14th saw the arrival of the 54th reinforcement of 16 men for the 52nd Light Infantry. At the end of July and in the early weeks of August 1916, the Regiment received reinforcements of a more irregular nature. The following two stories show a little of the reason why Lieutenant-Colonel Richard Crosse was such a popular and effective commanding officer. Indeed, at the Regimental reunions, from the 1920s-1960s, he was always to be found surrounded by an affectionate circle of his former soldiers, each of whom he knew by name and usually by their Regimental number as well. By 1916, many officers and men had been wounded in the earlier battles of the war. On recovery they very naturally wished to return to their own regiments. Unfortunately, the War Office had insisted that reinforcement drafts of men, who had recovered from their wounds, were deliberately posted to regiments other than their own. This was to establish an 'Army spirit' at the expense of 'Regimental esprit de corps'. Understandably, men treated in this cavalier fashion resented the transfer to a new regiment. Not a few battalions, at least temporarily, lost their fighting efficiency because of this rule. The War Office decision can only be described as crass. The Dominions, such as Australia, Canada, South Africa, and New Zealand always insisted that their men were returned to their own units after injury or illness. Possibly, this was one of the reasons that Dominion troops were consistently considered to be better fighting soldiers than the native Britons, despite the fact that they often had a common ancestry. Richard Crosse circumvented this state of affairs by arranging with Base for regular officers and soldiers of the Regiment to be posted to the 52nd either on first appointment or on rejoining from wounds. The following stories record how Crosse aided and abetted men, who wished to return to the 52nd, in an even more irregular fashion.

> During the last few days of July, while the Regiment was in action around Montauban, Longueval, and Delville Wood, there returned to the fold a poor exile of Erin in the person of Private Flanagan. I found him in a trench, inquiring for his old company. Fortunately I knew him – we had met several times in the romantic environment of the orderly room – or he might have suffered arrest or a worse fate, as a spy.

Earlier evacuated as wounded or sick, Flanagan had been caught up in a draft for the Manchester Regiment. As the Mancunians were not to his liking, he decided to find the 52nd. With what used to be called a 'nine inch grin' on his face, he told me as much, as no doubt, he thought it was necessary for me to know, about his adventure in escaping and, in his own words, 'coming home'. He was shown as a reinforcement, which indeed he was and, greatly to his satisfaction, was restored to his old company, without more ado.

Some weeks later one Private Phillips rejoined under escort, with another reinforcement. I perused about a score of papers of documentary evidence and papers prepared for a court-martial, which came with him, and on one of his periodical appearances at orderly room for a formal remand, I invited him to tell me his story, which I checked with the mass of documents above mentioned.

It appeared that while at Base Depot he had been detailed, with others, for a draft to be posted to an unpopular regiment – 'not our sort at all, sir'. Cap badges had been withdrawn and others issued and ordered to be worn. 'And you wouldn't like that yourself, would you, sir?'

There were great protests and commotion, in which our Phillips took no part. He gave the impression that he submitted meekly to whatever was in store for him. The daily draft paraded, was inspected and checked, and the order, 'pick up your kits', was given at the moment of marching off. At this point Private Phillips assumed the prone position in his place in the ranks, and remained motionless, despite all efforts to restore him to the vertical. The draft moved off, leaving him behind to be carried (on a stretcher) to the guard room.

It happened that, as soon as there had been time to accumulate the mass of papers with which I was now troubled, a draft was ordered for the 52nd, and, perhaps to get rid of him and place the court-martial in other hands, Private Phillips was included in it, greatly to his satisfaction. Thus he, too, 'came home'.

In a subsequent hurried move, one of the orderly room boxes became lost. It contained the Phillips papers. It was never traced: so nothing more could be done.

Private Flanagan's actions could have been construed as desertion, which was potentially a capital offence. He was lucky to meet a commanding officer like Richard Crosse, who would support any man wanting to return to his beloved 52nd. Private Phillips' dislike of changing his cap badge would certainly have appealed to Crosse, who was the very embodiment of regimental spirit. In World War II, Hitler's War, as Crosse called it, he had to wear the cap badge of the Pioneer Corps rather than that of the 52nd. It hurt. There can be little doubt that Crosse quietly destroyed Phillips' court-martial papers when he had the opportunity. Crosse saw the actions of Flanagan and Phillips in the same light as Privates Lewis and Tobin, in the Peninsular War of a hundred years before. In 1809, Lewis was caught filling his haversack with plunder and was about to be hanged when the French arrived. His life was spared and he was later to die gallantly. A year later, Tobin was taken by a French patrol, having fallen asleep after an excess of alcohol. His company commander knowing him to be a brave soldier reported him missing rather than having deserted. A few days later, Tobin escaped and returned to the 52nd. Nothing more was said about his recent adventures.

The 52nd spent August 15th resting and bathing before, the following day, marching to Montonvillers, a few miles north of Amiens. They were on the move once more on the 17th, route marching to Candas and, on the 18th, to Bus-lès-Artois. The village was to the north-west of Bertrancourt and south-west of Coigneux and Couin. There was a main dressing station as well as huts and tents. On August 19th, the 5th Brigade relieved the 3rd Guards Brigade in the Beaumont section. The 52nd went into brigade reserve, replacing the 1st Grenadier Guards, in new billets at Bus-lès-Artois, with the Regimental Headquarters under canvas close to the village. A welcome visitor, on the 20th, was Guy Blewitt, now Brigade Major 167th Infantry Brigade. He wrote in his diary: 'I motored to see the 52nd at Bus and I stayed to dinner, Buggins was in the trenches but Tiger Wyld came and dined and Richard Crosse. Whitfeld, Kite, Field, Thyritt Drake [sic], were there[447]. I was delighted to be with them'. Even for a staff officer Regimental ties remained strong. The next few days were spent in training and, on the 22nd, Richard Crosse together with the Adjutant, Ernest Whitfeld, and the company commanders reconnoitred the trenches of the left battalion in the Beaumont section. This was to be their first experience of the northern part of the Somme battlefields.

On August 23rd, the 52nd moved into the trenches viewed by their commanding officer the day before, in relief of the 17th Royal Fusiliers. They were to remain in these trenches for the next five days. The 55th reinforcement of 28 men arrived on the 23rd. After the loss of so many officers, on July 30th, near

---

[447] Diary entry for August 20th 1916. 'Buggins' was Charles Higgins. Ernest Whitfeld, Ralph Kite, George Field, Thomas Tyrwhitt-Drake.

Waterlot Farm, several officer replacements joined the Regiment. Second-Lieutenant Keith Peploe, rejoined on the 23rd; Second-Lieutenants A.S. Holiday[448] and Henry Davies, on the 25th; Second-Lieutenant Vivian Fanning, on the 26th; Second-Lieutenant Edward Vigars, rejoined on the 27th. The 26th saw three C Company men killed. On August 29th, most of the 52nd was relieved by the 17th Royal Fusiliers, and A plus C Company proceeded to Courcelles-au-Bois. Courcelles was a village some eight miles north of Albert, in the hilly country to the north-west of the Ancre. It had been shelled, but the damage was not as great as that done to nearby Colincamps, which was more exposed on the crest of a hill. B Company remained at the disposal of the 17th R.F., and D Company went to Ellis Square Redoubt and Fort Hoystead[449]. These were strong points on either side of the Mailly Maillet to Serre road.

On August 29th, Major Cuthbert 'Bingo' Baines, one of the heroes of Nonne Bosschen Wood, in the Autumn of 1914, returned to the Regiment from the 2/6th Warwickshire, as the senior major, and second-in-command. Although there is no documentary evidence, it is possible that Richard Crosse asked for his transfer to fill the gap left by the death of Reggie Owen. There was a distinct lack of experienced hands at the top of the Regiment, in case Crosse became incapacitated. Two days later, Ben Slocock, whilst commanding B Company with the temporary rank of captain, was wounded in the buttock and sent home to England. The last few days of August saw the arrival of further officer replacements: Second-Lieutenants F.S. Parsons and C.W. Fitt, on the 30th; Second-Lieutenant Morris Fielding rejoined, on the 31st, having been wounded in the eye, during the July 30th attack near Waterlot Farm.

On the first day of September, the 52nd was in position as the support battalion of the 5th Brigade. Regimental Headquarters and one company were based in huts and tents at Courcelles-au-Bois. A second company was in billets at Colincamps. By August 1916, Colincamps had been greatly damaged by shellfire, and its Sucerie or Sugar Factory lay in ruins to the south-east of the village. An Advanced Dressing Station was present as well. A third company was in Ellis Square Redoubt, just to the north of the Mailly Maillet to Serre road. The final company was in the trenches, at the disposal of the 17th R.F., who were holding the left Beaumont section. September 2nd saw the arrival of the 56th reinforcement of 25 men, and Second-Lieutenant Ronald Creswell reported for duty having been returned by the Royal Flying Corps. At 11.30 p.m. that

[448] Returned to England on October 21st 1916 with a gastric ulcer.

[449] In the *Regimental Chronicles* it was called Fort Horstead. Some of the 52nd's officers referred to it as Horsted or Hoysted. Trench maps mark the Fort as Hoystead and this spelling has been used in the text.

evening, a few shells were fired into Courcelles and landed in the area occupied by the Regimental Headquarters and the company based there. A man and a horse from another unit were killed, but despite the fact that shell splinters fell on their huts and tents, the 52nd were unharmed.

On September 4th, the Regiment relieved the 17th R.F., in the left Beaumont sub-sector trenches. This tour of the trenches proved to be a quiet one and the weather had improved. During one of these tours of the Beaumont trenches, the men of Captain Ralph Kite's D Company discovered the decomposed body of Private William Morgan of the 1/6th Warwickshire. The men had been part of a wiring party when the body was found. It was identified by photographs and a Christmas card with an address on it. The 1/6th Warwickshire had been decimated on July 1st and the corpse had lain there ever since. The 17th R.F. took over the 52nd's trenches on the 10th, and the 52nd went into divisional reserve, in huts in Coigneux Wood. The village of Coigneux lay behind the lines during the 1916 battles of the Somme, and was to the west of Hébuterne. Its wood, the Bois de Coigneux, lay to the south-west of the village.

The 57th reinforcement of seventeen men arrived on September 11th. That same day, Major-General Robert Fanshawe, who had served in the 52nd from 1883 to 1911, and was now commanding the 48th [South Midland] Division, visited the Regiment. He spoke to the men on parade and afterwards gave an address to the officers. Richard Crosse in his book *A Record of H.M. 52nd Light Infantry in 1914* has left an account of this visit.

> I remember the occasion well. I wanted the Regiment, now much changed in personnel[450], to see a very senior and distinguished 52nd officer, and I was determined to make the most of it.
>
> The General arrived, inspected the guard and walked quietly about, obviously happy and pleased. He wanted no fuss. He spoke to every officer in turn, and greeted his old comrades of the Indian Frontier of nearly twenty years past. I had taken care to have our few remaining old soldiers available; for these were men who remembered "D" or Captain R. Fanshawe's Company and "B" or Captain H.R. Davies' Company, and they had become very precious. But I wanted still more:
>
> Will you speak to the Regiment, sir?
>
> Yes, if you wish.
>
> We *do* wish, sir.

[450] As Crosse put it 'we had lately taken a battering on the Somme (30th July), and were shortly to take another (Beaumont Hamel, 13th Nov)'.

Very well.

R.F. was magnificent on these occasions. I knew that: and I did not mean to let the opportunity slip by. By sound of bugle-horn everyone was turned out in clean fatigue dress, and formed in fours facing to a flank, that is the head of each company in front – his favourite formation when he spoke to the Regiment on parade.

We were not disappointed. We were addressed, not at great length, but in a way that put heart into everybody. The General spoke of the Regiment's record, from Light Division days to 1914, that we must live up to, *as he understood it was being lived up to,* and not upon: how more than ever necessary it was for everyone to keep himself fit, so that when called on he could give the last ounce that was in him and a bit more: and how, to achieve this, no opportunity must ever be wasted to eat and sleep. With this, in the vulgar vernacular of to-day, the troops "couldn't agree more." And he reminded us that we belonged to each other, and belonged to the Regiment, and must never let it down.

It was a memorable occasion. After a simple meal such as he preferred, he drove away, leaving as quietly as he had come. I noted he had in his car, as always, his shaving kit and a haversack ration. I have seen tears in his eyes twice. This was the first occasion. The second was when he and I were leaving Whittington Barracks, Lichfield, in 1922, after having gone there from Oxford to say good-bye to the 52nd, soon to embark for India.

The next day, the 12th, the 52nd practiced co-operation with aeroplanes just to the north of Couin. From September 12th to the 15th, the Regiment was based at Coigneux and the time was used for training purposes. The young officers, many of whom could not ride a horse, attended a riding school, before breakfast each day, under the direction of Richard Crosse or Cuthbert Baines. In the era of World War I, it was considered essential for young officers to be proficient in the saddle.

In the last chapter, the first two chronological stages of the Somme battles of 1916 were described. September 15th saw the opening of the third stage, an attack on the German third position, which continued intermittently until November 11th. [Battles of Flers-Courcelette, Morval, Thiepval Ridge, Transloy Ridges, Ancre Heights]. Although, the 52nd was not directly involved in this third stage, it needs to be looked at briefly as it led into the fourth chronological stage, the Battle of the Ancre. In this, the final stage of the Somme battles of 1916, the 52nd were to play a prominent role.

On September 15th, Courcelette and Martinpuich, on either side of the Albert to Bapaume road fell, and finally High Wood was cleared of the enemy. That same day, the 32 tanks that managed to reach the starting line helped take the village of Flers to the north-east of Delville Wood. It was the first time that this new weapon had been used in battle. The next few weeks were spent in beating off German counter-attacks. During this period the French to the south had been advancing on either side of the Somme. Bouchavesnes, Vermandovillers, Berny, and Deniécourt fell into their hands. Wet weather hindered the Anglo-French efforts but, by September 25th, the date of the next general attack, it had improved. On the 25th, Lesboeufs and Morval were taken, and the following day Guedecourt was also captured. Combles had been abandoned by the enemy and the French were able to march in. The 27th saw the seemingly impregnable fortress of Thiepval finally cleared[451], and by the 30th, the Germans had been thrown out of their third position. October proved to be a very wet month which did not help offensive operations. Le Sars was captured on October 7th, and the Stuff and Schwaben Redoubts on October 9th and 14th respectively. These formidable enemy fortifications had proved to be tough nuts to crack.

Returning to the 52nd, on September 16th it was back to the familiar trenches in the Beaumont left section, in relief of the 17th R.F., which took place without incident. Here they remained until September 19th, although the Regimental Headquarters was shelled on most days. However, on the 19th, they were suddenly relieved by the 12th Sussex of the 116th Brigade, 39th Division, and retired to huts to the north of Bus-lès-Artois. The following day the whole of the 5th Brigade was relieved and the 52nd moved to good billets in Sarton. While at Sarton further officers joined the Regiment. Captain Rupert Brett was reappointed Transport Officer, a post he had held in the Autumn of 1914, before he was wounded; Lieutenants David Barnes was reposted to and John Slade-Baker joined D Company; Second-Lieutenants Octavius Hugh Mansfield 'Toby' Sturges and William Giles went to B Company; Second-Lieutenants Philip 'Blig' Booth and Harry Vernon were posted to C Company; Second-Lieutenants Frederick 'Bolo' Lowndes and Philip 'Slatcher' Whitehead joined A Company[452]. As Crosse wrote in the *Battalion War Diary:* 'The last 7 appear to be a very good

[451] The village of Thiepval fell on September 26th, but it took until the next day to clear it fully of fortified machine-gun nests and underground passages.

[452] Later Major Sir Philip Henry Rathbone Whitehead, Fourth Baronet. He was known as 'Slatcher' Whitehead. Whitehead gained this sobriquet while in his cups by repeating 'excellent man Private Slatcher, excellent man' several times.

type of regular officer, all Sandhurst educated and likely to be useful to the Regt. Several have family connections with the 52nd'. Yet another officer arrived, on September 23rd, he was Second-Lieutenant Geoffrey 'Gazeeka' Lyle. The Regiment was getting its number of officers up to something like a full complement.

The 52nd's stay at Sarton lasted until October 2nd. According to Richard Crosse, during this period of rest and training, some very useful work was carried out. Before breakfast, various forms of instruction took place, normally by lecture for the newly joined officers, and physical training for everybody else. After breakfast there were close-order and skirmishing[453] parades, attacks from trenches, wiring, bombing, and Lewis gun classes. Rupert Brett took over the officers' riding school. On October 1st, the Reverend William Dallas, who had been one of the 5th Brigade's Church of England chaplains for the last thirteen months, took his final Church Parade Service followed by a celebration of Holy Communion. Dallas was leaving to join the 165th Brigade in the 56th [1st London] Division, and he would be killed in action, on September 30th 1917, almost exactly a year later. Both the 2nd Division's commander, Major-General William Walker V.C., and the 5th Brigade's commander, Brigadier-General George Bullen-Smith, were present at the service. The 59th reinforcement of eleven men arrived.

On October 2nd, the 52nd left Sarton, at 10.33 a.m., for the march to Bus-lès-Artois, which proved to be unpleasantly wet. The latrines in the huts allotted to the Regiment, had been left 'in the most disgusting condition' by their unknown predecessors. It was a very different 52nd from that of the summer of 1916. Richard Crosse remained in command, with Cuthbert Baines as his deputy. Ernest Whitfeld continued in his post as adjutant, but there had been changes amongst the company commanders. Captain Nick Hill, commanded A; Captain George Field, commanded B; Captain John Littledale, commanded C; Captain Ralph Kite, commanded D. With the exception of George Field, who had been an experienced N.C.O. before gaining a commission, the other company commanders were inexperienced in comparison with their counterparts of August 1914. The first two years of the war had taken a heavy toll on the officer corps.

The night of October 3rd, a wet one, was further disturbed by an order issued by 5th Brigade at 2 a.m. and that reached the 52nd two hours later. The order required the Regiment to find two fatigue parties, consisting of two officers and 160 men, for rendezvous at 9 a.m. This required parading at 6.30 and 7 a.m. respectively. Unfortunately neither the *Regimental Chronicles* nor the *Battalion War Diary* recorded what the fatigue parties were to do. The Regiment moved

---

453 Fighting in small parties in an irregular manner.

via Bertrancourt and Beaussart to huts in Mailly Wood. The wood lay to the south-west of the village of Mailly Maillet, which was a bustling centre behind the British lines in 1916. The 52nd remained in Mailly Wood during the 4th and supplied further working parties. Second-Lieutenant Ronald Blackwell joined and was posted to D Company. The next day Richard Crosse took his company commanders [Ralph Kite being absent on leave in England] to visit the trenches in the Serre left sub-section, as they would shortly be responsible for them.

On October 6th, the 52nd relieved the 1st King's Royal Rifle Corps, in the trenches that had been reconnoitred the day before. The trenches extended 'from near Matthew Copse on the right to John Copse exclusive (Russian Sap just short of) on the left'[454]. The relief took place without incident. In the autumn of 1916, the lines of the two protagonists bent in a south-easterly direction, from Hébuterne and Gommecourt and, then turned to the south-west, in front of Serre and Beaumont Hamel. The villages of Gommecourt, Serre, and Beaumont Hamel had been heavily fortified by the Germans. In front of Serre, the British front line ran approximately along the bottom of a small valley, with the ground sloping upwards in the east towards the German line. To the west, the ground also sloped upwards towards the British reserve and support lines. The focal points of the Serre trenches were the four copses, named after the Apostles, from the north to the south, John, Luke, Mark, and Matthew[455].

The Serre trenches were unpleasant as they were overlooked by the enemy. On the morning of July 1st 1916, the 31st Division facing the village of Serre had a very great number of casualties inflicted upon them. The two Brigades involved, the 93rd and 94th, were made up of the so-called 'Pals Battalions', who were decimated. The men of whole communities had volunteered together and formed their own units, giving rise to the Leeds, Bradford, Durham and Accrington 'Pals' Battalions. All that was gained with mutual support and better morale was lost on July 1st when the men from whole streets were wiped out. The following month, on November 13th, the 52nd would participate in the attack on the German line between Serre and Beaumont Hamel. In fact Serre was never taken, and eventually the Germans evacuated it on February 24th 1917.

The Regiment discovered that the Serre trenches were a place of considerable trench mortar activity. Guns in the British lines were active with a

---

[454] Entry in the *Battalion War Diary.* A Russian sap was a narrow trench dug in the manner of a mine shaft, so that the surface of the earth was not disturbed. It helped raiding troops to approach the enemy's lines without being seen.

[455] The British front line ran along the south-eastern edge of Mark, Luke, and John Copses. However, Matthew Copse was slightly behind the front line.

view to wire-cutting, and this led to enemy retaliation causing a certain amount of damage. On October 6th, Second-Lieutenant C.W. Fitt returned to England, having been transferred to the Machine-Gun Corps. The following day was quiet, apart from the constant stream of officers from all units who wished to reconnoitre their trenches. During the afternoon of the 8th, the 52nd was relieved by old friends, the 4th Royal Fusiliers, under Lieutenant-Colonel E.B. North. The 4th R.F. was now part of the 3rd Division but, between 1911 and 1912, it had been brigaded with the 52nd[456]. The Regiment had a wet march to bivouac in Leavilliers.

On October 9th the officers were taken to inspect taped practice trenches to the south of Arquèves. This was the first indication that the Regiment was to be involved in a further assault. The next day, still at Leavilliers, Keith Peploe was given the temporary rank of captain, and he took over command of B Company, in the place of the injured Captain George Field who was admitted to hospital, having fallen in the trenches and sprained his ankle. A brigade conference was held in the morning, followed by further familiarisation with the taped practice trenches. The 60th reinforcement of seven men joined the 52nd. The following day, the 11th, the 61st reinforcement of eleven men arrived, and in the morning, another brigade practice took place over the same ground. On the 12th, yet another brigade practice was held over the now familiar practice ground. The next day, the practice was repeated once more, this time at divisional level. The 62nd reinforcement of 95 men, arrived under Second-Lieutenant Alfred Webster-Jones, who returned to the Reserve Army School on handing over. The men had transferred from the 6th Berkshire, and many of them were from a group called up in June 1916, and originally enlisted for the Royal Field Artillery. Richard Crosse was singularly unimpressed with their drill, especially the handling of arms.

October 14th proved to be a quiet day in camp, with an inspection of the draft, and the arrival of the 63rd reinforcement of ten signallers. The following day was also quiet with a Church Parade. Clearly it was a case of practice makes perfect as, on the 16th, there was a further divisional exercise over the taped trenches. The 17th saw the 52nd march independently to billets in Arquèves, where they were to remain until October 22nd. Second-Lieutenant Alfred Webster-Jones officially joined and was posted to A Company. On the 22nd, the Regiment replaced the 17th R.F. in billets in the village of Mailly Maillet. The 17th R.F. went to the trenches.

Three days later, on October 25th, the 52nd moved to trenches in the Redan Section, to the south of their previous position, in relief of the 24th R.F. on the left

[456] Part of the 5th Brigade.

and the 2nd H.L.I. on the right. Ultimately, on November 13th, the Regiment would assault the German line from here, on the opening day of the Battle of the Ancre. The next few days allowed them to become acquainted with the ground they would attack over. The Redan Ridge was a German strong point between Serre and Beaumont Hamel. John Masefield, the former Poet Laureate, described it in his book *The Old Front Line:*

> – no it was a question here, which side should hold the highest point of the spur. Right on top of the spur there was one patch of ground, measuring, it may be, two hundred yards each way, from which one can see a long way in every direction. From this path, the ground droops a little towards the English side and stretches away fairly flat towards the enemy side, but one can see far either way and to have this power of seeing both sides fought desperately.

On July 1st, the 4th Division had failed to take the Redan Ridge, and suffered many casualties. Both sides had undertaken a considerable number of mining operations prior to July 1st, and later in the summer and autumn. John Masefield has left a further description of the ground after the mining operations.

> – the whole of the summit (which is called the Redan Ridge) for all its two hundred yards, is blown into pits and craters from twenty to fifty feet deep, and sometimes fifty yards long.
>
> For many weeks, the armies fought for this patch of hill. It was all mined, counter-mined, and re-mined, and at each explosion the crater was fought for and lost and won. It cannot be said that either side won that summit till the enemy was beaten from all that field, for both sides conquered enough to see from. On the enemy side, a fortification of heaped earth was made; on our side, castles were built of sandbags filled with flint. These strongholds gave both sides enough observation. The works face each other across the ponds.

Such was the unpleasant spot that the Regiment was introduced to for the first time and which would become so familiar to its officers and men. The next day, October 26th, was a wet and moderately quiet one. At 7.45 p.m., that evening, two parties each consisting of an officer and fourteen men with blackened faces[457], went out on to the Redan, in order to take a sentry prisoner for identification purposes. The raid was to be supported by a box barrage to isolate the section of enemy front line trench that they hoped to snatch a German from[458]. Parties were detailed to form blocks in the flanks and communication trenches and bombers were to deal with the dug-outs. It was hoped that the raid would only take ten minutes, and in any case the men were scheduled to return to the British line, at zero hour plus twenty minutes, when the barrage ceased. Unfortunately, they failed to find the two gaps in the enemy's wire and so came back empty-handed, with several men slightly wounded. Five men were killed during the day. On the 27th, the 17th R.F. relieved the 52nd, who retired to the village of Mailly Maillet, where they would remain until November 9th. Their doctor Captain K.W. Mackenzie left the Regiment, for duties at the 2nd Division, and was temporarily replaced by Captain D.A. Cassidy. In a letter to his mother, Captain Ralph Kite, the D Company Commander, gave a few details of this period in Mailly Maillet[459].

> All goes well as can be expected here. It is wet and cold and the trenches are very muddy.
>
> We are billeted in a deserted village at the back of the front and are very comfortable. My company has a house to itself, less top storey which Fritz has demolished, and we have simply enormous logs on our fire and keep pretty warm. A little short-haired fox terrier also appeared yesterday and he also has been adopted. Fritz works up some frightfulness now and again but we merely repair to the cellars, with which most French houses are provided – by the Grace of Providence.

The 52nd remained in the same billets, in Mailly Maillet, for the next thirteen days. Initially, time was spent in bathing, inspections, and generally cleaning themselves up. From November 1st to the 8th, working parties of 200-300 men plus some officers were furnished every day. For most of the time the weather was wet, and the trenches and overland tracks very bad. On the 29th Captain J. McTurk relieved Captain D.A. Cassidy as their Medical Officer.

---

[457] The 5th *Brigade War Diary* recorded two officers and 30 other ranks for the two raiding parties. The *Regimental Chronicles* stated, 'two parties, each of an officer and 14 others'.

[458] German front line from Q.5.a.20.85 to K.35.c.19.00. [see trench map inside rear cover].

[459] Letter dated October 29th 1916. This was the last letter that he was known to have written, before being mortally wounded on the Redan Ridge on November 13th.

Cassidy's time with the Regiment had been brief. November 7th, saw the arrival of the 64th reinforcement of 43 men.

On November 9th, the 52nd returned once more to the Redan sector, in relief of the 24th R. F., and on this occasion occupied the whole brigade frontage that was normally held by two battalions. The right of the front line was held by Captain John Littledale's C Company, and the left of it by Captain Keith Peploe's B Company. In the support was Captain Nick Hill's A Company distributed along Chatham Line, and in reserve was Captain Ralph Kite's D Company along the Vallade Line, in Mountjoy Trench, and the communication trench 6th Avenue. The Regimental Headquarters were at White City with the 5th Brigade's Advanced Headquarters. The relief began down the 6th Avenue, at about 4 p.m., and was effected without difficulty.

Although the 9th was warm and sunny, much of the relief had to take place overland after dark as the trenches were in a terrible state and quite impassable in places. The Germans were obviously having similar problems with waterlogged trenches, parties of them being seen in the open, until scattered by Lewis gun fire. Enemy aircraft patrols were also very active. Tragedy struck at 9.20 p.m. that night, when Keith Peploe was visiting a bombing post on the north face of the Redan. The recently appointed B Company commander was shot at close range by a sniper lying out in no man's land for just such a purpose. The 23-year-old Peploe[460] was hit in the thigh of one of his legs and died a few minutes later while being brought in. Judging by the speed of his demise it is likely that his femoral artery had been ruptured and that he had rapidly exsanguinated. This was a fate that had befallen many a fighting man until the coming of modern surgical techniques. Peploe was succeeded in command of B Company by the 19-year-old Lieutenant Vivian Fanning, who would lead them in the coming battle.

November 10th was another fine day, although this made the mud in the trenches more sticky and heavy, and movement even more difficult. At 3 p.m., a conference of the 5th Brigade's battalion commanders was held at nearby Beaussart, at which Lieutenant-Colonel Richard Crosse attended on behalf of the 52nd. He learned the latest details of the amended scheme of operations for the forthcoming Battle of the Ancre. He wrote after the war that 'the coming battle was the most elaborately organized one on record'. No less than 35 typed pages of orders and amendments were delivered to the Regimental Headquarters during the days leading up to the action. It is surprising that Crosse managed to assimilate them in the time available and under the conditions of active service.

---

460 Keith Peploe was educated at Marlborough College and Trinity College, Cambridge. He had joined the 52nd in France in June 1915.

On November 11th, or "X" day, next but one to "Z" day, zero day, the onset of the assault, the 52nd was relieved by the 2nd H.L.I. The Regiment retired into billets in the Hotel de Ville area of the by now familiar Mailly Maillet.

The fourth and final stage of the Somme Battles of 1916, the Battle of the Ancre, was about to open. Strictly speaking it lasted from November 13th-18th, although Edmonds' *Official History* included the 19th as well. During the four months following July 1st, we have seen how the Franco-British forces had gradually advanced south of the Rivers Somme and Ancre, albeit with a great loss of life. However, by November there had been minimal progress north of the Ancre, where the Germans had continued to improve their defences. The northern-most point of the British line was just to the north of Le Sars, almost touching a straight line drawn on the map between Thiepval and Bapaume. As early as September 24th, Sir Douglas Haig had contemplated a tank-assisted attack on Serre from the Hébuterne sector, combined with an attack north-eastward from the Beaumont Hamel valley. Five days later, on the 29th, Haig instructed General Hubert Gough's Reserve Army to draw up plans to attack from the Thiepval Ridge through Irles to Miraumont, and from the Hébuterne - Beaumont Hamel front in the direction of Puisieux. The aim was to meet the southern thrust towards Miraumont, cutting off the enemy in the upper valley of the Ancre. Meanwhile, General Henry Rawlinson's Fourth Army, still further south, would push on towards the Thilloy - Warlencourt valley. The original intention was to attack on October 12th and Haig considered that, given normal autumn weather, it should be possible for his armies to achieve these objectives. Unfortunately, the weather in October 1916 was exceedingly wet and British plans had to be drastically revised.

The wet weather of October made mere existence on the Somme extremely trying without contemplating further offensive operations. Constant rain and mist made observation from the air difficult, so that it was impossible to identify new German trenches for the artillery to bombard. In mid-October, General Hubert Gough, in command of the Reserve Army [called the Fifth Army from October 30th 1916], discussed his options with Lieutenant-General Launcelot Kiggell, Chief of the General Staff, and it was decided that the conditions of the ground required a more limited offensive. The operation order for the three corps making up the Reserve Army was issued on October 15th. The attack was to take place astride the Ancre with V Corps assisted by XIII to the north of the river and II Corps to the south of it. The aim was to take the spur running north from Courcelette and Miraumont up to Serre, with a subsequent advance to Pys and Irles. A successful offensive would eliminate the large enemy salient from Beaumont Hamel to Serre.

The bad weather of October had repeatedly delayed operations north of the Ancre. The water in the trenches was knee-deep on average and in some parts it came up to a man's waist. The ground was pock-marked with shell holes, which were full of water. The constant traffic up and down the communication trenches had turned them into a quagmire. In 1917, Passchendaele would become infamous for its mud, but men who fought there as well as around the Ancre valley in October-November 1916, felt that the chalky mud of the latter was the more pernicious of the two.

The weather of early November was somewhat better and General Hubert Gough[461], commander of the newly named Fifth Army, was determined to start his attack on both sides of the Ancre. In a limited operation he hoped to take the head of the German salient between the Albert-Bapaume road and Serre and, if all went well, move into open country towards Irles and Pys. In effect this was a modification of the offensive first ordered on October 15th. No great changes to the plan of attack and the barrage schedule were necessary. On Friday November 10th, there was still some difference of opinion as to whether the ground was fit enough to launch an offensive or not. There had been no rain for two days and colder weather had set in. Having consulted his subordinate commanders widely, Gough made his decision to attack on Monday, November 13th, and zero hour would be at 5.45 a.m., an hour and a half before sunrise. Despite a full moon on the 9th, a night attack had been considered and then ruled out. Early on the 12th, Sir Douglas Haig, the Commander-in-Chief, sent word that he did not wish 'to bring on a battle in unfavourable conditions'. Gough took the view that the attack must go ahead as planned or he should withdraw his troops and rest them. In the afternoon of the 12th, Haig arrived in person, and with the preliminary bombardment already in progress, he reiterated that he did not want to risk too much. Haig was reassured and left Gough to carry on with his attack as arranged.

The commander of the V Corps during the Battle of the Ancre was Lieutenant-General Edward Fanshawe, a brother of the former Commanding Officer of the 52nd, Major-General Robert Fanshawe[462]. V Corps was to deliver the main attack, and Fanshawe had positioned his divisions from Serre in the

---

[461] General Sir Hubert Gough [1870-1963] or 'Goughie' was very much a Haig protégé. His rise to prominence during the Great War was meteoric, from a brigade to an army command, aged 44 years, in less than two years. Perhaps uniquely he was the son, brother, nephew, and cousin of V.C.s. Optimistic, energetic, amusing, a thrusting general, who was probably more suited to mobile rather than static warfare. Unfairly, he was made the scapegoat for the collapse of the Fifth Army, in front of a German onslaught, in 1918. He was replaced by General Henry Rawlinson.

[462] Edward Fanshawe had replaced yet another brother, Lieutenant-General Hew Fanshawe, in command of V Corps, on July 5th 1916. Hew Fanshawe would be sacked for a second time when in command of the 58th Division in October 1917.

north to the Ancre in the south. The order of the Divisions, from north to south, was the 3rd, 2nd, 51st [Highland], and 63rd [Royal Naval]. As was recorded earlier, little progress had been made against the original German defences north of the Ancre. However, since July 1st there had been a nibbling away of the enemy's line in some places, so that the average width of no man's land was less than 250 yards. The assault had three stages. Stage one's objectives were; from Beaucourt station, on the Ancre; up the Beaumont Hamel valley and to the eastern side of the village; across the Redan Ridge; to the slope in front of Serre. Three to four trench lines had to be taken, this representing an average advance of some 800 yards. The stage two objectives were; from the western edge of Beaucourt; along the eastern side of the Redan Ridge; crossing the valley south of Serre; then bending forward around the eastern side of the village of Serre. From here a defensive flank was to be thrown back westward, where XIII Corps would give them further protection to the flank. The third and final stage's objectives were; Beaucourt; with the left thrown back up the western slope of the valley leading to Puisieux. South of the Ancre, II Corps was to clear the enemy from between the Schwaben Redoubt and St. Pierre Divion, and end up with a line facing north-east abreast the village of Beaucourt. The river crossings at Beaucourt station and mill had also to be secured.

To have any chance of making a significant advance north of the Ancre, there would have to be an effective artillery barrage. General Hubert Gough was able to bring into play a proportionately greater weight of metal than had been used on July 1st. V Corps with its divisional field artillery had; 18 pounders, 364; 4.5 inch howitzers, 108. In addition, the heavy and siege artillery, in eight groups added; 15 inch howitzers, 2; 12 inch howitzer, 1; 9.2 inch howitzers, 28; 8 inch howitzers, 16; 6 inch howitzers, 56; 6 inch guns, 4; 60 pounders, 46; 4.7 inch guns, 8. Similar numbers of artillery pieces were available to II Corps south of the river. V Corps had a field gun or howitzer every 13.5 yards and a heavy gun or howitzer every 31 yards. On July 1st the distances had been 21 and 57 yards respectively.

At 5 a.m. on November 11th, the special bombardment preliminary to the attack commenced. V Corps' artillery bombardment had been planned to lull the Germans into a false sense of security with an intense barrage by the heavy artillery, starting about 30 minutes before dawn, when the night firing programme was completed. The barrage lasted for the best part of an hour and finished with intense fire in which the field artillery joined. On November 13th, it was hoped that the enemy would be so conditioned to this crescendo of fire, that they would not anticipate the assault, at 5.45 a.m., the onset of which was signalled by the sudden intensification of the fire. This attempt at subterfuge was somewhat of a

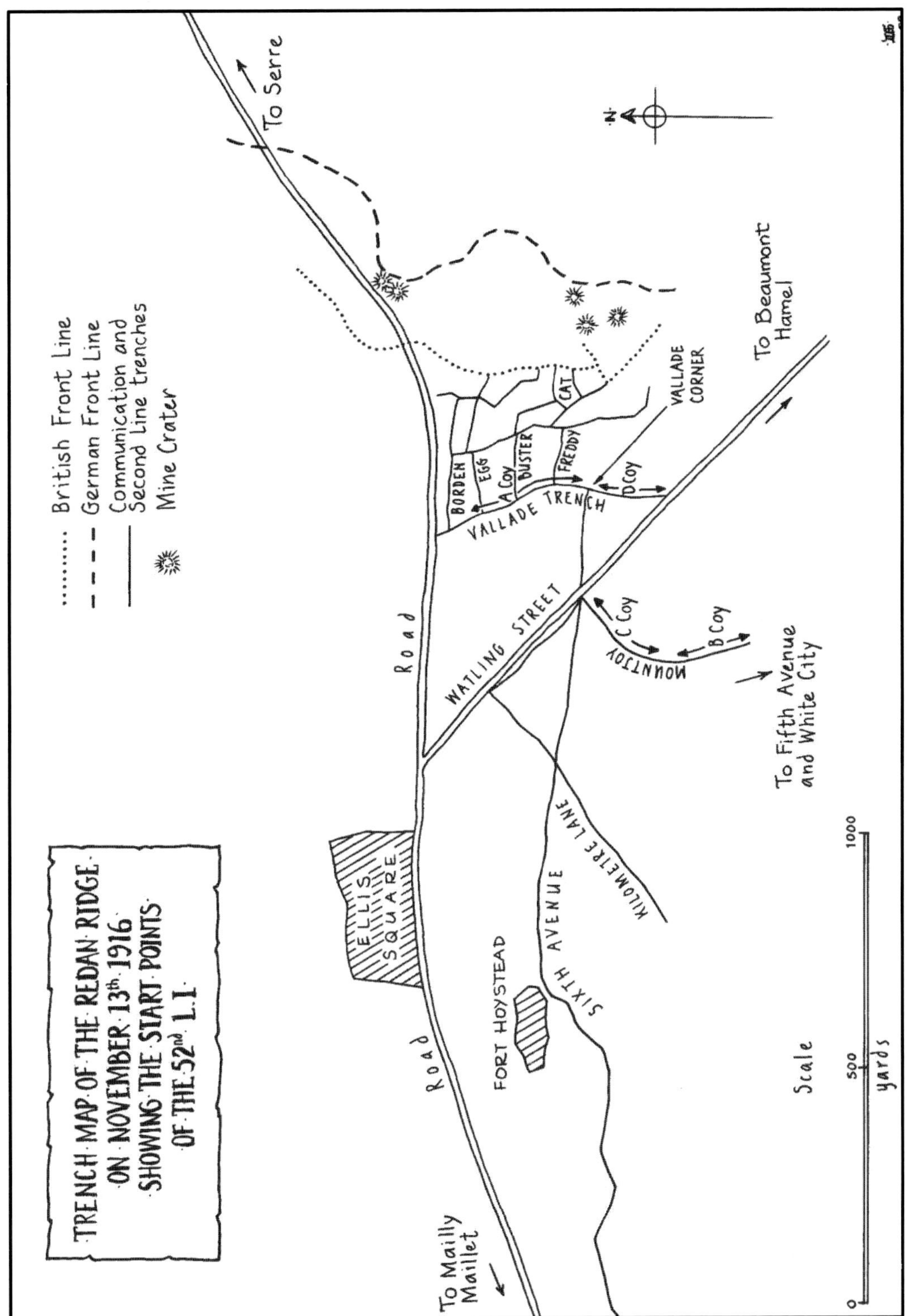
TRENCH MAP OF THE REDAN RIDGE ON NOVEMBER 13th 1916 SHOWING THE START POINTS OF THE 52nd L.I.
British Front Line
German Front Line
Communication and Second Line trenches
Mine Crater
To Serre
N
To Beaumont Hamel
VALLADE CORNER
CAT
FREDDY
BUSTER
EGG
BORDEN
A Coy
D Coy
VALLADE TRENCH
WATLING STREET
C Coy
B Coy
MOUNTJOY
To Fifth Avenue and White City
Road
Road
ELLIS SQUARE
KILOMETRE LANE
SIXTH AVENUE
FORT HOYSTEAD
To Mailly Maillet
Scale
0
500
1000
yards

failure as Crown Prince Rupprecht, commanding a group of armies had on October 28th, correctly anticipated the scheme.

At the opening of the attack, on November 13th, whilst the barrage concentrated on the German front line trenches, 25 per cent of the 18-pounders were to fire 50 yards short into no man's land to protect the advance of the British infantry. Unfortunately nobody informed the infantry of this fact and a number of men were caught in the British artillery fire. Six minutes after zero hour, at 5.45 a.m., the barrage would creep at a rate of 100 yards every five minutes with a pause beyond the reserve line of the enemy's front system. Originally, it had been arranged for the barrage to creep every four minutes, and a request from the general commanding the 3rd Division[463] asked for a 10 minute per 100 yards rate of lift. This was deemed to be inadequate although it would be used with success in 1917. The infantry were expected to be on their first objective in 56 minutes, and it was anticipated that they would move on the second objective an hour later. The creeping barrage, following five minutes of silence, would reopen with a rapid rate of fire as the signal to start the renewed assault. A consolidating barrage would also be put down 150 yards east of the Yellow Line [Frankfort Trench], to stop the enemy bringing up reinforcements.

We left the 52nd in their billets in Mailly Maillet on November 11th, "X" day. At 10 a.m., on the following day, November 12th, "Y" day, Major-General William Walker V.C., commanding the 2nd Division, met all the battalions' commanding officers at the 5th Brigade Headquarters to give them their final instructions. The 52nd spent the remainder of the day issuing stores and in general preparation for the coming action. One hundred and seventy rounds of small arms ammunition was to be carried on each man. The sites of the water dumps were noted. This may seem ironic as there was water everywhere, but of course the water in the sodden ground was potentially contaminated. A hot meal was served to all ranks at 7 p.m., the last hot food they would have for several days. A rum ration was distributed from brown jars with SRD printed on their sides. This stood for Special Rations Department, but the troops cynically claimed that it stood for 'Seldom Reaches Destination'. Rum blunted the men's fear before an attack. Stretcher bearers were to be at the Regimental Aid Post, which was the first organized point at which casualties could be treated.

The 52nd were due to leave Mailly Maillet for the trenches at 11.15 p.m., in the order A, D, C, B Companies. Two hours before he was due to leave the village, Serjeant-Major Fred Clare, of D Company, was one of the experienced men ordered to stay behind. They would provide a cadre to train the replacements following the inevitable casualties of the coming battle. Clare watched his

---

[463] Major-General C.J. Deverell.

Company move off and reported that his Company Commander, Ralph Kite was in the best of spirits as was everyone else. The Regiment was expecting to enter the long communication trench, 6th Avenue, for the front line, by a new entrance. It is not certain whether the 52nd used 6th Avenue on this occasion, as most units advanced across in the open, in view of the muddy state of the trenches. They were hidden from the enemy by a thick mist. In fact the 52nd left their billets a little early and were clear of Mailly Maillet by 10.15 p.m. They took up their assembly positions in the Redan trenches as follows. A Company in Vallade Trench, north of 6th Avenue; D Company in Vallade Trench, south of the communication trench 6th Avenue; C Company in the north end of Mountjoy Trench; B Company southwards towards White City. Mountjoy Trench lay to the west and approximately parallel to Vallade Trench. The 5th Brigade Headquarters had moved to their advanced position at White City, and it would remain here until the early hours of November 16th.

All these positions were occupied without difficulty, as the night was quiet and a thick mist had gradually come down. The men were enthusiastic about the coming operation, although the night before they had been disappointed to hear that the formidable new weapon, the tank, would not now be used. Tanks had been used for the first time, in the preceding September, at Flers, and had terrified the Germans, and boosted the morale of the British troops. However, the ground on the Redan Ridge was too waterlogged for tanks to be used, and waves were seen to flow along one enemy front line trench when shells fell into it. At 2 a.m., the *5th Brigade's War Diary* recorded; 'situation quiet – a large black retriever dog was captured. The dog had often been seen previously and is suspected of being a message carrier'. Both sides used animals to carry messages, although history does not record whether this was so in this instance. In fact it was not until September 1917 that the Germans were definitely shown to be using dogs to carry messages.

Around 3.45 a.m. on November 13th, "Zero" day, the code word 'Smith', indicating that the men were in position, came through to the Headquarters of the 2nd Division from all around the front. Major-General William Walker V.C. now knew that the assault of the German line could go ahead on schedule. November 13th was an auspicious day in the annals of the 52nd Light Infantry, as it was the anniversary of the birth, in 1761, of the greatest Colonel of the Regiment in their history, Sir John Moore of Peninsular War fame. There can be little doubt that Richard Crosse reminded his men of this fact before sending them into battle.

Although he had been dead for more than a century, Moore was still an inspiration to his regimental descendants[464].

On the 5th Brigade front, the 24th Royal Fusiliers on the left, and the 2nd H.L.I. on the right, were in the front line. Behind them, in the support trenches previously described, were the 52nd on the left and the 17th Royal Fusiliers on the right. To the north was the 3rd Division opposite Serre, with the 6th Brigade on the immediate left of the 5th Brigade. To the south were troops of the 51st [Highland], and 63rd [Royal Naval] Divisions facing Beaumont Hamel. At "Z" or "Zero hour", 5.45 a.m., the 24th R.F. and the 2nd H.L.I. were to assault the enemy's front system as far as Beaumont Trench, the Green Line [see trench map inside rear cover]. The 52nd and the 17th R.F. were to follow in support, and ultimately to pass through them and to attack the German trench system, still further to the east, up to Frankfort Trench or the Yellow Line. The Yellow Line in the area of operations of the 5th Brigade was Frankfort Trench. However, in the north it joined Munich Trench, close to Serre, and then circled that village to the east. In the south the Yellow Line joined Beaucourt Trench and then the village of that name. Under the curtailed plan, with its limited objectives, only in the southern sector was the V Corps to go beyond the Yellow Line to take Beaucourt. Frankfort Trench lay about 200 yards to the west of the Serre to Beaucourt road. A similar distance away, also to the west of Frankfort Trench, lay the inhospitable Munich Trench with its many dug-outs.

Facing the 5th and 6th Brigades of the 2nd Division were the tough and experienced men of the German 12th Division[465]. They were recruited from the mining and industrial areas of Upper Silesia and in the Battle of the Ancre they would fight well. On July 1st 1916, the 12th Division received the entire weight of the British attack, in the sectors Contalmaison to Hardecourt, and suffered losses of 61.5 per cent. Twelve days later, on July 12th, the Division was relieved and reorganized near Cambrai. The reorganization did not take long as, on the 20th, it was back to the Somme to the north-east of Pozières, and again suffered heavy losses. Finally, on August 9th, the 12th Division was relieved again, and retired to a quiet sector of the line south of Arras. From October 25th to November 19th, it played its part in the Battle of the Ancre, to the north of the river in the Beaumont Hamel sector. On November 13th, the 12th Division's 23rd Regiment, with its I and III Battalions, was facing the British 5th and 6th Brigades.

---

[464] In the 1950s, one former officer of the amalgamated 43rd and 52nd Light Infantry recalled that Moore was still an inspiration: 'with his portrait at the end of the mess glaring when we drank too much!'

[465] Between St. Pierre Divion and Serre were the 95th Regiment [38th Division, from the Thuringian States], 23rd, 62nd, 63rd Regiments [12th Division] and the 169th Regiment [52nd Division, from the Grand Duchy of Baden]. Each Regiment consisted of three battalions.

At 5.45 a.m., the British artillery bombardment increased its barrage with a greater weight of metal and a cacophony of sound. The men of the 24th R.F. and the 2nd H.L.I.[466], who had been lying out in no man's land since 4 a.m., moved forward up the slight incline through thick mud towards the German line, following closely behind the creeping barrage. They walked in half company, single file columns, in four waves, 100 yards apart, and with at least three paces between each man. The 52nd and 17th R.F. moved into the front line trenches as they were vacated, and followed their own officers across no man's land behind the leading British troops, in the same manner as before. Getting out of the trench was no mean feat as they were very deep and ladders were required. The thick mist reduced visibility down to 30 yards, which made it difficult to advance in the correct direction. The enemy's retaliatory artillery fire did not start until the troops were well into no man's land and was never heavy. Each man of the 5th Brigade, including the 52nd, had a red identification patch sewn on to his haversack to allow recognition from the air. A mine was fired, in no man's land opposite Cat Street, at 5.45 a.m. The crater was connected to the Cat Street Tunnel and eventually to the German front line trenches.

The 24th R.F., ahead of the 52nd, followed within 20 yards of the barrage, at a walking pace, and entered the German front line trench six minutes after the start of the attack. The enemy's wire was completely destroyed and the surprised Germans appeared from their dug-outs and surrendered without a fight. Much the same happened on the 24th R.F.'s right, where the 2nd H.L.I. advanced with élan behind a piper, with many of the men playing martial music on mouth organs. Recalling the unfortunate experience of some battalions on July 1st, the 2nd H.L.I. clearly did not trust the barrage to destroy the enemy's wire. Prudently, on the night before the attack, they sent out officers' patrols with Bangalore torpedoes[467] to blow up the wire for themselves. Both battalions were soon across the German second line, the Violet Line. The 2nd H.L.I. took 207 unwounded prisoners, two trench mortars, and a great deal of war material. However, they had suffered casualties of 14 officers and 255 other ranks in the action.

The 52nd advanced in four waves with Captain Nick Hill's A Company, and Captain Ralph Kite's D Company, on a two-platoon front, as the first two waves. The third wave consisted of Captain John Littledale's C Company and Captain Vivian Fanning's B Company, with two machine-guns, made up the fourth wave. We know that D Company went forward in the standard half-company wave, in single file, with the subalterns in the lead and Kite, the company commander, in the rear with his servant. It is likely that the other

[466] The 2nd H.L.I. had dug 'assembly trenches' one to two feet deep while they waited in the open.
[467] Cylinders full of explosive.

companies were organized in a similar fashion. Lieutenant-Colonel Richard Crosse, in a joint Headquarters with the 24th R.F.[468], watched his men go forward into the mist and, at least on the 5th Brigade's front, the beginning of the attack appeared to be progressing well. He had calculated that the average age of his officers going into action, excluding the Medical Officer at 35 years and himself at 28 years, was barely 21.

According to Richard Crosse, as far as Beaumont Trench, the Green Line, there was minimal opposition and the enemy appeared to be in a shocked state as a result of the British barrage. However, the *Official History* recorded that the 24th R.F. and the 2nd H.L.I., suffered considerable casualties from snipers and machine-gun fire between the German front line and Beaumont Trench[469]. Perhaps Crosse was mistaken or solely describing the experience of the 52nd. In the event, Beaumont Trench was soon taken by the 24th R.F. and 2nd H.L.I., and the position consolidated by these two battalions, the 52nd and the 17th R.F. The subsequent defence of Beaumont Trench was made more difficult by the fact that it was shallow and had no fire step or dug-outs. Over the next 24 hours a firestep was made facing east.

By 6.15 a.m., a mixture of the 24th R.F. and the 52nd held the Green Line from Crater Lane to a point about 70 yards south of Lager Alley. To their right were the men of the 2nd H.L.I. and the 17th R.F., and the first four lines of the enemy's trenches were being 'cleaned up'. The 24th R.F. established a strong point at the junction of Crater Lane and Serre Trench, and a major block of the original German front line, just south of K.35.c.24, to protect their open flank. The failure of most of the 6th Brigade to take their objectives had left the left flank of the 5th Brigade open to counter-attack. This particular block was very important as a number of Germans were still active in the Quadrilateral, and would remain so until the 15th, despite bombing attacks against them. The 52nd and the 24th R.F. were obliged to put further blocks on all trenches running to the north, and also to repel bombing attacks from this quarter. Also, to the south, further enemy bombing attacks, in the original German front line, were dealt with by four Stokes mortars. At 7.40 a.m., a platoon of the 10th Duke of Cornwall's Light Infantry had tried to connect the Cat Tunnel to the original German front line, but was hampered by machine-gun fire from the Quadrilateral. The Divisional Pioneers, the 10th D.C.L.I. and the 226th Field Company Royal

---

[468] The joint Regimental Headquarters with the 24th Royal Fusiliers was in Buster Trench. Crosse watched his men go forward from Chatham Trench at its junction with Buster Trench.

[469] Brigadier-General R.O. Kellett, in temporary command of the 2nd Division, reported on November 28th to V Corps that 'the two leading battalions (24th R.F. and 2nd H.L.I.) of this brigade appear to have reached the GREEN line according to programme but suffered considerable losses on the way'.

Engineers, also did excellent work in constructing strong points to protect the 5th Brigade's exposed left flank.

Now that the Green Line was in British hands, the 52nd's and 17th R.F.'s next goal was the seizure of Frankfort Trench, the Yellow Line, which ran up the hill from the north-eastern edge of Beaumont Hamel. At this juncture, there was no contact on the right with the 51st Division, who did not take the village of Beaumont Hamel until the afternoon. Around 7.30 a.m., about 120 men of the 52nd and the 17th R.F., plus a few members of the 13th Essex and 1st King's of the 6th Brigade, pushed on towards the Yellow Line, and met very considerable German resistance which had been less formidable west of the Green Line. The remnants of the German I Battalion of the 23rd Regiment reported that they had had difficulty in withdrawing to Munich and Frankfort Trenches. At 9 a.m., an officer of the 17th R.F. reported that there was heavy fighting in Munich Trench, and one company was held up by wire. By now the companies of the 52nd were mixed up. The advance should have taken them in an easterly direction across Wagon Road, into Munich Trench, and finally 200 yards further on, to their goal, Frankfort Trench.

The early morning mist had reduced visibility to 30 yards and compasses, carried by all officers and N.C.O.s, had to be used to keep direction. In the heat of the moment or in a maze of trenches this was not sufficient. At 5 a.m., on the 13th, the 2nd Division's *War Diary* described the weather, 'Fine: thick fog'. It was not surprising that their leading elements went too far to the north and found themselves assaulting Lager Alley, a communication trench, which ran west to east between Beaumont and Frankfort Trenches. In essence the 52nd had advanced at right angles[470] to the direction that was intended and had thought that Lager Alley was Frankfort Trench. Fortunately, their leader, Captain Nick Hill corrected their mistake and moved his men back towards the Yellow Line again. Hill remained at duty, although he was suffering from an injured foot, having accidently jumped on to a bayonet in the assault of Lager Alley.

The false move into Lager Alley was notified to 5th Brigade at 11.15 a.m. Eventually, on reaching Frankfort Trench, the men of the 52nd could not find any other British troops in the vicinity. Although, elements of the 17th R.F. had entered the trench to their right, the two parties did not meet. Neither of these small groups could withstand the German bombers and snipers, and both were forced to withdraw towards the Green Line, under cover of their Lewis guns and bombs. First they reached Munich Trench, then on the right, Wagon Road and

[470] The *Battalion War Diary* stated 'parallel to the real and correct line of advance'. By studying trench maps of the Redan Ridge, the error appeared to more of a 'right angled' course than a 'parallel' one.

Crater Lane, and on the left Beaumont Trench, the Green Line itself. On the left, Lager Alley became the defensive flank. At one point the forward party of the 52nd was virtually surrounded by the enemy. A counter-attack by two companies of the II Battalion of the German 23rd Regiment repulsed the British near the junction of Munich Trench and Lager Alley. No further troops were available for another counter-attack. Accounts of the British retirement from Frankfort Trench to the Green Line are not clear with their timings. However, by 9.30 a.m., it was reported that the 5th Infantry Brigade had passed 420 prisoners-of-war back to the cages.

During the advance to Frankfort Trench and their retirement from it, the men of the 52nd were involved in heavy hand-to-hand fighting in Munich Trench as well as Lager Alley. Many of their rifles were caked in mud and could not be fired. However, their attached bayonets were put to good use. An officer saw one soldier, Private E. Doulin throw 21 bombs in succession down the steps of a German Regimental Command Post in Munich Trench. This was typical of the work done to winkle the Germans out of their dug-outs. Having knocked the Command Post out, Doulin then carried a wounded officer to safety before returning with a fresh supply of bombs. Quite correctly, Doulin would receive the Military Medal [M.M.] for his exemplary actions.

Captain John Littledale, the C Company Commander, accompanied by Private Ernest Hawkes, attacked a dug-out containing nineteen Germans by firing his revolver into it. He ordered them to come out and surrender, which they did. Littledale was then wounded in the thigh by a shell and Hawkes[471] carried him down into the dug-out, dressed his wounds and looked after him for the next two days. The same shell rendered Company Serjeant-Major William Richardson unconscious, but on recovering, he carried on as if nothing had happened. Richardson reformed his company when they became mixed with the wave in front, and conducted its further advance. Littledale's luck ran out when he was wounded, on November 16th, for the second time. This time it was a gunshot wound to his neck which would put him out of the war for over a year. Richardson received the Distinguished Conduct Medal [D.C.M.][472] and Hawkes the M.M. for their actions.

Serjeant Cecil Bailey was the first man into Munich Trench when it was assaulted. When a withdrawal from Frankfort Trench and then Munich Trench

---

[471] Ernest Hawkes died of his wounds, aged 26 years, on November 26th 1916. He was a native of Redditch.

[472] William Richardson died of wounds on May 11th 1918, aged 30 years. His younger brother, Corporal Frederick Richardson, aged 23 years, had already been killed in action on July 30th 1916. They were both natives of Brighton and had been serving with the 52nd since the outbreak of the war.

Site of Waterlot Farm near Longueval.
September 1916.
[Imperial War Museum Q4261]

Wrecked waggons at Guillemont Station.
September 1916.
[Imperial War Museum Q1170]

ck Hardcastle: a slim man of reat promise who was killed action leading his company n the attack on Guillemont Station on July 30th 1916.
[Regimental Chronicles]

Initial grave marker for Jack Hardcastle and his men who were killed on July 30th 1916.
Now in Broughton Poggs Church.
[Author's Collection 2002]

T.G.C. Caulfield-Stoker who received a gunshot wound of the right forearm attacking Guillemont Station on July 30th 1916.
[Norfolk Record Office NRO NEV 7/32]

Morris Fielding M.C. who was wounded in the eye by a gunshot on July 30th 1916.
[St. Aidan's Church, Longueville, N.S.W., Australia]

View of the sites of Waterlot Farm and Guillemont Station from Ginchy. The arrow shows the direction of the 52nd's July 30th 1916 attack on Guillemont Station.
[Author's Collection 2002]

Ralph Kite M.C. was mortally wounded by a British shell shard at the Battle of the Ancre on November 13th 1916. He died after great suffering on December 10th 1916.
[Author's Collection]

British shell shard weighing nearly half a pound which mortally wounded Ralph Kite on the Redan Ridge.
[Kite Collection]

Keith Peploe was wounded in the leg by a sniper's bullet whilst visiting a bombing post on the Redan Ridge on December 9th 1916. He rapidly died from exsanguination.
[Regimental Chronicles]

German colonel, major and adjutant captured near Beaumont Hamel on November 13th 1916.
[Imperial War Museum Q 4503]

German barbed wire entanglements in the region of Beaumont Hamel during October 1916.
[Imperial War Museum Q1547]

Hubert Rawson, son of an admiral, whose defective eyesight precluded him from joining the Navy. Killed in action on November 15th 1916 during the Battle of the Ancre.
[Regimental Chronicles]

Alfred Webster-Jones, a Hastings solicitor, was killed in action at the Battle of the Ancre on November 13th 1916.
[Regimental Chronicles]

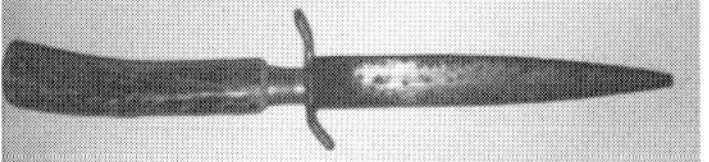

German trench knife captured by Ralph Kite.
[Kite Collection]

Theodore Ionides 'the Greek' was wounded in the arm and side at the Battle of the Ancre on November 13th 1916. He succumbed to his wounds on November 16th 1916.
[Regimental Chronicles]

John 'Bunjie' Littledale was wounded in the left thigh and neck at the Battle of the Ancre on November 13th and 16th 1916 respectively. He was killed in action near Vélu Wood on March 23rd 1918.
[Regimental Chronicles]

Nick Hill M.C. was highly intelligent, amusing and had the reputation of being a brilliant soldier. He was accidently wounded on November 13th 1916. On January 16th 1917 he was killed by a stray shell.
[NRO NEV 7/32]

Frederick 'Bolo' Lowndes M.C. was wounded in the right arm at the Battle of the Ancre on November 13th 1916. He was missing in a shell hole for 48 hours. On return to the British lines he consumed a large number of sardines.
[NRO NEV 7/32]

Bob FitzGerald, Dick Warren and Harry Vernon. Vernon received a gunshot wound of the scalp on November 13th 1916. He was wounded for a second time during the March retreat of 1918.
[NRO NEV 7/32]

Octavius 'Toby' Sturges was wounded in the right elbow at the Battle of the Ancre on November 13th 1916. He returned to the 52nd in 1918.
[Colvill Collection]

became necessary, he reformed his men and made a block at the command post. Despite being wounded himself, he held it to allow other wounded men to be taken back to the British lines. Bailey was captured and became a prisoner-of-war. Every surviving officer testified to his gallantry and to the great extent his example had affected the situation. Cecil Bailey was a highly intelligent, unambitious, unselfish man, and he too received the D.C.M. for his great bravery. Possibly, his actions were the most laudatory of many acts of valour by all ranks of the 52nd on November 13th 1916[473].

An intelligence report written by a member of the Royal Field Artillery gave valuable details about November 13th on the Redan Ridge[474]. He had spoken to some of the officers of the four battalions making up the 5th Brigade. Part of it reads as follows.

> Barrage: - Most of the Infantry Officers were pleased with our barrage. Some said that its irregularity had caused us no casualties and all stated that they were waiting just in front of the enemy front line at ZERO TIME and were in consequence caught by the 25% of our 18 pdrs which were firing short of the enemy front line. The barrage advanced too rapidly for the infantry who were held up by the mud which was, in places, quite impassable. The majority of our casualties were caused by our own R.A. The infantry had not been told that 25% of our guns would barrage 50 yards short of enemy front line.
> Wire. The Infantry had not [sic] trouble whatever with the enemy wire. It was laying around in large coils but there was hardly a strand that had not been cut. A considerable amount had been buried by the mud.
> Dugouts. The front line dugouts were nearly all blown in the 3rd and 4th support lines were mostly untouched. [sic].
> Prisoners. The enemy on the 5th Brigade front made little resistance. They were obviously taken by surprise as they left their dugouts in a semi-drowsy condition and mostly without arms and ammunition. They either retired rapidly into our barrage or surrendered. Boxes of

---

473 Although Cecil Bailey survived this war, he was to be killed in World War II, aged 44 years, on May 29th 1940, near Cassel, serving as a C.S.M. with the 4th Battalion Oxfordshire and Buckinghamshire Light Infantry. Shortly before his death he had dragged back to the British lines a wounded Lance-Corporal from under the noses of the Germans. He was a native of Henley-on-Thames.

474 Written on November 14th 1916. It is in WO 95 1294. The signature appended to it is not clear.

cigars or cigarettes were produced by prisoners after capture. The majority were very young although they were mixed with elder men. Casualties: - A number of casualties were caused by enemy snipers who had come out of dugouts to rear of GREEN LINE. The trench running from K35c6.0 to K35c4.2½ seemed to have been passed over by the infantry before the dugouts had been dealt with and in consequence the enemy had appeared in this trench with a machine gun and were active from 11 a.m. onwards.

The mud was a serious factor, at least 20 men were seen to be stuck fast, it was impossible to give them assistance owing to the bog. The enemy seemed to be very demoralized and shewed little fight.

We have seen how the units of Brigadier-General George Bullen-Smith's 5th Infantry Brigade had achieved a limited success by taking and consolidating positions in Beaumont Trench, the Green Line. However they had failed to hold Frankfort Trench, the Yellow Line, despite the fact that some men had entered it. Immediately, to their left, the 6th Brigade under Brigadier-General A.C. Daly, had fared still worse. The men of this brigade had advanced at 5.45 a.m., the same time as the 5th Brigade, closely following the creeping barrage into no man's land. The condition of the ground across which the 6th Brigade had to advance was even more treacherous for them than elsewhere, with some men sinking into the mud up to their waists. The mist was thick, the wire largely uncut, and the men floundering in deep mud could not see either the few gaps in the wire or firmer ground. The creeping barrage moved away, and then German machine-gunners in the vicinity of the untaken Quadrilateral opened fire. Some of the 13th Essex and the 1st King's, on the extreme right, reached the Green Line with the 5th Brigade, and helped protect its flank by making a block at the junction of Lager Alley and Beaumont Trench.

The 6th Brigade's units on the left, the 2nd South Staffordshire and the 17th Middlesex, in the fog, moved to the north-east, after running into units of the 3rd Division, supposedly on their left. Parties from all these units got into the German front line, but no further, with the uncut wire of the enemy's second line, the Violet Line, in front of them and, at the same time, being subjected to withering machine-gun fire. At 9 a.m., the remnants of the 6th Brigade were ordered to withdraw to the British front line. A further attack was considered but Brigadier-General A.C. Daly reported that his men were spent. The 2nd Division's reserve brigade, Brigadier-General R.O. Kellett's, 99th Brigade, was called upon instead, but the attack was cancelled in the afternoon.

The 99th Brigade had started to move forward at 7.30 a.m. and, an hour and half later, two companies of the 23rd R.F. were sent forward to support the 5th Brigade on the Green Line. Soon after 2 p.m., the 22nd R.F. was ordered to take up a position, in the captured trenches, facing north with its right on Beaumont Trench and the left facing the Quadrilateral. Such was the fear of the exposed flank of the 5th Brigade. It is possible that the reason for the Quadrilateral remaining in enemy hands for 48 hours, after the beginning of the attack, was because it was close to the junction of the two brigades, the 5th and the 6th, although the 6th Brigade had the primary responsibility for taking it. V Corps, at 3 p.m., gave orders for three battalions of the 99th Brigade to attack Munich Trench, but this was soon postponed until the following day, the 14th. At 5.35 p.m., an attack against the right of the 5th Brigade was reported, but did not materialize to any extent.

At night, on November 13th, on the front of the 5th Brigade, the 17th R.F. was holding an advanced position in Wagon Road and Crater Lane. The 2nd H.L.I., 24th R.F., and two companies of 23rd R.F. [detached from the 99th Brigade] were holding Beaumont Trench, the Green Line. The 2nd H.L.I. had by now made contact with the 51st Division on their right. Touch was first made on the German second line earlier in the day, but it was not until 7.35 p.m. that the 5th Brigade's and 51st Division's units were able to meet on the Green Line and Wagon Road. The 51st Division had taken the village of Beaumont Hamel during the afternoon. The 52nd plus a few men of the 1st King's and the 13th Essex of the 6th Brigade were in Lager Alley, forward of the Green Line, and in Serre Trench. From this position they were responsible for the left flank of the 5th Brigade. It is likely that some men of the 52nd were also in Beaumont Trench on the evening of the 13th. Later, at 3.20 p.m. on the 14th, the 5th Brigade had sent instructions for the 52nd and the 17th R.F. to hold the Green Line and the 24th R.F. to support them in the old German front line. Certainly a map in the 2nd Division's records shows this to be so for the 52nd on the following evening, the 14th. There is little doubt that the various units fighting on the Redan Ridge were thoroughly mixed up during the morning of the 13th.

The 52nd had suffered a considerable number of casualties on November 13th. Second-Lieutenant Alfred Webster-Jones, a 34-year-old Hastings solicitor in private life, was killed. He had been with the 52nd for less than a month. Second-Lieutenants Henry Davies, Ronald Creswell[475], and John Holland were all missing and later presumed to be dead. Holland was known to have been severely wounded. The wounded officers were: Captains Nick Hill [accidently wounded in the foot], John Littledale [gunshot wound left thigh and neck], Ralph Kite

[475] His body was found later and was buried in Munich Trench Cemetery.

[British shell shard right shoulder]; Second-Lieutenants Frederick Lowndes [gunshot wound right arm and trench feet], Octavius 'Toby' Sturges [gunshot wound right elbow], Harry Vernon [gunshot wound scalp] and Theodore Ionides [gunshot wound arm and right side]. Later, on November 14th, the 19-year-old commander of B Company, Lieutenant Vivian Fanning was killed in action, and on the 15th, Captain Hubert Rawson was also killed, whilst bringing up a carrying party[476]. In all during the period November 13th-17th, the 52nd suffered the following casualties; 13 officers and 235 other ranks, of whom 10 were killed, 149 wounded, and 76 were missing. The vast majority of the missing were in fact dead. The 2nd Division's losses from November 13th-16th were 129 officers and 2,767 other ranks, killed, wounded or missing.

Little is known of the circumstances of the deaths and wounding of the various officers. However, a description of the mortal wounding of Captain Ralph Kite has survived[477]. Kite was hit in the right shoulder by a piece of British shell in the vicinity of the Green Line. Kite found himself in a shell hole with Corporal Jack Ward of his own D Company. Ward had been hit in the hand by the same shell. Kite's only comment was; 'our own shell again, that's the second time!' Ward thought that Kite had been touched by a British shell on the Somme.

> A sniper had his eye on their shell hole and so Ward could not do much, but he set off and after a while and after searching round for some time discovered a trench full of unarmed German prisoners and English. He then went and brought Ralph in, carried him on his back and balanced him with Ralph's arm around his shoulder. On getting to the trench he got a stretcher and water and some brandy and a fresh bandage put on and then four German prisoners who were very plucky and worked hard, took the stretcher and they got on to the road. They got to a hospital in a house[478] where Ward was separated from Ralph who was operated on. Ward managed to smuggle Ralph's revolver past several police, but eventually had it taken from

---

[476] The 29-year-old Rawson was the son of Admiral Sir Harry Rawson, a Governor of New South Wales. In peace-time, defective eyesight kept him out of both the Navy and Army and he became a rubber planter.

[477] Account given by Lance-Serjeant Jack Ward to the Reverend Ben Ruck Keene, in March 1917. Kite was transferred in a French Ambulance train from No. 43 C.C.S. [Casualty Clearing Station] to Le Tréport and the British Red Cross Hospital No. 10 [Lady Murray's Hospital]. Here on December 10th 1916, he died of his wounds soon after the amputation of his arm. Recorded in *RBK A Very Parfit Gentil Knight* on page 126. Harry Vernon, who had been in the same house at Marlborough College as Kite, was in the No. 43 C.C.S. at the same time. It was situated at Warlencourt.

[478] The house was likely to have been Les Bieffes, Mailly Maillet. The cellar was used as a Dressing Station in 1916. It still stands and is now owned by the grand-daughter of its wartime occupants.

> him in the hospital. All the time Ralph never complained of his wound, only of being cld [sic] in his arm and leg. Ward covered him up in his greatcoat, Ward had a bullet from a sniper through the shoulder of his tunic whilst bringing Ralph in, but was not even scratched.

In the 52nd's *Battalion War Diary* and later, after the war, in his articles, Richard Crosse thought that Kite's mortal wounding was due to his getting too close to the British barrage. For example; 'stricken down by faithfully following only too closely behind our artillery barrage'[479]. The implication was that Kite was being a little foolhardy. However, this view does not stand closer inspection. The Fifth Army commander, General Hubert Gough, ordered 'the leading waves must always go as close up to the barrage as possible'. In a similar fashion the neighbouring 6th Brigade, the 24th R.F. and the 2nd H.LI. suffered a number of casualties from what is nowadays known as 'friendly fire'. It was essential to stay close to the barrage, so that as it crept forward, the enemy did not have an opportunity to get their bombs and machine-guns into play before they were overrun. Shells differed in their standard of manufacture and gun barrels lost a minute amount of rifling with each shot. In practice the barrage covered a belt of ground about 150 yards wide. Possibly, a key factor in the losses, illustrated by Kite, was the fact that 25 per cent of the 18-pounders were deliberately firing 50 yards short of the German front line without the ground troops having been informed of the fact.

Second-Lieutenant Theodore Ionides, 'the Greek', a D Company Platoon commander was fatally wounded on November 13th. His injuries to the right arm and side led to his death on November 16th. Lieutenant Robert Money Barnes described Ionides' last days[480].

> I am sending you a line just to tell you about the poor old Greek. He was brought to Corps Operating Station here about three days ago. There was no hope for him from the first, they said, he died the next day. I didn't see him at all as he was too bad. I hope the regt. had better luck than last time and that you are still alright. I feel such a shit to have been out of it for a second time.

---

479 *Regimental Journal* 12, 1936, page 179.

480 Letter from Lieutenant Robert Money Barnes to Captain Ralph Kite written on November 18th 1916. Barnes survived the war and went on to write books on military matters. *The Soldiers of London, Regiments and Uniforms of the British Army, The Uniforms and History of the Scottish Regiments* and *Military Uniforms of Britain and the Empire.*

At the end of November 13th, General Hubert Gough, commanding the Fifth Army, was reasonably satisfied with the partial success of the day. Early that morning, to the south of the Ancre, II Corps had taken St. Pierre Divion. North of the Ancre, the 63rd and 51st Divisions had also been successful, and Beaumont Hamel had fallen to the 51st Division during the afternoon. But to their left only the trenches in the vicinity of Beaumont Trench, the Green Line, had been taken and then held by the 5th Brigade. Even further to the north, the 6th Brigade and the 3rd Division, in front of the fortified village of Serre, had failed completely. Gough gave orders for V Corps to continue with their attack on the following day, the 14th. The 2nd and 51st Divisions were to renew the assault on Munich and Frankfort Trenches, and the 63rd [Royal Naval] Division was tasked with taking Beaucourt village.

The night of November 13th/14th was a cold one for the 52nd, in Lager Avenue and Serre Trench, and the next morning was slightly misty. Fortunately the mist cleared and air reconnaissance became possible once more. The heavy artillery had maintained a bombardment overnight and at 6 a.m. the fire became intense. At 6.20 a.m., units of the 2nd Division's 99th Brigade attacked Munich Trench. According to the records of the 2nd Division, the 52nd were sending as many men as could be spared to support this assault. Amongst much confusion the attack failed and the men fell back on Wagon Road. In the afternoon, units from the 112th Brigade [37th Division], who had been loaned to the 99th Brigade, were ordered to attack Frankfort Trench, in the belief that Munich Trench had already been taken. To their great surprise they were fired on from the supposedly captured trench, and retired in some confusion to Wagon Road, where they joined the unfortunate troops of the earlier attack in an embarrassing conglomeration of units. However, at least the 63rd [Royal Naval] Division had managed to capture Beaucourt by 10.30 a.m.

At about midnight, on the night of November 14th/15th, Lieutenant-Colonel Richard Crosse took his Regimental Headquarters across to the original German front line trenches[481]. However, that of the 24th R.F. remained in the British line. Crosse found 'in the captured trenches a remarkable combination of exuberance of spirits with physical exhaustion as few have been privileged to witness, whilst the arrangements for consolidation which were in progress under direction of youthful officers and junior N.C.O.s were as perfect as could be'. Amid the filth and disorder, the happiness of other days seemed to have returned

[481] At Q.5.a.5.7. in the German second line trench. If the 5th Brigade Headquarters had moved forward from White City, it would have moved to this site. In the event it did not move during the action.

when, in the early hours of November 15th, Second-Lieutenant Frederick 'Bolo' Lowndes, who had been reported missing, arrived at Regimental Headquarters wounded, after lying out in a shell hole for two days. Before being evacuated he gave a very clear and helpful account of the operation. As his Commanding Officer, Richard Crosse recorded: 'he was always remarkable for his good appetite and I never saw a man eat more sardines as he did, on his arrival with us on that misty November morning'. Lowndes would receive the Military Cross for his exploits on the Redan Ridge.

Operations were resumed on November 15th, when fresh units from the 51st Division attacked Frankfort Trench from New Munich Trench, some 500 yards ahead of the 2nd Division's troops in Beaumont Trench. The 2nd Division's 99th Brigade, using the remaining borrowed troops of the 112th Brigade, also attacked from their own position. Two tanks were to be used in the attack, but both got stuck in the mud, one before reaching the front line, the other in no man's land. The men of the 51st Division ran into their own barrage, and the troops of the 112th Brigade got lost in the morning mist. Needless to say, the attempt on Frankfort Trench had failed yet again. That morning, Lieutenant-General Launcelot Kiggell, Chief of the General Staff, had visited General Hubert Gough to inform him that Sir Douglas Haig disapproved of a renewed offensive. Later in the day, after discussions with his subordinate generals, who all felt there was a good chance of success, Haig sent Gough his blessing to continue with the offensive.

On the night of November 15th/16th, the lead troops of the 5th Brigade on the 13th, the 2nd H.L.I. and the 24th R.F., were withdrawn from the line to billets in Bertrancourt. At the same time the 52nd and the 17th R.F. moved back to the original British line, from Lager Alley, Serre Trench and Wagon Road, Crater Lane respectively. On the 17th, the 52nd and 17th R.F. retired to billets in Mailly Maillet, to recuperate from their exertions in battle.

Next morning, November 16th, a fine and cold one, Gough felt much less optimistic about the situation with Munich and Frankfort Trenches still untaken. Operations were to be principally left to II Corps, south of the Ancre. V Corps would be limited to supporting the left flank of this operation and again making an attempt on Frankfort Trench. To allow sufficient time to organize the attack, it was not planned to launch it until the early morning of November 18th. The weather on the 18th proved to be atrocious with sleet and the first snow of the winter. Although, over the next two days, II Corps made some gains to the south of the Ancre, to the north of the river, V Corps achieved little. Slight progress was made just to the north of the Ancre, and although units of the 32nd Division entered Frankfort and Munich Trenches, the by now familiar story of being unable to hold them was repeated. The Battle of the Ancre was closed down on November 19th. Beaumont Hamel, Beaucourt, and St. Pierre Divion had fallen to the British, but the Germans with great tenacity had held on to the Frankfort/Munich Trenches position on the Redan Ridge.

Quite properly a lengthy list of recommendations for gallantry awards was submitted on behalf of the 52nd for their part in the Battle of the Ancre. The eventual notification of the awards would take about two to three months. The M.C. was awarded to: Lieutenant Thomas Tyrwhitt-Drake; Second-Lieutenant [acting Captain] Nick Hill; Second-Lieutenants Morris Fielding[482] and Frederick Lowndes. The D.C.M. to: Company Serjeant-Major William Richardson and Serjeant Cecil Bailey. The M.M. to: Serjeants A. Boddington, E.J. Smith[483] and J.W. Wright[484]; Lance-Corporals W.J. Burford and J.Tilbury; Privates J. Bytheway, W. Cramp, E. Doulin, Ernest Hawkes, C. Norton, and J. Rogers.

At 8 a.m. on November 18th, 100 men of the 52nd turned out to evacuate casualties of the 99th Brigade from Lager Alley. Presumably they were chosen as they were familiar with the trench system in that vicinity. Later that day, the Regiment began a series of marches taking them away from the front line and eventually to a place for rest and training. The marches proceeded uneventfully. On the 18th, the 52nd marched to Bertrancourt; 19th[485], Amplier; 20th, Canaples; 21st, St. Ouen; 23rd, Le Ménage [Cramont]; 24th, Maison-Ponthieu; 25th, Canchy; 27th, Fontaine-sur-Maye. The last named, to the north-east of Abbeville, became the place of rest and training for the Regiment. In fact the whole of the 2nd Division had been taken out of the line and were based in the vicinity of Brailly. On the 26th, Lieutenant John Slade-Baker took over command of D Company from Second-Lieutenant Ronald Blackwell. D Company had lost its commander and several other officers on November 13th. The following day Blackwell took command of C Company. The 27th also saw an influx of officers from the Territorial Force reporting for duty. They were Second-Lieutenants H.E. Mann, J.J.G. Clarke, J.E. Ellis, Joseph Piperno, A.O.W. Kindell, and D.G. Rydings. Brigadier-General Archibald Eden, the former Commanding Officer of the 52nd until the summer of 1916, paid them a morale-boosting visit. Two days later, on the 29th, further officers and also the 65th reinforcement of one serjeant and 58

---

[482] Born at Paramatta, New South Wales in 1892 and won a scholarship to Merton College, Oxford in 1911. After the war he returned to Australia becoming the Rector, at Longueville, N.S.W. He died in 1972.

[483] He would win the D.C.M. and become the Regimental Serjeant-Major of the 52nd.

[484] Later he was commissioned into the Regiment and retired with the rank of Captain.

[485] Lieutenant R.E.A. 'Reggie' Webster is recorded as having received a gunshot wound of his left arm and back on this date.

men arrived. The officers were Second-Lieutenants W.G. Bacon, T.A. Coffin, J.N. Chapelle, and E.S. Fold.

The month of December was spent in billets at Fontaine-sur-Maye, and the standard forms of training ensued. On the 3rd, John Slade-Baker was off on his travels again with an attachment to the Headquarters of the 6th Infantry Brigade. Second-Lieutenant Geoffrey Lyle replaced him in command of D Company. Further reinforcements arrived; the 66th, of 87 men, on the 4th; the 67th, of 11 men, on the 7th; the 68th, of 113 men, on the 8th; the 69th, of one serjeant and 13 men, on the 12th; the 70th, of 10 men, on the 13th; the 71st, of 23 men, on the 17th; the 72nd, of 26 men, on the 26th.

The influx of new officers and men must have been difficult to assimilate into a battalion that had suffered so many recent battle casualties. Of course the quality of the new recruits was not as high as earlier in the war. However, a few officers with some experience returned to the 52nd. Lieutenant Clement Chevallier, on the 12th, and Second-Lieutenant Philip Booth returned to duty from hospital on the 25th. Booth had been suffering from bronchitis. Captain Rupert Brett took over command of C Company on the 14th, and Lieutenant Robert Money Barnes B Company on the 19th. That same day Second-Lieutenant D.G. Rydings transferred to England and the Machine-Gun Corps. The recently arrived Second-Lieutenants H.E. Mann and J.J.G. Clarke were reposted to the 13th Essex. Inexperienced Second-Lieutenants Edmond 'Jim' Neville and Harry Spurge came up from base on the 18th, and Christmas Day saw the arrival of Second-Lieutenant C.E. Cope for duty.

Jim Neville recorded some of his first memories of service with the 52nd and reflected on the coming active service[486].

> Christmas Eve! I am writing this in bed, in my small billet, most comfortable in every way. My window is open for it is a warm night. As in most French cottages, this room is mostly taken up by the bed. The room is about 6 foot by 6 foot and I can only lie at full length across the bed. The window looks on the inevitable manure heap. The inhabitants seem to recognize the muck heap as the family jewel, and that is why, I suppose they keep it so near to the house.
>
> There is very little news to tell you, I have been riding a lot since I came up. We all mount very queer steeds, some of them shaggy pack animals with very little life in them.
>
> As Harry Spurge and I were walking back from the glare of the mess lamps, plodding our way through the mud and slush, I said to

[486] Letter to his family written from Fontaine-sur-Maye on December 24th 1916.

him: "For all we are doing, we might be in England." He turned to me and pointed over to the right. I looked, and the sky and inky trees were lit up every other second by yellow flashes coming from far away. Flash, flash, flash; yet not a single sound to disturb the stillness of the night. And then, I seemed to realize, that probably, each one of those flashes might mean that some poor man, friend or foe, was being blown to bits. And there, over in the north-east, sitting in mud and water, are the men who have been fighting for us up till now; to them to-morrow means no more than to-day.

I know I have got to get through it, and all I pray is that I may stick it as well as the others before me.

On December 28th, the 5th Brigade Sports was held on the Noyelle Ground. The Regiment did creditably by winning the Boat Race and the Relay, and was second in the 'best turn out' both for the Heavy and Light Draught Pairs in Harness. The judge described Private Bunning's harness as the best he had seen all month. However, he was pipped to the prize by his limber. In the officers' scurry over four furlongs, the best Regimental performance was by John Slade-Baker who managed second place. Richard Crosse himself also rode in the race. The 52nd managed to win the Brigade Football Tournament. All in all the Regiment could be pleased with themselves.

The next day, the 28th, Second-Lieutenant J.D. Grover joined D Company. Second-Lieutenant Ronald Blackwell took over command of that Company again from Second-Lieutenant Geoffrey Lyle. The command of D Company was changing so frequently it was almost like musical chairs. On the last day of the year, the 2nd Division Sports was held on the Bois Grampus and Noyelle Grounds. Again the Regiment did well in winning the Light-weight Boxing with Private Smith; Best Turn-out, Limbered Wagon and Pair Light Draught Horses, Silver Cup, Private Bunning; The Pair Heavy Draught Horses was won by Private Weaving.

In the evening, the Deputy Chaplain-General, Bishop Llewellyn Gwynne, took a voluntary Evening Service, in a hut specially enlarged for the occasion, at the junction of Park Lane and Piccadilly[487]. The Bishop had travelled many miles to take the Service, and such was his popularity that everyone in the Regiment who could be fitted in attended. As he told his congregation, they were, 'the finest in the world – the British Expeditionary Force'. Later, through Lieutenant-Colonel Richard Crosse, he sent word to say, 'how pleased he was to see the Regiment again, and how much he would have liked to have gone all round the

[487] The main street of Fontaine-sur-Maye.

billets, as he used to do, to meet his old friends, some of whom he had recognized at the service'.

Nowadays it is possible to view and walk the 52nd's battlefield on the Redan Ridge. Coming off the D 919, the Mailly Maillet to Serre Road, is a track running to the old Frontier Lane and on to Beaumont Hamel. This is Watling Street and crosses the site of the old British trench systems from which the 52nd attacked on November 13th 1916. Standing on Watling Street and looking 350 yards to the east, up a gradual incline, can be seen two clumps of trees, which marks the sites of the Redan pits. These were mine craters in no man's land and are gradually being filled with the local community's rubbish. Nearby are two British cemeteries, Redan Ridge numbers one and three. Number one is in no man's land and has 154 graves from the July 1st and November 13th 1916 battles. Number three is inside the old German lines and has 67 graves. Number two cemetery is on the southern slopes of the ridge and has graves from both July 1st and November 13th.

Standing by the Redan pits and looking to the east, over gently undulating agricultural land, can be seen the sites of the trenches where the 52nd fought on November 13th-15th. This area of land is crossed north to south, by three roads or tracks. From west to east they are Frontier Lane at 400 yards, Wagon Road at 900 yards and the Serre to Beaucourt road at 1,500 yards. There are three British cemeteries in the area. They are Wagon Road, Munich Trench, and Frankfort Trench Cemeteries. Captains Vivian Fanning, Hubert Rawson and Second-Lieutenant Ronald Creswell lie in Munich Trench cemetery. To the north was Lager Alley, which the 52nd mistook for the Yellow Line in the mist.

So 1916 came to an end for the 52nd. The first part of the year had been spent in the relatively orderly arrangement of a system of trenches, before taking part in the rough and tumble of the Somme. The Regiment had given their utmost on July 30th, at Waterlot Farm, and had played a significant role in the partial success of November 13th, on the Redan Ridge, in the Battle of the Ancre[488], or as the 52nd called it, at Beaumont Hamel. 1917 would have new challenges for them.

[488] 44,000 British troops took part in the battle. This is greater than the number of British troops used either at the Battle of Waterloo, in 1815, or on the D-Day Normandy landings, in 1944.

Chapter XV

The Somme: Courcelette Sector and the Valley of Mud.

January 1st - March 31st 1917

[Maps: pages 315, 388, 390, 402, 409.]

Prior to their meeting at Chantilly, on November 15th 1916, the French Commander-in-Chief, General Joseph Joffre, and his opposite number, General Sir Douglas Haig, had already largely agreed the strategy to be employed in 1917. Joffre had proposed that the current lines of attack should be broadened, but he had no intention of selecting any new ones. Joffre suggested that the battle should be extended to the Oise in the south and to Arras in the north. The French would attack between the Oise and the Somme, and the British between Bapaume and Vimy. This would leave each ally with a front of about 25 miles, and an eight mile gap in the centre to be held defensively. In addition, Joffre would carry out two minor operations, one on the Aisne and the other in Alsace. The British agreed to extend their front to the south as far as Bouchavesnes. In December, an attempt to neutralize the U-Boat threat by breaking out from the Ypres sector, to clear the Belgium coast, in particular Ostend, was added to the original plan by the British. Joffre readily agreed to this proposal, suggesting a thrust towards Roulers - Thorout several weeks after the beginning of the main Allied offensive, with a follow up by the French along the actual coast. A naval attack on the coastal batteries, followed by a landing of troops was also envisaged.

Unfortunately, distasteful political manoeuvrings, in late 1916, led to the ridiculous position of Joffre being the French Commander-in-Chief with no powers of command. Wisely, on December 26th, he resolved this farcical situation by offering his resignation, which was duly accepted. The untimely fall of Joffre, with his imperturbability and common sense, was a great loss to the Allies. This was recognized by Haig who personally pointed out to Aristide Briand, the French Premier, the dangers of discarding such a man. Joffre was replaced by General Robert Nivelle, who leapfrogged more senior generals, Ferdinand Foch, Henri-Philippe Pétain, Franchet d'Espèrey and Noel de Castelnau. As in France, December saw a major change in those directing the war in Britain, with the replacement of Herbert Asquith as Prime Minister by the 'Welsh Wizard' David Lloyd George. Lloyd George's distrust if not frank contempt for the Chief of the Imperial General Staff, General William 'Wully' Robertson, and for Sir Douglas Haig complicated matters further. Lloyd George was an intriguer of the first order, and quite capable of taking the advice of Sir John French behind the back of his C.I.G.S. However, Lloyd George was much enamoured with General Robert Nivelle with his perfect English and his confidence that he had the solution to the stalemate in the trenches.

Robert Nivelle, a handsome artilleryman, was over 60-years-old with an English mother and consequently spoke the language fluently. He believed that with his 'new method' that he could rupture the German line in '24 hours' and then exploit the breakthrough. In essence this required an overwhelming artillery bombardment, followed by an unusually deep creeping barrage, and then the use of massive force to capture the enemy's whole system including his line of batteries. This 'mass of manoeuvre', was to be assembled close behind the front line, and ready to exploit the break-through. In late December, while Joffre was still nominally in charge, Nivelle outlined his plans to Haig. The enemy would be pinned down along the lines already agreed at Chantilly, by French forces between the Oise and the Somme, and by the British between Bapaume and Arras. The main assault would now come on the Aisne which had originally been seen as a subsidiary action. In order for French troops to be freed up for the 'attaque brusquée', the British would have to take over the trench line as far south as the Amiens - Roye road, a further 20 plus miles. Understandably, Haig was reluctant to occupy more trenches without additional forces from England, although it was eventually agreed that he would do so by early March. The British War Cabinet and Haig still considered that the operation to clear the Belgian coast, in 1917, was essential and looked to Nivelle to fulfil his verbal undertaking to use French troops to relieve men required for this northern offensive[489].

By 1917, Field-Marshal Paul von Hindenburg and General Erich von Ludendorff[490] had given up hope of obtaining victory on land, and intended to go on the defensive on the Western Front. At this juncture of the war, the only realistic means of a successful outcome was by unrestricted submarine warfare to starve the British into defeat. Unrestricted meant, sinking without warning, all ships, including neutral ones, in predetermined zones around Britain, France, Italy, and the Eastern Mediterranean. The danger to the Germans would be the probability that the United States of America would be drawn into the conflict on the side of the Allies. However, it was thought that six months all-out assault on merchant vessels, coming into British ports with food and war materials, would end the war before the enormous resources of the United States could come into

[489] On December 21st 1916, Nivelle wrote to Haig: 'if our attacks fail, it will still be possible to carry out in fine weather the operations projected in Flanders'.

[490] Paul von Hindenburg [1847-1934] and Erich von Ludendorff [1865-1937] were broadly in charge of the conduct of the war, after the fall of General Erich von Falkenhayn [1861-1922], as Chief of the General Staff, in 1916. Falkenhayn was removed by the Kaiser, in August 1916, after the failure of the German attacks at Verdun.

play. Unrestricted submarine warfare began on February 1st 1917, and on the 3rd, the German Ambassador to the United States was packing his bags and heading for home. In the event, the Royal Navy and the use of the convoy system for merchant vessels saved Britain from starvation. On April 6th, a formal proclamation declared that the United States and Germany were now at war. The threat posed by the vast resources of the United States proved to be, as we will see, a prime factor in the defeat of Germany in 1918.

At the end of the Battle of the Ancre, in November, the Germans still held much of the Ancre valley from Le Transloy to Grandcourt, and the first line of their defence lay along the lower northern slopes of the Thiepval Ridge. North of the Ancre, the enemy was still in possession of much of the spur above Beaumont Hamel. Beyond this the German front line ran past Serre, Gommecourt, and then north-east down the valley of the River Scarpe to the east of Arras. In addition to the fortified villages of the Ancre valley, the enemy had prepared a second line of defence along the forward crest of the ridge north of the Ancre valley. This consisted of a double line of trenches running north-west of Saillisel past Le Transloy to the Albert - Bapaume road, and then west close to Grevillers and Loupart Wood. Finally, it went past Achiet-le-Petit to Bucquoy. This strong defensive line became known as the Le Transloy - Loupart line. On the other side of the crest of the ridge, and parallel to it, was a third defensive system on the line of Rocquigny - Bapaume - Ablainzevelle. The first objective of General Douglas Haig [George V would promote him to the rank of Field-Marshal on December 27th 1916] in the Valley of the Ancre was to advance his trench line to within striking distance of the Le Transloy - Loupart line. These operations had actually been started on November 18th, but the inclement weather of the latter part of that month and, also in December, had brought operations to a virtual standstill. The New Year would see the offensive reopened with a view to taking the Le Transloy - Loupart line, as part of the greater scheme of things, in order to apply British pressure on the enemy between Bapaume and Arras.

We left the 2nd Division, including the 5th Infantry Brigade and the 52nd Light Infantry, undergoing rest and training to the north-east of Abbeville, in the vicinity of Brailly. The Division was to be transferred from the V Corps, under whose direction it had fought at the Battle of the Ancre, to II Corps [January 11th], commanded by General Claud Jacob[491], an Indian Army officer. The Regiment celebrated New Year's Day with a route march, and also inter-company football matches, played on a pitch that was half underwater. The newly arrived Second-Lieutenant Jim Neville got fearfully wet and muddy representing his company in

---

491 Sir Claud Jacob [1863-1948] in later life became a field-marshal [1926]. He commanded II Corps from May 28th 1916.

the football tournament, but managed to clean himself up with the aid of the Padre's bath. There was a torchlight procession down the main street of Fontaine-sur-Maye, known as Piccadilly, and the Divisional band played marches. A concert was held in a marquee, including a sketch taking off that comic genius Charlie Chaplin. Two Second-Lieutenants, M.S. 'Guillaume' Griffith-Williams and R.C. 'Dick' Warren joined the 52nd, having been reposted from the 6th Oxfordshire and Buckinghamshire on January 1st.

On January 2nd, Jim Neville rode over to the nearby battlefield of Crécy which had been fought over in 1346[492]. He was clearly impressed by it as he had visited before, on Christmas Day, and marvelled that over 500 years ago, a quarrel had been settled in a few hours, while the current conflict had already lasted two and a half years. On the 3rd, Captain Rupert Brett, the C Company commander, left the Regiment to return to England and the senior officers' course at Aldershot. It was obvious that this fine officer was destined for greater things than the command of a company. Other officer changes that day were: Lieutenant F.S. Parsons joined the Heavy Branch Machine-gun Corps [Tank Corps]. Lieutenant Ernest Whitfeld, the Adjutant, was temporarily seconded to the 5th Brigade. Richard Crosse used the recently decorated Lieutenant Thomas Tyrwhitt-Drake as the stand in for Whitfeld.

The 52nd left Fontaine-sur-Maye, at 9.30 a.m., on the 8th, and marched south-east to billets in Prouville. The trek took all day with several very cold halts on the way and only two men in B Company fell out during the march. The Regiment was on the move again the following day, this time to the east, and Gézaincourt, close to Doullens. The 10th was spent in their billets in Gézaincourt and then, on the 11th, the 52nd was on the move once more, this time to the south, to Talmas via Beauval. At 1 p.m., the following day, they marched a short distance to the east and Rubempré. Jim Neville rather enjoyed the ten or twelve miles marching that they were doing most days, and likened it to a walking tour, apart from the distant sounds of the guns. Every time the officers occupied a new mess the first thing that was brought out was the gramophone.

On January 13th, the 52nd paraded at 8.30 a.m. and 30 minutes later the first of the 41 black painted buses arrived to carry them to Wolf Huts, to the west of Pozières on the Albert - Bapaume road. Strictly speaking the huts were closer to Ovillers than Pozières and were just behind the old German second line. The final Company, B, was not 'embussed' until 2 p.m., for the journey which took them through Albert before reaching their destination at Wolf Huts. In Albert, the statue of the Virgin and Child, on top of the Basilica [church], was leaning over at

[492] On August 26th 1346, at the start of the 100 Years War, Edward III defeated the French, under Philip VI, at the Battle of Crécy. The fighting was over by midnight.

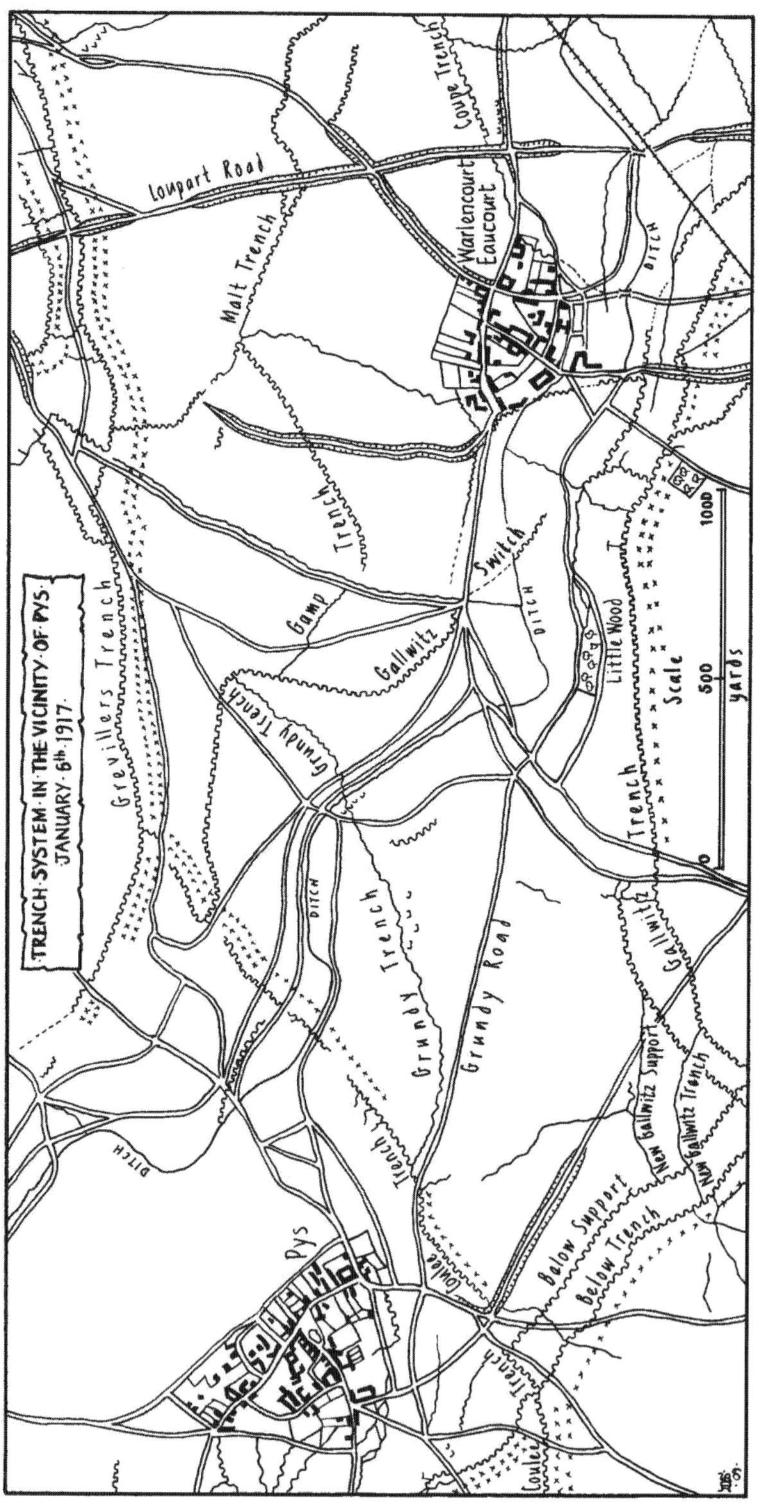
TRENCH·SYSTEM·IN·THE·VICINITY·OF·PYS·
JANUARY·6th·1917·
Loupart Road
Malt Trench
Coupe Trench
Warlencourt
Eaucourt
DITCH
Grevillers Trench
Gamp
Trench
Switch
Gallwitz
Grundy Trench
Little Wood
Trench
Scale
0
500
1000
yards
Grundy Trench
Grundy Road
Gallwitz
New Gallwitz Support
New Gallwitz Trench
Below Support
Below Trench
Pys
Coulee
Trench

a perilous angle, having been dislodged by a shell in 1915. The French believed that the war would end if the Virgin fell down. In 1918, when the British briefly lost Albert, they shot down the Virgin, but the war did not end. So much for the legend! It was getting dark by the time the final men of the 52nd reached Wolf Huts, which were situated just behind the old German front line of 1916. The linings of many of the huts had been stripped for fire-wood in what the locals described as the coldest winter for 30 years. Jim Neville spent a cold night in his sleeping bag and the next morning investigated his new surroundings. It was the first time in his life that he had seen a modern active battlefield[493].

> The whole place is simply torn up in a mass of shell-holes. I had a look at the German front line; there was practically nothing left of it; the communication trenches and parapets were blown to hell. The ground all round is littered with shell cases, bombs, grenades, and duds of every kind, and here and there a little wooden cross marks some poor chap's grave. There is one just outside the mess.
>
> As I was returning from my sight-seeing, I saw a boot sticking out of the ground. I kicked it and then saw a piece of khaki puttee attached. It gave me rather a nasty turn.
>
> You can see where little copses once stood by the presence of a few stumps and blasted tree trunks. A modern battlefield, though very interesting, is not very pleasant.
>
> Griffith-Williams and I made a tour of the battlefield. We found a few stumps of trees marking a copse of days gone by, a few ruins where a village once stood, a great many wooden crosses, and here and there an uncovered boot and leg protruding from the ground, a great many bits of shell, and much ammunition, both English and German. We also had a look at a derelict tank, which was very interesting. I tried to get inside, but my shoulders were too broad; and as the mud was over ankle-deep all round the brute, we came away. Next, we looked at the crater of the mine which was blown up on the German line on July 1st[494]. It took 10 months to make, and I am not surprised; and so far holds the record for the biggest exploded in this war. We reckoned that it was 120 feet across and nearly 80

[493] Firstly, a letter written to one of his sisters from Wolf Huts on January 14th 1917. Secondly, a letter to his father written on January 15th 1917.

[494] Lochnagar Crater, at La Boisselle, the largest mine crater on the Western Front. Since 1978 it has been privately owned by an Englishman, Richard Dunning.

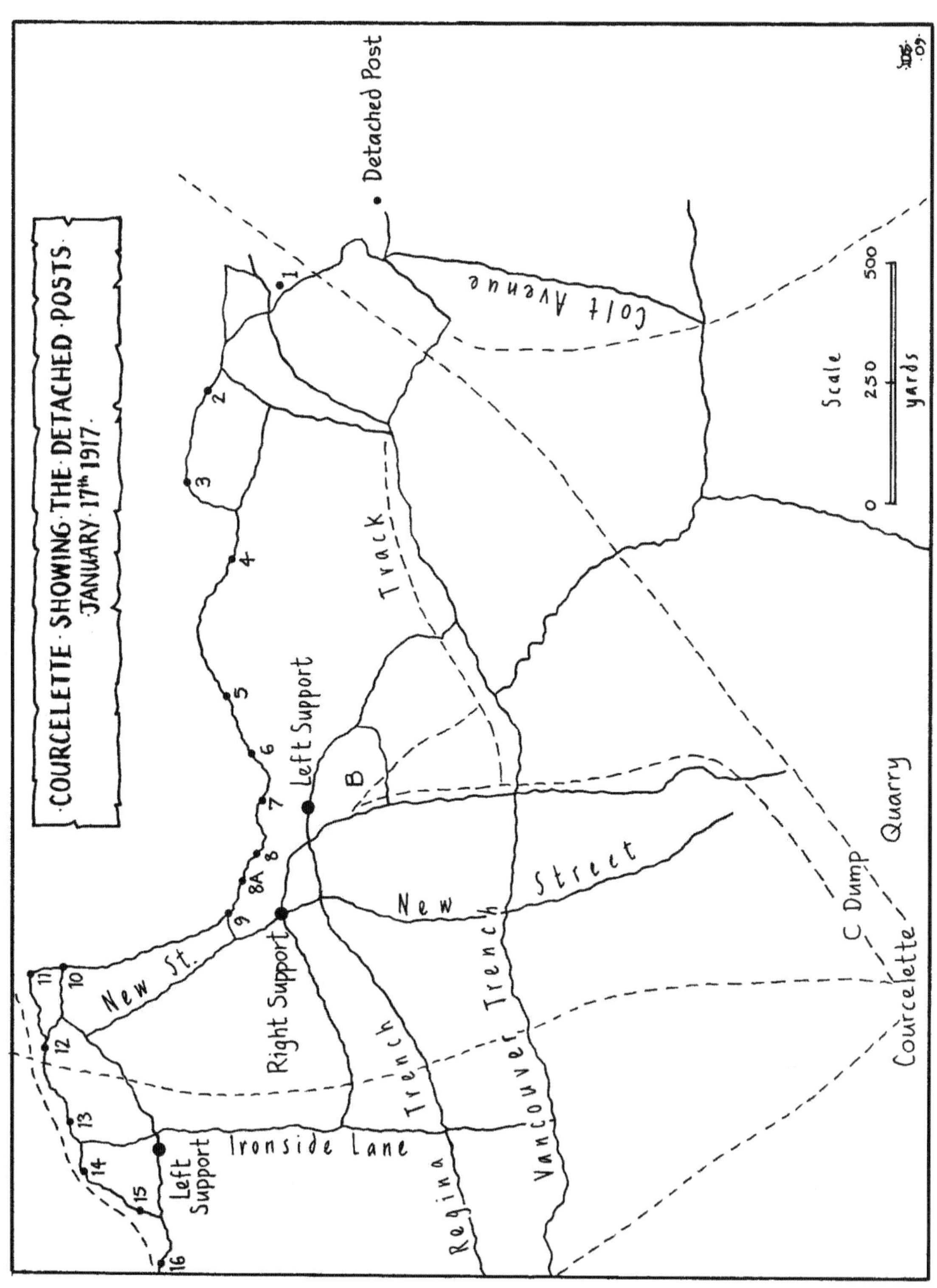
COURCELETTE · SHOWING · THE · DETACHED · POSTS ·
· JANUARY · 17th 1917 ·
Detached Post
Colt Avenue
Scale
0
250
500
yards
Track
Left Support
B
New Street
Quarry
C Dump
Courcelette
Vancouver Trench
Regina Trench
Ironside Lane
Left Support
Right Support
New St.
1
2
3
4
5
6
7
8
8A
9
10
11
12
13
14
15
16

> feet deep. Apparently, the mine was well below the German dug-outs. It is simply colossal.

The 52nd was acting as the support battalion of the 5th Brigade in the front of the 2nd Division, to the north-west of Courcelette [to the left of the Albert - Bapaume road]. The frontage was 2,500 yards, and the right of the British line was about 1,000 yards west of Le Sars, and the left a mile south of Miraumont, Pys was 1,200 yards north of the centre of the line. In fact, there was no continuous front line, the wire was inadequate, and the total number of posts was some seventeen in number[495]. No man's land was irregular in width, being broad in the centre, south of Pys, and much narrower on the right and left of the Divisional front. The only communication trench, Ironside Avenue, was in a shocking state, and for the most part impassable. Brushwood tracks to the line of posts were also in a poor state of repair and could only be used at night. The 5th Brigade had started relieving the 154th Brigade of the 51st [Highland] Division on January 12th. On the 15th, the 73rd reinforcement of 26 men arrived and, the following day, at 5 p.m., the 52nd began relieving the 24th Royal Fusiliers as the right battalion of the 5th Brigade in the 2nd Divisional front. In the front line, A Company was on the right, B Company was on the left, in each case holding a line of posts. The Regimental Headquarters was situated in Dyke Valley, C Company in Courcelette dug-outs, and D Company was at 5th Brigade Headquarters.

Jim Neville recorded his impressions of this relief in the dark, and his first time under fire[496]. Strangely neither he nor his company commander, Lieutenant Robert Barnes had been in action before. He gave a vivid account of the vicissitudes of trench relief, and patrolling the front line posts.

> Well we paraded on the 16th at 4.30 p.m., and marched up to a distributing hut near Pozières to draw thigh gum boots. Unfortunately, I could not get a pair quite big enough for me, so I had to content myself with a pair of nines. On the way up we were shelled with lachrymatory gas which had no ill effects, except to make our eyes water and cause a choking feeling at the back of one's throat, and to make breathing rather uncomfortable. I was carrying

[495] Taken from a map dated January 17th 1917, in the 2nd Division's archives. Everard Wyrall in *the History of the Second Division* shows only sixteen posts on his map of the area. Major-General Cecil Pereira's diary recorded eighteen posts. Unbelievably, it was not until January 29th, when photographs from the air were able to be taken that the exact position of the Posts became known with certainty. [see map on page 390].

[496] Letter to his father written from Bouzincourt on January 20th 1917.

besides my equipment, my ankle boots and a sandbag of rations for two days.

We had to halt for a good long time at a spot near the ruined village of Pozières while another regiment passed us. It was getting very late, and also it was freezing all the time.

It was while we were waiting here that a man in the passing regiment fell into a shell-hole full of water, and, being heavily equipped and having all his ammunition to weigh him down, very nearly went down for good. That is one of the dangers of going into the line at night; and sometimes, when it's very dark, you can't spot which hole the man has fallen into.

On moving off, we took a duckboard track which made marching much easier. The men were very heavily laden and had their rations to carry too. It was while we were going along this track that I nearly lost our (officers') loaf of bread which rolled out of the sandbag into a shell-hole. Luckily I was able to find it. Harry Spurge[497] and I were the only officers of "B" Company.

We left the duckboards at "C" Dump, which the Hun delights in shelling of a night, but he was quite quiet while we were passing, thank heaven. Up to this point progress had been pretty easy, but as soon as we got off the duckboards it was nothing more nor less than hell. The gum boots had no grip on the ground, and we went along floundering up to our waists in mud, slipping up and falling into shell-holes full of water, and all the while my ankle boots swung in between my legs, and the ration bag grew heavier with every step.

The guides of the regiment which we were to relieve missed the track and took us about half a mile out of our way. Men got stuck so deep in the mud that it took three others to pull them out, and as I was in the rear of the column, all these jobs devolved on me. More than once the men had their gum boots sucked off in the mud and continued in their socks! Then too, every time a man fell into a water-logged shell-hole his rations went with him, and these were often left at the bottom.

It was about 11 p.m. when we turned about and retraced our steps to try and find the right path. The difficulty of the going exhausted the men, and I, too, felt done up to the eyes. Luckily, I had your flask quite handy and took a swig which bucked me up a great deal. Just before we turned off on our track, I saw a body lying covered by

497 Lieutenant Harry Spurge. A man with a great sense of responsibility and duty.

a water-proof sheet. It was poor Nick Hill who had been killed by shrapnel leading "A" Company into the front line[498].

We finally reached our destination at about 3.30 a.m., having taken eleven hours on the way. Harry and I were in the Headquarters post and I crawled into the shelter which was about 12 feet long, 3 feet broad, and 4 feet high. To get in I had to go on hands and knees. It was made of semi-circular sheets of corrugated iron, had neither sandbags nor earth above it, and mud oozed from the joints. A whizz-bang or bullet would go straight through it.

At the far end Harry and I made shift for the night wedged in together so tightly that we could scarcely move.

Before turning in, we went round our posts. There was now a covering of snow on the ground which obliterated the shell-holes and concealed the track, as well as making the going rather treacherous.

The Hun, in this part of the line, is really quite friendly and never strafes us unless we strafe him. Here is an instance of this.

On our return journey from visiting the posts we completely lost our way in the snow. We came upon a post and Harry, thinking it was one of ours, gave the pass word. There was no answer. "Rum" Harry said again. As there was no answer I covered the sentry with my revolver. Then I noticed a couple of men dart towards what I took to be a machine gun, though I could not see for certain in the murk. I whispered to Harry that I thought it was time for us to go elsewhere, and we made off hastily. In my haste I tripped over something and fell flat on my face in the snow and found myself staring into the sunken eyes of a very old Boche. He was half covered in snow and very dead, but that sight gave me an awful shock. It turned out that we had visited a German post! How easily they could have shot us or made us prisoners.

It took us some time to find our line, for even our footmarks were covered by falling snow, so that we could not retrace our steps. It was a funny feeling to be lost in No Man's Land.

We eventually found our Headquarters and found that we had been away for two hours. I was amazed; it seemed as if we had been out for about half an hour.

The unfortunate Captain Nick Hill, commanding A Company, was the Regiment's only casualty during this tour of the trenches. He had an

[498] Captain Nick Hill.

instantaneous death as the shrapnel balls from a chance shell severed his carotid artery, penetrated his head, heart, and stomach. The 20-year-old Hill was one of the outstanding young officers, in the 52nd of his era, and he had recently been awarded the Military Cross. Charming, witty and with the reputation of being a brilliant soldier, he was sorely missed. His wit kept the mess going when there was a general depression. With the exception of Leslie Johnston, Hill was probably the most intelligent officer to serve with the 52nd during the whole war. He had been awarded scholarships to Winchester College and New College, Oxford. However, the onset of the war meant that he never went up to Oxford, but found himself at Sandhurst instead.

The constant rain from mid-November onwards, plus shellfire and traffic had turned the Somme battlefield into a quagmire. This was well illustrated by Jim Neville's description of moving through mud that was waist deep. Edmonds in his *Official History* wrote; 'the state of the ground of the Somme battlefield during December was such as was probably never surpassed on the Western Front - hardly even in the Ypres Salient. And if any part of that front was worse than another, it was the valley of the Ancre'. Apart from periods of heavy frost, matters had not improved during the following month. An experienced battalion and brigade commander compared the mud on the Somme with that of the Ypres Salient; 'possibly not quite so holding, but decidedly more slippery'. The horror of holding a line of posts 30-40 yards apart in a wilderness of mud was an experience that mere words cannot adequately describe.

Jim Neville managed to get lost in no man's land again, but this time he had taken the precaution of carrying a compass with him, and he had been able to get a bearing during daylight hours. The Germans were quite open in their movements during the day, sauntering from post to post with their hands in their pockets. On January 18th, a party of the enemy came quite close to the British line and waved their arms. At one post the Germans appeared to be offering the men of the 52nd a friendly drink by holding a beer bottle above their heads. The invitation seemed to be a genuine one as they were unarmed. Jim Neville longed to shoot at them, to settle a few scores, but feared the consequences of being sniped himself, or being taken prisoner, if perchance, he wandered into one of their posts. Neville believed that the Germans would guide you back to the British line if you got lost in no man's land! It is clear that the condition of the ground was so bad that it was enough just to survive rather than to try to kill the enemy as well.

On January 17th, further officer replacements, in the form of five second-lieutenants from the Territorial Force had joined the 52nd. They were J.D.M. Straith, E.H. Taylor, F.T. Gass, C.E. 'Church of England' Barnes, and D.E.

Haymen. Ten days later 'Church of England' Barnes would be admitted to hospital suffering from dysentery. On the 18th, C Company changed positions with A, and D with B. There was found to be insufficient room for B Company at Brigade Headquarters and they moved on to Courcelette dug-outs. Here they occupied fine former German accommodation, some thirty feet below the ground. Their beds were made of hard board, although the enemy had had feather mattresses. The 52nd were eventually relieved, on the afternoon of the 20th, by the 1st King's of the 6th Brigade, and retired to Bouzincourt, just to the north-west of Albert [see map on page 315]. The roads were icy and the men slipped and fell around like skittles. During this tour of the trenches only seven men had been wounded, and Captain Nick Hill was the only fatality.

From his billet in Bouzincourt Jim Neville reflected on his feelings when under fire[499].

> When we were going up, I had some doubts as to my sensations under fire, but I had none, strange to say. The only time I felt at all funny was at 6.30 a.m. on the 17th. We had no sleep all night, and the Huns started shelling us and our guns replied. The strafe lasted three quarters of an hour. I had a shivery feeling and, try as I would, I simply could not control that shivering! Harry said[500], "It's very cold, isn't it?" and I said, "Yes, I can't keep warm!!" We both had the wind up, but I don't think we betrayed it.

The *Battalion War Diary* has no entries for the period January 21st to the 27th, but it seems likely that the 52nd spent the period training and resting at Bouzincourt. The Regiment was certainly there on January 24th, when Jim Neville wrote a letter to his sister. On the 28th, the 52nd left Bouzincourt for Wolseley Huts in Ovillers, just to the south-west of their previous position at Courcelette. Here they relieved the 1st Royal Berks of the 99th Brigade, becoming the 'Work Battalion' of the 5th Brigade who had moved into support. Every day the 52nd supplied working parties which meant the whole Regiment was out from 5.30 a.m. until perhaps the early hours of the next morning. These fatigues were exhausting, and very unpopular with the men, who only got alternate nights in bed. One example of the type of work that they were undertaking was the salvaging of overturned railway trucks. Light railways carried revetting material, ammunition, and other supplies to the front. The trucks were inclined to come off the rails every 100 yards or so, and the men of the 52nd struggled to push them up

---

[499] Letter to his father written from Bouzincourt on January 20th 1917.

[500] Lieutenant Harry Spurge.

slopes, but then enjoyed free-wheeling down the other side until invariably the trucks came off the rails once more. An enormous amount of equipment was lying about and was salvageable. The work was made more difficult by intermittent shelling by the enemy and the bright moonlight making it as light as day.

For much of the time the weather was bitterly cold, with intermittent snow and an average of fifteen degrees of frost each morning. The ground became as hard as iron, and the snow on the surface became trodden into ice, making even walking very difficult. The men's boots were frozen stiff, and washing sponges so hard that football could be played with them. The servant of one officer, each night, filled his boots with paper, which was set fire to in the morning to make the boots supple enough for the officer to put on. Beer and Perrier were solid at mealtimes, and condensed milk just like ice cream. In fact everything froze except whisky and brandy. The water in their canvas buckets froze with an inch of ice every night, and the Royal Artillery had to blow holes in the Ancre to allow their horses water to drink. Sometimes, at night, it was so cold that a dew drop on the end of the nose turned into an icicle! The accommodation in Wolseley Huts, at Ovillers, left a great deal to be desired. The huts were draughty, the fire would not burn properly in the stove, and smoked whenever anything was put on it. There was no fuel allowance and wood had to be stolen. It was considered better to remain cold than be asphyxiated by the fire and have to wear gas respirators!

The health of the Regiment, which was usually excellent, suffered in the wet and from the low temperatures of the coldest European winter in living memory. Cooking in the forward posts was dependent on small quantities of solidified alcohol in Tommy cookers. Owing to the extreme conditions, the men found that it was impossible to rub whale oil into their feet, which resulted in many cases of trench foot. As a consequence the 52nd's fighting strength became sadly depleted. Trench foot led to an infected, macerated condition of the skin which arose from wearing boots for long periods in cold wet conditions such as flooded trenches. Occasionally death would ensue.

At 5 p.m. on February 5th, the new reserve brigade, the 99th, took over the working parties, and the 5th Brigade became responsible for the front line of the 2nd Division. The 52nd moved into the forward lines of Ovillers Huts, becoming the reserve battalion of the 5th Brigade. The weather remained very cold with a heavy frost, and the ground was iron hard. Two days later, on the 7th, four new officers joined the Regiment for duty, and the 74th reinforcement of seventeen N.C.O.s and men arrived. The officers were Lieutenant T.W.C Foreshew, and Second-Lieutenants H.A. Beaver, H. Miles, and G.C. Calloway. On the 9th,

Major Cuthbert 'Bingo' Baines, the second-in-command of the 52nd, was admitted to the No. 29 Casualty Clearing Station, at Gezaincourt, suffering from trench fever[501]. That same day the 52nd relieved the 24th R.F. in the right subsection of the line as before. This four days tour of duty had its eventful moments, with a trench raid made by the enemy on their left, and a heavy battery regularly shelling in the vicinity of four of the 52nd's posts. Despite repeated requests by Lieutenant-Colonel Richard Crosse, he was unable to get this so called 'friendly fire' stopped. At night the bright moonlight allowed movement and the visiting of posts to be conducted with ease. According to the *Battalion War Diary,* 'the attitude of the enemy on the whole [was] quiet', although the 52nd sniped and fired Lewis guns at the enemy's wire. On the 13th, the 52nd was relieved by the 24th R.F., and retired to Ovillers Huts, which they reached in the early hours of the following morning.

It is unlikely that Second-Lieutenants William Giles and Jim Neville, and their B Company would have agreed that the 'the attitude of the enemy on the whole [was] quiet'. Giles had taken over command of the company from Harry Spurge, who had been sent to hospital for surgery, having ruptured himself, jumping into a shell hole. A married man, Spurge would recover from his inguinal hernia operation, before becoming the Adjutant of the 5th Battalion, and eventually dying of his wounds on September 17th 1917, aged 24 years. Jim Neville described their experiences on the night of February 12th[502].

> It was thrilling to watch our guns cutting wire on the first day, the morning of the 12th. Our gunners were sending over some big stuff and shooting with good success. At dusk they all stopped. Then, at 7 p.m. Chevallier[503], the Regimental Lewis Gun Officer accompanied by the Brigade Intelligence Officer, came and warned us that we might be raided that night by the Hun. This information had been gleaned from a Hun prisoner captured a few days before. Shoveller, as we call Chevallier, talked so loud that I thought the Kaiser in Berlin would probably hear what he knew, and as the posts are very close to the Boche, it seemed that he wanted them to hear as well.

[501] This disease was caused by the organism Rickettsia quintana spread in infected faeces of the louse. Scratching of the skin forced the infected faeces into lesions caused by lice bites. After a week to a month, the infected soldier would suffer from a severe headache, muscle pains often of the shins, and fever. An alternative name was 'shin-bone fever'. The duration of the illness was five days; but it frequently relapsed. In the Great War there was no specific treatment. Nowadays antibiotics would be used.

[502] Letter to his father written from Fricourt on February 15th 1917.

[503] Lieutenant Clement Chevallier known as the 'Shoveller'.

Having delivered their messages, they buzzed back to Headquarters, and left Giles and me with the wind vertical! There was every possibility of the raid being made against us as our Headquarter post was slightly forward and flanked by a sunken road.

We prepared immediately, for the worst, and got out bombs and all manner of ammunition. The suspense of waiting was awful, and the time seemed to drag interminably. At 7.45 Giles decided to visit the other posts, and I was left in charge of Company Headquarters. Giles had not been gone a quarter of an hour when the Boches opened a barrage on our left where the H.L.I. held the line. The night was black as pitch, and very foggy, so that we could only see twenty yards in front of our parapet. We manned the trench and placed the Lewis gun in a coign of vantage.

Of course, as soon as the barrage started we knew that some raiders were coming over. A few seconds later, we saw the H.L.I. send up the S.O.S. rocket to tell our gunners to open fire. I must say I was relieved to see that rocket go up!

Before one rocket had flickered out, our guns opened simultaneously with a blasting barrage on the enemy's front line. It seemed that hell was let loose on the Germans. I looked over the parapet and saw our first shell burst, most beautifully timed. But the second – I saw a trail of fire go straight into the right hand corner of our trench with a fizzing noise – shrapnel!! The next thing I heard was a long-drawn out moan of agony and I knew that some poor devil had gone. Then, two more of our shells burst over the same corner, so we edged down to the left end of the post. It was while we were moving that another of our shells burst right over my head; I was knocked absolutely flat and my tin hat rolled down the trench. Luckily, there was a dug-out in our post, and I told the men to take cover while I and the Lewis gunner waited at the top and had a peep over the parapet every now and then. It seemed highly unlikely that the Boche would come our way as well, and if they had, our guns would have given them worse hell than they were actually giving us at the moment.

On the other side of the trench was a little shelter that Giles and I occupied. I heard the shrapnel ripping it up, and the bits rattling like peas. As the shelling got hotter, I thought I had better do something about it, so I sent through a message in clear on the power buzzer to say our guns were firing short. I thought the barrage had been blasting us for an hour, but when I looked at my watch I was dumbfounded to see it was only 8.15!

All through the bombardment I was as cool as a cucumber. I was quite surprised at myself, but then, we had no time to think about anything, and I felt frightfully excited and wished I had a rifle instead of an automatic.

Just as I had sent off this message, an officer descended the dug-out sweating from every pore. I have never seen anyone in such a malt. He had been caught in our barrage as well as the Boche. He said our guns were dropping shells from two to three hundred yards behind our front line, and he had crawled the whole way from shell-hole to shell-hole until he struck our post.

Next, I got a message to say that gas was being let off on our right. I took this to mean that the Boche was doing the letting off, because the wind was in the right direction for this; as it happened we were letting it off far away on our right beyond the salient where the wind was right for us. That message did not help matters!

The bombardment ended at 9 p.m., and we all got up into the trench where I found Giles, whom I never expected to see again. As a matter of fact the post he had stopped in was not touched by any of the shelling.

We found that two men had been killed in the right corner of the trench, and they were our two servants[504]. My servant was a gem. It was his first time in the line too. We also found a dud shell had fallen just where I had been squatting, and I think I had a narrow escape.

The Colonel[505] came up soon afterwards and cheered us up a lot. Chevallier had told us before the raid that he had been given the Legion of Honour, and when we congratulated him, he laughingly remarked: "Isn't it awful to think that I shall be a French Shoveller for the rest of my days!" He sent up four stretcher-bearers and our two servants were taken down and buried. That was the first time I had seen a man killed.

We were all pretty glad to get out of the trenches and to reach huts at 1 a.m. on the 14th. The raid was easily repulsed; only about 12 got

[504] Private Oliver John Hastings, aged 35 years, from Slough was Neville's servant. He had provided Neville's tutor, at Eton, with vegetables. Private Alfred Martin Crabbe, aged 24 years, from Oxford, was Giles' servant. They were both buried in Courcelette British Cemetery.

[505] Lieutenant-Colonel Richard Crosse.

> into our line of whom six were taken prisoners. The others managed to snaffle a Lewis gun team which had been pushed forward into No Man's Land on the express orders of the Brigadier. The raid started 70 strong and the enemy lost about 30 all told. So, it was a failure from their point of view.

The 2nd H.L.I., who had recently replaced the 17th R.F., in the line, were aware from information supplied by a German prisoner[506] that they were to be raided by 70 volunteer troops. The enemy raiding party came over wearing white, to blend with the snow, and endeavoured to raid the British line, held by the 2nd H.L.I., between Posts Nos. 9 and 10 [see map on page 390]. Here there was a 200 yard gap, with inadequate wire in front, covered by a single Lewis gun team. The enemy got into the British line where it was unoccupied, and were fired on by Post No. 10, before moving towards Post No. 9, and then away into no man's land. Five dead Germans, without documents of identification or badges, were found between Posts Nos. 9 and 10. One prisoner of the 90th Regiment was taken[507]. In reply, the Germans captured the Lewis gun detachment consisting of one N.C.O. and six men, positioned by Brigadier-General George Bullen-Smith in no man's land, between Posts Nos. 9 and 10. It is likely that they were all killed as they were never seen again.

On February 14th, the 52nd exchanged areas with the 99th Brigade, and became the 'Work Battalion' of the reserve brigade once more. Regimental Headquarters was situated at Aveluy, just to the north of Albert. The following day, B Company [less Second-Lieutenant Jim Neville and 50 men who were working at a railhead] was situated at Aveluy; C Company and 50 men from D at Donnet's Post, employed on the light railway; D Company less the 50 men with C, unloading ammunition; A Company with three platoons of 90 men working under the Chief Royal Engineer, at Wolseley Huts; the remaining men were making dug-outs with the 174th Tunnelling Company, near Pozières. Jim Neville and his 50 men were working at a railhead at Méaulte, just to the south of Albert. Although he was pleased to be away from the front line, Neville missed the camaraderie of the Regiment. He messed with the commanding officer of the railhead and two other officers. It was a comfortable existence with an open fire that reminded him of home in Norfolk. Neville found it pleasant to wear pyjamas

---

[506] German prisoner captured in a trench raid made by the 17th Royal Fusiliers, on February 10th 1917.

[507] The 90th Regiment was a part of the 17th Division, which had been recruited mainly in the Hanseatic towns and the Duchies of Mecklenburg. The 17th Division was considered to be a good one, with the officers and men of a higher intellectual capacity than was usual in the German Army. Many Danes were in its ranks.

again. In the line he recorded; 'During the hard frost no one dared to take off his pants except to change. It may sound unhealthy, but it was far too cold to wear only pyjamas, and we used to dress to go to bed, in cardigans, mufflers and Balaclava helmets. I would rather be warm and dirty than frozen and clean'[508].

The next day, the 16th, found the 52nd, as the 'Work Battalion', in the same locations. Sadly, shellfire killed a number of the regimental horses in their stables, at Aveluy. Willing hands toiled throughout the night to extricate the unfortunate animals, but to no avail. The older transport drivers felt the losses deeply. In all, five horses were killed, these being Richard Crosse's two [one being the black and white mare which had been with them since 1913, and had disturbed many a parade at Aldershot], the Adjutant's two [Lieutenant Ernest Whitfeld], and the Transport Officer's one [Lieutenant John Slade-Baker].

During January, the inclement weather had precluded serious offensive operations. But on February 17th II Corps undertook operations on both sides of the Ancre, in an attempt to gain possession of the high ground south of Miraumont. Its capture would allow the British to control the southern approaches to Miraumont and Pys, and additionally would enable them to observe the German's battery positions behind the fortified village of Serre. A subsidiary operation was to be undertaken north of the Ancre to still further improve the British positions, and to command Miraumont from the west. A further subsidiary attack to protect the right flank of the main assault was also to be undertaken. With luck, the operations as a whole should lead to the evacuation of Miraumont by the enemy and also make their position at Serre untenable. The main attack was to be carried out by the 2nd Division [Major-General Cecil Pereira[509]] on the right and the 18th Eastern Division [Major-General R.P.Lee] on the left [see map on page 402]. To the north of the Ancre, the 63rd Royal Naval Division [Major-General Cameron Shute[510]] would be responsible for this subsidiary operation.

Major-General Cecil Pereira used the 99th Brigade for the main assault towards Miraumont, and the 6th Brigade for the subsidiary operation, to protect

---

[508] Letter to one of his sisters written from Fricourt on February 18th 1917.

[509] Major-General Cecil Pereira, later Sir Cecil, [1860-1942], was wounded commanding the 85th Brigade, 28th Division, on May 26th 1915, in the Ypres Salient, and again on September 27th 1915, at the Battle of Loos. Pereira's two wounds, within a few months of each other, disproves the myth that Brigadier-Generals sat behind the lines in comfortable châteaux. He commanded the 2nd Division from December 27th 1916 until the end of the war.

[510] Major-General Cameron 'Tiger' Shute, later General Sir Cameron, commanded the 63rd Division from October 17th 1916–February 19th 1917, the 19th [Western Division] from May 24th–June 19th 1917 [temporary] and the 32nd Division from June 20th 1917–April 27th 1918. Later he commanded V Corps from April 28th 1918-19. An irascible, demanding, unendearing man, who disapproved of the state of the Royal Naval Division's latrines, and was ridiculed for it by the likes of Alan Herbert.

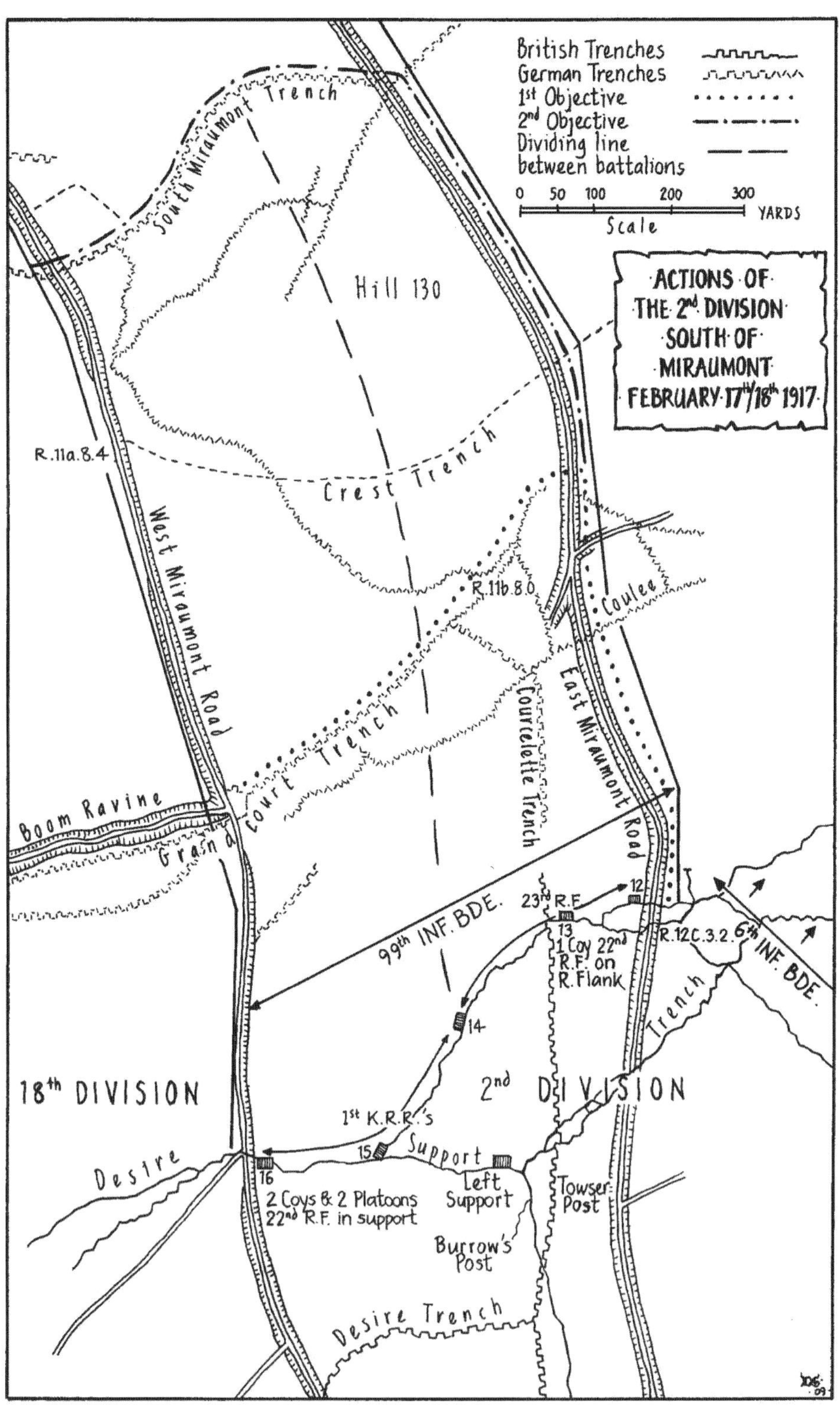

British Trenches
German Trenches
1st Objective
2nd Objective
Dividing line between battalions
0 50 100 200 300 YARDS
Scale
ACTIONS OF THE 2nd DIVISION SOUTH OF MIRAUMONT FEBRUARY 17th/18th 1917
South Miraumont Trench
Hill 130
R.11a.8.4
Crest Trench
West Miraumont Road
R.11b.8.0
Coulee
East Miraumont Road
Courcelette Trench
Grandcourt Trench
Boom Ravine
99th INF. BDE.
23rd R.F.
12
13
1 Coy 22nd R.F. on R. Flank
R.12C.3.2.
6th INF. BDE.
Trench
14
18th DIVISION
2nd DIVISION
1st K.R.R.'s
15
Support
16
Desire
Left Support
Towser Post
2 Coys & 2 Platoons 22nd R.F. in support
Burrow's Post
Desire Trench

the right flank of the main thrust. The 5th Brigade and the 52nd were not involved in this attack at all[511]. However, in order to follow the future movements of the 52nd, it is necessary to record a little of the events of February 17th 1917, and the days thereafter. The main assault suffered from a number of handicaps. Firstly, a thaw, which started on the 16th, turned the ground underfoot from being solid back into a quagmire. This made movement difficult, and the infantry had trouble in following the lifts of the artillery barrage, which had been calculated for frozen ground. Secondly, a captured British document, and then confirmation by a deserter of the time of the attack, put the Germans on their guard.

In the event, the 99th Brigade managed to take and hold its first objective, Grandcourt Trench, but was unable to take its second objective, South Miraumont Trench, or the key high ground of Hill 130, which lay between the two trenches. The 18th and 2nd Divisions [99th Brigade] had not advanced as far as had been hoped, but 500 yards had been gained on the right, 1,000 yards in the centre, and 800 yards on the left. In addition, the difficult ground at Boom Ravine, a 40 feet deep cleft, had been taken and was being firmly held. The 6th Brigade's attack on the Desire Support Trench, to protect the right flank of the main assault, failed completely, largely because the Germans were expecting it[512]. Consequently, the right flank of the 99th Brigade was left in the air, precluding the possibility of a further advance. To the north of the Ancre, the 63rd Division had been successful with their part of the operation.

The following day, the 18th, south of the Ancre, troops of the 18th Division and the 99th Brigade were engaged in the consolidation of the ground gained the previous day. Major-General Cecil Pereira, commanding the 2nd Division, proposed a further attack with fresh troops from the 99th Brigade, but this was vetoed by the II Corps. The 6th Brigade was ordered to relieve the 99th Brigade that night. To the north of the Ancre, at 11.25 a.m., the Germans, at about two battalions' strength, counter-attacked in a south-westerly direction. British artillery batteries broke the attack up, and the enemy retired in some disorder. Fog hampered observation from the air, although counter-battery fire was intermittently required throughout the day to stop the enemy from shelling the British trenches. The losses of the 2nd Division, for the two days, amounted to

---

[511] The 52nd was unable to claim the battle honour for the 'Actions of Miraumont February 17th and 18th', as they were outside the area 'Road Pys - Courcelette - Thiepval - Hamel - Beaucourt'. In fact some men, of the 52nd, were only just outside the defined area, making dug-outs near Pozières.

[512] According to Major-General Cecil Pereira's diary the deserter was from the 2nd South Staffordshire [6th Brigade]. His name is unknown. The British were heavily barraged and every machine-gun in the vicinity was turned on them. Pereira wrote 'what with the mist, mud and thrice accursed deserter we had every handicap against us'.

49 officers and 969 other ranks, and in the 18th Division to 54 officers and 1,135 other ranks.

On February 19th, the area occupied by the 2nd Division's 6th Brigade, was heavily shelled. The 13th Essex of the 6th Brigade was ordered to attempt to push forward patrols and posts. This they did on the night of the 20th/21st when some 50 yards of ground was gained. However, it was clear that unless the key point for observation, at Hill 130, to the south-east of Miraumont, was taken little further could be achieved. Major-General Cecil Pereira submitted plans to the II Corps, for an attack on the western portion of Crest Trench [about mid-way between Grandcourt and South Miraumont Trenches], with a view to securing at least part of the key position, Hill 130. This was agreed, but the matter was complicated further by the 6th Brigade's units needing to form up in the 18th Division's area. The weather stepped in with a steady downpour on the 20th, turning the ground underfoot into a bog. The operation having been set for February 22nd was postponed. Men were sinking into the mud up to their waists and required beams and pulleys to rescue them. It was clear that little further could be achieved under these dire circumstances. As we shall shortly see, the 5th Infantry Brigade relieved the 6th on the night of February 23rd/24th and their commander, Brigadier-General George Bullen-Smith, fully intended to attack Hill 130; but events would make this unnecessary.

The ground gained on February 17th, plus the minor gains since, had allowed British command of the German artillery positions in the upper Ancre Valley and threatened his defences around Pys and Miraumont. Constantly bombarded by the British artillery, and threatened by an infantry attack, the enemy gave up the unequal struggle and abandoned Pys and Miraumont.

On February 16th, we left the 52nd acting as 'Work Battalion' of the Reserve Brigade, with the Regimental Headquarters at Aveluy. The 5th Brigade was out of the fighting while the other two Brigades of the 2nd Division, the 6th and 99th, were involved in the heavy fighting on the 17th and 18th. On the 19th, two new officers, Second-Lieutenants Harold 'Fritz' Eagle and Leonard Bartlett reported for duty, and the 75th reinforcement of 45 N.C.O.s and men arrived. Two days later, on the 21st, the 52nd were finally relieved of their duties with working parties and retired to billets in Albert. A reconnaissance of the line that they were to take over was made on the 22nd. The following day the Regiment relieved the 1st King's of the 6th Brigade, in the right front sub-section, and had the 17th Royal Fusiliers on their left [see map on page 402]. This was a part of the general relief of the 6th Brigade by the 5th. The *Battalion War Diary* states that it was a troublesome relief, and not completed until 2 a.m. on the 24th[513]. Jim Neville has left a record of the difficulties of this relief[514]. From his account it is not difficult to see why offensive major operations had temporarily ceased. Also the beginnings of the German retreat to the Hindenburg Line are seen for the first time.

> Paraded at 5.30 p.m. for the line, an eight mile march. Picked up gum boots at the store at 7.15 and water in petrol tins at the junction of Artillery Lane. We then carried on by platoons to the cross roads where we met the guide from the 1st King's Liverpools. Then took the duckboard track on which I experienced the worst journey since I've been out here. Men were falling into shell-holes up to their armpits in wet mud, from which it was a labour of Hercules to extract them, and caused much delay. Marched down the valley and over the crest through a trench. Then the Huns started shelling the track to make confusion worse confounded. Mud was indescribable. I arrived at No. 9 Post with my servant, Platoon Serjeant and four men out of the whole platoon, the remainder being bogged at "B" Dump. I relieved and took over from a King's officer who was nearly off his head from being alone for six days under a piece of corrugated iron with bully beef and biscuits for grub. I assumed command at 12 midnight.
>
> Stragglers came in driblets all night up to "stand-to" at 5.30 a.m. Some of them had been badly stuck in the mud. Went over with Giles[515] to Company Headquarters in No. 8 Post. No signs of Germans in opposite trench. Also we noticed the enemy's Verey lights were going up a long way behind their front line. I remarked on this fact to Giles and suggested the Boche had evacuated his front line.
>
> Had breakfast in the dug-out and then tried to sleep. Went back to No. 9 Post at 7 p.m. to do my night duty with my platoon. A patrol went out to see if the Hun front line was still occupied.

[513] Neville [see below] recorded that it was 5.30 a.m. before everyone arrived.

[514] Letter to his father describing the events of February 23rd written in diary form from Albert on March 4th 1917.

[515] Lieutenant William Giles. Giles and Neville had been in the same company at Sandhurst in 1915. Neville would later describe Giles, in action, as courageous, imperturbable, and cool.

Brigadier-General George Bullen-Smith, commanding the 5th Brigade the first morning after the relief on February 24th, was faced with the problem of clearing up an awkward situation over very difficult country against an enemy liberally supplied with machine-guns and with whom contact had been lost. By 10 a.m., in a thick mist limiting visibility to 100 yards, some units of the 5th Brigade, with the 18th Division on the left and the 2nd Australian Division on the right, were moving forwards. The 17th R.F., to the left of the 52nd, began pushing forward with patrols and, a little later they had managed to take and hold Crest and Coulée Trenches. These two trenches lay just to the south of Petit Miraumont and Pys, and were roughly parallel [see map on page 402]. The support battalion, the 2nd H.L.I., went out in the darkness and proceeded, under cover of the early morning mist, to set up a line of outposts beyond and to the south of Pys.

Daytime for the 52nd was quiet, and they do not appear to have been involved in moving forward, or sending out patrols until the evening. It was only after dark that the 52nd received information to the effect that a patrol of the 18th Division, on the left of the 5th Brigade, had reported that the enemy was no longer occupying his front line. At once, orders were issued for the 52nd to send out patrols, to find out whether Guard Trench and Desire Support Trench were still being held by the enemy. Consequently, at 9 p.m., a patrol from A Company went out and, on return, reported that they thought Guard Trench and Desire Support Trench, to their front, were still held, although the enemy's posts could not be located. At 10.30 p.m., a further patrol, this time from B Company on the left, went out and subsequently reported that Desire Support Trench, on their front, was still being held by at least one enemy post. Later, more certain information became available, to the effect that the enemy was not holding his front system, apart from a few rearguard posts.

On the 24th, six Second-Lieutenants, H.A. 'Ginger' Smith, S.A.E. Miles, M.A. Simon, H.O.M. Herbert, A.E. Henley, and H.W.D. Palmer joined the 52nd. The last five were on attachment from the Royal Berkshire Regiment. During the following two days, the 25th and 26th, the Regiment continued to occupy the original British Line, except there were forward posts on the flanks, in order to keep in touch with the 2nd Australian Division on their right and the 17th R.F. on the left. The 52nd sent further patrols out on the 25th, and the 2nd H.L.I. continued to move forward, with two companies getting lost for a time.

Jim Neville continued with his narrative in diary form[516].

---

[516] Letter to his father describing the events of February 25th written from Albert on March 4th 1917.

The night seemed interminable. I did not dare to try to sleep because I might miss a visit to the sentries in the little posts. I sat up in between-whiles in the funny little shanty carving names of places I've been to over here, on my ashplant stick.

Went over to Company Headquarters at 5.15 a.m. to find the whole place astir. News had come through that the enemy was retiring and a patrol went out to verify it. Everyone was very excited, thinking "Here is a bit of open warfare at last." A Gunner Major turned up and went forward to lay a telephone wire. At 7.30 a.m. the H.L.I. arrived in force and went forward in pursuit and to make touch with the Boche. The Gunner returned with the news that we could occupy the enemy second line. Huge excitement! Next, the Serjeant in charge of the patrol returned and reported that he had been fired on by about twenty Germans when moving forward. The Gunner rather mistrusted this information and went forward again along his wire, accompanied by a patrol of six men of the H.L.I., and was never seen again. Presumably he was captured because the coil was found later and beside it, six rifles.

In the afternoon, I had orders to get in touch with the Fusiliers[517] who were in the second enemy line. Eagle[518] and I started off in daylight at 5.30 p.m. under direct observation of the enemy on the ridge behind the village of Pys. We got through the wire and were going along the Pys road, when the Hun, who had obviously spotted us advancing, put down an awful barrage on the road. We left the road which was too unhealthy, and got into a shell-hole and waited for the atmosphere to clear a bit; but we had to wait for about an hour before the shelling diminished sufficiently to allow us to advance. Gradually the shelling grew less and we went forward to try to find this trench which no one had seen before. By this time it was pitch dark. I took two platoons forward, and we got absolutely lost, so I thought it would be best to try and strike the road and adjust my bearings. By means of my compass I found the old German front line which we followed until we found the Pys road. Thus, I was back almost where I had started from!

However, on the road I found a messenger, who said that we had to go back to our old posts. Had no casualties, which was a miracle

[517] 17th Royal Fusiliers.

[518] Second-Lieutenant Harold 'Fritz' Eagle.

considering the amount of muck flying about. Dead beat and slept in Company Headquarters.

By February 25th, on other parts of the front between Guedecourt and Serre, the Germans had evacuated or been ejected from their front system of trenches. Warlencourt, Eaucourt, Pys, Miraumont, and Serre [evacuated by the Germans on February 24th] were now under British occupation. The German retirement to the Hindenburg Line or Siegfried-Stellung, as it was known to the enemy, officially started on March 14th and was completed by April 5th. In some places, such as on the Somme, the enemy retired as much as 30 miles. As we have seen, in the Ancre Valley, on the 2nd Division's front, in actuality it started on February 24th. The Germans' heavy losses in 1916 made it necessary for them to shorten their trench line. On February 9th, the enemy began the work of demolition in the large salient that they occupied between Arras and Soissons. Their scorched earth policy has been likened to the Spartan laying waste of Attica in the Peloponnesian war. As early as the autumn of 1916, British airmen had noticed trenches being constructed well to the rear of the then front lines. However, some months elapsed before work of this nature was identified elsewhere, and the significance of the constructions became known to the allies. The Hindenburg Line ran from the northern bank of the Aisne, to the east of Crouy, northwards, west of La Fere, west of St. Quentin, and then north-westerly to the southern bank of the Scarpe, east of Arras. The bloodshed and reverses, suffered by the Germans, on the Somme, in the summer and autumn, of 1916, led to the necessity of them shortening their line in early 1917.

On the morning of the 26th, the British artillery shelled Grevillers Trench, Loupart Trench, and Loupart Wood [see map on page 409]. This was a softening up process in preparation for a further advance. The enemy replied vigorously in kind, shelling Pys. Part of the 2nd H.L.I. pushed into Gallwitz Switch Trench, and patrols were ordered to reconnoitre Grevillers Trench, which was found to be held by the enemy in strength. It was clear that Grevillers Trench was part of a strongly fortified line of trenches running between Bapaume and Irles, making a formidable obstacle. The wire in front of the trench was in good condition, and appeared to be uncut, despite the best efforts of the artillery.

On February 27th, a lovely day, the 52nd relieved the 2nd H.L.I. in the forward position with A and B Companies in the new front line. This consisted of Gallwitz Switch Trench on the right, and a line of posts on the left extending to the outskirts of Pys, including the cemetery. D Company was in support in Grundy Trench, and C Company in reserve in shelters around the Regimental Headquarters in Aqueduct Road, the road between Le Sars and Pys. The relief of

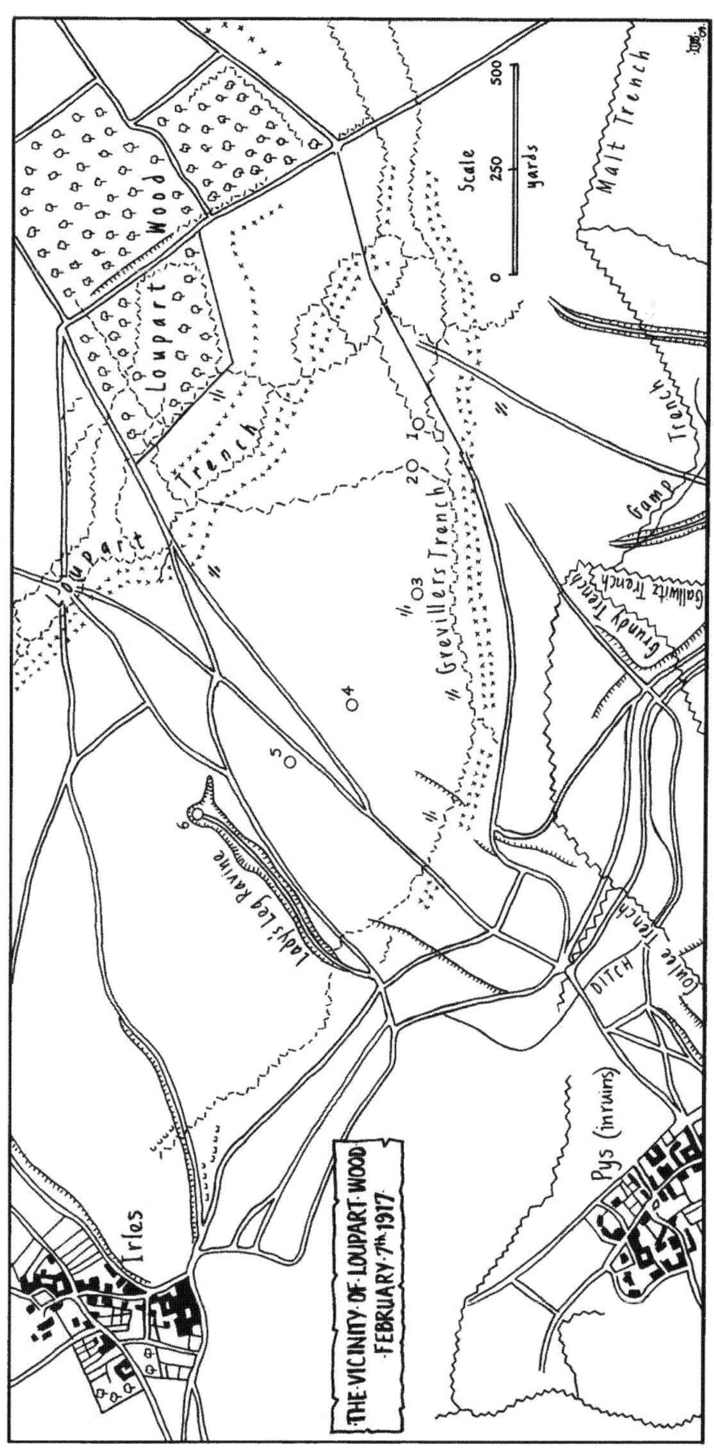
THE VICINITY OF LOUPART WOOD
FEBRUARY 7th 1917
Loupart Wood
Loupart Trench
Loupart
Grevillers Trench
Malt Trench
Gamp Trench
Gallwitz Trench
Grundy Trench
Ladys Leg Ravine
DITCH
Irles
Pys (in ruins)
Scale
0
250
500
yards
1
2
3
4
5
6

the 2nd H.L.I. proved to be difficult owing to the darkness, and was not completed until 3.20 a.m. the following morning.

Jim Neville described the relief of the H.L.I. in a letter[519].

> Paraded at 8.30 a.m. for the new front line. The going was infinitely easier after two days of drying sun. We reached our old Headquarters in No. 8 Post in splendid time; from there we turned right along the old front line to No. 3A Post where we picked up guides from the 74th[520], across No Man's Land, through the Boche first and second lines till we reached Regimental Headquarters in Aqueduct Road. Luckily the Huns kept fairly quiet and we had a rest outside the dug-outs. The last part of the journey was the stickiest, for we had to cross a ridge, which, by day, was under direct observation by the enemy. We could hear the snipers firing and my guide told me that they had a rifle "laid" on the track to and from the front. We wasted no time, crossing the crest by platoons, and then descended the valley, crossed a stream, and so reached the communication trench. The Boche knew all about the little bridge over the stream because rifle shots cracked like a whip lash at odd intervals, and put the fear of God into me! This was the first continuous piece of trench system I have been in, and the Company Headquarters were established in a dug-out with about five steps. The 74th were not sorry to quit.

That same day, the 27th, the 52nd received a rare admonition from their Divisional commander, Major-General Cecil Pereira. His chief staff officer, Lieutenant-Colonel C.P. Deedes sent the following message to the 5th Brigade. In retrospect the sentiments expressed seem to be a little harsh in view of the difficult relief of the 2nd H.L.I.

> There is [sic] still a large number of corpses to be buried and rifles etc to be salvaged in the area. Many of the bodies and much of the salvage lie near posts held by our troops. For instance there are twenty to thirty corpses lying quite close to the post number 6 which was held this morning by a company of the Oxfordshire and Buckinghamshire Light Infantry. The Divisional Commander thinks

---

[519] Letter to his father describing the events of February 27th written from Albert on March 4th 1917.

[520] 2nd Highland Light Infantry.

> that the O.C. Company should have taken steps to get the bodies buried and the rifles salved as the men were merely sitting still and doing nothing. Even if he had wished to avoid movement by daylight the hours of dawn and dusk could have been made use of.
>
> He wishes the habit of letting men sit idle to be put a stop to and would like you to bring to the notice of all regimental officers how important it is in the interests of moral [sic] and discipline to keep the men employed and the area cleared.
>
> He is very glad to see the good work that is being done by the 17th Royal Fusiliers in the matter of salvage.

February 28th was described in the *Battalion War Diary* as a quiet and misty day, although the enemy shelled the front line, and they were joined in this exercise by the British artillery endeavouring to cut the wire in front of Grevillers Trench. The 52nd undertook active patrolling.

Jim Neville also described the day[521], and undoubtedly he would not have agreed with the description of a 'quiet day'.

> The enemy started pasting the crossing of the stream on our left at 3 a.m. At noon they were still at it. Giles and I went over to "A" Company on the right. The trench had been very badly smashed in and we kept very low. We were occupying Gallwitz Switch, immediately under the crest on which Loupart Wood stands, and anyone in the trench in front of the wood could easily have spotted us darting along our trench. As we were leaving "A" Company, the enemy started shelling more furiously than ever, and two "wooly bears" (5.9 shrapnel) burst just behind us, so we returned to "A's" dug-out until the shelling slackened a bit. When once we started for our own line we scuttled like rabbits, I can tell you!
>
> The bombardment still continued. It was awful, and the Hun gunners were able to enfilade our bit of trench and they did so with excellent effect. Shrapnel bullets were falling all round us. I had one man killed in my platoon, concussed to death by H.E.[522] and rather a nasty sight. I thought the bombardment was never going to

[521] Letter to his father describing the events of February 28th written from Albert on March 4th 1917.

[522] High Explosive. The 52nd lost four men killed in action on February 28th 1917. They were Privates Charles Bond, George Morris, Herbert Pithers, and Edward Robins. One of these four is the man in question.

> end, and we were all a bit shaken after over twelve hours of it. It was really absolute hell. The two platoons on the left near the stream had the worst of it, and had one man killed, two wounded, and a Serjeant shell-shocked. All this time our guns had been silent until at 4 p.m., to our intense relief, we heard the twanging bark of our 18-pounders as they opened on the enemy front line. It was glorious to think that the Boche was having some of what he had given us. Our guns continued for an hour or so and at 6 p.m. the enemy stopped bombarding, and by that time we had had our bellyful.

So the month of February 1917 came to a close with the enemy driven back to the Le Transloy - Loupart line, except that he still held the village of Irles. Irles formed a salient in the German line, which was linked up to it by well protected trenches at Loupart Wood and Achiet-le-Petit.

On March 1st, the 52nd was relieved quickly and without incident by the 24th R.F. A and B Companies were in Coulee Trench; C and D in Below Trench; Regimental Headquarters in the Old British Front Line, Posts Nos. 8 and 9. The next two days were spent in general salvage and the unpleasant task of corpse retrieval.

Jim Neville and B Company had a scare on March 1st[523].

> I woke up at 12.30 a.m. and heard machine guns firing and also our men firing "rapid" away on the left. A second later the Huns opened a barrage. Giles [524]was on duty, and "Fritz" Eagle[525] and I in the dug-out. A machine gunner popped his head down our shaft and said: "They are coming over." We were up those steps like rats, but in the shemozzle "Fritz" pinched my automatic by mistake, and I did not know where his was!
>
> As I got to the top step two shells burst just over my head in an orange glare that lit up the inky darkness. Star shells were sailing up in the air all round; in fact the Germans had got the wind up badly and must have thought that we were coming over! By the light of each one of their star shells I peered into the night, but devil the sign of a moving thing could I see. From our side not a single Verey light

[523] Letter written to his father in diary form on March 4th 1917. B Company was either in Gallwitz Switch Trench or in a post towards Pys. As they were in a dug-out, it is likely to have been the former place.

[524] Second-Lieutenant William Giles.

[525] Second-Lieutenant Harold 'Fritz' Eagle.

> was fired, so whoever thought the Boche was coming must have been seeing things!
>
> But the chap who said they were coming over put the wind up me properly, and I was almost in a panic when I couldn't find my automatic. I had visions of being unable to defend myself.
>
> At 4 a.m. I led my platoon back, because our guns were going to cut wire in front of Loupart Wood. It was a lovely afternoon and a great relief to get out of the shell fire. Occupied old German dug-outs in the Miramont [sic] Road.

March 1st - 3rd was spent in the unpleasant task of burying the battlefield dead. They were mainly Canadian corpses and had been dead for five months. It was a ghastly experience as the bodies were much decomposed. As one officer put it; 'The dead were a detestable sight. Thank God, their dear ones can't see them like this'. At 8.30 p.m., after a lovely spring day, the 52nd was relieved by the 1st King's Royal Rifle Corps of the 99th Brigade. They marched well, in the bright moonlight, to billets in the vicinity of the Rue Carnot, Albert, which were reached at midnight. The next day, during the morning, the 52nd had baths in an establishment in the Rue Corbie. Many of them had not washed for the eight days that they had been in the line. For relaxation in the evenings, the officers watched the Australian Divisional Theatre almost every night, and particularly enjoyed a parody of "My Old Kentucky Home", in a lightly humorous manner, describing one of the enemy being blown up by a Mills bomb! The final two lines were;

'For the last bit of bomb landed right upon
His old Kentucky Home'.

On the 5th, the 76th reinforcement of eighteen N.C.O.s and men arrived, and Lieutenant Cyril 'Shiny' Horley rejoined the Regiment, replacing Lieutenant Clement 'Shoveller' Chevallier as the Lewis gun officer. For the next five days the 52nd undertook such training as the weather and state of the ground permitted.

Whilst in Albert, Jim Neville and Cyril Horley played a practical joke on the unfortunate Doctor, Captain J. McTurk. Horley had already crawled under the dining-room table to set fire to the bottom of the newspaper that Clement Chevallier, the 'Shoveller', was reading[526].

> Yesterday we played a trick on the Doctor, McTurk, who was standing in front of the fire holding forth at great length. "Shiny" Horley got hold of a Verey light cartridge which we cut open outside the mess. We then extracted the magnesium and powder, and I put

[526] Letter by Neville to his father written from Albert on March 8th 1917.

> the empty cartridge in my pocket. Unaware of a plot, the Doctor was still gassing when we returned. "Shiny" took cover behind the folding doors which divide the long mess room and which were half open, while I walked up to the fire which was practically out and, quite nonchalantly, dropped the cartridge into it and made for safety behind the doors!
>
> There was a loud explosion and clouds of embers and the grate were blown into the room and McTurk was enveloped in dust. For a second he was almost invisible. Then, roaring like a bull and spitting fury, he took up a book and hurled it at me just before I could reach cover. It was a good shot and caught me on the left ear with the point of the cover!
>
> Meanwhile "Shiny's" face was just visible round the corner of the folding doors wreathed in smiles. It was damned funny to see the Doctor. He took it jolly well, and it also had the desired effect of stopping him gassing! But though "Shiny" was the instigator and I merely the perpetrator, the Doctor went for me and left "Shiny" alone, and the latter did not even come to my help in the ensuing rough house.
>
> I had no idea there was such force in the ordinary cap of a Verey Light. The grate was not irreparably damaged. It was already broken before we blew it out, and it functioned all right afterwards.

In the early morning of March 10th, the 18th Division attacked the village of Irles, and the 99th Brigade of the 2nd Division assaulted Grevillers Trench [see map on page 409]. After a particularly effective artillery barrage, both objectives were taken. Only on the left, in a dangerous gully, known as Lady's Leg Ravine, and on the right, near Loupart Wood, did the 99th Brigade meet significant resistance. On the following day, the 11th, preparations were made to continue the attack, and the Loupart line was bombarded. The next day, the 99th Brigade was relieved by the 6th and retired to billets in Albert. The intention was to assault the Loupart line and final arrangements were to be completed by March 14th. In the event, on March 13th, units of the 6th Brigade, without opposition, occupied Loupart Trench and Wood. The Germans had virtually gone. Three of the enemy had been left behind in Loupart Wood with rations for a few days. Two of the men had bad trench foot, and the third only one leg. They had been ordered to send up Very Lights, and fire a machine-gun intermittently, so the British might still believe that the line was occupied. The 52nd had played no part in these operations. However, if the enemy had not withdrawn to the Hindenburg Line, the Regiment had been warned that, on March 15th, they were to attack Loupart Wood. It was not to be, and the 52nd was fortunate not to be put to the test, as this was a strongly fortified position.

The warm evening of March 11th, saw the 5th Brigade move into the support area, and the 52nd relieved one of the 6th Brigade's Battalions in Ovillers Huts. The following day was used for bathing and drill, and about ten of the 52nd's officers did a reconnaissance of the forward area. The 77th reinforcement of ten men joined from the base. The Regiment moved to the following positions: Regimental Headquarters at Dyke Valley; A Company, Chalk Mound; B and C Companies, Courcelette Dug-outs; D Company, old Brigade Headquarters. From March 13th until five days later, on the 18th, the Regiment was employed in road making: A and D Companies on the Pys - Le Sars road, and B and C Companies on the Warlencourt - Le Sars road, except on the 17th and 18th, when the whole Regiment worked on the latter road. Surprisingly, the men seemed to enjoy this work, perhaps, because they could see the fruits of their labour. Their road making was so good that they were congratulated by the 5th Brigade.

The general good humour of the Regiment was enhanced by news of the Russian Revolution. On the 17th, Major Cuthbert 'Bingo' Baines visited Bapaume, which the Germans had been burning with alacrity. The 52nd were on their guard when they went souvenir collecting, Germans being adept at leaving behind booby-traps as they moved towards the Hindenburg Line. In the dug-outs some steps and handrails had been mined. Souvenirs of an attractive nature such as revolvers, bayonets, helmets, and even artificial flowers or humble shell nose-caps had often been attached to explosives. Captain D.M. Rose of the 1/4th Battalion joined the Regiment for a temporary attachment, on the 17th.

Strangely, the fact that the 52nd was working on the Warlencourt - Le Sars road on March 17th, meant that under the rules of the *Report of the Battles Nomenclature Committee,* published in 1922, the Regiment was allowed to claim a part in the capture of Bapaume [March 17th], integral to the German retreat to the Hindenburg Line. The definition of geographical limits being; 'no more exact definition of the battle-area can be given than that the engagement took place "in the neighbourhood of" Bapaume'. The 52nd missed out on: Actions of Miraumont, February 17th-18th; Capture of the Thilloys, February 25th-March 2nd; Capture of Irles, March 10th, by not being present, in the correct geographical area, at the relevant time. In the case of the first two actions, only marginally not being eligible. Regiments based their claims for Battle Honours on the findings of the Battles Nomenclature Committee.

On March 18th, the 52nd moved forward to a position in the Lady's Leg Ravine, to the south-west of Loupart Wood. Here the Regiment came under the command of the 6th Brigade, in their forward area. Jim Neville took the opportunity to view the trenches in front of Loupart Wood that they had been expecting to attack on March 15th, until the German retirement made this unnecessary. He rightly thought that they were 'a very awkward objective'. At 8 a.m., on the next day, the 19th, the 52nd marched to the Bihucourt Line. Here they dug a defensive line 650 yards in length, and used the German wire as an obstacle in front. Ahead of them were fertile fields without a sign of a shell hole, which was a pleasant change from the desolation that they were used to. However, it was rumoured that the enemy had poisoned all the wells with arsenic during his retirement. The morale of the Regiment was greatly improved by the advance, after the many difficulties and slow progress of the last nine months. Later, at 4 p.m., they received orders to withdraw to Wolf Huts. Two days later, the 52nd moved to Bruce Huts on the Aveluy - Bouzincourt road[527]. On March 23rd, Serjeant A. McAlister, aged 43 years, left the Regiment having completed just over 22 years of service. He had undertaken vital work with the water-cart during the Retreat from Mons, and had been appointed as Pioneer Serjeant, in November 1914.

The German retirement, of March 1917, back to the Hindenburg Line, allowed them to shorten their line. Consequently, the British line, too, was reduced in length with the result that the 2nd Division was squeezed out, and the 18th Division, on their left, ended up holding a section of the front that was more appropriate for a platoon! In essence the British gained the services of a whole Army Corps. During this period, the 2nd Division's maximum advance from the old British front line was 14,000 yards. For the month of March, the 2nd Division's casualties, including those incurred in the taking of Grevillers Trench and the German retreat to the Hindenburg Line, numbered 23 officers and 466 other ranks killed, wounded, and missing. On March 23rd, the 2nd Division, including the 52nd, was transferred from the II to the XIII Corps [Lieutenant-General W.N. Congreve], part of the First Army. On leaving the II Corps, the commander, Lieutenant-General Claud Jacob, wrote to Major-General Cecil Pereira regretting the loss of the Division.

At the end of March, the 52nd set off on a series of stiff marches, taking them away from the Somme to the back areas of Arras, where they were to fight a month later. Fortunately, the weather, apart from one day, was fine. The journey, on foot, took the Regiment to; Hérissart, to the north of the Amiens - Albert road, 24th, for one day; Gézaincourt, just south-west of Doullens, 26th; Ligny-sur-

[527] March 21st was the day on which the 2nd Division finally came out of this section of the line. On March 18th, the commander of the II Corps, Lieutenant-General Claud Jacob, told Cecil Pereira that his corps had been 'squeezed out', and it was being relieved at 9 a.m. on March 21st.

Canche, east of Frévent, 27th; Héricourt and near-by Guinecourt, south-west of St. Pol, 28th, also for one day; Floringhem, just north of Pernes, 30th. The *Battalion War Diary* gave few details of this period. The final stage of the long march from Héricourt to Floringhem, some fifteen miles, was performed with style, and no man fell out. On the last day of the long march, the 52nd had a close-up view of a tank, crossing the road and climbing up a bank. One of the officers thought that it looked like 'a gigantic reptile'. On the 30th, Captain Rupert Brett left the Regiment, on appointment as the senior major of the 17th Royal Fusiliers. As the 17th R.F. was also a part of the 5th Brigade, he would not be far away from the Regiment. Further officer reinforcements joined the 52nd; Captain F.W.C. 'Chips' Chippindale; Second-Lieutenants R.G. Wilsdon, F. Southam, and Laurence 'Pullthrough' Fullbrook-Leggatt. The 31st was spent resting after their recent exertions on the march and generally cleaning themselves up.

This brought to an end the first three months of 1917, which the 52nd had spent on the Somme in the area bounded by Courcelette, Miraumont, Bihucourt, and Loupart Wood. In a sense it was a frustrating period for the 5th Brigade and the 52nd, as they had not been used in either the actions towards Miraumont, on February 17-18th, or the capture of Grevillers Trench, on March 10th. It did seem that the divisional commander, Cecil Pereira, favoured the use of the 99th Brigade over the 5th or 6th Brigades, when it came to assaulting the German line. During this period, the 52nd spent much of their time repairing roads or other duties of that ilk. However, from time to time, they did occupy the front line posts, and were scheduled to assault Loupart Trench and Wood, on March 15th, until the German's withdrawal to the Hindenburg Line made this a redundant operation. The Regiment were now in the back area of Arras, which was about to witness one of the great battles of 1917. The 52nd would show their mettle as part of that, between Arleux and Oppy, at the end of April.

Chapter XVI

The Battles of Arras 1917: the Battle of Arleux.

April 1st - May 2nd 1917

[Maps: pages 419, 424, 433.]

We have seen earlier of Sir Douglas Haig's plans for an offensive between Arras and the Somme, to be co-ordinated with the predominant assault of General Robert Nivelle's French forces on the Aisne. Both attacks were planned for the month of April with the French assault taking place a little after the British one. Nivelle had rashly proclaimed that he would capture the city of 'Laon in twenty-four hours and then break out'. Haig hoped, at the very least, to gain the vital Vimy Ridge, with its views over the plain of Douai, and preclude the German reserves being sent to the Aisne. The German withdrawal to the Hindenburg Line had forced him to make some small changes to his plans. In the south, from the valley of the Ancre, the Fifth Army, under General Hubert Gough, would follow up the German retreat to the Hindenburg Line, now without the necessity of fighting their way there. However, the scorched earth policy of the enemy had made the lines of communication of the Fifth Army problematical. Further north, the Hindenburg Line ended at the village of Tilloy-les-Mafflaines, to the south-east of Arras, so that the assault around Arras was not unduly affected by this obstacle.

Sir Douglas Haig had divided up the responsibilities of the four armies that he planned to use in the spring offensive as follows, from north to south: First Army [Horne], to take Vimy Ridge; Third Army [Allenby], to make the main assault from Arras in the direction of Cambrai; Fifth Army [Gough], to close up to the Hindenburg Line, and make a local attack at Quéant; Fourth Army [Rawlinson], to free up French troops for the major offensive on the Aisne by extending the British line down to the Amiens - Roye road.

At 5.30 a.m. on Easter Monday April 9th 1917, the British assault began, and in the region of Arras the men advanced into an unseasonal snow-storm. On the first day of battle, both at Arras and on the Somme in 1916, the British had used fourteen divisions. However, the frontage at Arras was a little narrower, at 25,000 yards, to that of the Somme at 27,000 yards. General Edmund 'the Bull' or 'Tin-Hat' Allenby, slow-moving and inarticulate, had wanted a short, sharp, barrage of 48 hours prior to the start of the assault, but Haig insisted on one lasting five days. More heavy artillery and a better quality of ammunition were available at Arras when compared with the Somme: 963 heavy guns, one every 21 yards compared to 455 heavy guns, one every 57 yards.

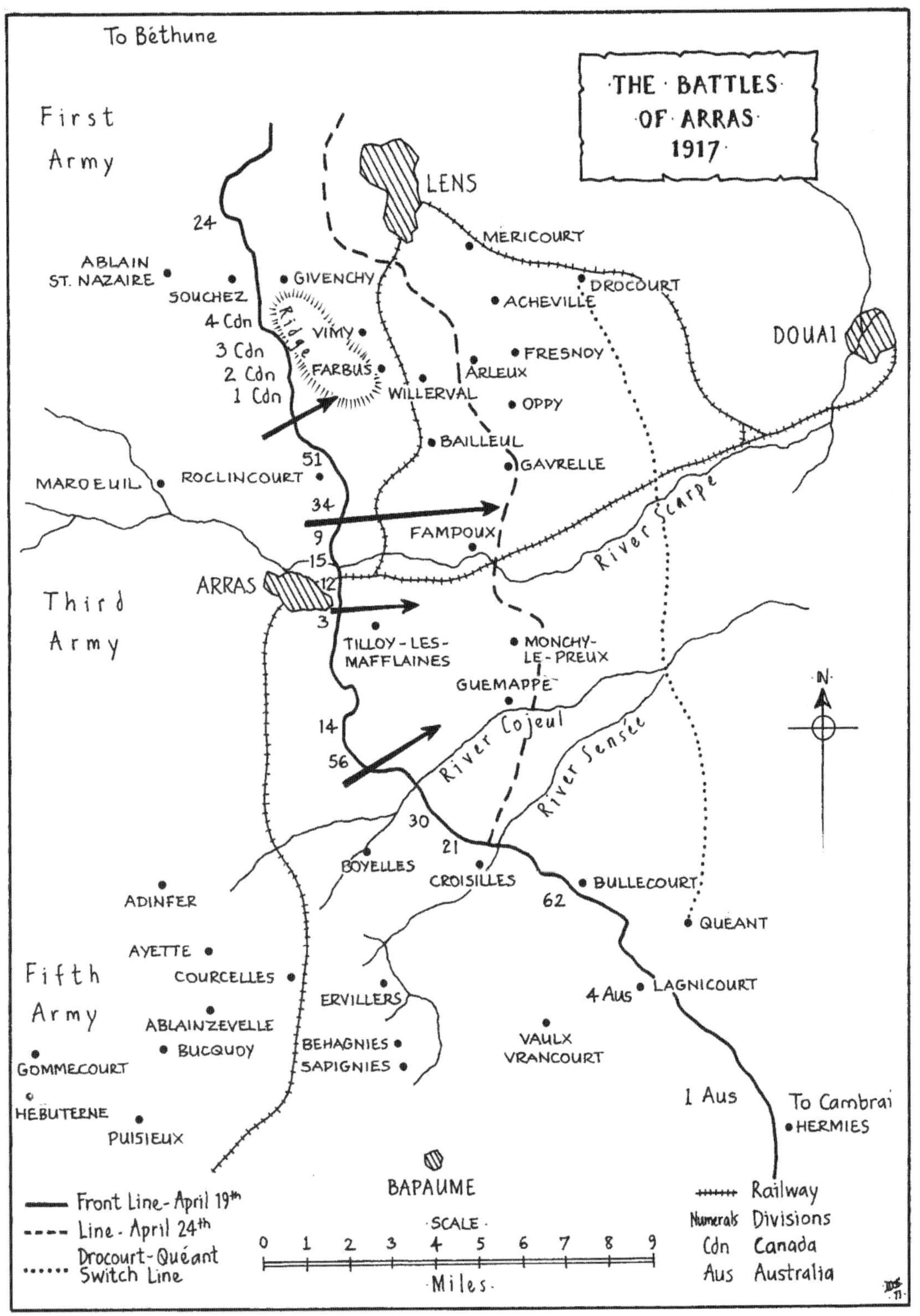
THE BATTLES OF ARRAS 1917
To Béthune
First Army
Third Army
Fifth Army
LENS
MERICOURT
DROCOURT
ACHEVILLE
DOUAI
FRESNOY
ARLEUX
OPPY
ABLAIN ST. NAZAIRE
SOUCHEZ
GIVENCHY
Ridge
VIMY
FARBUS
WILLERVAL
BAILLEUL
GAVRELLE
24
4 Cdn
3 Cdn
2 Cdn
1 Cdn
51
34
9
15
12
3
14
56
30
21
62
4 Aus
1 Aus
MAROEUIL
ROCLINCOURT
FAMPOUX
River Scarpe
ARRAS
TILLOY-LES-MAFFLAINES
MONCHY-LE-PREUX
GUEMAPPE
River Cojeul
River Sensée
N
BOYELLES
CROISILLES
BULLECOURT
QUEANT
ADINFER
AYETTE
COURCELLES
ERVILLERS
LAGNICOURT
ABLAINZEVELLE
BUCQUOY
BEHAGNIES
SAPIGNIES
VAULX VRANCOURT
GOMMECOURT
HEBUTERNE
PUISIEUX
To Cambrai
HERMIES
BAPAUME
Front Line - April 19th
Line - April 24th
Drocourt-Quéant Switch Line
SCALE
0 1 2 3 4 5 6 7 8 9
Miles
Railway
Numerals Divisions
Cdn Canada
Aus Australia

The Canadian Corps, of the First Army, made one of the most impressive assaults of the whole war in taking Vimy Ridge. This famous ridge was some four miles long and ran north-west to south-east, rising slowly from the west, before falling abruptly away to the plain of Douai. Although Vimy Ridge is at its most impressive at its highest point, where the Canadian War Memorial now stands, it actually runs down to the River Scarpe, just to the north of Arras. The Canadians constructed twelve tunnels, which allowed them to approach the enemy's front line under cover. Further south, units of the Third Army did equally well in what became known as the First Battle of the Scarpe. XVII Corps' impressive advance of some three and a half miles was the longest single day's advance since formal trench warfare began. VI Corps achieved two miles including the taking of numerous German guns in Battery Valley. VII Corps managed to advance over a mile, taking the strongly held Neuville Vitasse, and entered the Hindenburg Line. As with the Canadian Corps, the Third Army units used the cellars, sewers, caves, and two large underground tunnels to protect up to 24,500 men, and then get them to the front line under cover. Tanks were to play a part with both the Canadian and Third Army ventures.

As Cyril Falls recorded in the *Official History,* 'Easter Monday of the year 1917 must be accounted one of the great days of the War'. Sadly for the British the great successes of April 9th were not to be repeated. One of the main reasons for the British initial success was the failure of the German commander in the area, the 73-year-old Colonel-General Ludwig von Falkenhausen, to put into practice the new concept of elastic defence as drawn up by Erich von Ludendorff. Von Falkenhausen's reserves were kept too far in the rear to influence the battle. By April 10th and 11th, the enemy had brought up fresh troops and the British advance slowed down. General Edmund Allenby had misread the situation and thought that his men were pursuing a defeated enemy. The key village of Monchy-le-Preux was taken, and the Cavalry Corps was sent in, but the German artillery stopped any hopes of a breakthrough. Further to the south, at Bullecourt, Australian units of the Fifth Army took heavy casualties for very limited gains. Once again, the enemy's line had been broken into, but not through to allow the destruction of his communications and the rolling up of his line. 'Bull' Allenby was still keen to push on despite the protestations of his senior commanders, but Haig overruled him on April 14th, bringing operations to a temporary halt. On April 15th, the Germans undertook a spoiling attack on Lagnicourt, to the south of Bullecourt, and for a time managed to occupy the village. Their intention was to drive back the advanced posts, and to destroy guns, before retiring back to the Hindenburg Line. However, an Australian counter-attack restored the situation.

In reality, on April 14th, Haig should have closed down the British offensive, but the French were depending on him to pin down the German reserves, so that their own major assault, on the Aisne, could go ahead with a greater chance of success. On April 16th, Robert Nivelle's infamous offensive on the Chemin des Dames went ahead. Although nearly 30,000 prisoners and part of the enemy's trench system, sixteen miles wide and four miles deep, were taken, the French suffered large numbers of casualties and became disheartened. Sixty-eight French divisions mutinied, Nivelle was sacked, and General Henri-Philippe Pétain was brought in to restore order.

On April 23rd, at the Second Battle of the Scarpe, Haig loyally restarted his Arras offensive on a major scale. About one mile was taken on the Third Army's front, and the 63rd [Royal Naval] Division did brilliantly in taking Gavrelle to the north of Arras. In the south, Guémappe fell to the 15th Division after heavy fighting. As early as April 18th, there were fears that the French would call off their offensive on the Aisne, unless there was a likelihood of major material gains. Despite this serious development, the British decided to attempt the capture of Oppy and Arleux, which the First Army had been unable to attempt on April 23rd, as the enemy's wire was not sufficiently cut. On April 28th and 29th, the Battle of Arleux took place and very much involved the 2nd Division and the 52nd Light Infantry. The final significant action of the Battles of Arras began on May 3rd with limited objectives, but achieving very little. To make matters worse, the Australians suffered terribly in the second action at Bullecourt between May 3rd and 17th. The Battles of Arras had started so promisingly but had ended disastrously. The daily losses at Arras [1917], 4,076, were greater than those of the Somme [1916], 2,943, Passchendaele [1917], 2,323 and the Hundred Days Battles of 1918, 3,645. The total number of casualties for the Battles of Arras was in the order of 150,000.

Post-war, the Battles Nomenclature Committee defined the Battles of Arras as having taken place between April 9th and May 4th, 1917[528]. There was a further sub-division: the Battle of Vimy Ridge and the First Battle of the Scarpe [capture of Monchy-le-Preux and the Wancourt Ridge], April 9th-14th; Second Battle of the Scarpe [capture of Guémappe and Gavrelle], April 23rd-24th; the Battle of Arleux, April 28th-29th; the Third Battle of the Scarpe [capture of Fresnoy], May 3rd-4th. Based on this nomenclature, as will be shown, the 52nd was able to claim battle honours for Arras, April 9th-May 4th; Vimy, April 9th-14th; the Scarpe, April 9th-14th, April 23rd-24th[529], May 3rd-4th; and Arleux, April 28-29th. The 52nd Light Infantry were in support for Vimy on April 13th, and for the Scarpe

[528] The Arras Offensive was defined as running from April 9th–May 15th 1917.
[529] The 52nd was in the correct area for only the Second Battle of the Scarpe.

on April 23rd. However, the Regiment was one of the front line battalions for the Battle of Arleux on April 28th/29th.

At the beginning of April, the 52nd was still based at Floringhem, and three second-lieutenants reported for duty. They were Second-Lieutenants R.W.G. Creswell, Gordon Fuller, and Alfred Walter. The next day, the 2nd, 'summer time' began at rouse and, ironically, there had been an unexpected heavy fall of snow during the night, which continued into the day. Some of the Regiment's billets had to be evacuated, as their roofs leaked. Training was abandoned in favour of making the roads passable once more. The men enjoyed the unseasonal weather, and there were many snowball fights with the odd window being broken. In Arras, at the end of the day, the snow lay an inch thick. In further horse-play, Cuthbert 'Bingo' Baines, wearing an antimacassar on his head, 'married' Jim Neville to Philip 'Slatcher' Whitehead! This touching scene was further enlivened by the ribald comments of the other young officers. Second-Lieutenant B.J. Crewe joined for duty on the 3rd.

From April 4th-7th, the weather had improved considerably and training started once more. Particular attention was paid to the old Regimental method of bivouacking with a water-proof sheet. The old equipment of string, pegs, and sticks, carried on cookers, was completed. Major-General Cecil Pereira was so impressed with the method that it was adopted by the 2nd Division. On the 5th, the 78th reinforcement of thirteen men joined the Regiment, and Lieutenant J.E. Ellis was struck off its strength, returning to England with catarrhal jaundice. The 8th saw Captain D.M. Rose return to the 1/4th Battalion of the Oxfordshire and Buckinghamshire Light Infantry. That same day, the 52nd marched, as a part of the 5th Brigade, in a southerly and then south-easterly direction, to Hermin-Frevillers via Diéval and Bajus. A one hour halt for tea was held to the east of Diéval. The night was spent at Hermin-Frevillers before, the following day, the Regiment marched to the south-east and spent that night at Maroeuil, just to the north-west of the City of Arras.

Five officers, Captain F.W.C. Chippindale [D], Second-Lieutenants Philip Booth [C], C.E. Cope [A], T.W.C. Foreshew [C], and Jim Neville [B], plus 30 men who were specialists in bombing and the Lewis gun were based at Robecq away from the 52nd. An officer from each company was left behind by the Regiment, in case of casualties, in what was called a Divisional Reception Camp, commonly known as Conception Camp. Robecq was a nice little village to the north of Béthune, and representatives of the whole of XIII Corps were based there in the same capacity as the officers and men of the 52nd. The Regiment's officers messed with those of the 2nd H.L.I. and found them to be a very taciturn crowd. Jim Neville recorded an amusing incident on one of their parades[530].

> Booth[531] told me of a priceless thing he saw on parade the other afternoon. Old "Daddy" Foreshew was lecturing some reinforcements on gas respirators and gas drill. He explained to them how their lives might depend on the efficiency of their respirators, adding:-"I know that the satchel looks a useful receptacle for any odds and ends that you want handy and can't stuff into your haversack, but you must on no account put anything into the satchel. It is meant for the respirator and nothing else."
>
> "I will give you a demonstration. Having placed the satchel in the gas alert position, so, on the command 'Gas,' put your right hand into the satchel, grip the face mask and pull it out, so."
>
> And then, would you believe it, as he pulled out the face-mask, a couple of candles and a pair of socks tumbled into the road in front of the troops where they could not fail to see!!
>
> Booth was lucky, for he was behind the troops and did not have to conceal his smile!

Jim Neville and Philip Booth managed to get down to Arras to visit a friend serving with the 5th Oxfordshire and Buckinghamshire Light Infantry. Neville gave a vivid description of the conditions in the city, and its underground caves, at about the time of the start of the Arras offensive[532].

> It was a very interesting journey, and, when we actually got to Arras, we could easily observe our shells bursting in the Boche lines. The whole town was lousy with guns. In fact there were 18-pounders and 4.5 howitzers in the squares. The noise was redoubled by the echo resounding through the shattered houses. I have never heard such an awful noise since I've been in this god-forsaken land. I went with Philip Booth (do you remember him at the Savoy in September?).
>
> We found out, after some difficulty, where the 5th were. They were resting in the caves prior to "going over the lid." It proved to be an underground sewer. We walked about a mile along the side of this sewer till we reached a passage, leading off to the left, which had

[530] Letter to his sister written from Robecq on April 11th 1917.

[531] Second-Lieutenant Philip 'Blig' Booth.

[532] Letter to his sister written from Robecq on April 15th 1917.

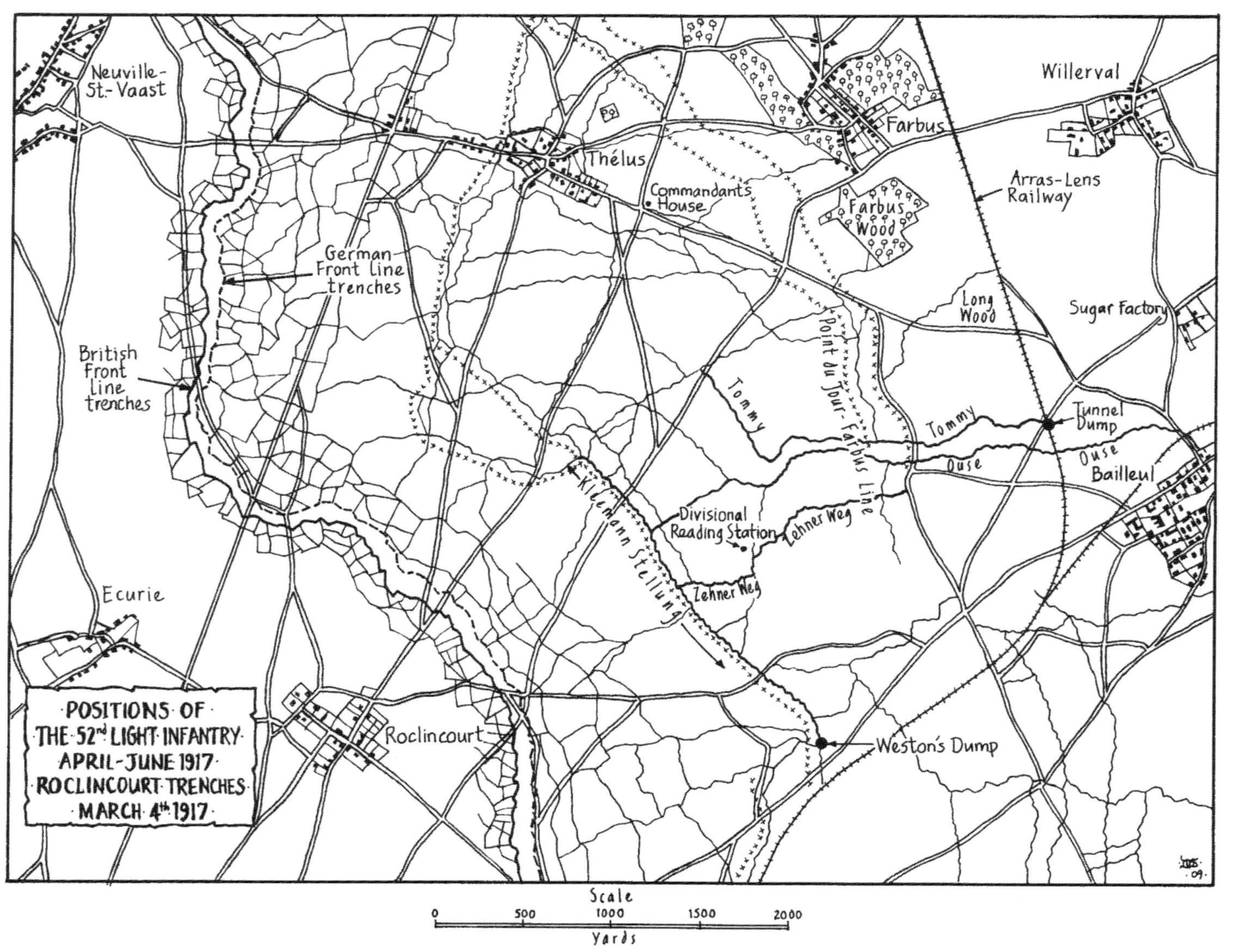

POSITIONS OF THE 52nd LIGHT INFANTRY APRIL-JUNE 1917. ROCLINCOURT TRENCHES MARCH 4th 1917.
Neuville-St.-Vaast
Thélus
Commandant's House
Farbus
Farbus Wood
Willerval
Arras-Lens Railway
German Front line trenches
British Front line trenches
Long Wood
Sugar Factory
Tommy
Point du Jour-Farbus Line
Tommy
Tunnel Dump
Ouse
Ouse
Bailleul
Kleemann Stellung
Divisional Reading Station
Zehner Weg
Zehner Weg
Ecurie
Roclincourt
Weston's Dump
Scale
0
500
1000
1500
2000
Yards

been hewn out of the chalk. Here we passed a policeman on the track of a Brigadier, of whom he was suspicious.

This passage was two miles long and debouched into the gigantic caves, which were lit by electric light, and which the Spanish slaves are supposed to have excavated in the middle ages. I have never seen anything quite so prodigious as these caves; they stretch for miles at a depth of 30 feet or more, are beautifully ventilated, and have water laid on!

On April 11th, the 2nd Division, including the 52nd, joined the Battles of Arras for the first time, by relieving the 51st Highland Division [VII Corps], in the area in front of Roclincourt. Thus the 52nd missed the great successes of the opening day, April 9th. The German first and second lines of trenches had been captured over the preceding two days by the 51st Division. To their left, on the 9th, the Canadian Corps had captured the major part of Vimy Ridge and, just to the north of the Scarpe, Fampoux had also fallen. The 52nd went into a position of support, in the former German second line or Kleemann Stellung, relieving the 6th Black Watch. This was a long trench to the east of Roclincourt, and running from the north-west to south-east. The relief took place in yet another unseasonable, blinding, snow-storm, which led to delays so that the relief was not completed until the early hours of the 12th. A Company of the 52nd in particular suffered badly, in view of the inadequate shelters available, as their section of trench was poorly provided with dug-outs and the men were forced to improvise shelters with small arms ammunition boxes. It was an unpleasant welcome to the trenches of the Arras sector.

The following day the 12th, all the 52nd's officers reconnoitred the forward area. The particular ground involving them lay across the southern end of Vimy Ridge, towards Bailleul and Oppy in the east. The 5th Infantry Brigade occupied the left sub-sector of the 2nd Division's area from a sunken road, 500 yards south-east of the Commandant's House, to a long communication trench, Zehner Weg [exclusive][533]. In their rear, the ground between the brigade and the old British front line was a maze of trenches and barbed wire. British, German, and even French dead littered the whole area. The French had been killed nearly two years before and were still unburied. One French skull still in its steel helmet, with bits of red breeches, femurs, boots, and fragments of feet projecting from the latter, disfigured the ground, awaiting burial.

The front line of the left sub-sector, part of the Farbus - Point-du-Jour line, consisted of two heavily wired trenches, with the wire still to the west, as

[533] Not including Zehner Weg.

there had been no time to transfer it to face the Germans in the east. On the extreme right of the 5th Brigade's sub-sector, to the east at about 1,400 yards, lay Bailleul. To the north-east of Bailleul, at 2,000 yards, were Oppy Wood and village. Other landmarks in the area were a sugar factory, 900 yards north of Bailleul; the Arras to Lens railway line; numerous sunken roads. Fortunately, the area of 5th Brigade's operations was on the southern and lower slopes of Vimy Ridge and, in the main, free from enemy observation behind the crest of the ridge. The 24th R.F. was in the forward trenches, the 52nd in close support [from Tommy Trench to Kleemann Stellung], the 2nd H.L.I. in reserve, and the 17th R.F. in the old German system. Thus the 5th Brigade had strength in depth. To the right of the 5th Brigade were units of the 99th Brigade, with the 6th Brigade in reserve. Captain John Southey of the 52nd, was posted to the 5th Service Battalion of the Regiment. For some time, he had been employed away from the Regiment at the Cadet School, General Headquarters.

In the early morning of April 13th, the 52nd received orders from the 5th Brigade that preparations were to be made for an attack on the Arras to Lens railway line, which crossed the 2nd Division's front. The railway was situated some 700 yards in front of the then British front line, the Farbus - Point-du-Jour Line. It was hoped to set up a line of posts in front of the railway in the direction of the line Bailleul - Willerval. A reconnaissance of the forming-up places was made by officers of the 52nd. However, during the afternoon, units of the 99th Brigade discovered that the railway line and Bailleul station had been vacated by the enemy and promptly occupied them. At about 3 p.m., the 24th R.F., having heard of the activities of the 99th Brigade, moved forward itself. The 24th R.F. advanced under heavy artillery fire to a line from the eastern edge of Willerval to Bailleul. The line covered a sugar factory, midway between the two villages, in the orchard of which a German naval six-inch gun was captured. At about 10 p.m., the 52nd moved forward in support, and the line was consolidated that night. A and D Companies were in the Farbus - Point-du-Jour Line, with B and C Companies and the Regimental Aid Post in Tommy Trench. This move, on the 13th, placed the 52nd within the confines of the Battle of Vimy Ridge, allowing the Regiment to qualify for it as a battle honour.

By 7 p.m. on the 13th, units of the 99th Brigade held Bailleul. That night two companies of the 1st King's Royal Rifle Corps [99th Brigade] pushed out towards Hill 80, the high ground between Bailleul and the Oppy Line. In this endeavour the Rifles were joined by the 23rd R.F. [also 99th Brigade] and by the 14th they had taken Hill 80. In the afternoon, the 24th R.F were sent forward to make contact with the enemy and then dig in. Their advance came to within 500-600 yards of the Arleux to Oppy Line, where the Fusiliers came under heavy fire from both the enemy's artillery and machine-guns, forcing them to dig front and support posts. Both flanks were refused[534] as the units on either side had not come up with them. One platoon, misinterpreting orders, attempted to capture Oppy, but after a spirited fight was taken prisoner. Patrols showed that the Oppy Line was occupied along its whole length, and Major-General Cecil Pereira, commanding the 2nd Division, ordered the Brigadiers of the 5th and 99th Brigades to push up to the line. Behind this line, guns were gradually being brought up, and those already in place began wire cutting, as the entanglements in front of the Oppy Line were formidable. By nightfall, the 2nd Division was occupying a linc running from 1,000 yards east of Willerval: south-east for 500 yards in front of the Oppy Line, to the railway between Oppy Wood and Bailleul; here the line turned back to the south-west across Hill 80 and then slightly east again to a point just west of Gavrelle. The intention was to push out posts to 300 yards from the German wire and then join them up to make a 'jumping off' place for the attack.

During April 14th, a gloriously sunny day, Major Cuthbert 'Bingo' Baines took over temporary command of the 52nd as Lieutenant-Colonel Richard Crosse was sick. At night the 52nd relieved the 24th R.F. in the front line. It was a troublesome relief, in view of the intense darkness of the night making it difficult to find the posts, and was not completed until after daylight on the 15th. Further problems related to the non-arrival of the ration and water carts whose guides had managed to lose themselves. The line now held by the 52nd ran parallel to and about 1,000 yards from the Arleux - Oppy and Arleux Switch Trenches[535], which were occupied by the enemy. The distribution of the 52nd was A, B, and D Companies, each with two platoons in the front line posts, and C Company in the environs of the Sugar Factory. The Regimental Headquarters was situated in a dug-out on the embankment of the Arras to Lens railway. Two men were killed during the day and three further wounded.

April 14th 1917, with the benefit of hindsight, was the day that Sir Douglas Haig could have closed down the Arras offensive to his own advantage, if he had not been committed to holding down the German reserves, so that the Nivelle offensive, on the Aisne, could have a better chance of success. By this juncture, to the north, the Canadians were occupying Vimy, Givenchy-en-Gohelle, Angres, and Liévin. South of the Scarpe, fierce fighting to the south-east of Arras had led to the fall of no less than seven miles of the Hindenburg Line. Haig reported that following six days of fighting the front had been pushed back four miles to the east, and the dominant features which were the immediate

---

[534] Turned back.

[535] Everard Wyrall in *The History of the Second Division* recorded the distance as 500–600 yards from the Arleux - Oppy line.

objective of his attack were now in his hands. In addition, 13,000 prisoners and over 200 guns had been captured and a wide gap driven through the prepared German defences.

The 52nd were now facing the Oppy Line, which in reality was a switch line from the Hindenburg Line south of the Scarpe. It ran from the northern bank of the river past the western outskirts of Fampoux, Gavrelle, Oppy, and finally Arleux. From close to the northern edge of Oppy Wood, a further switch line, the Oppy - Mericourt - Vendin Line ran away to the north. During April 15th, the enemy's artillery bombarded the 52nd in their sketchy front line posts, on either side of the Arleux - Bailleul road. Worse, German machine-gunners and snipers were very active, making life for the 52nd even more difficult as the men tried to dig themselves in more securely. That night B and D Companies of the Regiment were relieved by the 17th R.F., and retired to dug-outs, in the sunken road, between the Arras to Lens railway embankment and the Sugar Factory. Two men of the 52nd were wounded, and the long-serving Regimental Serjeant-Major Arthur Warnock returned to England and was put temporarily on the home establishment.

During April 16th, Second-Lieutenant R.W.G. Creswell was transferred to England with tonsillitis and one man was killed, another ten were wounded, and a further man was reported missing. At 6.40 p.m. that day, orders were received for the 52nd plus the 17th R.F.[536] in conjunction with the 63rd Division on the right, and the Canadian Corps on the left, to attack and capture the Arleux and Oppy Line with bombing parties. During the night of April 15th/16th, the 190th Brigade of the 63rd [Royal Naval] Division had replaced the 99th Brigade on the 5th Brigade's right. It was pointed out to the 5th Brigade that all reports of observers and patrols showed that on the front facing the 52nd, the enemy's wire was thick and had no gaps in it. The attack was postponed, at about 10.30 p.m., for further patrols to go out for another inspection of the two belts of wire. It rained all night and fortunately for the bombing parties, at 3.30 a.m. on the 17th, the operation was wisely cancelled by the 2nd Division.

---

536 On April 20th, Lieutenant-Colonel Charles 'Buggins' Higgins, formerly of the 52nd, now commanding the 17th Royal Fusiliers, left them to take command of the 174th Brigade. He said; 'I felt extremely elated. It was certainly one of the proudest moments of my life. I had always looked on command of a brigade as one of the best commands in the Army in France, and now I was one of the very youngest brigadiers in the Army [at 38 years]. I said "good-bye" to the 17th Royal Fusiliers with the greatest regret. I knew it was through them that I had really won my brigade'. Higgins' natural ambition to command a brigade was the reverse of that of his contemporary in the 52nd, Richard Crosse's, who declined to leave his beloved Regiment under any circumstances. Pressure in early 1917 to go on the staff or command a brigade was resisted and divisional and brigade commanders gave up trying to wean him from the Regiment.

A little later, the 52nd's D Company relieved A Company. Then A and B Companies were moved to Ouse Trench and also into cellars and dug-outs in the northern outskirts of Bailleul. During the afternoon, some of the cellars occupied by A Company were blown in by artillery fire and the men were transferred to a dug-out in the Sunken Road. At night, B and C Companies exchanged positions. It had not been a good day for the 52nd with five men killed, four wounded, and one missing. Amongst the wounded was Second-Lieutenant Laurence Fullbrook-Leggatt with gunshot injuries to his face and left hand. The redoubtable Company Serjeant-Major Fred Clare was appointed temporary Regimental Serjeant-Major in place of R.S.M. Arthur Warnock who had returned to England. A better man could not have been picked as Clare was the very essence of a fighting soldier.

The following day, April 18th, the 52nd was relieved by the 2nd South Staffordshire of the 6th Brigade, and retired to the old British and German front line dug-outs. Both the officers and men were in an exhausted state and needed to rest for a few days. One man was wounded on the 18th. Lieutenant-Colonel Richard Crosse returned to command the Regiment on the 19th, and five further men were wounded on the same day. The next day Lieutenant T.A. Coffin and Corporal Jones erected a bath-house, barber's shop, and shaving saloon at the Transport Lines. Each platoon was able to visit these establishments, and this did much to boost morale over the following two days. On the 21st, the 52nd exchanged positions with the 2nd H.L.I., with the Regimental Headquarters and C Company in Tommy Trench, and A, B, D Companies in Kleemann Stellung, the old German second line. On April 22nd, B and D Companies moved to the Farbus - Point-du-Jour Line, in relief of two companies of the 17th Middlesex [6th Brigade]. Two Second-Lieutenants, F. Southam and D.E. Haymen, were invalided to England, the former with a shell contusion to his back and right shoulder, and the latter with shell shock[537].

The French under General Robert Nivelle had launched their attacks on the Aisne, between Soissons and Reims, on the 16th, with a certain amount of success, although not the anticipated breakthrough. The heavy casualties and general disappointment would lead numerous divisions to mutiny and to Nivelle's summary dismissal. In the north, Sir Douglas Haig restarted his offensive primarily to take the pressure off the French and the enemy's reserves away from them, and on to his own forces in the vicinity of Arras. Consequently, on a most auspicious day, April 23rd, Saint George's Day, Sir Douglas Haig sent his First,

---

[537] Haymen would return to the 52nd in 1918. Clearly, his shell shock was not considered to be a stigma by the Regiment. In the *Regimental Chronicles* his name is spelt Haymen: in the 52nd's *Wounds and Movements* book Hayman.

Third and Fifth Armies into action, on a nine miles front, from Croisilles in the south to Gavrelle in the north. This series of actions became known as the Second Battle of the Scarpe. By the evening of the 24th, Gavrelle [on the 23rd], Guémappe, and the high ground overlooking Fontaine-lès-Croisilles and Cherisy had been taken. Some progress had been made east of Monchy-le-Preux, on the left bank of the Scarpe, and on Greenland Hill.

At dawn on Saint George's Day, a bright and sunny morning, the 63rd [Royal Naval] Division attacked and managed to capture the village of Gavrelle after heavy street fighting, but it was unable to progress the additional 300 yards to the east that had been intended. As we have seen, the attack further north on the Oppy Line had been cancelled in view of the uncut wire in front of it. Part of the reason for the uncut wire was the difficulty in finding suitable positions for the Field Artillery. Behind Vimy Ridge the guns were at the limit of their range, and in front of the Ridge they were exposed to the enemy's fire. In reality, the wire in front of Gavrelle also appeared to be uncut to the brigades about to undertake the assault. The Divisional Commander, Major-General C.E. Lawrie, refused to allow a postponement as air reconnaissance showed some gaps in the wire. In the event, he was proved to be correct and by a fine feat of arms the 63rd took the village of Gavrelle and held it. The officers and men of the 52nd, who were standing by in support of the 63rd Division, had a grandstand view of the action and the counter-attacks that continued the following day. The importance of Gavrelle to the enemy is shown by the fact that there were at least six separate attempts to retake the village. By the evening of the 23rd, 12 German officers and 350 other ranks had been captured by the Division.

Second-Lieutenant Jim Neville rejoined the Regiment on April 23rd after his sojourn with the Divisional Reception Camp. In two letters to his family, firstly, he described an aircraft attack on a balloon and a near miss to himself, and secondly, whilst watching the German counter-attack on Gavrelle, he gave a graphic description of the destructive power of the artillery against infantry in the open[538].

> I was very pleased to get back to the Regiment, which had been having a rotten time, for a fortnight on end, in the line. The Companies had to dig in under heavy artillery fire, and many men were blown up and buried, while our guns were not in a position to retaliate.

---

[538] The first a letter to his father and the second one to his sister both written from Bray on April 26th 1917.

I started for the support line at 2.30 p.m. on the 24th. On the way I watched a Hun aeroplane come over and attack one of our sausage balloons. He fired some tracer bullets which carry a little flame behind them and ignite petrol tanks of aeroplanes and balloon bags. I could see the track of the bullets quite plainly and then, the two observers jumped out in their parachutes and landed in a wood behind Arras. The Hun circled up, turned, and then potted the wretched chaps as they were floating down to the ground, until one of our machines turned up from nowhere and drove him off.

We managed to lose our way up to the support line in spite of it being a lovely sunny afternoon. While we were wandering about trying to find the particular old Hun trench, we stopped to watch some anti-aircraft guns fire, and we had a very lucky escape; a 4.2 shell landed quite close and practically on the battery. It was as close as if you were standing on the doorstep at 25 and the shell had landed on the pillar-box at the corner[539]. It was a dud by the grace of God! There would have been a pretty shambles if it had exploded.

Eventually I found "B" and we observed the plain between Oppy and Gavrelle through glasses and watched the Huns counter-attacking. Three times they attacked, and thrice they were scattered by our gunfire. There is an account of it in the *Daily Mail* of April 25th.

The view was simply magnificent. I could see all the mining towns, Lens on the left and Douai in the distance to our front, and the visibility was very good.

On the afternoon of the 24th there was a great deal of railway activity behind the enemy's line at Neuvireuil. We could see troops detraining, and telephoned through to our gunners to try and hurry them up a bit! The reply was that the map reference was out of range of the field guns. Eventually the heavies put a few good 'uns amongst them and they scattered like chaff. It was great fun to watch. But that was not all. About an hour later, we saw three waves of attacking troops advancing towards our front line at Gavrelle. We telephoned to the Field Gunners to give them hell, and were told by them, that they could not fire because the attack was being launched out of their group!! It was simply maddening as you

[539] The pillar-box has gone. The distance between No. 25 Eccleston Square and the corner is about 25 yards.

> can imagine. But when it seemed that the enemy was going to reach our line unmolested, there was a sudden and continuous roar of artillery on our right, and a curtain of devastating fire blotted out the advancing Huns. The next thing we saw were men, like ants, running away to the rear. The smoke rolled away, the firing ceased, the attack had been repulsed. Yet the Huns made two further efforts to reach our front line, and in each case they were caught by our guns and wiped out. I don't suppose I shall ever have another opportunity of watching an attack in complete safety. I felt quite sorry for the Huns, for they hadn't a ghost of a chance. We could even see their officers who follow behind their men, and don't lead them. It looked as if they were driving their men.

At 1.30 p.m. on April 25th, the Regiment received orders that they were to be relieved by the 17th R.F., and would proceed to Bray in the rear areas, near Ecoivres and Mont St. Eloi. The move was completed by 3 a.m. the next day. This gave the 52nd a short period to prepare for a continuation of the attack started on April 23rd by the 63rd Division.

On April 26th, Lieutenant-General Launcelot Kiggell, Chief of the General Staff, met with Generals Henry Horne [First Army] and Edmund Allenby [Third Army]. Kiggell informed them that Sir Douglas Haig intended to continue with operations in the vicinity of Arras, provided that the French on the Aisne did the same. The underlying reason for the attacks remained the necessity of tying down the enemy's forces so that the French in the south would have a greater chance of success. However, if the French closed down their assault on the Aisne, Haig would turn his attention to the submarine menace and open operations in the Ypres sector[540]. The secondary operation by units of the First Army against Arleux and Oppy, which had been unable to go ahead on April 23rd in view of the uncut wire, would start on the 28th. The Third Army would also attack both to the north and south of the Scarpe on the same day. The attacks on an eight-mile front would extend from Arleux in the north to Monchy-le-Preux in the south.

The First Army had been ordered to break through the Oppy Line, part of which at Gavrelle had already been taken on April 23rd by the 63rd Division. Straddling the Arras - Lille road, the original German third line made a large loop around the village of Arleux. On the eastern side of the loop a switch joined it to

---

[540] In Britain there was fear that the War might be lost if German U-Boats interrupted the supply of food and war materials by sinking merchant ships on a great scale. If the U-Boat bases in Belgium could be taken, the threat would be much reduced.

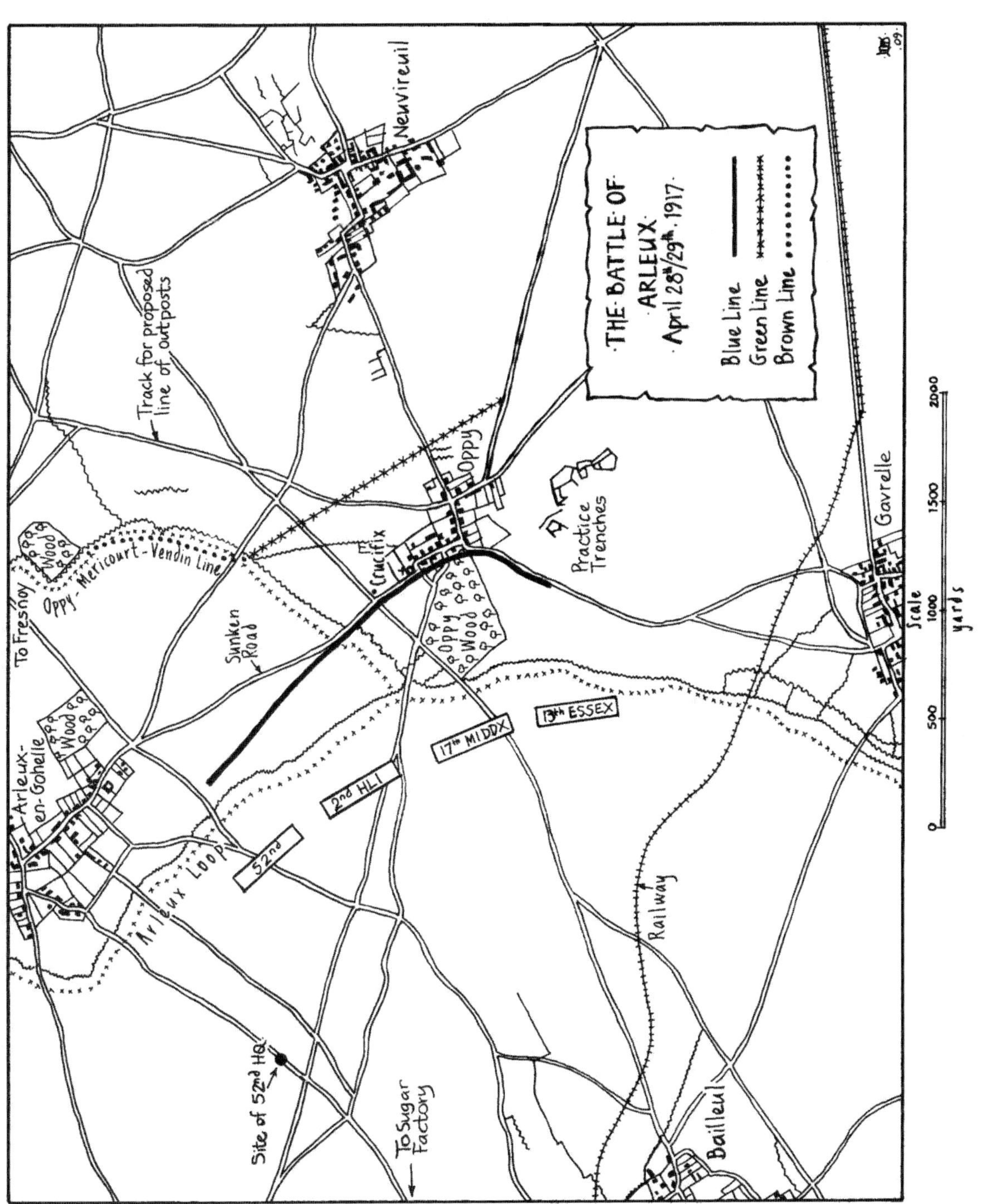
THE BATTLE OF ARLEUX April 28th/29th 1917
Blue Line
Green Line
Brown Line
Neuvireuil
Track for proposed line of outposts
Oppy
Crucifix
Practice Trenches
Oppy Wood
Wood
To Fresnoy
Oppy-Mericourt-Vendin Line
Sunken Road
Arleux-en-Gohelle
Wood
Arleux Loop
52nd
2nd HLI
17th MIDDX
13th ESSEX
Gavrelle
Railway
Bailleul
Site of 52nd HQ
To Sugar Factory
Scale
0
500
1000
1500
2000
yards

the next line of defence, this being to the west of Neuvireuil, the Rouvoy - Fresnes position. For the attack, units of the Canadian Corps would be on the left and XIII Corps on the right. In the XIII Corps' area the 2nd Division would be on the left and the 63rd [Royal Naval] Division on the right, around the salient that they had created at Gavrelle.

The 2nd Division was assigned a front of approximately 2,200 yards and with an average line of advance of 1,200 yards. Major-General Cecil Pereira decided to use his two numerically strongest brigades, the 5th and 6th, in the assault. All three brigades were short of manpower and the 5th and 6th could only muster a total of 3,518 men between them. The 5th Brigade was on the left opposite the gap between the village of Arleux and Oppy Wood, and the 6th Brigade was on the right facing Oppy Wood and village. The intended junction between the two brigades, in the enemy's trenches, was to be slightly to the north of Oppy Wood and village. The weakest in terms of numbers of men of the three brigades, the 99th, was held in reserve. The two front line brigades chose to use their strongest battalions in the attack. The 5th Brigade had the 52nd on the left and the 2nd H.L.I. on the right, and the 17th R.F. was to act as "mopper up" with the 24th R.F. in brigade reserve. The 6th Brigade positioned the 17th Middlesex on the left, next to the 2nd H.L.I., and the 13th Essex on the right with the 2nd South Staffordshire as "mopper up" or to provide "strong point parties".

The objectives of the 5th and 6th Brigades were three arbitrary lines named Blue, Green, Brown [see map on page 433]. The Blue Line, the first objective, ran from C.13.c.2.8 [map reference] - along the road past Oppy Church as far as the Crucifix - B.12.d.7.6 - thence along the German support line to the boundary of the 1st Canadian Division at B.12.a.3.9. It was the front and support German trenches. The Green Line, the second objective, ran from the trench junction at C.13.b.8.1 - trenches east of Oppy - to trench junction C.7.a.4.5. It was 300-400 yards east of the Blue Line. The Brown Line, the third objective [for the 5th Brigade only], ran from the trench junction at C.7.a.4.5. to the southern extremity of the wood south of Fresnoy C.1.a.4.1. Basically it ran along the Oppy Support Trench, thence the Mericourt - Vendin line, and then to the wood south of Fresnoy[541]. Also it was hoped to establish a line of Lewis gun posts along the track running through C.1.b and d. and C.7.b. on and south of Hill 60. On the left in front of the junction of the 52nd and the 1st Canadian Division, the Green and Brown Lines joined together. It was not intended to advance further than the Oppy Line and its villages, although if all the objectives were taken, strong

[541] Although documents in both the 2nd Division's and the 5th Brigade's records show this to be the extent of the third objective or Brown Line, a map in the latter's records shows the third objective extending to the east of Oppy.

patrols were to be pushed out to exploit the success, to seize tactical features and to maintain touch with the enemy. The 226th Field Company Royal Engineers was to assist the 5th Brigade in making strong points in order to retain the captured positions. The 2nd Division suggested that the lines of consolidation should be 100 yards in advance of the captured trench as the enemy would know the exact position of his trench, and consequently could shell it with great accuracy.

The 2nd Division's attack on the Oppy Line had been postponed on April 23rd because of uncut wire in front of the enemy. At a conference held by the Corps commander, Lieutenant-General Walter Congreve, on April 16th, it was recorded that there was 'a good supply of 106 fuzes available, and the wire was to be cut mainly by means of 4.5 inch howitzers using these fuzes'. '18-pounder ammunition was mainly to be saved for the attack'. The new 106 fuzes burst immediately on the slightest touch with any object. On making contact with barbed wire the shell splinters cut the wire and the blast dispersed it. It was an effective alternative to shrapnel for cutting wire. Nevertheless, as will be seen shortly, the two belts of wire in front of the 52nd were still ineffectively cut prior to their attack on April 28th.

The 2nd Division's orders for the attack on the Oppy Line on April 28th stated that 'the artillery barrage is the guiding factor to the pace of the infantry advance'. It continued 'it must be impressed on all ranks taking part in the attack that it is absolutely essential to advance close up to the barrage and they must assault any portion of the enemy trench or enemy position opposite them immediately the barrage lifts off it'. By 1917, the creeping barrages had become much more sophisticated compared with those of 1915-16. Often such barrages had got so far ahead of the attacking infantry that the enemy had recovered from its immediate effects and had been able to man his machine-guns. The artillery support for the 2nd Division in this operation was provided by its own divisional artillery, plus that of the CLXX Brigade of the 31st Division and the XXXIV, LXXXIV and CCCXV Brigades Royal Field Artillery. There was a double 18-pounder creeping barrage with one half firing high explosive shells 200 yards ahead of an inner one firing shrapnel. As was recorded earlier, artillery support was difficult in this area, as the crest of Vimy Ridge meant that either the guns were firing at long range from behind the crest, or were in an exposed position in front of it. There was concern that the 52nd and the 2nd H.L.I., on the open ground between Arleux and Oppy, would be particularly at risk from enfilade machine-gun fire. Hence it was arranged for the barrage on the flanks to be slightly ahead of that in the centre.

The barrage was arranged to creep forward at a set rate of 100 yards per four minutes, with regular pauses and isolation of the areas of trench that the infantry were assaulting. The barrage table allowed the infantry eight minutes to reach the German front line before it shifted on to the Blue Line. Thereafter there were regular lifts and pauses for the troops to reach the Green Line and eventually the Brown Line. The Blue Line was to be assaulted at sixteen minutes after zero hour; the Green Line at 78 minutes after zero hour; the Brown Line at 116 minutes after zero hour[542].

The 5th Brigade sent down further orders for the 52nd. Dress; the men were to be in fighting order without greatcoats. Considering that heavy snow had fallen earlier in the month the lack of greatcoats might have cost the troops dear. However, waterproof sheets were carried. The officers were to dress in exactly the same way as the men, although they would carry Very pistols and a packet of S.O.S coloured lights [to bring down defensive artillery fire][543]. Each battalion, excluding medical officers, was limited to sixteen officers in the attack. Every man would carry two No. 5 Mills bombs plus 120 rounds of small arms ammunition, except signallers, bombers, and Lewis and Vickers gunners who would carry 50 rounds only. As well as ammunition, each man would have a day's food rations about his person. Flares, sandbags and wire-cutters were also carried. All ranks were forbidden to carry into action documents, maps or sketches that might be of use to the enemy[544]. Watches were to be synchronized at 10 a.m., 2 p.m., and 10 p.m. on Y, the day before the assault or Z day, the day of zero. It was essential that all ranks and units were keeping the same time. Earlier, at the Battle of Festubert, we saw the difficulties created by a failure to synchronise all watches.

Communication between units was often difficult with telephone wires regularly being cut and the wireless at battalion level still being in its infancy. However, at this stage of the war, wireless stations were present at brigade, division, and corps level. For the attack on the Oppy line, telephone lines were laid out to the Sugar Factory where an exchange was to be set up. Lines were to be run up to the battalion headquarters on the road at B.10.b.8.2. Attacking companies would each take forward a telephone wire to allow communication with their commanding officers during the attack.

A Brigade Runner Post was established in the Sugar Factory consisting of one N.C.O. plus six men. These men would work both forwards and backwards.

---

542 Details of the barrage timetable can be found in the *Regimental Chronicles* for 1916-17 on pages 156 and 158. There appears to be a disparity in the timings given on the two pages.

543 Identical clothing would make it more difficult for the Germans to identify and preferentially kill officers in order to disrupt command and control.

544 Whether the rule prohibiting the carrying of sketches into battle was always followed is open to debate. Certainly, Captain Ralph Kite took a sketch of the layout of the British front line trenches with him in the major assault of the German line on the Redan Ridge in November 1916.

The 52nd was to have its own No. 1 Relay Post in the Arleux Loop as soon as it was captured. Again this would consist of one N.C.O. and six men. A further No. 2 Relay Post, consisting of the same number of men, was to be ready to go forward once the final objective had been taken. Each company officer was ordered to carry field message cards. The telephone lines discussed earlier were to be led into the Relay Posts. Power buzzers were to be placed in the forward battalion headquarters and they were to be manned by brigade signallers. The listening set was to be situated in the 5th Brigade Headquarters, allowing the 52nd to send messages directly back to Brigadier-General George Bullen-Smith. Basically, a power buzzer was an apparatus enabling the transmission of signals in morse code over a short distance[545]. A spare buzzer was to be kept in reserve in the Sugar Factory. A Wireless Station was to be established again in the Sugar Factory and would move forward as the attack progressed. There was a shortage of pigeons with only two birds per forward battalion available. A Divisional Reading Station was to be established at B.19.d.2.8., to monitor signals from the whole Divisional front. In the event of a misty day, a Brigade Station was to be set up at the Sugar Factory if there was a clear view from it. Thus there were no less than six methods of communication between the leading attacking troops and the brigade headquarters.

The 2nd Division also made additional administrative arrangements. Battle Straggler Posts were set up in the rear. Men who were found in areas away from their units were to be collected up, and it was to be noted whether they had discarded their arms or not, with a view to later disciplinary action. Well-led Regiments with high morale, such as the 52nd, seldom suffered from problems of this nature. Note was also to be made of the walking wounded, and whether it was thought that they had unnecessarily parted with their weapons. A Prisoner-of-War Cage was to be set up in Roclincourt, and one officer and ten men were to be delegated from 5th Brigade to act as guards for it. Captured officers were to be searched at once, but other ranks would not be until they reached the cage. Great care was to be taken to see that prisoners were taken to the appropriate divisional cage. If another division's cage was used receipts were to be taken. Presumably this was to stop other divisions from claiming the credit for the prisoners' capture!

In any battle the availability of further supplies of ammunition was always important. The 2nd Division's main ammunition dump was called Weston's dump and was situated at B.26.c.0.5. An advanced dump was set up in the railway tunnel to the north of Bailleul station, at B.15.c.6.3, and unsurprisingly was known as Tunnel dump. Individual brigades would decide the

[545] The power buzzer enabled signals to be transmitted through the earth to be picked up by an ordinary telephone receiver connected to widely separated earths.

necessity for and position of dumps in their forward positions. Here would be placed boxes of grenades and small arms ammunition, clearly marked with a notice cloth, either 'SAA' or 'Grenades'. The underlying principle was always automatic supply from the rear, rather than front line troops having to send back for more ammunition.

As well as ammunition, Weston's dump was to have a rations reserve in case normal food supplies failed to get through. No less than 2,500 cheese sandwiches were to be delivered to the 5th and 6th Brigades on Y day. Water dumps were to be set up in forward areas, and a reserve of 800 tins was to be held at Weston's dump. The officer in charge there was only to issue the reserve water sparingly. Carrying parties, to wear a yellow band on their left arms, were organised and a soup kitchen and coffee bar were set up at the beginning of the duck-boards at Roclincourt. Here free tea, coffee, biscuits and cigarettes could be obtained.

We left the 52nd in Bray on April 26th, where the day was spent in explaining the details of the forthcoming attack to the men. Only on the 27th was the Regiment informed that the attack on the Arleux Loop would go ahead on the following day, Z day, and that zero hour would be 4.25 a.m. At 11 a.m., the Regiment moved to the transport bivouac where they drew equipment and then moved to the assembly trenches after dark. The enterprise got off to a bad start on the night of the 27th/28th, when A Company was shelled near the 5th Brigade Headquarters, this resulting in the death of Second-Lieutenant Gilbert Calloway and six men. The 21-year-old Calloway had only been with the 52nd since February 7th, and had just got over a bout of chickenpox. A number of other men were wounded, and two Lewis guns were destroyed with their operators practically all becoming casualties. Matters were made worse on going up to the line, with further men, mainly members of the Regimental Headquarters, being wounded. The 2nd Division had a reputation for having fewer casualties than other divisions in XIII Corps, and one of their secrets was to take great care when going up to the line, if they could be seen by the enemy. Clearly on this occasion the 52nd was unlucky.

In the early hours of April 28th, the 52nd formed up and prepared to attack the Arleux Loop. The battalions of both the attacking brigades, the 5th and 6th, were in position by 3.30 a.m. The Regiment was to advance in four waves with support from companies of the 17th R.F. acting as 'moppers up' and carrying parties. The first wave was positioned on the parapet of the British front line trench, with two platoons of D Company on the left and two of B Company on the right. The second wave occupied the front line trench with two platoons of D Company plus their Company Headquarters [Captain David Barnes], and two platoons of B Company plus their Company Headquarters [Captain William Giles[546]]. Just behind the front line trench were two platoons from the 17th R.F. to mop up on the Blue Line once it had been reached. Immediately behind these men were the remaining two platoons of the attached company of the 17th R.F., who were to mop up the Arleux Loop itself. On a taped line, laid by the Royal Engineers [226th Field Company] 50 yards from the British forward trench, came the third wave of the 52nd consisting of two platoons of A Company [Second-Lieutenant Philip Whitehead] on the left and two platoons of C Company [Lieutenant Laurence Dowson] on the right. The fourth wave, consisting of the remainder of the two companies plus their headquarters, was situated a further 50 yards back. Twenty-five yards in the rear of the last 52nd man were the remaining two platoons of the attached company of the 17th R.F. who were to act as a carrying party. It is interesting to note that of the four company commanders of the 52nd, three of them had barely seven months experience of the trenches and their overall average age was 21 years. The relatively experienced man was Captain David Barnes. Lieutenant-Colonel Richard Crosse shared his Regimental Headquarters with the 2nd H.L.I., on the Bailleul to Arleux road, at B.10.b.8.2. He considered it a poorly sited Headquarters and, as will be seen, was correct in thinking so.

The plan envisaged that the first and second waves plus the 'moppers up' would closely follow the barrage, ready to rush the Arleux Loop the moment the barrage lifted off it. Some of the 'moppers up' would consolidate the Arleux Loop as the first and second waves continued to follow the creeping barrage towards the Blue Line. Compass parties on their right flank would help the 52nd advance in the correct direction. After the capture of the Blue Line by the first and second waves, the rest of the 'moppers up' would take over responsibility for it. The third and fourth waves would close up to the first and second waves, but not actually enter the Blue Line. Ultimately, the 52nd would advance in four waves on the Green Line and, following a halt in the barrage, advance to the Brown Line. In practice it seems unlikely that such a strict schedule, as this, could be followed, particularly under the inevitable retaliatory fire of the enemy.

Facing the 1st Canadian, 2nd and 63rd Divisions from north to south were units of the German 111th, 17th, and 1st Guard Reserve Divisions. The German 111th Division occupied positions from the north of Oppy to Acheville. In the forward trench of the Arleux Loop were two of its battalions, one of the 76th Regiment on the right, and one of the 73rd Regiment on the left. The 111th Division was considered to be a good unit in 1917, although it would be sorely tried in Flanders by the Franco-British attack on the following July 31st. The 73rd

[546] William Giles was a temporary captain. His substantive rank was Second-Lieutenant.

Regiment was recruited in Hanover, and the 76th from the Hanseatic cities. Further south of the 111th Division was the 75th Regiment of the 17th Division, which had not been in action on April 23rd and had remained in the line. Again the division was considered to be a good one, largely recruited from the Hanseatic cities and Mecklenburg. Next in the line was the 1st Guard Reserve Division, which had only one of its Regiments, the 64th Reserve, in the line. Like the rest of the Guard, the Division was recruited in the provinces of Prussia and its men would fight well in the ensuing battle. An officer of the 2nd Division described the 1st Guard Reserve Division as the most determined that he had seen.

At 4.25 a.m. on Saturday April 28th, the 52nd attacked the Arleux Loop, getting forward close to the artillery barrage which was pulverizing the German front line. The Regiment moved across the 300-400 yards of no man's land[547] in their four waves. Within a minute of the opening of the British artillery's fire, the enemy replied in kind with an intense artillery and minenwerfer[548] barrage about 150-200 yards behind the British front line. As the 52nd reached the German wire, intense machine-gun fire was brought to bear on the attacking troops. Despite the extra days of preparatory artillery fire with the new 106 fuze, the 52nd found only two gaps in the enemy's wire, fortunately one gap being in front of each company. Through the gap on the left Captain David Barnes' D Company went, and on the right Captain William Giles' B Company did likewise. Inevitably the Germans had machine-guns lined up on the two gaps, causing casualties[549]. Although the enemy was reported only to have a normal trench garrison, they had an unusually large number of machine-guns. After the attack, both Baines and Giles commented on the state of the German wire in front of their respective companies. Both officers described the barrage at zero hour as "weak".

> Left company [Barnes]: There was one gap in the wire on my Company frontage, and that was a very bad gap.
> Right company [Giles]: On my Company front there was only one proper gap in the wire, and that was on the right. The remainder of the wire had not been cut very much.

On the left of Barnes' D Company, the men of the Canadian 1st Division [8th Battalion] swept through the ruined village of Arleux driving all before

---

547 In front of the 6th Brigade, no man's land was only 250 yards wide in places.

548 See footnote 357 on page 247.

549 Although Richard Crosse could not see his men going through the gaps in the wire, he felt that the platoons must have passed through quickly and without losing direction, or the number of casualties would have been even higher.

Rare photographs of a named officer's funeral procession and burial.

On December 11th 1916, Captain Ralph Kite's funeral procession progressed down the hill from Lady Helen Stewart-Murray's Hospital [No. 10 British Red Cross Hospital] in the Golf Hotel, Le Tréport to the British Military Cemetery.
[Kite Collection]

The coffin is carried through the gates of the British Military Cemetery, Le Tréport. The tall figure in a dark coat is that of the Reverend Bertie Kite the deceased's father.
[Kite Collection]

The coffin is laid to rest close to the cemetery wall. Plot 2, row 0, grave 7. The woman in a dark coat and hat on the right of the funeral party is probably Lady Helen Stewart-Murray, a daughter of the 7th Duke of Atholl.
[Kite Collection]

Courcelette posts. The 52nd served here in the extremely cold weather of early 1917.
[NRO NEV 7/32]

Ernest 'Whitters' Whitfeld, an able soldier, was awarded the M.C. after annihilating a German machine-gun team at Richebourg l'Avoué in 1915. He succeeded Richard Crosse as Adjutant in March 1916.
[Colvill Collection]

Roger 'Bugler' Ames, B Company, singled out for his excellent patrol work, was seriously wounded in September 1917.
[NRO NEV 7/32]

Tom 'Twitt' Tyrwhitt-Drake was one of the outstanding officers in the 52nd and over the course of the war would be awarded the M.C. and two bars.
[Colvill Collection]

Germans in Oppy with the wood in the background. Photograph circa 1917.
[Private Collection]

Oppy Wood as the 52nd saw it in 1917.
[NRO NEV 7/31]

Dressing Station at the Sugar Factory used by the 52nd at the Battle of Arleux in April 1917.
[Author's Collection 2006]

David Barnes the senior 52nd officer present in the front line at the Battle of Arleux. In effect he had an independent command and was awarded a well-deserved D.S.O. for his efforts. Barnes was wounded in the ankle and became a prisoner-of-war during the March retreat of 1918.
[NRO NEV 7/32]

William Giles seated [on the right without cap] next to Harold 'Fritz' Eagle. Giles and David Barnes commanded the 52nd's front line troops at the Battle of Arleux in April 1917. He was awarded a M.C.
[Colvill Collection]

Fred Clare D.C.M. was made temporary R.S.M. in 1917, although he had to wait until 1920 for the substantive post. Serving continuously with the 52nd throughout the war, he has been likened to the legendary John Winterbottom of Peninsular War fame. There can be no greater compliment.
[Colvill Collection]

Reverend Edward 'Monty' Guilford M.C. had to be reminded of his ecclesiastical position so keen was he to join in the fighting at the Battle of Arleux.
[NRO NEV 7/32]

them[550]. On the immediate right of the 52nd was the 2nd H.L.I. who initially moved forward with them. Within an hour of the start of the assault of the Arleux Loop, Captain William Giles was able to report that his B Company had taken their section of the Blue Line, part of the enemy's support trench system, and that he was in touch on both his flanks with friendly forces. Here, excellent work was done by the Lewis gunners. At 6.45 a.m., Captain David Barnes, as the senior officer, took command of the front line of the Regiment and reported that his men had taken and consolidated the second objective, the Green Line[551]. By 8.10 a.m., Barnes' small force had managed to get into the Brown Line, but it was not in a position to remain there, and certainly not able to man outposts beyond the Brown Line which had been their intended final objective. A little later, the enemy appeared to be massing, apparently with a view to making a counter-attack. Throughout the day Barnes maintained contact with the Canadians on his left. In fact the Green and Brown Lines joined together approximately at the junction of the 52nd and the 1st Canadian Division.

Barnes' reports throughout the morning and afternoon of April 28th tell their own story.

> 5.30 a.m. My company has reached its objective[552] aaa 50 prisoners taken aaa We have a good many casualties aaa We are held up by M.G.s aaa Enemy made fair resistance aaa I am in touch with the 2nd Highland Light Infantry on my right and am in front of Canadians going towards Arleux.
> 6.45 a.m. Touch lost with Highland Light Infantry, though maintained with Canadians.
> 8.10 a.m. We cannot find the H.L.I. Our right flank is exposed. My company reached the Brown line but had to retire owing to the Boches being behind us on our right. Parts of all companies are with me, also Giles, Fuller, Wilsdon, Cope[553].
> 12.40 p.m. Still no signs of anyone on our right. The sniper mentioned in my DB 23 still worries us. We are being heavily shelled but most are falling on the Blue line. Prisoners taken by us

[550] The dividing line between the Canadian 1st Division and the 52nd ran a little to the south of Arleux, and to the southern point of a wood, to the east of the village, at C.1.a.3.1.
[551] An unidentified wounded officer of the 52nd reported at 7.20 a.m. that he was of the opinion that his Battalion was 'over the Green line'. He also confirmed that only one gap in the wire had been found and that the whole company had had to go through it.
[552] The Blue Line.
[553] Captain William Giles. Second-Lieutenants G.H. Fuller, R.G. Wilsdon and C.E. Cope.

> are: A Co. 20, B Co. 30, D Co. 30, C Co. not known. I am afraid that some of these may have gone to wrong cages.
> 3 p.m. Impossible to establish ourselves in Green line proper. I am going to establish a strong line of posts to join up with the H.L.I. (if they are in the Blue line) on right and Canadians on left with whom we are in close touch.

At this juncture Captain David Barnes and his small force dug in between the Blue and Green Lines, roughly corresponding to the Arleux to Oppy sunken road, with his right swung back towards the positions of the 2nd H.L.I[554]. The left of the 52nd was secure as the 8th Battalion of the Canadian 1st Division had crossed the German front line, taken the village of Arleux on its left and, on its right, to the south-west of the village, had pressed on over a rise in the land to cross the Arleux to Oppy road. In touch with the 52nd on their right, the Canadians had reached their final objective, consolidating a line through Arleux Wood, to the east of the village. The 52nd found itself with a front that was too long for their scanty numbers, and a company commander from the 8th Canadian Battalion took over a section of it of his own accord.

The 2nd H.L.I. had been less fortunate in their build up to the attack. The battalion headquarters had been established in a vacated German concrete gun-pit which was clearly visible to the enemy and was full of shells and cordite. The enemy opened heavy artillery fire on it, setting light to the cordite and making the stored shells explode, this leading to a fire and numerous casualties. Unfortunately one of the company commanders was killed trying to rescue the mess staff, who were trapped, and the Commanding Officer of the 2nd H.L.I., Lieutenant-Colonel John Grahame[555], was severely wounded. This disaster happened less than 24 hours before the onset of the attack, and the loss of their Battalion Headquarters cannot have helped their command and control in the coming battle. Major D.M. Murray-Lyon assumed command of the Regiment, and reorganized the remnants of the Headquarters. It was an inauspicious beginning to the 2nd H.L.I.'s assault on the Arleux Loop.

---

[554] At 1.35 p.m., Lieutenant-Colonel S.V.P. Weston, the newly appointed Commanding Officer of the 17th Royal Fusiliers, reported that the 2nd Highland Light Infantry had retired and joined his men in the old German front line. All communication with the 6th Brigade had gone.

[555] Lieutenant-Colonel John Grahame had recently replaced the now Brigadier-General Arthur Wolfe-Murray who has featured in these pages previously. Grahame had previously commanded the 9th, 10th, 10/11th, and 12th Highland Light Infantry. His devotion to the 2nd H.L.I. was said 'to border on the eccentric'. Pipers played each platoon in and out of the line. Grahame's wounds put him out of the war.

At 4.25 a.m., in a similar fashion to the 52nd, the 2nd H.L.I. advanced with two companies in front and immediately came under heavy fire. On reaching the enemy's wire, the men found little damage had been done to it. To the right, B Company found a gap in the wire and went through it. A Company, on the left, was delayed whilst the men cut their way through the barbed strands, and consequently lost touch with the barrage. Although by now much scattered, both companies pushed forward and the Green Line was eventually reached. Heavy enfilade fire from the vicinity of Oppy Wood precluded the 2nd H.L.I. from going further. By 10 a.m. they had been forced back to the vicinity of the Blue Line where measures were instantly taken to strengthen their exposed right flank. In this they were aided by men of the 17th R.F. who set up a defensive position. The 2nd H.L.I. and the 17th R.F. were in the nick of time as, at 11 a.m., the Germans launched a heavy counter-attack from Oppy Wood and followed it with an even heavier one in the afternoon. The 24th R.F. was ordered up from their support position and, by 11 p.m., had dug in to strengthen the defensive flank. Fortunately, the brave Scotsmen and the Fusiliers managed to hold on to their position until April 30th when they were relieved. Their casualties consisted of seven officers and 43 other ranks killed, and eight officers and 226 other ranks wounded.

On the right of the 2nd H.L.I. were units of the 6th Brigade whose attack was charged with taking Oppy Wood and village which stood directly to their front. The 6th Brigade had the 17th Middlesex on the left and the 13th Essex on the right with the 2nd Staffordshire as 'moppers up'. The 17th Middlesex had the principal responsibility for Oppy Wood and village. This was a problematic undertaking as previous experience had shown that a wood situated in front of a village made the latter difficult to capture. At 4.25 a.m. both of the two leading battalions chose to advance in three waves behind the barrage. The 17th Middlesex found the wire perfectly cut and were in the German front line trench eight minutes after zero hour. However, almost immediately, they lost touch with the 2nd H.L.I., on their left, who had been held up by uncut enemy wire in front of them. The Middlesex men moved forward through Oppy Wood and they managed to reach the east side of it, despite snipers firing from the trees. However, in the village itself, with the enemy firing through loop-holes in the walls, no progress was made. At this juncture very heavy fighting took place with the enemy attacking them from the flanks and rear. Most of the men were wiped out, although a few got back to the old British front line.

The 13th Essex also reached the German front line rapidly, except on the extreme right where they were held up by uncut wire. They maintained touch with the 17th Middlesex, but not with the units of the 63rd Division on their right, and eventually they reached the eastern side of Oppy Wood and to the south of the village of Oppy. However, the men of the 13th Essex were gradually overwhelmed and were forced back first to the German front line, and then small parties managed to return to the old British line. By the afternoon of the 28th it was clear that the 6th Brigade [17th Middlesex and 13th Essex] had failed to take their objectives, and its surviving men had been driven back to the old British front line. The 6th Brigade was replaced in the line by the 99th Brigade, whose Brigadier-General, R.O. Kellett, assumed command at 5.40 p.m. No part of the former German trench system was handed over to them. Later that evening, orders were issued by XIII Corps for the 99th Brigade to renew the attack on the untaken part of the Oppy Line at 4 a.m. the following morning.

The 63rd Division was supposed to be protecting the 2nd Division's southern flank with an attack from Gavrelle. The operation was carried out by the 188th Brigade using the 1st and 2nd Royal Marines[556]. In the south, the 2nd Royal Marines had a limited success but, in the north, the 1st Royal Marines failed and consequently were unable to protect the right flank of the 6th Brigade and the 13th Essex in particular. This led to the 13th Essex being attacked in the flank and rear. On the evening of the 28th, the 188th Brigade was ordered to join the 99th Brigade the following morning, in a further attempt on the untaken section of the Oppy Line.

At 8 a.m. on the 28th, the general situation was this: the Canadian 1st Division had taken Arleux village; the 5th Brigade on the left [52nd] held the Green Line, and on the right the Blue Line [2nd H.L.I.]; the 6th Brigade had got into both Oppy Wood and village, but had been unable to hold them and was being driven back to the old British front line; the 63rd Division had failed to protect the right flank of the 6th Brigade. Major-General Cecil Pereira felt that the lack of success of his 2nd Division troops was due to reduced numbers of men in his battalions, plus a long advance and the critical failure of the 63rd Division to protect the right flank of the 6th Brigade. A further factor was the lack of experience of his junior officers, some of whom were coming out to France only nine weeks after enlistment. Pereira was also impressed by the German infiltration tactics. The enemy moved rapidly up to the advanced British line, getting machine-guns and snipers into position, before dribbling small scattered parties through the line as a prelude to a counter-attack.

During the afternoon of the 28th, the 52nd set up their position between the Blue and Green Lines, roughly corresponding with the sunken Arleux to Oppy road, with their right turned back towards the 2nd H.L.I. in the Blue Line. A great

---

[556] Everard Wyrall in his history *The 17th (S) Battalion Royal Fusiliers 1914-1919* recorded that the 63rd Division did not leave their trenches. This is incorrect.

deal of initiative was shown by the platoon commanders in collecting together adjacent men, no matter to whom they originally belonged, and reorganizing them for further action. The recently arrived Second-Lieutenant B.J. Crewe was singled out as having done particularly good work in this respect. The trenches were heavily shelled by the enemy and some men were buried. Unfortunately there was a lack of dug-outs which might have protected a number of the men.

The battle that was being fought was controlled by the officers on the spot and in the case of the 52nd this was principally Captain David Barnes, who assumed command, with support from Captain William Giles. Their Commanding Officer, Richard Crosse, was way back at the Regimental Headquarters, on the Bailleul to Arleux road, and by his own admission little able to influence events. His Headquarters was often mistaken for an Aid Post and was crowded with wounded. For a time the power buzzer was covered in blood and could not be used! Crosse described the Battle of Arleux as a soldiers' battle similar to the Battle of Inkermann[557], where the junior officers had to make independent decisions on the battlefield without reference to higher authority. On the Redan Ridge, on November 13th 1916, Crosse had been able to watch his men advance from close to his Regimental Headquarters. Here, on the Arleux Loop, they were out of his sight.

Water, rations and stores for consolidation were brought up to the 52nd's new positions around the Arleux to Oppy sunken road by the 10th [Pioneer] Battalion of the Duke of Cornwall's Light Infantry. The backbreaking work of the Pioneers took place across areas swept by the enemy's artillery. The humanitarian Richard Crosse was concerned about the time taken to clear the battlefield of casualties. He recorded this entry in the *Battalion War Diary* for April 28th[558].

> As far as I could ascertain arrangements in accordance with Field Service Regulations Part II Ch. XI.(12) for clearing our part of the area of operations of the wounded had not been made sufficiently early for a clearing party to come up and begin work as early as they might have done. Guides were ready waiting, but after waiting some time these guides were taken off in error by the O.C. another carrying party, so that when the party officer and 100 other ranks did arrive for clearing the battlefield they had to be given other guides who went astray. The party appears to have passed Regt Hdqrs

[557] Battle of Inkermann [1854], known as the 'Soldiers' Battle', led to a Franco-British victory over the Russians during the Crimean War.

[558] It is not clear whether this applied to April 28th or 29th.

> (without reporting) on its return journey at 2 a.m., when 1 hours clearing could still have been done and no evacuation was thus carried out save by the Regt. Stretcher Bearers. The ground was reconnoitred in daylight. The next morning (which it might have been done 24 hrs previously) by the officer who was to bring up the party that night (29/30th) and such wounded as had not been brought in or killed by the barrages while lying out, were very satisfactorily brought in.

Soon after midnight and again at 9 a.m. on April 29th, Captain David Barnes continued with his reports from the position of the 52nd around the sunken Arleux to Oppy road.

> 29th April, 12.15 a.m. The Regiment is now organized but our strength is only about 180. We are digging in from B12 central to 12a66 and the Regimental front is from B12c87 to B12a66. We are in touch with the Canadians on left and the 24th on right[559].
> 9 a.m. Our line is now quite complete. The trench dug during the night is a very good one. Herewith pay book and civilian hat found on a dead Boche of the 76th Regt[560]. His pack contained a complete civilian outfit. I am sorry I did not send in a report for so long but I fell asleep and did not wake up till the attack on our right began, when I hoped that we might have to shift forward again. The men are hoping for relief to-night.

The attack David Barnes refers to in the penultimate sentence of his report was the 4 a.m. attack made by the 2nd and 63rd Divisions against the southern portion of the Oppy line, which they had failed to take the previous day. The 99th Brigade, supported by the 24th R.F. on their left, manfully attempted to take Oppy Wood and village and, although some improvised bombing attacks had a measure of success, the wood and village remained securely in German hands. Oppy Wood would not fall until June 28th. Further south, the 188th Brigade of the 63rd Division reached its objective but was driven out again. Meanwhile the 52nd sat tight in their positions under considerable shelling. However, no enemy

---

[559] Although the forward troops of the 52nd were supposed to have made their line in the vicinity of the sunken Arleux to Oppy road, these map references are further to the west. The 24th Royal Fusiliers, who had started the day in brigade reserve, had sent two companies to make contact with the 52nd in this sunken road.
[560] German 111th Division.

infantry counter-attacks were forthcoming and the 52nd continued to hold the ground that it had taken the previous day.

The devoted 10th D.C.L.I. again brought up to the front food and water. The remaining seventeen wounded men were at last evacuated, and the exhausted uninjured soldiers hoped for a relief that night. It was not to be. Many years later Richard Crosse wrote that it was intended to relieve the Regiment that night, but no troops were available and the unfortunate men had to remain in the line. Crosse felt that the sorely tested soldiers had shown the spirit of their ancestors on the Talavera road more than a century before. Here in 1809, the 52nd under Robert Craufurd, 'Black Bob', had marched 52 miles in 26 hours, believing the British at Talavera were hard pressed. Each man carried his arms, ammunition, and accoutrements, weighing between 50-60 pounds. In the event their supreme efforts were unnecessary. In the 52nd of 1917, reserve officers and N.C.O.s who had been left out of the battle, as was a routine precaution before major actions, were brought up from the transport lines. A welcome reinforcement of one serjeant and 73 other ranks arrived near Ecurie to the west of Roclincourt. Amongst the reserve officers of the 52nd who were called to the line was Second-Lieutenant Jim Neville. Neville recorded his experiences of April 29th[561].

> A lovely morning with bright sun. Whitfeld[562] went to the Division to get news of the fight. I was warned to go up and help. Paraded with ration party, and got up to the line without any trouble. A very quiet night. We made improvements in the trenches and dug deeper.

Captain David Barnes sent in another report in the early hours of April 30th. It is remarkable that the exhausted men were 'all now in ripping spirits'. It was a message treasured by Richard Crosse above all the rest.

> We are in touch with Blackfriars at B12d[563].
> We are in touch with Bickley at B12c85.
> My left is up to sunken road (inclusive). The Canadians have for the present agreed to take over as far as my left which is a L.G.[564] post at B12b36.
> I have got Lewis gun posts out to our front and one on the road.

---

561 Letter to his father written in diary form on April 29th 1917.

562 Captain Ernest Whitfeld, the Adjutant.

563 Blackfriars and Bickley are the code names for other units. One may be the 2nd Highland Light Infantry.

564 Lewis gun post.

I have got a bombing block at B12c78 in case Boche try to bomb up their communication trench.
I enclose rough sketch of line as now held by Regiment. We have reorganized the companies. The men are all now in ripping spirits. The officers and others sent up here bucked us up no end. The position is now very strong indeed. We have salved several Lewis Guns.
We have established dumps of bombs, SAA[565], shovels, picks and wire.
Rations are all right and have been issued.
Strength of Regt. now A 60
B 60
C 60
D 72
These numbers do not include men sent up tonight. The increase is due to the fact that men of all companies have joined us; men who lost direction in the attack.

The general situation on April 30th remained unchanged with Captain David Barnes commanding the 52nd's front line troops and Lieutenant-Colonel Richard Crosse, back in his headquarters on the Arleux to Bailleul road, unable to exert much influence on the situation. In the evening the four companies of the 52nd, A, B, C, D, were finally relieved by two composite companies, No. 1 formed from the 52nd [under Lieutenant R. Blackwell] and No. 2 from the 2nd H.L.I. [Captain D.G. Walker]. Each company of three platoons was made up of reserves and reinforcements of the two regiments. Crosse with the support of his Headquarters staff was left in command of the composite battalion, to hold the ground gained by the 52nd on the 28th until other arrangements could be made. This composite battalion took over the left of the 2nd Division's front, while the 24th R.F. held the right. The remainder of the Regiment retired to dug-outs in the original British and German front lines, near Roclincourt.

Amongst the reserves who helped form the composite battalion was Second-Lieutenant Jim Neville, who has recorded his memories of the day[566]. He had gone to the front line the day before.

"Stand-to" at 4 a.m. Our guns bombarded the Huns. Oppy Wood, which had been in full leaf and thick at that, when I last saw it on the

[565] Small arms ammunition.
[566] Letter to his father written in diary form from Camblain-Châtelain on May 6th 1917.

> 26th, had been distinctly thinned by shell fire. The enemy opened on our front line at 4.15, and never left us alone all day. They were crumping all round our dug-out, but not actually on it, as luck would have it. There was no communication open with Headquarters, so David Barnes sent off a carrier pigeon to try and get our guns to do a bit of counter-battery work, and also to ask for stretcher parties to come and remove the wounded still lying out.
>
> The candles in the dug-out were blown out every five minutes, and we had to "stand-to" with matches!
>
> Barnes and Giles led out the men who had done the attack, while Blackwell and I took over command of the front line with a draft of 52nd and 74th men. Considering the intensity of the shelling, very little damage was done. This was due to the fact that our trenches were very narrow and a difficult target. Shells seemed to burst short or over, but seldom in the trench.

May 1st saw the composite battalion of 52nd and 2nd H.L.I. men under the command of Richard Crosse still occupying their positions between Arleux and Oppy Wood. At this stage all three brigades in the 2nd Division were grossly depleted in manpower: the 5th Brigade had 1,237 men; the 6th Brigade 1,322 men; the 99th Brigade 1,088 men. At midday, in view of the lack of troops, a composite brigade under Brigadier-General R.O. Kellett was formed and, on the night of May 1st/2nd, one of its battalions relieved the composite battalion under Crosse plus his Regimental Headquarters. Kellett's composite brigade consisted of the remnants of the 5th, 6th, and his own 99th Brigades. Crosse and his weary men were able to retire to dug-outs in the old British and German front lines near Roclincourt. Once again, Jim Neville chronicled the events of May 1st[567].

> The enemy started shelling very early and bombarded us all day. It was perfectly awful. "Granny," way back in Roclincourt, started dropping 15-inch shells into Oppy Wood, which must have shaken Fritz up a bit. In spite of it all, we had no casualties until the evening. Great luck. Orders for our relief came at 6 p.m., and while we were preparing for it our guns put over a "Chinese bombardment[568]." The enemy, in retaliation, blew in our dug-out.

[567] Letter to his father written in diary form from Camblain-Châtelain on May 6th 1917.

[568] A feint barrage.

> One man was buried and when extricated, found to be dead[569]. Two orderlies were also wounded. The rest of us were untouched. A composite battalion relieved us at 11 p.m., and never have I been so glad to get back in all my life.

On April 30th, unbeknown to Richard Crosse and the 52nd, Sir Douglas Haig had held a conference of his Army Commanders and informed them that all hope of linking up with the French around Cambrai had gone. Also it was clear that General Robert Nivelle's days in command of the French armies were numbered[570]. Haig intended to go ahead with his offensive on May 3rd [the Third Battle of the Scarpe], partly in support of the French on the Aisne, whose latest offensive was scheduled for May 4th/5th, and partly to obtain a better defensive line for his own troops. He hoped to gain the line Lens, Acheville, Fresnoy, Greenland Hill, Bois du Vert, and Riencourt by May 15th. In essence this was a shallow arc to the east of Arras. In the likely event of the French closing down their front, Haig would switch his attention to clearing the Belgian coast to deal with the U-Boat menace.

The unfortunate 2nd Division found itself involved in the Third Battle of the Scarpe. It had already been given an extra 1,000 yards of front on April 30th, and the much depleted and exhausted force was now expected to take part in the offensive. Major-General Cecil Pereira, commanding the 2nd Division, explained 'that the only way the Division could do anything, now that we were so weak in numbers and so many of the men unfit for further operations, was by forming a Composite Brigade' of the remnants of his three brigades. 'It was resolved we should have to carry out our share of the attack'. This was Kellett's Composite Brigade and in the early morning of May 3rd, it took its place between troops of the Canadian Corps on its left and the fresh 31st Division on its right. So weak were Kellett's troops that Pereira extended the front of the 31st Division to 3,500 yards, leaving 1,100 for the Composite Brigade. The Canadians took Fresnoy village, and their right flank was just about protected by Kellett's troops, whose objectives were the rear of the Arleux Loop and then the Fresnoy-Oppy road. On the right, despite striving mightily, the 31st Division failed to take Oppy Wood or village. Once again the Canadians had taken a key village, and once more the 2nd Division found its right flank in the air.

On May 2nd, we left the remnants of the 52nd in the old British and German front line trenches near Roclincourt. About midday, the Regiment, as

---

569 This is likely to have been Private Albert Hardwick as the other three 52nd men who perished on May 1st, all died of their wounds.

570 He was replaced by General Henri-Philippe Pétain on May 15th 1917.

part of the 5th Brigade, received orders to move to Ecoivres. The move took place during the afternoon and the men were billeted in Y Hutments. Here the 52nd were able to count the cost of the Battle of Arleux and its aftermath. The total number of casualties was around 206; one officer was killed on the way up to the line on the night of April 27th/28th; six officers were wounded with two dying of their injuries; about 200 other ranks were casualties, of whom 130 were wounded and the remaining 70 killed or missing[571].

The officer killed by artillery fire in the assembly trenches was Second-Lieutenant Gilbert Calloway, and those who died of their wounds were the Second-Lieutenants Geoffrey La Warre Lyle, known as the 'Gazeeka', aged 25 years, and Alfred Walter. The unfortunate Lyle was shot in the abdomen/backside on April 28th, and died the next day at Aubigny. Walter had only been with the 52nd for less than a calendar month and initially it was thought that the gunshot wounds to his arm and leg were not serious. However, he lingered on until he died on May 13th[572]. The other wounded officers were Lieutenant Laurence Dowson [middle finger of left hand blown off and shrapnel wound right thigh], and Second-Lieutenants Philip Whitehead [gunshot wound left thigh], H.A. 'Ginger' Smith [gunshot wound right thigh], and Harold 'Fritz' Eagle [gunshot wound left hand]. Eagle returned to duty three days later. During this period, the 5th Brigade as a whole suffered 34 officers and 655 other ranks killed, wounded, and missing.

Captain David Barnes received an immediate and, in Richard Crosse's words, 'a more than well-earned' D.S.O., for his exemplary leadership on April 28th/29th. Initially, Crosse was told that Barnes' reward was to be an immediate M.C. Crosse replied that he would not insult his officer with such a decoration and would prefer to withdraw his recommendation altogether. He took a risk but the gamble came off. Barnes' fellow company commander, the 19-year-old Captain William Giles won a M.C. Corporal J.J. Abbey was awarded the D.C.M[573]. His citation read 'For conspicuous gallantry and devotion to duty, in rallying and retiring his company at a critical moment. He later held a difficult position for twenty-four hours under heavy fire'. Serjeant Henry 'Nicky' Lay

---

[571] As might be expected most men were killed on the first day of the battle. April 28th, 48 men killed in action; April 29th, 5 dead of whom 4 were killed in action and one man died of his wounds; April 30th, 3 dead of whom 1 was killed in action and 2 men died of their wounds; May 1st, 5 dead of whom 1 was killed in action and 4 men died of their wounds.

[572] The wounded Alfred Walter was evacuated to England and he was buried in Highgate Cemetery. Grave 61.40679.

[573] Crosse in an article written in the *Regimental Journal* in 1957 stated that 21455 Private Platt received a D.C.M. as well as Abbey. However, Platt's name does not appear in the Oxfordshire and Buckinghamshire Light Infantry section of *Citations of the Distinguished Conduct Medal in the Great War 1914-1920.*

received a bar to his M.M.; he would be awarded a D.C.M. in 1918. Despite wounds, Lay did not leave the 52nd throughout the war, and he has been described as 'the very best of best non-commissioned officers'. Serjeants Tunbridge, Smith, White and Privates Prescott and Law received the M.M. for their exploits in the recent battle.

Today, the 52nd's Arleux battlefield is easily followed on the ground. The villages of Arleux and Oppy have been rebuilt, and Oppy Wood has grown again on its original site. The sunken road around which the Regiment dug in on April 28th 1917 still exists, and the Dressing Station near to Richard Crosse's Battalion Headquarters stands as a shelter for grazing cattle. Here, the Reverend Edward Guilford had to be reminded of his ecclesiastical position so keen was he to join in the fighting!

In Ecoivres, on May 2nd, Lieutenant-Colonel Richard Crosse issued this Regimental Order.

> The conduct of the Regiment in action on and since 28th April last has been a fitting conclusion to its march to this battle area. The organisation of their commands by company commanders under very difficult circumstances, the cool acceptance of the situation by the junior commanders, and the quickness to put the right decision into effect by the leaders of small parties, from the moment when the wire was found to be improperly cut, onwards, reveal the real Light Infantry Training and a state of affairs of which every 52nd soldier may be justly proud, to make no mention of the steady pushing forward to our own front when the situation on the right flank was so uncertain, the final stubborn defence and consolidation, and maintaining touch with the flanks, without which other gains would have been lost.
>
> The work of the Regimental stretcher bearers, the R.A.M.C. personnel attached to the Regiment, and the Aid Post personnel, carried out with the usual untiring energy and unselfishness, must be gratefully remembered by all ranks.
>
> As usual, the rearward services, transport and supply, have fully played their part in contributing to success, and the ready and willing help of the carrying parties of the Pioneer Battalion must be remembered by us all.
>
> The good name and traditions of the 52nd must now be more than ever carefully guarded by all ranks of it.

The 52nd had certainly played their part in the Arras offensive. No praise can be too high for the Canadian Corps which had taken Vimy Ridge and the villages of Arleux and Fresnoy. Although the 52nd had not managed to achieve all their objectives on April 28th, they had protected the crucial right flank of the Canadian 1st Division, so that the village of Arleux might be captured and held. There is little doubt that the Canadians would have had to withdraw from Arleux if their right flank had been left unprotected. This had been achieved by the 52nd despite the fact that its own right flank was in the air. It was no mean achievement. Major-General Cecil Pereira, commanding the 2nd Division, wrote a letter of thanks to his opposite number Major-General Arthur 'Guts and Gaiters' Currie, commanding the 1st Canadian Division. Currie's reply was apposite[574].

> I confess that I did feel anxious concerning the flank, but it was only because I realized that you had been set a task which I considered an unfair one for a Division which had fought as hard and suffered as many casualties as the old 2nd Division. This Division will always be proud to fight beside them and to win their praise.

The Battles of Arras were coming to a close, but pressure on the Germans was to continue with a number of local offensives. Haig's final limited attack on May 3rd has been described as 'a ghastly failure, some thought the blackest day of the war'[575]. The associated flanking operation, the Second Battle of Bullecourt, May 3rd-17th, with large numbers of casualties on both sides would poison Britain's relations with Australia. France would have to become the junior partner to the British after the mutiny of so many of her troops as a result of the Nivelle offensive. The Battle of Arras was largely fought to assist the French, but there were still some positive results. Following the Battles of the Somme 1916, Germany could ill-afford a war of attrition with the loss of so many of its men. Britain and France, particularly with the United States of America entering the war, had a bigger manpower pool to train their armies from. On May 22nd, Sir Douglas Haig wrote in his diary 'I saw Sir Herbert Plumer Commanding Second Army at 9.45 am for a few minutes. He is in good spirits now that his Second Army occupies the first place in our thoughts!' Plumer commanded the Second Army which was based in the vicinity of Ypres. Haig was now switching his attention to the north and a means of neutralizing the U-Boat menace.

---

574 Letter written on May 8th 1917. WO 95 1345.
575 *The First World War* by Cyril Falls.

Chapter XVII

A Summer and Autumn in the Trenches: Roclincourt, Canal Zone, Givenchy, Cambrin.

May 3rd - November 22nd 1917

[Maps: pages 161, 424, 433, 463, 479.]

The remainder of 1917 would witness the predominantly British forces fighting in three major battles: the Battle of Messines [June 7th-14th]; the Battles of Ypres 1917, better known as the Third Ypres or simply as Passchendaele [July 31st-November 10th]; the Battle of Cambrai [November 20th-December 3rd]. The 52nd Light Infantry was not involved in the first or second battles, although at one point during the autumn of 1917, there was a strong rumour that it was to be sent to the Ypres Salient. As will be seen, the Regiment was to be intimately involved with the later stages of the final major action of 1917, the Battle of Cambrai. The Battles of Arras had been principally fought at the request of the French to allow General Nivelle's offensive on the Aisne a greater chance of success. With Nivelle's failure to make a significant breakthrough and the mutinies in the French army, the British would have to carry the main burden of the war. Their attention turned to Flanders and the necessity of clearing the coast of U-Boat bases. In the first six months of 1917 no less than 694 merchant ships had been sunk by submarines, and the British were in danger of being starved into defeat. No less a person than Admiral John Jellicoe, the First Sea Lord, stated to the War Cabinet, 'if the army cannot get the Belgian ports, the navy cannot hold the Channel and the war is lost'.

A successful offensive at Ypres, with an advance of only seven miles, would drive the enemy off the curved high ground surrounding the town. This would threaten the important railway junction at Roulers and potentially interrupt German logistics. The enemy might be forced to evacuate the area, and his hold on the U-Boats' bases would become untenable. Messines Ridge dominated the southern flank of the Ypres Salient and it was essential to take it prior to the main operation. With the aid of a massive artillery bombardment and the use of huge explosive mines General Herbert Plumer's Second Army succeeded in taking the ridge. On July 31st General Hubert Gough's Fifth Army began the Third Battle of Ypres, which would eventually end the following November with the capture of Passchendaele. Despite the loss of some 238,313[576] casualties the British were

[576] Figure taken from Edmonds' *Official History.* Later figures suggest a slightly higher total. For instance, Richard Holmes in his *Western Front* [1999] thought that both sides may have lost about 260,000 men.

never in a position to launch their amphibious landing on the Belgium coast. Subsequently Sir Douglas Haig was severely criticized for continuing his offensive in the appallingly wet and muddy conditions. However, Haig has pointed out that the French Commander-in-Chief, General Henri-Philippe Pétain, continually begged him to put in another effort against Passchendaele, such was the parlous state of the French army in 1917.

At the end of the year came the Battle of Cambrai which had originally been seen as a large scale tank raid. Sir Douglas Haig looked upon it as the final chance of 1917 to salvage something from his 1917 campaign. It might be possible to penetrate the Hindenburg Line and capture the important rail junction of Cambrai itself. As will be seen, the Battle of Cambrai started brilliantly, with the church bells of England ringing, but it fizzled out with most of the initial gains lost and the town of Cambrai never taken.

It is time to return to the detailed story of the 52nd Light Infantry's participation in the above events. The Regiment would spend the next six months in the trenches just to the north of Arras around Roclincourt and, in the environs of the La Bassée Canal. On May 5th, Major-General Cecil Pereira, commanding the 2nd Division, summoned his battalion commanding officers to a meeting at Bajus to see what lessons had been learned during the recent Battle of Arleux. It is almost certain that Lieutenant-Colonel Richard Crosse attended this meeting on behalf of the 52nd, although there is no documentary evidence.

Pereira wrote in his diary:

> I had a conference of COs at Bajus to discuss the recent operations. A point that I rubbed in was the necessity of getting snipers busy as soon as an objective was gained. They prevent close reconnaissance of our dispositions and do not permit Boche snipers to establish themselves close to our line, they also have great opportunities of killing Boche when there is great uncertainty as to where the opposing troops are placed.
>
> Some battns did this and held their front in comfort but in cases where they did not the Boche method of "infiltration" or gradually feeling the front and establishing themselves up against it soon began to tell and they found themselves soon troubled by Boche who had established themselves in vantage points where they could cause great annoyance and prevent freedom of movement.
>
> The only way is to follow up the advantage of having gained ground and got the enemy on the run by getting hold of all vantage points along the front and keeping the enemy at arms length without

any delay. Most likely there is an hour or two when this can be done at leisure and before there is a fear of hostile barrages. No doubt men are disorganized and tired after their recent advance and fighting, but it is fatal and costly not to seize the opportunity without delay.

I am going to form a Divl Rifleman's school to pass large numbers of men through and teach them the individual use of the rifle and the use of ground, sharpshooting and stalking, and confidence and reliance in themselves. The aim being that after any attack every coy will have some trained riflemen who will be available to go out and cover the front in an intelligent manner and with full confidence in their own powers and the power of their rifles, feeling the certainty that if they see a Boche within a reasonable range trying to find our line they can without disclosing their own position put him out of action.

I laid very great stress on the very great success that the Stokes T.M.s had had. I formulated a scheme of special platoons that would be specially trained and kept out of the trenches whose role in the offensive would be to exploit success or fill a threatened corner.

Out of this conference came the setting up of a Divisional Rifleman's School at Magnicourt in which the use of ground, the rifle, sharp shooting and stalking were taught. A Royal Fusilier, Captain Gore, a former Canadian trapper, was delegated to run the school. The infantry tactics of the Germans had become more sophisticated since 1916 and the British had to adapt to counter them. It is interesting to see how much was set in store by the Stokes mortar as it will be recalled that at Guillemont Station, on July 30th 1916, their failure had led to a large loss of life among the officers and men of the 52nd. As the Stokes mortar had only been invented in 1915, possibly its operators had become more experienced in its use.

We left the 52nd in Ecoivres on May 2nd, and the following day was spent in bathing and generally cleaning up. Second-Lieutenant Laurence 'Pullthrough' Fullbrook-Leggatt rejoined for duty having recovered from his recent wounds. On the 3rd the Regiment was on the move again, marching on the Arras - St. Pol road as far as the village of Villers Brûlin, to the north-west of Arras, where it was billeted. At about 10 p.m. orders were received to march at 8 a.m. the next day to Camblain-Châtelain. Their route took them via Frevillers - La Comté - Ourton, and on arrival the officers and men were very comfortably billeted in the region of the Mairie. The old hands of the Regiment knew the area well as they had been billeted here prior to entraining from Pernes, in July 1916, on the way to the Somme. In 1915, the men had called the village 'Charlie Chaplin', after the celebrated comic actor.

The Regiment would remain in Camblain-Châtelain until May 17th and the time was well spent in resting and training. Specialist classes of instruction were set up, and Lieutenant Philip Booth, Second-Lieutenants James Atkins, Gordon Fuller, B.J. Crewe and eight N.C.O.s attended a brigade bombing course run by Captain A.P. Young of the 17th R.F., in order to qualify as instructors. On Sunday May 13th, the Deputy Chaplain-General Bishop Llewellyn Gwynne was unable to take the morning service and he was replaced by the Reverend H.W. Blackburn, Assistant Chaplain-General to the First Army. A sports day was held on the 16th, which was deemed a great success despite the inclement weather. On the 6th, the irrepressible Irishman Second-Lieutenant Harry Vernon, 'with his highly developed sense of the ridiculous,' rejoined the Regiment having recovered from his injuries of the previous November.

Second-Lieutenant Jim Neville recorded his memories of the 52nd's time in Camblain-Châtelain. During this period he also managed two days of leave in Paris. As well as sightseeing, Neville was able to shop and eat his fill. His greatest pleasure was a proper full-length bath. 'It is the first time since I left home that I have had a bath in a big bath, and not had to hang my legs over the side'[577]. The six foot four inch Neville bathed both morning and evening! In addition he visited the Folies Bergère with its women 'rampant and abandoned'. Home leave was restricted, and according to Neville 'opened; only for the cavalry who have the soft time, and also the Staff who are nicknamed by the troops "----- in shatoos" or "velvet bottoms".

> We are now in a topping little village with very good billets. My billet is heavenly and so comfortable that I almost imagine myself at home when I wake up in the early morning. We are having a most awfully good time, like a pre-war holiday, and it is good to be alive and enjoy it all.
>
> Bruay is just over the hill, and we make jovial parties and go in there to see the show, which is the best I have seen out here. After it, we have a cheery dinner at the Hotel Cerniclet which is a very nice little place.

[577] Letter to his sister written from Camblain-Châtelain on May 10th 1917. Letters to his father written from the Hotel Continental Paris on May 19th and Roclincourt on May 21st 1917.

On Tuesday, "Bunjie" Rowe[578] came over from the aerodrome at Bruay and took three of us round the sheds. We stayed to tea, and afterwards we all three went for a joy ride. I had the wind up considerably, at first; we seemed to be mounting up at such a terrific speed, and the noise of the wind was simply deafening. I loathed banking round the corners; the whole ground tilted at an awful angle. The curious thing is that the height never affected me at all; the whole earth lay beneath me like a map, and as flat as a map; neither a rise nor a fall in the ground was visible, nor hills; everything absolutely flat.

We are being allowed two nights out of billets, so Grover[579] and I have applied to go to Paris. "Bingo" Baines and Giles went to-day, and we shall probably go next week. It ought to be good fun, although we shan't be able to see much in 48 hours. However, I hope to be able to get to Versailles.

I gave a small dinner in Bruay last night. I had asked "Bunjee" to bring two other R.F.C. officers, but he never turned up, because he had had a crash in the afternoon, and was in hospital badly shaken. Thank heaven, he escaped with his life; but no details of how it occurred had come through when I saw these officers.

This village is situated right at the bottom of a valley, and when we go on parade we wind up a narrow little path through a most delicious wood, on a hill where it is cool and refreshing. The wood is heavenly now, carpeted with a mist of wind flowers, cowslips, dog violets, white violets, blue bells and a few buttercups. How I wish there was no war on!

We have to enjoy ourselves when the opportunity occurs, and often the fun is spoilt by a wire to say the Brigade is to move on in two days. That always puts the damper on. However, we may have a week longer here, and I thoroughly hope so, because men are few and far between now, owing to our heavy casualties at Arras.

On May 17th, the 52nd marched via Divion - Houdain - Rebreuve - Gauchin Légal along the Chaussée Brunehaut to Bray. Here the Regiment was accommodated in huts and bivouacs for the night, before the following day marching via Anzin - St. Catherine's [suburb of Arras] to a camp at Les Quatre

[578] A contemporary of Neville's with the 3rd Battalion Oxfordshire and Buckinghamshire Light Infantry.

[579] Second-Lieutenant J.D. Grover.

Vents, between Arras and Roclincourt. The 52nd relieved the 2nd South Staffordshire of the 6th Brigade. During the period May 18th-23rd inclusive, the Regiment provided working and road-making parties of 200 men every 24 hours. Second-Lieutenant William Seale joined the Regiment.

On May 24th, the 5th Brigade relieved the 15th Brigade of the 5th Division, to the north of Arras, in the left brigade section of the 2nd Division's front. This entailed the 52nd taking over the position of support battalion to the east of Willerval from the 15th Warwickshire. On the 27th, British artillery bombarded the Germans' ration dumps with gas and lachrymatory shells. At this hour the dumps were likely to be full of soldiers.

The Regiment remained in support until the 28th, when it replaced the 2nd H.L.I. as right battalion of the left brigade. Their sector included the southern half of Arleux with the dividing line between the 52nd and the battalion on their left running from north-east to south-west through the centre of the village. Two companies, D on the right and C on the left, were in the front line to the east of the captured village of Arleux. To their front was the village of Fresnoy whose defences were being strengthened by the enemy who had retaken the village. The remaining companies, A and B, plus the Regimental Headquarters, were in the Arleux loop to the west of the village. The front line was described as very 'sketchy', and time was occupied in digging posts and wiring. During the day shellfire was intermittent, aircraft duels were common above the trenches and were watched with interest. Although the *Battalion War Diary* described this time as 'three quiet and uneventful days', Jim Neville might have disagreed[580]. He was 'completely flooded out' of his dug-out in the Arleux Loop, and also reconnoitred a site for a new trench amongst unburied, decomposing bodies.

> B Company is now in support, just behind the village, and I am writing this in a dug-out just behind the village while water is pouring down the steps. A thunderstorm is raging outside, and I am afraid we shall soon be flooded out. It is most unpleasant to hear a waterfall descending into one's home like it is at the moment! Up till now, we have had as good weather as we could hope for, and I trust this deluge will cease in due season.
>
> On the 30th I went out to reconnoitre ground for a new trench, and, incidentally to try and scupper any Boche knocking around. The whole of No Man's Land was carpeted with Canadians, killed in the attack of May 2nd. The stench was something frightful.

[580] Letters to his father written from Arleux on May 30th and June 1st 1917.

Late in the evening of May 31st, the 52nd exchanged with the 2nd H.L.I. and returned to their former positions that had been vacated on the 28th, in support to the east of Willerval. The move was not completed until about 1 a.m. on June 1st. Two men were wounded during the day. It was at Willerval that the intrepid Major Cuthbert 'Bingo' Baines was to be seen walking through the enemy's artillery barrage with no more concern than if he was crossing Piccadilly. The incoming H.L.I. spent the next three days in clearing out the trenches and posts which were now in a bad condition following the thunderstorm. On the night of June 1st/2nd Jim Neville was sent forward with a party to cover a sapper officer and corporal who were to lay a white tape in no man's land in front of Arleux to mark the jumping-off line for an attack. Many years later he recorded the event[581].

> When the two sappers arrived there was a clear sky and a bright full moon behind us. The sapper officer refused to leave the trench to be a silhouette target. I went down to Regt HQ to find out what I was to do. The use of field telephones was forbidden for security reasons as messages could be picked up by the Enemy and there was no code word for such a simple operation. At H.Q. the adjutant [Whitfeld] rang up the brigade major and asked him to go out and look at the sky. As we never saw any brigade or any other staff in the front line I never knew who the individual was anyhow, he inferred that our adjutant was mad but eventually he was persuaded to leave his dug out to look up at the heavens. He reported to our adjutant he could only see a full moon.
> Adjutant. 'The Sappers don't like it'.
> Staff officer. 'Don't like what?'
> A. 'What you have just seen'.
> S.O. 'Do you mean the moon – what of it'.
> A. 'Its bright'.
> S.O. 'Of course, its bright – what of it'.
> A. 'The Sappers refuse to lay the tape in it'.
> S.O. 'Oh! Well tell them to do it tomorrow night'.

The next night Neville led out his covering party and told the Sapper Officer he must do his stuff. The Sappers were not best pleased as there was still bright moonlight only broken by scudding clouds. Neville placed his men in shell

581 An account written by Neville in 1976 from the Special Collections Leeds University Library.

holes about 30 yards from the enemy's line. Finding one man missing he went back towards the British lines[582].

> I went back towards our line round the shell holes and found him sitting at the bottom of one. I whispered to him to get up and follow me. He did not move. He was scared immobile. So was I his fright gave me courage. I whispered 'I'm giving you an order – follow me'. Still he did not move. I pointed my automatic at his head. Still he would not move. This made me so angry that I forced the muzzle of my pistol between his teeth and said 'Get up or I'll press the trigger?' That did move him and he followed me to my position in the middle of the covering party.

Although the first three weeks of June were to be relatively quiet for the 52nd, the 2nd Division's battalion commanders must have had a harassing time as the Higher Command suspected that the Germans were about to effect an evacuation of their trenches, and a withdrawal similar to theirs to the Hindenburg Line. The 2nd Division's staff was suspicious that the trenches in front of Arleux were no longer occupied and it was difficult to convince them otherwise. Eventually, the 2nd H.L.I. personally conducted a party from divisional headquarters around the line one night. During their visit they experienced every kind of German "hate" available – rifle, machine-gun, pineapples, and whizz bangs. No doubt the Divisional Commander, Major-General Cecil Pereira was suitably impressed and allowed Richard Crosse and the other battalion commanders to get on with their own war.

On June 3rd/4th, the 52nd was relieved from its position of support near Willerval by the 1st King's of the 6th Brigade, and took over the camp at Roclincourt vacated by that Regiment. One man had been wounded on the 2nd and four more men were killed on the 3rd. On June 4th/5th, a working party 200 men strong was found from C and D Companies for the forward area. Several bombs dropped near the camp during the day. The Regiment moved to the support position of the right brigade, the 99th, on the 5th/6th. The companies were disposed from right to left: A in the railway embankment just south of the Tunnel; B astride the Arleux - Sugar Factory - Tunnel road [H.Q. in the old Brigade Battle H.Q. in the Sunken road]; C and D thence to the south end of Long Wood. [see maps pages 424 and 433]. Further working parties of 200 men were organized each night. On the 7th, one man was wounded and the 82nd reinforcement of a welcome 36 rank and file arrived. The next night, the 8th/9th, the 52nd was relieved

[582] An account written by Neville in 1976 from the Special Collections Leeds University Library.

by the 2nd H.L.I. and moved to Ecurie Wood Camp, and later that day Second-Lieutenant Frederick 'Bolo' Lowndes rejoined the Regiment. He had been wounded on the Redan Ridge on November 13th 1916, evacuated to England, and had been awarded a M.C. on January 1st 1917. Two days later, Second-Lieutenant Roger 'Bugler' Ames also joined the 52nd.

The Regiment would remain in Ecurie Wood Camp until June 14th. Their time was spent in working parties and undergoing training. Classes of instruction in bombing and the Lewis gun were undertaken by Lieutenant Cyril 'Shiny' Horley and Second-Lieutenant Harry Vernon. On the 12th, the 2nd Division's Horse Show took place, and in a cross-country race of about three to four miles, the 52nd finished second to the Royal Engineers with Serjeant Ernest Constable of the 52nd the individual winner of the race. As will be seen, in December 1917, Constable's athletic prowess would come to the fore. Two days later, A and C Companies held their sports, and then at 8.30 p.m. the 52nd moved to a camp east of Roclincourt, vacated by the 1st East Surrey of the 5th Division. Here the Regiment was one of six battalions from the division out of the line detailed to provide working parties in the forward area. A great deal of work was required in the camp itself and this was ably undertaken by the Sapping platoon.

The 52nd stayed at Roclincourt Camp until June 19th. Each night working parties 200 men strong, and on one occasion 400 men, worked mainly round Willerval Strong Point and Tommy Trench. Second-Lieutenant Jim Neville, who had just returned to the Regiment after leave in England, wrote 'we are under canvas just behind 6-in. howitzers, and I am not used to the noise of the guns yet'. 'The Commanding Officer is awfully pleased with the braces'. Evidently Neville had given the braces to Richard Crosse as a gift. On the night of June 19th/20th, the Regiment was relieved by the 10th Royal Dublin Fusiliers and moved to huts and billets in Mount St. Eloi, to the north-west of Arras. That day [20th] the XIII Corps' horse show was held.

On June 21st, the 52nd left the area to the north of Arras for the last time, as part of the 5th Brigade's and 2nd Division's transfers north to the region of Béthune. The Regiment travelled by bus and lorry to an old haunt, the Ecole de Jeune Filles, in Béthune. Just under two years before, the 52nd had been regularly billeted there. No doubt the longest serving members of the Regiment were welcomed by the local inhabitants as old friends. Richard Crosse was pleased to find so many familiar buildings in Béthune still relatively undamaged[583]. He enjoyed visiting places of relaxation such as the Café du Globe in the Place or the nearby Au Pane d'Or. Not to mention 'Madame Full-Up' where the whole British Expeditionary Force seemed to be parading for a haircut. She would stand

[583] Sadly, Béthune was virtually destroyed by German artillery in 1918.

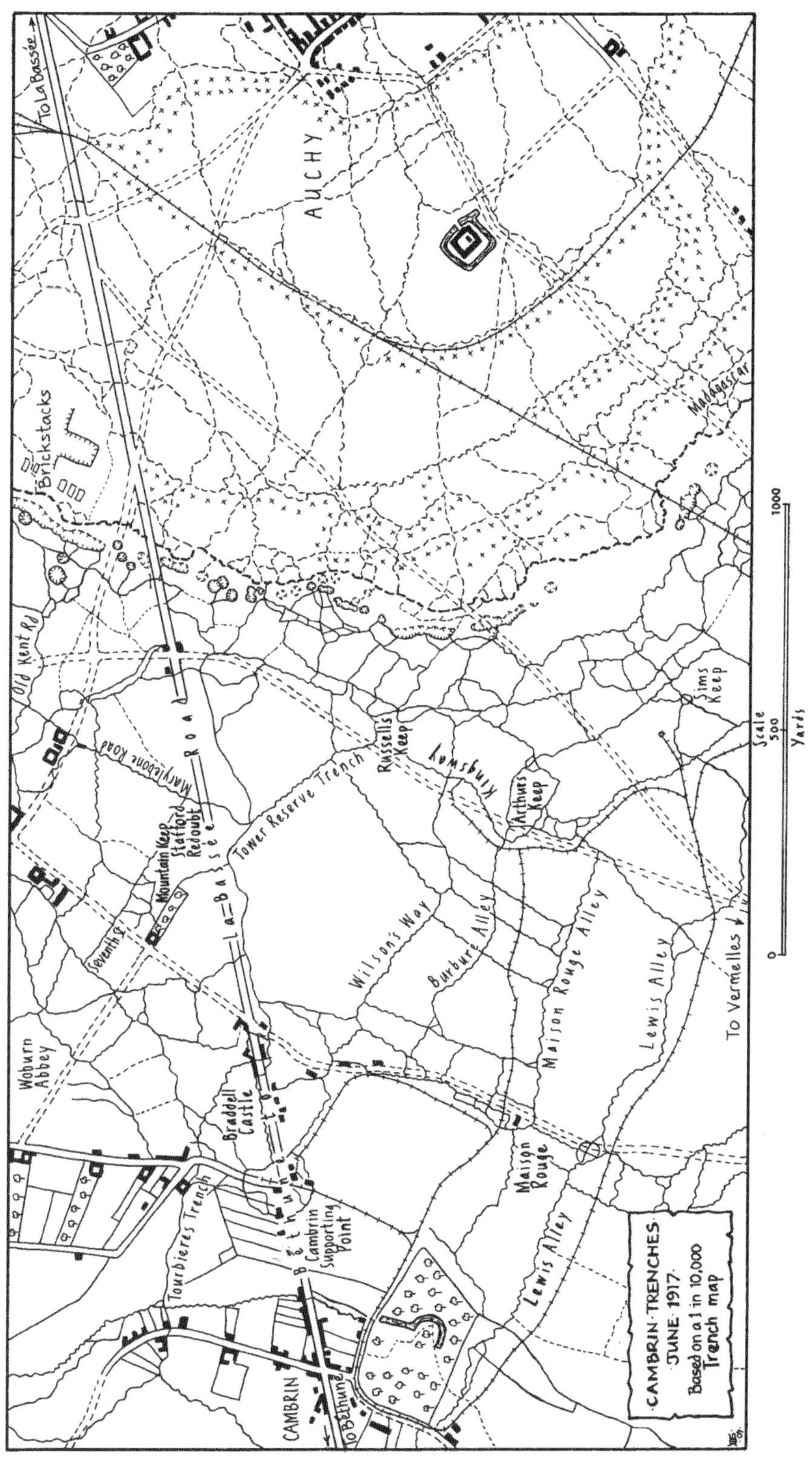

To La Bassée
AUCHY
Brickstacks
Madagascar
Old Kent Rd
Marylebone Road
Mountain Keep
Stafford Redoubt
Tower Reserve Trench
Russells Keep
Kingsway
Arthurs Keep
Sims Keep
Scale
0
500
1000
Yards
To Vermelles
Wilson's Way
Burbure Alley
Maison Rouge Alley
Lewis Alley
Woburn Abbey
Seventh St.
Braddell Castle
Cambrin Supporting Point
Tourbières Trench
Maison Rouge
Lewis Alley
CAMBRIN
To Béthune
CAMBRIN · TRENCHES · JUNE · 1917 · Based on a 1 in 10,000 Trench map

at the door crying "Full up, full up" while her assistants combed and cut feverishly inside. Jim Neville certainly thought that he had come to a better part of the line compared with Arras[584]. At this juncture, the front was quiet with the Battle of Messines coming to an end on June 14th and the Third Battle of Ypres still to start on July 31st.

The next day, the 22nd, the 52nd relieved the 2/4th East Lancashire of the 198th Brigade 66th Division[585] in the Canal right sub-sector [La Bassée Canal] of what had now become the 2nd Division's front. On their right, in the Cambrin left sub-sector were the men of the 23rd R.F. of the 99th Brigade, and to the left in the Canal centre sub-sector was the 2nd H.L.I. of their own Brigade. Still further to their left, in the Canal left sub-sector, was the 17th R.F. also of their own Brigade. Matters would be simplified on July 27th/28th when the centre sub-sector was amalgamated with those on either side.

The 5th Brigade had three battalions in the front line at a time and one in reserve, initially in Annequin and then in Le Preol, near Le Quesnoy, where the transport lines were situated. The reason for the move of one and a half miles further back was the quality of billet, and the periodic shelling of Annequin by the enemy. An additional advantage of Le Preol was the proximity of the Canal, allowing men to bath throughout the day in the particularly warm weather. Each battalion had two companies in the front line and two in support.

The 52nd's Canal right sub-sector extended from the La Bassée - Vermelles road [Burbure Alley] on the right, to the Béthune - La Bassée road on the left. The front line was taken over by B Company on the right, with C on the left. The trenches were described by Jim Neville as 'proper trenches, for the first time in my career out here'. In close support from Kingsway to Tower Reserve Trench was D Company, with C in support on the Village line, between its junctions with Maison Rouge Alley and Wilson's Way. The 52nd set up a regular system of reliefs whereby each company rotated, spending two days out of every eight in support in the Village line. In this way every man was able to slip away to Annequin for a bath and was re-underclothed every eight days. This was certainly an improvement on their habits in 1914 at Ypres, where circumstances dictated that clothing was not changed for weeks on end and there was communal underwear!

Major-General Cecil Pereira did not intend to let the enemy in his sector have a quiet time as he instructed his three Brigades, the 5th, 6th, and 99th, to undertake active patrolling. Each part of no man's land was to be systematically visited, and a patrol record book was to be kept in each sub-sector. This was to be

[584] Letter to his sister written from Le Quesnoy on June 26th 1917.

[585] According to a contemporary rumour the 66th Division had been lost in England for two years!

kept up to date and handed over to the incoming battalion. All three brigades were in the line, each with its own sector and carrying out inter-battalion reliefs in that sector. Hence individual battalions became familiar with the whole of their brigade front. In some parts of the Western Front, British patrolling of no man's land was so efficient that the enemy scarcely dared set foot in it at night.

The 52nd had gone into the Canal right sub-sector on June 22nd and it would remain there until July 6th rotating its companies in the manner described above. The *Battalion War Diary* recorded that this was a 'quiet and uneventful period' with the weather a mixture of the very hot and rainy. During this time, on the 25th, the highly experienced Captain George Field returned to the Regiment after having been injured on the Somme in October 1916, and was posted to command B Company. During the month of June, Second-Lieutenant H.A. Beaver was struck off the strength of the Regiment as he had been invalided back to England. In his few months with the 52nd he had been constantly ill with bronchitis, tonsillitis and a thigh strain. Second-Lieutenant Morris Fielding was another to fail his Medical Board in England and he too was struck off the strength having been found unfit for duty for one month on June 11th. The Australian Fielding had been seriously wounded in the eye at Waterlot Farm the previous July 30th and he had been awarded the Military Cross on January 1st 1917. The casualties during this time in the trenches were: five men wounded on the 24th; one man wounded on the 27th; a further man wounded, on the 28th, who subsequently died of his wounds.

In several letters during this period in the trenches, Second-Lieutenant Jim Neville gave his family at home a graphic account of his experiences both in the front line and in support. For the first time a degree of cynicism towards the war can be detected[586].

> We are now on a far better front where there is practically no shelling; on the other hand, there are no rest billets, and we shall be in the trenches for 28 days at a time, which is rather a ghastly prospect. I fear that there is little chance of a wound to bring me home, unless we do a raid or some stunt.
>
> My Company has been in the trenches for the last three days. I am commanding while Giles[587] is away on leave. We had to "stand-to" all Friday night, expecting a raid by the Boche. As I leant up against the parapet in the front line waiting, waiting, and waiting, my thoughts wandered back to those divine days at home; in front of us,

[586] Letter to his sister written from Le Quesnoy on June 26th 1917.
[587] Lieutenant William Giles.

the night was waning to a grey dawn. It really is wretched having to wait all night on the *qui vive* for a raid. It is really a hell of a strain, especially when you are responsible for the defence of the line and the lives of 100 men.

I am down at the Transport Lines for one night as my Company is in support. The gramophone is playing "Un peu d'amour," bringing back memories of Sloley[588] at Christmas 1914. Music is awful for reminding you of lovely times.

The shooting-stick gun is a great novelty. I am going to take it into the trenches with me and try to shoot some of the insolent rats, which sit on the parapet and positively laugh at me as I go my rounds at night. Some of them are as big as cats and fat as butter.

This land of France is most excessively boring, and I am fed up with the war. To think at this moment the last scene of "Bubbly" is being played, and everyone is preparing to go and try to find a cab. Time 10.45 p.m. All the fine ladies in their fine dresses, enjoying life to the full, and flirting with penniless subalterns to the detriment of both. The contrast is what amazes me. I never knew what war was like when I first came out; now I am bored and have seen enough. On the whole, I am glad I have had the opportunity of fighting for those who can't fight for themselves; but the way some of them talk, makes me doubt whether it is worth the candle.

This boredom is only temporary. I think I need a number 9.

The shortage of men in 1917 meant that, in the so-called quieter sectors, rest periods were reduced to the detriment of the troops' morale. For the first time, Neville's boredom and general disillusionment has come to the fore. Normally, an hour before dawn, the battalion in the line would 'stand to' in their battle position, as this was the most likely time for the enemy to attack. At the break of dawn the men would, apart from the sentries, 'stand down'. The same procedure would be repeated at dusk. However, as with the case here described by Neville, if a trench raid was expected the men might have to spend the whole night without sleep, ready to repel the enemy.

The Transport lines were the sphere of the Quartermaster and the Transport Officer, and might be as little as 100 yards behind the front line. The battalion's rations were brought as close to the front as the limbers[589] could reach, before being handed over to the company ration parties. However, it was not

[588] His family home in Norfolk which still belongs to the family nearly a century later.
[589] Detachable front part of a gun-carriage.

unknown for men to supplement their diet by dropping Mills bombs into the La Bassée canal and waiting for the dead fish to surface! The 17th R.F. was forbidden to use this unusual method of fishing. In the 2nd Division, Major and Quartermaster J. Taylor of the 2nd H.L.I., ran exemplary Transport lines, resplendent with whitewash and polish, and all the other Transport Officers were sent to him to be shown how transport lines should be run. The 52nd's Transport Officer at this juncture was Lieutenant John Slade-Baker.

Rats were a perennial problem in the trenches and thanks to the detritus of war and the ready availability of human corpses, they really could grow to be the size of cats. Neville's shooting-stick gun was a novel approach to rat infestation. Brigadier-General Archibald Eden, when in command of the Regiment, loved slashing at them on his morning round of the trenches, and the servant of a company commander brought a sackful of captured French cats to his officer for the same purpose. *'Bubbly'* was a revue at the Comedy Theatre in London, which opened in May 1917 and ran for 429 performances. The young Jack Hulbert was one of the stars of the show, and its songs included *'Reckless Reggie'*, and *'Keep on Loving Little Girlies'*. Musical Revues of this type were popular with the troops throughout the whole war. It is likely that Neville had seen the show on his recent home leave.

Second-Lieutenant Jim Neville wrote again to his father[590].

> I fear that I have been rather a long time in writing to you, the fact of the matter being that I have had more to do lately than I expected. We are now in the line opposite La Bassée. The Canal is on our left.
>
> We were rushed away from Vimy Ridge area in buses to come up here and take over from the 66th Division, which as rumour has it, was lost in England for two years!
>
> "B" went into the front line on the 22nd, and we came down to support here last night. This part of the line is an absolute rest cure compared to any I have been in so far. There are communication trenches right up to the front line. Up till now I have been accustomed to relieve over the top. I don't mind how long we stay here!
>
> On the night of the 23rd we were warned that the enemy might make a raid on the Regiment's front. As Giles is on leave I am in command of the Company. We stood-to-arms all night, but no raid was attempted. They would have got an awful hotting if they had tried.

---

590 Letter to his father written from the village line Canal right sub-sector on June 26th 1917.

I came up ahead of the Company, when we relieved the 2/4th East Lancashires on the 22nd, and while I was taking over, two Boche came and gave themselves up to the garrison of one of the sap-heads. They must have crawled up the mine crater into the post. They appeared in broad daylight, and seemed to be pleased as Punch to be in our lines. They were Alsatian conscripts, and only spoke German because they had been compelled by the Boche. They volunteered their hatred for the Boche, and when I asked them why, they gave as their reason, the scarcity of food. They showed me their ration which did look inadequate, yet they did not look thin; in fact they seemed to be able to thrive on what there was for them to eat.

I am amazed at the absence of shell fire. There are, however, certain things to be wary of, viz, "minnies," rifle grenades and "pineapples." The former are the deuce, and do a great deal of damage. They contain 120 lbs. of high explosive fired from a trench mortar, and are nicknamed "Rum Jars" from their appearance as they sail through the air. The latter are light trench mortar bombs like an aerial torpedo. They have vanes on their tails which keep them accurate in direction. They are so called because the body of the bomb is serrated into little squares. It is possible to have as many as 15-20 in the air at the same time, but our Stokes mortar can have more than that. Lastly, there is a terrible "minny" known as the "Flying Pig".

The Regiment will be here most probably for a long time holding the line, but, of course, you never know. We were badly swindled out of our rest by being sent here. I am not a thousand yards from the front line, yet behind me are cultivated fields and French men and women in Annequin beyond. Isn't that marvellous?

After the Franco-Prussian War of 1870-71, the two most eastern provinces of France, Alsace and Lorraine, were ceded to Germany. Many of the inhabitants of Alsace during the 1914-18 conflict felt a greater allegiance towards France than Germany. Hence Neville's description that the Alsatian deserters looked 'as pleased as Punch' is unsurprising under the circumstances. Two weeks later, there were further Alsatian desertions from the 65th Infantry Regiment of the 185th Division. The intelligence officer examining these men recorded that the 185th Division was to be relieved, as the number of Lorrainers meant that the division could not be trusted. The Germans were not alone when it came to the problem of desertion. In the British Army the desertion rate was said to be 10.26

per 1,000 men, which is equivalent to more than a division of troops for the average size of the army on the Western Front[591]. The majority of the men executed in the British Army, 266 out of 346, were for desertion.

Neville believed that the Alsatian deserters had crawled out of a mine crater to get into the British lines. Cuinchy Brickstacks had changed very little since the 52nd were last there in 1915, the only major difference being an almost continuous line of deep mine craters with the front line running approximately along their western lips. The mine craters extended south of the La Bassée to Béthune road where the 52nd was currently situated.

The Flying Pig was a very large British trench mortar which if one of its 150 pound bombs landed anywhere near an enemy post made it very unpleasant indeed for that post. However, the performances of the Pig were erratic, so much so that the line on either side of the mortar had to be cleared for a considerable distance, so common were the misfires. First produced in June 1916, the Pig shook the morale of the enemy until it was replaced by the six inch Stokes Mortar.

Jim Neville continued the description of his war[592].

> We are still in the trenches, and as far as I can see, we are likely to remain here some time longer. The weather has been atrocious too, and we are up to our knees in mud. ---.
>
> I spent last night in a detached post in the Mill Tunnel, garrisoned by thirty men. No one seemed to know the direction of the Hun trenches, so that I spent my time wandering about, trying to find our posts over the top, and fell into countless shell-holes full of water and mud. However, for duty in this particular post we are supplied with thigh gum boots which keep us dry, but also are very necessary because the bottom of the tunnel, which connects the posts, is at water level! You can imagine how hard it is to tell the direction of the enemy when you emerge from the tunnel into the posts. You cannot possibly tell which way you have travelled under ground [sic].

Despite the fact that it was early summer, it is interesting that the trenches were still water-logged. One of the main features of the area was the existence of four long tunnels, Wilson's, Robertson's, Lane, and Mill Tunnels.

---

[591] Quoted in *Tommy* by Richard Holmes. Page 564.

[592] Letter to his father written from Tower Reserve Trench on July 1st 1917.

The latter was situated just south of the Béthune - La Bassée road. The tunnels were lit by electric lights and were used mainly for getting safely up to the front line from support. During the day men in the front line could shelter in the tunnels away from the enemy's artillery and machine-guns. Indeed the 2nd H.L.I. set up a canteen in a dug-out under one of the Cuinchy Brickstacks. The main disadvantage of the tunnels was their height with men, particularly tall ones, having to bend to get through them.

Jim Neville recorded the use of oil shells[593].

> I have had a refreshing sleep in the Village Line. I watched a marvellous firework display last night. Our guns were bombarding the Boches on the left with our new blazing oil shells. I expect you have read about them in the papers. It is quite dark, and we could see the shells burst into a gorgeous flame, which sent long arms of fire shooting to the earth. Some shot the flaming liquid in a fan of fire, while others burst on percussion, producing the effect of a fountain of flame. The whole sky was lit up and it was a lovely sight to watch. The troops were tickled to death with the show; I heard a man say, "That's drumming Jerry up, not 'arf." I only hope the Boche has not got any stuff like it for us!

The projection of burning oil was a short-lived answer to the German flamethrower. Its concept is reminiscent of the use of boiling oil to deter those besieging castles in medieval times. Special Companies of Royal Engineers electrically discharged as many as 200-300 cylinders and fired them from mortars into the enemy's trench system. On impact with the ground, a fuse ignited them with the spectacular effect described by Neville[594]. Here, in 1917, the 2nd Division had a retaliation policy of six to one, which meant that for every shell or bomb sent at them, six must be fired in return. This was a very different state of affairs from 1915, when the supply of British shells and bombs was limited, so that the troops would often have to grin and bear an enemy bombardment.

On July 6th, the 52nd was relieved by the 24th R.F. and moved into billets at Le Preol, with the exception of the unfortunate D Company which was left to man Braddell, Stafford, and Mountain Keeps. These Keeps were strong points, to the north of the La Bassée to Béthune road; Braddell Keep at Burbure; Stafford

---

593 Letter to his father written on July 2nd 1917.

594 Everard Wyrall in the second volume of *The History of the Second Division 1914-1918* stated that burning oil was first used by the 2nd Division, prior to a trench raid on July 20th 1917. However, this is likely to be incorrect as Neville recorded witnessing its use nineteen days earlier on July 1st.

Keep close to Seventh Street; Mountain Keep to the south-west of Cuinchy village. Between July 7th and 11th, the 52nd rotated the other three companies through the Keeps, and did as much training as was feasible under the circumstances. The Lewis gun classes which had started two months previously were completed after carrying out range practices. A class to train privates to become lance-corporals was run by Captain Ernest Whitfeld, the Adjutant, and Regimental Serjeant-Major Fred Clare. The 5th Brigade also required the 52nd to provide a number of carrying and working parties. On the 10th and 11th, the Regiment greatly enjoyed Aquatic Sports in the nearby canal[595].

July 12th saw the 52nd return to the Canal right sub-sector of the Brigade front in place of the 24th R.F. A little after the completion of the relief at 11.30 p.m., misfortune was to strike the Regiment when their trenches were subjected to an unpleasant bombardment by gas shells. This was particularly heavy on the support and reserve lines. A gas shell struck the parados of Kingsway Trench, opposite the entrance to a dug-out occupied by personnel from B Company [see map page 463]. Unfortunately, the blast went straight down the steps and three longstanding soldiers of the 52nd died soon afterwards from its effects. The men who died were Lance-Corporal Edward Williams [Sanitary Corporal[596]], a Londoner aged 36 years; Private Arthur Burrows [stretcher-bearer], also a Londoner, also aged 36 years; Private Harry Tew [stretcher-bearer], born in Brackley, aged 37 years.

Over the next 48 hours a further fifteen to twenty men suffered from the effects of the gas. Evenings over the next two days seemed to be a particularly bad time for those suffering from gas inhalation. The Commanding Officer, Lieutenant-Colonel Richard Crosse, thought that had not the gas discipline been good, B Company could have had 85 per cent casualties. However, two men might have escaped the effects of the gas if they had been better trained. One of them was very badly affected, the other less so. The 52nd was not alone in suffering from this gas attack, as the 2nd H.L.I., which was in the line next to them, had no less than 153 gas shells fall in close proximity to their Regimental Headquarters. Gas masks had to be worn for an hour and a quarter and, of the seven men gassed, two died. Attacks of this type were all too common.

Second-Lieutenant Jim Neville, a member of B Company, witnessed at first hand the awful events of that night[597].

---

[595] On one occasion, a member of the 52nd swam underwater and surfaced in front of the grandstand exposing the 2nd Division's emblem [three eight-pointed stars] on his clothing. This was greatly appreciated by the watching divisional general!

[596] Inevitably known as the 'shit-wallah'.

[597] Letter to his sister written from Le Quesnoy on July 13th 1917.

> Last night the Boche tried to kill us all with gas shells, and it was my turn for duty too! They started popping them over about 12 midnight. The cry came down the trench, "Gas" "B" Company was in immediate support with gas sentries on duty, whom I had to visit during my tour of duty. The shelling went on for half an hour, and I stumbled round the trenches wearing my gas mask, running into the traverses and barking my knees on the revetting. It was pitch black and doubly hard to see with the respirator on, but I found all the men wearing their respirators and joking with each other.
>
> There were only four casualties at the time. A shell burst right outside a dug-out and gas went straight down the stairs and gassed our stretcher-bearers and sanitary corporal who were the oldest soldiers in the Company. One has since died. When I saw them in the Aid Post, one poor devil was coughing and spitting his very soul out. How blessed my box respirator.

Wisely, gas training was taken seriously, and there were gas chambers, such as the one at Ecurie which the 17th R.F. put all ranks through. The fact that Neville found his men joking with their respirators on says a great deal about the leadership and morale in the Regiment. The *Battalion War Diary* stated that the three old soldiers, Williams, Burrows, and Tew had 'died shortly afterwards'. This is not strictly accurate as Neville, writing on July 13th, recorded 'One has since died'. As the gas attack started around midnight on July 12th/13th, he was writing on the day in question. One other man must have died later on the 13th, after Neville had finished his letter, but the records show that Lance-Corporal Edward Williams did not die until the following day, the 14th. It does appear clear that all three of the old soldiers died from the effects of the gas rather than the initial blast of the explosion. Although terrifying, gas was a relatively ineffective weapon with only 3-4 per cent of its victims actually dying compared to the 25 per cent death rate with other weapons such as the shell, mortar bomb, and machine-gun.

For the 52nd, the period July 13th-20th proved to be quiet and the weather variable. Valuable patrol work was carried out amongst the mine craters in no man's land by Lieutenant Thomas 'Twitt' Tyrwhitt-Drake, Second-Lieutenant Dick 'Puff Ball' Warren and the Regimental scouts. On the night of July 20th/21st, the 23rd R.F. of the 99th Brigade, on the 52nd's right in the Cambrin left sub-sector, made a raid on Madagascar Trench, north of the Hohenzollern Redoubt, in the Germans' line [see map page 463]. This was a significant raid with three officers and 115 men taking part. A considerable number of the enemy were killed and two trench mortars destroyed before the raiding party returned to their own trenches at the appointed time. When Major-General Cecil Pereira went to congratulate the raiding party in person, one corporal paraded in his underpants having left his trousers on the German wire! The 52nd were subjected to retaliatory fire on their front line as a consequence of the raid.

No entries appear in the *Battalion War Diary* for the period July 22nd-25th, although the 52nd remained in the Canal right sub-sector. However, Second-Lieutenant Jim Neville recorded that he was out patrolling on the nights of July 22nd and 23rd. Despite the approbation of his Commanding Officer, Richard Crosse, the very tall Neville did not consider himself designed for patrol work. Neville found this period in the trenches particularly irksome with the hot weather turning the trenches into a fly-filled hot oven. He felt that he was living the life of a rat, only venturing forth at night[598].

> The last two nights I have spent on patrol, which does not amuse me much; it's too exciting. Our wire is most awfully hard to negotiate, and I get hung up and torn most unmercifully. I was never made for a boy scout to crawl on my belly, for my displacement is too great. Patrolling would be very good fun, if only the enemy had no rifles, bombs, or machine guns, which take the interest out of the whole affair.

It was the turn of the 5th Brigade to conduct a trench raid on the night of July 26th/27th, and the 2nd H.L.I. was the chosen battalion[599]. Originally it was intended that the 52nd undertook the raid, and Second-Lieutenant Jim Neville was to lead it. He had performed the necessary patrolling and had found a way across the craters in front of Cambrin. A single machine-gun lined up on the path could have obliterated the 52nd's raiders. But possibly for this reason the scheme was cancelled, and instead, the 2nd H.L.I. undertook their raid on the 52nd's right[600].

---

598 Letter to his sister written from Cambrin right front on July 24th 1917. Technically he was in the Canal right sub-sector and not the Cambrin trenches.

599 There is some confusion about the date of this raid. Everard Wyrall in *The History of the Second Division* stated that it took place on the night of July 27th/28th. Major A.D. Telfer–Smollett et al. in their *The 2nd Battalion H.L.I. in The Great War* gave the date as June 27th which is patently incorrect. This author has chosen to believe *The Battalion War Diary* and Jim Neville's letter which both independently gave the same date.

600 The *Battalion War Diary* stated that the 2nd H.L.I was on the right of the 52nd. This is a little odd as the raid would have taken place partially through the adjoining brigade's area.

At 12.40 a.m., the 2nd H.LI. attacked the German front and support trenches astride the Béthune - La Bassée road. The raid called 'Haggis' was led by two officers with 73 other ranks under them. An effective barrage including gas and burning oil was put down on the German line. The raid itself went like clockwork and many Germans were killed, although no prisoners were taken. The reason for the lack of prisoners was that part of the raiding party was held up on the wire, and the stampeding enemy narrowly escaped the two pincers of raiders closing on them. As a 'ruse de guerre', Lieutenant John Murray who was attached to the sapping platoon [later the pioneer platoon], set up a number of wooden figures in no man's land, to the front of the 52nd. According to Richard Crosse, the shortage of manpower with which to harass the enemy led to these Aldershot pole targets being used for special service to deceive the Germans in no man's land. The figures were made of half-inch wood with a hinged base and were of variable height. Each was secured by a screw picket and could be made to stand up or fall down by pulling a string running back to the trenches. At zero hour the figures were well and truly peppered by the enemy. The 52nd, led by Lieutenant Thomas Tyrwhitt-Drake, played their part in the 'ruse de guerre' by firing a large number of rifle grenades, as a feint.

Second-Lieutenant Jim Neville described the scene in his own words[601].

> On the night of the 26th the Regiment did a feint raid to draw fire from the 74th [2nd H.L.I.] astride the La Bassée road to our left. Murray's sapping platoon had made dummy figures which were put out in No Man's Land. These dummies were made in three sizes, big, medium and smallish, and were pulled into a vertical position by wires manipulated from the front line. The big ones were nearest the enemy wire and were the last to be elevated, the idea being that the Boche would get the illusion of men advancing.
>
> At the appointed time, we fired a torpedo[602] under the enemy's wire and then sent up the German S.O.S. signal. At the same moment, Murray pulled up the first set of dummies which were lying just in front of our parapet; down came the Boche barrage and up went the second line of advancing dummies!
>
> After the pucka [sic] raiding party had returned the dummies were collected from No Man's Land and found to be fairly riddled.

[601] Letter to his father written from the Mill on July 28th 1917.

[602] See footnote 467 on page 369.

The British army was suffering from a manpower crisis and this was the reason for the 52nd being kept in the line for such a prolonged period. The shortage was particularly acute in the Fusilier Battalions, of which the 5th Brigade had two, the 17th and 24th R.F. The month before, the commander of the 2nd Division, Major-General Cecil Pereira, recorded in his diary of his concern.

> Divisions not due for any offensive are being kept at 10,000 rifles, the full strength is 13,000. This sounds very satisfactory but there always 1,000 to 1,500 men away on leave at a time there are 350 on various employments, tunnellers etc, all of whom come out of our establishments. By the time one gets to trench strength battns go into the line very weak.
>
> All our Royal Fusilier battns are permanently weak owing to the large numbers of Fusiliers battns to be kept up.

On the morning after the raid made by the 2nd H.L.I., on the night of 26th/27th, Jim Neville and Thomas 'Twitt' Tyrwhitt-Drake travelled to Bruay to listen to an address by the Archbishop of York, Cosmo Lang[603]. Two officers from each Regiment in the Army in France plus numerous padres were packed into the small theatre. The Archbishop was introduced by General Henry Horne, the Army Commander, and proceeded to speak for an hour on self discipline and the duties of an officer after the war. According to Neville, Lang was an unimpressive speaker, and Horne summarised in five minutes all that the Archbishop had taken an hour to say, and the latter admitted it! It is possible that Lang was having an off day as he was a renowned orator, or that his criticism of the excesses of anti-German propaganda had antagonized his soldier audience. Previously he had recalled the Kaiser kneeling by the side of Edward VII at Queen Victoria's deathbed. Lang became the target of abuse and he aged appreciably by immediately losing all his hair.

About this time there was concern that some French civilians were spying for the enemy. A lance-corporal in B Company saw two carrier pigeons fly out of a house straight towards the German lines. The inhabitants, an elderly woman and a young man, came out and then went in again. The lance-corporal thought that they looked guilty and seemed to want to see if he had noticed anything. How the lance-corporal recognized the birds as carriers is odd. Perhaps there was a general paranoia, although French collaboration with the enemy was not unknown. For example at the Annequin coal mine which was close to the

---

[603] Cosmo Lang [1864-1945] was Archbishop of York from 1909-28 and Canterbury 1928-42. As he lay dying outside Kew Station, his final words were, 'I must get to the station'.

front, the French miners were thought to be communicating with the Germans underground.

On July 28th, the frontage of the 5th Brigade was altered, with the amalgamation of the Canal central sub-sector with those on its left and right. This meant that the 52nd, in the Canal right sub-sector, became responsible for the trench system to their left or north as far as Stirling Sap. Part of the group of Cuinchy brickstacks and the Old Kent Road Tunnel became within their sphere of influence. C Company under Captain M.S. 'Guillaume' Griffith-Williams were the first members of the Regiment to occupy the new trenches. In 1915 the Regiment had become all too familiar with this dangerous area. The main differences from nearly two years before were the greater number of mine craters and the tunnels, which allowed men to get into the front line without exposing themselves in the communication trenches to enemy fire. The changes meant one extra company of each battalion was in the front line, but now allowed one whole battalion to be in close support, and another in reserve in billets. The battalion rota was now: front line for six days; in close support for six days at Kingsclere; front line for six days; in reserve for six days at Le Preol. This method of holding the line was continued until the 52nd left the area later in the autumn. The next day, the 29th, was as Jim Neville put it: 'It is quiet enough for the King to come here now'.

The 52nd's Commanding Officer, Lieutenant-Colonel Richard Crosse, was on leave at this time having left the Regiment in the most capable hands of his second-in-command, Major Cuthbert 'Bingo' Baines. As has been recorded earlier, Crosse had some unusual views about taking leave, having tried to follow the example of his ancestor John Cross [no e], who declined any leave for the whole of the Peninsular War, a century earlier. In fact he took his first leave in early 1917 and was now enjoying another well-deserved one. Jim Neville has recorded his views on Crosse at this juncture[604].

> The Commanding Officer is now on leave, which is a great wonder. I think he enjoyed himself more on his first leave than he realized at the time. Apparently he spends all his leave in connection with the Regiment, either strafing the 3rd Battalion, or arranging for certain officers to come out to the 52nd. He is a perfectly amazing man.

Neville was not alone in thinking Richard Crosse 'a perfectly amazing man'. As Crosse was unmarried, the members of the 52nd and their dependants became a surrogate family to him. He was enormously supportive of the grieving

---

604 Letter to his sister written from the Mill on July 29th 1917.

relatives of fallen members of the Regiment. When on leave in England he travelled long distances to visit them and was a regular correspondent. In the case of one of his officers, Crosse was still writing regularly to the man's mother until she died 24 years after her son. While commanding his battalion at war, Crosse still found the time to give advice on what should be inscribed on a M.C. Nothing appeared to be too much trouble for him. Arrangements were made with base to return old 52nd officers back to the Regiment after recovering from their wounds. On one occasion Crosse was introduced to the clergyman cousin of one of his officers. Having been impressed by the man, he attempted to get him transferred to the 52nd[605]. If Crosse sometimes appeared to be treating the British Army as a private club, it was only to benefit his beloved 52nd Light Infantry.

During the month of July, one man had been killed, four men died of their wounds, and 26 were wounded, including sixteen by gas. July 13th saw Second-Lieutenant James Atkins, a former C.S.M., sent home to England with acute lumbago and myalgia. On the final day of the month, Lieutenant Percy Bobby rejoined the 52nd from the 3rd Battalion. Twelve months earlier, he had suffered an accidental gunshot wound to his leg.

On August 2nd, the 52nd was relieved by the 2nd H.L.I. and took up the position of the Reserve Battalion at Le Preol. That same day Second-Lieutenant C.B. Coleman joined the Regiment. The six days in reserve were spent in training, musketry, practicing for the Lewis gun competition, and generally resting. An interdenominational service was conducted in the 2nd Division's Theatre at Le Quesnoy by the Reverend Edward Guilford[606]. During August, a small chapel with an altar painted white, and a rest room were built, under Guilford's direction, in a trench called Wimpole Street, in the Cambrin sector. That same day, the 5th, the 83rd reinforcement of six buglers joined, and on the 7th, the 84th reinforcement of thirteen men also arrived.

On the 7th, the Regiment was visited by their former Commanding Officer, Brigadier-General Archibald Eden, plus Major Lancie Ruck Keene, whose ill-health had precluded his going abroad with the 52nd in August 1914[607],

[605] The clergyman was the Reverend Ben Ruck Keene who was killed at an Advanced Dressing Station, on September 17th 1917, during the battles for Passchendaele. Crosse wrote to the Deputy Chaplain-General, Bishop Llewellyn Gwynne, seeking a transfer of Ruck Keene to the Division and the 52nd if their own chaplain was promoted. In the event the transfer did not take place.

[606] A holder of the M.C.

[607] In 1914, the ill-health appeared to have been caused by a dental problem which continued into the following year. In an undated letter from Captain [later Admiral] William Ruck Keene R.N. to his wife Violet, apparently written in the early summer of 1915: 'Very poor news about Lancie he didn't pass the board and has been to another dentist who finds the 4 teeth Carter left in to be as

and Lieutenant-Colonel Earl Fitzwilliam[608] of the 3rd Battalion. The following day, the 8th, after their allotted six days in reserve, the 52nd relieved the 2nd H.L.I. in their former trenches, the Canal right sub-sector. Second-Lieutenant Ben Slocock rejoined for duty from the 3rd Battalion, and was attached to the Headquarters Company with a view to temporarily relieving Second-Lieutenant J.D. Grover as Signal Officer. Slocock had been Head of School at Radley when war broke out, and had been wounded in the buttock serving with the 52nd in August 1916. Grover was to be attached to the 2nd Signal Company Royal Engineers with a view to qualifying for the Army Signal Service. In this he was successful.

The six days in the line were uneventful, notable only for some further changes in personnel. The 85th reinforcement of 65 men arrived on the 10th, and the much-wounded Captain Billy Barnard rejoined from the 3rd Battalion, on the 11th. Barnard was described by a contemporary as 'a great chap, full of spirits and fun'. He had been made a captain backdated to August 1st. During this period eight men were wounded including one suffering from shell shock. August 13th was the third anniversary of the 52nd's embarkation for the Continent. On this date only four officers and 88 other ranks were still serving with the Regiment. One officer, Richard Crosse and, 59 rank and file had soldiered continuously in France for the full three years.

On August 14th, the 52nd was relieved by the 2nd H.L.I. and went back to the position of support battalion where, for the next six days, men were supplied for carrying and working parties. In essence, the 52nd's support positions were to the east of Cuinchy, to the south of the canal, and south-east of Givenchy, to the north of the canal. The length of the support line was much greater than their front line positions, as it was necessary to cover the battalion in the line north of the canal. The Regiment was distributed: Headquarters in Kingsclere, the remains of a house in the ruined village of Cuinchy; A Company in the village line and support line south of the Béthune to La Bassée road; D Company in the support line from the Béthune to La Bassée road to the junction of Esperanto Street and Marylebone Road trenches; C Company thence to the canal; B Company north of the canal in Orchard and Spoil Bank Keeps, Oxford and Cambridge Terraces, and Gunner Siding. The Quartermaster, Lieutenant Arthur Warnock was transferred to England sick with 'heart effect of strain' on the 19th. He was temporarily commissioned and transferred to pension.

---

bad as the others and they must come out. He seems to be in a wretched state and I can see Emmie is very upset'.

[608] William Charles De Meuron Wentworth-Fitzwilliam. 7th Earl.

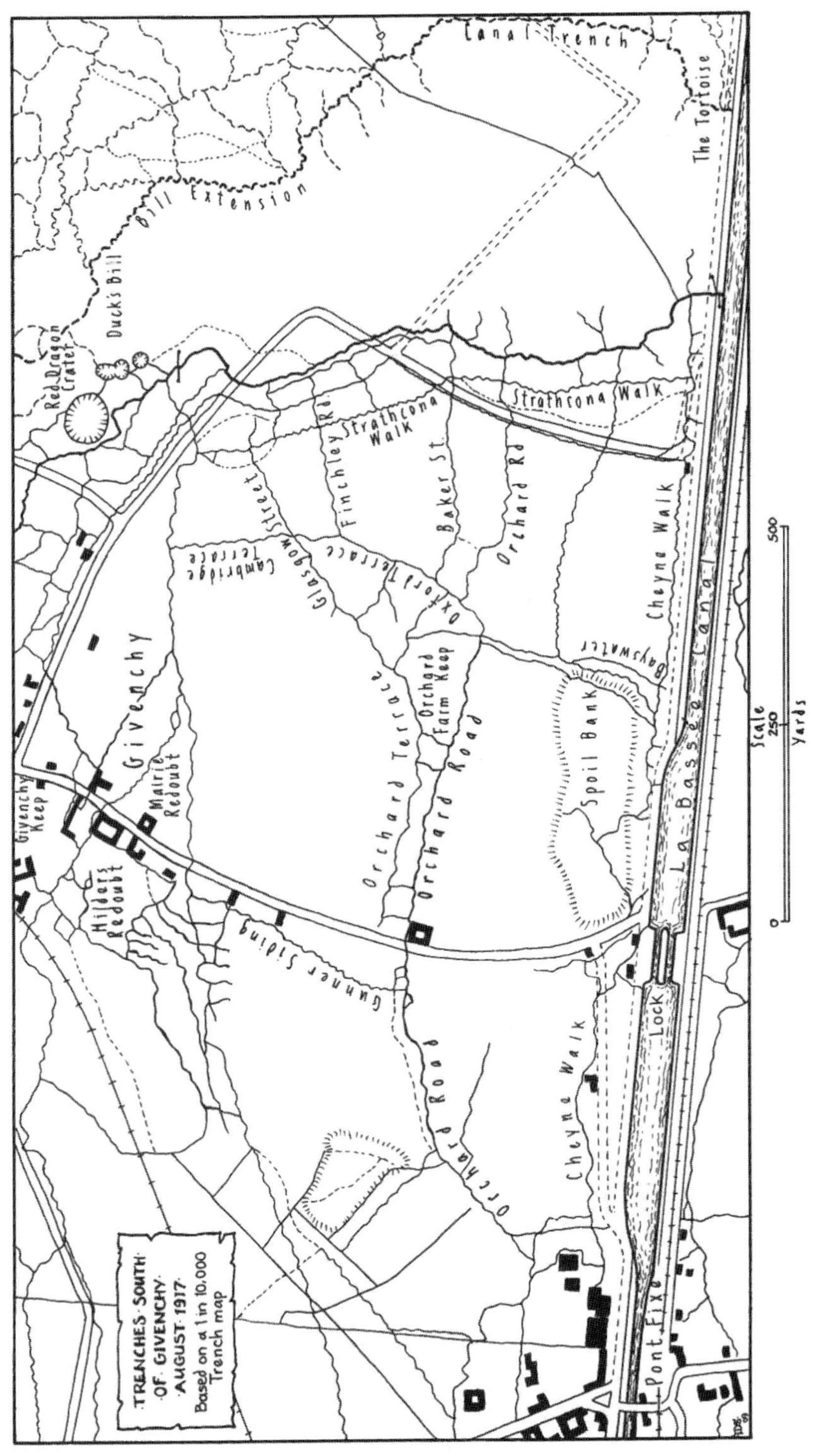
Canal Trench
The Tortoise
Duck's Bill Extension
Duck's Bill
Red Dragon Crater
Strathcona Walk
Finchley Rd.
Strathcona Walk
Baker St.
Orchard Rd
Cheyne Walk
Glasgow Street
Cambridge Terrace
Oxford Terrace
Orchard Farm Keep
Bayswater
Givenchy
Spoil Bank
Mairie Redoubt
Givenchy Keep
Hilders Redoubt
Orchard Terrace
Orchard Road
Gunner Siding
La Bassée Canal
Lock
Cheyne Walk
Orchard Road
Pont Fixe
Scale
0
250
500
Yards
TRENCHES SOUTH OF GIVENCHY AUGUST 1917
Based on a 1 in 10,000 Trench map

Billy Barnard and Jim Neville had made the most of their time in support with B Company, to the north of the canal, with a surreptitious swim[609].

> Billy Barnard and I have just had a bathe, which was spoilt by the Boche, who sent over some 5.9's, the bits of which splashed in the water close to us. Naked as I was, I felt doubly so, when the brutes began to shell. The water was very warm and we are thinking of having another try later on.

August 20th saw the 52nd return to their former Canal right sub-sector trenches once more, in place of the 2nd H.L.I. The enemy was extremely docile and lacked vigilance during this period of six days in the front line. Possibly their attention had been drawn to the north where the Third Battle of Ypres was now in full swing. Both in the *Battalion War Diary* and in his post-war articles, Richard Crosse singled out Second-Lieutenants Roger 'Bugler' Ames, Jim Neville, Dick 'Puff Ball' Warren and Lance-Corporal J. Tilbury for the excellence of their patrol work. The intrepid Warren entered the enemy's line in the same place, in broad daylight, on two consecutive days, and removed a loaded German rifle from a sniper's post. In turn Neville purloined a gas alarm bell from the German lines. Probably as a result of this active patrolling, which was very much part of the divisional commander's policy, reconnoitring parties of what looked like staff officers could be seen in the German lines.

On the 21st, the 86th reinforcement of one serjeant and fourteen other ranks arrived, and four days later it was the turn of the 87th reinforcement to join with eighteen other ranks from the 2nd Division's Draft School. Second-Lieutenant T.A. Coffin became Acting Quartermaster on the 21st, Lieutenant T.W.C. Foreshew proceeded to the Central Training School at Etaples on the 22nd, and Lieutenant N.G. Clarke was transferred to the 52nd from the 6th Battalion on the 24th. Yet more men arrived on August 25th in the form of the 87th reinforcement of eighteen other ranks.

Whilst in the Canal right sub-sector trenches, Jim Neville described a patrol on the night of August 21st/22nd, and sniping the enemy on the mornings of the 22nd and 23rd[610]. He looked upon night patrolling as a 'rather mouth-drying game, because there is always the possibility of a hostile patrol cutting off the line of retirement'[611].

---

609 Letter to his sister written from the Lock House Givenchy on August 19th 1917.

610 Letters to his sister and father written at Cuinchy Brickstacks on August 22nd and 23rd 1917.

611 Letter to his father written at Le Preol on August 27th 1917.

Last night I took a patrol out from Lunatic Sap, crossed the crater and our wire, and then made for the sap on the Boche side of the crater. We found it empty which was lucky! I told my men, by sign, to fan out and cover me while I had a look at the enemy's position. In the sap-head, I found a small hand-bell, probably used as a gas alarm bell. I wrapped my handkerchief round the clapper and stuffed it in my pocket. We then patrolled along his front line for about 100 yards: I, worming my way along his parapet. No sign of a Boche! So we waited a bit in case the "Verey Light Corporal" should come along, because lights are often sent up from his front line. Even he seemed to be off duty last night! The blinking bell in my pocket put the wind up me, because I was terrified that the "hankie" would work loose and the clapper would peal a clarion. So I kept my hand on it and prayed to heaven that I should not have to use my revolver. However, I got back safely with my souvenir in my pocket. I had to send it down to Headquarters as evidence of my route, and, I am told, the bell will have to be forwarded to Brigade. I should like it as a souvenir.

Then again this morning, I saw two Boche walking about in their support line, so I had a shot at them. They ducked, and I had another shot at them and they ran like hell. I wish I had killed them. I don't think I even hit one of them; I was a trifle excited, I think, because I wanted my Boche before breakfast. However, I am going to register some rifle grenades on that spot and see if I can't catch them tomorrow. Its great fun shooting human rabbits! I only hope they do not snipe me! We have the bulge on them in the very early morning, because the sky gets light behind them and they show up, while I imagine we don't show at all.

I had some good fun this morning. I spotted a Boche at "stand-to" and had a shot at him. There was one of our snipers observing for me, and he said that the Boche never moved from where he fell. To make sure of him, I put six rounds rapid with rifle grenades, so that, I think, if he was wounded by the bullet, he must have been put out of mess by the grenades.

Second-Lieutenant Jim Neville was up to more mischief on August 24th, leaving the unfortunate commander of the 5th Brigade, Brigadier-General George

'Humpty Dumpty' Bullen-Smith rather shaken up by his experience of the Canal right sub-sector trenches[612].

> I have told you about the Boche habit of walking about behind their lines at "stand-to." Yesterday Roger Ames and I had some awfully good fun. It was a glorious sunny morning, so we made a new emplacement for rifle grenades and registered them on the spot whence we had seen the Boche going to and fro at "stand-to." Probably there is a dug-out, because they appear between the brickstacks frequently in the light before dawn.
>
> Well, I crawled out over the parapet and sat in a very big shell-hole from which I could observe the fall and burst of the grenades through my glasses. Having found the range, we tried a salvo of six at a time, fired from one stand of rifles simultaneously.
>
> Now at breakfast George Field had told us that the Colonel had sent a message up to say that the Brigadier was coming to inspect the trenches. I am afraid that Roger and I were very naughty, and rather hoped that, if we badgered the enemy sufficiently, we might persuade him to retaliate about the time the Brigadier was due to come round.
>
> As it so happened, the old man arrived while we were doing a shoot. He said "good morning" to me from the trench, and asked what we were shooting at. I explained the situation, and that there had been a lot of movement round the spot where we were shooting, and that I suspected the presence of a dug-out.
>
> "Very good, my boy. But what can you see?"
>
> "Would you like to come and have a look, Sir?" said I.
>
> "Oh No. I must get on. I have got to be back at Division by 12.30."
>
> I caught the Colonel's[613] eye and thought I saw a twinkle of amusement in it.
>
> By the time the poor Brigadier had reached us he was exceedingly hot from having negotiated the long tunnels and many steps, and the sun, moreover, was hot. As a visible proof of this, there was a drop of sweat hanging on the tip of his nose.
>
> However, he seemed very pleased at the offensive spirit which Roger and I were manifesting to the troops, and him in particular, so

---

[612] Letter to his father written from Cuinchy Brickstacks on August 23rd 1917.

[613] Lieutenant-Colonel Richard Crosse.

we carried on and sent over two more salvos, each of 12 grenades, and hoped to have our efforts reported in the Brigade "Comic Cuts" as "B" Company, 52nd Light Infantry, carried out a shoot on a suspected enemy dug-out under No.1 Brickstack, firing in all fifty grenades, and achieve merit thereby.

Our plan could not have been more successful. From my coign of vantage, I could see four tin hats bobbing along the trench towards the entrance of the tunnel, and just as the first tin hat reached the steps, there was a boom from the enemy's guns and three whizzbangs burst in rapid succession around the spot. Thank heaven, they were wide of the entrance and the Commanding Officer.

We heard afterwards that the Brigadier was just about to descend the steps when the first shell arrived, and that he got from top to bottom in record time.

I don't know, but I think that the Commanding Officer knew that we were up to no good, and were having a game. He's a marvellous man.

On August 26th, the 52nd once again went back to become the reserve battalion at Le Preol. They marched from the front line in the Canal right sub-sector trenches wearing box respirators for practice purposes. The next day was spent in bathing and generally cleaning up. During the day No. 4 Company, 20th Battalion of the Portuguese Expeditionary Force, was attached to the Regiment, and split up by platoons amongst the various companies. It has to be said that from the Corps Commander down to the most inexperienced subaltern in the 52nd, no great faith was placed in the Portuguese contingent. The previous month, the Divisional Commander, Major-General Cecil 'Pinto' Pereira, of Portuguese extraction himself, had made his views clear in his diary[614]: 'Tamagnini the Portugese [sic] c-in-c was also present. He is commonly known as Tomato and he looks like it'[615]. 'The Portugese [sic] on the other hand abandon their posts and support line when ther[e] is heavy shelling with the idea of avoiding casualties and then counter attack. This is all very pretty in theory but I dont [sic] place any reliance on their boiling up a counter attack and they might continue with the idea of avoiding casualties whilst our left got more and more in the air'.

[614] Diary entry for July 6th 1917.

[615] General Tamagnini commanded the Portuguese Expeditionary Force. A surviving photograph shows a rather unprepossessing individual.

A few days later, Major-General Cecil Pereira, continued with his assessment of the Portuguese[616].

> The Corps Comdr told me he was having much trouble with the Portugese [sic]. They do no work, they sit up all night waiting for the Boche and are very weak in the day and slumber and consequently their trenches are all falling into disrepair. The Corps Staff are constantly round endeavouring to get them working. They have now been threatened that if they do not work they will be taken out of the line as incompetent to hold trenches and they will be disgraced.
>
> The men are good material but the officers are putrid and worthless. There are many political appointments and the Portugese [sic] Expeditionary Force is not worth the cost of their rations. There was a good bit of work done by a Portugese [sic] Cpl a few nights ago, he saw two Boche close to the wire and went out alone, he wounded one Boche with his bayonet and brought the other back prisoner.
>
> The Portugese [sic] camouflage their ignorance and idleness under the plea that they are a professional army whilst we are merely amateurs and must therefore be incapable of teaching professionals. Their motto is reputed to be "The night is for sleep, the day for repose".

Lieutenant-Colonel Richard Crosse recorded his own view on the attachment of the Portuguese to the 52nd.

> At this time a doubtful blessing was bestowed upon us by the attachment, for instruction in trench warfare, of the 20th Portuguese Infantry, which was believed to have derived some benefit. Our old allies' views on trench sanitation differed from our own. To a very good friend of the 52nd, a Rifleman on the staff of the 2nd Division, the Commanding Officer made an angry complaint, only to be asked: 'Why didn't you teach them better manners in the Light Division!'

---

[616] Diary entry for July 18th 1917.

But these were not the Cacadores[617], who doubtless, under 'Black Bob Craufurd'[618], behaved better.

A junior officer, Second-Lieutenant Jim Neville's perspective on the Portuguese was a little different. He was concerned about the language barrier, and was understandably irritated by the leave allocation being halved by their presence. Some of the 52nd's men had not been on leave since June 1916. To Neville and his colleagues, the Portuguese were known as 'geese' and orders forbade them from using the term 'those dagos'. The latter order described the Portuguese as 'gallant', which caused a certain amount of amusement. On August 29th, the 52nd with the attached No. 4 Company 20th Portuguese relieved the 2nd H.L.I., as the right battalion of the centre sector of the 2nd Division's front. The following day Second-Lieutenant David Chaigneau 'Charles' Colvill joined for duty from the 3rd Battalion, and on the last day of the month the 88th reinforcement of 40 other ranks arrived. In due course, Colvill would become a member of the select band who won gallantry awards in both world wars.

September 1st found the 52nd on the same battalion front. A Company was in posts 15-21 with its Headquarters in Old Kent Tunnel; B Company next on the right, with its Headquarters at the junction of the Lane and Tower Reserve Trench; C Company thence to No. 7 or Ipswich post with its Headquarters in Robertson's Tunnel; D Company had withdrawn to billets in Le Preol, on relief by A Company on the night of August 31st/September 1st, taking its attached Portuguese platoon with it. At 6 p.m. on September 1st, the attachment of the No. 4 Company of the 20th Portuguese came to an end and it returned to billets in Beuvry. On the 2nd, one company of the 2nd H.L.I. relieved A Company in the Old Kent Road Area, with the latter withdrawing to the Village Line. The 3rd saw the 20th Portuguese take over the front line from the Canal south to the Béthune - La Bassée road, and D Company undertook a ten mile route march from Le Preol with the buglers. The following day, the 52nd was relieved by the 2nd H.L.I. and moved into support, occupying the partially constructed Braddell Point [just to the east of Braddell Castle] and the surrounding area [see maps pages 237 and 463].

On September 2nd, Second-Lieutenant Jim Neville with B Company described an enemy raid on their right[619]. He gave a clear exposition of the German technique of raiding and the use of the box barrage.

---

617 Portuguese Light Infantry who combined with the British, in the Peninsular War, to form the Light Infantry Division.

618 Robert Craufurd [1764-1812] commanded the Light Infantry Division in the Peninsular War, until he was mortally wounded at the Siege of Ciudad Rodrigo.

619 Letter to his sister written from Braddell Castle, Cuinchy, on September 4th 1917.

> By the way the Boche made a raid just on our right on the 2nd. I was holding the Mill which is an isolated post just on the right of the La Bassée road. There is a tunnel underneath it, with exits to small posts, shallow and conspicuous. It always struck me as a potential death trap. At first, I thought we were going to come in for the raid, because we saw parties of Deutsches in the moonlight going out of one trench into another, just for all the world as if they were forming up for a raid. Then punctually at 5 a.m. they put down a barrage on the Mill, and I really thought I was in for a scrap with some Teutons. The little garrison "stood-to" on the steps of the tunnel, and I stood on the top ready to rush out when they came. I must say I never felt in a less pugilistic mood! The damnable thing about a raid is, that the Teutons put down a "box barrage" all round the area to be raided, to prevent the approach of supports from the rear or flanks. They follow close under the barrage and, as soon as it lifts are on you like lightning before you can man your trenches or posts. That is the idea. Not only do you have your front line plastered to hell with shells and "minnies" but also the "box" part of the barrage prevents you getting hold of fresh men to replace casualties, and the Boche can therefore outnumber your area, if he has a good barrage to follow under. I was damned thankful that they went and visited someone else and not us!!

From September 4th to the 8th, the 52nd had its Headquarters in Braddell Castle and its companies situated in the surrounding area. As the Regiment was in support it was a great relief not to have to undertake duty, night or day. The days were scorching hot although the early mornings became foggy, with the attendant risk of a German raid. Working parties were provided to improve the village and support lines. B Company spent one night burying cables forward from Fanshawe Castle. The place that the men were digging in was in the open and inclined to be swept by machine-gun fire. The bullets were spent by the time they reached them, and it was said that as long as a man was standing up straight it was unlikely that he would be severely injured! Four men were gassed on September 5th.

On the night of September 8th/9th, the 52nd once more relieved the 2nd H.L.I. and took over as the brigade's right battalion in the Canal right sub-sector. A special service for the Regiment was conducted by the Reverend Edward Guilford in commemoration of the Storming of the Cashmere Gate, Delhi, on

September 14th 1857, nearly 60 years earlier. Richard Crosse's uncle had been the first man through the gate[620], and no doubt with his intimate knowledge of its history and his great pride in the achievements of the Regiment he was the instigator of the service. It would have emphasized to the men of the 52nd what they had to live up to.

On the 9th, Major Cuthbert 'Bingo' Baines, one of the great heroes of Nonne Bosschen Wood in 1914, took his leave of the Regiment, having been promoted to the command of the 2/7th King's or 'Liverpuddlers'. The indomitable Baines had returned to the 52nd on August 29th 1916, as senior major and second-in-command to Richard Crosse, after the untimely demise of Major Reggie Owen earlier that month. The previous evening Baines had sadly gone around the companies to say his good-byes. Many a young subaltern owed him a debt of gratitude having been taken under his wing on first joining the Regiment. Rumour had it that Rupert Brett, then second-in-command of the 17th R.F., was to return to the 52nd as senior major, and he was considered to be the only suitable man to fill Baines' considerable boots. It was clear that Richard Crosse needed experienced support at the helm of the 52nd. Also on the 9th, Second-Lieutenant George Ashplant joined the Regiment; he had been a N.C.O. and had a M.M.

The rumour concerning Baines' successor proved to be correct and Rupert Brett rejoined the 52nd, as senior major, on September 10th. Three men were wounded during the day. On the following one, the Regiment received a welcome visit from their former Commanding Officer, the now Major-General Henry Davies of the 11th Division. Three men were incapacitated by gas. On the 14th, Captain J. McTurk the Medical Officer known as "McHaffey", left the 52nd and was replaced by Captain S. Murray. McTurk, who was considered great fun, had done his year of service and he was returning to civilian life[621]. The enemy was quiet during this time and did not show himself as much as in the past; perhaps the sniping and rifle grenading had taken its toll.

On September 15th, Serjeant A. Boddington of B Company, who had received a M.M. for his actions on the Ancre the previous autumn, was wounded in the head and was lucky to survive. Jim Neville described the scene[622].

> Yesterday my platoon Serjeant, Boddington by name, sniped through the head, but not killed, thank God. He was damned lucky, the

---

620 See footnote 178 on page 144.

621 As a balance had to be struck between civilian and military medical practice, in 1915, doctors had been able to sign a one year contract with the forces. Later in the war, military service for doctors effectively became compulsory.

622 Letter to his father written from Cambrin on September 16th 1917.

bullet, hitting a sandbag, ricocheted into three pieces, one of which hit him in the nose and the other two split his helmet. The latter undoubtedly saved his life. He had been looking over the top at two Boches, who had just thrown a bomb, and he was getting direction to fire a rifle grenade at them when the sniper pipped him. I had been doing exactly the same thing a little further to the left, and heard the bullet sing over my head soon after popping down behind the parapet, after getting the direction of the brutes. The Serjeant lost a lot of blood, but seemed quite cheery when I bid him good-bye in the Aid Post.

The next day, the 16th, it was Second-Lieutenant Roger Ames' turn to be wounded. This time it was a severe leg wound from a trench mortar which he would survive. Ames, a contemporary of Neville's at Eton, had been frustrated not to get a home leave as a result of a dictat from the 2nd Division that five months must be served before leave entitlement became due. Jim Neville again described the scene[623].

"Beg pardon, Sir, Mr Ames has had his leg blown off." I seized my helmet and rushed upstairs to find him stretched on the firestep. His right leg was shattered above the ankle. All he said was "Isn't this bloody." So he has got his leave after all!

He was hit in the right leg, and the bone is fractured in two places; his right cheek was badly burned, and his right eye affected; also a nasty cut on his right hand too.

A "pineapple" burst right at his feet, and it was damned lucky he was not blown off the face of the earth.

On the day of Second-Lieutenant Roger Ames' wounding, the 52nd was relieved again by the 2nd H.L.I and went into reserve in the by now familiar Le Preol. For the period September 16th to 22nd, a special programme of training was carried out. On the 19th, a low-powered Regimental Sports meeting took place near Le Preol. Various changes in personnel occurred during this period. First-Lieutenant E.F. Schmitz of the United States Medical Corps joined the 52nd in a temporary capacity as Captain S. Murray R.A.M.C. had transferred for duty in India and Mesopotamia. There was a significant shortage of British medical

[623] Letters to his father and sister written from Cambrin and Le Preol on September 16th and 18th 1917 respectively.

Quartermaster's Staff in May 1917. Back row from left: R.Q.M.S. F. Barnes, Sjt. W.G. Ward. Sitting: Pte. Walker, Hon. Lt. and Qr. A. Warnock, Pte. Jones. Each in possession of the Indian Frontier and Long Service and Good Conduct Medals.
[NRO NEV 7/32]

Harry Spurge, a man with a great sense of responsibility and duty. He served with the 52nd in early 1917, and as Adjutant of the 5th Battalion would die of his wounds in September 1917.
[NRO NEV 7/32]

M.S. 'Guillaume' Griffith-Williams. C Company Commander in 1917 until he went home in the October.
[Colvill Collection]

Lieutenant and Quartermaster Frederick Barnes M.C. Barnes was described: 'as a quartermaster in the field he was a brilliant success. He was hard, fit and fearless and his one thought was for the Regiment'. Photograph 1917.
[Regimental Chronicles]

Henry Lay D.C.M., M.M. and bar. He was described as 'the best of very best N.C.O.s'. Seen in later life as a R.S.M.
[Royal Green Jackets Museum]

Officers of 52nd Light Infantry in May 1917. Richard Crosse, the Commanding Officer, is seated in the centre left of the front row.
[Kite Collection]

Regimental Scouts in May 1917.
[NRO NEV 7/32]

David Colvill, known as 'Charles', was a member of a very select band of men who won gallantry awards in both World Wars. The M.C. in 1918 and the D.S.O. in 1940.
[NRO NEV 7/31]

The pre war construction of Lock 7 on the Canal du Nord. Site of the 52nd's operations in late 1917. [Private Collection]

Richard Crosse, Harry Vernon and Laurence 'Pullthrough' Fullbrook-Leggatt M.C. and bar [on the right of the picture]. The latter's A Company was responsible for Lock 6 during the British withdrawal of December 1917. [Colvill Collection]

Lock 6 on the Canal du Nord. Site of the action of the 52nd on December 6th 1917. The Canal du Nord was empty during the war. [Author's Collection 2008]

Dick 'Puff Ball' Warren M.C. and bar, an officer renowned for his bravery and night patrolling, gave the order for Lock 6 to be blown early during the British December 1917 retirement. [NRO NEV 7/31]

Jim Neville M.C., a fine officer who took over command of B Company in Kangaroo Alley on December 6th 1917 when Billy Barnard was wounded. He witnessed the blowing up of Lock 6. Author of the *History of the 43rd Light Infantry in WWI.* [NRO NEV 7/31]

Cyril 'Shiny' Horley, Lewis Gun Officer and consummate practical joker. [Colvill Collection]

John Slade-Baker, Transport Officer, transferred to the Indian Army in the autumn of 1918. [Colvill Collection]

William 'Billy' Barnard, the popular B Company commander, was wounded on no less than three occasions during the war. [NRO NEV 7/32]

Cyprien 'Ben' Slocock had been Head of School at Radley when war broke out. An intelligent officer who was acting as Adjutant, in March 1918, when he received the wounds which subsequently led to his death the following month. [NRO NEV 7/32]

Harold 'Fritz' Eagle the Hun. [Colvill Collection]

Clement 'Shoveller' Chevallier, acted as Lewis Gun and Intelligence Officer. He wrote an account of the 52nd at Cambrai in 1917. [Colvill Collection]

officers at this time. Schmitz was said to be 'not at all a bad kind of bloke and does not drawl over much either'[624]. The Doctor with the German-sounding name had an inauspicious start with the Regiment. On his second day in the line he was arrested by two men from the 2nd H.L.I. who were unfamiliar with the American uniform. They thought that he was a spy, and when asked his name they became even more convinced. Poor Schmitz was marched down to the 5th Brigade Headquarters with fixed bayonets!

On the 20th, Captain F.W.C. 'Chips' Chippindale was seconded to the Headquarters of the 11th Division to become A.D.C. to Major-General Henry Davies. Lieutenant Edward Vigars rejoined the Regiment from the Base also on the 20th, before two days later transferring to the Divisional Draft School. On this day the hard, fit, fearless Serjeant Frederick 'Old Alf' Barnes was discharged to a pension, appointed to a temporary Honorary Commission as Quartermaster and posted to the Regiment. During this period of relative rest Lieutenant Thomas Tyrwhitt-Drake received a bar to his M.C. and Second-Lieutenant Dick Warren the M.C. Warren received his award for a very daring daylight patrol. A contemporary described him as 'a wonderfully plucky little cove; in fact I don't think he knows what fear is'.

On September 22nd, the period in reserve came to an end and the 52nd relieved the 2nd H.L.I. in the Canal right sub-sector. The *Battalion War Diary* described this tour of duty as uneventful with active patrolling and destructive shoots being carried out. In the period September 17th- October 4th, the 2nd Division as a whole, fired no less than 6,720 Stokes bombs and 700,000 rounds of small arms ammunition mainly at night. These night shoots must have made movement for the enemy extremely unpleasant. On the 25th, Lieutenant T.W.C. Foreshew rejoined the Regiment from the Central Training School at Etaples. The next day, the 34-year-old Private Harry Stevens from Banbury was killed, and this unfortunate man's was the only Regimental death during the whole month[625].

On the 27th, Second-Lieutenant William Seale, on completion of his three weeks instruction with the 5th Light Trench Mortar Battery, was retained for a further period. The next day, September 28th, after their six days in the line, the 52nd was relieved by the 2nd H.L.I. and moved back into support with one company to the north of the La Bassée canal. That same day Second-Lieutenant

---

[624] Letter from Jim Neville to his sister written from Cuinchy Brickstacks on September 23rd 1917. It is salutary to remember that until the arrival of 'talkie' movies in the 1920s, very few English people knew how Americans spoke.

[625] Buried in Cambrin Military Cemetery. Grave L.21.

A.T. Charge joined for duty on his first appointment. Three months later he would depart for the Machine Gun Training Centre. On the 29th, about 110 men from all companies except C Company, who were in the front line, were employed in carrying up gas cylinders to the Brigade on their right. One man was wounded during the day.

Captain George Field handed over B Company to the experienced and popular Captain Billy Barnard on the last day of September. Field was going on leave and then joining the Senior Officers' Infantry School at Aldershot for instruction. The course would hold him in good stead, as the following summer he would temporarily command the 52nd when Richard Crosse was wounded at Triangle Copse. No reinforcements arrived during the month of September apart from C.Q.M.S. Newens and a number of casuals who rejoined.

October opened with the 52nd occupying the usual positions of the support battalion. D Company was positioned north of the La Bassée canal. First-Lieutenant E.F. Schmitz, the temporary Medical Officer, left the Regiment after a short stay, and was replaced by Captain B.L. 'Leech' Hutchence R.A.M.C. Second-Lieutenants William Creak and W.S. Moreton joined the Regiment from England on the following day. Three men were wounded in the Support Line on the 3rd and, on the 4th, the 52nd replaced the 2nd H.L.I. in the Canal right sub-sector once more. To their right, an integrated gas discharge and artillery bombardment took place.

Finally, on October 6th, the 52nd was relieved by the 11th Cheshire and moved to the familiar Montmorency Barracks in Béthune. Two days later the Regiment was on the move again, this time into poor billets in Marles-les-Mines. Matters were made worse by the lack of material to repair them. Second-Lieutenant G.W. Shaw reported for duty on his first appointment. The 9th saw the transfer of Lieutenant T.W.C. Foreshew and Second-Lieutenant C.E. Barnes to England for a six months tour, although they remained on the strength of the Regiment in the field. The next day it was the turn of Second-Lieutenant Herbert Windross to join the Regiment from the Foreign Office.

On October 11th, Major-General Henry Davies, commanding the 11th Division in the Ypres sector, instructed his men to erect a memorial on the site of the graves of the men of the 52nd who had been killed between October 21st-23rd 1914, the first time in the war that the Regiment had suffered major casualties. The memorial cross bore the inscription, 'In memory of the 5 officers and 70 N.C.O.s and men of the 52nd Light Infantry, killed in action, 21st-23rd October, 1914, some of whom are buried near this spot'. The cross was erected close to the St. Julien - Poelcappelle road, near to the line of trenches [map reference U30.d.40.55]. A day later, Captain M.S. 'Guillaume' Griffith-Williams handed over C Company, which he had led for nine months, to Lieutenant Percy Bobby, and proceeded on special leave for his urgent private affairs to England. The leave was subsequently extended to the end of the month and he was then struck off the strength of the Regiment. Mystery still surrounds this strange affair.

From October 13th - 16th, Lieutenant-Colonel Richard Crosse, Captain Billy Barnard, Captain Laurence Fullbrook-Leggatt, Lieutenant N.G. Clarke, and Lieutenant Percy Bobby attended a three-day's special "Battle Course" at the XVIII Corps School north of St. Omer. Five days earlier, Major-General Cecil Pereira, commanding the 2nd Division, had driven to Couthove Château, the Headquarters of XVIII Corps, to find out all the latest training developments in order to keep his division up to date. He wrote in his diary on October 8th, 'as we shall most likely be moved up north shortly------'.

Clearly at this juncture, the 2nd Division with the 52nd were expecting to join Lieutenant-General Ivor Maxse's XVIII Corps, which was about to take part in the Battle of Poelcappelle on October 9th, and the First Battle of Passchendaele on October 12th. Circumstances in the south at Cambrai would dictate that the 52nd did not go to the Ypres sector after all. Maxse, one of the few divisional commanders to distinguish themselves on July 1st 1916, on the Somme, was a renowned trainer of troops. Pereira listened to the emphasis placed on the combination of fire and movement, the importance of sound handling of small units such as platoons and sections, the earmarking of local reserves for special services, and the careful reconnaissance of ground. No doubt Richard Crosse and his men heard a similar story five days later. On the 16th Second-Lieutenant H.J. Ellam rejoined the Regiment after a year's absence.

On October 14th, the inter-battalion stage of the 2nd Division's competition for Fire Unit Commanders and Marksman was held. The 52nd came out a creditable second to the winners, the 17th R.F. The points scored were: 17th R.F. 1,090; 52nd 1,002; 24th R.F. 928; 2nd H.L.I. 694. Second-Lieutenant J.W. Bennett joined and the 90th reinforcement of 33 rank and file reported for duty. The long delayed Waterloo Sports which normally took place in June, were finally held in the presence of their Commanding Officer from 1911-15, Major-General Henry Davies. The 52nd's Commanding Officer from 1907-11, Major-General Robert Fanshawe, then currently commanding the 48th South Midland Division, visited the Regiment in the morning, but he was unable to remain for the afternoon Sports.

The period October 18th-November 5th was spent at Marles-les-Mines and the 52nd continued with its training programme. On the 23rd, a successful Torchlight Tattoo took place with the 52nd's buglers and the 2nd Division's band taking part. The Regiment was subjected to medical inspections during the final week of the month. It was recommended that 674 members of the Regiment should be reinoculated and this was carried out, apart from on thirteen men who declined to have the injection[626]. On November 4th, the Reverend H.L. Hornby conducted a voluntary service for the Regiment in the Marles-les-Mines Girls School.

By November 9th, the 2nd Division, and with it the 52nd, had been allotted to the II and not the XVIII Corps, and it was preparing to take part in operations in the Passchendaele sector. From the 6th-9th, the 52nd was regularly on the move. At 8.30 a.m. on the 6th, the Regiment marched the fifteen miles, via Lillers, to Les Ciseaux with its fairly scattered billets. On the march, the Regiment stretched out over half a mile of the road, it had not been so strong for some time. The countryside was different, flat with small dykes, and the houses were now two storied. At 9.30 a.m. on the 7th, it was a further fifteen miles via Hazebrouck to billets at Terdeghem. The 8th saw the 52nd cover the eight miles to Le Nouveau Monde on the Cassel - Wormhoudt road. The pretty village of Cassel was perched on the top of a hill, and the 52nd could see Mount Kemmel and the ruins of Ypres from it. Le Nouveau Monde was a straggling village with scattered farms, and the billets were too far apart, making the officers' rounds prolonged. The area covered was about two and a quarter miles by one and a quarter miles. Regimental Headquarters was established in Le Kaeper Ferme, just off the Cassel to Wormhoudt road. During the period November 9th-14th, the Regiment remained in the Le Nouveau Monde area undertaking training. A practice attack was carried out, at 5 a.m. on the 14th, in the fields around Clarke Farm. The rouse and turnout in the dark was well conducted. On the 13th, Second-Lieutenants Walter Bailey and Edward Barclay joined the Regiment. Both young men would be killed within a few months.

On the 15th, it was by cross-country tracks to a very bad camp at Winnezeele, where they stayed until the 23rd, being visited on the 18th by Brigadier-General Archibald Eden, their Commanding Officer from 1915-16, and by Captain John Boardman[627]. The men were under canvas in the midst of

---

[626] This was against typhoid. Possibly, the thirteen men declining the injection had previously suffered severe side-effects from the active vaccine. In addition, during 1915, a capricious campaign had been mounted by the British Union for the Abolition of Vivisection against inoculation. Immunisation against typhoid was first introduced in 1897. In the Boer War only a small number of soldiers were immunised and at least 8,000 men died from the disease, the same number as died in action. In the Great War, a mere 200 British and Dominion troops died of the disease. In World War II inoculation against typhoid was compulsory.

[627] John Hopwood Boardman was a former C Company commander in the 52nd in 1915, before being attached to the 5th Battalion in October 1917. The by then Major Boardman, second-in-command of the 9th Rifle Brigade, died of his wounds, aged 26 years, as a German prisoner after the great attack of March 1918. His grave is in Niederzwehren Cemetery, Germany.

interminable mud, although the officers were accommodated in comfortable billets. The distant roar of the guns at Ypres could be clearly heard, and the sky was lit up by their flashes. The officers of the 52nd began to think of their men's Christmas with the possibility of getting tinned pork and cigarettes from the Army and Navy Stores. Cigars were to be provided for the serjeants. At 4 p.m. on November 22nd the Regiment was put on two hours notice to move.

The destination of the 2nd Division and the 52nd was to be neither Ypres and the Battle of Passchendaele nor Italy, which was another possible destination. In the 52nd, there was a certain amount of relief that they were not going to Passchendaele where they expected to be decimated. On November 21st, Sir Douglas Haig heard that his request to stop the 2nd and 47th Divisions from going to prop up the Italian front, after the defeat at Caparetto, had been granted by the War Cabinet. Instead the 52nd was to play its part in the Battle of Cambrai.

Chapter XVIII

The Battle of Cambrai.

November 23rd - December 31st 1917

[Maps: pages 495, 501, 503, 620.]

The Battle of Cambrai began on November 20th and officially ended on December 3rd 1917, although operations continued throughout the first seven days of December. The 2nd Division with its 5th Infantry Brigade, including the 52nd Light Infantry, was not involved in the opening phases of the battle, but from late November onwards it would play a significant part. The origins of the battle went back to the summer of 1917 when an action involving the use of tanks in the region of Cambrai was first mooted. The Third Battle of Ypres had come to a halt on November 10th, and Sir Douglas Haig was reluctantly sending troops to prop up the Italian front after the Caporetto disaster. Haig believed that a limited attack in the region of Cambrai would reduce the number of Germans that might be used against the Italians, and would also make it less likely that the enemy would get up to mischief in other parts of the line. It was hoped to gain absolute surprise by launching the operation in great secrecy.

The 55-year-old General Julian Byng's Third Army was charged with the operation and, on October 26th, he laid out his plans to the corps commanders. It was to be his first battle as an army commander. Stage one consisted of smashing the Hindenburg Line [Siegfried Stellung] between the Canal du Nord and the St. Quentin Canal, with the whole tank force to support the infantry. Stage two would see the cavalry taking Cambrai and the crucial Bourlon Ridge, before swinging to the north and capturing the crossings over the River Sensée. This would have the effect of rupturing the lines of communication between Arras and Cambrai. Finally, if all went well, the German lines could be rolled up northwards. At conception the attack at Cambrai was seen as a large raid but it had progressed into something much bigger. However, its cardinal failing was the lack of reserves to exploit any success that might be forthcoming. Sir Douglas Haig had determined to shut down the operation at 48 hours if it did not start auspiciously.

The forces to be employed were: two infantry corps, the III [Lieutenant-General William 'Putty' Pulteney], the IV [Lieutenant-General Charles Woollcombe]; Cavalry Corps [Lieutenant-General Charles 'Black Jack' Kavanagh]; the Tank Corps [Brigadier-General Hugh Elles]. IV Corps was made up of the 36th, 51st and 62nd Divisions, and III Corps, which had the wider front, of the 6th, 12th, and 20th Divisions. The infantry divisions were to be supported by no

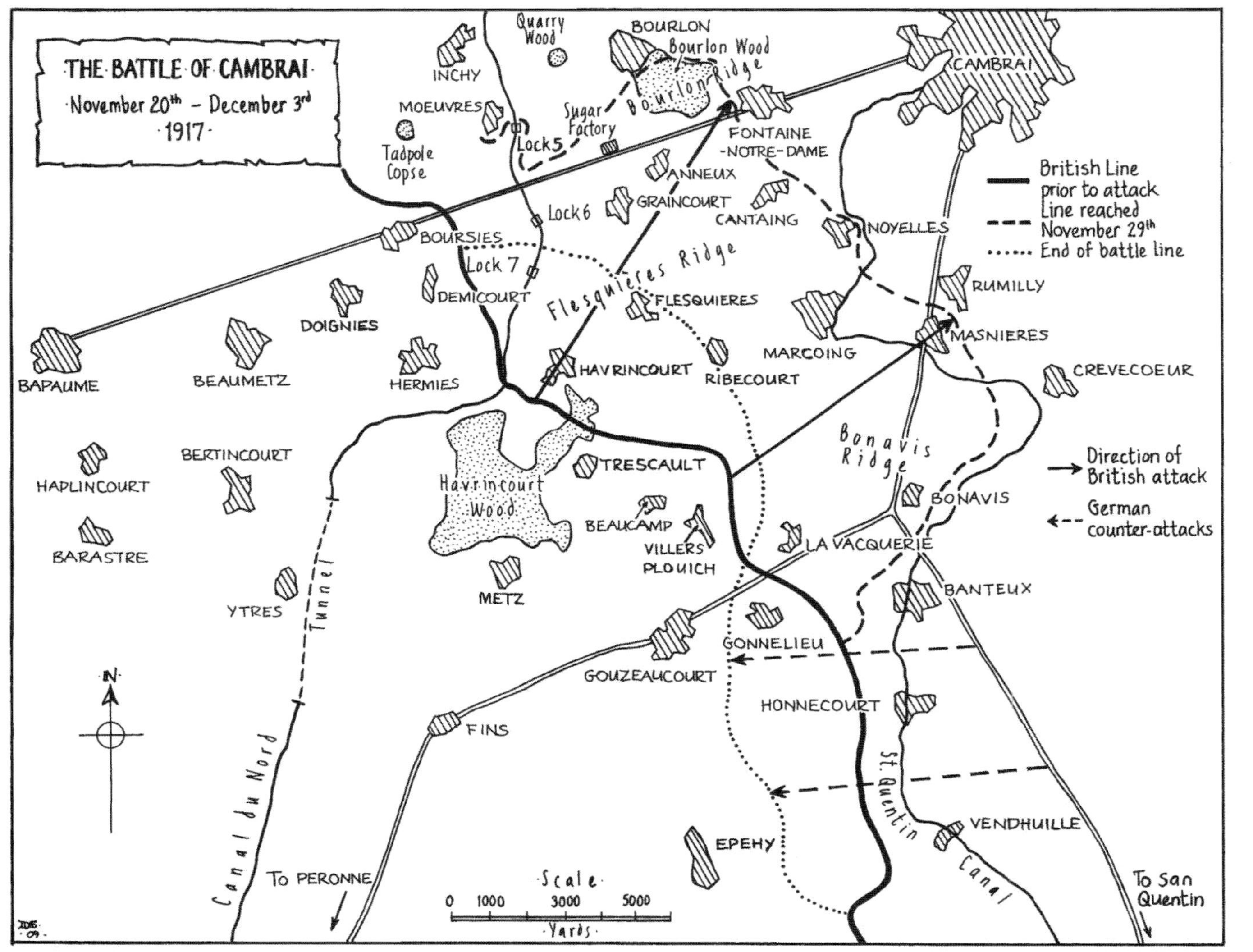
THE BATTLE OF CAMBRAI
November 20th – December 3rd
1917
British Line prior to attack
Line reached November 29th
End of battle line
Direction of British attack
German counter-attacks
INCHY
Quarry Wood
BOURLON
Bourlon Wood
Bourlon Ridge
CAMBRAI
MOEUVRES
Tadpole Copse
Sugar Factory
Lock 5
FONTAINE -NOTRE-DAME
ANNEUX
GRAINCOURT
CANTAING
Lock 6
NOYELLES
BOURSIES
Lock 7
DEMICOURT
Flesquieres Ridge
FLESQUIERES
RUMILLY
DOIGNIES
MASNIERES
MARCOING
CREVECOEUR
BAPAUME
BEAUMETZ
HERMIES
HAVRINCOURT
RIBECOURT
Bonavis Ridge
BERTINCOURT
TRESCAULT
HAPLINCOURT
Havrincourt Wood
BONAVIS
BEAUCAMP
VILLERS PLOUICH
LA VACQUERIE
BARASTRE
Tunnel
METZ
BANTEUX
YTRES
GONNELIEU
GOUZEAUCOURT
N
HONNECOURT
FINS
Canal du Nord
St. Quentin Canal
VENDHUILLE
EPEHY
To PERONNE
Scale
0 1000 3000 5000
Yards
To San Quentin

less than 476 tanks, led in person by the outspoken Hugh Elles. The attack was to be launched on a six-mile front from the Bapaume - Cambrai road to Vendhuile in the south. The order of divisions from left to right was; the 36th, 62nd, 51st, 6th, 20th, and 12th. The ground to be attacked to the south-west of Cambrai is best understood with reference to a map. The area over which the attack was to be made was rolling downland gradually falling from south to north, and divided by ridges into narrow valleys. To the north was the crucial Bourlon Ridge, partially covered by Bourlon Wood. West of Havrincourt village was the Canal du Nord connecting the Rivers Somme and Sensée. The Canal was 90 feet at its deepest and in places was as wide as 120 feet. In 1917, it had not been completed and was empty. To the east was the St. Quentin Canal or Canal de l'Escaut which linked St. Quentin with Cambrai and the River Sensée. This canal was 60 feet in width at the top and 33 feet at the bottom, with a depth of six to seven feet of water.

The Hindenburg Line of defences consisted of an outpost zone, front, and support trench systems. The front system was formidable with trenches ten to twelve feet wide at the top, and seven and a half feet deep. Supposedly they had been designed in this manner to make them tank-proof. There were no less than four rows of barbed wire, three feet in height and providing cover in depth over 100 yards. The system ran in a westward and then northward direction between the two canals, to the eastern side of Havrincourt Wood and into the village. Here it turned north crossing the Canal du Nord opposite Demicourt, before running along the western bank to Moeuvres. The immediate support trench was similar in character. Further to the east ran the support system proper, also consisting of a front and support system, each with three or four belts of wire. Even the main communication trenches were wired. Many of the batteries were situated behind the support system, which was backed by a further line of defences, making the depth of the whole area some six to eight thousand yards.

By the 1917 standards of the Western Front, a prolonged and intense artillery barrage would be required to have any hope of damaging the wire sufficiently to allow the infantry to advance. However, there was to be no preliminary artillery barrage prior to the attack, save for a single gun which fired at 6.20 a.m. on Tuesday November 20th, to indicate zero hour and the start of the operation. Then all the British artillery started to fire, first with smoke shells, followed by an intense barrage, the 'lifts' being kept 300-500 yards ahead of the tanks. That morning was dull, misty, with an overcast sky, as the troops followed the tanks into action. The tanks had a maximum speed of four miles per hour and the temperature inside them could reach 120 degrees Fahrenheit. They rolled over the wire defences of the Hindenburg Line flattening them or attaching hooks to drag the barbed wire away. Some of the tanks had fascines of wood on their hulls which were dropped into the wider trenches allowing them to be crossed.

The enemy was taken by surprise and was horrified to see the large number of tanks followed by infantry coming steadily towards them. By mid-morning the troops were in open country and, at dusk, a huge advance had been made, in some directions up to five miles. Anneux, Graincourt, Havrincourt, Ribécourt, Marcoing, Masnières, La Vacquérie, and Bonavis had all fallen. However, a check at Flesquières had cost Woollcombe's IV Corps the opportunity of taking the vital Bourlon Ridge on the first day.

The next day, November 21st, the British continued with their attack and the 51st Division assaulted the enemy in Bourlon Wood. Early in the morning, Flesquières Village was taken and then Cantaing, but it was to be the evening before Fontaine-Notre-Dame, the gateway to Cambrai, was entered. Much ground had been won, but Rumilly and Crèvecoeur were still in German hands, making it impossible to provide a stable right flank to allow further operations on Bourlon Wood. Sir Douglas Haig was in something of a quandary: to continue with the offensive or to withdraw to defend the Flesquières Ridge. Originally his intention had been to close down operations at 48 hours if matters were not progressing smoothly. However, his advance had gone so well, despite the failure of the cavalry to move through into open country[628], but the enemy was now bringing in reinforcements by train. With the benefit of hindsight, Haig made the mistake of continuing with his offensive.

November 22nd was spent in consolidating the gains and resting the troops. However, the enemy recaptured Fontaine-Notre-Dame. The following day Fontaine was entered again, but not cleared. The 40th Division took the whole of Bourlon Wood on the crucial ridge, and also part of Bourlon Village. The 36th Division had had some success around Moeuvres and Tadpole Copse. Although the Germans counter-attacked strongly, the British were able to hold their ground. From November 24th-30th, the battle swayed to and fro in the environs of Bourlon Wood and Village. On the evening of the 24th, the whole of Bourlon Village was in British hands, but much of it was lost again 24 hours later. It was clear that the enemy had brought up significant numbers of reserves, but Haig went ahead with his plans, on the 27th, to recapture the whole of the Bourlon Ridge and Fontaine-

[628] Lieutenant-General Charles Kavanagh, commanding the Cavalry Corps, was described by Lieutenant-Colonel J.C.F. 'Boney' Fuller, the tank expert, as 'probably the worst cavalry general in history'. Certainly there was a fatal lack of cavalry thrust in the first two days of the Battle of Cambrai. Fuller had drawn up the original plans for a tank raid at Cambrai. He had been commissioned into the 43rd L.I. in 1898.

Notre-Dame. Although Bourlon Village and Fontaine were briefly retaken, by the end of the day the gains were minimal.

This was to be the high water mark for the British. They had captured over 10,500 prisoners, 142 guns, 350 machine-guns, and 70 trench mortars, plus 60 square miles of countryside and ten villages. Sir Douglas Haig was fully aware of the Germans bringing to Cambrai large numbers of reserves and that a powerful counter-attack would be directed at his forces. He relieved as many of his tired troops as possible, replacing them with such fresh divisions as he was able to muster. Amongst the fresh divisions was the 2nd Division and with it the 52nd Light Infantry.

The blow came on November 30th, when the Germans counter-attacked in great force. It was to be their first offensive launched against the British on the Western Front since the Second Battle of Ypres in 1915. The northern side of the large salient that the British held towards Cambrai had three divisions in the line, and it was here that the 52nd was to be involved in the action. The 56th Division was on the left around Tadpole Copse, holding a defensive flank; the 2nd Division was situated between Moeuvres and Bourlon Wood; the 47th Division was on the right, in Bourlon Wood and to the west of it. The eastern face of the salient from Fontaine-Notre-Dame to Vendhuile was held by no less than five divisions. Although the German counter-attack was expected, the tactics employed were not. The enemy endeavoured to nip off the British salient by attacking it on either side of its base, thus isolating Byng's forces, before instituting a frontal assault. The enemy's counter-attack in the south-east started about two hours before that in the north.

In the south-east of the salient, the British line was broken between the Bonavis Ridge and Vendhuile. Although the enemy reached the rear of the 29th Division, at Masnières, that Division bravely held on to the village or a catastrophe might well have taken place. In the afternoon the Guards Division helped stabilize the situation by driving the Germans out of Gouzeaucourt, and a new line was formed. To the north, where the 52nd was in action, further heavy fighting took place around Moeuvres and Bourlon Wood. Although some outposts were lost to the north of the Cambrai - Bapaume road, the line was held. The loss of the ground in the south-east seriously destabilized the British positions around the Bourlon Wood, and Sir Douglas Haig, realising that he had insufficient forces to retake the Bonavis Ridge, in the south-east, resolved to withdraw his troops to a more sustainable line. The withdrawal started on the night of December 1st and continued on the 2nd and 3rd. To the north, in the Bourlon Salient, the retiral involving the 2nd Division and the 52nd began on the night of the 4th/5th. By December 7th a new line had been established which was about two and a half miles further forward than when the battle began on November 20th.

Sir Douglas Haig described his new line. "The new line taken up by us corresponded roughly to the old Hindenburg Reserve Line, and ran from a point about one and a half miles north by east of La Vacquérie, north of Ribécourt and Flesquières to the Canal du Nord, about one and a half miles north of Havrincourt". The British had taken sixteen square miles of ground, three villages, and 11,000 yards of the Hindenburg Line. The Germans had taken a small section of the old British front line, between Vendhuile and Gonnelieu, of some seven square miles in area. If the balance of achievement was in favour of the British, it might have been so much more.

We left the 52nd on November 22nd at Winnezeele. At 9.30 p.m. on November 23rd, the Regiment paraded at Winnezeele and marched to Cassel Station with orders to entrain at midnight for an unknown destination. It was rumoured that Gouy-en-Artois, seven miles to the south-west of Arras, was to be their destination. The men idled their time away by drinking tea and rum at the station. In the early hours of the next morning the French train moved off and at 9.30 a.m., after a very good journey, the 52nd found themselves at Achiet-le-Grand where the officers and men detrained. As usual the detrainment was slow and not completed until noon, and there was mystery in the air, largely because they had not expected to be back on the Somme again. The Regiment marched to Bapaume and then to Beaulencourt on the road towards Péronne. Here the 52nd was accommodated in excellent huts. On November 25th, they marched via Villers-au-Flos and Haplincourt to an unpleasant camp at Lebucquière. Conferences took place the following day and the 2nd Division moved from V to Woollcombe's IV Corps. It was understood that the 6th and 99th Brigades were going into the line in place of the 36th Division and that the 5th Brigade would be held in reserve. That night the 6th Brigade, on the left, and the 99th Brigade, on the right, went into the line that extended from south of Moeuvres to the west of Bourlon Wood.

On November 27th, the 52nd relieved the 1st Irish Fusiliers, the 'Faugh-a-ballagh Boys'[629], of the 36th Division, in the old British front line trenches, which straddled the Hermies - Havrincourt road between the Canal du Nord and the east of the village of Hermies. The Regiment was expecting to help hold the ground gained in the recent attacks. It was said that the last affair had 'put a vertical gust up the Boches'. The 27th was a worrying day as an attack by the 62nd and Guards Divisions on Bourlon Wood and Fontaine-Notre-Dame, initially successful, was gradually driven back, so that the 5th Brigade was ordered to stand by in a state of

[629] 'Clear the way'. The motto of the Royal Irish Fusiliers.

instant readiness. Grossly exaggerated reports of the battle, hinting at disaster, were circulating. That night, the 17th R.F. of the 5th Brigade was lent to the 99th Brigade which was hard pressed in its position to the north of the Bapaume – Cambrai road. On the 28th, the state of instant readiness was downgraded to a state of readiness to move at two hours notice, a situation that continued until the 30th.

Second-Lieutenant Jim Neville described their present positions[630].

> We are in putrid little shelters, which can easily be recognized by their proverbial lack of cover. There are four of us[631] in a little hole 6 foot by 5, and we eat and sleep and have our being in it. The obvious result is, that the mess stuff gets kicked about, and it is almost impossible to keep mud out of the butter and jam. It is an exact repetition of the posts at Courcelette, last winter. This is our third night in this place. We marched here along shelled roads whose surface was covered with liquid mud up to one's ankles. It rained hard the whole morning, before we began the whole march, but lucky it stopped soon after we moved off. The show seems to have been very successful by comparing the numbers of wounded to killed. We are some distance behind our line, but being on a ridge, can see our own front line being shelled to hell. I went on a reconnaissance yesterday to within 200 yards of our front line; though a good deal of muck was being hurled at the front line, nothing much fell on the south side of the Bapaume - Cambrai road, which was lucky for me.

Reconnaissance of the area was made by the officers of the 52nd over the following two days. The ground was largely virgin with few shell holes, and the British trenches were intact with excellent dug-outs and largely untouched wire. An excellent view of the ground to the east of the Canal du Nord as far as Fontaine-Notre-Dame could be obtained from a spoil heap, recently captured from the enemy, on the west bank of the canal, in which one of the companies of the 52nd was based. In the distance could be seen the spires and chimneys of Cambrai, which the 52nd found exhilarating.

The ground over which the 52nd would fight over the next week lay between the Hindenburg Front and Support systems. Between these two systems,

---

[630] Letter to his sister written from the Old British Front Line Hermies on November 28th 1917.

[631] The other officers were Captain Billy Barnard, and Second-Lieutenants G.W. Shaw and H.L. Windross.

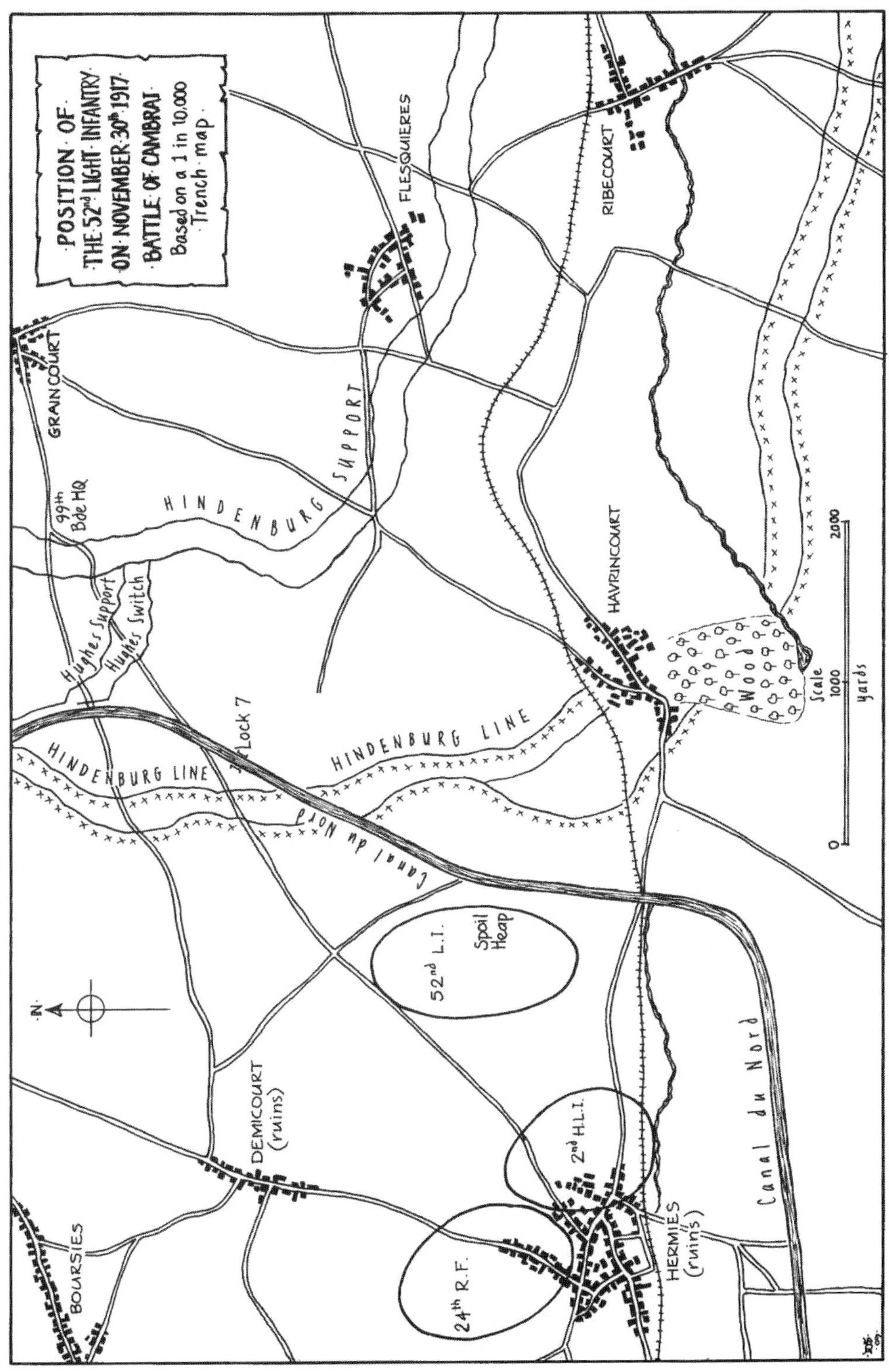
POSITION OF
THE 52nd LIGHT INFANTRY
ON NOVEMBER 30th 1917
BATTLE OF CAMBRAI
Based on a 1 in 10,000
Trench map
FLESQUIERES
RIBECOURT
GRAINCOURT
HINDENBURG SUPPORT
99th Bde HQ
Hughes Support
Hughes Switch
HAVRINCOURT
Wood
Scale
0
1000
2000
yards
Lock 7
HINDENBURG LINE
HINDENBURG LINE
Canal du Nord
52nd L.I.
Spoil Heap
N
DEMICOURT (ruins)
2nd H.L.I.
Canal du Nord
HERMIES (ruins)
24th R.F.
BOURSIES

closer to the front one, ran the partially completed Canal du Nord with its system of locks as it ran through the Agache Valley. Lock 5, just to the south of Moeuvres, was held by the 6th Brigade. Lock 6, to the south of the Bapaume - Cambrai road would be held by the 52nd during the December retirement. Lock 7, to the east of Demicourt was the Headquarters of the 5th Brigade on November 30th. A quarter of a mile to the north of Lock 7, the Hindenburg Front and Support systems were linked by Hughes Switch Trench. Eastward of Lock 6, Kangaroo Alley linked the Hindenburg Front system with the new British front line to the north of the Bapaume - Cambrai road. The roads from Graincourt - Demicourt and Hermies crossed the area north of Hughes Switch. At their junction, just east of the Hindenburg Support system, was the Headquarters of the 99th Brigade. Cutting both these roads at right angles, the road to the north from Havrincourt to Sains ran approximately parallel to the canal. As far as Kangaroo Alley the road was in good condition and little shelled, and was used for transport purposes. South of Lock 7, the empty Canal du Nord, with its brick bottom, provided an excellent roadway, apart from the parts subjected to enfilade fire.

November 30th was the start of the critical German counter-attacks, in the north and south-east, at the base of the new British salient. The 2nd Division was distributed as follows – 6th Brigade; south of Moeuvres, Lock 5, astride the Canal du Nord – 99th Brigade; holding the ridge from the Canal to the proximity of Bourlon Wood – 5th Brigade; in reserve occupying the trenches to the east of Hermies. On the left of the 2nd Division, the 56th had relieved the 51st [Highland] Division, which was holding the Hindenburg Front system as far as Tadpole Copse. To their right was the 47th [London] Division, which had replaced the 62nd Division and was occupying most of Bourlon Wood, including the crest line. Beyond them the line swung back with the 59th Division facing the heights of Fontaine-Notre-Dame.

The German forces opposing the 2nd Division were units from the 49th Reserve, 214th and 221st Divisions. In 1917, the 49th Reserve Division was considered to be a good division which recruited from Prussian Saxony and part of Thuringia. It was responsible for rolling up the Hindenburg Main system. The 214th Division was a composite division with many Poles and some Brandenburgers to counterbalance them. Nevertheless, it was considered to be a good division and had been rushed to Cambrai by rail on November 22nd, in response to the British attack. On November 30th, the 214th Division was responsible for sweeping down the old Hindenburg Support system and towards the Bapaume - Cambrai road. It would be sent to rest on December 4th at Valenciennes. The 221st Division was a mixture of men largely from Prussia, Westphalia, and the Rhine Province. It was also a division brought in by rail on

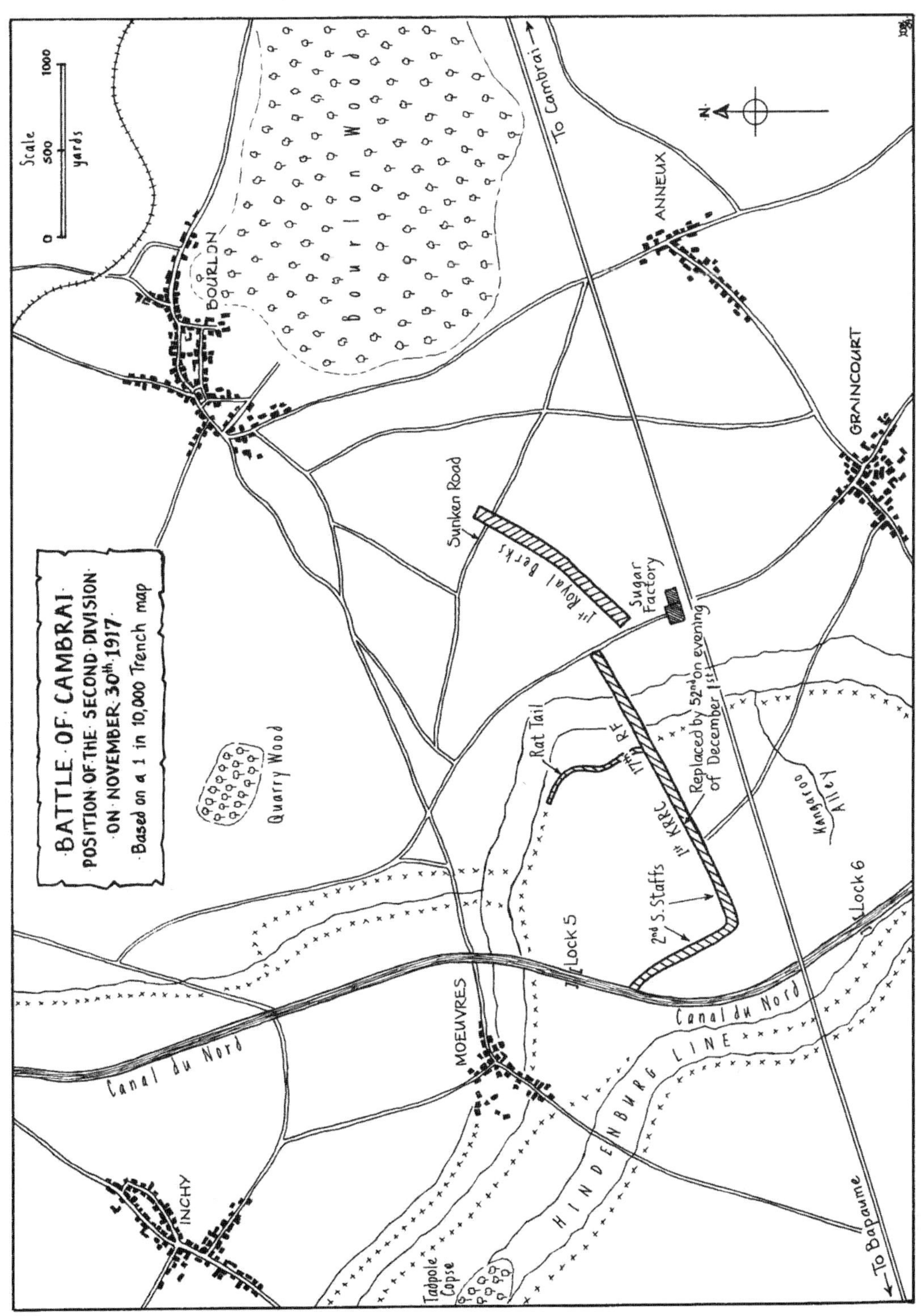
BATTLE·OF·CAMBRAI·
POSITION·OF·THE·SECOND·DIVISION·
·ON·NOVEMBER·30th·1917·
·Based on a 1 in 10,000 Trench map
Scale
0
500
1000
yards
Bourlon Wood
BOURLON
To Cambrai
N
ANNEUX
GRAINCOURT
Sunken Road
1st Royal Berks
Sugar Factory
Replaced by 52nd on evening of December 1st
17th RF
Rat Tail
1st KRRC
2nd S. Staffs
Kangaroo Alley
Lock 6
Lock 5
Quarry Wood
Canal du Nord
Canal du Nord
MOEUVRES
HINDENBURG LINE
INCHY
Tadpole Copse
To Bapaume

November 23rd, in view of the British offensive, and it would be relieved on December 7th. In November 1917, its morale was said to be good, and the general commanding the division and the major in charge of its 41st Infantry Regiment had both received the 'Pour le Mérite'. On November 30th, the 221st Division attacked to the west of Bourlon Wood and it was intended to capture Anneux and Graincourt.

The fine morning of November 30th started peacefully enough, but at about 8 a.m., there was an artillery bombardment to the west of Moeuvres which lasted until dusk, and heralded the German counter-attack on the three British Divisions between Moeuvres and Bourlon Wood. At 10 a.m., the enemy could be seen to the east and west of Quarry Wood, and men of the 99th Brigade were advancing over the open to the front line. Away to the south-east, the flashes and noise of a further artillery barrage could be seen and heard. This served as a prelude to the Germans' successful counter-attacks in the Gouzeaucourt area of which the 52nd was blissfully unaware at the time.

At 10.10 a.m., in their positions in the Old British Front Line to the east of Hermies, the Regiment received orders from the 5th Brigade to stack surplus kit not required for battle, and to report when it was ready to move forward. Lieutenant-Colonel Richard Crosse made certain that his men were given dinner before they left their current positions. As Crosse wrote many years after the war, he could not be certain when they would get another one. At 11.30 a.m., the Intelligence Officer, Captain Clement 'Shoveller' Chevallier was sent forward to find accommodation in Lock 7. Soon after noon, the 52nd with full stomachs were ready to go forward and, by 1.30 p.m., they had occupied quarters on the eastern side of the Lock. The western side was allotted to the 24th R.F., who arrived soon afterwards. These moves were in direct response to the German counter-attack. Major Rupert Brett plus the officers and men being kept out of the coming battle, were left to remove the remaining stores and carry them back to the Transport Lines, at the slag heap on the Hermies - Bertincourt road.

At 1.40 p.m., ten minutes after the 52nd reached Lock 7, there arrived from Brigade Headquarters, Hermies, in quick succession, two messages timed at 12.50 and 1 p.m. respectively. They were attached to a long message apparently originating from IV Corps Headquarters. This ordered the 59th and 47th Divisions to fall back on the Hindenburg Support system between Flesquières and Hughes Switch, where the 2nd Division was to conform westwards along Hughes Switch and across the canal. Richard Crosse described the two messages from 5th Brigade as 'remarkable'.

> 52nd and 24th R.F. will immediately counter-attack in direction of FACTORY in E29, OC 52nd will command this counter-attack which must be launched as soon as possible. 52nd will await arrival of 24th R.F. unless his judgement of the situation demands immediate action.
>
> Your objective is factory in E29a. Should enemy be met with you will press on and gain your objective. Should enemy not be met with you will get in touch with BGC 99th Bde and take up a line in support of his troops. Addressed 52nd L.I. repeated 99th IB, 2nd Divn.

The loss of Graincourt Sugar Factory was a surprise to the men of the 52nd, who had last seen the battle in progress to the north of it on the Bourlon Crest. If this was the case the Headquarters of the 99th Brigade was under an imminent threat. The origin of the report that the Sugar Factory had fallen when in reality the line was 400 yards further to the north of it is obscure. It was thought to have originated from the Headquarters of the 2nd Division, and possibly it came from the mistaken report of an artillery observer. Lieutenant-Colonel Richard Crosse, commanding the 52nd, was so perturbed by the apparent misunderstanding of the situation by Brigadier-General George Bullen-Smith at 5th Brigade, that he decided that it would be best to make contact with Brigadier-General R.O. Kellett of the 99th Brigade and to put the 52nd under the latter's command. It is clear from this and other occasions, such as the fiasco at Guillemont Station in July 1916, that Crosse did not hold Bullen-Smith in high esteem. However as will be seen, he had a high opinion of Kellett's powers of leadership and his tactical acumen.

At 1.50 p.m., Crosse sent his Intelligence Officer, Chevallier, on to Kellett's Headquarters with copies of the two orders. Kellett sent instructions to the 24th R.F. on the western side of Lock 7, who were awaiting the counter-attack, to proceed to his Headquarters. Crosse was about to follow suit with the 52nd when Bullen-Smith and his Brigade-Major arrived, but fortunately they allowed the move to proceed before setting up their own Headquarters on the eastern side of the Lock[632]. Bullen-Smith had had an eventful journey as he rode along the bed of the Canal du Nord, where his Staff-Captain's horse had fallen pinning the poor man to the ground. The 52nd moved off, with 100 yards between companies and 50 yards between platoons, from the base of the dry canal up the slight incline of its east bank, and then by the Graincourt road to Hughes Switch. The

[632] 'Dumpty rode to a Lock, Humpty Dumpty had a great shock. Bereft of his horses and most of his men, only Toc Emin[en]ces were left with Bullen'. Irreverent rhyme written by Richard Crosse in his copy of Wyrall's *The History of the Second Division.*

Regiment suffered a number of casualties from artillery fire, particularly Captain David Barnes' D Company. One wounded corporal was picked up by a passing ambulance and quite possibly was lucky enough to spend that night on a train for England. At 3 p.m., the 52nd remained in Hughes Switch whilst Crosse and Chevallier, who had returned from the 99th Brigade Headquarters, went forward to speak to Kellett.

Captain Clement Chevallier has described Brigadier-General R.O. Kellett seated at a table in a deep dug-out with his Brigade Major. Near the entrance was a single vacant chair for the officer being interviewed, whilst a line of Intelligence Officers, Artillery Liaison Officers, Signal Officers and others awaited their turn. He went on 'the cool and orderly working of the Brigadier and his staff could not but excite the admiration of those who witnessed it'. After the War, Richard Crosse described his meeting with Brigadier-General R.O. Kellett in similar laudatory terms.

> That imperturbable Irishman was easily found. He had not moved his headquarters after all. He had no intention of moving. Did the General wish the counter-attack to be carried out? No he did not. Was it true that some part of the front line had given way? Not at all. There was, said he, that ridge in front of his trenches, with the sky-line over which the grey masses must come, only to be mown down by his unbudgeable battalions. The front line ran nearly half a mile in front of that factory which two regiments had come to recapture. All was well and would remain so. It did. Meanwhile let the 52nd stay for the present where it was, as battalion in 99th Brigade reserve, and let the troops get what rest they could.
>
> With these instructions and feelings of great confidence in the brigade commander under whom he now found himself, the commanding officer made haste to rejoin the Regiment. There was so much about General Kellett that might be called the Fanshawe-Davies[633] touch.

Richard Crosse was clearly reinvigorated by his meeting with Kellett, who actually seemed to be enjoying the situation! The next day, December 1st, Major-General Cecil Pereira visited Kellett's Headquarters; 'Kellett was in tremendous form and his fighting spirit was fully aroused. His troops have been very heavily tried but they have laid out so many Boche that their tails are up'.

[633] Major-General Robert Fanshawe who was Commanding Officer of the 52nd from 1907-11. Major-General Henry Davies who was Commanding Officer of the 52nd from 1911-15.

On route to the 99th Brigade Headquarters, Crosse was able to make a quick reconnaissance of that Brigade's front line. He noted that the British front line was not just over the Bourlon Crest, as he had been led to believe, but about 100 yards short of it. Perhaps inspired by his recent interview, Crosse felt that should Kellett's Riflemen, like Craufurd's, fall back fighting, Bourlon might become another Busaco[634]. Three Novembers earlier, Nonne Bosschen brought back vivid memories of Waterloo. March 1918 was to raise up more than a memory of Corunna for him. Crosse the very epitome of a 52nd man gained fortitude by recalling his Regiment's exploits in the Peninsular War of a hundred years before. For Kellett's men to bear comparison with Robert Craufurd's was high praise indeed.

At the time the punctilious Richard Crosse was concerned that fiction might become history. In the *Battalion War Diary* he wrote 'Messrs Beach Thomas[635], Dewar[636] and probably other War Correspondents seem to have credited British troops with having retaken the Factory in E29a; the original orders to do so, addressed to the 24th R.F. and the Regt. are filed with the office copy of this diary, but no such attack was ever attempted which had it been would have resulted in the capture of our own supporting troops to the front brigades who never yielded the ground at all. It is very desirable that it should be converted into history that the Regt. was not in any way concerned in any "retaking" of the Sugar Factory'.

During the evening of November 30th, the 24th R.F. relieved the 17th R.F. in their position in the front line of the 99th Brigade. The 17th R.F. had been badly mauled and their heroic defence of the 'Rat Tail' sap was one of the outstanding actions of the war. Here the gallant Captain Walter Stone won a posthumous Victoria Cross, having refused to leave his rearguard, whose men were all killed holding up an overwhelming enemy force. The *5th Brigade's War Diary* recorded; 'the heroism of the Officers and men is unsurpassed in this war and a conservative estimate of the enemy killed and wounded by this Battalion is put down at 1000'. Richard Crosse returned to his Regiment in Hughes Switch where all ranks were cramped and uncomfortable with too few dug-outs. This led to a number of casualties particularly in B and D Companies with seven dead and

---

[634] The Battle of Busaco on September 27th 1810 was fought on a ridge. Robert Craufurd's Light Division was present at the battle. As the 52nd rose from the sunken road to attack General Louis Loison's Division, Craufurd said 'Now 52nd! Revenge the death of Sir John Moore'. With that cry ringing in their ears the 43rd and 52nd drove the French down the hill in confusion. The battle ended as a victory for the Duke of Wellington.

[635] William Beach Thomas [1868-1957], later knighted, was a journalist with the *Daily Mail*.

[636] G.A.B. Dewar, journalist who with Lieutenant-Colonel J.H. Boraston, Haig's private secretary, was responsible for *Douglas Haig's Command December 19th 1915–November 11th 1918.*

fourteen wounded. Second-Lieutenant Jim Neville's platoon was unfortunate with a direct hit from an eight-inch shell. He described the scene[637].

> We moved forward again, soon after, into Hughes Support Trench, which ran parallel to the Hindenburg Line. Here we remained from 5 p.m. until 2 a.m. The trench had been evacuated by some reserve troops of the 47th London Division, who had left their packs stacked high in the bays of the trench. We were packed like sardines, my platoon occupying half a traverse only. Some very heavy stuff was coming over at odd intervals, and one 8-inch shell laid out 20 men. As you know, you can hear these very heavy birds coming from a considerable distance; they seem to take ages to arrive, and there is always a second during their flight, when you know whether they are going to fall near or far from you. I heard this particular bird from afar, and felt relieved that he was going to plant himself away from us. Then I began to doubt my supposition; a second later, it was touch and go, and then I realized that it was probably going to blot me out. I lived through one agonizing second of uncertainty. There was no way of escape; we could not dodge the brute, as we were too cramped for space. With a rearing, rushing, mighty roar of an express train screaming at top speed through an enclosed station, it crashed in the next bay from me right in the middle of my platoon! I darted round the corner and found a shambles. It had fallen plumb in the centre of the trench, a magnificent shot from the enemy's point of view. Among the killed was Serjeant Archer, Platoon Serjeant of No. 7, and a damned good chap[638]. The only man who escaped untouched of all the men in that bay, was sitting on top of a pile of packs, at the foot of which the shell had landed. The packs were utterly destroyed and he was lifted off his perch but unhurt!
>
> As soon as it got dark, we collected some bits of men, put them in a sandbag, carried out the recognisable bodies over the top and dumped them in a shell hole, and Billy Barnard[639] said the Lord's Prayer over their remains. I think it was probably the only prayer he knows for certain.

---

637 Letter to his father written from Lebucquière on December 11th 1917.

638 Lance-Serjeant Sidney Archer, aged 31 years, from Reading died of his wounds before the day was out. He is buried in Hermies Hill British Cemetery.

639 Captain W.L. 'Billy' Barnard, B Company commander.

Major-General Cecil Pereira, commanding the 2nd Division, wrote in the *Divisional Diary* his opinion of the performance of his men on November 30th. Normally he was not a man to give unjustified praise.

> The subsequent story is one so brimful of heroism that it deserves to take its place in English History for all time and to be a proud day in the lives of all those splendid British soldiers who by their single hearted devotion to duty saved what would have been undoubtedly a catastrophe if they had given way.

Between 2.30-3 a.m. on December 1st, Brigadier-General R.O. Kellett moved the 52nd into the position of close support to his left battalion, the 1st King's Royal Rifle Corps of the 99th Brigade. The Regiment had A, B, and D Companies in Kangaroo Alley, C Company in the Hindenburg Support Trench and a shared battalion headquarters with the 1st K.R.R.C. slightly to the north-east of Kangaroo Alley. Richard Crosse recorded in the *Battalion War Diary* his admiration of his company commanders, who had guided their men through a complicated trench system on map references, without the benefit of a preliminary reconnaissance.

During the daylight hours of December 1st, the 52nd had an uneventful time although the brigades on their flanks were both attacked. On the right, in Bourlon Wood, the 47th Division held its own but, on the left the 6th Brigade had more difficulty repelling the enemy. It was here, to the west of the Canal, that Captain Allastair McReady-Diarmid of the 17th Middlesex [6th Brigade] won a posthumous V.C. in possibly the finest exhibition of single-handed bomb-throwing of the whole war. The official report stated; 'this officer killed and otherwise disposed of 88 of the enemy – 67 dead and 21 wounded were actually counted after the recapture of the trench, a feat which can hardly, if ever, have been equalled in the past'. The 2nd H.L.I. had been brought up and took over the left sub-sector of the 6th Brigade's front.

At 7.30 p.m. December 1st, the 52nd relieved the 1st K.R.R.C. in the front line with just two companies, its strength being double that of the battalion it was replacing. B Company took over the left front line and the strong points 4 and 5 which were in a partial state of construction. C Company took over the right front line and strong points 1, 2, 3, which were in a similar process of construction. These strong points were sited 150 yards behind the front line. A Company remained in Kangaroo Alley and D Company moved further west down the same trench. Battalion Headquarters remained in its spacious dug-out. The front line consisted of an untraversed, painfully broad, shallow communication trench. The strength of the position lay in the excellently sited posts to the rear which, with the aid of one company from the 10th D.C.L.I. [Pioneers], were eventually converted into a continuous line. According to the relevant trench map, the front line was situated just over the Bourlon Crest; in reality it was 100 yards short of it except on the left. The German lines were 300 yards away, and the position, though hidden from the enemy, allowed an excellent field of fire. The drawback was poor observation, but even this defect would soon be rectified.

On the right of Captain Percy Bobby's C Company was a mound from which the 1st K.R.R.C believed that it had been subjected to machine-gun and sniper fire. Shortly before their relief, two men had been sent out to reconnoitre the place, cries had been heard and the patrol was not seen again. At dawn on December 2nd, Lieutenant Edward Vigars and Serjeant H.W. Flower bravely undertook their own reconnaissance, and an old trench was opened up that led to the mound, along which the 24th R.F., on the right of the 52nd, had placed a bombing block. The mound had been the site of an old German observation and machine-gun post facing west of Moeuvres and the area south of it. The post was taken over by a platoon of C Company, and christened Vigars Post. Situated exactly on Bourlon Crest, it gave excellent views over the Agache Valley and the country as far as Quarry Wood. At 8.10 p.m. that night, at the instigation of Kellett and Crosse, an advanced trench was pushed forward to the north-west, the one direction that Vigars Post did not have a good field of fire over. Later Serjeant H.W. Flower would receive the M.M. for his actions that morning.

Apart from the taking of Vigars Post, the three days December 1st-3rd proved to be uneventful for the Regiment. On the night of the 2nd/3rd the 23rd R.F. of the 99th Brigade, on the right of the 52nd, recaptured some posts that had been lost on November 30th. Although the Regiment was not directly involved, 5th Brigade believed that it was heavily engaged and stopped the ration party coming up for more than four hours. To their left the 6th Brigade, including the temporarily attached 2nd H.L.I., was also heavily engaged but held the majority of its ground. As with the 99th Brigade, there was a general mix-up of troops from the constituent battalions. To the direct rear of their front line the Very lights of Gonnelieu were optimistically ignored. Second-Lieutenant Jim Neville gave an eye-witness account of the scene[640], including the attempt to rescue a company of the 13th Essex who had been cut off on November 30th just to the west of the Canal. It was reported that they would fight to the last man. The constant messages that Neville described were from the Royal Flying Corps [R.F.C.], who had supposedly spotted German infantry massing. Later oblique photographs showed that they were in fact piles of dead Germans!

[640] Letter to his father written from Lebucquière on December 11th 1917.

By 2 a.m. we were pretty hungry, as we had had nothing to eat since 7 a.m., but we moved forward again in the moon-light to Kangaroo Alley, a trench behind the Arras - Cambrai road. There was only desultory shelling at the time, and we were extraordinarily lucky in that respect.

We stayed in Kangaroo Alley till the evening of December 1st, when "B" Company went up to the front line for 48 hours. The trench was very shallow and broad, and the weather was excruciatingly cold, so much so that sentries could only watch on the fire step for half an hour. We were in the front line from the evening of the first till the evening of the third and had no casualties. Messages came with annoying regularity whenever we sat down to a meal in the dug-out, to say that the enemy was massing for an attack. Thereupon, we all went to our battle stations and stood-to-arms, waiting and ready for him, but he never came; not that he would have got far if he had tried. By the time we had "stood down," our meal was naturally stone cold. On the nights of the 1st and 2nd there were bombing attacks on our left, made by the 6th Brigade to try to extricate a Company of the 13th Essex which had been cut off at Lock 5 and Moeuvres and surrounded, when the Boche attacked on the 30th. This gallant handful of officers and men were still holding out in spite of their predicament and were annoying the enemy with great success, by sniping over the parapet and paradados. I am afraid the bombing attacks failed in both cases and the Essex had to surrender when their ammunition was exhausted.

We watched these attacks from our front line. It was very thrilling. We could see the shrapnel bursting over enemy trenches, and the smaller flashes of flame from Mills bombs. The darkness was continually lit up by Verey Lights which burst high in the frosty night and fell into rolling clouds of smoke. They were rather grim firework displays.

Officially the Battle of Cambrai ended on December 3rd, but there was still to be heavy fighting over the next few days. By the night of the 3rd, three of the battalions of the 5th Brigade were all in the front line and under the orders of other brigades. The 52nd and 24th R.F. were serving with the 99th and the 2nd H.L.I. was with the 6th Brigade. The withdrawal ordered by Sir Douglas Haig was both disappointing and certainly unexpected for the 52nd. Without sufficient forces to retake the Bonavis Ridge in the south-east, Haig had little choice in the matter or his positions on the exposed Bourlon Ridge would have become vulnerable. The plan to be followed was for the 2nd Division to form a defensive flank facing north and linking up the main line of resistance with the Old British Front Line north of Demicourt. So urgent was the evacuation of the Bourlon salient considered to be that the first instructions went out from the 2nd Division at 5.30 a.m. on December 4th. The operation was to be conducted in the greatest secrecy with no telephone conversations on the subject and the rank and file not told about it until the last possible moment.

The retirement from the Bourlon salient was to be the responsibility of the 5th Brigade under Brigadier-General George Bullen-Smith, who assumed command of the operation at 5 p.m. on December 4th. Battalions of other brigades were to be clear of the area to be evacuated by 2 a.m. on December 5th. The 2nd H.L.I. and the 17th R.F. from reserve were to occupy the old German trenches astride the Canal and those running west from Hughes Switch to extend them to the old British front line. East of the Havrincourt - Sains road, Hughes Switch was to be occupied by units from the 47th Division. This was to be the main line of resistance [A line]. In front of this line, Kangaroo Alley, Lock 6, and some observation posts west of it were to be held as the covering line by the 24th R.F. on the right, the 52nd in the centre, 51st Division on the left. On the right of the 24th R.F., the 47th Division around Graincourt extended the defensive position still further east [C line][641].

Lieutenant-Colonel Richard Crosse was given an inkling of the plan of withdrawal on the morning of December 4th. He briefed the officers of C and D Companies [D having replaced B in the line the night before]. Crosse conducted his briefing on the steps of a dug-out and 40 years later he recalled the occasion clearly. He took his instructions for great secrecy very seriously.

> This conference was held on the steps of an unfinished dugout which, being German faced the wrong way. As we talked, that model of military correctness, a British sentry shouted from above: 'Gentlemen, the -------s are coming over'. This proved to be a false alarm, though such event was not unexpected. I was at pains to find a means of destroying the secret message which I had with me about the withdrawal. As a non-smoker I never carried matches, and it did not occur to me to get a match from someone and burn it. Therefore I made haste to eat a page of Field Message Book A. B. 153;

[641] The B line consisted of outposts covering the main or A line.

fortunately finding it little more indigestible than some I have had to read.

Stores, ammunition, and bombs were sent to the rear or destroyed. The most important dug-outs were blown up by the 483rd Field Company R.E. and the remainder spoilt. In all, 65 dug-out entrances and dug-outs were dealt with by that company, who also left a booby-trap in the Sugar Factory to await the enemy. One unorthodox method of spoiling a dug-out, in fact the joint Headquarters of the 52nd/1st K.R.R.C., involved an unfortunate mule. On the night of December 3rd/4th, the 24th R.F. sent pack mules carrying stores up to the line. The leader of one of them mistook a sheet of corrugated iron for a bridge across the trench. The animal fell through into the trench, panicked by the fall and the site of a brazier, proceeded down the dug-out steps, before becoming firmly wedged half-way down. Unable to move him, the Commanding Officer of the 1st K.R.R.C., Lieutenant-Colonel Hugh Watson[642] shot the unfortunate beast. The following night, it was intended to drag the carcass out by means of ropes from the top of the trench. In view of the withdrawal, it was decided to leave the dead mule as an odoriferous obstacle and present for the Germans!

At 2 a.m. December 5th, the 52nd began to withdraw, leaving a rearguard of hand-picked officers and men. One platoon from both D and C Companies, under the experienced Lieutenants Ronald Blackwell and Edward Vigars respectively, remained. Their duty was to fire Lewis guns, rifles, and Very lights from the front line, in order to deceive the Germans into thinking that it was still occupied. The rearguard started to withdraw at 3.45 a.m. Meanwhile the Regiment took up its positions in the covering line. B Company [Captain Billy Barnard] occupied Kangaroo Avenue west of the Sains road, and maintained contact with the 24th R.F. A Company [Captain Laurence Fullbrook-Leggatt] occupied Lock 6 and the trenches of the Hindenburg Front System west of it. D Company [Captain David Barnes] was in support west of the bridge by which the Demicourt - Graincourt road crossed the canal. C Company [Captain Percy Bobby] was in the old German support line by that road, stretching southward towards the line of main resistance. Regimental Headquarters were close by, some half mile from Lock 6. The 52nd reached their positions by dawn, but the troops of the 51st Division who should have been to their left could not be found. At dusk, this forced D Company [from support] to move forward and refuse [turn back] their line to the south-west of Lock 6, to protect the 52nd's flank. D Company was now facing west in the Hindenburg Main system, in contact with A

[642] Later Major-General H.W.M. Watson [1881-1938], Inspector General of the Iraqi Army. He died in Iraq in 1938. In World War I he had the reputation of never having had a soft job.

Company on the right towards Lock 6. During the daytime on December 5th, D Company also sent one platoon to both A and B Companies as reinforcements.

A Company, occupying Lock 6, found that in front of them there was a rise in the ground blocking their view and making them vulnerable to a turning movement from the dead ground. In fact the Germans were cautiously moving forward, and it was not until 10 a.m. on December 5th that single men were seen coming over Bourlon Ridge. Later further parties moved south of Moeuvres and others were seen on the Bapaume - Cambrai road-bridge over the Canal du Nord. A Company reported the enemy as having been massing at a ruined house 100 yards south-west of the bridge, apparently intending to outflank the Lock. From 3 p.m. until dusk, the positions occupied by B, C, Companies and the Regimental Headquarters were heavily shelled by the enemy. B Company suffered the most from the shelling and the company commander, Captain Billy Barnard, was wounded by shrapnel in his left knee. His bugler and nine other men were also wounded. Lieutenant Jim Neville took over the command and, believing that an enemy attack was imminent, requested two Stokes mortars to break it up. In the event nothing happened and the night passed peacefully.

Once more Jim Neville recorded the scene[643].

> We went back into support from the night of the 3rd till 2 a.m. on the 5th, when the front line was evacuated, and we were left as the front line for 48 hours. "A" and "B" Companies were in the front line, the former holding Lock 6, where Dick Warren was in command, while we held about 400 yards of Kangaroo Alley on the right. This was a very long stretch and meant posting one man in every other bay for battle stations.
>
> We had a very quiet time until the morning of the 5th, when Fritz showed a lot of activity. We could see tin hats worming towards our line on the left, where there was a trench along the canal bank. At our end, this trench had been blocked and a bombing section posted under No. 8665 L/Cpl. Tilbury. We sent back this information to Headquarters, and Seale came up to see if he could get at them with his trench mortars. This he did, and discouraged the Boche a lot by lobbing over a few really good shots. However, early in the afternoon they started to creep forward again, and the bombing post was kept busy until at about 3 p.m. a whizzbang barrage came over. I was sitting in Company Headquarters with Billy Barnard when it opened. I rushed upstairs and along the trench to the right to get to

643 Letter to his father written from Lebucquière on December 11th 1917.

my platoon area. The shelling was pretty hot, the damned things kept bursting first in front of me and then behind me, so I expected to catch one all to myself in each bay. However, I reached my platoon safely and found the men "standing-to" in battle order. Scarcely had I sat down on the fire-step for a breather than an orderly popped his head round the corner of the trench and told me I was wanted at Company Headquarters as the Captain was hit. So back I had to go, running the gauntlet of the damned whizzbangs. I found Billy B sitting on the top step of the dug-out nursing his left knee. He had been hit by a piece of shrapnel. The stretcher-bearers were just contemplating the removal of his great bulk, when a man of the bombing post on the left reported that the enemy were in the trench. Billy B got up at once and hobbled down the trench towards the Canal, which was our only covered line of retreat and, incidentally towards the post which had reported the entry of the enemy into our trench! As it happened, the lad who brought the message was not telling the truth, thank God! He was a bit windy, for the Corporal had only told him to tell Billy B that the enemy were massing in the trench immediately opposite his post.

Billy's departure left me in command of the Company to carry out a rearguard action and a retirement later. I was taken by surprise, and had the wind up badly that I should make a mess of it.

All the afternoon, rumours came round that the enemy were massing at different map references. One report stated that the Lock had been captured on our left. This came just after Billy was wounded and put the wind up me badly. Thank heaven, it was also false, but all the same it was most alarming.

The Germans would make two attempts to take Lock 6 on December 6th. The first came at dawn, when the enemy was seen to be infiltrating Lock 6 from the west. A Company's Lewis gunners and riflemen claimed to have annihilated a party of 60, of whom 40 bodies could be counted when the mist lifted. The great advantage of the Lewis gun was fire-power with mobility. During the Battle of Cambrai, one battery of eight machine-guns, probably Vickers, from the 2nd Division, dealt with ten successive waves of Germans and fired 280 belts of ammunition into them. The machine-gun was a formidable weapon in the right hands, and did great execution as the enemy came over Bourlon Ridge. Before 9 a.m., the enemy began to build up about a house opposite Lock 6. Captain Laurence Fullbrook-Leggatt of A Company asked for Stokes mortars to be sent to break them up. Unfortunately the mortars did not arrive until the afternoon and the opportunity was lost.

Lock 6 had long tunnels, probably of German origin, running along either side at a low level. The eastern side of the lock was firmly held by the men of A Company. However, on the western side it was a different matter, as the Lock was more exposed. Failure to make contact with friendly troops on their left, meant that the 52nd had had to refuse or swing back their left flank. Along the western side of the upper Lock ran a trench, which acted both as a western defensive flank and as a sap to the north. Eighty yards to the north a trench ran obliquely back down into the Lock at a lower level. Where this trench left the tow-path a block, B, was established to stop the Germans getting down into the Lock and the dug-out below. Eighty yards back, at the northern end of the Lock, a second block, A, was established. A few yards behind this a staircase led directly down into the Lock dug-out. Block A overlooked the obliquely-running trench from block B down into the Canal, making it useless to the enemy unless A were taken. The Canal bed was securely covered from the eastern side of the Lock.

Captain Laurence Fullbrook-Leggatt, responsible for holding Lock 6 and its western perimeter, arranged his men accordingly. Second-Lieutenant Dick Warren held the most vulnerable area with No. 4 Platoon. This was both sides of the Lock itself, plus the A and B blocks. The other platoons, 3, 1 and 2, in that order, were used as flank protection in a trench running south-west from the Lock. The second attempt on the Lock came soon after 9 a.m. on the 6th, when the Germans attempted to bomb their way in. Block B fell to them, before they moved on to A, where a combination of riflemen and men with rifle grenades, under Lance-Corporal H. Easden, drove them back. Courageously Easden climbed on the parapet and pursued them with bombs back to Block B. Dick Warren brought up two men to re-establish the block which was then garrisoned by the bombing section of No. 3 Platoon. Lieutenant-Colonel Richard Crosse sent up Second-Lieutenant J.W. Bennett with No. 9 platoon from C Company to reinforce A, as he anticipated a larger attack by the enemy.

On the morning of December 6th, it was generally expected the final withdrawal to the main line of resistance would not be made until the following evening. However, on the right of the 52nd, the Germans had entered Graincourt earlier than had been anticipated and in consequence the covering force would have to be withdrawn. The right company of the 24th R.F. was to withdraw at 5.30 p.m. on December 6th, and the retirement was to be continued in succession from the right at five-minute intervals. The 52nd was to reform on the Old British Front Line where it crossed the Graincourt - Hermies road. On this occasion it was arranged that Captain Percy Bobby's C Company was to remain behind in close support and under command of the 17th R.F. Once the 24th R.F. had withdrawn from the covering line, B Company was to retire down the Canal. Then A Company was to evacuate Lock 6 and proceed along the trenches west of the Canal until striking the Graincourt - Hermies road, which it was to follow.

During the afternoon of the 6th, a party of Royal Engineers [226th Field Company R.E.] put a large charge of explosives, a 400 pounds mine, into the western part of Lock 6 so that it could be destroyed. The timing of the explosion was delegated by the 2nd Division to Brigadier-General George Bullen-Smith, who was responsible for the retirement and the main line of resistance. At 4.45 p.m. the enemy, having shelled the area west of the Lock since 10.30 a.m., attacked the Lock itself with bombs and members of A Company supported, by a Stokes mortar, returned fire. Lieutenant Dick Warren's No. 4 Platoon and Second-Lieutenant J.W. Bennett's No. 9 Platoon of C Company in support were both heavily engaged. By 5 p.m., Block B and the trench descending obliquely down the western side of the Canal had been lost to the enemy. Dick Warren described what happened next.

> I sent L-Cpl Easden and four men from the left and Serjt Constable ("C" Company) and four men around the right. The Germans were now coming across the open. Easden succeeded in reaching the steps but was driven down again. The Germans were now – 5.10 p.m. – in the Lock. I then gave the order for No 3 platoon to man the trench, and word was sent to "B" Company and to "A" Company headquarters. Bombing still continued up the trench to Block B. The Lock was now being occupied by Germans so I ordered the Corporal R.E. to blew it up and the Company to retire; which was done.

Unfortunately, the pincer attack made by Serjeant Ernest Constable and Lance-Corporal H. Easden and their men did not quite come off. As the enemy was actually in the Lock, Dick Warren had little choice in having the charges blown some fifteen to twenty minutes earlier than was intended. Unquestionably, Warren made the correct decision, having informed his company commander, Captain Laurence Fullbrook-Leggatt, and the Headquarters of nearby B Company where Lieutenant Jim Neville was now in command[644]. At 5.10 p.m., Warren

[644] This was taken from Captain Clement Chevallier's account in the *Regimental Chronicles 1919-1920* page 72. According to Jim Neville, Dick Warren told him after the explosion that Fullbrook-Leggatt had withdrawn A Company prior to the lock being blown up and without warning him. The

gave orders to the Royal Engineers for the fuse to be lit and this was done. Almost immediately word came that some 52nd men were still in the Lock. Instantly, Serjeant Ernest Constable with great courage ran down intricate passages and stairways, and across the basin of the Lock to make certain all his men were out. Fortunately, having risked his life from both enemy fire and a premature explosion, he returned safely and reported that the Lock was clear of men of the Regiment. It was thought that some twenty Germans were inside the Lock's buildings at the time of the explosion. The blowing up of the Lock delayed the enemy's advance, and facilitated the British withdrawal.

It is unclear whether the athletic Serjeant Ernest Constable was the last man out of the lock. The demolition party consisted of Second-Lieutenant W.E. Oliver and a small party from the 226th Field Company R.E. According to the *War Diary* of that Company, 'a six minute fuse was prepared, and also, in case the fuse did not work, an electric lead was laid to an explosion in [the] spoil bank. At 5 a.m. [sic] the enemy made a second attack on the lock, and it was evacuated. No. 134953 Lance-Corporal Grinnell and No. 81529 Sapper T. Barratt remained in the lock until the last of the British troops had gone, and then fired the fuse. Six minutes after, when the enemy were well in the lock, the charge blew up'. However, this diary entry was still consistent with Ernest Constable having gone back to check for the presence of his men, after Grinnell and Barrett had fired the fuse, presumably on the orders of Dick Warren.

Lieutenant Jim Neville was in Kangaroo Alley, close to Lock 6 when the charge was ignited. He also described the retirement of B Company[645].

> We held this position until the evening of the 6th. A message from Regimental Headquarters reached me early in the afternoon stating the time at which we were to withdraw, and I issued all orders accordingly so that there should not be any confusion or noise. But 20 minutes before the time, the Boches attacked Lock 6 and got into

---

words used were 'A Coy has bolted'. Already distressed by toothache, Neville rightly decided to withdraw early although he was 'terribly anxious about having evacuated the line 20 minutes before the stated orders'. The following morning Neville was ordered to make a written report, but before doing so Richard Crosse gave him Fullbrook-Leggatt's report which astounded him as Warren had told him that he had been left in the lurch at the lock. Neither Neville nor Warren [according to Neville] believed that Fullbrook-Leggatt deserved a M.C. on the strength of a fictitious report. This grave charge was recorded by Neville in 1976. Warren had been murdered by Sinn Feiners in 1921. Whatever may have happened on this occasion, Laurence Fullbrook-Leggatt or as he was known 'Pullthrough' was undoubtedly a brave man as he was to win a bar to his M.C. in 1918.

[645] Letter to his father written from Lebucquière on December 11th 1917.

it, so that "A" Company on my left, which was responsible for the Lock, was compelled to retire immediately.

I had no idea what was happening, until a terrific explosion rent the air and bits of the Lock sailed through space. It had been mined by the Sappers and was to have been blown by a time fuse after "A" Company had evacuated it, and when it was hoped there would be a big covey of Boche making themselves comfortable inside the Lockmaster's quarters.

A few minutes after the explosion, Dick Warren sauntered into my trench and told me that he had given the order to the Sappers to blow the mine, and that when it went up, there were about 20 of the enemy in it. So the covey was caught after all!

My left flank was now completely in the air, and the enemy was in a marvellous position to enfilade the whole length of my trench.

My original line of retreat down the Canal bed was now cut off, so I sent three platoons down a road[646] running towards our rear led by Windross[647], the only other officer left in the Company. This road was completely exposed and liable to be swept by machine gun fire at any moment, and I had visions of heavy casualties. The enemy, however, did not fire and the platoons got away safely. By this time, the other two platoons were ready in the trench, so I sent one off and a minute later sent out the last platoon, and marched in the rear of the Company with my Headquarters. We got back safely without a single casualty, which was extremely lucky, considering how Fritz had plastered that road the night before.

By 8 p.m. on December 7th, the 52nd assembled in a position on the Old British Front Line, south of Lock 7, with the Canal du Nord to the east, and the villages of Demicourt and Hermies to the west. The order of Companies from north to south was A, D, B, with Captain Percy Bobby's C Company under the auspices of the 17th R.F.s in Bullen Trench, supporting the main line of defence. Later, C Company was relieved and joined the rest of the Regiment in the old British trenches which were found to be in a particularly disgusting condition. On December 8th/9th, a miserably cold, wet, dark night, the 52nd was relieved by the 13th Essex of the 6th Brigade. As the relief was about to begin, it was interrupted by a commotion caused by the 17th R.F. losing an outpost to the enemy. The Regiment's A and D Companies were asked to retake the post, but in the event

[646] The Havrincourt – Sains Road. Originally B Company was to retire down the Canal bank.
[647] Second-Lieutenant Herbert Windross.

this was called off, and the whole exhausted, fully-laden Regiment marched well to Lebucquière. Here, it was accommodated in huts and tents in O'Shea camp. Lieutenant-Colonel Richard Crosse was pleasantly surprised to find how healthy his men were, despite the trials and tribulations of the last few days. The same had been true of the excellent health of the then 52nd, three years earlier, in the woods around Ypres. One man was wounded on the 8th, and the 91st reinforcement of 23 men arrived on the same day.

The Regiment was now able to take stock after the recent battle. Since November 30th, nine men of the 52nd had been killed and 33 more were wounded. Serjeant Sidney Archer had died of his wounds in hospital. Amongst the other wounded were Captain Billy Barnard and C.S.M. E. Ashby, both described by Richard Crosse as 'severely wounded'. However, it is difficult to accept, even by the medical standards of a bygone age, that Barnard's knee wound could be described as severe[648]. Apart from the afternoon of November 30th, the casualties during this period were light. Two of the dead were attached to the trench mortar battery and the remainder came from B and D Companies, killed in Hughes Switch Trench on the first afternoon. Most of the other casualties occurred during the shelling of December 5th. Surprisingly, on the 6th, during the fighting in Lock 6, only two men had been wounded, including C.S.M. E. Ashby. As at least 40 Germans had been killed by A Company on that same day, and some 20 more in the Lock explosion, the 52nd was considerably ahead of their foe in the killing stakes.

The excellent performance of all ranks of the 52nd in the Battle of Cambrai led to a considerable number of awards. Captain L.E.W.O. Fullbrook-Leggatt received the M.C.: Serjeant E. Constable the D.C.M.: Serjeants H.W. Flower, G. Williams; Lance-Corporals H. Easden, A. Foster, F. Imms, F. Taylor [who had been recommended for the D.C.M.], E.J. Wilden; Privates H. Carter, A. Gutteridge, C. Finch, F. Parker, P. Smith all received the M.M. It is likely that Second-Lieutenant Dick Warren would have also received an award for his exploits in Lock 6 if he had not already received the M.C. in September 1917. In fact a rumour circulated in the Regiment that he was to receive a bar to his M.C. However, it did not materialize and Warren would have to wait until 1918 for his bar. Serjeant Ernest Constable's exceptionally brave conduct on December 6th, at Lock 6, led his company commander to recommend him for his country's highest gallantry award. Captain Laurence Fullbrook-Leggatt wrote, 'I recommend Serjt. Constable for the Victoria Cross'. In the view of Lieutenant-Colonel Richard Crosse, Commanding Officer of the 52nd, 'he very richly deserved it'. The 2nd

[648] Barnard was also wounded in the left hand. This was the third time he had been wounded in the war.

Division's records described Constable's actions: 'he displayed the most magnificent gallantry and personal courage throughout'. The authorities downgraded the recommendation to the D.C.M. No member of the 52nd during the First World War was to be awarded the V.C.; perhaps Constable came closest to it. In the Spring of 1915, there were a number of occasions when members of the 52nd went out into no man's land, in broad daylight, to bring wounded men in. Certainly similar actions in other Regiments had led to the award of the V.C. Whether Serjeant Ernest Constable's actions matched those of the 2nd Division's two outstanding Cambrai V.C.s, Captain Allastair McReady-Diarmid and Captain Walter Stone is debateable.

Forty years after the Battle of Cambrai, Lieutenant-Colonel Richard Crosse wrote; 'A prophet is not without honour, save in his own country and in his own house. (St Matthew xiv, 57)'[649]. He explained himself.

> To one looking back forty years and recalling the events of 1916-17, it seems a remarkable thing that while scant credit was given, almost grudgingly to the Regiment, for its work in its own brigade (at any rate until April, 1918), generous appreciation came to it after attachment to other brigades of the Division; such as from the 6th Brigade (Brigadier-General Daly) in August, 1916, and from the 99th Brigade (Brigadier-General Kellett) in November-December 1917. The full text of these letters cannot be given here but, they are entitled to find a place in the archives of the 52nd in years to come[650].
>
> Thus it was pleasant to receive, and to publish in Regimental orders of 10th December, a kind letter in which General Kellett wrote to the Commanding Officer 'your splendid Battalion' and 'the great assistance you gave me at a very critical time'; going on to say that the knowledge he had the Regiment there 'made him feel quite secure and happy' about his left flank.

It is not difficult to interpret Crosse's comments. As has been intimated earlier, the man who did not appear to appreciate the 52nd was the commander of the 5th Brigade, Brigadier-General George Bullen-Smith, whose tenure of the post was from May 15th 1916 until March 25th 1918, when he was sent home exhausted. The new permanent incumbent, Brigadier-General W.L. Osborn took up his position on April 5th 1918. On July 30th 1916, as the brand new Commanding Officer of the 52nd, Crosse was singularly unimpressed with the

649 Crosse was wrong. It is St. Matthew xiii, 57.

650 The letters appear to have been lost.

plan of attack on Guillemont Station, and there were other occasions when he appeared to have been less than happy with Bullen-Smith's leadership of the 5th Brigade. Loyal man that Crosse unquestionably was, he did not allow his officers or men to be aware of his views of Bullen-Smith's limitations. There is no doubt that Crosse greatly admired and respected Brigadier-General R.O. Kellett, and he would have been much happier if his battalion had been in the 99th Brigade.

Today, the Canal du Nord is full of water and is a busy thoroughfare for barges. Lock 6 which was destroyed at the behest of Lieutenant Dick Warren has been rebuilt and there is no evidence of either the trench system on its western bank or of Kangaroo Alley. At the site of the Graincourt Sugar Factory, which the 52nd was erroneously asked to retake on November 30th 1917, there is broken ground and rubble.

The Battle of Cambrai had offered so much at its outset, with an enemy taken by surprise and then terrified by the massed ranks of tanks rolling towards them. The failure of the cavalry to push on aggressively on the first day, and the lack of reserves had cost Britain dear. For a time the rupture and rolling up of the German line had been a distinct possibility. The German counter-attacks on November 30th, attempting to cut off the British salient on both sides of its base, had been successful only in the south-east. To the north the 2nd Division, amongst others, had played a key role in stopping the enemy in his tracks. It was no fault of theirs that Sir Douglas Haig, in view of the situation to the south-east, had been forced to withdraw his units from the Bourlon Ridge to a more stable line.

The 2nd Division was not appreciably involved until the November 30th German counter-attack. Its 6th and 99th Brigades had fought heroically on November 30th and December 1st, as was manifested by the two outstanding Victoria Crosses that were awarded during the fighting to those serving with the two Brigades[651]. The 5th Brigade and the 52nd had been in reserve at the start of the enemy counter-attack. The 52nd was in the front line to the north of the Bapaume - Cambrai road on December 1st, and performed stoutly as part of the rearguard in the retirement to the main line of resistance. Technically, the retirement to a more stable line was not part of the Battle of Cambrai, which officially ended on December 3rd. It was no fault of the 52nd that fate decreed that they should play more of a supporting than starring role in the action.

Between December 9th-13th, the 52nd rested and all ranks took the opportunity to clean themselves and their equipment up. Baths were available in nearby Haplincourt. The three companies unfortunate enough to find themselves under canvas were moved into huts where they were much more comfortable. At about this time, the 52nd was given permission to use a piece of one-inch

[651] Captain Walter Stone of the 17th R.F. was attached to the 99th Brigade when he won his V.C.

Regimental ribbon to be sewn on to the sandbag covers of their helmets. The stripes, blue, buff, scarlet, blue were to be worn horizontally for identification purposes. In addition, quarter-sized camp colours to hang outside the Regimental and individual Companies Headquarters' were produced. Both the helmet cover ribbons and the pennants helped maintain the Regimental esprit de corps. On the 14th, the Regiment replaced two units of the 6th Brigade in the main line of resistance stretching from the north-west of Lock 7 on the right to the junction of Kellet, Walsh, and Bullen Trenches on the left [see map page 620].

The period December 15th-20th passed quietly enough, although the weather was cold with some snow. Jim Neville's sponge and nail brush froze together. It was so cold that he found that it positively hurt to do anything outside. The officers' latrine, a pole between sandbags over a hole, was immediately above their dug-out. Second-Lieutenant H.J. Ellam, an amusing man, had ascended the dug-outs steps to do his matutinal duty when a 5.9 shell landed close by. The unfortunate young man was blown off his perch and back into the dug-out still with his breeches around his ankles, but was able to join in the laughter of his comrades. During this period, the bombing posts 'Adam' and 'Eve' were improved as they had been found in a defenceless state. Two men were wounded on the 19th. On the night of the 20th/21st the 52nd was relieved by the 2nd H.L.I. and took up posts: Headquarters close to the Hermies - Graincourt road at K.13d.83; C Company in Hunt Avenue; D about the bridge over the Canal du Nord at K.15a.35; B and A in the Old British Front Line.

The Christmas period, December 21st-26th, was spent as Support Battalion to the Left Brigade of the 2nd Division. C Company was occupied for 48 hours making shelters to improve the lot of the Regiment. The weather was cold and dry and there was snow on the ground. On the 23rd, two men were killed and three more wounded, all from A Company. Christmas Day working parties were relaxed, and the Reverend Edward Guilford conducted morning and evening services at the Regimental Headquarters. The old Christmas hymns were sung and, because of the cramped space, the men had to kneel under the table for Holy Communion. Second-Lieutenant E.K. 'Jimmy' Blyth reported for duty.

Lieutenant Jim Neville described the officers' Christmas dinner[652]. His B Company was in reserve for the day and guests could be invited. There was one bottle of "fizz" amongst ten, just enough to take the grease out of their mugs.

> I must tell you how Christmas dinner went off. We all collected in our shack at 7.30, with a snow storm going on outside. It was devlish cold, and we were packed in like sardines, and every time the

[652] Letter to his sister written from Haplincourt on December 27th 1917.

servants came to the entrance and parted the canvas a drift of snow blew in! At the other end there was a blazing fire of huge logs. The fire-place was made by us and was a roaring success.

The Colonel[653] carved the chicken, or rather pulled it to pieces because, he said, he was not a married man. The plum pudding was excellent and came in in sheets of flame. Rum punch brought up the rear.

A rather funny thing happened which had not been pre-arranged; the shack had been made when there was eighteen inches of frost on the ground, and when the soil thawed, a great lump of mud fell down the Colonel's neck, at which we all shouted and cried for a speech, which was not forthcoming. After dinner, we had the tables and trestles taken out and a rough house in the dark as all our candles had been expended by that time. The Colonel and "Twitt"[654] had a good scrap.

We are now out of the line, thank heaven. But it has been almost impossible to sleep owing to the cold.

Richard Crosse was skilful, particularly if he deemed spirits to be low, to start a rough house in the mess after dinner, and then quietly vanish into the night leaving his officers to get on with it. The 52nd's mess was a very relaxed one with much laughter, and all the officers, with the exception of the commanding officer, on Christian name terms. The 3rd Battalion's mess, from which so many of the officers had originated, was strictly hierarchical.

On the night of the 26th/27th the 52nd was relieved by the 1st Royal Berkshire of the 99th Brigade and moved into huts on the Haplincourt - Barastre road. Christmas Day was officially celebrated by the men on the 28th, and Brigadier-General Archibald Eden, the 52nd's former Commanding Officer, 1915-16, visited the Regiment. The men had a royal feast of pork, beef, ham, and fresh vegetables[655]. The final three days of the year were spent in training, although there was one scare on the 30th, when the 52nd was ordered at one hour's notice to

[653] Lieutenant-Colonel Richard Crosse.

[654] Lieutenant Thomas Tyrwhitt-Drake.

[655] Jim Neville and William Giles were too well entertained by their men and became inebriated on neat whisky. The next day, the two young officers were marched in front of Lieutenant-Colonel Richard Crosse who admonished them quietly, until as Neville put it 'I was flayed with unutterable shame'. Crosse, having told them that they ought to be court-martialled, had the good sense to take the matter no further. Giles and Neville were two of his finest officers. Later, from 1940-42, Giles would command the 52nd Light Infantry.

be ready to move in support of the 63rd [Royal Naval] Division. However, the order was soon rescinded.

Lieutenant Jim Neville described a brush with death during this period. The Germans fired a 77 mm. shell or whizzbang at five minutes [sic] to each hour, but near the appointed time, 10.50 p.m., Neville was distracted by a group of Sappers[656].

> Suddenly there was a terrific explosion and a sheet of flame seemed to envelope me. The next thing that I knew, was that I was sprawling full length on the ground, just clear of the pieces of frozen earth that were falling all round. I felt myself all over, thinking I must be dead, picked up my tin hat and ran round the corner. There was not a graze on me. The explosion came from a whizzbang, which burst immediately behind my head. I saw the crater, the next morning. How it missed my head, Heaven only knows. Of course I never heard it coming; you never do hear the one that hits you. That shell must have arrived punctually at 10.50!

The fourth year of the War was at an end, and the 52nd Light Infantry could look back with pride on their part in the Battles of Arras and more recently the Battle of Cambrai. It was a very different Regiment from the one that had gone to war in August 1914. However, the 52nd was fortunate in having a commanding officer imbued with the ethos of the old Regiment to lead them into the challenges of the final year of the war.

---

[656] Letter to his sister written from Haplincourt on December 29th 1917.

Chapter XIX

The Trenches at La Vacquérie.

January 1st - March 20th 1918

[Maps: pages 495, 529.]

In the spring of 1918, Germany had a brief window of opportunity, a final chance to win the war. Russia was no longer a participant, allowing a large number of divisions to be switched from the Eastern to the Western Front. Italy had been soundly defeated at Caparetto and badly needed British and French divisions had to be sent to prop up the faltering Italians. The unrestricted U-Boat campaign had provoked the United States of America into joining the Allies, but her almost inexhaustible manpower would not be available to fight until the middle of the year. Ironically, on November 11th 1917, exactly a calendar year before the armistice, General Erich von Ludendorff met with the Chiefs of Staff of the Groups of Armies of Crown Prince Rupprecht of Bavaria and Crown Prince Wilhelm to discuss plans for the coming year. Surprisingly, neither the Kaiser nor Field-Marshal Paul von Hindenburg was present. Out of this conference came the basis of a plan, Operation Michael, to attack near St. Quentin and gain the Somme line, before carrying operations in a north-westerly direction to roll up the British front. The final decision for Michael was not made until January 21st 1918, when it was near certain that Russia was out of the war. Further operations against the British in the north were also planned. The overall spring offensive was called 'Die Kaiserschlacht' in honour of Kaiser Wilhelm.

By the end of 1917, it was clear to the British Commander-in-Chief, Sir Douglas Haig, that in the New Year manpower shortages would force him to go on the defensive on the Western Front. The Prime Minister, David Lloyd George, fearful of another Passchendaele with its attendant vast number of casualties, refused to release trained men from Britain to reinforce the armies in France[657]. In due course this would have catastrophic results. Haig was under no illusions that his forces were under a very real threat of a spring offensive by Germany using divisions brought back from the Eastern Front. That spring, Germany could deploy 192 divisions on the Western Front against an Anglo/French force of 156 divisions. Accordingly, Haig ordered his army commanders to organize zones of defence on their fronts. On January 10th, matters were further complicated for Haig when he was instructed to take over another 25 miles of the front from the

[657] Lloyd George had little confidence in Haig or the C.I.G.S. Field-Marshal Sir William Robertson. In October 1934, Lloyd George who had been writing his memoirs was quoted: 'was very sick that Haig and Robertson were not alive. He intended to blow their ashes to smithereens in his fifth volume. Unfortunately he could not get at them personally'.

French, so that his line now extended from the north of Ypres to five and a half miles east of the Oise. Some British battalions were so depleted in numbers that amalgamations of units were necessary, with the result that most brigades now consisted of three instead of four battalions, and consequently most divisions had only nine battalions. The changes did not apply to the Dominion troops of Australia, Canada and New Zealand.

In the early months of 1918, the British Expeditionary Force was responsible for some 126 miles of the Western Front. From north to south: Second Army [General Herbert Plumer], twelve divisions, 23 miles from north of Ypres to Armentières; First Army [General Henry Horne], fourteen divisions, 33 miles to Gavrelle; Third Army [General Julian Byng], fourteen divisions, 28 miles to just north of Gouzeaucourt; Fifth Army [General Hubert Gough], twelve infantry and three cavalry divisions, 42 miles to just south of Barisis. It can be seen from these figures that General Hubert Gough's Fifth Army was defending a long frontage with fewer divisions per mile than any other part of the line. Haig's troop dispositions were sensible in the circumstances that he found himself in. Firstly, at all costs, he must protect the Channel ports and his lines of communication with Britain. Secondly, if the centre of the line around Arras was pierced, the B.E.F. would be cut in two. Hence Haig placed his main strength in the north and centre. General Hubert Gough's Fifth Army was much further from the Channel coast and could afford to retreat without hazarding vital British interests. As well as the divisions described above, Haig had a General Headquarters Reserve of eight divisions, spread out behind the four armies, whose use was at his sole discretion.

At the end of 1917, a new flexible system of defence was drawn up by the British armies. This consisted of a Forward Zone, Battle Zone and Rear Zone. The Forward Zone was generally organized in three lines over 2,000-3,000 yards, with the third line often made up of small redoubts able to accommodate a company of infantry. Even the first two lines were not continuous, with mutually supportive outposts capable of firing over the intervening ground. The Forward Zone was expected to no more than delay the enemy's advance. A further 2,000-3,000 yards behind the Forward Zone was the Battle Zone where any enemy attack was expected to be held up and defeated. It too consisted of three defensive lines connected by switch lines. Parts of trenches and posts were positioned for all-round fire, but once more there was no longer a continuous trench line. The number of battalions placed into either the Front or Battle Zone was left to the discretion of local commanders. In the Rear Zones of the Third [in which the 52nd served] and Fifth Armies, where the might of the German army would fall on March 21st, little had been done to institute it and it was known as the Green Line.

The 52nd Light Infantry spent New Year's Day in huts on the Barastre - Haplincourt road. For the next two days training was undertaken, although the men had to be kept on the move in view of the very cold, fine weather. Second-Lieutenant Dick Warren, who had been wounded during the blowing up of Lock 6, was sent to hospital with an infected thumb. It was thought that the cause of his injury was a shell splinter and a little later he had to be sent back to England for further treatment. On the 3rd, the Regiment marched to Beaulencourt on the road from Bapaume to Péronne. Here, over the next two and a half weeks, the Regiment rested out of the line and continued with its training programme, including passing through the practice Gas Chamber. Captain George Field returned from his Senior Officers' Course at Aldershot and resumed command of B Company. Lieutenant-Colonel Richard Crosse decreed that the Company would be known as 'Captain G. Field's Company' reverting to a system of nomenclature which had been used in the pre-war era, where companies were identified by the name of the commanding officer rather than by a letter of the alphabet. On the 5th, the 52nd was notified that Lieutenant Jim Neville had been awarded a M.C.[658], and on the 11th, Lieutenants John Littledale and R.G. Wilsdon reported for duty. It had taken Littledale over a year to recover from wounds to his neck and thigh and, Wilsdon had been out of action since the previous July with an unexplained fever.

During this period of rest the 52nd were alongside the 2nd H.L.I., whose pipers invariably turned out to sound the Retreat in the evenings, constantly skirling 'The Shores of Argyll' as a slow march. Richard Crosse had increased the number of his buglers to 52, the regimental number. Towards the end of the period, the buglers turned out just before the official time of Retreat and sounded off with a terrific blast 'The Shores of Argyll' as they marched in slow time across the so-called parade ground. No more was that tune heard from the pipers![659]

---

[658] In letters to his family, Neville claimed not to know why he had received this award for gallantry. Undoubtedly it was for general good work over the whole of 1917 and, in particular, for a fine performance at the Battle of Cambrai. Richard Crosse wrote in a letter of congratulations: 'continuous good work over a long period illuminated by several specially fine pieces of work'.

[659] Stories of this sort were common in the pre-1914 army. Legend had it that when the 43rd marched out of Chatham on a change of station at the end of the 19th century, a crowd of women were at the barrack gates to watch the Regiment leave. In it were several women of easy virtue, one of whom shouted 'we've had enough of you' and in an immediate retort from the ranks came the cry 'and enough of us have had you!'

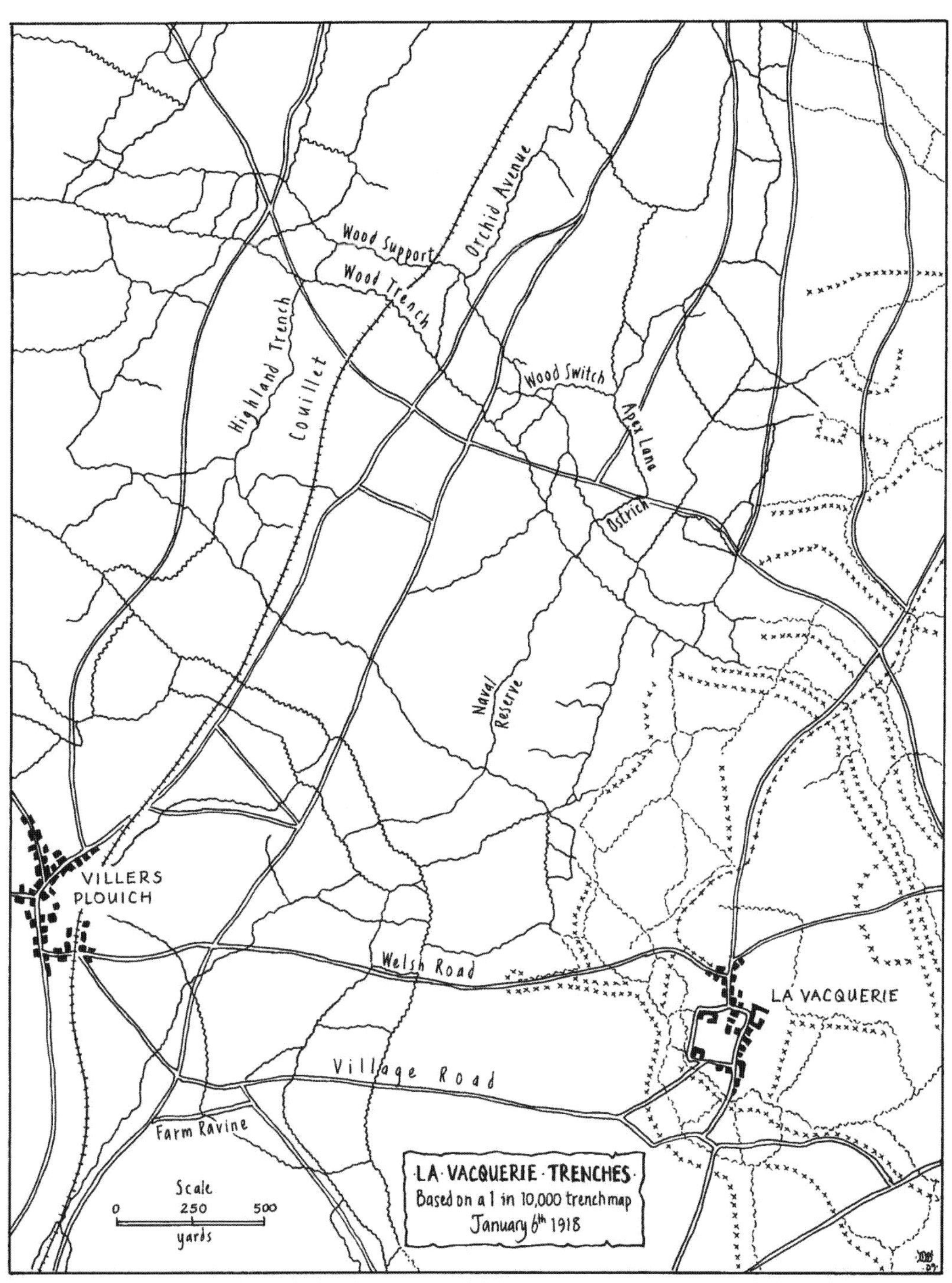
Orchid Avenue
Wood Support
Wood Trench
Highland Trench
Couillet
Wood Switch
Apex Lane
Ostrich
Naval Reserve
VILLERS PLOUICH
Welsh Road
LA VACQUERIE
Village Road
Farm Ravine
Scale
0
250
500
yards
·LA·VACQUERIE·TRENCHES·
Based on a 1 in 10,000 trench map
January 6th 1918

On January 22nd, the Regiment travelled by rail and relieved the Nelson Battalion of the 63rd [Royal Naval] Division in a camp in Havrincourt Wood. Conditions in the camp were very poor. The 2nd Division had taken over the La Vacquérie right and left sectors of the front, at the southern end of the Cambrai salient, from the 63rd Division. Initially the 5th Brigade and the 52nd were in reserve, but on January 25th, the Regiment went into the line in the left sub-section of the left La Vacquérie sector. The 10th Worcestershire [19th Division] was on their left and the 17th R.F. on the right. The 52nd remained in the line for the next three days. Although the relief was a quiet one, the enemy spent the night firing a machine-gun at the parapet, and would continue their fire over the next few days. The conditions in the shallow trenches were appalling with thigh-deep mud making getting around the line extremely difficult. At 6.30 p.m. on the 27th, the thick mud in the trenches would indirectly lead to the death of the nineteen-year-old Second-Lieutenant Edward Barclay, who was doing his rounds of the posts over the top when a machine-gun bullet tore out his intestines. The fog had cleared away at 5 p.m., possibly making him more visible. When the 52nd came out of the line, the unfortunate young man's impressive funeral was held at Fins with his body carried on a stretcher wrapped in a blanket. Later, Barclay's parents would discover that 12/6d had been deducted from their only son's pay to cover the cost of the blanket that he was buried in. A subaltern's life was not worth 12/6d to his country. Another soldier, Private Passey, in Field's Company, was wounded in the back facing the enemy! Such was the unpleasant situation of their salient.

Lieutenant Jim Neville gave a first-hand description of the La Vacquérie trenches at this juncture[660].

> We are in the front line, once more, and the conditions are far from being pleasant. There was sticky mud up to our thighs when we came in, but as it has not rained lately we have managed to get rid of some of it. There was some heavy fighting here in December, and out of the mud we have salved many things, from dead men to Lewis guns complete, besides rifles and much equipment. It is a foul position to hold, because, being the apex of a triangular salient, the Boche can enfilade us from three sides, while our own machine guns fire from behind. The sparks that fly from the stream of bullets would be a credit to any firework display. The trenches are very shallow, and we can only progress along the old firestep, for the mud in the trench is glutinous to a degree. We can only do the rounds of

[660] Letter to his sister written from Welsh Ridge Villers Plouich on January 27th 1918.

the sentry posts at night, and then their machine gun fire is almost incessant.

During the daytime of January 28th, a reconnaissance of the right La Vacquérie Sector's trenches, then held by units of the 99th Brigade, was made by the officers of the Regiment. The fortified village of La Vacquérie was in German hands with the British line several hundred yards to the west. Crossing no man's land at right angles and in parallel were Welsh and Village Roads, the latter the more southerly. For an hour in the afternoon, the enemy bombarded the 52nd's Support Line Posts with 5.9 inch [15 centimetre] shells. Fortunately there were no casualties. That evening a quiet relief was effected with the 1st King's of the 6th Brigade, and then the weary 52nd marched to billets and shelters in Metz-en-Couture. Here the Regiment remained until February 3rd, resting, bathing, supplying working parties for new transport lines north of Fins and in the improvement of the defences around Metz-en-Couture. No reinforcements had been forthcoming in January and the 52nd was hard pressed to find sufficient men to undertake these chores. Five men were wounded in January, and Lieutenant N.G. Clarke [debility after diphtheria], plus Second-Lieutenants Dick Warren [infected thumb], B.J. Crewe [debility] and W.S. Moreton [chronic nasal obstruction] were struck off the strength of the Regiment.

On February 3rd, the 52nd relieved the 23rd R.F. of the 99th Brigade, on the right of the Divisional front as far as Village Road, in trenches that they had inspected whilst last in the line. Regimental Headquarters were in Farm Ravine. The Companies were placed: D [Littledale] right front; A [Fullbrook-Leggatt] left front; C [Vigars] right support; B [Field] left support. Richard Crosse recorded that this six-day tour of the trenches was quiet apart from the shelling of shelters of B Company early on February 4th when three men were killed[661]. Two further men were wounded on the 6th. Lieutenant William Giles, who had served the Regiment with such distinction and had been awarded the Military Cross, was generally run down. He was suffering from the chronic skin condition psoriasis, and he was transferred to England for a rest. Technically, Giles was classified as being sick and he would return to action with the Regiment the following July.

---

[661] Both the *Regimental Chronicles* and the *Battalion War Diary* gave the date as the 5th. However, the Commonwealth War Graves' Records and the Soldiers Died in the Great War CD give the date of death as the 4th for all three men. There is a little doubt concerning the exact date. Lance-Corporal George Marsh, aged 30 years; Private Christopher Brooks, aged 19 years; Lance-Serjeant Frederick Groves, aged 22years. All three men were buried side by side in Metz-en-Couture Communal Cemetery, British extension. Graves. II.G.13-11.

Once more Lieutenant Jim Neville was on hand to describe the fate of his unfortunate men on February 4th[662].

> We are in the trenches again in a pretty quiet part of the line where the Boches are quite a long way away from us. We came up on the 3rd. "B" Company was in reserve for the first 48 hours, in Nissen huts beside Village Road which runs at right angles to our line across No Man's Land to the enemy line. These blinking huts are painfully exposed and nowhere near splinter proof. I did not feel at all comfortable in them and would have preferred a trench, for in any strafe the enemy would be bound to shell the road. The strafe came, just as I anticipated, at "stand to" on the 5th. A 5.9 shell landed on Company Headquarters. The result was a filthy sight. The hut was a shambles. Corporal Marsh and Private Brooks were blown to atoms, and Serjeant Groves, Lewis Gun Serjeant, though intact in body, was blue-black as a live lobster. The officers' hut escaped, but I liked occupying it still less after that episode. The only man to escape out of the Company Headquarters personnel was the Company Serjeant-Major, Smith by name, who had just gone out to "stand-to" with the troops.

On February 9th, the 52nd was relieved in the line by the 23rd R.F. of the 99th Brigade and withdrew to huts in Metz-en-Couture. That same day the 92nd reinforcement of transfers from the 6th Service Battalion arrived to replenish the 52nd's depleted ranks. Seven officers, eight serjeants and 129 other ranks made up the reinforcement. The officers were Lieutenants T. Walker, R.G. Pluckrose, and Second-Lieutenants J.E. Zeron, R.W. Sawers, C.R. Crosley, A.C. Bell, C.T. O'Neill. Pluckrose and Zeron were both holders of the Military Cross and the former had been wounded with the Regiment on July 30th 1916. The rank and file men were largely former members of the Headquarters and C Company of the now disbanded 6th Battalion[663]. Although some had previously served with the 52nd, many were elderly men and senior N.C.O.s. Richard Crosse was pleased to get the 6th's band of some eighteen performers plus six buglers. The disbandment of the 6th Battalion was related to the reorganisation, described earlier, whereby, from this time, most brigades consisted of three instead of four battalions. Thus

---

662 Letter to his father written from Riley Avenue La Vacquérie Sector on February 7th 1918.

663 The 6th Oxfordshire and Buckinghamshire Light Infantry was disbanded between February 2nd-9th 1918. Drafts of 36 officers and 700 other ranks went to the 2nd, 2/4th, and 5th Oxfordshire and Buckinghamshire L.I. with the surplus going to the 14th Entrenching Battalion.

on February 5th, the 5th Brigade lost the 17th R.F. which was transferred to the 6th Brigade.

In the early hours of February 11th, the men of the 52nd were shelled at 3.30 a.m. and 5.30 a.m. in their billets in Metz-en-Couture. Fortunately there were no casualties, although several shells fell close to where the soldiers were sleeping. Richard Crosse sought permission for the Regiment's position as reserve battalion to be moved to a safer location. The site selected was on the Equancourt - Metz cross-country track about three-quarters of a mile from Metz. A Company remained in Metz until the 12th, providing a working party. The following days were spent in improving their camp and in further training. The Lewis gunners practiced on a range near Metz. On the 15th, the 52nd relieved the 24th R.F. in the La Vacquérie centre sub-sector. C Company, left front; B Company, right front; D Company, in support; A Company, reserve; Regimental Headquarters, in Monument Ravine. On this date the London Gazette announced that Richard Crosse had been awarded a bar to his D.S.O. Six uneventful days passed and the improved weather allowed free movement in the trenches by day and made the dangerous overland journeys unnecessary. Consequently enemy shelling was reduced as there were fewer targets. The 52nd had found it particularly difficult to find their way around this system of trenches, partly as a result of a lack of signs, a defect which they were able to rectify. On February 19th, Lieutenant Victor Martin, who had served with the 52nd in January 1915, was transferred to the Regiment from the 6th Battalion.

On February 21st, the Regiment was relieved, after a further redistribution of the front, by part of the 1st King's, 1st Royal Berkshire, and the 17th R.F. [now 6th Brigade]. In turn the 52nd relieved the 2nd Royal Marine Light Infantry and part of the 1st R.M.L.I. [both 63rd Division]. The changes were made as a result of the reorganization of the divisional front from the old La Vacquérie right, centre and left sub-sectors into just two sub-sectors La Vacquérie right and centre. A new La Vacquérie left sub-sector was formed, which previously had been held by the right Brigade of the 63rd Division on the 2nd Division's left. This proved to be an indefinite front line with a support line from Apex Lane - Sailor [Naval] Reserve behind. This support line was over 2,000 yards long and was held by nine platoon posts. The 52nd became the Support Battalion in this new La Vaquérie left sub-sector, and was distributed about Wood Trench and Wood Support astride the Couillet Valley. Much work was required to improve the wire and fire steps in their new position. During this six-day tour in the line, the 52nd suffered seven men wounded.

The Regiment was relieved on February 27th by the 2nd H.L.I. and withdrew to billets in Metz-en-Couture, less C Company who went to undertake the construction of a camp in Winchester Valley [just in front of Metz] to accommodate one battalion. The following day Lieutenant-Colonel Richard Crosse presented the ribbon of the "1914 Star" to 70 of all ranks. Another 30 men serving with the 52nd were entitled to it although not able to be on parade that day[664]. Second-Lieutenant J.W. Bennett returned to England for six months service. The month of March began with the Regiment still in billets in Metz and Winchester Valley. A fortunate party of three officers and 29 other ranks proceeded to Paris on a refreshing four days of leave. Unfortunately five men were killed and another seven wounded by shellfire during the day. From March 2nd-5th, the weather was very bad, making difficult the building of the camp in Winchester Valley to replace the one in Metz.

On March 5th, the 52nd returned to the La Vacquérie left sub-sector with its 2,200 yards frontage and platoon posts in the front line. Each platoon post was about 50 yards from the next, and there was no covered communication between them. All this was typical of the new defence system's Forward Zone. The trenches were shallow and muddy and, as one officer put it 'a cock louse would be exposed crawling in them'. The remainder of the Regiment was deployed; three platoons in close support, one company in Sailor [Naval] Reserve Trench and another in Apex Lane. During the period 5th-11th, the positions of the Regiment were changed on an almost daily basis as part of a policy of holding the front more thinly. It was now considered to be an outpost line with firm arrangements for withdrawal if the need arose. Clearly, the front line could not be held with the number of men available at this time. There was considerable apprehension concerning the enemy's hostile intentions, and each morning the British artillery fired in order to break up the assembly of German forces. Lieutenant Jim Neville, on returning from leave in England, had presented Richard Crosse with a bugle to the Colonel's obvious delight. Neville had another narrow escape when, exasperated by the treacly mud on his round of inspection, he stood upright to get better purchase for his legs. The enemy spotted his tall figure and fired about fifteen mortar bombs at him in rapid succession. Lying flat in the mud he survived and vowed to take no chances in future.

At 4 a.m. on the 9th, a patrol from B Company under Lieutenant R.G. Pluckrose was sent out to attempt prisoner identification from Ostrich Sap which

---

[664] The 1914 Star was approved in 1917, and awarded to all those who had served in France and Belgium between August 5th and midnight on November 22nd/23rd 1914. In 1919, George V sanctioned the award of a bar to the previously issued 1914 Star to those who had been under fire during this period. The vast majority of the recipients of the 1914 Star were pre-war regulars known as 'The Old Contemptibles'.

was full of Germans. In addition, it was hoped to find out the date of the coming German offensive by interrogation of any prisoner that was taken. The wire was found to be thicker than had been anticipated, and the 6-inch Stokes mortars, manned by artillerymen, which had been expected to co-operate in the raid by cutting the enemy's wire, failed to do so. No prisoners were taken and indeed the German trench was not even entered. Lieutenant R.G. Pluckrose, the leader of the failed raid, and one other man were wounded. Pluckrose received gunshot wounds to his face and right leg. To make matters worse, Captain E.J. Osborne, commanding 5th Light Trench Mortar Battery, and Second-Lieutenant W.H. Seale, 52nd Light Infantry, attached to the 5th Light Trench Mortar Battery, were both wounded by the British 6-inch Stokes mortars when they were endeavouring to register prior to the raid. Osborne and Seale were in the 52nd's front line where they were laying their own mortars when 'friendly fire' wounded them. Sadly, on March 14th, William Seale was to die of multiple British inflicted wounds to his neck, shoulder, right arm and left thigh. Two months earlier he had been awarded a M.C.

Lieutenant Jim Neville temporarily in command of B Company watched the chaotic preliminaries to the raid[665].

> "B" Company made a raid last Saturday morning at 4 a.m., which was unsuccessful. We were told to get an identification because the Staff wanted to know when the Boche attack is to be launched. The cutting of the wire was left to the 6-in. Stokes Mortar Battery which is manned by gunners. They made a frightful hash of it. I watched the shoot from my Company Headquarters. The first round sailed well over into the Boche support line, and the second seemed to be an excellent shot into the enemy's wire. They had found the range.
>
> The Colonel warned me that they would cut wire early in the afternoon. They started just as the light trench mortars were making their emplacements in Ostrich Post. The latter were going to co-operate in the box barrage at zero. I watched the shoot again, and to my horror I saw the third bomb fall straight into Ostrich Post. The result was a shambles and poor Seale (52nd attached to the Light Trench Mortar Battery) was among the killed.
>
> I telephoned to Regimental Headquarters and asked the Colonel to stop the 6-inch Stokes firing. The latter reported to him that it could not possibly have been their shell which had fallen into my post. That is the stock reply of gunners when they are accused of

[665] Letter to his sister written from Highland Trench on March 12th 1918.

firing short. So after we cleared up the mess in Ostrich Post and I had a message to say that the damned 6-inch Stokes was going to try again, I asked the Colonel if a gunner officer might be detailed to observe the shoot and, at the same time, I withdrew the forward posts out of harm's way.

Just before the shoot began, a gunner officer arrived. We stood up on the fire step outside Company Headquarters and waited. The first bomb sailed over into Bocheland and the officer turned to me and said, "There you see; that is the range we were firing at before." The next one just cleared our front line parapet, and landed with a crash on our own wire.

"What about that one?" said I.

"That is the bracket," he replied.

I heard the pop of discharge of the third, and turned round to watch it sailing through the air. To me it was not at all obvious where the infernal thing was going to land until the last second of its flight, when I called to the gunner to dive for the dug-out. It landed just behind the parados approximately 150 yards from the front line.

After the exhibition the gunner hopped it back to his mortars and did not stop to argue.

An incandescent Lieutenant-Colonel Richard Crosse insisted that the wire cutting should be left in the hands of the Field Artillery and, unsurprisingly, the conclusion was reached that it was better to risk uncut wire than being shattered by their own mortars. Crosse was more than a little perturbed by the performance of the British artillery and uncharacteristically recorded these outspoken comments in the *Battalion War Diary*. He was particularly scathing about the operators of the medium trench mortars who had killed young Seale.

Considerable trouble was experienced during this period by the short shooting of our own artillery. Evidently in accordance with a general scheme of defence covering a large area, gun positions were far back and one felt there was a considerable decrease in the amount of support one might look for from this arm of the service. The same applied to the Trench Mortar Service, more especially the medium in which one ceased to have any confidence at all.

On the night of March 11th/12th, the 52nd completed its six days of occupation of the front line outpost system of the Forward Zone, and was relieved by the 2nd H.L.I., becoming the Support Battalion. The Regiment was distributed: D Company, Wood Trench and Support to the east of Orchid Avenue; C Company, also in Wood Trench and Support to the west of Orchid Avenue; B Company, in Highland Trench by day and standing to arms in the eastern part of Diarmid Trench; A Company, scattered about Loughborough Lane, but standing to arms in a battle position in the western part of Diarmid Trench; Regimental Headquarters, Village Support Trench. The 48 hours arrangement of sharing the Regimental Headquarters with another battalion did not work, and after the intercession of Brigadier-General George Bullen-Smith, the 52nd was able to reclaim the whole dug-out. Richard Crosse described the dual battalion headquarters as 'inconvenient and unworkable'.

During the nights of March 12th/13th and 13th/14th, the German enemy was very active with a mustard gas bombardment on the front and support areas, as part of his general softening-up of the line before the coming major offensive. Cool misty nights followed by sunny days were ideal for the purpose. The equanimity of the 52nd was further disturbed by the rumour that the Germans would use tanks in the imminent offensive. Each night the Regiment stood to arms and very little sleep was obtained. The pernicious mustard gas played havoc particularly with the ration parties and convoys of the 52nd. Villers Plouich became impassable in view of the gas fumes. About 100 gas casualties occurred on the two nights including the devoted Quartermaster Fred Barnes who refused to go sick until he was literally blind[666]. Fortunately Barnes regained his sight and was able to return to the Regiment on March 20th, just in time for the great retreat. Despite taking every precaution, it was found that even the brakes men of the ration limbers, despite protection from box respirators, still suffered from the gas permeating their clothing and then affecting them in their billets. Clothing had to be removed prior to entering accommodation, and men had to be stopped from sleeping in close proximity to one another for fear of the effects of gas. Virtually the whole of one platoon from C Company had to be transferred to hospital from Wood Trench suffering from gas inhalation. Minor whiffs of gas took 48 hours to manifest themselves with sore throats, laryngitis, coughs, and diarrhoea.

The night of March 17th/18th ended a thoroughly unpleasant twelve days in the La Vacquérie trenches with the relief of the 52nd by the 2nd H.L.I. The Regiment proceeded to an area outside Metz-en-Couture selected by Major Rupert Brett. B and D Companies, in Winchester Valley; A Company, west of Metz; C Company, the west end of Diarmid Fort. The 18th was a warm day, and some of the men of the 52nd were still suffering from runny noses and the loss of

[666] The actual figures for gas casualties were: March 11th, 1 man; 12th, 46 men; 13th, 10 men; 14th, 36 men; 15th, 3 men.

their voices as a direct result of the mustard gas. On March 20th, the Regiment was relieved by a battalion of the 47th [London] Division and marched to excellent, clean Nissen Huts in Vallulart Camp, Ytres. Although Crosse and his men were unaware of it at the time, here they were to await the coming German onslaught.

Chapter XX

The March Retreat.

March 21st - April 5th 1918

[Maps: pages 541, 543, 553, 562.]

Before considering the actions and movements of the 52nd Light Infantry in late March 1918, a brief overview of the First Battles of the Somme 1918, which included the March Retreat will be given.

Three German armies were employed in Operation Michael: General Otto von Below's Seventeenth Army faced Byng's Third Army in the vicinity of Arras; General Georg von der Marwitz's Second Army was positioned opposite the Flesquières Salient and the most northern part of Gough's Fifth Army; General Oskar von Hutier's Eighteenth Army was opposed by the southern part of the Fifth Army. In essence the German intention was to break open the British defences and then swing to the north and attack the British flank with a view to rolling it up against the English Channel. Later further attacks would be launched. Von Below's and von der Marwitz's forces were to capture the 1916 Somme battlefields before endeavouring to envelop Arras in the north. Von Hutier's roll was to act as a flank guard and to deal with French troops coming to the aid of Gough's Fifth Army in the south.

On March 21st, after a short intense barrage, German forces attacked the British Third and Fifth Armies. In the Fifth Army area most of the Forward Zone, twelve miles in depth, was overrun in the first hour. Two to three thousand yards behind it, much of the Battle Zone was lost during the afternoon. Further north, Byng's Third Army did better and was still holding its Battle Zone, although the retreat of the Fifth Army was exposing its flank. In particular, the Flesquières Salient, the sphere of influence of the 2nd Division and the 52nd Light Infantry, was in danger of envelopment. At nightfall on the 21st, the British Expeditionary Force had suffered its first serious defeat since trench warfare had begun three and a half years earlier. One man, the Kaiser, was so pleased with the successes of March 21st that he awarded Field-Marshal Paul von Hindenburg the Iron Cross with Golden Rays. The last recipient had been Field-Marshal Gebhard von Blücher in 1813[667]. He also gave the German schoolchildren a 'victory' holiday on March 23rd.

[667] Field-Marshal Gebhard von Blücher [1742-1819], the great Prussian soldier whose arrival at the Battle of Waterloo was decisive and allowed the Duke of Wellington his great victory. His medal was officially called the Star of the Grand Cross of the Iron Cross and was known as the 'Blücherstern'. Hindenburg's medal was the 'Hindenburgstern'. The Nazis intended to award a third Grand Cross to their leading general of World War II. Their defeat precluded the award. In

The following day, the 22nd, the German enemy renewed their attacks, continuing with them over the next few days. The 24th, 25th, and 26th, would prove to be the worst days for the British as the enemy continued to advance. On March 23rd, General Erich von Ludendorff switched the main focus of the attack from the north, where progress was slow, to the south. Von Hutier's forces were to have played the role of flank guard, but they were now to be made the main focus of the attack with the goal of driving a wedge between the British and French forces. This resulted in a dispersal of force rather than a concentration and was a major error. On March 26th, General Ferdinand Foch was made the de facto Anglo/French Generalissimo to synchronize the activities of the two nations' armies[668]. This stopped the possibility of the French concentrating on the defence of Paris to the exclusion of anything else, whilst the British protected their lines of communication. The unfortunate General Hubert Gough was held responsible for the apparent debacle and dismissed from his command of the Fifth Army on March 27th. This was a gross calumny and was at the behest of the Prime Minister, David Lloyd George. Although Gough had his limitations, his army had retreated, as it was bound to do with its limited manpower and in a manner agreed previously with Field-Marshal Sir Douglas Haig. It was not until 1936 that Lloyd George wrote a public letter of apology to Gough.

On March 29th, von Ludendorff, in the next phase of the offensive, Operation Mars, attacked with nine divisions to the north of the River Scarpe. General Julian Byng's Third Army dealt with them severely and von Ludendorff, not wishing another battle of attrition similar to Passchendaele, closed down operations against them. By now the Germans had reduced their grand ambitions to simply capturing Amiens. At Villers Bretonneux on April 4th/5th, Anglo/Australian forces brought the assault to a halt ten miles short of their goal. Von Ludendorff now closed down Operation Michael. His men had captured a large salient forty miles deep, which would subsequently prove difficult to hold. The British and French armies had not been separated, and although the British Fifth Army had been badly mauled, it had not been broken. The total number of British casualties in the period March 21st-April 5th was 177,739. The German casualties for the period March 21st-April 30th were 348,300, possibly with the lightly wounded excluded as was their custom.

Approximately at 4.40 a.m. March 21st, before dawn, the German artillery's five hour hurricane bombardment opened with a cacophony of sound

---

1945 Blücher's grave at Krobielowice was desecrated by Soviet troops, who played football with his skull.

[668] This was partly brought about by General Henri-Philippe Pétain's reluctance to come to the aid of Gough's Fifth Army.

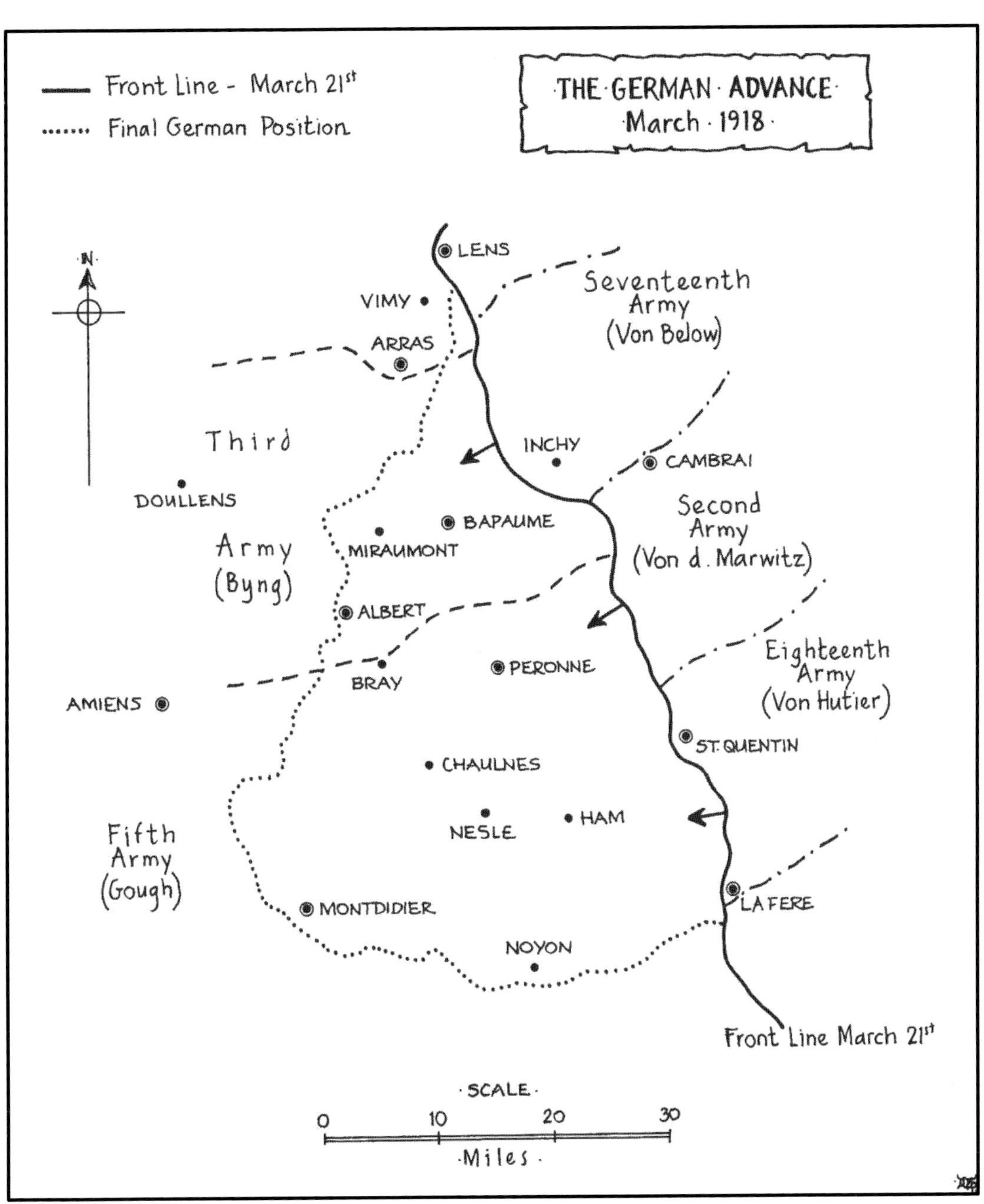
Front Line - March 21st
Final German Position
THE GERMAN ADVANCE
March 1918
N
LENS
VIMY
ARRAS
Seventeenth Army (Von Below)
Third Army (Byng)
INCHY
CAMBRAI
DOULLENS
BAPAUME
MIRAUMONT
Second Army (Von d. Marwitz)
ALBERT
PERONNE
BRAY
Eighteenth Army (Von Hutier)
AMIENS
ST. QUENTIN
CHAULNES
NESLE
HAM
Fifth Army (Gough)
MONTDIDIER
LA FERE
NOYON
Front Line March 21st
SCALE
0
10
20
30
Miles

on the whole of Gough's Fifth Army front and three quarters of Byng's Third Army front. The man behind the German artillery bombardment was Oberst Georg 'Durchbruck' [Breakthrough] Bruchmüller, who had an unique talent for estimating how much ammunition needed to be expended prior to an infantry assault. He had a particular interest in gas artillery fire. The total number of guns, 6,473, about half of all the enemy's artillery pieces on the western front, took part in the barrage. In fact, in the Flesquières Salient, where the 2nd Division had been relieved by the 47th [London] Division on the night of March 20th/21st, the bombardment started a little later, at 5.05 a.m., presumably to confuse the British commanders. With the benefit of hindsight, as the Director of Gas Services pointed out, the fact the enemy had used mustard gas in the salient for several days, made it unlikely that it would be subjected to a direct attack. The enemy intended to nip the salient off at its base to avoid a frontal assault. Mustard gas had a prolonged length of action and could hang around for days on end. The 2nd Division, including the 52nd, had had to be taken out of the line as so many of its men were suffering from its effects.

When the German artillery bombardment opened, Captain Percy Bobby had just led his C Company into Vallulart Camp, Ytres to join the rest of the 52nd there. Ahead of the 52nd, V Corps had in the nearly 14,000 yards of the Flesquières Salient, from north to south, the 17th [Northern], 63rd [Royal Naval] and the 47th [London] Divisions. The 52nd's 2nd Division, also part of V Corps, was in reserve. Thus the salient had a strong garrison compared with the rest of the line. The Battle Zone in the salient ran across its base.

Earlier in the month, Major-General Cecil Pereira, commanding the 2nd Division, had explained to his three brigadier-generals and to many of his battalion commanders the new concept of flexible defence. As elsewhere on the Third and Fifth Army fronts, the artillery had been kept well back and other than in response to S.O.S calls had remained silent, so that their positions were largely unknown to the enemy when the offensive started. Machine-gun positions had been placed in depth and Pereira was confident that the Germans could be held up. He was also concerned that the defensive positions of each corps had not been co-ordinated so that various disparate schemes had been put into practice. General Julian Byng, the commander of the Third Army, had thought that V Corps was holding the front line of the Flesquières Salient with too many men and measures had been taken to thin out this line. Byng had been reluctant to give up the Salient, after the hard graft of his troops at the Battle of Cambrai, however logical a step it might have been.

With the opening of the German barrage, the 52nd dressed quietly in the dark and stood to arms at about 5 a.m. The main bombardment appeared to be on

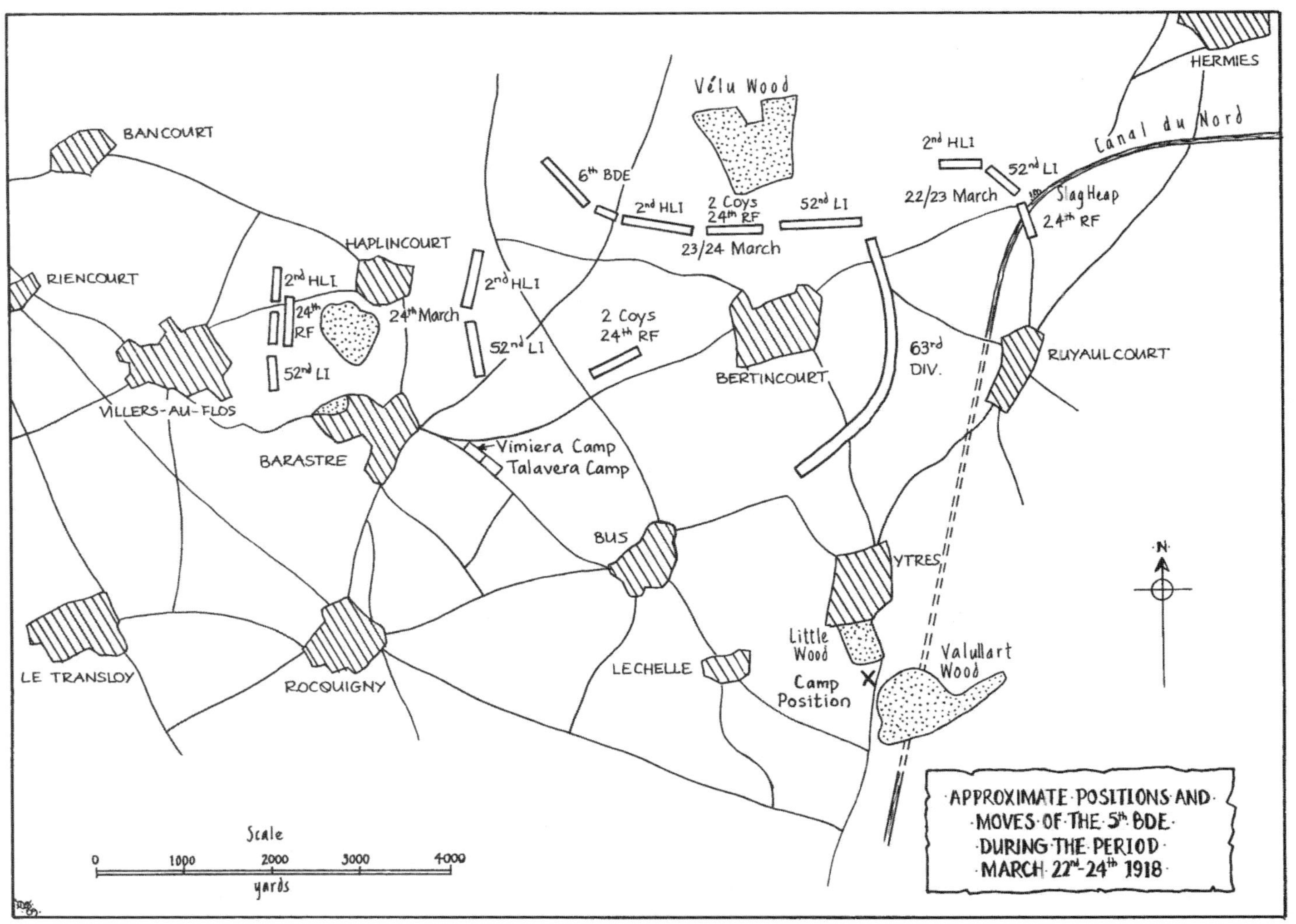
·APPROXIMATE·POSITIONS·AND·
·MOVES·OF·THE·5th·BDE·
·DURING·THE·PERIOD·
·MARCH·22nd-24th 1918·
N
HERMIES
Canal du Nord
Slag Heap
24th RF
52nd LI
2nd HLI
22/23 March
RUYAULCOURT
63rd DIV.
YTRES
Valullart Wood
Little Wood
Camp Position
52nd LI
Vélu Wood
2 Coys 24th RF
23/24 March
BERTINCOURT
2nd HLI
6th BDE
2 Coys 24th RF
LECHELLE
BUS
Vimiera Camp
Talavera Camp
2nd HLI
52nd LI
24th March
HAPLINCOURT
2nd HLI
24th RF
52nd LI
BARASTRE
ROCQUIGNY
BANCOURT
VILLERS-AU-FLOS
RIENCOURT
LE TRANSLOY
Scale
0
1000
2000
3000
4000
yards

the flanks of V Corps at Bullecourt and Gonnelieu and sounded like the beating of a colossal drum. The Regiment remained at 20 minutes notice to move throughout the daytime of March 21st until, late at night, this was increased to one hour. The news reaching the 52nd was scanty. IV Corps was heavily engaged to their left; V Corps to the front had not been heavily attacked and was holding its positions; VII Corps, part of Gough's Fifth Army, on the right was reported to have been pushed back two and a half miles. The 52nd slept fully dressed and in the early hours of the 22nd orders were received to be ready to move off at 4.30 a.m. The 2nd Division was to concentrate in the area Barastre-Haplincourt by 7 a.m., and the Regiment formed up on the Ytres road before marching the nearly two miles to Vimiera Barracks at Barastre via Lechelle and Bus. To be marching to the rear was something of a surprise for the 52nd who had been expecting to go in the opposite direction. It was a bitterly cold, foggy morning made more unpleasant by poor roads and constant halts for traffic going in all directions. Matters were made still worse by the continuation of the German artillery fire with 15-inch shells falling into Bus and Barastre.

By noon the fog lifted and the 52nd remained in their huts or lay in the warm sunshine. Their Commanding Officer, Lieutenant-Colonel Richard Crosse, was summoned to a meeting with Major-General Philip 'Blobs' Robertson of the 17th Division. The 5th Brigade, including the 52nd, was to report to the 17th Division as there had been a heavy attack on Hermies. Meanwhile at 2 p.m., the Regiment paraded under Major Rupert Brett and then set off across country following a circuitous route to the south of Bertincourt. They marched in open order with 100 yards between platoons and used the available dead ground as much as possible. Above them German aeroplanes seemed to have a mastery of the sky and brought down a heavy artillery barrage on the 2nd H.L.I. to the left of the 52nd.

At 4 p.m., Crosse rejoined his men with the serious news that they were to shore up a weak spot in the line where a brigade of the 17th Division was under pressure in the area of Hermies-Havrincourt. About 6.30 p.m., the 52nd reached their destination half-way between Bertincourt and Hermies, just to the west of the road and facing north-east. Fortunately there had been no casualties on route. To their left was the 2nd H.L.I. facing north and on the right the 24th R.F., close to the Slag Heap and straddling the empty Canal du Nord. Crosse had been instructed by the 5th Brigade to take command of the 2nd H.L.I., as well as his own battalion, if the situation demanded. At sunset the 52nd started to dig in and all ranks made themselves as comfortable as was possible on a bitterly cold night. The hours of darkness proved to be quiet and a forward reconnaissance was undertaken under the cover of darkness. Captain Ben Slocock took over as

Acting Adjutant from Captain Ernest Whitfeld who was going on leave. The unfortunate Whitfeld's leave was later cancelled in view of the German offensive. Lieutenant Victor Martin's leave suffered a similar fate as did that of some of the men.

Early on the morning of March 23rd, the 52nd was ordered to occupy and complete the digging of the forward loop of the so-called Green Switch Line around Bertincourt. The trigger for this move was the loss of ground by IV Corps to the north and that the enemy was advancing down the Bapaume - Cambrai road. The Green Line proper ran: to the east of Equancourt and Ytres; west of Bertincourt, where the switch line ran around the village; north-west to the Corps northern boundary a mile and a half west of Vélu. It was the corps Rear Zone of defence and was rudimentary. Its trenches were partially dug with up to four rows of wire in front of them in some places.

At 7 a.m. on a glorious spring morning, Richard Crosse called his company commanders together to inform them of their new positions. All four companies would have to go into the line to cover the 800 yards front allotted to them and this meant swinging back to the west Facing north, from right to left the Companies were in order C, A, D, B, with C at the apex of the loop, close to the railway[669]. The right of the Regiment's position was at the road/rail junction half a mile north of Bertincourt Station[670]. Vélu Wood was in front of them and the village of Bertincourt behind. Next to C Company was supposed to be a battalion of the 63rd Division, at right angles to the 52nd and facing eastwards. However, this unit of the 63rd Division, the 1st R.M.L.I., did not get into position until 2.55 p.m., only five minutes before they had been warned that, at 3 p.m., they would become the front line! To the 52nd's left in front of Vélu Wood were the 24th R.F. and then the 2nd H.L.I. Initially, Crosse could only see the H.L.I. and not the R.F. Soon the 24th R.F. took up their position astride the Bertincourt - Vélu road. Further still to their left was the 6th Brigade and then the 19th Division of IV Corps.

Lieutenant-Colonel Richard Crosse sent this message to 5th Brigade at 11.45 a.m.

> Am now in same dug-out with Colonel Goschen, R.F.A.[671], late H.Q. 17th Division. A.A.A. My line is partly dug in front of 2 companies

---

[669] In his diary entry for March 23rd, Jim Neville gave the order of companies from the right as C, D, A, B. This is contradicted by the *Battalion War Diary.*

[670] According to the *5th Brigade War Diary* the right of the 52nd's position was a little further south of this point. The position given in the text was taken from the *2nd Division's archives.*

[671] Colonel A.A. Goschen.

> only. A.A.A. We are digging platoon posts across remainder of front, through about P.1. central. A.A.A. No 24th R.F. as yet reported, but can see right of 2nd H.L.I. A.A.A. We very urgently need S.A.A., of which evidently no local resources.

The day proved to be a hot one, making the digging of the new trenches at maximum speed thirsty work. B Company had to dig their trenches from scratch and by 2 p.m. each man had a narrow hole with a small parapet and it was intended to link up the holes into a single trench line. Elsewhere the other companies found pre-prepared wide, shallow trenches, presumably as an anti-tank measure, which would prove to be useless in the coming attack. Certainly B Company felt safer in their small holes. The 52nd was fortunate in that the commanding officer of the Pioneer Battalion of the 17th Division supplied them with picks and shovels. At midday, a battery of field artillery took up a position between the 52nd and Vélu Wood, and commenced firing. Less than 30 minutes later it was subjected to machine-gun fire from Vélu Wood, limbered up and galloped away. Lieutenant Jim Neville described it as a thrilling sight and reminiscent of a picture by Lady Butler[672].

By 2 p.m., the 52nd could clearly see the enemy streaming over the skyline in pursuit of the retreating British troops made up of a heterogeneous mass from different regiments, divisions and even corps. The plan had been for the 17th Division to fall back through the 2nd Division to reform west of Villers-au-Flos. However, the retirement was conducted in good order, covered from behind by machine-guns and with Lewis guns on the flanks. Two officers of the 25th Machine-Gun Corps with their six men, all that remained of the original 50, took up a position in front of B Company and mounted their sole remaining gun. Lieutenant Jim Neville described these brave men and their pitiful state[673]. Despite the apparent orderly retirement, it was clear that on the Third Army Front, just below the surface, chaos reigned. Later the 52nd would see it at first hand.

> One of the officers came to me for some water and food as he had been without water and food for three days. I had to refuse his request for water, because we were already short, and did not know how long we might be compelled to subsist on our water bottles. I managed to find a tin of bully for him and some neat whisky, for which he was very grateful. He was in a pitiful state; his face was black from powder, his hands bleeding, his jacket ripped from

[672] Lady Elizabeth Butler [1846-1933], the leading military painter of the late 19th century.

[673] Diary entry for March 23rd 1918.

> shoulder to wrist by shrapnel, and his puttees and breeches torn to ribbons by wire. He said he had been blown up three times and had had three guns blown up under his hand. He had lost his Division which had retired early in the morning, and he informed me that he intended to stay with us and see it through. He was rather bitter about certain troops, who had retired without orders and left him and his guns in the lurch.

` On March 21st, the troops facing V Corps were the 24th and 53rd Reserve Divisions, all of XI Corps in von Below's Seventeenth Army. In addition they were faced by the 16th and 21st Reserve Divisions of XXXIXR Corps in von der Marwitz's Second Army. Both Armies were in Crown Prince Rupprecht's Army Group. The 24th Reserve Division took part in the initial attack and advanced through Hermies and Ruyaulcourt on March 23rd before being relieved that evening. It recruited in Saxony and by 1918 it was deemed to be only third class. This Reserve Division would have faced the 52nd during the night of March 22nd/23rd and during the daylight hours on the latter day. The 53rd Reserve Division was pulled out of the line on March 22nd prior to the actions involving the 52nd. The 16th Reserve Division attacked south of Marcoing on March 21st and was taken out of the line on the third day. It would not have come into contact with the 52nd. The 21st Reserve Division advanced from La Vacquérie to Beaumont Hamel which it reached on March 27th. The Division recruited from Hesse-Nassau and southern Westphalia. In 1917 it was considered to be a good division, but by 1918 it was in decline and was rated as only second class. There is little doubt that some of the men chasing the 52nd back to the Old Somme battlefields of 1916 were from this division. The 119th Division was used as an attack division on March 21st against the IV Corps to the north of the Flesquières Salient. It was withdrawn on the 23rd, but reappeared on the 25th, in the fighting to the south-east of Hébuterne and remained in the area until early April. As will be seen, it would have been in the sphere of the 52nd around March 26th. It recruited from Posen and Lower Silesia and was rated as second class in 1918.

At 3 p.m., the 52nd became the front line troops and the gaps in the wire in front of them were closed with movable chevaux-de-frise. The enemy followed up quickly but with caution and soon the Regiment was being peppered with machine-gun bullets from the direction of Vélu Wood. Although the Germans were not slow to follow up, they did so with caution, making use of the railway cutting and sunken roads to get within 50 yards of the 52nd. Further pressure was exerted by the enemy from the direction of Hermies. A Company, under Captain John 'Bunjie' Littledale, suffered the most casualties in their exposed position on a slope towards the railway embankment. Amongst the casualties was John Littledale who had gone forward to withdraw one of his posts at about 3.30 p.m. He had already been wounded on the Redan Ridge on November 13th 1916 and was an undoubted loss to the 52nd. The 22-year-old Littledale's contemporary at Eton, Jim Neville, described the former's demise[674].

> "A" Company on our immediate right had many casualties. The enemy worked a light machine gun forward along the railway embankment which ran through our front, and from a concealed position on top he was able to enfilade the trench. The piece of trench held by "A" Company was on a slope towards the railway embankment, and every movement in the trench could, thus, be spotted by the enemy. Also, as the trench was seven feet wide and three feet deep, there was absolutely no cover; in fact it was a death trap and nearly as bad as nothing at all.
>
> "B" Company was more fortunate. We were just over the crest and the only casualties which we suffered were due to indirect enfilade fire from the embankment.
>
> "A" Company had a forward post in our wire, which was well placed to snipe the enemy as he worked forward. However, this post was spotted by the light machine gun team, and its position rendered untenable. "Bunjie" Littledale, commanding "A" Company, went forward to withdraw this post, and was killed, hit through the heart and neck. Next, Colvill[675] ran the gauntlet of a hail of bullets and managed to get the men back and Littledale's body as well[676].

The Chaplain Reverend Edward Guilford was prevailed upon to go back to Gueudecourt to conduct funerals for Littledale, three of his men, and a Royal Fusilier.

By this stage it was clear that the enemy's attacks on the corps [IV and VII] on the flanks of the V Corps were making good progress. The situation on the right was more serious than on the left as VII Corps was retreating faster than IV Corps. Meanwhile, the Divisions of V Corps, 17th, 47th and 63rd, had extricated themselves from the Flesquières Salient. For a brief period both flanks of the 2nd Division seemed secure and the 17th Division had succeeded in retiring

---

[674] Diary entry for March 23rd 1918.

[675] Second-Lieutenant Charles Colvill, a hot-tempered Irishman who was brave and steadfast.

[676] Littledale's body is now buried in Bancourt British Cemetery. VII.C.17. Originally it was interred at Gueudecourt but was moved after the war.

'Shiny' Horley and 'Twitt' Tyrwhitt-Drake with a trench periscope. [NRO NEV 7/32]

J.D. Grover, Signal Officer. Circa 1918. [Colvill Collection]

Some 52nd officers in 1917.

Back row: R. Blackwell, Dick Warren, J.D. Grover.

Middle row: Jim Neville, B.J. Crewe.

Front row: 'Shiny' Horley, 'Fritz' Eagle.

[NRO NEV 7/32]

T.A. Coffin, stints commanding the Sapping Platoon, as Gas Officer and Acting Quartermaster. [NRO NEV 7/32]

In the early hours of March 24th 1918, the inspirational Commanding Officer of the 52nd, Richard Crosse, dreamt of the portrait of Sir John Moore that hung in the mess at Aldershot. Moore appeared to come alive and inspire his millitary descendant into the path of glory. Crosse awoke refreshed and led his men back from the German noose around Bertincourt. [Kite Collection]

The portrait of Sir John Moore by James Northcote that hung in the mess at Aldershot in 1914. [Royal Green Jackets Museum]

Jack Ward from Acton, London. Missing, presumed killed, near Villers-au-Flos, during the March retreat of 1918. [Kite Collection]

Germans in Villers-au-Flos. Photograph circa 1918. [Private Collection]

On March 27th 1918, the 52nd had a long halt at Martinsart Château to receive instructions from the 188th Infantry Brigade. Shortly afterwards the beautiful building was destroyed by shellfire. Photograph circa 1913.
[Private Collection]

Rupert Brett D.S.O. was one of the 52nd's finest officers in the war. In 1914, he was wounded as Transport Officer. From the autumn of 1917-1918 he was second-in-command to Richard Crosse. Brett's gaiety added to the magnetism of Crosse fostered the esprit de corps of the 52nd. His favourite parting was 'Good hunting old cock'.
[Regimental Chronicles]

George Field M.C. and bar shaving.
[NRO NEV 7/32]

Number 4 Platoon, A Company, 52nd Light Infantry in June 1918. The Platoon Commander, Charles Colvill, is seated in the middle of the second row from the front. [Colvill Collection]

The empty Canal du Nord which the 52nd got to know intimately during 1917, at the Battle of Cambrai and in 1918, at the Battle of Havrincourt. [Regimental Archives]

behind them. Information came to Major-General Cecil Pereira that the Germans were in Bus and as a consequence he wished to withdraw the right flank of the 5th Brigade. There was a very real risk that the Bertincourt Salient would be cut off from the south. However, V Corps would not permit the withdrawal.

The later afternoon of March 23rd was somewhat quieter with only the heavy artillery of both sides in action. The British heavy artillery concentrated on Vélu Wood to the front of the 52nd, whilst the enemy plastered the Bertincourt - Vélu road, about 100 yards behind the British line. Towards evening, a frost developed and the shelling increased in intensity, with the German field artillery again concentrating on the Bertincourt - Vélu road. Night came down, and the 52nd prepared for the inevitable attack on them the following morning by improving their trenches. At dusk, the shell dump at Ytres was set on fire by the retreating British soldiers to stop the ordnance falling into the hands of the enemy, and this led to a dull red glow in the sky with the constant thud of exploding shells. All round the Regiment, the enemy's Very Lights brightened up the sky, revealing more clearly than any map reference the unpleasant fact that they were well and truly 'bottled up' by the Germans. As the night progressed, so it became colder, making sleep impossible and there was a palpable tension in the air as the 52nd awaited daylight and all that would bring.

Towards evening, it had become clear to Lieutenant-Colonel Richard Crosse that the situation on their flanks was such that unless a withdrawal was carried out under cover of darkness, there was little chance of the 52nd escaping from the noose that the enemy was tightening around their necks. His Regiment was occupying incomplete trenches facing north from the Bertincourt to Vélu railway westwards with the 1st R.M.L.I. on their right and facing east. The two Regiments made an acute angled salient around the village of Bertincourt. The village had been badly damaged by shellfire and its destruction would be completed the next day. A cellar by the crossroads in the centre of Bertincourt became the joint Headquarters of the 52nd and the 1st R.M.L.I. It had recently been vacated by the 17th Division before being taken over by Colonel A.A Goschen R.A., as Crosse put it, 'an old friend' of the 2nd Division. Goschen too had moved out and the cellar was inherited by Crosse and the commanding officer of the 1st R.M.L.I. for a single night. During the 23rd Second-Lieutenant Harry Vernon received a gunshot wound of the right shoulder.

Richard Crosse awaited the anticipated order for the 52nd to retire from their present positions under the cover of darkness. Fully appreciating the seriousness of his situation, and believing every minute of delay would reduce the chances of his Regiment escaping from the clutches of the enemy, Crosse set in motion preliminary orders for their withdrawal to the west. At 11 p.m., he secretly notified his company commanders in writing that the order to retire would simply be CORUNNA followed by a map reference where the 52nd was to reassemble[677].

> RC. 93. 23rd. AAA. If we have orders to withdraw, a withdrawal is, as you know, only possible from our present position during darkness AAA with the present state of communications, it is very likely that, though the orders may be issued in time, they will not be received in time to carry them out AAA I shall therefore wire to you only CORUNNA followed by the map square in which the Regiment will reassemble, and perhaps the time of moving off AAA regard this as absolutely secret among your officers AAA carry shovels and SAA in bandoliers.

Shortly after midnight, Richard Crosse managed about an hour's sleep, and dreamt about Sir John Moore's portrait that hung on the wall of the 52nd's mess at Aldershot[678].

> I lay down in the cellar which was the Regimental headquarters and fell into a sound sleep. In what I can only describe as a dream, this picture appeared, exactly as I remembered it, but with the difference that Sir John Moore seemed to stand out from it, and to be alive. I noted particularly the left arm pointing, a gesture which I have always associated with the word in which William Napier has told how the first Colonel of the 52nd Light Infantry "urged all who came in contact with him onward in the path of glory along which he strode so mightily himself." At this moment he seemed to be calling on his Regiment to remember its traditions and its duty.
>
> I must have slept for an hour or more, but I woke very much refreshed, the dream very clear in my mind, and feeling, much as Charles Napier on the morning of Corunna, that I had seen him whose appearance I should have welcomed above all others at that time.

About 1 a.m., Richard Crosse received a verbal message from Brigadier-General George Bullen-Smith brought by the 52nd's Transport Officer,

---

677 Crosse's choice of CORUNNA as the code word was apt. Of course he was thinking of Sir John Moore's inspirational retreat in 1809.

678 Recorded as an addendum in the *Regimental Journal* of 1938.

Lieutenant Tom Tyrwhitt-Drake on horseback[679]. The message stated; 'Reinforcements were expected' and went on to say 'that the Brigade would put up the best all round fight using every available man', and that 'there would be no withdrawal'. The message was confirmed by wire; there was no mistake. Although he does not explicitly record his reaction, Crosse must have been incredulous at such an order. His flank cover did not exist and there could only be one end on the morrow. Encirclement followed by annihilation or at best captivity beckoned. Being the ever correct professional soldier that he undoubtedly was, Crosse merely recorded in the *Battalion War Diary* 'orders were issued accordingly'. His company commanders were simply told 'no change in positions will be made'. The Regiment stood to arms.

Earlier, it has been recorded that there appeared to have been an uneasy relationship between Crosse and his brigade commander, Bullen-Smith. At the very least Crosse felt that the 5th Brigade during Bullen-Smith's time in command never praised the actions of his Regiment. In fact on this occasion, the fault lay not at brigade or even at divisional level, but appeared to have been the decision of Lieutenant-General Edward Fanshawe, commanding V Corps and the brother of the 52nd's former commanding officer. Major-General Cecil Pereira, commanding the 2nd Division recorded: 'I explained to the Corps that we could easily carry out this retirement under the cover of darkness but that it would be costly by daylight. I had many conversations with the Corps about it but they would not believe that the Boche were in Bus and would not sanction it'. Fanshawe, described by Pereira as a kindly corps commander, did not believe that the enemy was seriously threatening the right flank of the 5th Brigade. He was wrong as, soon after 8.30 p.m. on the 23rd, the enemy's line was 200 yards to the west of Bus. It was a period of confusion and frenetic activity, and it is all too easy to be wise after the event.

At 2 a.m., Lieutenant Jim Neville was awoken by his Company Commander, Captain George Field, with a message to the effect that they might have to retire to another position in the rear. Presumably this was the CORUNNA message from Richard Crosse. The hours of darkness slipped by, and the tension grew with every minute. Dawn broke, a glorious spring morning but still no enemy attack. As it was getting light, two German officers crept forward to assess gaps made in the wire by the artillery. No. 8 Platoon of B Company allowed them to wriggle through the first row of wire before neatly shooting them.

---

[679] Crosse gave the time as 1 a.m. in the *Battalion War Diary.* In articles in the *Regimental Journals* of 1938 and 1958 he gave the time as 3.30 a.m. The contemporary timing of the former has been used in the text.

The 5th Brigade Headquarters moved back to Barastre at 5 a.m. on March 24th. Between 8-9 a.m. and almost certainly nearer to 9 a.m., Richard Crosse was called to the telephone and was given the first four paragraphs of orders from the 5th Brigade[680]. Subsequently he learnt that the orders ran to thirteen paragraphs but the telephone wire gave way after he had received the first four. Crosse had been told that the new line to be taken up would run O.5-O.11-O.17-O.23.-O.29 [map references], with the 52nd in a position on the right. This was a line running from north to south with Haplincourt, Barastre, Rocquigny to the west and Bertincourt, Bus to the east. Crosse immediately issued his own orders, 'CORUNNA O.22.', indicating a position to be taken up approximately behind the right of the new proposed line. O.22 was a map square, a little to the east of the mid-point between the villages of Barastre and Rocquigny. It is not clear why Crosse did not select part of the designated line. These orders were shouted down the telephone and backed up by an orderly. He felt that with a few minutes more delay the withdrawal would have been impossible. Subsequently, it was widely believed in the Regiment that Crosse's foresight had saved the 52nd from certain destruction. Crosse considered this day to be the worst of the whole war.

Soon after 9 a.m. on March 24th, the withdrawal of the 52nd got under way across the downs towards the high ground to the west, in the direction of Haplincourt and Barastre. The Regiment was now only about 160 men strong. On their right, the 63rd Division had got away a little earlier at 8.45 a.m. In theory the 2nd and 63rd Divisions were to withdraw through the 17th Division who were in positions behind them. The undulating countryside consisted of treeless open high land, sunken roads, old encampments, small shattered villages and here and there a stunted copse or tangle of crumbling trenches. Crosse led his Headquarters staff in two small columns of officers, signallers and orderlies through the dancing brickwork of Bertincourt, which as an Irish soldier commented 'was getting the father and mother of a beating'. On emerging from Bertincourt the matter of keeping direction was found to be very difficult. The retiral had been made particularly unpleasant by the long-range sweeps of enemy machine-guns and, from the direction of some of the fire, it appeared that Bus was certainly in enemy hands. Unfortunately, a gap of 800-1,000 yards developed in the line between the 5th and the 6th Brigades on the high ground to the east of Haplincourt. The cause of this was the failure of the 5th Brigade Staff, readily

[680] Much too late in the day, not appreciating how far the enemy had advanced, Lieutenant-General Edward Fanshawe's Headquarters at V Corps ordered the evacuation of the Bertincourt Salient at 8.15 a.m. on March 24th. The 2nd Divisional order was speedily issued at 8.20 a.m. and the evacuation was ordered to commence at 9.15 a.m.

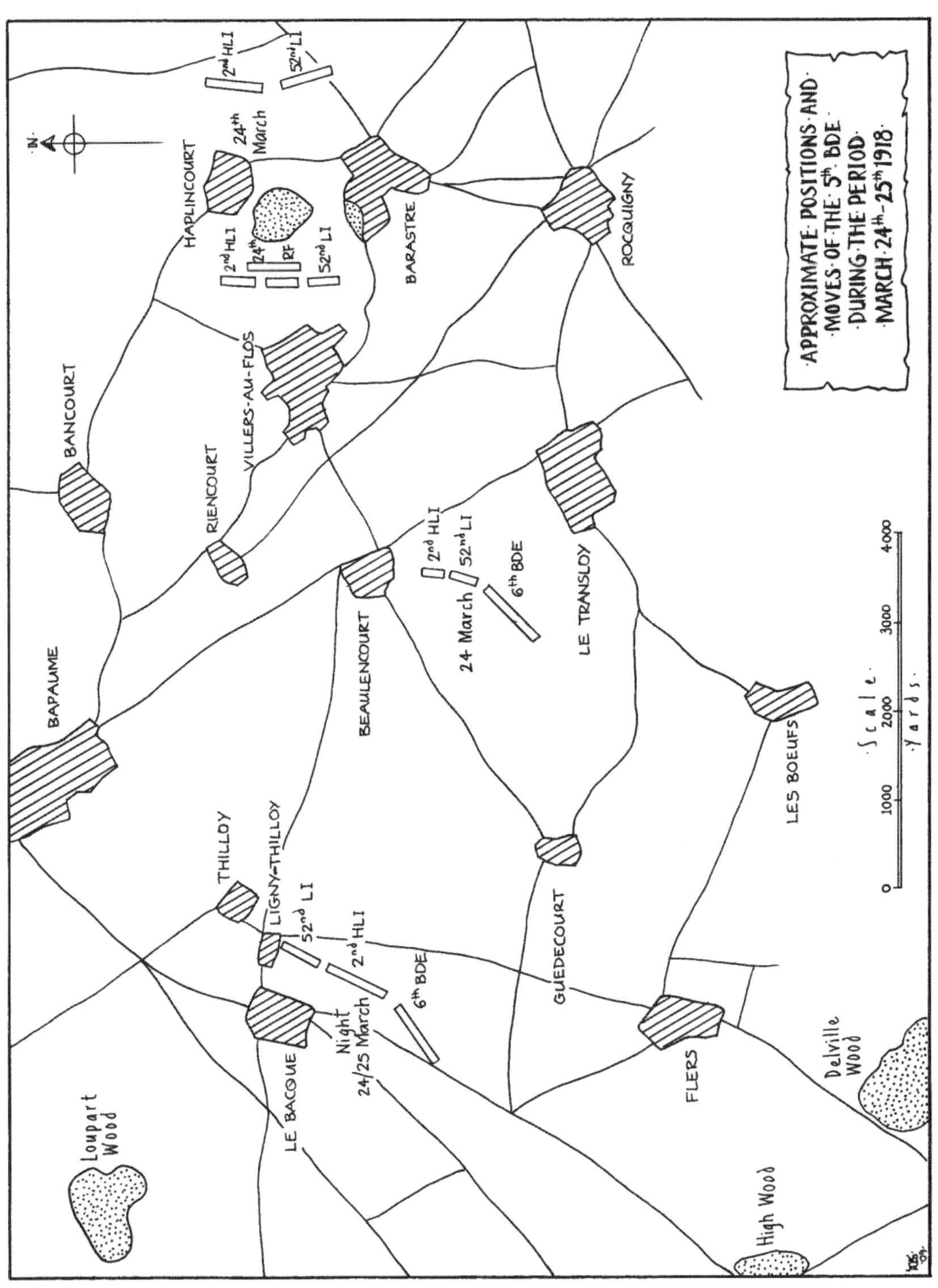
APPROXIMATE POSITIONS AND MOVES OF THE 5th BDE DURING THE PERIOD MARCH 24th–25th 1918
N
HAPLINCOURT
BARASTRE
ROCQUIGNY
VILLERS-AU-FLOS
BANCOURT
RIENCOURT
BEAULENCOURT
LE TRANSLOY
BAPAUME
THILLOY
LIGNY-THILLOY
GUEDECOURT
LES BOEUFS
FLERS
LE BACQUE
Loupart Wood
High Wood
Delville Wood
2nd HLI
52nd LI
24th March
2nd HLI
24th RF
52nd LI
2nd HLI
52nd LI
6th BDE
24 March
52nd LI
2nd HLI
6th BDE
Night 24/25 March
Scale
Yards
0
1000
2000
3000
4000

admitted by their Brigade Major, to identify the correct line on the ground, so that its northern flank lay where its southern flank should have been. The 2nd H.L.I. and a battalion from the 6th Brigade endeavoured to restore the break in the line.

Enemy pressure drove many of the 52nd, including their commanding officer, to the north of their destination in O.22. Others, including B Company, managed to reach O.22, further south, a little to the east of the mid-point between Barastre and Rocquigny. During the morning the main part of the Regiment held the high ground in front of the Barastre - Haplincourt road and made contact with the 2nd H.L.I. and the 24th R.F. Fortunately casualties were light for this part of the withdrawal.

After the publication of Everard Wyrall's *The History of the Second Division* in 1922, Richard Crosse was concerned by what he considered to be inaccuracies and omissions in the book's account of the 52nd on March 24th 1918. Wyrall had obtained his information from the *5th Brigade's War Diary* and a *Narrative of Operations* probably written by the commander of the 2nd Division, Major-General Cecil Pereira. In essence, Crosse was perturbed that Wyrall did not appear to realize that the 52nd had received only part of the retiral orders, and implied that Crosse had removed his Regiment too far to the rear. In the context of the nature of these operations, Crosse felt that 'this has an unpleasant sound'. At nearly a century's distance in time, it is understandable that Crosse should have these feelings but, in reality, he had no reason to reproach himself. It is extremely doubtful that Wyrall intended any offence[681]. In fact, Pereira recorded in his diary that the retiral of the right of the 5th Brigade [52nd] had been well-conducted. This was at a time when he was having trouble maintaining contact with V Corps and the adjoining divisions.

Lieutenant Jim Neville described the withdrawal of B Company on March 24th[682].

> However, at 8.50 an orderly came to me with a message, the one word "Corunna," the code word to retire. I went to Field[683] who gave me orders to retire with No. 8 Platoon from the extreme left. I was the only officer with a map of the area, and I was given the job

[681] In the 1920s, Richard Crosse felt so strongly about this subject that he wrote his own account of March 24th 1918 for the *Regimental Chronicles,* and had this account added to the *2nd Division's War Diary 1918,* which can be seen in the National Archives WO 95 1299 to this day. In addition, Crosse incorporated his article into the relevant section of his own copy of Wyrall's book, now owned by the author.

[682] Diary entry for March 24th 1918.

[683] Captain George Field.

of leading the Company. I handed over No. 6 Platoon to Serjeant Stevens and led out No. 8.

We started in single file through our wire, behind the trench. There was a stretch of 400 yards before we could reach the Bertincourt - Vélu road. No sooner were we all in the open than the enemy opened machine gun fire on us; we carried on steadily; and then, as it were, a thunderstorm seemed to burst over our heads in a deafening roar. The sun, which shone with all his might, was suddenly blotted out by yellow acrid smoke of shrapnel bursting overhead. The ground shot up all round in fountains of black smoke and earth. Everything on all sides was being heaved into the air. The Nissen huts bordering the road parallel to our line of retreat were flattened in one blast. Hell's fiery furnace was let loose.

I looked round and tried to collect the men together, because they were inclined to straggle, and even as I did so, a whizzbang caught the slanting roof of a Nissen hut but a few feet away on my right, and cut away Private Grey's legs. Another man and I tried to lift him, but he was too badly hit, and we had to leave him to the enemy.

We crossed the road and halted behind a manure heap for a breather. Field and Wilsdon[684] came up, and the former tried to shout orders to me; but it was not wise to wait too long in any one place, for five whizzbangs burst on the other side of the midden, showering manure all over us.

And so we retired in small parties to the Bertincourt-Haplincourt road, through some stables, and out again into the open.

Meanwhile Bertincourt was being plastered with every conceivable type of damnation, and the noise was terrific. I never expected to see any of the Headquarter [sic] officers again.

It was a great relief to be free of the roads and buildings, and to be in the open again. The heat seemed to be very intense, and the men were black and dripping with sweat; mostly battle sweat, for the sun was not hot enough to cause such perspiration. We marched on, through the Green Line, up the slope, and past some machine gunners who had dug in to cover our retreat.

During this retirement, it was possible to see what extent the British were, in fact, "bottled-necked." For miles I could see our troops filtering back across the rolling downs towards one spot, one narrow channel, while machine gun fire came from three sides.

[684] Second-Lieutenant R.G. Wilsdon.

On reaching the ridge in front of the Barastre-Bus road, we met Brett[685], and there we sorted out 52nd men, recognizable by the Regimental ribbon on their steel helmets, from the rabble of troops of all divisions of the 5th Corps, who were retiring through this narrow neck.

We formed up into Companies as the men came in, and having reformed, reported to Brett. "B" Company was ordered to go back to the original map reference [O.22] given in the "Corunna" message, and Field led the Company back to an old German line running between Rocquigny and Barastre.

By 10.30 a.m., the main party of the 52nd had collected on the high ground 1,000 yards to the east of the Barastre - Haplincourt road, with the 2nd H.L.I. on their left [north], and the 24th R.F. to their rear [west] behind Haplincourt Wood. At their backs the road went through a side arm of the main valley which ran south-west from Lebucquière to Villers-au-Flos. Their only protection was two belts of old German wire. Lieutenant-Colonel Richard Crosse had reported their position to the 5th Brigade, and that their flanks were doubtful. Here they were visited by Brigadier-General George Bullen-Smith who approved their positions and told them to hold on where they were, as they could do no better. About 11.30 a.m., it became necessary to throw back the right flank of the Regiment in an attempt to keep in touch with the 17th Division. At this juncture, Richard Crosse sent the following message to the 5th Brigade. Despite the general chaos of the retreat, he was trying to co-ordinate an orderly withdrawal of the line.

> 2nd H.L.I. effected touch with 1st King's on right of 6th Infantry Brigade. A.A.A. Latter repelled some attacks, but are now reported to be falling back. A.A.A. 17th Division went back about an hour ago, so I have now refused my right so as to keep touch with them and cover retirement of 2nd H.L.I. and 6th Infantry Brigade from ridge O.9.d.00. Regimental H.Q. 0.9.d.24.

However, despite the 52nd's best efforts, this southern flank was soon well and truly in the air, and a gap had also opened up once more, to the north, between the 5th and 6th Brigades, where the enemy's infantry, light trench mortars and machine-guns had pushed through. Their untenable position was maintained until soon after 2 p.m., when orders were received for the 52nd to fall back on the Red Line, a shallow trench running on the hillcrest in front of Villers-au-Flos.

685 Major Rupert Brett.

There was to be a tank presence to attract the attention of the enemy. Whilst these orders of retirement were being disseminated, the Acting Adjutant Captain Ben Slocock received the gunshot wounds to both thighs from which he subsequently died[686]. Lieutenant Cyril 'Shiny' Horley took his place.

We left Captain George Field's B Company of the 52nd on the old German line running between Barastre and Rocquigny and to the south of the rest of the Regiment. Lieutenant Jim Neville took up their story again[687].

> Having settled into the new position, we came under machine gun fire from Rocquigny on our right, and our own 4.5 howitzers mistook us for the enemy and started shelling us. Here the Company, about 40 strong, stayed until Field determined to go and join up with the 63rd Division, which was digging in on the next ridge behind Barastre, since there was no sign of the 52nd. Every moment we expected to see the remaining companies appear. At midday there was still no sign of them. I went off to try and find out if any of the neighbouring troops had seen them, but all my enquiries proved fruitless.
>
> While I was in Barastre, looking for the Regiment, I saw the tanks go into action to cover our troops retreat. It was very interesting to watch. The Germans had several field guns in close support to their infantry, and as the tanks waddled over the crest of the ridge the German gunners knocked them out one after the other.
>
> In Barastre, I gleaned the news that the 2nd Division was fighting a rearguard in conjunction with the 19th, between Haplincourt and Villers-au-Flos. I delivered my information to Field, who, thereupon, decided to go back to Beaulencourt and await the 52nd there.

The main party of the 52nd with their Commanding Officer, Lieutenant-Colonel Richard Crosse, fell back on the Red Line, the hindermost line of the Rear Zone to the east of Villers-au-Flos, which was reached at 2.30 p.m. To the south, the Red Line ran to the west of Barastre and to the east of Rocquigny. In front of Villers-au-Flos, the Red line consisted of an unwired, wide, shallow trench, but elsewhere it was reputed only to consist of a notice board or a mark on a map! To their left [north] were the 24th R.F. and then the 2nd H.L.I of their own

[686] Captain Cyprien Henry Benson 'Ben' Slocock died of his wounds in hospital at Boulogne on April 3rd 1918. He had been Head of School at Radley when war broke out.
[687] Diary entry for March 24th 1918.

5th Brigade. Crosse rapidly organized his men, formed from the remnants of A, C, and D Companies, into a defensive position. The missing B Company was still well to the south. Almost immediately, it was clear that their positions in front of Villers-au-Flos were untenable, as both flanks were unprotected and the Germans were rapidly advancing towards them. Having paused for breath, the 52nd made an almost instantaneous departure, not before 3 p.m., to the south-west of Beaulencourt, on the Bapaume - Péronne road. Richard Crosse found the retirement through Villers-au-Flos to be reminiscent of their experiences in Bertincourt earlier in the morning. The D Company Commander, Captain David Barnes, described the scene in front of Villers-au-Flos[688].

> All the time the Germans could be seen advancing, but we made them take more than considerable care, though I was worried about small arms ammunition. I must say that all the men in my sector behaved with great gallantry. There was not the slightest panicking and we were very puzzled as to why we had to retreat in the early morning[689]. Then from behind us we saw some of our tanks coming up. They came to our very great relief and joy, and crossed our front line to go forward to the Germans.
>
> In front were two small woods[690]. From each of these the Germans brought out two small guns and started firing point blank at the tanks. One was immediately knocked out and set on fire. A second was incapacitated when about 100 yards in front of me. The men in it jumped out and rushed back suffering casualties. Then from the woods machine gun cross-fire started sweeping all along our line and the Germans came on in great numbers. We waited calmly for them to get within range and then opened fire on them, inflicting plenty of casualties. They were being followed up by plenty of supports and so they got within 100 yards of us. I gave the signal to retire. We all turned round and started to run as hard as we

---

688 It is not certain when this account was written by David Barnes. Possibly he wrote to Crosse from his prisoner-of-war camp in Germany. The account does not appear in the contemporary *Regimental Chronicle,* but it is included in articles written by Richard Crosse in the *Regimental Journals of 1938 and 1958.*

689 At face value this seems to be an extraordinary comment for an experienced company commander to make. Failure to withdraw from the vicinity of Bertincourt on the morning of March 24th would have led to annihilation of the 52nd.

690 The relevant trench map shows two woods in the correct area. The first joining the south-western side of Haplincourt and had 'large trees planted close'. The second joining the western side of Barastre and was described as a 'thick wood'. The remnants of both woods are still shown on current maps.

> could. As I jumped up I got struck in the front of my ankle with a bullet and dropped into a shell hole. The Germans were up within a minute and so my fighting ended.

Captain David Barnes had been awarded a well-deserved D.S.O. after the Battle of Arleux in 1917. Barnes was a considerable loss to the Regiment as he was an able and experienced company commander who was thought highly of by his Commanding Officer, Richard Crosse. Barnes was lucky to be taken alive by the Germans as his men had killed many of the enemy shortly before he was taken prisoner. Under these circumstances men were often summarily executed. Many men from Barnes' D Company were posted missing after the remnant of the Company was cut off in Villers-au-Flos. Only Lieutenant Harold 'Fritz' Eagle and twelve men had managed to escape. Amongst the missing was Lance-Serjeant Jack Ward, who had carried back to the British lines Barnes' predecessor as D company commander, Captain Ralph Kite, who had been mortally wounded at the Battle of the Ancre, in 1916. The body of Ward from Acton in London was never found.

We left Captain George Field's B Company to the south of the remnants of the other companies, intending to make their way to Beaulencourt. Field led them back to the Le Transloy - Péronne road where they found the 1st K.R.R.C. of the 99th Brigade digging in. Field put his men under the command of this Regiment, and they proceeded to dig in for the third time that day on a ridge commanding the Bapaume - Péronne road. It was an area that the men had come to know well during their rests in divisional reserve during the last four months.

One of the most unpleasant features of this phase of the withdrawal was the pitiful sight of the wounded. Lieutenant Jim Neville gave water from his own water-bottle to a tank officer who was still operating his tank, this despite the fact that he was so badly burnt that the skin of his face hung around his neck like some macabre Elizabethan ruff. The poor man's hands were so raw that Neville had to hold the water bottle to his lips for him to drink. Wounded men from other units begged to be carried back to the Albert - Bapaume road, but they had to be refused as B Company's stretcher bearers were already fully occupied with their own men. One brave man with a shattered ankle set off dragging his ankle rather than fall into the enemy's hands.

At 5 p.m., when the Germans were in the outskirts of Le Transloy, B Company saw a small column of about 80 men, led by Richard Crosse and Rupert Brett, wearily marching up the slope. It was the first time since earlier in the morning that they had seen most of their comrades. Now all the survivors of the 52nd were together again.

From the south-west of Beaulencourt towards the outskirts of Le Transloy, all the available troops of the 5th and 6th Brigades began to prepare a new position with the 2nd H.L.I., 52nd, and units of the 6th Brigade stationed from north to south. The 24th R.F. had proceeded to Martinpuich independently. The two Brigadier-Generals of the 5th and 6th Brigades, G.M. Bullen-Smith and R.K. Walsh respectively, met and decided that, in view of the imminent risk of encirclement from the south, the retiral must continue immediately. At 5.45 p.m., this was done and the 5th Brigade was concentrated, and withdrew under the cover of dusk across the old Somme battlefields to Ligny-Thilloy. There an outpost line covering the village would be taken up later in the evening. During this latest retiral the 52nd acted as rearguard.

B Company were delegated to be the rear party of the 52nd, making them the very last troops to leave Beaulencourt which was now ablaze. Far on the left, at a distance of 2,000 or 3,000 yards, was a German column marching in the same direction as the 52nd. Neither side took any notice of the other! In the brilliant evening sunshine, the country over which they marched was full of old shell holes which were covered by grass and weeds. The exhausted troops constantly fell into the shell holes which were difficult to see and with the coming of dusk the last few miles seemed interminable. Eventually, at around 7 p.m., the 52nd halted at Ligny-Thilloy and the men had one hour's rest by the roadside. Never had a ditch seemed so soft and sleep came upon them as soon as they threw themselves down.

At 10 p.m., ammunition was distributed and the 52nd moved into the outpost line between the 24th R.F. and the 2nd H.L.I. The 6th Brigade continued the line on the right of the Highlanders, with the 99th Brigade still further to the right. To the left of the Fusiliers was the 19th Division. Earlier, the line had been partially dug by the available companies of Field Engineers. It was held by independent posts rather than as a continuous trench. The intention was to hold part of a line, from Ligny-Thilloy to High Wood, approximately one mile east of and parallel to the Albert - Bapaume road. The night was bitterly cold after the warmth of a beautiful spring day, and a freezing wind made life even more unpleasant for the 52nd. Miraculously, rations came up during the night, 'lunch' was taken and this consisted of only tea mixed with tobacco and boiled water. The shell hole water was much better than that brought up in petrol cans, as the latter proved to be one part petrol to three parts water. The hot tea did as much as anything to restore all ranks.

So March 24th 1918 came to an end. Richard Crosse later described it as the worst day of the whole war and Jim Neville looked upon it as the longest day of his life. Neville estimated that they had covered about eighteen miles in all, much of it under fire. The casualties suffered by the 52nd that day were: two other ranks known to have been killed; wounded, Captain Ben Slocock [he subsequently died from gunshot wounds to both thighs], Second-Lieutenant Harry Vernon a wild Irishman [gunshot wound right shoulder], 28 other ranks; missing, Captain David Barnes [gunshot wound ankle and became a prisoner-of-war], Second-Lieutenant Walter Bailey [assumed dead aged nineteen years], 23 other ranks[691]. Among the missing was Lance-Corporal F. Hubbard of C Company who had been taken prisoner, but would manage to escape and return to British lines on April 26th. In truth the losses of the 52nd were remarkably light under the circumstances. In later years Richard Crosse reflected on this March 24th and, as was his custom, looked at it in terms of the Peninsular War of a hundred years or so before. His ancestor John Cross [no e] who had served with distinction under the Duke of Wellington, had written a book[692]. For Richard Crosse, one paragraph in particular seemed to sum up the performance of his young officers of the 52nd in this later war on that fateful spring day.

> It may happen a little confusion in sounds or in orders may take place, and the officers commanding Companies may not know what to do: in this case they must be directed by their own judgement, and the general style of manoeuvring going on; but there can be no reason why each Company individually should not be kept perfectly in hand and in good order by the officer commanding it.

Thus did the captains of companies handle the situation on March 24th 1918. As Richard Crosse recorded in the *Battalion War Diary* 'the handling of companies and platoons by their officers' was beyond all praise'.

At 2 a.m. March 25th, the 52nd's rest was rudely interrupted when a mysterious order came to vacate the Ligny-Thilloy position and for the 5th and 6th Brigades to march down the main Albert - Bapaume road[693]. The march via Le Barque on to the main road was a silent one as it was rumoured that the enemy was in their rear and, in which case, they might be cut off. On reaching the Albert - Bapaume road there was a 30 minute halt for the 6th Brigade to catch up. The sky in the east had a streak of grey as the 52nd passed the Butte de Warlencourt,

---

691 This figure is given by Richard Crosse in the *Battalion War Diary.* The entry for March 24th, in the *Regimental Chronicles,* is 30 missing other ranks.

692 *A System of Drill and Manoeuvres as practiced by the 52nd Light Infantry* by Captain John Cross. Published 1823.

693 It is not clear where the order came from. Major-General Cecil Pereira, in his account, merely stated that the 5th and 6th Brigades retired at 5 a.m. Perhaps the local commanders considered their positions untenable.

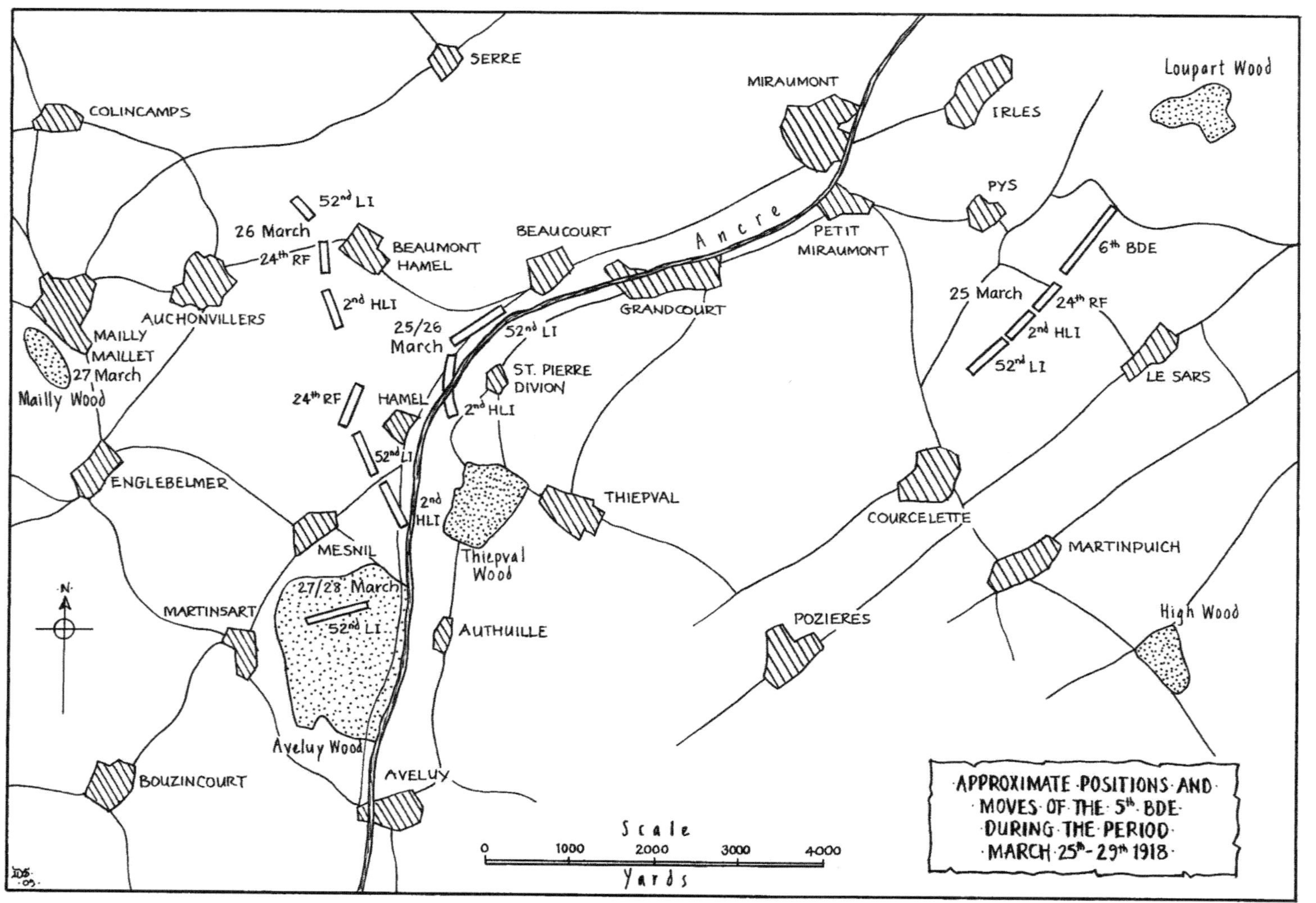
SERRE
COLINCAMPS
MIRAUMONT
IRLES
Loupart Wood
52nd LI
26 March
24th RF
BEAUMONT HAMEL
BEAUCOURT
Ancre
PYS
PETIT MIRAUMONT
6th BDE
25 March
24th RF
2nd HLI
52nd LI
AUCHONVILLERS
MAILLY MAILLET
27 March
Mailly Wood
2nd HLI
25/26 March
52nd LI
GRANDCOURT
ST. PIERRE DIVION
LE SARS
24th RF
HAMEL
2nd HLI
52nd LI
ENGLEBELMER
2nd HLI
Thiepval Wood
THIEPVAL
COURCELETTE
MARTINPUICH
MESNIL
27/28 March
52nd LI
MARTINSART
AUTHUILLE
POZIERES
High Wood
N
Aveluy Wood
BOUZINCOURT
AVELUY
Scale
0 1000 2000 3000 4000
Yards
APPROXIMATE POSITIONS AND MOVES OF THE 5th BDE DURING THE PERIOD MARCH 25th - 29th 1918

an old burial mound which projected like a pimple from the ridge. The march along the road was easy after the weed-covered shell holes of the previous day. It was galling to pass the well-known landmarks which had been taken with such a great loss of life in 1916-17. In 1917, the Regiment had actually repaired the road they were now marching down. At Courcelette the 52nd wheeled off the road into the ruined village. Here they met Brigadier-General George 'Humpty Dumpty' Bullen-Smith, their brigade commander. Lieutenant Jim Neville described the scene[694].

> Meanwhile, the poor old Brigadier was in a state of collapse. We had passed him on entering Courcelette, sitting on a blasted tree stump holding his head in his hands. Each Company had marched at attention, but he was far too weary to rise up and take the salute. Behind him, stood the Brigade-Major, looking like death; in this state, I saw the Brigade Staff for the first and last time, during these operations!

The 48-year-old Bullen-Smith was an exhausted and broken man who would shortly be sent home to England for six months. In fact that very day, the 25th, Major-General Cecil Pereira noted that Bullen-Smith was 'played out' and brought him back to the 2nd Division's Headquarters, giving the temporary command of the 5th Brigade to Lieutenant-Colonel Robert Pipon of the 24th R.F. However, the whereabouts of the 24th R.F. was unknown and 'it was impossible to contact him'! This took place at 7.30 p.m. and at 4.33 a.m. on the 26th, a by now frantic Brigade-Major asked Lieutenant-Colonel Richard Crosse to take command of the 5th Brigade. The anxiety of the poor Brigade-Major is quite palpable in the *Brigade War Diary's* entries. Crosse's interregnum was short-lived as Pipon resurfaced at about 7.30 a.m. on the 26th[695]. Several months later, Bullen-Smith confided in the wounded Jim Neville that 'a general should never be separated from his horse'. No doubt he was recalling the March retreat!

Bullen-Smith's sudden replacement was not to be the end of the poor man's indignities. An unauthorized car taking him to Amiens was stopped by the Military Police. Bullen-Smith and another officer, Lieutenant-Colonel Gregory

---

694 Diary entry for March 25th 1918.

695 Bullen-Smith, according to another entry in the *5th Brigade War Diary,* did not leave for the 2nd Division until 12.15 a.m. on the 28th. However, Pipon was officially in command of the Brigade from March 25th, despite his absence. In July 1944, Bullen-Smith's son, Charles, would be sacked from the command of the 51st Highland Division by Field-Marshal Bernard Montgomery in Normandy.

Knight of the 2nd H.L.I.[696], who was also being sent home to England, were locked up for several hours as spies! Major-General Cecil Pereira's troubles with the unauthorized Rolls Royce continued until June and, as he put it, 'metaphorically I had my trousers down to receive the rebuke of the Adjutant General for a gross irregularity'. The car was seized and Pereira was concerned that the cost of petrol and tyres would be taken from his private bank account, backdated to 1914! In the end he escaped by stating that the numerous changes in the staff of the 6th Brigade since the discovery of the car precluded finding out the cause of the impropriety and, in any case, higher authority had known about it since 1914.

From Courcelette the 5th Brigade turned northward and the 52nd was able to have a hot breakfast during a two-hour halt in Dyke Valley. Before falling out, Lieutenant-Colonel Richard Crosse formed the Regiment up in line and called it to attention. The 52nd had gone into action on March 23rd weak in numbers, and the trials of the last two days had further depleted their ranks. Consequently, Crosse temporarily reorganized his Companies: A and B became No. 1 Company under Captain George Field, and C and D became No. 2 Company under Captain Percy Bobby. Then Crosse said, 'when you fall out, I want to see every man get some wood and drum up at once'. Almost immediately equipment was thrown down, wood collected, and fires were going everywhere. By 7.15 a.m., everyone had had the hot meal mentioned earlier and most of the men were in a deep sleep.

At 8.45 a.m., the 52nd took up a strong position, facing east, along the ridge from Courcelette - Pys, overlooking Dyke Valley, and with commanding views over Le Sars and part of the Albert - Bapaume road. The position was about three-quarters of a mile north-west of the road. It was an excellent position, and the 6th Brigade continued the line to the left, with a battery of 18-pounders behind the 52nd. In front, the 99th Brigade was fighting a rearguard action and the plan was for them to retire through the 5th Brigade during the late morning. The one weakness of the Regiment's position was that there was no British unit on their right, this leaving their flank in the air. Here the 52nd remained for some hours under long-range, but uncomfortably accurate, enemy machine-gun fire. Some excellent shooting at the enemy was undertaken, particularly by the Regiment's Lewis gunners. As one officer put it: 'like shooting up rabbits'. Jim Neville described this period[697].

---

[696] On the 27th, a divisional car arrived at an early hour at the Regimental Headquarters of the 2nd Highland Light Infantry with instructions for Knight 'to reconnoitre positions and lines of the Reserve system'. Presumably this was a 'cover' for his going home.
[697] Diary entry for March 25th 1918.

> Here, however, was excellent scope for good and controlled fire, and through field glasses I could see every movement of the enemy. Though we only held here for half an hour, we had some good fun bringing down the enemy as they advanced across the open from Le Sars towards Courcelette. The Boches are no fools; they were well trained and made excellent use of ground and cover, and never exposed themselves unnecessarily. Their first consideration was, always, to manoeuvre the light machine guns forward, to cover the advance of the rest. Through my glasses, I picked up a man carrying one of these guns, and directed my Lewis gun on to him; that man never carried that or any other gun again! It was almost impossible to miss the enemy from this commanding position, and our Lewis guns were doing good execution and holding up the enemy's advance, when we, once again, received orders to retire, because the enemy, as was his cunning way, was crawling around our flanks.

By 1.30 p.m., all the troops ahead of the 52nd had withdrawn through them and shortly before 3.30 p.m. orders were received to fall back on the Pys-Miraumont line. The intention of the 2nd Division was that the retiral should be carried out in a leap-frog fashion across the once 'Promised Land' of 1917 towards Auchonvillers. It seemed clear that the enemy would advance up the valley of the Ancre. The Regiment set off across the Somme Plateau, past the ruins of Pys and retired from ridge to ridge, always with the German enemy on their heels and both of their flanks continually exposed. Later, in the absence of information or further orders, Lieutenant-Colonel Richard Crosse in conjunction with Lieutenant-Colonel Gregory Knight of the 2nd H.L.I., moved their battalions towards the River Ancre. For Major-General Cecil Pereira, commanding the 2nd Division, the moment of the 'worst depression' was when he heard that there had been practically no stay on the Pys line. Rapidly, he sent instructions for his brigades to hold the Old British Front Line, west of Beaumont Hamel and the crossings of the Ancre. This was done to gain time for reinforcing divisions to come up. His relief was 'unbounded' when he heard that this had been done.

Pereira's day had its moment of comedy when his aid, Lieutenant Frederick 'Bolo' Lowndes of the 52nd, was sent in a car with supplies to set up a new mess. In Albert, Lowndes ran into another member of the Divisional Staff who was in an excitable state over several cases of 'secret documents'. Jettisoning the rations he took the 'secret documents' to the new Divisional Headquarters, only to discover that they consisted of a lot of rubbish including very old *Vie Parisiennes.* Poor Lowndes was chastised for his mistake and the 2nd Division's Major-General and his Headquarters' Staff went hungry that night.

Eventually, a little after 6 p.m., the 52nd reached the eastern [left] bank of the Ancre opposite Beaucourt-sur-Ancre and here the second meal of the day, tea, was taken. Whilst tea was being devoured, British machine-gunners on the heights above Beaucourt, thinking that the 52nd was the enemy, opened fire on them. Fortunately their shooting was so poor that no one was hit and in any case all ranks were too exhausted to take any notice of them. Amazingly, the Regimental Transport managed to get rations to their men all through the retreat. Some less fortunate Regiments starved. One man, watching as the 52nd descended to the Ancre, recorded his impressions of them at this depressing moment[698]. It is remarkable that the Regiment showed such extraordinary discipline on the march in such trying circumstances. All ranks had been well trained in the traditions of the Light Infantry and their morale was excellent.

> The 2nd Oxfordshire Light Infantry and the 2nd H.L.I. retired a considerable time after the troops on their flanks had done so. The latter were lining the western slopes of the Ancre valley when troops were seen moving slowly in perfect artillery formation towards Beaucourt. It was considered that they must be German as it was thought that no British troops could, at this stage of the retreat, be in a fit state to maintain such fine march discipline. As they drew nearer it was possible, with glasses, to ascertain that they were British - they were the 52nd and the Highland Light Infantry.

At dusk, the 52nd led by Richard Crosse forded the river and took up a position between Beaucourt and Hamel. Here, on the heights above Beaucourt, on the western or right side of the Ancre, the Regiment pushed out guards to protect the ford plus two bridges across the river. After the events of the last three days it was a novel experience to have friendly forces on both flanks. Thus ended an exhausting day, one to be followed by a freezing cold night, as the wind whistled over the river from the direction of Thiepval. Their dug-outs had not been used recently and they were damp and musty. What was particularly depressing was the fact that they were occupying the same trenches that had been held by the Regiment in 1916. Jim Neville estimated that the 52nd had covered about fifteen miles during the day and Richard Crosse reflected on the day's losses. Nineteen men had been wounded and a further nineteen were missing,

---

[698] Quoted by Richard Crosse in his article of 1958 in the *Regimental Journal.* He does not record who the individual was.

most of the casualties having occurred on vacating the Courcelette - Pys ridge earlier in the day[699]. Amongst the wounded was Second-Lieutenant George Ashplant [gunshot wound right arm and left knee] who was attached to the 5th Trench Mortar Battery.

March 26th was a particularly difficult day for the 2nd Division, as the IV Corps, on their left, had melted away and their flank was now completely open. Fortunately, they were in contact with the 63rd Division on their right. In the early morning of this cold, foggy day, the 52nd came under the orders of the 6th Brigade, who ordered a withdrawal from the river crossings to a better position in the old British trenches. At one stage, B Company, as part of No. 1 Company, received orders to retire to Auchonvillers, but half-way there they met Major Rupert Brett who cancelled the orders and sent them back to their starting point. Erroneously, Brett had been told that Auchonvillers was reputed to be in German hands. Their journey back was enlivened by British 8-inch shells falling on the road at Beaucourt. Sensibly, the men took a short cut away from the road. No. 1 Company tried to improve their positions, but a British plane proceeded to shoot them up, fortunately without injuring them. Later they took up another position in the old British front line prior to the advance at Beaumont Hamel in 1916. However, the 52nd's left flank was now completely exposed and the ford across the Ancre could not be seen from here, although the German enemy could be clearly viewed wandering around on Thiepval ridge. Eventually the enemy would slip around the exposed left flank of the 5th Brigade beyond Hébuterne.

Within one and a half hours of arriving in their new position, enemy patrols entered the trench opposite. At 2 p.m. serious shelling of the 52nd took place and lasted for two hours. By this stage all ranks were desperate for relief and, after dark, orders came that the Regiment would withdraw through the New Zealand Division and bivouac in Mailly Maillet Wood. In the early hours of the 27th, a bright moonlight night, this withdrawal was carried out, and the 5th Brigade Headquarters was set up in a house in Mailly Maillet that had been used as the Headquarters of the 52nd in the autumn of 1916. Three men were wounded and three further men were reported missing during the day[700]. On the night of March 26th/27th, the enemy took the town of Albert. However, the relief of the 2nd Division by the New Zealanders, plus the 4th Australian Division plugging the gap to their left, somewhat stabilized the situation.

---

[699] Figures given by Richard Crosse in the *Battalion War Diary.* The figure for the missing, on March 25th, given in the *Regimental Chronicles,* was 21 other ranks.

[700] Figures given by Richard Crosse in the *Battalion War Diary.* The figure for the missing, on March 26th, given in the *Regimental Chronicles* was one.

In the early hours of March 27th, shells began to fall into the bivouac of the 52nd and a withdrawal of about 500 yards was made in the direction of Beaussart. At 7 a.m. permission was given for the Regiment to move to Boltun Camp, in the vicinity of the Bois Dauvillers, where a cold and generally miserable day was spent. Very little rest was forthcoming for the twelve officers and less than 200 men of the 52nd who were considered still to be fit for action. At 8 p.m., the 5th Brigade was ordered forward to support a brigade of the 12th [Eastern] Division in the vicinity of Martinsart. The 12th Division was a fresh one and was supposed to be holding the line of the Ancre. However, it was gradually being driven back, exposing the 2nd Division's positions. The 5th Brigade set off with their Brigadier-General[701] and the Regimental Headquarters at the head of the main body of troops. The march via Mailly Maillet, Englebelmer to Martinsart was an irritating one with constant checks. A long halt was made at Martinsart Château while the regimental commanders received instructions from the Headquarters of the 188th Brigade of the 63rd [Royal Naval] Division which the 5th Brigade had now been instructed to relieve[702].

Martinsart Château was a pleasant, beautifully furnished, little-damaged country house in a valley close to the road. Shortly afterwards it was destroyed completely by shellfire. A staff officer was sent out to ascertain the identity of the troops at the Château's gates. He inquired in the dark: 'who are you?' 'The Fifty second', came the quick reply from the ranks, in a tone more defiant than discrete. The Staff Officer returned to the Château to report there was halted outside: 'a battalion of light infantry, very weak in numbers, very strong in spirit, that called itself the Fifty second'[703]. Guides took the 52nd from the Château to their new positions in Aveluy Wood. On the way, there were numerous short halts, where the exhausted men fell asleep almost where they stood. So, by short stages, the Regiment made their way to Aveluy Wood where a battalion of the 63rd Division was relieved. The 52nd was positioned 500 yards from the wood's northern exits, and faced south. They had covered about ten miles in the last 24 hours.

The remainder of the night was quiet, but the next day the enemy attacked and broke the line, near Hamel, between the 6th East Kent and the 7th Sussex, both of the 12th Division. As usual the Germans pushed their light machine-guns well forward and inflicted heavy casualties on the Sussex. The position was only restored by a company of the 24th R.F. supported by the

[701] This is likely to have been the acting commander of the 5th Brigade, Lieutenant-Colonel Robert Pipon.

[702] The 12th Division was holding the long V Corps front, with the 63rd Division attached to it in support.

[703] This story was told to Richard Crosse by Major-General Henry Davies, with great satisfaction, some months later.

composite No. 1 and No. 2 Companies of the 52nd under Captains George Field and Percy Bobby respectively. They drove out the machine-gunners and captured some prisoners, including one man who had a British soldier's jacket under his own. Major-General Cecil Pereira of the 2nd Division, was scathing about the performance of the fresh troops of the 12th Division, some of whose brigades in the line, he had had to take over command of. He wrote forcibly to Lieutenant-General Edward Fanshawe of V Corps to complain about his own exhausted troops having to relieve men of this fresh division. His view of the parlous state of his men was reinforced by reports from the medical officers of all three battalions in the 5th Brigade, 'stating that the men were in a condition of exhaustion'.

In the afternoon of the 28th, the shelling of Aveluy Wood increased considerably and, after some casualties, the Regimental Headquarters was forced to move to gun pits near the edge of the wood on the Martinsart - Mesnil road. The enemy made a further minor attack which was completely repulsed. On the 28th, the casualties were: Captain George Field [slightly by a gunshot wound to his right hand], Lieutenant H.J. Ellam [seriously by a gunshot wound to his left thigh] and sixteen other ranks. Field was replaced in command of No. 1 Company by Lieutenant Tom Tyrwhitt-Drake.

During the very wet night of March 28th/29th, a side-step northward was ordered to be carried out by dawn to relieve the 6th East Kent. This was reconnoitred, carried out and completed by 4 a.m. Fortunately, the day, Good Friday, passed quietly as all ranks of the 52nd were exhausted, but few of them were able to rest. At night the Regiment was relieved by Z Company of the 10th D.C.L.I. [Pioneers] and withdrew to billets in and about Hedauville. There were no battle casualties on the 29th. The next day the 52nd marched the short distance west to the next village, Varennes, where Lieutenant Jim Neville who was seriously ill with food poisoning was sent down to Martinsart before being transported to hospital in Doullens by ambulance[704]. The unfortunate young man had found and eaten a half-opened tin of bully beef four days before. He was lucky not to die of the effects. The repose of the 52nd was disturbed by two shells falling into Varennes. On March 30th, the trench strength of the 52nd had risen to 17 officers and 314 other ranks.

[704] Neville recalled sitting in the latrine on a bucket and vomiting between his legs at the same time. Later, he became jaundiced. Neville was bitterly hurt by erroneous rumours that he had eaten the contaminated food deliberately to make himself ill. One of the 52nd's officers told his sister Angela that he had wangled his evacuation to England because his spirit was as yellow as his complexion. This was a cruel fallacy.

Reinforcements had begun to arrive for the 2nd Division and rather than being sent to their intended battalions, they were formed into a Composite Battalion under Colonel D.M. Murray-Lyon, late of the 2nd H.L.I., now of the 1st King's. Lieutenants Frederick Lowndes and John Murray commanded the 52nd's contingent and went into the line with it on the night of March 30th/31st. On March 31st, Easter Day, Major Rupert Brett, the 52nd's second-in-command, left the 52nd to take command of the 1st Royal Berkshire in the 99th Brigade. Brett was yet another great loss to the Regiment with his boisterous laughter and general gaiety which coupled with Richard Crosse's magnetism, did much to foster the esprit de corps of the 52nd[705]. Major Guy Blewitt, now an extra G.S.O. 2 with VII Corps rode over to Varennes to see the 52nd. He recorded: 'I was delighted to find Richard Crosse, Whitters, and "Twit" [sic] Drake all flourishing and the Regt. had had comparatively light casualties since March 21st'[706].

At 5 a.m. April 1st, acting on orders received late the night before, the 52nd stood to arms in anticipation of a further German attack which never came. Later in the day, the 52nd replaced the left company of the Composite Battalion in the line, marching from Varennes via Hédauville and Englebelmer. During the day, Lieutenant Frederick 'Bolo' Lowndes, who had given up his position as A.D.C. to Major-General Cecil Pereira of the 2nd Division to volunteer for front line duty, was slightly wounded. As one of his colleagues recorded 'his devotion was rewarded with a wound in the ankle which took him back to England'. The 2nd and 3rd proved to be quiet, uneventful and fine days. At about midnight on the 3rd, the 52nd was relieved by the 1/28th London [Artists' Rifles] and withdrew once more into Varennes. At 2.30 p.m. the following day, the Regiment, as part of the 5th Brigade, marched via Acheux-en-Amienois - Louvencourt - Marieux - Sarton. Their comfortable billets had previously been occupied by the Regiment in September and October 1916. That great stalwart of the Regiment, Lieutenant-Colonel Cuthbert 'Bingo' Baines, now commanding the 2/7th King's, visited them in their billets in Sarton. The 93rd reinforcement of 98 other ranks joined the 52nd. On April 5th, the Regiment marched from Sarton - Orville - Halloy - Lucheux - Le Souich and was billeted in the latter place. That same day Brigadier-General W.L. Osborn of the Royal Sussex Regiment assumed command of the 5th Brigade in place of Brigadier-General G.M. Bullen-Smith who was now in England.

[705] Two months later, on June 5th, a shell landed at his feet when he was leading a party consisting of his adjutant and four company commanders to reconnoitre a new position in the Ayette sector. He was the sole survivor of that party and although his shattered legs were saved, in later life they well-nigh crippled him.

[706] Diary entry for March 31st 1918. 'Whitters' was Ernest Whitfeld and 'Twit' [sic] Thomas Tyrwhitt-Drake.

The date April 5th brought to a close the First Battles of the Somme, 1918. They were officially deemed to have taken place from March 21st until April 5th. The 52nd was entitled to this as a battle honour and, in addition, also to others for the Battle of St. Quentin [March 21st-23rd] and the First Battle of Bapaume [March 24th-25th], both sub-divisions of the First Battles of the Somme, 1918. From March 21st-April 5th, the 52nd had lost – Officers: killed or died of wounds, three; wounded, three; wounded and prisoner-of-war, one. Other ranks: killed, five; wounded, 64; missing, 52.

Numbers from all ranks received decorations for gallantry during the March retreat. Bars to the M.C. were awarded to Captains George Field and Laurence Fullbrook-Leggatt. The M.C. was awarded to Captain Percy Bobby. M.M.s were awarded to Serjeant A.C. Smith; Lance-Serjeants A.H. Bennett, M. Shepherd, W. Wallis; Corporal W.H. Smith; Lance-Corporals A. Bazeley, H. Jackson, S. Kirby [third recommendation], J.H. Lloyd, F. Smith, H. Smith; Privates A. Jeffs, W. Peace, H. Southern, A.E. Tinson.

The performance of the 52nd in their twenty miles [as the crow flies] retiral from Bertincourt, which in some respects resembled that from near Mons four years earlier, had been exemplary. Their Commanding Officer, Lieutenant-Colonel Richard Crosse, aided by the celestial presence of Sir John Moore, had enabled most of the Regiment to escape from their exposed position. Major-General Cecil Pereira, of the 2nd Division, recorded in his diary: 'I heard in a roundabout way that the 17th Divn are considered "IT" in the Corps, that we are in high favour that the 47th and 63rd are nowhere and the 12th in absolute disgrace'. Elsewhere he wrote about his Division:

> Rearguard actions are recognised to be the severest test of the fortitude and ability of professional soldiers; and where the majority of officers and men have never known what it is to have 'a flank in the air', the moral and physical strain is greatly enhanced. Tired and unfit at the outset, the Division fought its way back with stubborn and unflinching courage; stopped to strike, then turned and limped back a few more miles; again and again would have stood at bay and held its ground, but for the restless tide to right and left, and the monotonous order to withdraw and to keep touch; till at last the men believed they were playing a part in an ingenious plan to lure the enemy into a fatal trap.

All this applied in equal measure to the 52nd Light Infantry during the long retreat back to Aveluy Wood. It has to be recognized that the advancing

Germans showed great skill; rapid mobility; enveloping movements; patrols that signalled immediately on discovering British positions; light machine-guns instantly in action; trench mortars with hand-carts of ammunition; aeroplanes that dropped lights to mark sites for the artillery. They were most worthy opponents.

Chapter XXI

The Hamelincourt and Ayette Sectors.

April 6th - August 20th 1918

[Map: page 574.]

The Germans were all too aware that their time of manpower superiority was fast running out with American Divisions beginning to come on line. Any chance that they had of winning the war was slipping away. No sooner had Operation Michael been closed down with its limited gains, the failure to take Amiens particularly rankling, than they attacked again in the north. During the period April 9th-29th the Germans assaulted across the plains of Flanders at what became known as the Battle of the Lys. This was followed by an attack on the French in the Champagne from May 27th-June 6th, who were forced back to Château-Thierry and Villers-Cotterêts. In mid-July, the French counter-attacked in the Battles of the Marne, 1918. Although some British Divisions were involved in these battles it was a predominantly French operation. During the four months from April 6th-August 8th, the beginning of the Battle of Amiens, the British Divisions undertook a plan of active defence whilst to replenish their numbers recruits were brought across the Channel and these men were trained for battle conditions.

The 52nd Light Infantry spent the first fortnight of April resting after the vicissitudes of the March retreat and in assimilating and training its reinforcements. There followed, as Lieutenant-Colonel Richard Crosse put it, 'a somewhat anxious month, one of many moves in parts of the line graded as quiet'. On April 6th, the Regiment marched out of Le Souich in a northerly direction via Ivergny - Beaudricourt - Estrée Wamin - Magnicourt and reached their destination at Gouy-en-Ternois. Their position was now north of Doullens and to the west of Arras and it was intended that the 52nd should spend the next week here. Second-Lieutenant E.K. 'Jimmy' Blyth returned from hospital having recovered from a fever and the 94th reinforcement of 62 other ranks arrived from base. The 7th was a quiet day and on the 8th four additional Lewis guns were distributed for anti-aircraft purposes, these to be manned by buglers and reserve transport drivers. The training of the new operators was to be undertaken as quickly as possible by the Lewis gun officer, Lieutenant Cyril 'Shiny' Horley.

At 2.30 p.m. April 9th, the 52nd was ordered to retrace its steps back to Le Souich and Brévillers. Here the men were distributed in billets between the two places. The following day Second-Lieutenants C.E. Barnes, F.W. Taylor and the 95th reinforcement of 268 other ranks joined the Regiment. Amongst the latter was Serjeant Rowe M.M. Lieutenant-Colonel Richard Crosse noted that the draft consisted mainly of inexperienced boys under the age of nineteen years, mostly

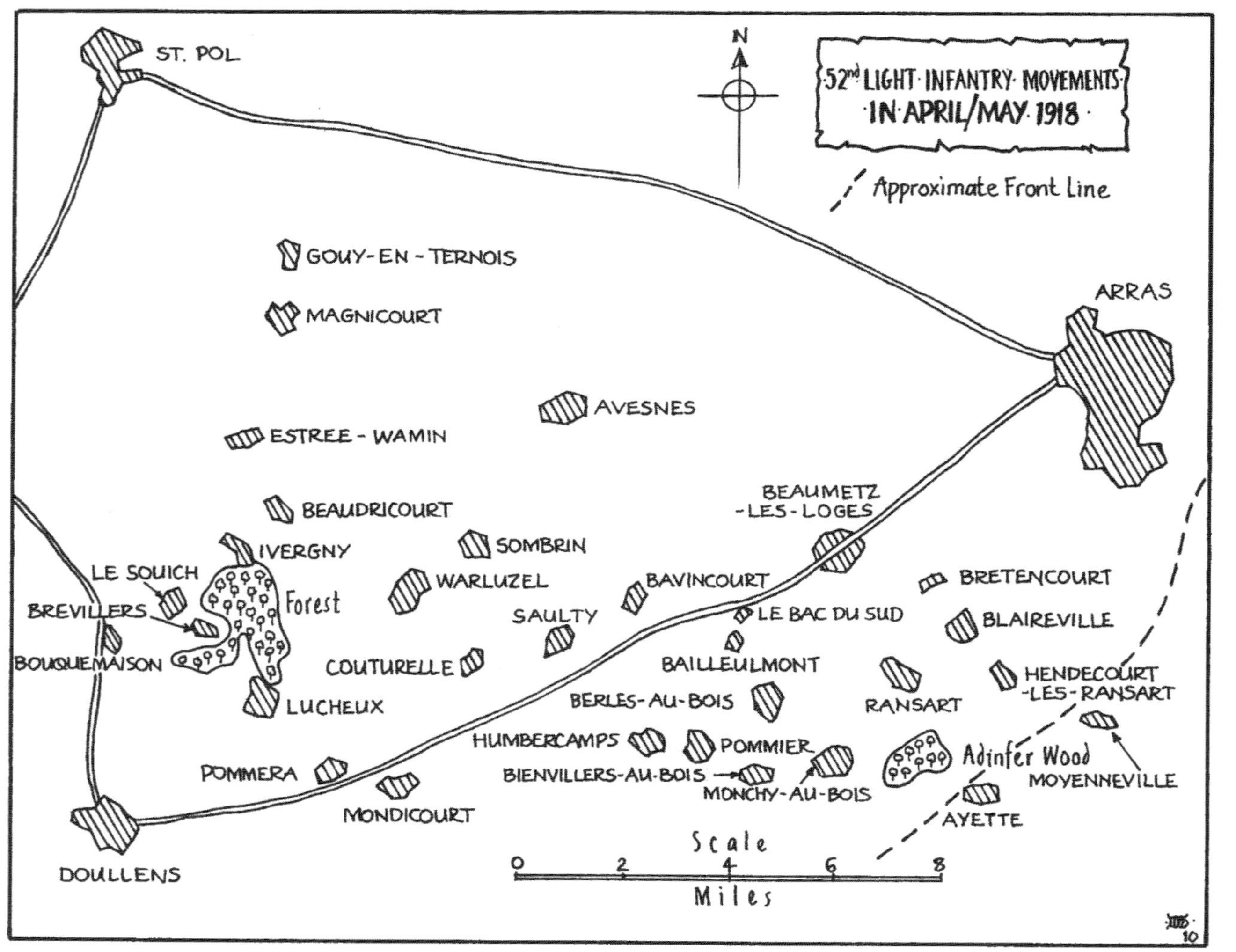
52nd LIGHT·INFANTRY·MOVEMENTS·
·IN·APRIL/MAY·1918·
N
Approximate Front Line
ST. POL
ARRAS
GOUY-EN-TERNOIS
MAGNICOURT
AVESNES
ESTREE - WAMIN
BEAUDRICOURT
BEAUMETZ
-LES-LOGES
SOMBRIN
IVERGNY
LE SOUICH
Forest
WARLUZEL
BAVINCOURT
BRETENCOURT
BREVILLERS
SAULTY
LE BAC DU SUD
BLAIREVILLE
BOUQUEMAISON
COUTURELLE
BAILLEULMONT
HENDECOURT
-LES-RANSART
LUCHEUX
BERLES-AU-BOIS
RANSART
HUMBERCAMPS
POMMIER
Adinfer Wood
POMMERA
BIENVILLERS-AU-BOIS
MONCHY-AU-BOIS
MOYENNEVILLE
MONDICOURT
AYETTE
DOULLENS
Scale
0 2 4 6 8
Miles

from the counties of Oxfordshire and Buckinghamshire. Unfortunately a number of the new recruits were measles contacts and Crosse wisely decided to segregate them from the Regiment. He received permission to set up a duplicate second battalion to be known as the 2/52nd and it was to be commanded by Captain Victor Martin[707] with Second-Lieutenant C.R. Crosley as Adjutant. The band which had been inherited from the 6th Battalion was added to this temporary unit. Crosse with his encyclopaedic knowledge of Regimental history, recalled that there had previously been a second battalion from 1804-16, when it finally became the 96th Foot. The 2/52nd was segregated at the nearby village of Bouquemaison. The new battalion officially remained in being until May 10th and rejoined the rest of the Regiment on May 17th at Saulty. The *Battalion War Diary* does not record if anyone actually developed the measles.

In the morning of April 11th, a commanding officer's parade took place with the 2/52nd returning from their billets for the occasion. In the afternoon, the 52nd marched in a south-easterly direction from Le Souich to good billets in Mondicourt, which was situated just to the south of the Arras to Doullens road. Their route took them through Lucheux, where each company used the baths, and Pommera. The next day Crosse took his company commanders to reconnoitre an outpost line to the south-west of Arras, in front of Hamelincourt between Boyelles and Moyenneville. It was currently held by the Guards Division and the 5th Brigade was due to take over part of it. The Purple Line and reserve line, Hendecourt-lès-Ransart, and in front of Blaireville[708] were also inspected. During the same day, the 52nd moved to billets in Saulty and also bivouacked in the park there. Saulty with its seventeenth century château lay a little to the north of the Arras - Doullens road and halfway between the two places.

At 2.30 p.m. April 13th, the 52nd left Saulty following the main road to Arras as far as Beaumetz-lès-Loges. Tea was taken at Le Bac du Sud and the Rearward Services were dispatched to Bailleulmont. From Beaumetz the Regiment marched via Bretencourt and Blaireville, before A and C Companies occupied part of the Purple Line relieving the 2nd Coldstream. The remainder of the 52nd occupied huts along the Blaireville - Hendecourt-lès-Ransart road. Unfortunately a heavy Royal Artillery Battery was situated close by and the enemy's attempts to destroy it led to rapid moves away from the area so that some rest might be obtained. The next day was very cold and B and D Companies exchanged positions with A and C at night. On the 15th two men were gassed and

[707] Martin had been acting as second-in-command of the 52nd until George Field could come up from Base.

[708] Spelt on French maps without the first e. On British trench maps it is spelt Blaireville.

the following day the 52nd moved into the part of the Brigade's front outpost line and two more men were wounded.

On April 17th, Richard Crosse narrowly escaped being taken prisoner whilst trying to follow the poorly delineated front outpost line. Crosse and Bugler Osborne ran into two N.C.O.s from A Company who were also out reconnoitring, and the whole party suddenly found themselves amongst some German posts. Firing followed and the party split into pairs. Bugler Osborne and Lance-Corporal Young were captured but Crosse and his companion safely found their way back to the British line. During the day, one man was killed, one died of his wounds and two more men were wounded. Second-Lieutenant C.F. Beeson joined on the 19th and, after a comparatively quiet six days in the line, the 52nd was relieved on the 22nd by the 24th R.F.

The 52nd's *Battalion War Diary* does not make it clear where the Regiment spent its period of relief, but it was back in the line on April 25th with its Headquarters at Boisleux-au-Mont. In this area the front line was continuous and the trenches quite good. On the 26th, notification of Lance-Corporal Hubbard's escape from German hands reached the Regiment. He had been captured on March 24th and a 2nd Division report recorded his experiences of a month in captivity.

> A N.C.O. of the 52nd Light Infantry, who was taken prisoner at Bertincourt last month, escaped to our lines on the front of the division on our left yesterday morning. He was employed at a German military veterinary school at Hordain, south of Denain. He was made to work on a forge of the school from 7 a.m. to 5.30 p.m. daily, and received one-fifth of a loaf and a little jam for breakfast and tea, and mangle-wurzels, or sometimes horse-flesh, for dinner. The food was too bad and insufficient for the amount of work that he was required to do. The German soldiers treated their prisoners very badly. French civilians were very good to British prisoners, but on one occasion a Frenchwoman was knocked down and kicked by three German soldiers for giving food to this N.C.O. Our aeroplanes have caused great loss amongst the already depleted transport of the Germans, and a bombing raid on Douai held up traffic for three days.

On April 28th, there was an intercompany relief of the men in the line. The next day saw an influx of officers from the Territorial Force which helped bring up the numbers lost in action. They were Lieutenants G.E. Pearson and J.P. Wayte M.C. and Second-Lieutenants C. Blick and E.A. Brown. The 52nd was relieved by the 24th R.F. on May 1st and moved back into Brigade reserve. During the relief, soon after 9 p.m., a party of eighteen guides under Captain Clement Chevallier left the Regimental Headquarters to proceed to the meeting point with the Fusiliers, at the bridge over the Cojeul River near Boisleux-au-Mont Station. Then they were subjected to some unpleasant shelling which killed three and wounded seven of the guides. Fortunately, despite a very dark night, there was little delay as the men of the 24th R.F. were familiar with the trenches they were to take over. Later Private Mount would receive a M.M. for his fine work in tending the wounded.

On May 3rd, the 52nd heard that Major-General Sir John Hanbury-Williams was to be the new Colonel of the Regiment in place of the recently deceased Major-General T.M. Bailie. The following day the 52nd went back into the line in place of the 2nd H.L.I. and there was considerable concern about a possible attack by the Germans. A section of the 6th Battalion of the Tank Corps was moved up in case the enemy made an assault. May 5th proved to be a quiet day, and part of the 2/52nd which was now out of isolation from measles returned to the Regiment and was billeted at Berles-au-Bois. The next day, having been inspected by Richard Crosse, those with full equipment joined their new companies in the line. At 9 p.m., the enemy attempted a raid on Captain Harold 'Fritz' Eagle's D Company and also on the 24th R.F. in the line to their left. By chance, in response to a false S.O.S. signal, the British put down a protective barrage. It was thought that a string of enemy lights had been mistaken for the signal. Both raids were beaten off, with the Germans taking some casualties, and further parties were discouraged from coming forward by the fortuitous barrage. One German's body was recovered inside the wire and his identity disc sent to the 2nd Division.

Earlier, at 4 p.m. May 6th, the Regimental Transport at Bailleulmont was inspected on behalf of Brigadier-General W.L. Osborn by Lieutenant-Colonel W.H. Greenley of the 2nd Division's Train. Greenley reported on the condition of the horses which were crucial for the resupply of the 52nd.

> The condition of the animals was generally fair. No less than 12 of them had been with the Battalion since 1914. They were clean and well groomed, except in one case which was pointed out by me. The shoeing was good. The harness was in good condition and the general fitting was correct. A few bits were too high in the mouth and there was no standard of fitting of the breechings[709]. These are

[709] Leather strap round shaft-horses' hind-quarters for pushing back.

minor faults easily remedied. --------------. The Transport generally shows signs of careful supervision and attention.

The relief of the 52nd on the evening of May 11th was delayed by a heavy gas bombardment in the vicinity of Blaireville. Eventually the relief by the 15th H.L.I. [32nd Division] was carried out. The 2nd Division, including the 52nd, was taken out of the line for rest and training. In the early hours of May 12th, the Regiment embussed at Blaireville and travelled back to Saulty where all ranks bivouacked in the village and park. Baths had been arranged to start at 9 a.m. for the whole of the 52nd. Unfortunately the arrangements broke down and there was a delay in the bathing until the Regiment used water from their own carts. Saulty was to be their home until June 7th. The next three and a half weeks were used to train up their new and inexperienced recruits to make them suitable for service in the front line. The Regimental Scouts were to be re-established in the manner of 1914 and their one serjeant, one corporal, and fifteen others were to be based at the Regimental Headquarters. The only difference from 1914 was that a further scout would be attached to each company's headquarters as 'Captain's observer'.

The training programme was to be drawn up and submitted weekly to the 5th Brigade. Training, under the supervision of the company commander, included bombing, the duties of an observer and semi-open warfare. The latter discipline was shortly to become extremely relevant. Early in the morning of May 15th, the Divisional Gas Officer's inspection of their box respirators, had almost finished when a message came through ordering them to carry out the 'Test Concentration' on the Arras to Doullens road. The Regiment was in position and ready to move by 1 p.m. On the 18th a Court of Enquiry was set up to consider the men who were missing on March 21st and the following days. Unfortunately, the *Battalion War Diary* makes no mention of its outcome.

On May 20th, Major-General Cecil Pereira, commanding the 2nd Division, inspected the companies while they were training and expressed dissatisfaction on several points. He raised three matters. Firstly, 'certain classes of instruction were working as such and not under platoon commanders'. Secondly, 'a platoon tactical exercise was not being carried out daily'. Thirdly, 'all training was to be carried out in steel helmets in future'. Pereira inspected the 52nd's billets and ordered that box respirators should be worn an hour daily until May 26th. This was done half an hour before breakfast and for half an hour after retreat. Bugle calls were used to indicate a gas attack. Presumably Pereira was concerned to see that the new recruits were familiar with their respirators when the real test came. Later, Brigadier-General W.L. Osborn, commanding the 5th

Brigade, judged the Transport Competition and then gave away the prizes. There were three classes: heavy draught pairs; light draught pairs; small horse turnout.

Captain John Blagrove joined the 52nd on May 22nd. The following day Lieutenant-General Aylmer Haldane, commanding the VI Corps, held a parade of the Brigade Group [5th, 6th, 99th] in the grounds of Saulty Château. On the 27th, Brigadier-General W.L. Osborn watched one of the 52nd's platoons carry out a tactical exercise in Saulty Park. Route marches were undertaken via the neighbouring villages of Couturelle - Warluzel - Sombrin.

The month of June opened with the 52nd still in billets in Saulty and bivouacked in the Château Park. June 2nd was a Sunday and it was possible to conduct a peace-time Church Parade. In the afternoon, bathing took place followed by the band playing in the Park. The next day the Regiment celebrated King George V's birthday. On the 4th, the 52nd conducted a practice Field Operation in the vicinity of Berles-au-Bois with Captain John Blagrove commanding the 52nd and Captain Harold Eagle's D Company playing the part of the enemy. In the evening a successful concert was organized by Captain Victor Martin. The following day the monthly sports' meeting was held with events both comic and serious. It was much enjoyed by all those who took part.

On June 6th, Richard Crosse, his company commanders: Captain C.E. Cope, A; Captain J. Blagrove, B; Captain P.A. Bobby, C; Captain H.S. Eagle, D; the Signalling Officer, Second-Lieutenant G.W. Shaw; the Officer Commanding the Sapping Platoon, Lieutenant J.B. Murray, reconnoitred the region of their new trenches in the vicinity of Adinfer Wood and thence towards Berles and Monchy. On the 7th, Lieutenant T.W.C. Foreshew returned to the Regiment from the 2nd Division and was made the Town Major at Pommier. The Regiment moved by the Light Railway from Chapel Dump Station at Saulty towards the line, intending to detrain at Monchy Siding. Unfortunately the third train carrying C Company had a truck derail, so that C and D Companies and part of the Regimental Headquarters had to march along the track to the rendezvous. Transport personnel with equipment such as cookers, which were required in the forward area, marched independently to this point. The 52nd relieved the 3rd Grenadier Guards in their positions near Adinfer Wood which they had previously reconnoitred. Initially the Rearward Services were split between Pommier and St. Amand. After 48 hours all these services were concentrated at Pommier.

About June 8th, influenza manifested itself in many members of the Regiment. A few cases had been seen in their time at Saulty, but now five officers and 60 other ranks had to be evacuated to hospital. Still more men were ill in their quarters and the effective strength of the 52nd was significantly reduced. The British were not the only ones to be suffering from the influenza pandemic, and their German foe were equally affected. A month later the Divisional commander, Major-General Cecil Pereira, referring to the enemy, wrote in his diary 'One rumour says the influenza has caused them so many casualties that they cannot do anything whilst it is raging'.

Apart from coming to terms with the influenza epidemic, the 52nd further reconnoitred their new area of action. On June 11th, the Regiment went into the front line near Adinfer Wood in place of the 2nd H.L.I., becoming the left front battalion, left brigade of the 2nd Division, right Division of VI Corps. In the front line was A Company on the right and D Company on the left, with B Company in Support and C Company in Reserve. The ground was undulating, and the front line was on the crest of a ridge, so that it was possible to walk behind it in the open. No man's land was wide here at about 800 yards. Post-war, Richard Crosse described this as 'a very untidy sector'. A number of enemy dead in no man's land were still unburied. Two of these bodies, very difficult to reach, yet near enough to make their presence particularly felt, were named 'Roger and Gallet' probably by Lieutenant Charles Colvill[710]. That night Colvill took out a patrol from A Company and brought back useful information on the state of the enemy's wire and positions. At 8.45 p.m. the following night, Captain Harold Eagle with Second-Lieutenant William Creak and two other ranks crawled from the British front line to make a reconnaissance. They were fired on and had to remain in a shell hole until it was dark enough for them to get back to their own lines.

The 52nd had been given notice, on June 13th, that an important patrol by two platoons would be undertaken on the night of June 17th/18th. Two platoons of D Company under Second-Lieutenant William Creak were selected to undertake the patrol and were withdrawn from the line to practice over taped ground on the 15th and 16th. Two platoons of C Company replaced them in the front line. Creak, in his early thirties, was older than his fellow subalterns although he fitted in well with them and was affectionately nicknamed 'The Old Firm'. The laying out of the practice tapes was supervised by a Royal Engineers' officer and by Brigadier-General W.L Osborn in person. The first few days were relatively quiet and some very active patrolling was undertaken both by Second-Lieutenant E.K. 'Jimmy' Blyth of D Company on the left, in preparation for the June 17th/18th patrol, and also by Lieutenant Charles Colvill of A Company on the right. During the day, on the 14th, a German messenger dog was unsuccessfully shot at before it escaped into a trench.

---

[710] Charles Colvill had a fine sense of humour. He and his fellow Irishman, Harry Vernon, were called the 'Kilkenny Cats' and they would keep the mess in fits of laughter.

The objectives of the minor operation, the raid to be carried out on the night of June 17th/18th, were to harass the enemy and to take prisoners from the German outpost line to the east of Adinfer Wood. The two platoons, No. 1 and No. 2, were to reach respectively the Ayette to Moyenneville road and the shell holes immediately to the north of them. On reaching its objective, each platoon was to 'left wheel' as if it was on the parade ground, before returning to its own lines! The whole operation was to last 45 minutes and covering fire was to be provided by the artillery, Stokes mortars and Vickers machine-guns. At zero hour the artillery would put down a straight barrage of 18-pounders and 4.5 howitzers, for two minutes on the outpost and main lines, followed by a box barrage for the remainder of the raid. The box barrage was intended to isolate the area under attack. Two Stokes mortars were to fire on the Ayette - Moyenneville road and its vicinity, with rapid fire for the first five minutes and thereafter one round per gun every two minutes, until the end of the raid. Two Vickers machine-guns from No. 2 Battalion of the Machine-Gun Corps were to fire along the flanks for the duration of the raid.

After the raid Lieutenant-Colonel Richard Crosse wrote a report.

> It is difficult to get a connected description of what occurred, but a summary of the results is as follows:-
>
> Identification obtained – NIL.
>
> Casualties – Wounded – 2nd Lieut. W.A. CREAK.
>
> 7 Privates.
>
> Missing – 4 Privates.
>
> There is evidence that some loss was inflicted on the enemy, but nothing to show that it was as great as the losses inflicted on us.
>
> Some time before and after ZERO hour a Machine Gun, said to be at A.2.b.10.40. [map reference] disturbed the forming up and subsequent movements of the party, causing our men to deviate to the right in advancing.
>
> Our barrage is described as good on the Left but poor on the Right. This was the view gained from outside Regtl. Headquarters also.
>
> While getting through the fairly thick wire in front of the line of shell holes, 2nd Lieut. CREAK was wounded in the eye and arm by a bomb.
>
> There was considerable bombing here and this largely appears to have caused our casualties.
>
> It does not appear that anyone reached the road.

> 7876. SGT. BENNETT, M.M.[711] and a party from both platoons must have done very well, and went along the line of the shell holes, driving Germans out of them. At least 5 dead were seen and reported. SGT. BENNETT shot one himself, one of his party is proved to have bayoneted another.
>
> The Germans were in considerable strength in their front system, to which they fell back from the shell holes.

Based on Lieutenant-Colonel Richard Crosse's report after the raid, Brigadier-General W.L. Osborn's account of it is to be found amongst the records of both the 5th Brigade and the 2nd Division.

> The raiders as arranged got out through their wire and lay down on the forward slope about 11.5 p.m. During this they appeared to have been seen by a forward German Post, and short bursts of M.G. fire were opened on them.
>
> At 11.35 p.m. when the barrage opened they advanced and came under close fire of one L.M.G.[712] which caused several casualties amongst the first platoon under 2nd Lieut. CREAK. The officer however led them forward, shooting a German on his way, but was wounded and put out of action by fragments of a bomb or shell when getting over some concertina wire.
>
> This party did not reach its objective on the AYETTE - MOYENNVILLE Road and had 11 out of total 12 casualties.
>
> The second party advanced and cleared their objective along the shell hole line, finding the Germans in shell holes between this line and our Front Line. Their leader SERGT. BENNETT accounted for several Germans by one of whom he was wounded with a bayonet in the knee as the German fell forward after being shot. L/CPL. WILSON also did good work with his leader - This party carried out their task well and as ordered.
>
> It is regretted that no identification was obtained, but there is no doubt that the Germans put up a good fight before clearing out, and Lieut. Col. CROSSE's estimate of 5 dead is within the mark. The enemy's system of changing his L.M.G.s from one shell hole position to another causes difficulty in making certain of them beforehand.

711 Lance-Serjeant A.H. Bennett.

712 Light Machine-Gun.

> Regarding casualties, seven out of 12 were from L.M.G. fire. One of the missing PTE. STOKES, crawled into our lines at 12 noon today so there are now three missing. Search will be made for these tonight.

Major-General Cecil Pereira, commanding the 2nd Division recorded his views on the morning after the raid.

> The Raiding Party of the 52nd Light Infantry made a most determined and courageous effort and I share their disappointment in not securing an identification.
>
> I congratulate them on the fine fighting qualities shown by Sgt Bennett's Party and on the casualties they know they inflicted on the Germans.

However well organized and courageously carried out the raid may have been, in the final analysis, it had failed in its single objective of obtaining the identification of the German unit facing them in the line. Serjeant A.H. Bennett later received a well-deserved bar to his M.M. Second-Lieutenant William Creak survived his wounds and lived to the ripe old age of 94 years. It is surprising that neither papers nor identity discs could be taken from any of the German bodies that the patrol had killed. To make matters worse, in all probability the 52nd suffered more casualties than they were able to inflict on the enemy. The raid can only be described as a failure.

On the night of June 18th, the 52nd sent out further patrols. Lieutenant C.E. Barnes of C Company took out a patrol and carefully searched the ground where the three men of the night before had vanished. There was no sign of them. Known as 'Church of England' or 'Sailor' Barnes, he preferred the command of a platoon and his second star had to be forced on him. 'More stars more trouble', he said. Also that night Second-Lieutenant F.W. Taylor went out on reconnaissance with two other ranks and on reaching the vicinity of the enemy's line encountered a German patrol which endeavoured to surround them. Rapid rifle fire was opened and the enemy retired in confusion.

On June 19th, the 52nd was relieved by the 24th R.F. and went back into reserve. Here the Regiment remained until the 23rd when it replaced the 2nd H.L.I. as the right battalion of the 5th Brigade to the east of Adinfer Wood. The Companies were distributed: A, left front; D, right front; C, support; B, reserve. On the 27th an inter-company exchange of positions allowed B and C their turn in the front line. Captain Ernest Whitfeld returned to the Regiment having completed his senior officer instructor course at Aldershot on the 30th. However, the very next day he left again for the 2nd Division Reception Camp. This tour of the front line trenches came to an end on the night of July 1st/2nd on relief by the 24th R.F. and it had been a quiet one. One man was killed on the 1st.

On July 1st, Lieutenant-Colonel Richard Crosse left the 52nd for two days in order to visit the Third Army's Infantry and Musketry Camp to see their training system. Captain John Blagrove briefly replaced Crosse in command before Captain George Field returned to the Regiment following a stint at D Infantry Base Depot. Field became an acting major and second-in-command of the 52nd. From July 1st-5th the Regiment undertook bathing and training. The latter comprised Lewis gun classes, rapid fire practices and instruction in gas warfare.

After dark on July 5th, the Regiment replaced the 2nd H.L.I. on the left battalion front. Three men were wounded on the 6th. The 7th started quietly; however towards evening there was some shelling just in the rear of the joint Headquarters of A and D Companies and this caused a number of casualties. The commander of A Company, Captain Gordon Fuller, went with the stretcher bearers to assist with the three wounded men when a further shell killed him and wounded another soldier. The 27-year-old from Streatham, a solicitor in private life, had been in France with the 52nd since April 1st 1917 and was highly thought of by his commanding officer. Fuller was buried at Bienvillers-au-Bois two days later[713]. That day seven more men were wounded.

On July 10th, the 52nd had a pleasant surprise with the return of Lieutenant William Giles who had been sent back to England for a six months tour in February. However, after only five months at home he had been returned to the Regiment without any explanation and was immediately posted to his old Company B. At 11.30 p.m., a patrol encounter took place in front of C Company on the right of the battalion line. Four men under the nineteen-year-old Corporal Joseph Ohren were covering a wiring party when they were attacked by an estimated eight-man German patrol and a hand-to-hand fight ensued. Ohren's men had been lying out 100 yards ahead of the wiring party. Several casualties were inflicted on the Germans and a prisoner was taken. Private Towner, one of the newly arrived measles contacts, described by Richard Crosse as 'an infant-in-arms', greatly distinguished himself in the action. The look-out man alone in a shell hole was attacked by three or more Germans. Towner immediately opened fire killing one of the enemy and driving off the rest, one of whom ran into the British lines and was captured. Richard Crosse considered that the actions of Ohren and his men reflected great credit on them. Unfortunately, Corporal Joseph

[713] Bienvillers Military Cemetery. Grave XIX.D.18.

Ohren was slain during the fighting[714]. Private Towner, received the M.M; a few mornings later, Crosse placed the medal ribbon on 'the little warrior's' chest halfway down a sap in front of his company officer and three comrades. The night before, Towner had been on fatigues carrying duckboards, and Crosse heard him say as he went round a traverse on his return journey, '— me if I haven't had duckboards on my back, all night, and the Commanding Officer puts one on my chest in the morning'. The Military Medal from the form of its ribbon was sometimes known as the duckboard.

The nineteen-year-old German captured during the action described above had actually run into the British line, whether through fear or disorientation is not known. He was from the 452nd Regiment of the 234th Division. So at last the 52nd had identification of the German units facing them. The next day under interrogation at the Headquarters of the 2nd Division, he gave some useful information. The prisoner was a Prussian by birth, fairly fluent in English and French, and had been a student at Berlin University until he was called up in 1917. The German patrol had been sent to capture a member of the wiring party for their own identification purposes. The prisoner had declined to give the date of his Regiment's relief as, following the capture of men from another unit, its ration party had been bombarded, giving the impression that the captured men had given away the date. Their relief had been delayed by a day. Morale was poor.

The period July 11th-13th was quiet although there was a good deal of rain particularly on the 11th. The wet weather made the tracks heavy and for a time they had to be closed. One man was wounded on the 11th. On the 13th the 52nd was relieved once more by the 24th R.F. and went back into battalion reserve. The usual training regime was carried out until July 17th when the Regiment returned to the trenches in place of the 2nd H.L.I. as the right battalion in the line. During this period there were several changes of personnel amongst the officers. On July 18th, Captain Victor Martin was struck off the strength of the Regiment by a medical board in England. That same day, the experienced Lieutenant Dick 'Puff Ball' Warren, who had performed so well at Lock 6 during the retiral from the Bapaume - Cambrai road in December 1917, and Lieutenant H.A. Smith rejoined the 52nd from the 3rd Battalion. 'Ginger' Smith had finally recovered from the thigh wound he had received at Arleux in 1917.

Two days later Lieutenant Jim Neville, happily recovered from his serious bout of food poisoning, returned to the fold. He was accompanied by Lieutenant R.A. 'Bob' FitzGerald and Second-Lieutenant Hugh Stokes. Neville was so keen to return to the 52nd that he actually wrote to Crosse asking him to

[714] Ohren was buried next to Captain Gordon Fuller in Bienvillers Military Cemetery. Grave XIX. D.19.

make a special application. When he was told that he was returning to the 52nd he 'thanked Allah'. On the 24th it was the turn of Captain Charles Bailie, son of the former Colonel of the Regiment, to join them on ceasing to be attached to the 2nd Rifle Brigade. One can detect the hand of Richard Crosse behind the scenes enabling the return of his 'old boys'. One man was killed on the 19th and a further two were killed with one wounded on the 24th.

On July 25th, the 24th R.F. relieved the 52nd in the trenches to the east of Adinfer Wood once again. The next day Lieutenant Harry Dashwood joined the Regiment; his brother Lionel had been killed with them at Richebourg l'Avoué in 1915. Training was seriously interfered with by the generally bad weather with heavy rain. As Crosse wrote, 'the accommodation in the Reserve Battalion area is all of the "fair weather" variety and very unsuited to wet weather conditions. Many men got little or no sleep their shelters being flooded out'. One man was wounded on the 25th. On the 28th, Richard Crosse returned to England on special leave to visit the 3rd Battalion. No doubt he thanked them for the return of Neville, Smith, Warren and the arrival of Dashwood, and he would have kept a weather eye open for other likely officers.

The Regiment returned to the line in place of the 2nd H.L.I. on the 29th. Their routine was broken by the fact that U.S.A. infantry was in the line with them. The newcomers from the 319th U.S.A. Infantry Division were being introduced to trench warfare. The part of the line normally held by two companies was now to be held by one company of the 52nd and three American platoons. Richard Crosse had been rather taken aback by a good-humoured American, 'say, are you the big noise of this outfit?' However, he was favourably impressed by them and felt that there were none of the problems that they had had the previous year with the Portuguese. The newly returned Jim Neville also commented on the performance of the Americans[715].

> The Americans are fearfully keen, but rather dangerous! They loose off at anything, and never wait to see who it is; even to fire at anyone going along the top between posts!! I'm afraid their discipline is not all it should be, but they will soon knuckle down and lose the keenness which almost amounts to suicide. They had three men knocked out by their own men. One officer, their intelligence bird, was shot through the neck by their Colour Serjeant Instructor in Musketry! And two privates were killed by some of their mates while cleaning rifles. Casualties from enemy action, NIL!! The Intelligence officer is not expected to live.

[715] Letter to his father written in the Front Line at Ayette on August 2nd 1918.

The month of August opened with the return of Lieutenant-Colonel Richard Crosse from England and the name of the Sapping Platoon under Lieutenant John Murray being changed to the Pioneer Platoon. The next day was a thoroughly wet and disagreeable one in the line, and Captain F.D.R. 'Dudley' Milne M.C. reported for duty from the 2nd Dragoon Guards. The 98th reinforcement of twenty other ranks joined on August 3rd and one man was killed on the 4th. This tour of the trenches lasted until the 6th when the Regiment was relieved by the 24th R.F. and withdrew into Battalion Reserve. On the night of August 9th, the usual routine of the 52nd was altered with a battalion of the 319th U.S.A. Infantry Division replacing them. The 52nd retired to the west of Pommier at Humbercamps and La Cauchie. Major George Field remained in the line with the Americans. The next four days were enjoyable and were used for generally cleaning themselves up and training. It was the first time since June 7th that the 52nd had occupied billets.

August 13th marked the fourth anniversary of the Regiment leaving Aldershot for France. Only three officers [Crosse, Field, F. Barnes] and 69 other ranks were still with the 52nd. Of this select group one officer [Crosse] and 44 others had served continuously. The occasion was marked by a commanding officer's parade in the morning, when the Regiment was reminded of the day's significance. A concert was given by the Divisional Troupe in the new theatre at Humbercamps which was particularly enjoyed by all. Richard Crosse used the anniversary to write to every 52nd prisoner-of-war.

> I have for some time wanted very much to write you a short letter from the Regiment, but you will understand how difficult it is to find something I shall be allowed to say.
>
> We have still many of the old soldiers left, and the younger ones are following in their footsteps, and they all keep up the good name and traditions of the Regiment. In the last three days over £50 has been collected in the companies towards parcels for the Prisoners of War, and we wish we could do more to make your life easier. This money has been sent to Mrs Davies[716].
>
> This picture is of Corporal Jackson and Private Heavens who collected frs. 175 at some Regimental Sports[717].

---

[716] The wife of Major-General Henry Davies former Commanding Officer of the 52nd.

[717] At the top of the letter was a photograph of two men in costume.

> Four years ago to-day we embarked for France, and wondered how long it would be before we returned. I don't think it will be very long now.
>
> We shall be very glad of any letter, or card, or message, to say how you are getting on.

At about 6 p.m. August 14th, the 52nd took over the reserve battalion area from the 2nd H.L.I. who in turn relieved the 319th U.S.A. Infantry Division in the line. The following day the 52nd went into the line as the left front battalion in place of the 24th R.F. The same day, the Reverend Edward 'Monty' Guilford, who had been chaplain to the Regiment and lived with it since November 1916, was transferred to the Headquarters of the 2nd Division in place of the Reverend H.L. Hornby who had been promoted to the Headquarters of the Third Army. Richard Crosse wrote in the *Battalion War Diary,* 'these two clergymen within their respective capacities as Regimental and Divisional Chaplains were greatly beloved by the troops and their work was deeply appreciated by all ranks'.

At about this time Lieutenant Cyril 'Shiny' Horley played a practical joke on the gullible Transport Officer Captain John Slade-Baker. Horley and some other officers had been celebrating the 21st birthday of Lieutenant Octavius 'Toby' Sturges. Jim Neville recounted the tale[718].

> Toby suddenly turned up on Tuesday to spend his 21st birthday with the Regiment. A party of six of us went to the 6th Corps Officers' Club at Bavincourt and had a rattling good dinner. We managed to get a lorry most of the way back, and on our return "Shiny" instigated a rag on S- B- , and gave him a bogus message to turn out the Transport at 4 a.m. He sucked it down most beautifully, and kept "Shiny" gassing about the reasons for the order and whether "Shiny" thought it was necessary to go in person.

During the period August 15th-20th, the 52nd undertook active patrolling every night and on one unfortunate occasion in the daytime. Major-General Cecil Pereira, of the 2nd Division, was very concerned about loose talk giving away the details of raids and he wrote firmly on the subject to his three brigades, warning all officers to be careful in what they said particularly in front of their servants. On the night of August 15th/16th, Lieutenant R.G. Wilsdon went out from 1.45 a.m.-3 a.m. with six other ranks in a southerly direction as far as the sunken road but did not see or hear any enemy movement. Lieutenant G.E. Pearson took out

[718] Letter to his sister written from Pommier on August 16th 1918.

his eight-man patrol to the south-west at the same time as Wilsdon going as far as the old enemy outpost line where they were sniped at.

The following night, August 17th/18th, Lieutenant Dick Warren and four other ranks left the British line at 11 p.m., and found the German outpost line unoccupied in front of the sunken road. However, stick bombs and shovels had been left in the outposts. Warren and his men proceeded towards Lone Tree, crossed Moyblain Trench with its deep dug-outs and found it empty. Leaving three men there, Warren moved on with a single man until the two of them reached an earthwork where they were challenged and shot at by a German sentry. Returning to Moyblain Trench, Warren found further dug-outs with evidence of occupation and he bombed one of them. After collecting the remainder of his men, Warren was challenged by a post garrison of at least four men who threw bombs, fragments of which hit the patrol without doing serious damage. Moving to the east, Warren and his patrol were then unfortunate enough to run into another six of the enemy in a further post. Bombs were thrown at them as they raced down the Ayette - Moyenneville road to the east, before leaving the road with two of the enemy continuing past them down the road. Eventually, on returning in the direction of British lines, their own artillery bombarded them. Such was life in mid-August 1918. At 3.30 a.m., Warren and his intrepid men were extremely lucky to get back to the British lines unscathed. At least they had conclusively demonstrated that the Germans had not retired to any degree.

On the night of August 17th/18th, it was the turn of Lieutenant William Giles and six other ranks to go out on patrol at 11 p.m. They were shot at by a light machine-gun, before proceeding down the road towards Moyenneville where they saw eight Germans lining the road. Some Very Lights were sent up and the enemy party vanished towards their own lines. The patrol returned at 1 a.m. to the British line. That same night Lieutenant Bob FitzGerald and eight other ranks were out, between midnight and 3 a.m., checking to see whether Moyblain Trench was still occupied or not. They were able to report that it was still occupied as they were shot at by a machine-gun from the trench in question. On the night of August 18th/19th, the incorrigible Lieutenant Dick Warren took out yet another six man patrol with the specific intention of seeking out and fighting enemy patrols. They were hampered by the bright moonlight and were unsuccessful.

The unfortunate daylight patrol took place on August 20th and had most unpleasant overtones. Richard Crosse gave a surprisingly long account of it in the *Battalion War Diary.* Uniquely, he wrote a complete page of the *Diary* on the young man's death. The young man in question was Second-Lieutenant Joseph Patrick Sears, born 24 years earlier at Bangalore, India and a student at Oxford. In his post-war articles Crosse made no mention of this incident.

> Patrolling on the Regt. front was necessarily very active: several very good patrols being carried out by Officers and NCOs of the front companies. One unfortunately cost the life of an officer T 2 Lt J.P. Sears who, about 9.45 a.m. asked permission to work forward from the line of the left front Coy (C Coy, Capt. Bobby M.C. which had relieved D Coy, Capt Eagle, the night before) to obtain better observation of the ground in the part. This was allowed and the objective to be reconnoitred was given as the outpost line and a covering party posted. About 11.15 a.m. the patrol was seen by the enemy who, contrary to expectation, were holding a post in the sunken AYETTE - MOYENVILLE Road which crossed the front. This post fired on our patrol and was engaged from a flank. The patrol withdrew slightly during which 2 Lt Sears was twice hit: he died from his wounds a few minutes later. The two NCOs (Cpl Hollyoake and L/C Lee) who went with him remained out until dark. His body was subsequently buried in the rear of our old front line[719].

Lieutenant Jim Neville recorded an account of the unfortunate Joseph Sears' demise in his diary entry for the day in question[720].

> Corporal Hollyoake and Lee came in from their daylight patrol and reported that Sears had been killed. It was his first time in the line. A nice officer. Had he been more experienced he would probably be still alive, but he would not listen to Corporal Hollyoake who told him to lie doggo in a shell-hole till nightfall, as soon as the enemy started firing at the party. He made a dart for the front line and was hit in the spine. Hollyoake and Lee pluckily left the shelter of their shell-hole and went to his help, experiencing a heavy fire as soon as they showed a sign of movement. They got to him unscathed, but nothing could be done for the poor chap. The Boches are very clever, for they allowed the patrol to cover half the distance of No Man's Land, which is 800 yards wide here, before they opened fire. The patrol ought never to have been allowed out and methinks a certain person ought to get into hot water for it, for he was out for personal kudos and sent another to reap it for him. I remember an

[719] Later he was reburied at Bucquoy Road Cemetery, Ficheux. Grave V.B.5.

[720] Diary entry for August 20th 1918.

order coming out in June 1917 forbidding daylight patrols. A waste of life.

This unsavoury affair was completely out of character for the 52nd Light Infantry of any era. It is inconceivable that Richard Crosse would have sent the young, inexperienced Sears out on a daylight patrol. Although, Neville did not name the individual concerned, the finger of suspicion must be pointed at Captain Percy Bobby, the C Company commander, whose company Sears had been posted to just fifteen days before. It would be fascinating to know what Crosse said to Bobby after the event.

The 52nd's Pioneer Platoon under Lieutenant John Murray, from Aberdeen, had built a church and recreation room in the Headquarters of the Reserve Battalion between Adinfer Wood and Monchy-au-Bois. The Church was dedicated to St. George by Bishop Llewellyn Gwynne, now the Deputy Chaplain-General of the British Armies in France, but an old and valued friend of the Regiment from 1914-15. The new Chaplain to the 52nd, the Reverend Ernest Gallop, was also present. Many years later, after his death aged 92 years, Gallop would be described thus: 'had the greatest gift of all, the gift of giving oneself in friendship, a lively, sparkling and infectious friendship, spreading gaiety and humour wherever he went, and it is by that gift that he will live in our memories'[721].

Officially the material used to build the Church had been supplied by the 5th Brigade. Later, Crosse would admit that he hoped that the use the materials were put to would absolve John Murray of some of the methods he had used to procure them. Murray was described as one of the characters of the wartime 52nd: as Crosse put it; 'a regulation in certain circumstances, such as when not in contact with the enemy, the health and comfort of the troops must be the first consideration, sometimes troubles the conscience of a commanding officer to reconcile what the troops need with what can be got officially. In 1918 it was found that the gap could best be bridged in the 52nd by using the experience of Lieutenant Murray to get what was wanted which he did very successfully'. Murray had inherited the Sapping Platoon from Lieutenant T.A. Coffin. Coffin had been a partner in a building firm and refused to leave the 52nd for promotion to field rank in a pioneer battalion. He was now the Gas Officer and Camp Commandant Rear H.Q.

[721] Reverend Edward Guilford. Taken from Gallop's obituary in the *Regimental Chronicles* of 1968.

Chapter XXII

The Second Battles of the Somme 1918: the Capture of Sapignies.

August 20th - August 25th 1918

[Maps: pages 593, 595, 597.]

The Battle of Amiens fought from August 8th-11th was the beginning of the end for Kaiser Wilhelm's German armies. General Henry Rawlinson's Fourth Army, using the Australian and Canadian Corps with a large force of tanks, made the longest advance in a single day of the war, some eight miles. No sooner had the enemy got over the Battle of Amiens than they were subjected to a series of British attacks: on August 21st, General Julian Byng's Third Army attacked over the old Somme battlefields on the opening day of the Battle of Albert; August 22nd, General Rawlinson's Fourth Army attacked again on the right of the Third Army; August 26th, it was the turn of General Henry Horne's First Army at the Battle of the Scarpe around Arras. On the night of August 26th/27th, the Germans began to pull back towards their position on the formidable Hindenburg Line. This had the effect of exposing their flank on the Lys battlefield in the north and led to them withdrawing once more.

As part of Byng's Third Army operations, orders from VI Corps [Lieutenant-General Aylmer Haldane] instructed the 2nd and Guards Divisions to take the Ablainzevelle-Moyenneville Ridge by surprise, in conjunction with an assault to the south by units of the IV Corps on Bucquoy and Ablainzevelle. Tanks from the 2nd Tank Brigade were to assist in the operation. Indeed tank officers came to lunch with the 52nd indicating that an action was in the offing. If the initial operation was successful the 3rd Division was to be pushed through the 2nd Division to take the line of the Albert-Arras railway in conjunction with units of the Guards Division. Subsequently, it was hoped to exploit any success in the general direction of Bapaume. On August 20th, Sir Douglas Haig told Major-General Cecil Pereira, commanding the 2nd Division that the battle starting on the morrow would extend from Arras to Soissons, an 85-mile front. Pereira commented 'some battle'.

At 6 a.m. August 20th, Lieutenant-Colonels Richard Crosse and Walter Brodie V.C., Commanding Officer of the 2nd H.L.I., were summoned to a meeting with Brigadier-General W.L. Osborn, of the 5th Infantry Brigade, to hear the operational plans and movements to be made the next day. It is likely that this was the last time that Crosse saw Brodie as three days later one man would be dead and the other seriously wounded. Both men had served their respective

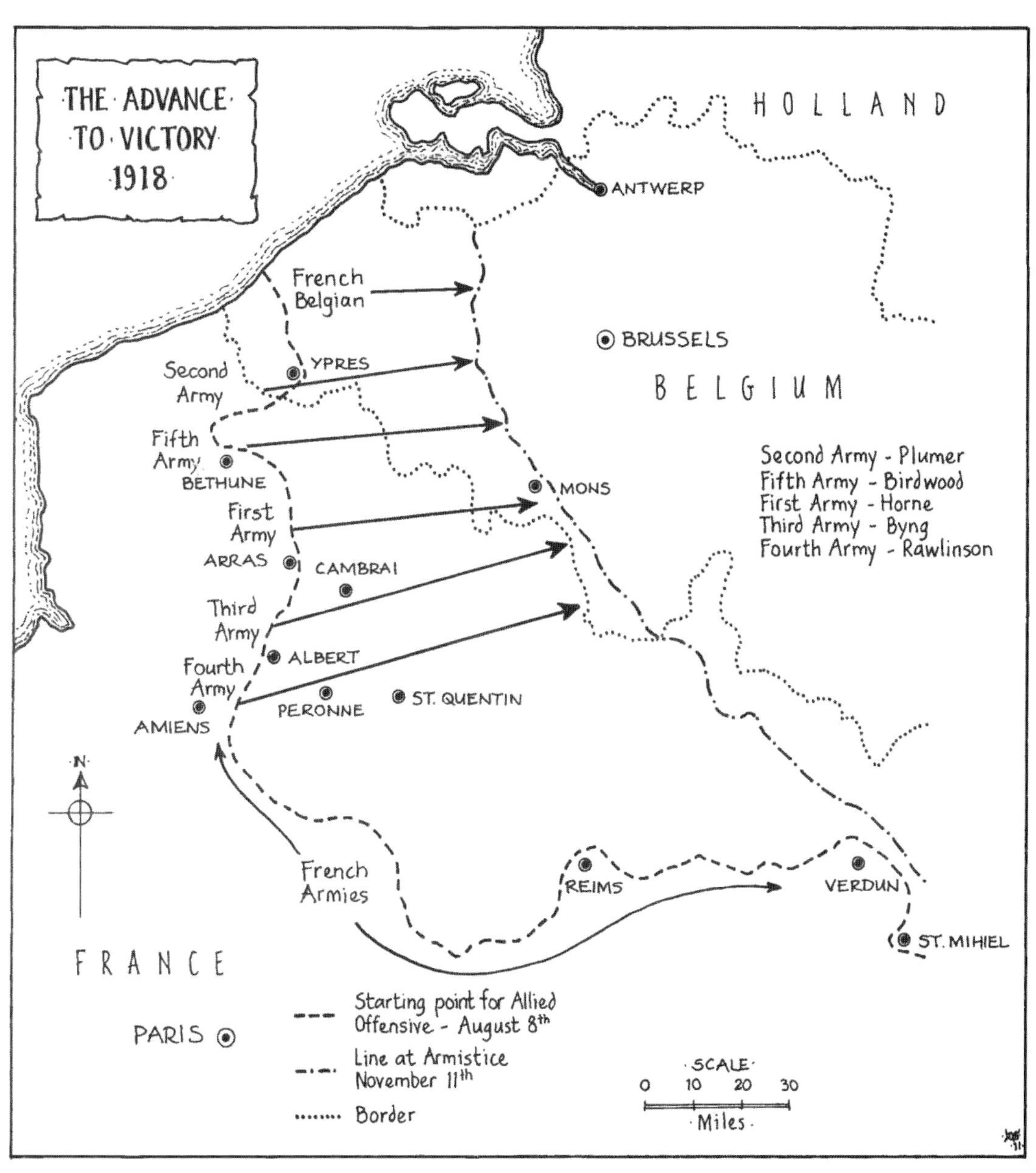
THE ADVANCE TO VICTORY 1918
HOLLAND
ANTWERP
French Belgian
BRUSSELS
YPRES
Second Army
BELGIUM
Fifth Army
BETHUNE
MONS
Second Army - Plumer
Fifth Army - Birdwood
First Army - Horne
Third Army - Byng
Fourth Army - Rawlinson
First Army
ARRAS
CAMBRAI
Third Army
ALBERT
Fourth Army
PERONNE
ST. QUENTIN
AMIENS
N
French Armies
REIMS
VERDUN
ST. MIHIEL
FRANCE
PARIS
Starting point for Allied Offensive - August 8th
Line at Armistice November 11th
Border
SCALE
0 10 20 30
Miles

regiments in the 5th Brigade with great distinction continuously since 1914, both rising to the command having started the war as lowly subalterns.

The 52nd Light Infantry was to be relieved prior to zero hour, 4.55 a.m. August 21st, by the attacking troops of the Guards Division positioned on the left of the 99th Brigade, who would be the lead troops of the 2nd Division. The 5th Brigade and the 52nd were attached to the Guards Division and would be in reserve for the duration of the operation. The 52nd had been warned, that if the necessity arose, they would be the first troops used from the reserve. It was envisaged that the 5th Brigade would either, in the event of great success, come between the 2nd Guards Brigade and the 3rd Division to protect the left of the advance, or relieve the 2nd Guards Brigade on the second night. On relief, the 52nd would occupy the area of trenches of the Hameau Switch front and support lines east of the Adinfer - Ransart road. Major George Field, Lieutenant Cyril 'Shiny' Horley and N.C.O.s representing their companies, reconnoitred the area and allotted accommodation. The move was effected without incident at about 3-5 a.m., with the Regimental Headquarters in Hameau Farm and a forward echelon of the transport situated in a valley behind them. Greatcoats were sent back to Pommier in bundles by section, and an extra bandolier of ammunition was issued to each man. Rations and water were brought up.

At 4.55 p.m. August 21st, the British barrage opened with a mighty roar and fell some 300 yards west of Moyblain Trench. Immediately, nine tanks moved forward through the assault troops of the 99th Brigade who then joined in the advance. On the flanks of the 99th Brigade the Guards Division on the left and the 37th Division on the right moved forward. The German enemy was taken completely by surprise on this foggy morning, and the Ablainzevelle-Moyenneville Ridge was soon in British hands. At about 5.50 a.m., the 3rd Division was launched through the attacking troops and pushed on to take Courcelles-le-Comte at around 11 a.m. This was followed by a further move forward towards the Albert-Arras railway line which proved to be strongly held by the enemy. Most of the railway line, bar 1,000 yards on the right, was captured by the 3rd Division. Operations were then closed down for the day.

About 10 a.m. August 21st, the 52nd received orders to move to a position of readiness on the sunken Ayette - Moyenneville road which a short time before had been regularly patrolled by them. This was in response to doubts about the junction of the Guards and 3rd Divisions where a gap was threatening to open up. The change of position took place via Adinfer and was completed by the early afternoon on an exceedingly hot day. Matters were made worse by the lack of shade and the Regiment gratefully received, in the later afternoon, orders to move into the old front line with its better shelter from the sun. Once the move

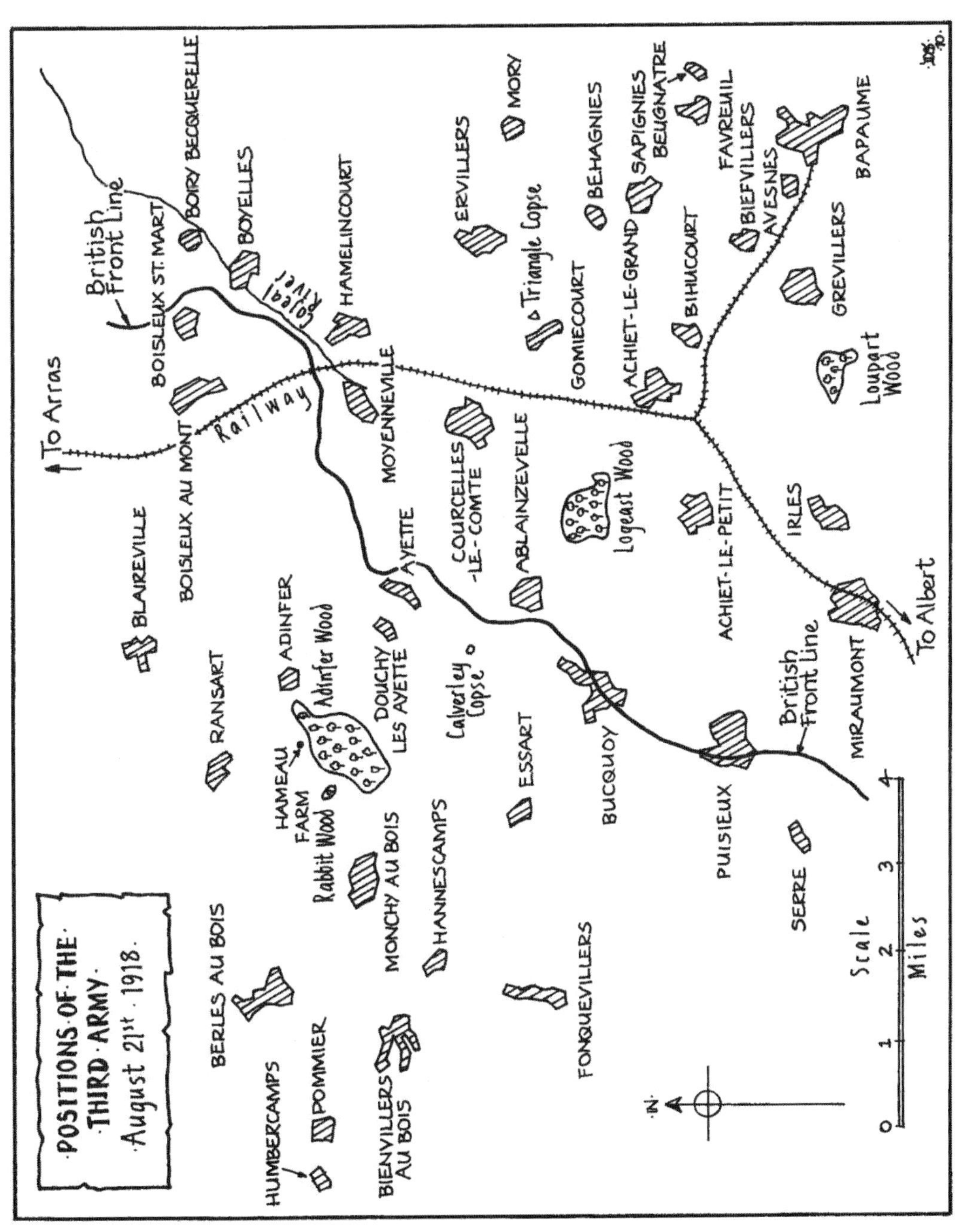
POSITIONS OF THE THIRD ARMY
August 21st 1918.
To Arras
British Front Line
BOIRY BECQUERELLE
BOYELLES
BOISLEUX ST. MART
HAMELINCOURT
Cojeul River
Railway
BOISLEUX AU MONT
MOYENNEVILLE
BLAIREVILLE
ERVILLERS
MORY
Triangle Copse
BEHAGNIES
SAPIGNIES
BEUGNATRE
FAVREUIL
BIEFVILLERS
AVESNES
BAPAUME
GOMIECOURT
ACHIET-LE-GRAND
BIHUCOURT
GREVILLERS
Loupart Wood
COURCELLES -LE-COMTE
ABLAINZEVELLE
Logeast Wood
ACHIET-LE-PETIT
IRLES
MIRAUMONT
To Albert
AYETTE
ADINFER
Adinfer Wood
DOUCHY LES AYETTE
Calverley Copse
RANSART
HAMEAU FARM
Rabbit Wood
ESSART
BUCQUOY
PUISIEUX
SERRE
MONCHY AU BOIS
HANNESCAMPS
BERLES AU BOIS
POMMIER
HUMBERCAMPS
BIENVILLERS AU BOIS
FONQUEVILLERS
N
Scale
Miles
0
1
2
3
4

was completed, water and rations were brought up and everyone settled down for a good night's sleep. In Lieutenant Jim Neville's case it was on a convenient stretcher.

The next morning, about 11 a.m., the 52nd received orders to move back and occupy accommodation between Adinfer Wood and the Monchy-au-Bois - Ransart road, in Rabbit Wood and Monchy Switch. The move and settling in was arduous as the day was again very hot and other units had also been allotted accommodation in the same area. The accommodation consisted of trenches and old gun pits, and part of D Company had to bivouac. Soon after 10 p.m. a brigade warning order came through for a change of position in the early hours of the following morning. By about 2 a.m. August 23rd, in perfect moonlight, the 52nd had reached their destination in Fox Trench and the nearest suitable ground at Calverley Copse [map reference F 16 a and c.]. It was the fourth anniversary of the action at Mons. The position lay a short distance from the Ayette - Bucquoy road, and slightly closer to the former than the latter. In their new position the Regiment was able to get a few hours of early morning sleep.

The plan on August 23rd was for the 3rd Division to assault the village of Gomiécourt at 4 a.m., and for the 52nd, 56th, and Guards Divisions to attack Boiry, Becquerelle, Boyelles and Hamelincourt a little later at 4.45 a.m. If the 3rd Division was successful, the 2nd Division would attack Ervillers, Behagnies and Sapignies. Once these three villages were taken, the attacking battalions were to consolidate at least 200 yards to the east of each village. The attack of the 2nd Division was to be assisted by ten relatively fast Whippet tanks from the 6th Tank Battalion acting as an advanced guard. After crossing the Gomiécourt - Sapignies road, three tanks would proceed to the north of Behagnies, three more would move between Behagnies and Sapignies, and a final four tanks would pass to the south of Sapignies. A Field Artillery barrage was to start at zero hour and move forward 300 yards every two minutes. The barrage would lift off Ervillers at zero plus 70 minutes, Behagnies at zero plus two hours and finally off Sapignies at zero plus two and a half hours. The 37th Division of IV Corps, to the south, would attempt to capture Achiet-le-Grand and Bihucourt.

At dawn, 4 a.m. August 23rd, the 3rd Division attacked from the line of the Albert-Arras railway and succeeded in taking Gomiécourt at around 6 a.m., so that it was possible to begin the second phase, namely the 2nd Division's attack on the villages situated on the Arras - Bapaume road. The 6th Brigade was to assault Ervillers, the 2nd H.L.I. of the 5th Brigade, Behagnies and the 24th R.F. also of the 5th Brigade, Sapignies. The H.L.I. would be the leading battalion with a gap of 500 yards to the R.F. The 52nd was to follow the other two regiments of the 5th Brigade at a distance of 1,200 yards, move into a reserve position, and act as

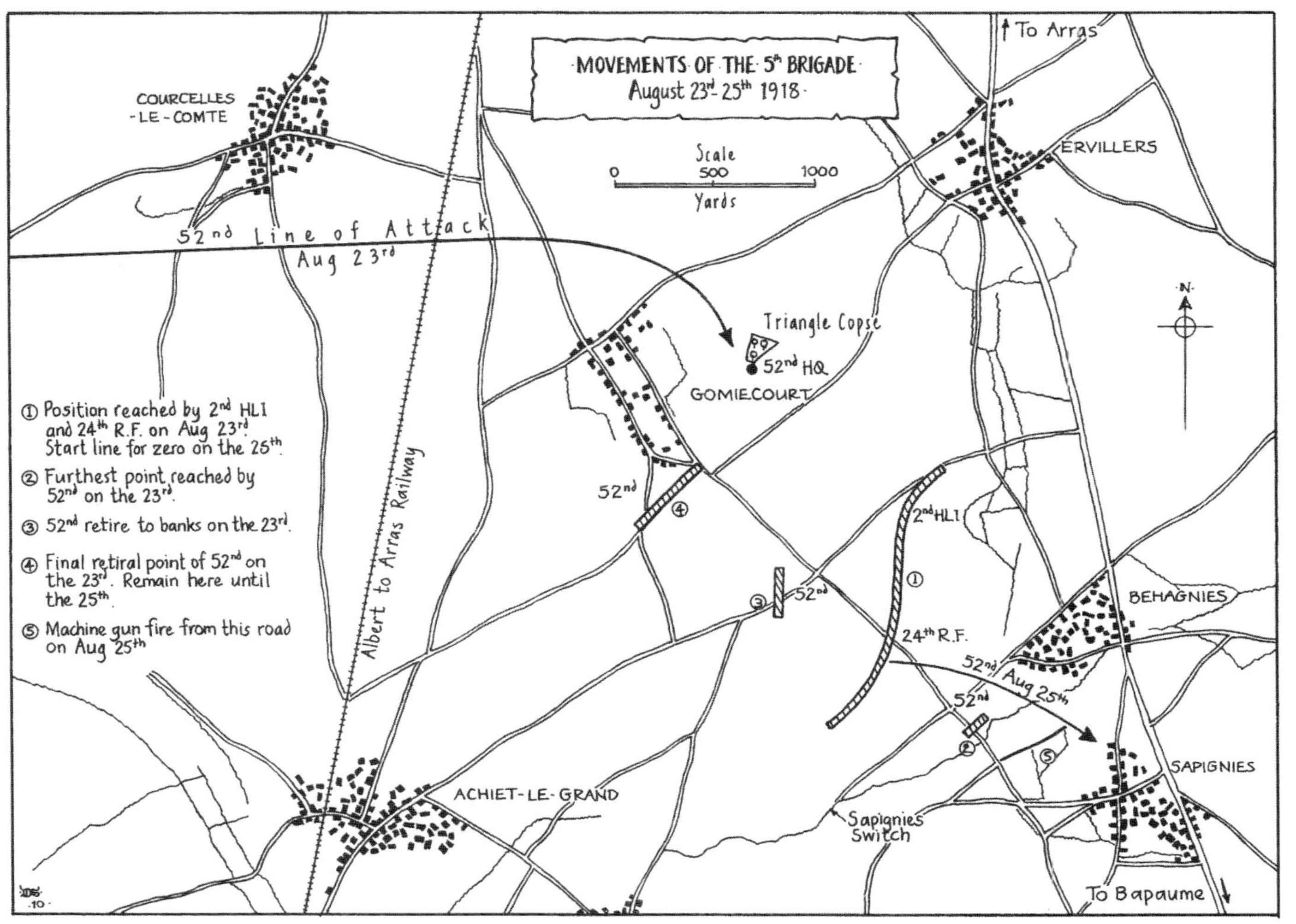
MOVEMENTS OF THE 5th BRIGADE
August 23rd-25th 1918
Scale
0
500
1000
Yards
N
To Arras
COURCELLES -LE-COMTE
ERVILLERS
52nd Line of Attack
Aug 23rd
Triangle Copse
52nd HQ
GOMIECOURT
Albert to Arras Railway
52nd
2nd HLI
24th R.F.
52nd
BEHAGNIES
52nd Aug 25th
52nd
SAPIGNIES
ACHIET-LE-GRAND
Sapignies Switch
To Bapaume
① Position reached by 2nd HLI and 24th R.F. on Aug 23rd. Start line for zero on the 25th.
② Furthest point reached by 52nd on the 23rd.
③ 52nd retire to banks on the 23rd.
④ Final retiral point of 52nd on the 23rd. Remain here until the 25th.
⑤ Machine gun fire from this road on Aug 25th

circumstances dictated. The plan intended that the 5th Brigade's battalions attacked on a two-company front of 700 yards. The 99th Brigade was to protect the southern flank of the operation with two battalions occupying the ridge between Sapignies and Bihucourt. By 8 a.m., all three brigades of the 2nd Division were assembled around Moyblain Trench and the Ablainzevelle-Courcelles Ridge. The 5th Brigade was in the centre with its left on Courcelles Alley. The 52nd got into artillery formation on a two-company front at 10 a.m. and followed the 24th R.F. to the east.

All the troops of the 2nd Division moved forwards to the line of the railway which they crossed at about 11 a.m. [Zero hour for the lead battalion, the 2nd H.L.I., to cross the railway was 11 a.m.[722]]. By now it was a very hot morning as the 52nd passed to the south of Courcelles-le-Comte. The advance was under a good artillery barrage with its lifts of 300 yards every two minutes and to which the enemy responded in kind. The retaliatory barrage did not interfere with the 52nd until it was approaching the line of Courcelles-le-Comte, where shells began to fall on the small columns or 'worms' in which the Regiment had been disposed. Jim Neville's spirits were raised when he met the Commanding Officer of the 24th R.F. wearing a brown 'gor blimey' hat and followed by his servant carrying his helmet. 'Good morning Sir, you have got a nice hat'. He said 'yes, there are no Generals to see what I have got on my head'[723].

On crossing the railway, the Regiment was subjected to machine-gun fire from the right flank and rear. At this stage the 52nd was particularly vulnerable as it had to wheel to the right and so exposed its flank. Down came the 5.9s and whizzbangs. C and B Companies were in the front line, followed and covered by A and D with the Regimental Headquarters bringing up the rear.

Lieutenant Jim Neville wrote an account of the opening of the operation in his diary[724].

> Packed up my superfluous kit and arranged as much as I could for the attack. Orders were expected at 8 a.m. It is horrible waiting to move – terrible needle.
>
> Moved at 10 a.m. in artillery formation past Courcelles. Then we came under artillery fire; got through that, though some heavy stuff was coming over. Ahead of us loomed the blasted railway cutting of the Bapaume-Arras line. Got through that safely, though the fire was

[722] Richard Crosse in an article written for the *Regimental Journal* in 1939 gave zero hour as 10 a.m. 11 a.m. is the time quoted in the *Battalion War Diary* and the *Regimental Chronicles.*
[723] Lieutenant-Colonel Robert Pipon.
[724] Diary entry for August 23rd 1918.

> getting worse and the railway cutting was being pounded. We ran like blazes across it! The Boche was shelling like hell with gas and sneezer. Once across the railway we made a right hand turn and had to halt in the open. Whizzbangs and 5.9's were dropping all over the place. My sections took cover in shell-holes. I got into one with my Platoon Serjeant, and had a cigarette.

Passing to the north of Gomiécourt, the 52nd set up a temporary Regimental Headquarters near the village, with a view to finding out the situation on their immediate right, where matters did not seem to be going according to plan. Richard Crosse was concerned that if the 52nd was called forward to support either the 2nd H.L.I. or the 24th R.F., the southern flank might be exposed. He sent out a pair of scouts to assess the situation; fortunately they reported that all was well on that flank so that the 52nd's advance could go forward. Eventually, the advance proceeded to a German Aid Post Dug-out on the edge of Triangle Copse to the north-east of Gomiécourt[725]. This was a little further north than the 52nd's intended reserve position in G.6.a. Crosse found the Post, situated at the southern corner of the Copse, occupied by a German Medical Officer with about 50 staff plus some wounded men and no less than nine machine-guns. The Germans' medical staff and patients were all taken prisoner. In the prisoner-of-war cages, the enemy prisoners were congratulating each other on being captured! They looked on bully beef as a delicacy and were full of praise for white English bread.

Lieutenant Jim Neville continued his account of the action[726].

> Shelling damned hard – moved on – enfiladed by Boche gunners with whizzbangs – Serjeant-Major Couldwell hit, two yards from me, very badly by one of those 106 fuse shells. He was literally lifted feet into the air and both his legs were cut away from under him. He was going on leave the day after to-morrow – damned bad luck. Then crossed the Gomiecourt - Sapignies road in front of triangle Copse. Whizz-bangs a b----- nuisance. Got into some old gun pits and waited. I could see the Boche gunners serving the guns that were firing on us, lined up on the skyline to the left of Behagnies. Having seen the flash of the guns through binoculars, we

[725] According to a document written by Brigadier-General W.L. Osborn, now in the records of the 5th Brigade in the National Archives, this was a regimental command post and much valuable material was found in it. Colonel von Poser, the Regimental Commanding Officer was described: 'he being a wise man was away on leave'.

[726] Diary entry for August 23rd 1918.

all crouched into the gun pits until the salvo had burst. Very little damage done by these guns, but damned annoying.

At about 1 p.m., a near-catastrophe was to strike the 52nd[727]. The dug-out on the edge of Triangle Copse had been divested of its German Medical Staff plus wounded and, had become the 52nd's Regimental Headquarters. Naturally, the dug-out's entrance faced east as it had been built by the enemy, and it was consequently exposed to artillery fire. This pleasant spot soon became the target for all types of unpleasant enemy fire, and within 30 minutes of its occupation was the subject of a direct hit by a German shell on the entrance of the 'verandah' of the dug-out. This lay at the top of the dug-out steps, about six feet below ground level, and was full of men. The explosion of the shell killed a number of soldiers, including an orderly of the 2nd H.L.I. who had come to report the instantaneous death of his Commanding Officer, Lieutenant-Colonel Walter Brodie V.C., some 30 minutes earlier. Brodie had been hit by a machine-gun bullet during the advance at 12.30 p.m. Amongst the wounded were Lieutenant-Colonel Richard Crosse, Captain Laurence Fullbrook-Leggatt, Lieutenant A.J. Smith U.S.A.M.C., and Serjeant-Major William Couldwell who had already had both his legs blown off. The exploding shell left the unfortunate Couldwell covered in dirt on a stretcher and also with further injuries. Earlier in the year this brave Yorkshire man had been awarded the D.C.M., and he would die of his injuries before the day was out[728]. Crosse had actually been speaking to the 2nd H.L.I.'s orderly when the shell killed the man, and wounded Crosse in the back and neck. The Regiment was in a state of shock on hearing that their charismatic Commanding Officer had been wounded. 'The news which ripped around the companies was received with consternation'. One officer described the wounding of Crosse as 'Damnable!' Crosse had led a charmed life and was thought to be indestructible.

Fortunately, Lieutenant A.J. Smith, the Medical Officer, had not been seriously wounded and was able to continue with his duties for a time, until he collapsed from exhaustion. Crosse's outstanding memory of the day was the magnificent work of the Medical Services known as 'Linseed Lancers' or 'Poultice Wallopers'. The shelling led to a delay in the evacuation of the 52nd's casualties from the dug-out on the edge of Triangle Copse where they had been

---

[727] This is the time recorded in the *Battalion War Diary.* The *Regimental Chronicles* stated that the 52nd reached the dug-out in Triangle Copse at about 1 p.m. and the shell exploded in the entrance of the dug-out towards 1.30 p.m.

[728] Richard Crosse commented on Couldwell as 'this fine soldier, one of the 1914 52nd, died later in the day. He would have gone far in the service'.

collected. Crosse took it as a compliment for the Regiment and a delicate tribute to Sir Charles Monro's old 2nd Division of 1914, when the weary 5th Field Ambulance, who had been following the 52nd into battle for the last four years, refused to let German prisoners carry the stretchers of the 52nd's casualties. 'No – Jerry should carry a 52nd officer'[729]. For the badly wounded Richard Crosse, who was one of the casualties on a stretcher, this was one of his most moving memories of the war.

Captain Laurence Fullbrook-Leggatt, the Adjutant, had been wounded in the face, but he remained at his post until later in the day when he went back for treatment. Whilst in the open after crossing the railway cutting, Second-Lieutenant Edgar Brown received the wounds from which he would die later in the day. It was the 21-year-old's first time in action. Lieutenant G.E. Pearson was amongst the wounded officers. In all, during the day, about eleven men were killed and five officers and 65 other ranks were wounded[730]. After Richard Crosse was incapacitated, Captain John Blagrove, as the most senior officer available, assumed command of the Regiment. As the 52nd and the 2nd H.L.I. had both lost their Commanding Officers in a short space of time, Lieutenant-Colonel Robert Pipon of the 24th R.F. temporarily assumed overall command and organized the infantry.

At 2.15 p.m., the leading battalions, the 2nd H.L.I. and the 24th R.F., were held up on a ridge to the west of their objectives, Behagnies and Sapignies, by machine-gun and point blank artillery fire. The 52nd was ordered to remain in reserve. Machine-guns to the north of Behagnies were particularly effective and operations locally became stationary. The 2nd H.L.I. was stuck at map reference B.25.c. and to their right, the 24th R.F. at H.1.a and G.6.d, with an open valley between them and the two villages [see map page 597]. Some of the Whippet tanks that were supposed to have supported the 5th Brigade had gone on a line too far to the south and were consequently no help in the attack. Others had been knocked out by the enemy. It became clear that there was little hope of taking Behagnies and Sapignies without further artillery softening up and reliable tank support.

At this point the 52nd were just in front of Behagnies at map reference H.1.c.9.1 and d.2.2 and then the Regiment moved slightly back towards Gomiécourt and the banks in G.6.b.0.4-8. [see map page 597]. At 6 p.m., C

---

[729] Crosse made this comment in the *Regimental Journal* of 1939. When he rewrote the article in 1958, the quote had changed slightly. 'No ---- Jerry should carry the 52nd wounded out of action that day'.

[730] Casualty figures taken from Crosse's article in the *Regimental Journal of 1958.* Major George Field recorded in the *Battalion War Diary* for August 23rd*:* 'wounded 63, killed 11, missing 1, died of wounds 1'.

Company reported that the 24th R.F. had withdrawn slightly from in front of Sapignies, putting three companies of the 52nd, A, B, D, in front of the support companies of the 24th R.F. Consequently, these three companies of the 52nd were withdrawn to a sunken road just south of Gomiécourt in A.29.d. and A.30.c. with revised orders for the 52nd to remain in reserve. Later two German aeroplanes bombed their positions and inflicted several casualties on A and D Companies. The fourth Company, C, was positioned on the high ground to the north of Triangle Copse at A.24. central. At midnight, the highly experienced second-in-command, Major George Field, came up from Base to take over command of the Regiment from Captain John Blagrove. Earlier in the day, at 12.30 p.m., the 6th Brigade had taken Ervillers with the support of light tanks. On August 24th, troops of the 99th Brigade would push beyond Ervillers and establish themselves to the west of the next village, Mory.

Lieutenant Jim Neville continued with his account of the later part of August 23rd[731].

> The Highland Light Infantry and the 24th Royal Fusiliers could not get forward. The 52nd took up a position under the lea of a steep bank about 400 yards in front of Gomiecourt, in support, and stayed there all afternoon.
>
> I did not have the foggiest idea what the time was. Had orders to retire to Regimental Headquarters near Triangle Copse, as the 52nd was too far forward. We got shelled on the road, so stayed where we were till dusk. Wilsdon of "B" Company got a bit of shell in his bottom as he was crossing the road, which made him hop!! We squatting under the cover of the bank, watched this proceeding and laughed like hell. His servant carried him back pick-a-back[732].
>
> I was apportioned a position among some gun pits to which the rest of the Company was to come, but the shelling was too great. Slept in a shelter with 5.9's [sic] falling all round. My Gawd! I could sleep for a week. I've never sweated so much in my life. The smoke and gas, as I write, are perfectly bloody – no other word.
>
> Later. Took up a position guarding the left flank of the Brigade, and consolidated shell holes. Slept fairly well, though terribly cramped, at the corner of Triangle Copse. Shelling has diminished, but the smell of dead men and horses is filthy.

[731] Diary entry for August 23rd 1918.

[732] The records of the 52nd suggested that the unfortunate Lieutenant R.G. Wilsdon had suffered a more discrete injury, a gunshot wound to his 'leg' and was also gassed.

The situation changed little overnight with the 52nd maintaining their position in reserve. A, B and D Companies remained in the sunken road to the south of Gomiécourt and made an arc to the south-east. C Company was just over a thousand yards away to the east of Triangle Copse and faced the north and north-east. The exposed Regimental Headquarters remained in the former dug-out at the southern corner of Triangle Copse. At 8 a.m. the new Commanding Officer Major George Field received orders to send out patrols, in conjunction with the 2nd H.L.I., and to endeavour to establish themselves on the north-east side of Behagnies. The rationale behind the patrolling was the vain hope that the enemy had relaxed his grip on Behagnies and Sapignies. Two platoons of A Company were told off for this and went forward to execute the orders but at 11 a.m. the order was rescinded and the men brought back. Other patrols reported that the villages were strongly held with many machine-guns and the wire was thick although with many gaps.

At 10 a.m., C and D Companies were ordered to relieve the 1st K.R.R.C. of the 99th Brigade, who were in position on the right of the 5th Brigade, and were to come under the orders of Lieutenant-Colonel Robert Pipon of the 24th R.F. Here the right company was made responsible for maintaining contact with the 37th Division to the south. At noon, B Company, to protect the 52nd's left flank, moved from the sunken road to the position previously occupied by C Company on the high ground to the east of Triangle Copse. C Company's Headquarters were in a narrow trench on the forward edge of Triangle Copse in full view of the enemy on the high ground of the Arras - Bapaume road. Lieutenant Jim Neville managed a little sleep despite being frequently awoken by shells in the vicinity. He felt that it was more of a 'coma' than a sleep. George Field reported that the rest of the day was quiet with four other-rank casualties.

Lieutenant Jim Neville of C Company had started the day in a narrow trench near Triangle Copse. At 10 a.m. his company was ordered to relieve the 1st K.R.R.C. of the 99th Brigade to the south. He recorded in his diary active patrolling towards Behagnies and Sapignies[733].

> We moved off at about midday, to take over the front line from the 60th Rifles[734], advancing in small parties to avoid detection from Behagnies ridge. The enemy was very quiet and never shelled us at all: we managed to take over the out-post line without any casualties. It was very interesting; we pushed forward patrols in conjunction

[733] Diary entry for August 24th 1918.

[734] 1st K.R.R.C.

with the 37th Division on our right, feeling for the enemy; one of these patrols reached the Sapignies Switch Line unmolested, crossed the Arras - Bapaume road, and established itself in shell-holes the other side. Another patrol, however, in trying to reach Behagnies got shot up badly and had to retire.

Our Company Headquarters was established in a Boche dug-out, on a slight ridge, from which we could see into the village of Sapignies. The whole afternoon was spent trying to advance still further, but Behagnies was tenaciously held: so Bobby and I had some tea, sitting at the top of the dug-out steps. A Major in the Rifle Brigade came up and spoke to Bobby, and I thought I recognized his face; he turned out to be Frank Gull who was at m'tutors[735], though long before my time. We had a short chat about our revered "Muggins,"[736] whilst he was having a cup of tea with us. I believed he was killed shortly after leaving us.

Later we heard that the 37th Division had occupied the village of Biefvillers, so we packed up and pushed forward. Our next Headquarters were practically in the Sapignies Switch, but we could go no further, because "D" Company on the left was held up by machine gun fire from our old friend, Behagnies.

We prepared to spend the night in our new Headquarters, and an excellent dinner was served by my faithful servant, Private Midwinter, from some extra rations which I had managed to scrounge from Bob FitzGerald[737], who had had them passed on to him by an unknown Colonel. We had soup, tinned salmon, rabbit, and toasted cheese!

Soon after nightfall, the Boches started shelling with their filthy sneezing gas; it was so damnably strong that there was nothing for it but to try and sleep in a gas mask, which is no easy feat. The outposts, too, came in for a pretty heavy strafe, but they were well scattered in shell-holes and the enemy could have no accurate idea of their positions. It amounted to random shelling by heavies, and did us little damage.

---

[735] 'm'tutors' in Etonian terms means house. Major Grancis [sic] 'Frank' Gull of the Rifle Brigade was the 28-year-old son of Sir William and Lady Gull. He was killed on the next day, August 25th.

[736] Hugh Macnaghten, a Housemaster at Eton from 1898-1920, when he became the Vice Provost. Both Gull and Neville were in his house.

[737] Lieutenant R.A. FitzGerald.

On the evening of August 24th, Major-General Cecil Pereira was told that his 2nd Division was to be relieved by the 62nd Division which would continue the advance, but that Behagnies and Sapignies must be taken first, by 9 a.m. the next day, 'at all costs'. On a bright moonlight night, Pereira rapidly rode up the shell-hole stricken tracks to meet Brigadier-General W.L. Osborn of the 5th Brigade and the local artillery commander. It was Pereira, himself, who came up with the plan to first take Behagnies direct, and then for a fresh battalion to assault Sapignies from the north in order to get behind the enemy's defences. As will be seen, this plan of attack on the two villages worked brilliantly and, for its conception, all the credit was Pereira's.

At about 1.40 a.m. August 25th, orders reached Major George Field that the 52nd must attack Sapignies in conjunction with the 24th R.F. and the 2nd H.L.I. who were to make a further assault on Behagnies. [see map page 597]. Zero hour was to be 3.30 a.m. for the R.F. and H.L.I., allowing only two hours for the units to move into position. The 52nd would directly follow the R.F., and were to wheel down into Sapignies for their own zero at 4.30 a.m. In fact Field was instructed by the 5th Brigade that the 52nd should not pass the junction of the sunken road with the Arras - Bapaume road at H.2.c.9.2. before zero hour and 60 minutes. Additionally, he was told to nominate a company to specifically clear the south-west of Sapignies. The plan envisaged the three battalions establishing positions to the east and south-west of the captured villages.

The 6th Brigade had carried Ervillers on the 23rd, and it was imperative that the 5th Brigade took the other two villages, Behagnies and Sapignies, through which the Arras - Bapaume road ran on a high ridge well above the current positions of the 52nd. Failure to take them would lead to a failure of the advance of VI Corps. Heavy artillery was to be used to soften the two villages up, and no less than seven brigades of field artillery would provide a creeping barrage for the attack. At 3.30 a.m., there would a six-minute period of artillery pounding of the German line, followed by a creeping barrage advancing at 100 yards every three minutes. This would include an individualized creeping barrage from the north for the 52nd at Sapignies.

The late arrival of his orders, and the fact that his companies were widely scattered, made it impossible for George Field to get all of his men to the point of assembly by 3.30 a.m., when the 24th R.F. and 2nd H.L.I. would lead the way forward. The plan was for the 52nd to follow the R.F. on the right, and the H.L.I. on the left, at a distance of 800 yards and then, at 4.30 a.m., to wheel into Sapignies from the north. When Field received his orders: B Company was 300 yards north-east of the Regimental Headquarters in Triangle Copse; A Company was 400 yards east of the Headquarters; C and D Companies were two miles away to the south, having relieved the 1st K.R.R.C. After being directly briefed by Field, B [Captain John Blagrove] and A [Lieutenant Charles Colvill] managed to reach the assembly point at about 3.40 a.m., just in time to follow the 24th R.F. at the correct distance. C [Captain Percy Bobby] and D [Lieutenant Bob FitzGerald] were sent messages and eventually arrived at 4.30 p.m. and 4.45 p.m. respectively[738].

At about 3.50 a.m., A, B Companies and the Regimental Headquarters set off after the 24th R.F. A and B had two platoons in front and the other two in support. Mustard gas and a thick mist made it difficult to keep direction and touch. Forty minutes later, C Company followed the leading companies and would eventually manage to catch them up. The last company to arrive at the point of assembly, D, was placed in reserve along the road to the west of Sapignies at H.7.b.55.35-H.7.b75.35. Initially George Field set up the Regimental Headquarters in front of Behagnies at H.1.a.23.65 before moving it forward at 6 a.m. to the south of Sapignies at H.7.d.3.8.

Taking the enemy completely by surprise, the 2nd H.L.I. and the 24th R.F. cleared Behagnies while it was still dark and then established themselves on a line 300 yards to the east of the village. Many of the enemy were found asleep in their dug-outs and surrendered at once. Others, attempting to escape, were shot down. One house on the northern edge of the village proved obdurate and a reserve company had to be brought up to deal with it but, by 6 a.m., Behagnies had been captured. During the assault, the enemy had fired gas and high explosive shells into the centre of the village on to both the 24th R.F. and their own troops.

As the 52nd moved forward, the enemy put down a heavy barrage of high explosive and mustard gas shells, through which the leading companies, A and B, advanced to the road running from the north-east to south-west [H.1.d to H.7.b] in front of the two villages. At this point the Germans opened a fairly heavy machine-gun fire but, owing to the mist, there were few casualties and the advance was continued. A party from B Company under Lieutenant Dick Warren dealt with the machine-gun in question, and two platoons of A Company under Lieutenant H.A. 'Ginger' Smith also went forward to clear the way. At this juncture, C Company arrived on the scene and moved to the left of the two leading Companies, A and B, who had gone a little too far to the south of the intended point. Thus, at about 4.30 a.m., the 52nd moved past the south side of Behagnies and followed their orders by wheeling down into Sapignies from the

[738] It is not clear where the rendezvous was situated. It was likely to have been at the point occupied by the 24th Royal Fusiliers, H.1.a. and G.6.d.

north with its left, C Company, on the Arras - Bapaume road[739]. This manoeuvre, taking the main German forces in flank and rear, was successful and resulted in the capture of most of the village by 7.15 a.m. At 8 a.m., the three companies made contact with Major George Field at Regimental Headquarters. Although, it was reported that Sapignies had been taken at 7.15 a.m., it was not until about 9 a.m. that the village was finally cleared of the enemy.

As the three companies of the 52nd went through Sapignies small parties became detached in the mist. Amongst them were Lieutenants Dick Warren and H.A. 'Ginger' Smith who, with a few men, captured several machine-guns and their crews, this greatly assisting in the taking of the village. A German officer was captured in the village as he ran to turn out his men and was commandeered to get them to surrender. Serjeant-Major E.J. Smith rounded up thirteen prisoners and four machine-guns from an enemy strong point. His great coolness and devotion to duty under very heavy shellfire would lead to the award of a D.C.M. to add to his M.M. At 8.50 a.m., another party of Germans was seen emerging from dug-outs to the south of Sapignies. They were fired upon and immediately put their hands up and surrendered to men of the 13th Rifle Brigade.

A little later, at 9.15 a.m., a brigade of the 62nd Division passed through Sapignies on its way to assault Beugnâtre. A 5th Brigade report recorded that the attack on Behagnies and Sapignies would have failed again, as a result of machine-gun fire, if it had been conducted once more in daylight. The Germans stated that they did not expect an attack so early in the morning and thought it was just an artillery bombardment.

Behagnies and Sapignies were held by Bavarian Reserve Regiment No. 16 of the 6th Bavarian Reserve Division. This was considered to be a second-class division in 1918 and was used by the Germans for 'follow up' work rather than for primary assaults. The No. 16 Regiment reported that 'few came back living from the murderous close fighting'. In a contemporary letter to Richard Crosse, Major George Field reported that the 52nd took Sapignies 'with very little opposition'. Judging by other reports his comment appears to be a considerable understatement.

At 4.30 p.m., the 52nd received orders to withdraw from Sapignies on the completion of relief by a regiment of the 62nd Division but, in the event, the withdrawal was not carried out until 9.20 p.m. owing to a heavy enemy barrage which lasted for four hours. George Field described it as one of the worst barrages he had experienced in the whole war. The Germans made a counter-attack against Behagnies and Sapignies, which was repulsed by the Guards and 62nd Division. Eventually, at 10 p.m., the 52nd bivouacked south of Courcelles-le-

[739] At least part of C Company crossed to the eastern side of the road.

Comte and to the west of the railway in A.21.d. Here they had a miserable night, being drenched by pouring rain during a terrible storm. Every man was soaked to the skin. The ground that the 2nd Division had taken had been reached by the Division the year before, on March 28th, when following up the Germans from Courcelette.

Lieutenant Jim Neville gave a vivid account of the action in his diary[740].

> At 3 a.m. Bobby[741] received orders to move at once to the Headquarters of the 24th Royal Fusiliers. Orderlies rushed off to the outposts to withdraw the platoons, and at 3.30, after the last of the Company had assembled, we marched off through a thick mist, by platoons at 100 yards distance. Meanwhile, our guns were barking like blazes just behind us, while the heavies and "grandmas," boomed in the distance still further behind; and in front, the woods of Behagnies were lit by the continual stream of bursting shells; a barrage had started in earnest.
>
> From the Headquarters of the 24th Royal Fusiliers we were led to our own Regimental Headquarters where George Field, now commanding the Regiment since Crosse had been knocked out, gave Bobby orders to attack Sapignies.
>
> We were the last of the Companies to arrive, and it was now well after 4 a.m., and our barrage had started at 3.30![742] The enemy's shelling with 5.9 sneezers was very heavy in front of us, and field guns were also putting down a curtain between us and the village. The filthy sneezers made us retch and spit and cough, but it was no earthly good putting on gas respirators, because the fog made it hard enough to see as it was. We started off in what we thought was the right direction for the village, but the mist and gas, hanging low on the ground, made it extremely difficult to determine with any accuracy. But we had not gone far, when we ran into "B" Company in the same plight; Bobby had a discussion with John Blagrove on the direction to take. They shouted at each other at the top of their voices to make themselves heard above the crash of shells.
>
> Eventually, we advanced with platoons in file towards the wood in front of us. There were plenty of dead and wounded Boches lying

[740] Diary entry for August 25th 1918.

[741] Captain Percy Bobby, commanding C Company.

[742] This is likely to be incorrect. Lieutenant Bob FitzGerald's D Company was the last to return and went into reserve.

in the first trenches we encountered, including one unfortunate man, shot through the carotid artery, spouting blood.

In the outskirts of Sapignies we put up a couple of Boches, who popped out of some huts and legged it like hell. I had a shot at one with my automatic. He fell forward with a crash and I was just congratulating myself on having, at last, killed a man with my pistol, when I realized that my Platoon Serjeant had dropped on his knee and fired simultaneously with me. After that there was little doubt whose bird the Boche was, for I knew what a good rifle shot Serjeant Brinsden was! Anyway, the shot blew the back out of the Boche's head. The other Boche was neatly floored by Corporal Hollyoake. So far, so good. It seemed almost too good to be true. Where are all the Boches?

We crossed the Arras-Bapaume road and occupied some trenches on the other side. My boots, puttees and socks were soaked through by the heavy dew, and it was cold squatting in the half-dug trenches. Bobby went off on his own to see if he could find "B" Company on the right; in the advance through the mist we had completely lost touch with them and at the moment had no troops on either flank; also, I think, he wanted to see if he could find any Boches, being of the fire-eating type.

While he was away I had a snack of food, there being no time like the present. It was an excellent breakfast, consisting of cold bacon and a hunk of bread covered with sugar!

Bobby, on his return said there was no sign of "B" Company anywhere, so I asked him if I could take a patrol and try to find touch. I was very cold and wet, and wanted some excuse to get warm, while there was always a chance of rounding up some Boches and picking up some useful souvenirs. Bobby agreed, and I called for some volunteers, and eventually chose a tough gang, including Serjeant Brinsden and Private James, who was thirsting to avenge the deaths of four brothers.

The mist was becoming filmy, with, now and again, beams of light from the rising sun, when my party set off. We hammered at the doors of all the dug-outs for lurking Boches but were unsuccessful until we reached the main road. Here I ran into a stretcher-bearer who put up his hands at once. He dumped his heavy equipment on the road, from which I took a jolly little Browning automatic. His equipment resembled a walking chemist's shop, and contained a mass of little bottles, pots, and glass vials; what we would call in Norfolk, a master-piece. I pointed to the shed where we had found him hiding, and shouted, as one generally does when one doesn't know a word of the language, "More Boches inside," he replied, "Nix" which was about the only word I did know!

Next we found a light gun, which we handed over to our prisoner to carry. We were doing quite well, when I was suddenly aware that Serjeant Brinsden had disappeared. A moment later, I caught sight of him through a rift in the mist, running down the road in pursuit of some Boches. The patrol had got a bit out of hand, and had not waited for me, nor had Serjeant Brinsden called my attention to the enemy down the road. All but one other man had followed the serjeant, like hounds on a breast-high scent. The Boches turned to the right off the road, straight in the direction of "B" Company, which suited me very well. I called back the nearest men, and formed them into line and made for the spot where I had last seen the Boches.

There was still no sign of "B" Company. This was rather awkward, because, by this time we had wandered far from the Company, and the thickness of the infernal fog prevented me from seeing exactly where I was. So we crossed the road and bore slightly to our right hoping that "B" Company might be a little behind us. I took out my whistle and blew it several times, and then bawled "B Company" at the top of my voice, but no answering call came back through the mist.

However, after a while, I heard considerable shouting ahead which I thought must have come from "B." I shouted back through the mist and thought I heard an answer. "Here we are." There was one man with me at the time, Private James, and the others were not far off, but invisible to me. James and I and the dog-like prisoner, who had followed patiently in our footsteps, went through the intervening hedge towards the sound of the shouting. At last we found them; sure enough I could see helmets, plenty of them, floating along the top of the fog. But seconds later, and then too late, I realized that these helmets contained Boche heads! Simultaneously there was a loud crack and my pistol fell out of my right hand, and I felt a numbing pain as if someone had hit me with a sledge hammer. I ran back to some cover, while the enemy streamed past me jabbering like monkeys. The rest of the patrol seemed to have

The spot in Sapignies where Jim Neville was wounded on August 25th 1918. The Arras to Bapaume road is in the foreground. Photograph circa 1920.
[NRO NEV 7/31]

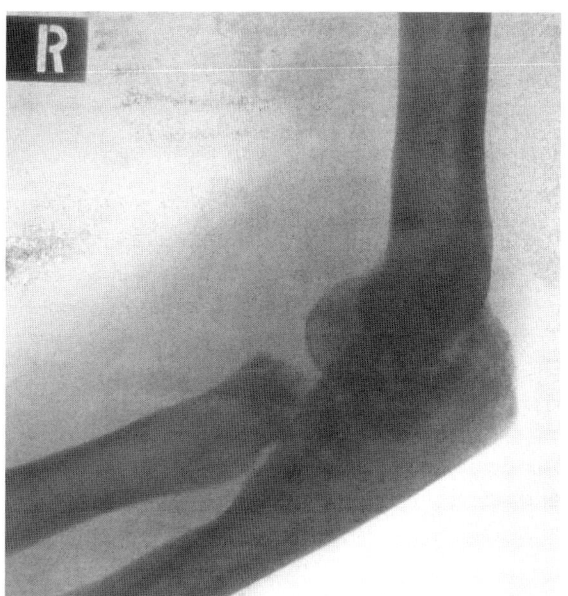

The original X ray of Jim Neville's wounded right elbow. After the war, his elbow remained slightly bent and his suits were adjusted accordingly.
[NRO NEV 7/32]

Jim Neville M.C.
[NRO NEV 7/32]

Looking up the hill towards the site of the Quarry at Mont-sur-l'Oeuvre from the railway where D Company were pinned down on October 1st 1918, during the Battle of the Canal du Nord. [Author's Collection 2008]

Sir Philip 'Slatcher' Whitehead served with the 52nd from 1916-18. He was severely wounded leading A Company at the Battle of Arleux in April 1917. Whitehead returned to the Regiment to lead A Company, once more, in their final battle, the Battle of the Selle, in October 1918. [Regimental Chronicles]

Percy Bobby M.C., an able and aggressive C Company commander, at the Battle of the Selle in October 1918. [NRO NEV 7/32]

This is believed to be Hugh Stokes M.C., the last 52nd officer to die in the war. [Townsend Collection]

Hugh Stokes' Military Cross. [Townsend Collection]

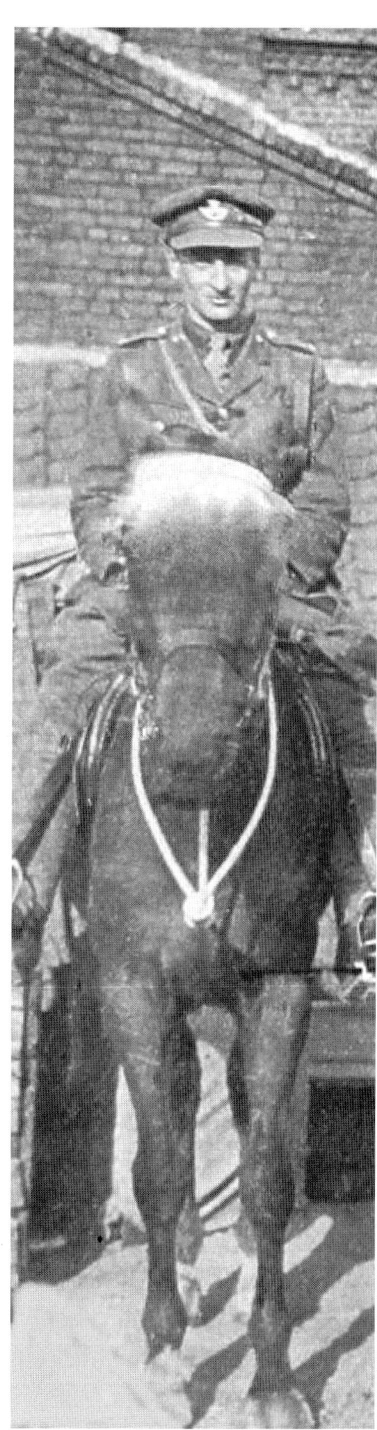

Gordon Fuller, A Company commander who was killed by shellfire on July 7th 1918. [NRO NEV 7/32]

Guy Blewitt's airedale terrier called D. When Blewitt left the 52nd, he gave the dog to George Field and it subsequently vanished in France. When Field was transferred to Egypt, he was surprised by the appearance of D in his tent at Suez, having apparently been adopted and transported overseas by another officer. [Blewitt's Diaries]

Ralph Kite's identity disc.
[Kite Collection]

Major-General Sir Cecil Pereira K.C.B., C.M.G. commanded the 2nd Division from December 1916 until March 1919. He was wounded twice in 1915, disproving the myth that Brigadier-Generals sat behind the lines in comfortable châteaux.
[Wyrall]

March 1st 1919, Major-General Cecil Pereira, commanding the 2nd Division, bids farewell to the 52nd at Zons.
[NRO NEV 7/32]

disappeared, and the chance of sailing into the retreating Boches with five rounds rapid was lost.

Then it occurred to me that there might be plenty more to come, in which case the patrol would be caught in an awkward predicament. I called to Private James to go and find Serjeant Brinsden, but received only moans in answer. To make things worse the fog chose that moment to lift and thus revealed us to the enemy, not more than 20 yards away. Why they took no notice of us, I cannot conceive; I can only suppose they were pre-occupied with their own safety. I went over to Private James to find him swearing like a good infantryman that he had been hit by an expanding bullet. His left arm was hanging by a thread from his shoulder, and, as only one shot was fired at us, I imagine the bullet which hit me must have turned from my elbow and torn off his arm.

Without achieving our object, I collected the patrol and tried to trace our way back to "C" Company; but this was no easy job, and I was terribly sick and shaken, and was also bleeding like a pig. So, I stopped and sat down for a bit while Corporal Hollyoake bound up my arm. The fog had come down again, and the Boches were shelling the road, while our guns were putting in a few playful shots into Sapignies, in case we had not captured it. I had almost given up hope of ever finding "C" again when suddenly the fog lifted once more, to the tune of machine gun fire. The lift was sufficient, for I saw two men coming towards us, and recognized the ever faithful Midwinter. I told Bobby what I knew, and roughly where the Boches had come from, and the direction of their retreat, and then set off down the line, wasting no time in passing through the village as our guns were shelling it.

On the other side of the village I met Dick Warren of "B" Company, leading his platoon forward. God knows what had happened to his Company. I suppose they had lost themselves too. He told me that he thought he had got a nice blighty one, but that, to his sorrow, he had found that that the machine gun bullet had merely taken the sole off his boot![743]

At forward Aid Post a stretcher bearer had a look at my wound, and sorrowfully remarked that he did not think the artery was

[743] In 1976, Neville recalled meeting Dick Warren. 'You lucky bugger. You have got a cushy one'. I said: 'well I have got one but it's not all that cushy'.

severed! Later, at the Regimental Aid Post, the Doctor confirmed his suspicions.

I was sorry to see the last of Midwinter, as I got into a horse-drawn ambulance. It seemed bad luck that he couldn't share my good luck. But orders are orders, and back he had to go. There was quite a hubbub at the Field Ambulance, near Courcelles. Somebody asked me where I had been hit, and when I said "in the elbow," he waxed rather wroth and wanted to know what part of the line. The one word, "Sapignies", seemed to have a magical effect, for the brass-hatted somebody popped off and came back with a still more brazen hat in tow, who, I believe, was our revered Corps Commander[744]. Their faces were wreathed in smiles, like the cats', when I told them that the 52nd – the accent on the 52nd – had captured the village at 4.30 a.m. It appeared that this infernal little village of ruins played a big part in the scheme of things.

They literally purred over the tidings, and I felt myself to be quite a hero, for I had never seen so many of the Staff before, and wondered where they had all come from. It seemed too close to the line!

The 52nd's casualties for the 25th were relatively light with five killed and 59 wounded[745]. No officers were killed during the day, but five had been wounded: Lieutenants Jim Neville [gunshot wound right elbow], Dick Warren [shrapnel wound hand], Bob FitzGerald [gunshot wound chest] and H.A. 'Ginger' Smith [gunshot wound right upper arm]; Second-Lieutenant R.W. Sawers [gunshot wound left leg]. The latter was slightly wounded but soon returned to duty. No doubt the reduced visibility secondary to the early morning mist was a significant factor in keeping casualties to a minimum. The next day, Dick Warren received a further gunshot wound of his head. The extraordinarily fortunate young officer was lucky not to lose his life, and travelled to hospital in the same train as Neville. Jim Neville wrote in a letter to his sisters[746]: 'He [Warren] had

---

[744] Lieutenant-General Sir Aylmer Haldane, commanding VI Corps.

[745] There is some doubt about these figures. The *Regimental Chronicles* gave a figure of 59 other ranks wounded; the *Battalion War Diary* stated total casualties of four officers and 36 other ranks for the August 25th entry. However, in a table at the end of the entries for August, 59 wounded have been recorded; Brigadier-General W.L. Osborn quoted casualty figures of one officer and 36 other ranks in his report.

[746] Letter to his sisters written from the No. 10 British Red Cross Hospital Le Tréport on September 2nd 1918. The hospital was better known as 'Lady Murray's' after Lady Helen Stewart-Murray, a daughter of the 7th Duke of Atholl, who ran it.

been hit though his helmet, which hung at the head of his cot with a huge hole blown out of the back of it'. Overall in the whole operation, the 5th Brigade had killed 180 Germans and captured 250-300 prisoners, 100 machine-guns and three field guns.

Later a number of gallantry awards were made to members of the 52nd following the recent operations. Lieutenant Dick Warren received a bar to his M.C. Lieutenants Charles Colvill, H.A. 'Ginger' Smith and Second-Lieutenant E. Hobson received the M.C. The American Medical Officer, First-Lieutenant A.J. Smith, was also awarded the M.C. Serjeant-Major E.J. Smith who had already received the M.M. was awarded the D.C.M. Serjeants Biggs, Brinsden, North; Corporals Stapeley, Hollyoake; Lance-Corporals Roberts, Williams; Private Hatchett all received the M.M.

Nowadays, the Albert-Arras railway still runs across the 52nd's former battlefield. Triangle Copse where Richard Crosse was seriously wounded has long since vanished and is merely marked by a darkening of the earth in a ploughed field. However, it is easy to see what easy pickings the German artillery had from the Bapaume to Arras road away to the east.

In 1920, the Battles Nomenclature Committee decided that the Second Battles of the Somme 1918 had taken place between August 21st and September 3rd. There were two sub-divisions: the Battle of Albert 1918, August 21st-23rd; the Second Battle of Bapaume, August 31st-September 3rd. The 52nd had been within the defined geographical limits for the Battle of Albert 1918 and, as will be seen in the next chapter, would become eligible for the Second Battle of Bapaume. However, the fighting had continued during the period August 24th-30th, including the action of the 52nd at Sapignies, and it was only covered by the general title of the Second Battles of the Somme 1918. In 1935, an attempt was made to extend the defined period of the Second Battle of Bapaume by six days to encompass August 24th-September 3rd. This seemingly sensible request was turned down by the Battles Nomenclature Committee.

In summary, the 52nd was able to claim the Battles of the Somme 1918, the Battle of Albert 1918, and the Battle of Bapaume as battle honours. However, there was no specific honour for their fine performance at Sapignies. In addition, the 52nd could only add one battle honour to its wartime total, for the Battles of Bapaume 1918, although the Regiment had taken part in both the First [March 24th-25th] and the Second [August 31st-September 3rd] Battles. The same rationale applied to the Battles of the Somme 1918, where the Regiment had taken part in both the First [March 21st-April 5th] and the Second [August 21st-September 3rd] Battles. There was only one battle honour to be added to the wartime total for the two actions.

Brigadier-General W.L. Osborn, of the 5th Brigade recorded the following comments about the recent actions in the *Brigade's War Diary.*

> ---- the splendid unflinching advance of the 5th Brigade at midday of the 23rd through an enemy heavy Artillery barrage on to BEHAGNIES and SAPIGNIES, the inability to capture the villages without further preparation and finally the gallant and highly successful capture of the two villages on the early morning of the 25th with its large haul of prisoners and booty. In this operation the enemy was completely out-manoeuvred.

Major-General Cecil Pereira, of the 2nd Division, was also impressed by the performance of the 5th Brigade on August 25th. He left these comments in his diary.

> The 5th Brigade have carried out a brilliant little exploit. It required exceptionally fine organizing and leading to carry out this coup against a strongly held place after the first attempt cost them considerable casualties. Without tanks the position was a most formidable one owing to a long glacis swept by M.G. fire. An attack before dawn got over this difficulty and Sapignies we got by surprise. Our heavy artillery bombarded both villages for an hour before Zero and were timed to carry it on until the Infantry were due on each objective.

The day after the 5th Brigade's success at Behagnies and Sapignies General Henry Horne's First Army attacked astride the River Scarpe. On August 26th, Wancourt, Monchy, Guémappe fell and the next day it was the turn of Roeux and Gavrelle. The Germans were given no respite and General Henry Rawlinson's Fourth Army took Combles and Morval on the 29th, whilst General Julian Byng's Third Army took Bapaume the same day. On the 30th, Horne was east of Eterpigny, Bullecourt and Vaulx-Vraucourt. The Germans were being pushed back in every direction including further south by the French.

The River Somme might have provided an excellent line of resistance, but on the night of August 30th Rawlinson's Fourth Army crossed the river, and the next morning stormed Mont St. Quentin, the key to the important city of Péronne. In a supreme feat of arms, the 2nd Australian Division captured this formidable position. General Erich von Ludendorff still believed that if he could get his armies back to the Hindenburg Line they might rest there for the winter.

However, to hold that line, von Ludendorff knew that he must hold Péronne at all costs. On September 1st, Rawlinson's Australians entered Péronne and, at the same time, Byng's forces pushed forward from Bapaume towards the Canal du Nord, north of Péronne. The German game was well and truly up.

Chapter XXIII

The Battles of the Hindenburg Line: Havrincourt, Canal du Nord, Cambrai 1918.

August 25th - October 12th 1918

[Maps: pages 620, 623, 630, 632.]

Sir Douglas Haig met Marshal Ferdinand Foch at a conference for the commanders-in-chief on August 29th, and came away with instructions to continue with the pursuit of the enemy. On September 2nd, General Henry Horne's First Army broke the Drocourt-Quéant Line south of Arras, and further to the south, General Julian Byng's Third Army was ordered to push on energetically, on the right of the First Army, towards the Canal du Nord. As part of the Third Army, Lieutenant-General Aylmer Haldane's VI Corps, in which the 2nd Division and the 52nd Light Infantry served, would play their part in forcing the enemy back to the Hindenburg Line.

In 1920, the Battles Nomenclature Committee decided that the Battles of the Hindenburg Line had taken place between September 12th and October 9th 1918. As will be seen shortly, the 52nd was actively involved in two of them: the Battle of Havrincourt on September 12th, and the Battle of the Canal du Nord from September 27th-October 1st. Although, the 52nd was in the correct geographical area for the Battle of Cambrai, 1918, which took place from October 9th-12th, and could therefore claim it as a battle honour, they did not fight in it.

It is time to return to the 52nd in their bivouacs to the south of Courcelles-le-Comte. Here the Regiment remained from August 25th-September 2nd, their time spent in resting, reorganizing and training. A number of officers reported for duty during this period: Lieutenant F.M. Cowell on the 28th; Second-Lieutenants C. Gray, L.M. Crosfield, on the 29th; Lieutenants L.S. Dowson [rejoining having been wounded at Arleux in 1917], A.H.B. Brooke, A. Cockshut, H.E. Wells, on the 30th; Second-Lieutenant C.H. Sheppard, also on the 30th. In addition the 99th reinforcement of 25 other ranks arrived on the 30th. A church parade was held on September 1st and a further reinforcement, the 100th, consisting of 22 other ranks, joined the same day.

On September 2nd, VI Corps used the 3rd and 62nd Divisions to attack the line Lagnicourt-Morchies with the 2nd Division in reserve. The 5th Brigade and the 52nd moved forward as part of the 2nd Division in case they were required. At 6 a.m., the 5th Brigade was put at one hour's notice and the 52nd set off at 11.30 a.m. from their camp near Courcelles-le-Comte, passing south of Gomiécourt and then by a track to the north of Behagnies. Finally, the Regiment reached its destination in map reference H4, between Sapignies and Vaulx-Vraucourt, and to the north of Favreuil. A and B Companies were accommodated in shelters and the unfortunate C and D in trenches. Unfortunately, the attack by the 3rd and 62nd Divisions was only partially successful, ending up some 2,000 yards short of their objective. The 52nd was not required to play a part in the action.

The following day, the 3rd, the 2nd Division which had replaced the 62nd Division in the front line was required to make a further attempt with the Guards Division, on Lagnicourt and Morchies. The 6th and 99th Brigades were to be used with the 5th Brigade now in divisional reserve. There was some hope that the Germans would have withdrawn, as their flank was now unprotected where XVII Corps had been successful around Quéant. In order to fulfil their responsibilities as part of the divisional reserve, the 52nd were on the move once more. The Regiment set off about 10 a.m. and reached the ridge close to the east side of Vaulx-Vraucourt by 1.30 p.m. Here the Regiment bivouacked facing the Bois de Vaulx in C.26.d.4.6, and their transport came up to the high ground to the east of the village. Second-Lieutenant E. Hobson was sent home to England suffering from piles. In the following December he would be awarded the M.C. By the end of the day, the Guards and 2nd Division had advanced nearly six miles until they came up against the Havrincourt-Moeuvres sector of the Hindenburg Line, made even more formidable by the Canal du Nord. The suspicion that the enemy might withdraw had proved correct.

On September 4th, the 6th Brigade reported that it was in contact with the enemy just to the west of the Canal du Nord. The 99th Brigade was to replace the 6th Brigade in the front line and the 5th Brigade would take the place of the 99th as the support brigade. At 5.30 p.m., the 52nd was scheduled to take the place of the 23rd Royal Fusiliers in support, but in the event no change in position took place. The order was cancelled as the Regiment was about to move off. The 52nd was saddened to hear of the death of Major Bertram Parr, a 43rd Light Infantry officer who had been serving as the second-in-command of the 2nd South Staffordshire, and had been killed the day before in the advance to the Canal du Nord. His body was buried in the British Cemetery close to Vaulx-Vraucourt Church on the 4th. The 34-year-old Parr was well known to the pre-war members of the 52nd, and he had escaped incarceration after Kut when he was serving with the West African Frontier Force.

A welcome visitor, on the 4th, was the 52nd's Commanding Officer, Lieutenant-Colonel Richard Crosse, who had managed to temporarily escape from hospital in Abbeville only twelve days after being seriously wounded. Crosse had been carried back on a stretcher to the Regimental Aid Post where he met 'our faithful padre, the Reverend E.M. Guilford M.C., whom I was glad to see'. At the Casualty Clearing Station, Crosse met another old friend, the Reverend Frank

Okell, a future Bishop of Stockport. Okell had been Crosse's dormitory captain at Rugby School. In No. 17 C.C.S., at Bourg, Crosse's wounds were properly cleaned and dressed: the dressing was unchanged for two weeks such was the pressure of work on the medical and nursing staff. Later, he was put on a train for Abbeville and the No. 2 Hospital there. Crosse was attended to by his bugler, Collier, the last of the 1914 buglers, who had attached himself to his commanding officer and was most attentive.

During the train journey, Crosse was handed a message from Major-General Cecil Pereira, commanding the 2nd Division. 'Deep personal sympathy aaa personal assurance that the command of the Regiment shall be kept open for Colonel Crosse From ADMS 2 Division'. Crosse described it as the 'best medicine'. 'Truly a kind act by General Pereira in sending it. I carried it with me always'. About September 10th, Crosse by irregular means got himself discharged from hospital. Two years before his death, he described the participants in this little pantomime[747].

> As several participants contributed to the humour of it; the parson whom I told would be torn to pieces if he talked to old soldiers as he did to me ("Are you prepared to meet your Maker?"), the orderly who would not lift me, Kathleen Mavcurneen (fictitious name) V.A.D.[748], 'Fanny fat legs', Slade-Baker's (of 52nd) father[749], Brooke Purdon[750] the Irish doctor. Several of these cooperated valiantly. Being Irish they were in their element when "agin the government".

In any case the ever charming and persuasive Crosse got himself to England on twenty days' sick leave 'suffering from debility'! If he had been granted longer leave 'he would have been struck off the strength of the Regiment in the field and that was too dreadful to think about'[751].

---

[747] Letter to Sir Edmond [Jim] Neville written in 1968.

[748] Possibly the name was based on the 1837 song *Kathleen Mavourneen*.

[749] The son Captain John Slade-Baker; the father Brigadier-General Arthur Slade-Baker R.A. and R.A.O.C.

[750] William Brooke Purdon [1881-1950]. Qualified in Belfast in 1913. From 1917-19 he served as an acting Lieutenant-Colonel in the Convalescent Depots Nos. 5, 6, 16. Purdon ended his military career as a Major-General in 1938.

[751] The quotes in this section concerning Richard Crosse are taken from Lieutenant-Colonel Sir Edmond [Jim] Neville's speech at the unveiling of a stained glass window, in memory of Crosse, in the Garrison Church, Winchester on June 18th [the anniversary of the Battle of Waterloo] 1971. The window depicted the Regimental crest which had been transported from Crosse's former home, Raven's Oak near Nantwich. He had died the year before. Sadly, the Garrison Church is now a cinema and the author could find no sign of the window in 2008.

On September 5th, the 5th Brigade ordered their battalion's officers to reconnoitre the forward area but, to go no further east than Demicourt and Hermies. The 52nd remained in their bivouacs facing the Bois de Vaulx. During the day, parties of officers reconnoitred as far as Doignies to the north-west of Hermies. On the morning of the 6th, the Regiment moved forward to the south of Morchies facing Chaufours Wood in I.11.d. and 12.c[752]. Officers and Scouts made a further reconnaissance of the forward area. From the point of view of the 52nd, little of consequence happened on September 7th. In the morning 9 a.m.-noon, company commanders supervised physical training and games for the men. As on the previous two days, officers and N.C.O.s reconnoitred the front area as far forward as Demicourt. During the day, the 101st reinforcement of 36 other ranks arrived and orders were received for the 5th Brigade to relieve the 99th Brigade on the night of September 8th/9th. As a part of this arrangement, the 52nd was put on notice that it would, with one company of the 24th R.F., relieve the 23rd R.F. as the front battalion.

At 10 a.m. September 8th, the 52nd sent forward advance parties to take over the stores of the 23rd R.F. and to arrange for the companies' positions that night. Later in the morning, the Regiment was warned to start making preparations for a minor operation on the 10th. The 52nd left their bivouac at 7.30 p.m. in the order of C Company plus two platoons of A, D Company plus two platoons of B, the remainder of A, the remainder of B and then the Regimental Headquarters with A Company of the 24th R.F. bringing up the rear. Two hundred yards was allowed between platoons and companies. The first company of the 52nd reached the Headquarters of the 23rd R.F. at 9 p.m. but the night was so dark and the guides unsure of the ground that the relief was not completed until 2.30 a.m. the following morning. The Regiment found themselves in the front line to the east of Demicourt. C Company with their contingent from A was in the front line on the left and D on the right. In support were the Regimental Headquarters, B Company and two platoons of A.

Shortly after the 52nd had taken up their new positions in the front line to the east of Demicourt, from 4 a.m.-5.30 a.m., the enemy started a bombardment with mustard gas on to part of A Company, the attached men of the 24th R.F., and the Regimental Headquarters. A further consignment of mustard gas was sent over at 8 a.m., and impregnated the ground and men's clothing. Unfortunately, a lack of accommodation precluded men being shifted out of the affected area and from noon-3 p.m. they began to show signs of distress. Further casualties were

---

[752] In the *Battalion War Diary* Major George Field has written 'about the area H.11.d.' which is clearly incorrect. A document entitled *A Narrative of Operations September 2nd-13th 1918* in WO 95 1346 gave the correct point.

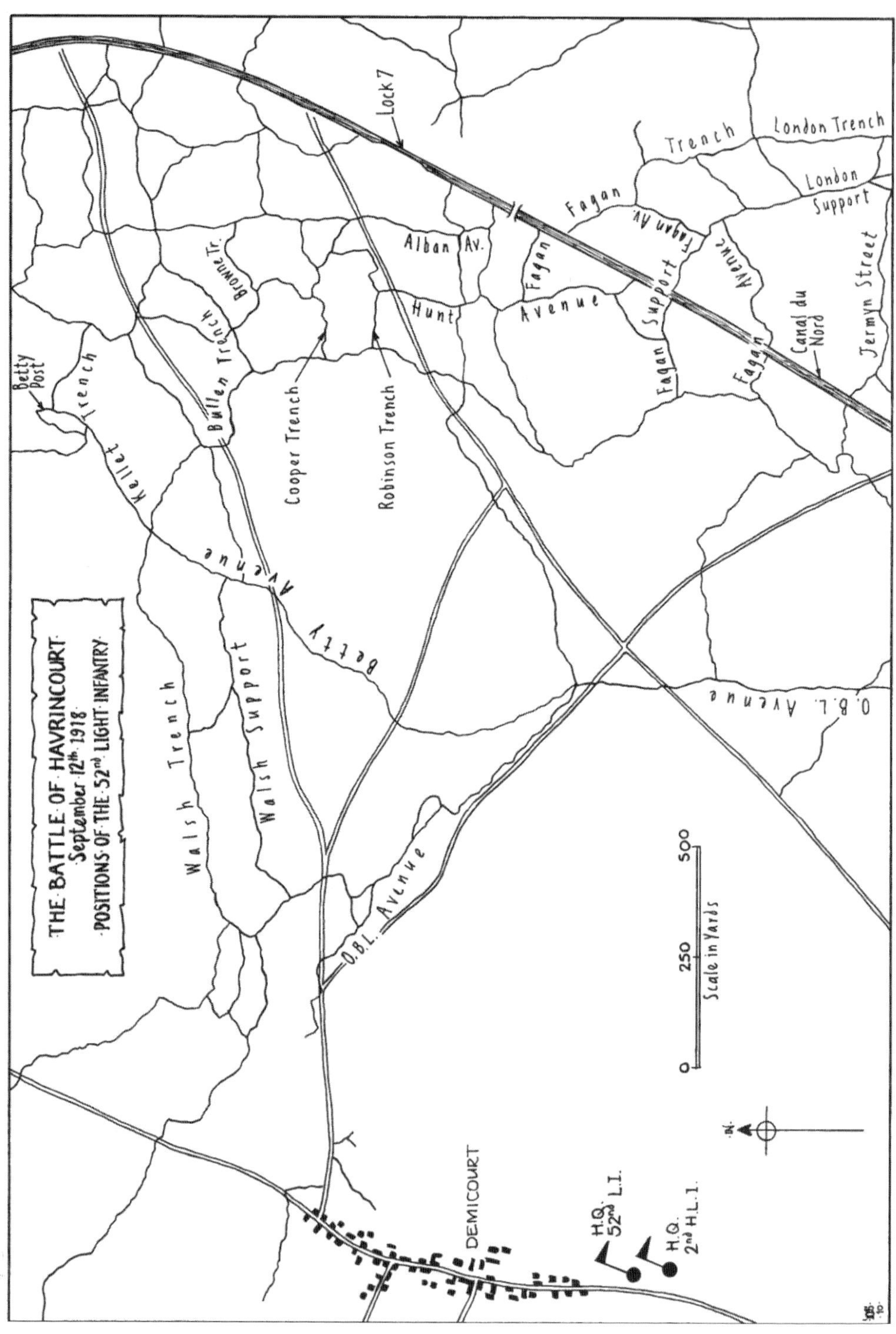
THE BATTLE OF HAVRINCOURT
September 12th 1918
POSITIONS OF THE 52nd LIGHT INFANTRY
Lock 7
London Trench
Trench
London Support
Fagan
Fagan Av.
Fagan Support
Fagan Avenue
Avenue
Jermyn Street
Canal du Nord
Alban Av.
Hunt
Browne Tr.
Bullen Trench
Cooper Trench
Robinson Trench
Betty Post
Kellet Trench
Betty Avenue
Walsh Trench
Walsh Support
O.B.L. Avenue
Scale in Yards
0
250
500
N
DEMICOURT
H.Q. 52nd L.I.
H.Q. 2nd H.L.I.

caused by British shells falling short. The total casualties for the day were three wounded and 40 more gassed [including 12 men from the attached 24th R.F.]. Lieutenant Charles Colvill, the A Company commander, was the only officer affected by the mustard gas, and he had to be sent to hospital[753]. Lieutenant Thomas 'Twitt' Tyrwhitt-Drake replaced Colvill as company commander. During the morning Major George Field began to make his arrangements for the minor operation to take place on the 10th. At about 2.30 p.m., he was informed by the 5th Brigade that the operation was postponed until the 11th, and the 2nd H.L.I. would take part in it with the 52nd.

On the morning of September 10th it rained heavily. Second-Lieutenant C.H. Sheppard was evacuated suffering from the effects of mustard gas. At 4.30 p.m., the 5th Brigade received definitive orders for the intended attack on the evening of the 11th, which were sent down to the 52nd for George Field to make his arrangements. In view of the impending operations, selected targets were harassed by both the Field and Heavy Artillery. The enemy replied in kind although, according to George Field, only a few shells on that particular day fell in the vicinity of the Regiment. The operation from the viewpoint of the 52nd would prove to be arduous and complicated in view of the heavy rain and consequent bad going. In addition, shelling and the fact that the Germans could readily follow their every move meant that the positions of assembly had to be taken up under the cover of darkness. Later the action on September 12th would be known as the Battle of Havrincourt.

On September 12th, VI Corps was ordered to advance on the important village of Havrincourt, which lay on the far side of the Canal du Nord. The 62nd Division was to capture Havrincourt, and the 5th Brigade was charged with a preliminary operation on the evening before, to secure the left flank of the 62nd Division. This involved taking the canal crossings between Hermies and Lock 7, and making a more forward line. At this stage, the 52nd had three companies in the front line along Betty Avenue and Kellet Trench; one company in close support behind them; two companies of the 24th R.F. in support to the south-east of Demicourt. On the right of the 52nd, the 2nd H.L.I. was positioned: three companies from the canal bank along West Trench and OBL Avenue; one company in support in Juniper and Kutno Trenches. The remainder of the 24th R.F. was in Brigade reserve around Beaumetz and to the north-west of Hermies. The trenches that the 52nd was occupying were all too familiar to them as the Regiment had helped construct them in late November/December 1917 during the

[753] Charles Colvill was awarded the M.C. in 1918 and the D.S.O. in 1940. He was one of the few officers to win gallantry awards in both world wars, and assumed command of the 43rd L.I. when Ernest Whitfeld was wounded at Comines in 1940.

earlier Battle of Cambrai. Thus three of the trenches bore the names, Bullen, Walsh, and Kellet [sic], those of the Brigadier-Generals G.M. Bullen-Smith, R.K. Walsh, and R.O. Kellett, commanding the 5th, 6th, and 99th Brigades of that era.

The detailed plan envisaged the 52nd, plus the two attached companies of the 24th R.F. in support, taking the enemy trench system from Fagan Avenue at K.15.c.3.3., due north along Alban Avenue, to K.9.a.3.9., and then making a defensive flank with Betty Post. To fulfil this order, part of the 52nd would have to cross the smooth, steep-sided but empty Canal du Nord. On the right of the 52nd was the 2nd H.L.I. who would endeavour to capture the line from K.26.b.0.5. to Fagan Avenue K.15.c.3.3. A party from the 10th D.C.L.I. was to be attached to the 52nd to make bombing blocks in the captured trenches.

Owing to the very bad state of the trenches and the fact that the enemy could observe their every movement, the 52nd decided to take up their battle positions on the night of September 10th/11th. This was carried out successfully without any casualties. On this night and the previous one, the 10th D.C.L.I. had deepened Betty Avenue so that it could be used as a jumping-off trench by the 52nd, and these Pioneers had also removed the bombing blocks in Walsh Trench and Walsh Support, the only available communication trenches for the 52nd to use.

For the 52nd the Battle of Havrincourt began with the minor operation whose zero hour was 6.15 p.m., September 11th. At 6.13 p.m., the field artillery fired smoke shells at a rapid rate to cover the exit of the assaulting troops. This barrage was extremely good, providing a screen from aimed fire and obliterating the view from German observation posts as far away as Bourlon Wood. From zero hour, 6.15 p.m., until zero plus four minutes, the barrage remained on the initial line and then crept forward at a rate of 100 yards every four minutes. At zero plus 36 minutes the barrage reached the line of protection where it remained until zero plus 90 minutes. This was to isolate the section of enemy line under attack in order to stop reserves being brought up. Three to four deep belts of Hindenburg Line wire had to be passed through by the advancing troops; fortunately, wire cutting barrages, over the last few days, had made suitable gaps in it. In addition to the field artillery, the heavy artillery, light trench mortars and machine-guns fired on selected points.

Both the 52nd and the 2nd H.L.I. required all four of their very weak companies in the front line when the officers and men left their trenches at 6.15 p.m. precisely. The Regiment's frontage was 1,500 yards wide, and each company advanced over the open on a two-platoon frontage in section worms, with 50 yards interval between worms, and 100 yards between the first and second lines. In the case of the 52nd, the two companies of the 24th R.F., which were attached to them, had been moved up into a close support position. The two

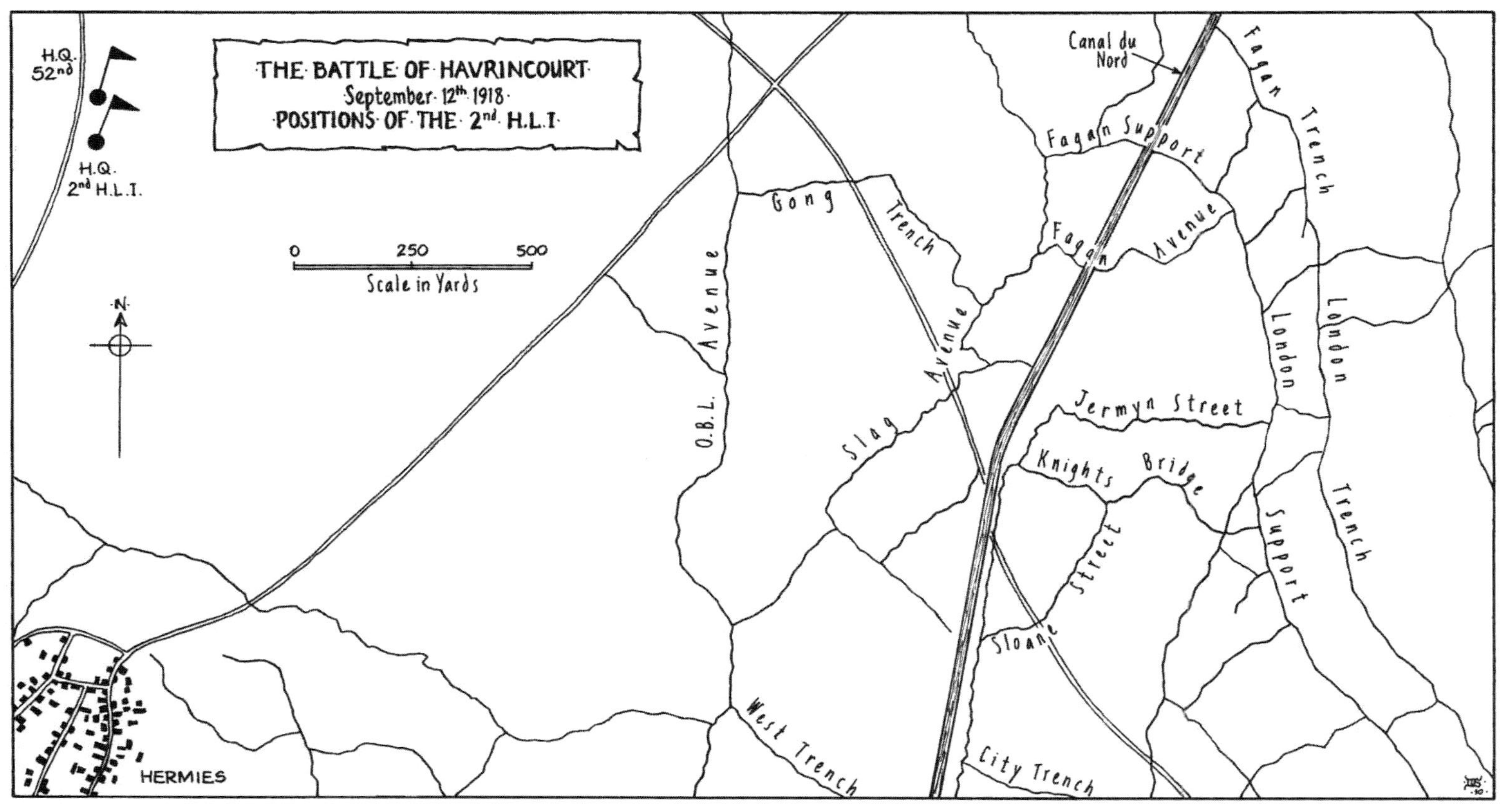
THE BATTLE OF HAVRINCOURT
September 12th 1918
POSITIONS OF THE 2nd H.L.I.
H.Q. 52nd
H.Q. 2nd H.L.I.
0
250
500
Scale in Yards
N
HERMIES
Canal du Nord
Fagan Trench
Fagan Support
Fagan Avenue
Gong Trench
O.B.L. Avenue
Slag Avenue
London Trench
London Support
Jermyn Street
Knights Bridge
Sloane Street
West Trench
City Trench

Regiments, the 52nd and the H.L.I., would have mixed fortunes over the next 24 hours.

On the right, the 2nd H.L.I. met with little opposition and by 8.10 p.m. reported that they had reached the Canal du Nord from Fagan Avenue to the Slag Heap and, shortly afterwards, that the canal bank further south was also in their hands. The H.L.I. pushed out posts beyond the canal and at 10.25 p.m. was able to report that their line was: the west bank of the canal from the divisional boundary; northwards to the Slag Heap; across the canal to Knightsbridge, Jermyn Street and Fagan Avenue. About 1 a.m. on the 12th, the H.L.I. had established posts in City Trench and Sloane Street, beyond their allotted objectives. However, they were ordered to abandon City Trench as it would interfere with the barrage for the 62nd Division's main operation at 5.25 a.m. that morning. The H.L.I. had been entirely successful and had taken all their objectives.

The 52nd was less fortunate than their Scottish comrades on the right who had met with little resistance from the enemy. Later a map captured from a German officer showed a hostile outpost line in Slag Avenue, and the main line of German resistance along Bear Trench, Hunt Avenue, across the canal, and down London Trench and Support. This was directly in the line of advance of the 52nd's C [Lieutenant J.P. Wayte], A [Lieutenant T. Tyrwhitt-Drake] and B [Captain J. Blagrove] Companies [from left to right] to the west of the canal. Hence progress for these three companies was slow with pockets of Germans resisting until they were killed or captured. Machine-gun fire from the front and left flank was particularly disruptive. Matters were made more difficult by the darkness of the night, the wet state of the ground and trenches and being subjected to a heavy barrage including a mixture of chlorine and mustard gas shells. It was clear that the 52nd's A, B, and C Companies had a formidable task ahead of them as they fought their way forward, yard by yard, with the bayonet and bomb.

At 6.45 p.m., the 52nd's supporting companies of the 24th R.F. were in position, and had established a defensive flank on the left. A little later, at 8.10 p.m., a report reached the 5th Brigade that part of the 52nd had reached their objective of Browne Trench but further south machine-gun fire had stopped the advance. By midnight it was clear that the Regiment was bogged down around Hunt Avenue which, as the enemy's main line of resistance, was strongly held with machine-guns untouched by the barrage. It was clear that a great deal of mopping up was required before daylight. Late on the 11th, the 52nd managed to establish themselves between Hunt Avenue and Alban Avenue. In the early hours of the 12th, units of the 3rd Guards Brigade, coming down from the north, relieved the 52nd's C Company and took over part of the line as far as Weston Trench and, by 5.a.m., it was occupying part of Hunt Avenue. Eventually, A and B Companies in conjunction with the battalion of the 2nd Grenadier Guards cleared Alban Trench as far as the flank of B Company.

Communications between the attacking battalions and Brigadier-General W.L. Osborn, at the Headquarters of the 5th Brigade, were very difficult. Telephone wires were soon cut by the artillery, orderlies acting as runners with messages were shot down, and the contours of the ground precluded direct visual signalling. To a degree, Osborn was able to follow the course of the action with the aid of a report from an aircraft whose pilot was able to see flares lit by the attacking troops. For instance, at 7.15 p.m., the pilot reported that there was strong resistance to the east of Alban Avenue.

The one success for the 52nd was by D Company, under Captain Harold 'Fritz' Eagle, on the extreme right of the Regiment's advance, which had a much easier time. There was little opposition in front of them and they succeeded in crossing the Canal du Nord, and made contact on the far side, in Fagan Avenue, with the 2nd H.L.I. D Company's advance was not without casualties, some of them caused by following the British barrage too closely. Unfortunately, a gap of 500 yards had opened in the line, between the right of B Company and the left of D Company, owing to a loss of direction of B which went too far to the left, and to enemy pressure. A party of Germans between the two companies stopped them from getting in touch.

At 5.25 a.m. September 12th, Major-General R.D. Whigham's[754] 62nd Division attacked on the right of the 2nd Division, whose 5th Brigade's action had been to protect the left flank of this, the major operation on Havrincourt village and the Hindenburg front system. Although the 5th Brigade's minor operation of the day before, using the 52nd and the 2nd H.L.I., had not been entirely successful, it had done just about enough to protect the 62nd Division's left flank. Whigham's Division had already captured Havrincourt on November 20th 1917 in the earlier Battle of Cambrai. His operation orders deliberately recalled this: 'the 62nd Division will recapture Havrincourt village'. The attack was made from the south-west and tapes were laid through Havrincourt Wood for the troops to follow. By 7.30 a.m., the Hindenburg front system had fallen, fresh units of the Division had pushed into the village itself and, by 11.30 a.m., it was in British

[754] Later, General Sir Robert Whigham [1865-1950], known inevitably as 'Whigwam'. He commanded the 62nd Division 1918-19. During the war he communicated with George V by writing letters via the Assistant Private Secretary Major Clive Wigram. A highly-rated general and considered by Cyril Falls, the military historian, as the best divisional commander with whom he served.

hands. A strong counter-attack by the enemy, at 6.30 p.m., was conclusively repulsed.

Meanwhile at 7.05 a.m. on the 12th, the 52nd's D Company, which was on the east side of the canal in Fagan Avenue, was ordered to attack with bombing parties down London Trench and Support in order to make contact with the 62nd Division to the south. However, their men met with little success as both trenches were strongly held, and a party of about 70 Germans in Fagan Support fired into them from the rear. At the same time, the 2nd H.L.I. was ordered to bomb down Jermyn Street and Knightsbridge [Knights Bridge on trench maps] and by 10.40 a.m. the party in Knightsbridge had made contact with the 62nd Division, although the one in Jermyn Street was still held up by machine-gun fire. The work of mopping up went on during the morning and at 2.05 p.m. it was reported that London Trench and Support were clear of the enemy and further contact made with the 62nd Division. Units of the 24th R.F. supported the H.L.I. and the 52nd's D Company in these two operations.

About 11 a.m., C Company, which had been replaced on the left of the 52nd's line the night before by the 2nd Grenadier Guards, was ordered to extend the line southwards from the right of Captain John Blagrove's B Company to fill the 500 yards gap to Captain Harold Eagle's D Company. A company of the 24th R.F. was ordered to assist the operation by working northwards from Fagan Support. In the event this did not work. The three depleted companies of the 52nd continued mopping up during the morning and they managed to clear Alban Avenue down to Robinson Trench. Lieutenant Thomas Tyrwhitt-Drake, commanding A Company, led a small party down Alban Trench towards the canal until he was held up by an enemy post he was too weak to tackle. At this point A and B Companies had a combined strength of 60 all ranks and began working as a single company. In the afternoon, the Regiment managed to clear Fagan Avenue and Support, but progress could not be made southward down their ends of London Trench and Support to meet the 2nd H.L.I. At this stage two pockets of the enemy remained: firstly, between Robinson Trench and the Canal; secondly, between Fagan Avenue and Jermyn Street.

The position on the west of the canal was not finally cleared of the enemy until the early morning of September 13th when, under an encircling pressure from the 2nd Grenadier Guards and the 24th R.F., they made off. One party, using the dry canal bed to escape, was caught by the 52nd's D Company's Lewis gun fire. At 9 p.m. on the 12th, the 2nd South Staffordshire of the 6th Brigade started the relief of the 52nd. Owing to the unstable situation between B and C Companies of the 52nd, the relief was not completed until 7.05 a.m. the next day. The 2nd South Staffordshire was instructed to fight for and clear up any part of the line that was not already in British possession. On relief, the 52nd marched independently to billets at Morchies, in a former German Casualty Clearing Station, where they rested and cleaned themselves up. The 52nd's total casualties for the period September 11th-13th were 96: killed, 17; wounded, 60; gassed, 12; missing, 7. Amongst the gassed were the American Medical Officer First-Lieutenant E.G. Huckin and the entire personnel of the Regimental Aid Post. Gas shells had been dropped on their position to the north-east of Demicourt on the night of September 12th/13th. It was the second time within one month that the medical officer had been gassed. Second-Lieutenants Thomas 'Little Bingo' Baines [gunshot wounds both knees] and R.W. Sawers [gunshot wound right thigh] were amongst the wounded on September 11th. Baines was seriously damaged in both knees.

The 5th Brigade, including the 52nd, took 80-100 prisoners during the operation. Approximately 60 machine-guns were captured, the men manning them having put up a stout defence. A captured machine-gun team was recognized as the one that had previously been seen bombing British wounded. One of them, killed by the 52nd, was found to be wearing a Red Cross brassard whilst working his machine-gun. The surviving members of the team were handed over to some Grenadier Guards 'to be suitably dealt with – which order was duly carried out'. Another German prisoner, on being disarmed, set about his captor with his fists. 'He was also suitably dealt with'[755]. On the whole, the enemy's infantrymen did not put up much fight. In several cases Germans refused to leave their dug-outs and 'much execution was done by bombing these'. Brigadier-General W.L. Osborn was able to write in his report: 'Thus the Brigade [5th] was able to hand over a completely established front line on relief that night by the 6th Brigade'. This was strictly true but, the 2nd Grenadier Guards and the 2nd South Staffordshire had played their part as well.

On September 14th, the 52nd spent their time improving their billets in the former German Casualty Clearing Station to the east of Morchies and in inspections of arms, equipment and billets. During the day, a new American Medical Officer, First-Lieutenant S.N. Trockey, joined the Regiment as a replacement for his gassed predecessor. At this stage of the war there was a distinct shortage of British doctors in the army, and the 52nd, as well as some other units, were well-served by American medical staff[756]. The following day, the Regiment was on the move once more, via poor tracks to the area between

---

[755] WO 95 1346: report by Brigadier-General W.L. Osborn. It is not difficult to guess 'what suitably dealt with' meant.

[756] British women doctors might have helped reduce the shortfall but they were not allowed near the front.

Gomiécourt and Courcelles-le-Comte, where they went into dug-outs in the railway embankment between map references A.22.d.3.2 to A.22.b.4.5. It was the same section of railway that the 52nd had advanced over on August 23rd. Their route took them to the south of Morchies, Vaulx-Vraucourt and Mory.

The 52nd remained in the Gomiécourt area with their accommodation in the railway embankment until September 26th. On the 16th, further shelters and dug-outs were made as there was insufficient cover for the whole Regiment. A further part of this near fortnight's rest after the Battle of Havrincourt was spent in general training. The training took the form of bombing, bayonet fighting, and skirmishing. The 17th/18th was used to watch tank demonstrations at Behagnies. On the latter day, a combined infantry and tank exercise was witnessed by the whole Regiment, with the 2nd H.L.I. taking the part of the infantry. On the 19th, a new second-in-command in the form of Major James Jervoise 'Alfonso' Powell reported for duty. Lieutenant-Colonel Richard Crosse was still recovering from his wounds, and there was a dearth of experienced officers serving in the companies of the 52nd to take the place of Major George Field, if he should become incapacitated. Two days later, the 103rd reinforcement of 77 other ranks arrived.

Once more it is time to look at events on a greater scale. Between August 8th and September 26th, the British First, Third and Fourth Armies, starting near Arras, Albert and Amiens had driven the enemy back roughly to the line occupied by the Third and Fifth Armies before the German offensive on March 21st 1918. To the south the French had also pushed the enemy back, whilst to the north, in August and September, the British Second and Fifth Armies had forced the Germans to give up the Lys Salient which they had gained in their offensive of the previous April. In addition, a limited American offensive from September 12th-13th had obliterated the St. Mihiel Salient.

As the end of September came, the German army was barely clinging on to its positions. At the beginning of October, in Berlin, the Kaiser met his generals. Field-Marshal Paul von Hindenburg said, 'I expect a full dress attack inside eight days and can accept no responsibility if a catastrophe or [correcting himself] at least the gravest consequences ensue'. Marshal Ferdinand Foch and Field-Marshal Sir Douglas Haig were now about to end the war with a series of attacks. Initially Foch wanted a limited offensive, but he was won over by Haig for a more expansive operation, and Foch's motto became 'Tout le monde à la bataille!'

The attacks on the German line followed one after another: the first to attack on September 26th, were the Americans and French in the Meuse-Argonne region; the next day, the British First [Horne] and Third [Byng] Armies attacked in the general direction of Cambrai; on the 28th, a combined Belgian, British, and French Army Group broke out of the Ypres Salient and moved beyond the Passchendaele ridge in a single day; finally on the 29th, the British Fourth Army [Rawlinson] with the French First Army attacked the Hindenburg Line. As part of the Third Army's attack on September 27th, the VI Corps [Haldane] was ordered to clear the Flesquières ridge and its spur running northwards to Graincourt and Anneux, and to clear the Hindenburg Support System which lay across the line of advance. The 2nd Division, whose commander, Major-General Cecil Pereira, thought that 'tomorrow the biggest battle in the worlds [sic] history begins', 5th Brigade, and the 52nd Light Infantry remained a part of the VI Corps for these operations. On their left would be XVII Corps with IV Corps to their right.

On September 26th, the 52nd received orders to move back to the south-west of Morchies. At 7.35 p.m., the Regiment left the railway embankment and their route took them to the north of Gomiécourt, south of Mory and Vaulx-Vraucourt to Morchies. Owing to a very wet, dark night, direction was lost east of Vaulx-Vraucourt, and they did not reach their destination in map reference I.11.c. until 1.15 a.m. on the 27th. Once more, in this position, the 52nd found itself facing Chaufours Wood.

The Battle of the Canal du Nord for Lieutenant-General Aylmer Haldane's VI Corps began at zero hour, 5.20 a.m., September 27th. Haldane had the Guards Division on the left and the 3rd Division on the right: their collective objectives were the Hindenburg Support and Graincourt Lines and Flesquières village. Once this had been achieved the 2nd Division on the left and the 62nd Division on the right would pass through the Guards and 3rd Divisions respectively. The final objectives for the two fresh divisions were Marcoing, Noyelles, Nine Wood, and the crossings of the Escaut River and the St. Quentin Canal. In essence, this involved taking the ground lying between the two canals, the Canal du Nord and the St. Quentin Canal[757]. Any success would be exploited by driving the Germans across the St. Quentin Canal, and by taking Masnières, Rumilly, and the railhead at Mont-sur-l'Oeuvre.

At 5.20 a.m. September 27th, the Guards and 3rd Divisions clambered up the smooth, high walls of the empty Canal du Nord and moved to the east. Forty minutes later, at 6 a.m., the brigades of the 2nd Division were set in motion. Heavy fighting took place as the Hindenburg Support system and Flesquières were stormed and eventually taken by the Guards and 3rd Division. Ribecourt also fell early in the day. On the left, there was serious resistance and the 63rd Division, to the north of the Guards, had significant problems on both sides of the

[757] Also known as the Schelde Canal or the Canal d'Escaut.

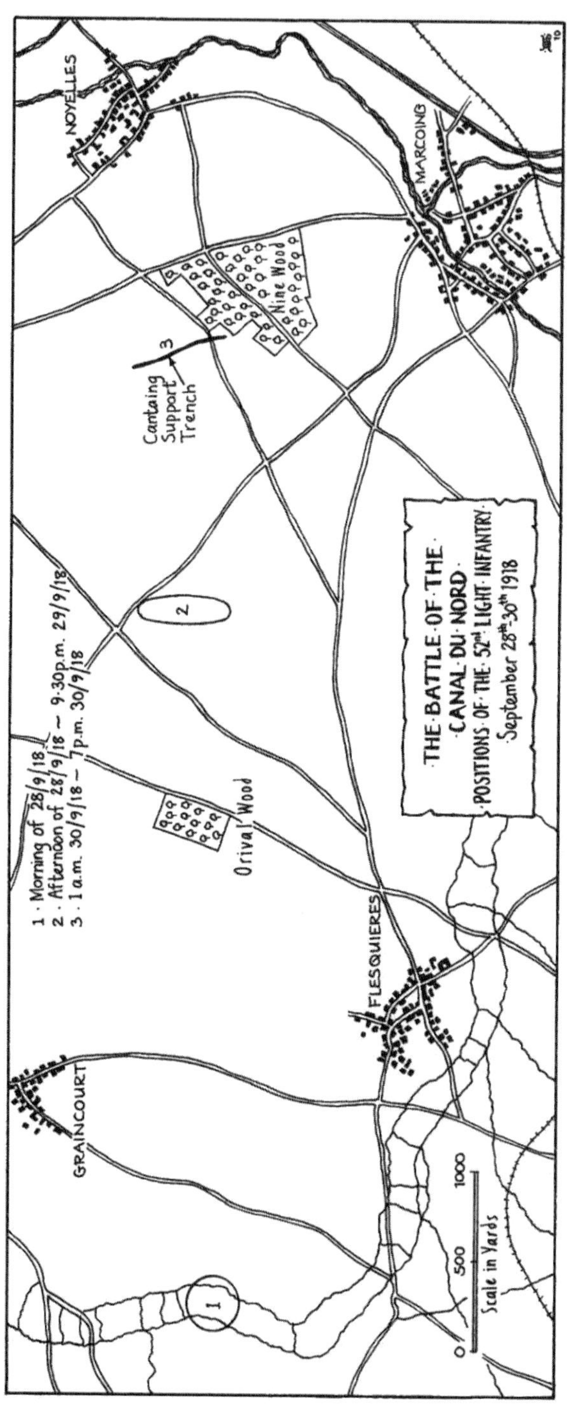
THE·BATTLE·OF·THE·
·CANAL·DU·NORD·
·POSITIONS·OF·THE·52nd·LIGHT·INFANTRY·
September 28th-30th 1918
1 · Morning of 28/9/18
2 · Afternoon of 28/9/18 ~ 9·30p.m. 29/9/18
3 · 1 a.m. 30/9/18 ~ 7p.m. 30/9/18
NOYELLES
MARCOING
Nine Wood
Cantaing Support Trench
Orival Wood
FLESQUIERES
GRAINCOURT
Scale in Yards
0
500
1000

Bapaume - Cambrai road. That night, British units were still 400-800 yards short of the Graincourt Line. Major-General Cecil Pereira had placed his Brigades in the order, 6th, 99th and 5th, and during the afternoon the 6th Brigade passed through the Guards Division as arranged. As reserve Brigade in the 2nd Division, the 5th moved up to the area west of the Demicourt - Hermies road, and was in position by 2.15 p.m. As part of this move, the 52nd left their bivouacs near Morchies and took up a position slightly to the north-west of Hermies before, at 5.45 p.m., going on to Lock 7 in artillery formation. The move was completed by 9 p.m. and here the Regiment spent the night on the eastern side of the canal. The Lock was all too familiar to them as they had held it briefly on November 30th 1917 during the earlier Battle of Cambrai.

At 5.15 a.m., September 28th, the attack recommenced from a line just to the east of Flesquières with the 2nd Division leading on the Corps' left. The advance continued with the 6th Brigade on the left and the 99th Brigade on the right. At the same time the 57th Division attacked to the north of the units of the 2nd Division, and, at 6.30 a.m., the 62nd Division joined in to the south. The objectives of the 2nd Division were: Cantaing Support; Nine Wood; thence the crossings of the San Quentin Canal; Mont-sur-l'Oeuvre; Rumilly. The attack progressed satisfactorily with Noyelles and Nine Wood falling during the morning, and later the fast-flowing River Escaut was crossed easily, and the units of the 2nd Division established themselves along the western bank of the St. Quentin Canal. Apart from those by two companies of the 6th Brigade, attempts to cross the Canal failed as the Germans held the eastern bank firmly with machine-guns. The enemy had made little attempt to stand and fight until the Canal was reached.

During the 28th, the 5th Brigade remained in the 2nd Division's reserve. At 6.15 a.m., the 52nd moved forward from their position on the east side of Lock 7 to trenches north-west of Flesquières at map reference K.10.d., and the move was completed by 8.15 a.m. In the afternoon, the Regiment went forward once more at platoon intervals to the area between Orival Wood and Nine Wood at map reference L.8.b. and d. From here, parties of officers and N.C.O.s were sent forward to reconnoitre the canal crossings east of Noyelles. Major-General Cecil Pereira, commanding the 2nd Division, visited the area of the 5th Brigade and recorded in his diary: 'The litter of the battle field is very thick all over this area. Dead men, dead animals, broken vehicles, equipment and ammunition all over the place. Cambrai is only 5 or 6 miles away and from here looks undamaged'. Next day he wrote: 'The swinish Boche have set fire to the latter [Cambrai] and dense clouds of smoke were rising from several parts of the town'.

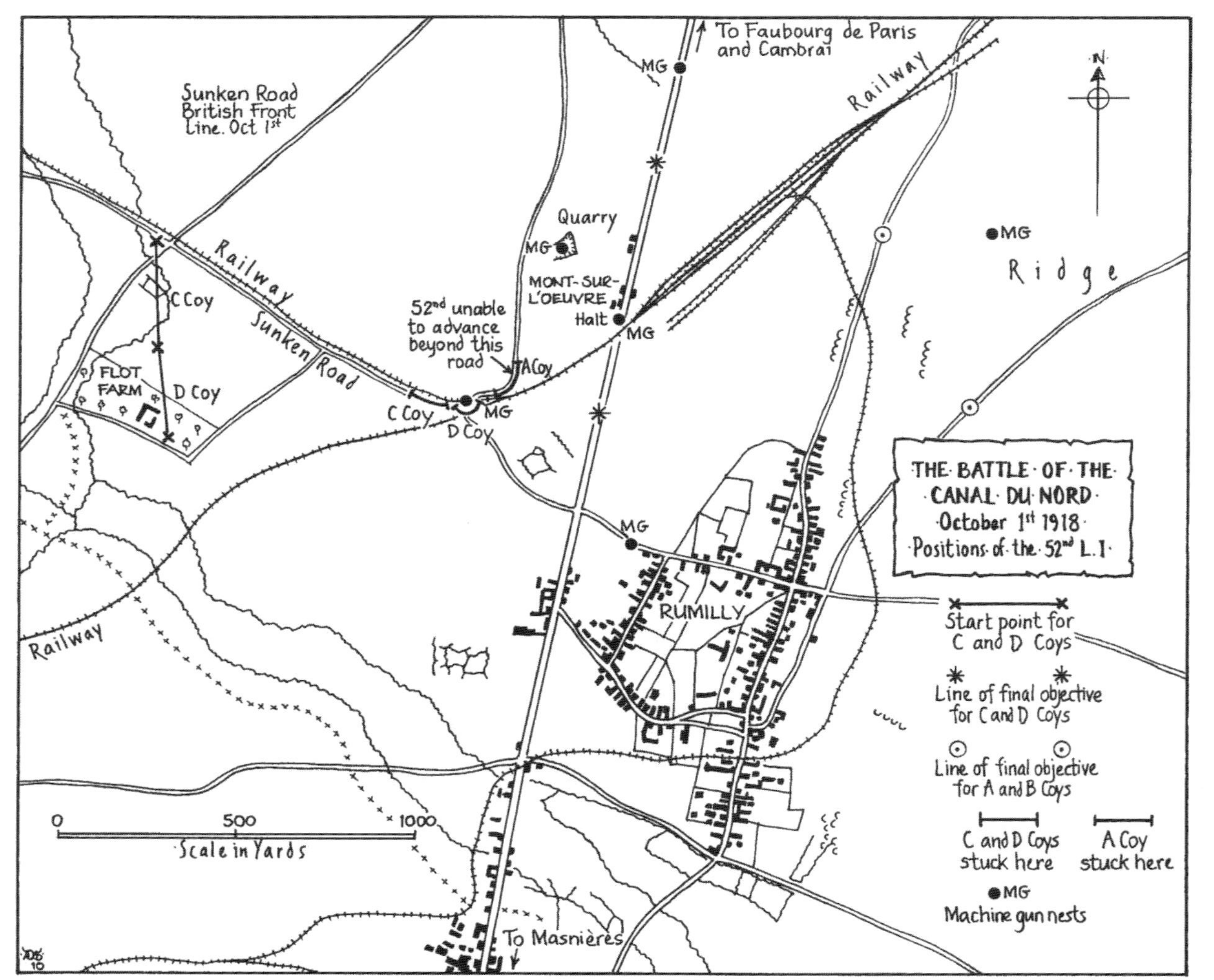
THE BATTLE OF THE CANAL DU NORD
October 1st 1918
Positions of the 52nd L.I.
Start point for C and D Coys
Line of final objective for C and D Coys
Line of final objective for A and B Coys
C and D Coys stuck here
A Coy stuck here
MG
Machine gun nests
N
To Faubourg de Paris and Cambrai
Railway
Ridge
MG
Quarry
MONT-SUR-L'OEUVRE Halt
52nd unable to advance beyond this road
A Coy
C Coy
D Coy
RUMILLY
To Masnières
Sunken Road British Front Line. Oct 1st
Sunken Road
FLOT FARM
0
500
1000
Scale in Yards

At 5 a.m. September 29th, units from the 99th Brigade established themselves across the St. Quentin Canal to the north and south of Flot Farm, and also in the sunken road to the north-east of it. On their right the 62nd Division had crossed the canal, which was being heavily shelled by the enemy. The 5th Brigade, including the 52nd, was put in a state of readiness to push on to the line Séranvillers-Niergnies. This proved to be much too optimistic as the units on the east of the Canal became bogged down, and a further advance was contingent on the taking of the village of Rumilly. That evening the 24th R.F. moved up to the line of the Canal, and the 2nd H.L.I. moved to trenches east of Nine Wood. The 52nd received orders at 9.30 p.m. to move to trenches in Cantaing Support Trench in an arc at L.10.a. and c. The move was completed by 1 a.m. on the 30th with one other rank killed during the day.

During the night of September 29th/30th, the 99th Brigade took over the whole of the 2nd Division's front with the 6th Brigade retiring to the area of Noyelles. The expectation was that the 99th Brigade would push forwards, on the 30th, to conform with the ground gained by the 63rd Division on their left. Also on the 30th, it was hoped that the 62nd Division, to the right of the 2nd, would capture the village of Rumilly, so that the advance could progress again. If the village was taken, the 5th Brigade would move on to Niergnies. Unfortunately, the 62nd Division was unable to take Rumilly and the 63rd Division also failed to progress. The 24th R.F. of the 5th Brigade had managed to get across the canal and it was ordered to advance two of its companies as far as the Cambrai - Masnières road, to the north of the Mont-sur-l'Oeuvre; the latter like Rumilly, was strongly held by the enemy with numerous machine-guns. It was deemed impracticable for the advance to continue that day.

The 52nd remained in Cantaing Support Trench, until 7 p.m. September 30th, when it was ordered to relieve the 1st King's Royal Rifle Corps [99th Brigade] in Noyelles. However, during the move, further orders were received and the Regiment moved to the area of Flot Farm[758] on the eastern side of the St. Quentin Canal. Here the 52nd relieved the 23rd R.F. of the 99th Brigade, prior to attacking the enemy the following day. Verbal orders for the assault were given to those concerned by 10.30 p.m. and all companies were in their appropriate positions by 11.30 p.m.

The enemy line ran from Rumilly to Mont-sur-l'Oeuvre and then on to Faubourg de Paris just to the south of Cambrai. It was a very strong line with numerous machine-gun posts. The 52nd, in co-operation with troops of the 3rd Division on their right, were charged with expelling the enemy from the ground

---

[758] It appeared on British trench maps as Flot Farm. However, in the *Battalion War Diary* of the 52nd it is called Flat Farm or Flat Foot Farm.

between Marcoing Switch and the ridge to the north-east of Rumilly at G.10.d. The primary objective of the 3rd Division was the village of Rumilly. The 23rd R.F. had attempted to take Mont-sur-l'Oeuvre on September 30th, and had failed after heavy machine-gun fire from Rumilly had broken the attack up. It was clear that simultaneous attacks on both places was required, and this was to be attempted by the 52nd and units from the 3rd Division on October 1st.

Major George Field, of the 52nd, chose C and D Companies to lead the assault with A and B in support. The points of assembly were: D Company in part of Flot Farm, from G.13.b.8.9. to G.7.d.8.4; C Company further to the north to the cross-roads, from G.7.d.8.4. to G.7.b.8.0; A and B Companies, in support in Marcoing Switch. The advance was to be made by companies in section worms with a first wave of two platoons, second wave of one platoon, and the third wave of one platoon with the company headquarters. The distance between waves and companies was 50 yards. C and D Companies were to take the ground as far as the Cambrai - Masnières road between G.9.c.2.0. to G.9.a.5.5. This included the fortified quarries at Mont-sur-l'Oeuvre, a formidable spot with an abundance of machine-guns. Later, after its capture, Major-General Cecil Pereira of the 2nd Division recorded in his diary: 'It is also a very commanding position. There were a number of dead Boche lying about. This place and Rumilly which is also on a spur just south across a valley gave each other great support and protection'. If the 52nd's leading two companies were successful, A and B Companies would pass through them to take the trench line on the ridge further to the east, between G.10.c.3.0. and G.9.b.8.0.

Between midnight and 5.30 a.m., the enemy's artillery and machine-gun fire was slight. At 6 a.m., zero hour, the British artillery opened fire with two minutes of smoke to hide the attacking force, and followed up with a further four minutes on the initial barrage line. During this period the two front companies moved out in worm formation as close up to the barrage as possible, getting ready to go forward at 6.06 a.m. The barrage then lifted and crept forward slowly in order to co-ordinate with the 3rd Division on their right, with lifts every six minutes from zero plus 6 to zero plus 108, as C and D Companies advanced with A and B in support. British machine-guns and trench mortars co-operated with the barrage. As will become apparent, the barrage failed to neutralize the carefully sited enemy machine-guns with catastrophic results for the 52nd. The enemy troops facing the 52nd were from the 9th, 19th Reserve, and 3rd Naval Divisions[759].

Initially the 52nd's attack progressed well, but soon they came under intense machine-gun fire from the Quarry at G.9.c.0.9, the high ground east of

[759] There is some doubt about exactly which German units opposed the 52nd on October 1st 1918.

Mont-sur-l'Oeuvre, at the Halt[760] on the Cambrai - Masnières road, the houses at G.3.c.7.0., the railway crossing at G.8.d.5.0, and the western end of Rumilly. Both this withering machine-gun fire and also British shells falling short led to numerous casualties. Nevertheless, C and D Companies advanced 400-500 yards. Then, owing to the large frontage to be occupied, plus their losses, combined with the fact that the left flank of the 3rd Division on their right had failed to get forward, the leading companies of the 52nd lost direction, and moved too far to the right. The result was that the Regiment only covered about half of their allotted frontage.

At this point the support Companies A and B came up and the whole Regiment pushed forward to the line of the railway about G.8.d.5.0., where they captured three enemy machine-guns with their teams and several other prisoners. The men of the 52nd were held up on the small road running from north to south through G.8.d., to the west of the Cambrai - Masnières road. A further advance to the east of this road was impossible as the enemy machine-gun nests in the Quarry, and also in the village of Rumilly, immediately opened fire on any movement. Captain Harold Eagle, commanding D Company, the senior officer present, after consultation with Lieutenant E.H. Cowell, commanding C Company, ordered all the companies to dig in. D Company dug in along the railway about G.8.d.5.0.; C Company on the sunken road facing north-east around G.8.d.3.1. with observation posts out; A Company on the small road from G.8.d.8.1. to G.8.d.8.5. The final position of B Company is not recorded. No doubt there was a degree of intermingling of the companies. On the left, touch was maintained with the 2nd H.L.I. by means of patrols. Communication with Major George Field at the Regimental Headquarters was very difficult, and the orderlies were forced to crawl as the positions of the 52nd were very much overlooked by the enemy. Meanwhile, the 3rd Division had taken a foot-hold in the south-western corner of Rumilly but could progress no further.

At noon, the 2nd H.L.I. made a gallant attempt to eradicate the German machine-gun nest at G.3.c.7.0. on the Cambrai - Masnières road but, failed owing to flanking machine-gun fire. At this point in the action, it was clear that in the vicinity of Mont-sur-l'Oeuvre and Rumilly the well-sited German machine-guns had the upper hand, preventing a forward movement of the attacking British troops. As will be seen, this situation was not to last much longer as the 2nd Division's artillery pounded their positions with shrapnel and high explosive rounds. The enemy's all-dominant machine-guns in the quarry at Mont-sur-l'Oeuvre and on the high ground to the east of the Cambrai - Masnières road were also subjected to a smothering attack by trench mortars.

---

[760] Railway level-crossing.

In the early evening of October 1st, Major-General Cecil Pereira, commanding the 2nd Division, came forward to arrange another attack by the 5th Brigade to clear the ground which the 52nd had failed to take earlier in the day. This was to be co-ordinated with an attack by the 52nd Division [XVII Corps] on Faubourg de Paris to their left[761], and a further assault by the 3rd Division on Rumilly to their right. The situation of the 52nd had remained unchanged for the whole day until, at 6 p.m., the 24th R.F. and the 2nd H.L.I. [both of the 5th Brigade] attacked the Germans from the west and north-west[762]. This took them completely by surprise, as the enemy clearly expected another attack from the same direction as the 52nd's. In a brilliant feat of arms, the 24th R.F. took the two quarries on the Mont-sur-l'Oeuvre[763], and found them to be honeycombed with an extensive network of tunnels plus large garrisons. Two hundred prisoners and no less than fifty machine-guns were taken. At the same time, the 3rd Division finally cleared the whole of the village of Rumilly, thus protecting the flanks of the 24th R.F. and 2nd H.L.I. However, the attack of the 52nd Division on Faubourg de Paris was unsuccessful. Later that night the 52nd Light Infantry became the support battalion of the 5th Brigade. The new British line now ran to the east of both the Cambrai railway and the village of Rumilly. The Germans' supposedly impregnable Hindenburg Line was now well and truly broken into.

On October 1st, the 52nd's casualties were 34 dead, 128 wounded and a further wounded man was missing. Lieutenant Leonard Bartlett, aged 20 years, from Dulwich, was the only officer to be killed that day. Amongst the wounded were Captain John Blagrove [gunshot wound abdomen] who had briefly taken charge of the 52nd when Richard Crosse was wounded on August 23rd 1918, Lieutenant A.H.B. Brooke [gunshot wounds left thigh and right leg][764], and Second-Lieutenant H.A.I.B. Stokes [gunshot wound right thigh with fractured femur]. Blagrove was lucky to survive a dangerous abdominal wound. The 24-year-old Hugh Stokes was awarded the M.C. and would die of his wounds in England on November 28th 1918[765].

In the early morning of October 1st, the 52nd had been unable to take the quarries at Mont-sur-l'Oeuvre, let alone the ridge behind them. Why was it

---

761 The attack by the 52nd Division began 45 minutes before that of the 24th R.F. and the 2nd H.L.I.

762 On October 1st, the British front line occupied by the 5th Brigade ran from Marcoing Support Trench-Sunken road in G.8.a. and G.2.d.-gun pits in G.3.a. The 24th R.F. was situated in the right sub-sector and the 2nd H.L.I. in the left sub-sector.

763 Accounts vary about whether there were one or two quarries on the Mont-sur-l'Oeuvre. If there were two they were close together.

764 Brooke was reputed to have been wounded three times in the war but he had never spent more than 36 hours in the front line.

765 Buried at Brookwood Military Cemetery near Pirbright. Grave VI.C.2.

possible, just a few hours later, for the 24th R.F. to succeed where the 52nd had so singularly failed, and with minimal casualties too? A number of reasons for this can be put forward. Firstly, the failure of the artillery barrage to neutralize the enemy's machine-gun positions prior to the 52nd's assault. The key to the German defensive position around Rumilly and Mont-sur-l'Oeuvre were the well-sited machine-gun nests, particularly on the high ground. On September 30th, the 23rd R.F. had also failed to take much the same ground owing to machine-gun fire particularly into its flanks. A further artillery and trench mortar barrage during the morning and afternoon of October 1st, undoubtedly dealt with a considerable number of the machine-gun sites before the 24th R.F.'s attack. Secondly, the 2nd Division came to the conclusion that the formidable quarries at Mont-sur-l'Oeuvre would only fall, if they were attacked simultaneously with Rumilly in order to protect the attacking forces' flank. Although the 3rd Division assaulted Rumilly on the morning of the 1st, it only achieved a foothold in the south-west of the village. That evening Rumilly was cleared completely as the quarries fell to the 24th R.F. Thirdly, there was the element of surprise with the 24th R.F.'s and the 2nd H.L.I.'s attack from a direction that the Germans were not expecting.

Later, Lieutenant-Colonel Robert Pipon temporarily in command of the 5th Brigade recorded some comments concerning lessons learned during the recent operation. In the Battle of the Canal du Nord he had commanded the 24th R.F.

> In the present phase all advances are confronted ultimately by a large number of machine guns grouped together in localities, which are exceedingly well chosen.
>
> In theory the way to deal with them is for the company or platoon, concerned to make a small attack employing the different arms at their disposal – rifle grenades, smoke grenades and L guns[766]. In practice I have been convinced that the better way is for the infantry to stick tight to their barrage – which I assume – and go straight for the M gun.
>
> The result, and the casualties incurred in obtaining it, must be the final test of all theories.
>
> The Coy of the 24th R.F. which took Mt sur l'Oeuvre had only 20 casualties. Other attempts to take it suffered very many times this number of casualties.
>
> I think the explanation is moral – the moral effect on the enemy of an attack which drives straight at them and conversely the moral

766 Lewis guns.

effect on our own troops of hesitation whilst more elaborate measures are carried out.

In my own experience there were no cases of single German M.G.s. They were always in clusters, that being so I do not think infantry should be asked to attack them without the aid of an additional factor which will put the German machine gunner off his aim. e.g. artillery barrage or darkness.

Today, the remains of Flot Farm lie in a wooded area close to a municipal refuse dump. The quarry at Mont-sur-l'Oeuvre which can be seen in outline in a spinney overlooking the positions of the 52nd's C and D Companies on October 1st 1918, was clearly a most formidable obstacle and it is easy to understand why the Regiment was pinned down by machine-gun fire.

We left the 52nd as the support battalion of the 5th Brigade on the evening of October 1st. The next day they remained in support and the railway close to the south of Flot Farm was shelled[767]. The Regiment was greatly heartened by the return of their Commanding Officer, Lieutenant-Colonel Richard Crosse, from sick leave following his serious injuries at Triangle Copse on August 23rd. He had sailed from England on September 30th and was to remain at rear headquarters for a further week recuperating from his wounds. Crosse had hated languishing in hospital and discharged himself with the wound still open. He had returned home to Cheshire where his mother dressed the wound. Hearing that the 52nd was to attack Rumilly, Crosse raced back to France before his wounds had healed. For several weeks he had to be lifted into the saddle of his horse because the pain was so great. In a letter to the mother of one of his fallen officers, Captain Ralph Kite, Crosse explained what had happened to him[768].

My Mother thanks you very much for your very kind letter of yesterday, inquiring after me. I am very nearly all right again, having been wounded on August 23rd by a shell which broke a rib and grazed and bruised my back particularly behind my right shoulder: I was only in hospital a fortnight in Abbeville, and was then given 3 weeks sick leave from France, specially so as not to lose

[767] The exact position of the 52nd in support is not recorded in the *Battalion War Diary's* entry for October 1st or elsewhere.

[768] Letter to Edith Kite written on September 28th 1918. Despite his unhealed wounds, Crosse had found the time to visit the recipient of his letter, and to travel to the medal specialists, Spinks, to find out the correct wording for engraving her late son's M.C.

command of the Regiment, which I rejoin on Sept 30th crossing from Folkestone on that day[769].

About 7.30 p.m. October 3rd, the 52nd was relieved by the 17th R.F., formerly of the 5th Brigade but now in the 6th, and moved its Headquarters to Noyelles on the west side of the St. Quentin Canal. A and D Companies were situated in the vicinity of the Lock on the Canal to the east of Noyelles, with B and C in trenches still further to the east. The move was completed by 9.30 p.m. The following two days were spent in the standard way after action, cleaning up, reorganization, and inspections of both clothing and arms. Unfortunately, continuous hostile shelling restricted movement and parades. During quiet periods, some physical training and even a lecture on the Regiment's History were undertaken by platoon commanders. The 2nd Division had advanced some 23 miles since August 21st.

Brigadier-General W.L. Osborn, of the 5th Brigade, was wounded by a splinter from a high explosive shell, on the morning of October 5th, which burst close to him whilst he was inspecting the billets of the 24th R.F. in Noyelles. Lieutenant-Colonel Robert Pipon and the Brigade Major who were with him had narrow escapes. Pipon assumed command of the Brigade. The unlucky Osborn was unable to return to his command until November 12th, one day after the Armistice.

On October 6th, Lieutenant A. Cockshut was slightly wounded in the left shoulder by shrapnel, and that night the Regimental Headquarters in Noyelles was hit by a shell which killed one man and wounded two others. The next day there was an influx of officers from the Territorial Battalions of the Regiment. Lieutenants A.N. Hunt and R.G.P. Howie, and Second-Lieutenants E.J. McAnsh and A.R. Price reported for duty. They were joined by a non-Territorial Officer, Second-Lieutenant F.H. Knight. On October 9th, the 2nd Division was relieved by the Guards Division, and the Regiment marched back to the west side of the Canal du Nord into an area, at K.8.b. and d, close to their start position for the Battle of Havrincourt, the previous month. Here they occupied trench and shelter accommodation. On the 11th, a new British Medical Officer, Captain W.A. Taylor joined the Regiment in place of the American First-Lieutenant S.N. Trockey. In addition, Lieutenant Frederick Lowndes and Second-Lieutenant C.H. Sheppard rejoined, having recovered from a foot wound and being gassed

[769] On the night before leaving England, in a Dover hotel, Crosse was aware that all was not well with his wound as an abscess burst. However, he still saw fit to travel and reached the Regiment on October 2nd.

respectively. Second-Lieutenants J. Thorne and F.C. Bobby also reported for duty.

The Battle of Cambrai, 1918, was fought from October 8th-9th. On the 8th, the 52nd was ensconced in the vicinity of Noyelles and to the east of the St. Quentin Canal, and on the 9th it moved back across the Canal du Nord. As recorded earlier, although the Regiment did not fight in the battle, its movements on the 9th took it into the defined geographical area, so that it might be claimed as a battle honour. Both Edmonds in the *Official History* and Wyrall in his *History of the Second Division* include the forthcoming attack on the Séranvillers-Niergnies Line under the heading of the Battle of Cambrai, 1918. As far as the 2nd Division is concerned, taking into account the criteria laid down by the 1920 Battles Nomenclature Committee, it is better deemed to be part of the pursuit to the Selle.

At zero hour, 4.30 a.m. October 8th, the 2nd Division used the 6th and 99th Brigades to assault the Séranvillers-Niergnies trench line, and Forenville, a collection of large farm buildings. The 3rd Division was on the right and the 63rd Division on the left. Despite the Germans' use of captured British tanks, the two objectives were taken. There had been stiff fighting and the Army commander, Julian Byng, was reported as saying, 'we had won by one wicket'. The 2nd Division's commander, Cecil Pereira thought otherwise 'we had a good many wickets in hand'. Early in the morning of October 9th, the Guards Division came through the units of the 2nd Division and continued the advance, meeting very little enemy resistance. The Guards pushed on to Solesmes producing a large salient as there had been no corresponding advance east of Vimy Ridge and the line to the south was well forward.

Cambrai had fallen and a few days later Major-General Cecil Pereira visited it. The 52nd had been gazing wistfully at its spires since late 1917.

> The town is much knocked about and houses appear to be denuded of furniture except the humbler ones. There has been a certain amount of damage from shell fire. The main square is a typical piece of Boche frightfulness; all the houses have been burnt and levelled to the ground and were still smouldering.
>
> The Town Hall, a modern renaissance, building is still standing but burnt out and roofless. The Mark of the Beast is upon the town. There are many senseless and groundless accusations against the Boche but there cannot be any justification for his criminal and spiteful destruction.

The following day, the 12th, in their positions to the west of the Canal du Nord, there was a Commanding Officer's Parade and Address conducted by Lieutenant-Colonel Richard Crosse. He was back and it was business as usual.

Chapter XXIV

The Battle of the Selle, the Armistice and the March into Germany.

October 13th - December 31st 1918

[Maps: pages 644, 646.]

The first weeks of October saw heavy fighting on many parts of the front, and a great deal of ground was reclaimed from the enemy who was now retiring in front of the Belgians in the north, and the French and Americans in the south. As we have seen, on October 8th, the British Third Army [Byng] and Fourth Army [Rawlinson] had broken through the last of the Hindenburg defences and captured Cambrai[770], while the French occupied St. Quentin. On the 9th, the advance continued and British cavalry was within a few miles of Le Cateau where General Horace Smith-Dorrien had fought his memorable battle in August 1914. The Hindenburg Line having been broken, the Germans were forced to take up a new defensive position along the River Selle. During the next week the British advanced to the west bank of the Selle, and the French to their south cleared the Oise-Sambre Canal.

On October 17th, Sir Douglas Haig's forces continued their advance with Rawlinson's Fourth Army attacking on a ten-mile front south of Le Cateau. Progress was slow and on the morning of October 20th, the First [Horne] and Third [Byng] British Armies widened the assault to the north of Le Cateau and managed to push forward for two miles. At 3.20 a.m. October 23rd, in darkness, Haig attacked with three of his Armies, the First, the Third, and the Fourth, and successfully advanced a distance of six miles. As a part of the Third Army's action, the 52nd Light Infantry was to play a significant role during the Battle of the Selle in the 2nd Division's action of October 23rd. The German enemy was in disarray and a new defensive line was formed between Valenciennes and the Sambre. On November 4th, this line was broken through at the Battle of the Sambre, and the pace of the Allied advance quickened up to the Armistice on November 11th.

Post-war, the Battles Nomenclature Committee decided that the Battle of the Selle had been fought from October 17th-25th. As will be seen the 52nd was to play an important part in it on October 23rd, in what would prove to be their last battle of the war.

---

770 The Germans' 18th Reserve Division held Cambrai and its rearguard evacuated the town at 2.30 a.m. on the 9th.

It is time to return to the 52nd in their build-up to the Battle of the Selle. On October 13th, the Regiment marched back to Rumilly via Flesquières and Noyelles, arriving at about 1.30 p.m. Their billets consisted of cellars and rooms in sufficiently undamaged houses, and all available men spent the next day improving them. On the 15th, Major George Field temporarily took over command of the wounded Captain John Blagrove's A Company. The following days were spent in route marching, and Lewis gun and rifle grenadier training classes. There was also time for football and the officers played a rugby match. Further replacement officers arrived on the 17th, the opening day of the Battle of the Selle. They were Lieutenants Bob FitzGerald, Philip 'Slatcher' Whitehead, Harry Vernon, and Second-Lieutenant F.C. Holland. The first three were old hands having recovered from their wounds, and Holland was a new boy. On the 19th, Lieutenant John Slade-Baker returned to England and transferred to the Indian Army[771].

During the afternoon of October 19th, the 52nd marched to Carnières via Séranvillers, Wambaix and Estourmel. The Transport, less cookers, water carts, and the officers' cart, which followed the Regiment, moved by another route, avoiding cross-country tracks. Their billets in Carnières, to the east of Cambrai, were structurally good although very dirty. At 8.15 p.m. that evening, instructions were received that, from 7 a.m. on the 20th, the 52nd would be at two hours notice ready to move to St. Hilaire, in view of the Third Army's advance on Le Quesnoy. About 8 a.m., orders were received for the Regiment to march to St. Hilaire at 10.16 a.m. The battalion leading them was late so that the 52nd did not pass the starting point until 10.30 a.m. The march via Boussières was a difficult one with poor surfaces, rain and many blocks. On arrival at St. Hilaire the Regiment found that it had not been allotted any billets, and the men spent over an hour waiting in the main street. Eventually they were given billets to the east end of the village. No sooner had the 52nd settled in than the enemy opened fire with a high-velocity gun, fortunately not causing any casualties. However, the area was thinned out and the most dangerous part vacated as a precaution. That evening the 105th reinforcement of 100 other ranks and casuals joined them, this requiring a further adjustment of the billeting arrangements.

Monday October 21st, Trafalgar Day, and the fourth anniversary of the 52nd's attack at Langemarck, was quiet. Lieutenant-Colonel Richard Crosse later recalled that there had been no time to get the names of the survivors of the 52nd, from the action of October 21st-23rd 1914, who were still with the Regiment. It

771 In January 1955, the then Colonel John Slade-Baker, whilst working for *The Sunday Times,* was the first British correspondent and only Englishman to enter the Yemen since 1896. He visited the Temples of Queen Bulkis near Marib.

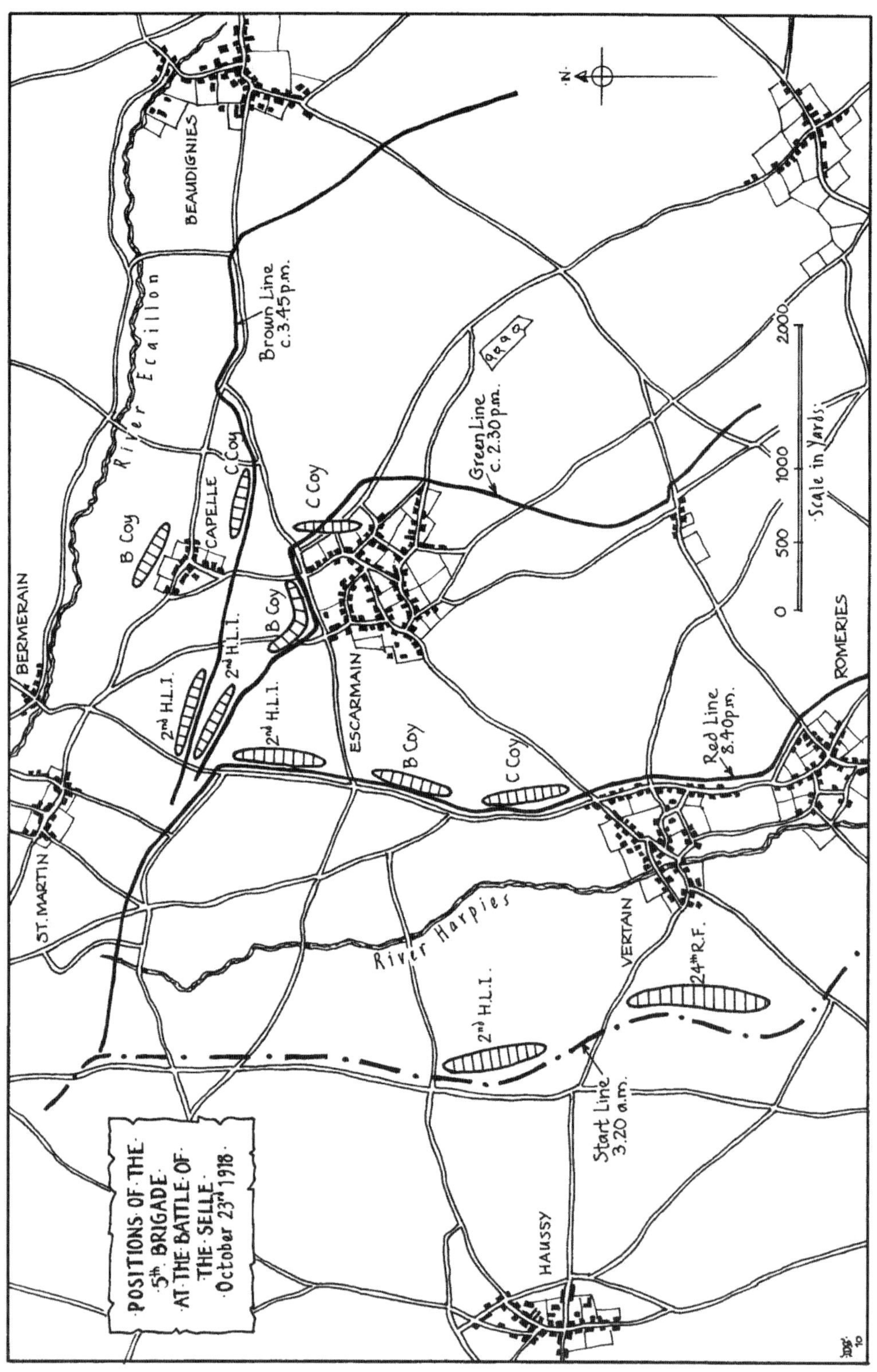
POSITIONS OF THE 5th BRIGADE AT THE BATTLE OF THE SELLE October 23rd 1918
N
BEAUDIGNIES
River Ecaillon
Brown Line c.3.45 p.m.
Green Line c.2.30 p.m.
BERMERAIN
CAPELLE
B Coy
C Coy
C Coy
B Coy
2nd H.L.I.
2nd H.L.I.
2nd H.L.I.
ESCARMAIN
B Coy
C Coy
Red Line 8.40 p.m.
ROMERIES
ST. MARTIN
River Harpies
VERTAIN
24th R.F.
2nd H.L.I.
Start Line 3.20 a.m.
HAUSSY
0 500 1000 2000
Scale in Yards

would have been a short list. At 6 p.m., orders were received for the resumption of the offensive, and two hours later these were communicated to the company commanders. The next morning, the 22nd, Major James Powell arranged accommodation in St. Hilaire for the rearward services and the nucleus to be left out of the coming battle. Arms and equipment were issued to the attacking companies and included one grenade per man, shovels, flares and wire cutters. Company commanders rode forward to reconnoitre the area where the night was to be spent.

The orders for the coming attack were promulgated by the 5th Infantry Brigade at 1 a.m. October 22nd. That evening, units of the 5th Brigade were to relieve the battalions of the Guards Division. On the right, the 24th R.F. was to relieve the 2nd Grenadier Guards and the 1st Irish Guards and, on the left, the 2nd H.L.I. was to relieve the 1st Grenadier Guards. The 52nd was to be in brigade reserve and to occupy positions in St. Python and its vicinity. The 2nd Division was using the 5th Brigade in the attack with the 3rd Division on their right and the 19th Division on their left. The important boundary, from the 52nd's point of view, would be the St. Python - Vertain - Escarmain road, which separated them from the 3rd Division. The 2nd Division had been given three objectives in the drive to the north-east, namely the Red, Green, and Brown Lines.

The 5th Brigade was ordered to take the first objective or Red Line with the 24th R.F. on the right and two companies of the 2nd H.L.I. on the left. The 5th Brigade's section of the Red Line ran along the road running from the north-east corner of Vertain cross-roads at W.3.b. - the northern divisional boundary at Q.33.b.3.6. Zero hour was 3.20 a.m. October 23rd. Once the Red Line was taken, the second objective or Green Line was to be attacked by the 52nd passing through the 24th R.F. on the right, and by two fresh companies of the 2nd H.L.I. on the left. The relevant part of the Green Line passed through the village of Escarmain cross-roads at W.4.b.7.7. - Q.34 central - junction of the Red Line with the northern divisional boundary. The time for this attack was to be Zero plus 5 hours and 20 minutes. Should exceptional progress be made by the 3rd Division on their right, the leading battalions [52nd and the 2nd H.L.I.] would advance to the third objective or Brown Line. The Brown Line, for the 5th Brigade, ran from the road junction at Q.36.c. - copse at Q.35.c. - the junction of the Red and Green Lines on the northern divisional boundary. The time for this attack was to be about Zero plus 9 hours. The order for this further advance was to be the code word BROWNING given by the 5th Brigade.

The assault conducted by the 5th Brigade was to be supported by an artillery barrage, sections of the 2nd Machine-Gun Battalion, and by the 5th Light Trench Mortar Battery. The machine-gunners would be attached to all three of

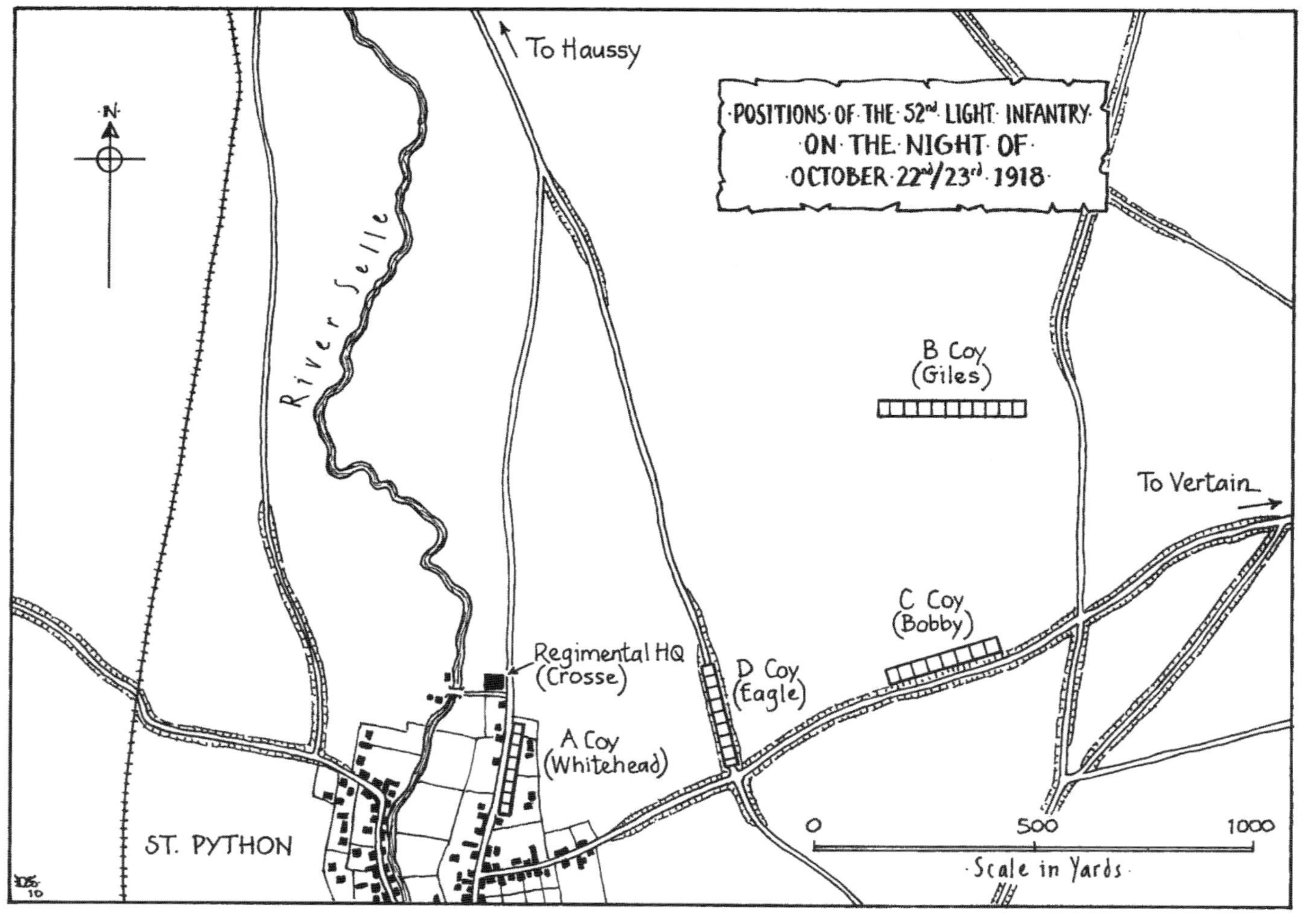
POSITIONS OF THE 52nd LIGHT INFANTRY
ON THE NIGHT OF
OCTOBER 22nd/23rd 1918
To Haussy
To Vertain
N
River Selle
B Coy (Giles)
C Coy (Bobby)
D Coy (Eagle)
Regimental HQ (Crosse)
A Coy (Whitehead)
ST. PYTHON
0
500
1000
Scale in Yards

the attacking battalions and would take up fixed positions as each objective was taken.

At 4.30 p.m. October 22nd, the 52nd, dressed in fighting order and jerkins, marched from St. Hilaire to St. Python via St. Vaast. Cookers followed the companies and tea or cocoa were issued on arrival at the preliminary assembly points before returning to St. Hilaire. Despite the fact that St. Python was being shelled by the enemy at frequent intervals, the Regiment reached its positions in and to the east of it without casualties. Regimental Headquarters were set up in a cellar on the St. Python - Haussy road, to the east of the River Selle at about V.30.a.50.17. A Company [Lieutenant Philip Whitehead] were in houses just to the south of Regimental Headquarters; D Company [Captain Harold Eagle] were along the sunken road in V.30.b. and d; C Company [Captain Percy Bobby] were in the former German trench north of the St. Python - Vertain road, about W.25.a.5.2.; B Company [Lieutenant William Giles] were in new trenches in W.19.c. During the night, the Germans shelled the whole of the area occupied by the Regiment with high explosive and gas shells. The unfortunate D Company in the sunken road suffered particularly and the 52nd was reported as having had fifteen gas casualties.

Two days later, Major-General Cecil Pereira commanding the 2nd Division gave his impressions of St. Python.

> The French inhabitants say that many Boche are getting into plain clothes and pulling out of the fight. There are about 100 inhabitants in St. Python, many women and children; the latter are playing about happily in the streets, but they have had a dreadful time living cooped upp [sic] in their cellars for about a fortnight whilst the village lay right in the midst of the fighting. They told me that the Boche fired M.G.s at their windows so as to break all the glass rapidly. In our office most of the glass that remains has got bullet holes through it.

The night of October 22nd/23rd was misty until bright moonlight forced its way through and helped the troops reach their points of assembly. Operations began at 3.20 a.m., when the artillery put down a barrage on the line of the Harpies River, and the 24th R.F. on the right and two companies of the 2nd H.L.I. [B and D] on the left assaulted the first objective – the Red Line. Their starting positions were to the west and south-west of the village of Vertain. The 24th R.F. crossed the River Harpies, a line heavily wired and garrisoned by the enemy with numerous machine-guns, and passed through the north-west of Vertain. Some men were forced to swim across the Harpies, which was four feet deep and eight feet wide but, by 5.10 a.m. the leading two companies, after stiff fighting, had established themselves on the eastern side of Vertain – the Red Line.

Meanwhile, the 2nd H.L.I., on the left, had less of a problem with the Harpies as it was shallower in their sector, but uncut wire in front of them had to be dealt with. Stiff opposition was encountered in a sunken road, which was rushed and its occupants were killed or taken prisoner. The Red Line was reached by 4.15 a.m. In the vicinity of the Red Line, the Highlanders noticed German S.O.S. Very light signals were being sent up from Rieux Farm in their rear, and a platoon from A Company was sent back to investigate. Under cover of Lewis gun and rifle fire, the farm was rushed, and one of the enemy was killed and 25 prisoners taken.

By 7.30 a.m., the 2nd H.L.I. and the 24th R.F. both reported that they had gained their objectives and were established on the Red Line. At this juncture, the 52nd was to pass through the 24th R.F. on the right, and with the aid of two fresh companies [A and C] of the 2nd H.L.I. on the left, assault the second objective or Green Line. The 24th R.F. became the 5th Brigade's reserve battalion. The section of the Green Line that the 52nd was to attack ran from the northern portion of Escarmain to a point to the north-west of the village at Q.34.d.1.7. Earlier, at 6.30 a.m., Captain E.J. Anderson who was performing the duties of second-in-command[772] and signals officer, with six orderlies, went forward to establish a Regimental Headquarters in the western outskirts of Vertain at a point selected from an aeroplane photograph. At 7.35 a.m., the Regimental Headquarters moved forward to this site and was established in a cellar by 8.30 a.m. while the village was being shelled. In view of the shelling and particularly the presence of gas, a forward headquarters was set up in a bank to the north of Vertain. At about this time Captain E.J. Anderson was wounded in the face and right knee by a shell that also killed Private William Wixey, a nineteen-year-old holder of the M.M.

At 8.40 a.m. October 23rd, the 52nd on the right, and the two companies of the 2nd H.L.I. [A and C] on their left, moved forward from their assembly positions on the Red Line towards the second objective – the Green Line. A creeping artillery barrage opened fire to smooth their way. Unfortunately some of the shells fell short, leading to British casualties. It was now a fine day after

---

[772] This is a little mysterious as Captain James Powell had become second-in-command on September 19th and, on October 22nd, was selecting men to be kept out of the battle on October 23rd. Perhaps he remained in the rear during the action. Where was Major George Field who had commanded the Regiment during Crosse's absence whilst wounded? Field was last mentioned on October 15th, temporarily commanding B Company. However, on October 23rd, Lieutenant William Giles commanded B Company. Possibly Field was sick. There is no doubt that Lieutenant-Colonel Richard Crosse was back in command of the Regiment on October 23rd.

several days of rain but movement across country was still very heavy. The two leading companies of the Regiment were B Company under Lieutenant William Giles, on the left, and C Company under Captain Percy Bobby, on the right. Percy Bobby had been unable to make contact with the units of the 3rd Division on his right and he called upon D Company for close support if necessary. In fact two platoons of Lieutenant Philip Whitehead's A Company had already been warned to be ready to cover the right flank of the C Company. Whitehead's men were to be established along the east bank of the Harpies River prior to following the leading companies forward. A Company became responsible for the Regiment's exposed right flank.

At 9 a.m., Lieutenant William Giles reported that his B Company was close to the west of the village of Escarmain, along a hedge line, and that they were held up by machine-gun fire from a strong point not yet identified. However, he was in touch with friendly units on both flanks. Thirty minutes later, at 9.30 a.m., Giles was able to report again that he was now in the village of Escarmain, although the unidentified enemy strong point had still not been neutralized. Lieutenant Philip Whitehead with his A Company started to move up to the western side of Escarmain at 10.45 a.m. Fifteen minutes later, at 11 a.m., Captain Percy Bobby reported that C Company had reached the Green Line on the eastern side of Escarmain and that 50 or so prisoners had been taken with little resistance. Casualties had been slight and he was in touch with B Company on his left, but still had made no contact with the 3rd Division on his right. Giles was able to report 45 minutes later, at 11.45 a.m., that his B Company had taken all their objectives, consolidation was proceeding on the Green Line, casualties were light, and many prisoners plus machine-guns had been taken. B Company had set up its Headquarters near the cross-roads to the north of Escarmain, in a sunken road. Contact was still being maintained on both flanks with British troops.

Meanwhile, the signal serjeant, Serjeant W.G. Older, with some orderlies, had been sent to Escarmain to lay a line and to establish a forward Regimental Headquarters on the western edge of the village. In the cellar which Older selected were four Germans with a machine-gun and a dump of new German kits. The large number of kits belonged to a division defending the place that had only come into the line the previous night[773]. Having taken possession of the four Germans, he opened up telephone communications with Vertain before 12 noon. By 1.15 p.m., the Regimental Headquarters had been moved to Escarmain. Later, Serjeant W.G. Older who had gone to France with the 52nd in August 1914 would be awarded a well-merited M.M.

---

[773] Most probably it was the 21st Reserve Division which was completing a relief when attacked. It had been in opposition to the 2nd Division on several previous occasions.

At 1 p.m., Lieutenant William Giles of B Company reported that British machine-guns had silenced a trench mortar which had been troublesome. About 1.15 p.m., an attack by the 3rd Division on the 52nd's right led to Escarmain being heavily shelled by the enemy. The Green Line had now been consolidated and, at 2.26 p.m., it was time for B and C Companies to attempt the third objective – the Brown Line. After the successful capture of the Green Line, the 5th Brigade suggested that the original Brown Line should be advanced to include the village of Capelle, and the Beaudignies - Bermerain road. The rationale for this was that it was a strong position to defend, giving command of the northern slopes of Capelle down to the River Ecaillon, and was also a good starting point for a further advance by the 99th Brigade the next day. Giles' B Company set off at the appointed hour but Bobby's C Company was delayed until 2.30 p.m. by the British barrage falling short. On the left, the 2nd H.L.I. also played their part in the advance on the Brown Line. From the high ground, just to the west of Escarmain, the Regimental scouts were able to watch the advance of the 52nd and the troops of the 3rd Division on their right.

Captain Percy Bobby reported with a message timed at 3.45 p.m. that he had taken the Brown Line with many prisoners, but that on attempting a further advance the whole line had come under heavy machine-gun fire from the high ground across the River Ecaillon. Casualties had been light. Helped by two platoons of Captain Harold 'Fritz' Eagle's D Company, C Company consolidated their part of the Brown Line. Lieutenant William Giles' B Company had done even better by taking the village of Capelle with numerous prisoners, machine-guns, and four trench mortars. The village was surrounded before the Germans were aware that they were being attacked in this area. Two orderlies from the 2nd H.L.I. had been taken prisoner earlier in the day; one of them was sent out by the Germans to find a British officer in order that the Battalion Headquarters could surrender to him. This was done and five officers and about 100 other ranks were taken. Later, Giles consolidated his position along a hedge to the north-east of the village[774]. At 4 p.m., Lieutenant Philip Whitehead reported that he was withdrawing his A Company slightly from W.4.b to W.4.c, on the western side of Escarmain, as the former position was under enemy observation. Lieutenant-

[774] In a report written after the battle, on October 29th 1918, Lieutenant-Colonel Robert Pipon temporarily commanding the 5th Brigade, recorded: 'Later the BROWN LINE was reached, during the advance a party of about 50 Germans walked into the attacking troops in the Sunken Road East of ESCARMAIN, both parties were surprised and the Germans opened rifle fire. A Lewis Gun was soon brought into action by this Battalion and several Germans were killed, the remainder bolting or scattering'. It is not clear from the records whether this applied to B or C Company of the 52nd. On balance, it was likely to have referred to Bobby's C Company from the position of the sunken road.

Colonel Richard Crosse at Regimental Headquarters was presented with something of a dilemma.

> It was then that the spirits of the soldiers seemed to rise very rapidly; indeed an almost un-52nd-like wave of excitement, quite unknown on such occasions as mobilization and armistice, swept over the Regiment. Breathless and beaming, a very young orderly of 'D' Company, fighting his first and perhaps last battle, arrived at Regimental headquarters after the capture of the Brown Line and told a shocked Commanding Officer, not only of the progress of the attack but of the appropriation of enemy personal property, about which there are vexatious regulations, thus; It's grand, sir. Just fresh in the line they are, and all new kits. Mr – 's platoon's souvenired eighteen watches. They're surrendering no end.

Not for the first time Richard Crosse cast his mind back to the Peninsular War of a century before for a precedent. 'I thought of that stern suppressor of looting, 'Black Bob' Craufurd, commanding the Light Division, and wondered what I ought to do: but I remembered the Irish soldier who, having added a pig to the temporary strength of the Division, met the General as he was removing the animal, and yet survived unpunished to enjoy a dinner of pork'. It is clear that even a well-led and disciplined Regiment such as the 52nd was capable of minor looting if the circumstances allowed.

The 52nd were not alone in reaching the Brown Line, as on their left the 2nd H.L.I. was also successful in taking their section of it. In fact, Major A.D. Telfer-Smollett and others wrote in their history *The 2nd Battalion Highland Light Infantry in The Great War.*

> Thus ended one of the most successful day's fighting which the Battalion experienced throughout the war. In all the Battalion had taken 300 prisoners, over 100 machine guns, 3 field guns and 2 trench mortars. Their casualties were 1 officer wounded, 3 other ranks killed and 33 other ranks wounded.

About 4 p.m. notification was received that the 5th Brigade was to be relieved that evening by the 99th Brigade. Half an hour later, officers of the 23rd R.F., the battalion relieving the 52nd, arrived to ascertain dispositions. As the 99th Brigade was to continue the advance the following day, the aggressive Captain Percy Bobby was instructed to establish a line of posts north of the road running through Q.35.b and Q.36.a, approximately parallel to that section of the Brown Line. This was effected after dark, when lack of visibility prevented the enemy opening machine-gun fire. Thus a good 'jumping off' line was handed over to the incoming 23rd R.F. Guides, one for the Regimental Headquarters and five per company [except for the reserve company, A, who were already in the vicinity] were sent to the cross-roads in W.3.b., to the west of Escarmain, at 8.30 p.m. The relief was complicated by the fact that the 23rd R.F. had only two companies to take over the positions of the four companies of the 52nd. However, by 11 p.m. the 52nd were moving back independently by companies to billets in Vertain. Blankets and hot food were sent up and issued by midnight. All ranks of the 52nd, tired but satisfied, settled down on the ground taken from the enemy in the last 24 hours. The Regiment had made its last attack of the war, although nobody was aware of this at the time. It had done remarkably well.

The then Lieutenant-Colonel Henry Davies wrote that 'the men had advanced splendidly' four years earlier on the Poelcappelle road. Richard Crosse felt that the same was true at the Selle action, although 'obviously the enemy was not what he had been, but the stubborn valour of the British soldier remained undiminished'[775].

About 4.30 a.m. October 24th, Vertain was shelled with high explosive and gas shells, so that box respirators had to be worn for some time. Two sections of D Company were buried in a cellar, but were dug out without injuries. The morning was spent in clearing up and in counting the cost of the previous day's battle. The 52nd's casualties on October 23rd had been remarkably light. One officer, Captain E.J. Anderson, was slightly wounded[776]. Other ranks: 8 killed; 36 wounded; 15 gassed. In exchange a large number of Germans had been killed, 200 were taken prisoner, and one 4.2 howitzer, four trench mortars, and 39 machine-guns were captured. During October 24th, the bodies of the eight men who had been killed the day before were found and buried in the British Cemetery, the Commanding Officer's two buglers sounding the last post[777]. In earlier battles the ground on which men had fallen was often not taken from the enemy, and many bodies were subsequently lost or blown to smithereens by the artillery. At 1.15 p.m. orders were received for the 52nd to move back to St.

---

[775] *Regimental Journal* of 1958.

[776] Anderson stayed on duty. Richard Crosse in the *Regimental Journal* of 1958 recorded: 'He was the fourth 52nd officer who, in the last three months fighting, might have been evacuated but refused to be : namely, on 23rd Aug, Capt. Fullbrook-Leggatt M.C.; 25th August, Lieut. Sawers (wounded again and evacuated 11th Sept.) and on 11th Oct. Lieut. Cockshut'.

[777] Of the records that can be traced of the men that were killed on October 23rd, some were buried in Vertain Communal Cemetery Extension and others in Escarmain Communal Cemetery Extension. Amongst the dead was Private William Wixey M.M. aged 19 years.

Python at 4 p.m. The march was very slow, the roads being congested with traffic, but the Regiment arrived at St. Python about 5.20 p.m. Transport, Rearward Services and the Reinforcement moved up simultaneously from St. Hilaire but, in view of another probable forward move, were billeted separately.

In the period October 23rd/24th, the 2nd Division captured 23 officers and 831 other ranks. The morale of the German prisoners was very low and they appeared to have lost interest in the war. They had been forbidden to pick up the leaflets showing the recent front line changes that the British had been dropping from balloons. However, many of the prisoners had these leaflets on their persons when they were captured. Their general feeling was: what is the point of continuing with the war when we are beaten? A large number of the prisoners believed that the British would shoot them in cold blood. Major-General Cecil Pereira felt that they did not really believe this as they surrendered so easily.

It is difficult to ascertain which German units fought against the 2nd Division and the 52nd in the Battle of the Selle. According to Edmonds in the *Official History* little is to be found in the German histories for October 23rd, although he does quote Lieutenant-General M. Schwarte's *Der deutsche Landkrieg*. One diary remarked that it was the day of 'heaviest fighting since the great defeat of 8th August with its direful results'. Practically every German regiment claimed that the British broke in elsewhere and either turned its flanks or got in the rear of it. In his diary entry for October, Major-General Cecil Pereira commented: 'we have captured men from the 21st R, 9th R, 4th, and 113th Divisions and from eight different Regts of these Divns'. Pereira went on: 'The 2nd Division has met the 21st R.D. on more than one occasion when holding the line and they used to be a fine Divn'.

The 21st Reserve Division recruited from Hesse-Nassau and the south of Westphalia, and intelligence assessments reported that it was a good division in 1917. But by 1918 it was considered to be second class in agreement with Pereira's estimate of it. In 1918, its 88th Reserve Regiment had been amalgamated with its 80th and 87th Reserve Regiments. However, at the time of the action, the 168th Reserve Regiment had just been transferred to it from 25th Reserve Division which had been broken up. Almost certainly units from the 21st Reserve Division encountered the 52nd in the environs of Escarmain and Capelle. Possibly the new kits referred to in the text belonged to the 168th Reserve Regiment who had recently joined the Division. The 9th Reserve Division recruited in Posen, the 4th Division in Pomerania, and the 113th Division in Prussian Saxony and part of Thuringia. The 4th Division was considered to be a very good one in 1918.

During the period October 24th-25th, the 99th Brigade continued the advance over the River Ecaillon, and towards the River Rhonelle, in the direction of Le Quesnoy and the Forest of Mormal. On October 25th, still in St. Python, the 52nd's chaplain, the Reverend Ernest Gallop left the Regiment on transfer to No. 3 Casualty Clearing Station. In his place a familiar figure, the Reverend Edward 'Monty' Guilford M.C., returned to the 52nd. The following Sunday, the 27th, a Church Parade was held in the School Yard at St. Python, followed by a football match in the afternoon. Their former Commanding Officer, Major-General Henry Davies, now commanding the 11th Division, visited the Regiment during the day. Two officers, Lieutenants R. Blackwell and J.W. Bennett rejoined the Regiment from their six months tours of duty in England.

At 4 a.m. October 29th, the 52nd received notification that later in the day the Regiment would move forward again. The starting point was passed at 2.45 p.m., the 52nd marching up the road to Vertain and then on to Escarmain. B and C Companies turned off to billets in Bermerain, and A and D with the Regimental Headquarters went forward to Ruesnes, in each case in relief of a company of the 1st Gordon Highlanders. The relief was completed by 6.55 p.m. During the day, Captain A.G. Cardy and Second-Lieutenant D.E. Haymen both rejoined the Regiment. Cardy had served with the Regiment in 1915 before being sent to the Mediterranean Expeditionary Force, and Haymen had been away since April 1917 suffering from shell shock. It is interesting that he was welcomed back to the 52nd and was not stigmatized for having suffered from shell shock. Major James Powell temporarily commanded the 52nd as Richard Crosse was sick. Whether this was related to his recent wounds or for some other reason is not recorded.

During the night and early morning, the enemy shelled Ruesnes with gas and high explosive shells. One private was wounded and another killed by the shelling. As Richard Crosse wrote forty years later: 'a cruel fate ordained that the latter should be 7785 Private Smith, cook of 'A' Company, a married man, a reservist who had served throughout the war'. Poor, unfortunate Charles Smith, aged 32 years, from Willesden Green in London, was the 52nd's last casualty of the war[778]. Captain A.G. Cardy who had only rejoined the Regiment the day before, and had been given command of B Company was admitted to hospital with bronchitis and later evacuated. On the last day of the month, Lieutenant-Colonel Richard Crosse returned from sick leave to fully resume command of the Regiment.

On November 2nd, the 52nd was relieved by the Coldstream and Irish Guards, and moved back again to billets in St. Python. Owing to the fact that the roads were blocked with traffic, it was midnight before the last company arrived

[778] Private Charles Smith was buried in Vertain Communal Cemetery Extension, grave E.5.

at its destination. The following day, Major James Powell temporarily took over command of the 17th R.F., and Captain E.J. Anderson replaced him as second-in-command of the 52nd. On the 4th, in anticipation of a big advance, packs, greatcoats, caps, and supplies were dumped in St. Python in order that the Regiment's mobility might be improved. In addition, Lewis gun numbers were cut from 36 to 20. Each man was to carry a blanket, jerkin, and a single flare. The 105th reinforcement of 70 other ranks arrived. Although the 52nd was on short notice to move during the day, nothing came of it.

On November 5th, the Regiment remained at short notice to move, and it rained continuously. That day, Lieutenant Harry Dashwood, having been absorbed into the Third Army Infantry School, was struck off the strength of the 52nd. In mid August 1918, Richard Crosse had been ordered to select an officer to become an instructor. The humanitarian Crosse, knowing that an attack involving his men, with its inevitable casualties, was about to take place, selected Harry Dashwood, as he knew that the young man had already lost three brothers in the war, two of them in May 1915 while serving with the Regiment[779]. The same day Lieutenant Octavius 'Toby' Sturges rejoined for duty from the Third Army Infantry School and on the 7th Lieutenant Laurence Dowson also rejoined the Regiment, having been away with a pyrexia of unknown origin since late August 1918. The experienced company commander Captain Harold 'Fritz' Eagle was admitted to hospital on the 8th with the same complaint as Dowson. It is likely that both men were suffering from influenza.

The Regiment marched from St. Python, at 9.08 a.m. November 8th, for Villers-Pol via Vertain - Escarmain - Capelle - Pont de Buat - Ruesnes - La Croisetta. Rain fell for a considerable portion of the march, and the going was very heavy. At one point, the Regiment was delayed for a long time by the leading battalion losing its way. This necessitated a long halt to regain the correct position on the line of march. Eventually, the 52nd reached its billets at 1.30 p.m. As part of the journey was across country, the Transport moved separately by road. Further officers were evacuated with influenza: Lieutenant Frederick Lowndes[780] and Second-Lieutenant C. Gray. By the late autumn of 1918, there was repeated evacuation of officers and men suffering from the influenza pandemic [Spanish 'flu] that was sweeping the world. Over a 24 week period

---

[779] From Lieutenant-Colonel Sir Edmond [Jim] Neville's address, on June 18th 1971 [Waterloo Day], at the unveiling of the Richard Crosse memorial window in the Garrison Church, Winchester.

[780] Lowndes subsequently served with the 43rd in North Russia, the Pioneer Corps in World War II and, in 1948, suddenly collapsed and died aged 50 years. In 1925, he changed his name to Belloc-Lowndes by deed poll. His father was F.S.A. Lowndes, a pillar of *The Times* editorial staff for many years and his mother, Marie Belloc Lowndes, a prolific English novelist. Hilaire Belloc the Anglo/French writer and historian was an uncle.

there were more than 300,000 cases of influenza in France and Flanders leading to a hospital admission rate of greater than 160 per 1,000 men. The Regiment spent November 9th cleaning roads.

November 11th 1918, Armistice Day, began in a very low-key fashion for the 52nd Light Infantry. At 9.30 a.m., the Regiment paraded at the Village Church of Villers-Pol for a route march taking them through Maresches where the 2/4th Battalion of the Oxfordshire and Buckinghamshire Light Infantry was based. Just as the 52nd was moving off, a wire was received from the 2nd Division and read out to the troops.

> Hostilities will cease at 1100[781] to-day, 11th November. Troops will stand fast on line reached at that hour, which will be reported by wire to Corps H.Q. Defensive precautions will be maintained. There is to be no intercourse of any description with the enemy. No Germans are to be allowed into our lines. Any doing so will be taken prisoner. All moves for 3rd Division for to-day, 11th November, are cancelled. 4th Cavalry Brigade will carry out its move to Boussois.

The 52nd showed no excitement at the announcement that the war was at an end, and the route march was carried out. About 3 p.m. that day, Lieutenant-Colonel Richard Crosse who had served in the 52nd throughout the war, firstly as Adjutant and latterly as the Commanding Officer, was sitting in the orderly room wondering what was to happen to them, when there was a loud explosion. A bomb in the garden of the house adjoining the orderly room had been thought to be harmless, but had 'gone bad' and hence the interruption to the peace and quiet. The divisional notice announcing the end of the war had been posted outside the orderly room. Immediately after the explosion one well-known 52nd voice was heard to say 'war's over; ain't yer read the notice?' Richard Crosse was amused by the comment and the ribald ones which followed. Of the 52nd which took the field in August 1914, there were serving with it at the Armistice 66 of all ranks of whom 39 had served continuously.

The 2nd Division, with the 5th Brigade and the 52nd, was selected to be part of the Army of Occupation, and would shortly start its long north-easterly march to the Rhine. The 52nd remained at Villers-Pol, making preliminary preparations for demobilization, repairing roads and burying dead animals, until November 16th, when they marched east to Preux-au-Sart. Their route took them

---

781 In late 1918, the 52nd and the British Army as a whole, started to use the 24 hour clock in orders and *War Diaries*. With this notable exception, the terms a.m. and p.m. have been substituted in the text to maintain consistency.

south of Wargnies Le Grand and Warngies Le Petit, and billets were reached at 11 a.m. On the 18th, the Regiment left Preux-au-Sart at 9 a.m. and, with slight snow falling at times, their march took them to billets in Douzies prior to 2 p.m., via Gommegnies - Amfroipret - Bermeries - Bavai - La Longueville. The 52nd had passed through Bavai twice before, firstly, on the way to Paris in 1815, and more recently on the retreat from Mons in 1914. Perhaps it was fitting that Major-General Henry Davies, who had led them back through Bavai on the latter occasion, visited them during the afternoon.

The march towards the Franco-Belgian border continued on November 20th, when the 52nd left Douzies at 8.10 a.m. and proceeded to Grand Reng through the nearby northern outskirts of Maubeuge - west of Elesmes - Vieux Reng. The roads were made slippery by mud and the going was heavy. Large numbers of escaped or repatriated Allied prisoners-of-war and civilian refugees were met on the roads. The Franco-Belgian border was crossed and billets reached in nearby Grand Reng at about 11.45 a.m. The inhabitants greeted the 52nd with cheering, flags and notices: 'Home to Our Heroes' and 'Welcome to Our Brave Allies'. Road clearing, bathing and washing of clothing was carried out on a company basis[782]. The 52nd marched from Grand Reng on November 24th, moving off at 8.30 a.m., on the way to Merbes St. Marie via Pleissant, and arrived in their billets at 10.50 a.m. They were on the move once more, at 8 a.m. the next morning, for Charleroi via Bienne lez Happart - Mont St. Geneviève - Plein Des Chênes - Fontaine l'Evêque. It was a miserable march in the rain, and the Regiment reached its billets at 2 p.m.

On November 27th, parties of seven officers and seventeen N.C.O.s, selected by the length of service with the Regiment, proceeded by lorry to the battlefield of Waterloo where, a little over a century before, their illustrious predecessors in the 52nd had made one of the key manoeuvres of the action. The day was spent walking and studying the battlefield. At 7.45 a.m. the next day, the Regiment left Charleroi for the easterly march to Sart-Eustache via Gilly - Châtelet - Presles. Once more, the journey was an unpleasant one with muddy roads, and billets were reached at about 12.15 p.m. However, Regimental Headquarters were in a red-bricked château with a moat and drawbridge surrounded by a beautiful park. Only one night was spent in Sart Eustache as, on the 29th, the Regiment paraded at 7.35 a.m. for the move to Bois De Villers via Le Roux - Vitrival - Fosses la Ville - Sart St. Laurent. Here, some of the N.C.O.s

[782] At Ypres in 1914, battalions had bathed and then changed into the washed underclothing of the previous unit, leaving their own garments for the next battalion. Here in 1918, matters had improved in that underclothes were laundered by company rather than taking on the underclothing of the last battalion on a communal basis.

and men had a fortunate escape from serious carbon monoxide poisoning from a stove in a poorly ventilated hut. The billets were appalling and were the subject of a later enquiry. Some leave parties were able to go to Namur.

During their four days in Bois De Villers rations were very short and a cow was bought to supplement them. Richard Crosse described his unfortunate purchase[783].

> On the 2nd December, to supplement the insufficient rations, a cow was bought from a farm, jointly by the commanding officers of the 52nd and 74th[784], to be shared between the two regiments. This, however, proved to be a failure, though an amusing one, the corpse being condemned by a veterinary officer. Fortunately, for the first time in several days bread and fresh meat came up with rations.

On December 4th, the Regiment marched to Nameche, crossing the River Meuse at Wépion by a German pontoon bridge and thence via Fort De Dave - Andoy - Fort D'Andoy - Lunay - Maizeret. The roads were good although in the Meuse Valley they were rather steep. The following day, the 5th, the Regiment moved on to Solières, their route taking them alongside the river via Sclayn - Andenne - Gives. Here the roads were bad and the hill from the Meuse Valley at Gives, exceptionally steep and trying. Billets were reached at 1.30 p.m. There was to be no respite as, at 8 a.m. December 6th, the Regiment marched to Seny via St. Léonard - Huy - La Sarte - Les Communes - Strée lez Huy - Tinlot. The next day the 52nd moved to Harzé via Warzée - Ouffet - Comblain Fairon - Comblain La Tour - Xhoris. A great many men had to sleep on stone floors. Early on the 7th, the Regiment passed the south end of Harzé on the march to Stoumont, via Houssonloge - Lorcé - the valley road along the north side of the railway - Stoumont Station - Targnon.

December 9th 1918 was an important day in the history of the 52nd Light Infantry; it was the day when the Regiment marched into Germany, until less than a month ago the land of the enemy. Their route took them from Stoumont to Malmedy via La Gleize - Roanne - Coo Station - road junction just north of Trois Ponts - Stavelot. The houses of Stavelot were festooned with Belgian flags. There was a long halt between Stavelot and the Belgium/Germany frontier. The roads were for the most part good, but the weather was bad, a cold wind blowing

783 Article in the *Regimental Journal* of 1959.
784 The 2nd Highland Light Infantry.

during the earlier part of the march changing to rain near the frontier. Lieutenant-Colonel Richard Crosse has left a description of the 52nd's entry into Germany[785].

> It seemed proper to make some ceremony of the crossing of the frontier into Germany on Monday, 9th December. It had been hoped that our General Davies[786], who led the 52nd into France fifty-two months gone by, would have been available to lead it into Germany, but this could not be.
>
> From the last halt before the border the band proceeded ahead, to be in position as the Regiment approached, to play the Regimental Marches of the 43rd and 52nd[787] while the whole column, led by the buglers, went by, in the order: 'A'(Capt. Bailie), 'B'(Lieut. Horley), 'C' (Capt. Bobby, M.C.), 'D' (Capt. Eagle), First Line Transport (Lieut. E.H. Vigars, D.C.M.), Second Line Transport, or 'Train' (Lieut F. Barnes, Quartermaster).
>
> Nobody who spent the last few years with the 52nd could watch the Regiment go by that day without being very much moved. There are emotions about a column of marching men with horses and wagons which no fleet of mechanized vehicles could stir up. Platoon after platoon went by at that step which is clearly light infantry, and which made possible a long tea break on every hard march. No less moving was the sight of the Regimental transport, men, horses, and vehicles, on each of the last a large 52 in white, displayed boldly on a ten-inch square painted rifle-green, with veteran horses as well as men: Botley and his greys; Weaving and his steady old pair; Bunning and his prize-winning light draught pair; Bunning who had served with the 43rd in South Africa eighteen years gone by, and with whose turnout even 'Old Pole-chain', a name bestowed irreverently on an exacting senior inspector of transport, could find no fault; shoeing-smiths, cold-shoers and brakemen, still rigidly at the trail despite heathen hints that they would look better at the slope; the good Padre's canteen cart and cooks, who served the Regiment so well on these marches and always.

---

[785] Article in the *Regimental Journal* of 1959.

[786] Major-General Henry Rodolf Davies. In the event Brigadier-General W.L. Osborn took the salute.

[787] The 43rd *Ein Schütze bin ich*; the 52nd *The Lower Castle Yard.*

At this moment of great emotion, Richard Crosse's thoughts turned to his support services, and he was particularly appreciative of the Regimental cooks. It must be recalled that the last 52nd man to be killed in the war was a cook. He singled out Joe Abery of C Company: 'universally approved as a cook, less unanimously agreed with as a football referee'. The cooks had less glamorous work to do than the buglers who led the Regiment into Germany. In order to keep his buglers together, Crosse had them trained as anti-aircraft Lewis gunners. Similarly, the company assistant accountants were employed in a dual role, as chiropodists, 'those cultured pruners of men's feet', as one 52nd poet so eloquently wrote.

The Regiment spent its first night in Germany, in Malmedy[788], sharing a factory with the 24th R.F. However, the officers were mainly billeted in houses or hotel rooms. As they were settling in that evening, a message was received from Brigadier-General W.L. Osborn, commanding the 5th Brigade, now recovered from his wounds.

> My congratulations to the 52nd Light Infantry on crossing the enemy frontier today as a result of the battles they have fought this last year. British Infantry throughout history have proved themselves to be second to none and I am proud to have the Regiment in the Brigade I command on such an historic occasion.

December 10th was spent standing fast in their Malmedy billets, with the usual cleaning up and refitting with the limited amount of serge clothing and boots that were available. Their leather boots, particularly, had been battered in the long march through Belgium into Germany. At 8.45 a.m. December 11th, the 52nd left Malmedy for Weywertz via Waimes, arriving at 12.30 p.m., just before it started raining. The following day, the 12th, the Regiment marched via Nidrum - Eisenborn - Kalterherberg - Monschau. The roads continued to be wet, muddy, and in a poor state of repair. Two men fell out but only because their boots had worn completely through. The long march continued on December 13th, via Imgenbroich - Simmerath - Strauch. Rain fell continuously, everyone was soaked to the skin, and many old soldiers said that it was the wettest day they had ever known. The men were billeted so that four to five men might dry themselves in front of a fire.

---

[788] Malmedy had been annexed by the Prussians in 1815. Following the First World War, after a plebiscite in 1925, it elected to join Belgium. On December 17th 1944, it was the scene of the infamous execution of 84 American prisoners-of-war by the S.S.

On the morning of December 14th, the 52nd marched for Niederau via Nideggen - Boich - Drove - Kreuzau, arriving after a journey of five hours. Some companies were billeted in a convent and others in a château. As Niederau was an easy train ride from Düren, a number of all ranks were allowed passes to visit it. The 15th and 16th were rest days and, on the 17th, the Regiment marched to Steinstrasse and Lich via Düren - Arnoldsweiler - Ellen - Oberzier - Niederzier. On all marches there was customarily a stop for tea which proved invaluable in restoring the men. The 5th Brigade column was led through the ancient city of Düren by the 2nd H.L.I. with pipes playing, bayonets fixed, and Colours flying. Major-General Cecil Pereira described the scene in his diary.

> The 5th Brigade marched through Düren. The 24th with fixed bayonets lead the way; the 74th[789] followed also with fixed bayonets and carrying their colours. It was quite an emotional moment when the 74th Pipers came along. The whole Brigade marched through the town as a Victorian Brigade should do, every man carried himself erect and they marched with a fine swing. The streets were crowded to see them go through. The transport were all very well turned out and the end of the column was brought up by the Bde Coy of the Train; the enormous sleek horses were looking their best and the Boche on-lookers were visibly impressed.

Lieutenant-Colonel Richard Crosse's 52nd was following the 2nd H.L.I. through Düren. He had endeavoured to send a party home to bring out their own Colours for an occasion such as this. Sadly, his request was turned down as the Colours were very precious to the Regiment and it was thought that there was no proper place to store them on their long journey through Belgium and Germany. In fact, the Colours were non-regulation ones and there was a collective wish not to draw this fact to the attention of the authorities[790]. Subsequently, Crosse had an Oxford firm make a quarter-sized painting of the Colours, which was sent out to Germany and used for lecturing purposes.

---

789 The 24th was the 24th Royal Fusiliers., and the 74th was the 2nd Highland Light Infantry.

790 The Colours were not of the 'battalion' or 1881 pattern bearing the joint honours of the 43rd and 52nd, but they were the Regimental Colours of the old 52nd. Normally, the Colours would have been replaced in 1881, however they had been hung on to and bore, with only one blemish which had been removed, only the eighteen battle honours of the old 52nd. Quebec had been forced on the 52nd in 1882 but, in 1913, the then Lieutenant-Colonel Henry Davies ordered Richard Crosse to remove the offending emblem. Crosse loyally carried out the order with a razor blade! No one outside the Regiment had noticed this gross irregularity.

The next day, the 18th, the Regiment was on the march once more. This time their destination was Rommerskirchen and Eckum via Elsdorf - Bergheim - Niederaussem - Huchelnoven. Notification was received that the 52nd would be spending Christmas in the area, prior to completion of the demarcation of the final region of Germany that their 5th Brigade would occupy. It was not until Christmas Eve that the Regiment was allotted Stommeln as its final destination. The same day some of the 52nd's officers had visited Cologne on a shopping trip for their companies. Unfortunately, they missed the last return train and spent an uncomfortable night on Cologne Station. A pleasant Christmas Day passed quietly with the usual services and celebrations. Richard Crosse had come to an agreement with the 2nd H.L.I. to exchange guard duties with them, to free the 52nd on Christmas Day, in exchange for a reciprocal arrangement on New Year's Day.

On December 27th, the 52nd marched to Stommeln, a village to the north-west of Cologne, and spent the rest of the day settling in. Lieutenant-Colonel Richard Crosse, in a Regimental Order, addressed his men. As always, he showed great pride in the history and traditions of his Regiment, and also in the young men of the current one, whose recent march over some 200 miles in five weeks was a great feat of endurance. The Retreat from Mons may have had the enemy snapping at their heels, and the blistering August sun on their backs, but the men of August 1914 were fit professional soldiers, unlike their successors of late 1918. These later young men, many of whom were conscripts, were war weary and suffering from the debilitating effects of the influenza epidemic. It says much for the traditions and spirit of the Regiment that Crosse had imbued in them that they did not fall by the wayside during the long march into Germany. In addition, Crosse told them to treat the German civilian population correctly.

> Now that the march to the Occupied Territory has been completed, the Commanding Officer wishes to record his great admiration of the way it has been carried out by the Regiment.
>
> Although unattended by the battle conditions which have been inseparable since August 1914, the march which began on 16th November last has not been without hardships in the matter of loads being extra to the normal marching order, and in many cases indifferent roads, steep hills, bad weather, and then bad billets, where washing arrangements have been difficult. At times leather for repairing boots has not been available; many men have had to march in new boots which there has been no chance to properly grease.
>
> There have been days when, until the railways could be got through, rations were bad and insufficient.

The Commanding Officer knows well what all this has meant. Cases are known to him where men who, from sickness or bad boots, have been given the chance of going on the lorries, but they have chosen to march in the ranks. Others, from sickness, might have had their packs carried, but they would not part with them. Others, again, have chosen not to join the ambulance or the "Slow Party" rather than spoil the Company's record.

Captains of Companies, Platoon Officers, and the Medical Officer have done their utmost by encouragement, by carrying rifles themselves, and by care and attention to men's feet, to keep men in the ranks, and the response has been worthy of the highest traditions of the Regiment.

It reveals a discipline more real than which is indicated by noisy handling of arms, stamping of feet, and loud clicking of heels.

The Light Infantry soldier does his duty at all times as quietly and steadily as he moves on parade or in battle, and there is no higher ideal.

Since August 21st last, when the final battles began, the Regiment has marched about 270 miles, exclusive of fighting; and from November 16th last, inclusive, about 200 miles.

Before the march to Germany began, all ranks were reminded in Regimental Orders of 13.11.18 how the good marching and soldierly bearing were required and expected as when, after Waterloo, the Regiment marched, in the Army of Occupation, to Paris; and if the same standard be maintained, and the same attitude of civility, with restraint, be observed towards our country's enemies – so as to leave them with feelings of respect and admiration for the British soldier, there will be no cause to be prouder of any chapter in the history of His Majesty's 52nd than of this one.

Chapter XXV

The Epilogue: Occupation of Germany and the Return Home.

January 1st - July 19th 1919

As the New Year of 1919 opened the 52nd Light Infantry's attention was settled on a programme of educational and recreational training. Classes were opened in English, drawing, shoe-making, tailoring, veterinary science, and horse-shoeing. For those men who wished to stay in the post-war Army, some 150 of them, preparations were made for entry into the Third Class Army School Certificate Examination. The classes were briefly interrupted by the final move to Zons on January 7th. January 16th 1919 was the 110th anniversary of the Battle of Corunna and the death of Sir John Moore, that greatest of all Colonels of the 52nd. Lieutenant-Colonel Richard Crosse arranged for lectures on the subject, and for the appropriate pages from the *Regimental War Tales* to be read in the Regimental school[791]. At Zons, on January 19th, the ribbon of the 1914-15 Star was presented to all those members of the Regiment who were entitled to it.

Amongst their other duties the 52nd kept a measure of control over the civilian population. The Commanding Officer, Richard Crosse, as Summary Court Officer, did his best to execute justice and maintain truth among Germans caught bicycling to work without lights, unlicensed vendors of potent and unwholesome beverages known as 'Red Biddy' and 'Fixed Bayonets'. There were also ladies of easy virtue, a bevy of whom were found to have established themselves in close proximity to a company headquarters. A raid on this hive of industry was conducted by Crosse, ably assisted by Lieutenant John Murray, an interpreter and a bugler. Just what part the bugler was intended to play is not clear!

Demobilization had begun in earnest at the end of the preceding December when, on the 28th, thirteen men were sent away as the first draft[792]. In January, two officers and 56 other ranks departed and, in February, it was the turn of four more officers and 150 other ranks. Sadness was always felt when a batch of old soldiers departed for demobilization. However, feelings ran high when some recent recruits, claimed for key posts in agriculture and industry, were demobilized before longstanding members of the Regiment. The whole process was laborious with five forms to be filled in, a medical inspection, and

[791] *Regimental War Tales* by Colonel A.F. Mockler Ferryman [First Edition] pages 53-57.

[792] The first man to be demobilized from the 52nd was Second-Lieutenant Herbert Windross, who was reclaimed by the Foreign Office on November 20th.

measurement for civilian clothes. The demobilization parties were usually played to the station by the band, and followed by the limber carrying three days' rations plus their packs. On average it took eight days from leaving the Regiment until the final dispersal. All the Regiment's drafts were collected at Concentration Camps, in Cologne or Düren, before being sent to the Base Ports for the voyage back to England. Finally, at Dispersal Camps, weapons were handed in, and the soldiers were then free to return home.

Thus January and February, 1919, passed in educational classes and demobilization. In the latter month, the 52nd were informed that they would be relieved by the 6th London, and reduced to a small cadre which would be transferred to England. On March 1st, Major-General Cecil Pereira addressed the Regiment for the last time, as he was giving up the command of the 2nd Division. The 6th London arrived in the vicinity on March 2nd, and the 52nd's residual cadre hopes were raised that they would soon be home. However, it would be three months before this happened. A further six officers and 129 other ranks were demobilized in March.

Other sad days followed. On the 8th, all the 52nd's men who had elected to or were required to remain in the army of occupation were transferred to the 9th Gloucestershire, there being no battalion of their own Regiment remaining in Germany. On March 16th, the remains of the 52nd left Zons for billets in Delrath, Nievenheim and Uckerath. At the end of March, the 52nd consisted of about 300 men and, at the beginning of April, all the regular subaltern officers were ordered home, to Aldershot, to join a composite battalion, to be known as the 1st Oxfordshire and Buckinghamshire Light Infantry. On April 7th, the Regiment made a short move to Gohr and Broich. April and May were filled with pseudo-educational classes on any possible subject an officer was familiar with: sports, football, hockey, bathing, dances, and whist drives were just some of the topics used to keep the men from becoming bored. Some leave was taken in Cologne. During the month of April, 193 other ranks were demobilized leaving only another twelve awaiting discharge.

On May 3rd, the 52nd's cadre stood in its final form of one company commanded by Captain Ernest Whitfeld and a small headquarters. In total, the 52nd now consisted of just seven officers and 75 other ranks. May 26th, saw the cadre starting on its journey home. It entrained at Düren on the 27th, arrived at Antwerp on the 28th, and embarked, finally arriving at Tilbury on June 1st. The weary men proceeded to Cambridge Barracks, Woolwich where they were not expected. Here the cadre was visited by Major-General Sir J. Hanbury-Williams, Colonel of the Regiment, and Lieutenant-Colonel Archibald Eden. The long-promised move to Oxford finally took place on June 12th, where Richard Crosse gave up the command to Archibald Eden[793]. It must have been a very difficult moment for Crosse to give up the command of his beloved Regiment to his immediate predecessor.

At Oxford Station there was a civic reception by the Mayor and Burgesses of the City of Oxford, and the small cadre marched to the Depot, at Cowley Barracks, with the buglers and their silver bugles to the fore. Many former and disabled 52nd men were in the watching crowd.

On July 9th, a Colour Party under Lieutenant Cyril Horley left the Depot, at Oxford for the Paris Victory March. This took place on the 14th, with a rouse at 2.45 a.m., an inspection by Field-Marshal Sir Douglas Haig at 8 a.m., followed by a six-miles procession, including the Arc de Triomphe and the Champs Elysées. The London Victory Parade took place on July 19th, with the Colours being carried from the Admiralty to Buckingham Palace. King George V took the salute at the Victoria Monument. That same day all the Battalions of the Regiment took part in a Victory March through Oxford. Fittingly, the parade was commanded by Major-General Sir Robert Fanshawe, a former commanding officer of the 52nd, whose training had been of inestimable value to the Regiment in the run up to the war.

So the Great War and its immediate aftermath came to an end. The 52nd Light Infantry had devotedly served their King and Country with great distinction. No doubt their greatest Colonel, Sir John Moore, would have been proud of the manner in which the Regiment had conducted itself. Twenty years would pass before the 52nd would be summoned, once more, to a major European battlefield, to defeat a Bohemian corporal[794] and his criminal Nazi regime. In the finest traditions of the Regiment they would not be found wanting.

---

[793] Eden had been a Brigadier-General for the final two years of the war and at its end he returned to the substantive rank of Lieutenant-Colonel.

[794] Adolf Hitler was called a 'Bohemian corporal' by Winston Churchill. President Paul von Hindenburg supposedly used the terms 'Austrian corporal', 'Bohemian corporal' and 'the Corporal'. In reality Hitler was Austrian.

Appendix 1
Battle Honours of the 52nd Light Infantry 1914-1918

The Battles Nomenclature Committee reported on July 9th 1920, and their report was accepted by King George V on September 4th 1922 as a basis for awarding battle honours. Regiments were to have no more than 24 battle honours emblazoned on their Colours, of which no more than ten might be Great War honours. A regimental committee representing the various battalions, decided that the ten battle honours for the Colours should be: 1) France and Flanders; Mons, Nonne Bosschen, Ypres [1914, 1917], Langemarck [1914, 1917], Somme [1916, 1918], Cambrai [1917, 1918]. 2) Italy; Piave. 3) Macedonia; Doiran [1917, 1918]. 4) Mesopotamia; Ctesiphon, Defence of Kut-al-Amara.

1914

Mons: August 23rd-24th. I Corps. [Lieutenant-General Douglas Haig].
Retreat from Mons: August 23rd-September 5th. I Corps. [Haig].
Marne, 1914: September 7th-10th. I Corps. [Haig].
Aisne, 1914: September 12th-15th. I Corps. [Haig].
Ypres, 1914: October 19th-November 22nd. I Corps. [Haig].
Langemarck, 1914: October 21st-24th. I Corps. [Haig].
Gheluvelt: October 29th-31st. I Corps. [Haig].
Nonne Bosschen: November 11th. I Corps. [Haig].

1915

Aubers: May 9th. I Corps, First Army. [Lieutenant-General Charles Monro, General Douglas Haig].
Festubert, 1915: May 15th-25th. I Corps, First Army. [Monro, Haig].
Loos: September 25th-October 8th. I Corps, First Army. [Lieutenant-General Hubert Gough, Haig].

1916

Somme, 1916: July 1st-November 18th. XIII Corps, Fourth Army. [Lieutenant-General Walter Congreve, General Henry Rawlinson].
Delville Wood: July 15th-September 3rd. XIII Corps, Fourth Army. [Congreve, Rawlinson].
Ancre: November 13th-18th. V Corps, Fifth Army. [Lieutenant-General Edward Fanshawe, Gough].

1917

Bapaume, 1917: March 17th. II Corps, Fifth Army. [Lieutenant-General Claud Jacob, Gough].

Arras, 1917: April 9th-May 4th. XIII Corps, First Army. [Congreve, General Henry Horne].

Vimy, 1917: April 9th-14th. XIII Corps, First Army. [Congreve, Horne].

Scarpe, 1917: April 9th-14th. April 23rd-24th. May 3rd-4th. XIII Corps, First Army. [Congreve, Horne].

Arleux: April 28th-29th. XIII Corps, First Army. [Congreve, Horne].

Cambrai, 1917: November 20th-December 3rd. IV Corps, handed over to V Corps on December 1st, Third Army. [Lieutenant-Generals Charles Woollcombe, Edward Fanshawe, General Julian Byng].

1918

St. Quentin: March 21st-23rd. V Corps, Third Army. [Edward Fanshawe, Byng].

Bapaume, 1918: March 24th-25th. August 31st-September 3rd. V Corps, Third Army [Edward Fanshawe, Byng] for the former and VI Corps, Third Army [Lieutenant-General Aylmer Haldane, Byng] for the latter.

Somme, 1918: March 21st-April 5th. August 21st-September 3rd. V Corps, Third Army [Edward Fanshawe, Byng] for the former and VI Corps, Third Army [Haldane, Byng] for the latter.

Albert, 1918: August 21st-23rd. VI Corps, Third Army. [Haldane, Byng].

Hindenburg Line: September 12th-October 9th. VI Corps, Third Army. [Haldane, Byng].

Havrincourt: September 12th. VI Corps, Third Army. [Haldane, Byng].

Canal du Nord: September 27th-October 1st. VI Corps, Third Amy. [Haldane, Byng].

Cambrai, 1918: October 8th-9th. VI Corps, Third Army. [Haldane, Byng].

Selle: October 17th-25th. VI Corps, Third Army. [Haldane, Byng].

This made a grand total of 29 battle honours for the 52nd Light Infantry in the Great War. Only one battle honour being allowed for each of the two periods of action around both Bapaume and the Somme in 1918.

Appendix 2
General Officers Commanding the 2nd Division and 5th Infantry Brigade during World War One

2nd Division

August 5th 1914	Major-General Charles Monro.
December 26th 1914 (acting)	Brigadier-General Robert Fanshawe.
January 1st 1915	Major-General Henry Horne.
November 5th 1915	Major-General William Walker V.C.
December 27th 1916	Major-General Cecil Pereira.

5th Brigade

August 5th 1914	Brigadier-General R.C. Haking (wounded 16/9/14).
September 16th 1914	Colonel C.B. Westmacott. (acting).
November 20th 1914	Brigadier-General R.C. Haking.
December 20th 1914	Lieutenant-Colonel H.R. Davies. (acting).
December 31st 1914	Brigadier-General A.A. Chichester.
July 13th 1915	Brigadier-General C.E. Corkran.
May 15th 1916	Brigadier-General G.M. Bullen-Smith.
March 25th 1918	Lieutenant-Colonel R.H. Pipon. (acting).
April 5th 1918	Brigadier-General W.L. Osborn. (wounded 5/10/18).
October 5th 1918	Lieutenant-Colonel R.H. Pipon. (acting).
November 12th 1918	Brigadier-General W.L. Osborn.

Commanding Officers of the 52nd Light Infantry

1911-1915	Lieutenant-Colonel Henry Davies. (17/9/11).
1915-1916	Lieutenant-Colonel Archibald Eden. (22/2/15).
1916-1919	Lieutenant-Colonel Richard Crosse. (8/7/16).

BIBLIOGRAPHY

Manuscript Sources

Lieutenant-Colonel D.C. Colvill's photograph album.

Imperial War Museum: MSS of Lieutenant-Colonel H. Dillon. 82/25/1.

The Kite Papers: Some 750 letters and documents concerning the life of Captain R.B. Kite. The majority are letters from R.B.K. to his mother.

The Leeds University Library Special Collections:

A.W. Middleditch's papers SC LC GS 1096; Sir J.E.H Neville's papers SC LC GS 1175; Sir J.E.H. Neville's audiotape.

The National Archives, Kew: 2nd Oxfordshire and Buckinghamshire Light Infantry War Diary: WO 95/1348.

5th Infantry Brigade War Diary: WO 95/1343, 1344, 1345, 1346.

2nd Division War Diary: WO 95/1283, 1284, 1285, 1286, 1287, 1288, 1289, 1290, 1291, 1292, 1293, 1294, 1295, 1296, 1297, 1298, 1299, 1300, 1301, 1302, 1303, 1304.

Service Records: Captain F.H. Beaufort. WO 339/6396; Second-Lieutenant R.E. Bull. WO 339/27611; Captain A. Carew Hunt. WO 339/2893; Second-Lieutenant L. A. Dashwood. WO 339/ 2550; Captain J. Hardcastle. WO 339/21163; Captain R.B. Kite. WO 339/14097 30186; Major R.M. Owen. WO 339/7882.

The Norfolk Record Office:

The Neville of Sloley catalogue: Photograph album 1914-1923, NEV 7/31; Photograph album 1914-c 1920, NEV 7/32; The War Letters of a Light Infantryman NEV 7/71; Letters NEV 7/72 589X9, NEV 11/43 592X3, NEV 11/44 592X3, NEV 11/45 592X3, NEV 11/46 592X3, NEV 11/47 592X3.

The Oxfordshire and Buckinghamshire Light Infantry Regimental Archives:

Diary of Private J. Cheshire.

Diaries of Lieutenant-Colonel Guy Blewitt. Volumes 1-5.

Diary of Sergeant [sic] H.C. Gutteridge.

The Titherington Papers: The war letters of Major Geoffrey Titherington.

Journals

Richard Crosse wrote a series of informative articles on the 52nd in The Great War, for the Regimental Journal, from January 1934 in Volume 10 to January 1939 in Volume 15. He repeated his articles with some changes from April 1953 in Volume 21 to May 1959 in Volume 26.

Bulletin of the Western Front Association. Another Fight for the Hohenzollern Redoubt. Peter Last. Number 71. February 2005. Pages 15-16.

Stand To! The Major "Minor Horror of War". Bob Wyatt. Number 23. 1980. Pages 29-30.

Stand To! A Policeman on board the Hampshire. R. McAdam. Number 50. September 1997. Pages 16-17.

Stand To! Military Medicine on the Western Front by Dr. Eric Webb. Number 65. September 2002. Pages 11-18.

Stand To! Trench Diseases of the Western Front by Dr. David Payne. Number 73. April 2005. Pages 15-16.

Books

Addison, A.C. and Matthews W.H. A Deathless Story or The Birkenhead And Its Heroes. 1906.

Atkinson, Capt. C.T. The Seventh Division 1914 - 1918. 1927.

Babington, Anthony. For the Sake of Example. 1983.

Barrow, Gen. Sir George. The Life of General Sir Charles Monro, Bt. 1931.

Battle Of The Aisne 13th-15th September, 1914. Tour Of The Battlefield. 1934.

Becke, Major A.F. Order of Battle. Divisions. Parts 1 - 4. 1934.

Bevan, Edwyn. A Memoir of Leslie Johnston. 1921.

Booth, Philip. The Oxfordshire and Buckinghamshire Light Infantry. 1971.

British Trench Warfare 1917-18. A Reference Manual. Reprinted 1997.

Carew, Tim. The Vanished Army. The B.E.F. 1914 - 1915. 1964.

Callwell, Major-General C.E. Field-Marshal Sir Henry Wilson His Life and Diaries. Volumes I and II. 1927.

Citations Of The Distinguished Conduct Medal In The Great War 1914 - 1920. Section 2 Part One. Line Regiments.

Cheyne, G.Y. The Last Great Battle of the Somme Beaumont Hamel 1916. 1988.

Clarke, Syd. Active Service in World War One. France May 1916 - June 1918.

Conan Doyle, Arthur. The British Campaigns In Europe. 1914 - 1918. 1928.

Coombs, Rose. Before Endeavours Fade. 1994.

Craster, J.M. Fifteen Rounds A Minute. 1976.

Craufurd, Rev. Alexander. General Craufurd and His Light Division.

Creagh, Sir O'Moore. The V.C. and D.S.O. Book. 1920.

Cron, Herman. Imperial German Army 1914 - 18. 2002.

Crosse, Lt.-Colonel R.B. A Record of H.M. 52nd Light Infantry in 1914. 1956.

Day, Roger. The Life Of Sir John Moore. 2001.

Debrett's Peerage, Baronetage, Knightage and Companionage. 1916.

Drake-Brockman, Brig.-Gen. D.H. With the Royal Garhwal Rifles in the Great War 1914 - 1917. 1934.
Drew, Lt.-Gen. Sir Robert. Commissioned Officers In The Medical Services Of The British Army 1660 - 1960. Volumes I - II. 1968.
Edensor, David. Wings Of The Morning. 2006.
Edgar, Capt. Miles. Editor. The Humph Letters 1910 - 1915.
Edmonds, Brig. James. Military Operations France and Belgium. Volumes for 1914, 1915, 1916, 1917, 1918.
Farndale, General Sir Martin. Western Front 1914 - 18. 1986.
Fox, Sir Frank. The Royal Inniskilling Fusiliers In The Great War. 1928.
Gliddon, Gerald. The Battle of the Somme. A Topographical History. 1994.
Gough, General Sir Hubert. Soldiering On. 1954.
Graves, Robert. Goodbye To All That. 1929.
Hallows, Ian. Regiment and Corps of the British Army. 1994.
Hamilton, Lord Ernest. The First Seven Divisions. 1916.
Hare, Maj.-Gen. Sir Steuart. The Annals Of The King's Royal Rifle Corps. Volume V. The Great War. 1932.
Harris, Ruth. Billie The Nevill Letters: 1914 - 1916. 1991.
Harris, Simon. RBK A Very Parfit Gentil Knight. 2004.
Hesketh-Prichard, Major H. Sniping In France. 1994.
Hogg, Ian. Hutchinson Dictionary of World War I. 1997.
Holmes, Richard. The Little Field Marshal. A Life of Sir John French. 1981.
Holmes, Richard. Tommy. 2004.
Holt, Tonie and Valma. Battlefields of the First World War. 1995.
Horne, Alistair. The Price of Glory. Verdun 1916. 1962.
Isselin, Henri. The Battle of the Marne. 1964.
Johnston, John Leslie. Some Alternatives To Jesus Christ. 1914.
Kearsey, Lt.-Col. A. 1915 Campaign In France. The Battles of Aubers Ridge, Festubert and Loos. 1929.
Kearsey, Lt.-Col. A., The Battle of Amiens 1918. 1950.
Keegan, John. The First World War. 1999.
Liddell Hart, Basil. History of the First World War. 1970.
List Of Etonians Who Fought In The Great War 1914 - 1919.
Loraine Petre, F et al. The Scots Guards In The Great War 1914 - 1918. 1925.
MacDonald, Lyn. The Roses of No Man's Land. 1984.
MacDonald, Lyn. 1915. The Death of Innocence. 1993.
MacDonald, Lyn. To the Last Man Spring 1918. 1998.
Mawer, Geoffrey. Editor. The War Letters of Jack Mawer.
Merewether, Lt.-Col. J.W.B. The Indian Corps In France. 1918.

Middlebrook, Martin. The Kaiser's Battle. 1978.
Middlebrook, Martin and Mary. The Somme Battlefields. 1994.
Mockler-Ferryman, Lt.-Col. A.F., The Oxfordshire and Buckinghamshire Light Infantry Chronicles. The Great War. Volumes I - V. Early 1920s.
Mockler-Ferryman, Lt.-Col. A.F., Regimental War Tales. 1741 - 1919. 1942.
Moore, William. Gas Attack. 1987.
Moorsom W.S. Editor. Historical Record of the Fifty Second Regiment (Oxfordshire Light Infantry). From the year 1755 to the year 1858. 1860.
Neville, Capt J.E. The War Letters of a Light Infantryman. 1930.
Neville, Capt J.E., History of the 43rd and 52nd (Oxfordshire and Buckinghamshire) Light Infantry in the Great War 1914 - 1919. Volume I. 1938.
Newbolt, Sir Henry. The Story of The Oxfordshire and Buckinghamshire Light Infantry. 1916.
Nicholls, Jonathan. Cheerful Sacrifice. The Battle Of Arras 1917. 1993.
Oatts, Lt.-Col. L.B. The Story of the Highland Light Infantry. 1882 - 1918. 1961.
Official History Of The Great War Principal Events. 1922.
O'Neill, H.C. The Royal Fusiliers in the Great War. 1922.
Ponsonby, Lieut.-Col. Sir Frederick. The Grenadier Guards In The Great War Of 1914 - 1918. Volumes I - III. 1920.
Powell, Geoffrey. Plumer The Soldier's General. 1990.
Putkowski, Julian and Sykes, Julian. Shot At Dawn. 1989.
Rickard, Mrs Victor. The Story Of The Munsters at Etreux, Festubert, Rue Du Bois and Hulloch. 1918.
Rodger, Alexander. Battle Honours of the British Empire and Commonwealth Land Forces 1662 - 1991. 2003.
Richter, Donald. Chemical Soldiers. 1994.
Sheffield, Gary. Forgotten Victory. 2001.
Sheffield, Gary and Bourne, John. Douglas Haig. War Diaries and Letters. 2005.
Stanley, Brig.-Gen F.C. The History of The 89th Brigade 1914 - 1918. 1919.
Statistics Of The Military Effort Of The British Empire During The Great War 1914-1920. 1922.
Taylor, A.J.P. English History 1914 - 1945. 1965.
Telfer-Smollett, Major A.D. The 2nd Battalion Highland Light Infantry in The Great War. Circa 1928.
Terraine, John. Mons The Retreat To Victory. 1960.

Terraine, John. To Win A War. 1918, The Year Of Victory. 1978.

Terraine, John. Douglas Haig The Educated Soldier. 1990.

Terraine, John. 1914 - 1918. Essays on Leadership and War. 1998.

Trythall, Anthony. 'Boney' Fuller The Intellectual General. 1977.

The Official Names Of The Battles And Other Engagements Fought By The Military Forces Of The British Empire During The Great War 1914 - 1919 And The Third Afghan War 1919. 1920.

United States War Office. Histories of two hundred and fifty one divisions of the German Army which participated in the war 1914 - 1918. 1989.

Warner, Philip. The Battle of Loos. 1976.

Wheeler-Holohan, Captain V. Divisional And Other Signs. 1920.

Whitehead, Ian. Doctors in the Great War. 1999.

Who Was Who 1897 - 1916.

Winter, J.M. The Experience of World War I. 1989.

Woollcombe, Robert. The First Tank Battle Cambrai 1917. 1967.

Wylly, Col. H.C. History Of The Queen's Royal Regiment In The Great War.

Wyrall, Everard. The History of the Second Division 1914 - 1918. 1922.

Wyrall, Everard. The 17th (S) Battalion Royal Fusiliers. 1914 - 19. 1930.

Wyrall, Everard. The History Of The Duke Of Cornwall's Light Infantry in 1914 - 1919. 1932.

INDEX